Industrial Organization

Industrial Organization

Competition, Strategy and Policy

Fourth edition

John Lipczynski, John O.S. Wilson and John Goddard

PEARSON

Harlow, England • London • New York • Boston • San Francisco • Toronto • Sydney
Auckland • Singapore • Hong Kong • Tokyo • Seoul • Taipei • New Delhi
Cape Town • São Paulo • Mexico City • Madrid • Amsterdam • Munich • Paris • Milan

PEARSON EDUCATION LIMITED

Edinburgh Gate
Harlow CM20 2JE
Tel: +44 (0)1279 623623
Fax: +44 (0)1279 431059
Website: www.pearson.com/uk

First published 2001 (print)
Second edition published 2005 (print and electronic)
Third edition published 2009 (print and electronic)
Fourth edition published 2013 (print and electronic)

© Pearson Education Limited 2001 (print), 2005 (print and electronic), 2009 (print and electronic), 2013 (print and electronic)

The Financial Times. **With a worldwide network of highly respected journalists,** *The Financial Times* **provides global business news, insightful opinion and expert analysis of business, finance and politics. With over 500 journalists reporting from 50 countries worldwide, our in-depth coverage of international news is objectively reported and analysed from an independent, global perspective. To find out more, visit www.ft.com/pearsonoffer.**

ISBN: 978-0-273-77041-1 (print)
      978-0-273-77042-8 (PDF)
      978-0-273-78085-4 (eText)

British Library Cataloguing-in-Publication Data
A catalogue record for the print edition is available from the British Library

Library of Congress Cataloging-in-Publication Data
Lipczynski, John.
  Industrial organization : competition, strategy, policy / John Lipczynski, John O. S. Wilson and John Goddard. – 4th ed.
    p. cm.
  ISBN 978-0-273-77041-1
  1. Industrial organization (Economic theory)   I. Wilson, John O. S. II. Goddard, John A. III. Title.
HD2326.L53 2013
338.6–dc23

2012043266

10 9 8 7 6 5 4 3 2 1
17 16 15 14 13

Print edition typeset in 10/12.5pt Times NR MT Std by 35
Print edition printed and bound in Great Britain by Ashford Colour Press Ltd, Gosport, Hampshire

NOTE THAT ANY PAGE CROSS REFERENCES REFER TO THE PRINT EDITION

For my family, Nicole, Sonya, Mark and Anna JL

In memory of my mother-in-law, Jean Angus JW

For Sarah, Aimée and Thomas JG

Contents

Part I: Theoretical Foundations

Part II: Structural Analysis of Industry

Part IV: Analysis of Public Policy

Appendices: Analytical Tools

Supporting resources

Visit www.pearsoned.co.uk/lipczynski to find valuable online resources

For instructors
- PowerPoints of book figures and tables for usage during lecturers
- Instructor's manual containing answers to book discussion questions

For more information please contact your local Pearson Education sales representative or visit www.pearsoned.co.uk/lipczynski.

List of tables

List of figures

List of boxes

List of case studies

Preface

Industrial Organization: Competition, Structure, Strategy and Policy, fourth edition, is a textbook on industrial organization. It provides coverage of the latest theories of industrial organization, and it examines empirical evidence concerning the strategies, behaviour and performance of firms and industries.

In selecting material for inclusion in *Industrial Organization: Competition, Structure, Strategy and Policy*, fourth edition, we have attempted to provide readers with a flavour of the historical development of industrial organization. The book reflects the development of this subject area from its origins in the classical theories of the firm, followed by its emergence as a recognized sub-discipline within economics around the mid-twentieth century, right through to the present. Today, industrial organization draws on an impressive array of contributions from fields of economic inquiry as diverse as game theory, information theory, organization theory, agency theory and transaction cost analysis. At various stages throughout the book, we examine the work of researchers in the closely related field of strategic management, in order to emphasize the relevance of industrial organization to readers who are approaching the subject primarily from a business or a management standpoint, rather than from a traditional economics perspective.

Industrial Organization: Competition, Structure, Strategy and Policy, fourth edition, contains 67 case studies, which are used to illustrate 'real world' applications of theoretical and empirical research in industrial organization. Many of the case studies have been selected from reports originally published in the *Financial Times*; while others have been compiled from alternative sources. Many of the case studies have been chosen not only for their relevance to industrial organization, but also because they are lively, newsworthy and topical. The case study material certainly bears little or no resemblance to the subject matter of a traditional industrial economics research agenda of 20 or 30 years ago, when much greater emphasis would have been placed on traditional manufacturing and heavy industry. Instead, the case studies focus on key sectors of the modern-day economy, such as banking and financial services (commercial banking, the credit union movement); sport and leisure (Hollywood movies, English Premier League football); and online products and services (social networking, music apps).

Industrial Organization: Competition, Strategy and Policy, fourth edition, is aimed primarily at undergraduate students. The book is intended for use on modules in industrial organization, industrial economics or business economics, by students studying for degrees in economics, business and management studies, and other related disciplines. It can also be used as a preparatory, background or reference text by students taking graduate courses in the same subjects. The only prior experience of economics that is assumed is the completion of an introductory Principles of Economics module, or a one-semester module in Microeconomics.

The style of presentation is non-technical throughout. No knowledge of calculus is required. However, for readers requiring a more rigorous treatment of certain topics, a Mathematical Methods appendix provides formal derivations (using calculus) of a selection of the most important theories and results presented in the main text. Empirical research in industrial organization is also presented throughout the text in a non-technical style. No knowledge of statistics or econometrics is assumed. For readers requiring a primer in the fundamentals of regression analysis, an Econometric Methods appendix provides a brief and non-technical introduction to some of the basic tools, such as regression coefficients, t-statistics and goodness-of-fit.

Structure of the book

Industrial Organization: Competition, Strategy and Policy, fourth edition, is divided into four parts. In Part I, Theoretical Foundations, Chapter 1 introduces some of the key elements of industrial organization, starting with the structure–conduct–performance paradigm, which provided the intellectual foundation for the early development of industrial organization as a separate sub discipline within economics. Chapters 2 and 3 review the core microeconomic theory from which many of the early and modern theories of industrial organization have developed. Chapters 4 and 5 examine a number of alternative theories of firm behaviour, including the neoclassical, managerial and behavioural theories, as well as perspectives drawn from transaction cost analysis, agency, knowledge- and resource-based theories. Chapter 6 examines issues related to corporate governance.

Part II, Structural Analysis of Industry, discusses the approach within the field of industrial organization which emphasizes the role of the structural attributes of an industry in explaining the conduct of the industry's constituent firms. Chapters 7 and 8 examine non collusive and collusive theories of oligopoly, a market structure whose most important characteristic is the small number of interdependent, competing firms. Chapter 9 examines practical aspects of industry definition, and the measurement of the number and size distribution of an industry's constituent firms, summarized by measures of industry or seller concentration. Chapter 10 examines the determinants of seller concentration. Chapter 11 examines another important structural attribute of industries: barriers to entry. Finally, Chapter 12 provides a link between Parts II and III of the book, by describing the evolution of industrial organization beyond the confines of the structure–conduct–performance paradigm, and the development of new approaches and methods, which are conveniently summarized under the banner of the 'new industrial organization'.

In Part III, Analysis of Firm Strategy, the focus shifts away from industry structure, and towards the newer theories of industrial organization that emphasize conduct or strategic decision-making at firm level. Chapter 13 examines a number of pricing practices, including price discrimination and transfer pricing. In recognition of the growing use of auctions as a method for allocating resources and awarding contracts in the commercial and public sectors, Chapter 14 examines the economic theory of auctions. In the rest of Part III, the emphasis shifts towards various non-price strategies that can be adopted by firms, in an attempt to improve their profitability or gain a competitive advantage over their rivals. Chapters 15 and 16 examine product differentiation and advertising. Chapter 17 examines research and development and technological progress. Chapters 18 examines horizontal mergers. Chapters 19 and 20 examine vertical integration and vertical restraints. Chapter 21 examines the economics of network goods and services. Chapter 22 examines diversification and conglomerate merger.

Part IV, Analysis of Public Policy, concludes the book, by drawing together the implications for public policy of many of the key findings of Parts I, II and III. Chapter 23 examines competition policy, including government policy towards monopolies, restrictive practices and mergers. Chapter 24 examines the topic of regulation, with particular emphasis given to public scrutiny of the activities and business practices of the recently privatized utilities and other natural monopolies.

Changes for the fourth edition

We have been gratified and encouraged by the responses to the first, second and third editions we have received from instructors and students. However, a new edition provides a welcome opportunity to make improvements and to update and extend the material that was covered previously. For the fourth edition, the number of chapters has increased from 22 to 24. Part I of the book has been increased via the inclusion of a new chapter on Corporate Governance resulting in the number of chapters increasing from five to six. The number of chapters in Part II remains the same. In Part III of the book, Chapter 21 on Network Goods and Services is new. In addition to the two new chapters, we have revised and updated our coverage of many theoretical and empirical topics in industrial organization throughout the book.

The previous editions' extensive bibliography has turned out to be a highly popular feature with instructors, and with students wishing to read beyond the confines of a core textbook, perhaps with a view towards choosing a dissertation topic, or towards studying industrial organization at graduate level. Accordingly, in the fourth edition we have taken the opportunity to extend and update our previous bibliography.

We have retained or updated the most interesting and relevant case studies from the first, second and third editions, and we have added many more completely new case studies to the fourth edition. Most of the new case studies describe recent events, which have occurred since the publication of the first edition in 2001. We have revised the end-of-chapter discussion questions.

Finally, we have extended our website **www.pearsoned.co.uk/lipczynski**, which contains supporting material for instructors in the form of PowerPoint slides and outline answers to discussion questions. The website also contains links to other relevant websites, and a glossary of key terms, for instructors and students.

Authors' acknowledgements

We would like to thank colleagues and students at the School of Management at the University of St Andrews, and Bangor Business School at Bangor University for their direct and at times unknowing help towards the development of this project. We would like to give special thanks to John Hart, Donal McKillop, Phil Molyneux and Ian Williams for all of their advice, support and helpful comments. In addition to the people who helped in earlier editions John Lipczynski would like to thank Mark Scibor-Rylski and Ann Marsden for their contributions to this fourth edition.

Thanks are due to a number of staff at Pearson Education who have provided excellent support at all stages as this project has progressed. We are especially indebted to Rufus Curnow, Kate Brewin, Gemma Papageorgiou, Geoffrey Chatterton, Summa Verbeek, Michelle Morgan and Jennifer Sargunar for all of their advice, encouragement, for keeping things on track and reminding us of deadlines during the editing, typesetting and production stages. We are also grateful for the assistance provided by Jenny Oates (Copy Editor), Mary Dalton (Proof Reader) and Gary Hall (Indexer). Any remaining errors are, of course, the authors' joint responsibility.

Finally and most importantly, we would like to thank our families, for their patience, encouragement and support.

We are also grateful to those who have allowed the reproduction of copyrighted material.

Publisher's acknowledgements

Our thanks go to all reviewers who contributed to the development of this text:

- Caroline Elliott, Lancaster University

- Taimur Sharif, London South Bank University

- Alex Dickson, University of Strathclyde

We are grateful to the following for permission to reproduce copyright material:

Figures

Figure 1.2 adapted from *Competitive Strategy: Techniques for Analysing Industries and Competitors*, The Free Press (Porter, M. 1990) p. 4, Copyright 1980, 1998 by The Free Press. All rights reserved; Figure 5.3 from The theory of the firm as governance structure: from choice to contract, *Journal of Economic Perspectives*, 16, pp. 171–95 (Williamson, O.E. 2002); Figure 6.1 from Recent developments in corporate governance: an overview, *Journal of Corporate Finance*, 12, p. 383 (Gillian, L. 2006), with permission from Elsevier; Figure 10.3 adapted from *The Competitive Advantage of Nations*, The Free Press (Porter, M. 1990) p. 72, Copyright 1990, 1998 by Michael E. Porter. All rights reserved; Figure 18.1 adapted from the Office for National Statistics Data 2008, licensed under the Open Government Licence v.1.0; Figure 18.2 from Equity alliances take centre stage, *Business Strategy Review* (Pekar Jr, P. and Margulis, M.S. 2003), © London Business School [2003]. The definitive, peer reviewed and edited version of this article is published in Business Strategy Review [volume 14, pages 50–65, 2003], www.london.edu/bsr.

Tables

Table 10.4 adapted from *Economic Trends* Number 635, October 2006. Appendix 1. National Statistics © Crown Copyright 2000, Office for National Statistics licensed under the Open Government Licence v.1.0; Table 10.5 adapted from Eurostat (2011) *Key Figures on European Business*. Luxembourg: Office for Official Publications of the European Communities. Table 2.2, p. 34., *Key Figures on European Business with Special Features on SMEs*, Eurostat, Table 2.2 page 34, http://epp.eurostat.ec.europa.eu, © European Union, 2011; Table 10.6 adapted from European Commission (2000) Panorama of EU Business. Luxembourg: Office for Official Publications of the European Communities. Selected table entries, Chapters 2–21., Panorama of European Business. Industry Data 1989–1999, Eurostat, http://epp.eurostat.ec.europa.eu, © European Communities, 2000. Responsibility for the adaptation lies entirely on the Pearson Group; Table 10.7 adapted from Eurostat (2011) *Key Figures on European Business*. Luxembourg: Office for Official Publications of the European Communities. Table 2.2, p. 34, *Key Figures on European Business with a Special Feature on SMEs*, Eurostat, Table 2.6, page 41, http://epp.eurostat.ec.europa.eu, © European Union, 2011. Responsibility for the adaptation lies entirely on the Pearson Group; Table 10.8 adapted from Eurostat (2009) *European Business Facts and Figures*. Luxembourg: Office for Official Publications of the European Communities. Table 1.4, p. 23., *European Business. Facts and Figures*, Eurostat, Table 1.3, page 23, http://epp.eurostat.ec.europa.eu, © European Communities, 2009. Responsibility for the adaptation lies entirely on the Pearson Group; Table 10.9 adapted from European Commission (2002b) *Regional Clusters in Europe, Observatory of European SMEs 2002*/No. 3, p. 28., Table 4.1 © European Communities, 2002; Table 11.1 adapted from Pratten (1988), Table 5.5, pp. 88–92., © European Union, 1995–2012; Table 12.1 from Industry structure, market rivalry and public policy, *Journal of Law and Economics*, 16, 6 (Demsetz, H. 1973), Table 2, University of Chicago Press; Table 13.1 adapted from How do UK companies set prices?, *Bank of England Quarterly Bulletin*, May, Vol. 36, pp. 180–92 (Hall, S., Walsh, M. and Yates, A. 1996); Table 16.1 from *The European Advertising and Media Forecast*, National Data Sources, NTC Publications Ltd. Reproduced from Advertising Association (2009) *Advertising Statistics*

Yearbook 2003, Table 19.4, p. 183 and Advertising Association (2009) *Advertising Statistics Yearbook 2009*, Table 19.4, p. 221. Oxford: NTC Publications. Reprinted with permission; Table 16.2 adapted from *Advertising Statistics Yearbook 2009*, Advertising Association (2009) Table 18.1, pp. 206–12, researched and compiled by WARC (http://www.warc.com); Table 16.3 adapted from *Advertising Statistics Yearbook 2009*, The Neilsen Company (*Advertising Association 2009*) pp. 251–52; Table 18.1 from The effects of mergers: an international comparison, *International Journal of Industrial Organisation*, 21, pp. 625–53 (Gugler, K., Mueller, D.C., Yurtoglu, B.B. and Zulehner, C. 2003); Table 22.1 adapted from Rondi, L., Sembenelli, A. and Ragazzi, E. (1996) Determinants of diversification patterns, in Davies, S. and Lyons, B. (eds) *Industrial Organisation in the European Union*. Oxford: Oxford University Press, p. 171; Table 24.3 from www.doingbusiness. org/economyrankings (data from *Doing Business 2011*).

Text

Case Study 2.1 from Companies and productivity – small is not beautiful: why small firms are less wonderful than you think, *Economist*, 03 March 2012, © The Economist Newspaper Limited, London; Case Study 4.1 from We should be talking about the market economy, *Financial Times*, 10 January 2012 (Kay, John), © The Financial Times Limited. All Rights Reserved; Case Study 4.2 from Cable under fire over executive pay plans, *Financial Times*, 14 March 2012 (Groom, Brian and Burgess, Kate), © The Financial Times Limited. All Rights Reserved; Case Study 5.1 from Outsourcing everything, *Financial Times*, 24 January 2008 (Harford, Tim), © The Financial Times Limited. All Rights Reserved; Case Study 5.2 from How to encourage managers to act more like owners, *Financial Times*, 07 July 2009 (Stern, Stefan), © The Financial Times Limited. All Rights Reserved; Case Study 6.1 from Reaction to Governance Code divided, *Financial Times*, 27 May 2010 (Sanderson, Rachel, Burgess, Kate and Masters, Brooke), © The Financial Times Limited. All Rights Reserved; Case Study 6.2 from Apple has incentive to worry about workers' rights, *Financial Times*, 15 February 2012 (Waters, Richard), © The Financial Times Limited. All Rights Reserved; Case Study 6.3 from How 'good' does a shampoo need to be?, *Financial Times*, 03 February 2012 (Tett, Gillian), © The Financial Times Limited. All Rights Reserved; Case Study 7.1 from Indian airlines lose altitude in price war, *Financial Times*, 04 October 2011 (Kazmin, Amy), © The Financial Times Limited. All Rights Reserved; Case Study 7.2 from *The Evolution of Co-operation*, Perseus Books Group LLC (Basic Books) (Axelrod, Robert 1984), Copyright © 1984 Robert Axelrod. Reprinted by permission of Basic Books, a member of the Perseus Books Group; Case Study 8.1 from Whiter than white?, *Economist*, 11 December 2011, © The Economist Newspaper Limited, London; Case Study 9.1 from Break up Britain's uncompetitive big banks, *Financial Times*, 12 December 2010 (Myners, Paul); Case Study 9.2 from The media concentration debate, *Financial Times*, 31 July 2003 (Noam, E.), © The Financial Times Limited. All Rights Reserved; Case Study 9.3 from Andersen's collapse results in a fee bonus for Big Four rivals, *Financial Times*, 29 April 2008 (Hughes, J.), © The Financial Times Limited. All Rights Reserved;

Theoretical Foundations

Industrial organization: an introduction

Learning objectives

This chapter covers the following topics:

- static and dynamic views of competition
- the structure–conduct–performance paradigm
- the Chicago school approach to the study of competition

Key terms

Austrian school
Chicago school
Collusion hypothesis
Distinctive capabilities
Efficiency hypothesis
Five forces model

Market equilibrium
New industrial organization
Structure–conduct–performance
   paradigm
Value chain

1.1 Introduction

This book deals with the economics of industrial organization. Specific topics that are covered include theory of the firm, oligopoly, concentration, barriers to entry, pricing and auctions, product differentiation and advertising, research and development, mergers, vertical integration, diversification, competition policy and regulation. The aim of this introductory chapter is to provide an overview of some of this subject material, for both the specialist and the non-specialist reader.

The chapter begins in Section 1.2 by examining static and dynamic views of competition in economic theory. The view of competition found in the neoclassical theory of the firm (incorporating the textbook models of perfect competition, monopolistic competition, oligopoly and monopoly) is essentially static.

In contrast, a more dynamic approach can be found in the writings of Schumpeter and economists identified with the Austrian school. Section 1.3 describes the structure–conduct–performance (SCP) paradigm, which laid the foundation for the original development of industrial organization as a separate sub-discipline within economics. The key elements of structure, conduct and performance are introduced, and some of the main limitations of the SCP paradigm are discussed. Finally, Section 1.4 makes a short diversion into the related sub-discipline of strategic management and identifies several further themes that will be pursued in more depth thoughout this book.

1.2 Static and dynamic views of competition

In microeconomics, the neoclassical theory of the firm considers four main theoretical market structures: perfect competition, monopolistic competition, oligopoly and monopoly. These underpin much of the subject matter of industrial organization. A perfectly competitive industry has six main characteristics: there are large numbers of buyers and sellers; producers and consumers have perfect knowledge; the products sold by firms are identical; firms act independently of each other and aim to maximize profits; firms are free to enter or exit; and firms can sell as much output as they wish at the current market price. If these conditions are satisfied, a competitive equilibrium exists in which all firms earn only a normal profit. If any particular firm is unable to earn a normal profit, perhaps because it is failing to produce at maximum efficiency, this firm is forced to withdraw from the market. In this way perfect competition imposes discipline: all surviving firms are forced to produce as efficiently as the current state of technology will allow.

In reality, however, competition often gives rise to a market or industry structure comprising a relatively small number of large firms. Each firm has sufficient market power to determine its own price, and some or all firms are able to earn an abnormal profit in the long run. One reason competition tends to lead to a decrease in the number of firms in the long run is that as firms grow, they realize economies of scale and average costs tend to fall. In the most extreme case of natural monopoly, a single firm can produce at a lower average cost than any number of competing firms. Among others, Marshall (1890) and Sraffa (1926) formulated the theory of monopoly. The tendency for average costs to fall as the scale of production increases might be a beneficial aspect of monopoly, if the cost savings are passed on to consumers in lower prices. However, if a monopolist exploits its market power by restricting output and raising price in order to earn an abnormal profit, then monopoly may have damaging implications for consumer welfare.

Influenced by Marshall and Sraffa, Chamberlin (1933) and Robinson (1933) brought together the previously separate theories of monopoly and perfect competition, to formulate the theory of imperfect competition, which can be subdivided into the cases of monopolistic competition and oligopoly. The theory of monopolistic competition retains the assumption that the number of firms is large, but emphasizes non-price as well as price forms of competition. In the theory of oligopoly it is assumed the number of firms is small (but greater than one). The firms recognize their interdependence: changes in price or output by one firm will alter the profits of rival firms, causing them to adjust their own prices and output levels. Forms of competition under oligopoly vary from vigorous price competition, which can often lead to substantial losses, through to collusion, whereby the firms take joint decisions concerning their prices and output levels.

Essentially, the neoclassical theory of the firm is based on a static conception of competition. In all of the models outlined above, the main focus is on long-run equilibrium.

> In the end-state conception of equilibrium, the focus of attention is on the nature of the equilibrium state in which the contest between transacting agents is finally resolved; if there is recognition of change at all, it is change in the sense of a new stationary equilbrium of endogenous variables in response to an altered set of exogenous variables; but comparative statics is still an end-state conception of economics.

> *(Blaug, 2001, p. 37)*

In the twentieth century, some researchers rejected this static view of competition, and sought to develop a more dynamic approach. According to both Schumpeter (1928, 1942) and the **Austrian school** of economists, the fact that a firm earns an abnormal (monopoly) profit does not constitute evidence that the firm is guilty of abusing its market (monopoly) power at the expense of consumers. Instead, monopoly profits play an important role in the process of competition, motivating and guiding entrepreneurs towards taking decisions that will produce an improved allocation of scarce resources in the long run. Schumpeter and the Austrian school both recognize that knowledge or information is always imperfect.

According to Schumpeter, competition is driven by innovation: the introduction of new products and processes, the conquest of new markets for inputs or outputs, or the reorganization of existing productive arrangements (for example, through entry or takeover). By initiating change by means of innovation, the entrepreneur plays a key role in driving forward technological progress. Innovation destroys old products and production processes, and replaces them with new and better ones. The successful innovator is rewarded with monopoly status and monopoly profits for a time. However, following a brief catching-up period, imitators are able to move into the market, eroding the original innovator's monopoly status and profits. Alternatively, another innovator may eventually come along with an even better product or production process, rendering the previous innovation obsolete. According to this dynamic view of competition, monopoly status is only a temporary phenomenon, and is not capable of sustaining a stable long-run equilibrium, as is assumed in the neoclassical theory of the firm.

The Austrian school also views competition as a dynamic process, and sees the market as comprising a configuration of decisions made by consumers, entrepreneurs and resource owners (Kirzner, 1973, 1997a,b). Entrepreneurs play a crucial role by noticing missed opportunities for mutually advantageous trade. Entrepreneurs discover and act upon new pieces of information. By observing the actions of entrepreneurs, other decision-makers are able adjust their trading plans and arrive at improved outcomes. Disequilibrium reflects imperfect information or ignorance on the part of buyers and sellers. The entrepreneurial function adds to the flow of information, and helps lubricate the process of adjustment towards a new and superior allocation of scarce resources. Whereas the Schumpeterian entrepreneur actively initiates change, the role of the entrepreneur in Austrian thinking is more passive: the Austrian entrepreneur merely responds more quickly than other agents to new information that is generated exogenously. According to Austrian economists, a monopoly position is attained through the originality and foresight of the entrepreneur; and, as Schumpeter suggests, monopoly profits are unlikely to be sustained indefinitely. As information arrives and new trading opportunities open up, other entrepreneurs appear, who by their actions help propel the economy towards a further reallocation of resources (Young *et al.*, 1996; Roberts and Eisenhardt, 2003).

1.3   The structure–conduct–performance paradigm

The static and dynamic theories discussed above have found an empirical counterpart in the field that has become known as industrial organization. Early work in this area, based predominantly on the **structure–conduct–performance (SCP) paradigm**, concentrates on empirical rather than theoretical analysis (Bain, 1951). In the main, the field of industrial organization analyzes empirical data and, by a process of induction, develops theories to explain the behaviour and performance of firms and the industries to which they belong (Schmalensee, 1988; Caves, 2007).

Outline of the structure–conduct–performance paradigm

Seminal early contributions in industrial organization include Mason (1939, 1949) and Bain (1951, 1956, 1959). Mason and Bain are credited with the development of the SCP paradigm. According to this approach, the structure of a market influences the conduct of the firms operating in the market, which in turn influences the performance of those firms. The field of industrial organization is concerned with the investigation of 'the size structure of firms (one or many, "concentrated" or not), the causes (above all the economies of scale) of this size structure, the effects of concentration on competition, the effects of competition on prices, investment, innovation and so on' (Stigler, 1968, p. 1).

The SCP paradigm is useful in a number of ways:

■ It allows the researcher to reduce all industry data into meaningful categories (Bain, 1956).

■ It is consistent with the neoclassical theory of the firm, which also assumes there is a direct link between market structure, and firm conduct and performance, without overtly recognizing this link (Mason, 1949).

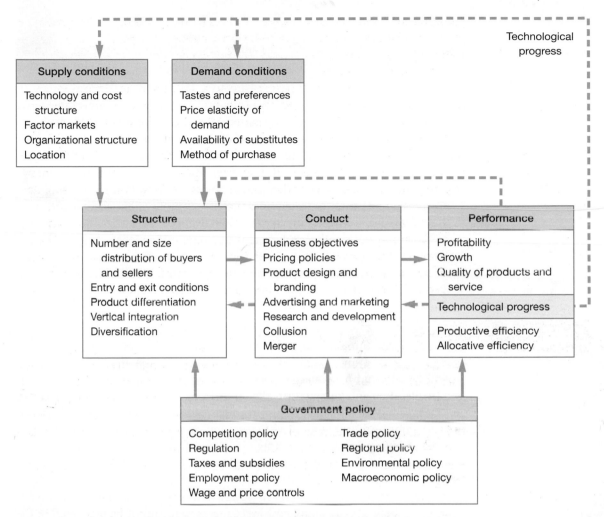

Figure 1.1 The structure–conduct–performance paradigm

- By defining a workable or acceptable standard of performance, it may be possible to accept an imperfect market structure, if such a structure produces outcomes that are consistent with the acceptable standard (Clark, 1940). By implication, market structure can be altered in order to improve conduct and performance (Sosnick, 1958).

A schematic representation of the SCP paradigm is presented in Figure 1.1. In accordance with the fundamental logic of SCP, the main linkages are shown as running from structure through conduct to performance. However, various feedback effects are also possible: from performance back to conduct; from conduct to structure; and from performance to structure (Phillips, 1976; Clarke, 1985). These are represented in Figure 1.1 by dotted arrows. Several specific types of feedback effect are identified in the following discussion of the main components of the structure, conduct and performance categories.

Structure

Structural characteristics tend to change relatively slowly, and can often be regarded as fixed in the short run. Some of the more important structure variables are as follows:

■ *The number and size distribution of buyers and sellers* is an important determinant of the market power exercised by the leading firms in the industry and the discretion these sellers exercise over their own prices. In consumer goods industries it is normally the case that there are large numbers of small, atomistic buyers. Accordingly, the main focus is on the number and size distribution of sellers. Seller concentration is typically measured using data on the share of total industry sales, assets or employment accounted for by the largest firms in the industry. In capital goods industries, however, it is possible that the number of buyers is also small. If so, there may be market power on the demand side, as well as on the supply side: buyers may exercise discretion over the prices they pay. In such cases, a full assessment of the distribution of market power might require measurement of buyer concentration as well as seller concentration.

■ *Entry and exit conditions* include barriers to entry, which can be defined loosely as anything that places a potential entrant at a competitive disadvantage relative to an incumbent firm. The important issue is the relative ease or difficulty that firms may experience when entering an industry: if entry is difficult, then incumbents are sheltered from outside competition (Neven, 1989). Entry barriers may derive from basic characteristics of the product or production technology and cost structure; or from deliberate actions taken by incumbent firms to discourage or prevent entry. The analysis of entry barriers has shifted from the simple classification developed by Bain (1956) to complex models of strategic behaviour which incorporate threats and irreversible commitments (Dixit, 1982). Irreversible commitments involve an incumbent making sunk cost investments that cannot be recovered in the event of subsequent withdrawal from the market. By raising barriers to exit in this way, an incumbent can signal its intention to stick around and fight in order to preserve its market share. The signal may in itself be sufficient to deter a potential entrant from proceeding.

■ *Product differentiation* refers to the characteristics of the product. How similar is each firm's product to those of rival firms? To what extent is each firm's product unique? Any change in the characteristics of the product supplied by one firm, whether real or imagined, may affect the shares of the total market demand that each firm is able to command.

■ *Vertical integration and diversification.* Vertical integration refers to the extent to which a firm is involved in different stages of the same production process. Diversified firms produce a variety of goods or services for several distinct markets. The extent to which a firm is vertically integrated or diversified is likely to have implications for conduct and performance. Vertically integrated firms have greater certainty in obtaining supplies of raw materials, or guaranteed distribution outlets. They have opportunities to engage in certain types of anticompetitive practice (vertical restraints), which may be damaging to non-integrated rivals. Diversified firms may benefit from economies of scope, and are less exposed to risk than their non-diversified counterparts, because losses realized in one market can be offset against profits earned elsewhere. In the long run, of course, firms make their own choices concerning vertical integration and diversification; therefore in the long run these can also be interpreted as conduct variables.

Conduct

Conduct refers to the behaviour of firms, conditioned, according to the SCP paradigm, by the industry's structural characteristics identified above. Conduct variables include the following:

- *Business objectives.* The objectives that firms pursue often derive from structural characteristics of the industry, in particular the firm size distribution. The neoclassical theory of the firm assumes profit maximization; while managerial theories, developed primarily with large corporations in mind, emphasize the maximization of non-profit objectives such as sales revenue, growth or managerial utility (Baumol, 1959; Williamson, 1963; Marris, 1964).

- *Pricing policies.* The extent of a firm's discretion to determine its own price depends to a large extent on the industry's structural characteristics. Possible pricing policies include cost plus pricing, marginal cost pricing, entry-deterring pricing, predatory pricing, price leadership and price discrimination (Phlips, 1983). For oligopolists, in particular, it may be imperative to avoid direct price competition leading to mutually destructive price wars.

- *Product design, branding, advertising and marketing.* Natural or inherent characteristics of the firm's basic product are likely to influence the scope for non-price competition centred on product design, branding, advertising and marketing. Although product differentiation is cited above as a structural characteristic, to some extent this is an oversimplification: the extent of product differentiation is at least partly endogenous, influenced or determined by strategies consciously implemented by incumbent firms.

- *Research and development.* Together with advertising and marketing, investment in research and development provides an outlet for non-price competition between rival firms. The extent and effectiveness of research and development investment, and the pace of diffusion (the speed at which a new idea is adopted by firms other than the original innovator), are critical determinants of the pace of technological progress (Kamien and Schwartz, 1982).

- *Collusion.* Another option open to firms wishing to avoid direct forms of price or non-price competition is to collude with one another, so as to reach collective decisions concerning prices, output levels, advertising or research and development budgets. Collusion may be either explicit (through an arrangement such as a cartel), or implicit or tacit (through a less formal agreement or understanding).

■ *Merger*. Horizontal mergers (between firms producing the same or similar products) have direct implications for seller concentration in the industry concerned. Vertical mergers (between firms at successive stages of a production process) affect the degree of vertical integration. Conglomerate mergers (between firms producing different products) affect the degree of diversification. Therefore each type of merger decision provides an example of a conduct variable that has a feedback effect on market or industry structure.

Performance

Important indicators of performance, the final component of the SCP trichotomy, include the following:

■ *Profitability*. The neoclassical theory assumes high or abnormal profits are the result of the abuse of market power by incumbent firms. On the other hand, it has also been argued by the **Chicago school** (see below) that abnormal profit may be the consequence of cost advantages or superior productive efficiency on the part of certain firms, that have consequently been able to achieve monopoly status by cutting price and driving rivals out of business. If this is the case, it is not obvious that market power and abnormal profit should be viewed as detrimental to consumer interests. Similarly, according to the Schumpeterian or Austrian views, abnormal profit is a reward for successful past innovation, or the exercise of superior foresight or awareness by an entrepreneur. To the extent that profitability influences firms' decisions to continue or exit from a market, this performance indicator has direct implications for future structure (the number and size distribution of sellers).

■ *Growth*. Profitability is a suitable performance indicator for a profit-maximizing firm, but may be less relevant for a firm that pursues other objectives, such as sales, growth or managerial utility. Growth of sales, assets or employment might represent a useful alternative performance indicator, by which the performance over any period of firms that were unequal in size at the start of the period can be compared.

■ *Quality of products and service* might be considered an important performance indicator by individual consumers or consumer groups, regulators or governments.

■ *Technological progress* is a consequence of the level of investment in research and development, and the pace of technological progress may be considered a relevant performance indicator. In the long run, technological progress produces perhaps the most fundamental type of feedback effect shown in Figure 1.1, due to its impact on the basic conditions of demand (consumer tastes and preferences change when new products are introduced) and supply (technology and cost structures change when new and more efficient production processes are developed).

■ *Productive and allocative efficiency*. Productive efficiency refers to the extent to which a firm achieves the maximum technologically feasible output from a given combination of inputs, and whether it chooses the most cost effective combination of inputs to produce a given level of output. Allocative efficiency refers to whether social welfare is maximized at the **market equilibrium**. Productive and allocative efficiency are both regarded by economists as important performance indicators.

The role of government policy

As Figure 1.1 suggests, government policy can operate on structure, conduct and performance variables. According to the SCP paradigm, if an industry comprises only a few large firms, the abuse of market power is likely to lead to the level of output being restricted, and prices being raised. This stifling of competition is likely have damaging implications for consumer welfare. This suggests there is a role for government or regulatory intervention to promote competition and prevent abuses of market power.

■ Competition might be promoted by preventing a horizontal merger involving two large firms from taking place, or by requiring the break-up of a large incumbent producer into two or more smaller firms. Such measures operate directly on market or industry structure.

■ Intervention might instead be targeted directly at influencing conduct. A regulator might impose price controls, preventing a firm with market power from setting a profit-maximizing monopoly price. Legal restrictions on permissible forms of collusion might be strengthened, or punishments for unlawful collusion might be increased.

■ Finally, a wide range of government policy measures (fiscal policy, employment policy, environmental policy, macroeconomic policy and so on) may have implications for firms' performance, measured using indicators such as profitability, growth, productive or allocative efficiency.

Box 1.1 provides a brief account of some of the important contributors to the development of industrial organization. Case Study 1.1 provides an application of the structure–conduct–performance paradigm to the European banking industry.

Box 1.1

Contributors to the development of industrial organization

This box gives a brief account of 15 key contributors to the development and shape of industrial organization, in chronological order. Their writings cover a wide range of topics in economics, and it is impossible to distil all of their ideas into a few sentences. This box focuses their key contributions to industrial organization. In several cases, these contributions drew on the ideas of other, lesser-known past or contemporary economists.

Adam Smith (1723–90)

Adam Smith is widely regarded as the father of modern economics. Many of his key ideas are found in his book *The Wealth of Nations* (1776). Smith believed that through the exercise of self-interest and competition, the market would produce just the right amount of goods to satisfy both consumers and producers. They would be led, as if by an 'invisible hand', to maximize the welfare of both. Smith lived at a time when new inventions, such as the flying shuttle and the spinning jenny, were revolutionising manufacturing; and he believed that economic growth could be achieved through mechanization and the division of labour. The division of labour is illustrated by means of a description of Smith's visit to a Nottinghamshire pin factory. Ten workers, by dividing the tasks of manufacturing a pin, could produce 2,000 times as many pins as one worker performing all of the tasks. Smith also advocated control over monopolies and restrictive practices, which he viewed as unconducive to good management and free trade, and likely to lead to a misallocation of resources.

Augustin Cournot (1801–77)

Cournot was a French mathematician, who applied his skills to economic ideas and wrote a major contribution to economics, *Recherches sur les principes mathématiques de la théorie des richesses* (1838) (known as *The Researches*). He was the first economist to develop the concept of the downward-sloping demand curve which, when combined with supply, determines a market equilibrium. He was also instrumental in identifying variable and fixed costs, and in defining marginal cost, marginal revenue and profit maximization. Although he contributed much to the formulation of the theories of perfect competition and monopoly, he is best known for the development of the duopoly model, a precursor to future developments in oligopoly theory. Cournot argued that the output decision of one firm affects the market price, which then leads to the rival reacting with its own output decision. This reaction, in turn, causes a further adjustment to the output decision of the first firm, and so on. An equilibrium is achieved when neither firm can improve its profit through further output adjustments.

Alfred Marshall (1842–1924)

Marshall was highly instrumental in establishing economics as an academic discipline. Prior to 1903, when Marshall established a degree in economic science at Cambridge, economics had been taught in conjunction with moral philosophy and history. Marshall's *Principles of Economics* (1890) established many of the methods and concepts still in use today. Although not the first to do so, Marshall identified the laws of demand and supply, linking them in the now familiar Marshallian Cross diagram. He also developed concepts such as price elasticity of demand (noting the important effect of substitute goods), consumer surplus and quasi-rents. In *Industry and Trade* (1870) he recognized the power of monopolies, moderated by competition and the contribution of enthusiastic new managers. However, Marshall did not provide a formal analysis of perfect competition, other than as a driver for the equality of price with unit cost of production. Although a good mathematician, having studied maths at Cambridge, he relegated most of his mathematical analysis to appendices in order to make his books accessible to business managers and informed laypersons.

Joseph Schumpeter (1883–1950)

Schumpeter is famous for two contributions to economics on macroeconomic cycles, and the role of innovation in capitalist economies. In his early years he developed the theory that the level of innovation, so important to the growth of an economy, is determined from within the firm by risk-taking entrepreneurs. Since consumers are naturally conservative, their preferences do not lead directly to the supply of new goods and services; instead, the firm attempts to shape and alter consumer tastes so as to create demand for new products. These ideas were further refined in his book *Capitalism, Socialism and Democracy* (1942), in which he argued that the process of 'creative destruction' provides a powerful dynamic underpinning the growth and development of capitalism. Firms and the economy grow and prosper not only because of successful innovation, but also because weak, inefficient firms are rooted out and destroyed by their innovative competitors. Schumpeter recognized that as successful firms grow, they become increasingly reliant on a professional class of technocratic managers charged with running what are increasingly complex and bureaucratic organizations. Professional managers tend to be risk-averse, and not imbued with the entrepreneurial spirit. Pessimistically, Schumpeter believed accordingly that the dynamic of innovation and the development of the capitalist economy are destined to stagnate in the long term.

Edward Chamberlin (1899–1967)

Chamberlin taught economics at Harvard (1937–67) and was responsible for important contributions to microeconomics, especially areas of competition theory and consumer choice. In explaining how a producer in a competitive market can set a price higher than perfect competition will allow, he first introduced the term 'product differentiation'. His PhD thesis, *The Theory of Monopolistic Competition*, was later revised and published in 1933. Prior to this, mainstream economists had focused on the polar cases of perfect competition and monopoly, ignoring market structures occupying the large middle ground. Chamberlin argued that few markets are truly competitive. He identified two intermediate market structures. The first was the small group case, where firms choose between myopic competition and the ability to achieve joint profit maximization. The second was the large group case, where firms strive to alter consumers' perceptions by differentiating their products from each other, allowing the opportunity to charge a higher price or increase market share. Chamberlin's analysis was influential in the development of the structure–conduct–performance paradigm in industrial organization.

Joan Robinson (1903–83)

Robinson was a Cambridge economist who helped to shape some of Keynes' ideas in the *General Theory*. Her principal contribution to industrial organization, *The Economics of Imperfect Competition*, was published in 1933, almost simultaneously with Chamberlin's *The Theory of Monopolistic Competition*. Using the concept of marginal revenue Robinson argued that in imperfect competition, firms faced downward-sloping marginal revenue functions. If they reduce their prices, they may eventually face a fall in total revenue if marginal revenue is zero or negative. The only logical response would then be to reduce production. In industries characterized by imperfect competition, there may be an underutilization of resources, notably labour. A new theory of price determination was required for imperfect markets. Unlike perfect competition, oligopolies are able to set mark-up prices above their variable costs. The less intense the competition and the greater the demand for internal funding for growth, the greater the mark-up. Robinson argued that the concept of equilibrium, as suggested by supply and demand analysis, is unsuitable for explaining the dynamics of imperfect markets.

John Von Neumann (1903–57)

Von Neumann, a Hungarian–American mathematician, was involved in several fields of study, including quantum mechanics, computers, geometry and statistics. In economics he is primarily identified with the development of game theory. After studying Walrasian supply and demand equations based on an interplay of calculus and classical mechanics, von Neumann argued that this analysis failed to address the issue of interdependence between agents: each agent's decisions have implications for other agents. Game theory addresses this shortcoming in economic theory. In the context of industrial organization, game theory is the study of the choices faced by firms in the pursuit of their optimal outcomes. In 1944, with the help of his colleague Oskar Morgenstern, von Neumann developed a formal analysis based on two players, decision sets and payoff matrices, enabling each player to calculate his best course of action or strategy. Von Neumann extended the analysis to games involving more than two players, with relevance for the theory of oligopoly.

Ronald Coase (1910–)

The British economist Coase, resident in the US for 60 years, made a key contribution to the field of industrial organization in a seminal article, 'The nature of the firm' (1937), while still studying as an undergraduate at London University. The article explains why organizations known as firms are formed in order to coordinate resource allocation decisions, instead of individuals relying on market transactions coordinated via the price mechanism. Coase argued that when the transactions executed using market mechanisms prove costly, producers seek to reduce these costs by allocating resources internally by 'diktat', rather than by relying on the price mechanism. Firms exist, therefore, in order to internalize market transactions. Examples of transaction costs that arise when using markets to allocate resources include search and information costs, bargaining costs that become onerous owing to contractual complexity, and the costs of monitoring compliance with the terms of market transactions. Coase's article was the forerunner of a new branch of industrial organization and management strategy known as transaction cost economics. Coase's other major contribution to economics was in the field of social costs resulting from externalities. Coase's seminal article, 'The problem of social cost' (1960) described externalities as arising from the costs of transacting over rights to undertake actions that affect others. High transaction costs inhibit the internalization of social costs, and so increase the impact of externalities.

George Stigler (1911–91)

Based at the University of Chicago, Stigler's main contribution to Industrial Organization was in the areas of the economics of information and oligopoly theory. He also contributed much to the analysis of barriers to entry, economies of scale, antitrust issues and the measurement of industrial concentration. The economics of information focuses on price dispersion found in many markets, though it could be applied to almost any other variable present in a market transaction. Economic theory suggests that over time price discrepancies should iron themselves out and if they do not, the fault lies with market imperfections. Stigler pointed out that market information is costly to collect and disseminate. Buyers may consider that seeking the lowest price is not worth their time and effort. Another important contribution, in the area of oligopoly theory, was also concerned with the dissemination of price information. Firms' sales are not only affected by their rivals' price changes but also by changes in the market. The time it takes for a firm to unravel these effects and respond has important implications for the functioning of markets. Stigler is known for developing the theory of regulatory capture, which describes the tendency for producers and other interest groups to attempt to gain control over regulatory arrangements, so as to reshape them in their own interests.

Joseph Bain (1912–91)

Bain was a Harvard economist, and a key figure in the development of Industrial Organization as an important sub-field within economics. The American Economic Association described him as the 'father of modern Industrial Organization'. His major contribution was the development, with Edwin Mason (his PhD supervisor), of the structure, conduct and performance (SCP) paradigm, which argues that industry structure indicators such as the level of concentration, the degree of product differentiation and entry conditions are key determinants of firm or industry performance indicators such as profitability, efficiency and technological change. Bain introduced new concepts, such as the classification of entry barriers, potential competition and limit pricing. He regarded product differentiation, notably advertising, as the most potent of entry barriers, enabling firms to develop market power and maintain high prices. He also contributed much to the development of empirical research methodologies for testing hypotheses derived from the SCP paradigm. An important innovation was the examination of cross-country variation in structure and performance indicators for the same industry, used as a means of verifying SCP relationships.

Herbert Simon (1916–2001)

Simon is best known in economics for his research into decision-making in the modern organization, and the introduction of the term 'bounded rationality'. In his 1947 book, *Administrative Behavior*, he argued that economic optimization was an impossible goal. If managers were to make rational decisions they had to identify all possible alternatives, determine their consequences and calculate the impact of such consequences. He suggested an alternative approach, known as 'satisficing', whereby managers search for actions that achieve reasonable rather than optimum payoffs. These fresh insights into organizations were influential in the development of the behavioural theory of the firm. Simon later suggested that both economics and psychology could contribute to understanding decision-making in an organization. Simon's scientific interests extended to several other fields, including cognitive psychology, computer science and artificial intelligence.

William Baumol (1922–)

Baumol, a Princeton economist, has written widely on many topics. His articles and books cover areas as diverse as the transactions demand for money, the labour market, the service industries and the history of economic thought. His contribution to industrial organization is focused on the theory of the firm, contestable markets, regulation and various industry studies. An early contribution to the theory of the firm was the sales revenue maximization hypothesis, based on his observation and experience as a consultant to many US corporations. Baumol argues that because of the divorce of ownership from control, managers in control of large corporations are attracted to the maximization of total revenue, which determines their remuneration and status. This objective is subject to a minimum profit constraint sufficient to placate shareholders. The theory of contestable markets, which Baumol developed with his colleagues John Panzar and Robert Willig, is based on the idea that firms operating in highly concentrated market structures may nevertheless behave competitively if the industry is characterized by low entry and exit barriers. Incumbents are, in effect, constrained from exercising their market power by the presence of potential, rather than actual competitors.

John Nash (1928–)

Nash completed a PhD in mathematics at Princeton in 1950. This work contained his major contribution to economics in the field of game theory: the derivation of an equilibrium solution for non-cooperative games. In a Nash equilibrium, taking the other players' current actions as given, no player can improve his own payoff by changing his own actions. He demonstrated that a Nash equilibrium exists for a broad class of games, provided players are allowed to adopt mixed strategies whereby they choose randomly from several actions, with a specific probability assigned to each action. The Nash equilibrium bears close affinities to the solution to the duopoly model that was proposed by Cournot more than a century before. One of the best known examples of a Nash equilibrium is the prisoner's dilemma, where two players recognize the strategies that will lead to an optimal outcome for both and yet, rationally, select strategies leading to a sub-optimal outcome. Another key contribution to economics was Nash's discussion of the bargaining problem, concerning the utility-maximizing division of the gains from a bargain between two parties. Nash's contributions as a mathematician and game theorist also found important applications in fields as diverse as computing, evolutionary biology, politics and military strategy.

Harold Demsetz (1930–)

Another member of the Chicago school, Demsetz has contributed much to the theory of the firm, the theory of property rights and antitrust policy. In developing some of the ideas introduced by Coase, Demsetz argued that the act of assigning and enforcing a property right bears a cost. Property rights will be assigned if the gains outweigh the costs. For example, the Montagne Indians of Quebec established property rights over beavers when the fur trade became profitable during the eighteenth century, internalizing the externality created by hunting. The hunting of grazing animals with little commercial value continued without the creation of property rights, however, because the limited gains from internalization would have been outweighed by the high costs of tracking the animals. The existence of clearly defined and marketable property rights, whether imposed by government or through 'promises' made by individuals, leads to efficient markets. Another important contribution was Demsetz's extension of transaction cost analysis. Demsetz extended the scope of transaction costs economics by examining market frictions that can occur independently of organizational structure.

Oliver Williamson (1932–)

Williamson's major contribution is the development of transaction cost economics (TCE), which he first outlined in 1975. This approach has had a great influence not only in economics, but also in organization theory and contract law. Williamson was concerned with the problem of market failure in markets that had, traditionally, been assumed always to adjust towards equilibrium. This analysis led him to investigate many topics in economics, including market structure, monopoly, vertical integration and public utility regulation. TCE was constructed on the triad of opportunism, bounded rationality and asset specificity. Opportunism refers to what happens when certain players in a market, motivated by self-interest, are dishonest and willing to exploit other players. Bounded rationality refers to decision-makers having only limited information regarding the environment in which they operate, most likely concerning the activities closest to their own sphere of operations. This situation gives rise to uncertainty and the possibility of taking incorrect decisions that may prove costly. Asset specificity refers to the value of a productive asset being greater in a certain application than in others. This tends to bind the seller and the buyer of the asset together, giving either or both the chance to engage in opportunitsic behaviour. A solution might be to pursue a strategy of vertical integration, so that the integrated firm economizes on the transaction costs that otherwise arise when the seller and buyer are separate entities.

Structure, conduct and performance in European banking

The banking system is of central strategic importance for economic growth, capital allocation, financial stability, and the competitiveness and development of the manufacturing and service sectors. In Europe in 2006, bank assets were valued at the equivalent of 350 per cent of Europe-wide GDP (Molyneux and Wilson, 2007).

The nature of competition in European banking has changed significantly since 1990. Following deregulation (via the Second Banking Directive), the creation of the EU single market in financial services, and the launch of the euro, barriers to trade in financial services have been significantly reduced. Banks are able to trade not only in their own countries but also elsewhere throughout Europe. Banks have increased the range of products and services they offer to customers, leading to the distinction between banks, building societies, insurance companies and other financial institutions becoming blurred. The arrival of foreign-owned banks in many European banking markets has caused competition to intensify. Furthermore, a wide range of non-bank institutions, including supermarkets and telecommunications firms, now offer financial products and services as well. This has placed additional pressure on established banks to lower costs, limit their risk exposures, improve their management and governance structures, and find new ways of generating revenues from new forms of banking business (Goddard *et al.*, 2007, 2010).

Structure

During the period 1990–2009, there was a decline in the number of banks trading in most European countries. This trend is similar for mutual savings banks, cooperative banks and commercial banks. Table 1 shows data on the total number of banks (domestic and foreign-owned) trading in selected European countries in various years. In most (but not in all) countries, there has been a pronounced decline in bank numbers. Over the same period, branch numbers have also declined, as banks have sought to rationalize their branch networks.

This is part of an overall trend towards consolidation in financial services, which has been accompanied by an increase in seller concentration. In 2009, seller concentration measured by the five-firm concentration ratio (the share of the five largest banks in the total assets of the banking industry) exceeded 60 per cent in Belgium, Denmark, Greece, the Netherlands, Portugal, Finland and Sweden. Concentration has also increased, but has remained at lower levels, in Italy, Germany and the UK.

However, the number of foreign-owned banks trading in every country included in Table 1 increased over the period 1990–2009, leading to an intensification of competition. There are several ways in which a bank might operate across national borders within an integrated European banking market. The bank might establish either a branch or a

Table 1 Number of banks by country (selected countries, 1990–2009)

Country	1990	1995	1998	2002	2006	2009
Austria	1,210	1,041	898	823	809	790
Belgium	157	145	123	111	105	104
Denmark	124	122	212	178	191	164
Finland	529	381	348	369	361	349
France	2,027	1,469	1,226	989	829	712
Germany	4,720	3,785	3,238	2,363	2,050	1,948
Italy	1,156	970	934	821	807	801
Luxembourg	177	220	212	184	154	147
Netherlands	111	102	634	539	345	295
Portugal	260	233	227	202	178	166
Spain	696	506	402	359	352	352
Sweden	704	249	148	216	204	180
UK	624	564	521	451	401	389
EU total	12,582	9,896	9,260	7,751	6,926	6,397

Source: Central Bank reports, European Central Bank (various).

subsidiary in another European state; or it might provide banking services directly (without establishment) across national borders. The bank might enter into a strategic partnership with an institution in another state; or it might locate different functions in different states. Recent years have seen the emergence of several large cross-border institutions within the EU: in 2009, the 14 largest cross-border banking groups accounted for almost one-third of total EU bank assets.

Conduct

In response to competitive pressure (brought about by the entry of foreign banks and new financial services providers), many banks have consolidated by means of merger and acquisition. This strategy has enabled some banks to achieve the large size (or critical mass) required to operate effectively throughout the European single market. Recent mergers between large banks from different EU member states suggest an increased propensity for large cross-border mergers. Examples of significant cross-border mergers include Unicredito (Italy) and HVB (Germany); Credit Agricole (France) and Emporiki (Greece); BNP Paribas (France) and Banco Nazionale de Lavaro (Italy); and Banco Santander (Spain) and Alliance and Leicester (UK). This suggests that barriers to cross-border mergers arising from difficulties in selling generic products across borders, differences in competition, employment, regulatory and supervisory policy across countries, political interference, and a lack of consumer trust in foreign banks are diminishing. Major cross-border banking groups have adapted their organizational structures, risk management and strategic planning functions to deal with pan-European activity in a range of areas, including traditional commercial banking as well as treasury and trading activities.

Many banks have also implemented strategies of product diversification and financial innovation. Examples include online share dealing, letters of credit, pensions and insurance, and a wide range of investment services. For European banks, revenue from non-interest-bearing business as a proportion of the total revenue increased from 28 per cent in 1992 to over 50 per cent in 2009.

Performance

Table 2 shows that the average profitability (measured by return on equity) of banks in most European countries improved between 1990 and 2006, but declined sharply during the financial crisis of 2007–9 (see below). Given that competition has become more intense, it seems likely that increased profitability is a consequence of revenues having been generated from a wider variety of sources (diversification), and of the more efficient use of technology (such as consumer databases and call centres). This means that banks are able to offer a wider variety of products at lower cost than was previously the case. Some of the increase in profitability was driven by aggressive cost-cutting strategies, including branch closures and reductions in staffing. Overall competition between banks, and between banks and other financial service providers, has become more intense. Deregulation and technological progress have lowered entry barriers, making banking more highly competitive. At the same time, as a consequence of continued consolidation the proportion of industry assets held by the largest banks has increased.

Bank competition and the global financial crisis

The failure in 2007 of Northern Rock, a UK retail bank, preceded a serious financial crisis that afflicted the banking industry worldwide, but most notably in the US and

Table 2 Return on equity, 1990–2009 (various European countries, %)

Country	1990	1995	1998	2001	2006	2009
Austria	8.63	8.15	9.48	11.29	16.31	1.63
Belgium	8.29	12.89	14.76	15.31	19.36	6.89
Denmark	3.34	18.5	14.6	16.53	16.84	−6.90
Finland	5.61	7.93	9.86	17.21	10.92	7.92
France	10.15	3.63	9.93	11.76	14.77	8.36
Germany	11.93	12.57	17.38	5.12	11.02	3.57
Italy	16.4	5.91	13.17	14.01	10.5	3.47
Luxembourg	6.17	19.95	24.67	18.5	19.22	8.24
Netherlands	12.3	15.81	14.3	15.23	16.96	9.41
Portugal	12.54	7.65	7.56	6.31	13.4	4.57
Spain	13.58	9.17	11.07	9.26	15.22	1.74
Sweden	3.65	22.08	17.33	19.48	15.7	9.98
UK	14.45	28.59	28.31	20.05	16.1	4.37

Source: Various Central Bank reports, Bankscope.

many western Europen countries. Many banks, both large and small, incurred heavy losses and defaults on their loans portfolios, resulting in numerous bank failures and rescues through the intervention of central banks and governments. Initial responses to the financial crisis of 2007–9 included: government purchase of distressed assets (loans made by banks that are unlikely to be repaid, or loans on which the borrower has already defaulted); changes to the rules concerning the types of asset accepted as collateral; nationalization or part-nationalization of financial institutions considered too-big-to-fail; and government guarantees of consumer deposits and bank liabilities. Factors widely cited as having contributed to the financial crisis include: global imbalances in trade and capital flows; excessively expansionary monetary policy; misalignment of the incentives facing investors, banks and credit-rating agencies; inadequate financial disclosure and the adoption of inappropriate accounting rules; lax lending standards; loopholes in regulation and supervision; and individual fraud.

Signs of recovery in the banking industry have been apparent since 2009. The wider economic recovery has stalled, however, owing to the onset of a sovereign debt crisis that has afflicted several European countries (most notably Greece, Ireland, Italy, Portugal and Spain) and remains unresolved at the time of writing in 2012. In some cases, earlier steps to bail out distressed banks during the financial crisis have merely fuelled the sovereign debt crisis, by transferring distressed assets from bank balance sheets into public ownership. In an effort to reconfigure their balance sheets, banks in Europe and many other jurisdictions have adopted conservative lending policies, so as to reduce the size of their loans portfolios and strengthen their capitalization and liquidity. Small and medium-sized enterprises have been hard hit by the reluctance of banks to lend. Economic recovery has been further stymied as governments have sought to reduce their own budget deficits through swingeing cuts in public-sector spending. Speculation that the sovereign debt crisis might precipitate the break-up of the European single currency, the euro, was commonplace during the latter months of 2011 and throughout 2012. The possibility of future default by governments on their borrowings raises fresh concerns over the solvency of banks that are among the principal investors in euro-denominated sovereign bonds.

European governments initially responded to the 2007–9 financial crisis by implementing policies aimed at improving disclosure and transparency, and reducing the potential for deliberately reckless lending on the part of large banks in anticipation of a government bailout in the event of the bank becoming financially distressed. Specific actions include: extension of the scope of bank regulation based on economic substance rather than legal form; requirements for banks to hold more capital, serving as a buffer capable of absorbing future losses on their loans portfolios; requirements for banks to strengthen their capitalization (ratio of capital to total loans or total assets) during economic upturns, rather than succumb to the natural tendency for bank capitalization to be depleted through increased lending when economic growth is strong; enhanced regulation and supervision of bank liquidity; enhanced supervision of credit-rating agencies; introduction of more prescriptive codes of conduct for executive remuneration and benefits; improved arrangements for regulation of the activities of cross-border banks; reform of accounting rules concerning financial disclosure; and the establishment or strengthening of consumer protection agencies.

Large European banks are subject to new arrangements for macro- and micro-prudential supervision, including a new European Systemic Risk Board (ESRB) to monitor and assess systemic risks in the EU financial system. Some individual EU member states have taken further measures. In the UK, for example, an Independent Banking Commission was established to consider reforms to the banking industry to promote financial stability and competition. The Commission's final report, published in 2011, included the following recommendations:

■ Retail banking should be ring-fenced from wholesale and investment banking;

■ Different arms of the same bank should have separate legal entities, each with their own boards of directors;

■ Systemically important banks and large UK retail banks should maintain a minimum shareholder capital-to-assets ratio of 10 per cent.

In common with the Austrian school, the Chicago school argue vehemently against government intervention in markets in order to promote competition (Reder, 1982). The Chicago school is a group of prominent academic lawyers and economists, whose pro-market, pro-competition and anti-government views were perhaps at their most influential during the 1970s and 1980s. The Chicago school is identified with the argument that large firms are likely to have become large as a result of having operated efficiently, and therefore more profitably, than their smaller counterparts. Therefore, punishing the largest firms because they are also the most profitable firms is tantamount to punishing success. Even if certain abuses of market power do take place in the short run, these are likely to be self-correcting in the long run, when competition will tend to reassert itself. For example, there is little point in passing laws against collusive agreements, since such agreements are inherently unstable and are liable to break down in the fullness of time (Posner, 1979). Markets and industries have a natural tendency to revert towards competition under their own steam, without the need for any intervention or assistance from government.

The strident views of the Chicago school have not gone unchallenged. Blaug (2001), for example, accuses the Chicago school of promoting ideology rather than science.

> The Chicago school does not deny that there is a case for antitrust law but they doubt that it is a strong case because most markets, even in the presence of high concentration ratios, are 'contestable'. How do we know? We know because of the good-approximation assumption: the economy is never far away from its perfectly competitive equilibrium growth path! Believe it or not, that is all there is to the 'antitrust revolution' of the Chicago school.

(Blaug, 2001, p. 47)

Beyond structure–conduct–performance

Although the SCP paradigm was highly influential in the early development of industrial organization as a sub-discipline within economics, SCP has been subject to fierce criticism from a number of different directions. Below, we provide a checklist of criticisms of the SCP paradigm. Many of these points recur, and will be examined in greater depth, in later chapters of this book.

■ The SCP paradigm draws heavily on microeconomic theory and the neoclassical theory of the firm. However, the theory does not always specify precise relationships between structure, conduct and performance variables. For example, oligopoly theory is largely indeterminate, and sometimes fails to produce clear and unambiguous conclusions.

■ It is often difficult to decide which variables belong to structure, which to conduct and which to performance. For example, product differentiation, vertical integration and diversification are structure variables, but they are also strategies that firms can consciously choose to adopt, and can therefore also be interpreted as conduct variables.

■ What exactly do we mean by performance? Performance is some measure of the degree of success in achieving desired goals. Is it possible to have a set of uniform performance indicators? Differences between the objectives of different firms may render SCP relationships tenuous. For example, if firms are sacrificing potential profits in order to reduce risk by making more secure investments, researchers should be more concerned with variability in profitability than with the profit rate as such (Schwartzman, 1963).

■ As indicated above, the definition of market or industry structure has a number of dimensions. However, many empirical studies based on the SCP paradigm measure structure solely by seller concentration. This is mainly because concentration is easier to measure than other dimensions of structure, such as entry barriers and product differentiation. Consequently, there is a danger of overemphasizing the role of concentration. More generally, many of the variables in all three categories of structure, conduct and performance are difficult to measure (Grabowski and Mueller, 1970). How do we quantify the degree of vertical integration in an industry? How do we quantify the extent of collusion, or how do we even know if collusion is taking place? How do we measure the pace of technological progress? How do we determine whether firms are achieving maximum productive efficiency?

> We have concentration measures for most manufacturing markets in many economies for instance, but little comprehensive information is available on more subtle aspects of market structure, and essentially no systematic data aside from accounting profit rates is available on conduct and performance. This leaves a factual vacuum in policy debates that is quickly filled by beliefs and assumptions.
>
> *(Schmalensee, 1990, p. 138)*

■ Empirical research based on the SCP paradigm often finds associations in the anticipated direction between structure, conduct and performance variables. However, such relationships are often quite weak in terms of their statistical significance. Much of the early SCP literature examines the relationship between industry structure and performance, taking conduct as given. For example, in industries with only a few large firms, collusion was simply assumed to take place.

■ The SCP paradigm has been criticized for overemphasizing static models of short-run equilibrium (Sawyer, 1985). No explanation is offered as to the evolution of the structure variables, and the influence of current conduct and performance on future structure. This criticism echoes the earlier discussion of feedback links within the SCP framework. At best the SCP paradigm is capable of providing only a snapshot picture of the industry and its constituent firms at one particular point in time.

■ Most early empirical research based on the SCP paradigm focused on the relationship between seller concentration and profitability. According to the **collusion hypothesis**, a positive association between concentration and profitability was interpreted as evidence of collusion or other abuses of market power designed to enhance profits. Later researchers emphasized the possibility that high profitability was achieved through the exploitation of economies of scale, or other cost savings achieved by the managers of large firms. According to the **efficiency hypothesis** (which is closely identified with the Chicago school, discussed above), a positive relationship between concentration and profitability reflects a natural tendency for efficient firms to be successful, and to become dominant in their industries. During the 1970s and 1980s, a large body of literature attempted to resolve the collusion-versus-efficiency debate using tests based on empirical data.

Several of these criticisms, especially the realization that a number of conduct and performance variables have feedback effects on structure, and that causality within SCP is a two-way and not just a one-way process, led eventually to a shift away from the presumption that structure is the most important determinant of the level of competition. Instead, some economists argued that the strategies (conduct) of individual firms were equally, if not more, important (Scherer and Ross, 1990). Theories that focus primarily on strategy and conduct are subsumed under the general heading of the **new industrial organization** (NIO) (Schmalensee, 1982). According to this approach, firms are not seen as passive entities, similar in every respect except size. Instead they are active decision-makers, capable of implementing a wide range of diverse strategies. Game theory, which deals with decision-making in situations of interdependence and uncertainty, is an important tool in the armoury of the NIO theorists. Theories have been developed to explore situations in which firms choose from a plethora of strategies, with the choices repeated over either finite or infinite time horizons. Some economists believe game theory has strengthened the theoretical underpinnings of industrial organization (Tirole, 1988). Others, however, are highly critical of the game theoretic approach. Schmalensee (1990), for example, complains that just about 'anything can happen!' when game theory is used to analyze competition:

Game theory has proven better at generating internally consistent scenarios than at providing plausible and testable restrictions on real behaviour . . . Until game-theoretic analysis begins to yield robust, unambiguous predictions or is replaced by a mode of theorizing that does so, any major substantive advances in industrial organization are likely to come from empirical research.

(Schmalensee, 1990, p. 141)

1.4 Strategic management: a short diversion

A number of tools developed in the industrial organization literature have contributed to the growth of the sub-discipline of strategic management. Highly influential in the early development of this literature is Porter (1979a, 1980, 1985, 1996), whose **five forces model** of the firm's competitive environment is heavily SCP-influenced. Porter's five forces are: the extent and intensity of competition; the threat of entrants (new competitors); the threat of substitute products and services; the power of buyers; and the power of suppliers. The five forces are illustrated schematically in Figure 1.2.

- *Extent and intensity of competition.* The intensity of competition depends on the number and size distribution of the industry's incumbent firms. If there are large numbers of similarly sized firms, competition is expected to be more intense than it is if one or a few firms are dominant. Other influences on the extent of competition include the rate of growth of industry sales; incumbent firms' cost structures; and the availability of spare capacity to meet potential increases in demand.

- *Threat of entrants.* Incumbent firms that are threatened by entry behave differently to those in industries that are sheltered from competition. The perceived

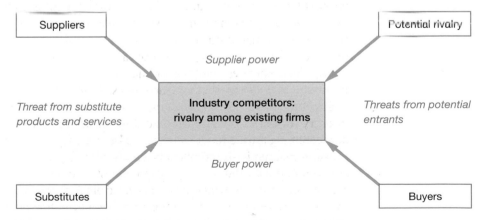

Figure 1.2 Porter's five forces model
Source: Adapted with the permission of Free Press, a Division of Simon & Schuster, Inc., from Competitive Strategy: Techniques for Analyzing Industries and Competitors by Michael E. Porter. Copyright © 1980, 1998 by The Free Press. All rights reserved.

threat of entry is likely to be higher in industries where incumbents are highly profitable, and incumbents may search for ways of raising entry barriers. Government regulation also plays a part in determining the ease of entry. The size of the entry threat depends on the importance of economies of scale, the extent of product differentiation and brand loyalty, the level and specificity of capital investments, and the availability of access to distribution outlets.

■ *Threat of substitute products and services.* The availability of substitute products and services naturally tends to increase the intensity of competition. The availability of substitutes increases the price elasticity of demand for existing products, reducing the market power of incumbent firms. Incumbents may respond by seeking to differentiate their products more strongly from those of rivals, through branding or advertising. The attractiveness of substitute products to consumers depends on the prices and quality of the competing products, and the size of any switching costs.

■ *Power of buyers.* The power of buyers of a firm's product depends on their number and size distribution, and their level of dependence on the firm's output. If there are only a few buyers, or if close substitutes are available, buyers are likely to wield significant market power. In order to secure their own supplies, large buyers may seek to integrate backwards (by taking over an input supplier), reducing their reliance on external suppliers.

■ *Power of suppliers.* If suppliers of important inputs into a firm's production process are large in size and small in number, these suppliers can exercise market power by raising price, reducing quality, or even threatening to withhold supplies.

Porter's five forces identify the sources of competition that may confront a firm at any point in time. The firm's strategies and conduct are conditioned by the presence and strength of the five forces. In common with the SCP paradigm, however, Porter's approach is essentially static, and perhaps tends to underemphasize the problem of uncertainty caused by change in the competitive environment.

In contrast to many economists, management strategists tend to emphasize the distinctive internal characteristics of firms, in order to explain how a competitive advantage can be acquired and sustained. In the strategic management literature, the focus is on maximizing firm value through the choice of effective management strategies, rather than minimizing or eliminating abnormal profit in pursuit of wider public policy goals (Spulber, 1992, 1994; Ghemawat, 2002). Competitive advantage is measured by the value a firm is able to create in excess of its costs. Porter (1980) introduces the concept of the **value chain**, which disaggregates the firm into its strategically relevant activities. Primary activities are those associated with the physical creation of the product or service. Support activities are those that support primary activities and each other: for example, activities associated with the purchase of inputs, the management of human resources or the improvement of technology through research and development. Once the firm's activities are disaggregated in this way, appraisal of their individual contributions can begin. Each support activity is linked to each primary activity to a greater or lesser extent. This approach examines how these links can be improved in order to increase margins on each of the firm's products.

Porter argues that a firm must select and follow a generic strategy in order to add value and gain a competitive advantage over rivals. Generic strategies include cost leadership, differentiation and focus. Under a cost leadership strategy, the firm attempts to keep its costs lower than those of competitors. The firm must be able to identify cost savings at some point in its value chain, or alternatively change the structure of the value chain; for example, by striking an exclusive deal with a supplier of an essential input. Under a differentiation strategy, the firm's product has some unique characteristic that appeals to its customers, leading to higher margins and profits. Finally, focus can apply to both cost leadership and differentiation. The firm focuses its efforts on a particular market segment. In the case of differentiation, for example, this may involve identifying a particular group of customers and gearing the firm's product towards its tastes or needs.

Kay (1993) argues that each individual firm is inherently different, and therefore dismisses the notion of generic strategies. Instead, firms develop **distinctive capabilities** in an attempt to achieve a competitive advantage. This shift of emphasis away from analyzing the characteristics of the firm's external environment, and towards examining each firm's unique attributes and strategies, mirrors the shift of emphasis away from structure and towards conduct that is implicit in much of the NIO (new industrial organization) literature. According to Kay, the main sources of distinctive capability include innovation, architecture and reputation.

- *Innovation.* Successful innovation provides a firm with advantages over its competitors. However, this advantage only lasts for the time before imitation takes place. Even patents lapse eventually, or are vulnerable to being superseded by further technological change. Advantages from innovation can only be maintained if the firm has other capabilities that make imitation of the technology on its own insufficient to erode the firm's competitive advantage.

- *Architecture.* Architecture refers to the firm's internal organization. For example, Liverpool Football Club's famous boot room, from which several coaches were promoted in succession to the position of team manager, ensured long periods of continuity and success throughout the 1970s and 1980s. If the market changes, however, such advantages can be rapidly eliminated (Kay, 1993, 2003). Arguably, Liverpool failed to adapt as successfully as rivals such as Arsenal and Manchester United to the internationalization of the footballers' labour market that took place during the 1990s.

- *Reputation.* If a firm has a reputation for providing good quality and service, this helps add value and generate sales. Once having been acquired, a positive reputation can be sustainable for long periods, making it difficult for entrants to compete on equal terms with a reputable incumbent.

According to the strategic management literature, the strategic choices and decisions taken by firms are the main determinants of performance. Firms can only maintain a competitive advantage if they can protect their strategies from imitation. The ease of imitation is influenced by institutional and economic factors. For example, restrictive employment contracts, which prevent individuals from using any firm-specific knowledge if they move to a rival firm, may help impede imitation. An organization's corporate culture may be important; for example, a firm that offers secure employment may obtain a greater level of commitment from its workforce than one that relies heavily on temporary workers. Some aspects of corporate culture can be difficult for rivals to imitate. Economic factors affecting the speed of imitation include profitability and risk. Rapid imitation is more likely if the expected profitability from imitation is high, and if the risk is perceived to be low.

The strategic management literature provides many important insights into how firms can obtain and sustain competitive advantages over rivals. Some of these insights have been neglected in much of the industrial organization literature, especially in empirical studies. This is partly due to difficulties in quantifying key variables from the strategic management literature. The strategic management approach has been criticized for placing insufficient emphasis on the interactions between firms at the level of the market or industry. Instead, the focus is mainly on the strategic options available to the individual firm. In this sense, many of the insights derived from strategic management are complementary to those of the more traditional market-oriented microeconomic theory of the firm. This complementarity is reflected at a number of points throughout the course of this book.

Discussion questions

1. Why is the structure–conduct–performance paradigm so widely used to study the conduct and performance of firms and industries?

2. List the factors that describe market structure. Give examples of ways in which market structure affects conduct.

3. Explain the logic of forward and reverse causation between structure, conduct and performance.

4. What are the limitations of the structure–conduct–performance paradigm?

5. How does the Chicago school view of competition differ from the structure–conduct–performance paradigm?

6. Compare the explanations for differences in firm profitability that are suggested by the collusion and efficiency hypotheses.

7. Compare the neoclassical conception of competition with the views advanced by Schumpeter and the Austrian school.

8. In what ways does the new industrial organization contribute to our understanding of firm behaviour?

9. In what ways does the strategic management literature contribute to our understanding of the decision-making and performance of firms?

10. Outline Porter's five forces model of the firm's competitive environment.

11. What are distinctive capabilities and why are they important?

12. With reference to Case Study 1.1, assess the extent to which competition has increased in European banking in recent years. What effect has this had on the performance of banks? To what extent did excessive competition in the banking industry cause the global financial crisis of the late 2000s?

Further reading

Bresnahan, T.F. and Schmalensee, R.C. (1987) The empirical renaissance in industrial economics: an overview, *Journal of Industrial Economics*, 35, 371–8.

Caves, R.E. (2007) In praise of the old IO, *International Journal of Industrial Organization*, 25, 1–12.

Einav, L. and Levin, J. (2010) Empirical Industrial Organization: a progress report, *Journal of Economic Perspectives*, 24, 145–62.

Ghemawat, P. (2002) Competition and business strategy in historical perspective, *Business Strategy Review*, 76, 37–74.

Kirzner, I. (1997) Entrepreneurial discovery and the competitive market process: an Austrian approach, *Journal of Economic Literature*, 35, 60–85.

Neven, D.J. (1989) Strategic entry deterrence: recent developments in the economics of industry, *Journal of Economic Surveys*, 3, 213–33.

Pakes, A. (2003) Common sense and simplicity in empirical industrial organization, *Review of Industrial Organization*, 23, 193–213.

Porter, M.E. (1979) How competitive forces shape strategy, *Harvard Business Review*, July–August, 1–10.

Posner, R. (1979) The Chicago school of anti-trust analysis, *University of Pennsylvania Law Review*, 127, 925–48.

Reder, M.W. (1982) Chicago economics: permanence and change, *Journal of Economic Literature*, 20, 1–38.

Roberts, P. and Eisenhardt, K. (2003) Austrian insights on strategic organization: from market insights to implications for firms, *Strategic Organization*, 1, 345–52.

Schmalensee, R.C. (1982) Antitrust and the new industrial economics, *American Economic Review*, Papers and Proceedings, 72, 24–8.

Schmalensee, R.C. (1988) Industrial economics: an overview, *Economic Journal*, 98, 643–81.

Schmalensee, R.C. (1990) Empirical studies of rivalrous behaviour, in Bonanno, G. and Brandolini, D. (eds) *Industrial Structure in the New Industrial Economics*. Oxford: Clarendon Press.

Spulber, D.F. (1992) Economic analysis and management strategy, a survey, *Journal of Economics and Management Strategy*, 1, 535–74.

Spulber, D.F. (1994) Economic analysis and management strategy, a survey continued, *Journal of Economics and Management Strategy*, 3, 355–406.

Young, G., Smith, K.G. and Grimm, C.M. (1996) Austrian and industrial organization perspectives on firm-level activity and performance, *Organization Science*, 7, 243–54.

Production, costs, demand and profit maximization

Learning objectives

This chapter covers the following topics:

- the Law of Diminishing Returns
- short-run and long-run production functions
- the relationship between production and costs
- returns to scale and the minimum efficient scale
- demand, revenue and elasticity
- profit maximization

Key terms

Abnormal profit	Economies of scope	Opportunity cost
Advertising elasticity of demand	Elasticity	Pecuniary economies of scale
	Fixed cost	Price elasticity of demand
Average cost	Increasing returns to scale	Price elasticity of supply
Average fixed cost	Isocost	Production function
Average product of labour	Isoquant	Profit maximization
Average revenue	Law of Diminishing Returns	Real economies of scale
Average variable cost	Long run	Returns to scale
Complements	Marginal cost	Short run
Constant returns to scale	Marginal product of labour	Substitutes
Cross-price elasticity of demand	Marginal revenue	Total cost
Decreasing returns to scale	Market demand function	Total revenue
Diseconomies of scale	Minimum efficient scale	Variable cost
Economies of scale	Normal profit	

2.1 Introduction

This chapter reviews the core elements of production and cost theory and demand theory. The chapter begins in Section 2.2 with a review of production and cost theory. A key distinction is drawn between the **short run** (when some inputs are variable and others are fixed) and the **long run** (when all inputs are variable). The short-run relationship between inputs, output and production costs is governed by the **Law of Diminishing Returns**, and the long-run relationship is governed by **economies of scale** or **diseconomies of scale**.

Section 2.3 reviews the essentials of demand theory, including **price elasticity of demand**, a standard measure of the responsiveness of quantity demanded to a change in price. Other **elasticity** measures, including cross-price elasticity of demand, advertising elasticity of demand and price elasticity of supply, are defined. Finally, a very general rule for profit maximization is developed. The profit-maximizing firm should produce the output level at which its marginal revenue *equals* its marginal cost.

2.2 Production and costs

Microeconomic theory assumes firms combine factor inputs through an efficient method of production in order to produce output. Economists distinguish between factors of production that the firm can vary in the short run, and factors of production that cannot be varied in the short run but can vary in the long run. For example, by offering overtime to its current workforce or by hiring more workers, a firm might easily increase the amount of labour it employs in the short run; similarly, by reducing overtime or by laying workers off, a firm might easily reduce the amount of labour it employs. However, it is not possible for the firm to change the amount of capital it employs at short notice. New factories or offices take time to construct. New capital equipment has to be ordered in advance, and orders take time to be completed. Accordingly, for a firm that employs two factors of production, labour and capital, it is usual to assume labour is variable in the short run, and capital is fixed in the short run but variable in the long run.

A general expression for the long run **production function** of a firm that uses a labour input and a capital input is as follows:

$$q = f(L, K)$$

where L = units of labour employed, K = units of capital employed and q = units of output produced.

In the short run, labour is variable and capital fixed. Accordingly, the expression for the firm's short-run production function, obtained by rewriting the long-run production function, is as follows:

$$q = g(L)$$

For example, if the long-run production function is $q = f(L, K)$, but in the short run K is fixed at $K = 100$, the short-run production function is $q = f(L, 100)$. By incorporating '$K = 100$' into the structure of a newly defined function, the short-run production function can be rewritten $q = g(L)$.

Short-run production and costs

Production theory

The short-run relationship between the quantity of labour employed and the quantity of output produced is governed by the Law of Diminishing Returns, sometimes alternatively known as the Law of Diminishing Marginal Product. As increasing quantities of labour are used in conjuction with a fixed quantity of capital, eventually the additional contribution that each successive unit of labour makes to total output starts to decline. The Law of Diminishing Returns is illustrated in Columns 1 to 4 of Table 2.1. According to Column 1, the firm can employ between $L = 1$ and $L = 11$ workers per week. Column 2 shows the total weekly output in each case. Column 3 shows the **marginal product of labour** (MPL). MPL is the quantity of additional output the firm obtains by employing each additional worker. If one worker is employed, $L = 1$ and $q = 7$. But if two workers are employed, $L = 2$ and $q = 26$. Effectively, the first worker contributes MPL = 7 units of output, but the second worker contributes MPL = 26 − 7 = 19 units. Similarly, if three workers are employed, $L = 3$ and $q = 54$, so effectively the third worker contributes MPL = 54 − 26 = 28 units. One worker can produce relatively little by themselves because the factory is severely understaffed. However, two workers combined are more effective than one in isolation, and three are more effective than two. This is reflected in Column 4, which shows the **average product of labour** (APL). APL is the ratio of total output to quantity of labour employed. As L increases from 1 to 2 to 3, APL increases from 7 to 13 to 18.

However, as more and more workers are employed, the point is eventually reached when each additional worker's contribution to total output starts to fall. Once the full contingent of workers that the factory can comfortably accommodate and occupy has been hired, employing even *more* workers will not result in very much more output being produced. If the factory becomes overstaffed, either some of the workforce will be idle for most of the time, or most of the workforce will be idle for some of the time. In Table 2.1, diminishing returns begin to set in after $L = 6$ workers are employed. The sixth worker contributes MPL = 37 units of output, but MPL = 34 for $L = 7$, and MPL = 28 for $L = 8$. Eventually average productivity, measured by APL, also starts to fall. Average productivity reaches its peak of APL = 28 for $L = 7$ or $L = 8$, but APL = 27 for $L = 9$ and APL = 25 for $L = 10$. Eventually, the point is reached where the factory becomes so overcrowded that output starts to fall if more workers are taken on. If a tenth worker is employed, total output increases from $q = 243$ to $q = 250$, so MPL (= 7) is small but still positive. But if an eleventh worker is employed, total output falls from $q = 250$ to $q = 242$, so MPL (= −8) becomes negative.

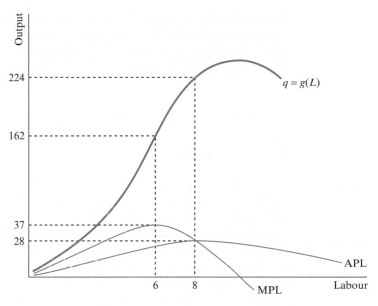

Figure 2.1 Short-run relationship between total, marginal and average product of labour

Figure 2.1 illustrates the relationship between MPL and APL. It is important to notice that APL is increasing whenever MPL > APL, and APL is decreasing whenever MPL < APL. This implies APL reaches its maximum value at the point where MPL = APL.

- If the marginal contribution to total output of the last worker employed is higher than the average output per worker (MPL > APL), the last worker must be pulling the average up (so APL is increasing).

- If the marginal contribution to total output of the last worker employed is lower than the average output per worker (MPL < APL), the last worker must be pulling the average down (so APL is decreasing).

This relationship between MPL and APL is also visible in the numerical example shown in Columns 1 to 4 of Table 2.1.

Cost theory

The short-run relationship between inputs and output, governed by the Law of Diminishing Returns, has direct implications for the firm's cost structure in the short run. Before examining the mechanics of cost theory, it is important to notice that the economist's idea of items that should count towards a firm's 'costs' differs from that of an accountant when preparing a set of company accounts. For an economist, costs encompass 'rewards' as well as monetary payments, since in many cases the supply of an input involves no formal cash or monetary transaction. For example, the owners of a business might not pay themselves for their own time and effort, or for ploughing their own money into the business. Nevertheless, the owners will soon contemplate the closure of the

Table 2.1 Short-run production and costs: numerical example

(1) Quantity of labour employed (number of workers per week) L	(2) Total output (units per week) q = g(L)	(3) Marginal product of labour (units per week) MPL	(4) Average product of labour (units per week) APL	(5) Variable cost (£ per week) VC	(6) Fixed cost (£ per week) FC	(7) Total cost (£ per week) TC	(8) Short-run marginal cost (£ per unit of output) SRMC	(9) Average variable cost (£ per unit of output) AVC	(10) Average fixed cost (£ per unit of output) AFC	(11) Short-run average cost (£ per unit of output) SRAC
1	7	7	7	200	1,000	1,200	28.6	28.6	142.9	171.4
2	26	19	13	400	1,000	1,400	10.5	15.4	38.5	53.8
3	54	28	18	600	1,000	1,600	7.1	11.1	18.5	29.6
4	88	34	22	800	1,000	1,800	5.9	9.1	11.4	20.5
5	125	37	25	1,000	1,000	2,000	5.4	8.0	8.0	16.0
6	162	37	27	1,200	1,000	2,200	5.4	7.4	6.2	13.6
7	196	34	28	1,400	1,000	2,400	5.9	7.1	5.1	12.2
8	224	28	28	1,600	1,000	2,600	7.1	7.1	4.5	11.6
9	243	19	27	1,800	1,000	2,800	10.5	7.4	4.1	11.5
10	250	7	25	2,000	1,000	3,000	28.6	8.0	4.0	12.0
11	242	−8	22	2,200	1,000	3,200	–	–	–	–

business if the reward or profit from such a personal investment is insufficient to compensate them for their own time and effort *and* match the **opportunity cost** of the financial investment: the return that the owners could have achieved had they invested their financial resources elsewhere. Accordingly, returns that an accountant might consider as part of the firm's 'profit' would be considered by an economist to be part of the 'costs' the firm needs to cover if it is to remain in business. An economist would include in the firm's cost functions an allowance for the reward the firm's owners require in order to remain in business. This reward is known as **normal profit**. Finally, any additional return over and above the normal profit is known as **abnormal profit**.

Columns 5 to 11 of Table 2.1 illustrate the implications of the Law of Diminishing Returns for the firm's cost structure in the short run. The previous discussion notwithstanding, for the purpose of constructing this simple numerical example, the firm owner's reward or normal profit is not included explicitly within the cost function (although this could be considered as part the firm's fixed costs). In addition to the short-run production function data contained in Columns 1 to 4 of Table 2.1, two further pieces of information about costs are used to construct Columns 5 to 11:

- the firm's weekly cost of employing each worker is £200;

- the firm also incurs a fixed cost of £1,000 per week. This is the cost associated with the fixed (capital) factor of production. This fixed cost does not vary with the number of workers employed.

Accordingly, columns 5, 6 and 7 of Table 2.1 show the firm's **variable cost, fixed cost** and short-run **total cost**, VC, FC and TC, respectively. Column 8 shows the firm's short-run marginal cost, SRMC. **Marginal cost** is the additional cost the firm incurs in order to produce one additional unit of output. For the purposes of Table 2.1, marginal cost is calculated by dividing £200 (the cost of employing each additional worker) by MPL (the additional output contributed by each additional worker). For example, by spending £200 to employ the first worker, the firm obtains MPL = 7 units of output. Therefore at $q = 7$, the firm's marginal cost (per additional unit of output) is SRMC = 200/7 = 28.6. By spending another £200 to employ the second worker, the firm obtains MPL = 19 additional units of output. Therefore at $q = 26$, the firm's marginal cost (per additional unit of output) is SRMC = 200/19 = 10.5. It is important to notice that when MPL is rising SRMC is falling, but once diminishing returns set in and MPL starts falling (beyond $q = 162$), SRMC starts rising. The increase in SRMC beyond this point is a direct consequence of the Law of Diminishing Returns. As each additional worker employed becomes less productive, the cost to the firm of producing each additional unit of output inevitably increases.

Columns 9 and 10 of Table 2.1 show the firm's **average variable cost** and **average fixed cost**, AVC and AFC, respectively. These are calculated by dividing the total variable and fixed costs (columns 6 and 7) by total output (column 2). Comparing Columns 4 and 9, it is important to notice that when APL is rising AVC is falling, but once APL starts falling (beyond $L = 8$ and $q = 244$) AVC starts rising. Therefore AVC is 'U-shaped'. If the average productivity of labour is rising, the average labour cost incurred per unit of output produced must be falling. Likewise, if the average productivity of labour is falling, the average labour cost incurred per unit of output produced must be rising. Meanwhile, AFC is decreasing over all values of L and q that are shown in Table 2.1. Reading down Column 10, the total fixed cost is spread over larger and larger volumes of output in order to calculate AFC. Therefore AFC falls as q increases. Finally, Column 11 of Table 2.1 shows the firm's short-run average cost, SRAC, calculated by summing AVC and AFC. The 'U-shaped' appearance of AVC ensures SRAC is also 'U-shaped'. As q increases, a point is eventually reached at which the downward pull of AFC on SRAC is exceeded by the upward pull of AVC on SRAC. Before this point SRAC is decreasing as q increases, but beyond this point SRAC is increasing as q increases.

Figure 2.2 illustrates the relationship between the firm's marginal and average cost functions, SRMC, AVC, AFC and SRAC. It is important to notice that while the MPL and APL functions shown in Figure 2.1 are drawn with labour on the horizontal axis, the SRMC, AVC, AFC and SRAC functions shown in Figure 2.2 are drawn with output on the horizontal axis. It is also important to notice that AVC is decreasing whenever SRMC < AVC, and AVC is increasing whenever SRMC > AVC. This implies AVC reaches its minimum value at the point where SRMC = AVC.

■ If the marginal cost of producing the last unit of output is lower than the average labour cost per unit of output (SRMC < AVC), the cost of producing the last unit must be bringing the average down (so AVC is decreasing).

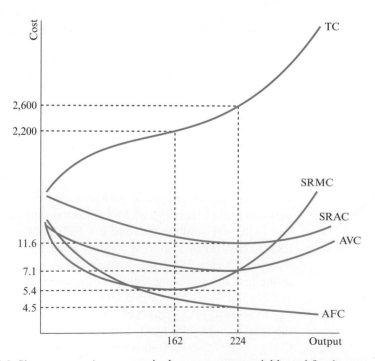

Figure 2.2 Short-run total cost, marginal cost, average variable and fixed cost and short-run average cost

- If the marginal cost of producing the last unit of output is higher than the average labour cost per unit of output (SRMC > AVC), the cost of producing the last unit must be pulling the average up (so AVC is increasing).

This relationship between SRMC and AVC is also visible in Columns 8 to 9 of Table 2.1. This relationship is very similar to the relationship between MPL and APL shown in Figure 2.1. In fact, the SRMC and AVC functions in Figure 2.2 can be interpreted as a 'mirror image' of the corresponding MPL and APL functions in Figure 2.1.

Long-run production and costs

In the long run, the firm has the opportunity to overcome the short-run constraint on production that is imposed by the Law of Diminishing Returns, by increasing its usage of *all* inputs. In addition to employing more workers, it can acquire more plant and machinery and move into a larger building. In other words, it can alter the scale of production.

The long-run relationship between the firm's inputs and output is governed by **returns to scale**. This refers to the proportionate increase in output that is achieved from any given proportionate increase in all inputs. Three types of returns to scale are identified schematically in Figure 2.3. Although the three cases are shown separately, firms can pass through all three phases as they expand the scale of their operations.

- **Increasing returns to scale** occurs when output increases more than proportionately to the increase in inputs. For example, a doubling of all inputs leads to more than a doubling of output. In this case there are **economies of scale**.

- **Constant returns to scale** occurs when output increases proportionately with an increase in inputs. A doubling of all inputs leads to a doubling of output.

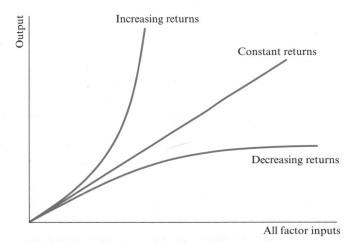

Figure 2.3 Increasing, constant and decreasing returns to scale

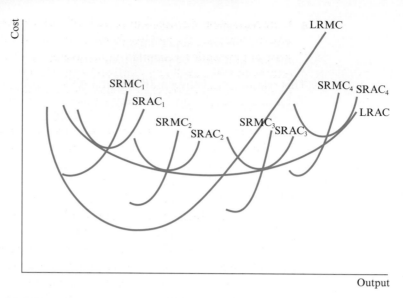

Figure 2.4 Long-run average cost and long-run marginal cost

- **Decreasing returns to scale** occurs when output increases less than proportionately to the increase in inputs. A doubling of all inputs leads to less than a doubling of output. In this case there are diseconomies of scale.

The sources of economies of scale and diseconomies of scale are considered in some detail below.

In order to derive the firm's long-run cost functions, it is assumed initially that the firm faces a choice between four possible values for the capital input, denoted K_1 to K_4. Therefore the firm can choose between four different scales of production. For each of the four values of K, the appropriate short-run production function (treating K as fixed in each case and allowing L to vary) is used to derive the firm's short-run cost function. Figure 2.4 shows the four short-run average cost functions, $SRAC_1$ to $SRAC_4$, and the corresponding short-run marginal cost functions, $SRMC_1$ to $SRMC_4$.

Reading Figure 2.4 from left to right, each successive short-run average cost curve refers to a larger scale of production.

- Initially, by moving from K_1 to K_2 and $SRAC_1$ to $SRAC_2$, a larger scale of production generates lower average costs. This is due to increasing returns to scale, or economies of scale. Output increases more than proportionately to the increase in inputs, so the average cost (per unit of output produced) decreases.

- At some point, however, the opportunities for reducing average costs by increasing the scale of production are exhausted. By moving from K_2 to K_3 and $SRAC_2$ to $SRAC_3$, a larger scale of production has no effect on average costs. This is the case of constant returns to scale. Output increases in the same proportion as the increase in inputs, so the average cost (per unit of output produced) remains unchanged.

■ If the scale of production is increased still further, average costs may eventually start to increase. By moving from K_3 to K_4 and SRAC$_3$ to SRAC$_4$, a larger scale of production generates higher average costs. This is due to decreasing returns to scale, or diseconomies of scale. Output increases less than proportionately to the increase in inputs, so the average cost (per unit of output produced) increases.

In the long run, the firm can choose from a continuous range of possible values for the capital input. Therefore SRAC$_1$ to SRAC$_4$ in Figure 2.4 can be interpreted as representative of an infinite number of possible short-run average cost functions. The smooth 'envelope' that enfolds these curves from below is the firm's long-run average cost function, denoted LRAC. LRAC represents the lowest cost of producing any given output level when the firm can vary both the capital and labour inputs in the long run.

It is important to notice that in order to produce any given level of output at the lowest long-run average cost, the firm does not usually operate at the lowest point on the short-run average cost function. For example, in Figure 2.5 the minimum average cost of producing q_1 units of output is C_1, obtained by operating on SRAC$_1$. If the firm were to increase its output from q_1 to q_2, enabling it to adjust to the minimum point on SRAC$_1$, it could produce at a lower average cost of C_2. However, if the firm really wants to produce q_2 rather than q_1, it can do better still by increasing its scale of production, and shifting onto a new short-run average cost function, SRAC$_2$. By doing so, it produces q_2 at an average cost of C_3, which is lower than C_2 at the minimum point on SRAC$_1$. However, the same argument applies here as well, and the firm does not operate at the minimum point on SRAC$_2$. Only if the firm selects the output level at the lowest point on LRAC does it also operate at the minimum point on the corresponding SRAC function.

The firm's total cost and LRAC functions can also be derived more directly from the production function, using the apparatus of isoquants and isocost functions. This apparatus emphasizes the fact that in order to produce any

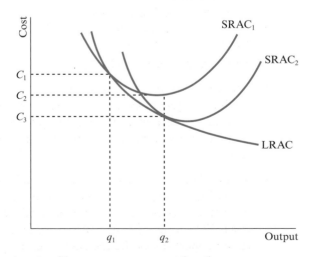

Figure 2.5 Short-run and long-run average cost functions

given quantity of output at the lowest possible cost, the firm needs to select the most cost-effective combination of inputs. This decision will depend not only on the technological conditions embodied in the production function but also on the prices of the inputs. In other words, there is both a technological dimension and an economic dimension to the firm's decision as to its choice of inputs.

Suppose a firm that employs two inputs, labour and capital, wishes to identify the combination of these inputs that will produce a given quantity of output, say $\bar{q}$, as cheaply as possible. By substituting $\bar{q}$ into the production function $\bar{q} = f(K, L)$ and rearranging, a relationship is identified between all the combinations of L and K that could be combined in order to produce $\bar{q}$ units of output. This relationship is represented by the function $K = h(L, \bar{q})$, known as the **isoquant** for $\bar{q}$ units of output. $h()$ is a new function, obtained by rearranging $f()$. In Figure 2.6, which has L and K on the axes, this isoquant is depicted as a downward sloping and curved function. Assuming L and K are substitutable in production to some extent, the downward sloping isoquant implies $\bar{q}$ units of output could be produced either in a capital intensive manner (large K and small L), or in a labour intensive manner (small K and large L), or using some intermediate combination of K and L.

The set of three downward sloping lines shown in Figure 2.6 are the firm's **isocost** functions. Each isocost function shows all combinations of L and K the firm can hire which incur an identical total cost. The further away from the origin, the higher the total cost represented by each successive isocost function. The positions and slope of the isocost functions depend on the prices per unit of L and K, which can be denoted w (the wage rate per unit of labour) and r (the rental per unit of capital), respectively. Finally, Figure 2.6 shows that the most cost-effective method of producing $\bar{q}$ units of output is to hire L_1 units of labour

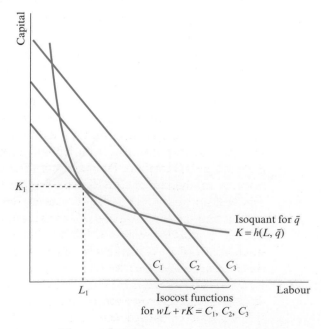

Figure 2.6 Isoquant and isocost functions

and K_1 units of capital, at a total cost of $C_1 = wL_1 + rK_1$. At any other point on the isoquant for $\bar{q}$, the firm would be located on a higher isocost function than at this point of tangency. This analysis establishes that the lowest possible total cost of producing $\bar{q}$ units of output is C_1. The corresponding LRAC (long-run average cost) is $C_1/\bar{q}$. A complete description of the firm's cost structure is obtained by repeating a similar analysis for all other possible output levels.

The LRAC function can be used to derive the firm's long-run marginal cost function, denoted LRMC in Figure 2.4. The relationship between LRMC and LRAC is rather similar to the relationship that exists between the firm's short-run marginal cost and average variable cost functions.

- LRAC is decreasing when LRMC < LRAC. If the marginal cost of producing the last unit of output is lower than the average cost per unit of output, the cost of producing the last unit must be pulling the average down, so LRAC is decreasing. In this case there are economies of scale.

- LRAC reaches its minimum value at the point where LRMC = LRAC. At this point there are constant returns to scale.

- LRAC is increasing when LRMC > LRAC. If the marginal cost of producing the last unit of output is higher than the average cost per unit of output, the cost of producing the last unit must be pulling the average up, so LRAC is increasing. In this case there are diseconomies of scale.

Economies of scale

This sub-section examines in some detail *why* long-run **average costs** should either decrease or increase as the firm alters its scale of production in the long run. In other words, the *sources* of economies of scale and diseconomies of scale are examined.

Economies of scale can be classified as either real or pecuniary. Real economies of scale are associated with savings in average costs due to changes in the quantities of physical inputs. Pecuniary economies of scale are associated with savings in average costs due to changes in the prices paid by the firm for its inputs or factors of production. These categories can be further subdivided according to the specific element of the firm's operations from which the cost savings arise (for example, from labour, technology, marketing, transport or the managerial function). Economies of scale can be realized at the level of the plant, or (in the case of a multi-plant firm) at the level of the firm. Some of the principal sources of economies of scale are described below.

As a firm increases its scale of production, it can benefit from specialization through a greater division of labour. Individual workers can be assigned to specialized tasks. As workers become more specialized, their knowledge and skills increase and they become more productive. Furthermore, less time is wasted through workers having to switch from one task to another. Accordingly, the firm's average costs are reduced. Similar benefits are also derived from specialization in management. A manager of a small firm may have to perform many tasks (financial planning and control, bookkeeping, marketing, personnel management and so on). The manager may well lack the necessary expertise to perform some or all of these functons effectively. In contrast, a large firm benefits by employing specialist managers to perform each separate function.

Real economies of scale arise from various technological relationships between inputs and output that underlie the firm's long-run production function. Some examples are as follow:

■ *Large-scale production* may simply be more cost-effective than small-scale production. By producing at large volume, the firm can make use of large machines that would not be feasible for a small-scale producer. One large machine may produce more output from any given quantity of inputs than two smaller machines combined.

■ *Indivisibilities* of capital and labour inputs are also an important source of economies for the large firm. Some types of capital equipment are 'lumpy' or indivisible. The firm either purchases a whole machine or it does not do so; it cannot acquire 10 per cent or 50 per cent of the machine. A combine harvester is a highly productive input in agriculture, but only a large farm operates at a sufficient scale to justify the purchase of such equipment. The usage of some inputs does not necessarily increase at all as the scale of production increases. A factory perhaps requires one receptionist and one photocopying machine, regardless of whether it produces 5,000 or 10,000 units of output per week. The same might apply to functions such as accounting, finance or health and safety. As the scale of production increases, the total cost of each indivisible input is spread over a larger volume of output, causing average costs to fall.

■ *Learning economies* are another important source of cost savings (Spence, 1981). Over time, workers and managers become more skilled as they repeat the same tasks. The length of the production run is therefore an important determinant of the extent to which the firm may benefit from learning economies. For example, Alchian (1963) identifies a learning curve in aircraft production: labour productivity in the manufacture of frames was a function of the cumulative number of frames already assembled.

■ *Geometric relationships* between inputs and outputs can result in cost savings as the scale of production increases. In some cases, costs may be proportional to surface area while outputs are proportional to volume. In Figure 2.7, a square tank of dimensions 1 m × 1 m × 1 m has a surface area of 6 m² (square metres) and a storage capacity of 1 m³ (cubic metres). A tank of dimensions 2 m × 2 m × 2 m has a surface area of 24 m² and a capacity of 8 m³. A fourfold increase in surface area is associated with an eightfold increase in volume. Accordingly, the capacity of an oil tanker increases more than proportionately with an increase in its surface area. Similarly, doubling an oil or gas pipeline's circumference more than doubles its capacity. Some costs (for example, the costs of materials) might be proportional to surface area, while output is proportional to volume. In the oil industry, a '0.6 rule of thumb' is sometimes used by engineers to indicate that a 100 per cent increase in capacity should require only a 60 per cent increase in costs.

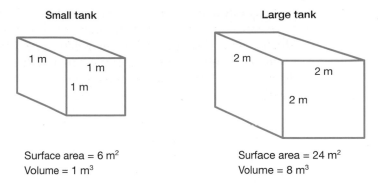

Figure 2.7 Surface area and volume of small and large storage tanks

Pecuniary economies of scale arise if large firms find it easier than small firms to raise finance. A large firm may be able to offer lenders stronger security guarantees than a small firm. A large firm may have access to sources of finance unavailable to a small firm, such as the stock market or its own bond issues. Lenders may believe a large firm poses a lower risk, perhaps because a large firm can spread its risks through multi-plant operations or diversification, or because a large firm benefits from a reputation effect.

Large firms can buy and sell in bulk, benefiting from *purchasing and marketing economies*. Suppliers of raw materials or other inputs may be willing to offer discounts for large-scale orders. Retailers or distributors may be willing to offer more favourable terms or service to a large-scale producer. A large firm may be able to benefit from using large-scale forms of advertising, such as television advertising, which would be beyond the means of a smaller firm. A large firm that services a national market may be able to realize *transport economies*, by operating separate plants that produce and sell in different regions. A small firm that services a national market from a single plant may incur significant transport costs.

All of the economies of scale described above (both real and pecuniary) are *internal economies of scale*. In every case, cost savings are generated directly by the firm, through its own decision to increase its scale of production. In contrast, *external economies of scale* refer to cost savings that are generated not through expansion on the part of any one firm individually, but through the expansion of all of the industry's member firms collectively. As the size of an industry increases, all firms may realize benefits including: increased specialization of labour; the availability of industry-specific education and training programmes; the availability of specialist facilities, support services or physical infrastructure; the growth of publicly or privately funded research centres; the development of expertise and knowledge of the industry's requirements within banks or other financial institutions; and so on. As the scale of the industry's aggregate production increases, external economies of scale tend to reduce average costs for all of the industry's member firms, large and small.

Diseconomies of scale

Diseconomies of scale arise when long-run average costs tend to increase as output increases for plants or firms operating beyond a certain scale. Managerial diseconomies, arising from difficulties encountered in managing large organizations effectively, are perhaps the most widely cited explanation for diseconomies of scale. Sources of managerial diseconomies include the following:

- Strained communications between different tiers of management, or between different parts of the organization generally.

- Long chains of command and complex organizational structures.

- Low morale among the workforce, who may sense a lack of personal involvement or interest in the performance of the organization.

- Poor industrial relations, due to the complexity of relationships between the workforce and management, or between different groups of workers.

Case study 2.1

Companies and productivity
Small is not beautiful
Why small firms are less wonderful than you think

PEOPLE find it hard to like businesses once they grow beyond a certain size. Banks that were 'too big to fail' sparked a global economic crisis and burned bundles of taxpayers' cash. Big retailers such as Walmart and Tesco squeeze suppliers and crush small rivals. Some big British firms minimise their tax bills so aggressively that they provoke outrage. Films nearly always depict big business as malign. Tex Richman, the oil baron in the latest Muppets movie, is so bad he reads *The Economist*. Small wonder that whenever politicians want to laud business they praise cuddly small firms, not giants.

It is shrewd politics to champion the little guy. But the popular fetish for small business is at odds with economic reality. Big firms are generally more productive, offer higher wages and pay more taxes than small ones. Economies dominated by small firms are often sluggish.

Consider the southern periphery of the euro area. Countries such as Greece, Italy and Portugal have lots of small firms which, thanks to cumbersome regulations, have failed lamentably to grow. Firms with at least 250 workers account for less than half the share of manufacturing jobs in these countries than they do in Germany, the euro zone's strongest economy. A shortfall of big firms is linked to the sluggish productivity and loss of competitiveness that is the deeper cause of the euro-zone crisis. For all the boosterism around small business, it is economies with lots of biggish companies that have been able to sustain the highest living standards.

Big firms can reap economies of scale. A big factory uses far less cash and labour to make each car or steel pipe than a small workshop. Big supermarkets such as the villainous Walmart offer a wider range of high-quality goods at lower prices than any corner store. Size allows specialisation, which fosters innovation. An engineer at Google or Toyota can focus all his energy on a specific problem; he will not be asked to fix the boss's laptop as well. Manufacturers in Europe with 250 or more workers are 30–40% more productive than 'micro' firms with fewer than ten employees. It is telling that micro enterprises are common in Greece, but rare in Germany.

Big firms have their flaws, of course. They can be slow to respond to customers' needs, changing tastes or disruptive technology. If they grew big thanks to state backing, they are often bureaucratic and inefficient. To idolise big firms would be as unwise as to idolise small ones. It's what you do with it that counts.

Rather than focusing on size, policymakers should look at growth. One of the reasons why everyone loves small firms is that they create more jobs than big ones. But many small businesses stay small indefinitely. The link between small firms and jobs growth relies entirely on new start-ups, which are usually small, and which by definition create new jobs (as they did not previously exist). A recent study of American businesses found that the link between company size and jobs growth disappears once the age of firms is controlled for.

Rather than spooning out subsidies and regulatory favours to small firms, governments should concentrate on removing barriers to expansion. In parts of Europe, for example, small firms are exempted from the most burdensome social regulations. This gives them an incentive to stay small. Far better to repeal burdensome rules for all firms. The same goes for differential tax rates, such as Britain's, and the separate bureaucracy America maintains to deal with small businesses. In a healthy economy, entrepreneurs with ideas can easily start companies, the best of which grow fast and the worst of which are quickly swept aside. Size doesn't matter. Growth does.

Source: © The Economist Newspaper Limited, London, 3 March 2012.

Williamson (1967) elaborates on the causes of managerial diseconomies of scale. The firm can be viewed as a coalition of various teams or groups who are responsible for specialist activities such as production, marketing and finance. Since much of the firm's activity requires teamwork, as in any team there are incentives for opportunistic behaviour such as shirking or free-riding on the part of individuals. This creates a need to monitor the performance of team members. Traditionally, monitoring has been the role of the entrepreneur, but in the modern corporation the entrepreneur has been replaced by salaried managers. Each layer of management is monitored by a higher tier of managers, who in turn are monitored by another tier, and so on. At the apex of the hierarchical structure is the final control exercised by the firm's owners.

An essential function of the hierarchy is to handle, transmit and process or interpret information as it flows between different levels of the organization. This information is subject to two distortions. First, deliberate distortion (information impactedness) occurs when managers, supervisors and team members at lower levels misrepresent their efforts or abilities, so as to appear in the best possible light. Second, accidental distortion (serial reproduction) occurs whenever information has to flow through many channels. Williamson draws an analogy with the children's party game of 'Chinese whispers':

> Bartlett (1932) illustrates this (serial reproduction) graphically with a line drawing of an owl which, when redrawn successively by eighteen individuals, each sketch based on its immediate predecessor, ended up as a recognizable cat; and the further from the initial drawing one moved, the greater the distortion experienced. The reliance of hierarchical organizations on serial reproduction for their functioning thus exposes them to what may become serious distortions in transmission.
>
> *(Williamson, 1967, p. 127)*

If decision-makers do not have access to accurate information, errors tend to occur, and the firm's average cost tends to increase.

The managerial function is not necessarily the only source of diseconomies of scale. As the firm or plant expands, transport costs may tend to increase. As the firm's demand for raw materials or other inputs increases, these may have to be shipped in from further afield. Similarly, in order to find sufficient customers, the firm's end product may need to be transported over longer geographic distances. External diseconomies of scale might also arise, if the expansion of all of the industry's member firms causes all firms' average costs to increase. This could happen if growth of the industry leads to shortages of raw materials or specialized labour, putting upward pressure on the costs of these essential factors of production.

Some economists have questioned whether diseconomies of scale are inevitably encountered beyond a certain scale of production (Sargent, 1933). At plant level, there may be a natural tendency for average costs to increase as the plant size becomes large and unwieldy. Therefore it seems reasonable to assume the plant's LRAC function is U-shaped. However, a multi-plant firm might be able to circumvent the tendency for LRAC to increase at plant level, simply by opening more plants and allowing each one to operate at the minimum point on its own LRAC function. In this case, the firm's LRAC function might be L-shaped rather than U-shaped (see Figure 2.8). Eventually, of course, managerial diseconomies at firm level may prevent what might otherwise be potentially limitless expansion of the firm through proliferation of plants. However, even in this case the inevitability of diseconomies of scale has been questioned. The development of decentralized organizational structures, with managers of separate divisions within the firm given considerable individual responsibility and decision-making autonomy, can be interpreted as an attempt to avoid managerial diseconomies that might otherwise arise under a structure of excessive centralized control (see also Section 5.3).

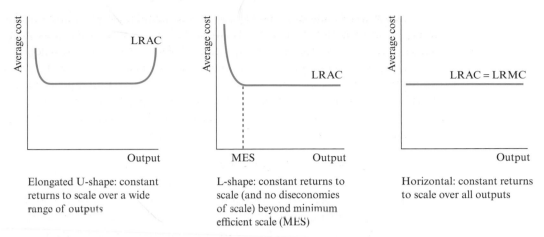

Figure 2.8 Long-run average cost functions with constant returns to scale

Economies of scope

Economies of scope are cost savings that arise when a firm produces two or more outputs using the same set of resources. Diversification causes average costs to fall if the total cost of producing several goods or services together is less than the sum of the costs of producing them separately. Economies of scope can be realized by bulk-purchasing inputs that are used in the production of several different products. For example, the same microchips may be used in the manufacture of several different consumer electronics products. Economies of scope can also be realized by spreading the costs of specialist functions, such as finance, marketing or distribution, over a range of products or services. Computing and telecommunications may provide an important source of economies of scope. Data on the characteristics of customers who have already purchased one product can be stored electronically, and analyzed in order to devise targeted marketing strategies for the promotion of other products or services.

Minimum efficient scale

The **minimum efficient scale** (MES) is defined as the output level beyond which the firm can make no further savings in LRAC (long-run average cost) through further expansion. In other words, the MES is achieved when all economies of scale are exhausted. Textbook microeconomic theory suggests a U-shaped long-run average cost function: as soon as economies of scale are exhausted, the firm immediately experiences diseconomies of scale. In practice, however, once MES has been achieved, it is possible that a firm may be able to produce at the minimum attainable LRAC over a wide range of output levels. For any range of output levels over which the LRAC function is flat, the firm experiences constant returns to scale. Accordingly, a more realistic LRAC function might have an elongated U-shape, or (as suggested by our earlier discussion of the possible avoidance of diseconomies of scale) an L-shape. These possibilities are shown in the left-hand and middle diagrams in Figure 2.8.

In some of the theoretical models that are widely used in industrial organization, a convenient simplifying assumption is that firms encounter constant returns to scale over all possible output levels they can choose. In other words, it is sometimes convenient to simplify the assumed cost structure by ignoring economies of scale and diseconomies of scale altogether. In this case, the LRAC and LRMC functions are both horizontal and identical to each other, over all possible values of q. For example, suppose the total cost of producing 10 units of output is £100, the cost of producing 20 units is £200, and the cost of producing 30 units is £300. In this case LRAC = £10 (= £100/10 or £200/20 or £300/30) for any value of q. Similarly LRMC = £10 for any value of q, because each additional unit of output always adds exactly £10 to the firm's total cost. This case is shown in the right-hand diagram in Figure 2.8.

For any firm seeking to minimize its costs over the long term, it is important to be able to identify the shape of the LRAC function, or at least identify the output level at which MES is achieved and all possible cost savings arising from economies of scale have been realized. With reference to a textbook LRAC function, identifying the MES is a trivial task. However, in practice a firm's managers may have little or no idea of the true shape of the LRAC function, and may have to rely on estimates.

2.3   Demand, revenue, elasticity and profit maximization

Demand, average revenue and marginal revenue

The **market demand function** for a product or service shows the relationship between market price and the number of units of the product or service consumers wish to buy at that price. In many of the models that are presented in this book, a linear market demand function is assumed. Table 2.2 presents a numerical illustration of a linear market demand function. Columns 1 and 2 show that the maximum price any consumer would be prepared to pay is £2. When $P = £2$, $Q = 1$ unit is sold. However, if the market price is reduced below $P = £2$, more buyers are attracted: when $P = £1.8$, $Q = 2$ units are sold; when $P = £1.6$, $Q = 3$ units are sold; and so on. If the market price is reduced as low as $P = £0.2$, $Q = 10$ units are sold; and if (hypothetically) the product or service were being given away for free, $Q = 11$ would be the quantity demanded when $P = 0$.

Suppose the product or service is being supplied by one firm only, so the industry structure is monopoly. The theory of monopoly is developed in full in Section 3.3. At this stage, however, there is sufficient information to evaluate the monopolist's **total revenue** function, TR. By definition, total revenue *equals* price × quantity, so each entry in Column 3 of Table 2.2 is obtained by multiplying the corresponding entries in Columns 1 and 2. Notice that the monopolist's TR function has an inverted U-shaped appearance: TR = 0 for $Q = 0$ and $Q = 11$, and TR attains its maximum value of TR = 6 for $Q = 5$ and $Q = 6$.

Columns 4 and 5 of Table 2.2 show the monopolist's **average revenue** and **marginal revenue** functions. The average revenue function, AR, shows the average revenue per unit of output sold, and is calculated by dividing total revenue

Table 2.2 Demand, revenue, price elasticity and profit maximization: numerical example

(1) Market price (£ per unit of output) P	(2) Quantity demanded (Units per week) Q	(3) Total revenue (£ per week) TR	(4) Average revenue (= Price, £ per unit of output) AR	(5) Marginal revenue (£ per unit of output) MR	(6) Price elasticity of demand |PED|	(7) Short-run marginal cost (£ per unit of output) SRMC	(8) Total cost (£ per week) TC	(9) Profit (£ per week) π
2.2	0	0					1.0	−1.0
2.0	1	2.0	2.0	2.0	21.00	0.5	1.5	0.5
1.8	2	3.6	1.8	1.6	6.33	0.2	1.7	1.9
1.6	3	4.8	1.6	1.2	3.40	0.5	2.2	2.6
1.4	4	5.6	1.4	0.8	2.14	0.8	3.0	2.6
1.2	5	6.0	1.2	0.4	1.44	1.1	4.1	1.9
1.0	6	6.0	1.0	0.0	1.00	1.4	5.5	0.5
0.8	7	5.6	0.8	−0.4	0.69	1.7	7.2	−1.6
0.6	8	4.8	0.6	−0.8	0.47	2.0	9.2	−4.4
0.4	9	3.6	0.4	−1.2	0.29	2.3	11.5	−7.9
0.2	10	2.0	0.2	−1.6	0.16	2.6	14.1	−12.1
0.0	11	0.0	0.0	−2.0	0.05	2.9	17.0	−17.0

Illustrative calculations at $(P = 1.8, Q = 2)$, Columns 3 to 6:

$TR = PQ = 1.8 \times 2 = 3.6$

$AR = TR/Q = 3.6/2 = 1.8$

$MR = \Delta TR = TR(Q - 2) - TR(Q - 1) = 3.6 - 2.0 = 1.6$

$PED = \dfrac{\Delta Q}{\Delta P} \times \dfrac{P}{Q} = \dfrac{2 - 1}{1.8 - 2.0} \times \dfrac{1.9}{1.5} = -6.33 \quad \Rightarrow \quad |PED| = 6.33$

(Column 3) by quantity demanded (Column 2). Since $TR = PQ$, $AR = TR/Q = PQ/Q = P$. In other words, average revenue is identical to price. Therefore Column 4 of Table 2.2 is the same as Column 1. The marginal revenue function, MR, shows the additional revenue generated by the last unit of output sold, and is calculated as the change in total revenue achieved as a result of each one-unit increase in quantity demanded. For $Q \leq 5$, TR increases as Q increases, so MR > 0. Between $Q = 5$ and $Q = 6$, TR does not change as Q increases, so MR = 0. For $Q \geq 7$, TR decreases as Q increases, so MR < 0. Figure 2.9 illustrates the monopolist's TR, AR and MR functions.

Elasticity

Price elasticity of demand

What is the effect of a reduction in price on a monopolist's total revenue? Table 2.2 and Figure 2.9 demonstrate that the monopolist could experience either an increase, or no change, or a decrease in its total revenue, depending on the point on the market demand function from which the price reduction is introduced.

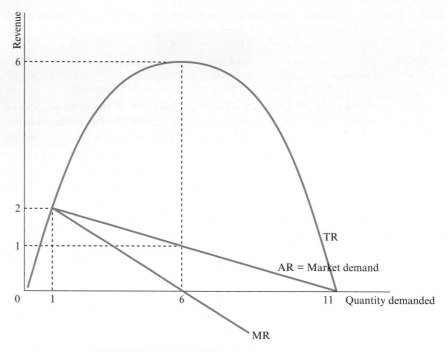

Figure 2.9 Total, average and marginal revenue

By definition, TR = PQ. As P falls, Q rises, so the overall effect of a reduction in P on TR could be positive, zero or negative. More specifically:

■ If the (positive) quantity effect dominates the (negative) price effect, TR increases as P falls.

■ If the quantity effect just balances the price effect, TR remains unchanged as P falls.

■ If the quantity effect is dominated by the price effect, TR decreases as P falls.

The effect of a reduction in P on TR therefore depends upon the responsiveness of quantity demanded to a change in price. **Price elasticity of demand**, PED, provides a convenient measure of this responsiveness. The formula for calculating PED is as follows:

$$\text{PED} = \frac{\text{Proportionate change in quantity demanded}}{\text{Proportionate change in price}}$$

Let ΔP denote the change in price between any two points on the market demand function, and let ΔQ denote the corresponding change in quantity demanded. The proportionate change in quantity demanded is $\Delta Q/Q$, and the proportionate change in price is $\Delta P/P$. The values of P and Q used in the denominators of these expressions are usually taken as the values midway between the two points on the market demand function over which PED is being calculated.

$$PED = \frac{\left(\frac{\Delta Q}{Q}\right)}{\left(\frac{\Delta P}{P}\right)} = \left(\frac{\Delta Q}{\Delta P}\right)\left(\frac{P}{Q}\right)$$

Because the changes in P and Q are in opposite directions ($\Delta Q > 0$ if $\Delta P < 0$, and $\Delta Q < 0$ if $\Delta P > 0$), the formula for PED produces a negative value. However, when economists discuss price elasticity of demand, it is quite common to ignore the minus-sign and refer to the corresponding positive value. Therefore a 'price elasticity of demand of 2' refers to the case PED $= -2$. The mathematical notation used to convert a negative value into its corresponding positive value is the absolute value function, written $|PED| = |-2| = 2$. Column 6 of Table 2.2 shows the values of $|PED|$ calculated over each successive pair of values for (P, Q) shown in Columns 1 and 2.

The previous discussion of the effect of a reduction in P on TR has the following implications:

- If $|PED| > 1$, TR increases as P falls. The quantity effect dominates the price effect. The demand function is *price elastic*. Quantity demanded is sensitive to the change in price.

- If $|PED| = 1$, TR remains unchanged as P falls. The quantity effect just balances the price effect. The demand function exhibits *unit price elasticity*.

- If $|PED| < 1$, TR decreases as P falls. The quantity effect is dominated by the price effect. The demand function is *price inelastic*. Quantity demanded is insensitive to the change in price.

Another useful interpretation of price elasticity of demand is obtained by demonstrating the relationship between PED and MR. By definition:

$$MR = \frac{\Delta TR}{\Delta Q}$$

where ΔTR denotes the change in total revenue achieved as a result of a change in quantity demanded, denoted ΔQ. Using the definition TR $= PQ$ and a mathematical rule known as the Product Rule, an expression for MR in terms of P, Q, ΔP and ΔQ is as follows:

$$MR = \frac{\Delta TR}{\Delta Q} = \frac{\Delta(PQ)}{\Delta Q} = P \times \frac{\Delta Q}{\Delta Q} + \frac{\Delta P}{\Delta Q} \times Q$$

Since $\Delta Q/\Delta Q = 1$:

$$MR = P + \frac{\Delta P}{\Delta Q} \times Q = P + P \times \left(\frac{\Delta P}{\Delta Q} \times \frac{Q}{P}\right) = P + P \times \frac{1}{\left(\frac{\Delta Q}{\Delta P} \times \frac{P}{Q}\right)}$$

$$= P\left(1 + \frac{1}{PED}\right) = P\left(1 - \frac{1}{|PED|}\right)$$

See Appendix 1 for a more formal mathematical derivation of this result. The interpretation of the expression $\text{MR} = P\left(1 - \dfrac{1}{|\text{PED}|}\right)$ is as follows:

- If $|\text{PED}| > 1$, $1/|\text{PED}| < 1$ and $\text{MR} > 0$. When the demand function is price elastic, $\text{MR} > 0$.

- If $|\text{PED}| = 1$, $1/|\text{PED}| = 1$ and $\text{MR} = 0$. When the demand function exhibits unit elasticity, $\text{MR} = 0$.

- If $|\text{PED}| < 1$, $1/|\text{PED}| > 1$ and $\text{MR} < 0$. When the demand function is price inelastic, $\text{MR} < 0$.

It is possible to define price elasticity of demand either at market level, or at firm level. This distinction was irrelevant in the preceding discussion, which referred to a monopolist. However, in a competitive market in which an identical product is sold by many firms, there might be a big difference between the sensitivity of the total quantity demanded to a change in the market price (assuming all firms make the same price adjustment), and the sensitivity of one individual firm's quantity demanded to a change in its own price (assuming other firms keep their prices unchanged).

Price elasticity of demand is only one of several elasticities used by economists to measure the sensitivity of one variable (in the case of PED, quantity demanded) to changes in another variable (in the case of PED, market price). Other elasticities, defined in a similar manner to PED, will be encountered at various points throughout this book. At this stage, however, three examples will illustrate the wide range of applications of the concept of elasticity. In each case, the symbol 'Δ' in front of a variable denotes the change in this variable.

Cross-price elasticity of demand

Cross-price elasticity of demand, CED, measures the sensitivity of the quantity demanded of Good 1 to a change in the price of Good 2.

$$\text{CED} = \frac{\text{Proportionate change in the quantity demanded of Good 1}}{\text{Proportionate change in the price of Good 2}}$$

$$\text{CED} = \frac{\Delta Q_1}{\Delta P_1} \times \frac{P_2}{Q_1}$$

where Q_1 denotes the demand for Good 1, and P_2 denotes the price of Good 2. CED provides an indication of whether Goods 1 and 2 are **substitutes** or **complements** in consumption, or whether the demand for Good 1 is unrelated to the price of Good 2:

- If $\text{CED} > 0$, an increase in P_2 leads to an increase in Q_1. This suggests Goods 1 and 2 are substitutes: as the price of Good 2 increases (and the demand for Good 2 decreases), consumers tend to switch from Good 2 to Good 1, causing the demand for Good 1 to increase.

- If CED < 0, an increase in P_2 leads to a decrease in Q_1. This suggests Goods 1 and 2 are complements: as the price of Good 2 increases (and the demand for Good 2 decreases), consumers also reduce their consumption of Good 1, causing the demand for Good 1 to decrease.

- If CED = 0, an increase in P_2 has no effect on Q_1. This suggests Goods 1 and 2 are neither substitutes nor complements: the demand for Good 1 is independent of the price of good 2.

Advertising elasticity of demand

Advertising elasticity of demand, AED, measures the sensitivity of quantity demanded to a change in advertising expenditure.

$$AED = \frac{\text{Proportionate change in quantity demanded}}{\text{Proportionate change in advertising expenditure}}$$

$$AED = \frac{\Delta Q}{\Delta A} \times \frac{A}{Q}$$

where Q denotes quantity demanded, and A denotes advertising expenditure.

AED is a measure of the effectiveness of advertising. Normally AED should be positive: an increase in advertising leads to an increase in quantity demanded. Calculated or estimated at the level of the individual firm, AED might be an important indicator of the level of resources the firm should allocate to its advertising budget. If AED is large, the firm might decide to advertise heavily; but if AED is small it might be more cost-effective to look for alternative methods of increasing the demand for its product.

Price elasticity of supply

Price elasticity of supply, PES, measures the sensitivity of quantity supplied to market price.

$$PES = \frac{\text{Proportionate change in quantity supplied}}{\text{Proportionate change in price}}$$

$$PES = \frac{\Delta Q_S}{\Delta P} \times \frac{P}{Q_S}$$

where Q_S denotes quantity supplied, and P denotes price. The s-subscript on Q_S distinguishes the formula for PES from the (otherwise identical) formula for PED. While an increase in price should be associated with a *decrease* in quantity demanded, an increase in price should be associated with an *increase* in quantity supplied. Therefore, PED should be negative and PES should be positive.

This section has focused on the relationship between price and quantity demanded. For most products, however, price is not the only determinant of the level of demand. Case Study 2.2 examines a wide range of factors that influence the level of demand for spectator attendance at professional football matches.

The demand for spectator attendance at professional football

The determinants of the level of demand for spectator attendance at professional team sports matches have been the subject of attention from economists since the 1970s. Some of the earliest contributions to this literature include Demmert (1973), Hart *et al.* (1975) and Noll (1974). The literature is reviewed by Dobson and Goddard (2011) and Sandy *et al.* (2004). This case study examines some of the main factors that influence spectator demand.

Price

Economic theory suggests a professional sports club should price its tickets in order to maximize its revenue or profit. In practice, however, there is some empirical evidence to suggest that many clubs fail to achieve this.

Suppose initially the club's marginal cost (the direct cost incurred by attracting one additional spectator into the stadium) is zero. Figure 1 shows the club's demand function for spectator attendance at one match: the number of spectators it would attract at each (uniform) ticket price. In this case, the club maximizes its revenue by charging £20 per ticket and attracting 30,000 spectators: this is, equivalent to maximizing the area of the rectangle beneath the market demand function.

- At prices above £20, price elasticity of demand |PED| is greater than one.

- At prices below £20, |PED| is less than one.

- At a price of £20, at the very centre of the demand function, |PED| *equals* one.

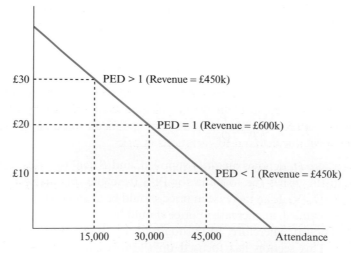

Figure 1 Uniform ticket pricing for profit maximization – zero marginal cost
Maximum revenue/profit = 20 × 30,000 = £600k

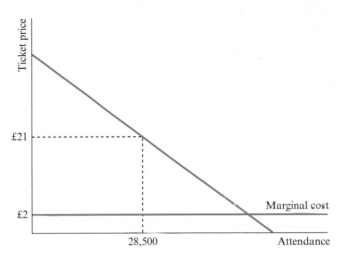

Figure 2 Uniform ticket pricing for profit maximization
Maximum profit − 21 × 28,500 − 2 × 28,500 = £541.5k

Suppose, instead, the club's marginal cost (cost of stewarding or policing) is £2 per spectator. Figure 2 shows the club's marginal cost, and the same demand function. In this case profit maximization requires charging £21 per ticket and attracting 28,500 spectators: this is equivalent to maximizing the area of the rectangle between the market demand and marginal cost functions.

Therefore a profit-maximizing club should always operate on a section of the demand function where $|PED| \geq 1$. However, several econometric studies have found that the actual $|PED|$ for football attendance is less than one. There are several possible explanations:

- Football clubs may not be profit maximizers, as the theory assumes.

- The econometric studies could be wrong. It is difficult to estimate price elasticities accurately, because football clubs do not change their prices very often. In recent years, many stadia are regularly sold out, so it is difficult to obtain good data on the sensitivity of spectator demand to variations in price.

- Alternatively, the clubs may be operating more sophisticated pricing policies, for which operating with $|PED| < 1$ may be consistent with profit maximization. (This is the subject of Case Study 13.1.)

- Finally, interrelationships between the demand for match tickets, and the demand for related products or services such as live television broadcasts, merchandise or catering could explain why it is profitable for clubs to price their match tickets so that $|PED| < 1$.

City population and *per capita* income

There is a natural tendency for the strongest teams to be located in the cities with the largest population and/or largest *per capita* incomes. Teams with the largest potential or actual markets tend to generate the most income. In the long term this usually translates into playing success.

In the North American major league sports (baseball, American football, basketball and hockey), membership of the major leagues is closed: there is a fixed number of franchise-holding teams. In the longer term, franchises tend to gravitate towards the largest cities that can afford to pay the highest subsidies. In Europe, membership of the top divisions is regulated through the promotion and relegation system:

- If a small market team is promoted to the top division, its lack of spending power often ensures speedy relegation.

- If a big market team is relegated to a lower division, its high spending power will usually guarantee promotion back to the top division sooner or later.

Uncertainty of outcome and competitive balance

It is widely assumed by sports economists that spectator interest in sport depends on uncertainty of outcome. There are three (related) types of uncertainty of outcome:

- Degree of uncertainty concerning the result of an individual match.

- Degree of uncertainty concerning the end-of-season outcome of a championship race or a battle to avoid relegation.

- Degree to which championship success is concentrated in the hands of a few teams, or spread among many teams, over a number of years.

In today's English Premiership, there is less of all three types of uncertainty of outcome than in the equivalent competition (the Football League) 20, 30 or 50 years ago. There has been extensive debate concerning the usefulness of policy measures designed to promote competitive balance and increase uncertainty of outcome:

- Capping of teams' total expenditure on players' wages or salaries.

- Sharing or pooling of gate or television revenues.

- The US draft pick system, whereby the weakest teams from the previous season get first choice of new players turning professional for the first time.

Television and newspaper publicity

In most countries, professional sports such as football probably could not survive without the free publicity they receive through newspaper, television and radio coverage.

Equally, sports coverage is essential for the ability of the print and broadcasting media to attract readers, viewers, listeners and, thereby, advertising revenue.

For a long time, it has been assumed by sports administrators and academics that if a sports fixture is the subject of live television coverage, spectator attendance may be adversely affected. However, the statistical evidence for a negative impact of television coverage on attendance is rather mixed: some studies find such an effect, while others find no effect.

Other relevant factors include the following:

■ Even if attendance is affected, the loss of gate revenue might be compensated by direct income from the broadcaster, or indirect income from advertising or sponsorship within the stadium.

■ The broadcasting rights might be more valuable if the stadium is full, due to the improved atmosphere created by a capacity crowd. Consequently, there might be a case for offering cheaper ticket prices to spectators attending televised matches.

Geographic market segmentation

Fifty years ago, the markets served by each English football club were local: most spectators lived within walking distance or a short bus or train journey from the stadium. Today, the most successful clubs attract a national audience. Factors that have contributed to reduced geographic market segmentation have included:

■ growth in private car ownership;

■ improvements in the road transport system;

■ demographic change (population is more mobile geographically);

■ increased media coverage of star players and leading teams.

Stadium facilities and hooliganism

In England, anecdotal evidence suggests that hooliganism and the antiquated, delapidated physical condition of many football stadia made a major contribution to the long-term decline in football attendances between the late 1940s and mid-1980s. Aggregate attendances for English league football fell from 41.0m in the 1948–9 season to 16.5m in the 1985–6 season, before recovering to reach 29.5m in the 2010–11 season.

Since the mid-1980s, incidents of hooliganism affecting English football at club level have become much less frequent. Over the same period, the stadia of most leading clubs have been significantly upgraded or completely rebuilt. Since the mid-1990s, Premiership clubs have been required to provide seated viewing accommodation only; many lower-division clubs have done so as well.

Profit maximization

Returning to Table 2.2, Columns 7 and 8 summarize the monopolist's short-run cost structure. In accordance with the discussion in Section 2.2, the monopolist's short-run production function is subject to the Law of Diminishing Returns, and SRMC eventually increases as output (Q) increases. As before, total cost is the sum of the firm's variable cost (which can be inferred from the SRMC function) and fixed cost (assumed to be £1 per week). Column 9 shows the monopolist's profit function. Profit, denoted π, is total revenue *minus* total cost, or $\pi = TR - TC$.

In order to maximize its profit in the short run, the monopolist should select its output level so that marginal revenue *equals* short-run marginal cost, MR = SRMC. It is worthwhile to increase output as long as the additional revenue gained by doing so exceeds the additional cost incurred. Once the point is reached at which the additional revenue *equals* the additional cost (and beyond which the additional cost would exceed the additional revenue) the firm should not increase its output any further. In Table 2.2, this can be demonstrated by starting from the lowest possible output level of $Q = 0$ and increasing Q in steps of one:

■ Increasing from $Q = 0$ to $Q = 1$ increases revenue by MR = £2, and increases costs by SRMC = £0.5. Therefore profit increases by £1.5, from $\pi = -1.0$ to $\pi = 0.5$.

■ Similarly, increasing from $Q = 1$ to $Q = 2$ increases profit by £1.4, from $\pi = 0.5$ to $\pi = 1.9$; and increasing from $Q = 2$ to $Q = 3$ increases profit by £0.7, from $\pi = 1.9$ to $\pi = 2.6$.

■ Increasing from $Q = 3$ to $Q = 4$ increases revenue by MR = £0.8, and increases costs by SRMC = £0.8. Therefore profit remains unchanged, at $\pi = 2.6$. Between $Q = 3$ and $Q = 4$ MR = SRMC, and $\pi = 2.6$ is the maximum profit the monopolist can earn.

■ Increasing from $Q = 4$ to $Q = 5$ increases revenue by MR = £0.4, and increases costs by SRMC = £1.1. Therefore profit falls by £0.7, from $\pi = 2.6$ to $\pi = 1.9$. Any further increase beyond $Q = 5$ also causes profit to fall.

The profit-maximizing rule 'marginal revenue *equals* marginal cost' is quite general, and applies not only to monopolists, but also to firms operating in other market structures such as perfect competition and monopolistic competition. Furthermore, this rule is valid not only for profit maximization in the short run (MR = SRMC, as in Table 2.2), but also for profit maximization in the long run (MR = LRMC).

2.4 Summary

This chapter has reviewed the core elements of microeconomic theory that are required for an understanding of the economic models of firms and industries that are developed throughout the rest of this book.

In production and cost theory, an important distinction is drawn between the short run and the long run. For a firm that uses two factors of production, labour and capital, labour is assumed to be variable and capital fixed in the short run. In the long run, both labour and capital are assumed to be variable. The short-run relationship between inputs, outputs and costs of production is governed by the Law of Diminishing Returns. As increasing quantities of labour are used in conjunction with a fixed quantity of capital, eventually the additional contribution made by each successive unit of labour to total output starts to decline. Consequently, as the quantity of output increases, the marginal cost of producing any further output starts to increase.

The long-run relationship between inputs, outputs and costs of production is governed by economies of scale and diseconomies of scale. Returns to scale describes the proportionate increase in output achieved from any given proportionate increase in all inputs. Returns to scale are increasing, giving rise to economies of scale, if output increases more than proportionately to the increase in inputs. Returns to scale are decreasing, giving rise to diseconomies of scale, if output increases less than proportionately to the increase in inputs. A firm attains its minimum efficient scale by producing an output level beyond which no further savings in long-run average costs are possible; or, in other words, at which all possible opportunities for cost savings through economies of scale have been exhausted.

The market demand function for a product or service shows the relationship between market price and the number of units consumers wish to buy at that price. Price elasticity of demand is a measure of the responsiveness of quantity demanded to a change in market price. It is possible to define price elasticity of demand either at the market level, or at the firm level. Other useful elasticity measures include cross-price elasticity of demand, advertising elasticity of demand and price elasticity of supply.

A profit-maximizing firm should produce the output level at which its marginal revenue *equals* its marginal cost. It is worthwhile to increase output as long as the additional revenue gained by producing one additional unit of output exceeds the additional cost incurred. Once the point is reached at which the additional revenue *equals* the additional cost, the firm should not increase its output any further.

Discussion questions

1. Distinguish between returns to a variable factor of production, and returns to scale.

2. Sketch a typical total product function for a firm with one variable factor of production (labour). At what point on the total product function is the marginal product of labour at a maximum? At what point on the total product function is the average product of labour at a maximum?

3. Relying on your own research from textbooks, newspaper articles or the internet, identify the most important inputs to the production function of a specific industry.

4. Explain why a firm's short-run average cost function may be U-shaped. Explain why a firm's long-run average cost function may be U-shaped.

5. With reference to Case Study 2.1, explain why large firms may be able to operate with lower average costs than small firms in the long run.

6. With reference to Case Study 2.2, assess the relative importance of ticket prices and factors other than price in determining the level of spectator demand for attendance at professional football matches.

7. With reference to a large firm or other organization which is familiar to you, give examples of the possible causes of diseconomies of scale.

8. How might the concept of cross-price elasticity of demand be useful when attempting to identify the impact of an increase in the price of petrol on the demand for cars, or the impact of a reduction in the price of butter on the demand for margarine?

9. Explain why a profit-maximizing firm would never operate on the portion of its demand function where the price elasticity of demand is below one.

Further reading

Holmes, T.J. and Schmitz, J.A. (2010) Competition and productivity: a review of evidence, *Annual Review of Economics*, 2, 619–42.

Syverson, C. (2011) What determines productivity? *Journal of Economic Literature*, 49, 326–65.

Van Reenan, J. (2011) Does competition raise productivity through improving management quality? *International Journal of Industrial Organization*, 29, 306–16.

3

The neoclassical theory of the firm

Learning objectives

This chapter covers the following topics:

- historical development of the neoclassical theory of the firm
- perfect competition, monopoly and monopolistic competition
- allocative and productive efficiency
- welfare properties of perfect competition and monopoly

Key terms

Allocative efficiency
Barrier to entry
Consumer surplus
Deadweight loss
Economic efficiency
Imperfect competition
Interdependence
Lerner index

Monopolistic competition
Monopoly
Natural monopoly
Oligopoly
Perfect competition
Price taking behaviour
Producer surplus
Product differentiation

Production function
Productive efficiency
Profit maximization
Tangency solution
Technical efficiency
Welfare
X-efficiency

3.1 Introduction

This chapter reviews the body of microeconomic theory known as the neoclassical theory of the firm, including the models of perfect competition, monopoly and monopolistic competition. Section 3.2 begins by providing a brief description of the early historical development of the neoclasical theory.

The models of perfect competition, monopoly and monopolistic competition describe how firms should set their output levels and prices in order to maximize their profits, under various sets of assumptions concerning market structure.

The most important characteristics of market structure are the number of firms, the extent of **barriers to entry** and the degree of **product differentiation**.

The two most extreme cases considered by the neoclassical theory of the firm are **perfect competition** (the most competitive model) and **monopoly** (the least competitive). These models are developed in Section 3.3, and their efficiency and welfare properties are compared in Section 3.4. Finally, Section 3.5 develops the model of **monopolistic competition**. This model describes an industry with large numbers of sellers and no entry barriers (as in perfect competition), but some product differentiation affording the firms some discretion over their own prices (as in the case of monopoly). Accordingly, monopolistic competition represents an intermediate case, falling between the two polar cases of perfect competition and monopoly.

3.2 The neoclassical theory of the firm: historical development

It is difficult to decide precisely when the first theory of the firm emerged which was judged to be sufficiently coherent to be acceptable as the 'general' theory. Some people would claim that the credit should go to Edward Chamberlin and Joan Robinson in the 1930s. Others tend to look back further, to the contributions of Alfred Marshall in the 1890s, or perhaps even Augustin Cournot in the 1830s or Adam Smith in the 1770s. Nevertheless, it is possible to identify a coherent body of theory that claims to explain the determination of price and output, for both the industry and the individual firm, based on assumptions of **profit maximization** on the part of each individual firm. This body of theory is known as the neoclassical theory of the firm.

In *The Wealth of Nations*, Adam Smith (1776) argues that the value of the firm's output is related to its costs of production (a notion which constituted the orthodox view at that time). Costs include an allowance for profit, interpreted as a reward to the firm's owner. Owners maximize profit by attempting to minimize the other costs incurred by the firm. One of the most widely quoted passages is a description of Smith's visit to a Nottingham pin factory, where he observed the potential for the division of labour to increase labour productivity and generate large cost savings.

> To take an example, from . . . the trade of a pin maker; a workman not educated to this business . . . nor acquainted with the use of the machinery employed in it . . . could scarce, perhaps, with his utmost industry, make one pin in a day, and certainly could not make twenty. But in the way in which this business is now carried on, not only the whole work is a peculiar trade, but it is divided into a number of branches, of which the greater part are likewise peculiar trades. One man draws out the wire, another straights it, a third cuts it, a fourth points it, a fifth grinds it at the top for receiving the head . . . ten persons, therefore, could make among them upwards of forty-eight thousand pins in a day.
>
> *(Smith, 1776, pp. 4–5)*

Augustin Cournot (1838) was one of the first economists to attempt a formal mathematical analysis of the behaviour of monopolists and duopolists. Although Cournot was a mathematician by background, he was the first to apply calculus to an analysis of the pricing decisions of firms. Cournot's analysis is considered in detail later on (see Chapter 6).

The idea that the value of a firm's output is dependent on production costs survived until the late nineteenth century, when this notion was seriously challenged for the first time. According to the new view, the value of the product determines the rewards paid to the factors of production. Firms earning high profits by selling products that are in demand for a high price can pay higher rents, wages and interest. The price and therefore the value of the product depends ultimately on the level of demand. Stanley Jevons (1871) argued that the value a consumer places on a product depends on utility at the margin, which implies value is judged against all other past units of the product consumed. If marginal utility declines as consumption increases, price reductions are required to induce an increase in the quantity demanded. This relationship provides an explanation for the downward sloping demand function.

Alfred Marshall (1890, 1892) is considered to have been the first economist to draw the link between costs of production and market demand. Accordingly, value is determined by interactions between the conditions surrounding both supply and demand. Marshall developed the tools of economic analysis that are still familiar to first-year undergraduates: the upward sloping supply function and downward sloping demand function which combine, scissor-like, to determine an equilibrium price and quantity demanded and supplied. If price is set above or below this equilibrium, then firms are faced with excess supply or excess demand. In the case of excess supply or a glut of goods, price tends to fall, encouraging more buyers into the market. Some firms that are no longer able to cover their costs of production are forced to reduce their supply or leave the market. In the case of excess demand or a shortage of goods, price tends to rise, discouraging some buyers who withdraw from the market. Some incumbent firms respond to the price signal by increasing their production, and some entrants are attracted into the market for the first time.

Marshall also introduced the concept of price elasticity of demand, and drew the distinction between the short run and the long run. Like Smith, Marshall recognized that in the long-run firms benefit from economies of large-scale production. However, this does not necessarily lead to the emergence of monopoly, because other producers may still be able to compete with a large incumbent, by exploiting distinctive entrepreneurial skills or external economies of scale. Marshall recognized the importance of rivalry, and that this creates the potential for collusion. However, Marshall viewed oligopoly as a form of quasi-monopoly, and therefore as an exception to the normal competitive market structure.

The theory of perfect competition was developed by John Bates Clark (1899), who believed that competition is fundamentally a force for good in the economy. In competitive markets, everyone receives a reward equivalent to their marginal contribution to production. Accordingly, Clark analyzed those forces that have the potential to frustrate competition, especially monopoly and associated restrictive practices. The theory was refined by Frank Knight (1921), who lists a number of conditions required for a market to conform to the model of perfect competition. Most importantly, no one buyer or seller is sufficiently powerful to influence prices; entry barriers do not impede the flow of resources into the market; and all agents have perfect knowledge. Knight explains why perfect competition does not necessarily eliminate abnormal profit in situations of *uncertainty*. According to Knight, uncertainty implies the probabilities that should be assigned to possible future events are unknown. Risk, on the other hand, describes the case where the probabilities are known and future events can be insured against. Knight argues that, even in long-run equilibrium, firms might earn an abnormal profit as a payoff for dealing with uncertainty.

In the 1930s, Joan Robinson and Edward Chamberlin coined the term **imperfect competition** to describe the middle ground between perfect competition and monopoly (see Box 1.1). Robinson (1933) introduced the concept of marginal revenue and showed that in perfect competition marginal revenue *equals* price. For a firm in imperfect competition, the marginal revenue function is downward sloping. At some levels of production (where marginal revenue is negative), it may be possible to increase total revenue by producing and selling less output. Robinson argues that the tendency for imperfectly competitive firms to restrict production and operate below full capacity helps explain the high unemployment experienced in the UK in the 1930s. In contrast, high unemployment is inconsistent with the theory of perfect competition. Robinson's analysis of price discrimination represents another important contribution to the theory of the firm. Chamberlin (1933) developed the theory of monopolistic competition to describe a market in which many firms produce goods that are similar but not identical. Accordingly, the firms have some discretion in setting their prices. Chamberlin also contributed to the theory of oligopoly. Oligopolists recognize that their actions are interdependent: a change in output by one firm alters the profits of rival firms, perhaps causing them to adjust their output as well. Forms of competition under oligopoly vary from vigorous price competition to collusion.

3.3 Theories of perfect competition and monopoly

Within the neoclassical theory, different models describe price and output determination for different market structures. The most important characteristics of market structure are the number of firms, the extent of barriers to entry, and the degree of product differentiation. Table 3.1 shows a standard typology of market structures. The two most extreme cases are **perfect competition** (the most competitive model) and **monopoly** (the least competitive). Section 3.3 examines these two cases, and Section 3.4 draws some comparisons between their efficiency and welfare properties. Occupying a large swathe of territory between perfect competition and monopoly is imperfect competition, which subdivides into two cases: **monopolistic competition** (the more competitive variant of imperfect competition) and **oligopoly** (the less competitive variant). This chapter concludes in Section 3.5 by examining the first of these two cases: monopolistic competition. Oligopoly theory forms a much larger sub-field within microeconomics and industrial economics, and requires its own separate and more

Table 3.1 The neoclassical theory of the firm: typology of market structures

	No. of firms	Entry conditions	Product differentiation
Perfect competition	Many	Free entry	Identical products
Imperfect competition			
Monopolistic competition	Many	Free entry	Some differentiation
Oligopoly	Few	Barriers to entry	Some differentiation
Monopoly	One	No entry	Complete differentiation

extensive treatment. Accordingly, oligopoly theory is covered in detail later (see Chapters 7 and 8).

Perfect competition

In the neoclassical theory of perfect competition, the industry is assumed to have the following characteristics:

- There are large numbers of buyers and sellers. It is sometimes said that buyers and sellers are atomistic. An important implication is that the actions of any individual buyer or seller have a negligible influence on the market price.

- Firms are free to enter into or exit from the industry, and a decision to enter or exit does not impose any additional costs on the firm concerned. There are no barriers to entry and exit.

- The goods or services produced and sold are identical or homogeneous. There is no product differentiation.

- All buyers and sellers have perfect information. There are no transaction costs, such as costs incurred in searching for information or in negotiating or monitoring contracts between buyers and sellers.

- There are no transport costs. Therefore, the geographical locations of buyers and sellers do not influence their decisions on where to buy or sell.

- Firms act independently of each other, with each firm seeking to maximize its own profit.

These assumptions ensure each individual buyer and seller is a price taker. **Price taking behaviour** implies each buyer and seller operates under the assumption that the current market price is beyond his or her personal control. Each firm recognizes its market share is sufficiently small that any decision to raise or lower its output would have a negligible impact on the industry's total output and, therefore, a negligible impact on the market price. Therefore, each firm believes it can sell whatever quantity of output it wishes to sell at the current market price. An important implication of price-taking behaviour is that any attempt on the part of an individual firm to increase or decrease its own price directly would be ineffective. If the firm set a higher price than its competitors, all of the firm's customers would immediately switch to its competitors and the quantity of output sold by the firm would fall to zero. On the other hand, it would be pointless for the firm to set a lower price than its competitors because the firm can already sell as much output as it wishes at the current market price.

With price-taking behaviour, each firm faces a horizontal firm-level demand function, located at the current market price. A very small proportionate reduction in price would induce a very large proportionate increase in quantity demanded. This implies the perfectly competitive firm's price elasticity of demand (PED) is infinite. Recall $PED = PED = \dfrac{\Delta Q}{\Delta P} \times \dfrac{P}{Q}$. Accordingly, if ΔP is infinitely small (and negative) and ΔQ is infinitely large (and positive), $PED = -\infty$ or $|PED| = \infty$. The firm's demand function is also its average revenue (AR) function (see Section 2.3). Finally, given that the firm's demand or AR function is horizontal, the same function is also the firm's marginal revenue (MR) function. The equivalence between marginal revenue and price when $|PED| = \infty$ can be demonstrated as follows:

$$ MR = P\left(1 - \frac{1}{|PED|}\right) = P\left(1 - \frac{1}{\infty}\right) = P(1 - 0) = P $$

The analysis of the perfectly competitive firm's short-run and long-run cost structure was described earlier (see Section 2.2). The firm's profit-maximizing output decision can be analyzed, both in the short-run case, and in the long run. In order to keep the analysis as simple as possible, in the short run it is assumed that each firm is already using the quantity of the fixed factor of production (capital) that will eventually be consistent with the minimization of long-run average costs, or production at the minimum efficient scale (MES), in the long run. For simplicity, it is assumed that fixed costs are zero, so the firm's AVC and SRAC functions are the same. Figure 3.1 shows the determination of the pre- and post-entry market price and the output levels for one representative firm and for the industry as a whole. In order to understand Figure 3.1, it is important to follow the construction of the firm- and industry-level diagrams in the correct sequence, as follows:

■ The upper left-hand diagram shows the firm's SRAC and SRMC functions. The firm's MR function is horizontal and equivalent to the market price (P). Profit maximization requires MR = SRMC, so the firm's profit-maximizing output level for any given value of P will be found by reading from the SRMC function. To produce any output at all, the firm must at least cover its SRAC. Therefore, the minimum price the firm is willing to accept is determined by the intersection of SRMC and SRAC. The section of SRMC above this intersection is the representative firm's supply function.

■ The upper right-hand diagram shows the market demand function, and the industry supply function. The industry supply function is constructed by summing horizontally the SRMC functions over all N_1 firms in the industry. (Each individual SRMC function is a supply function for one firm; therefore the horizontal sum of the SRMC functions is the supply function for the entire industry.) The pre-entry market price of P_1 is determined by the intersection of the market demand and industry supply functions. Pre-entry industry output is Q_1.

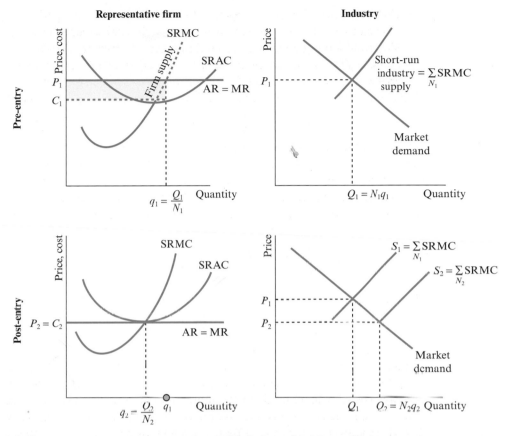

Figure 3.1 Short-run pre-entry and post-entry equilibria in perfect competition

■ Returning to the upper left-hand diagram, the representative firm's demand, AR and MR functions are shown by the horizontal line at P_1. The firm maximizes profit by producing q_1 units of output, at which MR = SRMC. By construction $q_1 = Q_1/N_1$, or $Q_1 = N_1q_1$. At the pre-entry profit-maximizing equilibrium represented by P_1 and q_1, the representative firm earns an abnormal profit shown by the shaded area between P_1 and C_1, the firm's average cost.

■ The availability of abnormal profits attracts entrants, so (P_1, Q_1) cannot represent a final or stable equilibrium. Entry increases the number of firms from N_1 to N_2, and in the lower right-hand diagram shifts the industry supply function to the right from S_1 to S_2. Consequently, price falls from P_1 to P_2, and industry output increases from Q_1 to Q_2.

■ In the lower left-hand diagram, the representative firm's post-entry demand, AR and MR functions are shown by the horizontal line at P_2. The firm maximizes profit by producing q_2 units of output, at which MR = SRMC. By construction $q_2 = Q_2/N_2$, or $Q_2 = N_2q_2$. At the post-entry profit-maximizing equilibrium represented by P_2 and q_2, the representative firm earns a normal profit only, because P_2 coincides with C_2, the firm's average cost. The fall in

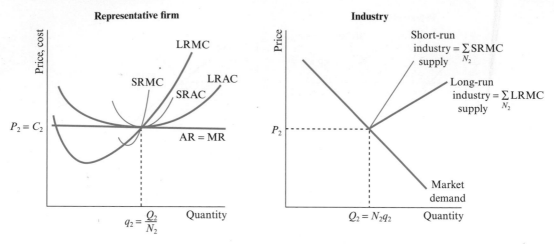

Figure 3.2 Long-run post-entry equilibrium in perfect competition

market price caused by entry and the increase in industry supply eliminates the pre-entry abnormal profit. Post-entry, each individual firm produces less output than it did pre-entry, but total post-entry industry output increases due to the increase in the number of firms.

Figure 3.2 shows the equivalent long-run analysis. For simplicity, Figure 3.2 shows only the final (post-entry) equilibrium, corresponding to (P_2, Q_2) in Figure 3.1. In Figure 3.2, all short-run functions are identical to those in Figure 3.1. In addition, the left-hand diagram shows the representative firm's long-run marginal cost (LRMC) and long-run average cost (LRAC) functions. Notice that SRAC is nested within LRAC, as in Figure 2.4. In the right-hand diagram, the long-run industry supply function is constructed by summing LRMC horizontally over all N_2 firms, in the same way as before. The equilibrium market price of P_2 is located by the intersection of both the short-run and long-run supply functions with the market demand function.

Monopoly

In the neoclassical theory of monopoly, the industry is assumed to have the following characteristics:

■ There are large numbers of atomistic buyers, but there is only one seller. Therefore the selling firm's demand function is the market demand function, and the firm's output decision determines the market price.

■ Barriers to entry are insurmountable. If the monopolist earns an abnormal profit, there is no threat that entrants will be attracted into the industry.

■ The good or service produced and sold is unique, and there are no substitutes. There is complete product differentiation.

■ The buyers and the seller may have perfect or imperfect information.

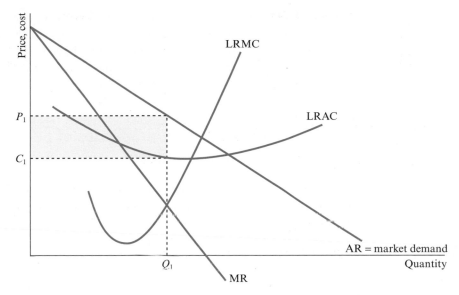

Figure 3.3 Long-run equilibrium in monopoly

- Geographical location could be the defining characteristic which gives the selling firm its monopoly position. In a spatial monopoly, transport costs are sufficiently high to prevent buyers from switching to alternative sellers located in other regions or countries.

- The selling firm seeks to maximize its own profit.

As before, the analysis of the monopolist's short-run and long-run cost structure is as described earlier (see Section 2.2). Figure 3.3 shows the determination of price and output. In order to understand Figure 3.3, it is important to note the following points:

- Since there is only one firm, Figure 3.3 does not distinguish between the firm and the industry. By definition, the monopolist's private price and output decisions immediately establish the market price and the industry output. This means that for a monopoly, there is no industry supply function. Industry output depends on the monopolist's private profit-maximizing output decision, which in turn depends on the shape of the monopolist's cost and revenue functions. In contrast to the case of perfect competition, it is not possible to express this decision in the form of a direct supply relationship between market price and industry output.

- Since there is no entry, Figure 3.3 does not distinguish between the pre-entry and post-entry equilibria.

- For simplicity the analysis in Figure 3.3 is limited to the long-run case: the monopolist's short-run average and marginal cost functions are not shown.

The monopolist's profit-maximizing output level of Q_1 is located at the intersection of the marginal revenue (MR) and the SRMC and LRMC functions. The market price of P_1 is established by reading from the market demand or average revenue (AR) function at Q_1, and the monopolist's average cost of C_1 is established by reading from the average cost functions at Q_1. In this case, the monopolist earns an abnormal profit represented by the shaded area between P_1 and C_1. See Appendix 1 for a mathematical derivation of the monopolist's profit-maximizing equilibrium for the case where LRAC and LRMC are horizontal.

<table>
<tr><td>3.4</td><td></td></tr>
</table>

3.4   Efficiency and welfare properties of perfect competition and monopoly

In much of the academic, political and media discussion about the role of market forces and competition in allocating resources in a free-market economy, there is a strong presumption that competition is a desirable ideal, and monopoly is a state of affairs to be avoided if possible. Figure 3.4 presents a comparison of the long-run industry equilibrium under perfect competition and monopoly for the special case of constant returns to scale, in which the LRAC and LRMC functions are horizontal and identical (see Section 2.2).

Under perfect competition, the industry supply function is a horizontal summation of the firms' horizontal LRMC functions, and is also horizontal. Industry price and output is (P_C, Q_C), at which $P = \text{LRAC}$ and abnormal profit is zero. Under monopoly, the profit-maximizing price and output is (P_1, Q_1), at which $\text{MR} = \text{LRMC}$ and abnormal profit is positive.

Figure 3.4 indicates that, under monopoly, market price is higher and output is lower than under perfect competition. The monopolist earns an abnormal profit in the long run, while the perfectly competitive firm earns only a normal profit. In the more general case of an L- or U-shaped LRAC function, the monopolist fails to produce at the minimum efficient scale (MES), and therefore fails to produce at the minimum attainable LRAC (see Figure 3.3). In contrast, the perfectly competitive firm produces at the minimum attainable LRAC (see Figure 3.2).

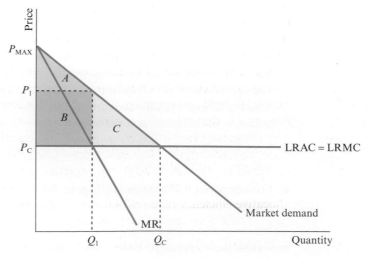

Figure 3.4 Allocative inefficiency in monopoly

In perfect competition, price *equals* (short-run or long-run) marginal cost. This suggests that the degree to which price exceeds marginal cost provides a useful indicator or measure of market power. Accordingly, Lerner (1934) proposes the following measure of market power, known as the **Lerner index**:

$$L = \frac{P - MC}{P}$$

The Lerner index is subject to a minimum value of zero, and a maximum value of one. In perfect competition, $P = MC$ so $L = 0$. In monopoly $P > MC$, and if $MC > 0$, $0 < L < 1$. After some simple manipulations, the Lerner index can also be expressed in terms of price elasticity of demand:

$$MR = P\left(1 - \frac{1}{|PED|}\right) = P - \frac{P}{|PED|} \Rightarrow P - MR = \frac{P}{|PED|} \Rightarrow \frac{P - MR}{P} = \frac{1}{|PED|}$$

For a profit-maximizing firm, $MR = MC$. Therefore:

$$\frac{P - MC}{P} = \frac{1}{|PED|}, \text{ or } L = \frac{1}{|PED|}$$

The Lerner index is the reciprocal of the firm's price elasticity of demand. In perfect competition, $|PED| = \infty$ for each firm, so $L = 0$ (as above). In monopoly, if $MC > 0$ then $MR > 0$ and $|PED| > 1$, so $0 < L < 1$ (as above).

The Lerner index provides a convenient measure of a firm's market power based on the relationship between its price and marginal cost. However, does it actually matter that market price and profit are higher under monopoly than under perfect competition? This might be bad news for consumers, but it is also good news for producers. In practice, a slightly more sophisticated comparison is usually required, taking account of both the efficiency and **welfare** properties of the two models. On the basis of this kind of comparison, it can be shown that perfect competition is usually preferable to monopoly, because the long-run competitive equilibrium has several desirable properties that are not satisfied by the corresponding long-run monopoly equilibrium. However, the first task is to define the relevant notions of efficiency.

Allocative efficiency is achieved when there is no possible reallocation of resources that could make one agent (producer or consumer) better off without making at least one other agent worse off. A necessary condition for allocative efficiency is that the marginal benefit (to society as a whole) of an additional unit of output being produced *equals* the marginal cost of producing the additional unit of output. The market price (the price at which the most marginal consumer is prepared to buy) is interpreted as a measure of the value society as a whole places on the most marginal unit of output produced. Accordingly, allocative efficiency requires that the total quantity of output produced should be such that price *equals* marginal cost.

- If price exceeds marginal cost, the value that society would place on an additional unit of output (measured by the price the most marginal consumer is prepared to pay) exceeds the cost of producing that unit. Therefore, the industry's output is currently too low. Welfare could be increased by producing more output.

■ If price is below marginal cost, the value that society places on the last unit of output produced (again measured by the price the most marginal consumer is prepared to pay) is less than the cost of producing that unit. Therefore, the industry's output is currently too high. Welfare could be increased by producing less output.

Quite distinct from allocative efficiency is the notion of **productive efficiency**, which consists of two components. First, a firm is **technically efficient**, also known as **x-efficient**, if it is producing the maximum quantity of output that is technologically feasible, given the quantities of the factor inputs it is currently employing. In other words, a technically efficient firm operates on (and not within) its own **production function** (Leibenstein, 1966). Second, a firm is **economically efficient** if it has selected the combination of factor inputs that enable it to produce its current output level at the lowest possible cost, given the prevailing prices of the factor inputs available to the firm (Leibenstein, 1966; Comanor and Leibenstein, 1969). A firm might be technically efficient but economically inefficient, if it uses its selected inputs to produce as much output as is technologically feasible, but it could produce the same quantity of output more cheaply by selecting a different combination of inputs.

Figures 3.5 and 3.6 draw a comparison between the efficiency properties of the perfectly competitive equilibrium and the profit-maximizing equilibrium under monopoly. In common with Figures 3.3 and 3.4, Figures 3.5 and 3.6 are based on an assumption of constant returns to scale, and a horizontal long-run average cost (LRAC) and long-run marginal cost (LRMC) function. Figure 3.5 compares perfect competition and monopoly on allocative efficiency criteria, while Figure 3.6 also incorporates productive efficiency criteria.

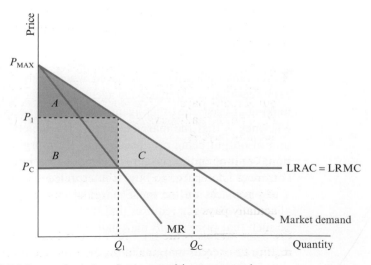

Figure 3.5 Monopoly and perfect competition compared

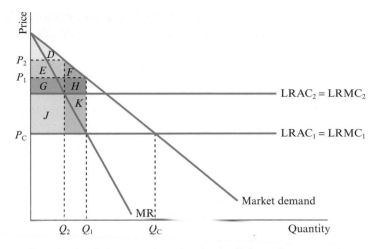

Figure 3.6 Allocative inefficiency and productive inefficiency in monopoly

In Figure 3.5, the horizontal LRMC function is also the industry supply function under perfect competition, and the equilibrium market price and output are P_C and Q_C, located at the intersection of the industry supply and market demand functions. Since P_C = LRMC, the condition for allocative efficiency is satisfied. The profit-maximizing monopolist chooses a price and output level of P_1 and Q_1, located at the intersection of the MR and LRMC functions. Since P_1 > LRMC, the condition for allocative efficiency is not satisfied. Welfare would be increased by producing more output than Q_1. The superior welfare properties of the perfectly competitive equilibrium can also be demonstrated with reference to the welfare economics concepts of consumer surplus and producer surplus.

Consumer surplus is the sum over all consumers of the difference between the maximum amount each consumer would be prepared to pay and the price each consumer actually does pay. Imagine consumers arrayed along the horizontal axis of Figure 3.5 in descending order of their willingness to pay (reading from left to right).

■ At the perfectly competitive equilibrium (P_C, Q_C) consumer surplus is represented by the triangle $A + B + C$. The first consumer is willing to pay P_{MAX} but actually pays P_C. The second consumer is willing to pay slightly less than P_{MAX} but actually pays P_C. The last consumer (at Q_C) is willing to pay P_C and actually pays P_C.

■ At the monopoly equilibrium (P_1, Q_1) consumer surplus is represented by the triangle A. As before, the first consumer is willing to pay P_{MAX} but actually pays P_1, and so on. The last consumer (at Q_1) is willing to pay P_1 and actually pays P_1.

Producer surplus is the total reward producers receive beyond the reward they require to cover their costs of production, including their normal profit. In the present case, producer surplus is equivalent to abnormal profit.

■ At the perfectly competitive equilibrium (P_C, Q_C), producer surplus is zero because there is no abnormal profit.

■ At the monopoly equilibrium (P_1, Q_1), producer surplus is represented by the rectangle B, equivalent to the monopolist's abnormal profit.

Under perfect competition, consumer surplus is $A + B + C$ and producer surplus is nil. The sum of consumer surplus and producer surplus is $A + B + C$. Under monopoly, consumer surplus is A and producer surplus is B. The sum of consumer surplus and producer surplus is $A + B$. The triangle C is known as the **deadweight loss** associated with monopoly. It represents the total welfare loss resulting from the fact that less output is produced under monopoly than under perfect competition. It is important to notice that the transfer of surplus of B from consumers to the producer does not form part of the critique of monopoly from a welfare economics perspective, because welfare economics does not make distributional judgements as to *whose* welfare should be maximized. However, the existence of a deadweight loss does form part of this critique, since it implies the welfare of at least one agent could be increased without reducing the welfare of any other agent or agents. For example, if the market structure were changed from monopoly to perfect competition, and the consumers gave the monopolist a compensating side payment of B, the consumers would be better off (their surplus net of the side payment having risen from A to $A + C$) and the producer would be no worse off (the loss of producer surplus of B having been compensated by the side payment).

Figure 3.5 makes the case that monopoly is less desirable than perfect competition using an allocative efficiency criterion. The possibility that monopoly might also be less desirable based on a productive efficiency criterion rests on the suggestion that a monopolist shielded from competitive pressure (emanating either from rival firms or from actual or potential entrants) may tend to become complacent or lazy, and therefore inefficient in production. A complacent monopolist may not strive to make the most efficient use of its factor inputs (technical inefficiency), or it may not identify its most cost-effective combination of factor inputs (economic inefficiency). Consequently the monopolist may operate on a higher LRAC and LRMC function than it would attain if the full rigours of competition forced it to produce as efficiently as possible.

Figure 3.6 identifies the further welfare loss resulting from productive inefficiency on the part of the complacent monopolist. $LRAC_1 = LRMC_1$ is the same as $LRAC = LRMC$ in Figure 3.5, and (P_1, Q_1) is also the same in both diagrams. $LRAC_2 = LRMC_2$ represents the complacent monopolist's cost functions. The complacent monopolist's profit-maximizing price and output are P_2 and Q_2. Examining the welfare implications of shifting from (P_1, Q_1) to (P_2, Q_2), the following conclusions emerge:

■ Consumer surplus falls from $D + E + F$ ($= A$ in Figure 3.5) to D.

■ Producer surplus falls from $G + H + J + K$ ($= B$ in Figure 3.5) to $E + G$.

■ Therefore (consumer surplus *plus* producer surplus) falls by $F + H + J + K$.

■ J represents the increase in the cost of producing Q_2 units of output resulting from productive inefficiency.

- $F + H + K$ represents the increase in the deadweight loss resulting from the reduction in output from Q_1 to Q_2.

Is monopoly always inferior to perfect competition on efficiency and welfare criteria? This section concludes by examining one special case for which the comparison is not clear-cut. A **natural monopoly** is a market in which LRAC is decreasing as output increases over the entire range of outputs that could conceivably be produced, given the position of the market demand function. In other words, there is insufficient demand for any firm to produce the output level at which all opportunities for further savings in average costs through economies of scale are exhausted, or at which the minimum efficient scale (MES) is attained. In a natural monopoly, monopoly is always a more cost-effective market structure than competition. LRAC is lower if one firm services the entire market than if two (or more) firms share the market between them. Industries where the costs of indivisibilities represent a large proportion of total costs, and where total costs do not increase much as output increases, are most likely to exhibit the characteristics of natural monopoly. Perhaps the most widely cited examples are the utilities, such as gas, electricity and water. A vast and costly physical infrastructure is required in order to distribute these products but, once this infrastructure is in place, fluctuations in the quantities traded cause only relatively minor variations in total costs.

The case of natural monopoly is illustrated in Figure 3.7.

- In order to maximize profit, the monopolist produces Q_1 units of output, and charges a price of P_1. Average cost is C_1, and the monopolist earns an abnormal profit, represented by area A.

- If the monopolist were forced to produce Q_2 units of output, then price would fall to $P_2 = C_2$ ($< C_1$) and the monopolist would earn only a normal profit.

- In order to achieve allocative efficiency (price *equals* marginal cost), the monopolist would have to produce Q_3 units of output. Average cost would fall to C_3 ($< C_2 < C_1$), but price would fall to P_3 and the monopolist would realize a loss, represented by area B.

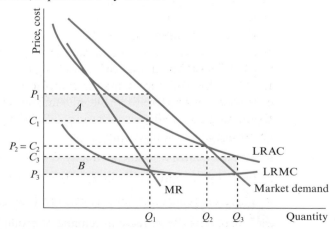

Figure 3.7 Natural monopoly

In the case of natural monopoly, allocative efficiency might not be attainable because the monopolist would rather go out of business altogether than operate at (P_3, Q_3). However, on efficiency and welfare criteria, it would be preferable for the monopolist to operate at (P_2, Q_2) rather than at the monopolist's preferred (profit-maximizing) position of (P_1, Q_1). This suggests a possible justification for the regulation of natural monopolies by the competition authorities (see Chapters 23 and 24).

3.5 Theory of monopolistic competition

The theory of imperfect competition attempts to draw together the polar cases of perfect competition and monopoly. Imperfect competition encompasses both oligopoly (see Chapters 7 and 8) and monopolistic competition, described here in this final section of Chapter 3. In the neoclassical theory of monopolistic competition, the industry is assumed to have the following characteristics:

■ There are large numbers of atomistic buyers and sellers.

■ Firms are free to enter into or exit from the industry, and a decision to enter or exit does not impose any additional costs on the firm concerned. In other words, there are no barriers to entry and exit.

■ The goods or services produced and sold by each firm are perceived by consumers to be similar but not identical. In other words, there is some product differentiation. There could be real differences between the goods or services produced by each firm, or the differences could be imagined, with consumers' perceptions of differences reinforced by branding or advertising.

■ The buyers and the sellers may have perfect or imperfect information. If the product differentiation is perceived rather than real, this suggests that the buyers' information is in some sense imperfect.

■ Geographic location could be the characteristic that differentiates the product or service produced by one firm from those of its competitors. In this case, transport costs may to some extent deter buyers from switching to alternative sellers located elsewhere. However, each firm's market is not completely segmented geographically. Any firm that raises its price too far will find that its customers start switching to other sellers.

■ Each selling firm seeks to maximize its own profit.

These assumptions ensure each individual firm has some discretion over its own price. Due to product differentiation, each firm can exercise some market power. In contrast to the perfectly competitive firm, a firm in monopolistic competition that raises its price does not immediately lose all of its customers, and a firm that lowers its price does not immediately acquire all of its competitors' customers. Therefore, non-price-taking behaviour is assumed on the part of each firm. Each firm faces a demand function that is downward sloping (not horizontal as in perfect competition). However, the firm's discretion over its own price is limited by the fact that its product is quite similar to its competitors' products. If the firm does increase its price, it tends to lose customers to its competitors rapidly; similarly, by cutting its price the firm can attract customers rapidly. Therefore, the firm's demand function is relatively price elastic, more so than the market demand function faced by the monopolist.

The assumption that buyers and sellers are atomistic under monopolistic competition has implications for the way in which equilibrium is determined. Under atomistic competition, each firm believes its market share is sufficiently small that any decision to raise or lower its own price or output has a negligible impact on its competitors' individual demand functions, and therefore a negligible impact on their price and output decisions. The firms are sufficiently small and plentiful that the issue of **interdependence** can be ignored: the possibility that any one firm's profit-maximizing price and output decisions carries implications for all of the other firms' decisions.

Figure 3.8 shows the determination of the pre- and post-entry market price and output levels for one representative firm in monopolistic competition.

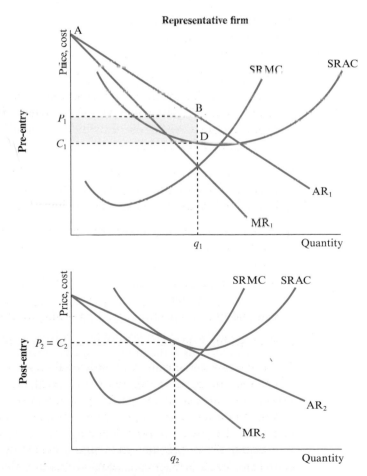

Figure 3.8 Short-run pre-entry and post-entry equilibria in monopolistic competition

Because each firm sells a differentiated product, there is no market demand function and no industry-level analysis. The upper diagram shows the firm's SRAC and SRMC functions. In accordance with the previous discussion, the firm's AR and MR functions are downward sloping. The firm maximizes profit by producing q_1 units of output, at which $MR = SRMC$. At the pre-entry profit-maximizing equilibrium represented by P_1 and q_1, the representative firm earns an abnormal profit shown by the shaded area between P_1 and C_1.

As in perfect competition, the availability of abnormal profits attracts entrants, so (P_1, q_1) cannot be a final or a stable equilibrium. Entry increases the number of firms, and in the lower diagram causes the representative firm's AR and MR functions to shift to the left. The firm maximizes profit by producing q_2 units of output, at which $MR_2 = SRMC$. At the post-entry profit-maximizing equilibrium represented by P_2 and q_2, the representative firm earns a normal profit only. The fall in market price caused by entry has eliminated the pre-entry abnormal profit. Post-entry, each individual firm produces less output than it did pre-entry. (P_2, q_2) represents the **tangency solution** to the model of monopolistic competition, so called because the firm's AR function is tangential to its SRAC function. There is a similar tangency solution to the long-run model (not shown in Figure 3.8).

Using the criteria developed in Section 3.4, the efficiency and welfare properties of the long-run equilibrium under monopolistic competition are as follows:

■ The representative firm under monopolistic competition fails to produce at the minimum efficient scale (as is usually the case in monopoly), and therefore fails to produce at the minimum attainable long-run average cost.

■ The representative monopolistic competitor earns only a normal profit in the long run (as in the case of perfect competition).

■ The representative monopolistic competitor sells at a price that exceeds its marginal cost. Accordingly, there is allocative inefficiency (as in the case of monopoly). Each firm's output, and the total industry output, is lower than is required for the maximization of welfare. There is a deadweight loss.

■ The market power enjoyed by the representative monopolistic competitor, thanks to its differentiated product, might enable the firm to operate without achieving full efficiency in production (as in the case of monopoly). Monopolistic competition might be compatible with either technical inefficiency (x-inefficiency) or economic inefficiency, or both. However, in contrast to the monopolist, the monopolistic competitor is not fully shielded from the rigours of competition. A monopolistic competitor that is producing inefficiently is vulnerable to the threat of competition from incumbents or entrants. An efficient incumbent or entrant might imitate the inefficient firm's product characteristics, and be capable of undercutting the inefficient firm on price, because its costs are lower. Therefore, the degree to which the monopolistic competitor can operate at less than full efficiency is severely constrained by the lack of entry barriers and the threat of actual or potential competition.

3.6 Summary

Chapter 3 has traced the historical development of the neoclassical theory of the firm, and has reviewed several important neoclassical models of the firm, including perfect competition, monopoly and monopolistic competition.

In the model of perfect competition, there are large numbers of atomistic buyers and sellers, firms are free to enter into or exit from the industry, and there is no product differentiation. All buyers and sellers are assumed to have perfect information, and there are no transaction or transport costs that could otherwise protect individual firms from the full rigours of competition. At the long-run equilibrium, each firm produces at the minimum point on its long-run average cost function, and earns only a normal profit. There is allocative efficiency because the market price *equals* each firm's marginal cost. Competitive discipline ensures that all firms must either achieve full efficiency in production, or fail to realize a normal profit at the long-run equilibrium market price and face being forced out of business.

In the model of monopoly there is only one seller, there are insurmountable barriers to entry, and there is complete product differentiation in the sense that no other firm produces a substitute product that could undermine the monopolist's market power. At the long-run equilibrium, the monopolist charges a higher price and produces less output than would occur if the monopolist were relaced by (or broken down into) a large number of small, perfectly competitive firms. The monopolist typically fails to produce at the minimum point on its long run average cost function, but it can earn an abnormal profit in the long run. The monopolist charges a price higher than its marginal cost, so there is allocative inefficiency. The lack of competitive discipline suggests that the monopolist may be able to operate without achieving full efficiency in production.

The model of monopolistic competition falls between the polar cases of perfect competition and monopoly. The industry comprises many firms and entry is possible, but product differentiation affords the firms a degree of market power that is not available to their perfectly competitive counterparts. The absence of barriers to entry ensures the firms are only able to earn a normal profit in the long run. The firms also fail to produce at the minimum efficient scale and fail to achieve allocative efficiency, because price exceeds marginal cost at the long-run equilibrium. It is possible that the firms' market power may permit them to operate without achieving full productive efficiency. However, the degree of inefficiency that is sustainable is constrained by the threat of competition from incumbents and entrants.

Discussion questions

1. Comment on the realism of the assumptions of the theoretical model of perfect competition. Suggest real-world industries or markets that might approximate to the ideal of perfect competition.

2. If a representative firm in perfect competition earns an abnormal profit, explain why this situation is unstable, and explain how an industry equilibrium in which all firms earn only normal profits is achieved.

3. With reference to cost theory, explain why the long run industry supply function in perfect competition is more price-elastic than the short-run industry supply function.

4. Compare the productive and allocative efficiency properties of the long-run profit-maximizing equilibria under perfect competition, monopoly and monopolistic competition.

5. Are all monopolies necessarily bad for social welfare?

6. Is allocative efficiency ever attainable by a natural monopoly?

7. Like a monopolist, a firm in monopolistic competition faces a downward-sloping demand function and enjoys some market power. Unlike a monopolist, a firm in monopolistic competition cannot earn an abnormal profit indefinitely. Explain why not.

Managerial and behavioural theories of the firm

Learning objectives

This chapter covers the following topics:

- critique of the neoclassical theory of the firm
- the separation of ownership from control in the large modern corporation
- managerial theories of the firm
- the behavioural theory of the firm

Key terms

Austrian school	Organizational slack
Bounded rationality	Satisficing
Cost plus pricing	Side-payments
Managerial utility	Valuation ratio
Minimum profit constraint	

4.1 Introduction

Previously, we examined the neoclassical theory of the firm, and the models of perfect competition, monopoly and monopolistic competition (see Chapter 3). In the neoclassical theory, the role of the firm is to allocate resources and organize production in such a way as to satisfy consumer wants, driven by the desire to maximize profits. Chapter 4 describes the development of several alternative theories of the firm. The objective of introducing more realism into the theory of the firm motivates the development of most, if not all, of the alternative theories described in this and the next chapter.

Section 4.2 motivates the development of alternatives to the neoclassical theory of the firm by discussing some of the main limitations and criticisms of the neoclassical theory. Some of the earliest challenges to the neoclassical theory developed in the light of growing evidence of the increasing complexity of firms and the separation of the ownership of large corporations (in the hands of shareholders) from control (in the hands of salaried managers). While the neoclassical theory assumes that firms operate so as to maximize the interests of their owners, some economists started to acknowledge that managers' objectives may differ from those of the shareholders. Section 4.3 examines the managerial theories of sales revenue maximization, growth maximization and managerial utility maximization. Section 4.4 examines a behavioural theory of the firm that has its roots in both economics and organizational science.

4.2 Critique of the neoclassical theory of the firm

A common criticism levelled at the neoclassical theory of the firm is that it is insufficiently realistic. The theory is largely based on outdated views of competition and entrepreneurial activity. In the eighteenth and early nineteenth centuries, the rise of the textile industry and the growing international trade in staples provided early economists with concepts which dominated economic thought. During this era, price competition was both intense and instantaneous, goods produced by competing suppliers were usually similar or identical, there were few trade secrets, and markets were populated by large numbers of buyers and sellers. In later periods, however, the theoretical model of the firm that was developed against this background became subject to several forms of criticism:

■ *Organizational goals.* The neoclassical theory assumes that firms seek to maximize profit. In reality, however, the managers of a firm may pursue other objectives, such as the maximization of sales, growth or market share, or goals related to their own status or job security, or perhaps the enjoyment of a quiet life. Simon (1959) argues that the firm's managers may aim for a satisfactory profit, or a profit that is sufficient to allow them to pursue other objectives.

■ *Uncertainty and imperfect information.* In practice, all economic decisions are based on assumptions or predictions about near or future events. Implicit in the neoclassical theory is an assumption that the firm's decision-makers can make accurate predictions, or at least be able to assign probabilities to various possible future events. Decision-makers must be able to anticipate changes in consumer tastes, changes in technology, changes in factor markets and the likely reactions of rivals. In practice, such events are extremely difficult to foresee.

■ *Organizational complexity.* Modern firms are complex hierarchical organizations, bound together by complex communications networks. In practice, breakdowns in communications occur frequently. The larger the size of the organization, the greater the likelihood that information is distorted, either deliberately or accidentally. Misinformation reduces the ability of the firm's decision makers to reach correct decisions.

- *Decision-making.* According to the neoclassical theory, the firm's decision-makers decide which inputs to purchase and how much output to produce by applying rules such as marginal revenue *equals* marginal cost. However, empirical evidence suggests that many businessmen and women do not employ such methods. Instead, they often rely on simpler decision-making conventions or rules-of-thumb. In a seminal article, Hall and Hitch (1939) report the outcomes of interviews with decision-makers at 38 firms. Very few had even heard of the concepts of marginal cost and revenue, or price elasticity of demand. Instead, many set their prices by calculating their average cost, and adding a mark-up that included a margin for profit. This pricing method, known as **cost plus pricing**, is examined in Chapter 13. Neoclassical profit maximization requires that both demand and costs are taken into account in determining price and quantity, while cost plus focuses on average cost.

In defence of the neoclassical theory, Friedman (1953) argues that some critics miss the point by attacking the validity of the assumptions on which the theory is constructed. The objective of any science is to develop theories or hypotheses which lead to valid and accurate predictions about future outcomes. The only relevant test of the validity of a theory is whether its predictions are close to the eventual outcome. Friedman argues that the proper test of an assumption such as profit maximization is not whether it is realistic, but whether it enables accurate predictions to be generated from the theory on which it is based (Rotwein, 1962; Melitz, 1965).

Machlup (1946, 1967) argues for the essential validity of the profit maximization assumption, even if it does not provide a literal description of reality. Most decision makers have an intuitive feel for what is required to come close to a profit-maximizing outcome, even if they are unable to articulate their practices using the same terminology or with the same precision as economists. The practical implementation of marginal analysis should not require anything more difficult than an ability to formulate subjective estimates, hunches and guesses. By analogy, motorists execute complex manoeuvres such as overtaking intuitively, rather than by using precise and complex mathematical formulae to judge the speeds and distances needed in order to overtake successfully. Using similar reasoning but adding a Darwinian slant, Alchian (1965) argues that firms that survive in the long run are those that have come close to long-run profit maximization, either deliberately or intuitively or perhaps even inadvertently. Accordingly, the neoclassical theory accurately describes the behaviour of surviving firms.

An essentially static conception of competition is emphasized in the neoclassical models of perfect competition, monopolistic competition and monopoly. In the neoclassical theory, the entrepreneur is the personification of the firm, but otherwise plays a rather unimportant role. Price competition is the only form of rivalry. In contrast, Schumpeter (1942) and the **Austrian school** give the entrepreneur a central role within a more dynamic model of competition. By initiating technological change by means of innovation, the Schumpeterian entrepreneur is the main driving force behind economic progress. Innovation revolutionizes economic conditions by replacing old production methods with new and superior ones. Successful innovation is the fundamental source of monopoly status and abnormal profit. Abnormal or monopoly profit is only a temporary phenomenon, however, because eventually the market for a new product will be flooded by imitators, or the original innovation will be superseded by further technological progress. The Schumpeterian view of the entrepreneur as innovator is examined in more detail in a later chapter (see Chapter 17).

The Austrian school also emphasizes the role of the entrepreneur. Here the entrepreneur plays a crucial role in facilitating the spread of information among consumers and resource owners. The entrepreneur spots missed opportunities for trade or investment, by acquiring and processing new information more quickly than other decision-makers. Through their actions, entrepreneurs contribute to the spread of information, enabling other market participants to adjust their trading plans accordingly.

> The overambitious plans of one period will be replaced by more realistic ones; market opportunities overlooked in one period will be exploited in the next. In other words, even without changes in the basic data of the market (i.e. in consumer tastes, technological possibilities, and resource availabilities), the decisions made in one period of time generate systematic alterations in the corresponding decisions for the succeeding period. Taken over time, this series of systematic changes in the interconnected network of market decisions constitutes the market process.
>
> *(Kirzner, 1973, p. 10)*

The entrepreneur is constantly alert to new and unexploited opportunities to earn a profit, and initiates the changes that propel the economy towards a new equilibrium. 'The entrepreneur . . . brings into mutual adjustment those discordant elements which resulted from prior market ignorance' (Kirzner, 1973, p. 73). Essentially, disequilibrium results from the ignorance of buyers and sellers. Potential buyers are unaware of potential sellers and vice versa. Scarce resources are sometimes used to produce goods for which there is no market, and resources that could be used to produce goods for which a market exists are sometimes left idle. The alert entrepreneur intervenes and remedies the situation by bringing the potential buyers and sellers together.

Casson (1982) develops a synthesis of several of these theories of entrepreneurship. The entrepreneur's main function is the management, coordination and allocation of other scarce resources, using key or privileged information. If this is done efficiently, and the key information remains secret, the entrepreneur is rewarded with profit or income. However, as in the Schumpeterian and Austrian views, in the long run there is a tendency for the entrepreneurial reward to be dissipated. Casson models the entrepreneurial function using a neoclassical-style demand and supply framework. The demand for entrepreneurs depends most crucially on the pace of technological change, which determines the level of opportunity for entrepreneurial initiative. The supply of entrepreneurs depends on the educational system and qualifications, social networks, institutions and the general culture of the society, all of which influence the propensity for entrepreneurial behaviour and the availability of capital to finance new ventures. Entrepreneurial rewards tend to be higher when the demand for entrepreneurs is high (due to a high level of technological opportunity) and when the supply of active entrepreneurs is scarce.

4.3 Separation of ownership from control: managerial theories of the firm

As shown earlier (see Section 3.2), by the first half of the twentieth century, the foundations for an economic theory of the firm were well established. The theory referred to firms that were managed by their owners, which specialized in clearly defined activities. During the late nineteenth and early twentieth centuries, however, reality was already changing. The largest and most successful firms were evolving into increasingly complex organizations, buying their inputs and selling their products in many different markets. Some economists became increasingly conscious that these evolving institutions bore little resemblance to the simple conception of the firm according to the neoclassical theory. There were two important implications. First, increasing organizational complexity made it impossible for the largest firms to be managed solely by a single entrepreneur or owner. Instead, there was a tendency for firms to employ large teams of managers, including specialists in functions such as marketing, finance and human resource management. Second, it became impractical for the individual entrepreneur or owner to finance the growth of the largest firms from personal financial resources. Large firms in need of finance looked increasingly to the capital markets. Consequently, ownership became more widely dispersed, among large numbers of individual or institutional shareholders. Not only did the number of shareholders grow, but the nature of share ownership was also changing and becoming more complex. Many large individual shareholdings were effectively broken up by progressive taxation; there were new demands for share ownership from individuals who became newly affluent as patterns of income and wealth distribution evolved throughout the course of the twentieth century.

As share ownership became increasingly dispersed, the control of firms, vested in the ownership of shares, became increasingly diluted. In many cases, a type of power vacuum was created, which was filled by an increasingly dominant cadre of managers. This so-called separation or divorce of ownership from control provided ammunition for the critics of the neoclassical theory of the firm, who argued that there was no reason to suppose that the theory's assumed objective of profit maximization would necessarily coincide with the objectives of the managers of large firms, the individuals actually taking the decisions. Managers might well be tempted to pursue objectives other than profit maximization, such as maximizing their own income, status or job security. Furthermore, given that shareholders are large in number, widely dispersed and perhaps poorly informed and poorly organized, the shareholders' ability in theory to hire and fire their own managers might not be sufficient to force the latter to act in accordance with the shareholders' interests.

Berle and Means (1932) are widely credited with having first identified and measured the extent of this separation of ownership from control, although the same issue is discussed by Veblen (1923). Classifying a shareholding of between 20 per cent and 50 per cent held by any individual or group as effective control, Berle and Means found that 88 out of 200 large US non-financial corporations surveyed in 1929 were management controlled. No one individual owned more than 5 per cent of the total stock of any of these 88 firms. Some 30 years later, Larner (1966) replicated the Berle and Means study, but adjusted the ownership threshold from 5 per cent to 10 per cent of shares in the hands of a single owner. Of the 200 top firms, 84 per cent could be regarded as management controlled. The managerial revolution, already in progress in 1929, was close to complete by the mid-1960s. Applying similar methodology (but with a different definition of an owner-controlled firm) to a UK data set, Florence Sargent (1961) reports that only 30 of a sample of 98 of the largest UK firms could be classed as owner controlled. In another sample of smaller firms, only 89 of 268 firms were owner controlled.

Prais (1976) and Nyman and Silbertson (1978) question the results, as well as the research methodology, of these studies. First, the presence of interest groups or individuals owning large proportions of shares, does not necessarily imply there are no effective constraints on management. Second, Berle and Means ignore interlocking directorships: an important means of representing the interests of other firms at board level. Third, Berle and Means classify firms according to their ultimate control. If firm A has majority control over firm B and A is management controlled, B is also regarded as management controlled. This method of classification is contentious. Finally, statistical criteria alone are insufficient to determine the extent of ownership or managerial control. It is important to examine the nature of the shareholdings and their inter-relationships including, for example, similar or near-similar interest groups such as kinship. Nyman and Silbertson advocate studying the nature of control on a case by case basis. This approach suggests owner control was much stronger than had previously been realized: 55 per cent of the top 250 UK firms had some degree of owner control, using a 5 per cent threshold for a firm to be classed as owner controlled. Using the same ownership threshold, Leech and Leahy (1991) find 91 per cent of 470 large UK industrial firms were owner controlled using 1983–5 data. Using a 20 per cent threshold, only 34 per cent were classified as owner controlled.

Although some of the early research concerning the separation of ownership from control has been qualified, the original hypothesis that share ownership in many large corporations is widely dispersed remains essentially valid, even at the start of the twenty-first century. Does this imply that the managers of these organizations enjoy the freedom to pursue goals and objectives different from those of the owners? In practice, there are several reasons why the managers might not wish to depart too far from the owners' objectives:

■ If the managers are perceived to be running the organization badly, in principle the shareholders can mobilize themselves to dismiss the managers at a shareholders' general meeting. In practice, however, this may be difficult to organize. First, some shareholders might not wish to disrupt continuity by voting for wholesale dismissals. Second, shareholders might not necessarily be able to assess the degree to which the managers are failing in their duties. Third, even knowledgeable shareholders may be unable to disseminate the relevant information, due to the costs incurred in printing leaflets, arranging meetings, dealing with the press and so on. Finally, disaffected shareholders can often be outvoted at a general meeting by proxy votes held by the chair. Shareholders not wishing to attend a meeting, normally the majority, can nominate a proxy to vote on their behalf, but proxy votes are often assigned to the firm's managers. Ultimately, disaffected shareholders may only be able to influence the management by selling their shareholdings, depressing the firm's market valuation. Case studies 4.1 and 4.2 discuss two contrasting examples of the exercise of shareholder power.

■ Although shareholders may lack clear information concerning the performance of management, managers of other firms may not be subject to the same constraints. Rival management teams, who perhaps face similar demand and cost conditions, may be in a good position to detect underperformance. If the market valuation of a firm's shares is relatively low but its financial structure is sound, the firm may be vulnerable to a takeover bid. Recognition of this danger reduces the managers' incentives to pursue non-profit-maximizing objectives.

■ If the firm relies on external sources of finance, its managers may face additional constraints in the form of scrutiny by lending institutions such as merchant banks or investment companies. On the whole, UK firms tend not to rely heavily on external sources of finance. Nevertheless, investment banks often arrange new issues, secure external finance and provide advice; and a number of large UK companies have investment bank representation on their boards.

Let's talk about the market economy

The *Financial Times* is debating capitalism, but what it is really debating is the future of the market economy. Karl Marx never used the word capitalism. But after the publication of *Das Kapital*, the term came to describe the system of business organisation which had made the industrial revolution possible. By the mid-19th century that system was central to the economic landscape. Werner Siemens in Germany, Andrew Carnegie and John D. Rockefeller in the US, and in Britain Richard Arkwright's successors. As individuals or with a small group of active partners, they built and owned both the factories and plants in which the new working class was employed, and the machinery inside them.

While the fascia labelled Barclays Bank tells you only the name of the company you are dealing with, the sign that said Arkwright's Mill told you that Sir Richard owned it. And no one who passed forgot that. The economic and political power of business leaders derived from their ownership of capital and the control that ownership gave them over the means of production and exchange.

The political and economic environment in which Marx wrote was a brief interlude in economic history. Yet the terminology devised by 19th-century critics of business continues to be used by both supporters and opponents of the market economy, although the industrial scene has been transformed. Legislation passed in Marx's time permitted the establishment of the limited liability company, which made it possible to build businesses with widely dispersed share ownership. This form of organisation did not become popular until the end of the 19th century, but then expanded rapidly. By the 1930s, Berle and Means would write of the divorce of ownership and control. At the same time, Alfred Sloan at General Motors demonstrated how a cadre of professional managers might wield effective control over a large and diversified corporation.

So the business leaders of today are not capitalists in the sense in which Arkwright and Rockefeller were capitalists. Modern titans derive their authority and influence from their position in a hierarchy, not their ownership of capital. They have obtained these positions through their skills in organisational politics, in the traditional ways bishops and generals acquired positions in an ecclesiastical or military hierarchy.

If the first half of the 20th century was a time of fundamental change in the nature of business organisation, the second half was a time of fundamental change in the nature of business success. The value of raw materials is only a small part of the value of the production of a complex modern economy, and the value of physical assets is only a small part of the value of most modern businesses. The critical resources of today's company are not its buildings and machines but its competitive advantages – its systems of organisation, its reputation with suppliers and customers, its capacity for innovation. These attributes are not, in any relevant sense, capable of being owned by anyone at all.

The typical reader of this article works in front of a computer at a desk in an office block. He or she probably does not know who owns any of these things. It is quite likely that each is owned by someone different – a pension fund, a property company or a leasing business – none of whom is their employer. People do not know who owns their work tools because the answer does not matter. If your boss pushes you around, exploits you or appropriates your surplus value, the reasons have nothing to do with the ownership of capital. While control over the means of production and exchange matters a great deal to the organisation of business and the power structures of society, ownership of the means of production and exchange matters very little.

Sloppy language leads to sloppy thinking. By continuing to use the 19th-century term capitalism for an economic system that has evolved into something altogether different, we are liable to misunderstand the sources of strength of the market economy and the role capital plays within it.

In the 1960s, several new theoretical models were developed to examine the contribution of managers to decision-making within the firm. The rest of Section 4.3 describes the best known of the managerial theories of the firm.

Baumol (1959) suggests that the managers of a large firm are primarily interested in maximizing their organization's sales revenue, subject to satisfying a **minimum profit constraint**. There are three reasons why the managers might pursue a sales revenue maximization objective. First, sales are widely regarded as a good general indicator of organizational performance.

> [S]urely it is a common experience that when one asks an executive, 'How's business?', he will answer that his sales have been increasing (or decreasing), and talk about profit only as an afterthought, if at all.

> *(Baumol, 1959, p. 46)*

Second, executive remuneration, as well as the power, influence and status executives can command, tend to be closely linked to their organization's sales performance. Third, assuming lenders tend to rely on sales data as a reasonably simple and visible indicator of organizational performance, a reduction in sales gives cause for concern because it gives rise to difficulties in raising finance from capital markets. The need to satisfy a minimum profit constraint is included in the managers' objective function, because sufficient profit is required to provide finance for future expansion, and to satisfy current shareholders and the capital markets. If shareholders are dissatisfied, they might vote to dismiss the managers at a general meeting; or they might sell their shares, causing the company's market valuation to fall and rendering the company vulnerable to takeover. A new group of owners might wish to bring in its own management team. Therefore, if profit falls too low, the managers' job security is jeopardized.

> In practice minimum acceptable profit is a rough attempt to provide completely acceptable earnings to stockholders while leaving enough over for investment in future expansion at the maximum rate which management considers to be reasonably marketable.

> *(Baumol, 1959, p. 53)*

Case study 4.2

Cable under fire over executive pay proposals

Business secretary Vince Cable has come under fire from the CBI employers' group and corporate chiefs after outlining proposals to give shareholders in quoted companies an annual binding vote on future executive pay policy. FTSE bosses are alarmed by the business secretary's proposal that boards must achieve a 'supermajority' of 50–75 per cent for the policy to be approved, which they fear would hand power to a 'Machiavellian minority' of shareholders.

Mr Cable, launching a consultation on Wednesday, said: 'Directors' pay goes up when times are good, and yet it still goes up when performance is poor. I want shareholders to feel empowered to prevent rewards for mediocrity or failure.' One FTSE 100 chairman called the supermajority idea 'completely insane'. He added: 'My sense is that No. 10 will realise that 50 per cent is as far as they want to go.' A 75 per cent threshold was first proposed by Fidelity Worldwide Investment. Mr Cable's document does not specify a figure, but makes clear that the government wants to go beyond a straight majority.

The document, recognising that in some companies a sole shareholder holds a quarter or more of shares, says a threshold of 50–75 per cent might be 'more appropriate'. If a company failed to achieve the required majority, it would have to stick with its existing policy or put a revised proposal to a general meeting within 90 days. The binding vote would approve variable remuneration including salary increases and the level and criteria of performance-related pay for the year ahead. Shareholders already have a binding vote on long-term incentive schemes. Mr Cable plans to give shareholders a binding vote on pay-offs to executives that exceed the equivalent of one year's base salary.

John Cridland, CBI director-general, said businesses did not believe that binding shareholder votes were the right way to ensure reward reflected performance. 'The consultation's proposal for up to a 75 per cent shareholder vote approval threshold would be damaging, leaving decision making about company strategy in the hands of a minority of shareholders who may not represent the wider group,' he said. But he was relieved that any binding vote would be aimed at an organisation's general remuneration policy, rather than specific directors' pay packages.

The National Association of Pension Funds said it supported the government's 'general direction'. Votes should be used to block policies where there was a failure to connect boardroom pay to a company's long-term success, it added.

Source: Cable under fine over executive pay proposals, © The Financial Times Limited. All Rights Reserved, 14 March 2012 (Groom, B. and Burgess, K.).

Baumol's sales revenue maximization model is illustrated in Figure 4.1. The analysis uses short-run cost functions and, for simplicity, it is assumed that the fixed cost is zero. The profit function, denoted π, is the difference between total revenue (TR) and total cost (TC). Therefore $\pi = 0$ at the points where TR = TC. Profit maximization is achieved by producing the output level q_1, at which the vertical distance between TR and TC is maximized. In the absence of any effective shareholder control, the firm's managers might attempt to maximize sales revenue. Sales revenue maximization is achieved by producing the output level q_3, at which the TR function is maximized. However, the need to satisfy the minimum profit constraint shown by the horizontal line π_{MIN}, prevents the managers from increasing output as far as q_3. Sales revenue maximization subject to a profit constraint of π_{MIN} is achieved by producing q_2, the highest output level that is consistent with $\pi \geq \pi_{MIN}$.

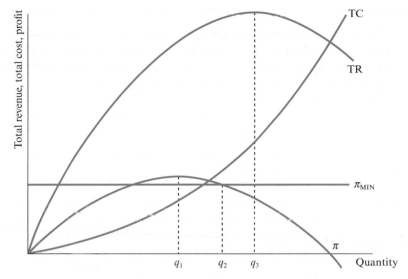

Figure 4.1 Baumol's sales revenue maximization model

Needham (1978) develops a long-run or multi-period version of the same model. The long-run analysis is motivated by the observation that current profit is a key source of finance for a firm seeking to expand. And, by definition, growth is required for the firm to increase its sales revenue in the future. Therefore, if managers have long-time horizons, it is not obvious that in the short run they should produce a level of output greater than that which would maximize current (short-run) profit.

For a firm with a planning horizon of n years, the present value of future sales revenue, denoted PV, depends on current sales revenue, denoted TR_0; the annual rate of growth of sales revenue, denoted g; and the discount rate employed to convert future sales revenue flows into present values, denoted r:

$$PV = \frac{TR_0(1 + g)}{1 + r} + \frac{TR_0(1 + g)^2}{(1 + r)^2} + \cdots + \frac{TR_0(1 + g)^n}{(1 + r)^n}$$

The growth rate g depends on current profit, which is used to finance future growth. By maximizing profit in the short run, the firm also maximizes g. However, as shown in Figure 4.1, short-run profit maximization implies sales revenue is lower than it could be. By increasing output beyond its short-run profit-maximizing level, the firm achieves an increase in current sales revenue TR_0 at the expense of a reduction in g. Accordingly, in order to maximize PV, the firm's managers must decide on an optimal trade-off between current sales revenue and future growth in sales revenue.

The short-run profit that is required to deliver the chosen long-run growth rate might be interpreted as the short-run profit constraint. If so, the main difference between the short-run model and the long-run model is that, in the former, the profit constraint is determined exogenously (by the managers' job security requirement), while in the latter it is determined by the trade-off between current sales revenue and future growth. This in turn is determined by the short-run trade-off between current sales revenue and current profit.

Not all economists accept Baumol's sales revenue maximization hypothesis. Peston (1959) suggests that the hypothesis might be applied to cases where firms are uncertain about their revenue or demand functions. In an uncertain world, rather than risk producing too little output, firms prefer to produce too much, and overproduction may at least enable the firm to realize economies of scale.

Marris's theory of growth maximization

In view of the separation between ownership and control, Baumol (1962), Marris (1964) and Williamson (1963) suggest managers may wish to pursue a strategy of maximizing the growth of the firm. Growth maximization might be achieved at the expense of maximizing the present value of the firm's future profit streams, reflected in the firm's current stock market valuation.

In Marris's model, the managers' salaries and status depend on the size of their departments. Managers are judged by their peers, subordinates and superiors for professional competence. Since each manager's individual contribution to profit is difficult to assess, some other method of evaluation has to be determined. A manager's ability to get on with other people and run their department smoothly is often used as a performance indicator. However, managers need to do more than this to increase their esteem, especially in the eyes of superiors and peers. Expanding the activities under their own command, and the activities of the firm in general, is a natural way for managers to enhance their reputation. By so doing, the manager also enhances his or her own job security, and that of subordinates. The firm naturally tends to reward those who contribute most toward its own growth and security.

Therefore, managers tend to strive for growth rather than profit maximization. Successful pursuit of a growth maximization objective necessitates achieving balance between the rate of growth of demand for the firm's products and the rate of growth of the firm's capital.

In the short run, growth of demand for the firm's existing product range might be achieved through measures such as price adjustments, new marketing campaigns, or small changes in product design. However, for any given range of products, there are limits to the effectiveness of such measures in increasing demand; or at the very least, continued reliance on these measures may have damaging and unacceptable consequences for profitability. Eventually, further price reductions become counter-productive as the firm moves onto the price inelastic section of its demand function; or diminishing returns to further advertising or research and development expenditure are encountered. Therefore, in order to grow continually over the long run, the firm cannot rely solely on existing products: it must diversify. By adopting a strategy of diversification, the firm can overcome the inevitable constraint on growth of demand imposed by exclusive reliance on any one product or on a fixed product range.

However, even for a firm that is willing to exploit opportunities for diversification into new markets, there are limits to the rate of growth of demand that can be achieved without causing profitability to decline. This is because there are limits to the number of diversification opportunities the firm's management team can successfully handle at any one time. If too many new projects are taken on, the firm's managerial resources become too thinly spread. The decision-making and organizational capabilities of the firm's management team become overstretched, mistakes are made, some projects fail and the firm's capacity to produce begins to exceed the demand for its products. Consequently, profitability starts to decline. Attempts to overcome this problem by recruiting more managers may not succeed. It takes time for new recruits to become familiar with the organization's practices and methods of operation and, in the short run, the need to provide training for the newcomers may make matters worse by diverting the attention of the firm's existing managers. In summary, there is a *managerial constraint on growth*: if a firm attempts to grow too quickly through diversification, profitability will eventually tend to decline

Firms have available three means of financing growth of capital: borrowing; the issue of new share capital; and the use of retained profits. However, there are limits to the use of all three sources, which give rise to a *financial constraint on growth*:

■ If the firm borrows too heavily, its balance sheet debit–equity ratio or gearing ratio (the ratio of long-term debt to share capital) increases. The level of risk faced by lenders and shareholders also increases: earnings may be insufficient to meet the interest payments on the debt, and the higher the fixed charge on earnings required to cover interest, the more volatile (proportionately) is the residual component of earnings that accrues to shareholders.

■ Issuing new share capital is effective as a means of financing expansion only if the financial markets are willing to invest. In order to sell new shares, the firm needs to be able to demonstrate an acceptable rate of current and future profitability.

■ Finally, growth can be financed from retained profit. However, this creates a dilemma for the firm's managers, who must consider the trade-off between using retained profit to finance growth on the one hand, and paying dividends to shareholders on the other. If the shareholders believe that the new investments funded from retained profit will be profitable, they may be content to sacrifice dividends. But if the shareholders are dissatisfied, they may vote to dismiss the managers or sell their shares. In both cases the managers' job security is jeopardized, for the reasons discussed earlier with reference to Baumol's minimum profit constraint.

As a measure of shareholder contentment, Marris suggests using the **valuation ratio**, defined as the ratio of the firm's stock market value to the book value of its assets. The stock market value represents the market's assessment and expectations of present and future performance, while the book value represents the value of assets employed by the firm. If investors are dissatisfied with the managers' performance, and feel that the firm is not producing an adequate return on the assets it employs, the stock market value will be low relative to the book value of assets, and the valuation ratio will be depressed. The firm is vulnerable to takeover when the valuation ratio falls so low that potential bidders

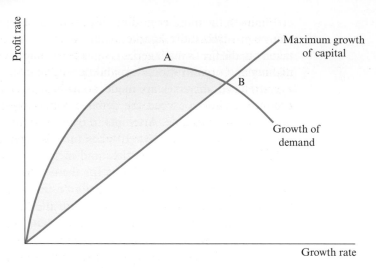

Figure 4.2 Marris's growth maximization model

believe they could acquire the firm's assets and then earn a higher return, producing a capital gain through an increase in the share price, market value and valuation ratio.

Marris's model of growth maximization is illustrated in Figure 4.2. The growth of demand function reflects the relationship between the firm's chosen rate of growth of demand (shown along the horizontal axis) and its profitability (shown on the vertical axis). This function is read in an anti-clockwise direction (from the horizontal to the vertical axis). As the rate of growth of demand is increased, at first profitability increases, because it is possible for the firm's managers to identify and successfully exploit profitable diversification opportunities. If the rate of growth increases beyond a certain point, however, profitability starts to fall as the managerial profit constraint on growth begins to bite.

The maximum growth of capital function shows the relationship between the firm's rate of profit (shown along the vertical axis) and the maximum rate at which the firm is able to increase its capital (shown on the horizontal axis). This function is read in a clockwise direction (from the vertical to the horizontal axis). Marris assumes there is a linear relationship between the rate of profit and the maximum growth rate that can be sustained. Implicitly, the retention ratio (the ratio of retained profit to total profit) is assumed to be constant. In accordance with the preceding discussion of the financial constraint on growth, the higher the profit rate, the higher the maximum rate of growth of capital the firm can sustain. The feasible combinations of profit and growth open to the firm are represented by the shaded area between the growth of demand and maximum growth of capital functions. The shareholders, whose objective is profit maximization, would prefer the firm to operate at A. But the managers, whose objective is growth maximization, choose instead to operate at the highest attainable balanced growth rate (at which growth of demand *equals* growth of capital), located at B.

Figure 4.2 and the preceding discussion capture the essential features of the Marris growth maximization model. As with the Baumol sales revenue maximization model, a few refinements have been suggested, which tend to narrow the distinction between the profit-maximizing and growth-maximizing outcomes. For example, shareholders might be willing to sacrifice some current profit in order to achieve faster growth, if the growth is expected to deliver higher profits in the future. Similarly, managers might be willing to sacrifice some growth in order to achieve higher current profit, if this produces an increase in the firm's valuation ratio, reducing the likelihood of takeover and enhancing the managers' job security. In both cases there is a trade-off between current profitability and growth, suggesting that an equilibrium might be established somewhere along the section of the growth of demand function between the polar cases of profit maximization at A and growth maximization at B.

The Marris model suggests a few testable hypotheses. First, owner-controlled firms achieve lower growth and higher profits than managment-controlled firms. Radice (1971) finds that despite differences in average profitability between the two types of firm, owner-controlled firms enjoyed faster growth. Second, a low valuation ratio increases the likelihood of the firm being taken over. Using data for some 3,500 UK firms between 1957 and 1969, Kuehn (1975) finds evidence to support this hypothesis. However, Singh (1971) and Levine and Aaronovitch (1981) do not find any such evidence.

Williamson's theory of managerial utility maximization

In Baumol's model, the managers' interests are tied to a single variable, namely sales revenue, the growth of which the managers seek to maximize, subject to a minimum profit constraint. Williamson (1963) incorporates several variables into the managers' objective or utility function. Managers are assumed to adopt expense preference behaviour, by undertaking large amounts of discretionary spending. This yields satisfaction or utility to the managers, which they seek to maximize. Effectively, expense preference behaviour implies managers divert some of the firm's productive resources for their own uses.

The **managerial utility** function can be represented as follows:

$$U = f(S, M, \pi_D)$$

U denotes managerial utility. S denotes expenditure on staff. It is assumed the manager derives utility from the prestige or power obtained by empire-building (increasing the number of staff who report to the manager). M denotes expenditure on managerial emoluments (fringe benefits or perks), such as large offices, expense accounts and company cars. π_D denotes discretionary profit, defined as net profit (after tax and expenditure on managerial emoluments) over and above the minimum level of profit that is required to pay an acceptable level of dividend to shareholders. Again, it is assumed the managers derive utility from discretionary profit: the higher the value of π_D, the greater the managers' job security.

Let π denote operating profit (before expenditure on managerial emoluments), T denote tax, and π_0 denote the shareholders' minimum acceptable profit level:

$$\pi_D = \pi - M - T - \pi_0$$

Operating profit, π, is a function of staff expenditure, S. As the level of staff expenditure increases, operating profit initially increases as well. However, eventually diminishing returns set in, and staffing costs start to rise faster than the extra revenue additional staff are capable of generating. As the level of staff expenditure continues to increase, operating profit eventually starts to decrease:

$$\pi = \pi(S) \Rightarrow \pi_D = \pi(S) - M - T - \pi_0$$

The problem of managerial utility maximization involves selecting the values of S, M and π_D that maximize the utility function $U = f(S, M, \pi_D)$, subject to the constraint $\pi_D = \pi(S) - M - T - \pi_0$. A diagrammatic representation of this constrained optimization problem can be obtained by assuming, for simplicity, M is constant, and examining the trade-off between S and π_D. This is shown in Figure 4.3. The relationship between S and π_D implied by diminishing returns to additional staff expenditure is represented by the inverted U-shaped function $\pi_D = \pi(S) - M - T - \pi_0$. The indifference curves U_1, U_2 and U_3 represent the trade-off between π_D and S that is implied by the managerial utility function.

In Figure 4.3, a profit-maximizing firm selects staff expenditure S_1, and earns discretionary profit π_{D_1}. This produces managerial utility of U_1. A managerial firm, whose managers seek to maximize their own utility function, selects a higher staff expenditure S_2 and earns a lower discretionary profit π_{D_2}. This produces higher managerial utility of U_2.

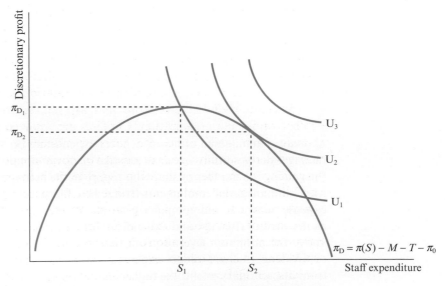

Figure 4.3 Williamson's managerial utility maximization model

Williamson concludes that a managerial firm tends to overspend on its staff in comparison with a profit-maximizing firm. This result demonstrates the preference of managers for staff expenditure. If M is also made variable rather than fixed (as assumed in Figure 4.3), a similar conclusion emerges in respect of managerial emoluments. At the respective equilibria, $M = 0$ for a profit-maximizing firm and $M > 0$ for a managerial utility-maximizing firm.

4.4 The behavioural theory of the firm

The behavioural theory of the firm is most closely associated with Cyert and March (1964). This theory defines the firm in terms of its organizational structure and decision-making processes. The boundaries of the firm are defined quite loosely, to include all individuals or groups with influence or interests in the organization's activities. Relevant groups include the firm's managers, shareholders, employees, customers and suppliers of inputs, as well as other parties such as trade unions, consumer organizations, local residents (whose living environment may be affected by the firm's operations), government departments (with interests in the implications of the firm's activities for tax revenues, employment or the balance of payments) and so on. In more recent terminology, these interest groups have been referred to as stakeholders. Group definitions can be formulated at several different levels; for example, the firm's management team might be subdivided into its constituent parts with responsibilities for marketing, sales, production, stock-keeping, finance, human resources and so on, with each group tending to emphasize its own priorities and objectives.

The behavioural theory recognizes that all decision-making takes place in an environment of uncertainty, or **bounded rationality** (Simon, 1959). No individual or group has complete information about every aspect of the firm's activities and operating environment. But all groups and individuals have some information, and the information they have tends to be most complete in the immediate vicinity of their own activities. Accordingly, decision-making is based on bounded rationality rather than global rationality. All decisions are influenced by the beliefs, perceptions and aspirations of the individuals and groups involved. Differences in beliefs, perceptions and aspirations create the potential for conflict within the organization. Conflicts are resolved through a bargaining process, from which corporate goals or objectives emerge. Organizations themselves do not have goals or objectives: corporate goals are the outcome of bargaining within the organization. Agreements between groups or individuals bond the interested parties into coalitions. Corporate goals or objectives are always subject to change, as aspirations change over time. Periodically, the parties compare the performance of the firm in the areas in which they are interested with their own aspirations. If performance is consistently above or below aspirations, then aspiration levels may be revised, and new goals or objectives may emerge. Therefore, corporate goals and objectives are themselves dependent on past performance.

Corporate goals cannot be reduced to a simple formula, such as profit maximization. In an environment of complexity, imperfect information and uncertainty, it is impossible to identify the precise set of actions required to maximize profit. Instead, the firm's managers may settle for a satisfactory profit, following rules-of-thumb and decision-making conventions that depend on past experience. Simon (1959) used the term **satisficing** to refer to the idea that the firm aims for a satisfactory profit, instead of seeking to maximize profit. Rules-of-thumb might include conventions such as 'we must spend 5 per cent of revenue on advertising' or 'we must capture 50 per cent of the market' or 'we must play a lead role in research and development'.

The resolution of conflict through bargaining between groups of stakeholders is achieved using **side-payments**. For example, managers may be keen to adopt a new technology, while individual employees, or the trade union that represents them, may be reluctant. The adoption of new technology might be achieved by increasing wages or bonuses. Side payments need not necessarily be in monetary form. For example, it might be sufficient to allow the workforce some representation at board level. Managers can also bargain over side payments. For example, more resources might be allocated to the department of a key manager who is threatening to leave in order to join a competitor, in an attempt to retain the manager within the firm.

The successful firm holds together, by making side payments that are sufficient to prevent essential individuals or groups from withdrawing. If the side payments are insufficient, workers may go on strike, key personnel may leave, shareholders may sell their shareholdings, suppliers may cease to supply the firm, banks may refuse to grant loans, or local residents may take legal action to force the closure of a plant or factory. Side payments, which exceed what is strictly necessary to hold the firm together, are possible when there is **organizational slack**. Normally, most parties benefit from organizational slack. For example, shareholders receive dividends above those strictly necessary to prevent them from selling their shares; products are priced at a level some distance below the point at which most customers would switch to a rival firm's product; wages are above the level at which most employees would resign; and executives receive remuneration or fringe benefits that are more than sufficient for their services to be retained. When the firm is enjoying increasing sales and profitability, organizational slack expands and side payments increase. In times of falling demand and low profitability, organizational slack provides a cushion, enabling cuts or economies to be made without prompting key parties to withdraw from the organization.

The behavioural theory of the firm recognizes the complexity of organizational decision-making. There is no definitive behavioural theory, since the organizational structure of every firm is different. Accordingly, behavioural theory is strong on explanation, but weak on prediction. In an environment of complexity, imperfect information and uncertainty, it is unlikely that the goals or objectives of the organization can be reduced to simple formulae such as profit maximization. Instead, decisions emerge from bargaining between numerous individuals and groups, pursuing multiple and often conflicting objectives. The emphasis on bargaining over side payments and the resolution of conflict implies that the behavioural theory is primarily concerned with decision-making in the short run. Accordingly, the theory can be criticized for offering little more than broad generalizations as to how firms tend to develop and grow in the long run.

4.5 Summary

Chapter 4 has shown how, over the years, economists have attempted to develop alternatives to the neoclassical theory of the firm that may be more realistic in describing and explaining the essential or fundamental characteristics of firms. Paradoxically, it has been argued that the neoclassical theory of the firm is not really an analysis of the firm at all, but rather a theory of resource allocation at the level of the market. The neoclassical theory devotes little attention to internal decision-making within the firm; instead, the firm is viewed almost as a 'black box'. The firm pursues its goal of profit maximization by converting inputs into outputs in highly mechanical fashion.

Some of the earliest challenges to the neoclassical theory of the firm were developed in the 1950s and 1960s, in the light of growing evidence of the increasing complexity of firms, and the separation of the ownership of large corporations (in the hands of shareholders) from control (in the hands of salaried managers). Where previously it had been assumed that firms were run so as to maximize the interests of their owners, economists began to acknowledge that managers' objectives may differ from those of the shareholders.

In Baumol's theory of sales revenue maximization, managers are assumed to maximize the size of the firm measured by its sales revenue, since managers' compensation and prestige are assumed to depend more on firm size than on profitability. Profit cannot be ignored altogether, however, because the managers' job security depends upon their ability to earn a satisfactory rate of return for the firm's shareholders. Marris develops a more dynamic model of long-run growth maximization, emphasizing the need for balanced growth in the demand for the firm's products and the firm's capacity to supply. The managers' pursuit of a growth strategy is subject to both a managerial and a financial constraint. Williamson develops a model based on the maximization of managerial utility, which depends on staff expenditure, managerial emoluments and discretionary profit.

The behavioural theory of the firm of Cyert and March defines the firm in terms of its organizational structure and decision-making processes, involving all individuals or groups with influence or interests in the organization's activities. Decision-making takes place in an environment of uncertainty or bounded rationality, as individuals and groups bargain in an attempt to secure rewards that meet their own aspirations. The resolution of conflict is facilitated by the existence of organizational slack which, in normal conditions, allows parties to receive rewards over and above the level necessary to prevent them from withdrawing their participation and support from the organization.

Discussion questions

1. Outline the strengths and limitations of the neoclassical theory of the firm in enhancing our understanding of firm behaviour.

2. With reference to Case studies 4.1 and 4.2, discuss the extent of separation of ownership from control in the modern firm and assess the extent to which shareholders can influence corporate objectives.

3. Assess the contribution of the managerial theories of the firm of Baumol, Marris and Williamson to our understanding of the conduct and performance of firms.

4. Suggest possible methods for testing Baumol's sales revenue maximization hypothesis.

5. What is bounded rationality and why is it important?

6. With reference to Cyert and March's behavioural theory of the firm, give examples of groups and coalitions within a specific organization with which you are familiar. Identify the possible conflicts between these groups, and suggest ways in which such conflicts can be resolved.

Further reading

Cowling, K. and Sugden, P. (1998) The essence of the modern corporation: markets, strategic decision-making and the theory of the firm, *The Manchester School*, 66, 1, 59–86.

Moss, S. (1984) The history of the theory of the firm from Marshall to Robinson and Chamberlin: the source of positivism in economics, *Economica*, 51, 307–18.

Stigler, J. (1957) Perfect competition, historically contemplated, *Journal of Political Economy*, 65, 1–17.

Transaction costs, agency and resource-based theories of the firm

Learning objectives

This chapter covers the following topics:

- the Coasian view of the firm
- transaction costs and the theory of the firm
- the firm as team-based production; the firm as a nexus of contracts; agency theories of the firm
- property rights and the theory of the firm
- resource-based theories of the firm

Key terms

Adverse selection
Agency theory
Asset specificity
Governance
Incomplete contracts
Moral hazard

Principal–agent problem
Quasi-rent
Residual rights
Specific rights
Sunk cost
Transaction costs

5.1 Introduction

Over time, increasing awareness of the limitations of both the neoclassical theory of the firm that is described in Chapter 3, and the managerial and behavioural alternatives that are described in Chapter 4, have motivated further efforts to develop yet more realistic economic and organizational theories of the firm. These approaches are examined in Chapter 5.

An early paper by Coase (1937) provides a natural point of departure for the transaction costs approach to the theory of the firm, described in Sections 5.2 and 5.3. Coase questions why centrally planned institutions called 'firms' exist in market-based economies. Coase's answer is that by implementing certain transactions or taking certain resource allocation decisions consciously (within the domain of the firm) rather than unconsciously (through the medium of the market), a saving in **transaction costs** can be realized. Transaction costs can be defined loosely as costs incurred when using market mechanisms to allocate resources in a world of imperfect information. The firm is viewed as an institution which economizes on transaction costs, or the costs of processing information. Resources are allocated in response to the firm's interpretation of information flows. The firm organizes governance structures that provide protection from the threat of opportunistic behaviour made possible by informational asymmetries.

Coase's insights have also influenced a number of approaches to the theory of the firm based on agency theory, which are reviewed in Section 5.4. Echoing the earlier managerial approach, agency theory emphasizes the conflicts that can arise between principals (owners or shareholders) and agents (managers). Under conditions of incomplete contracts and uncertainty, opportunities may arise for agents to act against the best interests of principals, unless the incentive structures confronting principals and agents are properly aligned. In the property rights approach, reviewed in Section 5.5, a key distinction is drawn between specific rights defined explicitly in the terms of contracts, and residual rights which accrue to the owner once all specific rights have been assigned. In a world of incomplete contracts the ownership of the residual rights is of paramount importance. The ownership of residual rights gives control over access to physical assets, or less tangible assets such as brands or reputation.

Dissatisfaction within the fields of management science and strategic management with both the neoclassical theory of the firm and its more modern alternatives has led to the development of resource-based theories of the firm. This approach, which characterizes the firm in terms of the resources or knowledge it embodies and commands, is examined in Section 5.6. Resources include both physical inputs and intangible resources such as technical expertise, knowledge and organizational structure. A number of insights are borrowed from the transaction costs literature, relating to the boundaries of the firm and decision making under bounded rationality. Some writers emphasize knowledge as perhaps the most important of a firm's intangible resources. Firms exist in order to coordinate and protect the unique knowledge that is the firm's key strategic asset.

5.2 The Coasian firm

Although the transaction costs approach to the theory of the firm has developed mainly since the 1970s, a natural starting point is a much earlier paper by Coase (1937). Coase observes that in a market economy, many resource allocation decisions are taken unconsciously, through the operation of the price mechanism. Resources tend to flow to wherever they command the highest price. Excluding the possibility of market imperfections, if the price of a factor of production is higher in industry X than in industry Y, the factor moves from Y towards X, until the price differential disappears. However, there is another large class of resource allocation decisions that are not decided in this manner. For resource allocation decisions that are taken internally within firms, the price mechanism is suspended. When workers move from one department to another, for example, they do so not because there has been a price signal, but because they have been told to do so. Within the firm, something similar to centralized economic planning is observed: the conscious coordination of the firm's resources by the entrepreneur or manager. Accordingly, Robertson likens the position of firms within markets to 'islands of conscious power in this ocean of unconscious cooperation' (Robertson, 1930, p. 85).

Why do these 'islands' of conscious power exist? In other words, why should the task of coordination or resource allocation be assigned to the market in some cases, and to the firm in other cases? Coase points out that **transaction costs** are incurred when using markets to allocate resources. Transaction costs include:

- the search costs associated with gathering information about relative prices;

- the costs incurred in negotiating the contract that specifies the terms of the transaction; and

- costs that are created artificially by the government, through the levy of sales taxes or the imposition of quotas.

Coase's explanation as to why some transactions are removed from the domain of the market, and are instead decided consciously within organizations called firms, is that this method of coordination creates a saving in transaction costs.

- It is not necessary for a factor of production to search for a price signal in order to transfer from one department to another within the firm. The transfer is decided consciously by the entrepreneur or manager.

- The costs associated with negotiating contracts with suppliers of factors of production may be greatly reduced. For example, instead of hiring labour on a daily basis in a spot market, the firm can hire workers on long-term employment contracts. The precise details of the worker's contractual obligations over the entire duration of the contract are not specified; instead, the employee is expected to comply (within certain limits) with instructions issued by the entrepreneur or manager. The contract needs only specify the limits to the obligations of the contracting parties.

- Sales tax liabilities or other restrictions on economic activity imposed by the government may be circumvented if transactions take place internally within the organization, rather than externally through the market.

According to the Coasian analysis, a firm expands when additional transactions are removed from the sphere of the market and are decided instead within the boundaries of the firm. A firm declines when it ceases to organize some transactions, which are returned to the sphere of the market. Naturally, a critical question is: what determines the boundaries that separate the firm from the market? If the removal of transactions from the market and their incorporation within the firm reduces or eliminates transaction costs, why does the market survive at all as a medium for coordination or resource allocation? Why is there not just one very large firm? Fundamentally, the answer is that there are also costs associated with the supply of the entrepreneurial or organizing function. The entrepreneur may be more skilled in organizing some types of transaction than others, and for some transactions it may be better to rely on the market and bear the associated transaction costs. Furthermore, the marginal cost of incorporating additional transactions within the firm increases as the number of transactions already incorporated increases. Due to diminishing returns to the entrepreneurial or organizing function, a point is reached at which it would be counter-productive to extend the boundaries of the firm any further. Case Study 5.1 discusses the policy of outsourcing: using the market to supply essential resources, rather than producing them internally.

Cowling and Sugden (1998) challenge the Coasian view that the analysis of the firm should rest exclusively on identifying the boundaries between market and non-market transactions. Coase (1991) himself draws attention to the fact that within some large organizations, internal markets or quasi-markets are created deliberately in order to settle certain resource allocation decisions, and to introduce an element of competitive pressure or discipline. Coase suggests that, in such cases, the firm's competing departments might be viewed as if they were effectively separate firms. However, Cowling and Sugden argue that the market versus non-market (or some intermediate combination) characterization of transactions and resource allocation decisions is largely a superficial construct. The analysis of the firm should concentrate on the nature of the productive activity itself, rather than the method of coordinating this activity. Nevertheless, Coase's interpretation of firms as 'islands of conscious planning' is highly insightful, especially in view of the modern emphasis on strategic decision making within the firm (see Section 5.4).

Case study 5.1

Outsourcing everything

Michael Munger has written the most lucid essay you're likely read for a while on the theory of the firm:

'Then one day, in one firm, one manager, perhaps on a whim, outsources the computer services or janitorial services or the legal advice. Not to India or Ireland but simply to another company across town or across country. The boss signs a contract, after taking bids from several companies that provide similar services. These companies are forced by

the scolding winds of market competition to provide excellent service at low cost. By looking at the different prices in the bids offered in this competition, the boss learns something. He learns how much the service costs to provide. And he learns how much money he saves by laying off the employees who used to provide the service in-house.

It's hard to fire employees, particularly since most employees are smart enough to work hard enough to get acceptable performance reviews. The boss also has a hard time motivating the in-house staff, because watching each employee is expensive and tiresome. But it's easy to fire contracted employees, because you just sign a new contract with a competitor. Why not let the market system do your motivation work? Let's suppose that our outsourcing boss sees the company's profits rise dramatically, and the stock price goes up 18% in six months. Life is good, for the boss.

So, one day the boss has this crazy thought. He asks himself a question that has never occurred to him before: Why have any employees at all? Why have a building? Why not just sit home, wearing his jammies and bunny slippers, sipping a nice cup of tea, and outsource everything? He can write contracts to buy parts, he can pay workers to assemble the parts, and he can use shipping companies to box and transport the product.'

You can tell that this parable is not going to end happily ever after. As Munger argues, there's a balancing act: too little outsourcing and a firm becomes a socialist state, denied incentives or price signals; too much and the problem of coordinating all the contracts becomes impossible. It's worth thinking about how changing technology may alter this balancing act. The answer is not obvious. Some outsourcing decisions are made much easier to coordinate thanks to the internet and all the rest. At the same time, inter-firm communications also improve. And if the world is full of firms making more complex, intangible products, that may favour more implicit contracts and therefore larger firms. I simply don't know the answer and I'm not sure anyone else does either.

Source: Outsourcing everything, © The Financial Times Limited. All Rights Reserved, 24 January 2008 (Harford, T)

5.3 Transaction costs and the theory of the firm

Coase's ideas regarding the nature of the firm spawned a number of further contributions to the theory of the firm, which can be grouped under the heading of transaction costs economics. Some of the key ideas are advanced by Cheung (1983), Klein *et al.* (1978) and most notably Williamson (1975, 1985). Coase's original emphasis was on transaction costs incurred before contracts are concluded. These include costs associated with searching for information and negotiating contracts. In contrast, the later transaction costs literature focuses on costs incurred after contracts are concluded. These costs arise from difficulties in monitoring and enforcing compliance, and punishing non-compliance. This section focuses on Williamson's approach.

Agency theory (see also Section 5.4) examines the **principal–agent problem**, which is central to the transaction costs approach to the theory of the firm. The principal–agent problem refers to the difficulties that arise when a principal hires an agent, due to imperfect information. The principal–agent problem affects most employer–employee contracts, including the relationship between a firm's shareholders (principal) and its managers (agent), and the relationship between the firm as employer (principal) and its employees or workers (agent).

Most contracts between a principal and an agent are **incomplete contracts**, in the sense that the parties to the contract cannot identify in advance every contingency that might affect their contractual relationship. There is bounded rationality, rather than global rationality. The parties to a contract may find it impossible to foresee all events that could possibly occur in an uncertain world. Even if the range of possible future events can be foreseen, the parties may disagree over the probabilities that should be assigned to different events. And even if events can be foreseen and probabilities assigned, this information may be difficult to translate into a meaningful and enforceable contract. Such a contract would have to be exhaustively specified, so as to eliminate all possible ambiguities that could otherwise give rise to expensive litigation.

Contracts that have already been agreed can give rise to unforeseen consequences. The parties may incur renegotiation or switching costs if alternative partners or production technologies are discovered. An important issue, which may create a need for the renegotiation of contracts, is **asset specificity**. A contract between two parties may involve the creation of an asset that is specific to that relationship, and which has little or no value outside that relationship. This gives rise to the creation of a **quasi-rent** (Klein *et al.*, 1978), reflecting the difference between the asset's value in its present use and its value in its next best use (or its salvage value). After the contract has been concluded, the parties can act opportunistically by asking to renegotiate the incomplete contract, in an effort to appropriate the quasi-rent.

For example, a principal–agent relationship might involve extensive **sunk cost** investment in the agent's human capital by both parties, with neither party able to recoup the sunk costs if the relationship breaks down. This situation could arise if the principal incurs substantial training costs, and the agent also invests effort in the acquisition of skills that are specific to this particular relationship. Once the specific human capital embodied in the agent has accumulated, on each occasion the contract is renegotiated both parties have an incentive to seek to appropriate a larger share of the return that the principal–agent relationship generates. In a spot market for agents' services, recontracting might take place on a daily or weekly basis. In each renegotiation, the agent can threaten non-renewal causing the principal to incur the training costs all over again with a new agent. But, equally, the principal can threaten non-renewal, forcing the agent to sell his services to a new principal with whom the agent's productivity, and therefore his remuneration, might be much lower. As each party issues threats and counter-threats, the costs of renegotiating tend to become prohibitively high. If either party can foresee the possibility that the other party might behave in this manner, the party with foresight might be reluctant to enter into such a relationship in the first place.

The alternative is for the contract between the principal and agent to be integrated or internalized within the sphere of a firm. As discussed by Coase, the employee becomes bound by a long-term employment contract, which does not specify every detail of both parties' obligations over the entire duration of the contract, but which does impose some limits on permissible behaviour. The need for recontracting on a daily or weekly basis is eliminated, and the scope for opportunistic behaviour in an attempt to appropriate quasi-rents is reduced but perhaps not eliminated altogether: threatened strike action or resignation by employees, or threatened dismissal of employees by the employer, are still powerful bargaining instruments once the sunk cost investment in specific human capital has been incurred by both parties. The internalization of market transactions proceeds up to the point where the marginal governance cost associated with running the transaction internally (within the firm) *equals* the marginal transaction cost associated with contracting (via the market).

Although the internalization of transactions is a common remedy according to much of the transaction costs literature, there are some exceptions. Milgrom and Roberts (1988) suggest that under some conditions a series of short-term contracts may be preferable to the internalization of transactions, especially in situations where market conditions and production technologies are subject to change. The empirical transaction costs literature is surveyed by Shelanski and Klein (1995) and Boerner and Macher (2001). Some of this literature explores the relationship between the degree of asset specificity within firms and governance structures, vertical integration and the types and duration of contracts. In a study of subcontracting in the UK engineering industry, for example, Lyons (1996) finds that the degree of asset specificity influences not only the duration of contracts, but also the decision whether a firm should subcontract or not. Where firms are more vulnerable to opportunistic behaviour on the part of subcontractors, formal contracts are more likely to be adopted in preference to flexible and informal agreements.

The transaction costs approach has been used to explore the question of the most effective organizational structure. Figure 5.1 illustrates the unitary or U-form organizational structure, in which the firm's key activities are subdivided into functional areas, such as marketing, finance, production, personnel and so on. Each department is run by a middle manager, who reports to the firm's chief executive. An advantage of the U-form is that by specializing, the

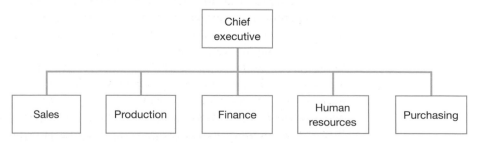

Figure 5.1 Unitary or U-form organizational structure

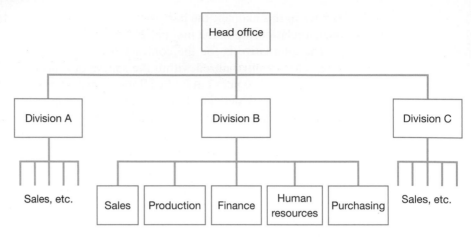

Figure 5.2 Multidivisional or M-form organizational structure

departmental managers develop functional expertise, allowing the clustering of particular skills or talents within departments. This is particularly useful when a firm produces a single product. Consequently, this organizational structure is common among small and medium-sized firms. The U-form is less suited to large organizations that supply a diversified range of goods and services because, in this case, each department has to deal with a more diverse range of tasks and functions. Effective coordination of resource allocation decisions and the transmission of information between departments become more difficult as the organization increases in size, and transaction costs increase. The departmental managers' workloads become more demanding, and conflict between departments tends to increase.

Figure 5.2 illustrates the multidivisional or M-form organizational structure, in which the firm is divided into a number of quasi-independent operating divisions. The M-form was first developed in the US in the 1920s and 1930s, as the scale and scope of large firms such as General Motors grew to such an extent that management structures based on the U-form became overloaded and unable to operate effectively (Chandler, 1977). Within an M-form organizational structure, the operating divisions can be organized geographically (within regional, national or international boundaries), or by product type. Each division is a quasi-firm, comprising all of the key functional areas required to deliver the product or service. Divisional managers exercise considerable decision-making autonomy. The head office is responsible for the longer-term strategic direction of the organization, and plays a supervisory role with respect to the activities of the divisions: the head office monitors performance, allocates finance and sets the parameters within which the divisional managers are permitted to operate. A closely related variant is the holding company or H-form organizational structure, in which a holding or parent company has a significant ownership stake (normally a controlling interest) in other companies or subsidiaries. Again, the managers of the subsidiaries may be granted considerable decision-making autonomy with respect to operational matters. The H-form is especially common among multinational companies.

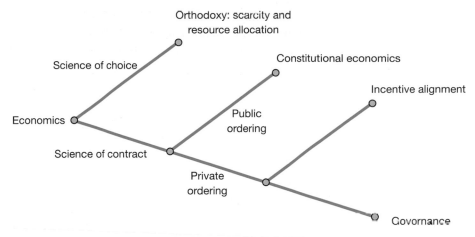

Figure 5.3 The science of choice and the science of contract
Source: Adapted from Williamson (2002), p. 181.

Synthesizing a number of insights drawn from his earlier work, Williamson (2002) proposes a theory of the firm as governance structure. The orthodox approach to economics, popularized by Robbins (1932), can be interpreted as the science of choice on the part of rational utility or profit-maximizing agents. However, this approach is not the only source of insight into economic relationships: there is also the science of contract. Figure 5.3 shows schematically this division between the two sciences. The science of contract branch subdivides into public ordering, covering collective action to secure goods and services which the market fails to deliver; and private ordering, covering issues associated with the alignment of incentives and governance. The alignment of incentives is addressed by agency theory and the economics of property rights (see Sections 5.4 and 5.5). **Governance** addresses the ways in which organizations can best manage their contractual relationships. Williamson draws the following lessons from organization theory:

- Bounded rationality is a fact of organizational life, and complex contracts are always incomplete. Parties to a contract have to be ready to adapt to unexpected events, not only because of their lack of information or foresight, but also because of the potential for opportunistic behaviour that may take place due to unanticipated events. The potential for breakdown in contractual relationships encourages the organization to search for the most appropriate governance structures.

- Governance structures should be designed in the light of all possible outcomes or significant behavioural regularities, both intended and unintended.

- The most pertinent unit of analysis in the firm is the transaction. The three essential characteristics of transactions which affect the nature of governance are: first, the degree of asset specificity; second, the potential disturbances to which the transaction may be subject; and, third, the frequency with which the transaction recurs.

■ Organizational structures are adaptable in the light of changing conditions. With market transactions, agents modify their behaviour in response to price signals. In contrast, organizations rely on skilled or specialized managers to take decisions as to how the organizational structure should adapt and evolve.

5.4   Agency theory

Agency theory is the body of theory that analyzes the conflicts that may arise between principals and agents (see also Section 5.3). The relevance of agency theory to the understanding of the modern firm or corporation derives partly from the separation of ownership from control in modern corporations (see Section 4.3), and the observation that managers as agents may not always act in the best interests of shareholders as principals (Jensen and Meckling, 1976).

Adverse selection and moral hazard

With reference to conditions of incomplete contracts and uncertainty, adverse selection and moral hazard are two of the key issues that are addressed by agency theory. The possibility of **adverse selection** arises when a principal is unable to verify an agent's claims concerning the agent's own ability or productivity. There is **moral hazard** when the possibility exists for the agent to act opportunistically in the agent's own private interests, but against the principal's interests as stipulated in the contract that binds the agent to the principal.

The terms adverse selection and moral hazard both originate in the insurance industry. Suppose an insurer wishes to sell health insurance policies to individuals, some of whom are at high risk of sickness while some are at low risk. Suppose the insurer cannot easily distinguish between high-risk and low-risk applicants when the policy is taken out, and therefore decides to charge a premium based on the average sickness rate. This practice is likely to be disastrous for the company, because low-risk applicants will realize it is not worthwhile for them to take out insurance (priced at an average rate that is higher than their own sickness rate). In contrast, high-risk applicants will realize that insurance priced at the average rate (below their own sickness rate) is a bargain, and will buy a lot of insurance. The company suffers an adverse selection effect, because it finishes up with a loss-making portfolio of high-risk policyholders.

The term moral hazard refers to the tendency for policyholders to become less careful about protecting an interest once it has been insured. If one's house is insured against burglary, when leaving the house one might not bother to lock the doors and windows. If one's car is insured against theft and vandalism, one might not worry about parking in an unsafe part of town. Once insured, the policyholder has little incentive to act in the best interests of the insurer, since it is the insurer who pays the price for the policyholder's carelessness or recklessness.

The implication for the theory of the firm is that a fixed wage contract may not be the best way of organizing the relationship between a principal and an agent. At the point of hiring, a fixed wage offer may result in the principal hiring a group of agents whose actual productivity is lower than the remuneration on offer, because high-productivity agents are unwilling to work for less than their actual productivity (an adverse selection problem). Having been hired, an agent may lack sufficient incentive to work to the full limit of their capabilities, since the remuneration is the same regardless of the intensity of effort (a moral hazard problem).

A remuneration structure that is performance-related might offer a solution to both types of problem. Establishing a link between effort and reward reduces or eliminates adverse selection if agents know at the point of hiring that they will be rewarded in proportion to their productivity. The same link reduces or eliminates moral hazard if agents know they will pay a price for shirking, in the form of lower remuneration. However, a number of problems still remain. Difficulties involved in monitoring individual contributions to team performance may prevent the design of a remuneration structure that fully reflects individual ability and effort. Furthermore, principals and agents may have different attitudes concerning the trade-off between risk and return. In pursuit of a higher short-run return, managers (agents) may impose higher risks on shareholders (principals) than the latter would prefer. For example, part of the managers' remuneration package might take the form of stock options, allowing the holder the right to buy equity in the company for a set price at a future date. Options provide an incentive for managers to act in a way that increases the firm's market value, helping to align the agent's incentives with the principal's interests. However, in order to maximize the value of their options, managers might be tempted to pursue exceptionally risky ventures in the short run, to the possible detriment of the firm's long-run profitability and stability.

The firm as team-based production

The development of theories of the firm focusing on contractual relationships between the parties who comprise the organization can be traced back to Alchian and Demsetz (1972). Two important issues are addressed. First, why should the gains from specialization and the coordination of activities be greater if activities are organized within the firm rather than through the market? Second, how can the internal organizational structure of the firm be explained? Alchian and Demsetz challenge the Coasian notion that firms possess the ability to resolve coordination issues by diktat. An employer has no more power over an employee than a customer has over their shopkeeper. All the employer can do is assign various tasks to the employee on terms that are acceptable to both parties. As in the case of the shopkeeper and the customer, there is no contractual requirement for the employer and the employee to maintain their relationship permanently. The contract between the parties is renegotiated continually, and can be terminated by either party at any time.

However, the employer–employee relationship within the firm is different from the shopkeeper–customer relationship in one crucial aspect. The firm is characterized by teamwork, which requires coordination and cooperation between large numbers of suppliers of inputs. A central contracting agent, employer or owner carries out this essential coordinating function. To ensure the various inputs are combined effectively, it must be possible for the coordinator to measure and monitor the contribution made by each input, and reward each supplier appropriately. This is known as the metering problem. In many cases, metering works effectively through the medium of decentralized, competitive markets. A consumer who wishes to buy apples can easily establish which supermarket, grocer or fruit seller offers the best deal. For some transactions, however, effective metering may be more difficult to achieve. When hiring a plumber, it is not always straightforward to establish whether the work has been completed properly or whether the price being charged is fair. In cases where the metering of productivity and rewards is weak, effective coordination through the medium of markets may be more difficult to achieve, since one or more of the parties may lack the necessary incentives to comply with their contractual obligations.

With respect to the metering problem, team production poses a number of challenges for the firm. Technically, team production within the domain of the firm may be more efficient than contracting between independent suppliers. With team production, however, it may be difficult to measure accurately each team member's individual contribution to the firm's total output. If individuals are self-employed, any increase in productivity is rewarded directly by an increase in the relevant factor payment. For a team of n members among whom the rewards are divided equally, any increase in effort produces a reward to the individual of only $1/n$ *times* the extra effort. Consequently, there is temptation for individual members of a team to shirk or free-ride. Shirking by team members is dealt with by the central contracting agent, employer or owner, who monitors performance and disciplines non-performing team members. The employer's incentive to carry out the monitoring function effectively is provided by his or her claim on the organization's residual return. Essentially, the Alchian and Demsetz argument is as follows. If the total output that can be achieved by organizing team production within a firm exceeds the output that can be produced by contracting between independent suppliers through the market, and if the additional output exceeds the costs of monitoring the team members' individual efforts, team production within the firm supersedes production coordinated through market mechanisms.

The firm as a nexus of contracts

Jensen and Meckling (1976) argue that Alchian and Demsetz's emphasis on team production and monitoring is too narrow, and perhaps even misleading. Instead, the essence of the firm is the entire set of contractual relationships which bind together the firm's owners, employees, material suppliers, creditors, customers and other parties with contractual involvement in the firm's activities. The contractual relationships that bind the parties together raise the issues of agency, incentives and monitoring discussed by Alchian and Demsetz. Therefore, the firm encompasses a much wider set of relationships than those defined purely in terms of team production. Jensen and Meckling claim most firms are simply legal fictions, which possess an artificial identity created by law, and serve as a nexus (or link) for the contractual relationships between the individual parties. This wider definition of the firm encompasses non-profit, mutual and public sector organizations.

Jensen and Meckling seek to understand why different sets of contractual relationships develop for different firms, and how these relationships change in response to exogenous changes to the firm's external environment. This approach makes redundant the attempt to distinguish between contractual relationships within the firm on the one hand, and those within the market on the other. Viewing the firm simply as a nexus of contractual relationships renders the personification of the firm analytically misleading. The firm is not like an individual that pursues its own distinct set of objectives. Rather, the firm acts like a clearing house for the multitude of (often conflicting) objectives pursued by the parties linked together by the nexus of contracts.

5.5 Property rights and the theory of the firm

Transactions can be viewed as an exchange of rights over various assets such as labour, capital and the use of land. The rights that are exchanged may include the right to use, modify, transfer or extract an income from the asset concerned. Transactions are normally effected through contractual agreements. A distinction is drawn between **specific rights** defined explicitly in the terms of a contract, and **residual rights** that accrue to the owner once all specific rights have been assigned. The property rights approach to the theory of the firm is based on this distinction (Hart and Moore, 1990; Hart, 1995a) In a world of incomplete contracts, where there is insufficient information or foresight to define a complete contract covering all specific rights, the ownership of the residual rights is of paramount importance. The owner of the asset has the final or *default* control over the asset, and the right to dispose of a good or asset as they see fit.

In contrast to the Alchian and Demsetz (1972) approach, which suggests firms have relatively little control over their employees, the property rights approach emphasizes the control that is vested in the firm as holder of the residual rights. In cases where an asset such as group of skilled employees are in their most valued use in an organization, they may be willing to follow orders or directions, since the firm, as owner of the residual rights, can appropriate their quasi-rent or even deny them access to the firm's physical assets by dismissing them. It is the ownership of the residual rights that gives the firm control over access to physical assets, or less tangible assets such as brands or reputation.

Suppose two firms, a textbook publisher A and a printing firm B, have a long-term contractual agreement. An unforeseen change to the terms of the original contract is now required: A wishes to switch from two-colour to four-colour ink production. If both firms hold the property rights to their own assets, and both have sufficient leverage to damage the other party, it is likely that a mutually acceptable renegotiated contract can be agreed, enabling B to obtain a higher price for its printing services and A to sell more books. However, ownership of the residual rights affects the rewards accruing to the two parties, which may in turn affect the willingness of the parties to commit themselves to specific investments. Firm A may be reluctant to invest in the expensive, specialized software required for the new printing process, as this investment will increase B's bargaining power over A in future contract negotiations. However, if A and

B are fully integrated, the change to four-colour ink production is organized by the owner of the integrated firm, who instructs the manager of the print division to implement the change. The integrated firm neither has to negotiate a new contract, nor increase the manager's remuneration. Furthermore, in the integrated firm the owner has no fear that the benefits of the specific investment will be diluted by opportunistic behaviour. Therefore, integrated ownership may encourage specific investment (Grossman and Hart, 1986; Bolton and Scharfstein, 1998).

5.6 The resource-based theory of the firm

As shown earlier (see Section 4.2), critics have suggested that the neoclassical theory of the firm is not really an analysis of the firm as such, but rather a theory of resource allocation in the market. The neoclassical theory pays little attention to internal decision-making within the firm. The firm is like 'a black box operated so as to meet the relevant marginal conditions with respect to inputs and outputs, thereby maximizing profits, or more accurately, present value' (Jensen and Meckling, 1976, p. 307). In contrast, Sections 5.2 to 5.4 of this chapter have described the transaction cost and agency theory approaches, which view the firm as an institution which minimizes or economizes on transaction costs, or the costs of processing information. Resources are allocated in response to the firm's interpretation of information flows. The firm organizes governance structures that create incentives and protect the organization from the threat of opportunistic behaviour arising from informational asymmetries.

However, dissatisfaction with both the neoclassical approach and the transaction cost and agency approaches has led researchers in the field of management science and organization theory to develop alternative theories of the firm which emphasize the strategic choices facing the firm's decision-makers. The firm is characterized primarily in terms of the resources or knowledge it embodies or commands. 'It appears obvious that the study of business strategy must rest on the bedrock foundations of the economists' model of the firm . . . [the] economic concepts [of Coase and Williamson] can model and describe strategic phenomena' (Rumelt, 1984, p. 557). Therefore development of a completely new body of theory is not required. The resource-based theory is best seen as a complement rather than as a substitute for the economic theories of the firm, adding further detail and texture to an understanding of the modern organization (Penrose, 1959; Wernerfelt, 1984; Phelan and Lewis, 2000).

The resource-based view of the firm extends further than the technological relationship between physical inputs and outputs embodied in the neoclassical production function. For example, Grant (1991) distinguishes between tangible and intangible resources, and Barney (1991) distinguishes between physical capital, human capital and organizational capital resources. Miller and Shamsie (1996) argue that each firm's uniqueness derives from the resources it controls, which are unavailable to other firms. More generally, resources are either property based or knowledge based. Property-based resources are legally defined property rights held by the firm, such as the right to use labour, finance, raw material inputs and new knowledge. Other firms are unable to appropriate these rights unless they obtain the owner's permission. Property-based resources are protected by contracts, patents or deeds of ownership. In contrast, knowledge-based resources such as technical expertise or good relationships with trade unions, are not protected by law, but they may still be difficult for other firms to access.

'A firm's competitive position is defined by a bundle of unique resources and relationships' (Rumelt, 1984, p. 557). These resources and relationships generate rents; and the more unique a resource, the more valuable it is to the firm. In a competitive market, rents arise because the initial owner and the firm have different expectations as to the value of the resource. To the owner, the value of a resource is its opportunity cost, or its value in its next best use. To the firm, however, value is added by combining and coordinating the resource with other firm-specific resources. The fact that the firm can use the resource in ways the owner cannot envisage creates a differential between the initial owner's valuation and the firm's valuation of the resource.

The term 'capability' defines the specific, unique outcomes when a set of resources are combined and coordinated in complex ways. Foss and Eriksen (1995) and Langlois and Foss (1997) suggest resources can be distinguished from capabilities in two ways. Resources are tradeable and uniquely tied to individuals within the organization. Capabilities are not tradeable, and are not necessarily embodied in any particular individual. Capabilities might include a good track-record in research and development, a reputation for using only high-quality inputs, a reputation for good customer service, or other aspects of the firm's culture and traditions. Through continued use, these capabilities become stronger, more profitable and more difficult for competitors to imitate. The firm acts as a repository for the skills, knowledge and experience that have accumulated over time.

Conner and Prahalad (1996), Grant (1996), Kogut and Zander (1992) and Liebeskind (1996) elaborate on the idea that firms apply knowledge to the production of goods and services, and that knowledge is strategically the most important of a firm's resources. An important distinction is drawn between tacit and explicit knowledge. Tacit knowledge cannot be conveyed sufficiently quickly to be appropriated immediately by the learner. For example, learning to ride a bicycle involves observation and practice, and cannot be done immediately simply by reading a manual. Tacit knowledge is held by individuals and not by the organization as such (Grant, 1996). To be useful, this knowledge must be coordinated. The firm exists because its management is better able to perform this coordinating function than the market.

Explicit knowledge, in contrast, is easily absorbed, and can be transferred to various uses immediately. A trade secret might be regarded as explicit knowledge: as soon as the secret is revealed, anyone can make use of the relevant knowledge. Liebeskind (1996) suggests that firms exist in order to protect explicit knowledge. Employment contracts may specify exclusivity and confidentiality clauses, preventing the transfer of economically advantageous knowledge to rival organizations. Firms can protect their explicit knowledge by threats of dismissal of staff who pass on information, making their departure costly through the loss of bonuses, pensions, stock options and promotion opportunities. The firm may try to ensure that its staff have access to no more information than is strictly necessary for them to perform their functions.

As suggested above, the boundaries of the firm can be defined by the ownership of resources. The boundaries of the firm define which activities or transactions are organized within firms, which are organized by intermediate organizations such as joint ventures, and which remain within the sphere of the market. Strategies of vertical or horizontal integration, franchising, forming strategic alliances and so on, all involve redefining the boundaries of the firm.

Due to indivisibility of certain inputs, the firm may find itself with spare capacity, which offers the potential for the development of new activities. However, growth is constrained by the limits to the ability of managers to conceive and control movements into new products and markets. In other words, there are cognitive limits to growth. Similar productive activities require similar capabilities, so economies of scale and scope can be realized when firms expand into similar activities. Complementary activities require different capabilities but, as the degree of complementarity increases, the need for greater cooperation and coordination becomes more important. Joint ventures, strategic alliances or full-scale integration may assist towards achieving sufficient cooperation and coordination. If managers are rent seekers, growth is constrained by their ability to transfer the firm's resources and capabilities into these new areas.

The neoclassical theory assumes firms have complete information. In reality, firms are neither fully informed about the best use of resources, nor do they know if they are properly equipped to face future contingencies. It is difficult to predict future changes in market demand, how best to respond to these changes, and what the payoffs are likely to be. Consequently, there is no point in attempting to estimate with any precision a production function of the type associated with neoclassical theory. Instead, the resource-based theory focuses on how firms can develop and improve their capabilities in order to adapt to a changing market environment. Success depends on the extent to which the firm's managers can nurture adaptive capabilities. Firms whose managers are slow to innovate will eventually tend to decline. Managers' decisions depend on their technical skills, knowledge, interpersonal and leadership skills. Different managers use similar resources in different ways. Accordingly, over time the capability of different firms tends to diverge, as does their performance.

Case study 5.2

Managers who act like owners

What would your customers say if they could see your expenses claim? The abstemious can rest easy. But extravagant restaurant receipts, first-class travel and accommodation, huge taxi fares – such things might not endear you to the people you are supposed to be serving. You should expect a tough conversation about the prices you charge if customers get the impression you are enjoying the high life with their money. That is why smart business leaders advise their colleagues to imagine they are spending their own money when they are out on company business. Act like an owner, the adage goes. Be responsible. Think before you splash the company's cash about.

This is a micro-level example of what has been called the 'principal-agent problem'. Even the most senior managers are not, usually, the owners of the business they are working for. It may not be easy for them to think and act like an owner. At the same time, can owners be confident that managers are working in the company's best interests and not simply pursuing their own selfish agenda? This question was explored by two academics, Michael Jensen and William Meckling, in a famous 1976 paper ('Theory of the firm: managerial behaviour, agency costs and ownership structure'), which popularised so-called agency theory. Their answer to the problem? Among other things, try to align the interests of managers and shareholders. Use share options to give managers 'skin in the game', a personal interest in the success – or failure – of the company. Incentives work: they should be deployed to get people working towards the same end.

There have been, to put it at its gentlest, regrettable unintended consequences to the spread of this theory. It turns out that the simple solution of share options does not solve the complicated problem of how to encourage and reward effective, re-sponsible management. For one thing, senior managers may not have the same time horizons as owners. A chief executive might reasonably calculate that he or she will be given no more than three or four years to run the business before their time is up. You would under-stand it if that CEO worked pretty hard to get the share price up fast in order to make those share options more valuable. And the longer-term consequences for the business in engineering such a rapid share price rise? Not necessarily the CEO's problem.

The shareholder base will, in any case, reflect a wide range of characters with varying priorities. There will be long-term institutional investors and hedge funds working in their own unique way. You can't easily be aligned with all of these people at the same time. Prof Jensen conceded in 2002, in the wake of the dotcom crash, that the incentives he regarded as crucial could do terrible harm. 'In the bubble, the carrots (options) became managerial heroin, encouraging a focus on short-term prices with destructive long-term consequences,' he said. 'It also encouraged behaviour that actually reduced the value of some firms to their shareholders.'

Stewardship – steady, long-term leadership that may not be reflected in rapid rises in the share price – is harder to reward with remuneration schemes based on stock markets. In an important critique published in 2004 ('Bad management theories are destroying good management practices'), Sumantra Ghoshal condemned agency theory as an example of all that was wrong with modern management. Amoral theories taught in business schools, he said, had 'actively freed their students from any sense of moral responsibility'. Agency theory served to convert 'collective pessimism about managers into realised pathologies in management behaviours'.

According to this critique, the theory seems to launch a cycle of distrust. Managers are knaves, out for themselves, who have to be tied in with share options. But managers who feel regarded in this way can become unmotivated and in the end untrustworthy. Why has executive pay exploded over the past 20 years? Partly, Prof Ghoshal suggested, because managers have sunk to reach the low expectations people have for them.

Source: Managers who act like owners, © The Financial Times Limited. All Rights Reserved, 7 July 2009 (Stern, S.). Abridged.

5.7   Summary

Chapter 5 has examined a number of approaches to the theory of the firm that represent alternatives to the neoclassical theory (reviewed in Chapter 3), and the managerial and behavioural theories (reviewed in Chapter 4). Coase provides a natural point of departure for many of the more recent, alternative theories of the firm, by asking why institutions known as firms exist at all. Why should the task of coordination or resource allocation be left within the sphere of the market in the case of some transactions, but handled within the domain of the firm for others? Coase's answer is that the firm's conscious method of coordination creates a saving in transaction costs: the costs incurred when using market mechanisms to allocate resources in a world of imperfect information. Coase's original emphasis was on transaction costs incurred before contracts are concluded, such as the costs of negotiation. The later transaction costs literature, to which Williamson is perhaps the most influential contributor, focuses on costs incurred after contracts are concluded, arising from bounded rationality, asset specificity and difficulties in monitoring and enforcing compliance. The transaction costs approach has been used to explore the question of what constitutes the most effective organizational structure. With a U-form structure, the firm's activities are subdivided into functional areas (marketing, finance, production, personnel), each of which is run by a specialist manager. However, effective coordination becomes more difficult as the U-form firm increases in size. In the twentieth century, such problems were addressed by the development of the M-form structure, in which the firm is divided into a number of quasi-independent operating divisions. Organizational structures are adaptable in the light of changing conditions. With market transactions, agents modify their behaviour in response to price signals. In contrast, organizations rely on skilled or specialized managers to take decisions as to how the organizational structure should adapt and evolve.

Coase's original insights have also influenced approaches to the theory of the firm based on agency theory. Echoing the earlier managerial approach, agency theory emphasizes the conflicts that can arise between principals (owners or shareholders) and agents (managers). Under conditions of incomplete contracts and uncertainty, opportunities may arise for agents to act against the best interests of principals, unless the incentive structures confronting principals and agents are properly aligned. Alchian and Demsetz view the firm as an efficient structure within which to organize team production. A central contracting agent (the employer or owner) carries out essential coordinating and monitoring functions, which cannot be performed effectively through the medium of markets. Jensen and Meckling's nexus of contracts approach focuses attention on the entire set of contractual relationships which bind together the firm's owners, employees, material suppliers, creditors, customers and so on. The firm encompasses a wider set of relationships than those defined purely in terms of team production.

In the property rights approach, a key distinction is drawn between specific rights defined explicitly in the terms of contracts, and residual rights which accrue to the owner once all specific rights have been assigned. In a world of incomplete contracts the ownership of the residual rights is of paramount importance. The ownership of the residual rights gives control over access to physical assets, or less tangible assets such as brands or reputation.

Recently, resource-based theories of the firm have been developed in the fields of management science and strategic management. The resource-based approach defines firms in terms of the resources and knowledge they embody and command. Resources include both physical inputs and intangible resources including technical expertise and organizational structure. The firm's resources combine to produce distinctive capabilities, and the firm acts as a repository for all of the skills, knowledge and experience that have accumulated over time. Some writers emphasize knowledge as perhaps the most distinctive and important of all the firm's resources.

Many of these theories have provided new insights and superior analytical tools with which to understand the modern organization. What seems clear is that no single theory can, by itself, adequately capture the essence of what a firm is, how it acts and how it evolves. Therefore, it would be wrong to select one single characteristic and expect a general theory to emerge from a partial analysis. A more productive approach is draw insights from each of the theories, so as to develop as broad an understanding as possible.

Discussion questions

1. Explain why Coase believed that the defining characteristic of the firm was the supersession of the price mechanism.

2. In what ways do transaction costs influence the design of the most efficient organizational structure?

3. With reference Case Study 5.1, examine the limits to outsourcing.

4. With reference Case Study 5.2, discuss how firms might encourage their managers to behave more like owners.

5. Some economists claim the firm is a collection of contracts. If so, in what ways does the firm differ from the market?

6. Assess the contribution of agency theory to our understanding of firm behaviour.

7. Discuss the extent to which the strategic- and knowledge-based theories of the firm can be regarded as substitutes for the neoclassical and alternative economic theories of the firm.

Further reading

Bloom, N. and Van Reenen, J. (2010) Why do management practices differ across firms and countries? *Journal of Economic Perspectives*, 24, 203–24.

Bolton, P. and Scharfstein, D.S. (1998) Corporate finance, the theory of the firm and organisations, *Journal of Economic Perspectives*, 12, 95–114.

Cowling, K. and Sugden, P. (1998) The essence of the modern corporation: markets, strategic decision-making and the theory of the firm, *The Manchester School*, 66, 1, 59–86.

Foss, N.J. (2003) The strategic management and transaction cost nexus: past debates, central questions, and future research possibilities, *Strategic Organization*, 1, 139–69.

Hart, O. and Holmstrom, B. (2010) A theory of firm scope, *Quarterly Journal of Economics*, 125, 483–513.

Kaplan, S., Schenkel, A., von Krogh, G. and Weber, C. (2001) Knowledge-based theories of the firm in strategic management: a review and extension. *MIT Sloan Working Paper 4216-01*, www.management.wharton.upenn.edn/kaplan/documents/KBV-SbanWP-4216-01.pdf.

Kay, J.A. (1999) Mastering strategy, *Financial Times*, 27 September www.johnkay.com/strategy/135.

Koppl, R. (2000) Fritz Machlup and behavioralism, *Journal of Industrial and Corporate Change*, 9, 4.

Shelanski, H.A. and Klein, P.G. (1995) Empirical research in transaction cost economics: a review and assessment, *Journal of Law, Economics and Organisation*, 11, 335–61.

Corporate governance

Learning objectives

This chapter covers the following topics:

- Corporate ethics
- Corporate governance
- Corporate social responsibility
- Governance codes of practice
- Links between corporate governance, executive compensation and performance
- Links between corporate social responsibility and performance

Key terms

Asset-stripping	Junk bond
Business ethics	Perquisites
Call option	Residual rights to control
Chairman–CEO duality	Stakeholder
Corporate governance	Synergy
Corporate social responsibility	Tobin's q
Empire-building	Tournament theory
Executive compensation	

6.1 Introduction

Corporate governance refers to the systems by which firms are directed and controlled. More specifically, corporate governance describes the arrangements that ensure the firm operates in accordance with the objectives of its own stakeholders, and the mechanisms that deal with conflicts of interest between various stakeholder groups. Agency theory, and its treatment of the possible conflicts that may arise between the owners or shareholders acting as principal, and its management acting as agent, is central to any discussion of corporate governance. A key issue concerns whether the maximization of shareholder value is the only legitimate objective of a privately owned enterprise, or whether the firm should accept a wider range of responsibilities towards a broader constituency of **stakeholders** including some or all of the following: employees, customers, suppliers, retailers, taxpayers, and society in general. Public awareness of the importance of corporate governance has risen to new heights during the early twenty-first century, after fraudulent accounting and various other forms of corporate malpractice contributed to several high-profile bankruptcies at the start of the 2000s. Various shortcomings in procedures for the management of risk, and compensation packages that created perverse incentives for short-termism or excessive risk-taking on the part of executives, are widely acknowledged as significant contributory factors towards the financial crisis of 2007–9.

The first four sections of this chapter examine a number of aspects of corporate governance. Section 6.2 describes several agency problems that arise through conflicts of interest between key investors, which create a need for governance mechanisms to mitigate conflict. Section 6.3 details the principal instruments of corporate governance, by outlining the roles and responsibilities of the board of directors, shareholders and bondholders, chief executive officer and other senior management. The constraints on discretionary behaviour on the part of the firm's management that are imposed by non-executive directors, various shareholder types (institutional, large and small), the dividend policy, the market for corprate control, and product market competition, are examined. The role of executive compensation in shaping behaviour is also considered. Section 6.4 outlines the international code of practice for good corporate governance that has been developed by the Organization for Economic Cooperation and Development (OECD), and describes the evolution of the UK's code of conduct that is currently articulated in the Financial Reporting Council's (FRC) Corporate Governance Code. Section 6.5 provides a brief historical overview of the implementation of corporate governance, and a selective review of academic research on the relationship between corporate governance and financial performance.

Adopting the broadest possible stakeholder definition, interest and awareness of the social responsibilities of firms has grown dramatically over the past forty years, stimulated in part by high-profile cases of corporate misbehaviour such as the explosion at Union Carbide's chemical plant at Bhopal in 1984, the oil spillage from the Exxon-Valdez tanker in 1989, and BP's Deep Horizon oil rig explosion in 2010. These events led to an increase in the activities of pressure groups, and aroused the interest and indignation of households, governments and the media. Section 6.6 provides a brief introduction to the topic of business ethics, centred on the contrasting views of three famous historical thinkers from the fields of economics and philosophy: David Hume, Adam Smith and Milton Friedman. Section 6.7 examines the **corporate social responsibility** (CSR) movement, which has gathered momentum as increasing numbers of firms have embraced the challenge of formulating and implementing explicit policies designed to satisfy stakeholder expectations and fulfil social responsibilities beyond the narrow pursuit of shareholder value.

6.2 Agency problems and the need for corporate governance

A narrow definition of the **corporate governance** of a firm might refer to the instruments or mechanisms available to the providers of finance that their investments are either safe, or that they will yield the maximum possible return. This definition assumes, implicitly, that the objective of the firm is the maximization of shareholder value. A broader definition refers to mechanisms that ensure management runs the firm in accordance with the objectives of several relevant groups of **stakeholders**. Relevant stakeholders might include shareholders as well as other groups such as employees, customers, suppliers, retailers, and so on. The most general definition might cover all specific legal obligations, as well as general responsibilities to society as a whole.

In the US and the UK, there exists a presumption in company law that the firm's net assets are the private property of its shareholders, and that shareholder interests of profit or shareholder value maximization should define the firm's objective function. In some continental European countries, including Germany, there is explicit provision in company law for legitimate pursuit of the objectives of other stakeholders. In recent years, however, there has been a tendency in continental Europe for convergence towards the shareholder-oriented Anglo-Saxon model. Compliance with company law is obligatory, while organizations such as the OECD have developed various codes of conduct for corporate governance, to which adherence is voluntary. Apart from compliance with company law, a fundamental reason why firms pay attention to governance issues is that by doing so, they develop and strengthen the trust of their investors.

> The economics of governance. . . . [is] that the immediate parties to
> an exchange are actively involved in the provision of good order and
> workable arrangements.
>
> *(Williamson, 2005, p. 1)*

Figure 6.1 shows at its core the 'internal' governance of the firm where the firm's management, acting on behalf of its shareholders, decides how best to raise funds for investment. This function is overseen by the board of directors, who are responsible for the general oversight of the managers, and setting their terms of employment and remuneration. In the UK the Cadbury Report (1992), one of the earliest codes of practice for corporate governance, placed heavy emphasis on the responsibilities of the board of directors for ensuring good governance. Adopting a broader perspective, Figure 6.1 shows the core 'internal' governance of the firm surrounded by an 'external' governance based on a nexus of contracts definition of the firm (see Section 5.4). The most important element in this

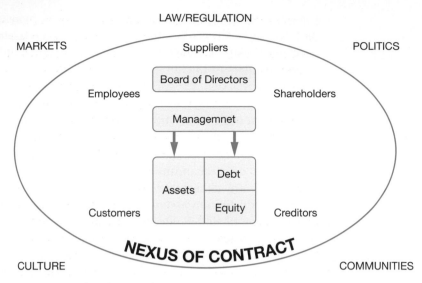

Figure 6.1 Internal and external governance
Source: Gillan, L. (2006) Recent developments in corporate governance: an overview, *Journal of Corporate Finance*, 12, p. 383.

sphere is the shareholders, who elect the board of directors. Shareholders are joined by employees, suppliers, customers and creditors who have contractual relationships with the core. This nexus of contracts is positioned within a larger environment encompassing markets, law, regulation, and the culture of the society in which the firm is located.

Agency theory, introduced in Section 5.4, is integral to any discussion of corporate governance issues. An agency problem arises when there is a separation within the firm of ownership from control (see also Section 4.3). Managers apply the funds contributed by investors to productive activities that are expected to generate returns, and investors rely upon the managers' specialist skills to generate a return on their investments. In the terminology of agency theory, the management is the agent, contracted by the shareholders or principal to generate a return on the shareholders' investment. In a world of imperfect or asymmetric information, however, the managers cannot always be relied upon to act in the shareholders' best interests, and the shareholders might not always be able to monitor the managers' actions effectively, owing to a lack of information. In other words, an agency problem arises from the potential conflict of interest that characterizes the relationship between principal and agent.

The two most common sources of agency problem that arise from the principal–agent relationship between shareholder and manager are first, **perquisites**, also known as discretionary or expense-preference behaviour; and second, **empire-building**. Perquisites refers to diversion of the resources of the firm to support on-the-job consumption by the managers, through means such as luxury offices, expense accounts, foreign travel, and so on. Empire-building consists of the pursuit of growth for its own sake, rather than growth that is targeted at increasing shareholder value. A merger and acquisition deal that fails to generate efficiency savings or **synergy** (see also Chapter 18), but which enhances the status or reputation of the management team that brokered the deal, is a typical example of empire-building behaviour on the part of management that fails to advance, or might be damaging to, shareholder interests.

One solution to the separation of ownership and control might be for the parties to enter into a legally binding complete contract, which specifies what actions the managers must take, and the rewards they will receive, under every possible contingency or state of the world (Shleifer and Vishny, 1997). In a world of uncertainty and asymmetric information, however, it is difficult to draw up complete contracts that are capable of anticipating every possible future contingency. Accordingly, agreements are required on the allocation of **residual rights to control** under the contingency that the firm goes into liquidation. At one extreme one could imagine a contract that assigns the residual rights to control to the shareholders who supplied the finance, and who enjoy the residual property rights in the assets that remain after all other prior obligations and debts have been settled. However, shareholders are not necessarily best placed to make decisions on how to make best use of their own funds when unexpected events occur. After all, they hired the managers to do just that! Consequently, the managers are typically assigned most of the residual rights to control, and are therefore afforded a large amount of discretion. Corporate governance attempts to impose limits on this discretionary behaviour.

Other agency problems within the firm may arise from conflicts of interest between large (majority) and small (minority) shareholders, or between bondholders (holders of debt) and shareholders (holders of equity). The potential conflict of interest between large (majority) and small (minority) shareholders arises from the possibility that the former use their controlling interest to expropriate the value of the latter's shareholding. For example, a shareholder with a majority interest in Company A and a 100 per cent interest in Company B faces an incentive to transfer assets from Company A to Company B, or to overcharge Company A for services provided by Company B.

In the event of bankruptcy bondholders have the prior claim to recovery of the debt by realizing the remaining value of the firm's assets. In conditions of uncertainty, the maximum payoff to bondholders is recovery of the full value of the debt, while the downside risk to bondholders is the loss of the debt. By contrast, the maximum payoff to shareholders is unbounded, while the downside risk is the loss of the value of the equity. The current value of the equity is the difference between the value of the firm's assets and the value of its debt. If the current value of the equity is small, there is a risk-shifting incentive for the shareholders to sanction investments in high-risk projects, because the upside benefit is unlimited while the downside risk to shareholders (loss of the value of the equity) is small. On the contrary, bondholders prefer low-risk investments, because the upside benefit is the same regardless of the level of risk while the downside risk to bondholders (loss of the value of the debt) is large.

Jensen and Meckling (1976) point out that in a firm part-financed by equity and part by debt, the equity has characteristics similar to those of a **call option** on the ownership of the firm. A call option on any asset gives the holder the right, but not the obligation, to purchase the asset at a pre-determined price on a specified future date. Suppose a firm has a bond issue outstanding, calling for a single payment to redeem the bond (repay the debt) on maturity. At maturity the shareholders have the following choice: either repay the debt and retain ownership of the firm; or fail to repay the debt, file for bankruptcy and sacrifice ownership. The equity is like a call option: when the debt matures the shareholders can either pay a fixed sum to retain the ownership of the firm (exercise the option), or do nothing and sacrifice ownership (allow the option to lapse). The distinction between the original shares, and options on those shares, becomes somewhat blurred. The fact that the value of any option is a positive function of the volatility of the underlying asset explains shareholders' risk-shifting incentive for investment in high-risk projects. The bondholders, who are effectively the counterparty to the call option, prefer low-risk investments.

Myers (1977) identifies a second type of debt agency problem, known as the underinvestment incentive. Shareholders bear all of the cost of investment in positive net present value (NPV) projects, but only realize part of the benefit. The rest accrues to bondholders, in the form of a reduced probability of failing to recover their investments. Therefore shareholders face an incentive to under-invest. Recognizing both the risk-shifting incentive and the underinvestment incentive, investors in bonds will demand a higher return on their investments, imposing an agency cost on the firm.

6.3   Instruments of corporate governance

Corporate governance comprises a number of instruments or mechanisms that mitigate the conflicts of interest that may arise between the shareholders acting as principal and the managers acting as agent, or between different groups of investor (large *versus* small shareholders, or bondholders *versus* shareholders), or more generally between various other stakeholder groups. The principal instruments of corporate governance, described in full by Goergen (2012), are identified in this section.

Boards of directors

Boards of directors may be either one-tier or two-tier. Membership of a one-tier board comprises both executive and non-executive directors. Executive directors include the chief executive officer (CEO) and other senior members of the management team. Non-executive directors are appointed to represent the interests of all of the shareholders collectively, and (sometimes) other investors or other stakeholders. In firms that operate under a board structure of **chairman–CEO duality**, the CEO is also the chairman of the board. In other cases, chairman of the board and CEO are separate roles. Duality may bring advantages of decisive leadership, with the leadership of the firm clearly vested in one individual. However, duality may tend to give rise to a lack of independence of the board from the senior management. Separation of these two roles might allow for more robust, independent oversight of management performance by the board, but separation might also lead to situations of conflict between the chairman and CEO.

Firms in the US, UK and several other countries operate with one-tier boards of directors. In some other countries, including Germany, a two-tier board structure operates. A supervisory board comprising non-executive directors is constituted separately from the management board, comprising the CEO and other senior members of the management team. In a two-tier system, individual members of the supervisory board might represent the interests of particular shareholders, or other stakeholders such as employees, customers or suppliers. A two-tier board structure might strengthen the supervisory capability of the non-executive directors, by affording them greater independence from the CEO or the firm's senior management in general. In some cases, however, lack of information or lack of expertise might limit the effectiveness of non-executive directors' supervisory contribution.

Shareholders

Significant shareholdings in many firms are in the hands of institutional investors, such as banks, insurance companies and pension funds. It is difficult to generalize as to whether share ownership by institutional investors tends to create a more or a less effective supervisory regime for monitoring managerial performance and constraining discretionary behaviour. Some studies report that institutional investors are relatively passive, perhaps lacking the expertise, resources or motivation to become closely involved in monitoring the performance of the firms in which they hold shares. Institutional investors may prefer to sell their shares, rather than attempt to intervene in the running of the firm, in the event of perceived underperformance on the part of management. There are some recorded instances, however, of institutional investors having adopted a more hands-on approach. Clear evidence is scarce, since any intervention on the part of the institutional investors is likely to take place in private, beyond the glare of publicity.

Shareholder activism, or mobilization of small shareholders to attend annual general meetings or extraordinary general meetings, in order to use their voting rights to create pressure or achieve policy changes, has been advocated by some as a promising tool for improving corporate governance. It has also been suggested, however, that intervention by small shareholders only tends to gather sufficient momentum to enforce change in extreme adverse circumstances. If so, small shareholder activism is more likely to operate as a vehicle for punishing management that has already failed, rather than as a means for promoting good management performance.

Firms whose share ownership is widely dispersed might experience a form of free-rider problem. No single shareholder has sufficient incentive to devote effort to monitoring, because the most of the benefit would accrue to other shareholders, who gain by free-riding. By contrast, firms with large individual shareholders might benefit from superior corporate governance, since a large shareholder gains more of the benefit from their own monitoring effort. It has been suggested, however, that large shareholders might be drawn to intervene excessively in tasks that are best left in the hands of professional managers. Collectively, empirical studies that examine the relationship between the

as an indirect instrument of corporate governance. Intense competition reduces the extent to which any inefficiencies in the firm's production that raise average or marginal costs may be offset by charging a higher price for the firm's product or service. Intense competition may also assist the monitoring of the managers' performance, enabling direct comparisons to be drawn with the performance of similar firms in close competition.

6.4 Corporate governance codes of practice

Since corporate governance is essential for the development and success of private business activity, most countries around the world have introduced and developed guidelines or recommendations for good corporate governance (Hart, 1995b). An OECD (1998) report identified four key principles: fairness, transparency, accountability and responsibility. *Fairness* refers to the protection of shareholders' rights. Shareholders hold property rights in the corporation, and participatory rights which involve them in the employment of managers and making their views known over a range of general business strategies. *Transparency* refers to the need to make all relevant information available to shareholders and other investors, who are then able to make informed decisions. Company accounts should be accurate and competently audited, and information regarding ownership, voting rights, board composition and the remuneration of managers should be disclosed. *Accountability* refers to the responsibility of boards to monitor the performance of managers, and generally be accountable to shareholders for their actions. The board has a duty to the firm's owners, and should try to avoid conflicts of interest. The board should not be too close to the managers, so as not to hinder its monitoring function. The recruitment of non-executive and independent directors can further strengthen accountability. *Responsibility* refers to corporations not only abiding by a country's laws, but also meeting culture-driven expectations of ethical behaviour towards stakeholders. Corporations should avoid socially harmful actions, even when there is no legal obligation to do so. Such responsibilities may vary from country to country, and corporate governance should reflect societal culture.

Revised subsequently, the OECD (2004) Principles of Corporate Governance have become internationally accepted as a benchmark for good corporate governance. The Principles are organized under six headings:

1. *Ensuring a basis for an effective corporate governance framework*. The framework should promote transparent and efficient markets and compliance with the rule of law, and should define the responsibilities of supervisory, regulatory and enforcement agencies.

2. *The rights of shareholders and key ownership functions*. The framework should protect and facilitate the exercise of shareholder rights.

3. *The equitable treatment of shareholders*. All shareholders, including minority and foreign shareholders, should be treated equitably and should have redress if their rights are violated.

4. *The role of stakeholders in corporate governance.* The framework should recognize the rights of stakeholders established by law or mutual covenant, and encourage cooperation between firms and stakeholders in creating wealth and jobs and promoting financially stable enterprise.

5. *Disclosure and transparency.* The framework should promote timely and accurate disclosure on relevant matters including financial situation, performance, ownership and governance.

6. *Responsibilities of the board.* The framework should ensure effective strategic leadership, monitoring and accountability to shareholders.

The OECD has acknowledged that the financial crisis of 2007–9 exposed some serious weaknesses in corporate governance in many countries. OECD (2009) identifies several areas of concern. In the field of executive compensation, managers typically have too much influence over performance-related pay. The governance process for compensation should be more clearly defined, and the role of non-executive directors should be strengthened. The link between performance and compensation is often weak, and hard to identify. Compensation schemes are opaque, impose limited downside risk, and thereby encourage excessive risk-taking by managers. Greater transparency in compensation structures is needed, and compensation should be linked more closely to long-term performance.

The financial crisis raised further concerns over the quality of risk management. The latter requires an enterprise-wide approach, and should not be confined to individual business units within the firm. Reporting of risks to the business, and risk management strategies, to the board of directors should be strengthened. The board should understand the nature of risk, and take responsibility for the integration of risk management into the overall corporate strategy. The firm's attitudes to risk, and its risk management processes, should be made explicit, and adequately disclosed to the market.

Finally, the financial crisis exposed several weaknesses in the areas of board composition and shareholder engagement. Competence, as well as independence, should be a key criterion in the selection of non-executive directors. Board member responsibilities should be specified and disclosed. Chairman–CEO duality is generally discouraged, but exceptions are possible depending upon circumstances. The shareholders' role in nominating and appointing board members should be strengthened, and companies should do more to engage their own shareholders. Institutional investors in particular should play a more active role in corporate governance.

In the UK the Cadbury Report (1992) was the first published code of practice for corporate governance, targeted primarily at companies with a London Stock Exchange listing. Its main recommendations were: the roles of chairman of the board of directors and CEO should be separate (no duality); board membership should include a significant number of independent, non-executive directors; a nomination committee, composed mainly of non-executives, should oversee nominations of executives and non-executives to the board; a remuneration committee, also composed mainly of non-executives, should scrutinize executive compensation; an audit committee should oversee financial reporting and disclosure; and institutional investors should disclose their voting policy.

Subsequently, the Greenbury Report (1995) contained recommendations that strengthened the independence and reporting responsibilities of the remuneration committee, introduced provisions for the disclosure of executive compensation on an individual basis, and requirements for the alignment of executive compensation with company performance. The Hampel Report (1998), which consolidated the recommendations of the earlier reports into a Combined Code, further emphasized the responsibility of institutional investors to use their voting power constructively, and recommended a strengthening of systems for internal control to protect shareholder interests. A revised Combined Code was published in 2006, consolidating a number of additional recommendations on matters such as the composition of the audit, nomination and remuneration committees, and the frequency and content of reporting and disclosure, which appeared in the Turnbull Report in 1999, the Myners Report in 2001, and the Higgs Report and Smith Report, both in 2003.

The current UK Corporate Governance Code was published by the Financial Reporting Council (FRC) (2010). The FRC identifies five main principles: leadership, effectiveness, accountability, remuneration and relations with shareholders. These cover territory similar to the OECD Principles described above. The FRC states that the Code should not be interpreted too rigidly or mechanistically, and any departures should not automatically be seen as breaches of the Code. The ethos is to encourage dialogue, rather than confrontation. An important principle is the 'Comply or Explain' approach, whereby a firm is required to either follow the Code, or explain to shareholders why it has not done so. A key feature is that the Code should not be over-prescriptive, and should not burden every firm with regulations that might not be applicable to some. Alternatives to the Code may be implemented, subject to the proviso that they are explained and justified. Exceptions might apply to smaller listed and unlisted firms, as well as firms with different board structures.

Case study 6.1

Reaction to Governance Code divided

Reaction to the revised UK Corporate Governance Code was divided following, as it did, months of strongly felt debate about one of the key issues of the financial crisis: the responsibility of company boards. The code's most controversial addition was the annual re-election of company directors.

The Confederation of British Industry had already warned that the move could be disruptive and might discourage directors from speaking out in the board room. David Tyler, chairman of Logica and J Sainsbury, has said it will present shareholders 'with a charter for mischief-making'. Speaking on behalf of the Institute of Directors, Roger

Barker, head of corporate governance, said the institute remained opposed to yearly re-election, but he thought the impact on boards would be slight as shareholders were unlikely to use the powers very significantly. 'Which raises the question "Why bother with it anyway?"', he added.

Encouraging boards to appoint more women – the code's other controversial move – was also 'not helpful'. 'Our women want to achieve a position on the board through their own merit and own abilities. When this artificial mechanism is used it undermines their own legitimacy, people will now question why they have come to be on a board,' Mr Barker said.

Philip Richards, a partner at law firm Freshfields, said board friction could also arise as each director must be voted separately, so there will be an 'opportunity for the shareholders to indicate who they do and who they don't like'. He added that 'it has the possibility to turn into an annual popularity contest between the directors, which is a slight downside'. However, George Dallas, director, corporate governance at F&C, the fund management group, said investors understood the concerns of those opposed to annual director elections. Moreover, he believed that 'long-term shareholders, which account for the vast majority of institutional shareholders, will exercise these additional voting rights responsibly and will use their shareholder rights to preserve and build the long-term value of their investments.'

Inclusion of more diversity on boards, with particular reference to gender, also attracted praise from investors. Although the UK has not gone so far as Norway, which has set quotas for increasing the number of women on boards, supporters saw it as a positive step. 'Board diversity is more likely to bring a breadth of opinions and provide the best leadership for a business,' said Benjamin McCarron, responsible investment analyst at The Co-operative Asset Management. In a riposte to those critics who have said there is insufficient female talent to serve at board level, Cranfield University School of Management has produced a list of more than 2,000 women who are on executive committees of FTSE 100 or 250 companies, which the institution described as 'poised and ready for a board position'.

Source: Reaction to governance code divided, © The Financial Times Limited. All Rights Reserved, 27 May 2010 (Sanderson, R., Burgess, K., Masters, B.).

6.5 Corporate governance: implementation and empirical evidence

Throughout the twentieth and early twenty-first centuries, financial crises and corporate scandals have repeatedly stimulated scholarly interest and public awareness of corporate governance issues. It is probably no coincidence that Berle and Means' (1932) seminal monograph 'The modern corporation and private property' was published only three years after the Wall Street Crash of 1929. Not long afterwards, Coase's (1937) article 'The nature of the firm' introduced the concept of transaction costs as a framework for understanding the reasons for the formation of firms, and the ways in which they operate (see Sections 4.3, 5.2 and 5.3).

During the three decades following the end of the Second World War, the large multinational corporation appeared to have established an unassailable position for itself as the predominant form of privately owned productive organization, staffed by a technocratic layer of professional management. Accordingly, much of the academic literature of the 1950s and 1960s was concerned with analyzing the decisions and actions of large corporations governed by an autonomous managerial class (see Section 4.3). Plender (2003) discusses reasons for the failure of past corporate governance to constrain the activities of managers and boards of directors. Prior to the 1980s, a cadre of strong and entrenched managers exercising considerable autonomy, together with weak accounting practices, led to empire-building and the pursuit of growth to the detriment of shareholder profits. However, a range of unacceptable practices, such as hostile takeovers followed by **asset-stripping**, excessive executive compensation, and the issue of **junk bonds**, led eventually to the growth of a 'shareholder value movement', which succeeded, temporarily, in constraining managerial discretion.

By the 1990s and early 2000s, the pendulum had swung gently but inexorably back in the direction of management. As noted above, the issue of call options to provide incentives for managers to target growth in the firm's share price, offering prolific rewards for those who succeeded by the time their options expired, was not treated in the US as an accounting expense. Consequently, options became an attractive boardroom currency, because their use allowed managers to be remunerated in a manner that left profit-and-loss accounts undisturbed. This led to an increase in option-leveraged ownership, providing managers with rewards far in excess of their true productivity. In order to mitigate the consequent dilution of existing equity, firms would borrow in order to buy back their own shares. The net effect was a transfer of wealth from shareholders to managers. Another factor was a tendency to interpret the share price as the only valid measure of a firm's performance, leading to excessive 'short-termism' on the part of managers. Some were tempted to adopt 'creative' accounting techniques allowing, for example, the maintenance of high earnings to mask underlying weaknesses in the business. When the danger increased that the bubble might burst, a hastily arranged merger and acquisition deal might further inflate the firm's share price in the short term. In some instances, creative accounting would shade into illegal practice. CEOs with their large executive compensation packages and status to match, operated increasingly in a self-contained world of hubris or 'self-attribution' (Monbiot, 2011) or 'wilful blindness' (Heffernan, 2011).

The collapse of Enron Corporation in 2001 is widely regarded as a defining moment in the history of corporate governance (Asad and Hoje, 2010). Enron was a US conglomerate that traded in electricity, natural gas, water, communications, and pulp and paper, with 20,000 employees and revenue of over $100 billion in 2000. Enron filed for bankruptcy protection in late 2001, when it was revealed that its financial position had been sustained by fraudulent accounting practices over a period of years during which the firm had pursued an aggressive growth strategy. Enron had created a number of offshore entities known as special-purpose units, which enabled the firm to maintain the illusion that it was highly profitable, when it was actually realizing large losses that were transferred to the offshore entities and not reported. Anticipated future profits were systematically reported as if they had already been realized, while the firm's executives focused obsessively on maintaining a high share price. Investors were unaware of the existence of the offshore units that were hiding the firm's losses, while several executives who were aware of the true situation were trading illegally in the firm's stock on the basis of insider information. The firm's auditors Arthur Andersen, at the time one of the world's 'big five' accounting firms, were heavily implicated in the Enron scandal. The reputational damage was terminal, and in 2002, Arthur Andersen voluntarily surrendered its licence to practise in the US. The Enron case was quickly followed by several other accounting and corporate governance scandals, the largest of which involved the collapse of the telecommunications firm WorldCom in 2002, where, once again, revenues had been inflated and losses disguised through fraudulent accounting practice.

Enron, WorldCom and several other US corporate scandals of the early 2000s strengthened the motivation for the passage of the 2002 Sarbanes-Oxley Act, which contained a range of provisions to strengthen corporate governance and address the weaknesses revealed by the previous scandals. The Act defines standards for auditor independence, and strengthens the independent oversight of public accounting firms providing auditing services. Stricter reporting requirements for financial transactions, including off-balance-sheet transactions, are imposed. Senior executives are held directly accountable for the accuracy of financial statements, and the management and auditors are required to produce an internal control report and comment on the soundness of the financial reporting. Criminal penalties for white-collar crime are strengthened, and some incentives are provided for whistle-blowers. Responsibilities are imposed on lawyers acting on behalf of the firm to report any irregularities to the CEO in the first instance, or to the audit committee and board of directors if the situation persists. There are provisions for the regulation of financial analysts by stock exchanges, and for disclosure of conflicts of interest that may arise from the dual role of financial analysts as advisors and traders. While there have been complaints from the corporate sector concerning the costs of compliance with Sarbanes-Oxley, there is also evidence that firms that have improved their internal controls and financial reporting have benefited from an improvement in investor confidence, through reduced borrowing costs or an increase in share-holder value.

There exists an extensive academic literature on the relationship between corporate governance and financial performance. This section concludes by reviewing a few selected studies. A dilution of shareholder rights would enable the firm's managers to pursue policies designed to protect and entrench their own positions. Gompers, Ishii and Metrick (GIM) (2003) investigate the relationship between a measure of shareholder rights known as the G-Index, and long-term stock returns and market value of the firm. The G-index is based on 24 corporate governance provisions for 1,500 US firms. A point is awarded for each provision that restricts shareholder rights. For example 'classified boards' which stagger elections to the board, calling special meetings, altering bylaws, or suing directors can, if used injudiciously, afford increased powers to managers. The highest decile of the index, comprising firms with the most powerful management, is referred to as the 'dictatorship portfolio'; the lowest decile is the 'democracy portfolio'. Between 1990 and 1999, the democracy portfolio outperformed the dictatorship portfolio by a statistically significant 8.5 per cent per year. In 1999 a one point difference in the index was associated with an 11.4 per cent difference in **Tobin's q**, a measure of market value of the company compared to the replacement value of the firm's assets. Weak shareholder rights were associated with lower profitability and lower sales growth.

Since the choice of corporate governance arrangements is not random, GIM consider three hypotheses that might explain the difference in performance between the two groups. Hypothesis 1 is that at the start of the period, shareholders failed to recognize that a reduction in their rights would lead to higher agency costs and the inability to replace poor managers. Hypothesis 2 is that there is no relationship between governance and performance, and the observed differences arise from managers fearing poor performance at the start of the period, and introducing provisions to weaken shareholder rights, affording the managers enhanced protection. This hypothesis recognizes the possibility of reverse causality between performance and governance. Hypothesis 3 is that the differences are explained by omitted variables such as the size of firm or the level of institutional ownership. GIM find some evidence to support hypothesis 1, but none for hypothesis 2. In accordance with hypothesis 3, up to one-third of the variation in performance can be attributed to other factors.

The G-index is used by Malmendier and Tate (2009) to examine the performance of award-winning CEOs featured in US magazines including *Forbes*, *Fortune* and *Time*. Performance typically fell after an award was conferred, and was weaker on average than in similar firms with non-award-winning CEOs. Award-winning CEOs tend to secure increased remuneration, and spend more time on public and private diversions. Underperformance and rent extraction by award-winning CEOs is strongest in firms characterized by weak governance according to the G-Index. Award winners in firms with strong governance achieve performance that was marginally stronger than the performance of firms with non-award winning CEOs.

Pissaris *et al.* (2010) ask whether the relationship between pay disparity, the difference in the remuneration of CEOs and managers at a lower level in the corporate hierarchy, and financial performance is best explained by agency theory (corporate governance) or **tournament theory**. The latter interprets high CEO remuneration as a 'prize', which provides incentives for junior executives to compete against each other in an effort to emerge as the top performer and become eligible for future promotion to the rank of CEO. The larger the firm, the greater is the pay disparity. Tournament theory suggests a positive relationship between pay disparity and financial performance. By contrast, agency theory suggests that in firms with weak governance, shareholders are less effective in monitoring management. Accordingly, agency theory points to a negative association between pay disparity and financial performance.

> . . . (T)he results suggest that firms characterized by weaker monitoring and transparency suffer from lower performance in the presence of high pay disparity than strongly governed firms. In other words, while pay disparity can provide incentives for better performance, consistent with tournament theory, it can become destructive in the absence of other governance measures and exacerbate agency conflict.
>
> *(Pissaris* et al., *2010, p. 307)*

The corporate governance of banks and other financial institutions has been subject to intense scrutiny by politicians, the media and the general public since the onset of the financial crisis of the late 2000s (Mehran *et al.*, 2011). Box 6.1 provides an overview of academic research on the corporate governance of banks before and during the financial crisis.

Box 6.1

The corporate governance of banks

Financial institutions, and particularly banks, are subject to control mechanisms, which differ from those of non-financial firms, owing to the unique role played by banks in the wider economy (Adams and Mehran, 2003). Depositors, shareholders and regulators maintain a shared interest in the corporate governance mechanisms of banks. The added regulatory dimension makes the analysis of corporate governance more complex than in the case of non-financial firms.

Board size and composition, executive compensation, bank ownership and cross-holdings, and the market for corporate control are key elements of the system of bank corporate governance (Allen and Gale, 2000). Executives' personal and professional attitudes towards power, entrenchment and ethics, play a role in determining the degree of alignment between executive and shareholder interests, and the extent to which executives pursue the maximization of shareholders' value. Governance is further shaped by prudential regulation and mechanisms of market discipline, which can give rise to further difficulties. Prudential regulation relies heavily on accounting data, which may be opaque and misleading. Errors or even fraud in financial reporting could prevent regulators from carrying out effective supervision. Market discipline varies widely across countries, depending on factors such as the legal framework, the level of stock market development, and the market for corporate control.

The incentive for shareholders to monitor banks depends on how effectively their rights are protected (Levine, 2004; Adams and Mehran, 2008; Adams *et al.*, 2010). This perhaps explains why banks with dispersed (unconcentrated) ownership structures tend to be more prevalent in countries with stronger laws for shareholder protection.

Corporate governance and financial performance

A number of studies of corporate governance in banking examine how risk and performance are affected by factors such as laws concerning investor protection, bank regulation, and the extent of ownership concentration. Much of the evidence refers to the US. Elyasiani and Jia (2008) find that stable institutional ownership improves the performance of US bank holding companies. Vyas (2011) finds banks with strong corporate governance (measured as an index of attributes including board structure and composition and executive compensation practices) tend to recognize and write off delinquent loans in a more timely fashion. Panthan (2009) finds that US bank holding companies whose CEOs exercise greater influence over board decisions tend to be riskier. Cornett *et al.* (2010) examine corporate governance mechanisms and the performance of publicly traded US banks before and during the financial crisis of the late 2000s. The linkage between CEO pay and financial performance, and the extent of insider ownership, weakened significantly around the financial crisis. Stronger corporate governance was associated with stronger financial performance. Berger *et al.* (2012) examine the relationship between board composition (age, gender and education) and risk-taking behaviour on the part of German banks. Boards with higher proportions of younger and female executives tend to accept more risk, while boards with a higher proportion of members with PhD qualifications accept less risk.

Several cross-country studies present comparative evidence on the corporate governance of banks. In a study of 244 banks in 44 countries, Caprio *et al.* (2007) find that concentrated ownership, often in the hands of families, foundations or the state, tends to increase shareholder value. Weak shareholder protection law has the opposite effect. Laeven and Levine (2009) find that risk is higher in banks with concentrated ownership. This effect is weaker, however, in countries with strong shareholder protection. Concentrated ownership is therefore helpful in mitigating the negative effect on shareholder value of weak shareholder protection. Beltratti and Stulz (2012) find that banks with more shareholder-friendly boards performed worse during the financial crisis of the late 2000s. Banks in countries with stricter capital regulation, and with more independent supervision, typically performed better.

Executive compensation and financial performance

The structure of executive remuneration is likely to be a key determinant of corporate strategy and performance (Houston and James, 1995; Bolton *et al.*, 2010).

Managerial ownership of equity and options in the firm, as well as other incentive features in managers' compensation structures (such as performance-related bonuses and performance-contingent promotions and dismissals), serves to align managerial incentives with shareholder interests.

(John and Qian, 2003, p. 109)

Several recent studies examine whether there is any empirical relationship between executive remuneration and bank conduct or performance, focusing especially on measures of the value of executive share options, or the ratio of share options to total executive compensation. Chen *et al.* (2006) find a higher proportion of share options in total compensation is associated with increased risk-taking. Mehran and Rosenberg (2008) and DeYoung *et al.* (2012) find share options encourage CEOs to undertake riskier investments. Fahlenbrach and Stulz (2011) find banks with CEO incentives more closely aligned with shareholder interests typically performed poorly during the financial crisis of the late 2000s.

Cheng *et al.* (2009) investigate the relationship between compensation and risk-taking among financial institutions during the period 1992–2008. Payouts to top executives were positively related to risk. Balachandran *et al.* (2011) find equity-based compensation (in the form of stock options) increased the probability of default during the period 1995–2008, while non-equity compensation (cash bonuses) reduced the default probability. With reference to bank holding companies during the period 1993–2007, John *et al.* (2010) find the sensitivity of bank CEO compensation to financial performance decreases with leverage (the ratio of debt to equity). Further, this sensitivity increases with outside monitoring by subordinated debt holders and regulators.

A few studies examine the link between financial performance and executive turnover. Erkens *et al.* (2012) find CEOs of banks with boards comprising high proportions of independent directors and institutional investors are more likely to be replaced following financial losses, than their counterparts in banks with boards dominated by insiders. Schaeck *et al.* (2012) examine the determinants of executive turnover in US banks. Executives of banks that are risky or have incurred losses are more likely to be dismissed, but dismissals often fail to deliver improved performance.

6.6 Business ethics

Business ethics can be defined as a philosophical analysis of moral issues seen from the perspective of companies and other forms of business organization (Brenkert and Beauchamp, 2010). It is a practical application of ethics in the domain of business firms. Some firms attempt to train their employees in ethical behaviour such as integrity and responsible practice. Ethics are not necessarily the same in different countries and cultures. Philosophers view ethics as having three components: metaethics, normative ethics and applied ethics. *Metaethics* describes how ethical standards or moral behaviour come into existence, through individual emotions and social interaction. *Normative ethics* defines moral standards that classify conduct as either good or bad, identify what constitutes duty, and examine the consequences of actions for other individuals and groups. *Applied ethics* concerns specific issues, such as war, abortion, euthanasia or the environment. It is clear that the application of ethics to business involves elements of both normative and applied ethics.

David Hume, Adam Smith and Milton Friedman

The foundations of business and corporate ethics are built on the ideas of several philosophers and economists. The eighteenth-century philosopher David Hume (1711–76) provides a useful starting point. Hume was primarily concerned with issues of justice. Justice is a set of rules that define and bind society together, and a virtue in its own right. Without the rules of justice, it is impossible to have the virtue of justice. The rules of justice define the stability of possession, its transference by consent, and the performance of promises. These rules provide the foundations for all social interaction, including commerce and business, making people better off than if acting as individuals. Society enables people to cooperate, achieving outcomes that would be beyond their capabilities as individuals, through the division of labour. Society also allows people to develop formal and informal insurance arrangements, whereby the risks of individual misfortune are shared or pooled. The benefits of such a society rest on the rules of property, trade and contract, and the underpinnings of society are largely economic. Hume recognizes, however, that self-interest may dissuade everyone from obeying all of these rules all of the time.

The potential contradiction between ethical behaviour and the pursuit of self-interest is integral to the writings of Hume's close contemporary, the economist and philosopher Adam Smith (1723–90) (see Box 1.1). Smith is most famously credited for introducing the notion of the 'invisible hand', whereby society is best served by the pursuit of self-interest by consumers and producers, and the absence of state coercion.

> It is not from the benevolence of the butcher, the brewer or the baker, that we expect our dinner, but from their regard to their own interest. We address ourselves, not to their humanity but to their self-love, and never talk to them of our own necessities but of their advantages.

(Smith, 1776, p. 19)

Prior to his contributions to economics, Smith (1759) discusses the idea that morality is largely based on the ability to sympathise with others and to garner social respectability. This can be achieved through benevolent actions aimed at various groups: first, family and other relatives; second, friends whom we respect and who may have helped us previously (a form of reciprocal altruism); and third, others on whom we bestow benevolence without any expectation of reciprocity. Through acts of kindness and compassion we earn respectability. Does this extend to business life? Although business people interact with others from outside their circle of benevolent concern, they do not do so soullessly, but instead they collaborate with each other (Bragues, 2009). This collaboration is obvious within a firm, but also extends to business relationships with suppliers and customers, fostering networks that may draw on the managers' benevolence. According to Smith individuals, and by extension business managers, have just one moral duty: to follow the system of natural liberty and to obey the rules of justice. Justice differs from benevolence, in that the latter is a choice for which individuals may receive plaudits or a loss of esteem. Justice, on the other hand, is a moral compunction as it is concerned with an avoidance of harm. Without benevolence markets can still function; but without justice, business is severely threatened.

By contrast, the University of Chicago economist Milton Friedman (1912–2006) expresses the seminal case for the incompatibility of free-market economics with social responsibility.

> When I hear businessmen speak eloquently about the 'social responsibilities of business in a free-enterprise system . . .' [They] believe that they are defending free enterprise when they declaim that business is not concerned 'merely' with profit but also with promoting desirable 'social' ends, that business has a 'social conscience' and takes seriously its responsibilities for providing employment, eliminating discrimination, avoiding pollution and whatever else may be the catchwords of the contemporary crop of reformers . . . Businessmen who talk this way are unwitting puppets of the intellectual forces that have been undermining the basis of a free society these past decades.
>
> *(Friedman, 1970, p. 33)*

To Friedman, the only moral responsibility within the law is the maximization of shareholder returns. In a personal capacity a manager might wish to pursue worthy causes; but in such cases he acts as a principal and not as an agent. Any money spent or effort exerted should be his own, and not the property of shareholders or the effort the manager has been contracted to supply. For a manager to be socially responsible in his professional capacity as an agent would mean that he is acting to the detriment of the principal. Friedman argues further that 'socially responsible' managers are no experts at how best to invest funds in ethical projects. Their expertise is limited to their function as corporate managers. From a different perspective, Baumol (1991) argues that firms in perfect competition or in imperfect markets which, because of low entry barriers, are 'contestable' (see Section 11.5), suffer a loss of market share if they invest in socially responsible activities. Such actions are only possible when firms enjoy market power. Furthermore, some Marxist philosophers would agree with Friedman's position, that the linking of capitalist business and ethical behaviour is inherently contradictory (Shaw, 2009).

The ethics versus business objectives debate: further considerations

A resolution of the potential conflict between business and ethical objectives is proposed by several writers who examine the relationship between business objectives and concepts of duty and obligations to stakeholders and the wider society. For example, Frederiksen (2010) discusses the ethical basis for corporate behaviour. Four possible ethical approaches are egoism, libertarianism, utilitarianism and commonsense morality.

■ Moral egoists take actions that maximize the good for themselves. A firm should act in its own best interest, which would normally be understood as profit maximization. Socially responsible behaviour is not because the firm feels socially obligated to do so, but because such policies are in the firm's self-interest. For example, it is in the firm's self-interest to enter into some form of social contract that will guarantee the safety and success of the organization.

■ Libertarianism as a moral theory emphasizes 'negative' rights such as free speech. People have an obligation not to impinge on the rights of others, by doing physical harm or preventing others from expressing their opinions. There is no duty, however, to act in a proactive way, such as giving support to the arts or charity.

■ Utilitarians argue that a moral action is one that attempts to determine the best outcome from an impartial point of view: the maximization of total utility. Firms have a moral duty to implement policies that maximize overall happiness. Firms should not, for example, discriminate in favour of their own employees over others. In practice it may be difficult to identify which actions promote the greater good, or to define the relevant constituency of beneficiaries.

■ Commonsense morality, located somewhere between the extremes of libertarianism and utilitarianism, accommodates both negative rights and positive duties. A firm has a moral obligation not to interfere with the rights of others, and a duty to help others proactively. Beneficiaries may be defined more narrowly than under a utilitarian approach, and perhaps limited to employees, shareholders, customers and the local community. Van de Ven (2005) questions whether some stakeholders' appeal to 'human rights' can override the claim of corporate self-interest, as well as the claims of other stakeholders. Human rights are seen as universally valid, imposing universal moral obligations on firms. According to Van de Ven, the size of the stakeholder constituency influences which groups should be prioritized. Those stakeholders with most influence over self-interest of the firm have the strongest claim for priority.

Sen (1993) develops a critique of Smith's arguments. The famous quotation concerning the 'benevolence of the butcher . . .' focuses on the motivation for the *exchange* of products, where there is no ethical dimension. Smith, however, would almost certainly consider certain issues that arise in production and distribution as subject to ethical concerns. If the producer, motivated by self-interest, attempts to defraud consumers and suppliers, then ethical issues do arise. Sen argues that self-interest is an insufficient condition for exchange to operate efficiently. What is needed is some form of institutional structure, which fosters implicit trust and mutual confidence in the ethics of all parties. Where there are no such institutions, or where they function inefficiently as in some developing countries, people are less likely to engage in market exchange transactions. In some cultures 'motivational structures' are very different from those that characterize the free market. In Japan, for example, a particular code of business ethics, influenced by the Samurai tradition and Confucianism, is prevalent. This differs greatly from the neoliberal promotion of self-interest as the foundation for a successful capitalist economy.

Contrary to Friedman's view that managers are bound solely by their contractual obligations to shareholders, Kolstad (2007) points out that an agreement between two parties does not necessarily invalidate their responsibilities to other human beings. In addressing Friedman's argument that the pursuit of goals other than profit maximization imposes a 'tax' on shareholders, Kolstad argues that the key question is not whether managers should redistribute wealth from shareholders to society, but whether shareholders should sacrifice some of their returns for socially desirable ends. Friedman's view that managers become less efficient by focusing on activities beyond their core areas of expertise is deemed to be less than universally applicable: some firms do have the skills and capability to marshal resources in the provision of social goods. The argument that by incurring additional costs the firm may jeopardize its own survival prospects does not find strong empirical support: few, if any, firms have been bankrupted solely by their commitment to social investments. Friedman's position is also challenged by the widely held belief that good ethics are good for business. Firms may be rewarded when their managers make ethical decisions. For example, if employees, suppliers, customers and investors are treated well, then improved productivity, favourable contracts, customer loyalty and further investments may ensue. 'Reputational capital' leads to higher revenues or lower costs.

The argument that good ethics is good business has been criticized from a philosophical and economic perspective (Burton and Goldsby, 2009). Any definition of ethical standards is conditioned by societal or cultural norms. For example, discrimination in an organization's hiring policy might, in some cases, be viewed as permissible or morally neutral. If individuals differ in their interpretations of the same actions, then the rewards to the organization may also differ. It would be contentious to assume that the general public rewards managers' moral decisions with any precision. Disapproval of unethical behaviour may be stronger than approval of ethical behaviour. Unethical behaviour might be construed as those actions that lie below a 'moral floor', and some individuals might refrain from entering into business relations with managers who fall below this floor. Managers' actions that lie on or above the floor may elicit different responses from different stakeholder groups. Some investors may punish managers who rise above the floor for their pursuit of ethical deeds, while others may reward such actions. Others may take a morally neutral view, and focus solely on the firm's financial performance.

6.7 Corporate social responsibility

By adopting a **corporate social responsibility** (CSR) policy, a firm embraces a range of economic, social and environmental responsibilities over and above its duty to shareholders to maximize profit or shareholder value. The firm also monitors its own compliance with ethical standards, on matters such as fairness and justice. Much of the discussion of CSR refers to stakeholder theory (Freeman, 1984; Freeman *et al.*, 2004). The broadest stakeholder definition includes any group that has the capability to influence or exert pressure on the firm's management. The implementation of a CSR policy requires management to strike a balance between its responsibilities towards non-investing stakeholders, and its agency duties to shareholders. The stakeholder theory has been criticized by Orts and Strudler (2009), who claim that the connection between the theory and ethical considerations is weak. The main practical application of stakeholder theory is to identify groups that have an interest in the organization. Precise identification of who qualifies as a stakeholder is ambiguous. Even if the relevant stakeholders can be identified, the theory offers little guidance on how to balance their interests. How, for example, does a firm balance the needs of a shareholder's investment to provide a pension with the needs of a low-paid employee to feed their children?

Several forces have shaped the growth of the CSR movement since the 1980s (Azer, 2002). Growing affluence has heightened interest and awareness of ethical issues: poor societies are less likely to penalize businesses for unethical behaviour. Globalization and improvements in communications technology have increased the speed of dissemination of information concerning ethical misconduct around the globe. Groups of consumers, employees, community activists and shareholders have discovered that challenging the corporate status quo can often deliver change. A firm's reputation is built, in part, on the foundation of stakeholder views and the firm's responses to their concerns. CSR has increased in importance as governments have reduced their role in the regulation of business by liberalizing markets and trade. This trend has resulted in some loss of public accountability, creating impetus for pressure groups to bypass government and engage directly with firms. Equally, firms are less likely to rely entirely on government codes of practice, and more likely to develop their own CSR policies. A demand for greater accountability throughout the supply chain has led to firms being held increasingly accountable for their suppliers' practices on issues such as child employment, payment of low wages or operation in countries with corrupt governments. The ethical investment movement, especially in Europe, has strengthened scrutiny of firms' ethical standards and behaviour. Finally, the growth of the CSR movement reflects, in part, an increased public awareness and concern over environmental issues.

More specifically, a sequence of high-profile cases of corporate misconduct with devastating environmental consequences has served as a focus of attention for pressure groups, the media, households and governments. In December 1984, a leakage of poisonous gases from the Union Carbide pesticide plant in Bhopal, India resulted in 3,787 deaths among the population in the immediate vicinity of the plant, according to official figures released by the Madhya Pradesh state government. The total number of deaths since 1984 that were related to the incident exceeds 10,000 according to some estimates, and between 100,000 and 200,000 people are believed to have suffered permanent injury. In the aftermath, numerous deficiencies were uncovered in the firm's management and operational procedures, including poor working conditions, inadequate training, poor maintenance of equipment, inadequate safety policies, inadequate emergency procedures and processing of dangerous chemicals in a densely populated area.

In March 1989, a spillage of crude oil from the Exxon-Valdez oil tanker off the coastline of Alaska resulted in a spillage of between 11 million and 32 million gallons of crude oil, contaminating a stretch of coastline and ocean that was a prolific habitat for marine wildlife. Exxon was adjudged responsible for providing insufficient supervision and rest periods for the captain and crew, and for failings in the maintenance of a radar system that could have averted the disaster. Exxon-Valdez was the largest oil spillage in US waters until the Deepwater Horizon oil spill in the Gulf of Mexico, which continued for three months between April and July 2010 following an explosion at a BP oil rig that killed 11 employees and injured 17 others. Over 200 million gallons of crude oil were released into the ocean, with devastating consequences for marine habitats and the local fishing and tourism industries. Once again, a catalogue of management failures on the part of BP and its contractors Halliburton and Transocean were found to have contributed to the disaster. These included the prioritization of cost-cutting measures over health and safety, technical failure in the testing of equipment, inadequate risk management policy, and inadequate safety and emergency procedures.

One of the most influential early contributions to the academic literature on CSR was provided by Carroll (1979), who classifies the constituents of a CSR policy into a four-level pyramid: economic, legal, ethical and discretionary or philanthropic responsibilities.

- The lowest level is the firm's economic responsibility in meeting the needs of its customers. Everything else is predicated on the firm's success in fulfilling this basic responsibility. Aspects of economic responsibility include the maximization of the value of the firm, the development and maintenance of competitive advantage, and efficiency.

- The second level is the responsibility for compliance with the law of the countries in which the firm operates. The law reflects society's ethical view as to the minimum standards of behaviour expected of firms and other organizations, as well as efforts to ensure fair competition or a 'level playing field' in the market.

■ The third level is the ethical responsibility, over and above a strict inter-pretation of economic and legal responsibilities, to act in a manner that is considered fair by society, even though not codified in law. The firm's treatment of shareholders, employees, suppliers and customers is scrutinized with reference to society's ethical norms as to what constitutes moral behaviour.

■ The highest level is the philanthropic responsibility that defines the firm as a good 'corporate citizen', covering discretionary acts and behaviour that actively promote society's well being. Philanthropic responsibilities extend beyond society's expectations regarding ethical behaviour. Whether activities such as charitable donation and sponsorship of artistic events are truly altru-istic, or motivated by the prospect of an economic return by strengthening the firm's brand, is often ambiguous.

Having identified the various levels at which a CSR policy may operate, Carroll emphasizes the practical importance for management of identifying the issues for which a social responsibility existed, and of articulating a specific strategy for responding to these issues. Four generic motives for the adoption of a CSR policy that are widely cited in the literature are moral obligation, sustainability, licence to operate and reputation. *Moral obligation* concerns the need for firms to be 'good citizens', and follow moral imperatives. Many moral decisions are straightforward and pose no conflicts of interest, such as the filing of correct tax returns. Some decisions, however, involve conflicts that, in the absence of a 'moral calculus', are difficult to resolve. *Sustainability* refers to actions in pursuit of long-term economic, social and environmental objectives, rather than short-term goals. *Licence to operate* refers to a more pragmatic approach to CSR, whereby firms attempt to avoid interference in their affairs from regulators or governments, by taking voluntary steps that pre-empt intervention in areas such as health and safety, environmental protection or equal opportunities. Finally, *reputation* covers actions that aim to placate third parties in 'stigmatized' industries such as petrochemicals. Such actions provide insurance against possible disasters, but it is difficult to measure accurately the benefit to the firm. Porter and Kramer (2006) suggest, however, that the four generic motives are framed at a level that is too general to provide guidance for action in specific cases.

In what ways might the adoption of a CSR policy be value-enhancing for the firm, rather than detrimental to the narrowly focused corporate objective of shareholder value maximization? Kurucz *et al.* (2008) identify four aspects of the business case for CSR: cost and risk reduction; competitive advantage; reputation and legitimacy; and synergistic value creation.

■ A firm might invest in CSR as a means of reducing costs or risk, thereby enhancing its economic value. According to Friedman, spending on CSR dilutes the firm's ability to work in the best interests of shareholders. If the firm earns more than a normal profit, there might be a trade-off between the maximization of shareholder value, and the direction of some resources towards CSR. By contrast, an 'enlightened value maximization' hypothesis suggests that the demands of all stakeholders need to be managed so as to reduce the risk of conflict, so investment in CSR is not necessarily incompatible with shareholder value maximization.

- Investment in CSR for competitive advantage involves viewing stakeholder demands for socially responsible policies less as a constraint, and more as a positive opportunity for the firm to create value by orienting and directing resources towards the perceived demands of stakeholders.

- Investment in CSR might increase shareholder value by improving the firm's reputation and legitimacy. This is achieved by aligning the interests of stakeholders with those of the firm by incorporating a commitment to social investment into the marketing strategy.

- Synergistic value creation through CSR refers to a deliberately created market where the interests of stakeholders are aligned by developing new perceptions of value. The linking of communities, social networks and organizational stakeholders with new thinking and new paradigms can lead to a united concept of what is valuable. Once achieved, a virtuous circle is created leading to further CSR investment.

According to Aguilera and Jackson (2003), institutional theory is better than agency theory in explaining national differences in corporate governance. Institutions are characterized by norms, incentives, rules, stability and patterns of behaviour. Agency theory fails to recognize cross-national differences between stakeholders and their interests. By contrast, institutional theory considers the motives of managers and stakeholders in determining governance arrangements, which should be analyzed within different national, cultural and institutional contexts. Different national approaches to CSR depend on institutional arrangements. Some commentators have identified differences between the typical approaches towards CSR of US and European firms. For example, Matten and Moon (2008) characterize the US approach as explicit, and the European approach as implicit. Firms that adopt an explicit approach view CSR as deliberate, voluntary and strategic, and use CSR terminology to communicate their policies to stakeholders. Firms that adopt an implicit approach view CSR as an involuntary policy that adjusts to prevailing societal norms, and tend not to communicate their policies using CSR terminology explicitly.

The volume of empirical research into the relationship between CSR and financial performance has grown explosively in recent years. On the EBSCO database there are 135 references to CSR between 1945 and 1980, 122 between 1981 and 1990, 232 between 1991 and 2000, and 5,463 between 2001 and 2010. Research in this field faces the challenge of devising a meaningful metric for CSR (Turker, 2009). The Kinder Lydenberg and Domini (KLD) database scores 3,000 US firms on a range of criteria including community relations, employee relations, treatment of women, treatment of minorities and military contracts. Other databases include the FTSE4Good, covering 1,000 European firms; and SIRIS covering 300 firms listed on the Australian Stock Exchange. A drawback of this approach is that the choice of criteria may lack objectivity, and may be relevant for a particular country or region only. An alternative approach is to focus on single-issue indicators such as pollution control or treatment of women. Some studies use textual analysis to examine the CSR content in a firm's publications. A difficulty is that the CSR content in a firm's publications might not accurately reflect the reality of CSR activity. Another approach is to investigate the perceptions of individuals to a firm's CSR policies. Several studies adopt Carroll's (1979, 1991) four-level pyramid as a framework. Difficulties may arise, however, from a tendency for questionnaires with limited choices to impose the investigator's preconceptions on an individual's responses.

Chih *et al.* (2010) investigate the conditions under which a corporation is likely to behave in a socially responsible manner, with reference to financial performance, competition, state regulation, private regulation, existence of power groups, business education, trade associations and employee relations. Testable hypotheses include the following. First, financially weak firms are less likely to adopt responsible policies. Second, where competition is intense, firms may seek to reduce costs by acting in a socially irresponsible manner, within or even outside the law. Where competition is weak and profit margins are high, firms may seek to enhance their reputations by adopting responsible policies. A monopolist facing little or no competitive threat might not be fearful of a loss of reputation, and there might be limited incentive to behave responsibly. Chih *et al.* examine a sample of 520 financial firms from 34 countries between 2002 and 2005, drawn from the Compustat Global Vantage database. Firm size is used to control for any tendency for larger firms to be subject to greater scrutiny than smaller ones. Macroeconomic controls include the inflation rate, and indices of industrial production and consumer confidence. There is support for the hypothesis of a positive relationship between financial performance and social responsibility. Large firms are more likely to implement CSR policies. There is also support for the proposition that firms are less likely to invest resources in socially responsible projects if there is either too much or too little competition.

Dowell *et al.* (1999) use a sample of MNEs in manufacturing and mining, drawn from the Investor Responsibility Research Centre's corporate environmental profiles, to examine whether shareholder value is linked to environmental policy. There is no support for the notion that that the adoption of global environmental standards depresses shareholder value. King and Lennox (2001) find evidence of a negative relationship between TRI (Toxic Release Inventory) emissions and shareholder value, for 652 firms in 1997 and 1998. Brammer and Millington (2005) examine factors that encourage charitable donations, as well as the size of donations. For 550 firms quoted on the London Stock Exchange in 1999, firm size and advertising intensity positively influence the probability of making donations, whilst strict governance and managers' remuneration have a negative association. The size of donations is positively related to R&D expenditure, managers' remuneration and profitability, and negatively related to the firm's debt.

For a range of CSR policies implemented by a sample of firms drawn from the KLD database, Bird *et al.* (2007) attempt to identify policies with a negative impact on financial performance, and those with a positive impact that do not conflict with the objective of shareholder value maximization. CSR policies in the areas of employee relations, diversity, community, environment and product are examined. Employee relations covers policies such as profit-sharing schemes, pensions and health and safety; diversity refers to the firm's activities in recruiting minorities; community refers to discretionary actions such as charitable donation; environment refers to pollution control and recycling; and product refers to the production of high-quality goods, and innovation. The empirical analysis reveals few policies that produce conflicts between the interests of shareholders and other stakeholders; it is suggested, however, that the stock market punishes firms that spend above legally required environmental standards.

Simpson and Kohers (2002) analyse the Community Reinvestment Act ratings of 385 US banks for the period 1993–4. A higher rating is associated with higher profitability and lower loan losses. Scholtens and Dam (2007) examine whether the adoption by banks of a set of principles for managing environmental and social risk in project finance transactions, known as the Equator principles, had any immediate effect on the share prices of the banks concerned. There is no evidence of any significant effect. Shen and Chang (2012) find no relationship between the adoption of CSR policies and financial performance for Taiwanese banks during the period 2002–6.

The results from much of the empirical research into the relationship between CSR and financial performance are varied, and sometimes contradictory. A key methodological issue concerns the correct identification of the direction of causation. It seems just as plausible to argue that it is the most successful firms that can afford to adopt socially responsible policies, as it is to argue that firms reap financial rewards from being socially responsible. For example, better industrial relations may not necessarily lead to greater shareholder value; rather, profitable firms can afford to reward their employees in a way that reduces the likelihood of industrial conflict. Any observed relationship between the adoption of CSR policies and financial performance may simply reflect the quality of the firm's management, which impacts upon both. In the empirical literature, conflicting results and weak relationships derive partly from definitional and measurement issues. In 95 CSR studies reviewed by Vogel (2005), financial performance was measured in 70 different ways using 27 different data sources. KLD, the most popular CSR database (see above), includes measures of community relations, industrial relations, environment, diversity and product safety; but the weightings attached to different variables are undisclosed and probably subjective. Studies that examine narrower aspects of CSR may have greater focus and clarity, but the results are not directly comparable with those of other studies that adopt a different focus.

Finally, in recognition of the importance of consumer attitudes to socially responsible behaviour on the part of business, some research examines directly the impact of CSR policies on consumer purchasing decisions. For example, Öberseder *et al.* (2011) use interviews to examine how consumers respond to CSR initiatives. The key factor in determining consumer purchasing decisions is price, and a perception that ethical goods are more expensive might have a negative impact. Smith *et al.* (2010) investigate consumers' knowledge of CSR, and the extent to which they act on this knowledge. Awareness of a firm's CSR policies influences the perception of the firm in its other activities through 'halo effects'. For example, consumers aware of a firm's environmentally friendly policy might assume the firm also supports diversity and local communities. Halo effects might be used strategically to make unsubstantiated claims about the beneficial social attributes of unrelated products. The term *greenwashing* describes the misleading promotion of ethical or environmental actions. In the 1980s the American environmentalist Jay Westervelt characterized the practice on the part of some hotels of asking customers to re-use their towels, while doing nothing else to promote recycling, as a cynical ploy to economize on laundry bills. Another example is the decision of McDonald's to alter the theme colour of its European outlets from the traditional red and yellow to green.

> Now that the interiors of most restaurants have been modernized and redesigned, it's time to take on the exteriors, with green instead of red. The colour was chosen because it invokes respect for the environment.

> *(Holger Beek, vice-president of McDonald's German operation,*
> *quoted in* Deutsche Welle, *2009)*

Case study 6.2

Apple has incentive to worry about workers' rights

Imagine a company generating an extra $1.5bn in sales every week compared to what it earned only a year ago – and nearly all of that coming from products that it had dreamt up from scratch within the last half decade. These were things the world didn't know until recently that it needed.

That would be like General Motors conjuring up its entire North American sales – all the Chevrolets, Cadillacs, Buicks and GMC trucks – from nothing, in the space of just a year.

That gives some idea of the enormity of Apple's recent success on the back of the iPhone and iPad. Without those inventions, it would be a struggling computer-maker trying to fill the gap left by shrinking iPod sales. Instead, it is a world-beater with a share price that surged past $500 this week and didn't stop to catch breath. It was only with the launch of the iPad that Apple's stock market value topped that of Microsoft, a company that once seemed unassailable: it is now worth nearly twice as much. But this latest surge has consequences. When Microsoft's sales jump on the back of new software releases, it only needs to ship more bits. Apple has an altogether different problem. In late 2010, it was shipping 1.8m shiny new iPhones and iPads a week. A year later, it had upped that weekly quota by nearly 1.5m – and still couldn't satisfy demand.

This has created one of the great historic challenges of manufacturing. The supply chain of the electronics industry, with its hub in south China, was already one of the most impressive manifestations of the forces that have brought a new, globally distributed workforce into play. But this system is now being tested in the extreme.

This is not just about iPads and iPhones: with the advent of true mobile computing, an industry that once counted its sales in the hundreds of millions will soon be counting it in the billions.

That makes Apple's handling of the supply chain labour issues that continue to dog it a central concern not just for its own future but for the industry at large. Its scale and conspicuous brand have brought it unwelcome attention. But it is already ahead of its main rivals in trying to grapple with the underage labour, excessive forced overtime and inadequate safety standards that continue to be alleged against it, and the new standards it is helping to set will be felt across the industry.

One implication is that costs will rise. According to one tech industry veteran who has been closely involved with supply chain labour issues in the past, Foxconn, the immense Chinese manufacturer that supplies much of Apple's output, 'clearly has optimised around cost and speed rather than worker rights'. Changing that will take money. For a company that can charge premium prices, like Apple, that may not present a problem. It is also unlikely to hurt the lowest-cost makers of consumer electronics based in the emerging world, many of which will feel no obligation to meet the new, higher, voluntary standards that are likely to emerge. But the same will not be true for consumer electronics brands based in the US or Europe: without Apple's premium brand, they will have little price protection, but they will still need to conform to raised expectations.

All of this presumes, of course, that Apple actually has the power to influence how its suppliers treat their own workers. Transparency appears to be one problem. Apple executives argue strenuously that they audit suppliers thoroughly and have identified any problems. Tim Cook, chief executive, says that he gets weekly data on the working hours put in by 500,000 workers around the world – surely giving him a far better understanding than his counterparts in the automobile industry had nearly a century ago when they first introduced mass manufacturing. Yet independent investigations – most recently one by the *New York Times* – continue to point to significant shortcomings.

Apple's leaders certainly have plenty of incentive to get to the root of this problem. The consequences of failing to deal with it would be significant. It is not just a question of appeasing the NGOs that make themselves a nuisance about such issues. As Nike and Reebok found a decade ago, customers can rebel against brands associated with sweatshop practices. Steve Jobs, for whom the Apple brand experience was a big part of delighting his customers, would have understood what is at stake.

Of course, this could also have consequences that reach far beyond the Apple brand. Unlike the recent stream of young internet idealists who have made a show of their desire to make the world a better place – most recently Mark Zuckerberg of Facebook – Mr Jobs never set his sights beyond pleasing his customers as he sought to 'put a dent in the universe'. But for Apple's brand to thrive as it moves into its new phase of global manufacturing superpower, his heirs will have to show that their company is dedicated to the betterment of a large slice of the world's working population.

Case study 6.3

How 'good' does a shampoo need to be?   FT

Until recently, I thought that Unilever was a company whose primary purpose was to make products such as shampoo. No longer. Last week, I chaired a panel of business leaders on the sidelines of the World Economic Forum in Davos. And during that debate, entitled 'The Future of Business', it became clear that most business leaders do not really want to talk about the grubby financial realities of business these days, or, at least, not at Davos. Instead, Keith Weed, the charming head of marketing at Unilever, earnestly outlined the social and environmental initiatives that Unilever is now pursuing to help the 2 billion consumers who apparently buy its products each day. Whereas the company used to think of corporate social responsibility (CSR) programmes as separate from core business, he said, these days CSR is at the core of everything it does.

Similarly, Novartis, the pharmaceutical giant, is now devoting considerable energy to bringing health initiatives to poor people around the world, even at a loss. Daniel Vasella, its chairman, told the panel that this makes him 'very proud' (never mind the commercial side of Novartis's work). Meanwhile, T.K. Kurien, the head of Wipro, the Indian technology group, explained that his company is also expanding its social programmes in response to employee demand. 'Young people in India used to be happy to have a job. But now they are aware [of social issues] – they don't want to work in something such as defence, but [in] something like health.' And these companies are not alone: a senior employee at Bloomberg revealed that CSR pages are now one of the fastest-growing sections of its data terminals. That is apparently because investors are clamouring for information about companies' CSR programmes, be that in relation to 'responsible' shampoo – or anything else.

Is this a good thing? Some observers think it is. Nadine Hack, executive-in-residence at IMD business school in Lausanne, for example, firmly believes that companies should be applauded for being more socially engaged. After all, she argues, companies are so powerful these days that there is little hope of addressing societal problems – environmental, economic or anything else – without their support. Conversely, when corporate muscle is engaged, the outcomes can be powerful: when, for example, Coca-Cola started battling Aids in Africa, it had an extraordinary impact.

But there is a powerful counter-argument, too: some business leaders retort that companies would actually do better to focus on their primary function – namely the business of making money – and leave governments to worry about those bigger social goals. After all, governments are elected to make countries better, so why do unelected company executives feel any duty to reach into other areas of life? 'The fact that companies are doing all this CSR stuff just shows that government has failed,' muttered one British manufacturing executive. My views lie somewhere between these extremes: I think that companies should recognise their wider impact on society, but I also think that it is primarily up to governments – not companies – to set the rules and pursue wider social aims. In other words, I don't want Unilever to trash the environment with high-margin shampoo, but I expect the government, not Unilever, to set environmental standards, penalise miscreants – and tax Unilever to help the poor.

But whatever I (or anybody else) thinks of the merits of CSR, my experience of Davos suggests its strategic importance can only grow right now. That is partly because governments are blatantly failing to pursue many of their core responsibilities, forcing companies to step in. But a second, related, factor is that company executives themselves are getting scared of wider social strains. Just before this year's Davos meeting, for example, a survey from the World Economic Forum showed that 'income disparity' heads the list of issues that Davos Man thinks will threaten global stability this year. That is stunning, since income disparity never even featured on that list until this year (it was previously dominated by concerns such as the 'asset price collapse', 'oil shock' or 'fiscal crisis').

Corporate executives do not have any easy answers to this. As Wipro's Kurien observed, with commendable honesty: 'We [in business] can all see the problem of income disparity, we just don't know what to do about it.' But, in today's world, nobody wants to sit on their hands; somehow, they need to be seen to be doing something. Hence the appeal of CSR, in Davos and beyond; in today's world, it has become a useful salve for a troubled corporate conscience, if not a quasi amulet that companies like to wear as a protection against the evil eye (or, at least, future social strife).

And somewhere along the way, CSR is delivering some genuine good for people who need help – at least, I fervently hope so. Either way, it provides something else to ponder on the next time you buy a bottle of commercial shampoo.

Source: How 'good' does a shampoo need to be?, © The Financial Times Limited. All Rights Reserved, 3 February 2012 (Tett, G.).

6.8 Summary

Corporate governance describes the arrangements put in place to ensure that a firm operates in accordance with the objectives of its own stakeholders, together with the mechanisms that deal with conflicts of interest between various stakeholder groups. Agency theory is central to any discussion of corporate governance issues. The separation within the firm of ownership from control creates an agency problem and a potential conflict of interest between the firm's shareholders acting as principal, and its management acting as agent. In a world of imperfect or asymmetric information, management cannot always be relied upon to act in the shareholders' best interests, and shareholders might not always be able to monitor management's actions effectively. Another crucial issue in the design of corporate governance mechanisms concerns whether the maximization of shareholder value should be the firm's sole legitimate objective, or whether the firm recognizes a wider set of responsibilities towards a broader constituency of stakeholders, including some or all of employees, customers, suppliers, retailers, taxpayers and society in general.

Corporate governance comprises a number of instruments or mechanisms that mitigate the various conflicts of interest that may arise between stakeholder groups.

- *Boards of directors.* A one-tier board comprises both executive and non-executive directors. Chairman-CEO duality, where the CEO is also the chairman of the board, is practised by some firms that operate a one-tier structure, but is not recommended in official corporate governance codes of conduct. A two-tier structure comprises a supervisory (non-executive) board and a management (executive board).

- *Shareholders.* It is unclear whether institutional share ownership creates a more or a less effective monitoring regime In recent years, mobilization of small shareholders to use their voting rights to sanction poorly performing management has been advocated as a tool for improving corporate governance. Firms with widely dispersed share ownership might find that no single shareholder perceives sufficient incentive to devote effort to monitoring. On the other hand, large shareholders might be tempted to intervene excessively.

- *Dividend policy and debt finance.* By paying dividends, managers reduce the resources available to fund their own discretionary behaviour. Similarly, a high ratio of debt to equity finance imposes constraints on managerial discretion, owing to the legal obligation to pay interest on the debt.

- *Executive compensation and share ownership.* The design and structure of executive compensation packages is a key determinant of the alignment or misalignment of the incentives of top managers with shareholder interests. Relevant constituents of executive compensation packages include cash bonuses related to financial performance, share ownership, and call options.

- *The market for corporate control.* The share price of an underperforming company is likely to fall, leaving the firm vulnerable to hostile takeover by new owners who expect to be able put the firm's assets into more productive use, and are likely to replace the firm's existing management. This threat acts as a disciplining device.

- *Competition in the market for products or services* may also impose limits on the scope for discretionary behaviour on the part of management.

The OECD's Principles of Corporate Governance have become internationally accepted as a benchmark for good corporate governance. The Principles specify provisions for the promotion of transparent and efficient markets and compliance with the rule of law, protection of the rights and equitable treatment of shareholders, protection of the rights of other stakeholders, timely and accurate disclosure and transparency, and detail the responsibilities of the board of directors. In the UK, the Financial Reporting Council's (FRC) (2010) Corporate Governance Code identifies five main principles for good governance: leadership, effectiveness, accountability, remuneration and relations with shareholders.

Public awareness of corporate governance issues attained new heights following several high-profile scandals associated with corporate bankruptcies in the early 2000s, including Enron in 2001 and WorldCom in 2002. In the US the Sarbanes-Oxley Act of 2002 aimed to strengthen corporate governance in several key respects. Shortcomings in procedures for the management of risk, and executive compensation packages that were excessive or created perverse incentives, are widely cited among the causes of the financial crisis of 2007–9. This suggests that the development of robust systems for corporate governance remains work-in-progress in the aftermath of the crisis.

Business ethics is defined as a philosophical analysis of moral issues from the perspective of companies and other forms of business organization. David Hume and Adam Smith, key thinkers in eighteenth-century philosophy and economics, provide key insights concerning the application of the concepts of ethics and justice to corporate behaviour. This historical discussion is contrasted with the views of Milton Friedman on the primacy of shareholder value maximization as the sole legitimate corporate objective. A resolution of the potential conflict between business and ethical objectives is proposed by several writers who examine the relationship between business objectives and concepts of duty and obligations to stakeholders and the wider society.

Adopting a broad stakeholder definition that encompasses societal interests in the activities of privately-owned firms, public awareness of the social responsibilities of firms has grown dramatically, leading to the adoption by many companies of explicit corporate social responsibility (CSR) policies. Carroll provides a widely recognized typology of the constituents of a CSR policy, encompassing the firm's economic, legal, ethical and discretionary/philanthropic responsibilities. Forces that have shaped the emergence of the CSR movement include a greater willingness on the part of consumers, employees, community activists and shareholders to challenge the corporate status quo, and a simultaneous retreat of governments from their role in the regulation of business. Academic research into the relationship between the adoption of CSR policies and financial performance has proliferated as the CSR movement has gathered momentum. Empirical research in this field has produced mixed findings, which partly reflect confusion over definitional and measurement issues, and difficulties in disentangling the direction of causality between a firm's financial performance and its adoption of socially responsible policies.

Discussion questions

1. To what extent does greater shareholder activism offer a promising direction for mitigating agency problems affecting the principal–agent relationship between shareholders and managers?

2. In what ways can executive compensation packages be structured to improve the alignment of managers' incentives with shareholder objectives?

3. With reference to Case Study 6.1, examine the arguments in favour of board diversity.

4. Explain how the threat of hostile takeover might constrain discretionary behaviour on the part of the management of firms with stock market listings.

5. For what reasons do the principal corporate governance codes of practice recommend separation of the roles of chairman of the board of directors and chief executive officer?

6. Some large firms have ethics training programmes, but can ethics be 'learnt'?

7. Discuss reasons why many areas of social responsibility are left to voluntary compliance.

8. Discuss potential reactions of investors when a corporation wishes to increase spending on socially responsible initiatives. Will reactions vary with different sectors of business activity?

9. Corporate philanthropy has always existed. To what extent do you believe that the modern approach to corporate social responsibility is any different?

10. With reference to Case Studies 6.2 and 6.3, discuss the importance of social responsibility as part of the modern firm's core objectives.

Further reading

Adams, R., Hermalin, B. and Weisbach, M. (2010) The role of boards of directors in corporate performance: a conceptual framework and survey. *Journal of Economic Literature* 48, 58–107.

Adams, R. and Ferreira, D. (2009) Women in the boardroom and their impact on governance and performance, *Journal of Financial Economics*, 94, 291–309.

Frydman, C. and Jenter, D. (2010) CEO compensation, *Annual Review of Financial Economics*, 2, 75–102.

Gillan, L. (2006) Recent developments in corporate governance: an overview, *Journal of Corporate Finance*, 12, 381–402.

Goergen, M. (2012) *International Corporate Governance*. Harlow: Pearson.

Orlitzky, M., Schmidt, F.L. and Rynes, S.L. (2003) Corporate social and financial performance: a meta-analysis, *Organization Studies* 24, 403–41.

Shleifer, A. and Vishny, R.W. (1997) A survey of corporate governance, *Journal of Finance*, 52, 737–83.

PART

II

Structural Analysis of Industry

Oligopoly: non-collusive models

Learning objectives

This chapter covers the following topics:

- interdependence and the analysis of price and output determination in oligopoly
- the Cournot, Chamberlin and Stackelberg models of output determination in duopoly
- the Bertrand and Edgeworth models of price determination in duopoly
- the models of the kinked demand curve and price leadership
- game theory and the analysis of decision-making in oligopoly

Key terms

Barometric price leadership
Bertrand model
Collusion
Conjectural variation
Constant-sum game
Cournot–Nash equilibrium
Dominant price leadership
Dominant strategy
Duopoly
Edgeworth model
Experimental economics
First-mover advantage
Game theory
Independent action
Interdependence
Isoprofit curve
Joint profit maximization
Kinked demand curve

Mixed strategy
Multiple-period game
Nash equilibrium
Non-constant-sum game
Oligopoly
Payoff
Price leadership
Price rigidity
Prisoner's dilemma
Pure strategy
Reaction function
Repeated game
Sequential game
Simultaneous game
Stackelberg equilibrium
Strategy
Tit-for-tat
Zero-sum game

7.1 Introduction

Oligopoly theory rests on recognition of the importance of the number of firms in the industry, and the nature of the product. These two characteristics are closely related. An industry is defined by the nature of the product it supplies. Firms producing highly differentiated products may not even see themselves as being in direct competition with others. The more similar or homogeneous the products of different firms, however, the greater the awareness of competitors. In all oligopolistic markets, a few sellers account for a substantial proportion of total sales. The fewness of the firms is the chief identifying characteristic of an oligopoly.

As a result of the fewness of firms within a clearly defined industry, producing a similar product or service, the central problem of oligopoly focuses on the recognition of the firms' mutual dependence or **interdependence**. Interdependence means a firm is aware that its own actions affect the actions of its rivals and vice versa. Profit maximization and survival in an oligopoly depend on how effectively each firm operates in this situation of interdependence.

This chapter begins in Section 7.2 with a general discussion of the key issues of interdependence, conjectural variation, independent action and collusion in oligopoly. Subsequently, the structure of the chapter reflects the development of theories of independent action in oligopoly, as they have tackled the central issue of interdependence. Section 7.3 examines Cournot's original model of output determination in a duopoly, based on a simple assumption that two firms take their output decisions sequentially, each in the expectation that its rival will not subsequently react. Other models that recognize the importance of interdependence include Chamberlin's model of joint profit maximization, in which 'mutual dependence was recognized'. Although this recognition involved some broad theorizing, the process was invaluable in the sense that it asked the right questions concerning short- and long-run reactions, time-lags, imperfect knowledge, irrational conduct and so on. Stackelberg's leader–follower model builds in an assumption that one firm learns to anticipate its rivals' reactions to its own decisions, and exploits this foresight to increase its own profit at its rivals' expense.

The Cournot, Chamberlin and Stackelberg models focus mainly on the firms' output decisions in duopoly or oligopoly. Section 7.4 examines the complementary models developed by Bertrand and Edgeworth, which focus on price-setting. The Bertrand model provides a theoretical justification for the idea that intense price competition might occur in markets with few firms producing a similar or identical product. The Edgeworth model focuses on the possibility that oligopolistic markets might be permanently unstable, with no long-run equilibrium price or output level ever being achieved.

Another attempt to introduce a greater degree of reality into oligopoly theory is Sweezy's **kinked demand curve** model, examined in Section 7.5. Although challenged on empirical grounds, this model rests on the core assumption that firms' behaviour is determined by expectations as to what actions rivals are most likely to take. In this respect, it represents a major contribution to the development of more realistic models of oligopoly. This section also considers models of **price leadership** in oligopoly, in which one firm takes decisions on price and the others simply follow the lead of the price-setting firm.

Finally, Section 7.6 focuses on **game theory**. Game theory is the study of decision-making in situations of conflict. It has many applications throughout the social, behavioural and physical sciences; and accordingly, its remit is much wider than just economics. Nevertheless, its focus on uncertainty, interdependence, conflict and strategy makes it ideally suited to the analysis of decision-making in oligopoly. Game theory shows how situations can arise in which firms take decisions that may appear rational from each firm's individual perspective, but lead to outcomes that are sub-optimal when assessed according to criteria reflecting the collective interest of all the firms combined. Theoretically, in many respects game theory is the strongest of all the approaches examined in Chapter 7 as regards its treatment of the key issue of interdependence.

7.2 Interdependence, conjectural variation, independent action and collusion

At the beginning of the twentieth century, classical microeconomic analysis focused on the models of perfect competition and pure monopoly in its attempt to describe the behaviour of firms. While no one pretended what was being presented was an exact copy of real business behaviour, it was felt the two extremes sufficiently defined a spectrum on which reality could be conveniently located. It almost seemed what was being argued was that defining the colours white and black would somehow enable other colours, such as yellow and purple, to be described simply by mixing white and black together in the correct proportions. It soon became apparent, however, that these two models were unable to explain many aspects of business conduct in the real world, such as product differentiation, advertising, price wars, parallel pricing and collusion. An additional theory was required to deal with the vast area of industry structure that lies between the two polar cases of perfect competition and monopoly. This middle ground, known as imperfect competition, can be subdivided into two: monopolistic competition, occupying the analytical space closest to perfect competition; and oligopoly, taking up the remaining large portion of the spectrum.

Interdependence provides the main challenge for the analysis of oligopoly. Each firm's behaviour depends on its assumptions about its rivals' likely reactions.

> 'I' (an oligopolist) cannot define my best policies unless I know what 'You' (my rival) are going to do; by the same token, however, you cannot define your best move unless you know what I will do.
>
> *(Asch, 1969, p. 54)*

Faced with this situation of interdependence, the firms must make some guesses or conjectures as to the likely actions of rivals. Each firm must determine its price or output, while making assumptions about its rivals' likely reactions to its own actions. The term **conjectural variation** refers to the assumptions a firm makes about the reactions it expects from its rivals in response to its own actions.

It is sometimes suggested that the solution to the oligopoly problem is one of two extremes: either pure **independent action** or pure **collusion**. Under pure independent action, each firm reaches a unilateral decision on a course of action, without any prior contact with its rivals. Under collusion, two or more rival firms recognize their interdependence, creating the potential for bargaining to take place with a view to formulating some plan of joint action. In some ways, however, the dichotomy between pure independent action and pure collusion is artificial. Independent action could produce outcomes similar to those achieved through collusion, if the firms were subsequently to revise their initial decisions in the light of their rivals' reactions. Furthermore, collusion could take the form of a careful sequence of recognized moves and counter-moves, in which the firms effectively reveal their own positions and react to their rivals' positions, without entering into any explicit discussions or negotiations. In reality, both independent action and collusion are usually a matter of degree. While examples may be found that conform to these two polar cases, most cases fall somewhere between the two extremes. Nevertheless, despite this ambiguity, the structure of Chapters 7 and 8 of this book adheres to the dichotomy between independent action and collusion. The remaining sections of Chapter 7 discuss theories of oligopoly that focus primarily on independent decision-making Chapter 8 examines theories of collusion.

7.3 Models of output determination in duopoly

Cournot's duopoly model

Cournot's (1838) model of output determination in oligopoly was the first successful attempt to describe an oligopoly equilibrium. The type of solution that Cournot proposed almost two centuries ago still plays a central role in many present-day models of oligopoly.

Cournot's original formulation assumes a two-firm oligopoly, known as a **duopoly**, operating at zero marginal cost. Cournot analysed a market comprising two proprietors or firms, A and B, both selling mineral spring waters. To ensure both firms operate at zero marginal cost, it is assumed the two firms are located side by side next to the spring and customers arrive at the spring with their own bottles. The firms are assumed to make their trading plans in turn or sequentially. It is also assumed, when making its own trading plans, that each firm expects the other firm to maintain *its* output at its current level. In other words, each firm assumes the other firm's reaction (in terms of adjustment to output) is always zero. In the terminology introduced in Section 7.2, this is tantamount to an assumption of zero conjectural variation.

It is assumed the market demand or AR function is linear. For simplicity, the units of measurement for price and quantity are both chosen so that both axes are drawn on a scale of 0 to 1. The market demand or AR function is illustrated

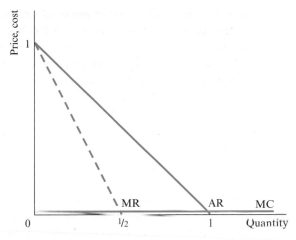

Figure 7.1 Market average revenue, marginal revenue and marginal cost functions, Cournot's duopoly model

in Figure 7.1. In order to understand the derivation of the Cournot model, it is important to note that if the AR function is linear, the marginal revenue (MR) function is also linear, and intersects the horizontal axis at the mid-point between the origin and the intersection of the AR function. In Figure 7.1, this implies if the AR function intersects the horizontal axis at a value of $Q = 1$, the MR function must intersect at a value of $Q = 1/2$. Finally, in accordance with the assumption of zero marginal cost, in Figure 7.1 the MC function is shown running horizontally along the quantity axis.

In the Cournot model, the market equilibrium is reached through a sequence of actions and reactions on the part of the two firms. This is illustrated in Figure 7.2.

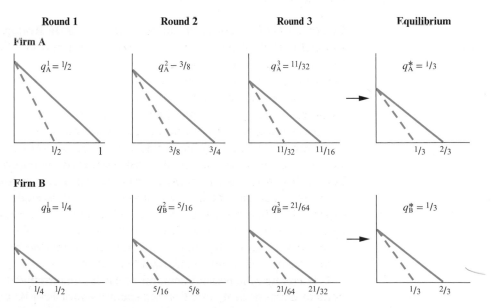

Figure 7.2 The Cournot model: sequence of actions and reactions

Assume firm A is the first to open for business. In Round 1, firm A fixes its output and price at the point where MR = MC = 0. Firm A's output in Round 1 is $q_A^1 = 1/2$, and the correponding price is 1/2. Before firm B starts producing, firm A operates as if it were a monopolist.

Now firm B enters the market. B sees A is supplying $q_A^1 = 1/2$. According to the zero conjectural variation assumption, B assumes that whatever B does, A will continue to produce $q_A^1 = 1/2$. Therefore B's effective or residual demand function is the segment of the market demand function that is not currently serviced by A. This is the segment of the market demand function that lies to the right of $q_A^1 = 1/2$. If B charges a price of 1/2, B sells zero output. However, if B were prepared to allow the price to fall to 0, B could sell an output of 1/2. In Round 1, therefore, B's AR function runs from $P = 1/2$ to $q = 1/2$, and B's MR function intersects the horizontal axis at $q_B^1 = 1/4$. This is B's profit-maximizing output in Round 1, because at this output MR = MC for B. At the end of Round 1, total industry output is $q_A^1 + q_B^1 = 1/2 + 1/4 = 3/4$. Accordingly, using the market demand function, price is $P = 1/4$.

Before B entered, A was maximizing profit at $q_A^1 = 1/2$ and $P = 1/2$. However, B's intervention causes price to fall to $P = 1/4$, which means A is no longer maximizing profit. According to the zero conjectural variation assumption, A assumes whatever A does, B will continue to produce at $q_B^1 = 1/4$. Therefore A's residual demand function is the segment of the market demand function that lies to the right of $q_B^1 = 1/4$. In Round 2, A's AR function runs from $P = 3/4$ to $q = 3/4$. A's MR function intersects the horizontal axis at $q_A^2 = 3/8$, A's new profit-maximizing output in Round 2.

At the end of Round 1, B was maximizing profit at $q_B^1 = 1/4$ and $P = 1/4$. However, A's adjustment causes price to rise to $P = 3/8$, so B is no longer maximizing profit at $q_B^1 = 1/4$. According to the zero conjectural variation assumption, B assumes whatever B does, A will continue to produce at $q_A^2 = 3/8$. Therefore, B's new residual demand function is the segment of the market demand function that lies to the right of $q_A^2 = 3/8$. In Round 2, B's AR function runs from $P = 5/8$ to $q = 5/8$. B's MR function intersects the horizontal axis at $q_B^2 = 5/16$, B's new profit-maximizing output in Round 2. At the end of Round 2, total industry output is $q_A^2 + q_B^2 = 3/8 + 5/16 = 11/16$, and using the market demand function, price is $P = 5/16$.

By this stage, the mechanics of the sequence of actions and reactions should be clear. The Round 3 adjustments are shown in Figure 7.2, but they are not described in full here. At the end of Round 3, total industry output is $q_A^3 + q_B^3 = 11/32 + 21/64 = 43/64$, and price is $P = 21/64$. Of more importance is the equilibrium towards which the industry is converging as each round of actions and reactions takes place. This is shown on the right-hand side of Figure 7.2, where both firms produce identical outputs of $q_A^* + q_B^* = 1/3$. Total industry output is $q_A^* + q_B^* = 1/3 + 1/3 = 2/3$, and price is $P = 1/3$.

With this set of outputs, neither firm has an incentive to make any further change to its trading plans. For example, A assumes B's output is fixed at $q_B^* = 1/3$. Therefore A's residual demand function runs from $P = 2/3$ to $q = 2/3$, so A maximizes profit at $q_B^* = 1/3$. The same is true for firm B. Both firms maximize their own profit subject to the constraint that the other firm's output is fixed at its current level; or equivalently, both firms maximize profit subject to the zero conjectural variation assumption.

Isoprofit curves and reaction functions

The zero marginal cost assumption is an obvious limitation of the version of the Cournot model that is described above. As shown in this sub-section, however, it is straightforward to rework the Cournot model so that it can be applied to the case where marginal costs are non-zero. Therefore, the zero marginal cost assumption is not a fundamental limitation. In order to rework the Cournot model, a new diagrammatic representation of the model, known as an isoprofit diagram, is developed. In order to do so, the assumptions of identical firms and a linear industry demand function are retained. In the following discussion non-zero marginal costs are assumed, although the derivation is similar if marginal costs are zero.

In Figure 7.3, the output levels of firms A and B are shown on the horizontal and vertical axes, respectively. Begin by selecting a certain combination of outputs represented by point F, located somewhere towards the bottom-left-hand corner of Figure 7.3. At F, both q_A and q_B are relatively small. Total industry output is also relatively small. Let π_A^1 denote A's profit at F, and consider what happens to A's profit if A increases its output by a small amount, while B holds its output constant. This adjustment is represented by a horizontal shift from F to G. It can be inferred that A's profit at G *increases* to π_A^2, for two reasons:

- Total industry output at F is small. The industry is operating on a relatively price-elastic section of the market demand function. Therefore an increase in q_A (and the corresponding fall in market price) produces a large increase in A's revenue.

- q_A at F is small, and A's marginal cost is relatively low. Therefore, an increase in q_A produces only a small increase in A's costs.

Now consider what happens to A's profit if B increases its output by a small amount, while A holds its output constant. This adjustment is represented by

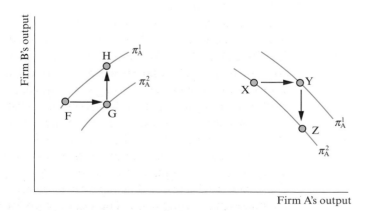

Figure 7.3 Derivation of firm A's isoprofit curves

the upward vertical shift from G to H. It can be inferred that A's profit *decreases*, back to π_A^1. The fall in market price caused by B's increase in output produces a decrease in A's revenue, while A's output and costs are unchanged.

Firm A's **isoprofit curves** show all combinations of q_A and q_B which produce identical profit for firm A. Comparing the values of A's profit at points F, G and H, it is evident that firm A's isoprofit curves are upward-sloping in this region of Figure 7.3.

The exercise can be repeated by selecting a new combination of outputs represented by the point X, located somewhere towards the bottom-right-hand corner of Figure 7.3. At X, q_A is relatively large, but q_B is relatively small. Because q_A is large, total industry output is also relatively large. Assume A's profit at X is π_A^2, and consider what happens to A's profit if A increases its output by a small amount, while B holds its output constant. This adjustment is represented by a horizontal shift from X to Y. It can be inferred that A's profit at Y *decreases* to π_A^1, for two reasons:

■ Total industry output at X is large. The industry is operating on a relatively price-inelastic section of the market demand function. Therefore an increase in q_A (and the corresponding fall in market price) produces only a small increase, or perhaps even a decrease, in A's revenue.

■ q_A at X is large, and A's marginal cost is relatively high. Therefore an increase in q_A produces a large increase in A's costs.

Consider what happens to A's profit if B decreases its output by a small amount, while A holds its output constant. This adjustment is represented by the downward vertical shift from Y to Z. It can be inferred that A's profit *increases*, back to π_A^2. The increase in market price caused by B's decrease in output produces an increase in A's revenue, while A's output and costs remain unchanged. Comparing the values of A's profit at points X, Y and Z, it is evident that firm A's isoprofit curves are downward-sloping in this region of Figure 7.3.

The concave curves shown in Figure 7.4 represent firm A's complete set of isoprofit curves. In accordance with the preceding discussion, successive isoprofit curves represent higher levels of profit for A as they approach the horizontal axis. Furthermore, for any given value of q_B, the profit-maximizing value of q_A can be found by identifying the isoprofit curve that attains a peak at that value of q_B. For example, if $q_B = \bar{q}_B$ in Figure 7.4, A's profit-maximizing output level is q_A^*, where the horizontal line at $\bar{q}_B$ is tangential to the isoprofit curve for π_A^2, the highest isoprofit curve that is attainable by A anywhere along this horizontal line. At any other point on the line, A's profit is less than π_A^2.

Reading Figure 7.4 from top to bottom, as firm A's profit increases, the peaks of successive isoprofit curves lie further to the right. The lower the value of q_B, the more of the market there is available for A to exploit, and so the higher the profit-maximizing value of q_A. Firm A's **reaction function**, denoted RF_A, shows, for each value of q_B (assumed fixed), the profit-maximizing value of q_A. In Figure 7.4, RF_A is the line connecting the peaks of successive isoprofit curves.

The next stage in the analysis involves the construction of isoprofit curves and a reaction function for B. Firm B's isoprofit curves show all combinations

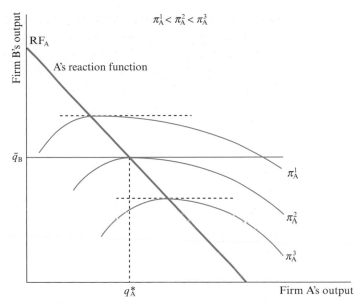

Figure 7.4 Firm A's isoprofit curves and reaction function

of q_A and q_B which produce identical profit for firm B. Firm B's reaction function shows, for each value of q_A (assumed fixed) the profit-maximizing value of q_B. Based on the earlier assumption that the firms are identical, this task is straightforward. B's isoprofit curves and reaction function have exactly the same appearance relative to the vertical axis as A's isoprofit curves and reaction function relative to the horizontal axis. Figure 7.5 shows one (representative) isoprofit curve for each firm, together with the two firms' reaction functions, on the same diagram.

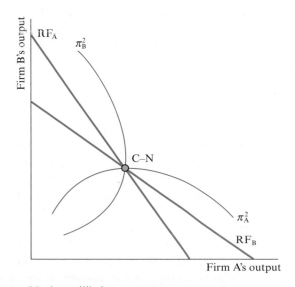

Figure 7.5 Cournot–Nash equilibrium

Cournot–Nash equilibrium

Using the apparatus of isoprofit curves and reaction functions, the outputs q_A and q_B, that represent an equilibrium solution to the duopoly model, can be located. Using the same reasoning as in the derivation of Cournot's model, assume both firms seek to maximize their own profit, subject to the constraint that the other firm's output is fixed at its current level. In other words, both firms maximize profit subject to the zero conjectural variation assumption. In the terminology of this sub-section, this is equivalent to assuming that both firms seek to operate on their own reaction functions (recall, each firm's reaction function shows its profit-maximizing output treating the other firm's output as given). The point in Figure 7.5 at which both firms are simultaneously located on their own reaction functions is the point where RF_A and RF_B intersect, denoted C–N. C–N denotes a **Cournot–Nash equilibrium**, named after Cournot and the American mathematician John Nash. The centrepiece of Nash's PhD thesis, prepared in 1950, was a solution to the problem of determining an equilibrium in a non-cooperative game (see Section 7.6), based on similar principles to the solution to the two-firm duopoly model proposed by Cournot more than a century before. Nash was eventually awarded the Nobel Prize in economics in 1994 for his contributions to game theory (see Box 1.1).

It is interesting to note that the previous description of the Cournot model can also be represented (more concisely) using reaction functions. Figure 7.6 shows a pair of reaction functions derived under the zero marginal cost assumption; as noted above, assuming MC = 0 does not change the general shape of the isoprofit curves and reaction functions, although it does affect their precise locations. Figure 7.6 represents the process of convergence towards the market equilibrium at C–N as a process of 'zigzagging' between points located on RF_A and RF_B.

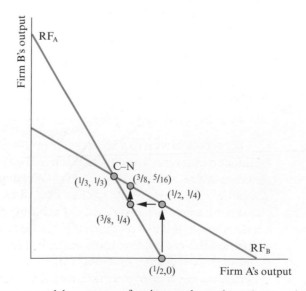

Figure 7.6 Cournot model: sequence of actions and reactions shown using reaction functions

- In Round 1 before B has entered, A's profit-maximizing output is $q_A^1 = 1/2$, at the very bottom of RF_A (where $q_B = 0$). When B does enter, B's profit-maximizing output subject to $q_A^1 = 1/2$ is $q_B^1 = 1/4$, at the point on RF_B corresponding to $q_A = 1/2$. Therefore at the end of Round 1, $(q_A^1 = 1/2, q_B^1 = 1/4)$ is attained, as before.

- In Round 2, A's profit-maximizing output subject to $q_B^1 = 1/4$ is $q_A^2 = 3/8$ (the point on RF_A corresponding to $q_B = 1/4$). Similarly, B's profit-maximizing output subject to $q_A^2 = 3/8$ is $q_B^2 = 5/16$ (the point on RF_B corresponding to $q_A^2 = 3/8$). At the end of Round 2, $(3/8, 5/16)$ is attained.

- At the end of Round 3, $(11/32, 21/64)$ is attained (not shown in Figure 7.6).

- Equilibrium is attained at $(q_A^* = 1/3, q_B^* = 1/3)$, represented by the point C–N in Figure 7.6 located at the intersection of RF_A and RF_B.

The Cournot–Nash solution can also be derived for cases in which an oligopoly consists of more than two firms. Under the zero conjectural variation assumption in an N-firm model, each firm sets its output so as to maximize its own profit, treating the outputs of the other $N - 1$ firms as fixed at their current levels. A general formula for the market equilibrium is:

$$Q_n = Q_C \frac{N}{N + 1}$$

where Q_n represents total industry output at the Cournot–Nash equilibrium and Q_C represents total industry output if the industry structure was perfectly competitive.

In Figure 7.1, the maximum value of market demand (when price *equals* zero) is one, and marginal cost is zero. The perfectly competitive industry output level is $Q_C = 1$, because $P = MC$ implies price is driven down to zero. The formula for Q_n (above) implies the following:

- $N = 1$ corresponds to the case of monopoly. In Round 1 before B enters, A maximizes profit by producing the monopolist's output, $Q_n = q_A^1 = 1/2$.

- $N = 2$ corresponds to the case of duopoly. $Q_n = q_A^* + q_B^* = 2/3$ is consistent with $(q_A^* = 1/3, q_B^* = 1/3)$ at the Cournot–Nash equilibrium.

- As N increases and approaches infinity, Q_n increases and approaches $Q_C = 1$.

What conclusions can be drawn from the Cournot model? The model can be criticized in several ways. First, it is based on a naive and unrealistic assumption that each firm believes its rival will not change its output (the zero conjectural variation assumption), in spite of each firm continually observing behaviour that contradicts this assumption. Each time either firm adjusts its own output, it does so on the basis of the zero conjectural variation assumption. But on each occasion this assumption turns out to be false, because the other firm does react and does also change its output. It is natural to wonder why the firms fail to learn from experience to anticipate each other's reactions.

In defence of the Cournot model, it can be argued that the solution to the problem of oligopoly is more important than the story about how this equilibrium is attained. This story does not need to be taken too literally: in practice there are many ways for the two firms to arrive at C–N, where both are maximizing their own profits subject to the constraint that the other firm's output is treated as fixed.

Cournot can be criticized for ignoring the possibility that firms may seek cooperative or collusive solutions, in order to maximize their joint profits. This is, and almost certainly was in Cournot's time, a fact of economic life in oligopolistic markets. Cournot has also been criticized for focusing on output-setting, and ignoring price-setting decisions. Price adjustments in the Cournot model are the consequence of output decisions, rather than being primary courses of action.

Nevertheless, the theory does makes make several important positive contributions. It introduced the use of mathematical techniques for the solution of economic problems, and it subsequently provided economists with important tools of analysis, such as conjectural variation, isoprofit curves and reaction functions. It identifies an oligopoly equilibrium that is located reassuringly between the extremes of perfect competition and monopoly. It can be used as a benchmark for all further discussion of decision-making under oligopoly, including decisions concerning intellectual property, research and development, mergers, international trade and the financial structure of the firm (Daughety, 2008).

Chamberlin's solution: joint profit maximization

The apparatus of isoprofit curves and reaction functions developed in the previous sub-section can be used to identify several solutions to the duopoly model other than the one proposed by Cournot. Chamberlin (1933) suggests an alternative solution, in which the firms recognize their interdependence when making their output decisions. Accordingly, Chamberlin departs from the zero conjectural variation assumption. No longer does each firm set its output so as to maximize its own profit, while treating the other firm's output as fixed. Instead, the firms recognize it is in their mutual interest to produce and share equally among themselves the output that would be delivered if the market was serviced by a single monopolist. In this way, the firms also share equally among themselves the monopoly profit.

Starting from the Cournot–Nash equilibrium C–N in Figure 7.7, it is apparent that if both firms were to simultaneously reduce their output, both firms could simultaneously achieve an increase in profit. In other words, moving 'south-west' from C–N, it is possible for both firms to simultaneously move onto isoprofit curves representing higher levels of profit than at C–N. In fact, starting from any point above and to the right of the line $Q_M Q_M$, it is always possible for both firms to simultaneously increase their profits by moving 'south-west' in Figure 7.7. $Q_M Q_M$ is the line identifying all points of tangency between the isoprofit curves of firms A and B.

The points at which $Q_M Q_M$ cuts the horizontal and vertical axes of Figure 7.7 are labelled Q_M because these points represent the profit-maximizing outputs if either firm were operating as a monopolist. For example, along the horizontal axis $q_B = 0$, firm A operates as a monopolist with a profit-maximizing output of Q_M. Similarly, along the vertical axis $q_A = 0$ firm B's profit-maximizing output is also Q_M. $Q_M Q_M$ is simply a 45-degree line linking these two points. At any

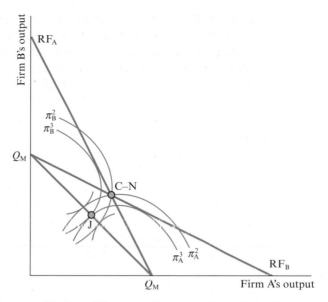

Figure 7.7 Cournot–Nash equilibrium and joint profit maximization

intermediate point on $Q_M Q_M$, total output is Q_M, and this output is shared between firms A and B. At point J, at the middle of this line, the monopoly output of Q_M is shared *equally* between firms A and B. Point J represents Chamberlin's **joint profit maximization** solution to the duopoly model.

In Chamberlin's formulation, both firms recognize their interdependence and realize that sharing the monopoly profit is the best they can do. It is important to note that Chamberlin does not suggest firms achieve this solution through collusion. The outcome rests on the assumption that each firm recognizes that the monopoly ideal can be achieved through independent action; and this view is shared by its rival. In this way, both firms achieve a higher payoff than in Cournot's formulation.

Chamberlin's solution allows for no unilateral aggression, cheating or back-sliding on the part of the two firms. Starting from point J, A may be aware that if it were to unilaterally increase its output (moving 'east' in Figure 7.7 towards RF_A) it could achieve an increase in profit, provided B does not react by also increasing its output. However, moving 'east' from J causes B's profit to fall, so it seems unlikely B would fail to react. Similarly at J, B is aware that if it were to increase its output (moving 'north' towards RF_B) it could increase its profit provided A does not do the same. But, again, moving 'north' from J causes A's profit to fall and it seems unlikely A would fail to react. Therefore, Chamberlin's solution is always liable to break down, if either or both firms succumb to the temptation to act unilaterally and ignore their interdependence.

Stackelberg's solution: the leader–follower model

Stackelberg (1934) suggests yet another solution to the Cournot duopoly model. The Cournot model assigns equal status to both firms as they progress towards the final equilibrium. Both firms operate according to the zero conjectural variation assumption, and each firm fails to anticipate the other's reaction on each occasion it adjusts its own output. Suppose, however, the zero conjectural variation assumption is dropped for firm A, but retained for firm B. B continues to select its profit-maximizing output by treating A's output as fixed at its current level. But A learns to recognize that B behaves in this manner. A therefore learns to take B's behaviour into account whenever A makes its own output decisions.

How should firm A select its own output, given that it has this insight into firm B's behaviour? A's awareness of B's behaviour is tantamount to A's recognition that whatever output A selects, B always reacts by selecting an output that returns the two firms to an output combination that lies on B's reaction function, RF_B. A should therefore select the output that maximizes A's profit, subject to B's expected reaction. Accordingly, A should select q_A^L and aim for S_A in Figure 7.8: the point on RF_B where A's profit is maximized. A anticipates, correctly, that B will react by producing q_B^F. S_A is the point of tangency between RF_B and the highest isoprofit curve A can attain, given that the final equilibrium must lie on RF_B. At any other point on RF_B, A's profit is lower than it is at S_A.

By learning to anticipate and take account of firm B's behaviour, firm A earns a higher profit than at C–N, while B earns a lower profit. A is rewarded, and B is punished, for the fact that A has insight into B's behaviour, while B does not have corresponding insight into A's behaviour. An alternative (but only slightly different) interpretation of Stackelberg's solution is as a model of **first-mover advantage**. Returning to Cournot's original story of sequential decision-making, if A recognizes that B always follows the zero conjectural variation assumption, in Round 1 A should produce q_A^L, in the knowledge that B will react by producing q_B^F. Accordingly, the two firms arrive directly at the **Stackelberg equilibrium** at the end of Round 1, with A producing the higher output and earning the higher

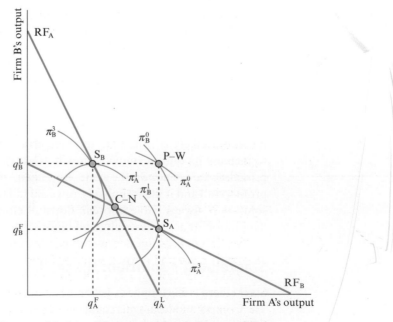

Figure 7.8 Cournot–Nash equilibrium and Stackelberg equilibria

profit. In this interpretation, A is the leader and B is the follower, and A is rewarded for its first-mover advantage.

Generalizing the preceding discussion, four possible outcomes are identified in Figure 7.8:

- At S_A, firm A is the leader and firm B is the follower, as discussed above.

- S_B represents the opposite case, where B is the leader and A is the follower. A follows the zero conjectural variation assumption. B recognizes A behaves in this way, and aims for S_B, the point on A's reaction function RF_A that maximizes B's profit.

- If both firms are followers, C–N, the Cournot–Nash equilibrium, is achieved as before.

- Finally, and quite realistically in many oligopolistic markets, both firms might similtaneously attempt to be leaders. If both simultaneously produce the higher level of output $q_A^L = q_B^L$, the result is a Stackelberg disequilibrium or price war at P–W. At this conflict point there is overproduction, and the firms are forced to cut their prices in order to sell the additional output. Accordingly, both firms earn less profit than at C–N. A costly price war might eventually determine a winner and a loser, but it is also possible the firms may realize the futility of conflict and search for a more cooperative solution.

Section 7.3 identifies a number of possible solutions to the problem of output determination in duopoly. A mathematical derivation of these results can be found in Appendix 1. To conclude this section, it is useful to return to the numerical example that was used to introduce the Cournot model at the start of this section, and compare the numerical values of price and quantity for each of the solutions to the model. Consider a duopoly in which the market demand function is linear and the units of measurement for price and quantity are scaled from 0 to 1; and both firms produce at zero marginal cost. Figure 7.9 shows the numerical values of q_A and q_B at the Cournot, Chamberlin and Stackelberg equilibria. The following table contains the same numerical data, and also compares the equilibrium prices and profits of the two firms.

	P	Q	q_A	q_B	π_A	π_B
Cournot–Nash	1/3	2/3	1/3	1/3	1/9	1/9
Chamberlin	1/2	1/2	1/4	1/4	1/8	1/8
Stackelberg – A as leader	1/4	3/4	1/2	1/4	1/8	1/16
Stackelberg – B as leader	1/4	3/4	1/4	1/2	1/16	1/8
Stackelberg disequilibrium (price war)	0	1	1/2	1/2	0	0

The Chamberlin joint profit maximization equilibrium corresponds to the monopoly price and output, with the firms sharing the monopoly profit equally between them, with $\pi_A = \pi_B = 1/8$. Both are better off than at the Cournot–Nash equilibrium, where price is lower, total output is higher, and $\pi_A = \pi_B = 1/9$. At the Stackelberg equilibrium with A as leader, price is lower still and total output is higher. A does better ($\pi_A = 1/8$) and B does worse ($\pi_B = 1/16$) than at the

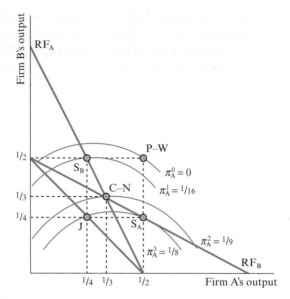

Figure 7.9 Equilibrium values of q_A, q_B, π_A, π_B: duopoly with linear market demand and zero marginal cost

Cournot–Nash equilibrium. At the Stackelberg equilibrium with B as leader, these positions are reversed. Finally, the Stackelberg disequilibrium (price war) corresponds to the perfectly competitive price and output, with price driven down to zero (equal to marginal cost), output raised to one, and both firms earning zero profit.

<table>
<tr><td>**7.4**</td><td>**Models of price determination in duopoly**</td></tr>
</table>

The Bertrand model: price competition

In another famous and influential contribution to duopoly theory, Bertrand (1883) criticizes Cournot's emphasis on output-setting. Bertrand argues that price, rather than output, is the key decision variable for most firms. In Cournot's model, the firms decide their output levels and then allow the market price to adjust accordingly. In the **Bertrand model** each firm sets its own price, and then sells as much output as it can at the chosen price. Bertrand uses a zero conjectural variation assumption concerning prices: each firm assumes its rival will stick to the rival's current price. The model rests on implicit assumptions that the output of the two firms is identical and there are no transaction or search costs. Therefore, customers flow effortlessly to the firm that is currently offering the lowest price.

To locate the equilibrium in the Bertrand model, assume, as in the Cournot model, that the firms take their price decisions sequentially and that both firms face a horizontal marginal cost function $MC_A = MC_B$. In Round 1, firm A sets its price initally at the monopoly level, P_M, and earns the monopoly profit. Then firm B arrives. How should B react to A's initial price decision? By setting its price fractionally below P_M, say at $P_M - \varepsilon$ where ε is a very small amount, B undercuts A and gains all of A's customers. By doing so, B earns a profit fractionally below the monopoly profit.

In Round 2, how should A react to B's intervention in Round 1? Using the same reasoning, by setting its price fractionally below $P_M - \varepsilon$, say at $P_M - 2\varepsilon$, A undercuts B and gains all of B's customers. Firm A earns a profit a little further below the monopoly profit. Then, by setting its price at $P_M - 3\varepsilon$, B undercuts A again and regains all of A's customers. B's profit is now a little further still below the monopoly profit.

Similar reasoning also applies in Round 3 and in subsequent rounds, when further price-cutting takes place. Is there ever an end to the price-cutting sequence? The answer to this question is yes. When price has fallen to the perfectly competitive level $P_C - MC$, there is no incentive for either firm to cut price any further. Although by so doing, either firm could still gain all of the other's customers, this would not be worthwhile if it required setting a price below marginal cost, at which normal profit would not be earned. If firm A is the first to reach P_C, at the next decision point firm B simply follows firm A, and also charges P_C. Because consumers are indifferent between the two firms at this price, it is assumed each firm captures a 50 per cent share of the market at P_C. The solution is illustrated in Figure 7.10. At the equilibrium price $P_C = MC$, both firms produce output levels of $q_A = q_B = 1/2Q_C$.

Previous criticism of the zero conjectural variation assumption applies to the Bertrand model, as it does to the Cournot model. Each firm might be expected to learn from experience to anticipate its rival's reactions to its own price-cutting decisions. Furthermore, Bertrand's conclusion that, in equilibrium, the two duopolists finish up charging the perfectly competitive price may seem surprising. In contrast to the Cournot model, the Bertrand model appears to suggest there is no intermediate case lying between the polar cases of monopoly and perfect competition. In fact, this conclusion is due to Bertrand's assumption that the two firms produce an identical product. Chapter 15 develops a model

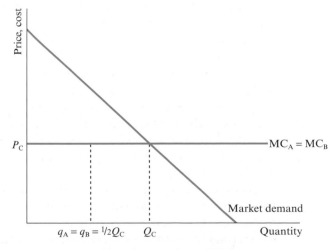

Figure 7.10 Equilibrium in the Bertrand duopoly model

of Bertrand competition with product differentiation, in which a price cut by one firm allows it to gain some, but not all, of its rival's customers.

However, in the case described above, where the firms produce identical products, there is no option other than to compete on price. Equilibrium is only achieved when price is driven down to the perfectly competitive level. It has been suggested that price competition in the airline industry, especially since the arrival of low-cost airlines, may approximate to Bertrand competition. Although the number of airlines is small, from the customer's perspective they offer essentially an identical product. Intense price competition on many routes has driven down fares to levels close to marginal cost, which (in an industry with high fixed costs and low variable costs) is quite close to zero.

The Edgeworth model: price competition with a production capacity constraint

Edgeworth (1897) modifies Bertrand's model of price competition in duopoly to allow for the possibility that the firms are subject to a production capacity constraint. At relatively low prices, this constraint precludes each firm from gaining all of the other firm's customers by implementing a further small price cut. Edgeworth retains Bertrand's zero conjectural variation assumption as regards prices: each firm assumes its rival will stick to the rival's current price. In this capacity-constrained case, the conclusions are very different from those of Bertrand. In fact, Edgeworth shows that there is *no* stable equilibrium solution to the capacity-constrained duopoly model.

Figure 7.11 illustrates **Edgeworth's model**. The horizontal marginal cost function of Figure 7.10 is replaced with a vertical section located at $1/2Q_C$, which is assumed to represent each firm's full-capacity output level. Suppose through a process of Bertrand competition, the two firms have arrived at the Bertrand equilibrium, with each firm producing an output of $1/2Q_C$ and selling at a price

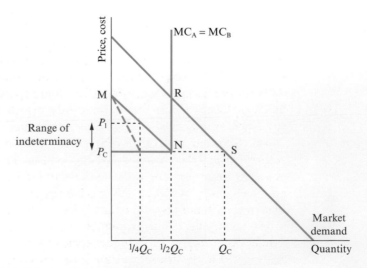

Figure 7.11 Price-setting in the Edgeworth duopoly model

of P_C. Why is this no longer a stable equilibrium if the firms are capacity constrained? The answer is that either firm can now consider raising its price without the fear it will lose all its customers to the other firm. For example, if A is incapable of producing more than $1/2Q_C$, B can set a price anywhere between P_C and M, and still sell some output to those customers whom A is incapable of servicing. These customers are forced to pay the higher price charged by B. In Figure 7.11, MN represents B's residual demand function. The triangle P_CMN is the segment of the market demand function that cannot be serviced by A (equivalent to the triangle NRS). To maximize profit using B's residual demand function, B should charge a price of P_1, at which B produces and sells an output of $1/4Q_C$.

However, a situation where A produces $1/2Q_C$ and charges P_C, and B produces $1/4Q_C$ and charges P_1, is also not a stable equilibrium. Firm A now has an incentive also to raise its price to P_1. By doing so, A can still produce and sell its full-capacity output of $1/2Q_C$. However, A now sells twice as much output and earns twice as much profit as B. But B then realizes that, by reducing its price slightly, say to $P_1 - \varepsilon$, B can undercut A, increasing its own output to B's full-capacity level of $1/2Q_C$, and reducing A's output to (slightly more than) $1/4Q_C$. A then realizes that if A reduces its price further, it can once again increase its own output and profit, at B's expense. The sequence of price-cutting continues until the price returns to P_C and both firms produce their full-capacity output levels of $1/2Q_C$. At this point, however, one of the firms realizes it can do better by raising its price, and the entire cycle begins all over again! And so it goes on, prices fluctuating continually between P_1 and P_C. The model is inherently unstable and the solution is indeterminate.

As before, Edgeworth's model can be criticized for its reliance on the zero conjectural variation assumption. The model seems to be built on the idea that firms' conjectures are *always* wrong. The model can also be criticized for the assumption that firms can continually and effortlessly adjust their prices and outputs. A charitable assessment of the model is to see it as an improvement on some of the previous models discussed, because it identifies the possibility of *instability* in oligopoly. Some economists believe that oligopolies are inherently unstable. Although prices may at times appear stable, often the stability is imposed, either by tacit or explicit collusion. Perhaps the temptation to collude is irresistible, if the alternative is perpetual instability as Edgeworth suggests. Solberg (1992) suggests that Coca-Cola and Pepsi Cola, both subject to capacity limits in local markets, have frequently resorted to aggressive price-cutting strategies, as suggested by the Edgeworth model.

The Bertrand and Edgeworth models are among the earliest attempts to theorize about the behaviour of oligopolists. The one major drawback these models have in common with the Cournot model, but not with the Chamberlin and Stackelberg models, is the zero conjectural variation assumption: the belief that rivals will not respond to any price or output change by altering their own prices or outputs, *despite* continually observing behaviour that contradicts this assumption. Section 7.5 examines some other models in which this assumption is relaxed, and the firms are aware their actions will prompt rivals to reconsider their own decisions.

Indian airlines lose altitude in price war   FT

India's private airlines began the year optimistically, as soaring passenger numbers raised hopes that profits were finally on the horizon. But while Indians are flying in record numbers, the airlines are still bleeding red ink, wounded by surging fuel prices and fierce price wars with ailing state carrier Air-India. Already burdened with years of accumulated losses, the private airlines are battling for survival, and some of the weaker ones could be forced out of business even as Air-India – the most indebted of all – is kept aloft by a taxpayer-funded lifeline. 'Some of these airlines are at a critical stage,' said Kapil Kaul, the south Asia chief executive of the Centre for Asia Pacific Aviation.

Air-India, which has estimated debts exceeding $9bn and is expected to lose another $1.5bn this year, was forced by a pilot strike to ground most of its domestic flights for 10 days earlier this year. Since then it has fought back by cutting its domestic fares by between 15 per cent and 20 per cent.

Industry executives say the fare-slashing by Air-India – which received $425m in government handouts in the past two years and is looking for more – has pressured private airlines to hold down their own fares even as more crowded planes should have brought them greater pricing power.

'In the current calendar year, Brent crude went from $80 to $125 per barrel, while Air-India decided to halve their fares to justify their huge capacity expansion,' says Ravi Nedungadi, chief financial officer for the UB Group, the parent company of Kingfisher Airlines.

Mr Kaul said Air-India is playing 'the most lethal, below-the-belt pricing games' by selling tickets below cost while counting on the cushion of government funds. 'It's going to turn out to be a disastrous year for everyone,' he says. 'When fuel is at a peak, and you are pricing below cost, the damage on your balance sheet is going to be of a very significant order.' That was evident in airlines' earnings for April to June, the first quarter of India's financial year. Analysts warn that the second quarter, a traditionally lean season for domestic travel in India, will probably be worse.

Kingfisher, owned by Indian liquor baron Vijay Mallya, lost Rs 2.6bn ($52m), compared with a net loss of Rs 1.87bn in the same period last year. Jet Airwayslost Rs 1.23bn compared with a net Rs 35m profit previously, while low-cost carrier SpiceJet lost Rs 719m, far worse than analysts' forecasts. Indian airlines do not lack for demand. Domestic passenger numbers have rebounded strongly since the 2008 global financial crisis, rising 19 per cent in 2010 to an all-time high of 52m and surging another 18 per cent in the first half of 2011. But that has failed to translate into financial reward in an industry that New Delhi still views – and taxes – as a decadent luxury sector rather than an integral part of a growing economy.

Source: Indian airlines lose altitude in price war, © The Financial Times Limited. All Rights Reserved, 4 October 2011 (Kazmin, A.). Abridged.

The kinked demand curve

This famous model was developed almost simultaneously by Sweezy (1939) and Hall and Hitch (1939). The model seeks to explain an observed tendency for price to be rather inflexible or 'rigid' in many oligopolistic markets. The idea behind the kinked demand curve model is that each firm in an oligopoly may be reluctant to initiate either a price increase or price cut, for the following reasons:

- The firm believes if it increases its price, its rivals will not follow, but will seek instead to take advantage by encouraging the firm's customers to switch to them. Consequently, the firm stands to lose a sizeable portion of its market share if it increases its price.

- The firm also believes, if it cuts its price, its rivals will follow in order to protect their own market shares. Consequently, the firm does not stand to gain market share if it cuts its price.

In other words, the firm tends to take a rather cautious or pessimistic view of its rivals' likely reaction to any decision to either increase or reduce its own price. If all firms think in this way, prices throughout the industry tend to be inflexible or rigid, because no firm wishes to be the first to implement a price change in either direction.

Sweezy's model is shown in Figure 7.12. P_1 is the firm's current price. dd is the firm's demand function, drawn on the assumption that if it raises or lowers its price from P_1, its rivals do not follow. dd is relatively price elastic, because if the firm is the only one raising its price, it loses most of its customers; and, if it is the only one cutting its price, it gains customers rapidly from its rivals. DD is

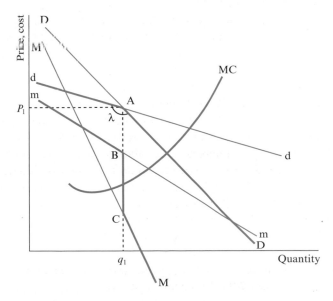

Figure 7.12 Sweezy's kinked demand curve model

the firm's demand function, drawn on the assumption that if it raises or lowers its price from P_1, its rivals follow and do the same. DD is less price elastic because, if all firms simultaneously raise or lower their prices, they only gain or lose sales to the extent that total industry sales rise or fall; the firms do not tend to gain or lose customers from one another.

In Figure 7.12, the firm faces two possible demand functions, drawn on differing assumptions about rivals' reactions to any price change. What is the firm's perceived demand function? On the pessimistic assumptions described above, dd is considered to be the demand function applicable for a price rise above P_1 (or for quantities less than q_1). DD is the demand function applicable for a price cut below P_1 (or for quantities greater than q_1). Therefore, dAD is the firm's perceived demand function. There is a kink at point A, which identifies the current price and quantity, P_1 and q_1.

What is the shape of the firm's perceived marginal revenue (MR) function? Applying similar logic, mm is the MR function associated with the demand function dd, applicable for quantities less than q_1. MM is the MR function associated with the demand function DD, applicable for quantities greater than q_1. Therefore, mBCM is the firm's perceived MR function. There is a discontinuity between points B and C located at the current quantity q_1, at which point a switch between the two MR functions takes place.

Profit is maximized where MR = MC. MR > MC to the left of q_1, and MR < MC to the right of q_1. Therefore profit is maximized at P_1 and q_1, because MC intersects the discontinuous section of the perceived MR function at q_1. Even if MC rises or falls slightly, as long as the point of intersection remains within the discontinuity BC, the profit-maximizing price and quantity are unchanged. This provides a more formal demonstration of the property of price rigidity or 'sticky prices'.

The degree of price rigidity depends on the length of the discontinuity in the MR function, BC. This in turn depends on the angle of the kink (λ), which has been called the barometer of **price rigidity**. Stigler (1947) identifies several factors that might affect the angle of the kink:

■ If there are very few rivals, both price increases and price cuts are *more* likely to be followed, since the firms are highly conscious of their interdependence. The perceived demand function may approach DD. If there are many rivals, price increases and price cuts are *less* likely to be followed, as competition approaches the atomistic case in which each firm's actions have a negligible effect on its rivals. Stigler thought an intermediate number of firms would generate the most acute λ, and the longest discontinuity in the MR function.

■ The size of the rivals may also affect the size of the kink. If there is one large firm, or a clique of firms, it may act as a price leader, with others following its price decisions. In this extreme case there may be no kink. The same applies if there is collusion.

■ Product homogeneity (or a large and positive cross-elasticity of demand) produces an acute λ and a long discontinuity, as customers are more likely to shift when facing a price differential.

This list is extended by Cohen and Cyert (1965, p. 251):

- If entrants are unsure about the market structure, or incumbent firms are unsure about the intentions of entrants, firms may adopt a wait-and-see attitude and be reluctant to initiate price rises.

- The same may also be true in a new industry, where firms are learning to understand each other's behaviour.

- If there is substantial shareholder control, risk-averse managers may decide to play safe by avoiding actions that could provoke damaging reactions from rivals.

The kinked demand curve model can be criticized for not explaining how price is formed at the kink. The model begins with the price as given; it does not explain how price is determined. It explains the existence of the kink but not its location. Furthermore, price rigidity might be explained in other ways. Firms may be reluctant to raise price for fear of alienating their customers. Firms may wait for a convenient time to introduce one large price rise, rather than revise prices continuously, the latter being a strategy that might annoy customers. Levy *et al.* (1997) suggest that changing price is itself a costly and complex operation. Accordingly, in businesses where menu costs are high, price changes are less frequent.

Stigler (1947) finds little empirical evidence of price rigidity. Having examined the evidence in seven oligopolistic markets (cigarettes, automobiles, anthracite, steel, dynamite, refining and potash) he claims price changes were quite frequent, although there is some evidence to suggest that the smaller the number of firms, the less frequent are the changes in price.

> But is this adverse conclusion really surprising? The kink is a barrier to changes in prices that will increase profits, and business is the collection of devices for circumventing barriers to profits. That this barrier should thwart businessmen – especially when it is wholly of their own fabrication – is unbelievable.
>
> *(Stigler, 1947, p. 435)*

In a later article, Stigler commented that he was amazed at the continuing popularity of the model. 'The theory has received no systematic empirical support and virtually no theoretical elaboration in these decades, but these lacks have been no handicap in maintaining its currency' (Stigler, 1978, p. 183). Freedman (1995) argues that Stigler was instinctively hostile to the kinked demand curve model, because it adopts a methodological approach different from that of the neoclassical theory of the firm.

For some years, macroeconomists have used aggregate data to identify the implications of price rigidity for the behaviour of output and inflation over time (Blinder *et al.*, 1998). More recently, micro-level data sets have become available that allow detailed analysis of price-setting behaviour. For example, Kashyap (1995) examines price changes for 12 retail goods over 35 years, and finds that prices were typically fixed for more than a year. In a study based on 80 industries, Domberger and Fiebig (1993) find that price cuts were more readily followed than price increases in tight oligopolies. Some recent research focuses on the way in which prices respond to changes in costs and demand. Overall, there is evidence of asymmetric price adjustment, with quicker adjustment to increases in cost and reductions in demand than to changes in the opposite directions (Peltzman, 2000; Genovese, 2003; Bils and Klenow, 2004; Álvarez and Hernando, 2005; Davis, 2007). There is also evidence of a positive relationship between industry concentration and price rigidity (Carlton, 1986; Eucaouna and Geroski, 1986).

Sweezy's basic assumption that price increases will not be followed and that price cuts will, has been challenged. A price cut need not send signals to rivals that a firm is aggressively seeking to capture a larger market share. Rivals may reason that the firm's product is of lower quality, or the firm has financial problems. Rivals react according to how they interpret the price cut. Likewise, price increases may be followed if firms believe market conditions warrant such an increase, or if they face temporary capacity shortages and are unable to meet increases in demand. In times of increasing demand and possible price inflation, producing any additional output increases costs substantially for a firm approaching capacity (Bronfenbrenner, 1940; Efroymson, 1955). Accordingly, a capacity-constrained firm may be eager to follow a rival's price rise and reluctant to follow a price cut, which would only increase demand further.

Price leadership

Models of price leadership or parallel pricing are yet another type of oligopoly model, in which the firms recognize their interdependence. It is frequently observed that firms in oligopolistic markets change prices in parallel. One firm announces a price change, and the other firms rapidly follow.

Dominant price leadership

In one class of price leadership model, **dominant price leadership**, it is assumed that the industry is dominated by one firm, owing to its superior efficiency (lower costs), or perhaps its aggressive behaviour. The firm sets the price and other firms follow passively, whether through convenience, ignorance or fear. In fact there is no oligopoly problem as such, since interdependence is absent.

In Figure 7.13, it is assumed that there is one large dominant firm, and a competitive 'fringe' comprising a large number of small firms. The dominant firm is the price leader, and sets the market price. The competitive fringe are the followers. These firms are price takers and each firm faces a perfectly elastic demand function at the price set by the dominant firm. It is assumed that the dominant firm has complete information regarding its own demand and cost functions, as well as those of its smaller competitors.

In Figure 7.13, D_{TOTAL} is the market demand function. S_{FRINGE} is the total supply function of the competitive fringe, obtained by summing the marginal cost functions of each firm in the competitive fringe horizontally. Each firm in the competitive fringe maximizes profit by producing the quantity at which

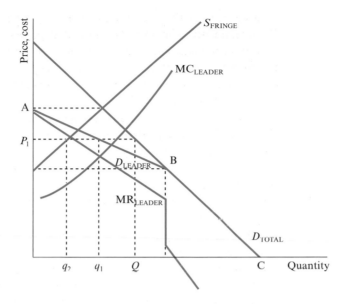

Figure 7.13 Dominant firm price leadership

price *equals* marginal cost. Therefore the horizontal sum of all of the marginal cost functions represents the total quantity supplied by the competitive fringe at any price. In order to obtain D_{LEADER}, the residual demand function of the dominant firm, subtract the quantity supplied by the competitive fringe at any price from the total market demand function at that price. Therefore $D_{LEADER} = D_{TOTAL} - S_{FRINGE}$. Notice at A, $S_{FRINGE} = D_{TOTAL}$, so $D_{LEADER} = 0$. At B, $S_{FRINGE} = 0$, so $D_{LEADER} = D_{TOTAL}$. Beyond B, the leader operates along D_{TOTAL}, so over the entire range of output levels the leader's demand function is ABC. The kink in this demand function at B implies the leader's marginal revenue function (MR_{LEADER} above B) has a discontinuity at B.

The dominant firm maximizes profit by choosing the output at which MR_{LEADER} *equals* MC_{LEADER}, the dominant firm's marginal cost function. The dominant firm's price and output are (P_1, q_1). At a price of P_1, the output of the competitive fringe is q_2. Total industry output *equals* $Q = q_1 + q_2$. By construction, $q_2 = Q - q_1$, because the horizontal distance between D_{TOTAL} and D_{LEADER} *equals* S_{FRINGE}.

Barometric price leadership

Barometric price leadership exists where a firm announces a price change that would, in time, be set by the forces of competition. It is simply the first to announce the price change. The leader is not necessarily the dominant firm, and the leader does not necessarily have any market power with which it could impose its will on others, as in the dominant firm price leadership model. Indeed, one would expect the identity of the leader to change from time to time. The leader acts as a barometer for the market and, if it fails to interpret market signals correctly, leadership will soon pass to some other firm.

Markham (1951) suggests barometric price leadership is of two types: the competitive type and the (more dangerous) monopolistic type, known as effective or collusive price leadership. The more benign, competitive type is characterized by:

■ Frequent changes in the identity of the leader;

■ No immediate, uniform response to price changes: followers take their time to consider the suitability of a price change implemented by the leader;

■ Variations in market share.

Effective or collusive price leadership is characterized by:

■ A small number of firms, all relatively large;

■ Substantial entry barriers;

■ Limited product differentiation, reinforcing the firms' awareness of their interdependence;

■ Low price elasticity of demand, deterring price-cutting;

■ Similar cost functions.

These characteristics are not too dissimilar to the characteristics of successful cartels (see Chapter 8). When the agreed price leader changes its price, the other firms immediately follow. There is no overt or explicit collusion: all firms act independently. However, they realize it is better to cooperate tacitly in an orderly market than to slide into the anarchy of a price war. Nevertheless, the effect is similar to explicit price fixing. 'The monopolistically barometric form of price leadership is dire, and it may serve all the ends of a strong trade association or a closely knit domestic cartel' (Bain, 1960, p. 198).

7.6 Game theory

Game theory is an approach to decision-making under conditions of uncertainty developed by the mathematicians John von Neumann and Oskar Morgenstern (1944). A game is a situation in which two or more decision-makers, or players, face choices between a number of possible actions at any stage of the game. A game that is played only once is a single-period game. A game that is played more than once is a **multiple-period** or **repeated game**. A multiple-period game can be repeated either infinitely, or a finite number of times. A player's **strategy** is a set of rules telling him which action to choose under each possible set of circumstances that might exist at any stage in the game. Each player aims to select the strategy (or mix of strategies) that will maximize his own **payoff**. The players face a situation of interdependence. Each player is aware that the actions of other players can affect his payoff, but at the time the player chooses his own action he may not know which actions are being chosen by the other players. A game in which all players choose their actions simultaneously, before knowing the actions chosen by other players, is a **simultaneous**

game. A game in which the players choose their actions in turn, so that a player who moves later knows the actions that were chosen by players who moved earlier, is a **sequential game**. The outcome of a game is the set of strategies and actions that are actually chosen, and the resulting payoffs. An equilibrium is a combination of strategies, actions and payoffs that is optimal (in some sense) for all players.

In a **constant-sum game**, the sum of the payoffs to all players is always the same, whatever strategies are chosen. In a **non-constant-sum game**, the sum of the payoffs depends on the strategies chosen. A **zero-sum game** is a constant-sum game in which the sum of the gains and losses of all players is always zero. A game of poker is a zero-sum game: one player's winnings are exactly matched by the losses of rival players.

In many ways, the property of **interdependence** is the key defining characteristic of a game, and it is this property that makes game theory relevant to an understanding of decision-making for firms in oligopoly. In most of the game theory examples that are discussed in Section 7.6 and elsewhere in this book, the players are two or more oligopolistic firms. Strategies and actions concern the decisions the firms have to take about price or output, or other commercial decisions on matters such as advertising, product differentiation, research and development, entry, location, and so on. Payoffs are usually defined in terms of the implications for the firms' profitability of the strategies and actions that are chosen. However, it is worth noting that game theory has many applications other than decision-making under oligopoly. Examples include strategy and tactics in sports, military strategy and nuclear deterrence.

Dominant strategy equilibrium and Nash equilibrium

As an initial game theory example, Figure 7.14 shows the payoff matrix for two firms, A and B, that have to decide simultaneously whether to produce low or high levels of output. Firm A's strategies are denoted **Low** and **High** and, similarly, firm B's strategies are denoted *Low* and *High*. The elements in the matrix represent the payoffs (for example profit) to the two firms. Both firms' payoffs depend on their own output level and on the output level of the other firm, since market price is a function of the combined output levels of both firms. Within each cell of Figure 7.14, the first figure is A's payoff and the second figure is B's payoff. For example, if A selects **High** and B selects *Low*, A's payoff (profit) is **3** and B's payoff is *2*.

First, consider the choice between strategies **Low** and **High** from firm A's perspective. One method A could use in order to make this choice would be to examine which of **Low** and **High** is best for A if B selects *Low*, and which of **Low** and **High** is best for A if B selects *High*:

- If B selects *Low*, **Low** yields a payoff of **4** for A, while **High** yields a payoff of **3**. Therefore, if B selects *Low*, it is best for A to select **Low**.

- If B selects *High*, **Low** yields a payoff of **2** for A, while **High** yields a payoff of **1**. Therefore, if B selects *High*, it is best for A to select **Low**.

Firm B's strategies

		Low	High
	Low	**4** *4*	**2** *3*
Firm A's strategies			
	High	**3** *2*	**1** *1*

Figure 7.14 Payoff matrix for firms A and B

In this game, no matter what strategy B selects, it is best for A to choose **Low** rather than **High**. **Low** is said to be a **dominant strategy**, because it is the best strategy for A no matter what strategy B selects.

Second, consider the choice between strategies *Low* and *High* from B's perspective, using a similar approach:

■ If A selects **Low**, *Low* yields a payoff of *4* for B, while *High* yields a payoff of *3*. Therefore, if A selects **Low**, it is best for B to select *Low*.

■ If A selects **High**, *Low* yields a payoff of *2* for B, while *High* yields a payoff of *1*. Therefore, if A selects **High**, it is best for B to select *Low*.

Accordingly, no matter what strategy A selects, it is better for B to select *Low* rather than *High*. Therefore *Low* is B's dominant strategy. Following this approach, it appears A should select **Low** and B should select *Low*, so that both firms earn a payoff of 4. This outcome, denoted (**Low**, *Low*), is known as a **dominant strategy** equilibrium. In fact, the game shown in Figure 7.14 is rather trivial, in the sense that 4 is the best payoff achievable by either player under any circumstances. It seems natural that the players should choose the combination of strategies that produces this payoff for both of them. Below, it is shown that not all games are structured in a way that always produces such a pleasing outcome for the players!

There is one further desirable and important property of the current example. At the dominant strategy equilibrium (**Low**, *Low*), neither firm can improve its payoff given the current strategy of the other firm. Given that B selects *Low*, if A switches from **Low** to **High**, A's payoff falls from *4* to *3*. And given that A selects **Low**, if B switches from *Low* to *High*, B's payoff also falls from *4* to *3*. Therefore, if A selects **Low** and B selects *Low*, both firms maximize their own profit, subject to the constraint that the other firm's output is fixed at its current level. Therefore both firms maximize profit subject to a zero conjectural variation assumption. An equilibrium of this kind has been identified previously, in the discussion of the Cournot duopoly model. In the terminology of Section 7.3, this kind of solution is known as a Cournot–Nash equilibrium. In the terminology of game theory, it is known simply as a **Nash equilibrium**. In a Nash equilibrium, neither firm can improve its payoff given the strategy chosen by the other firm.

Firm B's strategies

	Low	*High*
Low	3 *3*	1 *4*
High	4 *1*	2 *2*

Firm A's strategies

Figure 7.15 Payoff matrix for firms A and B: prisoner's dilemma example

Prisoner's dilemma ✓

Figure 7.15 presents a second example, with a similar structure but a different set of payoffs. Applying the same reasoning as before, from A's perspective:

- If B selects *Low*, **Low** yields a payoff of **3** for A, while **High** yields a payoff of **4**. Therefore, if B selects *Low*, it is best for A to select **High**.

- If B selects *High*, **Low** yields a payoff of **1** for A, while **High** yields a payoff of **2**. Therefore, if B selects *High*, it is best for A to select **High**.

And from B's perspective:

- If A selects **Low**, *Low* yields a payoff of *3* for B, while *High* yields a payoff of *4*. Therefore, if A selects **Low**, it is best for B to select *High*.

- If A selects **High**, *Low* yields a payoff of *1* for B, while *High* yields a payoff of *2*. Therefore, if A selects **High**, it is best for B to select *High*.

Therefore, **High** is a dominant strategy for A and *High* is a dominant strategy for B. Accordingly, it seems that A should select **High** and B should select *High*, in which case both firms earn a payoff of 2. As before, the dominant strategy equilibrium (**High**, *High*) is also a Nash equilibrium. Given that B selects *High*, if A switches from **High** to **Low**, A's payoff falls from **2** to **1**; and given that A selects **High**, if B switches from *High* to *Low*, B's payoff also falls from *2* to *1*. However, this time something appears to be wrong. If both firms had selected the *other* strategy (**Low**, *Low*), either by cooperating or perhaps by acting independently, both firms would have earned a superior payoff of 3 each, rather than their actual payoff of 2 each.

Figure 7.15 is an example of a special class of single period non-constant-sum game, known as the **prisoner's dilemma**. In a prisoner's dilemma game, there are dominant strategies for both players that produce a combined payoff that is worse than the combined payoff the players could achieve if they cooperate, with each player agreeing to choose a strategy other than his dominant strategy. In other words, in a prisoner's dilemma, gains can be made by both players if they cooperate or collude.

To see why this type of game is known as a prisoner's dilemma, consider a situation where the police hold two prisoners, Alan and Brian, who are suspected of having committed a serious crime together. However, the police have insufficient evidence to secure a conviction unless one or both prisoners confesses. The prisoners are separated physically and there is no communication between them. Each is told the following:

■ If you both confess to the serious crime, you both receive a reduced punishment of five years in prison.

■ If neither of you confesses to the serious crime, you are both convicted of a minor crime and you both receive the full sentence for the minor crime of two years in prison.

■ If you confess to the serious crime and your fellow prisoner does not confess, you receive a reduced sentence of one year in prison for the minor crime (and your punishment for the serious crime is cancelled).

■ If you do not confess to the serious crime and your fellow prisoner confesses, you receive the full sentence for the serious crime of ten years in prison.

The payoff matrix is shown in Figure 7.16, with all payoffs shown as negative numbers (because in this case a large payoff or prison sentence is bad, not good). Alan's reasoning might be as follows: if Brian confesses, I should confess because five years is better than ten years; and if Brian does not confess, I should confess because one year is better than two years. Therefore I will confess. Brian's reasoning is the same, because the payoffs are symmetric between the two prisoners. Therefore both confess, and both receive sentences of five years. But if they had been able to cooperate, they could have agreed not to confess and both would have received sentences of two years. Even acting independently, they might be able to reach the cooperative solution. Alan knows that if he does not confess, he receives a two-year sentence as long as Brian does the same. However, Alan is worried because he knows there is a big incentive for Brian to 'cheat' on Alan by confessing. By doing so, Brian can earn the one-year sentence and leave Alan with a ten-year sentence!

Brian is in a similar position: if he does not confess, he receives the two-year sentence as long as Alan also does not confess. However, Brian also knows there is a big incentive for Alan to cheat. The cooperative solution might be achievable, especially if Alan and Brian can trust one another not to cheat, but it is also unstable and liable to break down.

		Brian's strategies	
		Not confess	*Confess*
Alan's strategies	**Not confess**	−2 −2	−10 −1
	Confess	−1 −10	−5 −5

Figure 7.16 Payoff matrix for Alan and Brian: classic prisoner's dilemma

Section 7.3 analyzed the choices of output levels by two duopolists. Comparing the Cournot–Nash and the Chamberlin solutions to the duopoly model shown in Figure 7.9, it is apparent that if the two firms operate independently according to the zero conjectural variation assumption, and each firm produces a relatively high output level of 1/3, the Cournot–Nash equilibrium is attained. In the terminology of the present section, this is a non-cooperative outcome. If, on the other hand, the two firms recognize their interdependence and aim for joint profit maximization, and each firm produces the lower output level of 1/4, the Chamberlin equilibrium is attained. In present terminology, this is the cooperative outcome.

Figures 7.17 and 7.18 show that if the two duopolists have to make their output decisions simultaneously, without knowing the other firm's decision, effectively they play a prisoner's dilemma game. The assumptions underlying Figures 7.17 and 7.18 are the same as in the original Cournot model developed in Section 7.3, with one exception. The two duopolists are assumed to produce an identical product and incur zero marginal costs. The one change involves a rescaling of the quantity axis for the market demand function, so that the maximum quantity that could be sold if the price falls to zero is 144 units (rather than one unit). As before, the price axis for market demand function is on a scale of $P = 0$ to $P = 1$, so when $P = 0$, $Q = 144$ and when $P = 1$, $Q = 0$. (Rescaling of the quantity axis avoids the occurrence of fractional prices, quantities and

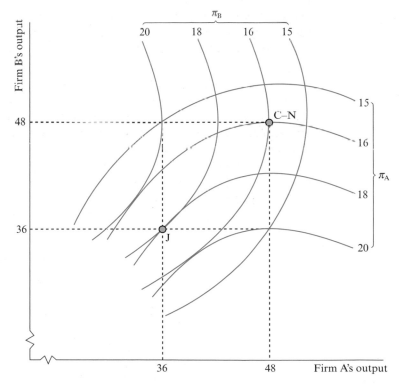

Figure 7.17 Isoprofit curves for firms A and B: Cournot–Nash versus Chamberlin's prisoner's dilemma

Firm B's strategies

		Low	High
Firm A's strategies	**Low**	**18** *18*	**15** *20*
	High	**20** *15*	**16** *16*

Figure 7.18 Payoff matrix for firms A and B: Cournot–Nash versus Chamberlin's prisoner's dilemma

profits.) You can verify that the prices, quantities and profits or payoffs shown in Figures 7.17 and 7.18 are equivalent to their counterparts in Figure 7.9 multiplied by a factor of 144.

In Figure 7.17, it is assumed that each firm has to choose between producing a high output of 48 units, or a low output of 36 units. If both firms select high, the Cournot–Nash equilibrium is attained, and both firms' profits are 16. If both firms select low, the Chamberlin joint profit maximization equilibrium is attained, and both firms' profits are 18. If one firm selects low while the other selects high, the low-producing firm suffers and earns 15, while the high-producing firm prospers and earns 20. Figure 7.18 represents these outcomes in the form of a payoff matrix. Applying the same reasoning as before, from A's perspective:

■ If B selects *Low*, **Low** yields a payoff of **18** for A, while **High** yields a payoff of **20**. Therefore, if B selects *Low*, it is best for A to select **High**.

■ If B selects *High*, **Low** yields a payoff of **15** for A, while **High** yields a payoff of **16**. Therefore, if B selects *High*, it is best for A to select **High**.

Accordingly, it is best for A to select **High**, no matter what strategy B selects. The same is also true for B, because the two firms are identical. (**High**, *High*) is the dominant strategy equilibrium, and is also a sub-optimal non-cooperative Cournot–Nash outcome. As before, the cooperative or collusive outcome (**Low**, *Low*) might be achievable if the firms can trust each another to stick to the low output strategy and not defect and produce high output. However, as before, this outcome is unstable and liable to break down. For the cooperative solution to hold in an oligopoly, any agreement between the firms might have to be accompanied by an enforceable contract (legal or otherwise).

Not all prisoner's dilemma games generate sub-optimal outcomes, especially when the assumptions are relaxed. First, the optimal (cooperative) outcome might be achieved if there is good communication between the players. If firms meet frequently, they can exchange information and monitor each other's actions. If the two prisoners, Alan and Brian, were not segregated, they could determine their best strategies by a continual examination of their options. The nuclear deterrence 'game' played by the United States and the Soviet Union in the 1960s and 1970s was likened to a prisoner's dilemma game. The choices were whether to attack the rival with a pre-emptive strike, or abide by the 'non-first use' agreement. Perhaps one reason why the optimal outcome (sticking to the agreement) was achieved was that the installation of a telephone hotline between Washington and Moscow permitted rapid communication and exchange of information at the highest levels of government. Alternatively, it might be possible to achieve a cooperative outcome if the players are able to recognize trustworthiness in other players through visual signals (Janssen, 2008).

Second, in practice an important characteristic of any game is the length of the reaction lag: the time it takes for a player who has been deceived to retaliate. The longer the reaction lags, the greater the temptation for either player to act as an aggressor. If Brian cheats on Alan, Alan may have to wait ten years to take revenge, unless he has friends outside the prison who are prepared to act more quickly. In cartels, the main deterrent to cheating is immediate discovery and punishment. In the nuclear deterrence game, short reaction lags were crucial to ensuring both sides kept to the agreement. Each side boasted that it could retaliate within minutes if attacked by the other, ensuring there was no first-mover advantage. This policy became known as mutually assured destruction (MAD).

Third, the dynamics of rivalry may also be relevant. Is the rivalry continuous, or 'one-off'? If rivalry is continuous in a repeated game, players learn over time that cooperation is preferable to aggression. Professional criminals have no problem with the prisoner's dilemma: experience has taught them that silence is the best option. In an oligopoly, firms change prices, alter product lines, determine advertising strategies, continuously. The firms may learn over time that aggressive behaviour leads to hostile (tit-for-tat) reactions from rivals, that tend to cancel out any short-term gains (see Case Study 7.2). Repeated or multiple-period games are examined in more detail below.

Relationship between dominant strategy equilibrium and Nash equilibrium

In the game theory examples that are presented in Figures 7.14, 7.15, 7.16 and 7.18, there is an exact correspondence between the dominant strategy equilibrium and the Nash equilibrium. In fact, it can be shown that a dominant strategy equilibrium in any game is always a Nash equilibrium. If both players are selecting their dominant strategies, then it is impossible for either to improve its own payoff by changing its strategy given the current strategy of the other player. However, it is possible to conceive of games in which there exists a Nash equilibrium, but there are no dominant strategies and no dominant strategy equilibrium. In Figure 7.19, for example, firms A and B must decide simultaneously their advertising expenditures. They have a choice between three levels of expenditure: low, medium or high. Both firms' payoffs from the advertising campaign depend on their own expenditure and on the expenditure of the other firm.

As before, consider firm A's choices:

- If B chooses *Low*, A's best choice is **Low**.

- If B chooses *Medium*, A's best choice is **Medium**.

- If B chooses *High*, A's best choice is **High**.

Firm B's budget

		Low	Medium	High
	Low	**40** 40	**35** 45	**10** 25
Firm A's budget	**Medium**	**35** 35	**45** 30	**15** 20
	High	**30** 25	**25** 15	**20** 30

Figure 7.19 Payoff matrix for the advertising budgets of firms A and B

Similarly, consider firm B's choices:

■ If A chooses **Low**, B's best choice is *Medium*.

■ If A chooses **Medium**, B's best choice is *Low*.

■ If A chooses **High**, B's best choice is *High*.

Therefore there are no dominant strategies for either firm A or firm B.

Although there is no dominant strategy equilibrium in Figure 7.19, by inspection it can be confirmed that (**High**, *High*) is a Nash equilibrium. If B chooses *High*, then **High** is also A's best choice; and if A chooses **High**, then *High* is also B's best choice. Unfortunately, in the absence of dominant strategies, there is no simple decision-making procedure that will enable the two firms to reach the Nash equilibrium easily. If the Nash equilibrium is achieved by some means, however, it is stable in the sense that there is no incentive for either firm to depart from it, given the zero conjectural variation assumption.

As in the prisoner's dilemma examples, firms A and B could both made be better off by cooperating or agreeing to choose (**Low**, *Low*) in Figure 7.19, rather than remaining at the Nash equilibrium of (**High**, *High*). However, in contrast to the Nash equilibrium this cooperative solution is unstable. If A chooses **Low**, B has an incentive to 'cheat' and choose *Medium* instead of *Low*. But if B chooses *Medium*, A would also prefer **Medium**; and then if A chooses **Medium**, B would prefer *Low*; and so on. Therefore the cooperative solution is vulnerable to defection by one or both of the firms, and is likely to break down.

Mixed strategies

In some games, there is neither a dominant strategy equilibrium nor a Nash equilibrium. Consider the case of two firms that need to decide simultaneously their advertising budgets (low or high). As before, both firms' payoffs from the advertising campaign depend both on their own expenditure and on the other firm's expenditure. The payoff matrix is shown in Figure 7.20. This is a constant-sum game. Whatever combination of strategies is chosen, the sum of the payoffs

Firm B's strategies

		Low	*High*
Firm A's strategies	**Low**	1 *4*	3 *2*
	High	4 *1*	0 *5*

Figure 7.20 Payoff matrix for firms A and B: mixed strategy example

to both firms is 5. However, there is no dominant strategy for either firm. From firm A's perspective:

- If B chooses *Low*, A's best choice is **High**.

- If B chooses *High*, A's best choice is **Low**.

And from B's perspective:

- If A chooses **Low**, B's best choice is *Low*.

- If A chooses **High**, B's best choice is *High*.

There is no simple solution to this game because there are no dominant strategies. A is in a difficult position. If A selects **Low**, B might select *Low* and A only earns a profit of 1. But, on the other hand, if A selects **High** and B selects *High*, A earns a profit of 0. Of course, B also faces a similar dilemma.

The solution lies in the concept of a **mixed strategy**, developed by von Neumann and Morgenstern (1944). A player follows a mixed strategy by choosing his action randomly, using fixed probabilities. Each player's optimal mixed strategy involves the selection of probabilities that maximize his expected payoff, regardless of the strategy that is being employed by the other player. In contrast, previous examples have resulted in the choice of a **pure strategy** by both players. According to the non-cooperative solution to the prisoner's dilemma game shown in Figure 7.15, for example, A should only select **High** and B should only select *High*, because **High** and *High* are dominant strategies.

Returning to Figure 7.20, suppose firm A assigns a probability of x to the choice of **Low**, and a probability of $(1 - x)$ to the choice of **High**. A's expected payoffs (in terms of x) are as follows:

- If B chooses *Low*, A's possible payoffs are **1** (if A chooses **Low**, with a probability of x) and **4** (if A chooses **High**, with a probability of $1 - x$). A's expected payoff is $1x + 4(1 - x) = 4 - 3x$.

- If B chooses *High*, A's possible payoffs are **3** (if A chooses **Low**, with a probability of x) and **0** (if A chooses **High**, with a probability of $1 - x$). A's expected payoff is $3x + 0(1 - x) = 3x$.

The left-hand diagram in Figure 7.21 plots firm A's expected payoffs against all possible values of x, for each of the two possible choices available to firm B.

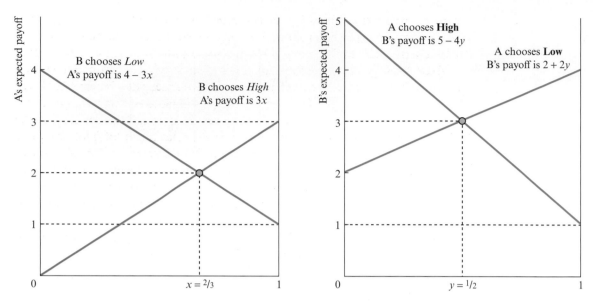

Figure 7.21 Expected payoffs for firms A and B in mixed strategy Nash equilibrium

Setting $x = 1$ is equivalent to 'A always chooses **Low**'. In this case, the worst A can do is earn a profit of 1 (if B chooses *Low*). Similarly, setting $x = 0$ is equivalent to 'A always chooses **High**'. In this case, the worst A can do is earn a profit of 0 (if B chooses *High*). However, according to Figure 7.21 A can improve on the worst possible outcomes under both of these pure strategies by selecting a mixed strategy of $x = 2/3$. In this case, A earns an expected profit of 2, whichever of *Low* and *High* is chosen by B. In fact, it can be shown that A still earns an expected profit of 2 if B selects any mixed strategy which involves choosing randomly between *Low* and *High*, no matter what probabilities B assigns to these two choices.

B's optimal mixed strategy can also be evaluated with reference to Figure 7.21. Let B assign a probability of y to the choice of *Low*, and a probability of $(1 - y)$ to the choice of *High*. B's expected payoffs (in terms of y) are as follows:

■ If A chooses **Low**, B's possible payoffs are *4* (if B chooses *Low*, with a probability of y) and *2* (if B chooses *High*, with a probability of $1 - y$). B's expected payoff is $4y + 2(1 - y) = 2 + 2y$.

■ If A chooses **High**, B's possible payoffs are *1* (if B chooses *Low*, with a probability of y) and *5* (if B chooses *High*, with a probability of $1 - y$). B's expected payoff is $1y + 5(1 - y) = 5 - 4y$.

The right-hand diagram in Figure 7.21 plots B's expected payoffs against all possible values of y, for each of the two possible choices available to A. Setting $y = 1$ is equivalent to 'B always chooses *Low*'. In this case, the worst B can do is earn a profit of 1 (if A chooses **High**). Similarly, setting $y = 0$ is equivalent to 'B always chooses *High*'. In this case, the worst B can do is earn a profit of 2 (if A chooses **Low**). However, B improves on the worst possible outcomes under both of these pure strategies by selecting a mixed strategy of $y = 1/2$. In this case, B earns an expected profit of 3, whichever of **Low** and **High** is chosen by A. In fact, B earns an expected profit of 3 for any mixed strategy selected by A.

If A sets $x = 2/3$ and B sets $y = 1/2$, the game shown in Figure 7.20 achieves a **mixed strategy** Nash equilibrium. Each firm selects the probabilities that maximize its own expected payoff, given the mixed strategy that is being employed by the other firm. In fact, by selecting the probabilities in this way, each firm guarantees its own expected payoff, whatever the probabilities selected by the other firm. Selecting $x = 2/3$ guarantees A an expected payoff of 2 for any value of y selected by B; selecting $x = 2/3$ makes A indifferent to B's selection of probabilties. Likewise, selecting $y = 1/2$ guarantees B an expected payoff of 3 for any value of x selected by A; selecting $y = 1/2$ makes B indifferent to A's selection of probabilities. Although the mathematics is beyond the scope of this text, it has been shown that for any game with a fixed number of players, each of whom chooses between a fixed number of possible actions, a Nash equilibrium involving either pure strategies or mixed strategies always exists.

Sequential games

In the games examined so far in Section 7.6, the players act simultaneously and decide their strategies and actions before they know which strategies and actions have been chosen by their rivals. However, there are other games in which the players' decisions follow a sequence. One player makes his decision, and the other player observes this decision before making his response. For example, firm A decides to launch a new brand and firm B then decides how best to respond. Should B imitate A and launch a brand with identical characteristics, or should B aim for a segment in the market that is not serviced by A and launch a brand with different characteristics? For a **sequential game**, it is convenient to map the choices facing the players in the form of a game tree.

Assume two breakfast cereal producers are both considering a new product launch. They each have a choice of launching one of two products: one product's appeal is 'crunchiness' and the other's appeal is 'fruitiness'. Assume the crunchy cereal is more popular with consumers than the fruity cereal. Figure 7.22 shows the payoff matrix in the same form as before, assuming both firms move simultaneously, ignorant of what their rival is planning. According to Figure 7.22, it is better for both firms if they each produce a different product than if they both produce the same product. The structure of the payoffs is such that there is no

| | | Firm B's strategies | |
		Crunchy	*Fruity*
Firm A's strategies	**Crunchy**	**3** *3*	**5** *4*
	Fruity	**4** *5*	**2** *2*

Figure 7.22 Sequential game: strategic form representation

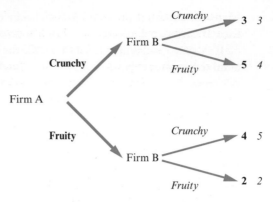

Figure 7.23 Sequential game: extensive form representation

dominant strategy for either firm. If B produces *Crunchy* it is better for A to produce **Fruity**, but if B produces *Fruity* it is better for A to produce **Crunchy**. Using the methods of the previous sub-section, you can verify that the mixed strategy Nash equilibrium requires both firms to choose their actions randomly, with probabilities of 3/4 assigned to crunchy and 1/4 assigned to fruity.

In a sequential game, however, where A is the first to launch its new product and B then responds after having observed A's action, the outcome is different. Using the same figures for the breakfast cereals example, Figure 7.23 shows the game tree representation of the payoffs, also known as the *extensive form representation*. (The equivalent terminology for the payoff matrix used previously is the *strategic form representation*.) Consider A's decision:

■ If A produces **Crunchy**, B's *Fruity* payoff of *4* exceeds B's *Crunchy* payoff of *3*, so B will produce *Fruity* and A will earn a profit of **5**.

■ If A produces **Fruity**, B's *Crunchy* payoff of *5* exceeds B's *Fruity* payoff of *2*, so B will produce *Crunchy* and A will earn a profit of **4**.

In fact, A realizes that whatever product A launches, the rational response of B is to launch the alternative product. A's best action is to produce **Crunchy**, and A earns the higher payoff of **5**. B produces *Fruity* and earns the lower payoff of *4*. A finishes up with the higher payoff because A benefits from a first-mover advantage, as in the case of the Stackelberg duopolist examined in Section 7.3.

Repeated games

In the previous discussion of single-period prisoner's dilemma and other games, it is assumed that the game is played only once. However, some games may be played repeatedly by the same players. Suppose firms A and B are hotdog sellers located outside a sports stadium. If the occasion is a one-off event such as the Olympics, and the two hotdog sellers are unlikely to ever see each other again, the game between them is a single-period game. In this case, the two hotdog sellers are less likely to cooperate. Suppose, however, the event is one that is repeated at regular intervals. Suppose the stadium is Old Trafford, the event is

Manchester United home matches and the hotdog sellers see one another at regular, fortnightly intervals. In this case, it is more likely that cooperative behaviour will evolve as the two sellers observe and learn from each others' behaviour. In a **repeated** or **multiple-period game**, each firm may attempt to influence its rival's behaviour by sending signals that promise to reward cooperative behaviour and threaten to punish non-cooperative behaviour.

With reference to the prisoner's dilemma game shown in Figure 7.15, (**High**, *High*) is the (sub-optimal) non-cooperative solution, which produces payoffs of 2 for firms A and B; and (**Low**, *Low*) is the (optimal) cooperative choice, which produces payoffs of 3 for both firms. In a single-period game, in which the firms act independently, **High** and *High* are the dominant strategies, and the non-cooperative outcome is likely to occur. However, suppose the game is to be repeated over an indefinite number of periods. Firm A could adopt the following strategy, known as **tit-for-tat**, in an attempt to encourage firm B to always select the cooperative choice:

■ In period 1 A chooses **Low**.

■ If B chose *Low* in period $t - 1$, in period t (for $t > 1$) A chooses **Low**.

■ If B chose *High* in period $t - 1$, in period t (for $t > 1$) A chooses **High**.

In each period after the first, provided B chose the cooperative strategy last time, A rewards B by choosing the cooperative strategy this time. But if B chose the non-cooperative strategy last time, A punishes B by choosing the non-cooperative strategy this time. For as long as B cooperates, A also cooperates and the (optimal) cooperative solution is achieved. But if B attempts to exploit A's cooperation for short-term gain by defecting from *Low* to *High*, A punishes B in the following period by also switching, from **Low** to **High**. However, B's punishment does not necessarily have to be long-lasting. Provided B learns from his error and switches back from *High* to *Low*, A also switches back from **High** to **Low** and cooperation is restored.

Since it is difficult to observe situations which replicate the structure of many theoretical games in practice, a sub-field of economics known as **experimental economics** has been developed in order to test the predictions of game theory. Laboratory experimentation allows economists to determine the structure of games and test relevant hypotheses. Some economists are particularly optimistic about the future of this development:

> [A] hundred years from now, game theory will have become
> the backbone of a kind of microeconomics engineering that will
> have roughly the relation to the economic theory and laboratory
> experimentation of the time that chemical engineering has to
> chemical theory and bench chemistry.
>
> *(Roth, 1991, p. 107)*

In the present context, experiments have shown the adoption of a tit-for-tat strategy by one or both players is a highly effective method for ensuring adherence to cooperative behaviour in repeated games with a prisoner's dilemma structure. Usually, both players rapidly learn it is best for them to adhere to the cooperative strategy on each occasion the game is repeated.

However, there is one important caveat. Tit-for-tat is effective in infinitely repeated games, in which there is no period when the game is played for the last time. Tit-for-tat may also be effective in games that are repeated only a finite number of times, but on each occasion neither player knows whether or not this *is* the last time the game will be played. However, tit-for-tat is likely to be ineffective in games that are repeated only a finite number of times, and on the final occasion the players know they will not play the game again.

Suppose the game is played for the last time in period T. In period T, B knows 'defecting' from *Low* to *High* will go unpunished, because the game will not be played again in $T + 1$. Therefore there is no deterrence and B defects. Realizing that B will behave in this way, A may as well abandon tit-for-tat in T, and also defect from **Low** to **High**. Therefore the non-cooperative outcome occurs in T.

From this reasoning, it might be supposed that the usefulness of the tit-for-tat strategy now finishes in period $T - 1$. In fact, however, the situation is actually worse than this, because in period $T - 1$ the same difficulty occurs. In $T - 1$, B knows 'defecting' from *Low* to *High* will go unpunished, because non-cooperation is going to happen anyway in T. Therefore there is no deterrence in $T - 1$ either, and B defects. Realizing that B will behave in this way, A may as well abandon tit-for-tat in $T - 1$, and also defect. Therefore the non-cooperative outcome also occurs in $T - 1$.

Similar reasoning will also apply in periods $T - 2$, $T - 3$ and so on, all the way back to the start of the game. In other words, the usefulness of tit-for-tat as a means for ensuring adherence to cooperative behaviour unravels completely due to the finite lifetime of the repeated game. A has no means of punishing B for non-cooperative behaviour in period T, so the tit-for-tat strategy fails in period T. But if tit-for-tat fails in period T, it also fails in $T - 1$; and if it fails in $T - 1$, it also fails in $T - 2$; and so on.

Case study 7.2

The prisoner's dilemma in practice: tit-for-tat in the First World War trenches

The original prisoner's dilemma story involves two criminals who are arrested after committing a serious crime. The police have no proof of their involvement except for a minor infraction. The prosecutor offers them a deal whereby the one who implicates the other escapes all punishment and the other gets a heavy prison sentence. If both implicate the other, both end up in prison for a long time. The dominant strategy is for each criminal to implicate the other. Consequently, they both end up getting relatively heavy prison sentences. When the game is repeated, however, co-operation can be sustained implicitly through dynamic strategies. In his classic book, *The Evolution of Co-operation*, University of Michigan political scientist Robert Axelrod studied empirically and experimentally the strategies that lead players involved in prisoner's dilemma situations to co-operative outcomes. His starting point was an unexpected experimental result. When experts were asked to submit strategies for repeated prisoner's dilemma games and these strategies were matched with each other in a computer tournament, tit-for-tat, the simplest strategy, won. This was a strategy under which each player started by co-operating, and then did to the other player what that player had done to him previously. Axelrod's analysis of the data found tit-for-tat had four properties making a strategy successful. A successful strategy should be nice: confronted with a co-operative player, it should reciprocate. It should also be provocable: faced with an uncalled defection, it should respond. It should be forgiving: after responding to a defection, it should go back to co-operation. And it should be easy to understand: other players should be able to anticipate the consequences of their actions. Axelrod presents a surprising example of the usefulness of a variant of this strategy: First World War trench warfare. Here is a summary of his account.

The historical situation in the quiet sectors along the Western Front was a (repeated) prisoner's dilemma. At any time, the choices of two small units facing each other are to shoot to kill or deliberately to shoot to avoid causing damage. For both sides, weakening the enemy is important because it promotes survival. Therefore, in the short run it is better to do damage now, whether the enemy is shooting back or not. What made trench warfare so different from most other combat was that the same small units faced each other in immobile sectors for extended periods of time. This changed the game from a one-move prisoner's dilemma in which defection is the dominant choice, to an iterated prisoner's dilemma in which conditional strategies are possible. The result accorded with the theory's predictions: with sustained interaction, the stable outcome could be *mutual co-operation* based upon *reciprocity* [emphasis added]. In particular, both sides followed strategies that would not be the first to defect, but that would be provoked if the other defected. As the lines stabilized, non-aggression between the troops emerged spontaneously in many places along the front. The earliest instances may have been associated with meals served at the same times on both sides of no-man's land. An eyewitness noted that: 'In one section the hour of 8 to 9 a.m. was regarded as consecrated to private business, and certain places indicated by a flag were regarded as out of bounds by the snipers on both sides.' In the summer of 1915 [a soldier noted that] 'It would be child's play to shell the road behind the enemy's trenches, crowded as it must be with ration wagons and water carts, into a bloodstained wilderness but on the whole there is silence. After all, if you prevent your enemy from drawing his rations, his remedy is simple: he will prevent you from drawing yours.' The strategies were provocable. During the periods of mutual restraint, the enemy soldiers took pains to show each other they could indeed retaliate if necessary. For example, German snipers showed their prowess to the British by aiming at spots on the walls of cottages and firing until they had cut a hole.

7.7 Summary

The fewness of the firms is the chief defining characteristic of oligopoly. The central problem of oligopoly focuses on the recognition of the firms' interdependence when they are few in number. Interdependence implies each firm is aware its actions affect the actions of its rivals. There are as many different models of oligopoly as there are assumptions about how firms behave when faced with this situation of interdependence. It is often suggested that the solution to the oligopoly problem is one of two extremes: either pure independent action, or pure collusion where all scope for independent action is extinguished. In reality both independent action and collusion are matters of degree and the great majority of cases fall somewhere between these two extremes. However, Chapters 7 and 8 are structured in accordance with this traditional dichotomy. Chapter 7 dealt mainly with models of independent action; in Chapter 8 the emphasis shifts towards collusion.

The Cournot duopoly model is the earliest theory of output determination in oligopoly. Cournot assumes the firms maximize their own profit subject to the constraint that the other firm's output is fixed at its current level; or, equivalently, both firms select their outputs so as to maximize profit subject to a zero conjectural variation assumption. Zero conjectural variation is equivalent to the behavioural assumption that leads to what is known in game theory terminology as a Nash equilibrium. Under this assumption, the Cournot duopolists achieve a market equilibrium that lies somewhere between the polar cases of monopoly and perfect competition. Other possible solutions to the model of output determination under duopoly include Chamberlin's model of joint profit maximization; Stackelberg's leader–follower model; and Stackelberg disequilibrium, in which both firms simultaneously behave aggressively, leading to overproduction and a price war.

In the Bertrand and Edgeworth models of price determination under duopoly, there is a zero conjectural variation assumption with respect to price. Both firms maximize their own profit subject to the constraint that the other firm's price is fixed at its current level. In Bertrand's model, the firms' output levels are unconstrained. Edgeworth considers the implications of a production capacity constraint. These models recognize the possibility that oligopolistic markets may deliver outcomes such as intense price competition (Bertrand) or perpetual instability with no determinate market equilibrium (Edgeworth). In contrast, the kinked demand curve model suggests price under oligopoly may become 'sticky'; while models of price leadership suggest that one way for oligopolists to deal with their situation of interdependence is to delegate responsibility for price-setting to a single dominant firm or price leader.

Game theory is an approach to decision-making in which two or more decision-makers or players face choices between a number of possible courses of action or actions at any stage of the game. The property of interdependence is the key defining characteristic of a game. Although game theory has many applications throughout the social and physical sciences, it is the treatment of interdependence that makes game theory relevant to an understanding of decision-making in oligopoly. Game theory shows how situations can arise in which players take decisions that appear rational from an individual perspective, but lead to outcomes that appear sub-optimal when assessed according to criteria reflecting the players' collective interest. However, games do not always generate unique solutions, since strategic decisions and outcomes are dependent on sociological and psychological as well as economic behavioural patterns and conventions. For this reason, game theory is often better at explaining observed patterns of behaviour after the event than it is at predicting behaviour in advance.

It should be apparent from Chapter 7 that oligopoly can generate many possible outcomes. It seems that almost anything can happen in oligopoly, from outright collusion to bitter price wars. As a result some economists (for example, Rothschild, 1947) have suggested that oligopoly theory is indeterminate. The consensus, however, is still largely in favour of developing better theory and better models.

> But it would be misleading to conclude that we cannot develop theories which predict oligopolistic conduct and performance with tolerable precision. A more constructive interpretation is this: to make workable predictions we need a theory much richer than the received theories of pure competition and pure monopoly, including variables irrelevant to those polar cases. In our quest for a realistic oligopoly theory we must acquire Professor Mason's 'ticket of admission to institutional economics', at the same time retaining the more sharply honed tools with which economic theorists have traditionally worked.
>
> *(Scherer, 1980, p. 152)*

Nevertheless, it is still the case that there is no clear and unambiguous solution to the central issue of interdependence. Firms and individuals may react in many different ways, and this is reflected in the large number of models examined in this chapter.

Discussion questions

1. Explain the relevance of the concepts of interdependence, conjectural variation, independent action and collusion to our understanding of oligopoly.

2. Does Cournot's original duopoly model have any relevance to our understanding of price and output determination under oligopoly?

3. Explain the role played by the assumption of zero conjectural variation in the derivation of the Cournot–Nash equilibrium.

4. Compare and contrast the Cournot, Chamberlin, Stackelberg and Edgeworth models of price and output determination for a duopoly.

5. Suggest examples from the real world that approximate to each of the classical theories of oligopoly.

6. With reference to Case Study 7.1, identify the characteristics of the Indian Airline industry that may have been instrumental in leading to a price war.

7. Quote real-world examples of oligopolistic firms that have benefited from a first-mover advantage.

8. With reference to Sweezy's model of the kinked demand curve, explain the reasons why we might expect price to be unresponsive to small variations in cost in the case of oligopoly. What are the main limitations of the kinked demand curve model?

9. Explain the distinction between dominant and barometric price leadership. How are price leaders chosen?

10. Explain the relationship between Cournot's solution to the problem of output determination in duopoly and the game theory concept of the Nash equilibrium.

11. In repeated games, it is often assumed that rivals are more likely to cooperate with one another than to compete. Under what conditions might competition be likely to break out in a repeated game?

12. With reference to Case Study 7.2, outline the contribution of the model of the prisoner's dilemma to our understanding of strategic behaviour.

Further reading

Álvarez, L.J., Dhyne, E., Hoeberichts, M.M., Kwapil, C., Bihan, H., Lunnemann, P., Martins, F., Sabbatini, R., Stahl, H., Vermeulen, P. and Vilmunen, J. (2006) Sticky prices in the euro area: a summary of new micro evidence, *Journal of the European Economic Association*, 4, 575–84.

Asch, P. and Seneca, J. (1976) Is collusion profitable?, *Review of Economics and Statisitics*, 58, 1–10.

Binmore, K. (2007) *Game Theory: A very short introduction*. Oxford: Oxford University Press.

Hall, R.L. and Hitch, C.J. (1939) Price theory and business behaviour, *Oxford Economic Papers*, 2, 12–45.

Haskel, J. and Scaramozzino, P. (1997) Do other firms matter in oligopolies? *Journal of Industrial Economics*, 45, 27–45.

Kashyap, A. (1995) Sticky prices: new evidence from retail catalogues, *Quarterly Journal of Economics*, 110, 245–74.

Machlup, F. (1952) *The Economics of Sellers' Competition*. Baltimore, MD: Johns Hopkins University Press.

Robinson, J. (1969) *The Economics of Imperfect Competition*, 2nd edition. London: Macmillan.

Roth, A.E. (1991) Game theory as a part of empirical economics, *Economic Journal*, 101, 107–14.

Stigler, G.J. (1978) The literature of economics: the case of the kinked oligopoly demand curve, *Economic Inquiry*, 16, 185–204. Reprinted as Reading 10 in Wagner, L. (ed.) *Readings in Applied Microeconomics*. Oxford: Oxford University Press (1981).

Oligopoly: collusive models

This chapter covers the following topics:

- the tendency for firms to collude in oligopoly
- forms of collusion
- collusive institutions
- economic models of collusion and cartel behaviour
- factors conducive to cartel formation
- influences on cartel stability

Key terms

Buyer concentration
Cartel
Explicit collusion
Forms of collusion
Joint venture
Seller concentration

Semi-collusion
State-sponsored collusion
Switching costs
Tacit collusion
Trade association

8.1 Introduction

Collusion between firms attracts much attention from the public, the press and government. One manifestation of collusion is price-fixing, which is easily recognized as having adverse consequences for consumer welfare.

> [P]eople of the same trade seldom meet together, even for merriment and diversion, but the conversation ends in a conspiracy against the public, or in some contrivance to raise prices.

> *(Smith, 1776, p. 128)*

However, price-fixing in order to boost profitability is not the only reason for firms to collude. For a group of oligopolists, collusion may represent a way of dealing with the uncertainties that would otherwise arise due to their situation of interdependence. Collusion may be simply a means of easing competitive pressure and creating a manageable operating environment through unified action, rather than necessarily a strategy for maximizing joint profits. A central theme of this chapter is that many collusive agreements are highly unstable. History is littered with examples of cartels that have eventually broken down, often because individual members have succumbed to the temptation to act selfishly in pursuit of private interests, rather than adhere to arrangements aimed at furthering the collective interest of group members.

The chapter begins in Section 8.2 with a discussion of the principal forms that collusion may take. Section 8.3 focuses on the institutions that help shape and determine collusion. To assume that all collusion is organized through the medium of cartels is an oversimplification. Alternative vehicles, including trade associations, joint ventures and state-sponsored collusion, are considered. Section 8.4 examines economic models of cartel behaviour. Some models are based on assumptions of joint profit maximization. Others focus on issues arising when cartel members bargain over the allocation of production quotas or the distribution of joint cartel profits. Section 8.5 considers factors other than joint profit maximization that may motivate firms to explore avenues for cooperation. Section 8.6 discusses aspects of market structure that are conducive to collusion and the formation of cartels. Finally, Section 8.7 examines factors that affect cartel stability or instability. As well as standard market structure variables, these include the effectiveness of mechanisms for monitoring compliance and punishing non-compliance on the part of cartel members, and some sociological and psychological factors that are sometimes ignored in the economics literature.

8.2 Collusive action and collusive forms

In the idealized free market, all firms are assumed to act independently in their desire to seek the highest economic return. However, as we saw previously (see Chapter 7), in oligopolies characterized by interdependence and uncertainty, firms may seek to avoid taking independent action. The uncertainties and risks associated with independent action provide a spur for the firms to participate in some form of collusive arrangement.

> Unlimited competition may be a fine thing from the point of view of the political philosopher speculating about the welfare of people, but surely it is a nuisance from the point of view of most businessmen. There may be a few hardy individualists among them who enjoy vigorous competition as long as they are stronger than their opponents,

can take pride in their success, and make enough money for comfort. But those that are losing ground and those that are losing money, or fear that they may lose, and all those who prefer an easy life to one of strain and strife – the majority, I dare say – regard unrestrained competition as an uncivilized way of doing business, unnecessarily costly of nervous energy and money, and disruptive of friendly relations with their fellow men.

(Machlup, 1952a, p. 434)

Collusion is best seen as a way of easing competitive pressure through unified action, rather than purely as a strategy to maximize joint profits. It has been claimed that the collusive solution to the oligopoly problem is often the most obvious solution.

Collusion eliminates the uncertainties of independent action and reduces the complexities of interdependence: firms no longer need to speculate about the likely reactions of rivals. Throughout the world, competition authorities are never short of work in investigating the sharper end of collusive practices. It therefore seems probable that the weaker forms of collusion are widespread. **Tacit collusion** is a term often used to describe a collusive outcome that requires no formal agreement and no direct communication between firms. Tacit collusion may develop through personal contacts, a group ethos, or live-and-let-live attitudes. Personal and social contacts among competitors lessen rivalrous attitudes: perhaps one does not undercut or poach customers from people with whom one socializes. Social groupings, whether by social class, ethnic origin or even religion, may help stabilize an otherwise potentially unstable collusive arrangement. This feeling of belonging can be strengthened by the existence of trade associations, trade journals, conferences, social activities and passive investments in rival firms (Gilo *et al.*, 2006). Tacit collusion may also develop through deliberate pricing strategies such as price leadership models discussed in Section 7.5, and low-price guarantees. Arbatskaya *et al.* (2006), by examining the retail price of tyres, test whether tacit collusion is facilitated by the existence of low-price guarantees as a way of discouraging rivals from cutting their prices. Where 'price-matching' guarantees exist, prices tend to be higher than where an alternative 'price-beating' guarantee is used. The former is interpreted as conducive to tacit collusion to keep prices relatively high.

Forms of collusion based on explicit agreements include verbal and written agreements. A widely quoted example of the former is the so-called Gary Dinners, hosted by Judge Gary, president of US Steel, between 1907 and 1911. Leaders of the steel industry met socially, but also used the opportunity to negotiate verbal agreements concerning pricing and production strategies. The colluders believed that they were operating within the law, as long as no formal agreement existed. Written agreements can be regarded as forms of **explicit collusion**. These may be characterized as formal contracts, stipulating rights and obligations, sanctions, fines, deposition of collateral and so on. Case Study 8.1 provides an example of a cartel.

Whiter than white?

FRANCE'S competition regulator, the Autorité de la concurrence, has fined three of the world's biggest consumer goods firms, Procter and Gamble (P&G), Henkel and Colgate-Palmolive, €361 million for colluding to fix the price of laundry powder, tablets and liquids in France between 1997 and 2004. A fourth, Unilever received immunity for coming forward first. This follows the European Commission's decision in April to fine P&G and Unilever €315.2 million for a similar but apparently unrelated pan-European detergent cartel that operated between 2002 and 2005. In that case Henkel had received immunity.

There is some fantastic detail in the 177 page report on the French cartel. The executives involved went to elaborate lengths to cloak their plans (both from their bosses and the regulators) to fix the prices charged to supermarkets. Each of the companies had a code name: 'Pierre' for P&G, 'Laurence' for Unilever, 'Hugues' for Henkel and 'Christian' for Colgate-Palmolive. The conspirators met in suburban Paris hotels for meetings termed 'store checks'.

But the report also illustrates how difficult it was to maintain cooperation. Executives had been meeting in some form since the 1980s to share price information, but in the early 1990s a price war broke out. Following this, a formal cartel was contrived in 1996 and stricter controls were implemented. Special offers were banned and cost savings were not to be passed on. In the end, however, the scheme unravelled: while fixing prices was easy, monitoring special offers proved difficult. In 2004 Unilever launched a 10% discount that proved terminal. A cascade of deals and special offers from the others followed. An anonymous manager reminisces in the report about chaotic meetings where recriminations flew about.

How the two cartels are connected is equally interesting – and will be the subject of significant legal wrangling in a Paris court for months to come. Henkel contends the French case is 'directly linked' to the European Commission case in which the firm is protected. On the surface the two cartels look similar: they involve the same product. But both regulators argue that that the European cartel emerged out of an agreement not to cut prices when reducing packaging sizes (under the auspice of an environmental initiative called 'AISE'). This, they say, is entirely unrelated to the longer running and more complex scheme the Paris managers had cooked up.

The chain of events leading to the uncovering of the cartels is also notable, in particular because it determined why Henkel received immunity in one case and Unilever in the other. In 2006 the French economy ministry inspected Unilever under the guise of another investigation in a market 'close to detergents'. Around the same time (though it is unclear which came first) a Unilever employee, possibly spooked by the raid, came forward with a 283-page document he had stashed at home detailing the cartel. Yet it was not before 4th March 2008 that Unilever did submit a leniency application to the French competition authority, which implies full subsequent cooperation.

Leniency regimes, which have been widely adopted around the world, aim not only to destabilise cartels, but also to reduce investigation and legal costs. The first member to come forward receives full immunity from fines and prosecution. Subsequent cooperation from other members can warrant discounts on fines.

Shortly after, on the 28th April 2008, Henkel came forward to apply for clemency to the French. And a couple of weeks later, on 13th May 2008, the firm submitted an immunity application to Brussels (following an internal audit) that triggered an investigation into the separate pan-European cartel. Later P&G came forward to cooperate with the Commission and received a 50% discount. Unilever however did not submit a leniency application until 2nd October 2009. It is unclear why it held out for so long while cooperating with the French regulator from the beginning.

'It is a rather odd situation to have a French case and an EU case covering the same companies, in overlapping years, in the same country whether or not they relate to the same cartel,' said one competition lawyer. It is odder still to have a company fully cooperating with one investigation and holding out in another.

In a further twist, Henkel has complained that the European commission refused to hand over information to the French competition authority that could have been helpful to the firm in the French case. Others note that claims of any disadvantage are almost certainly puffed up for the benefit of an appeal against this week's fine.

The European Commission had the power to solely investigate both cases but this case is part of a broader trend to let individual countries take charge. This may end up complicating matters where there is any European dimension. It is certainly bad for companies that face the legal costs of separate inquiries and doubts regarding their universal immunity if they come forward. Those doubts may mean fewer cartels are uncovered in the future.

Source: © The Economist Newspaper Limited, London, 11 December 2011.

8.3   Collusive institutions

This section examines various institutions that have been set up to promote and organize cooperation between producers. These include **cartels**, **trade associations**, **joint ventures**, **semi-collusion** and **state-sponsored collusion**.

Cartels

The term **cartel** derives from the German word *Kartelle* meaning a producers' association. Perhaps the simplest and most concise definition is suggested by Liefmann (1932), who views cartels as associations with monopolistic aims. The notion of monopolistic intent has caused much controversy. The term monopoly has emotional connotations, which may blur a reasonable description of collective action. The monopolistic intent of cartels may be seen simply as a corollary of any restrictions imposed upon unfettered competition (Piotrowski, 1932).

Cartels are associations of independent firms in the same industry that impose restraint upon competition. Cartels are often associated with actions taken by small groups of firms determined to exploit their market power to the full; alternatively, firms join cartels mainly for reasons of self-defence or protection (Hunter, 1954). Agreements tend, on the whole, to impede entry or the development of new products that might threaten the profitability or survival of incumbent firms. Price-fixing seems only to be of secondary importance, usually as a means to support the less efficient members. Profits are not spectacularly higher than one would suppose (Fog, 1956; Asch and Seneca, 1976).

Some observers have tried to classify types of cartel. For example, OECD (1965) identifies no fewer than seven types: price cartel, quota cartel, allocation cartel, standardization agreement, specialization agreement, costing agreement and rebate agreement. Wilcox (1960) identifies four main categories according to the methods employed: cartels that control the conditions surrounding a sale; cartels that control costs, prices and profit margins; cartels that allocate territories or customers; and cartels that award members fixed shares in the industry's total productive capacity. Many cartels fall under more than one of these headings.

Trade associations

A cartel is an organization formed by firms in an oligopoly in an attempt to foster cooperation. Many cartels seek to enhance the market power of a group of producers through combined action. There is a fine dividing line between a cartel and a **trade association**. Trade associations that attempt to improve the economic situation of their members do not necessarily require market power in order to achieve their aims.

> Trade associations can be enormously helpful to their memberships. They can expand and upgrade education and consumer information programs, launch new research and development programs, encourage ethical business practices and communicate the viewpoint of business in the political forum.
>
> *(Clanton, 1977, p. 307)*

One of the chief functions of a trade association is to provide members with industry data on sales, productive capacity, employment, creditworthiness of customers, quality of products and innovation. They also promote activities intended to reduce inefficiency and promote better relations with customers, trade unions and government. To achieve this goal they publish trade journals, stimulate cooperative research programmes, instigate market research surveys, define trade terms and recruit lobbyists.

The dividing line between legitimate and collusive action is open to interpretation. For example, moves to standardize output could be interpreted either as a legitimate policy to improve product quality, or an illegitimate vehicle for price-fixing by reducing the ability of firms to price differentially. The popularity of price reporting systems or open price associations, through which members inform each other, as well as outsiders, of current and future product prices, reached a peak in the US in the early years of the twentieth century through the formation of open price associations, defined as follows:

> an organization which provides a medium for the exchange of business information among members of a given industry whereby they may arrive at an intimate acquaintance with competitive conditions as they exist among themselves and in the whole industry.

(Nelson, 1922, p. 9)

Nelson (1922) sees these organizations as distinct from other trade associations, characterized by fairly loose structures and more general aims. Nelson quotes the case of the American Hardwood Manufacturers' Association, which was quite open in its price deliberations, inviting customers, the press and any other interested parties to its meetings. Price reporting schemes or open price associations might be justified on the grounds that they promote fair competition: information is an essential lubricant for competitive markets. But on the other hand, a price-reporting agreement could simply provide a form of cover for price-fixing.

If a price-reporting scheme is intended to promote competition, it should be neither doctored, nor prevented from being disclosed to all parties including buyers. Comments or suggestions as to likely future pricing policy should not accompany such reports, which should be neutral and informative. In practice, it is doubtful whether trade associations can always divorce themselves from self-interest in this manner. Mund and Wolf (1971) suggest agreements can be tolerated if they are limited to closed transactions. Reported prices should be actual prices. To report quoted prices could increase pressure from the more dominant or militant members to standardize all prices. If waiting periods are stipulated (so each member undertakes to maintain the price for a given period), open price agreements are tantamount to price-fixing (Machlup, 1952b). A waiting period allows firms to set a price, confident in the knowledge that rivals will not immediately reduce their prices. Marshall *et al.* (2007) examine price announcement effects in the vitamin industry during periods when a cartel operated and at other times when there was no cartel. When the cartel operated there was typically a time-lag between the public announcement and the implementation of a price change, but in the absence of the cartel there was typically no delay.

In general, the impact of trade associations on competition is uncertain. If a trade association does not itself help foster collusion, it might provide a convenient stepping-stone towards full-blown collusion, perhaps by gathering, processing and disseminating the information that subsequently forms the basis of an agreement. However, any advantages stemming from the circulation of information on prices may be undermined by the use of price data to reinforce and police collusion. It is difficult to generalize, and a case-by-case approach is required to establish the direction taken by any particular trade association.

Joint ventures, semi-collusion and state-sponsored collusion

A **joint venture** is an association between two or more otherwise competing firms. Joint ventures might take the form of a consortium or a syndicate, although the latter is generally limited to the fields of banking and insurance. Consortia are usually established when firms undertake speculative activities, for which the risk is sufficiently high to discourage individual involvement. In so far as joint ventures prevent or distort competition by coalescing the interests of several firms, they are similar to cartels. In some cases, however, joint ventures may stimulate innovation, by enabling projects to proceed that would not otherwise be feasible. Alternatively, joint ventures may enable a group of new firms to band together and overcome entry barriers.

Joint ventures have often been sponsored by governments and international bodies. '[European] Community action must . . . create an environment or conditions likely to favour the development of cooperation between undertakings' (European Commission, 1985, p. 34). In a later report, however, the European Commission (1997a) is concerned that this type of cooperation could inhibit competition. It identifies three main reasons why firms are keen to form joint ventures: to combine their resources in such a way as to increase efficiency; to enter a new market; and to develop joint research and development programmes. Only the latter motive appears justified on efficiency grounds. Not all joint ventures result in cooperation. Partnerships such as joint ventures and strategic alliances may encounter difficulties when managers behave non-cooperatively, so as to advance the private interests of their own firms (Minehart and Neeman, 1999). The issue is how best to design contracts that encourage managers to maximize joint (partnership) profits.

Semi-collusion occurs in cases where it is difficult to formulate specific agreements covering all aspects of the firms' behaviour. For example, agreements covering research and development, advertising and capital investment strategies may not be possible, because it is too difficult to monitor compliance. Accordingly, it has been suggested that firms may opt to collude in some activities and compete in others. Matsui (1989) argues that if collusion takes place in the product market, but there is competition in other areas of activity, firms may be worse off and consumers better off. In a study of Japanese cartels in the 1960s, Matsui argues that firms accumulated excess capacity in the belief that cartel quotas would be based on capacity. The combination of cartelization and excess capacity led to increased output and reduced profits. Similar conclusions are reached by Steen and Sørgard (1999) and Roller and Steen (2006), with reference to the Norwegian cement industry. However, Brod and Shivakumar (1999) show that where the non-production (competitive) activity is research and development, the welfare effects might be either positive or negative.

The discussion of cartels has concentrated on private, voluntary organizations that are free of government control or intervention. **State-sponsored collusion** is a further variation. Governments may either meet the demands of a group of producers, or they may impose cartelization on reluctant firms. The justification might be to promote rationalization, as in Britain and Germany in the 1930s, or to encourage 'orderly marketing': the objective behind the UK's Agricultural Marketing Acts of 1931 and 1933.

Profit-maximizing models of price and output determination for a cartel

Suppose all of the firms in an industry are members of a centralized cartel, which has complete control over price and output decisions. It is assumed that each firm produces an identical product. However, the firms' cost functions need not necessarily be identical. Finally, it is assumed that entry is successfully deterred. The maximization of the cartel members' combined profit is essentially a problem of joint profit maximization, with the cartel firms seeking to act collectively as if they were a single monopolist.

Figure 8.1 shows a three-firm model. The cost functions of firms A, B and D are shown in the first three diagrams, reading from left to right. The industry marginal cost function shown in the right-hand-side diagram is obtained by summing the three firms' marginal cost functions horizontally. Joint profit maximization is achieved by choosing the industry output at which marginal revenue derived from the industry average revenue function *equals* the industry's marginal cost. This output level is Q_M, and the corresponding price is P_M. The individual production quotas of firms A, B and D are q_A, q_B and q_D, and by construction $Q_M = q_A + q_B + q_D$. The total cost of producing Q_M is minimized by allocating quotas in such a way that the marginal costs of each firm, when producing its own quota, are the same (Patinkin, 1947). Suppose the quotas were such that the cost to firm D of producing its last unit of output was higher than the cost to firm A of producing its last unit of output. Then it would be profitable to reallocate some of firm D's quota to firm A. This would be true until the marginal costs are brought into equality. It can be seen from Figure 8.1 that the least efficient producer with the steepest marginal cost function, firm D, is assigned a smaller quota than the more efficient producers, firms A and B.

A second joint profit-maximizing model examines the case where an industry consists of two groups of firms: a group that forms a cartel, and a group of non-cartel firms. The total number of firms is N, and the number of firms that form the cartel is K; therefore there are $N - K$ non-cartel firms. There are assumed to be large numbers of small firms in both groups. In this model, it is assumed that all firms produce an identical product, all firms have identical cost functions and entry is successfully deterred. Finally, price-taking behaviour on the part of

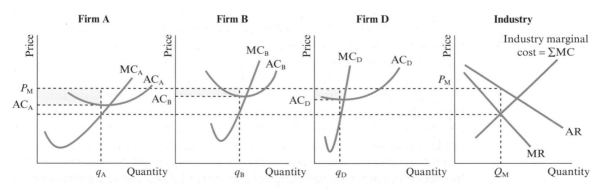

Figure 8.1 Joint profit maximization in a three-firm cartel

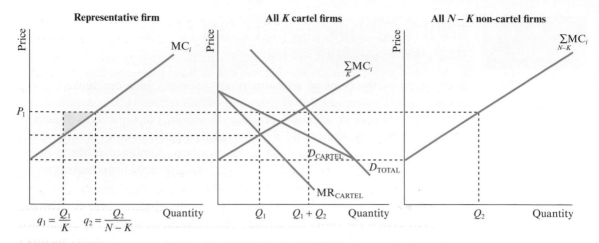

Figure 8.2 Equilibrium with K cartel firms and $N - K$ non-cartel firms

the non-cartel firms is assumed. The model is similar to the dominant firm price leadership model that was introduced in Section 7.5.

The diagram on the right-hand-side of Figure 8.2 shows the non-cartel firms' collective marginal cost function, obtained by summing the non-cartel firms' individual marginal cost functions horizontally. Because the non-cartel firms are price-takers, their collective marginal cost function can be interpreted as their supply function. The middle diagram shows the cartel firms' collective marginal cost function, also obtained by summing their individual marginal cost functions horizontally. The middle diagram also shows the residual demand function for the cartel firms, obtained by subtracting the non-cartel firms' total supply at each price from the industry demand function. The cartel firms maximize their joint profit by choosing the output level Q_1, at which the residual marginal revenue *equals* the cartel firms' collective marginal cost. The cartel firms' output decision also determines the industry price, P_1, obtained from the cartel firms' residual demand function at Q_1. Returning to the right-hand-side diagram, the non-cartel firms' total output when the price is P_1 is Q_2. Total industry output is $Q_1 + Q_2$, which by construction *equals* the industry demand when the price is P_1.

Finally, the diagram on the left-hand-side of Figure 8.2 compares the outputs and profits of an individual cartel firm and a non-cartel firm. These can be drawn on the same diagram because it is assumed that both firms have identical cost functions. As shown in the middle diagram, for the cartel firm the joint profit-maximizing price of P_1 exceeds marginal cost. Each individual cartel firm produces $q_1 = Q_1/K$ units of output. Each non-cartel firm is a price-taker, and produces $q_2 = Q_2/(N - K)$ units of output, at which price *equals* marginal cost. This means the non-cartel firm produces more output than the cartel firm. The non-cartel firm also earns a higher profit than the cartel firm. In the diagram on the left-hand-side of Figure 8.2, the difference in profit is represented by the shaded area between P_1 and MC_i over the output range q_1 to q_2.

This comparison between the profits of the cartel and non-cartel firms has important implications for the theory of cartels. In Figure 8.2, the cartel firm deliberately reduces its output in order to raise price and earn a higher profit. However, the non-cartel firm also benefits from the increased price, but without bearing any burden in the form of profit foregone as a result of producing a reduced output. Essentially, there is a free-rider problem. The free-riding non-cartel firms earn higher profits than the cartel firms, thanks entirely to the sacrifices made by the latter.

This situation may have serious implications for the viability or the stability of the cartel. Why should any firm agree to join the cartel if, by doing so, it earns a lower profit than it would earn by remaining outside? Clearly, it is better to let others bear the burden of reducing their outputs and, meanwhile, sit back and enjoy the benefit of the increased price. Of course, the difficulty is that if all potential cartel members think in this way, the cartel may never be formed. Moreover, even if the cartel has already been formed, its stability is threatened by the possibility of defection or cheating. In Figure 8.2, each cartel member knows that by increasing its output from q_1 to q_2, it can increase its profit by an amount represented by the shaded area. If the number of cartel members is large and only one firm defects, the effect of this additional ouput on the profits of the remaining loyal cartel members might be quite small. The remaining cartel members may be prepared to tolerate the situation, since the costs of disciplining the recalcitrant firm might exceed the profits that would be recouped. However, it is possible that more than one firm could defect, in which case the cartel could quickly disintegrate. If all cartel members simultaneously increase their outputs, the market ends up at the competitive price and output, with all firms earning only a normal profit.

> And this is the first difficulty of forming a cartel. Every firm would prefer to be the outsider, and yet if enough stay outside, the cartel becomes futile: a large group of free riders will find that the streetcar won't run.
>
> *(Stigler, 1966, p. 233)*

D'Aspremont *et al.* (1983) discuss an important qualification to these conclusions concerning the free-rider problem and cartel instability. In the model shown in Figure 8.2, suppose N, the number of firms, is small rather than large (see also Donsimoni *et al.*, 1986). In this case, any decision by a cartel firm to break the cartel agreement has a non-negligible effect on the profits of both the cartel firms that remain loyal and the non-cartel firms. In the model shown in Figure 8.2, a decision by one cartel firm to withdraw from the cartel and produce q_2 rather than q_1, would shift the non-cartel supply function to the right and the cartel residual demand and marginal revenue functions to the left. This would reduce the equilibrium price, and reduce the profits of both the cartel and the non-cartel firms. Before any defection takes place, the profit of a non-cartel firm always exceeds the profit of a cartel firm. However, this does not rule out the possibility that the post-defection profit of the cartel firm that defects is less than its pre-defection profit when it was still part of the cartel.

Accordingly, for a firm considering leaving the cartel or defecting, the relevant comparison is not between the current profits of a cartel firm and a non-cartel firm. Instead, the relevant comparison is between the current profit of a cartel firm and the adjusted (post-defection) profit of a non-cartel firm. There are two conditions for the stability of the cartel. First, there is internal stability if no cartel member can increase its profit by leaving the cartel; and second, there is external stability if no non-cartel firm can increase its profit by joining the cartel. D'Aspremont *et al.* (1983) show that a cartel that is both internally and externally stable can always be achieved if the number of firms is finite. A corollary is that the greater the number of firms in the industry, the smaller the effect of any one firm's actions on price and profits, and the greater the likelihood that any cartel agreement will turn out to be unstable.

Apart from the free-rider problem and cartel instability, two remaining difficulties may be encountered in forming a cartel (Stigler, 1966). The first, which also derives from the free-rider problem, is that of potential or actual entry. If entry is not successfully deterred, and outside firms are attracted by the relatively high cartel price, industry output increases and price falls, destroying the cartel. The cartel may have to modify its pricing policy in order to exclude potential entrants; or alternatively, seek some form of accommodation with actual entrants (Patinkin, 1947).

The other difficulty is administrative: how should the output quotas be determined and profits divided? In theory, and as shown in Figure 8.1, the quotas should be determined so as to ensure the marginal costs of all cartel firms are equal. However, this implies that each firm earns a different profit. Low-profit firms might not be willing to accept such an outcome. One solution might be to introduce a system of side-payments to compensate low-profit earners. This solution implies complex negotiations, monitoring and sanctions for non-compliance. The administrative costs might outweigh the benefits. Alternatively, quotas could be set at sub-optimal levels (different from those necessary to maximize joint profits) in order to make mutual compliance more likely. For example, quotas might be fixed as a percentage of each firm's capacity, or quotas might be fixed as a percentage of pre-cartel output levels. This type of arrangement might also lead to instability. Firms might invest unnecessarily in spare capacity, or they might increase their outputs unnecessarily shortly before the agreement takes effect, in order to obtain a larger quota.

8.5 Other motives for collusion

Section 8.4 shows that the higher profits resulting from the exercise of near-monopoly power by a cartel can be described by traditional microeconomic models of the firm. This section examines a number of other motives for collusion in general, and for the formation of cartels specifically.

Risk management and the enhancement of security

In some cases, the reduction of risk may be the principal motive for collusion. Some of the earliest writers emphasize this point. '[I]t is the pressure of risk which first arouses producers to the possibilities of another method of organization'

(MacGregor, 1906, p. 46). The nature of risk is twofold. First, risk arises from changes in consumer tastes.

> No method of industrial organization will standardize the consumer. His demand for even such routine goods as food and clothing changes both quantitatively and qualitatively by accidents of time, place and value of money. Even a whole industry must face these changes, and provide whatever defences may lessen their influence.
>
> *(MacGregor, 1906, p. 51)*

Second, risk results directly from competition between producers. In the absence of any central control, firms may tend to overproduce, driving price below average cost.

> The market may be able to bear the increment of supply caused by himself [the firm]; but not an equivalent increment from all his rivals, if they retaliate by his own means, or if even they communicate panic to each other. This is the road which leads to crises.
>
> *(MacGregor, 1906, p. 52)*

The firm might attempt to escape from these risks by developing market power independently through product differentiation, product innovation or vertical integration (strategies that are explored in subsequent chapters of the book). However, all such strategies are costly and uncertain. Collusion represents an alternative method for reducing risk.

Liefmann (1932) sees the development of collusion as resulting from the increased divergence between what he calls the 'risk of capital' and the 'profit of capital'. Mass-production technology raises the risk to entrepreneurs' fixed capital, if they are unable to keep their plants in continuous operation. Entrepreneurs also risk their working capital if they are unable to find sufficient customers for their finished goods. Due to these pressures, entrepreneurs had experienced a steady erosion of profit. This divergence reached a critical point when the capital risks could no longer be offset by profit. However, neither the pre-war nor the more recent evidence necessarily supports this view. Industries prone to rigorous competition are not always made up of sickly firms, limping their way towards collusive agreements. '[C]laims that competition has cut-throat and destructive propensities, and hence that cartelization [collusion] is warranted, deserve to be taken with several grains of salt' (Scherer and Ross, 1990, p. 305).

Another possible source of risk and uncertainty is a firm's reliance on large orders that are placed infrequently (Scherer and Ross, 1990). Such orders may make tacit collusion more difficult, and force firms to consider explicit collusion. Any price reduction from some tacitly agreed norm involves a cost in the form of lower future profits, owing to retaliation from rival firms. This cost is independent of the size of the order, but the short-term gain depends on the order size. Undercutting is more likely if orders are large and irregular than if they are small and regular. Furthermore, firms that operate with short time horizons are likely to accept the immediate gain from a price reduction and be unconcerned about future retaliation. Firms with large overheads or excess capacity may also be tempted to break ranks and breach a tacit price agreement. In the US cast-iron pipe, electrical equipment and antibiotics industries, large and infrequent orders led to the formation of 'bidding cartels to restrain industry members' competitive zeal' (Scherer and Ross, 1990, p. 307).

The degree of collusion attributable to risk in an industry is difficult to measure. High risk may bring about collusion, but the intended result of collusion is the reduction of risk. Ambiguity as to the direction of causation is inevitable. Asch and Seneca (1975) measure risk as the standard deviation of the residuals from a time trend fitted to each firm's time-series profit data, but find little evidence of causation in either direction.

An alternative view is that the firm attaches importance to its relative position when all producers in the industry are ranked in descending order of their market shares. Any move towards the guarantee of position through collusion is attractive. Perfect competition and monopoly, as polar cases, are not concerned with positioning. In contrast, an oligopolist may be acutely aware of its own market share, which may define its status within the industry. The oligopolist may wish to increase its market share, or at least ensure that its market share is not eroded. Maintaining or improving position is therefore a central objective in the oligopolist's strategic decision-making.

Exchange of information

Many of the factors that motivate collusion are associated with uncertainty. Accordingly, such concerns might be reduced by the provision of useful market information, which may itself be a powerful motive for collusion. O'Brien and Swann (1969) develop a theory of information exchange. All firms require information on which to base their decisions. The importance of information depends on the degree of interdependence, or on the extent to which firms are vulnerable to damage by the actions of rivals. Firms are most vulnerable when undertaking investment, which involves long-term, and possibly irreversible, financial commitments. It may be in the interests of all firms that each firm invests wisely, since miscalculations that create excess capacity may lead to price-cutting or other panic measures, threatening industry stability.

The type of information required, its timing (pre- or post-notification) and the means of communication (oral or written; trade gossip or more formal, detailed memoranda) depend on the required degree of stability. Regular, strict pre-notification agreements, identifying individual parties and their terms of sale, produce greater uniformity and stability than information that is supplied informally or intermittently. Information exchange reduces firms' vulnerability and increases industry cohesion, enabling firms to react more consistently and efficiently when some potentially destabilizing event occurs. Firms become more sensitive to one another and more aware of their positioning in terms of market share. By itself, sharing information may drive firms towards more cooperative forms of behaviour. Firms that cooperate in this manner may not wish to threaten industry stability with overtly competitive behaviour.

Unsatisfactory performance

Firms are naturally concerned with profitability. Years of poor profitability, perhaps caused by intense competition and frequent price-cutting, may eventually prompt firms to explore the possibility of establishing an accommodation with rivals. This type of pressure forced the American Plumbing Fixtures Manufacturers to develop price-fixing agreements in the 1960s. The price conspiracy was rationalized by the executives of the 15 companies involved as not '"gouging" the public, just seeking an adequate profit' (*Fortune*, 1969, p. 96). Profits may also be low as a result of depressed demand conditions for a particular product or industry. The frequently quoted price agreements in the American bleachers, electrical equipment and pipe industries all followed periods of decline and poor performance at industry level. 'Certain economic conditions – depressions, recessions, or downward movements in industry demand – provide both a favourable climate and a powerful incentive for conspiracy' (Erickson, 1969, p. 83).

Asch and Seneca (1976) estimate the effect of collusion on the profitability of US manufacturing corporations between 1958 and 1967. They also reverse the causation, to examine the effect of profitability on the level of collusion. They find an inverse relationship between the level of collusion and profitability. This is consistent with the hypothesis that unsatisfactory profits encourage collusion. However, an alternative explanation is that their sample was largely made up of collusion-prone firms. Since the data were based on unsuccessful examples of collusion, poor collusive performance was likely to be discovered. The bleacher manufacturers earned low profits during the Second World War, owing to their inability to obtain steel and other materials. Collusive price and tendering agreements could not resolve the underlying problem of supply shortages. Consequently, these agreements were unstable.

A firm's growth record can also reflect its profitability. Asch and Seneca (1975) suggest that growth and profits can be correlated, and growth might be included among the factors encouraging firms to collude. Firms in a declining industry are perhaps more likely to collude in an attempt to restore profitability to some historical level. Declining industries may also see the breakdown of orderly marketing, or other forms of tacit collusion, as firms attempt to undercut rivals in a desperate bid to maintain their own profitability. This sudden indiscipline may encourage firms to search for more explicit or specific **forms of collusion**.

8.6　Factors conducive to cartel formation

This section identifies factors that influence whether the firms in an industry are likely to be able to succeed in forming a cartel. These include the degree of **seller concentration** and the number of firms in the industry, the degree of similarity in the firms' cost structures, product characteristics and market shares, and the extent to which firms are vertically integrated. Finally, under a transaction costs approach to the theory of the firm, the ease with which firms are able to collude depends primarily on the nature of the transaction costs incurred in negotiating and policing a collusive agreement.

Seller concentration and the number of firms

A common hypothesis is that firms find it easier to collude in industries with small numbers of firms, or high levels of concentration. This hypothesis is based on theories of group and coalition behaviour which suggest that, as numbers increase, the unanimity of goals diminishes. With a dilution of unanimity, the group incurs heavier bargaining, monitoring and enforcement (or transaction) costs.

Phillips (1962) and Scherer and Ross (1990) provide a theory of the effect of numbers on the extent of collusion. First, as the number of firms increases, the contribution of each firm to total output decreases, and the firms become more likely to ignore their interdependence. Second, as the number of firms increases, there is more temptation for a rogue firm to undercut the agreed price, as it perceives a low risk of detection. Finally, since firms often have different views as to the optimal cartel policy, communication and negotiation between firms is required to reconcile differences. Coordination becomes more difficult as numbers increase. In the absence of a central agency or trade association, the number of channels of communication is $N(N - 1)/2$. One channel will suffice for two firms, but six are required for four firms, and 15 for six firms. A breakdown in any one channel may precipitate retaliation, and the resulting disruption may extend far beyond the two parties originally responsible.

The importance of concentration and the number of firms seems to be confirmed by the empirical evidence. Levenstein and Suslow's (2006) survey indicates that there is widespread empirical evidence of an association between high concentration and the extent of collusion. However, a difficulty that arises with any empirical study is that the instances of collusion that are identified may be the 'inefficient' ones, which are caught and prosecuted. Other cases may remain undetected, either by the antitrust authorities or by researchers. High concentration indicates that the fringe of non-colluding firms is relatively small, and may be tolerated. If the non-colluding fringe makes serious inroads into the cartel members' market shares, however, defensive strategies such as price-cutting may be instigated. In the case of Laker Airways, an early low-cost airline which failed in 1982, the liquidator alleged (and for the most part was subsequently vindicated by the US courts) that the major airlines (British Airways, Lufthansa, Swissair, Pan Am and TWA) had conspired to drive Laker out of business by cutting fares.

If a sizeable fringe of firms cannot be induced to join a cartel, there is little chance of success in maximizing joint profits. Armentano (1975) finds that price-fixing conspiracies in the electrical equipment industry were always threatened by a fringe of low-quality producers, which regularly undercut the nationally agreed price. There are many cases in which high seller concentration did not lead to collusion, or there was no significant relationship between the number of firms and the level of collusion (Asch and Seneca, 1975; Dick, 1996; Symeonides, 2003). Although very high concentration might lead to tacit collusion, at slightly lower levels of concentration a more explicit form of collusion is required as numbers increase. An industry comprising only three or four firms may be able to organize itself informally, but if new firms enter, tacit collusion may no longer suffice. Fraas and Greer (1977) suggest that in the polar case of two firms with an identical product, explicit collusion is possible but hardly necessary. At the opposite extreme, with many firms selling differentiated products, explicit collusion is desirable (for joint profit maximization) but hard to achieve. Explicit collusion is most likely in intermediate cases.

Similar cost functions

Firms with similar cost structures find it easier to collude than those with pronounced differences in costs. A firm faced with an average cost function that decreases as output increases may be reluctant to restrict its output as a condition of cartel membership. In the absence of side-payments to offset the opportunity cost incurred by membership, the firm may be reluctant to join the cartel in the first place. Furthermore, a requirement to restrict output might run counter to a smaller firm's ambition to eventually overtake the larger producers. Obviously, this can only be achieved by growth in sales, and not by moves to restrict sales (Rothschild, 1999). If quotas are determined by the cartel on the basis of equal percentage reductions from prior competitive output levels, unequal shares of cartel profits will accrue to firms with different marginal cost functions. The formation of the uranium cartel in 1980 rested on recognition that there was a wide variety of deposits, of different depths and thicknesses, and consequently widely differing marginal costs (Rothwell, 1980). Quotas, devised to ensure an equitable distribution of cartel profits, were an important precondition for the formation of a cartel.

Similar market shares

MacGregor (1906) suggests that if most of the firms in an industry are similar in size, the likelihood of successful collusion is enhanced. Other symmetries conducive to collusion might include similar patterns of firm evolution, similar technologies, similar product ranges and similar productive capacities. If market shares are symmetric, it is possible that the large firms have already eliminated the smaller firms through competition. Asymmetric market shares, on the other hand, are likely to be associated with a divergence of views between the large and the small firms (Schmalensee, 1987; Harrington, 1989, 1991). Small firms may be reluctant to adopt quotas based on existing market shares, while large firms may collude with each other to enhance their (collective) dominance. Compte *et al.* (2002) consider a situation in which colluding firms have similar costs and produce similar goods, but have different capacities. Firms with spare capacity are tempted to defect from a price-fixing agreement, while firms with limited capacity are unable to issue credible threats to punish defectors.

However, asymmetry in market shares could enhance the ability of a few large firms to initiate and enforce a profitable agreement by means of price leadership (see also Section 7.5). Phillips (1962) suggests that unequal market shares can help create a degree of stability and order. Price leaders have the authority to enforce cooperative behaviour, while followers are aware that as higher-cost producers, they can easily be punished by the leaders through price cuts. Vertically integrated leaders can also punish the followers by impeding their access to inputs or markets.

Similar products

Similar products (or a lack of product differentiation) may be another factor conducive to successful collusion. Firms selling similar goods need only focus on a narrow range of pricing decisions. If many characteristics contribute to (either real or perceived) product differences, it becomes difficult to achieve agreement over price.

Switching costs are costs incurred when a buyer switches between suppliers, but not incurred when remaining with the original supplier. Effectively, switching costs make similar products more heterogeneous, as a buyer is no longer indifferent between the two suppliers. Switching costs include transaction costs incurred when changing a bank or internet service provider; compatibility costs incurred when changing products that are linked to one another, such as Microsoft Windows and Office; and the learning costs incurred in using a new product or service (Klemperer, 1995). Switching costs reduce the incentive for producers to join or adhere to cartel agreements (NERA, 2003).

Even similar products may be supplied under varied conditions and specifications. For example, while a product such as steel springs for upholstery seems to be fairly homogeneous, the price list used by the Spring and Interior Springing Association (Office of Fair Trading Register, Agreement 1132) records over 400 separate prices, according to height, thickness of spring, alloys used, status of buyer and so on (Lipczynski, 1994). Negotiating, monitoring and renewing such an array of prices is inevitably a complex task. Furthermore, if product characteristics are subject to change over time, perhaps due to technological progress or evolving consumer tastes, a price agreement is more difficult to negotiate and sustain.

Measuring the relationship between the degree of product differentiation and the level of collusion is a difficult task. Asch and Seneca (1975) distinguish between producer and consumer goods industries, on the grounds that the former are more homogeneous than the latter. The expectation is that collusion is more likely in producer goods industries. Symeonides (1999) suggests product differentiation achieved through investment in advertising or research and development tends to frustrate collusion, since low-quality producers are less likely to collude with high-quality producers.

Kantzenbach *et al.* (1995) modify the general conclusion that product differentiation inhibits successful collusion. High product differentiation may have implications primarily for the form of collusion, rather than the ability to conclude an agreement at all. Firms might abandon price-fixing, but still segment the market by product type or geography. In this case successful collusion is possible, because in segmented markets price elasticity of demand tends to be low, and punishment is not costly if price cuts are required in only a few market segments (Davidson, 1983; Ross, 1992).

Vertical integration

A successful cartel requires member firms to be reassured that fellow members are abiding by the terms of the agreement. Effective monitoring is important. If one member is vertically integrated downstream, perhaps with ownership of retail outlets, it may be able to undercut the cartel price by reducing its transfer price to its own retailers. Unless other cartel members are fully aware of the true cost structure of the retail business, they may be unaware that the cartel agreement is being undermined.

Transaction costs and collusion

Under Williamson's (1975) transaction costs approach to the theory of the firm (see also Box 1.1 and Section 5.3), collusion is viewed primarily as a problem of contracting. Collusive agreements may or may not be lawful, but in either case participants cannot rely on the courts to enforce agreements. Therefore firms must develop their own armoury to ensure compliance and punish non-compliant behaviour. The ease with which collusion can be established and sustained through contractual arrangements depends on a number of factors:

- *The ability to specify contractual relations correctly*. It is difficult to formulate a comprehensive statement of obligations and responsibilities. Any such statement requires information on the production costs of each firm, the nature of the product, the permitted levels of expenditure on research and development or innovation, as well as the 'interaction effects between the decision variables within and between firms' (Williamson, 1975, p. 244). Not only is this information expensive to gather, interpret and transform into specific policies for each firm, but it is also necessary to formulate these policies for an unknown future context. If the contract is to be comprehensive, all future contingencies must be anticipated.

- *The extent to which agreement can be reached over joint gains*. Even if joint profit maximization can be specified contractually, a number of problems immediately arise. Joint profit maximization might require the reduction of some firms' output and the expansion of others. Those firms faced with demands to reduce their output may be reluctant to agree to, or tolerate, any reduction in their market share. These firms may fear that if the agreement were to break down, they would be left in a less powerful position than the position they occupied before the agreement.

- *Uncertainty*. The agreement is also subject to uncertainty. Firms must agree on how to adapt to changes in the economic environment. This may require costly renegotiation if the firms subsequently discover new opportunities to profit from such changes.

- *Monitoring*. Individual firms may not be able to detect fellow conspirators' price cuts. In Williamson's terminology, information is impacted, giving rise to opportunistic behaviour. Monitoring is necessary to detect and deter non-compliance with the cartel arrgement. Monitoring and policing an agreement are more complex in cases where there are non-price forms of competition.

■ *Penalties*. Successful collusion must eventually rest on the availability of effective sanctions against firms that fail to comply with the terms of the agreement. In the absence of legal protection, the cartel must impose its own penalties through the market. For example, cartel members might retaliate by reducing their own prices to the level set by the non-compliant firm; or by ceasing inter-firm cooperation; or by head-hunting the non-compliant firm's key employees. The success of such penalties depends on the effectiveness of the deterrent as well as the willingness of the loyal firms to impose penalties. The enforcers (the loyal cartel members) also incur costs by introducing sanctions. Indeed, some of these firms might also defect and secretly assist the non-compliant firm, if they feel the benefits of so doing outweigh the costs they incur through enforcement.

Some theorists view collusion as an attempt to increase market power, and to treat successful cartels as effective monopolies. In contrast, Williamson's approach clearly emphasizes a key distinction between monopoly and oligopoly, with the former avoiding but the latter incurring transaction costs of contracting in order to achieve market power.

> The monopolist . . . enjoys an advantage over oligopolists in adaptational respects since he does not have to write a contract in which future contingencies are identified and appropriate adaptation thereto devised. Rather, he can face the contingencies when they arise; each bridge can be crossed when it is reached, rather than having to decide *ex ante* how to cross all bridges that one may conceivably face.
>
> *(Williamson, 1975, p. 245)*

8.7 Influences on cartel stability

Impermanence appears to be a characteristic of most, if not all, cartels. Ironically, those agreements that have lasted for longer durations may have been among the least effective in promoting joint profit maximization. The fundamental reason so many cartels fail to live up to expectations is that what appears optimal for the group as a whole may not be optimal for each member individually. Therefore, bargaining is required to find a form of agreement that reconciles this divergence of interests.

Fellner (1965) believes the fundamental reason for the instability of coordinated action is that the bargaining strengths of members tend to change in unpredictable ways. For an agreement to remain effective, the group must create outlets for these changes. Individual firms might be permitted some freedom to introduce new product lines or experiment with new cost-saving technologies; but mutually damaging competition might still break out from time to time. Since firms are aware of this possibility, they might decide to maintain some spare productive capacity. However, this might directly contravene one of the requirements for joint profit maximization, namely the elimination of spare capacity. This section examines factors that tend to frustrate long-term cooperation.

Seller concentration and the number of firms

Section 8.6 argued that high seller concentration and small numbers of firms are factors conducive to cartel formation. The same factors may also affect the stability of a cartel after it has been formed, particularly if effective communication and monitoring are easier when numbers are small. With small numbers, in the event that non-compliance is detected, retaliation is likely to be quicker and more effective. If there are long time-lags prior to retaliation, the short-term gains from non-compliance may outweigh the long-term costs; if time-lags are short, the opposite applies. Experimental research suggests that cartel stability is affected by the number of firms (Huck *et al.*, 2001).

It is widely assumed that cartels are threatened by competition from outside firms. Non-cartel firms earning profits higher than those of cartel members may tempt members to desert the cartel, undermining its existence (Posner, 1976; Kleit and Palsson, 1999). In an analysis of agreements at the Office of Fair Trading (OFT), however, Lipczynski (1994) finds that some cartels are able to tolerate sizeable portions of the industry remaining outside the cartel.

Different goals of members

If a cartel comprises a heterogeneous collection of firms, it is probable that individual members have differing goals. Conflicting objectives might remain lightly buried in the interests of group solidarity but might resurface at any time. Members may disagree over issues such as the balance between short-run and long-run profit maximization, the regard that should be paid to potential competition, or how best to respond to changes in government policy. The literature on cartels contains numerous examples of conflict among members.

Fog (1956) suggests that larger firms often tend to seek stable, long-run policies, while smaller firms are more interested in exploiting short-run opportunities. Pindyck (1977) finds that some members of the International Bauxite Association in Australia, faced with high transport costs and excess capacity, were tempted to sell bauxite outside the cartel. In US Major League Baseball, some team owners appear to be less concerned with profit maximization than others:

> Agreement within the cartel is also hampered by the fact that not all members are profit maximizers. Some owners view baseball as largely a sporting activity, with profitability at most a secondary concern. Even today, teams like the Red Sox and the Cubs behave quite differently from teams like the Dodgers. Given the relatively small size of the cartel and the protected positions of its members, this divergence of goals tends to produce instability.
>
> *(Davis, 1974, p. 356)*

The process of cartel formation and the assignment of quotas

It is possible that the process of cartel formation might have implications for stability. Prokop (1999) develops several game-theoretic models of cartel

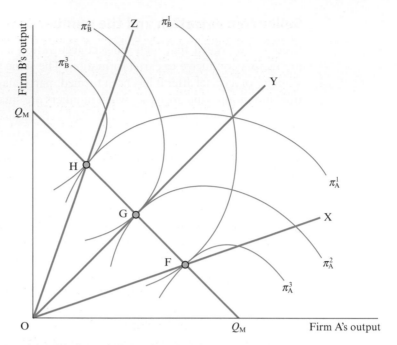

Figure 8.3 Osborne's model of cartel stability and instability

formation, in which firms decide whether to join the cartel or remain on the non-cartel fringe either sequentially or simultaneously. Cartel stability is shown to be more likely if decision-making is sequential rather than simultaneous. A similar conclusion was reached in the discussion of the likelihood of players behaving cooperatively in a sequential game in Section 7.6.

Osborne (1976) argues that the assignment of production quotas when the cartel is established can have important implications subsequently for its stability. This argument is illustrated in Figure 8.3, based on the isoprofit curves and reaction functions diagrams that were developed previously (see Section 7.3). At any point on the line $Q_M Q_M$, the combined output of firms A and B *equals* the profit-maximizing output for a monopolist, Q_M. At all points on $Q_M Q_M$, the firms maximize their joint profits, but the quotas assigned to each firm vary between different points on $Q_M Q_M$. At F, firm A takes the larger share of output; at H, B takes the larger share; while G is an intermediate case. If the two firms are identical and the model is symmetric, at G both firms are assigned an equal quota of $1/2 Q_M$.

Starting from any of points F, G and H, there is an incentive for either firm to cheat by raising its output, if it believes the other firm will not retaliate. If firm A increases its output while firm B's output is unchanged (moving 'east' from F, G or H), A increases its profit; or if B increases its output while A's output stays unchanged (moving 'north' from F, G or H), B increases its profit.

Suppose, however, the rules or established practices of the cartel are such that if one firm cheats by increasing its output, the other firm punishes it by also increasing its output, until the market shares implied by the quota agreement are restored. In this case, a decision by either firm to cheat would invite retaliation, resulting in a diagonal shift up the rays OX, OY or OZ, along which the market shares of both firms are the same as at points F, G and H respectively.

An examination of the implications of diagonal shifts up the rays OX, OY and OZ demonstrates the importance for cartel stability of the initial quota assignment. Beginning from G and moving up OY, both firms experience a decrease in profits. Therefore, if retaliation of the kind described above is anticipated, neither firm has an incentive to cheat. If the quotas are assigned such that the firms locate at G, the cartel is stable. However, beginning from either F or H, the cartel is unstable. Beginning from F and moving up OX, A's profit increases while B's decreases, so A has an incentive to cheat. Similarly, beginning from H and moving up OZ, B's profit increases while A's profit decreases, so B has an incentive to cheat.

Notice that at F and H, it is the firm with the larger initial quota (firm A at F, and firm B at H) that has the incentive to cheat. This is because the retaliation always restores the original quotas. For example, beginning from F, at which A has the larger market share, a large increase in output by A only provokes a small increase by B, so overall A gains and B loses. Diagrammatically, the condition for cartel stability is that the ray from the origin should be tangential to the two isoprofit curves at their point of tangency on the line $Q_M Q_M$. This condition is satisfied at G, but it is not satisfied at either F or H.

In a comment on Osborne's study, Holahan (1978) demonstrates that when there are differences between the firms' profit functions, retaliation along the lines suggested by Osborne to restore the original quotas may leave the retaliating firm worse off. Rothschild (1981) examines further the conditions under which retaliation is damaging to the retaliating firm. Retaliation may be damaging even in the case where the firms have identical profit functions. Osborne's prescription of retaliation to restore the original quotas in the event of cheating is effective only under certain conditions, which depend on the number of firms, their initial output levels, and the size of the increase in output by the firm that decides to cheat.

Non-price competition

A cartel is likely to be unstable if there are significant opportunities for non-price competition. Little purpose is served by agreeing to fix prices if, soon afterwards, intense non-price competition between cartel members breaks out in the form of expensive rival advertising campaigns, or the simultaneous launch of new and competing brands. Symeonides (2003) reports evidence for the UK of a negative relationship between the level of advertising and the degree of collusion.

Monitoring and detection of cheating

Stigler (1964) argues that collusion is successful when it is accompanied by efficient mechanisms for monitoring compliance with the agreement. The most effective method for detecting secret price-cutting might be to check transaction prices in the market. Stigler argues that evidence of cheating can be inferred by observing unexpected changes in the market shares of individual firms. If a firm discovers that it is systematically losing business it would normally expect to secure, it might infer that another cartel member is guilty of price-cutting. The greater the degree of regular variation in the cartel firms' market shares, the greater the potential for secret price-cuts, since it is more difficult for loyal firms to detect suspicious changes in their market shares. Collusion is more effective where actual transaction prices are correctly reported, as in government contracts. Collusion is less effective where the identity of the buyers changes frequently. Effectiveness varies inversely with buyer and seller numbers.

Stigler's approach can be criticized in several respects. Implicitly, Stigler assumes the threat of detection is a sufficient deterrent. The non-compliant firm incurs no penalty other than that of having to discontinue its non-compliance (Yamey, 1970). By concentrating on the detection of non-compliance, many other aspects of collusion are ignored.

> [Stigler] takes as given that the collusive agreement has already been reached. Attention is focused instead on cheating and on statistical inference techniques for detecting cheaters. While this last is very useful and calls attention in an interesting way to aspects of the oligopoly problem that others have neglected, it is also incomplete . . . monitoring is only one of a series of contracting steps, and not plainly the one that warrants priority attention.
>
> *(Williamson, 1975, p. 244)*

Levenstein and Suslow (2006) suggest that the existence of a joint sales agency plays an important role in determining the success of a cartel. An agency reduces the discretionary powers of individual firms with respect to pricing, output and distribution.

Sanctions

The ability of a cartel to impose effective sanctions if cheating occurs is another important determinant of cartel stability. If additional profits can be realized through non-compliance, then non-compliance probably will occur unless some policy of deterrence is adopted. 'It is surely one of the axioms of human behaviour that all agreements whose violation would be profitable to the violator must be enforced' (Stigler, 1968, p. 42). The ability of a cartel to discipline its own members for breaches of agreement is essential, as the courts cannot be used to enforce an illegal contract. Punishment can be effected either by taking action that reduces the demand for the non-compliant firm's product, or by increasing its costs (Ayres, 1987). Increasing costs may be difficult, but reducing demand is often straightforward. Accordingly, a common sanction is the matching of price cuts.

Rees (1993a) finds that in a British salt-producers' duopoly, any gain from cheating was outweighed by losses from credible short-term price cuts. Levenstein

(1996, 1997) also observes the effective use of short-term price-cutting in the bromine cartel prior to the First World War. However, in some cases the cartel members may not wish to disturb the market by instigating a retaliatory price war, and would instead prefer to accommodate cheats and absorb any loss of rent (Bergenstock *et al.*, 2006).

Sealed bidding provides a useful mechanism for ensuring detection if a firm breaks a cartel agreement. Sealed bid competition occurs when a buyer (frequently the government) requests bids for a contract, and subsequently announces the result publicly. The firms submit their bids secretly. The bidding firms might decide to meet in order to consider their bids, and perhaps decide which firm will win the contract. If a firm should cheat by submitting a lower bid than has been agreed, it will be detected when the winning bid is announced.

In a study of restrictive practices in the food trade, Cuthbert and Black (1959) document the use of fines and expulsion as direct sanctions for firms in breach of a cartel agreement. Fines were sometimes heavy, while expulsion implies the loss of any advantage from cartel membership. This might be serious if, for example, raw material suppliers cooperate with the cartel and agree not to supply non-members. A cartel might use the services of third parties to deter cheating. A joint sales agency through which all output is channelled should prevent price-cutting, although problems of allocating the proceeds between the cartel members might surface. Finally, the threat or use of physical force might be an effective means of encouraging compliance (Kuhlman, 1969).

Buyer concentration

It seems plausible that cartel stability should be enhanced if buyers lack market power or if **buyer concentration** is low. Buyers with market power may threaten agreed prices by switching to alternative suppliers, or by suggesting reciprocal transactions with individual producers. '[T]he better organized and more efficient are the other groups with which an interfirm organization has conflict relations, the greater the tendency for rivalry within the interfirm organization' (Phillips, 1962, p. 35).

Snyder (1996) and Dick (1996) find evidence that large buyers encourage suppliers to deviate from cartel agreements. When an industry supplies a small number of large buyers, orders are often large and infrequent. Under these conditions, it is tempting for parties to a collusive agreement to defect by offering secret price reductions, in an effort to secure these valuable contracts. In such cases it may be difficult for other cartel members to detect and punish defection.

> The relevance of big buyers to coordinated interaction does not stem from their sophistication or self-proclaimed ability to protect themselves. Instead, the issue is whether sellers will have the incentive to deviate from terms of coordination because the gains from securing a large long-term contract outweigh any losses from being caught after the fact.
>
> *(Dennis, 1992, p. 9)*

On the other hand, if buyers are atomistic, defection becomes more difficult: the more buyers there are, the greater the chance of being found out. 'No one has yet invented a way to advertise price reductions which brings them to the attention of numerous customers but not to that of any rival' (Stigler, 1968, p. 44).

Fluctuations in demand

A reduction in total demand may place strains on a cartel agreement (Haltwanger and Harrington, 1991; Briggs, 1996; Fabra, 2006). As demand falls, firms are tempted to undercut the cartel price in a bid to protect their sales volumes. This temptation need not affect all firms equally. Some may regard the drop in sales as temporary and may urge others to keep their nerve; others may view the decline as a real threat to their futures and will consider any strategy for survival. A climate of mutual suspicion and uncertainty may eventually cause the cartel to break apart. In the sense that they must adapt to fluctuating demand, cartels are no different from individual firms. If they fix prices, they have to make accommodating changes in production and employment. If they fix output quotas, they have to accept the burden of fluctuating prices. No cartel has complete control over demand, and history is full of instances of cartels and agreements that collapsed in the face of fluctuating demand.

If cartel members have spare capacity or if fixed costs are a large proportion of total costs, the cartel is likely to be unstable. If demand is falling, the temptation to cut price in an attempt to increase output and cover the fixed costs is strong. The existence of spare capacity might allow for greater stability, so long as the capacity is under the control of loyal cartel members. By adjusting production and price as demand conditions fluctuate, a dominant cartel member can use spare capacity to maintain order and discipline in the market. The behaviour of Saudi Arabian crude oil producers has been quoted as evidence for this hypothesis (Youssef, 1986). For such a strategy to be effective, however, the costs of maintaining spare capacity must not be excessive. It is questionable whether such a strategy is often applied in practice.

Posner (1976) argues collusion may be more difficult to enforce in times of increasing demand. In an expanding market, a firm being undercut by rivals may not immediately detect that cheating is occuring, since its own sales are rising (Ellison, 1994; Bagwell and Staiger, 1997; Rotemberg and Saloner, 1986). Rey (2002) suggests collusion is easier in times of expanding demand, as current profits are lower than future profits. In this case, the long-term costs imposed by rivals' retaliation should exceed the short-term benefits gained from non-compliance with the agreement.

Porter (1983) and Green and Porter (1984) argue cartel breakdowns occur when there is an unanticipated change in demand, evidenced by unusually low market shares for at least one firm, rather than a general long-term decline in demand. Demand can vary for a number of predictable reasons. However, at some critical level, when no rational explanation can be deduced for the falling sales, firms will take action. If the price drops below a certain level (a trigger price), firms that have previously been maximizing joint profits may revert, for a time, to Cournot-type competition (see Section 7.3).

Entry

In the long run, the stability and profitability of collusion depends on the ease or difficulty of entry. If a cartel shelters behind effective entry barriers, it may enjoy the necessary time and space to prosper and resolve the conflicting demands of its members. If entry barriers are low, the cartel faces competitive pressure from potential entrants. If a cartel has agreed to fix the price above the competitive level, there is an incentive for an entrant to move in and set a price just below the cartel price, encroaching on the profits of group members. In the most extreme case, unrestricted entry will lead to the destruction of the cartel. The survival of the cartel may therefore require implementation of measures to raise entry barriers, or policies that increase the time required to achieve successful entry. Entry barriers are examined in Chapter 11. Entry-type threats to cartel stability need not emanate only from rival firms, and the development of new products could have similar destabilizing implications.

Competition law

In most countries, competition law threatens the stability of cartels (see also Chapter 23). Since price-fixing is illegal, an effective cartel pricing strategy should not create suspicions on the part of customers and the authorities that coordinated action is taking place (Harrington, 2004). Detection of anti-competitive practices can result in heavy fines and possible loss of public goodwill. Aubert *et al.* (2006) discuss the deterrent effects of leniency programmes, which offer reduced fines for firms that present evidence of cartel activities and cooperate with the authorities. Rewards may also be offered to individuals for providing information. In the US, the reward is a share of the fines collected, sufficient to compensate an employee for any loss of future earnings. A system of rewards might be structured so that the cost to the cartel of inducing employees to remain loyal becomes greater than the benefit of collusion. It has been argued that the prohibition of cartels could result in a market being dominated by an incumbent monopolist. Prohibition reduces the threat of entry, as potential entrants will not expect to be able to participate in profitable collusive action (Haan, 2007).

Case study 8.2

Predicting cartels

In March 2005, the UK's Office of Fair Trading published a report which identifies factors that are conducive to the formation of cartels. The objective of the report is to direct regulatory scrutiny towards those markets in which cartels are most likely to exist. The report's case studies focus primarily on two industries, shipping and basic chemicals, which are examined under a number of themes.

Theme 1: Demand, capacity and intensity of competition. Although demand affects the formation and success of cartels, it is often difficult to determine whether demand operates directly, or through related factors such as excess capacity and falling market prices. For example, cross-Channel ferry operators colluded on price after a sterling devaluation in 1992 had reduced revenues for the five operators. Although the impact on revenues was different, all five responded with an identical 'currency surcharge'. In petrochemicals in 1994, as a result of persistent falling demand, a cartel was organized to tackle excess capacity and the exit of vulnerable firms. Products for which cartels were formed as a response to intense competition include citric acid in 2002, methionine in 2003, soda ash in 2003, and vitamins in 2003.

Theme 2: Barriers to entry. Although the report does not provide any direct evidence concerning the relationship between entry barriers and successful collusion, it does suggest that entry may have a disruptive effect on a cartel. The cartel of vitamins producers was terminated as a result of strong competition from Chinese importers, who disrupted the cartel with low pricing and high volumes. In shipping, the emphasis had always been on preventing entry. The 'liner service', which transports goods at regular times and on specified routes, faces competition from the irregular and non-advertised 'tramp vessel service'. In 1993 the Cewal, Cowac and Ukwal (Shipping Conferences), representing liners serving France and West Africa, set up a 'Fighting Committee' to determine who should sail close to the dates offered by the tramp vessels, at reduced, 'fighting' rates. Members of the Conferences met the costs of these 'fighting ships'.

Theme 3: Transparency and communication. A cartel might be considered as a driver for greater transparency and enhanced communication concerning sales and prices. In the organic peroxide case, frequent meetings were organized by the Swiss consultancy Treuhand. They produced 'pink' and 'red' papers detailing market shares, which were not to be removed from Treuhand offices, and the travel expenses of the attendees were reimbursed to cover the tracks of the conspiracy.

Theme 4: Size. The case studies confirm the notion that the smaller the number of firms in the industry and the higher the level of seller concentration, the easier it becomes to set up and sustain a cartel. A cartel is more likely to form if output is homogeneous; if turnover is stable over time; and if the leading firms in the industry are relatively large and membership of the leading group is stable. For a successful cartel, at least two of these three conditions should score highly.

Theme 5: Asymmetry. It is often assumed that differences in the sizes and other characteristics of cartel members tend to create instability; however, the opposite turned out to be the case. In citric acid, methiodine and the ferry operators' cartels, for example, cartel participants were drawn from a wide variety of social and commercial backgrounds.

Source: Grout, P.A. and Sonderegger, S. (2005) Predicting cartels, *Office of Fair Trading* OFT773.

Non-economic influences on cartel stability

In a classification of influences on cartel stability, non-economic factors such as leadership, trust and social background may be relevant (Yamey, 1973). Many economists are reluctant to recognize the importance of leadership, which perhaps sits more comfortably in the domain of disciplines like organizational behaviour or sociology. However, the formation of a cartel requires that someone takes the lead and organizes discussions and negotiations. People need to be persuaded, coaxed or even threatened to join the cartel, and leadership qualities are necessary to create and sustain a successful agreement. Likewise, a strong personality hostile to the notion of cooperation might prevent the formation of a cartel. Trust between cartel members is another important requirement for successful collusion. Through the medium of his famous dinners, Judge Gary, president of US Steel in the early 1890s, attempted to develop a spirit of cooperation. A firm considering a significant change of strategy would feel duty-bound to inform the other firms.

If the participants to an agreement share the same social background, group stability is likely to be enhanced. Consider the following account of an American electrical equipment conspiracy:

> The industry is tightly-knit with many friendships among the executives of competing firms; indeed, officials of smaller firms sometimes are former General Electric or Westinghouse Electric executives. The men involved oftentimes had similar educational backgrounds — college graduates in engineering with a rise through technical ranks into the world of sales. And the friendships were not only professional but often quite personal. Trade association meetings fostered these. It was perhaps easy in the camaraderie of these meetings at upper bracket hotels, amid speeches typical of any association lauding the industry's members and 'mission', to draw even closer than business and background indicated.
>
> (Wall Street Journal, 10 January 1962)

If most owners and managers come from a similar and preferably closely knit social background, stability is likely to be enhanced. To cheat on one's peers is to run the risk of suffering not only economic retaliation but also social stigmatization. The cheat is branded as an outsider, and denied the support and comfort of the social group.

Even where collusion would seem to be unenforceable, a common social background can help establish effective joint action. Common value systems are also built on efficient communications, so that potential or actual conflict can be quickly resolved through the auspices of trade association meetings, clubs, lodges and so on. However, Phillips (1972) suggests the importance of class and social background may tend to diminish over time. Eventually competing firms' value systems tend to converge because they are producing similar products, attracting similar customers or encountering similar technical problems. Consequently, rivalry decreases and cooperation increases.

8.8 Summary

This chapter has discussed the various methods used by groups of firms to facilitate cooperative or collusive actions in pursuit of their collective interests. Collusion is best seen as a means of easing competitive pressure and reducing the uncertainty that stems from oligopolistic interdependence by taking unified action, rather than solely as a strategy for maximizing joint profits. Collusion might be effected though the medium of a cartel, but might alternatively take place through mechanisms such as trade associations, joint ventures or state-sponsored agreements.

The prescription in terms of output quotas and pricing policy for cartel members to maximize their joint profits is easy to define in theory but often harder to implement in practice. For example, the less efficient firms might be required to accept relatively low production quotas, and may demand a share of the profits emanating from elsewhere in the cartel as the price that must be paid for their compliance. This raises numerous questions about the bargaining process between the prospective cartel members, the outcome of which may be theoretically indeterminate. Furthermore, if the cartel does succeed in reducing total industry output, this creates a free-rider problem in the sense that non-cartel firms reap the benefits of a higher price, without bearing any of the costs of having to produce a lower output. If it is obviously more profitable for an individual firm to remain outside the cartel, this misalignment of private and collective interests might prevent agreement from ever being reached, or might cause the cartel to break down.

The success or failure of collusive arrangements depends on many factors, some of which are beyond the direct control of the group of colluding firms. In the absence of legal sanctions, what are the factors most likely to determine the success or failure of collusion?

- Fewness of numbers helps in the handling and evaluation of information.

- Similarity of cost conditions reduces a potential source of conflict.

- Demand that is relatively inelastic at the pre-cartel price ensures that revenues can be increased significantly by reducing output levels and raising price.

- An equitable and fair mechanism for determining the allocation of production quotas and distribution of profits helps make an agreement possible.

- The smaller the number of decisions required to conclude an effective agreement, the greater is the likelihood of success.

- Members must perceive that the gains from cooperative action outweigh the benefits of private action.

- Mechanisms for detecting and punishing non-compliance with the terms of the agreement should be effective.

- Higher prices and improved profitability should not attract non-cartel entrants into the industry.

- The cartel must guard against other external threats to its stability, including significant changes in demand or technology.

- The quality of leadership and the degree of mutual trust and social cohesion among cartel members may be important influences on stability.

Discussion questions

1. Explain why trade associations can be useful as vehicles for facilitating collusion.

2. Using a suitable theoretical model, show how the divergent interests of the members of a cartel can be resolved through a process of bargaining.

3. Are there ever any motives for collusion other than the desire to maintain prices at a level higher than would be achieved in a competitive market?

4. Why is it often necessary to police cartel agreements? Who polices OPEC?

5. Typical characteristics of industries that are prone to collusion include high concentration, high entry barriers, price-inelastic demand, large numbers of buyers, homogeneous products and static demand. Explain why each of these characteristics may help foster collusion. Give real world examples of industries that exhibit some or all of these characteristics.

6. Auctions in which participants are required to submit sealed bids often seem to be prone to collusion among bidders. Why?

7. Explain why producers in certain industries set recommended retail prices.

8. Given the difficulty in detecting acts of collusion, suggest evidence that might provide investigators with proof of collusive behaviour.

9. In what ways might the assignment of production quotas when a cartel is first established have important implications for its subsequent stability?

10. Quoting examples drawn from Case studies 8.1 and 8.2, discuss factors that may tend to help or hinder collusion.

Further reading

Asch, P. and Seneca, J. (1975) Characteristics of collusive firms, *Journal of Industrial Economics*, 23, 223–37.

Grout, P.A. and Sonderegger, S. (2005) Predicting cartels, *Office of Fair Trading*, OFT773.

Harrington, J. (2008) Detecting cartels, in Buccirossi, P. (ed.) *Handbook of Antitrust Economics*. Cambridge: MIT Press.

Jacquemin, A. and Slade, M.E. (1989) Cartels, collusion and horizontal merger, in Schmalensee, R. and Willig, R.D. (eds) *Handbook of Industrial Organization*. Cambridge, MA: MIT Press.

Levenstein, M. and Suslow, V. (2006) What determines cartel success?, *Journal of Economic Literature*, 44, 43–95.

Osborne, D.K. (1976) Cartel problems, *American Economic Review*, 66, 835–44.

Phlips, L. (ed.) (1998) *Applied Industrial Economics*. Cambridge: Cambridge University Press, Sections II and III.

Podolny, J.M. and Scott Morton, F.M. (1999) Social status, entry and predation: the case of British shipping cartels 1879–1929, *Journal of Industrial Economics*, 47, 41–67.

Shepherd, W.G. (1997) *The Economics of Industrial Organization*. Englewood Cliffs, NJ: Prentice Hall, Ch. 11.

Concentration: measurement and trends

Learning objectives

This chapter covers the following topics:

- market and industry definition
- schemes for industry classification
- measures of concentration
- interpretation and application of concentration measures

Key terms

Aggregate concentration	Herfindahl–Hirschman index
Complements	Industry concentration
Concentration measures	Lorenz curve
Concentration ratio	Market concentration
Cross-price elasticity of demand	Numbers equivalent
Entropy coefficient	Product market definition
Geographic market definition	Seller concentration
Gini coefficient	Substitutes
Hannah and Kay index	

9.1 Introduction

Any analysis of a firm's competitive environment involves identifying the key elements of industry structure. Usually, the most important characteristics of industry structure include the number and size distribution of firms, the existence and height of barriers to entry and exit, and the degree of product differentiation. **Seller concentration** refers to the first of these elements: the number and size distribution of firms. In empirical research in industrial organization, seller concentration is probably the most widely used indicator of industry structure. Any specific seller **concentration measure** aims to reflect the implications of the number and size distribution of firms in the industry for the nature of competition, using a relatively simple numerical indicator. Both the number of firms and their size distribution (in other words, the degree of inequality in the firm sizes) are important. For example, the nature of competition in an industry comprising ten equal-sized firms might be very different from the nature of competition in an industry comprising one dominant firm and nine smaller firms. A useful concentration measure should be capable of capturing the implications of both the number of firms, and their relative sizes, for the nature of competition.

In view of the importance of concentration in empirical studies of competition, two chapters are devoted to this topic. Chapter 9 focuses on the measurement of concentration, while Chapter 10 focuses on the factors that determine the levels and trends in concentration in particular industries.

Before producing concentration measures for specific markets or industries, it is necessary to take decisions concerning the boundaries of the markets or industries that are being measured. Section 9.2 discusses the issues involved in market and industry definition, from both a theoretical and a practical perspective. Section 9.3 describes the schemes that are used to classify industries for the purposes of compiling the official UK and EU production and employment statistics. Section 9.4 describes the calculation of a number of alternative concentration or inequality measures, assuming individual size data are available for the firms that are members of the industry. The concentration or inequality measures include the n-firm concentration ratio, the Herfindahl–Hirschman index, the entropy coefficient and the Gini coefficient. Worked examples are used to illustrate the method of calculation for each measure, and to compare the properties and limitations of the various measures. Finally, Section 9.5 discusses some of the issues that should be considered when interpreting seller concentration measures.

9.2 Market and industry definition

Markets and industries

In the calculation of any specific concentration measure, the definition of the relevant market is likely to be a crucial decision. The definition of a market is straightforward in theory, but often more problematic in practice. Serviceable theoretical definitions can be found in the works of the earliest, nineteenth-century economists. For example, Cournot defined a market as:

> the entire territory of which parts are so united by the relations of unrestricted commerce that prices there take the same level throughout, with ease and rapidity.

> *(Cournot, 1838, pp. 51–2Fn)*

Similarly, Marshall defined a market as an area in which:

> prices of the same goods tend to equality with due allowance for transportation costs.

(Marshall, 1920, p. 270)

For practical purposes, the definition of any market contains both a product dimension and a geographic dimension. The **product market definition** should include all products that are close substitutes for one another, both in consumption and in production. Goods 1 and 2 are substitutes in consumption if an increase in the price of Good 2 causes consumers to switch from Good 2 to Good 1. The degree of consumer substitution between Goods 1 and 2 is measured using the **cross-price elasticity of demand**. Good 1's elasticity of demand with respect to a change in the price of Good 2 is:

$$CED = \frac{\text{Proportionate change in quantity demanded for Good 1}}{\text{Proportionate change in price of Good 2}}$$

$$CED = \left(\frac{\Delta Q_1}{\Delta P_1}\right) \times \left(\frac{P_2}{Q_1}\right)$$

A large and positive cross-price elasticity of demand indicates that the two goods are close **substitutes** in consumption (for example, butter and margarine). If the price of Good 2 rises, the demand for Good 1 also rises. Goods 1 and 2 should therefore be considered part of the same industry. But how large does the cross-elasticity have to be; or, in other words, how close is 'close'? Presumably Coca-Cola and Pepsi are very close substitutes, and Coca-Cola and Tango are quite close substitutes. But what about Coca-Cola and mineral water, or Coca-Cola and coffee?

In contrast, a large and negative cross-price elasticity of demand indicates that the two goods are close **complements** (for example, personal computer and printer). However, this could also imply that they should be considered part of the same industry. Compact disc players and speakers might be grouped together as part of the consumer electronics industry. But what about cars and petrol? These goods are also complementary, but would it be sensible to include motor manufacturers and oil companies in the same industry group?

Good 1 produced by firm A, and Good 2 produced with similar technology by firm B are substitutes in production if an increase in the price of Good 1 causes firm B to switch production from Good 2 to Good 1. In this case, firms A and B are close competitors, even if from a consumer's perspective Goods 1 and 2 are not close substitutes. For example, Good 1 might be cars and Good 2 might be military tanks. No consumer would decide to buy a tank simply because there has been an increase in the price of cars. But on receiving the same price signal, a tank producer might decide to switch to car production. The degree of producer substitution between Goods 1 and 2 can be measured using the cross-price elasticity of supply. Good 1's elasticity of supply with respect to a change in the price of Good 2 is:

$$\text{CES} = \frac{\text{Proportionate change in quantity supplied of Good 1}}{\text{Proportionate change in price of Good 2}}$$

$$\text{CES} = \left(\frac{\Delta Q_1^S}{\Delta P_2}\right) \times \left(\frac{P_2}{Q_1^S}\right)$$

A negative value for CES would suggest that Goods 1 and 2 are substitutes in production: if the price of Good 2 rises, the supply of Good 1 falls, as producers switch from Good 1 to Good 2. In this case, as well, there can be difficulties in implementation. For example, if 'engineering' is defined as 'a process using lathes', aerospace and bicycle manufacturers might be classified as direct competitors.

The **geographic market definition** involves determining whether an increase in the price of a product in one geographic location significantly affects either the demand or supply, and therefore the price, in another geographic location. If so, then both locations should be considered part of the same geographic market. In principle, a similar analysis involving spatial cross-price elasticities could be used to determine the geographic limits of market boundaries.

In practice, however, the problems are similar to those that arise in defining product markets. Should any specific market be defined at the local, regional, national, continental or global level? Substitution in consumption or production is always a matter of degree, but any operational market definition requires specific boundaries to be drawn, not only in 'product space', but also in geographic space. Elzinga and Hogarty (1973, 1978) suggest a practical procedure for defining geographic boundaries. This requires data on the extent to which consumers in a regionally defined market purchase from regional producers (internal transactions) and from producers outside the region (external transactions). A regional market exists if the ratio of internal to total transactions is high; Elzinga and Hogarty suggest a critical value of 75 per cent.

National Economic Research Associates (NERA) (1992) and Bishop and Walker (2002) describe the methodology used to determine market definitions in the application of UK and EU competition policy (see also Chapter 23). The SSNIP (small but significant non-transitory increase in price) test is widely used. For product markets, this test assesses whether a (hypothetical) monopolist producing Good 1 would find it profitable to increase price by between 5 per cent and 10 per cent. If so, Good 1 occupies a market by itself. If not, this suggests the producers of other goods constrain the monopolist's pricing policy. Therefore the market definintion should include Good 1 and related Goods 2 and 3. A similar procedure is used to define a geographic market: would a (hypothetical) monopolist located in geographic area X find it profitable to increase price by between 5 per cent and 10 per cent? If so, X is a geographic market; if not, a wider geographic market definition is required. In order to implement the SSNIP test, various price and cross-price demand elasticity measures are used (Stigler and Sherwin, 1985; Werden and Froeb, 1993; OFT, 1999).

Throughout much of microeconomics and industrial organization, the terms *market* and *industry* tend to be used rather loosely and, sometimes, interchangeably. Although the distinction is not rigid, it seems natural to use the term *industry* to refer specifically to a market's supply side or productive activities, while the term *market* encompasses both supply/production and demand/consumption. This book will usually adhere to this terminological convention. However, this convention is not universal. Kay (1990a) sees markets as representing demand conditions, while industries represent supply conditions. In Kay's terminology, the *strategic market*, defined as the smallest geographic or product area in which a firm can successfully compete, brings the industry and market together.

> The characteristics of the strategic market are influenced both by those demand factors which determine the economic market which the firm serves, and by those supply factors which determine the boundaries of the industry within which the firm operates.
>
> *(Kay, 1990a, p. 3)*

Nevertheless, in this book the term 'industry' will usually to refer to a group of firms producing and selling a similar product, using similar technology and perhaps obtaining factors of production from the same factor markets. A focus on factor markets might provide a yardstick for grouping firms into industries that differs from the criteria for market definition discussed above. However, once again there are practical difficulties. This type of classification might suggest that soap and margarine belong to the same industry, while woollen gloves and leather gloves belong to different industries. Finally, in order to emphasize the degree of overlap between markets and industries, it is interesting to note that Stigler's (1955) industry definition provides a succinct summary of the criteria for identifying the boundaries of markets:

> An industry should embrace the maximum geographical area and the maximum variety of productive activities in which there is strong long-run substitution. If buyers can shift on a large scale from product or area B to area A, then the two should be combined. If producers can shift on a large scale from B to A, again they should be combined. Economists usually state this in an alternative form: All products or enterprises with large long-run cross elasticities of either supply or demand should be combined into a single industry.
>
> *(Stigler, 1955, p. 4)*

9.3 Official schemes for industry classification

Although in principle the definition of markets and industries may raise a number of difficult issues, for the practical purpose of compiling official production and employment statistics, some specific scheme for defining and classifying industries is required. In 1992, the European Commission introduced the current classification system that is used throughout the European Union (EU), known as *Nomenclature générale des activités économiques dans les communautés Européennes* (NACE). At the same time, the UK's Standard Industrial Classification, originally introduced in 1948 and revised in 1980, was revised to achieve consistency with NACE. The objective was to standardize industry definitions across member states, making inter-country comparisons easier and providing a statistical basis for the harmonization of competition and industrial policy within the EU. The UK's 1992 SIC (SIC 1992) is based on a four-digit numbering system, while NACE adds a fifth digit in some cases. There are 17 sections, labelled alphabetically from A to Q. These are reproduced in Table 9.1, which provides a comparison with the earlier SIC 1980.

Although there is consistency between the industry definitions used in the UK's SIC 1992 system and the EU's NACE system, there are minor differences in the numerical presentation of the various levels of both systems. For example, NACE contains more levels in total than SIC 1992. Most of the NACE sections are subdivided into subsections by the addition of a second letter. Not all sections are subdivided: for example, section B, Fishing, has no sub-sections. In contrast, section D, Manufacturing, has 14 sub-sections. Sub-sections are then subdivided into divisions, which correspond to a two-digit classification. The full list of NACE divisions is reproduced in Table 9.2. Divisions are further subdivided into three-digit groups, four-digit classes and, in some cases, five-digit sub-classes. For example, Table 9.3 shows all layers of classification between the most general 'Manufacturing' section D, and the most specific 'Bacon and ham' sub-class 15.13/1.

Table 9.1 The UK's SIC 1992 and the EU's NACE, by section

Section (SIC 1992/NACE)	Description	Division (SIC 1980)
A	Agriculture, hunting and forestry	0
B	Fishing	0
C	Mining and quarrying	1, 2
D	Manufacturing	1, 2, 3, 4
E	Electricity, gas and water supply	1
F	Construction	5
G	Wholesale and retail trade; repair of motor vehicles and household goods	6
H	Hotels and restaurants	6
I	Transport, storage and communication	7, 9
J	Financial intermediation	8
K	Real estate, renting and business activity	8, 9
L	Public administration and defence, compulsory social security	9
M	Education	9
N	Health and social work	9
O	Other community, social and personal service activities	9
P	Private households with employed persons	9
Q	Extra-territorial organizations and bodies	9

Table 9.2 The EU's NACE, by division

NACE division (two-digit) code	Description
A.1	Agriculture, hunting and related service activities
A.2	Forestry, logging and related service activities
B.5	Fishing; operation of fish hatcheries and farms; service activities incidental to fishing
CA.10	Mining of coal and lignite; extraction of peat
CA.11	Extraction of crude petroleum and natural gas; service activities incidental to oil and gas extraction
CA.12	Mining of uranium and thorium ores
CB.13	Mining of metal ores
CB.14	Other mining and quarrying
DA.15	Manufacture of food products and beverages
DA.16	Manufacture of tobacco products
DB.17	Manufacture of textiles
DB.18	Manufacture of wearing apparel; dressing and dyeing of fur
DC.19	Tanning and dressing of leather; manufacture of luggage, handbags, saddlery, harness, footwear
DD.20	Manufacture of wood, wood and cork products except furniture
DE.21	Manufacture of pulp, paper and paper products
DE.22	Manufacture of publishing, printing and reproduction of recorded media
DF.23	Manufacture of coke, refined petroleum products
DG.24	Manufacture of chemicals and chemical products
DH.25	Manufacture of rubber and plastic products
DI.26	Manufacture of non-metallic mineral products
DJ.27	Manufacture of basic metals
DJ.28	Manufacture of fabricated metal products, except machinery and equipment
DK.29	Manufacture of machinery and equipment not elsewhere classified
DL.30	Manufacture of office machinery and computers
DL.31	Electrical machinery and apparatus not elsewhere classified
DL.32	Manufacture of radio, television and communication equipment and apparatus
DL.33	Manufacture of medical, precision and optical instruments, watches and clocks
DM.34	Manufacture of motor vehicles, trailers and semi-trailers
DM.35	Manufacture of other transport equipment
DN.36	Manufacture of furniture, manufacture not elsewhere classified
DN.37	Recycling
E.40	Electricity, gas, steam and hot water supply
E.41	Collection, purification and distribution of water
F.45	Construction
G.50	Sale, maintenance and repair of motor vehicles; retail sale of automotive fuel
G.51	Wholesale trade and commission trade, except motor vehicles and motorcycles
G.52	Retail trade, except motor vehicles and motor cycles and repairs of household goods
H.55	Hotels and restaurants
I.60	Land transport; transport via pipelines
I.61	Water transport
I.62	Air transport
I.63	Supporting and auxiliary transport activities; activities of travel agencies
I.64	Post and telecommunications
J.65	Financial intermediation

Table 9.2 (*continued*)

NACE division (two-digit) code	Description
J.66	Insurance and pension funding
J.67	Activities auxiliary to financial intermediation
K.70	Real estate activities
K.71	Renting of machinery and equipment without operator and of personal and household goods
K.72	Computer and related activities
K.73	Research and development
K.74	Other business activities
L.75	Public administration and defence; compulsory social security
M.80	Education
N.85	Health and social work
O.90	Sewage and refuse disposal, sanitation and similar activities
O.91	Activities of membership organization n.e.c.
O.92	Recreational, cultural and sporting activities
O.93	Other service activities
P.95	Activities of households as employers of domestic staff
P.96	Undifferentiated goods producing activities of private households for own use
P.97	Undifferentiated services producing activities of private households for own use
Q.99	Extra-territorial organizations and bodies

Table 9.3 Comparison between the UK's SIC 1992 and the EU's NACE

SIC 1992	NACE	Description
Section D	Section D	Manufacturing
n/a	Subsection DA	Manufacture of food products; beverages and tobacco
Division 15	Division DA.15	Manufacture of food products and beverages
Group 151	Group DA.151	Production, processing and preserving of meat and meat products
n/a	Class DA.1513	Production of meat and poultry products
n/a	Subclass 15.13/1	Bacon and ham

9.4 Measures of seller concentration

Seller concentration, an indicator of the number and size distribution of firms, can be measured at two levels:

1. For all firms that form part of an economy, located within some specific geographical boundary.

2. For all firms classified as members of some industry or market, again located within some specific geographical boundary.

The first type of seller concentration, known as **aggregate concentration**, reflects the importance of the largest firms in the economy as a whole. Although in practice data are relatively hard to come by, in principle aggregate concentration is relatively straightforward to measure. Typically, aggregate concentration is measured as the share of the *n* largest firms in the total sales, assets or employment (or other appropriate size measure) for the economy as a whole. The number of firms included might be $n = 50$, 100, 200 or 500. Aggregate concentration might be important for several reasons:

- If aggregate concentration is high, this might have implications for levels of seller concentration in particular industries.

- Aggregate concentration data might reveal information about the economic importance of large diversified firms, which is not adequately reflected in indicators of seller concentration for particular industries.

- If aggregate concentration is high, this might indicate that the economy's largest firms have opportunities to exert a disproportionate degree of influence over politicians or regulators, which might render the political system vulnerable to abuse, or the regulation system vulnerable to regulatory capture.

The second type of seller concentration, known as **industry concentration** or (alternatively) **market concentration**, reflects the importance of the largest firms in some particular industry or market. In some cases, it may also be relevant to measure buyer concentration, in order to assess the importance of the largest buyers. This might arise in the case of an industry which supplies a specialized producer good, for which the market includes only a very small number of buyers.

The rest of Section 9.4 focuses on the measurement of seller concentration at industry level. Clearly, the number and size distribution of the firms is a key element of industry structure. Any specific measure of seller concentration at industry level aims to provide a convenient numerical measure reflecting the implications of the number and size distribution of firms for the nature of competition in the industry concerned. In empirical research in industrial organization, concentration is probably the most widely used indicator of industry structure.

Economists have employed a number of alternative **concentration measures** at industry level. To assist users in making an informed choice between the alternatives that are available, Hannah and Kay (1977) suggest a number of general criteria that any specific concentration measure should satisfy if it is to adequately reflect the most important characteristics of the firm size distribution:

- Suppose industries A and B have equal numbers of firms. Industry A should be rated as more highly concentrated than industry B if the firms' cumulative market share (when the firms are ranked in descending order of size) is greater for industry A than for industry B at all points in the size distribution.

- A transfer of market share from a smaller to a larger firm should always increase concentration.

- There should be a market share threshold such that if a new firm enters the industry with a market share below the threshold, concentration is reduced. Similarly, if an incumbent firm with a market share below the threshold exits from the industry, concentration is increased.

- Any merger between two incumbent firms should always increase concentration.

Table 9.4 Firm size distribution (sales data): six hypothetical industries

	I1	I2	I3	I4	I5	I6
Firm 1	5,066	1,644	2,466	7,412	3,564	5,066
Firm 2	3,376	1,644	2,466	3,706	3,564	3,376
Firm 3	2,250	1,644	2,466	1,854	3,564	2,250
Firm 4	1,500	1,644	2,466	926	1,500	1,500
Firm 5	1,000	1,644	2,466	464	1,000	1,000
Firm 6	666	1,644	2,466	232	666	666
Firm 7	444	1,644		116	444	938
Firm 8	296	1,644		58	296	
Firm 9	198	1,644		28	198	
Total	14,796	14,796	14,796	14,796	14,796	14,796

As shown below, not all of the seller concentration measures that are in use satisfy all of the Hannah and Kay criteria. This section examines the construction and interpretation of the most common measures of seller concentration. These are the n-firm concentration ratio, the Herfindahl–Hirschman index, the Hannah–Kay index, the entropy coefficient, the variance of the logarithms of firm sizes and the Gini coefficient.

In order to demonstrate the calculation of the various concentration measures that are described below, Table 9.4 shows sales data for six hypothetical industries, I1 to I6, all of which have the same total sales.

■ The nine firms in I1 have a typically skewed distribution of sales figures.

■ The nine equal-sized firms in I2 all have the same sales figures.

■ In I3, the number of equal-sized firms is six (rather than nine).

■ I4 is similar to I1, except the size distribution is more heavily skewed (with the largest firm in I4 taking a larger market share than its counterpart in I1, and the smallest firm in I4 taking a smaller market share than its counterpart in I1).

■ I5 is the same as I1 except for the three largest firms, which are equal-sized in I5.

■ Finally, the six largest firms in I1 are the same as their counterparts in I6, but the three smallest firms in I1 have been merged to form a single firm in I6.

For each of I1 to I6, Table 9.5 shows the numerical values of the concentration measures that are presented below. For I1, Tables 9.6 to 9.10 show the calculations for each concentration measure in full.

n-firm concentration ratio

The n-firm **concentration ratio**, usually denoted CR_n, measures the share of the industry's n largest firms in some measure of total industry size. The most widely used size measures are based on sales, assets or employment data. The formula for the n-firm concentration ratio is as follows:

$$CR_n = \sum_{i=1}^{n} s_i$$

where s_i is the share of the i-th largest firm in total industry sales, assets or employment.

In other words, $s_i = x_i / \sum_{i=1}^{N} x_i$, where x_i is the size of firm i, and N is the number of firms in the industry. There are no set rules for the choice of n, the number of large firms to be included in the calculation of CR_n. However, CR_n for $n = 3$, 4, 5 or 8 are among the most widely quoted n-firm concentration ratios.

For most practical purposes, both the choice of n and the choice of size measure may not be too crucial. For example, Bailey and Boyle (1971) find that n-firm concentration ratios for several values of n are highly correlated. In practice, an attractive property of the n-firm concentration ratio is that it requires size data on the top n firms only, together with the corresponding aggregate size measure for the entire industry. In other words, the data requirements are less demanding than for the other concentration measures that are described below, each of which requires individual size data for all of the industry's member firms. However, the use of data for the top n firms only is also a limitation, in the sense that no account is taken of the number and size distribution of firms that are outside the top n. Furthermore, no account is taken of the size distribution within the top n firms.

These points are illustrated in Tables 9.4 and 9.5 by I5 and I6, both of which have the same CR_3 as I1. However, I5 might well be regarded as *less* highly concentrated than I1, and I6 as *more* highly concentrated:

Table 9.5 Seller concentration measures: six hypothetical industries

	I1	I2	I3	I4	I5	I6
n-firm concentration ratio						
CR$_3$	.7226	.3333	.5000	.8767	.7226	.7226
CR$_4$	.8240	.4444	.6667	.9393	.8240	.8240
CR$_5$	.8916	.5556	.8333	.9707	.8916	.8916
Herfindahl–Hirschman and Hannah–Kay indexes						
HK(1.5)	.4376	.3333	.4082	.5485	.4236	.4440
HH = HK(2)	.2108	.1111	.1667	.3346	.1924	.2133
HK(2.5)	.1076	.0370	.0680	.2158	.0906	.1084
Entropy and relative entropy						
E	1.7855	2.1972	1.7918	1.3721	1.8236	1.7191
RE	.8126	1.0000	1.0000	.6245	.8299	.8835
Numbers equivalent						
n(1)	5.96	9.00	6.00	3.94	6.19	5.58
n(1.5)	5.22	9.00	6.00	3.32	5.57	5.07
(I/HH) = *n*(2)	4.74	9.00	6.00	2.99	5.20	4.69
n(2.5)	4.42	9.00	6.00	2.78	4.96	4.40
Variance of logarithms of firm sizes						
VL	1.0960	0	0	3.2223	1.1040	.4669
Gini coefficient						
G	.4482	0	0	.6035	.4101	.3219

Table 9.6 Calculation of three-, four- and five-firm concentration ratios

	I1
Firm 1	5,066
Firm 2	3,376
Firm 3	2,250
Firm 4	1,500
Firm 5	1,000
Firm 6	666
Firm 7	444
Firm 8	296
Firm 9	198
Total	14,796

$$CR_3 = \frac{5{,}066 + 3{,}376 + 2{,}250}{14{,}796} = 0.7226$$

$$CR_4 = \frac{5{,}066 + 3{,}376 + 2{,}250 + 1{,}500}{14{,}796} = 0.8240$$

$$CR_5 = \frac{5{,}066 + 3{,}376 + 2{,}250 + 1{,}500 + 1{,}000}{14{,}796} = 0.8916$$

- The top three firms in I5 are equal-sized, while the size distribution of the top three in I1 is skewed, making I5 more competitive than I1.

- The three smallest firms in I1 have been merged in order to form one larger firm in I6, making I6 less competitive than I1.

These comparisons show that the n-firm concentration ratio fails to meet several of the Hannah and Kay criteria for a satisfactory concentration measure. For example, a transfer of sales from a smaller to a larger firm does not necessarily cause CR_n to increase; and a merger between two or more industry member firms does not necessarily cause CR_n to increase.

Herfindahl–Hirschman (HH) index

Working independently, Hirschman (1945) and Herfindahl (1950) both suggested a concentration measure based on the sum of the squared market shares of all firms in the industry. The **Herfindahl–Hirschman (HH) index** is calculated as follows:

$$HH = \sum_{i=1}^{N} s_i^2$$

where s_i is the market share of firm i, and N is the total number of firms in the industry. For an industry that consists of a single monopoly producer, $HH = 1$. A monopolist has a market share of $s_1 = 1$. Therefore $s_1^2 = 1$, ensuring $HH = 1$. For an industry with N firms, the maximum possible value of the Herfindahl–Hirschman index is $HH = 1$, and the minimum possible value is $HH = 1/N$.

- The maximum value of HH = 1 occurs when the size distribution of the N firms is highly skewed. In the most extreme case, one dominant firm has a market share only fractionally smaller than 1, and $N-1$ small firms each has a market share only fractionally larger than zero. Essentially, this is the same as the case of monopoly, for which HH = 1 as shown above.

- The minimum value of HH = $1/N$ occurs when the industry consists of N equal-sized firms. In this case, each firm has a market share of $s_i = 1/N$. Therefore

$$s_i^2 = (1/N)^2 \text{ for } i = 1 \ldots N, \text{ and } HH = \sum_{i=1}^{N}(1/N)^2 = N(1/N)^2 = 1/N$$

In Tables 9.4 and 9.5, I2, I1 and I4 each have $N=9$ firms, and the respective size distributions are equal sized, skewed and highly skewed. HH = 0.1111 (or 1/9) for I2, HH = 0.2108 for I1 and HH = 0.3346 for I4. This confirms that HH increases as the size distribution becomes more unequal. It is important to notice also that HH succeeds where CR_3 fails in identifying I5 as less concentrated than I1, and I6 as more concentrated than I1. For I5, I1 and I6, the values of HH shown in Table 9.5 are 0.1924, 0.2108 and 0.2133, respectively. Of all the concentration measures considered in this section, the HH index and the closely related **Hannah and Kay index** (see below) are generally the most satisfactory in respect of their ability to satisfy the Hannah and Kay criteria.

A practical difficulty with the HH index is its requirement for individual size data on all of the industry's member firms. In contrast, CR_n only requires individual data on the top n firms, and an industry total. However, it can be shown that even if individual data are not available for the smaller firms, a reasonable approximation to HH is obtained using data on the larger firms only. For I1, suppose individual sales data are available for firms 1 to 6 only, and an industry total sales figure is also available. Suppose also that the total number of firms in I1 is unknown. Then the maximum value HH could take (if one other firm accounted for all of the remaining sales) is HH = 0.2133. The minimum value HH could take (if a large number of very small firms accounted for the remaining sales, each with a very small share) is HH = 0.2093. The actual value of HH for I1 is 0.2108. Therefore, the range of values that HH could conceivably take is small. No matter what assumptions are made about the missing individual firm size data, a reasonably close approximation to the true value of HH is obtained.

A reciprocal measure, known as the **numbers equivalent** of the HH index, is defined as (1/HH). The numbers equivalent is an inverse measure of concentration. For an industry with N firms, the minimum possible value of the numbers equivalent is (1/HH) = 1, and the maximum possible value is (1/HH) = N.

- The minimum value of (1/HH) = 1 occurs when HH = 1, and corresponds to the case of one dominant firm and $N-1$ small firms.

- The maximum value of (1/HH) = N occurs when HH = $1/N$, and corresponds to the case of N equal-sized firms.

Table 9.7 Calculation of Herfindahl–Hirschman and Hannah–Kay indexes

Firm	Sales	s_i	$s_i^{1.5}$	s_i^2	$s_i^{2.5}$
1	5,066	.3424	.2003	.1172	.0686
2	3,376	.2282	.1090	.0521	.0249
3	2,250	.1521	.0593	.0231	.0090
4	1,500	.1014	.0323	.0103	.0033
5	1,000	.0676	.0176	.0046	.0012
6	666	.0450	.0095	.0020	.0004
7	444	.0300	.0052	.0009	.0002
8	296	.0200	.0028	.0004	.0001
9	198	.0134	.0015	.0002	.0000
Sum	14,796	1.0000	HK(1.5) = 0.4376	HH = HK(2) = 0.2108	HK(2.5) = 0.1076

Numbers equivalent: $\quad n(1.5) = 0.4376^{1/(1-1.5)} = 0.4376^{-2} = 5.22$

$\qquad\qquad\qquad\quad (1/\mathrm{HH}) = n(2) = 0.2108^{1/(1-2)} = 0.2108^{-1} = 4.74$

$\qquad\qquad\qquad\quad n(2.5) = 0.1076^{1/(1-2.5)} = 0.1076^{-0.666\,7} = 4.42$

Accordingly, the numbers equivalent is useful as a measure of inequality in the firm size distribution. For an industry with N firms, the minimum possible value, $(1/\mathrm{HH}) = 1$, corresponds to the most unequal size distribution; and the maximum possible value, $(1/\mathrm{HH}) = N$, corresponds to the most equal size distribution. In Tables 9.4 and 9.5, I2 with $N = 9$ equal-sized firms has $(1/\mathrm{HH}) = 9$, and I3 with $N = 6$ equal-sized firms has $(1/\mathrm{HH}) = 6$. I1 with $N = 9$ firms and a skewed size distribution has $(1/\mathrm{HH}) = 4.74$, and I4 with $N = 9$ and a highly skewed distribution has $(1/\mathrm{HH}) = 2.99$. However, even I4 falls some way short of the maximum inequality case of $(1/\mathrm{HH}) = 1$.

Hannah and Kay index

It is possible to interpret the Herfindahl–Hirschman index as a weighted sum of the market shares of all firms in the industry, with the market shares themselves used as weights. A general expression for a weighted sum of market shares is $\sum_{i=1}^{N} w_i s_i$, where w_i denotes the weight attached to firm i. Setting $w_i = s_i$ reproduces the Herfindahl–Hirschman index:

$$\mathrm{HH} = \sum_{i=1}^{N} w_i s_i = \sum_{i=1}^{N} s_i^2.$$

Therefore HH is a weighted sum of market shares, with larger weights attached to the larger firms and vice versa.

Hannah and Kay (1977) suggest the following generalization of the HH index:

$$\mathrm{HK}(\alpha) = \sum_{i=1}^{N} s_1^{\alpha}$$

where α is a parameter to be selected. α should be greater than zero, but not equal to one, because HK(1) = 1 for any firm size distribution. In terms of the 'weighted sum' interpretation of the HH index, the choice of α in the HK(α) index enables the relative weights attached to the larger and small firms to vary from the proportions used in the HH index. For the HK(α) index, the weights can be defined $w_i = s_i^{\alpha-1}$.

Accordingly, $\text{HK}(\alpha) = \sum_{i=1}^{N} w_i s_i = \sum_{i=1}^{N} s_i^{\alpha-1} s_i = \sum_{i=1}^{N} s_1^{\alpha}.$

- If $\alpha = 2$, the Hannah–Kay index is the same as the Herfindahl–Hirschman index, or HK(2) = HH.

- If $\alpha < 2$, HK(α) attaches relatively more weight to the smaller firms and relatively less weight to the larger firms than HH.

- Conversely, if $\alpha > 2$, HK(α) attaches relatively more weight to the larger firms and relatively less weight to the smaller firms than HH.

The last two points are illustrated in Table 9.7. For I1 the contribution to the HK(1.5) index of firm 1 (the largest firm) is 45.8 per cent (0.2003 out of 0.4376). But firm 1's contribution to the HK(2.5) index is 63.8 per cent (0.0686 out of 0.1076). Previous comments about the favourable properties of the HH index apply in equal measure to the HK(α) index. Furthermore, the larger the value of α, the smaller the degree of inaccuracy if the HK(α) index is calculated using accurate individual data for the largest firms, but estimated data for the smaller firms.

The expression for the corresponding inverse concentration measure, the numbers equivalent of the Hannah–Kay index, is as follows:

$$n(\alpha) = \left(\sum_{i=1}^{N} s_1^{\alpha} \right)^{1/(1-\alpha)}.$$

Notice that when $\alpha = 2$, $n(2) = \left(\sum_{i=1}^{N} s_i^2 \right)^{1(1-2)} = \left(\sum_{i=1}^{N} s_i^2 \right)^{-1} = 1 \Big/ \sum_{i=1}^{N} s_i^2 = 1/\text{HH}$, as before.

The numbers equivalent can be defined for any value of α that is greater than zero apart from $\alpha = 1$. The properties and interpretation of the numbers equivalent are the same as before. For an industry with N firms, the minimum value is 1 (one dominant firm and $N - 1$ small firms); and the maximum value is N (all N firms are equal-sized). In Tables 9.4 and 9.5, $n(\alpha) = 9$ for I2 (with $N = 9$ equal-sized firms) and $n(\alpha) = 6$ for I3 (with $N = 6$ equal-sized firms), no matter what value is chosen for α.

Entropy coefficient

The **entropy coefficient**, E, is another 'weighted sum' concentration measure. In this case, however, the weights are inversely related to the firms' market shares. The weights are the natural logarithms of the reciprocals of the firms' market shares. E is defined as follows:

$$E = \sum_{i=1}^{N} s_i \log_e(1/s_i)$$

Table 9.8 Calculation of entropy coefficient

Firm	Sales	s_i	$1/s_i$	$\log_e(1/s_i)$	$s_i \log_e(1/s_i)$
1	5,066	.3424	2.9206	1.0718	0.3670
2	3,376	.2282	4.3827	1.4777	0.3372
3	2,250	.1521	6.5760	1.8834	0.2864
4	1,500	.1014	9.8640	2.2889	0.2320
5	1,000	.0676	14.7960	2.6944	0.1821
6	666	.0450	22.2162	3.1008	0.1396
7	444	.0300	33.3243	3.5063	0.1052
8	296	.0200	49.9865	3.9118	0.0783
9	198	.0134	74.7273	4.3138	0.0577
Sum	14,796	1.0000			$E = 1.7855$

Relative entropy: $\quad RE = E/\log_e(N) = 1.7855/\log_e(9) = 1.7855/2.1972 = 0.8126$

Numbers equivalent: $\quad n(1) = \exp(E) = \exp(1.7855) = 5.96$

E is an inverse concentration measure: E is small for a highly concentrated industry, and E is large for an industry with low concentration. In Tables 9.4 and 9.5, E is 1.3721 (for I4), 1.7855 (I1) and 1.8236 (I5). Therefore E correctly identifies I4 as more concentrated than I1, and I1 as more concentrated than I5. The minimum possible value is $E = 0$, for an industry comprising a single monopoly producer. The maximum possible value is $E - \log_e(N)$, for an industry comprising N equal-sized firms. Because the maximum value of E depends on the number of firms, it may be inconvenient to use entropy coefficients to compare concentration for two different-sized industries. However, it is straightforward to define a standardized entropy coefficient, whose maximum value does not depend on the number of firms. This is known as the relative entropy coefficient, RE, defined as follows:

$$RE = E/\log_e(N) = [1/\log_e(N)]\sum_{i=1}^{N} s_i \log_e(1/s_i)$$

The minimum possible value is $RE = 0$ for a monopoly, and the maximum possible value is $RE = 1$ for an industry comprising N equal-sized firms.

Finally, as noted above, both E and the numbers equivalent of the HK index are inverse concentration measures. Hannah and Kay (1977, pp. 56–7) demonstrate the mathematical relationship between them. The numbers equivalent of the HK index, $n(\alpha) = \left(\sum_{i=1}^{N} s_i^\alpha\right)^{1/(1-\alpha)}$ is not defined for $\alpha = 1$. However, it can be shown that as α approaches one, the limiting value of $n(\alpha)$ is $\exp(E)$ or $e^E = \prod_{i=1}^{N}(1/s_i)^{s_i}$.

Therefore $\exp(E)$ can be interpreted as a numbers equivalent-type measure that corresponds to the case $\alpha = 1$.

Variance of the logarithms of firm sizes

In statistics, a variance provides a measure of dispersion or inequality within any data set. In the case of data on the sizes of firms in an industry, the statistical

Table 9.9 Calculation of variance of logarithmic firm sizes

Firm	Sales, x_i	$\log_e(x_i)$	$\log_e(x_i) - \bar{x}(\bar{x} = 6.9078)$	$[\log e(x_i) - \bar{x}]^2$
1	5,066	8.5303	1.6225	2.6325
2	3,376	8.1244	1.2167	1.4802
3	2,250	7.7187	0.8109	0.6575
4	1,500	7.3132	0.4054	0.1644
5	1,000	6.9078	0.0000	0.0000
6	666	6.5013	−0.4065	0.1652
7	444	6.0958	−0.8120	0.6593
8	296	5.6904	−1.2174	1.4821
9	198	5.2883	−1.6195	2.6229
Sum	14,796	62.1072		9.8643

$$\bar{x} = \text{mean value of } \log_e(x_i) = (1/N)\sum_{i=1}^{N}\log_e(x_i) = 62.1072/9 = 6.9078$$

$$VL = (1/N)\sum_{i=1}^{N}[\log_e(x_i) - \bar{x}]^2 = 9.8643/9 = 1.0960$$

property of dispersion or inequality is closely related to (but not identical to) the economic property of seller concentration. In Table 9.4, dispersion in I2 is zero (because all firm sizes are the same), but dispersion in I4 is much higher (due to the inequality in the firm size distribution). Clearly, seller concentration is higher in I4 than in I2. Accordingly, the variance of the logarithms of firm sizes, VL, can be included among the list of concentration measures (Aitchison and Brown, 1966). VL is defined as follows:

$$VL = (1/N)\sum_{i=1}^{N}[\log_e(x_i) - \bar{x}]^2 \quad \text{where} \quad \bar{x} = (1/N)\sum_{i=1}^{N}\log_e(x_i)$$

and x_i is the size of firm i (as before, measured using sales, assets, employment or some other appropriate size indicator).

For the purposes of calculating VL, the firm size data are expressed in logarithmic form for the following reasons:

■ Most industries have a highly skewed firm size distribution, with large numbers of small firms, fewer medium-sized firms and very few large firms. The variance of the (untransformed) firm size data would tend to be unduly influenced by the data for the largest firms. The log-transformation reduces or eliminates the skewness in the original distribution, enabling VL to provide a more reasonable measure of inequality across the entire firm size distribution.

■ The variance of the (untransformed) firm size data would be influenced by the scaling or units of measurement of the data. VL, in contrast, is unaffected by scaling. For example, if inflation caused the reported sales data of all firms to increase by 10 per cent, the variance of the (untransformed) sales data would increase, but VL would be unaffected. In this case, there is no change in concentration or dispersion because the sales of all firms are increased in the same proportions. VL reflects this situation accurately.

Although VL has occasionally been used as a measure of seller concentration, it is more accurate to interpret VL as a measure of dispersion or inequality in the firm size distribution. The distinction can be illustrated using the following examples taken from Tables 9.4 and 9.5:

- Both I2 and I3 have VL = 0 because in both cases all firms are equal-sized, so there is no inequality. From an industrial organization perspective, however, it seems clear that I3 is more highly concentrated than I2. I3 has fewer firms than I2, making it more likely that a cooperative or collusive outcome will be achieved.

- An economist would regard I6 as more concentrated than I1. However, the merger between the three smallest firms in I1 to form I6 implies I6 has a lower degree of inequality in its firm size distribution than I1. Accordingly VL is smaller for I6 than for I1. Switching from I1 to I6, VL moves in the opposite direction to HH and HK(α), and in the wrong direction from the economist's perspective.

Lorenz curve and the Gini coefficient

A **Lorenz curve** (named after Lorenz, 1905) shows the variation in the cumulative size of the n largest firms in an industry, as n varies from 1 to N (where N is the total number of firms). Figure 9.1 shows a typical Lorenz curve. The firms are represented in a horizontal array, from the largest to the smallest (reading from left to right) along the horizontal axis. The vertical axis shows the cumulative size (the sum of the sizes of all firms from firm 1 to firm n, as a function of n)

- If all of the firms are equal-sized, the Lorenz curve is the 45-degree line OCA. At point C, for example, exactly half of the industry's member firms account for exactly half of the total industry size, represented by the distance OD.

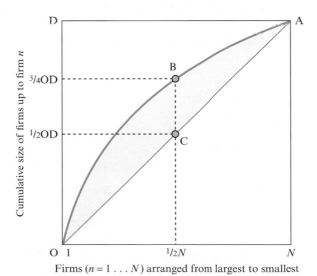

Figure 9.1 The Lorenz curve

■ If the firm size distribution is skewed, the Lorenz curve is the concave curve OBA. At point B, exactly half of the industry's member firms account for three-quarters of the total industry size, represented by OD.

The Lorenz curve can be used to define a concentration measure due to Gini (1912), known as the **Gini coefficient**. With reference to Figure 9.1, the Gini coefficient is defined as follows:

$$G = \frac{\text{area of the crescent between OBA and OCA}}{\text{area of the triangle ODA}}$$

■ The maximum possible value of $G = 1$ corresponds to the case of one dominant firm with a market share approaching one, and $N - 1$ very small firms each with a negligible market share. In this case the Lorenz curve approaches the line ODA, so the numerator and denominator in the formula for G are the same.

■ The minimum value of $G = 0$ corresponds to the case of N equal-sized firms. In this case the Lorenz curve is the 45-degree line OCA, so the numerator in the formula for G is zero.

The formula definition for the Gini coefficient is as follows:

$$G = \left\{ \frac{\sum_{n=1}^{N} \sum_{i=1}^{n} x_i}{0.5(N+1)\sum_{i=1}^{N} x_i} \right\} - 1$$

where x_i is the size of firm i (as before, measured using sales, assets, employment or some other appropriate size indicator) when the firms ranked in descending order of size.

Table 9.10 Calculation of Gini coefficient

Firm, n	Sales, x_i	Cumulative sales, up to firm n, $\sum_{i=1}^{n} x_i$
1	5,066	5,066
2	3,376	8,442
3	2,250	10,692
4	1,500	12,192
5	1,000	13,192
6	666	13,858
7	444	14,302
8	296	14,598
9	198	14,796
Sum	$\sum_{i=1}^{N} x_i = 14,796$	$\sum_{n=1}^{N} \sum_{i=1}^{n} x_i = 107,138$

$$\text{Gini coefficient, } G = \left\{ \frac{\sum_{n=1}^{N} \sum_{i=1}^{n} x_i}{0.5(N+1)\sum_{i=1}^{N} x_i} \right\} - 1 = \left\{ \frac{107,138}{0.5 \times 10 \times 14,796} \right\} - 1 = 0.4482$$

Like the variance of logarithmic firm sizes measure, the Gini coefficient is most accurately interpreted as a measure of inequality in the firm size distribution. In fact, elsewhere in economics one of the best known applications of the Gini coefficient is for the measurement of inequality in household incomes. Tables 9.4 and 9.5 show that both I2 and I3 have $G = 0$, because in both cases all of the firms are equal-sized. As before, however, an industrial economist might regard I3 as more highly concentrated than I2. Furthermore, I6 has $G = 0.3129$, smaller than $G = 0.4482$ for I1, but an industrial economist would regard I6 as more concentrated than I1.

Section 9.4 concludes with three case studies that focus on the relevance of seller concentration for policy debates concerning competition. Case Study 9.1 examines UK banking, Case Study 9.2 examines US newspapers and broadcasting and Case Study 9.3 examines the pricing of auditing services.

Case study 9.1

Break up Britain's uncompetitive big banks

The Independent Commission on Banking, chaired by Sir John Vickers, has the task of balancing bank competition with stability, and of weighing reforms to the structure of the market alongside changes to the banks themselves. If handled correctly, it can shape a new era for British banking.

Historically, such regulatory interventions have created immediate benefits. The US crash of 1907 produced the Federal Reserve; the 1929 crash created both America's Glass-Steagall Act and its Securities and Exchange Commission; and the 1930s depression produced the Investment Company Act. Now we have the Basel III rules.

To ensure a further contribution, Sir John should note that Britain's banks are too concentrated and that each individually represents too great a portion of gross domestic product. Indeed its high operating margins and return on equity suggest the UK has one of the world's most concentrated and least competitive banking systems. Two lines of inquiry follow. First, is such concentration good for banking and its customers, given there is no compelling evidence that scale provides economic or service gains? Second, after Sir John's commission, will any of the banks remain too big to fail, financially or socially?

Concentration affects relative performance and strategic behaviour. In general it produces less competition. This is also a long-standing problem: the tendency for banks to merge, rather than divest, has triggered 21 separate inquiries since Don Cruickshank's review in 2000. Few industries require such consistent attention. Worse, consolidation has accelerated over the past decade, with the crisis leading to yet more mergers, increasing the power of existing banks. The implicit support the most important of these receive from government is now a competitive advantage and barrier to new entrants. Yet some argue it follows that these large, concentrated banks create a more stable system than a market filled with numerous, smaller competitors.

This is not necessarily the case. In fact, competition is not the opposite of stability or security – because stability emanates not just from size and status, but also from diversity and pluralism. Inadequate competition can produce excess profits, poor customer service and a dearth of innovation, none of which are likely to create a stable system.

Now Sir John must decide what to do next. At the tactical level it is not necessary to separate the retail and 'casino' parts of Britain's three biggest banks. The problems associated with unified banks can be controlled instead by rules regarding capitalisation, subsidiarisation, limits on cross-funding and resolution processes. Instead, the Vickers commission's main opportunity is to embrace the reasonable view that a failure in the banking system has more widespread social consequences than a failure in other British oligopolies, such as sugar and tobacco. Money moves faster than labour, or raw materials. If the banks mess up, society suffers. The future lies in less monolithic institutions, with more fluid entries into and out of the banking sector. And this, in turn, may mean undoing existing bank mergers.

In practice the banking commission must therefore give proper consideration to splitting one or both of Lloyds Banking Group and the Royal Bank of Scotland. It would do so on the grounds of increasing competition and reducing barriers to new entrants. But new entrants alone will take too long to change industry concentration – particularly because of the dominance of the six major banks in current accounts, the entry product for most customers. Sir John will need to examine the practicalities of undoing one or both of the mergers. But I am told neither group has irreversibly integrated their systems, so demerging is possible.

In general we also need smaller banks, supported by more capital. The commission should examine the case for government sponsoring (in concert with private equity) a new category of bank for small- and medium-sized enterprises – and using the huge financial gains arising to the taxpayers from the interventions of 2008 and 2009 to fund it. The commission should also consider requiring existing banks to provide new entrants and building societies with access to their payment and other critical systems. In parallel the government needs to bring forward plans to return Northern Rock to the private sector as a mutual.

As the banking commission weighs its options, it might finally acknowledge that stability, as an end in itself, is a mirage in a world of rapid change. Instead we need a banking system that is agile, robust and flexible. Only this less monolithic, more collaborative and at the same time more competitive structure can produce the dynamic equilibrium from which economic growth can flow, without fear of unmanageable systemic failure.

Source: Break up Britain's uncompetitive big banks, *Financial Times*, 12 December 2010. Reproduced with kind permission of Lord Paul Myners.

Case study 9.2

The media concentration debate

One of the most rancorous political battles in Washington today is over the rules limiting media concentration. Michael Powell, chairman of the Federal Communications Commission, has narrowly pushed through a set of rules that relax ownership restrictions. The share of population that can be reached by the television stations owned by any one company was raised from 35 to 45 per cent. The cross-ownership limits of newspapers and television stations in the same market were rescinded or reduced, depending on the size of the market. And local ownership ceilings for television stations were raised. The result has been a political firestorm, in which the political right and left have joined forces against free-market advocates, resulting in a lopsided congressional vote of 400:21. The Senate is in no better a mood. The White House has threatened a veto if such a law is passed. It would be President George W. Bush's first veto; and judging from the congressional vote tally and the desertion of the FCC's Republican allies, an uphill struggle. Powell, meanwhile, seems disgusted enough to contemplate departing.

Opponents of the FCC's new rules view themselves as a last line of defence against homogenized news controlled by five giant media conglomerates: AOL Time Warner, Disney, General Electric, News Corporation and Viacom. They fear a situation like that of Italy, where Silvio Berlusconi has used his media empire to achieve power and office. Defenders of the FCC argue that new technologies have made the media market wide open and reduced the importance of broadcasting stations. Both sides project themselves as defenders of the first amendment, protecting media from government, or, alternatively, shielding the public from communications empires.

The American media concentration debate and the principles that are at stake were cogently analysed in June by my fellow New Economy Forum columnists Tom Hazlitt and Richard Epstein. This column, in contrast, will be empirical. It is useful to step back and look at the facts. Are American media more concentrated today, nationally and locally, than they were in the past? This is largely an empirical question. It is true that large media companies have become larger; but so has the entire sector. The answer is therefore not as obvious as it seems.

Fortunately for its readers, the FT Online New Economy Forum is in possession of the world's best data set on media ownership and market shares, covering about 100 information sector industries and going back about 20 years. We are therefore able to provide some real but still preliminary empirical findings. What follows might be dry but it is directly relevant to the debate in Washington.

It is important to understand the difference between national and local media concentration. A newspaper company may own 25 papers that give it in the aggregate a moderate national market share among newspaper companies; but each of these papers may be the only local paper in its town, giving it substantial powers there over local news coverage and advertising prices. Other media are national rather than local, for example most magazines, books, music, and content network of television and cable. It is therefore necessary to look at both national and local concentrations.

What is market concentration? We use an index known as 'CR$_4$', which is the share of the top four companies in a market. Just to be sure, we also look at another index, the 'HH' used by the US Government to define concentration for antitrust purposes. We compare concentration trends over the past 20 years.

The concentration of broadcast television is the most contentious issue in the debate. Let us therefore look at the facts. For local television station ownership, the national share of the top four companies just about doubled, from 12 per cent in 1984 to 21 per cent in 2001/2. But by the standards of the US antitrust authorities, this leaves the industry still firmly in the range of 'unconcentrated'. During that period, market concentration also declined for television networking, which provides the bulk of broadcast station evening and weekend programmes, from a three-network oligopoly of nearly 100 per cent to a four-company share of 92 per cent, still very high but dropping. If we combine networks for broadcast television and for cable television, as most viewers would, national network concentration declined from 82 per cent to 68 per cent.

At the same time, the local concentration of broadcast television stations, based on an analysis of 30 representative markets, did not increase as many have feared, but actually declined, owing to the shift of viewership away from the affiliates of three networks to a wider range of broadcast stations. Whereas the largest four stations in a local market accounted for 90 per cent of audiences in 1984, that number had declined to 73 per cent 20 years later. Furthermore, most of that decline took place in the past five years. If we put all these elements together into a composite index, the results show a decline in the overall concentration of broadcast television over the past 20 years.

In contrast, market concentration grew considerably for radio stations, where the ownership rules until the 1990s kept any company from owning more than a few stations, in an industry of 12,000 stations. Today, with no national ownership ceilings, the top four station groups, led by Clear Channel and Viacom, account for 34 per cent of stations by revenues. This is more than four times the 8 per cent of two decades ago, and marks a growth unparalleled by any other medium; but even this, in terms of the US government's guidelines on market concentration, is well within the 'unconcentrated' range. Furthermore, most of that growth has taken place between 1992 and 1996 and has slowed down more recently. Local radio concentration is perhaps the most important issue to worry about. It has grown from an average of 44 per cent of an audience held by the top four station owners in each local market 20 years ago to 84 per cent, and falls definitely within the range of 'highly concentrated industries'.

For multi-channel television (cable and satellite), the four-company concentration tripled nationally from 21 per cent to 60 per cent, an increase that is more troubling than that of broadcast television. Most important is the extent of local concentration. Here, cable used to be for a long time the only option, wielding considerable gatekeeper power. Today, with satellite television a viable option for national programmes, cable's share has declined to 78 per cent and keeps sliding.

It is interesting to look at which local medium is most concentrated: newspapers. While their national concentration is moderate but rising (27 per cent, up from 22 per cent), local concentration levels are astonishingly high. Whichever index one uses, local newspapers are at the top for local media concentration.

Finally, to get an overall picture, we aggregated the trends for all mass media: television, cable and radio but also print, music, and film. On average their concentration is low by the definition of the US antitrust authorities but steadily increasing, especially after 1996. Average four-company concentration in each of the industries rose from 31 per cent to 46 per cent, to a level that is still unconcentrated (but barely) by the government's guidelines.

Contrast this with the higher concentrations in the telecom services sector (76 per cent) or even the internet sector, whose wide-open fragmentation increasingly exists more as a founding myth than as a reality (up from 63 per cent in 1996 to 73 per cent in 2001/2).

We can also look at the presence of the top four mass media companies in the entire mass media sector. Their revenues tripled from $26bn in 1984, in today's money, to $78bn last year. The share of these companies in the overall mass media sector has doubled from about 11 per cent in 1984 to 21 per cent in 2001/2. This is a considerable relative increase – but the absolute level would be considered low in most sectors of goods and services. The low percentages, defying conventional wisdom, are explainable by the sheer size and diversity of the mass media market and its segments: about $400bn, if one adds up the revenues of print, music, broadcasting, cable, and film.

These dry numbers are relevant to the hot debate in Washington, assuming that evidence has a role besides the rhetoric. Outside of radio, the data do not show a rapid trend to media concentration and dominance. This should not suggest that media concentration is low or that there is no need for vigilance. But it is quite another matter to call it a crisis, as many have done in the heat of the battle. Congress has clearly signalled its unwillingness to see the radio scenario replay itself for television. Society is entitled to determine the proper balance between the economic and speech rights of media companies and the public's right to diverse sources of information. And economics is not the only factor to consider. The ownership of news and entertainment media is important to the health of democracy. But the debate over it must be healthy, too, and relate to facts rather than be driven by some dark fear that a handful of media giants (liberal or conservative, take your pick) are taking over nationally and locally, a fear which is not supported by the data.

Source: The media concentration debate, © The Financial Times Limited. All Rights Reserved, 31 July 2003 (Noam, E.).

Case study 9.3

Andersen's collapse results in a fee bonus for Big Four rivals

The dominance of the Big Four auditors has directly raised the fees companies pay to have their accounts verified, according to a study that is likely to trigger a new row about the effects of audit concentration.

Research due to be published today concludes that the reduction to four big firms after the collapse of Arthur Andersen in 2002 led to an average 2.4 per cent increase in the fees paid – excluding the impact of other factors such as changes in regulation.

While the concentration-related increase might appear small given that statutory audit fees have almost doubled in the past five years, the fact a direct link has been made is potentially explosive given the debate about the risks of having so few firms responsible for verifying the accounts of all the biggest companies. It could also raise competition concerns in regulatory circles far outside the financial world.

The report was sponsored by BDO Stoy Hayward, a rival to the Big Four, but carried out independently by the London School of Economics. 'This is not about price as such, it is about whether the market is distorted – and this market is not operating the way other markets do,' said Jeremy Newman, managing partner of BDO, who has long contended that the audit market suffers from barriers to entry and is distorted as a result. 'People have said "prove it", and if we can show, like this, that there are distortions in pricing, that's evidence the market isn't operating freely,' he added.

It is not the first time the link between concentration and fees has been made; the Oxera consultancy said similar things in its own 2006 study into the audit industry, sponsored by the Department for Trade and Industry. It looked at audit fees before and after the 1998 merger of Price Waterhouse and Coopers & Lybrand – the move that shrank the Big Six to the Big Five. But the Big Four firms attacked the data used and proved they were unreliable. After that, the matter was largely dropped.

The Big Four – PwC, Deloitte, KPMG and Ernst & Young – audit all FTSE 100 companies between them and almost all the FTSE 350 businesses. Intriguingly, the LSE study found no evidence of a link between concentration and fees prior to Andersen's collapse. 'There is a difference between five firms and four at the top and it does change the competition dynamic,' said BDO's Mr Newman. 'Underlying profitability at the Big Four has improved since Andersen left, for example, but we are not seeing margins increase on our audit work.'

The report also found that over the period of the study – 1998 to 2006 – there was an average 'premium' in Big Four fees of 13 per cent. However, this rose to 20 per cent after 2002 – the year that Andersen disappeared. The sharp rise in audit fees since 2002 has so far been largely attributed to the effects of new regulation such as the switch to international accounting standards and the introduction in the US of Sarbanes-Oxley.

Mariano Selvaggi, who conducted the study that he says is entirely independent of any outcome BDO might have wanted, said his analysis of the data did not support the theory that added regulatory work had driven fee inflation. Instead, the concentration of audit work had had a quantifiable impact.

Audit work accounts for roughly one-third of the income of the biggest firms and all the top firms acknowledge their reputation in this area is the core of their business. Last year PwC's total fee income – including its tax advisory and consulting businesses – topped the Big Four table at £2.1bn. At the bottom of the Big Four was E&Y at £1.2bn – still a long way ahead of the £317.4m of BDO and £315m of Grant Thornton, BDO's close rival. UK regulators such as the Financial Reporting Council have long been concerned about the risks posed by the Big Four's dominance, but they have so far been less concerned about the price of audits than their availability – particularly should one of the firms abruptly collapse as Andersen did. A collapse would leave companies suddenly bereft of the services they depend upon and – more importantly for investors – scrambling to get their accounts properly verified, with the added risk of unnoticed accounting fraud as new auditors get to grips with their new clients.

Source: Andersen's collapse results in a fee bonus for Big Four rivals, © The Financial Times Limited. All Rights Reserved, 29 April 2008 (Hughes, J.).

9.5 Interpretation of concentration measures

Subject to the availability of data, the calculation of any of the concentration indicators detailed above is straightforward. Some of the technical limitations of individual measures have already been identified and discussed. However, even if the technical issues are disregarded, the broader interpretation of concentration indicators can still be problematic, due to inherent difficulties in defining the boundaries of the relevant industry or market (Curry and George, 1983). Some of the key issues are as follows:

- *Choice of appropriate industry definition.* A concentration measure is specific to an industry, but any industry definition is arbitrary to some extent. Industry definitions should allow the calculation of concentration measures that sensibly reflect market power. Therefore a properly defined industry should include producers of all substitute products. But how close does an alternative product have to be in order to count as a substitute? Substitution is a matter of degree, and the difficulty lies in knowing where to draw the line. By defining the limits very tightly, almost any firm could be considered as a monopolist. In one case in the US, the relevant market was described as 'the industry supplying paint to General Motors'. Since DuPont was at the time the only supplier of paint to General Motors, DuPont immediately achieved monopoly status. In general, the more refined the industry definition (the greater the number of digits), the higher measured concentration is likely to be. The choice of suitable industry or market definitions for decision making in competition policy is discussed in Chapter 23.

- *Defining the boundaries of the market.* The selection of the cohort of firms whose size data are to be used to measure concentration also includes a geographical dimension. The relevant market for one firm might be local; another firm might service an international market. Naturally, concentration measures calculated from international or national data tend to suggest lower levels of concentration than regional or local measures. For example, public transport services by bus are provided by small numbers of carriers in each city. Therefore, locally, seller concentration tends to be high. Measured at national level, however, concentration tends to be much lower.

■ *Treatment of imports and exports.* If (as is likely) producers of imported goods are excluded from the calculation of a concentration measure for an industry in the national economy, measured concentration might either overstate or understate the true importance of the largest firms. For example, if a single foreign firm imported goods that accounted for 40 per cent of the market, making it the largest single producer, CR_n calculated using data on domestic firms only would seriously understate the true degree of concentration. If on the other hand the imported goods' 40 per cent market share was accounted for by a large number of small foreign producers, CR_n would overstate true concentration. Similar issues arise if (as is likely) the reported sales of domestic firms include sales in export markets. One firm might have extremely high sales relative to all the rest, but if these sales are dispersed across several highly competitive export markets, the firm does not have much market power. But a high concentration ratio might easily be misinterpreted to suggest the opposite. These and other similar issues are discussed by Utton (1982).

■ *Multi-product operations.* Concentration measures based on a firm's reported company accounts data might not take account of diversification: many larger firms sell goods or services across a wide range of separate markets. Typically, a plant or firm is classified as part of the census industry to which its main product belongs. If 60 per cent of a firm's sales revenues are derived from an industry A product, and 40 per cent from an industry B product, then all of that firm's sales (or other firm size data) may be attributed to industry A. Concentration measures calculated from data of this kind might tend to overstate or understate concentration in both industries. Only by pure chance (if all of these 'diversified firm' effects cancel each other out) will concentration be measured accurately.

Although at first sight the choice between the various concentration measures might seem almost bewildering, this decision often turns out not to be too crucial in practice. Most of the measures described above tend to be highly correlated with each other (Davies, 1979; Kwoka, 1981). However, in the final analysis it may be impossible to quantify all relevant aspects of an industry's competitive nature in a single numerical measure. For example, the number of firms in an industry might be small, but if their objectives and modes of operation differ fundamentally, they may disregard their interdependence and behave like atomistic competitors. Even the narrower and purely 'economic' characteristics may be hard to pin down. '[N]o single concentration measure effectively considers the three underlying determinants of competition: sector size, inequality of market shares and coalition potential' (Vanlommel *et al.*, 1977, p. 15).

9.6 Summary

Seller concentration, the number and size distribution of firms in a industry, is one of the key characteristics of industry structure. Chapter 9 has examined the measurement of seller concentration. Any specific measure of seller concentration aims to reflect the implications of the number of firms and their size distribution for competition in the industry concerned.

In measuring seller concentration for any industry or market, it is necessary to take decisions concerning industry or market definition. The definition of any market contains both a product dimension and a geographic dimension. The product market definition should include all products that are close substitutes for one another, both in consumption and in production. The geographic market definition involves determining whether an increase in the price of a product in one location significantly affects demand or supply elsewhere. Price and cross-price elasticities can be used to determine the limits of product and geographic market boundaries. In practice, however, substitution is always a matter of degree, and decisions concerning boundaries are always arbitrary to some extent. The UK's Standard Industrial Classification and NACE, its EU counterpart, are currently the official standard used in the compilation of government statistics.

The most widely used seller concentration measures include the n-firm concentration ratio, the Herfindahl–Hirschman index, the Hannah–Kay index, the entropy coefficient, the variance of the logarithms of firm sizes, and the Gini coefficient. The method of calculation for all of these measures has been described in detail, and their strengths and limitations have been assessed.

Discussion questions

1. Explain the terms substitutes in consumption, and substitutes in production. What is the relevance of these terms to the issue of market definition?

2. With reference to Case Study 9.1, examine the case for and against breaking up large banks into smaller units.

3. Examine the issues involved in defining the geographic boundaries of a market. With reference to Case Study 9.2, illustrate your answer with reference to issues that have arisen in the political debate concerning media concentration in the US.

4. With reference to Case Study 9.3, it is alleged that the collapse of the auditors Arthur Andersen in 2002 led to a significant increase in the market power of the surviving Big Four auditors. Which seller concentration measures are best equipped to reflect this increase in concentration and market power?

5. What is the distinction between a market and an industry?

6. What is a strategic market?

7. Explain the distinction between aggregate concentration and industry concentration.

8. Outline Hannah and Kay's (1977) general criteria for a concentration measure to adequately reflect the most important characteristics of the firm size distribution.

9. Examine the main advantages and disadvantages of the n-firm concentration ratio as a measure of seller concentration.

10. Does the Herfindahl–Hirschman index provide a more satisfactory method for measuring seller concentration than the n-firm concentration ratio?

11. Explain the distinction between concentration and inequality. How accurately does an inequality measure such as the variance of the logarithms of firm sizes reflect the characteristics of market structure?

12. Explain the construction of the Gini coefficient as a measure of inequality in an industry's firm size distribution.

Further reading

Carranza, J.E. (2008) Concentration measures, in Durlauf, S.N. and Blume, L.E. (eds) *The New Palgrave Dictionary of Economics*, 2nd edition. London: Palgrave Macmillan.

Curry, B. and George, K. (1983) Industrial concentration: a survey, *Journal of Industrial Economics*, 31, 203–55.

Davies, S.W. (1989) Concentration, in Davies, S. and Lyons, B. (eds), *The Economics of Industrial Organisation*. London: Longman.

Davies, S.W. and Lyons, B.R. (1996) *Industrial Organisation in the European Union*. Oxford: Clarendon Press.

Utton, M.A. (1970) *Industrial Concentration*. Harmondsworth: Penguin.

Determinants of seller concentration

Learning objectives

This chapter covers the following topics:

- systematic determinants of seller concentration
    - economies of scale
    - barriers to entry
    - sunk costs
    - regulation
    - industry life cycle
    - distinctive capabilities, strategic assets and core competences
- the random growth hypothesis
- trends in seller concentration
- seller concentration and the location of industry

Key terms

Cluster
Core competences
Distinctive capabilities
Geographic concentration
Gibrat's law
Industrial district
Industry life cycle
Law of Proportionate Effect

Porter's Diamond Model
Regional concentration
Sample selection bias
Specialization
Sunk cost
Survivorship bias
Type 1 industry
Type 2 industry

10.1 Introduction

Chapter 10 examines some of the important determinants of seller concentration, and identifies patterns and trends in the data on seller concentration across regions and countries, and over time. Why do some industries tend to become more highly concentrated than others? What factors cause seller concentration to vary over time?

Section 10.2 identifies the principal theoretical determinants of seller concentration, and the role that these factors play in influencing the historical evolution of industry structure. Relevant factors include economies of scale, entry and exit barriers, regulation, the scope for discretionary sunk cost investment on items such as advertising and research and development, the stage reached in the industry's life cycle, and the firm's distinctive capabilities and core competences.

Section 10.3 describes an alternative approach towards explaining the evolution of industry structure, based on the notion that the growth of individual firms is inherently unpredictable. According to the random growth hypothesis, there is a natural tendency for concentration to increase gradually over the long term, even if the growth patterns of individual firms are completely random.

Finally, Section 10.4 presents some facts and figures concerning patterns and trends in seller concentration in the UK and EU. Patterns of specialization and geographic concentration, reflected in spatial patterns of firm and industry location within the EU, are also considered.

10.2 Seller concentration: systematic determinants

This section examines the main systematic determinants of seller concentration. These factors include economies of scale, entry and exit barriers, regulation, the scope for discretionary **sunk cost** expenditure on items such as advertising and research and development, the stage reached in the industry's life cycle, and the firm's distinctive capabilities and core competences.

Economies of scale

The structure of costs may have important implications for industry structure and the behaviour of firms. Economies of scale result from savings in the long-run average cost (LRAC) achieved as a firm operates at a larger scale. The output level at which the firm's LRAC attains its minimum value is the firm's minimum efficient scale (MES) of production. The comparison between the total output that would be produced if each incumbent firm operates at its MES, and the total demand for the industry's product at the price required in order for at least normal profit to be earned, has important implications for the number of firms that the industry can accommodate. This in turn has implications for seller concentration and industry structure.

If the total demand for the product *equals* the MES, the most cost-efficient arrangement is for the industry to be serviced by a single firm, and industry structure is most likely to be monopolistic. If the total demand for the product is 1,000 times as large as the MES, then the industry can accommodate 1,000 firms all producing at the MES, and the industry structure might approximate perfect competition. However, if average costs are approximately constant over a range of output levels beyond the MES, the actual number of firms might be less than the number that could be accommodated if all were operating at (but not beyond) the MES.

Barriers to entry

Microeconomic theory views entry (and exit) as an important driver in the process by which markets adjust towards equilibrium. The more dynamic Schumpeterian and Austrian schools emphasize the innovative role of entry in driving industry evolution. There is plentiful empirical evidence to show that entry is higher in profitable or fast-growing industries (Baldwin and Gorecki, 1987; Geroski, 1991a,b), and exit is higher from low-profit industries (Dunne *et al.*, 1988). Other things being equal, entry is likely to reduce concentration, assuming the average size of entrants is smaller than that of incumbent firms. However, the effect could be the opposite if entry takes place at a large scale, perhaps as a result of a diversification strategy on the part of a large established firm from some other industry or geographic area. Meanwhile, by reducing the numbers of incumbent firms, exit is likely to increase concentration. In practice, entry and exit rates themselves tend to be correlated (Caves, 1998). For example, Dunne *et al.* (1988) report evidence of a negative relationship between annual entry and exit rates for US manufacturing industries over the period 1963–82. Barriers to entry are examined in detail in Chapter 11.

Scope for discretionary, sunk cost expenditures

Sutton (1991, 1998) examines the implications of a long-run increase in market size for the market shares of individual firms and for seller concentration. Sutton identifies two basic industry types, classified according to the nature of their sunk costs. In a **Type 1 industry**, also known as an *exogenous sunk cost industry*, each firm incurs a fixed sunk cost in order to enter the industry. This expenditure might include the cost of establishing a plant, or the cost of achieving some threshold level of advertising expenditure. Sunk costs are exogenous, in the sense that the firm has limited discretion in choosing the levels of such expenditures. There are no other entry barriers. In a **Type 2 industry**, also known as an *endogenous sunk cost industry*, the amount of sunk cost expenditure allocated to items such as advertising and research and development is discretionary. Some sunk cost expenditure may be required in order to enter, but further substantial sunk cost expenditures are incurred subsequently, as incumbents compete to maintain or increase their own market shares. Advertising and research and development are important vehicles for discretionary sunk cost investment in Type 2 industries.

The following summary of Sutton's argument draws on Bagwell's (2007) survey. Consider first a Type 1 industry with a homogeneous product. For any given level of total industry sales, the profit earned by each individual firm is assumed to be inversely related to N, the number of firms, and influenced by θ, an industry-level parameter reflecting the intensity of price competition. The polar cases for θ are joint profit maximization, in which the firms operate a cartel, setting their prices as if they were a single monopolist; and Bertrand competition, in which price is driven down to the perfectly competitive level. Costs comprise a variable component that is linear in output; and a fixed component σ, the exogenous sunk cost.

In this model, N adjusts so that each firm earns only a normal profit in the long run. The equilibrium condition can be written $S \times \pi(N, \theta) = \sigma$, where S denotes total consumer expenditure in the market, and $S \times \pi(N, \theta)$ is each firm's operating profit (revenue *minus* variable costs). Each firm must earn sufficient operating profit to cover its fixed cost. This analysis has two implications. First, for any given N, an increase in S increases $S \times \pi(N, \theta)$, enabling each incumbent firm to earn an abnormal profit. This tends to encourage entry. Therefore an increase in S leads an increase in N. As S increases, seller concentration, measured by $1/N$, tends towards zero. Therefore there is a tendency towards the fragmentation of industry structure as the size of the market increases.

The second implication follows from the assumption that $\pi(N, \theta)$ is dependent on θ. This implies a relationship between θ and the equilibrium value of N. With joint profit maximization, the operating profit per unit of output is at its maximum. Many firms can earn a normal profit, so N is large and industry concentration is relatively low. With Bertrand competition, the operating profit per unit of output is at its minimum. Fewer firms can earn a normal profit, so N is small and concentration is high. Within any Type 1 industry, the performance of all firms is similar; but when comparisons are drawn between firms in different Type 1 industries, variations in the industry-level parameter θ are the main drivers of differences in firm performance.

Then consider a Type 2 industry with vertical product differentiation. This means the products of different producers are differentiated by product quality: some producers concentrate on the high-quality end of the product range, while others produce lower-quality lines for a mass market. Each firm's product is defined by a vertical attribute u, which reflects product quality. Suppose by advertising, each firm can increase consumers' perceptions of u. In a Type 2 industry, the tendency towards fragmentation as the market expands is offset by a competitive escalation in advertising expenditures. By advertising sufficiently heavily relative to its competitors, a firm can always induce a certain proportion of consumers to buy its product at a price that exceeds its variable cost. Therefore, as the market expands, at some point a firm that deviates from the established equilibrium by incurring an increased advertising outlay can earn sufficient operating profit to cover its (increased) sunk cost. At that point, it becomes profitable for a firm to deviate, resulting in the creation of a new equilibrium. Each time there is an escalation in sunk cost expenditure, the deviating firm's market share attains at least some minimum value (which does not change over time). Therefore concentration does not tend towards zero, and industry structure does not fragment, as the size of the market increases. Over time, the industry's member firms become increasingly dispersed in size, with each firm's relative position dependent on its historical record of achievement in ratcheting up its sunk cost expenditures.

Several attempts have been made to classify Type 1 and Type 2 industries. Type 1 industries include household textiles, leather products, footwear, clothing, printing and publishing. Type 2 industries include motor vehicles, tobacco, soaps and detergents, pharmaceuticals and man-made fibres (Bresnahan, 1992; Schmalensee, 1992; Davies and Lyons, 1996; Lyons *et al.*, 1997). Lyons *et al.* (1997), Robinson and Chiang (1996) and Dick (2007) test Sutton's hypothesis empirically, and report some supporting evidence. The European Commission (1997b) examines the evolution of concentration in 71 industries between 1987 and 1993. Average concentration was found to be significantly higher in Type 2 than in Type 1 industries, in accordance with Sutton's hypotheses.

Regulation

Government policy can also influence levels of concentration. Competition policy and regulation are primarily aimed at correcting market failure, increasing competition and giving consumers a wider choice of products and services. Policies aimed at increasing competition by discouraging restrictive practices or disallowing mergers on grounds of public interest tend to reduce concentration, or at least prevent concentration from increasing. Conversely, policies that restrict the number of firms permitted to operate in certain industries, or grant exclusive property rights to selected firms, tend to increase concentration. Competition policy and the regulation of industry are examined in Chapters 23 and 24.

The industry life cycle

The stage that has been reached in the **industry life cycle** may have implications for seller concentration (Dosi *et al.*, 1997; Klepper, 1997; McGahan, 2000). Figure 10.1

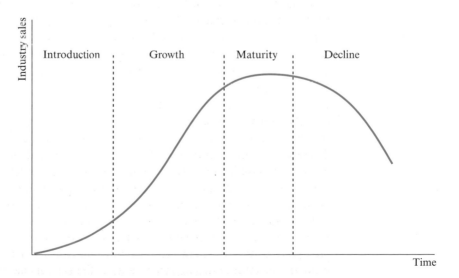

Figure 10.1 The industry life cycle

illustrates the four stages of a typical industry life cycle: the introduction, growth, maturity and decline stages. Case Study 10.1 provides an application to the credit union sector.

During the introduction phase, firms invest heavily in research and development in order to develop a completely new product. The firms that are initially successful in bringing the product to market benefit from a first-mover advantage. Although they are able to charge high prices, sales volumes may be relatively small, and there is no guarantee that revenues will be sufficient to recoup the initial research and development expenditures. Competing producers may offer similar products with incompatible technological specifications. At this stage, there may be lack of awareness or confusion on the part of consumers as to the usefulness of the product. Seller concentration is likely to be relatively low.

During the growth phase, a particular technological specification becomes established as the industry standard. The market starts to expand, and by producing at higher volumes, successful producers whose brands become established start to realize cost savings through economies of scale. Prices fall rapidly, stimulating further growth in consumer demand. Success may also attract entry, with new firms seeking to imitate the successful specification, perhaps by introducing brands embodying only minor or superficial variations in product characteristics. The consequent increase in industry supply and competition places further downward pressure on prices. However, because consumer demand is expanding rapidly, incumbent firms can tolerate the presence of entrants, and seller concentration remains relatively low.

During the maturity phase, growth of sales and profitability level off as consumer demand for the industry's product approaches the saturation level. Opportunities for additional growth in demand, through further price-cutting or further introduction of minor variations in product characteristics, are eventually exhausted. Incumbent firms may respond more defensively to threatened or actual competition from entrants by seeking to raise entry barriers, perhaps by undertaking large-scale advertising campaigns or through brand proliferation. Merger and takeover is likely to be the principal means by which incumbents can achieve further economies of scale or further growth. At this stage, seller concentration increases to levels higher than those seen during the introduction and growth stages, as production at high volume becomes essential if firms are to maintain acceptable levels of profitability.

Finally, during the decline stage, the sales and profits of incumbent firms begin to fall. Collusion or mergers between incumbent firms may well take place, primarily for defensive purposes: to eliminate competition and strengthen the parties' market power, thereby providing some compensation for the decline in consumer demand. Some firms may decide to withdraw from the industry altogether, perhaps having identified new opportunities in alternative markets. Incumbents that are unable to implement effective defensive strategies may be faced with a loss of investor confidence, a falling share price and eventual bankruptcy. With the market only capable of sustaining a declining number of producers, seller concentration remains relatively high.

Stigler (1951) examines the interaction between the industry life cycle and the extent of vertical integration, and considers the implications for concentration in vertically linked industries. Before the market has achieved sufficient volume to sustain specialist suppliers of raw materials and specialist distribution channels, producers may seek to ensure their own input supplies and provide their own sales service, through backward and forward integration. Accordingly, concentration in the supply of raw materials and in distribution may be relatively high during the introduction stage. As the market starts to expand, however, specialist suppliers of raw materials and specialist distribution services begin to appear, and concentration in these adjacent sectors tends to decline. In the later maturity and decline stages of the industry life cycle, vertical integration may form part of the incumbents' defensive strategies. Accordingly, concentration in the raw materials and distribution sectors may tend to revert back towards higher levels. Klimenko (2004) elaborates on the nature of vertical integration towards the end of the industry life cycle:

> [A]t mature stages of industry evolution, firms rarely introduce new products and most of the time routinely produce standardized goods and services. The existence of stable interface standards between segments of the industry's value chain implies that upstream firms can mass-produce intermediate products to satisfy standardized downstream demands instead of customizing them to individual specification of downstream firms. At the same time, the downstream firms are able to pick standardized inputs 'off the shelf' without worrying how well they fit in the assembly of the final product.
>
> *(Klimenko, 2004, p. 178)*

The mobile phone industry provides a recent example. At the birth of the industry, mobile phone manufacturers were required to have expertise in designing radio chips, batteries, software, the assembly of electronic components, and the design of cases. Incumbent firms such as Nokia, Motorola and Ericsson integrated vertically to produce base stations in order to provide mobile phone coverage. However, as the industry has evolved and matured, specialist producers have entered the market, producing radio chips, software and handsets. Consequently, a process of vertical disintegration is taking place as incumbent firms outsource the manufacturing of component parts (*The Economist, 2004a*).

Case study 10.1

Industry life cycle for the credit union sector

Credit unions are cooperative, member owned, not-for-profit financial institutions, which are based on the underlying principle of self-help. Credit unions offer loans to their members out of a pool of savings that is built up by the members themselves. Credit unions are constituted according to provisions set out in their common bond statutes, which define (and restrict) their target membership. Consequently, credit unions in different categories may exhibit differences in the membership characteristics, operational structure and the subsidies that are available. Common bond categories include the following: community; associational; educational; military; federal, state and local government; manufacturing; service; and low income.

The interwoven relationship that exists between a credit union's members, who are the customers for its financial products, the suppliers of its funds, and in some cases its managers and shareholders, has led to credit unions being described by Croteau (1963) as the purest form of cooperative institution. In many countries, credit unions are viewed as playing a crucial role in tackling financial exclusion, by providing low-cost financial services to groups often excluded from obtaining credit from banks, or access to other banking services. It is estimated that more than 177 million people in 92 countries belong to a credit union. The total assets of credit unions worldwide are estimated at US $1,181bn. However, the pace of development of the credit union movement differs widely between different countries. Ferguson and McKillop (1997) detail four discrete stages in the development of a credit union sector:

■ *Nascent stage*. In this stage, credit unions are run by volunteer workers, and receive financial aid and other forms of assistance from local government agencies and charitable organizations. This model still characterizes the relatively underdeveloped credit union sector in many African and Asian countries.

■ *Transition stage*. Once a particular critical mass has been achieved, the industry moves into the second, transition stage of development. At this stage, objectives of saving costs by achieving economies of scale are largely forgone in favour of maintaining smallness as a defining credit union attribute. However, in the transition stage credit unions tend to hire paid employees (full-time or part-time) rather than rely solely on volunteers. They have professional management, but retain volunteer directors. They may offer a range of financial services, rather than just one or two basic products. Membership becomes more socially diverse, including some middle-class income earners. This model characterizes the credit union sector in the UK, Poland, Lithuania and Latvia.

■ *Mature stage*. At the mature stage, a more business-like philosophy tends to prevail. Mature credit union sectors are characterized by much larger asset and membership sizes. Concentration within the sector tends to increase, as dominant institutions begin to emerge. This trend is strengthened by means of consolidation, in the form of horizontal mergers between some individual institutions. Professional staffs operate multi-product services, and state-of-the-art information technology is employed in marketing and administration. Mature credit union sectors include those in Ireland, Canada and Australia.

■ *Post-mature stage*. During the post-mature stage, the distinctiveness of the credit union movement tends to be eroded or lost, as the largest and most successful institutions become increasingly similar to market-oriented financial services competitors. In the US, a small number of credit unions have recently been converted into banks.

While the industry life cycle approach is a useful tool to analyze the development of the credit union sector, there are some limitations:

■ Not all credit union sectors pass through the four stages identified above. Changes in general economic conditions or technology might significantly influence the development of a particular credit union sector.

■ The importance of strategic decisions taken by the managers of individual credit unions may influence the path taken by a credit union sector. As a sector reaches maturity, credit unions are unlikely to remain passive spectators while the demand for their products and services stagnates or declines. Instead, they may decide to invest in financial innovation, or diversify into new product or geographic areas, or acquire others.

■ A credit union sector might comprise several distinct strategic groups (see Section 12.3). These may reach each stage in the life cycle at different times. In the case of credit unions, the common bond may be an important determinant of strategic group formation.

Distinctive capabilities and core competences

According to Kay (1993), the performance of firms depends on **distinctive capabilities**. Distinctive capabilities include architecture, innovation and reputation. Architecture refers to the firm's internal organization, its relationships with suppliers, distributors and retailers, and its specialized industry knowledge, all of which may allow the firm opportunities to maintain a competitive edge over rivals or entrants. Innovation, combined with mechanisms to protect intellectual property, provides some firms with assets that can be used to maintain high levels of performance. A firm that has established a name, reputation of brand associated with high quality and service may also enjoy a decisive advantage over competitors. Accordingly, firms that can draw on distinctive capabilities may be able to grow and sustain a large or dominant market share over long periods.

In the terminology of Prahalad and Hamel (1990), a firm's **core competences** are the key to its performance. Core competences derive from the firm's specialized knowledge, and the ways in which this knowledge is used in order to establish and maintain an edge over competitors. The key to staying ahead of the competition is being able to protect the firm's specialized resources and competences from imitation. Especially in industries where technological change occurs at a rapid pace, incumbent firms must be capable of adapting quickly, and initiating change themselves. Only firms with sufficient ambition ('strategic intent') and sufficient flexibility or adaptability ('strategic stretch') are likely to succeed (Hamel and Prahalad, 1994).

This approach emphasizes the firm itself, rather than industry characteristics, as the ultimate source of a competitive advantage that may eventually have major ramifications for industry structure indicators such as seller concentration or barriers to entry. Singh *et al.* (1998) attempt to identify the types of strategy that were most frequently used by UK firms in the food, electrical engineering, chemicals and pharmaceuticals industries. Questionnaire data obtained from marketing executives suggest that research and development and advertising are among the most common instruments employed with long-term strategic objectives in view. There was little indication of reliance on price-based strategies or the patenting of new products.

10.3 The random growth hypothesis

Section 10.2 emphasizes the importance of a number of systematic factors in determining the structure of an industry. All of these explanations assume that observable characteristics of an industry or its incumbent firms are the ultimate source of the competitive advantages that will determine the performance of the industry's most successful firms. In turn, the most successful firms' performance has major implications for the number and the size distribution of firms the industry is ultimately capable of sustaining. In Section 10.2, the emphasis on *observable* characteristics of the industry and its constituent firms is crucial.

An alternative school of thought within industrial organization emphasizes the role of chance or random factors in determining the growth of individual firms and their eventual size distribution (Cabral and Mata, 2003). According to the random growth hypothesis, individual firms' growth over any period is essentially random, as if determined by means of a draw in a lottery. Some firms do well and some do badly, but the distribution of strong and weak growth performance between firms is essentially a matter of chance. Furthermore, past growth is no reliable indicator of the rate at which a firm will grow or decline in the future. The growth of individual firms cannot be foreseen, any more than the winners of next Saturday's lottery can be predicted from the characteristics of last week's winners and losers, the strategies they employed when selecting their numbers, or their past records of success or failure.

It is important to note that the random growth hypothesis does not rule out the possibility that *ex post* (with the benefit of hindsight), strong growth performance can be attributed to 'systematic' factors such as managerial talent, successful innovation, efficient organizational structure or favourable shifts in consumer demand. Rather, it implies that growth originating from these factors cannot be predicted *ex ante* (before the event). 'Systematic' factors of this kind may determine growth, but these factors are themselves distributed randomly across firms. As before, their effects cannot be foreseen or predicted in advance using data on the firms' observable characteristics.

If successful growth performance is essentially a matter of luck or chance, is the tendency to hero-worship successful entrepreneurs (Bill Gates, Richard Branson) in certain quarters of society (some sections of the business press, for example) fundamentally misconceived? In support of this view, Schwed's (1955) analogy of the 'great coin flipping contest' is worth quoting at length.

The referee gives a signal for the first time and 400,000 coins flash in the sun as they are tossed. The scorers make their tabulations, and discover that 200,000 people are winners and 200,000 are losers. Then the second game is played. Of the original 200,000 winners, about half of them win again. The third game is played, and of the 100,000 who have won both games half of them are again successful. These 50,000, in the fourth game are reduced to 25,000, and in the fifth to 12,500. These 12,500 have now won five straight without loss and are no doubt beginning to fancy themselves as coin flippers. They feel they have an 'instinct' for it. However, in the sixth game, 6,250 are disappointed and amazed they have finally lost, and perhaps some of them start a Congressional investigation. But the victorious 6,250 play on and are successively reduced in number until less than a thousand are left. This little band have won nine straight without a loss, and by this time most of them have at least a local reputation for their ability. People come from some distance to consult them about their method of calling heads and tails, and they modestly give explanations of how they have achieved their success. Eventually there are about a dozen men who have won every single time for about fifteen games. These are regarded as the experts, the greatest coin flippers in history, the men who never lose, and they have their biographies written.

(Schwed, 1955, pp. 160–1, quoted in Sherman, 1977, p. 9)

Kay (2004) makes a similar observation.

When you buy a lottery ticket, you make a mistake – you almost certainly should not bet at such poor odds. But if the winning ticket is yours, chance redeems your mistake. When people succeed in risky situations, the outcome is a mixture of good judgment and good luck, and it is impossible to disentangle the elements of the two. This is of central importance to considering successful businesses and successful business people. To what extent were Henry Ford, William Morris and Bill Gates people who had the judgment to choose the right number, or lucky people whose number came up?

(Kay, 2004, p. 402)

What are the implications of random growth for the long-run trend in seller concentration? The fact that the growth or decline of individual firms cannot be predicted using data on the firms' observable characteristics does not imply the trend in seller concentration is also purely a matter of chance. Proponents of the random growth hypothesis have developed simulation models to show that there is a natural tendency for industry structure to become increasingly concentrated over time, even if the growth of the industry's individual member firms is random. These models involve tracing the effects on seller concentration of the imposition of a sequence of random 'growth shocks' upon simulated (hypothetical) firm size data. This random growth hypothesis is embodied in the **Law of Proportionate**

Table 10.1 Trends in seller concentration with random firm growth

	Year 1	Year 2	Year 3	Year 4
Firm 1	100	200	400	800
2	100	200	400	200
3	100	200	100	200
4	100	200	100	200
5	100	50	100	50
6	100	50	100	50
7	100	50	25	50
8	100	50	25	12.5
CR3	.375	.6	.72	.768
HH	.125	.17	.231	.314

Effect (LPE). The LPE is also known as **Gibrat's law** after the French statistician Gibrat (1931), who is credited with the first discussion of the implications of the random growth hypothesis for seller concentration (Mata, 2008).

A simple and highly stylized illustration of the implications of a random growth process for the trend in seller concentration is shown in Table 10.1. Suppose in year 1 an industry comprises eight equal-sized firms, each with sales of 100. The assumed random growth process is as follows: in any subsequent year, each firm has an equal chance of either doubling or halving its sales. For simplicity, it is assumed that no other outcome is possible. It is important to emphasize that this is only one of many possible ways in which a random growth process could be specified. A more realistic formulation might select the individual firms' growth rates randomly from some continuous range of values, rather than allowing only two (extreme) outcomes. However, the binary formulation keeps the arithmetic as simple as possible.

In Table 10.1 it is assumed that, every year, half of the firms in each size category grow and the other half decline. Therefore four of the eight equal-sized firms in year 1 double in size in year 2, and four halve in size. From each group of four equal-sized firms in year 2, two double in size and two halve in size in year 3, and so on. The CR_3 and HH seller concentration measures (see Section 10.4) are reported at the bottom of Table 10.1. These reflect a progressive increase in concentration, with the firm size distribution becoming increasingly skewed in successive years. By year 4, only one firm has experienced the good fortune of three consecutive years of positive growth. Accordingly, this firm (firm 1) achieves a market share of more than 50 per cent in year 4.

Hannah and Kay (1977) use a gambling analogy to illustrate the same point.

> [I]f a group of rich men and a group of poor men visit Monte Carlo, it is likely that some of the rich will become poor and some of the poor become rich: but it is also probable that some of the rich will get richer and some of the poor will get poorer, so that the extent of inequality within each group and over the two groups taken together is likely to increase. The process works to increase industrial concentration in much the same way.
>
> *(Hannah and Kay, 1977, p. 103)*

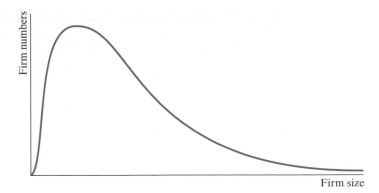

Figure 10.2 Distribution of firm sizes

Therefore if firms' growth rates are determined randomly, the firm size distribution tends to become skewed, with the industry comprising a few very large firms and a much larger number of smaller firms. This pattern is illustrated in Figure 10.2. Furthermore, the degree of skewness tends to increase progressively over time.

The long-run implications of the random growth hypothesis for seller concentration have been analyzed using more realistic and less highly stylized simulation models. For example, Scherer (1980) traces the evolution of a firm size distribution for a hypothetical industry initially comprising 50 equal-sized firms. Each firm's growth rate in each year was drawn from a normal probability distribution, whose parameters (mean and variance) were calibrated using data on a sample of 369 of the 500 largest US firms over the period 1954–60. The evolution of industry structure over a 140 year time period was simulated 16 times, and the average four-firm concentration ratio calculated. The results showed that the concentration ratio increased from 8 per cent in period 1 to approximately 58 per cent in period 140. McCloughan (1995) develops a more elaborate stochastic growth model that also incorporates entry and exit.

Table 10.2 reports the average results across 20 replications of a simulation over 50 time periods of an industry comprising 20 firms. The firms are equal-sized (each with a size value of 1 unit) at period 0. In each subsequent period, their logarithmic growth rate is drawn randomly from a normal distribution with zero mean and a standard deviation of 0.1. Over 50 periods, the average market share of the largest firm increases from 5 per cent to 15.1 per cent, and the average market share of the top five firms increases from 25 per cent to 49 per cent. Table 10.2 also shows the corresponding adjustments in the HH index and the numbers equivalent of the HH index.

Some of the earliest empirical research on the random growth hypothesis examines whether the actual size distribution of firms is consistent with the size distribution that would be expected if firm growth is truly random. Quandt (1966), Silberman (1967), Clarke (1979), Stanley *et al.* (1995) and Growiec *et al.* (2008) all report tests which assess how accurately certain theoretically skewed statistical probability distributions describe observed firm size distributions. Although these studies are unable to identify any specific theoretical distribution

Table 10.2 Simulated evolution of industry structure and concentration under the random growth hypothesis

Period	Mean size	St. dev. of size	CR_1	CR_2	CR_5	HH	Numbers equivalent, $n(2)$
0	1.00	–	.050	.100	.250	.050	20.0
1	1.00	.10	.060	.117	.282	.050	20.0
2	1.00	.14	.064	.124	.291	.051	19.6
5	1.02	.23	.075	.142	.324	.052	19.2
10	1.03	.33	.087	.161	.354	.055	18.2
15	1.05	.41	.096	.177	.383	.058	17.2
20	1.10	.49	.105	.191	.400	.060	16.7
25	1.14	.59	.117	.208	.419	.063	15.9
30	1.18	.67	.127	.218	.435	.066	15.2
35	1.21	.74	.133	.226	.454	.068	14.7
40	1.22	.78	.138	.236	.462	.070	14.3
45	1.22	.83	.143	.245	.471	.072	13.9
50	1.26	.91	.151	.257	.490	.076	13.2

that always provides the best description of reality, the tendency for observed firm size distributions to be highly skewed, and therefore amenable to representation using these types of distribution, is almost universal.

An alternative approach to testing the LPE is based on the idea that if growth is random, there should be no relationship between the size of a firm at the start of any period and its growth over that period. In other words, firm size should have no predictive capability for future growth. Furthermore, past growth should also have no predictive capability for future growth. Regression analysis can be used to test for these non-relationships. A typical specification is as follows:

$$(x_{i,t+T} - x_{i,t}) = \alpha + \beta_1 x_{i,t} + \beta_2(x_{i,t} - x_{i,t-T}) + u_i$$

where $x_{i,t}$ represents the natural logarithm of the size of firm i in year t. Growth is observed over the T-year period between years t and $t + T$, and $(x_{i,t+T} - x_{i,t})$ represents firm i's logarithmic growth rate over this period. Similarly $(x_{i,t} - x_{i,t-T})$ represents firm i's logarithmic growth over the previous T-year period between years $t - T$ and t. The disturbance term u_i represents the random component of firm i's growth for the period t to $t + T$. According to the random growth hypothesis, the regression coefficients β_1 and β_2 should both be zero. $\beta_1 = 0$ implies there is no relationship between firm size in year t and growth over the period t to $t + T$; and $\beta_2 = 0$ implies there is no relationship between growth over the period $t - T$ to t, and growth over the period t to $t + T$. Using firm size data for a sample of firms observed at points $t - T$, t and $t + T$, the model can be estimated as a cross-sectional regression. The hypotheses $\beta_1 = 0$ and $\beta_2 = 0$ can be tested in order to determine whether the data support the random growth hypothesis.

In the event that the random growth hypothesis is not supported by the data, two of the most likely alternatives are as follows.

- If $\beta_1 < 0$, there is a negative relationship between initial size and subsequent growth. In other words, $\beta_1 < 0$ implies the smaller firms tend to grow faster than the larger firms. Over the long run, there is a tendency for *convergence* in firm sizes. In this case, there would be some eventual limit to the tendency for concentration to increase over time. Accordingly, the long-run implications for the trend in seller concentration of $\beta_1 < 0$ are very different from the implications of $\beta_1 = 0$.

- If $\beta_2 > 0$, there is a positive relationship between growth in consecutive T-year periods. In other words, a firm that grew relatively fast over the period $t - T$ to t is likely to do so again over the period t to $t + T$. Such a pattern could reflect distinctive capabilities on the part of the firm, enabling it to deliver above-average growth consistently. In this case, the tendency for concentration to increase over time would be strengthened relative to the case in which growth is completely random.

Empirical research that tests the LPE has produced mixed results. Several early studies, based on data up to and including the 1970s, report either no relationship or a positive relationship between firm size and growth. A number of more recent studies find a consistent tendency for small firms to grow faster than large firms. As we have seen, a growth pattern that is in accordance with the LPE ($\beta_1 = 0$) implies seller concentration tends to increase over time. A tendency for small firms to grow faster than large firms ($\beta_1 < 0$) implies no long-term increase in seller concentration. Broadly speaking, the results of the empirical literature are consistent with what is known about trends in seller concentration (see Section 10.4). Until the 1970s concentration tended to increase consistently, but since the 1970s there has been no consistent trend.

Table 10.3 summarizes a number of empirical studies of the LPE. This section concludes with some comments on the general features of this literature. As noted above, much of the recent LPE literature reports a tendency for small firms or plants to grow faster than their larger counterparts (Evans, 1987a,b; Dunne and Hughes, 1994; Hart and Oulton, 1996, 1999; Blonigen and Tomlin, 2001). While this might reflect genuine growth patterns, it has also been suggested that a negative size–growth relationship might, at least in part, be an artifact of the way in which many empirical tests are constructed. Specifically, their reliance on data for firms that survived over the sample period raises the possibility that a type of **sample selection bias** or **survivorship bias** might be responsible for a negative reported size–growth relationship. Some of the earliest literature recognized that the validity of the LPE might be limited to firms operating above a certain size threshold, or minimum efficient scale (MES) (Simon and Bonini, 1958). The long-term survival of small firms depends upon their ability to achieve at least the MES, so that they can realize the full benefits of economies of scale. For example, constraints on access to external finance may create difficulties for small firms in achieving the MES (Beck *et al.*, 2005). Firms that fail to achieve the MES reasonably quickly are likely to exit. Therefore an

Table 10.3 Tests of the Law of Proportionate Effect (LPE): a selective review

Study (chronological order)	Sample characteristics	Results
Hart and Prais (1956)	UK firms, 1885–1950. London Stock Exchange valuation size measure	No size–growth relationship before 1939. Negative size–growth relationship for 1939–50
Hart (1962)	UK brewing, spinning and drinks firms, 1931–54. Gross profit depreciation size measure	No size–growth relationship. Large brewing firms have more variable growth than small firms
Hymer and Pashigian (1962)	1,000 large US manufacturing firms, 1946–55. Assets size measure	No size–growth relationship. Variability in growth greater for small firms
Mansfield (1962)	Varying numbers of US steel, petroleum and tyre firms, 1916–57. Firm output size measure	Reports tests for all firms, for survivors, and for firms operating above industry MES (minimum efficient scale). No size–growth relationship above MES
Samuals (1965)	322 UK manufacturing firms, 1951–60. Net assets size measure	Larger firms grew faster than smaller firms, due to economies of scale
Samuals and Chesher (1972)	2,000 UK firms from 21 industry groups, 1960–69. Net assets size measure	Large firms grew faster than small firms. Variability in growth greater for small firms. Departures from LPE greatest in oligopoly. Some evidence of persistence of growth
Utton (1972)	1,527 UK firms from 13 manufacturing industries, 1954–65. Net assets size measure	Large firms grew faster than small firms in five industries; small firms grew faster in one industry
Aaronovitch and Sawyer (1975)	233 quoted UK manufacturing firms, 1959–67. Net assets size measure	No size–growth relationship
Singh and Whittington (1975)	Approx. 2,000 UK firms in 21 industry groups, 1948–60. Net assets size measure	Large firms grew faster than small firms. Variation in growth rates declines with firm size. Some evidence of persistence of growth
Chesher (1979)	183 UK manufacturing firms, 1960–9. Net assets size measure	No size–growth relationship. Some evidence of persistence of growth
Kumar (1985)	UK firms, 1960–76. Three sub-periods are: 1960–5 (1,747 firms), 1966–71 (1,021 firms), 1972–6 (824 firms). Net assets, fixed assets, total equity, employees and sales size measures	Negative size–growth relationship for 1960–5 and 1972–6. No size–growth relationship for 1966–71. Some evidence of persistence of growth
Evans (1987a)	42,339 small US firms, 1976–80. Employees size measure	Failure rates, growth and variability of growth decrease with age. Overall, rejects LPE in favour of an inverse relationship between size and growth
Evans (1987b)	17,339 small US manufacturing firms, 1976–82. Employees size measure	Finds an inverse relationship between firm size and firm growth. Strong evidence of an inverse relationship between age and growth
Hall (1987)	Varying numbers of US firms, 1972–83. Three sub-periods are: 1972–83 (962 firms); 1972–9 (1,349 firms); 1976–83 (1,098 firms). Employees size measure	Negative size–growth relationship. Variability of growth greater for small firms

Table 10.3 (*continued*)

Study (chronological order)	Sample characteristics	Results
Dunne *et al.* (1988)	200,000 US manufacturing plants, 1967–77. Employees size measure	Negative size–growth relationship, and negative age–growth relationship for multi-plant firms. Variability of growth declines with plant size
Contini and Revelli (1989)	467 small Italian manufacturers, 1973–86. Employees size measure	Negative size–growth relationship. LPE holds for largest firms in the sample
Acs and Audretsch (1990)	408 four-digit US industries, 1976–80. Employees size measure	No size–growth relationship in the majority of industries (245 out of 408)
Reid (1992)	73 small UK firms, 1985–8. Sales and employees size measures	Negative size–growth relationship. Younger firms have faster growth
Wagner (1992)	7,000 small German firms, 1978–89. Employees size measure	No size–growth relationship. Some evidence of persistence of growth
Dunne and Hughes (1994)	2,149 UK firms, 1975–85. Assets size measure	Accepts LPE for majority of size classes in 1980–5, but rejects in all classes 1975–80, finding that small firms had faster and more variable growth than larger counterparts
Hart and Oulton (1996)	87,109 small independent UK firms, 1989–93. Net assets, employees and sales size measures	Negative size–growth relationship. This pattern is robust with respect to size category and size measure
Hart and Oulton (1999)	29,000 small independent UK firms, 1989–93. Employees size measure	Negative size–growth relationship, except for the very largest firms
Wilson and Morris (2000)	264 manufacturing and 163 service firms, UK, 1991–5. Net assets size measure	Negative size–growth relationship. Small firms had more variable growth. Persistence of growth for manufacturing
Wilson and Williams (2000)	400 European banks, 1990–6. Total assets and equity size measure	Small Italian banks grew faster than large ones. No size–growth relationship for France, Germany and the UK
Blonigen and Tomlin (2001)	Japanese-owned US manufacturing plants, 1987–90. Employees size measure	Small plants grew faster than large plants
Goddard *et al.* (2002a)	443 Japanese manufacturing firms, 1980–96. Total assets size measure	Some evidence of convergence in firm sizes towards firm-specific average values
Goddard *et al.* (2002b)	7,603 US credit unions, 1990–9. Assets and membership size measures	Large credit unions grew faster than small credit unions
Geroski *et al.* (2003)	147 quoted UK firms, 1948–77. Net assets size measure	Growth among surviving firms is mainly random. Little evidence of long-run convergence in firm sizes
Lotti *et al.* (2001, 2003)	New Italian start-ups, 1987–93. Employees size measure	New small firms initially grow rapidly. Initial fast growth not sustained
Audretsch *et al.* (2004)	1,170 Dutch service firms, 1987–9. Sales size measure	In contrast to recent manufacturing evidence, no size–growth relationship
Goddard *et al.* (2006)	96 large, quoted UK firms, 1972–2001. Net assets size measure	Evidence of non-random growth
Coad (2007)	Sample of 10,000 French manufacturing firms, 1996–2002. Sales size measure	Small firms subject to negative correlation between successive annual growth rates. Large firms subject to positive correlation

empirical study based on a sample of firms that were in existence both at the start and at the end of a certain period might observe rapid average growth at the lower end of the firm size distribution. However, this observation does not imply that *all* small firms achieve rapid growth. Rather, the study is subject to a form of survivorship bias, because growth data are observed and recorded only for those firms that survived from the start to the end of the observation period. Data for those small firms that failed to achieve rapid growth and exited would not have been recorded.

In most instances, empirical tests of the LPE are based on a cross-sectional regression of logarithmic growth rates over a given period on initial log sizes. However, Gibrat's original formulation and many subsequent interpretations of the LPE emphasize the implications for trends in the size distribution of firms and seller concentration over the long run. In view of recent improvements in the time coverage of firm-level databases, and advances in econometric methods for analyzing time-series data sets and panel data sets (containing both a cross-sectional dimension and a time dimension), it is unsurprising that empirical tests of the LPE based on time-series or panel models, rather than on cross-sectional regression, have recently started to appear. For example, Goddard *et al.* (2002a) test the validity of the LPE for a Japanese manufacturing sample with 15 years of annual size and growth data for more than 300 firms. Some evidence of a negative size–growth relationship is reported. For the majority of the 147 large, quoted UK firms in Geroski *et al.*'s (2003) 30-year study, there is little or no evidence of any relationship between size and growth. Accordingly, the study comes down strongly in favour of the random growth hypothesis.

> Our results suggest that the growth rates of firms who survive long enough to record 30 years of history are random . . . Among other things, this means that there is no obvious upper bound on levels of concentration in individual industries or across the economy as a whole. A metaphor for convergence might tell a story of ships all reaching the same harbour despite coming from different directions. In fact, the metaphor that describes our data is ships passing in the night.
>
> *(Geroski* et al.*, 2003, p. 55)*

Several researchers develop models in which growth is part-random, but partly influenced by systematic factors. For example, Davies and Lyons (1982) include firm numbers, economies of scale and barriers to entry among the systematic determinants of growth. Small firms need to grow rapidly in order to achieve the MES. The systematic influences are most important in determining growth, and (implicitly) concentration, up to the point at which economies of scale are exhausted. Once the MES has been attained, however, growth is mainly random. Geroski and Mazzucato (2001) examine the extent to which corporate learning (which can be either systematic, arising from technological innovation and spillovers, internal resources and learning economies of scale; or random) is evident in the growth patterns of large US car manufacturers over an 85-year period. There is only limited evidence of any systematic learning effect on observed growth. Learning effects appear to be mainly random.

Davies and Geroski (1997) apply a variant of the random growth model to firm-level market share data on 200 large UK firms within 54 manufacturing industries. The empirical model is as follows:

$$\Delta \mathrm{MS}_{i,j} = \alpha_j + \beta_j \mathrm{MS}_{i,j} + \gamma_1 x_{1,i} + \gamma_2 x_{2,i} + \cdots + \gamma_k x_{k,i} + u_{i,j}$$

$\mathrm{MS}_{i,j}$ represents the market share of firm i in industry j at the start of the observation period, and $\Delta \mathrm{MS}_{i,j}$ the change in firm i's market share in industry j over the course of the observation period. $u_{i,j}$ is a disturbance term that incorporates the random element in variations in the firms' market shares. The regression coefficients α_j and β_j play a similar role in this model to their counterparts in the random growth model (as specified previously in this section). However, the j-subscripts indicate that the values of these coefficients are permitted to vary between industries. Davies and Geroski use a number of industry characteristics to model the variation in α_j and β_j. These include estimates of the MES, growth in industry sales, the advertising-to-sales ratio, the research and development expenditure-to-sales ratio, and the initial level of concentration. The additional covariates $x_{1,i}, x_{2,i}, \ldots, x_{k,i}$ represent a number of firm-specific determinants of growth. $\gamma_1, \gamma_2, \ldots, \gamma_k$ are the regression coefficients on these covariates. Indicators of expenditure on advertising and research and development that are specific to the firm itself and its nearest rivals are found to be significant determinants of changes in market share. The model suggests that relative stability in an industry's concentration ratios can conceal significant 'turbulence', or turnover, in the identities and rankings of the firms with the largest market shares.

10.4   Trends in concentration and the location of industry

Section 10.4 describes patterns and trends in seller concentration at the aggregate level and for particular industries, and examines influences on the geographical location of industry.

Trends in aggregate concentration

Hart and Prais (1956) examine trends in aggregate concentration for the UK (by examining the distribution of firm sizes of all quoted companies, measured by stock exchange valuation) for the period 1895–1950. Aggregate concentration increased throughout most of the pre-Second World War period up to 1939. Subsequently, aggregate concentration appears to have declined between 1940 and 1950. Evely and Little (1960) report similar findings. Hannah and Kay (1977) examine trends in aggregate concentration (measured by the proportion of assets accounted for by the top 100 firms) between 1919 and 1969. Aggregate concentration appears to have increased over the period 1919–30, declined during 1930–48, but then increased again during the 1950s and 1960s. Merger activity appears to have contributed significantly to the rise in concentration both during the 1920s, and during the 1950s and 1960s. The fall in concentration during the period 1930–48 is attributed to the faster growth of medium-sized firms, relative to their larger counterparts.

Large-scale mergers and an improvement in the competitiveness of large manufacturing firms appear to have contributed to a further increase in aggregate concentration in the UK during the 1970s (Hart and Clarke, 1980; Clarke, 1985). During the 1980s, however, the long-term trend was reversed, and aggregate concentration began to decrease (Clarke, 1993). At the start of the 1980s, the UK's manufacturing sector was subjected to an unprecedented squeeze from a combination of high interest rates and a high exchange rate. Faced with a sharp fall in demand in both the domestic market (as the UK economy became mired in recession) and in export markets (as the high exchange rate damaged competitiveness), many manufacturing firms were forced out of business altogether. Many of those that survived did so only by shedding labour and downsizing. This led to a reduction in average firm size, and a fall in aggregate concentration.

Davies *et al.* (2001) examine changes in aggregate concentration at the European level (measured by the aggregate market shares of the 100 largest European manufacturing firms) over the period 1987–93. Aggregate concentration fell slightly from 29.6 per cent to 28.6 per cent. While concentration remained relatively stable, there was a substantial turnover (entry and exit) among the top 100 firms. Between 1987 and 1993 there were 22 exits from the top 100. In nine cases, this was caused by slow internal growth, bankruptcy or takeover by firms from outside the top 100. In four cases, it was caused by takeover by other top 100 firms. In the remaining nine cases, it was caused by a relative decline in sales, resulting in these firms slipping from the top 100. Of the 22 entrants, two were created by divestment of assets by existing top 100 firms, and 13 achieved top 100 status through relative sales growth. The remaining seven firms were classified as completely 'new' entrants.

Pryor (2001a,b, 2002) examines the trend in aggregate concentration in the US, over the period 1960–97. Aggregate concentration appears to have declined over the period 1962–85. However, this trend was reversed and aggregate concentration began to increase from the late 1980s onwards. Deconcentration during the 1980s is attributed to factors such as an increase in import penetration, deregulation, stronger competition policy and technological change which tended to lower the minimum efficient scale (MES). During the 1990s, phenomena such as globalization, improvements in information technology and e-commerce appear to have pushed in the direction of further deconcentration. However, this tendency has been more than offset by an increase in merger activity, which caused aggregate concentration to increase during the 1990s.

Trends in industry concentration

Naturally, seller concentration varies considerably from industry to industry. Economists have often been most concerned with concentration in manufacturing, in which large-scale production techniques became prevalent during the 1920s and 1930s (Chandler, 1990). For example, Shepherd (1972) reports that average four-digit, five-firm industry concentration ratios were lower for UK (52.1 per cent) than for US manufacturing (80.3 per cent) for the period 1958–83. This pattern is attributed to differences in technologies, more intense competition and a more rigorous competition policy regime in the UK. Table 10.4 shows CR_5

Table 10.4 Five-firm concentration ratios for UK business by industry in 2004

Industry	Five-firm concentration ratio Output	Five-firm concentration ratio Value added
Agriculture	n/a	n/a
Forestry	48	39
Fishing	16	14
Coal extraction	79	71
Oil and gas extraction	57	59
Metal ores extraction	n/a	n/a
Other mining and quarrying	43	45
Meat processing	17	22
Fish and fruit processing	36	39
Oils and fats	88	84
Dairy products	32	37
Grain milling and starch	31	44
Animal feed	36	42
Bread, biscuits, etc.	17	17
Sugar	99	100
Confectionery	81	88
Other food products	39	42
Alcoholic beverages	50	68
Soft drinks and mineral waters	75	76
Tobacco products	99	100
Textile fibres	29	34
Textile weaving	26	31
Textile finishing	14	11
Made-up textiles	17	17
Carpets and rugs	27	35
Other textiles	15	19
Knitted goods	32	30
Wearing apparel and fur products	14	10
Leather goods	30	27
Footwear	25	31
Wood and wood products	9	7
Pulp, paper and paperboard	21	24
Paper and paperboard products	34	21
Printing and publishing	12	12
Coke ovens, refined petroleum and nuclear fuel	66	67
Industrial gases and dyes	57	77
Inorganic chemicals	57	51
Organic chemicals	69	55
Fertilizers	72	70
Plastics and synthetic resins, etc.	24	27
Pesticides	75	71
Paints, varnishes, printing ink, etc.	37	42
Pharmaceuticals	57	63
Soap and toilet preparations	40	43
Other chemical products	18	28
Man-made fibres	79	85
Rubber products	45	40

Table 10.4 (*continued*)

Industry	Five-firm concentration ratio Output	Five-firm concentration ratio Value added
Plastic products	4	5
Glass and glass products	26	28
Ceramic goods	31	33
Structural clay products	68	70
Cement, lime and plaster	71	74
Articles of concrete, stone, etc.	25	24
Iron and steel	61	48
Non-ferrous metals	14	25
Metal castings	13	14
Structural metal products	6	6
Metal boilers and radiators	45	51
Metal forging and pressing	4	3
Cutlery, tools, etc.	11	10
Other metal products	14	11
Mechanical power equipment	29	26
General purpose machinery	8	9
Agricultural machinery	26	34
Machine tools	26	27
Special purpose machinery	20	15
Weapons and ammunition	77	70
Domestic appliances	44	51
Office machinery and computers	37	61
Electric motors and generators	21	17
Insulated wire and cable	58	51
Electrical equipment	13	14
Electronic components	21	28
Transmitters for TV radio and phone	51	48
Receivers for TV and radio	27	24
Medical and precision instruments	14	17
Motor vehicles	34	34
Shipbuilding and repair	43	48
Other transport equipment	59	46
Aircraft and spacecraft	44	56
Furniture	5	5
Jewellery and related products	16	13
Sports goods and toys	23	27
Miscellaneous manufacturing and recycling	26	20
Electricity production and distribution	55	64
Gas distribution	82	100
Water supply	55	57
Construction	5	5
Motor vehicle distribution and repair	15	18
Wholesale distribution	6	10
Retail distribution	20	21
Hotels, catering, pubs, etc.	13	13
Railway transport	41	50

Table 10.4 (*continued*)

Industry	Five-firm concentration ratio Output	Five-firm concentration ratio Value added
Other land transport	13	18
Water transport	41	45
Air transport	n/a	n/a
Ancillary transport services	13	32
Postal and courier services	65	74
Telecommunications	61	69
Banking and finance	n/a	n/a
Insurance and pension funds	n/a	n/a
Auxiliary financial services	n/a	n/a
Owning and dealing in real estate	n/a	n/a
Letting of dwellings	n/a	n/a
Estate agent activities	n/a	n/a
Renting of machinery	10	13
Computer services	19	17
Research and development	37	51
Legal activities	9	9
Accountancy services	36	40
Market research, management consultancy	10	13
Architectural activities and technical consultancy	8	12
Advertising	10	12
Other business services	5	6
Public administration and defence	n/a	n/a
Education	10	8
Health and veterinary services	17	17
Social work activities	11	11
Sewage and sanitation	31	36
Membership organizations	n/a	n/a
Recreational services	47	26
Other service activities	4	5
Private households with employed persons	n/a	n/a

Source: Adapted from Economic Trends Number 635, October 2006. Appendix 1. National Statistics © Crown Copyright 2000. See Mahajan (2005, 2006) for an extended discussion of concentration in the UK.

(five-firm concentration ratios) for selected UK industries in 2004, calculated on a total output basis and on a value added basis.

All EU member countries experienced a pronounced shift in the distribution of economic activity away from manufacturing and towards services towards the end of the twentieth century. Over the period 1991–2004, GDP in services (distribution, hotels and restaurants, transport, financial intermediation, real estate and public administration) grew at an average rate of around 3 per cent per annum, while GDP in industry (mining and quarrying; manufacturing; and electricity, gas and water supply) grew at around 1.5 per cent per annum (European Commission, 2003a). By 2005, industry accounted for 18 per cent of

GDP in the EU, services accounted for 71 per cent, agriculture accounted for 2 per cent and utilities and construction accounted for 8 per cent. In all EU member countries, with the exception of Portugal, more than 80 per cent of the labour force was employed in services (European Commission, 2007). Table 10.5 provides a snapshot of the industrial structure of the EU-27 countries as a whole in 2008, excluding the financial sector.

The trend towards increasing seller concentration was repeated in many service sector industries towards the end of the twentieth century. Table 10.6 summarizes the size distribution of firms by industry classification across all EU member countries in 1997. Table 10.6 suggests there is considerable variation in patterns of concentration between industries, with the largest employers (firms of 250 employees or more) accounting for the largest shares of sales in motor manufacturing and financial services, and the smallest shares of sales in hotels and restaurants, construction and real estate.

The location of European industry

Specialization reflects whether a country's production is composed mainly of a small number of products or services, or whether the country's production is widely dispersed across a broad range of goods and services. **Geographic concentration** (or **regional concentration**) reflects whether a large share of an industry's total output is produced in a small number of countries or regions, or whether the industry is widely dispersed geographically (Aiginger, 1999).

Table 10.5 Industrial structure of EU-27 excluding the financial sector, 2008

Industry	Enterprises (000s)	Person employed (000s)	Turnover (euro million)	Value added (euro million)	Investment (euro million)
Non-financial business economy	21,004	136,281	24,915,339	6,155,686	–
Mining and quarrying	20	670	250,000	100,000	21,000
Manufacturing	2,123	32,961	7,136,428	1,669,537	240,078
Network energy supply	–	1,200	1,100,000	199,849	–
Water supply, sewerage, waste and recycling	60	1,266	218,103	–	32,426
Construction	3,285	15,047	1,907,138	604,362	97,287
Distributive Trades	6,144	32,816	9,117,514	1,153,272	132,683
Transportation and storage	1,118	10,863	1,305,077	476,619	126,012
Accomodation & food services	1,696	9,612	461,343	194,131	29,112
Information & Communication	797	5,798	1,141,269	502,495	57,279
Real Estate Activities	1,097	2,500	420,000	220,000	140,000
Professional, scientific & technical activities	3,392	10,752	1,168,753	573,128	42,594
Administrative & support services	1,054	11,864	810,000	390,000	70,000
Repair, computers, personal and household goods	176	377	26,227	10,569	–

Source: Adapted from *Key Figures on European Business with a Special Feature on SMEs*, Eurostat, Table 2.2, page 34, http://epp.eurostat.ec.europa.eu, © European Union, 2011.

Table 10.6 Firm size distributions for selected industries, EU, 1997 (distribution of sales by employment size class)

NACE two-digit code	Description	Micro	Small	Medium	Large
13 and 14	Mining of metal ores; other mining and quarrying	21.1	29.6	22.4	26.9
15 and 16	Manufacture of food products and beverages; manufacture of tobacco products	7.8	14.0	23.5	54.6
17, 18 and 19	Manufacture of textiles; manufacture of wearing apparel; dressing and dyeing of fur; manufacture of tanning, leather; luggage, handbags, saddlery, harness, footwear	11.8	27.8	30.3	30.1
20, 21 and 22	Manufacture of wood, wood and cork products except furniture, manufacture of pulp, paper and paper products, manufacture of publishing, printing and reproduction of recorded media	12.5	20.4	23.5	43.5
24 and 25	Manufacture of chemicals and chemical products; manufacture of rubber and plastic products	3.7	9.9	20.1	66.3
26	Manufacture of non-metallic mineral products	8.8	20.7	26.2	44.2
27	Manufacture of basic metals	1.7	7.6	15.4	75.3
28	Manufacture of fabricated metal products, except machinery and equipment	14.8	29.5	25.9	29.9
29	Manufacture of machinery and equipment not elsewhere classified	5.7	15.5	22.5	56.3
30, 31 and 32	Manufacture of office machinery and computers; electrical machinery and apparatus not elsewhere classified; manufacture of radio, television and communication equipment and apparatus	4.2	7.9	13.4	74.6
33	Manufacture of medical, precision and optical instruments, watches and clocks	11.3	18.6	23.3	46.8
34 and 35	Manufacture of motor vehicles, trailers and semi-trailers; manufacture of other transport equipment	1.3	3.5	6.1	89.1
36	Manufacture of furniture, manufacture not elsewhere classified	16.2	26.2	26.4	31.2
40	Electricity, gas steam and hot water supply	5.9	4.2	28.3	61.7
45	Construction	33.9	28.9	18.4	18.8
50, 51 and 52	Sale, maintenance and repair of motor vehicles; retail sale of automotive fuel; wholesale trade and commission trade, except motor vehicles and motorcycles; retail trade, except motor vehicles and motor cycles and repairs of household goods	29.1	24.7	19.7	26.5
55	Hotels and restaurants	49.7	20.2	10.7	19.4
60, 61, 62 and 63	Land transport; transport via pipelines; water transport; air transport; supporting activities; travel agencies	23.5	18.9	14.9	42.8
64 and 72	Post and telecommunications; computer and related activities	11.4	9.1	11.5	68.1
65	Financial intermediation	4.1	7.3	23.6	65.0
66	Insurance and pension funding	6.6	6.1	15.2	72.2
67	Activities auxiliary to financial intermediation	8.1	13.2	9.2	69.4
70	Real estate activities	53.6	20.3	20.2	6.0
71, 73 and 74	Renting of machinery and equipment without operator and of personal and household goods; research and development; other business activities	33.3	20.5	16.8	29.4

Notes: Size bands: Micro: 0–9 employees; Small: 10–49 employees; Medium: 50–249; and Large: 250+ employees.

Source: Adapted from *Panorama of European Business. Industry Data 1989–1999*, Eurostat, adaptation of selected table entries from Chapters 2–21, http://epp.eurostat.ec.europa.eu, © European Communities, 2000. Responsibility for the adaptation lies entirely on the Pearson Group.

A study by European Commission (2000) compares patterns of specialization in Europe, the US and Japan. While Europe tends to specialize in traditional industries such as building materials, tiles, footwear and textiles, Japan and the US specialize in technology-oriented industries such as electronic components and motor vehicles. Cockerill and Johnson (2003) suggest this is due to the higher absolute and relative expenditures on research and development in the US and Japan. For example, in 2001 private sector research and development expenditure as a percentage of GDP was 1.28 per cent for the 15 states that were EU members at the time (the EU-15), 2.11 per cent for Japan, and 2.04 per cent for the US. Within Europe, Sweden and Finland had the highest percentages (2.84 per cent and 2.68 per cent, respectively), and Portugal and Greece had the lowest (0.17 per cent and 0.19 per cent, respectively). The UK figure was 1.21 per cent (European Commission, 2003a).

According to European Commission (2007), there is an inverse relationship between country size and sectoral specialization. Large countries such as France, Germany, Italy and the UK tend to have a highly diversified sectoral distribution of economic activity, while small countries such as Malta, Luxembourg and Finland tend to be more specialized. Table 10.7 presents by member state, the most specialized activity within the non-financial business economy. Table 10.8 reports the EU-27 member countries with the largest and second-largest absolute levels of value added for selected industrial sectors in 2004, and the countries in which each sector's share in total economy-wide value added (excluding the financial sector) was the largest and the second largest.

Observed patterns of specialization and geographic concentration in European industry are rather complex, and often dependent on definitions and methods of measurement. Consequently, different studies have drawn different conclusions as to the existence or direction of any long-term trends in these patterns. Amiti (1997, 1998) examines changes in specialization and geographic concentration for 27 European manufacturing industries over the period 1968–90.

Table 10.7 Relative specialization by member state in terms of value added in 2008

Country	Industry	Industry
Belgium	Administrative & support services	7.1
Denmark	Mining & quarrying	7.1
Finland	Manufacturing	36.4
France	Repair, computers, personal & household	0.3
Germany	Real estate activities	5.2
Italy	Construction	12.1
Netherlands	Mining and quarrying	3.0
Spain	Construction	17.8
Sweden	Real estate activities	7.5
UK	Mining & quarrying	4.3

Source: Adapted from *Key Figures on European Business with a Special Feature on SMEs*, Eurostat Eurostat, Table 2.6, page 41, http://epp.eurostat.ec.europa.eu, © European Union, 2011. Responsibility for the adaptation lies entirely on the Pearson Group.

Table 10.8 Largest and most specialized EU member countries in 2007

Industry	Largest	Second largest	Most specialized	Second most specialized
Food, beverages and tobacco	Germany	UK	Poland	Ireland
Textiles, clothing, leather and footwear	Italy	Germany	Romania	Blugaria
Wood and paper	Germany	Italy	Finland	Estonia
Chemicals, rubber and plastics	Germany	France	Luxembourg	Czech Republic
Other non-metallic mineral products	Germany	Italy	Czech Republic	Cyprus
Metal and metal products	Germany	Italy	Slovakia	Slovenia
Machinery and equipment	Germany	Italy	Germany	Italy
Electrical machinery and optical equipment	Germany	France	Finland	Hungary
Transport equipment	Germany	France	Germany	Czech Republic
Furniture and other manufacturing	Germany	Italy	Lithuania	Estonia
Non-energy mining and quarrying	UK	Germany	Bulgaria	Poland
Energy	UK	Germany	Poland	Lithuania
Recycling and water supply	Germany	UK	Bulgaria	Slovakia
Construction	UK	Spain	Spain	Cyprus
Motor trades	Germany	UK	Latvia	Greece
Wholesale trade	Germany	UK	Greece	Latvia
Retail trade and repair	UK	Germany	Greece	Cyprus
Accommodation and food services	UK	France	Cyprus	Greece
Transport services	Germany	UK	Latvia	Lithuania
Communications and media	UK	Germany	Bulgaria	Ireland
Business services	UK	Germany	UK	Luxembourg

Notes: Largest and second largest refer to absolute levels of value added. Most and second most specialized refer to the share of a particular activity in non-financial business economy average.

Source: Adapted from *European Business. Facts and Figures*, Eurostat, Table 1.3, page 23, http://epp.eurostat.ec.europa.eu, © European Communities, 2009. Responsibility for the adaptation lies entirely on the Pearson Group.

Specialization increased for Belgium, Denmark, Germany, Greece, Italy and the Netherlands, but decreased for France, Spain and the UK. A similar exercise for selected countries using a more disaggregated industry classification finds that Belgium, France, Germany, Italy and the UK all became more specialized. Geographic concentration increased in 17 out of 27 industries, predominantly those in which producers were heavily reliant on intermediate inputs from suppliers, and where there were significant economies of scale. Brulhart (1998) reports geographic concentration increased throughout Europe during the 1980s. However, Aiginger and Davies (2000) report that while specialization in European manufacturing increased during the period 1985–98, geographic concentration decreased. A number of smaller countries overcame historical disadvantages and increased their shares of production in specific industries.

Hallett (2000) measures specialization and geographic concentration in order to examine changes in the spatial distribution of 17 economic activities within Europe for the period 1980–95. Southern (peripheral) regions were more highly specialized than their northern counterparts. Specialization tended to increase in poorer regions, and in regions that underwent major change in industrial structure. Geographic concentration is captured using four measures:

■ The extent to which production is spatially dispersed.

■ The extent to which production is concentrated at the EU's core or periphery.

■ The degree of 'clustering', reflected by the geographic distance between branches of similar activity.

■ The extent to which production is concentrated in high- or low-income regions.

Manufacturing industries with significant economies of scale tend to be geographically concentrated. Production in sectors such as agriculture, textiles and clothing takes place predominantly at the EU's periphery, while sectors such as banking and financial services are concentrated at the centre. Production of a number of products, including ores and metals, chemicals and transport equipment, is clustered around specific locations, perhaps due to historical links to raw material suppliers. Finally, labour-intensive sectors tend to be located in low-income regions, while capital-intensive or technology-oriented sectors are concentrated in the higher-income regions.

Clusters are groups of interdependent firms that are linked through close vertical or horizontal relationships, located within a well defined geographic area (European Commission, 2002). Porter (1998a) provides a more detailed definition:

> a geographically proximate group of inter-connected companies and associated institutions in a particular field, linked by commonalities and complementarities. The geographic scope of a cluster can range from a single entity or state to a country or even a group of neighbouring countries. Clusters take varying forms depending on their depth and sophistication, but most include end-product or service companies; suppliers of specialized inputs, components, machinery and services; financial institutions; and firms in related industries. Clusters also often involve a number of institutions, governmental and otherwise, that provide specialized training, education, information and technical support (such as universities, think tanks, vocational training providers); and standard setting agencies. Government departments and regulatory agencies that significantly influence a cluster can be considered part of it. Finally, many clusters include trade associations and other collective private sector bodies that support cluster members.
>
> *(Porter, 1998a, p. 254)*

Some researchers use the term **industrial district** to refer to a production system 'characterized by a myriad of firms specialized in various stages of production of a homogeneous product, often using flexible production technology and connected by local inter-firm linkages' (Jacobson and Andréosso-O'Callaghan, 1996, p. 116). For example, several well-known clusters or industrial districts are located in northern Italy and southern Germany. A tendency for many firm owners to originate from similar social backgrounds facilitates communication, and tends to blur the boundaries between individual firms and the communities in which they are based. This phenomenon has been documented in Italy, where there are several clusters or industrial districts comprising networks of small, specialized firms that are internationally competitive in the production of goods such as furniture, ceramic tiles and textiles (Markusen, 1996; Becattini *et al.*, 2003). Case Study 10.2 examines the importance of industrial clusters.

Clusters typically include distributors and retailers, suppliers, banks and firms producing related products and services. They can also include public or semi-public bodies such as universities, voluntary organizations and trade associations. Relationships are most effective if the firms are in close geographical proximity to one another, and if there is effective communication. Firms within a cluster do not always always compete, but sometimes cooperate by serving different niches of the same industry. However, they face the same competitive threats and opportunities. Because clusters are made up of what often seem to be a collection of disparate firms, standard industry classifications may not be useful in identifying them (Porter, 1998b).

Case study 10.2

Clusters flustered
Global competition seems to be weakening the benefits of being in a cluster

OPENED in 1845, the Cantoni cotton mill in Castellanza went on to become the country's biggest but, burdened by debt, it closed in 1985. A large cluster of producers centred on the town, once called the Manchester of Italy, also perished. In Como, about 20 miles (32km) to the north-east, a cluster of silk firms is ailing, and so is a woollens cluster around Biella, 50 miles to the west, victims like Castellanza of low-cost competition.

Michael Porter, a guru on clusters at Harvard Business School, has said they help productivity, boost innovation and encourage new firms. For Mr Porter, firms' geographical proximity, their close competition with each other and the growth of specialised suppliers and production networks around them make a winning combination. Globalisation has, however, made this far less certain. More open trade and improved transport links may mean that bunching together in a cluster no longer offers such a strong defence against cheaper foreign rivals. Indeed, as Italy's medium-sized industrial firms adapt to the threat from China, the benefit they get from being bunched together in a cluster seems to be weakening.

More than 100 such clusters speckle the boot of Italy: tiles in Sassuolo, food machinery in Parma, sofas in Matera, footwear in Fermo and clothing in Treviso, to name just some. A few owe their existence to local natural assets – marble is quarried in the mountains behind Carrara, for example. But mostly they are the result of skills built up over successive generations. The packaging-machinery firms around Bologna grew out of the region's tradition of precision engineering, and the area around Belluno, where the first ever spectacles factory was built in 1878, is still home to a cluster of eyewear makers.

San Maurizio d'Opaglio, midway between Castellanza and Biella, is the world's largest centre for working brass. Workers there once made bells; now the cluster has around 380 firms that together employ about 10,000 people making valves and taps, businesses that took off with reconstruction after the second world war and the building boom that followed. About 19,000 are employed in small satellite firms involved in parts of the production process.

Founded in 1951, now employing 850 people who make brass valves, connectors and manifolds and turning over €165m ($218m) last year, Giacomini is a giant of the cluster. However, quality certification, precision production and a catalogue of 6,000 products will not safeguard its future. 'Germans saw us in the 1950s and 1960s as we now see Chinese products – low quality, low cost. Long-term, brass fittings are not enough. We cannot expect to survive on these,' admits Corrado Giacomini, the chairman. The firm began diversifying into electronic controls and heating and air conditioning systems ten years ago, and this move away from its traditional business means that its links to the cluster look increasingly less relevant to its future.

Zucchetti, a tapmaker in the nearby town of Gozzano, has also changed strategy. As well as buying a maker of luxury baths and basins, it has shifted production upmarket, with smaller production runs and a larger product range. How Zucchetti performs in the future depends less on being in the cluster than designing smart products and defending its brand. A recent report from Intesa Sanpaolo, a bank, notes how competition is forcing firms to innovate, improve quality and build brands.

Firms in a jewellery cluster in Valenza, in southern Piedmont, hope to protect their businesses with help from the regional authorities, the creation of a group trade mark and peer pressure to keep skills in the cluster. Bruno Guarona, chairman of the jewellers' association, moans about unfair competition from China, where labour regulations are lax and firms enjoy tariffs and duties that undercut those his members face. But he reserves special bitterness for jewellers from Valenza who have moved production abroad, 'traitors who have committed a crime'.

Indeed, fragmentation of production and outsourcing abroad, clear signs that firms have become less competitive, weaken the networks on which clusters are built and may even destroy their competitive advantage, warns Rodolfo Helg, an economics professor at the university in Castellanza, which occupies the buildings that were once the town's large cotton mill. He believes successful clusters in the future will be very different from those of the past. Britain's large manufacturing clusters withered and died. The risk for Italy is that the decline of its clusters will prove as terminal elsewhere as it was in Castellanza.

Source: © The Economist Newspaper Limited, London, 14 April 2011.

European Commission (2002) surveys 34 clusters located in the EU-15 plus Norway. The clusters are characterized as traditional (transactions are based on long-term market relationships; collaboration is between service suppliers and government bodies; innovation takes place through product development and distribution), and science-based (transactions are based on temporary and long-term relationships; collaboration is between research and development institutions and government bodies; innovation takes place through new product and process development and new organizational forms). Table 10.9 reports the locations of some of these clusters.

Enright (1998) discusses the importance of clusters for firm-level strategic decision-making and performance. Many regions contain vital resources and capabilities that can be exploited by individual firms in order to gain a competitive advantage. However, firm-level strategy and performance are affected

Table 10.9 Location of EU science-based (S) and traditional (T) clusters

Country	Cluster name
Austria	Cluster biotechnology and molecular medicine science in Vienna (S); wooden furniture cluster, upper Austria (T)
Belgium	Flanders multimedia valley (S); Flemish plastic processing (T)
Denmark	Communication cluster in northern Jutland (S); Herning-Ikast textiles and clothing industry (T)
Finland	Technology cluster in Oulu (S); shipbuilding in Turku (T)
France	Evry Genopole (biotechnologies), Evry (S); Technic Valle (screw-cutting and mechanics), Haute-Savoie (T)
Germany	Chemical industry, northern Ruhr area (S); Enterprise – information – system, Lower Saxony (S); media cluster, north Rhine-Westphalia (T)
Greece	Industrial district of Volos (sundry metal products and foodstuffs) (T); industrial district of Herakleion (foodstuffs, non-metallic minerals) (T)
Ireland	Dublin software cluster (S); dairy processing industry (T)
Italy	Biomedical cluster in Emilia-Romagna (S); eye-glass cluster in Belluno country (T)
Liechtenstein	Financial services (T)
Luxembourg	CASSIS (IT and e-business consultancy for SMEs) (S); Synergie (technical facilities industries) (T)
Netherlands	Dommel valley (information and communication technology), Eindhoven/Helmond (S); Conoship (shipbuilding), Freisland and Groningen (T)
Norway	Electronics industry in Horten (S); shipbuilding at Sunnmore (T)
Portugal	Footwear cluster with several geographical concentrations in northern and central parts of the country (T); manufacture of metallic moulds in Leiria (T)
Spain	Machine-tools in the Basque country (S); shoe manufacturing in the Vinapolo valley (T)
Sweden	Biotech valley in Strangnas (S); recorded music industry in Stockholm (T)
United Kingdom	Cambridgeshire (high-tech) (S); British motor sport industry, Oxfordshire/ Northamptonshire (T)

Source: *Regional Clusters in Europe*, Observatory of European SMEs 2002, No. 3, Table 4.1 page 28, © European Communities, 2002.

by interdependence, cooperation and competition between firms within the same cluster (Gilbert *et al.*, 2008). Efficiency or productivity gains are realized if firms can access resources and inputs (skilled personnel, raw materials, access to customers, training facilities for staff) from elsewhere within the cluster, or take advantage of complementarities such as joint marketing and promotion, or accumulate specialized information and knowledge (Porter and Sovall, 1998). The formation of new firms may be encouraged and entry barriers kept low. If firms diversify within a cluster they not only take advantage of firm-specific economies of scope, but can also draw on the human capital or other resources that already exist elsewhere within the cluster. Clusters foster a sense of trust (or 'social glue') that helps bind participants together (Morosini, 2004).

Porter (1990) identifies clusters as key to the interactions between location, competition and national competitiveness. The competitive environment influences the way in which firms use their endowments of resources in order to formulate their strategies, which in turn determine performance. Innovation and technological spillovers are crucial to the development of firms. **Porter's Diamond Model** (1990) illustrates the determinants and dynamics of national competitive advantage. Competitive rivalry, factor and demand conditions, and the existence of related and supporting industries are the key determinants of the extent to which firms can develop and maintain a competitive advantage over rivals.

Porter's Diamond is illustrated in Figure 10.3. Domestic competitive interaction and rivalry stimulates firms to innovate and improve efficiency. For example, the Japanese car manufacturing and consumer electronics industries were intensely competitive within Japan, before the most successful firms also became dominant players at the international level. Changes in demand conditions provide an important stimulus for innovation and quality improvement. German firms are the dominant producers of high-speed cars, partly because there are no speed limits on the autobahns. Belgian and Swiss chocolate makers service discerning, up-market customers. The varied preferences of consumers allow firms and

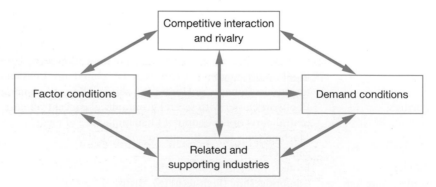

Figure 10.3 Diamond framework of competitive advantage
Source: Adapted with the permission of Free Press, a Division of Simon & Schuster, Inc., from The Competitive Advantage of Nations by Michael E. Porter. Copyright © 1990, 1998 by Michael E. Porter. All rights reserved.

industries to transfer locally accrued advantages to a global arena. Factor conditions comprise natural, human and capital resources, and the quality of the physical, administrative and technological infrastructures. Some of these resources are natural, but others, such as concentrations of specialized labour or capital, have developed in tandem with the historical growth of specific industries in particular locations. The quality and quantity of specialized high-quality inputs influence national competitiveness. Clusters of related and supporting industries, which engage in complementary or support activities, often strengthen successful industries. Examples of mutually supporting clusters include semi-conductors, computers and software in the US, and chemicals, dyes, textiles and textile machinery in Germany.

Porter's Diamond has stimulated academic and policy-maker interest in regional clusters of small and medium-sized firms. A number of schools attempt to explain the emergence of clusters. Many of the ideas date back to the work of Marshall (1890), who identifies a number of positive externalities that arise when firms are located in close proximity. These include benefits from the exchange of knowledge, sharing of labour and access to suppliers. Locational advantages or agglomeration economies accumulate through the growth of related industries and the development of specialized labour markets. The availability of agglomeration economics means that, over time, specialization is likely to increase.

According to organization theory, during the last two decades of the twentieth century technological change and the changing nature of production tended to push in the direction of smaller-scale production. Another common theme has been the fostering of long-term relationships between buyers and suppliers, and the development of cooperative networks of firms. Specialized knowledge is a crucial determinant of firm performance. Consequently, firms tend to cluster in specific geographic areas, in order to take advantage of learning opportunities and the sharing of knowledge (Lundvall and Johnson, 1994).

Industrial organization and strategic management literature views clusters as a consequence of specialized firms coming together in order to reduce transaction costs (see Chapters 5 and 19). According to this approach, an industry is most accurately defined by identifying commonalities across firms situated at different stages of the production process or value chain. This might involve the grouping together of raw material, intermediate input suppliers, end-user manufacturers and retailers into a single cluster (Porter and Sovall, 1998; Enright, 1998, 2000; Porter, 1998a,b, 2001).

The economic geography literature emphasizes the effect of agglomeration economies on the dynamics of growth and trade (Harrison *et al.*, 1996; Martin and Sunley, 1997). In seeking to explain geographic concentration, Krugman (1991, 2000) observes that much trade that takes place is intra-industry (between firms within the same industry). Trade theory based on notions of comparative advantage has little to say about this phenomenon. The geographic location of industry is driven primarily by regions seeking to exploit agglomeration economies. The initial location of trade is partly a product of historical accident but, as the gains from trade are realized, spatial patterns of location, specialization and trade become entrenched. Transport costs are an important influence on the location of industry but, even if transport costs are low, early patterns in the location of production (which may initially have been partly accidental) tend to persist. The role of forward and backward linkages is also important, and can lead to the appearance of vertically integrated clusters of firms. However, increased specialization can leave non-diversified regions highly exposed to business cycle fluctuations.

Kay (2004) notes that the location of industry and clusters is the result of historical accident and the co-evolution of capabilties and specialization.

> Since mutually reinforcing capabilities and specialisms depend on past choices, forgotton or now irrelevant historical events still influence the location of production today. Film producers in the 1920s sought the light of southern California. Films are rarely made in California anymore, but Hollywood remains the centre of the world film industry. London is still a marketplace for shipbroking and marine insurance because of Britain's historical past. Similar accidents of history – the site of Leland Stanford's University and Xerox Corporation's research facility – made Silicon Valley the centre of the international software industry.
>
> *(Kay, 2004, p. 73)*

Porter (1998a) argues that the advantages of locating within a cluster might represent a countervailing factor that helps check the widespread tendency for the international relocation of production, a pervasive feature of the globalization phenomenon. Globalization has resulted in improvements in communication, transport and distribution networks, enabling firms to switch productive activities between countries in order to reduce labour costs or tax liabilities. However, many low-cost locations are unable to offer adequate supplies of essential factor inputs or business support facilities; such locations may also fail to provide a suitable environment for innovation. Therefore, savings in labour costs or tax liabilities can be more than offset by losses in productivity. By locating within a cluster, firms can attract and retain key factor inputs and exploit opportunities for innovation. Steiner (2002) argues that current and future improvements in information technology and telecommunications may eventually permit the development of clusters that are not confined to specific geographic locations.

> Clusters are a system of production which is more than just a territorial concentration of specific firms working in the same sector, but one which involves complex organizations with tight trans-sectorial relationships implying a change from 'industrial district' to 'network' forms of organization at the interregional and international level. Instead of interpreting the globalization process as an external constraint and a risk to their survival, the increasing regional production systems is viewed as the gradual extension to the international level of tight inter-firm relationships, which have traditionally existed at the local and interregional level.
>
> *(Steiner, 2002, p. 208)*

10.5 Summary

Chapter 10 has examined some of the main theoretical determinants of seller concentration. Why do some industries tend to become more highly concentrated than others, and what are the factors driving trends in seller concentration over time? Theoretical determinants of seller concentration include the following:

- *Economies of scale.* The comparison between the total output that would be produced if each incumbent firm operates at minimum efficient scale, and the total demand for the industry's product, has major implications for the number of firms the industry can profitably sustain.

- *Entry and exit.* Entry tends to reduce concentration if the average size of entrants is smaller than that of incumbents. However, the effect could be the opposite if entry takes place at a large scale, perhaps as a result of a diversification strategy on the part of a large established firm from some other industry. By reducing the numbers of incumbents, exit usually tends to increase concentration.

- *Scope for discretionary, sunk cost expenditure.* Advertising, product differentiation and research and development are more important vehicles for discretionary investment in some industries than others. In industries which provide scope for these forms of sunk cost expenditure, incumbent firms tend to respond to an increase in demand by increasing their discretionary expenditures, leading to raised entry barriers, a larger minimum efficient scale and increased seller concentration. In industries without scope for significant sunk cost expenditures, any increase in demand may create opportunities for entrants, and seller concentration may tend to decrease.

- *Regulation.* Government competition policy directed towards monopolies, mergers or restrictive practices may have direct implications for seller concentration. Policies that restrict the number of firms permitted to operate may tend to increase concentration.

- *The industry life cycle.* New and rapidly expanding industries may be capable of sustaining large numbers of firms, with small firms able to prosper by innovating or finding niches. Mature and declining industries are likely to accommodate smaller numbers of firms, as incumbents attempt to offset the effects on profitability of slow growth in demand by realizing economies of scale, and eventually by eliminating competition through collusion or merger.

- *Distinctive capabilities and core competences.* According to the resource-based theory of the firm, the successful firm itself, rather than the industry structure, is the ultimate source of the strategies and capabilities that will eventually determine structural indicators such as seller concentration.

According to the random growth hypothesis that is expressed by the Law of Proportionate Effect (also known as Gibrat's law), strong or weak growth performance is distributed randomly across firms. In any given period some firms may perform well and others perform badly, but the distribution of strong and weak growth performance between firms is essentially a matter of chance. Furthermore, past growth is no reliable indicator of the rate at which a firm will grow or decline in the future. According to this view, the growth performance of individual firms can neither be explained by specific identifiable characteristics of the firms themselves, nor foreseen or predicted in advance. If individual firms' growth is random, there is a natural tendency for industry structure to become increasingly concentrated over time.

Inspection of empirical data on trends in seller concentration suggests that the trend towards increased seller concentration in manufacturing, which was evident throughout much of the twentieth century, was repeated in many service industries towards the end of the century. Complex patterns of specialization and geographic concentration influence the spatial distribution of production within the EU. In particular, the phenomenon of clustering, whereby groups of interdependent firms located within a specific geographic area realize economies by establishing close vertical or horizontal relationships, is a locational pattern that has received much attention in the industrial organization, strategic management and economic geography literatures.

Discussion questions

1. What are the implications of the relationship between MES (the minimum efficient scale of production) and the level of market demand for the degree of seller concentration in an industry?

2. Explain Sutton's (1991) distinction between Type 1 and Type 2 industries. If there is a sustained increase in market size in the long run, how is the trend in seller concentration expected to differ between these two industry types?

3. Outline the model of the industry life cycle. For what reasons might the degree of seller concentration be expected to change as an industry progresses through the four stages of its life cycle?

4. With reference to Case Study 10.1, consider the extent to which the historical development of the US credit union sector conforms to the industry life cycle model.

5. What are distinctive capabilities, and what are core competences? Why are they important?

6. Explain the implications of the random growth hypothesis (Gibrat's Law, also known as the Law of Proportionate Effect) for the long-run trend in seller concentration.

7. Explain how the random growth hypothesis might be subjected to empirical scrutiny.

8. Explain the distinction between specialization and geographic concentration.

9. What factors may give rise to the appearance and disappearance of clusters of related and supporting industries in particular geographic areas? Illustrate your answer with examples drawn from Case Study 10.2.

10. Outline the main elements of Porter's Diamond Model. To what extent does this model shed light on the sources of national competitive advantage?

Further reading

Beck, T., Demirguc-Kunt, V. and Maksimovic, V. (2005) Financial and legal constraints to growth: does firm size matter?, *Journal of Finance*, 60, 137–77.

Bell, G.G. (2005) Clusters, networks and firm innovativeness, *Strategic Management Journal*, 26, 287–95.

Campbell, J.R. and Hopenhayn, H.A. (2005) Market size matters, *Journal of Industrial Economics*, 53, 1–25.

Caves, R.E. (1998) Industrial organization and new findings on the turnover and mobility of firms, *Journal of Economic Literature*, 36, 1947–82.

Coad, A. (2009) *The Growth of Firms: A survey of theory and evidence*. Cheltenham: Edward Elgar.

Curry, B. and George, K. (1983) Industrial concentration: a survey, *Journal of Industrial Economics*, 31, 203–55.

Davies, S.W. (1989) Concentration, in Davies, S. and Lyons, B. (eds) *The Economics of Industrial Organisation*. London: Longman.

Davies, S.W., Rondi, L. and Sembenelli, A. (2001) European integration and the changing structure of EU manufacturing, 1987–1993, *Industrial and Corporate Change*, 10, 37–75.

Dosi, G., Malerba, F., Marsila, O. and Orsenigo, L. (1997) Industrial structures and dynamics: evidence interpretations and puzzles, *Industrial and Corporate Change*, 6, 3–24.

Geroski, P.A. (2003) *The Evolution of New Markets*. Oxford: Oxford University Press.

Mata, J. (2008) Gibrat's law, in Durlauf, S.N. and Blume, L.E. (eds) *New Palgrave Dictionary of Economics*. London: Palgrave Macmillan.

Porter, M.E. (2001) Regions and the new economics of competition, in Scott, A.J. (ed.) *Global-city Regions*. Oxford: Oxford University Press.

Sutton, J. (1991) *Sunk Costs and Market Structure*. London: MIT Press.

Sutton, J. (1997) Gibrat's legacy, *Journal of Economic Literature*, 35, 40–59.

Winter, S.G. (2003) Understanding dynamic capabilities, *Strategic Management Journal*, 24, 991–5.

Learning objectives

This chapter covers the following topics:

- definition and classification of barriers to entry
- entry-deterring strategies
- potential entry and the theory of contestable markets
- entry and the evolution of industry structure
- empirical evidence concerning barriers to entry

Key terms

Absolute cost advantage
   entry barrier
Bargain-then-ripoff pricing
Barriers to entry
Barriers to exit
Committed incumbent
Conjectural variation

Contestable market
Economies of scale entry
   barrier
Geographic entry barrier
Hit-and-run entry
Legal entry barrier
Limit pricing

Network externalities
Passive incumbent
Predatory pricing
Product differentiation entry
   barrier
Sunk costs
Switching costs

11.1   Introduction

Barriers to entry are defined by Bain (1956) as conditions that allow established firms or incumbents to earn abnormal profits without attracting entry (see Box 1.1). Stigler (1968, p. 67) defines entry barriers as 'a cost of producing (at some or every rate of output) which must be borne by a firm which seeks to enter an industry but is not borne by firms already in the industry'. Spulber (2003, p. 55) defines an entry barrier as 'any competitive advantage that established firms have over potential entrants'.

Section 11.2 identifies the principal types of barrier to entry. These include *Bain's framework* barriers that arise from economies of scale or from an absolute cost advantage held by an incumbent over an entrant, or from product differentiation. Other barriers to entry include legal barriers and geographic barriers, which create difficulties for foreign firms attempting to trade in the domestic market. Many of the factors that give rise to the barriers to entry may be beyond the direct control of the incumbent firms. However, sometimes incumbents are able to take steps that increase the difficulties that new entrants will have to over-come if they are to establish themselves on a profitable basis. In other words, incumbents can implement entry-deterring strategies in an attempt to increase the size or height of barriers to entry. The entry-deterring strategies discussed in Section 11.3 include limit pricing, predatory pricing, and brand proliferation.

Paradoxically, the extent of **barriers to exit** may be an important factor deter-mining the incentive for new firms to enter. It is costly to exit if production requires sunk cost investment expenditures. **Sunk costs** are costs that cannot be recovered if the firm subsequently decides to close down or exit. For example, expenditure on capital equipment that can only be used to manufacture the product in question and will be scrapped if the firm exits, is an example of a sunk cost expenditure. Entry is therefore riskier in cases where the entrant is unable to recover its costs if its decision to enter subsequently turns out to be unsuccessful.

Even if the entrant is confident it can succeed, perhaps because it knows it can produce at a lower average cost than an incumbent, barriers to exit facing the incumbent may still be an important consideration for the entrant. If the incumbent has already incurred significant levels of sunk cost expenditure (for example, by building excess capacity), so its exit barriers are high, the incumbent is likely to resist attempts by the entrant to capture part or all of its market share, perhaps by initiating a price war. If there has been no sunk cost expenditure and exit barriers are low, the incumbent threatened by com-petition from a low-cost entrant might simply prefer to withdraw quietly. If entrants take account of the probable reaction of incumbents before deciding whether or not to enter, the extent of exit barriers facing incumbents may be an important factor influencing the entry decision. Section 11.4 examines ways in which incumbents can signal commitment to defend an estab-lished position of market dominance by deliberately increasing their sunk cost expenditure.

Contestable markets theory is examined in Section 11.5. In industries where barriers to entry are surmountable, the threat of entry may keep prices close to the competitive level, even if there are few firms and the industry appears to be highly concentrated. Contestable markets theory breaks the direct link between the number and size distribution of sellers and the extent of market power or the discretion incumbents have in setting their own prices. Section 11.6 examines a more dynamic view of entry and market evolution over the long run. Entry is seen as a disequilibrating force that plays a central role in shaping the evolu-tion of market or industry structure in the long run. The chapter concludes in Section 11.7 with a brief review of some of the empirical evidence on the determinants of entry and the main sources of barriers to entry.

11.2 Types of barrier to entry

The types of barrier to entry examined in this section are economies of scale, absolute cost advantage, product differentiation, switching costs, network externalities, and legal and geographic barriers to entry. Carlton (2004) and McAfee *et al.* (2004) provide further discussion on classifying and measuring entry barriers.

Economies of scale

Economies of scale can act as a barrier to entry in two ways. First, there is an entry barrier if the MES is large relative to the total size of the market. As shown earlier, MES is the output level at which all potential economies of scale have been exploited, and the firm is operating at the lowest point on the LRAC function (see Section 2.2). The nature of the technology may be such that firms must claim a large market share in order to produce at the MES. A natural monopoly, in which long-run average costs decrease as output increases over all possible output levels the market can absorb, is the most extreme case. In a natural monopoly average costs are minimized if one firm occupies the entire market (see Section 3.4). This situation tends to arise in industries where fixed costs are high relative to variable costs.

The second way in which economies of scale can act as an entry barrier is when average costs associated with a production level below the MES are substantially greater than average costs at the MES. This is illustrated in Figure 11.1. In both industry A and industry B, the penalty for producing at 50 per cent of the MES is $C_1 - C_2$. This penalty is much greater in industry B than in industry A, due to the difference in slope between the two LRAC functions.

Economies of scale present the potential entrant with a dilemma. Either the entrant accepts the risk associated with large-scale entry in order to avoid the average cost penalty; or the entrant enters at a smaller scale and absorbs the average cost penalty. Large-scale entry is risky because the expansion in industry

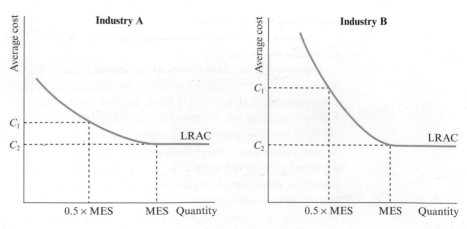

Figure 11.1 Economies of scale as a barrier to entry

Table 11.1 Economies of scale as a barrier to entry

Industry	Increase in average cost if operating at 50% of MES
Motor vehicles	6–9%
Chemicals	2.5–15%
Metals	> 6%
Office machinery	3–6%
Mechanical engineering	3–10%
Electrical engineering	5–15%
Instrument engineering	5–15%
Paper, printing and publishing	8–36%
Rubber and plastics	3–6%
Drink and tobacco	1–6%
Food	3.5–21%
Footwear and clothing	1%

Source: Adapted from Pratten (1988), Table 5.5, pp. 88–92, © European Union, 1995–2012.

capacity might disrupt an established industry equilibrium, depressing prices and inviting retaliatory action from incumbents. On the other hand, small-scale entry may not be viable, because the average cost penalty may make it impossible for the entrant to operate profitably alongside incumbents already producing at (or beyond) the MES.

Pratten (1988) provides some empirical estimates of the extent to which economies of scale acted as a barrier to entry for a number of European industries in 1986. Table 11.1 shows estimates of the additional average cost that would be incurred by operating at 50 per cent of the MES, in comparison with the average cost incurred when operating at the MES expressed as a percentage of the latter.

Absolute cost advantage

An incumbent has an **absolute cost advantage entry barrier** over an entrant if the LRAC function of the entrant lies above that of the incumbent, and the entrant therefore faces a higher average cost at every level of output. This situation is illustrated in Figure 11.2.

There are several reasons why an entrant may operate on a higher LRAC function. First, an incumbent may have access to a superior production process, hold patents, or be party to trade secrets. For example, the Monopolies and Mergers Commission (1968) estimated that it would take an entrant to the cellulose fibre industry between five and seven years to catch up with state-of-the-art production technology. Patenting involves the deliberate creation of a property right for new knowledge, intended to protect an innovator from imitation by rivals. From a public policy perspective, the motive for allowing patents may be to increase consumer welfare. Patents encourage firms to invest in research and development, with the promise of monopoly profits for successful innovators, as well as increased choice and utility for consumers.

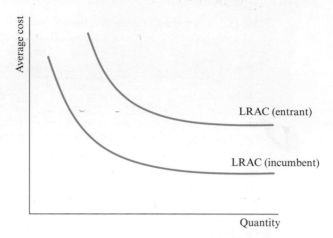

Figure 11.2 Absolute cost advantage as a barrier to entry

However, patenting can also be used by an incumbent strategically, in an attempt to deter entry. For example, a firm in possession of a new technology may apply for multiple patents to cover all possible spin-offs, so as to deny rivals the opportunity to invent around the new technology. In chemicals, for example, minor variations in molecular structure can easily lead to the creation of new product spin-offs (Needham, 1976). In the defence industry, new firms incur substantial entry costs related to technology and research and development expenditure in order to produce sophisticated defence equipment (Hartley, 2003). Langinier (2004) presents a theoretical model that assesses the extent to which patents and patent renewals act as a barrier to entry. In cases of low demand and asymmetric information regarding market demand, patent renewal is shown to deter entry. However, if market demand is high, patent renewals do not discourage entry. The economics of patenting is examined in more detail later (see Section 17.5).

Second, incumbent firms may have exclusive ownership of factor inputs. They may control the best raw materials, or have recruited the most qualified or experienced labour or management personnel. Consequently, entrants are forced to rely on more expensive, less efficient or lower-quality alternatives. For example, British Airways exercises influence over landing slots at London's Heathrow Airport, forcing competitors to use less attractive airports. However, through a variety of innovative strategies low-cost entrants have been able to overcome this entry barrier and operate profitably. For example, low-cost airlines have: unbundled their core product by charging separate prices for the flight itself and extras such as meals; reduced costs by using cheaper airports; simplified ticket purchase and check-in arrangements; reduced airport turnaround times; and made more intensive use of their aircraft (Johnson, 2003).

Third, incumbents may have access to cheaper sources of finance, if they are viewed by capital markets as less risky than new firms. For example, in pharmaceuticals, large incumbents with well-established research and development programmes are deemed less likely than their smaller counterparts to develop products that subsequently go on to fail drug trials. Lower risk means that preferential financial backing is easier to attain (Nightingale, 2003). If the new firm's management is previously unknown, any funds loaned are likely to carry a risk premium.

Finally, the presence of vertically integrated incumbents in industries such as biotechnology, brewing, iron, mobile telephones, steel or chemicals may force an entrant to operate at more than one stage of production if it wishes to overcome the incumbents' absolute cost advantage. In European brewing, for example, any new firm would not only manufacture beer, but also be able to source supplies, promote the finished product and establish an efficient network of distribution outlets (Lawler and Lee, 2003). Denying rivals access to inputs or markets through various forms of vertical exclusion may be subject to legal challenge under competition law (see Chapter 23), but this is not to say that such practices never take place.

It is worth noting that an absolute cost differential need not always work in favour of the incumbent. It is possible that an incumbent has overpaid for its assets, in which case the entrant may be favoured. This might be true in industries reliant on rapidly changing technologies, such as computer hardware or software, whose costs fall rapidly over time. In some cases the entrant may be spared the costs of persuading consumers to accept a new idea or a new product, such costs having already been incurred by incumbents.

Demsetz (1982) argues that Bain's absolute cost advantage does not reflect the abuse of market power by incumbents, but simply reflects the scarcity of resources and the associated rents. However, this comment does not invalidate the preceding discussion, in so far as it concerns structural barriers to entry. These additional costs are real enough to potential entrants, and they do not necessarily derive from the exploitation of market power.

Product differentiation

A barrier to entry exists if customers are loyal to the established brands and reputations of incumbents. A successful entrant will need to persuade customers to switch from their existing suppliers. This might be achieved either by selling the same product at a lower price, or launching advertising, marketing or other promotional campaigns (Comanor and Wilson, 1967). Due to price-cutting or increased costs (or both) the entrant is faced with a squeeze on profit, at least during the initial start-up phase. **Product differentiation entry barriers** include the following:

- High advertising imposes additional costs upon entrants. In order to overcome existing brand loyalties or customer inertia, the entrant must spend proportionately more on advertising for each prospective customer. This is an absolute cost advantage barrier. For example, in the brewing industry it is estimated that the establishment of a leading European brand through advertising takes around 20 years (Competition Commission, 2001; Lawler and Lee, 2003).

- If entry takes place on a small scale, the entrant will not benefit from economies of scale in advertising. Large-scale advertisers may benefit from an increasingly effective message, and decreasing average advertising costs.

■ The funds needed to finance an advertising campaign may incur a risk premium, as this type of investment is high risk. Furthermore, it creates no tangible assets that can be sold in the event of failure.

In some cases, incumbents may deliberately seek to increase the degree of product differentiation through brand proliferation, in order to raise barriers to entry. Product differentiation or brand proliferation as a form of entry-deterring strategy is examined in Section 11.3.

Switching costs

Switching costs are incurred when customers face additional costs if they decide to change the supplier of a product or service. Switching costs may include: search costs incurred in acquiring information about alternative products or services; the costs of learning how to use a different product or service; and installation or disconnection charges. Switching costs raise barriers to entry into markets for a wide range of products such as credit cards, computer software, utilities (supplies of gas, electricity and water), phones and banking services.

For example, consumers wishing to change a mobile phone may have to purchase a new handset, master a new interface, pay a disconnection charge, and set up new billing arrangements. Further switching costs may be incurred when a good or service is tied to an aftermarket, through servicing or the need to purchase refills or replacement components. Tying makes it difficult for users to switch to alternative suppliers. Users become locked in to an existing supplier, which acquires *ex post* market power. **Bargain-then-ripoff pricing**, a policy of offering new customers a low price to attract their custom and then charging existing customers a high price in order to extract increased revenue or profit, works best when locked in customers can be separated from new ones: for example, in markets where users are tied into buying complementary products, such as ink refills or spare parts for cars; or in markets where prices are individually negotiated. If there is only one price, the supplier must compromise between a low price to attract new users and a high price to exploit locked in users.

To what extent do switching costs distort competition? Barriers to entry arising from switching costs due to incompatability of technological standards can result in the segmentation of a market into sub-markets or segments, such that an incumbent within a particular segment concentrates on charging high prices to its existing customers, and does not even attempt to attract customers from rival producers. Klemperer (2008) suggests that in view of the anti-competitive and entry-deterring effects of switching costs, regulatory attention should focus on situations where incompatibility is a matter of strategic choice, rather than governed by the nature of the technology.

Network externalities 网络外部性 例: giffgaff

Network externalities arise when the value of a product or service to a consumer depends upon the number of other consumers using the same product or service

(Katz and Shapiro, 1985; Economides, 1996; Farrell and Klemperer, 2007; Klemperer, 2008). Each consumer purchases the product or service for their own benefit, but by doing so they (unintentionally) create a benefit for other users who gain extra value as the size or coverage of the network of users increases. Network externalities make it difficult for new firms to enter when an incumbent has already established a large or comprehensive user network. As more users buy into the network, an effective monopoly might be created, raising formidable barriers to entry for any entrant wishing to challenge the dominance of the established product, service or technological standard. Chapter 21 examines the economics of markets that are subject to network externalities.

Markets subject to network externalities include those in which users are linked through communication systems such as telephones or the internet. Computer operating systems and widely used applications, such as Microsoft Windows and Microsoft Office, are subject to network externalities. For example, the value to a job seeker of acquiring the skills required to use Microsoft products increases with the number of employers that use the same products. The ability to share files that are specific to Microsoft products depends on the number of other users of the same products. Stock and derivatives exchanges are also subject to network externalities. As the number of traders in an established exchange increases, liquidity increases and transaction costs decrease. A new exchange might face a formidable barrier to entry in attempting to overcome these advantages.

Direct network externalities exist when the network becomes *more* attractive to new users as the level of adoption increases. Indirect network externalities arise when increased adoption affects a related market. Bandwagon effects are characteristic of successful networks. Success in establishing a network depends on users' expectations as to which network will achieve dominance, and on the coordination of users' choices. In the early stages of the commercial development of a new technological standard, producers tend to compete aggressively, knowing that success depends not on the tastes of individual consumers, but also on their expectations as to the most likely winner.

With compatible technological standards, consumers may be able to enjoy full network benefits without having to buy from a single producer. If consumers are willing to pay a higher price for this benefit, then firms might be encouraged to supply compatible products. However, an incumbent might still prefer incompatibility, because this serves as a barrier to entry. Incompatibility might damage consumers in several ways. Competing standards may result in market fragmentation, in which case the benefits of network externalities fail to materialize. On the other hand, if the market 'tips' towards one technological standard, it is possible that a later and technologically superior standard fails to become established. Competition between producers seeking to become the established standard might encourage bargain-then-ripoff pricing. Producers may initially compete aggressively in order to become the standard, but the winner may subsequently abuse its market power in order to earn abnormal profits (Salop and Stiglitz, 1977).

Legal barriers to entry

Legal barriers to entry are erected by governments and enforced by law. Both the Chicago and Austrian schools view legal barriers as highly damaging to competition. Examples of legal barriers include:

■ *Registration, certification and licensing of businesses and products.* Some industries are characterized by the need to seek official permission to trade, for example pubs, taxis, airlines and defence equipment (Hartley, 2003). For pharmaceuticals, legal barriers to entry facing new firms or products are high, arising from the framework of safety rules and regulations requiring products to satisfy a myriad of standards and tests (Nightingale, 2003). In some cases, incumbents may press for more stringent regulation, in an attempt to keep out firms that do not meet industry standards. Under this guise of maintaining standards, low-cost entrants may be denied access to the market.

■ *Monopoly rights.* Monopoly rights may be granted by legislation. The government might allow certain firms exclusive rights to produce certain goods and services for a limited or unlimited period. An example is franchised monopolies in industries such as the railways, mobile telephones and television broadcasting. Franchised monopolies are often awarded in situations of natural monopoly, where average costs are minimized when one firm occupies the entire market, or in cases where firms require the guarantee of a relatively large market share in order to invest in technology and product development.

■ *Patents.* As noted above, patenting involves the deliberate creation of a property right, enforced by law. Ownership of a patent confers monopoly rights and the potential to earn an abnormal profit, usually for a fixed period. The intention is to encourage research and development and innovation, by enabling successful innovators to appropriate the returns from their original investment. The disadvantage, from a public policy perspective, is that by granting an incumbent exclusive rights to use a piece of technology or produce a particular product, competition is impeded and the pace of diffusion of a technology is inhibited.

■ *Government policies.* Government policies can also create legal barriers to entry directly. Friedman (1962) suggests tariffs, tax policies and employment laws may all impede entry, either directly or indirectly. For example, in several European countries car tax is related to engine capacity. This has the effect of increasing the price of cars imported from the US, which have greater engine capacity on average.

Klapper *et al.* (2004) examine ways in which regulation hampers entry, especially in industries where start-up costs are low and high rates of entry would normally be expected. Value added in naturally 'high-entry' industries tends to grow more slowly in countries with high entry barriers.

Geographic barriers to entry

Geographic barriers to entry include restrictions faced by foreign firms attempting to trade in the domestic market. Geographic barriers affect the extent and type of entry (for example, greenfield investments, acquisitions or joint ventures) undertaken by foreign firms (Elango and Sambharya, 2004). Examples of geographic entry barriers include:

- *Physical barriers.* Frontier controls and customs formalities create administrative and storage costs, and lead to delays in transactions being completed.

- *Technical barriers.* Technical barriers include requirements to meet specific technical standards, employment regulations, health and safety regulations and transport regulations.

- *Fiscal barriers.* Aspects of a country's fiscal regime may disadvantage foreign firms. Exchange controls may impose costs on foreign firms that need to convert currencies in order to trade. Tariffs, quotas or subsidies to domestic producers may place foreign producers at a disadvantage relative to domestic producers.

- *Preferential public procurement policies.* Purchasing policies practised by national governments may give preferential treatment to domestic firms, placing foreign competitors at a disadvantage.

- *Language and cultural barriers.* Language or other cultural differences between countries may also be considered as a geographic barrier to entry (Ghemawat, 2003).

Case study 11.1

Barriers to entry in retail banking

New entrants to the retail banking sector face significant challenges in attracting customers and expanding their market shares, an OFT review has found. The review of barriers to entry, expansion and exit in retail banking was launched in May 2010 to identify any obstacles blocking firms from entering the sector or from successfully competing against existing firms, as well as factors preventing inefficient firms from exiting the market and being replaced by more efficient ones.

The OFT has established a body of evidence relating to the size and significance of potential barriers, based on extensive consultation with the industry, including established incumbent banks and building societies, new and prospective entrants and consumer and industry groups. A copy of the review will be submitted to the Independent Commission on Banking which is examining issues of competition and stability in the banking market.

The OFT examined four aspects of personal and small and medium-sized enterprise (SME) banking to identify possible barriers: 1. the regulatory process; 2. access to essential inputs necessary to offer retail banking products such as IT systems, payment schemes, information and finance; 3. the ability of new entrants to grow by attracting new customers; 4. issues around exiting the market.

While the review found that most prospective entrants are able to meet regulatory requirements, and source the necessary inputs to offer retail banking services, new providers face difficulties in attracting customers and expanding market share. This is because of the reluctance of personal and small business customers to switch providers, their loyalty to established brands, and preference for banks with a local branch. This was most marked for personal and business current account customers, whereas personal customers were more likely to shop around for loan products.

The other major findings were that:

■ Some firms reported problems around the process of becoming authorised by the FSA to accept deposits, with a lack of transparency and uncertainty causing delays and difficulties in raising funds. The FSA has recently revised its authorisation process and this should lead to greater transparency and certainty.

■ Existing capital requirements may disproportionately affect new entrants and smaller banks by requiring them to hold proportionally more capital than incumbents. As capital and liquidity requirements are updated, it may be appropriate for the prudential regulators to consider and monitor their impact on competition.

■ Entering the market involves significant IT investment, often in the form of sunk costs, which can account for up to two-thirds of start-up costs. This makes it all the more important for firms to be able to grow quickly, to spread those costs over a larger customer base.

■ New entrants are able to access industry-wide payment schemes such as CHAPS and BACS, and information on personal and SME customer risk profiles is widely available. However, credit risk information about micro-enterprises is limited, which may make it harder for new banks to lend to the smallest firms.

■ Following the financial crisis, the ability of some firms to expand could be constrained by the current lack of interbank lending.

■ There is no evidence to suggest that the regulatory framework dealing with how a failing bank exits the sector prevents inefficient firms leaving the market, but the OFT encourages the authorities to give due consideration to competition issues when these arrangements are operated.

The review also explored whether there are specific issues around barriers to entry, expansion and exit in England, Scotland, Northern Ireland and Wales. While the review did not find significant differences in relation to most of the themes covered, it did find that brand loyalty to incumbent national brands in Scotland and Northern Ireland may be greater than elsewhere in the UK and that new entrants' choice of location is largely driven by the size of the potential customer base, with highly populated urban areas seen as more attractive than rural areas.

Clive Maxwell, OFT Executive Director for Goods, Services and Mergers said:

> Vigorous competition in retail banking is vital for personal and small business customers and helps support growth and productivity in the economy. If firms

face significant difficulties in entering and competing in the market, incumbents have less incentive to reduce costs, innovate and price competitively.

A number of firms have recently entered the market, and more are expected to follow. While we found few barriers to setting up, new firms trying to grow in this market face difficulties due to customers' low levels of switching, loyalty to incumbent providers, and attachment to a local branch.

We hope that this review will be of value to the Independent Commission on Banking, and contribute to the wider debate on the future of banking.

Source: Office of Fair Trading (2010) *Review of Barriers to Entry, Expansion and Exit in Retail Banking.* London: HMSO.

Case study 11.2

Don't get boxed in by a cloud

Does your company attract customers and keep them happy via adept use of analytics and online data? Then your business may be among the first to be affected by the seldom-discussed restrictions that can happen when adopting popular cloud computing. Yet it behoves top management in any company to understand how to manage one of the worst potential constraints – getting locked into one particular service that limits a firm's ability to compete over time. For example, how can you avoid huge data switching costs if you want to migrate to another cloud vendor?

Alternatively, rather than rapidly manipulating a lot of data, does your business need to allocate additional computing resources to manage routine peak season or monthly closing computing tasks? You have been told that the 'cloud' is your best way to manage those regular peak usage periods. You may need to develop new capabilities to capture that capacity. How do you implement new software to take advantage of enabling features of one cloud without becoming inextricably linked to it?

As enterprises invested more and more money in enterprise software architectures and massive database platforms, the C-suite developed a healthy fear of being locked-in to outmoded technologies. The truth of the matter is that most enterprises are more locked in to their current IT providers than they might desire. Now, with cloud computing, a new wild frontier in IT is emerging and standards are again not yet set, so lock-in risks arise in a new form. On the other hand, by anticipating the risks, enterprises have a new opportunity to increase the ability to move flexibly from one IT provider to another as they move more of their operations to cloud platforms.

Here are five key concepts related to lock-in to consider so that you can capture the enormous potential upside of cloud capabilities while not being constrained by the downsides:

1. If you want to move to a different cloud, your firm's computing style – say with Java or .Net – could be in conflict with the way a new cloud provides computing services. In addition, different clouds have different billing models and other enabling services. These differences influence the architecture of what and how your firm can build on the cloud. When changing to another cloud, differing styles may mean that you may not be able to recreate the same architectural structure. The choices you make will have a huge effect on your firm's organisational processes around software development, testing and deployment. The longer you operate within one cloud the higher the stakes in attempting to move.

Changing clouds should involve not just IT, but the C-suite's strategic review. You will want to ensure that IT is designing a service oriented architecture that will facilitate accessing all or parts of your IT needs from one or more cloud service providers, as well as movement from one provider to another. It needs to be flexible and adaptable enough to support services needed by your firm that you will use on that cloud, whether your company directly implements them or they come from a third party. Use of services means you have a better chance of cleanly separating user interfaces from business rules, as most IT people know. Consequently you will be able to move to one or more clouds with less pain.

2. What does not appear to be lock-in today can quickly become lock-in by tomorrow. Big data – data that comes in large volumes, grows quickly, and lives long – can make it quite difficult to move between clouds. The time it takes to move data over a network connection could prove prohibitive. For example: 100 terabytes would be moved over a 1000 Base T network in about 12 days; 100 petabytes over the same network would take about 12,000 days; and 100 exabytes transferred over the same network would take about 12,000,000 days. That's why it is essential to know how quickly your cloud data will grow, and how easily and quickly your prospective cloud vendor can both manage the transfer of your data between your firm and the cloud and handle ongoing capacity during your use of that cloud. At the core of your cloud data management strategy within a particular vendor is your ability to partition data in that cloud in ways that make its movement easier, should you need to move it, and also easier to analyse in parallel.

3. Clouds provide different, specialised capabilities and resources. One provides the ability to query and analyse large distributed data sets. Another implements functionality complementary to e-commerce purposes, whereas others don't but they provision access to CRM/ERP (customer relationship management/enterprise resource management) application platforms, or they more easily integrate public and private clouds. Some may invest more in global delivery of content into and out of clouds (sometimes called cloud fronts), whereas others do far less in this area.

4. Storing huge amounts of data in a cloud represents a significant business risk. It must be safe and recoverable. Consequently your IT leader should be convinced that the cloud vendor has a secure disaster recovery system for your data. Cloud vendors implement disaster recovery quite differently than the ways to which we've been accustomed. For example, redundant storage is the cloud default for new types of cloud storage, so you can be less worried about multiple recoverable copies than about where the redundant copies are stored. Be sure that the geographical location of both your primary and

redundant data meets your safety and business regulatory requirements. Cloud vendors may be trustworthy with data, but the potential size your data could reach means that data safety, data encryption, and disaster recovery may all be performed differently by your prospective vendors. Understand how they perform these tasks, and how they meet your particular need. For example, how one vendor does 'backup' might complicate how you move the data to a new site that has quite different backup or redundancy strategies.

5. What you cannot see you cannot manage, and what you cannot manage you cannot move easily. The management capabilities of your legacy system and your potential cloud vendors' management platforms may lead you to choose one cloud vendor over another. To avoid lock-in, ensure that your new cloud and your legacy systems are designed for management, independent of cloud-specific management interfaces. That means your management instrumentation should interoperate with theirs, but you also should be able to make it interoperate with other management interfaces easily. Business and operational policies are often embedded within legacy software; however they need to be made explicit to make their enforcement possible, using cloud management capabilities.

All these considerations represent different kinds of capabilities that are often not discussed when talking about avoiding lock-in. They are sometimes considered more as a bias or enticement to choose one cloud over another. Yet, top management would be well served to explicitly address the risks that each represents.

The competitive stakes are high. Moving to clouds equates to factoring control in ways that differ substantially from how IT has operated in the past. The C suite should be involved in such discussions since it is precisely these control points that affect a company's ability to swiftly innovate. Changing APIs (application programming interfaces) and moving from one ERP to another, for example, could feel like a walk in the park in comparison to undoing the damage of a cloud lock-in.

Source: Don't get boxed in by a cloud, *Financial Times*, 26 July 2011. Reproduced with kind permission of Hagel, J. and Seely Brown, J.

Case study 11.3

Confusion at a price

The UK energy secretary wants to reform the way suppliers charge customers. But his plans seem unlikely to give a dramatically better deal. Are we living in a confusopoly?

You know what I mean: trying to figure out whether it's cheaper to use one phone company's 'Armadillo Everyday 500' tariff or another's 'Supersava B', with a special concessionary price for the first 15 minutes of the 25-year contract. (The term confusopoly was, I believe, first coined by Scott Adams, the creator of 'Dilbert'.) Chris Huhne, the UK energy secretary, fears the confusopoly in energy prices, and in a speech last month, he announced his plans to do something about it.

Huhne has a point: we know that a well-functioning, competitive market is a good way to get prices down. If such a market is feasible it's far more likely to deliver good results than regulatory diktats, with all their inevitable loopholes and unintended consequences. Yet if consumers are confused about prices then competition is unlikely to produce such glorious results. But the story is – surprise, surprise – not quite as simple as Huhne suggested in his conference speech. There are two separate issues here: people feel that it's a hassle to switch suppliers, and they are uncertain about whether they'd be better off if they did.

The first problem, switching costs, is less serious than it seems. Paul Klemperer, an economics professor at Oxford University, says that switching costs need not be bad for consumers or particularly good for companies. In a market with switching costs, what every company wants is a fat share of captive customers to exploit. But how to acquire those customers? The obvious solution is to offer fantastic deals, attract the suckers, and then gouge them for all they're worth. (This is why your phone company will happily give you a £500 phone 'free'; nobody has yet offered me a free laptop computer.) The early bargains partially – and sometimes fully – compensate for the later price gouging.

What every company wants is a fat share of captive customers to exploit. Perhaps we should not worry too much, as long as the introductory bargains are generous enough. I wonder what to make of the fact that Huhne has branded them 'predatory pricing' and declared that the bargains will stop. I fear it will be hard to implement that policy sensibly. For instance, Michael Waterson of the University of Warwick reckons that a recent effort by the energy regulator to stop some kinds of predatory pricing simply backfired: the deals dried up but lower everyday prices did not materialise.

The second problem, confusion pricing, seems to be the curse of our age. There is certainly reason to worry: I've written in this column before about the research of the economists Catherine Waddams Price and Chris Wilson, who studied customers who had overcome whatever switching costs they faced and were determined to find a cheaper electricity supplier. Most people missed the lion's share of the savings they might have achieved, and a quarter managed to make themselves worse off. And yet, and yet. Eugenio Miravete of the University of Texas at Austin studies what he calls 'foggy pricing' and reckons that competition is a pretty good antidote to the fog: new entrants typically have an incentive to offer simple prices to cut through the confusions, while incumbents do not retaliate by complicating their own offers.

Bain (1956) argues that barriers to entry arising from economies of scale, absolute cost advantage and product differentiation are generally stable in the long run. However, this does not imply these barriers should be regarded as ~~forever~~ permanent. The same comment applies to entry barriers arising from switching costs and network externalities, and legal and geographic barriers. Market structures can and do change eventually, and the importance of any entry barrier can vary over time. For example, new technology may re-shape the LRAC functions of both incumbents and entrants, transforming the nature of economies of scale. New deposits of a raw material may be discovered, reducing the absolute cost advantage enjoyed by an incumbent. One highly innovative marketing campaign might completely wipe out long-established brand loyalties, or other product differentiation advantages of incumbents.

The Chicago school regards Bain's definition of barriers to entry, which includes any obstacle a new firm must overcome to enter a market, as too general to be useful. Stigler's preferred definition is limited to factors that impose a higher long-run production cost on the entrant than on the incumbent. The Chicago school argues that it is rare for such a cost differential to endure in the long run. Therefore the most important issue is not the existence of barriers to entry, but rather the speed with which entry barriers can be surmounted (Stigler, 1968; Demsetz, 1982).

11.3   Entry-deterring strategies

The barriers to entry examined in Section 11.2 stem from underlying product or technological characteristics, and cannot be changed easily by incumbent firms. In contrast, entry-deterring strategies are barriers to entry that are created or raised deliberately by incumbents through their own actions. Relevant actions might include changes in price or production levels, or in some cases merely the threat that such changes will be implemented if entry takes place. A credible threat of this kind may be sufficient to deter potential entrants from proceeding. The extent to which it is possible for an incumbent to adopt entry-deterring strategies depends on the degree of market power exercised by the incumbent (Cabral, 2008).

This section examines three types of entry-deterring strategy. The first two are pricing strategies: **limit pricing** and **predatory pricing**. The third is strategic product differentiation or brand proliferation, whereby incumbents employ advertising or other forms of marketing activity in order to strengthen brand loyalties.

Limit pricing

Suppose a market is currently serviced by a single producer but entry barriers are not insurmountable. The incumbent therefore faces a threat of potential entry. According to the theory of limit pricing, the incumbent might attempt to prevent entry by charging a price, known as the limit price, defined as the highest price the incumbent believes it can charge without inviting entry. The limit price is below the monopoly price, but above the incumbent's average cost. Therefore the incumbent earns an abnormal profit, but this abnormal profit is lower than the monopoly profit (Martin, 2008).

In order to pursue a limit pricing strategy, the incumbent must enjoy some form of cost advantage over the potential entrants. In the limit pricing models developed below, this is assumed to take the form of *either* an absolute cost advantage *or* an economies of scale entry barrier. It is therefore assumed that a structural barrier to entry exists, but this barrier may be surmountable unless the incumbent adopts a pricing strategy that makes it unattractive for entrants to proceed.

A critical assumption underlying models of limit pricing concerns the nature of the reaction the entrants expect from the incumbent, if the entrants proceed with their entry decision. A key assumption of these models is that entrants assume the incumbent would maintain its output at the pre-entry level in the event that entry takes place. Therefore the incumbent is prepared to allow price to fall to a level determined by the location of the combined post-entry output (of the incumbent and entrants) on the market demand function (Sylos-Labini, 1962). Notice that this assumption (which has been termed the Sylos Postulate in the barriers to entry literature) is equivalent to the zero **conjectural variation** assumption that we have encountered previously in the development of the Cournot duopoly model (see Section 7.3).

Figure 11.3 shows the limit pricing model in the case of an absolute cost advantage entry barrier. It is assumed there is a single incumbent and a fringe comprising a large number of small competitive potential entrants. $LRAC_1$ is the incumbent's average cost function, and $LRAC_2$ is the entrants' average cost function. In order to concentrate solely on the effects of absolute cost advantage (and exclude economies of scale), it is assumed both LRAC functions are horizontal, and therefore equivalent to the long-run marginal cost (LRMC) functions. The incumbent's monopoly price and output are (P_M, Q_M). At all output levels, the entrants' average cost is below P_M. Therefore, if the incumbent operates at (P_M, Q_M) initially, entry takes place subsequently. The entrants produce $Q^* - Q_M$, reducing the price to P^*, and reducing the incumbent's abnormal profit from BP_MEG (pre-entry) to BP^*FG (post-entry).

Suppose instead the incumbent pursues a limit pricing strategy in the short run. This involves operating at (P^*, Q^*) initially. If entry takes place, industry output is increased above Q^*, causing price to fall below $P^*(= LRAC_2)$. The entrants' residual demand function shows the relationship between industry price and the entrants' output, assuming (in accordance with the zero conjectural variation assumption) the incumbent maintains its output at Q^*. The residual demand function is equivalent to the segment of the market demand function

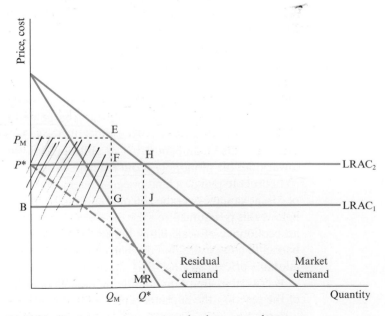

Figure 11.3 Limit pricing to deter entry: absolute cost advantage

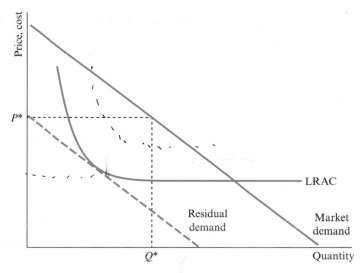

Figure 11.4 Limit pricing to deter entry: economies of scale

that lies to the right of Q^*. Since the residual demand function lies below $LRAC_2$ at all output levels, the entrants conclude they cannot earn a normal profit and abstain from entry. The incumbent's position at (P^*, Q^*), and its abnormal profit of BP^*HJ, are sustainable in both the pre-entry and post-entry periods. BP^*HJ exceeds BP^*FG, the long-run abnormal profit in the previous case where the incumbent starts at (P_M, Q_M) and allows entry to take place.

Figure 11.4 shows the limit pricing model in the case of an economies of scale entry barrier. In this case, it is more natural to consider the case of a single incumbent and a single entrant (rather than a fringe of small competitive entrants), because both firms would need to operate at a reasonably large scale in order to benefit from economies of scale. For simplicity, only the limit pricing solution (and not the comparison with the monopoly pricing solution) is shown. LRAC is the average cost function of both the incumbent and the entrant. The incumbent can prevent entry by operating at (P^*, Q^*). As before, the residual demand function is the entrant's effective demand function when the incumbent is producing Q^*, equivalent to the section of the market demand function to the right of Q^*. The residual demand function lies below LRAC at all output levels. If the entrant produces a low output, it fails to benefit from economies of scale. If the entrant produces a high output, it benefits from economies of scale, but the extra output causes price to drop to a level that is unprofitable. Therefore the entrant concludes it cannot earn a normal profit at any output level, and abstains from entry.

There is limited empirical evidence concerning the use or effectiveness of limit pricing strategies. Much of the evidence that is available is anecdotal. For example, Scherer and Ross (1990) observe that the pricing policy of the Reynolds Pen Corporation, manufacturers of the first ballpoint pens, invited entry on a large scale. In 1945 the price was between US$12 and US$20, but by 1948 the price had fallen to 50 cents and Reynolds' market share was close to zero. In the 1960s Xerox implemented a strategy of charging low prices to low-volume users (less than 5,000 copies per month). An alternative technology (wet copying) was available, and Xerox's pricing strategy was designed to deter low-volume users from switching to this alternative product. Yamawaki (2002) examines how incumbent firms in the US luxury car market responded to threatened or actual entry from Japanese manufacturers during the period 1986–97. There was a tendency for incumbent firms to reduce prices and mark-ups. However, surveys by Smiley (1988) and Singh *et al.* (1998) find limited evidence of the use of limit pricing as an entry-deterring strategy.

Stigler (1968) and Yamey (1972) criticize the theory of limit pricing on the following grounds:

- Why is it more profitable to attempt to restrict all entry rather than retard the rate of entry?

- Why should the entrant believe the incumbent would not alter its pricing and output policies if entry takes place?

- If an industry is growing, it may be difficult to persuade a potential entrant that there is no market available if entry takes place.

- Market structure is ignored. Applied to the case of oligopoly, the theory assumes all incumbent firms would implement a limit pricing strategy. For this strategy to succeed, a high level of coordination or collusion would be required.

- Limit pricing implies perfect information regarding the market demand function, the incumbent's own costs, the entrants' costs and so on. These would be impossible to estimate with any degree of precision. Predatory pricing (see below) might offer an easier alternative: the incumbent would simply set a price below that of the entrant until the entrant withdraws.

- The status of the entrant is all-important. An incumbent may wish to seek an accommodation with a large potential entrant.

Predatory pricing

A strategy of **predatory pricing** on the part of an incumbent firm involves cutting price in an attempt to force a rival firm out of business. When the rival has withdrawn, the incumbent raises its price. The incumbent adopts the role of predator, sacrificing profit and perhaps sustaining losses in the short run, in order to protect its market power and maintain its ability to earn abnormal profit in the long run. For example, Bresnahan and Reiss (1991), Joskow *et al.* (1994) and Marion (1998) report evidence of price-cutting by incumbents, following entry into the tyre, airline and grocery industries respectively. Strictly speaking, predatory pricing is a post-entry strategy. However, an incumbent faced with threatened entry might attempt to ward off the threat by convincing the potential entrant it would implement a predatory pricing policy in the event that entry takes place (Myers, 1994; Ordover, 2008).

Faced with the threat or the actuality of price-cutting on the part of a predator, how might an entrant or other rival firm respond? The rival might be able to convince the predator it is in their mutual interest to merge, or find some other way of sharing the market between them. Alternatively, the rival might be able to convince customers it is not in their interest to accept price cuts from the predator in the short run, if the consequence is that the predator achieves monopoly status in the long run.

Another possible response would be for the rival firm to reduce its output, forcing the predator to produce at an even higher volume than it might have planned, in order to maintain the reduced price. If the reduced price is below the predator's average variable cost, the predator's losses are increased, and the length of time over which it can sustain the price-cutting strategy might be reduced. If the rival firm does not have large sunk costs, it might be able to redeploy its assets to some other industry and (temporarily) withdraw altogether, in the expectation that it will return when the predator raises its price.

The (anti-interventionist) Chicago school is rather sceptical about the reality of predatory pricing. First, the predator's gain in profit in the long run must exceed the loss resulting from price-cutting in the short run. It may be difficult for a predator to be certain this condition will be met. Second, for a predatory pricing strategy to succeed in deterring entry, the predator has to convince the entrant it is prepared to maintain the reduced price and sustain losses for as long as the entrant remains in business. It may be difficult or impossible for the predator to signal this degree of commitment to the entrant. Third, as suggested above, for a predatory pricing strategy to be worthwhile, the predator has to be sure that having forced its rival out of business and raised its price, the entry threat will not return, either in the form of the same rival or some other firm. In order to prevent this from happening, the predator might attempt to acquire the rival's assets. Finally, if an incumbent and an entrant have identical cost functions, a predatory pricing strategy could just as easily be used by the entrant against the incumbent as the other way round. Therefore, predatory pricing is not necessarily or solely an entry-deterring strategy.

For regulators, it is often difficult to determine whether a specific price-cutting campaign constitutes predatory pricing, which is likely to be unlawful under competition legislation, or whether it constitutes a legitimate strategy to acquire market share that will also benefit consumers. From 26 proven cases of predatory competition in the US, in only six was there clear economic evidence of predatory pricing (Koller, 1975).

Case study 11.4

Predatory competition

Buses

Predatory competition can come in many forms and is by no means merely confined to pricing. For example, firms can adopt predatory strategies in relation to the quantity or quality of products and services supplied. In 1994, the Office of Fair Trading investigated two bus companies in Scotland suspected of non-price forms of predatory competition.

In 1990, Moffat & Williamson (M&W) won a contract to operate bus services that were subsidized by Fife Regional Council. On some of the routes M&W faced a competitor, Fife Scottish, which operated a commercial service. In 1992 Fife Scottish duplicated the subsidized service provided by M&W, by running additional bus journeys. This had the effect of reducing the demand for M&W services. The OFT found that, as a dominant local operator, Fife Scottish was guilty of cross-subsidizing loss-making services that were introduced purely in order to compete directly with M&W.

In 2008, 2 Travel entered into the Cardiff Bus Market with a new no-frills bus service. The dominant firm in the market, Cardiff Bus introduced its own no-frills bus service (the 'white service', or 'white services'). Cardiff Bus' white service buses ran on the same routes and at similar times of day as 2 Travel's no-frills services. Competition Commission found clear evidence that Cardiff Bus had run its new service at a loss with the intention of diverting customers away from the new entrant.

Newspapers

In 1996, after launching a free weekly newspaper, the *Aberdeen and District Independent* newspaper complained to the Office of Fair Trading about the actions of its rival, *Aberdeen Herald and Post* (part of the Aberdeen Journals newpaper group). The *Herald and Post* was accused of predatory competition, by reducing advertising rates for its own newspaper in order to discourage customers from buying advertising space in the *Aberdeen and District Independent*. In July 2001, the *Aberdeen Herald and Post* was found guilty of predatory competition: deliberately incurring losses in order to eliminate its rival from the market.

Internet broadband

In 2003, the European Commission examined the pricing practices of Wanadoo Interactive (a subsidiary of France Telecom) in the high-speed internet access for residential customers in France. The Commission found that Wanadoo had a dominant position in this market, and had used its position to charge prices that were below cost over the period March 2001 to October 2002. This stratey was found to have restricted market entry, and resulted in Wanadoo's market share increasing from from 46 per cent to 72 per cent. The European Commission considered this an abuse of dominant position and imposed a fine of €10.35 million on Wanadoo Interactive for predatory pricing.

Sources: Buses: Based on an article in the the *Independent* newspaper 24 December 1995 and Office of Fair Trading Bus Case Review CA98/01/2008. Newspapers: Based on Office of Fair Trading (2002b), *Predation by Aberdeen Journals Limited*, CE/127-02. Internet broadband: Based on European Commission (2003b) *High-speed Internet*, press release July 2003, IP/03/1025.

Brand proliferation

For many product types, a certain amount of product differentiation is quite natural, in view of basic product characteristics and consumer tastes (see Section 11.2). In some imperfectly competitive markets, however, incumbents may employ advertising or other types of marketing campaign in order to create or strengthen brand loyalties beyond what is natural, in order to raise the start-up costs faced by entrants. A firm wishing to establish a new brand would incur significant sunk costs in the form of advertising and other promotional expenditure.

Brand proliferation, or spurious product differentiation, refers to efforts by an incumbent firm to crowd the market with similar brands, denying an entrant the opportunity to establish a distinctive identity for its own brand. This form of entry-deterring strategy is common in markets for products such as detergents and processed foods. From the incumbent's perspective, however, a strategy of brand proliferation could simply cannibalize existing brands. The incumbent firm might also raise its own average costs relative to those of an entrant (Spulber, 2003).

Advertising can help raise barriers to entry. An incumbent firm may benefit from an absolute cost advantage in advertising if its past advertising investment has helped establish name recognition or brand loyalty among consumers. Consumer familiarity makes current advertising more effective than it is for an entrant attempting to establish a presence in the market for the first time. Economies of scale in advertising may also make it difficult for small-scale entrants to compete effectively with incumbents who are already producing and advertising on a large scale.

Using a sample of 800 advertising managers, Paton (2008) investigates the extent to which managers perceive actual or potential entry in determining the level of advertising. Nearly 25 per cent of the firms in the sample stated that they attributed importance to entry deterrence as an aim of their advertising. In addition, over 20 per cent of firms responded that they would increase advertising expenditure in response to the entry of a rival product or service.

Existing brand loyalties, and therefore entry barriers, are strengthened in cases where consumers incur significant switching costs associated with switching to another supplier. Customers with high switching costs are committed to remaining with their existing suppliers, and cannot easily be lured elsewhere (see Section 11.2).

Loyalty discounts, exclusive dealing and refusal to supply are all strategies intended to deny entrants access to supplies of inputs or access to customers. For example, the London radio station Capital Radio's practice of offering exclusivity deals to advertisers was investigated by the UK's Office of Fair Trading in 1994. In return for agreeing to advertise exclusively on Capital Radio, the advertiser received a discount. The effect of these agreements was to exclude Capital's competitors from a significant segment of the radio advertising market (OFT, 1994). A similar case involved petrol retailing in the UK in the 1960s, when many independent retailers signed long-term contracts to receive petrol supplies from a sole supplier. Vertical relationships of this kind are examined in Chapter 20.

Signalling commitment

Dixit (1982) uses a game-theoretic model to describe a situation in which an incumbent firm attempts to deter entry by deliberately increasing its sunk cost expenditure before entry takes place. The incumbent creates and signals a commitment to fight entry by engaging the entrant in a price war, in the event that entry subsequently occurs.

A **passive incumbent** does not pre-commit to fighting the entrant, in the event that entry subsequently takes place. In other words, a passive incumbent waits to see if entry occurs, before investing in the additional productive capacity or the aggressive marketing campaign that will be required in order to fight a price war. In contrast, a **committed incumbent** does pre-commit, by incurring the sunk cost expenditure that will be required in order to fight in advance, before it knows whether or not entry will actually take place. Figure 11.5 shows the array of possible outcomes in a sequential game (see also Section 7.6) played by an incumbent and an entrant, in the form of realized final profits or losses for each firm. These depend upon whether the incumbent is passive or committed, and upon whether entry actually does occur.

Passive incumbent

Suppose the incumbent is passive. If the entrant stays out, the incumbent earns the monopoly profit and the entrant earns zero. In Figure 11.5, this outcome is denoted $(P_m, 0)$. If entry does occur, the incumbent can either fight a price war, or accommodate the entrant by sharing the market. In the event of a price war, both firms earn a loss of P_w. This outcome is denoted (P_w, P_w). In the event that

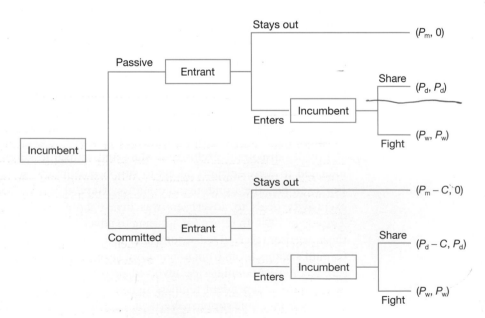

Figure 11.5 Sequential entry game

the firms share the market, both earn duopoly profit and the outcome is (P_d, P_d). It is assumed $P_d > 0$, $P_d \leq \frac{1}{2}P_m$ and $P_w < 0$.

In this case, the incumbent might attempt to threaten the entrant with the prospect of a price war in the event that entry occurs. However, if the entrant has perfect knowledge of the array of outcomes shown in Figure 11.5, the entrant will realize this threat is not credible. Suppose entry actually does occur. At that point, the incumbent is faced with the choice of fighting, in which case it suffers a loss of P_w, or accommodating, in which it earns a profit of P_d. In other words, if entry actually does take place, it makes no sense for the incumbent to carry out the threat to fight. Realizing this and attracted by the prospect of a profit of P_d, the entrant proceeds, and (P_d, P_d) is the final outcome.

Committed incumbent

Suppose the incumbent is committed rather than passive, and incurs sunk cost investment expenditure of C. In this case, if the entrant stays out, the incumbent's monopoly profit is reduced as a result of having incurred the sunk cost expenditure. As before the entrant earns zero. In Figure 11.5, this outcome is denoted $(P_m - C, 0)$. If entry does occur, as before the incumbent can either fight a price war, or accommodate and share the market. In the event of a price war, the outcome is (P_w, P_w). Crucially, the fact that the sunk cost expenditure needed to fight was incurred in advance does not affect the incumbent's realized losses if the price war occurs. In the event that the firms share the market, the outcome is $(P_d - C, P_d)$. It is assumed $C > 0$, $P_m > C > P_d$ and $P_d - C < P_w$.

In this case, the incumbent's threat to launch a price war is credible. Suppose entry actually does occur. At that point, the incumbent is faced with the choice of fighting, in which case it earns a loss of P_w, or accommodating, in which it earns an even greater loss of $P_d - C$. This time, if entry actually takes place, it makes sense for the incumbent to carry out the threat to fight. Faced with the prospect of suffering a loss of P_w if it proceeds, the entrant is deterred, and $(P_m - C, 0)$ is the final outcome.

For a numerical illustration of this model, let $P_m = 100$, $P_d = 20$, $P_w = -20$, and $C = 60$. Summarizing the logic of the previous paragraphs, if the incumbent is passive and entry takes place, the incumbent realizes -20 by fighting and 20 by accommodating. Therefore, post-entry, it is in the incumbent's interests to accommodate. Faced with the prospect of realizing a profit, the entrant proceeds and the final outcome is $(20, 20)$. If the incumbent is committed and entry takes place, the incumbent realizes -20 by fighting and -40 by accommodating. Therefore, post-entry, it is in the incumbent's interests to fight. Faced with the prospect of realizing a loss, the entrant does not proceed and the final outcome is $(40, 0)$.

Are there any circumstances in which the incumbent could remain passive (avoiding incurring the sunk cost expenditure), but still be successful in deterring entry? Dixit (1982) discusses the case in which the game described in Figure 11.5 is repeated an infinite number of times. In this case, it might be in the interests of an incumbent who is passive in each period (as defined above) to fight whenever entry actually occurs, in order to establish a reputation for fighting. Observing that the incumbent always reacts by fighting, the entrant learns from experience that there is nothing to be gained by entering, and abstains from doing so. As shown in Section 7.6, however, this type of model unravels if there is a limit to the number of times the game is repeated. Reputation then becomes unimportant in the final period, when there is no incentive for the incumbent to fight. Knowing this, the entrant proceeds in the final period. But this implies reputation also becomes unimportant in the penultimate period, so the entrant proceeds then as well, and so on.

In the setting of a repeated entry game, another case in which a passive incumbent might succeed in deterring entry (without incurring sunk cost expenditure) occurs if there is imperfect knowledge, and the entrant does not know whether the incumbent is passive or committed. An incumbent who is actually passive might attempt to deceive the entrant into believing the incumbent is committed, by launching a price war in the event that entry takes place. After observing a fighting response in one period, and knowing that a committed incumbent always fights, the entrant's subjective probability that the incumbent is committed increases, making it less likely that the entrant will decide to proceed in subsequent periods.

Alternatively, incumbent firms can attempt to deter potential entrants by announcing new versions of existing products well in advance of their actual launch. This deters potential entrants from developing similar products, as they may anticipate it will be unprofitable to do so. Haan (2003) cites a number of instances of so-called vaporware (excessively early announcement of a new version of a product) in the information technology industry. These include Microsoft's Windows 2000 (promised in 1997 but not launched until 2000), and Intel's 64-bit Itanium chip (promised in early 2000 but not launched until 2001).

11.5 Potential entry and contestability

The theory of **contestable markets**, originally developed by Baumol *et al.* (1982), considers an industry comprising a small number of incumbent firms or a single incumbent, whose market power is constrained by the threat of potential entry. Despite the fact that the incumbents are few in number, the entry threat forces them to keep their prices at a relatively low level, and constrains their ability to earn abnormal profits. Accordingly, even in highly concentrated industries, it is possible that incumbent firms can earn only a normal profit, because of threatened competition from potential entrants. The presence of a large number of competing firms is not a necessary condition for industry price and output to be set at a level consistent with perfect competition; threatened competition from potential entrants may be sufficient to produce the same effect.

For a market to be perfectly contestable, there must be no significant entry or exit barriers. The theory of contestable markets therefore excludes structural entry barriers, entry-deterring strategies on the part of incumbent firms, and sunk costs. Baumol *et al.* introduce the idea of **hit-and-run entry**, based on the following assumptions:

- A potential entrant can identify consumers who will purchase its output at or below the current market price.

- The entrant has sufficient time to sell to these consumers before the incumbent has time to react.

- At the prices quoted, the entrant earns sufficient revenue to cover its fixed and variable costs.

For unrecoverable investments, the length of time for which the asset is employed is important. If the asset can be used solely in the current period, the sunk costs are essentially a current fixed cost. The ability to recover all costs quickly is a defining characteristic of a contestable market, because if sunk costs cannot be recovered quickly, the incumbent has the opportunity to respond to the entrant's presence strategically. By cutting price aggressively, the incumbent might be able to make the entrant's continuing operation unprofitable. If hit-and-run entry is profitable, however, the entrant can move in and realize its profit before the incumbent has time to react.

Goolsbee and Syberson (2008) use data from the US Department of Transportation to assess how established firms respond to the threat of entry of competitors in the US Airline Industry. The evolution of Southwest Airlines' route network is examined to identify routes where the probability of future entry rises abruptly. Incumbents on threatened routes cut prices significantly when threatened by Southwest's incursion into their markets.

Graham *et al.* (1983), Call and Keeler (1985), Moore (1986) and Morrison and Winston (1987) discuss some of the limitations of the theory of contestable markets.

- The exclusion of sunk costs is generally unrealistic, as entry into most markets requires a significant amount of sunk cost investment. There are some possible exceptions (see below), but in most industries 'sunk costs are found to weaken the support for "strong" interpretations of the contestable market hypothesis and thus yield a wide diversity of dynamic patterns of market performance' (Coursey *et al.*, 1984, p. 69).

- By restricting the analysis to the short-run period within which the incumbent does not have sufficient time to respond, the reaction of the incumbent to attempted hit-and-run entry is excluded by assumption. Schwartz and Reynolds (1983) argue that an analysis of entry should focus not on the existing price charged by incumbents before entry, but on the post-entry price. 'The theory is naïve and static, with only one price. It ignores possible strategic price discrimination by the incumbent, which would decisively defeat entry while permitting excess profits' (Shepherd, 1997, p. 220).

- The assumption that the potential entrant faces no cost disadvantage relative to the incumbent is unrealistic. The latter may have acquired technical expertise and built up goodwill in the past.

Commercial airline services and bus services on specific routes have been viewed as promising testing grounds for contestable markets theory. While the construction of an airport or a bus station represents a form of sunk cost investment (since these assets cannot be moved geographically), the purchase of a fleet of aircraft or buses by a service provider does not entail sunk costs. Such assets can easily be transferred from one route to another, making hit-and-run entry (on the part of service providers) a realistic possibility.

Several researchers have subjected contestable markets theory to empirical scrutiny using data on commercial airlines. Hurdle *et al.* (1989) test for contestability in 867 airline routes in 1985. Regression analysis is used to examine the effects of potential entry and industry concentration on the level of fares charged on any specific route. Industry concentration, and not potential entry, is found to be the most important determinant of fares. Similarly, Strassmann (1990) tests for contestability using data on 92 US airline routes in 1980. If contestable markets theory is relevant, there should be no relationship between industry concentration and fares, or between entry barriers and fares. In a regression analysis, structural variables such as concentration and entry barriers are found to be the most significant determinants of fares. Therefore, both of these studies find that factors other than potential entry have the greatest influence on price. Neither study provides much support for the contestable markets theory. More recent evidence suggests established airlines benefit from learning economies of scale and brand loyalty advantages, which result in barriers to entry (Button and Stough, 2000; Johnson, 2003).

Accordingly, the practical relevance of contestable markets theory is questionable. Although the theory provides some insights concerning the possible behaviour of incumbents threatened by potential entry, early predictions that the notion of contestability might revolutionize the theory of the firm were wide of the mark.

> As often happens, a bright idea has been exaggeratedly oversold by its enthusiastic authors. The ensuing debate trims the concept and claims to their proper niche, taking their place among all the other ideas. In this instance, contestability offers insights, but it does not affect the central role of market structure.
>
> *(Shepherd, 1997, p. 220)*

Case study 11.5

Nabucco pipeline will rely on government intervention

Sir, Your report on the state of the Nabucco pipeline misses a key point ('Transit states ease tension on Nabucco pipeline', July 10). To be sure, as the article implies, the project attempts to turn pipeline economics on its head. Normally gas is found and the pipeline is built. In the case of Nabucco, it appears the pipeline is to be built and then gas supplies secured. This could eventually work in commercial terms but only if some way is found to involve Iran with its huge gas potential in the process. While recent developments in US–Iranian relations appeared to improve the prospects of such involvement, the aftermath of the hijacking of the Iranian presidential elections and a de facto coup makes this much less likely.

There is, however, another logic to building Nabucco. A big problem with all transit pipelines is to persuade transit countries to behave. Demands to renegotiate transit terms (as, for example, between Russia and Ukraine) inevitably lead to conflict with the potential to disrupt supplies. Here the economist's concept of 'contestable markets' might help. If a monopolist faces potential competition from easily achieved entry as in a 'contestable market', theory argues it will behave as though in a competitive market.

Given the flow of gas into western Europe, the presence of Nabucco as a real, relatively instant alternative might ensure other pipelines are less affected by transit disputes. Once built, even if operating below capacity, its threat as an existing alternative route would be a powerful deterrent to bad transit behaviour by a number of other countries.

However, such concerns cut little ice with commercial companies, which is why Nabucco must rely heavily on government intervention if it is to happen.

Source: Nabucco pipeline will rely on government intervention, *Financial Times*, 17 July 2009. Reproduced with kind permission of Stevens, Professor P.

11.6   Entry and industry evolution   *dynamic view of entry*

Most of the models of entry and exit that have been examined in this chapter are static, in the sense that they are based on direct comparisons between a pre-entry and a post-entry market equilibrium. Essentially, entry is modelled either as a once-and-for-all game, or an equilibrating mechanism whose principal economic function is the elimination of abnormal profit. This approach is criticized by Carlton (2005), on the grounds that the abnormal profits that are earned in the short run (before entry takes place) may be of greater practical relevance than the long-run (post-entry) equilibrium in which only normal profits are realized.

> The usual discussions of barriers to entry typically focus on the long run and ignore adjustment costs. In the short run, the concept of an entry barrier is not meaningful (since, by assumption, entry is not possible). But why is the long run of interest? Only because economists often slip into ignoring dynamics and go back to our simple models of short and long run. But as a practical matter, the long run may be of no interest whatsoever. It may take so long to get there that the persistence of supracompetitive profits until then turns out to be the fact of practical importance, not that these excess profits are eliminated in some far-off future year.
>
> *(Carlton, 2005, p. 10)*

In an attempt to address this kind of critique, and echoing some of the insights of Schumpeter (1928, 1942), Geroski (1991a) positions entry within a dynamic model of competition. In this context, entry and exit play a central role in shaping the evolution of industry structure in the long run. Geroski discusses two types of entry:

■ *Imitative entry*, which occurs when the entrant can earn a profit by copying an incumbent's product or method of production. Imitative entry is primarily an equilibrating force, in the sense that it helps propel the industry towards an equilibrium whose location and characteristics remain fundamentally unaltered. The incumbent's abnormal profit is reduced or eliminated as part of the adjustment process.

■ *Innovative entry*, which occurs when an entrant introduces a product with new characteristics, or finds a new method of producing an existing product more cheaply than before. Innovative entry is primarily a disruptive or dis-equilibrating force, in the sense that it changes the location and characteristics of an existing market equilibrium, and propels the industry in a new direction.

Innovative entry in particular makes a crucial contribution to the formation and growth of new industries and the decline of old ones. Entry by more innovative or more efficient outsiders encourages incumbent firms to improve or replace their existing product lines, or reduce their costs. Competition will eventually force the withdrawal of incumbents that fail to innovate.

> Entry can also play a more creative role in markets, serving as a vehicle for the introduction and diffusion of innovations which embody new products or processes that fundamentally alter conditions of supply and demand. Further, the mere threat of entry of this type may induce incumbents to generate new innovations or to adopt existing ones more rapidly.
>
> *(Geroski, 1991a, p. 210)*

The turnover of firms due to entry and exit is likely to be higher in technology-oriented industries such as electronics and pharmaceuticals, in which non-price competition tends to prevail. In these industries, variation in firm-level profit rates may be extreme, due to the uncertainties associated with the outcomes of innovation. Successful entrants may benefit significantly from first-mover advantages, which arise in several ways:

> The first springs from its headstart in travelling down learning functions and exploiting economies of scale . . . The second comes from the fact that first movers have an opportunity to monopolize scarce inputs . . . Third, the purchase decisions of early consumers are effectively investments in learning about the product – what it does and how to use it – and when consumers have made such investments and are content with how the product works for them, they will be reluctant to try alternatives . . . Fourth and finally, first movers who bring a winning product to the market often enjoy an enhanced brand identity and status.
>
> *(Geroski, 2003, pp. 194–5)*

For example, Berger and Dick (2007) examine first-mover advantages for entrants into localized US banking markets during the period 1972–2002. The earlier a bank entered, the larger was its eventual market share relative to other banks. Long-lasting first-mover advantages were secured by building capacity through investment in branch networks.

11.7 Empirical evidence on entry

There is a substantial empirical literature on the determinants of entry in manufacturing (Siegfried and Evans, 1994). Typical findings are that rates of entry are relatively high in profitable industries and fast-growing industries (Baldwin and Gorecki, 1987; Geroski, 1991a,b). Rates of entry are relatively low in industries where incumbents have absolute cost advantages over potential entrants, or where entrants' capital requirements are substantial (Orr, 1974). However, evidence concerning the relationship between rates of entry and factors such as scale economies, excess capacity and incumbents' pricing practices (such as limit and predatory pricing) is both limited and inconclusive.

As discussed above, the size of barriers to exit depends on the level of sunk costs. A complete absence of sunk costs is unusual, given that many assets are specific, and cannot easily be transferred to other uses (Harbord and Hoehn, 1994). There is some manufacturing evidence to suggest that exit is higher when profits are low and sunk costs are insignificant (Dunne et al., 1988); although Schary (1991) finds no relationship between profitability and exit. Other characteristics of the firm's financial and operational structure may have more influence on the decision to exit. Deutsch (1984) suggests conflicts of objectives between owners and managers may make it difficult to achieve a decision to exit. It is also possible that there is a direct association between entry and exit rates, if there is a tendency for entrants to displace some incumbents. However, using US manufacturing data for the period 1963–82, Dunne et al. (1988) find a negative correlation between annual entry and exit rates.

In a well-known study, Orr (1974) examines the determinants of entry into 71 Canadian manufacturing industries for the period 1963–7. The regression model is as follows:

$$E = \beta_1 + \beta_2 \pi_p + \beta_3 Q + \beta_4 X + \beta_5 K + \beta_6 A + \beta_7 R + \beta_8 r + \beta_9 C + \beta_{10} S$$

E is the average number of entrants in the sample period; π_p is the average industry profit rate; Q is past industry growth; X is the ratio of MES to industry sales (representing an economies of scale barrier to entry); K is an estimated fixed capital entry requirement; A is advertising intensity (ratio of advertising expenditure to industry sales); R is research and development intensity (ratio of research and development expenditure to industry sales); r is the standard deviation of industry profit rates (representing business risk); C is the level of industry concentration (measured on an ordinal scale: low = 1, high = 5); and S is total industry sales.

Orr finds a positive relationship between each of π_p, Q and S, and E. Therefore, high values of profitability, growth and industry size are all associated with high rates of entry. Orr finds a negative relationship between each of X, K, A, R, r and C, and E. This constitutes evidence of entry barriers resulting from economies of scale, capital requirements, high advertising or research and development intensities, business risk and high industry concentration.

Smiley (1988) and Bunch and Smiley (1992) examine entry-deterring strategies adopted by incumbents in new and established product markets. A total of 293 completed questionnaires were obtained from product managers, brand managers, directors of product management, division managers and marketing managers. Respondents were asked to identify the types of entry-deterring strategy they employed, and how frequently. In new product markets, entry-deterring strategies include:

■ Charging low prices and spending heavily on advertising and promotion.

■ Building excess capacity as a signal that incumbents are able to meet future demand.

■ Pre-emptive patenting in order to prevent entrants from producing identical or similar products.

■ Using the media to signal that entry would provoke retaliation.

■ Engaging in limit pricing to make entry unprofitable.

Additional strategies used in established product markets include:

■ Brand proliferation, intended to occupy product space, so that entrants cannot establish their own differentiated products or brands.

■ Masking the profitability of any single product line through the use of appropriate reporting practices in company accounts.

For new products, advertising (78 per cent of firms) and pre-emptive patenting (71 per cent) were the most widely used entry-deterring strategies. Limit pricing was rarely used. There was little systematic difference between manufacturing and services, except that manufacturers were significantly more likely to use pre-emptive patenting.

For existing products, brand proliferation (79 per cent of firms), advertising (79 per cent) and masking the profitability of individual product lines (78 per cent) were the most widely used entry-deterring strategies. Building excess capacity was rarely used. Manufacturers were more likely than service firms to mask the profitability of product lines, and to use pre-emptive patenting. Service firms typically concentrated on advertising and promotions and product differentiation to create brand loyalties.

Khemani and Shapiro (1990) argue that entry is expected if an incumbent's current profit, denoted π_0, exceeds the expected long-run profit, denoted $\hat{\pi}_p$. Exit is expected if current profit is below the expected long-run profit. Expressions for entry and exit are as follows:

$$\text{ENT} = \alpha_1 + \gamma_1(\pi_0 - \hat{\pi}_p)^R + \beta_1 \log_e(N) + \varepsilon_1$$
$$\text{EXT} = \alpha_2 + \gamma_2(\pi_0 - \hat{\pi}_p)^R + \beta_2 \log_e(N) + \varepsilon_2$$

ENT and EXT are the logarithms of the numbers of firms entering or exiting an industry; N is the number of firms in the industry; and R is an indicator variable for positive or negative values of $(\pi_0 - \hat{\pi}_p)$. Observed patterns of entry and exit are found to correspond to this model specification.

Geroski (1991b) examines the extent of entry by domestic and foreign firms in 95 UK manufacturing industries for the period 1983–4. The number of entrants per industry was similar in both years, but the market share of entrants was relatively small (the average across industries was between 7 per cent and 8 per cent of total industry sales). On average, domestic entrants succeeded in capturing a higher market share than foreign entrants. Exit rates were relatively stable over time, but entry and exit rates were positively correlated, suggesting a displacement effect. High profitability and large industry size are reported to have encouraged entry, but (surprisingly) there was a negative relationship between industry growth and entry. The significance of these effects is greater for domestic entrants than for foreign entrants.

Sleuwaegen and Dehandschutter (1991) examine the determinants of entry for 109 Belgian manufacturing industries for the period 1980–4. Schwalbach (1991) does the same for 183 German manufacturing industries for the period 1983–5. In these studies, entry rates are positively related to expected profits and industry growth, but negatively related to barriers in the form of initial capital requirements, and product differentiation advantages accruing to incumbents. For the early 1980s, Cable and Schwalbach (1991) report entry and exit rates for Belgium, Canada, Germany, Korea, Norway, Portugal, UK and US averaging at around 6.5 per cent of the relevant population of firms. Entry and exit rates also tend to be positively correlated with each other.

Rudholm (2001) assesses the determinants of entry to 22 Swedish pharmaceutical markets between 1972 and 1996. Entry is higher in markets where incumbent firms earn high profits. Entry is lower in markets where incumbent firms enjoy long periods of patent protection. Overall, entrants tend to enjoy a high probability of survival.

Roberts and Thompson (2003) examine the population of Polish manufacturing firms drawn from 152 three-digit industries over the period 1991–3 to assess the determinants of entry and exit. Concentration, profitability, capital requirements and state ownership all tend to reduce entry. There is a positive association between the rate of entry and industry size, and the rate of previous exit of incumbent firms. Exit is less likely when concentration, industry growth and profitability are high, but more likely in large industries or in those with a past history of high entry and exit.

Disney *et al.* (2003) examine the Annual Business Inquiry Respondents Database (ARD) for evidence on entry, exit and survival for UK manufacturing establishments over the period 1986–91. The results suggest small entrants are more likely to fail than their larger counterparts, but this danger recedes if fast growth is achieved. The rate of exit is higher for single establishments than for those that form part of a larger group.

Using data on the market for tourist accommodation in Texas, Conlin and Kadiyali (2006) examine whether firms use excess capacity to deter entry. There is evidence of higher investment in capacity relative to demand in markets with higher concentration, and by firms with a larger market share. These findings are consistent with the hypothesis that firms with the most incentive to deter entry do so through the creation of spare capacity.

Jeon and Miller (2007) examine the evolution of the population of US banks over the period 1978–2004. Entry of small banks occurred frequently, but only a small minority of these banks survived. Furthermore, exit of established banks (typically by merger) exceeded entry.

Geroski (1995) presents a series of stylized facts on entry, based on accumulated past theoretical and empirical research:

■ Rates of entry by new firms are often high (relative to the numbers of incumbents), but new entrants rarely capture large market shares.

■ Entry often leads to the displacement and exit of some incumbent firms.

■ Small entrants are less likely to survive than large entrants.

■ Entry by new firms is more common than entry by existing firms by means of diversification. However, diversified entrants are more likely to succeed.

■ Entry rates tend to be high during the early stages of an industry's development, when consumer preferences are unsettled, and core brands, products and processes are not yet established.

■ Entry by new firms leads to increased competition, stimulates innovation and encourages incumbents to make efficiency savings.

■ Incumbents tend to prefer non-price strategies to price strategies in order to deter entry.

■ Large or mature entrants are more likely to succeed than small or young entrants.

11.8　Summary

There are some barriers to entry over which neither incumbents nor the entrants have direct control. Economies of scale can act as an entry barrier in two ways. First, there is an entry barrier if the minimum efficient scale (MES) of production is large relative to the total size of the market. Second, economies of scale can act as an entry barrier when average costs associated with a production level below the MES are substantially greater than average costs at the MES. Economies of scale present the potential entrant with a dilemma. Either the entrant accepts the risks associated with large-scale entry in order to avoid the average cost penalty; or the entrant enters at a smaller scale and absorbs the average cost penalty.

An incumbent has an absolute cost advantage over an entrant if the long-run average cost function of the entrant lies above that of the incumbent, and the entrant therefore faces a higher average cost at every level of output. An absolute cost advantage might arise in several ways. The incumbent might have access to a superior production process, hold patents or be party to trade secrets. The incumbent might have exclusive ownership or control over factor inputs. The incumbent might have access to cheaper sources of finance. Finally, the entrant might incur costs in the form of expensive advertising or marketing campaigns, in an effort to create a reputation or establish its own brand identities and brand loyalties.

Other barriers to entry include: product differentiation in the form of customer loyalties to established brands and reputations of incumbents; switching costs; network externalities; legal barriers to entry; and geographic barriers, which create difficulties for foreign firms attempting to trade in the domestic market.

Entry-deterring strategies are barriers to entry created or raised by incumbents through their own actions. The extent to which it is possible for incumbents to adopt entry-deterring strategies is likely to depend on the degree of market power in the hands of the incumbent. Under a limit pricing strategy, the incumbent seeks to prevent entry by charging the highest price possible without inviting entry. To do so, it exploits either an absolute cost advantage or an economies of scale advantage, in order to set a price such that if entry takes place, the entrant is unable to earn a normal profit.

A strategy of predatory pricing on the part of an incumbent involves cutting price in an attempt to force an entrant to withdraw from the market. When the entrant has withdrawn, the incumbent raises its price. The incumbent sacrifices profit and perhaps sustains losses in the short run, in order to protect its market power in the long run. An incumbent faced with threatened entry might attempt to ward off the threat by convincing the potential entrant that it would implement a predatory pricing policy in the event that entry takes place.

For many product types, a certain amount of product differentiation is quite natural, in view of basic product characteristics and consumer tastes. In some imperfectly competitive markets, however, incumbent firms may employ advertising or other types of marketing campaign in order to create or strengthen brand loyalties beyond what is natural to the market, raising the initial costs entrants will incur in order to establish a presence. In this case, product differentiation becomes a strategic entry barrier. Finally, it is suggested that incumbents may attempt to deter entry by deliberately increasing their sunk cost investment expenditure before entry takes place. The incumbent signals a commitment to fight entry by engaging the entrant in a price war.

Contestable markets theory considers an industry comprising a small number of incumbent firms or a single incumbent, whose market power is constrained by the threat of potential entry. Even though the incumbents are few in number, and the industry appears to be highly concentrated, the threat of hit-and-run entry keeps prices close to the competitive level. A large number of competing firms is not a necessary condition for industry price and output to be set at the perfectly competitive level. Threatened competition from potential entrants may be sufficient to produce the same effect. Contestable markets theory breaks the direct link between the number and size distribution of sellers and the amount of discretion exercised by incumbents in determining their own prices.

A more dynamic view of entry and market evolution over the long run regards entry not as an equilibrating mechanism, as assumed in the neoclassical theories of perfect and monopolistic competition, but rather as a disequilibrating force which, by changing and disrupting established market equilibria, plays a central role in shaping the evolution of industry structure in the long run.

Most of the empirical evidence on the determinants of entry in manufacturing confirms that high industry profitability and growth are effective stimulants to entry. There is also some empirical evidence that, in accordance with the theory, entry barriers resulting from economies of scale, heavy capital requirements, high advertising or research and development intensities, high levels of business risk and high levels of industry concentration are effective in slowing the rate at which entry takes place.

Discussion questions

1. With reference to Case Study 11.1, examine barriers to entry in the UK retail banking industry.

2. With reference to Case Study 11.2 examine the barriers that can arise for firms wishing to adopt cloud computing technologies.

3. With reference to Case Study 11.3 explain how switching costs can act as a barrier to entry.

4. How might the height of entry barriers to a particular industry be measured in practice?

5. To what extent does the theory of limit pricing provide a useful contribution to the theory of entry deterrence?

6. Is limit pricing preferable to monopoly pricing on social welfare criteria?

7. With reference to Case Study 11.4, explain how a strategy of predatory pricing might be used to eliminate competition.

8. What factors are likely to influence the credibility of a threat by an incumbent to engage an entrant in predatory competition, in the event that entry takes place?

9. Explain how an incumbent might attempt to deter entry by increasing its own sunk cost investment.

10. What factors are relevant for a firm in deciding whether to be a pioneer in a new market, or to enter an established market at a later stage?

11. Explain the theory of contestable markets. To what extent do the empirical evidence and Case Study 11.5 justify the idea that potential competition is an important influence on pricing behaviour?

12. Examine the role of entry and exit in determining the evolution of industry structure.

13. According to the empirical evidence, what are the most commonly used entry-deterring strategies adopted by incumbent firms in new and established product markets?

Further reading

Bain, J.S. (1956) *Barriers to New Competition*. Cambridge, MA: Harvard University Press.

Baumol, W.J., Panzer, J. and Willig, R.D. (1982) *Contestable Markets and the Theory of Industry Structure*. New York: Harcourt Brace Jovanovich.

Berry, S. and Reiss, P. (2007) Empirical models of entry and market structure, in Armstrong, M. and Porter, R. (eds) *Handbook of Industrial Organization*, Vol. 3. Amsterdam: Elsevier.

Bresnahan, T.F. and Reiss, P.C. (1994) Measuring the importance of sunk costs, *Annals of Economics and Statistics*, 34, 181–217.

Cabral, L.M.B. (2008) Barriers to entry, in Durlauf, S.N. and Blume, L.E. (eds) *The New Palgrave Dictionary of Economics*, 2nd edition. London: Palgrave Macmillan.

Cabral, L.M.B. and Ross, T.W. (2008) Are sunk costs a barrier to entry?, *Journal of Economics and Management Strategy*, 17, 97–112.

Djankov, S. (2009) The regulation of entry: a survey, *The World Bank Research Observer*, 24, 183–203.

Geroski, P.A. (1995) What do we know about entry?, *International Journal of Industrial Organization*, 13, 421–40.

Martin, S. (2008) Limit pricing, in Durlauf, S.N. and Blume, L.E. (eds) *The New Palgrave Dictionary of Economics*, 2nd edition. London: Palgrave Macmillan.

Neven, D.J. (1989) Strategic entry deterrence: recent developments in the economics of industry, *Journal of Economic Surveys*, 3, 213–33.

Ordover, Janusz A. (2008) Predatory pricing, in Durlauf, S.N. and Blume, L.E. (eds) *The New Palgrave Dictionary of Economics*, 2nd edition. London: Palgrave Macmillan.

Siegfried, J.A. and Evans, L. (1994) Empirical studies of entry and exit: a survey of the evidence, *Review of Industrial Organisation*, 9, 121–55.

Spulber, D.F. (2003) Entry barriers and entry strategies, *Journal of Strategic Management Education*, 1, 55–80.

Market structure, firm strategy and performance

Learning objectives

This chapter covers the following topics:

- empirical controversies surrounding the use of the structure–conduct–performance paradigm
- the strategic groups approach
- variance decomposition of firm-level profitability
- the new empirical industrial organization
- persistence of profit

Key terms

Accounting rate of profit	New empirical industrial organization
Business unit effects	Persistence of profit
Collusion hypothesis	Price–cost margin
Corporate effects	Revenue test
Efficiency hypothesis	Strategic group
Industry effects	Tobin's q
Mark-up test	Variance decomposition analysis

12.1 Introduction

This chapter discusses empirical research in industrial organization that has examined the links between market structure and the conduct and performance of firms and industries. The SCP (structure–conduct–performance) paradigm (which was introduced in Chapter 1) represents a natural starting point for empirical research in this area. However, the SCP approach has been subject to intense criticism, and later empirical research in both industrial organization and strategic management has sought to shift the focus of attention away from industry structure and towards conduct or strategic decision-making at firm level.

This chapter begins in Section 12.2 by reviewing some early empirical research based on the SCP paradigm, which sought to identify the impact of structural industry-level variables such as concentration, economies of scale, and entry and exit conditions on firm performance, usually measured by profitability indicators. A powerful critique of the SCP paradigm was developed in the 1970s by the Chicago school, which suggested a positive association between concentration and profitability might reflect not an abuse of market power, but an association between firm size and efficiency: the most efficient firms are the most profitable, and also tend to grow and achieve large market shares. This suggests the analysis of performance should be based less on industry structure, and more on the conduct and strategic decision-making of the individual firm.

The strategic management literature on strategic groups is reviewed in Section 12.3. A strategic group is a group of firms whose conduct is similar, and which tend to view other members of the same group as their main competitors. The members of a strategic group recognize their interdependence, and this recognition conditions their behaviour. Mobility barriers impede the rate at which non-members can join a strategic group. In some respects, strategic groups theory represents a middle way between the competing industry- and firm-oriented approaches of the industrial organization literature.

Section 12.4 reviews variance decomposition studies of firm-level profitability data, which involve the decomposition of the variation in profit rates into components specific to the industry, the parent corporation and the line of business. This approach is capable of providing further insights into the debate as to whether the industry or the firm is the most appropriate unit of observation in industrial organization. Section 12.5 reviews a body of research known as the new empirical industrial organization, which attempts to draw inferences about market structure and competitive conditions from direct observation of conduct at firm level. Finally, Section 12.6 examines the persistence of profit literature, which analyzes the process of adjustment towards equilibrium by observing patterns of persistence and convergence in firm-level profit rate data. In this literature, the degree of persistence of profit is interpreted as another indicator of the nature of competitive conditions.

12.2 Empirical tests of the SCP paradigm

The performance of firms is one of the central research themes in industrial organization. There is a substantial body of empirical research that seeks to explain variations in performance between firms, most commonly measured by profitability. Early research within the SCP tradition developed and extended frameworks to analyze competitive conditions in industries. According to much of the earliest empirical literature, based on the SCP paradigm, industry-level variables such as concentration, economies of scale, and entry and exit conditions are the main determinants of firm performance. Caves provides a useful summary of this early research.

Most research in this line proceeded without any formal theoretical model of imperfect competition. It rested on the proposition, following from nearly every model of oligopoly, that the fewer the sellers in a market, the higher is the equilibrium price and the smaller is industry output. For this reason, and because measures of fewness or concentration were not wholly exogenous to patterns of conduct and levels of performance, no unbiased estimates of theoretically founded parameters resulted. What did emerge, however, was a large body of stylized facts – relationships found with some regularity in numerous cross-sections of markets.

(Caves, 2007, p. 2)

The literature has subsequently been criticized for providing (at best) limited explanation as to why profitability varies between firms. For example, the Chicago school argues that market power deriving from monopolization is only temporary, except perhaps in the case of monopolies that are created and maintained by government. A positive association between concentration and profitability may reflect a positive association between productive efficiency and firm size: the most efficient firms earn the highest rates of profit, and their success enables them to grow and achieve a relatively large market share. Consequently, the relationship between market structure and profitability has nothing to do with the exploitation of market power by large firms; instead, it is due to the association between efficiency, profitability and firm size. If differences in efficiency between firms are important in determining the performance of individual firms, the firm rather than the industry is the most appropriate unit of analysis. This view, which is in contrast to the SCP paradigm, has been termed *revisionist* by Schmalensee (1985) and Amato and Wilder (1990).

The debate between the revisionist and traditional schools can be summarized in terms of their differences regarding the appropriate unit of observation in industrial economics. The revisionist view is a story of industries consisting of both successful and unsuccessful firms, implying that there are important inter-firm differences in profitability. The traditional view focuses on industry effects which are assumed to be measured by concentration. The revisionist view thus focuses on the firm and firm-level efficiencies, while the traditional view focuses on the market and industry-specific sources of market power.

(Amato and Wilder, 1990, p. 93)

These opposing views have motivated an extensive empirical debate. Many of the earlier studies suggest concentration and other industry-level variables are important in determining performance, the **collusion hypothesis**. Many later studies emphasize the importance of efficiency differences between firms, the **efficiency hypothesis**. Naturally, for all of these studies the measurement of profitability is an important methodological issue. This topic is examined in Box 12.1.

Box 12.1

Measurement of profitability

Profitability is perhaps the most relevant and certainly the most widely used performance measure in empirical studies based both on the SCP paradigm and on most of the other empirical methodologies that are reviewed in Chapter 12. However, the measurement of profitability is not always a straightforward task. For example, measures of profitability based either on company accounts data or on stock market data do not always correspond precisely or even closely to the theoretical concepts used by economists in the neoclassical theory of the firm, such as normal profit or abnormal profit.

Measure 1: Tobin's q

Tobin's q is the ratio of the firm's stock market value to the replacement cost of its capital:

$$q = \frac{M_c + M_p + M_d}{A_r}$$

M_c and M_p are the market values of the firm's ordinary and preference share capital, respectively, M_d is the firm's outstanding loan capital, and A_r is the firm's total assets valued at replacement cost.

$q = 1$ implies the market value of the firm is equal to the book value of the assets owned by the firm, while $q \neq 1$ indicates the market value diverges from the book value of the firm's assets.

If $q > 1$, the firm's market value exceeds its book value. This situation exists when a firm has resources or advantages that contribute positively to its market value (in other words, from which it can expect to earn a positive return in the future), but which do not feature among the assets valued in the firm's balance sheet. Such advantages might stem from intangible assets that rival firms are unable to replicate, or from the exercise of market power that enables the firm to earn a return in excess of the normal profit the assets deployed by the firm would ordinarily be expected to yield.

If $q < 1$, the firm's market value is below its book value. This situation exists when the firm fails to earn a return equivalent to the normal profit the firm's assets would ordinarily be expected to yield. This might be due to lazy or incompetent management. A firm whose stock market value is significantly lower than its book value is usually considered to be vulnerable to being taken over. Outside investors (other than the firm's current shareholders) might believe they can make more profitable use of the firm's assets, and might therefore bid for the firm in the hope of acquiring it at a price from which they can subsequently realize a capital gain by increasing the firm's profitability.

A stock market-based profitability measure might be attractive for several reasons. Under assumptions of capital market efficiency, a firm's current market value should reflect all currently known information about its future profitability. An allowance for the level of risk is automatically incorporated, eliminating distortions arising from the fact that company accounts-based measures of returns or profits are not risk-adjusted. Stock market valuations should be unaffected by distortions to company accounts arising from the treatment of items such as tax and depreciation. One obvious limitation, however, is that stock market valuation data are, by definition, only available for listed firms. Furthermore, the firm's stock market valuation depends on expected future profitability. This tends to be subjective, and likely to fluctuate with investor sentiment, making stock market performance measures rather volatile. Finally, the denominator of Tobin's q is based on company accounts data, and is therefore subject to all of the limitations associated with the use of such data. In particular, the replacement cost of assets can be difficult to assess or measure.

Measure 2: price–cost margin

The price–cost margin is the ratio of profit to sales revenue:

$$\text{PCM} = \frac{\text{TR} - \text{TC}}{\text{TR}} = \frac{P \times Q - \text{AC} \times Q}{P \times Q} = \frac{P - \text{AC}}{P}$$

where TR = total revenue, TC = total cost, P = price, Q = quantity and AC = average cost. If AC is constant so AC = MC, PCM is equivalent to the Lerner index, $L = (P - \text{MC})/P$ (see Section 3.4). In perfectly competitive equilibrium, PCM = 0. If the firm exercises some market power, and can elevate price above average cost, PCM > 0.

The price–cost margin is not an accurate proxy for the Lerner index in the absence of constant returns to scale. Consequently, the greater the positive or negative difference between average cost and marginal cost, the greater the tendency for the price–cost margin to overstate or understate the Lerner index.

Measure 3: accounting rate of profit

An accounting rate of profit (ARP) is usually defined as the ratio of profit (before or after tax) to capital, equity or sales. Discretionary expenditure, depreciation, debt, tax, inflation and mergers can all cause difficulties for the calculation and interpretation of company accounts-based profitability measures.

Bain (1951) tests the relationship between concentration and profitability, using data for 42 US manufacturing industries between 1936 and 1940. Profitability is measured using return on equity, and concentration is measured using the eight-firm concentration ratio CR_8. Average profitability is significantly higher in industries with CR_8 above 70 per cent (at 9.2 per cent) than in those with CR_8 below 70 per cent (at 7.7 per cent). These results are interpreted as indicating that exploitation of market power leads to enhanced profitability. Numerous other studies from the 1950s and 1960s report similar results. This literature, reviewed by Weiss (1974, 1989), was influential in shaping the direction of competition policy in many countries.

In a representative study based on the SCP paradigm from the 1960s, Collins and Preston (1966) examine the relationship between concentration (measured using CR_4) and a **price–cost margin** profitability measure, for a sample comprising 32 US four-digit (SIC) food manufacturing industries observed in 1958. There is evidence of a quadratic relationship between concentration and profit. There are no systematic increases in the price–cost margins accompanying increases in concentration when concentration is low ($CR_4 < 0.3$). For $0.3 < CR_4 < 0.5$, concentration and the profitability appear to increase in similar proportions. For $CR_4 > 0.5$, profitability increased at an accelerating rate.

Demsetz (1973, 1974) points out that if the positive relationship between market concentration and profitability reflects the exercise of market power, then it should affect all firms equally. However, if the profitability of large firms in concentrated industries is higher than the profitability of small firms in concentrated industries, then the correlation between profitability and concentration is due to a relationship between efficiency and profitability. Demsetz's empirical results, based on 1963 US Internal Revenue Service data for 95 manufacturing industries, are summarized in Table 12.1. The profitability of firms in size classes R1, R2 and R3 does not appear to be related to concentration. However, in the largest size class, R4, profitability and concentration are positively related, lending support to the efficiency hypothesis. Demsetz argues against Bain's view that highly concentrated industries are uncompetitive. An implication is that specific government policies intended to promote competition directed at highly concentrated industries are not required. Overall, the empirical evidence does not adjudicate definitively between the collusion and efficiency hypotheses (Weiss, 1989). Below, a representative selection of studies is reviewed.

Table 12.1 Rates of return by size and concentration (weighted by assets)

CR_4 (%)	Number of industries	R1 %	R2 %	R3 %	R4 %	All firms %
10–20	14	7.3	9.5	10.6	8.0	8.8
20–30	22	4.4	8.6	9.9	10.6	8.4
30–40	24	5.1	9.0	9.4	11.7	8.8
40–50	21	4.8	9.5	11.2	9.4	8.7
50–60	11	0.9	9.6	10.8	12.2	8.4
Over 60	3	5.0	8.6	10.3	21.6	11.3

Notes:

CR_4 is the four-firm concentration ratio measured on industry sales in 1963.

R1 is average rate of return for firms with assets < US$500,000.

R2 is average rate of return for firms with US$500,000 < assets < US$5 million.

R3 is average rate of return for firms with US$5 million < assets < US$50 million.

R4 is average rate of return for firms with assets > US$50 million.

Source: Demsetz, H. (1973) Industry structure, market rivalry and public policy, *Journal of Law and Economics,* 16, p. 6, Table 2, University of Chicago Press.

Using US data, Ravenscraft (1983) finds price–cost margins are positively associated with lines-of-business market shares, but negatively associated with seller concentration. However, Ravenscraft's regression only explains about 20 per cent of the variation in profits. Scott and Pascoe (1986) test for the importance of firm and industry effects by allowing for firm- and industry-specific coefficients on variables such as concentration, market growth and market share. Both firm and industry effects are important determinants of profitability, although much of the variation in profitability remains unexplained.

Smirlock et al. (1984) use Tobin's q (see Box 12.1) to test the collusion and efficiency hypotheses, using US data. The independent variables are market share, CR_4, indicators of the height of entry barriers (classed as high, medium or low), and the growth of the firm's market share. If the efficiency hypothesis is valid, there should be a positive relationship between profitability and market share, and no relationship between profitability and concentration. Conversely, if the collusion hypothesis is valid, there should be a positive relationship between profitability and concentration, and no relationship between profitability and market share. The results support the efficiency hypothesis. There is a positive relationship between profitability and growth, perhaps because growth influences investors' expectations of future profitability reflected in the firm's valuation ratio; but entry barriers appear unrelated to profitability.

Clarke et al. (1984) test the validity of the collusion and efficiency hypotheses, using UK data. Little difference is found between the average profitability of large and small firms within highly concentrated industries. This finding lends support to the collusion hypothesis. Eckard (1995) uses US data for five cohorts of firms (based on size) to examine the relationship between changes in profitability (measured by the price–cost margin) and changes in market share. Under the efficiency hypothesis, there should be a positive relationship between changes in profitability and changes in market share, assuming the more efficient firms are more profitable and grow faster. The empirical results are consistent with this hypothesis.

The collusion and efficiency hypotheses have been investigated extensively in the banking literature. Berger (1995) compares the validity of two variants of the collusion hypothesis and two variants of the efficiency hypothesis, using US banking data. According to the collusion hypothesis, banks exploit their market power either by charging higher prices for differentiated banking products, or by colluding in order to raise prices. Large banks produce at lower average cost either by becoming more efficient through superior management or by being innovative; or by realizing economies of scale. In both cases, according to the efficiency hypothesis, the most efficient banks are likely to have the largest market shares. In the empirical model, the dependent variable, profitability, is measured using both return on assets and return on equity. Independent variables include concentration, measured using the HH index (see Section 9.4); measures of the effect on average cost of economies of scale; and measures of the efficiency implications of managerial talent. The efficiency measures were significant determinants of profitability, but there was little association between economies of scale and profitability. Profitability was positively related to market share, but not to concentration. These results suggest product differentiation contributes positively to profitability, but collusion does not do so.

Berger and Hannan (1998) examine the relationship between operational efficiency and concentration. According to the *quiet life hypothesis*, market power may enable banks to operate without achieving full efficiency in production; in other words, there may be x-inefficiency. The relationship between concentration and efficiency is examined using data on a sample of 5,263 US banks, with controls included for differences in ownership structure and geographic location. Banks in more highly concentrated markets are found to be less efficient. This finding lends some support to the quiet life hypothesis.

Slade (2004) examines the relationship between concentration, market share and profitability from both a theoretical and an empirical perspective. Concentration in the metal, mining and refining industries is positively related to profitability, but there is no relationship between market share and profitability. The results are consistent with the collusion hypothesis. Yoon (2004) finds a negative relationship between market growth and profitability in Korean manufacturing, and between concentration and profitability. There is a positive relationship between expenditures on advertising and research and development, and profitability.

12.3 Strategic groups

The **strategic groups** approach steers a middle way between the original industry-level and the later firm-level approaches discussed in Section 12.2. A strategic group can be defined as a group of firms whose conduct is similar, and which tend to view other firms from the same group as their main competitors (Oster, 1999). The members of a strategic group recognize their interdependence, and this recognition conditions their behaviour. For strategic groups, mobility barriers play a role similar to entry barriers, by preventing non-members from joining the group. For example, entry barriers to the UK pharmaceutical industry depend on whether an entrant wishes to compete with branded or generic products; and an existing generic producer would face mobility barriers if it were to attempt to move into branded products. Mobility barriers can account for a tendency for some groups of firms consistently to earn higher rates of profit than others within same industry (Caves and Porter, 1977; Newman, 1978). More specifically, the amount of variation in average profitability between firms in different strategic groups depends on the following factors:

- *The number and size of groups.* If the strategic groups are numerous and similar in size, competition is likely to be more intense than if there is a small number of strategic groups that are heterogeneous in size.

- *The extent to which groups follow different strategies.* If strategic groups differ in respect of their propensities to invest in discretionary expenditures such as advertising and research and development, differences in average profitability are likely to be magnified.

- *The extent to which groups are interdependent.* If the markets served by different strategic groups tend to be segmented, differences in profitability are likely to be larger than in the case where the groups tend to compete to attract the same customers.

According to McGee and Thomas (1986), strategic groups can be delineated on the basis of similarities in market-related strategies (similarities in product quality or design, pricing, extent of product differentiation, branding and advertising); firm-specific characteristics (firm size, ownership structure, the extent of vertical integration or diversification); or industry characteristics (reliance on economies of scale or scope, production technologies used, types of distribution methods and networks).

If the strategic group is a meaningful or useful concept, there should be greater variation in profitability between groups than within groups. Porter (1979b) aims to identify strategic groups using US data for 38 consumer good industries. Leaders are defined as firms accounting for at least 30 per cent of industry sales revenue. For the leader group, profitability is positively related to concentration, economies of scale, advertising-to-sales ratio, capital requirements and industry growth. For the follower group, profitability is inversely related to concentration, but there is a positive association between industry growth and capital requirements and profitability. The differences between the two groups is cited as evidence for the existence of strategic groups.

An obvious difficulty with the strategic groups approach is the subjective element involved in the definition of a strategic group. Barney and Hoskisson (1990) argue there is no theoretical basis for choosing a set of variables that could be used to identify strategic groups, or for determining the weightings to be attached to any given set of variables. Nevertheless, it seems likely that the strategic group is a meaningful concept in many industries, even though it is impossible to define a list of objective criteria that can be used to identify strategic groups. The strategic groups approach has received relatively little attention from economists, but this approach is popular in the field of management science.

12.4 Sources of variation in profitability: industry, corporate and business unit effects

In the literature reviewed in Sections 12.2 and 12.3, it is assumed various industry-level and firm-level variables can be used to explain the variation in firms' performance measured using profitability data. However, in many studies only a relatively low proportion of the total variation in profitability is explained by the independent variables. In a seminal paper, Schmalensee (1985) suggests an alternative approach, known as **variance decomposition analysis**, which involves the decomposition of the variation in profitability data into a component that is specific to the industry, a component specific to the corporation, and a component specific to each line of business of a diversified corporation. A statistical technique known as analysis of variance (ANOVA) is used to determine the proportions of the total variation in profitability that can be explained by **industry effects**, **corporate effects** and **business unit effects**, and the proportion that is left unexplained by each type of effect.

Schmalensee's sample contains 1975 data on 456 diversified US corporations, with lines of business that are classified into 261 different industry groups.

A diversified corporation reports separate accounts data for each of its lines of business, and a separate **accounting rate of profit** is available for each line of business. The following equation is estimated:

$$\pi_{i,k} = \mu + \alpha_i + \beta_k + \eta S_{i,k} + \varepsilon_{i,k}$$

The dependent variable, $\pi_{i,k}$, is the accounting rate of profit reported for corporation k's line of business in industry i. μ is the overall mean profit rate, across all firms and all industries (or lines of business). α_i is the component of $\pi_{i,k}$ that is specific to industry i. α_i is the same for all lines of business (across all corporations) that are classified under industry i. In other words, α_i is the average deviation of the profit belonging to industry i from the overall mean profit rate, μ. α_i can therefore be interpreted as the effect that is specific to industry i. β_k is the component of $\pi_{i,k}$ that is specific to corporation k. β_k is the same for all of corporation k's lines of business. In other words, β_k is the average deviation of the profit rates belonging to corporation k from the overall mean profit rate, μ. $S_{i,k}$ is corporation k's share of total sales in industry i. This market share variable is included in order to obtain an approximation to the effect that is specific to corporation k's line of business in industry i; or, in other words, to obtain an effect that corresponds to the interaction between the industry effect α_i and the corporate effect β_k. η is the coefficient on $S_{i,k}$. Finally, $\varepsilon_{i,k}$ is a disturbance term that captures any variation in $\pi_{i,k}$ that is not attributed to any of the other effects.

Although the variance decomposition approach is mainly descriptive, it is capable of providing powerful insight into the fundamental debate as to whether the industry or the firm is the most appropriate unit of observation in industrial organization. If the industry effects account for a larger proportion of the variation in profitability than the firm (corporate or line of business) effects, this suggests the industry is more important; conversely, if the firm effects dominate the industry effects, this suggests the firm is more important. Schmalensee's empirical results suggest industry effects are more important than firm effects; however, a number of later studies based on a similar empirical methodology came to the opposite conclusion.

Schmalensee's analysis, based on data for a single year, is exclusively cross-sectional. However, a number of subsequent contributions draw on panel data sets comprising several annual profitability observations on each line of business within each firm. If the data set includes both a cross-sectional and a time-series dimension, an analysis of the sources of variation in profitability richer than the one developed by Schmalensee becomes possible. Specifically, it is possible to identify the following effects:

- Industry effects that are common to all corporations operating a line of business in any particular industry. There is a unique effect pertaining to each industry. These effects derive from industry characteristics such as seller concentration, the extent of entry and exit barriers, and product differentiation.

- Corporate effects (or firm effects in Schmalensee's original terminology) common to all lines of business operated by any particular corporation. There is a unique effect pertaining to each corporation. These effects reflect the impact of strategic decisions taken at head office level, concerning matters such as the firm's scale and scope, horizontal and vertical integration and other forms of long-run investment or divestment.

- Line of business or business unit effects that are specific to each line of business operated by each corporation. These effects capture the impact of operational decisions on performance within each of the corporation's lines of business, concerning matters such as production levels, resource allocation across departments, research and development and marketing.

- Year effects capture the effects of macroeconomic fluctuations and changes in government policy or taxation that impact equally on the profitability of all lines of business for all corporations. In addition, it is possible to include interactions between year effects and industry effects, and between year effects and corporate effects. These allow for the presence of a transitory component within each of these effects. For example, macroeconomic fluctuations or government policy changes might have a different impact on different industries; therefore the industry effects should be time-varying. Alternatively, it might be that strategic decisions confer only a temporary rather than a permanent competitive advantage; therefore the corporate effects should also be time-varying.

One of the first panel studies was published by Rumelt (1991), who takes Schmalensee's sample of 1975 data on 1,775 business units, and appends 1974, 1976 and 1977 data for the same business units, thereby obtaining a panel data set. The following equation is estimated:

$$\pi_{i,k,t} = \mu + \alpha_i + \beta_k + \gamma_t + \delta_{i,t} + \varphi_{i,k} + \varepsilon_{i,k,t}$$

Time-subscripts are added to the dependent variable and the disturbance term, $\pi_{i,k,t}$ and $\varepsilon_{i,k,t}$ respectively, to identify the year to which each observation belongs. μ, α_i and β_k are interpreted in the same way as before. The year effect γ_t allows for year-to-year variation in the overall mean rate of profitability. The industry–year interaction term $\delta_{i,t}$ allows for these year-to-year variations to differ by industry. Finally, the industry–corporate interaction term $\varphi_{i,k}$ incorporates a business unit effect: an effect that is specific to corporation k's line of business in industry i. This term replaces the market share variable $S_{i,k}$ in Schmalensee's formulation. The panel structure of Rumelt's data set enables a separate effect to be estimated for every business unit, without the need for any assumption that the business unit effects are proportional to market share. By fitting this model, Rumelt obtains an industry effect that explains 17.9 per cent of the variation in profitability; the industry–year interactions explain a further 9.8 per cent; the corporate effects explain 14.8 per cent; and the business unit effects explain a further 33.9 per cent. Accordingly, Rumelt infers the business unit effect is actually very much larger than the one reported by Schmalensee.

A number of later contributions have reported similar models estimated using more recent or more extensive data sets; similar models for alternative performance indicators; or models with extended specifications that incorporate various refinements. As alternative performance indicators, Wernerfelt and Montgomery (1988) use Tobin's q; Chang and Singh (2000) use business unit market share data; and Hawawini *et al.* (2003) use residual income. McGahan (1999) reports analyses of accounting profitability and Tobin's q, observed at corporate rather than at business unit level. This study includes an analysis of the effect of corporate focus (the extent to which a corporation is diversified) on performance. Corporate focus is found to be unimportant in explaining variations in profitability at corporate level.

Several contributors, starting with Roquebert *et al.* (1996), have suggested that Schmalensee and Rumelt may have understated the importance of the corporate effect. In a simulation study, Brush and Bromiley (1997) show that even if the corporate effect is of a similar magnitude to the one reported in the earliest studies, it still has a non-negligible influence on the averages of their simulated business unit profit rates. The simulations suggest the statistical techniques used in most variance decomposition studies lack sufficient power to identify the smaller effects on performance accurately. It may be possible to improve the power of the tests by estimating non-linear transformations of the effects. Bowman and Helfat (2001) argue that the inclusion of single business units in many samples deflates the estimated corporate effect for corporations comprising multiple business units. If corporate strategy exerts a varying effect on different businesses within the corporation, the effect may be incorrectly attributed to business rather than corporate level. According to Ruefli and Wiggins (2003), a small estimated corporate effect may be due to the importance of corporate strategy, rather than the opposite: if the performance of management improves in all corporations, competitive forces may tend to erode the magnitude of the corporate effect. Adner and Helfat (2003) estimate a time-varying corporate effect, using press reports to identify the timings of major strategic decisions by US petroleum corporations.

Using accounting profitability data, McGahan and Porter's (2002) reported industry, corporate and business unit effects turn out to be smaller when estimated over a 14-year period than when estimated over a seven-year period. This suggests these effects may contain a temporary component, which may be present for several successive years, but which may disappear in the long run. Therefore the industry, corporate and business unit effects appear bigger when estimated using short-duration data sets (where any temporary effect is more prominent) than when they are estimated using longer-duration data sets (where temporary effects are likely to have disappeared). Accordingly, McGahan and Porter (1997) and Chang and Singh (2000) incorporate an adjustment for persistence, or first-order autocorrelation, in the disturbance term of their profitability models. Persistence or first-order autocorrelation is present when there is non-zero correlation between successive values of the disturbance term for the same firm: a likely feature if the industry, corporate or business unit effects contain a temporary component, as described above.

McGahan and Porter (1999) develop a more general analysis of the persistence or sustainability over time of the industry, corporate and business unit effects. Estimates of these effects are split into a fixed component, and a time-varying, incremental component. The empirical analysis allows for different degrees of persistence in each of the incremental components. This approach appears more informative than modelling persistence solely through the disturbance term, because persistence can be directly related to questions concerning the sustainability of competitive advantage at different levels (industry, corporation or business).

According to the view that the industry is the most appropriate unit of observation in industrial organization, an industry's structural characteristics are more stable than the fortunes of individual firms. Greater persistence should be found in in incremental industry effects than in incremental corporate or business unit effects. According to the view that the firm is the most relevant unit of observation, entry and exit to and from industries should eliminate inter-industry differences rapidly; but the incremental corporate or business unit effects should be more persistent. McGahan and Porter's empirical results generally tend to favour the industry view: the incremental industry effects turn out to be more persistent than the incremental corporate and business unit effects. McGahan and Porter (2003) test for the presence of asymmetries in these results. For example, they find both the magnitude and the persistence of industry effects is greater for above-average performers than for below-average performers; conversely, business unit effects are more important for low-performers.

The empirical studies reviewed above draw exclusively on US data, and the profitability variance decomposition literature includes relatively limited evidence from outside the US. Furman (2000) reports comparisons between four countries using 1992–8 data: Australia, Canada, the UK and the US. Khanna and Rivkin (2001) examine the effects of business group membership on profitability for a sample of firms drawn from 14 developing countries. Business group and industry membership are important determinants of the variation in profitability. In a study using 1994–8 data on Spanish manufacturing firms, Claver et al. (2002) report a business unit effect of around 40 per cent, together with very small industry and year effects. Spanos et al. (2004) analyze Greek data for 1995–6, and find business unit and industry effects account for 15 per cent and 6.5 per cent of the variance in profitability, respectively. Goddard et al. (2009) use a variance decomposition analysis to examine the importance of the country, industry, corporate group and firm effects on profitability and growth for European manufacturing firms. They find differences between industries in the comparative advantage offered by different countries, reflecting a tendency for specialization and geographic concentration. However, as in several previous studies, the firm-level effects are found to be the most important class of effect in explaining the variation in performance.

12.5　The new empirical industrial organization (NEIO)

Empirical research based on the SCP paradigm has been widely criticized for placing too much emphasis on industry structure, while the analysis of firm conduct is often underemphasized. However, the observed relationship between commonly used SCP structure and performance indicators, such as concentration and profitability, is often quite weak. These considerations have motivated a number of attempts to collect direct empirical evidence on the nature of competition, by observing conduct directly (Lau, 1982; Panzar and Rosse, 1982, 1987; Bresnahan, 1982, 1989). This approach has become known as the **new empirical industrial organization** (NEIO). One of the major strengths of NEIO is that it is grounded firmly in microeconomic (oligopoly) theory. SCP measures structure–performance relationships across a number of industries, and draws inferences about what these relationships might mean for conduct. In contrast, NEIO makes direct observations of conduct in specific industries, and draws inferences about what these observed patterns of conduct might mean for structure.

Empirical research in the NEIO strand attempts to estimate the behavioural equations that specify how firms set their prices and quantities. However, a behavioural relationship such as marginal revenue *equals* marginal cost cannot be estimated directly, because data on marginal revenue and marginal cost are not observed. Such a relationship might be estimated indirectly, by specifying a model in which the application of a pricing rule such as marginal revenue *equals* marginal cost has implications for the observed patterns of variation in other variables. For example, one of the approaches described below compares variations in the prices of the firms' factor inputs with variations in their total revenues. If the firms are profit maximizers, this comparison produces different results under market conditions of perfect competition, monopolistic competition and monopoly. One of the main methodological challenges for NEIO research is to find ways of transforming behavioural relationships that are unobservable in their original theoretical form into relationships involving variables that can be observed, so that tests are available that can be implemented in practice. Two such approaches, the revenue test and the mark-up test, are reviewed in the next two sub-sections.

The Rosse–Panzar revenue test

Rosse and Panzar (1977) develop a test that examines whether firm conduct is in accordance with the models of perfect competition, imperfect or monopolistic competition, or monopoly. The Rosse–Panzar test is also known as the **revenue test**. This test is based on empirical observation of the impact on firm-level revenues of variations in the prices of the factors of production that are used as inputs in the production processes of a group of competing firms. Built into the test is an explicit assumption of profit-maximizing behaviour on the part of the firms.

Rosse and Panzar show that the H-statistic, defined as sum of the elasticities of a firm's total revenue with respect to each of its factor input prices, differs under perfectly competitive, imperfectly competitive and monopolistic market conditions. The intuition is straightforward in the polar cases of perfect competition and monopoly, but more complex in the intermediate case of imperfect or monopolistic competition. The following discussion focuses on the two polar cases. In each of these, the impact of a simultaneous equiproportionate increase in all of the firm's factor input prices is considered. This implies an equiproportionate increase in the total cost of producing any given level of output, and an upward shift in the positions of the LRAC (long-run average cost) and LRMC (long-run marginal cost) functions.

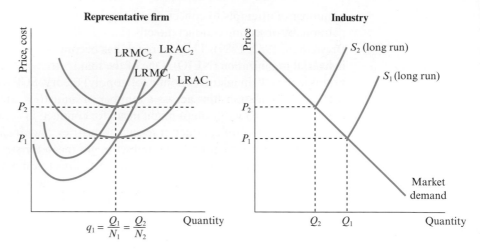

Figure 12.1 Effect of an increase in factor input prices on long-run post-entry equilibrium in perfect competition

Figure 12.1 illustrates the adjustment under perfect competition. As each firm's LRAC and LRMC functions shift upwards (LRAC$_1$ to LRAC$_2$; LRMC$_1$ to LRMC$_2$), the market price must increase in exactly the same proportion, so that each firm continues to earn only a normal profit when long-run equilibrium is restored. The increase in market price implies a reduction in the level of demand. The required adjustment in the total quantity of output (from Q_1 to Q_2) is achieved by a reduction in the number of firms (from N_1 to N_2). However, for those firms that survive, total revenue increases in the same proportion as total cost; and in the same proportion as the original increase in factor prices. Therefore in perfect competition, the H-statistic (the sum of the elasticities of revenue with respect to each factor price) is one.

Figure 12.2 illustrates the adjustment under monopoly. For simplicity, in this case horizontal LRAC and LRMC functions are assumed. As these functions shift upwards, the monopolist's profit-maximizing price and output adjust from (P_1, Q_1) to (P_2, Q_2). Note that a monopolist with non-zero costs always operates on the price-elastic portion of the market demand function. This must be so, because for profit maximization, marginal revenue *equals* marginal cost, so if LRMC > 0, then MR > 0. And if MR > 0, price elasticity of demand, $|\text{PED}| > 1$. This implies the shift from (P_1, Q_1) to (P_2, Q_2) causes a reduction in the monopolist's total revenue (if $|\text{PED}| > 1$, an increase in price causes total revenue to fall). Therefore, in monopoly, the H-statistic (the sum of the elasticities of revenue with respect to each factor price) is negative.

The Rosse–Panzar revenue test is implemented by estimating the following linear regression using firm-level data:

$$\log_e(\text{TR}_{i,t}) = \beta_0 + \beta_1\log_e(w_{1,i,t}) + \beta_2\log_e(w_{2,i,t}) + \beta_3\log_e(w_{3,i,t})$$

where $\text{TR}_{i,t}$ = total revenue of firm i in year t; $w_{j,i,t}$ = price of factor input j paid by firm i in year t. In this formulation, it is assumed there are three factors of production (for example, labour, capital and land). If the prices of the factor

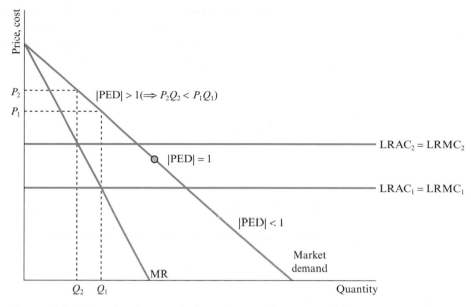

Figure 12.2 Effect of an increase in factor input prices on equilibrium in monopoly

inputs cannot be observed directly, they are usually imputed, using the ratio of the quantity of each factor employed (number of employees, for example) to the level of expenditure on the same factor (expenditure on wages and salaries).

An advantage of specifying this revenue equation in log-linear form is that the coefficients can be interpreted as elasticities. Therefore, with three factor inputs, the Rosse–Panzar H statistic is defined as:

$$H = \beta_1 + \beta_2 + \beta_3$$

The estimated version of the revenue equation can be used to obtain an estimated value of H, and the numerical value of H leads to inferences about the firms' conduct. The interpretation is as follows:

- If $H = 1$, conduct is in accordance with the model of perfect competition.

- If $H < 0$, conduct is in accordance with the model of monopoly.

- $0 < H < 1$ represents the intermediate case of conduct in accordance with imperfectly competitive market conditions.

Bresnahan and Lau's mark-up test

Another method for examining the nature of firm conduct, known as the **mark-up test**, is suggested by Bresnahan (1982, 1989) and Lau (1982). This test involves estimating a structural model incorporating demand and cost equations, together with the profit-maximizing condition marginal revenue *equals* marginal cost. The parameters of the model can be estimated using data either at industry level or at firm level.

This sub-section provides a detailed description of the construction of one such model, which is employed by Shaffer and DiSalvo (1994) to test for the nature of competitive conduct in a banking market in south central Pennsylvania. Although this model is implemented using banking data, the model specification is quite general, and the same model can be used for other industries. To describe the mark-up test, the style of presentation is more technical than in the previous sub-section.

Shaffer and DiSalvo begin by specifying a market demand function in log-linear form, to be estimated using industry time series data:

$$\log_e(P) = a_0 + a_1\log_e(Q) + a_2\log_e(Y) + a_3\log_e(Z) + a_4t$$

where P = market price; Q = total industry output; Y = aggregate income; Z = price of a substitute product; t = linear time trend. This market demand function is specified in inverse form (with price on the left-hand-side and quantity demanded on the right-hand-side). However, the expression can easily be rearranged to provide an expression for quantity demanded in terms of price:

$$\log_e(Q) = -a_0/a_1 + (1/a_1)\log_e(P) - (a_2/a_1)\log_e(Y) - (a_3/a_1)\log_e(Z) - (a_4/a_1)t$$

As before, by specifying the market demand function in log-linear form, the coefficients can be interpreted as elasticities. Therefore, PED (price elasticity of demand) *equals* $(1/a_1)$. The income elasticity of demand *equals* $-(a_2/a_1)$, and the cross-price elasticity of demand *equals* $-(a_3/a_1)$. If $a_1 < 0$, $a_2 > 0$ and $a_3 > 0$, PED is negative, and the income and cross-price elasticities are both positive, as the relevant theory suggests. Furthermore, since $PED = \dfrac{1}{a_1}$, it follows that $\dfrac{1}{PED} = a_1$.

Having specified the market demand function, Shaffer and DiSalvo also specify a marginal revenue and a marginal cost function for each firm. An expression for the total revenue of firm i is:

$$TR_i = Pq_i$$

where q_i = output of firm i, such that $\sum_i q_i = Q$.

Therefore firm i's marginal revenue can be written as follows:

$$MR_i = P + q_i\frac{\Delta P}{\Delta q_i}$$

This expression says that if firm i increases its output by one unit, the effect on firm i's total revenue consists of two components. First, firm i obtains the current market price, P, for the additional unit of output produced and sold. Second, if the extra output causes the market price to fall, firm i loses some revenue over each unit of output it is already producing. Firm i's current output level is q_i, and the rate at which price falls as firm i's output increases is $\Delta P/\Delta q_i$. In perfect competition, firm i does not expect price to change when it increases its output, so $\Delta P/\Delta q_i = 0$. In imperfect competition or monopoly, however, firm

i expects price to fall as it increases its output, so $\Delta P/\Delta q_i < 0$. Some simple algebraic manipulation of the previous expression yields:

$$\text{MR}_i = P + q_i\frac{\Delta P}{\Delta q_i} = P\left(1 + \frac{q_i}{P} \times \frac{\Delta P}{\Delta q_i}\right) = P\left(1 + \frac{1}{\text{PED}_i}\right)$$

where PED_i is firm i's price elasticity of demand.

What is the relationship between PED and PED_i? The answer depends on firm i's conjectural variation: how does firm i expect its competitors to react if firm i implements a small increase in output? Shaffer and DiSalvo introduce a parameter λ_i to represent firm i's conjectural variation.

$$\text{PED}_i = \frac{\text{PED}}{1 + \lambda_i} \Rightarrow \frac{1}{\text{PED}_i} - \frac{1 + \lambda_i}{\text{PED}} = a_1(1 + \lambda_i) \rightarrow \text{MR}_i = P[1 + a_i(1 + \lambda_i)]$$

The numerical value of the parameter λ_i provides important information about the nature of competition that is perceived by firm i:

- Under perfect competition, when firm i increases its output level, it assumes there will be no impact on the market price. In order to represent this in the model, $\lambda_i = -1$ is required. This ensures $\text{PED}_i = \infty$, and $\text{MR}_i = P$.

- Under joint profit maximization, the firms set their prices as if they were a single monopolist. When firm i increases its output level, it assumes the market price will adjust in accordance with the market demand function. In order to represent this case in the model, $\lambda_i = 0$ is required. This ensures $\text{PED}_i = \text{PED}$, and

$$\text{MR}_i = P\left(1 + \frac{1}{\text{PED}}\right)$$

- Finally, intermediate values of the parameter λ_i such that $-1 < \lambda_i < 0$ correspond to various forms of imperfect competition, including Cournot competition (each firm chooses its profit maximizing output level, treating other firms' output levels as fixed at their current levels).

Next, Shaffer and DiSalvo specify firm i's marginal cost function:

$$\text{MC}_i = \text{AC}_i[b_0 + b_1\log_e(q_i) + b_2\log_e(w_{1,i}) + b_3\log_e(w_{2,i}) + b_4\log_e(w_{3,i})]$$

where AC_i = firm i's average cost; $w_{j,i}$ = price of the j'th factor input used by firm i (as before, firm i is assumed to use three factors of production). This type of specification is commonly used to estimate cost functions. The numerical values of the parameters of the total cost function from which this marginal cost function is derived can be chosen to allow for diminishing returns to each factor input; and either increasing, constant or decreasing returns to scale. For present purposes, the following features of the marginal cost function are important:

- Marginal cost, which cannot be measured or observed directly, is expressed as a function of average cost, which can be measured and observed.

- If $b_1 > 0$, $b_2 > 0$, $b_3 > 0$ and $b_4 > 0$, marginal cost increases as output increases, and marginal cost increases as each factor input price increases.

Firm i's condition for profit maximization is $MR_i = MC_i$:

$$MR_i = P[1 + a_1(1 + \lambda_i)] = MC_i \Rightarrow P = MC_i - Pa_1(1 + \lambda_i)$$

Unfortunately, this expression contains MC_i, which cannot be observed. Some further algebraic manipulation is therefore required, in order to express firm i's profit-maximizing condition in terms of variables that are observed and measured. Divide all three terms in the second expression (above) by AC_i; multiply top and bottom of the first term by Q; and multiply top and bottom of the third term by q_i, to obtain:

$$\frac{PQ}{Q \times AC_i} = \frac{MC_i}{AC_i} - \frac{Pq_i a_i(1 + \lambda_i)}{q_i AC_i} \Rightarrow$$

$$\frac{TR}{Q \times AC_i} = [b_0 + b_1 \log_e(q_i) + b_2 \log_e(w_{1,i}) + b_3 \log_e(w_{2,i}) + b_4 \log_e(w_{3,i})] - \frac{TR_i a_i(1 + \lambda_i)}{q_i AC_i}$$

where TR = industry total revenue = $PQ = \sum_i TR_i$. This final expression is a rearranged statement of firm i's profit-maximizing condition $MR_i = MC_i$, expressed entirely in terms of variables that can be observed and measured. In order to implement the mark-up test, the following linear regressions are estimated using time-series data at industry and firm level. For clarity, all firm and time-subscripts are included.

Market demand function (one equation, based on industry-level time-series data):

$$\log_e(P_t) = a_0 + a_1 \log_e(Q_t) + a_2 \log_e(Y_t) + a_3 \log_e(Z_t) + a_4 t$$

Profit-maximizing condition (one equation for each firm, based on firm-level time series data):

$$y_{i,t} = b_{0,i} + b_{1,i} \log_e(q_{i,t}) + b_{2,i} \log_e(w_{1,i,t}) + b_{3,i} \log_e(w_{2,i,t}) + b_{4,i} \log_e(w_{3,i,t}) + \beta_i x_{i,t}$$

where $y_{i,t} = \dfrac{TR_t}{Q_t AC_{i,t}}$; $x_{i,t} = \dfrac{TR_{i,t}}{q_{i,t} AC_{i,t}}$; $\beta_i = -a_i(1 + \lambda_i)$

The estimated versions of these equations can be used to obtain an estimated value of λ_i for each firm. The value of λ_i (within the range $-1 \leq \lambda_i \leq 0$) provides an indication of the nature of firm i's conjectural variation. This in turn indicates whether price-setting conduct by each firm is based on perfectly competitive, imperfectly competitive or monopolistic (joint profit-maximization) assumptions.

Empirical evidence

The revenue and mark-up tests have been applied extensively using banking data. Using the revenue test for a sample of New York banks, Shaffer (1982) finds $0 < H < 1$, and infers competition is in accordance with the model of monopolistic competition. Although the New York banking sector is highly concentrated, entry and exit conditions are relatively free. Nathan and Neave (1989) run similar tests for Canadian banks, trust companies and mortgage companies with data for the period 1982–4. In each case the results indicate $0 < H < 1$. Using European banking data for the period 1986–9, Molyneux *et al.* (1994) obtain $0 < H < 1$ for France, Germany, Spain and the UK, and $H < 0$ for Italy. In a later study using 1992–6 data, De Bandt and Davis (1999) obtain $0 < H < 1$ for France, Germany, Italy and the US. Competition appears to be most intense in the US, while French and German small banks have a certain degree of market power.

The results of many of these empirical studies tend to be consistent: commonly, price-setting behaviour in accordance with the intermediate competitive models (imperfect or monopolistic competition) is detected. Accordingly, some critics have argued that while NEIO models are 'potentially useful if there is concern over the specification of the structural model, or if data required to estimate the structural model are not available', they are also limited in the sense that they offer 'a determination of only what the market structure of degree of monopoly is not, and do not suggest what it is' (Church and Ware, 2000, p. 450).

Furthermore, the revenue test in particular is based on assumptions that markets are observed in a state of long-run equilibrium.

> Where available data are sufficient to implement it, the Bresnahan–Lau technique is superior to the Rosse–Panzar approach in terms of econometric identification and ability of the estimated conduct parameter to map into specific oligopoly solution concepts. Moreover, the Rosse–Panzar statistic is not reliable for samples that are not in long run equilibrium, but may exhibit a downward bias in that case.
>
> *(Shaffer, 2001, p. 82)*

Goddard and Wilson (2009) identify the implications for the H-statistic of misspecification bias in the revenue equation, arising when adjustment towards market equilibrium is partial and not instantaneous. Using simulation techniques, it is shown that fixed effects estimation produces a measured H-statistic that is severely biased towards zero. A dynamic formulation of the revenue equation is required for accurate identification of the H-statistic and the level of competition.

12.6 The persistence of profit

The SCP and NEIO approaches are based on microeconomic theory, in which optimizing behaviour is assumed. The main focus is on equilibrium, and little is said about the process by which equilibrium is reached. Problems such as imperfect information and uncertainty are ignored. Another strand in the empirical literature, known as the **persistence of profit** (POP) approach, examines the time-series behaviour of firm-level profit data.

POP constitutes a departure from the static, cross-sectional methodology that is prevalent in most of the literature based on the SCP paradigm. It can be argued that the SCP view of competition is typically based on a snapshot, taken at one particular moment in time, and does little to explain the dynamics of competition (Geroski, 1990). There is no certainty that a profit rate, or any alternative performance measure observed at some specific moment in time, represents a long-run equilibrium value of the variable in question. An empirical association between concentration and high profitability may simply appear by chance, from observation during a period when the relevant market is in a state of disequilibrium. If so, cross-sectional data do not capture (unless by luck) the long-run equilibrium relationship. Furthermore, cross-sectional data usually do not contain enough information on which to base reliable policy decisions. For example, an abnormal or monopoly profit realized in one period could disappear in the next, rendering intervention by government or other regulatory organizations unnecessary.

Brozen (1971) criticizes Bain's (1951) study, suggesting that a disequilibrium phenomenon was being observed (in the data used). If high profitability is the result of the exercise of market power by a monopolist in long-run equilibrium, then similarly high returns should be realized over a number of years. Brozen replicates Bain's empirical analysis over a later period (1953–7), and finds that in highly concentrated industries, average profitability was only 0.6 per cent above the average; and in unconcentrated industries, average profitability was 0.5 per cent below the average. This suggests that over time, profitability in the more profitable industries tends to fall, and profitability in the less profitable industries tends to rise. In other words, there is a tendency for profit rates to converge towards a common long-run average value. This finding lends support to the disequilibrium hypothesis.

Brozen's findings motivated a body of empirical research that has examined patterns of industry and firm performance over an extended period. Research at industry level suggests industry profits tend to converge quite slowly, over periods of several years' duration. Significant correlations between past and present profit rates are therefore observed. Firm-level studies suggest there are significant differences between firms in long-run equilibrium profit rates, and differences in the speed of convergence. The remainder of this section provides a selective review of this literature.

Industry-level studies

Using US data, Levy (1987) develops a model in which expectations of future profitability are formed with reference to market structure variables such as entry barriers, concentration, advertising intensity and industry growth; and anticipated changes in these variables. If current profitability is higher than expected, entry should take place, causing profitability to fall. The same process should happen in reverse if current profitability is lower than expected. The results suggest the process of adjustment towards long-run equilibrium takes about four years. Industry-level variables such as entry barriers, concentration and growth in demand are important in determining the speed of adjustment. These results provide support for Brozen's critique. Coate (1989) reports a tendency for profits above or below the long-run equilibrium to converge towards a long-run equilibrium within ten years. These results provide partial support for Brozen's critique. Keating (1991) finds that profitability in highly concentrated US industries was less persistent than profitability in unconcentrated industries. There is no evidence of long-run persistence in industry-level average profitability.

Droucopoulos and Lianos (1993) investigate convergence in industry-level average profit rates using Greek manufacturing data. In most cases, the speed of adjustment towards long-run equilibrium is slow: 90 per cent of any abnormal return earned in year t persists into year $t + 1$. High concentration or high advertising intensity tend to slow the speed of adjustment. Similarly, Bourlakis (1997) reports evidence of a tendency for profitability to persist, especially in highly concentrated Greek industries.

Firm-level studies

At the firm level, the POP literature focuses on the persistence of a firm's standardized profit rate, defined as the difference between the firm's actual profit rate and the average profit rate across all firms in each year. If firm i's standardized profit rate in year t is denoted $\pi^s_{i,t}$, then $\pi^s_{i,t} = \pi_{i,t} - \bar{\pi}_t$, where $\pi_{i,t}$ is firm i's actual profit rate in year t and $\bar{\pi}_t$ is the average profit rate in year t. The standardization eliminates from the analysis the effects of any macroeconomic fluctuations, which tend to impact equally on all firms' profit rates, causing $\bar{\pi}_t$ to vary from year to year.

Firm-level POP studies investigate two forms of persistence in $\pi^s_{i,t}$. First, short-run persistence refers to the degree of correlation between consecutive values of $\pi^s_{i,t}$ for the same firm: in other words, the correlation between $\pi^s_{i,t-1}$ and $\pi^s_{i,t}$.

- In perfectly competitive markets with no barriers to entry, abnormal profit is only a very temporary (short-run) phenomenon, which is rapidly eliminated by the forces of competition. Therefore any abnormal profit (positive or negative) should disappear quickly. This implies there should be little or no correlation between consecutive values of any firm's standardized profit rate, or between $\pi^s_{i,t-1}$ and $\pi^s_{i,t}$.

- If competition is anything less than perfect, and there are barriers to entry (which may or may not be surmountable in the long run), it may take some time for any abnormal profit to be eroded by the forces of competition. This means if an abnormal profit (positive or negative) is realized by a firm in one year, it is more than likely the same firm will earn a similar abnormal profit the following year. There should be a positive correlation between consecutive values of the standardized profit rate, or between $\pi^s_{i,t-1}$ and $\pi^s_{i,t}$.

The second type of persistence of profit, long-run persistence, refers to the degree of variation in the long-run average standardized profit rates between firms.

■ In competitive markets with no barriers to entry, or with entry barriers that are surmountable in the long run, short-run abnormal profits are eventually competed away. Each firm's profit rate should eventually converge towards a common value that is the same for all firms. In other words, all firms should earn only a normal profit in the long run.

■ In markets where barriers to entry are permanent and insurmountable, there is no convergence of firm-level profit rates towards a common long-run average value. Differences in firm-level average profit rates may persist permanently or indefinitely.

The POP model can be formulated using a first-order autoregressive model for each firm's standardized profit rate:

$$\pi_{i,t}^{s} = \alpha_i + \lambda_i \pi_{i,t-1}^{s} + \varepsilon_{i,t}.$$

The parameters α_i and λ_i have i-subscripts to denote that it is usual to estimate a separate version of this model for each firm. λ_i represents the strength of short-run persistence in firm i's standardized profit rate. $\lambda_i = 0$ implies there is no association between $\pi_{i,t-1}^{s}$ and $\pi_{i,t}^{s}$, and therefore corresponds to the case of perfect competition. $0 < \lambda_i < 1$ implies there is a positive association between $\pi_{i,t-1}^{s}$ and $\pi_{i,t}^{s}$, or positive short-run persistence of profit.

In the first-order autoregressive model with $0 \leq \lambda_i < 1$, there is a tendency for firm i's standardized profit rate to converge towards an average or equilibrium value of $\mu_i = \alpha_i/(1 - \lambda_i)$ in the long run. The sign of the parameter α_i determines whether firm i's long-run average standardized profit rate is positive or negative; in other words, whether firm i's actual long-run average profit rate is above or below the average for all firms. If $\mu_i = 0$ for all firms, then all firms' profit rates converge to the same long-run average value. In this case there is no long-run persistence of profit. If $\mu_i > 0$ for some firms and $\mu_i < 0$ for others, there is long-run persistence: there is variation between the long-run average profit rates of different firms.

The implications of different patterns of short-run and long-run persistence for some typical time series plots of firm-level profit rates are illustrated in Figure 12.3. The graphs show stylized plots of standardized profit rates for two firms (1 and 2) when short-run persistence is either zero or positive; and when long-run persistence is either zero or non-zero. Figure 12.3 illustrates the following features:

■ When short-run persistence is zero ($\lambda_i = 0$), the time-series plots of the standardized profit rates are jagged. The value of $\pi_{i,t-1}^{s}$ (above or below zero) conveys no information about whether $\pi_{i,t}^{s}$ will be above or below zero, because the year-to-year variation in $\pi_{i,t}^{s}$ is essentially random. In contrast, when short-run persistence is positive ($\lambda_i > 0$), the time-series plots of the standardized profit rates are smoother. If $\pi_{i,t-1}^{s}$ is above zero, it is likely $\pi_{i,t}^{s}$ will also be above zero (and vice versa), because sequences of positive or negative standardized profit rates tend to persist over several consecutive time periods.

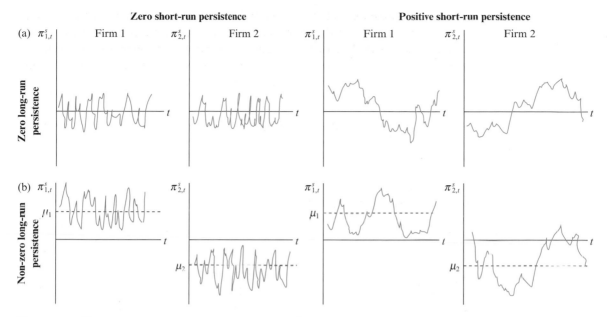

Figure 12.3 Short-run and long-run persistence of profit

■ When long-run persistence is zero ($\mu_i = 0$ for all i), the standardized profit rates of all firms tend to fluctuate around the same long-run average value of zero (Figure 12.3(a)). When long-run persistence is non-zero ($\mu_i \neq 0$ for all i) the standardized profit rates tend to fluctuate around different long-run average values ($\mu_1 > 0$ and $\mu_2 < 0$ in Figure 12.3(b)).

The idea that by observing patterns in the time-series variation of firm-level profit rate data, inferences can be drawn about the nature of competition (whether barriers to entry exist and, if so, whether they are temporary or permanent), has motivated a body of research that was first pioneered by Mueller (1977, 1986). The hypothesis tested in these studies is that (potential and actual) entry into and exit from any market are sufficiently free to bring any abnormal profits quickly into line with the competitive rate of return. In other words, competitive forces are sufficiently powerful to ensure no firm persistently earns profits above or below the norm. Firms never achieve a stable equilibrium in the conventional sense, however, because each period brings new random shocks. If the market is responsive to excess profits and losses, returns tend to gravitate towards the competitive level. But if some firms possess and are able to retain specialized knowledge or other advantages, these firms may be able to earn profits that remain above the norm persistently, in the long run.

In the empirical POP literature, the average value (over a number of sample firms) of the estimated short-run persistence parameter λ_i provides a useful indicator of the strength of persistence, which has been reported on a consistent basis in most studies. Most researchers have obtained a value of this statistic in the range 0.4–0.5. Most studies have also reported evidence of significant differences between firms in long-run average profit rates. In other words, it appears all firms' profit rates do not tend to converge towards the same equilibrium or

Table 12.2 Summary of firm level persistence of profit studies

Study	Country	Sample period	No. of firms	Mean λ_i
Geroski and Jacquemin (1988)	UK	1949–77	51	0.488
	France	1965–82	55	0.412
	West Germany	1961–81	28	0.410
Schwalbach *et al.* (1989)	West Germany	1961–82	299	0.485
Mueller (1990)	US	1950–72	551	0.183
Cubbin and Geroski (1990)	UK	1950–72	243	0.482
Jenny and Weber (1990)	France	1965–82	450	0.363
Odagiri and Yamawaki (1990)	Japan	1964–82	376	0.465
Schohl (1990)	West Germany	1961–81	283	0.509
Khemani and Shapiro (1990)	Canada	1964–82	129	0.425
Goddard and Wilson (1996)	UK	1972–91	335	0.458
Waring (1996)	US	1970–89	12,986	0.540
Goddard and Wilson (1999)	UK	1972–91	335	0.450
Marayuma and Odagiri (2002)	Japan	1964–82	376	0.464
		1983–97	357	0.543
Glen *et al.* (2001, 2003)	Brazil	1985–95	56	0.013
	India	1982–92	40	0.229
	Jordan	1980–94	17	0.348
	Korea	1980–94	82	0.323
	Malaysia	1983–94	62	0.349
	Mexico	1984–94	39	0.222
	Zimbabwe	1980–94	40	0.421
Villalonga (2004)	US	1981–97	1,641	0.284

average value in the long run. Cuaresma and Gschwandtner (2008) use a threshold autoregression applied to US profitability data. There is statistical evidence of non-linear adjustment for many firms in the sample. Goddard *et al.* (2008) apply three panel unit root tests to UK firm size, growth and profit rate data. There is strong and consistent evidence of mean-reversion in profit rates. A summary of empirical POP studies is shown in Table 12.2.

12.7 Summary

The performance of firms is one of the central research themes in industrial organization. There is a now a substantial body of empirical research that seeks to explain variations in performance between firms, most commonly measured by profitability. Early research, based mainly on the SCP (structure–conduct–performance) paradigm, identified structural industry-level variables such as concentration, economies of scale, and entry and exit conditions as the most important determinants of firm performance. However, this approach has been subject to intense criticism. Many of the structure–performance relationships identified in SCP-based empirical research are weak. Some economists, including those associated with the Chicago school, argue that market power deriving from monopolization is only a temporary phenomenon. A positive association between concentration and profitability may reflect an association between productive efficiency and firm size: the most efficient firms earn the largest profits, enabling them to grow at the expense of their competitors. If efficiency differences between firms are more important than industry structure in determining performance, attention should presumably be directed less towards the industry and more towards the individual firm. Accordingly, later empirical research in both industrial organization and strategic management has sought to shift the focus of attention towards conduct or strategic decision-making at firm level.

The strategic management literature on strategic groups perhaps offers a middle way between the industry-level and firm-level approaches discussed above. A strategic group is a group of firms whose conduct is similar, and which tend to view other members of the same group as their main competitors. The members of a strategic group recognize their interdependence, and this recognition conditions their behaviour. For strategic groups, mobility barriers play a role similar to entry barriers, by preventing non-members from joining the group. The variation in average profitability between firms in different groups depends on the number and size of groups; the extent to which groups follow different strategies; and the degree of interdependence between groups. Cluster analysis is often used to identify groups of firms with similar characteristics, but the strategic groups approach can be criticized for failing to provide a clear theoretical basis for deciding group membership. The strategic groups approach has been more influential in the strategic management literature than in the industrial economics literature.

A variance decomposition analysis of firm-level profitability data involves the decomposition of the variation in profit rates into components specific to the industry, the parent corporation and each line of business within a diversified corporation. It is possible to identify the proportions of the total variance in profitability that are explained by each type of effect. The variance decomposition approach is mainly descriptive. However, it is capable of providing powerful insights into the debate as to whether the industry or the firm is the most appropriate unit of observation in industrial organization, by comparing the relative contributions made by the industry effects or the corporate and business unit effects in explaining the variation in profitability. Some of the earliest studies of this kind found industry effects to be more important than firm-level effects; however, this finding has been challenged by several later researchers. Recently, several researchers have explored the persistence or sustainability over time of the industry, corporate and business unit effects. Estimates of these effects are split into a fixed component and a time-varying, incremental component. The notion of persistence can be directly related to questions concerning the sustainability of competitive advantage at different levels (industry, corporation or business).

In industrial organization, empirical research based on the SCP paradigm has been widely criticized for placing too much emphasis on industry structure, while the analysis of conduct is underemphasized. This critique has motivated several attempts to assess the nature of competition by observing conduct directly. This approach is known as the new empirical industrial organization

(NEIO). NEIO makes direct observations of conduct and draws inferences about market structure. The revenue test of Rosse and Panzar involves estimating the sum of the elasticities of revenue with respect to each of the firm's factor input prices. The sign and magnitude of this statistic indicate whether firms' price-setting behaviour is consistent with the theoretical models of perfect competition, monopolistic competition or monopoly. The mark-up test of Bresnahan and Lau involves estimating a structural model incorporating demand and cost equations, linked by the profit-maximizing condition marginal revenue *equals* marginal cost. An estimate of the firm's price elasticity of demand again provides evidence about the nature of competition the firm perceives.

Both the SCP and NEIO methodologies are based on assumptions of profit maximization and long-run equilibrium. In contrast, the persistence of the profit strand in the empirical industrial organization literature focuses on the process of adjustment towards equilibrium, by analyzing time-series data on firm-level profit rates. Short-run persistence refers to the degree of correlation between consecutive values of a firm's standardized profit rate (in successive years). In perfectly competitive markets with no barriers to entry, abnormal profit is rapidly eliminated by competition, so there is little correlation between consecutive profit rates. In imperfectly competitive markets, with high barriers to entry, abnormal profits may tend to persist for several years. Therefore, consecutive profit rates tend to be more highly correlated. Long-run persistence refers to the degree of variation between firms in the long-run average (standardized) profit rates. Empirical studies at industry and firm level consistently report evidence of significant short-run and long-run persistence of profit.

Discussion questions

1. Distinguish between the traditional and revisionist views of the ultimate source of profitability.

2. To what extent is it reasonable to infer that high profits earned by firms in highly concentrated industries are the result of these firms abusing their market power?

3. Examine the strengths and limitations of company accounts-based measures of firm profitability.

4. In order to calculate a reliable measure of a firm's performance, why is it important to adjust a profit rate calculated from company accounts data for risk?

5. Explain carefully the construction and interpretation of Tobin's q as a measure of performance.

6. Explain the construction of an empirical test for the relative merits of the collusion and efficiency hypotheses as explanations for variations in firm profitability.

7. What are strategic groups? What criteria might be used to identify strategic groups in practice? With reference to an industry of your choice, attempt to identify two or three strategic groups.

8. Compare and contrast the SCP (structure–conduct–performance) and the NEIO (new empirical industrial organization) approaches to empirical research in industrial organization.

9. Explain how the application to firm-level profitability data of variance decomposition techniques such as analysis of variance can shed new light on the long-standing debate as to whether performance depends primarily on industry-level or on firm-level factors.

10. Summarize the intuition underlying the following tests that are used to draw inferences about market structure and competitive conditions, based on observation of firms' conduct under assumptions of profit maximization: the Rosse–Panzar revenue test, and Bresnahan and Lau's mark-up test.

11. What can be inferred about the intensity of competition by observing patterns of variation in firm-level time-series profit rate data?

12. Explain the distinction between short-run and long-run persistence of profit.

Further reading

Bresnahan, T.F. (1989) Empirical studies of industries with market power, in Schmalensee, R. and Willig, R.D. (eds) *Handbook of Industrial Organization*, Vol. 2. Amsterdam: Elsevier, 1011–58.

Caves, R.E. (1986) *American Industry: Structure, Conduct and Performance*, 6th edition. Englewood Cliffs, NJ: Prentice Hall.

Caves, R.E. (2007) In praise of the old I.O., *International Journal of Industrial Organization*, 25, 1–12.

The Economist (1998) The economics of antitrust, May.

Glen, J., Lee, K. and Singh, A. (2003) Corporate profitability and the dynamics of competition in emerging markets: a time series analysis, *Economic Journal*, 113, F465–84.

Martin, S. (2002) *Advanced Industrial Economics*, 2nd edition. Cambridge, MA: Blackwell, Chs 5, 6 and 7.

McGee, J. and Thomas, H. (1986) Strategic groups: theory, research and taxonomy, *Strategic Management Journal*, 7, 141–60.

Mueller, D.C. (ed.) (1990) *The Dynamics of Company Profits: An International Comparison*. Cambridge: Cambridge University Press.

Neuberger, D. (1998) Industrial organization of banking: a review, *International Journal of the Economics of Business*, 5, 97–118.

Scherer, F.M. and Ross, D. (1990) *Industrial Market Structure and Economic Performance*, 3rd edition. Boston, MA: Houghton Mifflin, Ch. 11.

Schmalensee, R.C. (1989) Inter-industry studies of structure and performance, in Schmalensee, R.C. and Willig, R.D. (eds) *Handbook of Industrial Organization*, Vol. 2. Amsterdam: North-Holland, Ch. 16.

Weiss, L.W. (1974) The concentration–profits relationship and antitrust, in Goldschmid, H., Mann, H.M. and Weston, J.F. (eds) *Industrial Concentration: The New Learning*. Boston, MA: Little Brown, 183–233.

Weiss, L.W. (1989) *Concentration and Price*. Boston, MA: MIT Press.

White, L.J. (2013) Market power: how does it arise? How is it measured? in Thomas, C.R. and Shughart, W.F. (eds) *Oxford Handbook of Managerial Economics*. Oxford: Oxford University Press.

Young, G., Smith, K.G. and Grimm, C.M. (1996) Austrian and industrial organization perspectives on firm-level activity and performance, *Organization Science*, 7, 243–54.

Learning objectives

This chapter covers the following topics:

- cost plus pricing
- first-degree, second-degree and third-degree price discrimination
- price discrimination in practice
- peak-load pricing
- transfer pricing under various market conditions
- price dispersion

Key terms

Cost plus pricing	Perfect price discrimination
Dumping	Price dispersion
First-degree price discrimination	Second-degree price discrimination
Intertemporal price discrimination	Third-degree price discrimination
Metering	Transfer pricing
Peak-load pricing	Two-part tariff

13.1 Introduction

Price determination is an essential component of most of the theories of decision-making and resource allocation at firm and industry level that have been developed in the previous chapters of this book. For example, price formation in perfectly competitive, imperfectly competitive and monopolistic market conditions is one of the central themes of Chapters 3, 7 and 8. Chapter 13 examines a number of further aspects of pricing behaviour, from both a theoretical and a practical perspective.

The neoclassical theory of the firm can be criticized by questioning whether firms have sufficient information in practice to determine their prices by applying the profit-maximizing rule marginal revenue *equals* marginal cost. Section 13.2 examines an alternative pricing rule known as cost plus pricing, whereby price is determined by adding a percentage mark-up to average variable cost. The mark-up includes a contribution towards the firm's fixed costs, and a profit margin. The relationship between profit-maximizing pricing and cost plus pricing is considered, and the conditions are identified under which both methods produce similar outcomes.

The pricing models developed earlier in this book are based on an assumption that firms set uniform prices that are identical for all consumers, and are identical no matter what quantity each consumer buys. Section 13.3 examines a pricing policy known as price discrimination, under which a firm either sells at different prices to different consumers, or makes the price per unit each consumer pays dependent on the number of units purchased. For such a policy to be possible, the firm must enjoy some degree of market power, and the market must be divisible into sub-markets between which secondary trade or resale is not possible. Three types of price discrimination, known as first-, second- and third-degree price discrimination, are considered. Several examples of price discrimination commonly encountered in practice are identified. Section 13.4 examines the related (but conceptually distinct) practice of peak-load pricing, in which a supplier facing a level of demand that varies at different times of the day or on different days of the year can vary its prices accordingly, but must also decide on a fixed capacity level that is the same for all periods.

In multidivisional organizations, the choice of transfer prices at which intermediate products are traded internally between divisions affects the imputed divisional profitability. Decisions taken at divisional level with a view to the maximization of divisional profits do not necessarily ensure the maximization of the firm's aggregate profits. Section 13.5 develops several profit-maximizing models of transfer pricing. The analysis suggests that incentives for divisional managers, and decisions concerning the viability of loss-making divisions, should not be based solely on imputed divisional profitability, but should reflect the implications for the profitability of the firm as a whole.

The growth of online retailing has stimulated interest in the topic of price dispersion. Given that online consumers can shop around and compare the prices of similar or identical products at the click of a mouse, how much scope remains for different retailers to charge different prices for the same product or service? This chapter concludes in Section 13.6 with a review of a number of recent empirical studies of price dispersion in traditional and online retailing.

13.2 Cost plus pricing

According to the neoclassical theory of the firm, under the assumption of profit maximization price is determined through the application of the behavioural rule marginal revenue *equals* marginal cost (MR = MC). As shown in Section 4.2, from an early stage in the development of the neoclassical theory, some economists questioned whether firms have sufficient information to apply this rule in practice. In a highly influential study, Hall and Hitch (1939) report the results of interviews with the managers of 38 businesses, 30 of whom reported the use of some form of **cost plus pricing** formula. Under cost plus pricing, the firm calculates or estimates its AVC (average variable cost), and then sets its price by adding a percentage mark-up that includes a contribution towards the firm's fixed costs, and a profit margin:

Price = AVC + % mark-up

or $P = (1 + m)$AVC

where P denotes price, and the mark-up (expressed as a percentage) is $100 \times m$ per cent. A number of advantages are claimed for cost plus pricing over pricing using the profit-maximizing rule MR = MC.

- The cost plus pricing formula is simple to understand, and can be implemented using less information than is required for profit-maximizing pricing. For the latter, the firm requires detailed information about its MC, MR and AR (demand) functions. For cost plus pricing, the firm only requires an estimate of its AVC, and a decision concerning the size of the mark-up.

- Cost plus pricing may produce greater price stability than profit-maximizing pricing. The latter implies price should change every time there is a minor variation in demand. In contrast, with cost plus pricing, provided AVC is relatively flat over the relevant range of output levels, minor variations in the level of demand need not lead to changes in price. Price stability may be valued by consumers, as it reduces their search costs, and by producers, as it reduces the likelihood that destructive price competition may break out.

- Cost plus pricing appeals to a sense of fairness: in determining its mark-up, the firm can claim to allow for a reasonable profit margin, rather than the maximum profit. Price changes can be attributed solely to changes in costs, rather than fluctuations in market demand.

However, in some cases these claimed advantages might be open to question. Fluctuations in demand can only be ignored safely when setting price if AVC is constant over the relevant range of output levels. If AVC varies with output, the firm needs to know its output level before it can determine its price. This means it needs to estimate its demand function. Cost plus pricing does not imply price stability if costs are changing, or if there are fluctuations in demand and AVC varies with output. Cost plus pricing may not be simple to implement for a multi-product firm, since it may be difficult to apportion fixed and variable costs accurately between a number of product lines (Hanson, 1992).

Finally, the question arises as to what profit margin to include in the mark-up. If the size of the profit margin varies with market conditions, the difference between cost plus pricing and pricing for profit maximization using the rule MR = MC might not be as large as it first appears. Suppose the cost plus pricing firm always selects approximately the same profit margin as a profit-maximizing firm would achieve by applying the rule MR = MC. Naturally, this profit margin tends to be higher when demand conditions are strong, and lower when demand is weak. In this case, cost plus pricing and profit-maximizing pricing would both yield approximately the same outcome. The widespread reported use of cost plus pricing might suggest that it serves as a convenient rule-of-thumb for firms that are really profit maximizers, even if they do not themselves explicitly recognize this form of behaviour.

Under what conditions do cost plus pricing and profit-maximizing pricing using the rule MR = MC produce identical results? In Section 2.3, it is shown that MR can be written as follows:

$$MR = P\left(1 - \frac{1}{|PED|}\right)$$

where $|PED|$ is the absolute value of the firm's price elasticity of demand. A necessary condition for MR > 0 is $|PED| > 1$, or PED < −1. Rearranging the previous expression:

$$MR = P\left(\frac{|PED| - 1}{|PED|}\right)$$

Under the profit-maximizing rule MR = MC:

$$MC = P\left(\frac{|PED| - 1}{|PED|}\right) \Rightarrow P = \left(\frac{|PED|}{|PED| - 1}\right)MC$$

If it is assumed that AVC is approximately constant over the range of output levels within which production takes place, then MC ≅ AVC. Under this assumption:

$$P = \left(\frac{|PED|}{|PED| - 1}\right)AVC$$

Using the cost plus pricing formula $P = (1 + m)AVC$:

$$1 + m = \frac{|PED|}{|PED| - 1} \Rightarrow m = \frac{1}{|PED| - 1}$$

Therefore, cost plus pricing is equivalent to profit-maximizing pricing if AVC is approximately constant, and the mark-up is set to a value of $1/(|PED| - 1)$. Note that this formula for the mark-up only produces a positive (and therefore meaningful) value for the mark-up in the case $|PED| > 1$, the same condition that is required for MR > 0. The more price inelastic the firm's demand, the larger the mark-up required for profit maximization. When economic conditions are depressed, $|PED|$ is likely to be high, in which case the mark-up consistent with profit maximization is small. When economic conditions are more buoyant, the mark-up consistent with profit maximization is larger. Similarly, when competition is intense, |PED| is likely to be high, in which case the mark-up consistent with profit maximization is small. When competition is weaker, the mark-up consistent with profit maximization is larger.

Since Hall and Hitch's (1939) original paper on cost plus pricing, several researchers have investigated firms' pricing practices, mostly using survey methods. In a survey of 728 UK manufacturing firms, Shipley (1981) asked respondents to assess the importance of various objectives that might be considered when formulating prices: these included target profitability; target sales revenue; target market share; price stability; stability of sales volume; comparability of own prices with those of competitors; and prices perceived as fair by customers. Many firms reported considering multiple objectives when pricing their products. While profitability was important, it was not the only consideration. Firms were more likely to be profit-oriented in industries where competition (measured by the number of competing firms) was more intense. Large firms (measured by the number of employees) were more likely than small firms to admit to profit-maximizing behaviour. However, only 16 per cent of all firms considered profit maximization to be an overriding objective.

Hall *et al.* (1996, 2000) report a survey of 654 UK firms, which were asked to assess the most important factors they consider when setting prices. The results are summarized in Table 13.1. Market conditions were the most important factor, especially in the case of firms in the construction industry. Competitors' pricing policies were also important, especially in retailing. Around 40 per cent of the firms surveyed reported the use of a cost plus pricing method. Smaller firms in particular were unlikely to have collected sufficient data on demand conditions to be able to use a profit-maximizing (MR = MC) pricing rule.

Álvarez and Hernando (2006) classify pricing practices as either: (i) cost plus pricing; (ii) prices set according to competitors' prices; and (iii) other, where the pricing decision is taken by a third-party stakeholder such as a government department or quango, a corporate parent company, the main customers, or the suppliers. Table 13.2 summarizes the results of a survey of euro area firms. Fifty-four per cent of respondents used cost plus pricing, setting their prices by applying a mark-up to average cost; 27 per cent based their prices on those of

Table 13.1 How UK firms set their prices

Pricing method	All	Manufacturing	Construction	Retail	Other services
Reference to market conditions	39	41	51	18	48
Competitor prices	25	26	11	30	23
Direct cost + variable mark-up	20	20	22	21	17
Direct cost + fixed mark-up	17	16	19	24	14
Customer set	5	6	3	0	6
Regulatory agency	2	1	0	0	3

Note: Data are percentages of sample firms reporting use of the method shown in the left-hand column. Percentages may exceed 100 per cent because firms are permitted to indicate more than one choice.

Source: Adapted from Hall, S., Walsh, M. and Yates, A. (1996) How do UK companies set prices?, *Bank of England Quarterly Bulletin*, May, 36, 180–92, Table A, 13.

Table 13.2 Price-setting strategies of firms in the euro area

Country [1]	Cost plus pricing	Rivals' prices	Other
Belgium:			
All firms	45.9	36.4	17.7
Low competition	–	–	–
High competition	–	–	–
France:			
All firms	40.0	38.0	22.0
Low competition	49.8	24.4	25.9
High competition	36.0	47.6	16.4
Germany:			
All firms	73.0	17.0	10.0
Low competition	78.9	9.4	11.7
High competition	69.8	22.5	7.6
Italy:			
All firms	42.4	31.7	25.9
Low competition	57.6	14.5	27.9
High competition	33.6	42.6	23.7
Netherlands:			
All firms	56.4	22.3	21.3
Low competition	56.6	15.3	28.2
High competition	56.5	25.4	18.1
Portugal:			
All firms	64.5	12.6	22.9
Low competition	78.7	2.9	18.4
High competition	59.9	17.6	22.4
Spain:			
All firms	51.9	26.6	21.5
Low competition	61.3	11.8	27.0
High competition	44.1	40.5	15.3
Euro area			
All firms	54.3	27.1	18.7
Low competition	63.6	14.7	21.7
High competition	49.8	35.1	15.1

[1] *Sources*: Álvarez, L.J. and Hernando, I. (2006) Competition and price adjustment in the euro area, Bank of Spain Working Paper, No. 0629, p. 14. Data derived for individual country level studies of price setting strategies for Belgium (Aucremanne and Druant, 2005); France (Baudry *et al.*, 2004); Germany (Hoffman and Kurz-Kim, 2005); Italy (Veronese *et al.*, 2005); Netherlands (Jonker *et al.*, 2004); Portugal (Dias *et al.*, 2004); and Spain (Álvarez and Hernando, 2005).

competitors; while 19 per cent claimed they had no autonomy in determining their prices. Pricing practice often depends upon whether a firm operates in a highly competitive market, or in an uncompetitive market. Where competition is less intense, cost plus pricing tends to be prevalent, and firms are less likely to take competitors' prices into account. These results are consistent across most euro area countries.

Fabiani *et al.* (2006) examine the processes and information used by euro area firms when reviewing their pricing policies, in response to changes in cost and demand conditions. For example, is the decision to review prices state-dependent (in response to a large shock to demand or costs) or time-dependent (with reviews held at regular intervals)? Around two-thirds of the firms surveyed held state-dependent reviews, while the remainder held time-dependent reviews. Around half of the firms surveyed stated that past and expected future economic developments were taken into account when reviewing prices, but only one-third used past data to inform current decisions. Prices were reviewed rather infrequently (between one and three times per year), with more frequent reviews being typical where competitive pressure was most intense and in service industries. Cost plus pricing was the dominant pricing method, followed by pricing with reference to competitors' prices.

13.3 Price discrimination

In most of the theoretical models of firms' production and pricing decisions that have been considered previously in this book, it is assumed the firm sets a uniform price which is the same for all consumers, and the same no matter how many units of the product each consumer buys. In practice, however, a firm that enjoys some degree of market power might consider adopting a more complex pricing policy. Consider a product that is produced under uniform cost conditions. It might be in the firm's interest to sell at different prices to different consumers, or to make the price per unit that any consumer pays dependent on the number of units purchased. The policy of selling different units of output at different prices is known as price discrimination (Pigou, 1920; Phlips, 1983).

Price discrimination is possible only in cases where there are variations in the prices charged for a product that is supplied under an identical cost structure no matter who the buyer is, or how many units are produced and sold. For example, a petrol retailer who charges different prices at an inner-city petrol station and at a remote rural petrol station does not adopt a policy of price discrimination if the price differential is proportional to the difference in costs (transport costs perhaps being higher in the rural location). Conversely (and perhaps paradoxically), a petrol retailer who charges the same price in two locations where there *is* a cost difference *does* practice price discrimination, favouring consumers in the high-cost location who under a uniform pricing policy would pay a higher price to reflect the cost difference. This pricing practice is known as free-on-board pricing (see below).

There are three types of price discrimination, as follows:

- **First-degree price discrimination**, also sometimes known as **perfect price discrimination**, involves making the price per unit of output depend on the identity of the purchaser *and* on the number of units purchased. First-degree price discrimination is a theoretical construct that is encountered only rarely in practice. A possible example would be a private doctor in a small village who does not operate a fixed price structure, but instead simply charges their patients on the basis of an assessment of their ability to pay.

■ **Second-degree price discrimination** involves making the price per unit of output depend on the number of units purchased. However, the price does not depend on the identity of the purchaser: all consumers who buy a particular number of units pay the same price per unit. Discounts for bulk purchases are a common form of second-degree price discrimination. Other examples of industries that adopt this type of pricing structure include the utilities (water, gas and electricity) and some high technology industries such as mobile phones and internet services.

■ **Third-degree price discrimination** involves making the price per unit depend on the identity of the purchaser. However, the price does not depend on the number of units purchased: any consumer can buy as few or as many units as they wish at the same price per unit (Schmalensee, 1981). Common examples of third-degree price discrimination include the practice of offering discounts to children, students or senior citizens for products such as transport or entertainment. Firms that trade internationally sometimes adopt this type of price structure. The term **dumping** describes the practice of charging a lower price to consumers in poorer countries than to those in richer ones.

For a policy of price discrimination to be possible, two conditions must be satisfied. First, the price discriminating firm must enjoy some degree of market power, so that it has the discretion to choose its own price structure. For a perfectly competitive firm, a policy of price discrimination is not possible. If the firm attempts to charge a price in excess of its marginal cost to any segment of the market, entry takes place and the increase in supply forces price down until price *equals* marginal cost at the perfectly competitive equilibrium. The successful exercise of price discrimination is sometimes interpreted as proof of market power.

The second necessary condition for successful price discrimination is that the market for the product must be divisible into sub-markets, within which there are different demand conditions (or different price elasticities of demand). These sub-markets must be physically separate either through space or time, so that secondary trade or resale between consumers in different sub-markets is not possible. A firm cannot force Jack to pay more than Jill if it is possible for Jill to purchase at the lower price on Jack's behalf. For example, in the markets for accounting, legal and medical services, there is often simultaneity between production and consumption, making it difficult or impossible for consumers to resell the service between themselves. Similarly, simultaneity between production and consumption enables a cinema to offer discounted admission to children, because it is not possible for a child to purchase the right to watch the movie at the cheaper price and then pass on or resell this right to an adult. But, on the other hand, the cinema does not allow children to buy ice cream at a discounted price, because it would be easy for children to buy ice cream on their parents' behalf.

Simultaneity between production and consumption is not the only way in which effective separation of sub-markets can be achieved. Some newspapers are made available to students at a discounted price, despite the fact that resale would be possible in theory. However, in practice it would not be worthwhile incurring the transaction costs involved in organizing the resale of a newspaper for which a cover price discount of (say) 50 per cent represents a saving of only a few pence. Significant transport costs can also help achieve an effective physical separation of sub-markets. For example, the practice of dumping surplus agricultural produce in poorer countries relies on transport costs being prohibitive if the consumers in poorer countries attempted to resell to their counterparts in the richer countries.

First-degree price discrimination

Figure 13.1 illustrates a policy of **first-degree price discrimination**, exercised by a monopoly supplier. First, consider the polar case where the market demand function represents a large number of consumers. Depending on the price, each consumer either buys one unit of the good, or abstains from buying altogether. Each consumer's reservation price is the maximum price the consumer is willing to pay. It is helpful to imagine the consumers arrayed along the horizontal axis of Figure 13.1, in descending order of their reservation prices or willingness to pay. Therefore the first consumer has a reservation price of P_1; the second consumer has a reservation price of P_2; and so on. In the standard case where the monopolist charges the same price to each consumer, the profit-maximizing price and quantity is (P_M, Q_M). Notice that if the monopolist did not have to offer the same price to all consumers, it would be worthwhile to supply the consumer located just to the right of Q_M, whose reservation price or willingness to pay is slightly lower than P_M but still higher than the monopolist's marginal cost. But, in the standard case, the monopolist would have to offer the same price cut to all of its existing Q_M consumers who are located to the left of this point. The loss of revenue this would entail exceeds the benefit the monopolist would gain by attracting the additional customer. By implementing a policy of first-degree price discrimination, however, the monopolist can exploit the

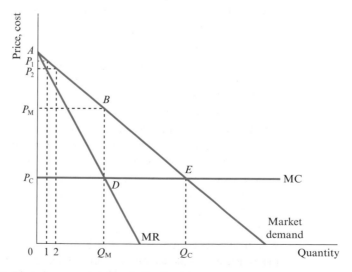

Figure 13.1 First-degree price discrimination

differences in willingness to pay, by charging each consumer their own reservation price. Therefore the first consumer pays a price of P_1, the second consumer pays a price of P_2 and so on. It is worthwhile for the monopolist to supply all consumers whose reservation prices exceed the monopolist's marginal cost. Therefore total output is Q_C and the most marginal consumer pays a price of P_C.

It is also possible to implement a policy of first-degree price discrimination in a second polar case, where the market demand function represents one consumer, who is prepared to buy any number of units of the good, but whose willingness to pay decreases as the number of units purchased increases. If the monopolist offers a price of P_1, the consumer buys only one unit. But if the monopolist offers to sell a second unit at a reduced price of P_2, the consumer buys two units. If reductions in the prices of further units are offered, the consumer is induced to buy three, four or five units, and so on. The monopolist could continue in this way until the price of the last unit sold *equals* the monopolist's marginal cost. As before, the monopolist's total output is Q_C, and the selling price is P_C. At (P_C, Q_C) the monopolist obtains a surplus of P_CAE.

An alternative way in which the monopolist could obtain the same surplus is by charging a **two-part tariff**. The monopolist offers the consumer a price structure requiring the payment of a fixed fee (which is mandatory if the consumer wishes to make any purchases at all) and an additional uniform price for each unit that is purchased. In Figure 13.1, the monopolist's optimal two-part tariff is to charge a fixed fee of P_CAE, and a uniform price per unit of $P_C = MC$. As before, the total quantity of output produced and sold is Q_C, and the most marginal unit is sold at a price of P_C. A two-part tariff price structure is often used by golf, tennis or bowling clubs, which charge a fixed annual membership fee, and make an additional charge for use of the facilities on each occasion. Two-part tariffs are also used by amusement parks and theme parks, such as Disneyland, where there is a fixed entry fee and an additional price charged for each ride (Oi, 1971).

Figure 13.1 can be used to compare the efficiency and welfare properties of the monopolist's standard profit-maximizing equilibrium at (P_M, Q_M), and the equilibrium that is achieved with first-degree price discrimination. With first-degree price discrimination, the total output of Q_C is higher than Q_M in the standard case of monopoly. In fact, Q_C is the total output that would be produced if the monopolist were replaced by a large number of perfectly competitive producers. Furthermore, the equilibrium achieved with first-degree price discrimination satisfies the necessary condition for allocative efficiency (see Section 3.4), that the price of the most marginal unit of output produced *equals* the marginal cost of producing the last unit.

For a non-discriminating monopolist operating at (P_M, Q_M) consumer surplus is represented by the triangle P_MAB (triangle in Figure 3.4); producer surplus is the monopolist's abnormal profit of P_CP_MBD; and the deadweight loss is DBE. With first-degree price discrimination there is no consumer surplus, because each consumer pays a price equivalent to their maximum willingness to pay for each unit. There is a producer surplus of P_CAE, which represents the total abnormal profit earned by the monopolist by selling each unit at a varying price. Finally, the deadweight loss that exists in the non-discriminating case is eliminated.

This analysis leads to what might at first sight seem a rather paradoxical conclusion. The monopolist who adopts a policy of first-degree price discrimination earns an even higher abnormal profit than the monopolist who charges a uniform price but, on allocative efficiency criteria, the outcome under first-degree price discrimination is preferable to the outcome in the case of monopoly with uniform pricing. The policy of first-degree price discrimination allows the monopolist to convert all of the consumer surplus that exists in the non-discriminating case into producer surplus and to eliminate the deadweight loss. In other words the monopolist extracts all of the available surplus and earns an even higher abnormal profit. However, this outcome is superior on allocative efficiency criteria, for the following reasons:

- In the non-discriminating case, it is possible to make someone better off without making anyone else worse off, because there is a consumer who is willing to pay a price for an extra unit that would exceed the cost of producing this extra unit.

- With first-degree price discrimination it is not possible to make someone better off without making anyone else worse off, because price *equals* marginal cost for the most marginal unit produced and sold.

The paradox is resolved by noting that, for allocative efficiency, it does not matter whether the surplus accrues to consumers or to producers. Welfare economists do not make value judgements as to whether monopoly profits are good or bad. All that matters is that there should be no unexploited opportunities for welfare gains that could be achieved without causing losses elsewhere. As shown above, such opportunities do exist at the non-discriminating monopoly equilibrium (which is therefore allocatively inefficient), but no such opportunities exist at the equilibrium under first-degree price discrimination. First-degree price discrimination is sometimes known as perfect price discrimination, because all of the available surplus is extracted by the monopolist. As shown below, this is not the case with either second-degree or third-degree price discrimination.

Second-degree price discrimination

In the case where the market contains a number of consumers with different demand functions (or differences in willingness to pay), first-degree price discrimination requires the monopolist to be able to sell to different consumers on different terms. However, while the monopolist may be aware that different consumers have different demand functions, the monopolist may have no practical method for distinguishing between individual consumers. How is the monopolist to tell which consumer has which demand function? The consumers themselves are not likely to be willing to reveal this information, since doing so enables the monopolist to extract all of their consumer surplus. In the case where the monopolist cannot distinguish between consumers, the best policy is to offer the same menu of prices and quantities to all consumers, and allow the consumers to self-select. In other words, the monopolist designs a menu of prices and quantities such that each consumer chooses a price–quantity

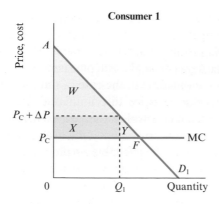
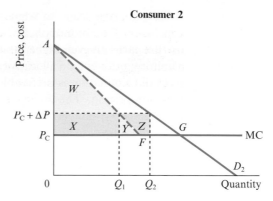

Figure 13.2 Second-degree price discrimination (two-part tariff)

combination that is optimal for the consumer, but which also allows the monopolist to discriminate profitably between consumers.

The two-part tariff that was discussed above can be used to implement a policy of **second-degree price discrimination**. Suppose there are two groups of consumers with different demand functions and different price elasticities of demand. In Figure 13.2, Consumers 1 and 2 are representative consumers from each group (and for simplicity it is assumed that there are equal numbers of consumers in each group). Consumer 2 buys more units than Consumer 1 at any price, and at any given price Consumer 2 has a higher price elasticity of demand than Consumer 1. For simplicity, it is assumed that the maximum price any consumer is prepared to pay is the same for both groups; in other words, the demand functions of Consumers 1 and 2 touch the vertical axis at the same point. With a policy of first-degree price discrimination, the monopolist would set a fixed fee of $P_C AF$ for Consumer 1; a fixed fee of $P_C AG$ for Consumer 2; and a uniform price of P_C per unit purchased for both consumers. For second-degree price discrimination, however, the monopolist must offer both consumers the same menu of prices. Suppose the monopolist continues with the uniform price of P_C per unit. Which fixed fee should the monopolist set?

- If the fixed fee is set at the larger value of $P_C AG$, the monopolist extracts all of Consumer 2's surplus, but Consumer 1 drops out of the market altogether, and the monopolist fails to extract any surplus from Consumer 1.

- On the other hand, if the fixed fee is set at the smaller value of $P_C AF$, the monopolist extracts all of Consumer 1's surplus and extracts the same amount of surplus from Consumer 2, but fails to extract FAG of Consumer 2's surplus.

In fact, it can be shown that in some cases neither of these two options is optimal for the monopolist. Suppose the second of the two options is preferred to the first and the monopolist chooses to supply to both consumers (in which case $2P_C AF > P_C AG$). Using Figure 13.2, it can be shown that the monopolist can earn a producer surplus higher than $2P_C AF$ by setting a fixed fee slightly lower than $P_C AF$, and charging a uniform price per unit slightly higher than P_C. Suppose the monopolist increases the price per unit from P_C to $P_C + \Delta P$. In order for Consumer 1 to remain in the market, the fixed fee must be reduced from area $W + X + Y (= P_CAF)$ to area W. Consumer 1 purchases Q_1 units, and the producer surplus earned from Consumer 1 is $W + X$. Previously, the producer surplus earned from Consumer 1 was $W + X + Y$. Therefore the producer loses Y from Consumer 1. However, Consumer 2 purchases Q_2 units, and the producer surplus earned from Consumer 2 is $W + X + Y + Z$. Previously the producer surplus earned from Consumer 2 was $W + X + Y$. Therefore the producer gains Z from Consumer 2. By construction, area Z exceeds area Y. This ensures that the monopolist gains overall by increasing the price per unit from P_C to $P_C + \Delta P$ and by reducing the fixed fee from $W + X + Y$ to W.

The analysis illustrated in Figure 13.2 establishes that in the case where it is profitable for the monopolist to supply both consumers, the optimal two-part tariff includes a uniform price that is set at a level higher than the monopolist's marginal cost. The precise determination of the optimal two-part tariff is a rather complex mathematical problem and beyond the scope of this book. The complexity is even greater in the more realistic case in which there is a large number of consumer types, each with their own demand functions. However, one important result is that with second-degree price discrimination, the monopolist cannot extract as much surplus as is possible with a policy of first-degree price discrimination. In Figure 13.2, if the monopolist sets a uniform menu of prices which does not vary between the two consumers, no uniform two-part tariff will enable the monopolist to extract a surplus as large as $P_CAF + P_CAG$. It is natural to expect that a policy of first-degree price discrimination, which is based on perfect information about consumers' preferences, is more profitable than second-degree price discrimination, which is based on imperfect information.

Third-degree price discrimination

In the case of second-degree price discrimination, the monopolist cannot segment the market by distinguishing between consumers, and must offer the same menu of prices to each consumer. However, the menu of prices is constructed in such a way that the price per unit that each consumer pays depends on the number of units purchased. This is true even in the case of the two-part tariff: if a larger quantity is purchased, the average price per unit is lower because the fixed fee is spread over a larger number of units. In contrast, with a policy of **third-degree price discrimination**, the price per unit that each consumer pays is constant, but the monopolist can segment the market by offering different prices to different consumers.

In practice, the monopolist is unlikely to have sufficient information to achieve complete market segmentation, since this would require perfect information about each consumer's individual demand function. However, partial market segmentation may be achieved quite easily in cases where consumers can be divided into groups based on easily identifiable characteristics, such as age or membership of particular groups such as students or pensioners. For partial market segmentation to be effective, the nature of the individual's demand function must be correlated with the identifying characteristic. This condition is often satisfied. A child's demand for admission to a cinema is likely to be more price elastic than that of an adult. A pensioner's demand for bus travel, or a student's demand for a newspaper, is more price elastic than that of other adults.

Therefore, with third-degree price discrimination, the monopolist segments the market into groups, charges the same price per unit sold within each group, but charges different prices to members of different groups. Figure 13.3 illustrates the case where there are two groups of consumers. As before, Consumers 1 and 2, shown in the two left-hand diagrams, are representative consumers from each group. It is assumed that Consumer 2's demand is more price elastic than that of Consumer 1. Since the price must be uniform within each sub-market but the sub-markets are perfectly segmented, it turns out that the monopolist's optimal pricing policy is to operate as a monopoly supplier to each sub-market. The monopolist should select the price–quantity combination for each sub-market at which the sub-market's marginal revenue *equals* the monopolist's marginal cost. Therefore, in Figure 13.3, the monopolist charges a relatively high price of P_1 to Consumer 1 whose demand is price inelastic, and a relatively low price of P_2 to Consumer 2 whose demand is price elastic. For reference, in Figure 13.3 the right-hand diagram shows the market demand function (obtained by summing the consumers' individual demand functions horizontally), and the profit-maximizing price–quantity combination (P_M, Q_M) in the standard case, where the monopolist charges a uniform price to all consumers.

It is not possible to draw many general conclusions about the welfare effects of third-degree price discrimination. In comparison with the non-discriminating case (where the monopolist charges a uniform price to all consumers regardless of sub-group membership) the sum of producer surplus and consumer surplus may be higher, lower or the same, depending on the exact positions of the sub-market demand functions. However, two unequivocal conclusions are possible. First, the monopolist's abnormal profit (producer surplus) is always higher in the case of third-degree price discrimination than in the non-discriminating case. The monopolist does not segment the market and charge different prices to different sub-markets unless it is profitable to do so. Second, in the case where there are two sub-markets, one price will always be higher and the other price lower than the uniform monopoly price in the non-discriminating case. Consumers in the sub-market with the higher price have less consumer surplus

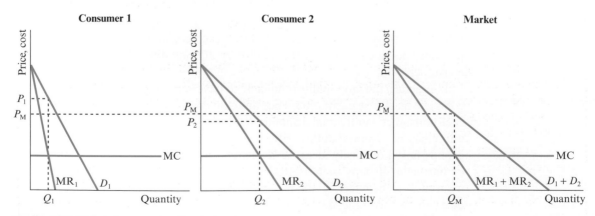

Figure 13.3 Third-degree price discrimination

and are always worse off than in the non-discriminating case; conversely, consumers in the sub-market with the lower price have more consumer surplus and are always better off than in the non-discriminating case (Yamey, 1974; Layson, 1994). Appendix 1 contains a mathematical derivation of profit maximization under third-degree price discrimination.

Examples of price discrimination

Section 13.3 concludes by identifying a number of examples of price discrimination other than those that have been discussed previously in this section, and Case Study 13.1 identifies some practical applications to ticket pricing in football's Premier League.

Intertemporal price discrimination

With **intertemporal price discrimination**, the supplier segments the market by the point in time at which the product is purchased by different groups of consumers. Video games, mobile phone handsets, books, CDs and DVDs are examples of goods that are often more expensive if they are purchased earlier, but cheaper for consumers who are prepared to delay purchase. In the case of books, there is a physical difference between the expensive hardback edition that is available when the book is first published, and the cheaper paperback edition that appears several months later. However, the retail price differential is usually much larger than the difference in production costs between hardbacks and paperbacks. Therefore despite the physical difference, this case conforms to the model of intertemporal price discrimination. Case Study 13.2 describes an empirical study of intertemporal price discrimination in the book publishing industry.

Case study 13.1

Price discrimination in ticket price structures for English Premier League football

In Case Study 2.2, it was shown that understanding the determinants of spectator demand is important to clubs when making decisions about stadium capacity and ticket pricing. In a survey of English Premier League football clubs carried out during the 1998–9 season, Clowes and Clements (2003) find clubs use a wide range of sophisticated ticket-pricing structures.

In accordance with the economic theory of price discrimination, several of these price structures are designed to extract more value from spectators with differing degrees of willingness-to-pay than would be possible with a uniform ticket price structure. Several examples can be found of both second-degree price discrimination (charging different prices depending on the number of matches attended) and third-degree price discrimination (charging different prices to different spectators or groups of spectators).

Season tickets

Buying an annual season ticket normally offers three benefits:

- A guaranteed seat for every home match.

- Priority allocation of tickets for away matches, cup finals, and so on.

- An effective discount on the price of buying tickets for each match individually (second-degree price discrimination).

In the 1998–9 survey, the size of the discount varied from zero to about 35 per cent. Two clubs charged season ticket premiums: a policy that might be justified in economic terms if the stadium is regularly filled to capacity.

Membership schemes

Membership schemes that require payment of a fixed membership fee, but then allow members to purchase match tickets at a discounted price, are a form of two-part tariff (second-degree price discrimination).

Some clubs run separate membership schemes for juniors, with separate prices. Some junior membership schemes give members the right to receive a package of 'free' merchandise.

Personal seat licence (PSL)

In the US, some major league teams charge a fee that guarantees the right to purchase a season ticket for a particular seat over the long term (20 or 30 years). PSLs typically lapse if the holder dies or fails to renew the season ticket (Sandy *et al.*, 2004). A PSL is also a form of two-part tariff (second-degree price discrimination).

In the US, PSLs are common among new (expansion) teams or teams that have relocated to a new city. Unsurprisingly, the idea has been more difficult to sell to the existing season ticket holders of established teams. Several attempts to introduce similar schemes by English football clubs in the early 1990s were unpopular with spectators, and the idea failed to take off.

Price concessions

Price concessions to specific groups are a form of third-degree price discrimination. The 1998–9 survey found that all Premier League clubs that responded offered discounts on season tickets or match-day tickets (or both) to juniors, pensioners and people with disabilities. Some (but not all) clubs offered discounts to students and the unemployed. However, perhaps surprisingly only a small number of clubs offered discounts to family groups.

Price banding

In the 1998–9 survey, seven English Premier League clubs indicated that ticket prices were dependent on the attractiveness of the opposition, with home fixtures classified into two or three price bands.

This practice is consistent with profit maximization. If the PED (price elasticity of demand) is lower for a fixture against Manchester United than for a fixture against average Premier League opposition, the profit-maximizing club should charge a higher price for the more attractive fixture. This policy is not price discrimination, since different prices are charged for different matches with different characteristics.

Good and bad seats

Most English football clubs charge different prices for seats in different locations within the stadium. This policy is not price discrimination, since different prices are charged for what are essentially different products.

The demand functions for seats in different locations are likely to be interdependent:

- If the club sets too large a price differential, there is likely to be excess demand for the cheaper seats.

- If the price differential is too small, demand will tend to switch towards the dearer seats.

Most clubs tend to rely on experience or trial-and-error in order to determine the most appropriate price differential.

Price bundling

In the 1998–9 survey, eight English Premier League clubs operated a policy of bundling. Either tickets for two or more matches must be bought simultaneously; or proof of purchase of a ticket for one match is required to purchase a ticket for another match.

A common practice is to bundle a sell-out match together with a match that is unlikely to sell out. Bundling is also justified as an attempt to reduce the possibility of away supporters of popular teams purchasing tickets in the home sections of the stadium.

Source: Clowes, J. and Clements, N. (2003) An examination of discriminatory ticket pricing practice in the English football Premier League, *Managing Leisure*, 8, 105–20. Reprinted by permission of the publisher, Taylor & Francis Ltd, http://www.tandf.co.uk/journals.

Figure 13.4 shows the market demand function in the case where there is a large number of consumers, each of whom either buys one unit of the good, or abstains from buying altogether (as in Figure 13.1). Each consumer's reservation price is the maximum price the consumer is willing to pay, and as before it is helpful to imagine the consumers arrayed along the horizontal axis of Figure 13.4 in descending order of their reservation prices or willingness to

to the triangle Q_1AB. MR_2 is the marginal revenue function associated with the residual demand function, and in period 2 the profit-maximizing price and output combination is $(P_2, Q_2 - Q_1)$. The $Q_2 - Q_1$ consumers who purchase in period 2 pay a lower price than the Q_1 consumers who purchase in period 1. If the model were extended over further periods with similar assumptions, more consumers (to the right of Q_2) could be induced to make purchases by means of further price cuts.

Coase (1972) points out that the ability of a monopolist to practise inter-temporal price discrimination may be limited by strategic behaviour on the part of consumers. If the monopolist acquires a reputation for price-cutting, even those consumers with a high willingness to pay may decide to delay their consumption, so as to obtain an increased surplus by purchasing at the reduced price at a later date. The extent to which consumers are prepared to do so depends on the durability of the good (is it worth the same tomorrow as it is worth today?) and the discount rate consumers use to evaluate the present value of future consumption. In an extreme case in which the good is perfectly durable and the discount rate is zero (consumers are indifferent between present and future consumption), the monopolist is forced to charge the competitive price in all periods. Anticipating that the monopolist will eventually reduce the price to the perfectly competitive level, all consumers decide to delay purchase rather than pay more than the perfectly competitive price. This forces the monopolist to charge the perfectly competitive price from the outset.

Brand labels

The practice of charging different prices for similar or identical goods differenti-ated solely by a brand label can be interpreted as a form of price discrimination. In supermarkets, value brands sell at a substantial discount relative to the brands of recognized manufacturers, even though in some cases the difference in quality is small or non-existent. In the clothing market, some consumers are willing to pay £20 or £30 more for a small badge or emblem sewn onto an otherwise identical T-shirt or pair of jeans. But it can be argued that branding does not conform to the model of price discrimination, because the status or prestige conferred by the purchase or ownership of the branded product should be recognized as a genuine product characteristic, for which suppliers of branded products are entitled to charge if consumers are willing to pay.

Loyalty discounts

Major airlines offering airmiles schemes that can be used by frequent travellers to earn free tickets, practise a form of second-degree price discrimination. Consumers who travel frequently pay a lower average price per journey than consumers who make only single or occasional journeys. Many airlines allow airmiles to be earned from purchases of other products, making it possible to travel without ever paying directly for a ticket. Supermarkets, such as Tesco, which operate loyalty or bonus points schemes providing coupons or rebates to regular customers, operate a similar form of second-degree price discrimination.

Coupons

Some retailers supply coupons that provide price discounts, perhaps through advertisements printed in the newspapers or through leaflets delivered directly to people's homes. In principle, the price discount is available to any consumer but, in practice, only those consumers willing to spend the time and make the effort required to cut out, retain and present the coupon will obtain the discount. This practice can be interpreted as a form of price discrimination, favouring those consumers with more time or lower opportunity costs, who are prepared to make the effort to collect and present the coupon.

Stock clearance

A department store that conducts a sale in which the price of merchandise is successively reduced until all sale items have been purchased exercises a form of price discrimination, if this practice results in different consumers paying different prices on different days for identical goods. This pricing practice can be interpreted as a form of intertemporal price discrimination. For a single item that is successively reduced in price until it is eventually sold, this procedure for finding a buyer is known as a Dutch auction. The theory and practice of auctions is discussed in Chapter 14.

Metering

Metering price discrimination is the practice of charging consumers a relatively low price for a primary product, and a relatively high price for a secondary product that is tied to the primary product (Oi, 1971; Schmalensee, 1981; Rosen and Rosenfield, 1997; Ellison, 2005; Gil and Hartmann, 2008). Consumers who are highly price-sensitive, and who would not be willing to pay for the primary product if it were priced at a higher level, can purchase the primary product but abstain from purchase of the secondary product. Consumers who are less price-sensitive, and who would be willing to pay a higher price for the primary product, may be willing to purchase both products. The seller is compensated for the low profit margin on the primary product by realizing a high margin on the tied secondary product. Effectively, the two groups of consumers are charged at different levels for the package that each chooses to purchase: either the primary product alone, or the primary and secondary products in combination.

Examples of metering price discrimination include tickets for concerts or sporting events (the primary product) that might be priced competitively so that the stadium is filled, while food and drinks concessions located inside the stadium charge prices much higher than the local supermarket that is located outside. Retailers of white goods (electronic domestic appliances such as refrigerators and washing machines) might offer the basic product at a highly competitive price in order to attract consumers into the store, but then attempt to persuade customers to purchase an extended warranty or guarantee that provides the retailer with a large profit margin. Case Study 13.3 examines the practice of metering price discrimination by cinemas.

Free-on-board pricing

In some markets, producers or distributors absorb transport costs, so that all buyers within a specific geographic area (country or region) pay a uniform price, despite the variation in transport costs within this area. This pricing system is known as free-on-board pricing. As noted above, even though all prices are the same, free-on-board pricing is a form of price discrimination, which favours buyers in the more remote locations where transport costs are higher. The difference in costs means these buyers should pay more. Therefore the policy of charging the same price is a form of price discrimination. From the point of view of suppliers, a uniform pricing policy may be attractive because, by eliminating price discrepancies, it reduces the risk that price competition may break out among suppliers. Free-on-board pricing removes any temptation for an individual supplier to implement a price cut, which might be justified to competitors on grounds of reduced transport costs, but might actually be motivated by an attempt to capture an increased market share.

Case study 13.3

Metering price discrimination by cinemas

Cinemas are notorious for charging consumers top dollar for concession items such as popcorn, fizzy drinks and sweets. Are moviegoers just being stung?

New research from Stanford and the University of California, Santa Cruz suggests that there is a method to cinemas' madness – and one that in fact benefits the viewing public. By charging high prices on concessions, cinemas are able to keep ticket prices lower, which allows more people to enjoy the silver-screen experience.

The findings empirically answer the age-old question of whether it's better to charge more for a primary product (in this case, the film ticket) or a secondary product (the popcorn). Putting the premium on the 'frill' items, it turns out, indeed opens up the possibility for price-sensitive people to see films. That means more customers coming to cinemas in general, and a nice profit from those who are willing to fork it out for the Gummy Bears.

Indeed, cinemas rely on concession sales to keep their businesses viable. Although concessions account for only about 20 per cent of gross revenues, they represent some 40 per cent of cinemas' profits. That's because while ticket revenues must be shared with film distributors, 100 per cent of concessions go straight into an exhibitor's coffers.

Looking at detailed revenue data for a cinema chain in Spain, Wesley Hartmann, associate professor of marketing at the Graduate School of Business, and Ricard Gil, assistant professor in economics at University of California, Santa Cruz, proved that pricing concessions on the high side in relation to admission tickets makes sense.

They compared concession purchases in weeks with low and high film attendance.

The fact that concession sales were proportionately higher during low-attendance periods suggested the presence of 'die-hard' cinema-goers willing to see any kind of film, good or bad – and willing to purchase high-priced popcorn to boot. 'The logic is that if they're willing to pay, say, $10 for a bad movie, they would be willing to pay even more for a good movie,' said Hartmann. 'This is underscored by the fact that they *do* pay more, even for a bad movie, as is seen in their concession buying. So for the times they're in the theater seeing good or popular movies, they're actually getting more quality than they would have needed to show up. That means that, essentially, you could have charged them a higher price for the ticket.'

Should cinemas flirt with raising their ticket prices then? No, says Hartmann. The die-hard group does not represent the average film-goer. While the film-o-philes might be willing to pay, say, $15 for a ticket, a cinema that tried such a pricing tactic would soon find itself closing its doors.

'The fact that the people who show up only for good or popular movies consume a lot less popcorn means that the total they pay is substantially less than that of people who will come to see anything. If you want to bring more consumers into the market, you need to keep ticket prices lower to attract them.' Cinemas wisely make up the margin, he says, by transferring it to the person willing to buy the $5 popcorn bucket.

The work of Hartmann and Gil substantiates what movie exhibitors have intuited all along. 'The argument that pricing secondary goods higher than primary goods can benefit consumers has been circulating for decades, but until now, no one has looked at hard data to see whether it's true or not,' says Hartmann.

In another study examining Spanish cinemas, the researchers discovered: Moviegoers who purchase their tickets over the internet also tend to buy more concession items than those who purchase them at the door, by phone, at kiosks, or at ATMs (the latter option has not yet hit the United States). More research is needed to figure out why, but for now this suggests that cinemas may want to be sure to partner with an internet service to make such ticketing available – or even take the function in-house.

People who come to the cinema in groups also tend to buy more popcorn, fizzy drinks and sweets, Hartmann and Gil found. While this, too, merits more investigation, it may be that such groups comprise families or teenagers. 'If that turns out to be the case, it may be that cinemas will want to run more family- or adolescent-oriented movies to attract a more concession-buying crowd,' Hartmann says.

Analyzing data along the lines suggested by Hartmann and Gil can also support other pricing schemes for businesses that sell concessions, such as baseball parks. Taking the kids to a ball game can be a pricey proposition for many families, once you take into account all the hotdogs and memorabilia. 'If we found the current pricing scheme turns away such a group, theory suggests that the firm might want to throw in a free baseball cap or bat,' Hartmann says. 'That raises the quality of the experience and provides an incentive for families to show up.'

Source: Gil, R. and Hartmann, W.R. (2008) Empirical analysis of metering price discrimination: evidence from concession sales at movie theaters, *Marketing Science*, 28, 1046–62. Reproduced with kind permission of the Institute for Operations Research and the Management Sciences (INFORMS).

13.4 Peak-load pricing

In some markets, demand varies at different times of the day or on different days of the year. Examples of products or services for which demand is variable include: gas and electricity; public transport services; roads, tunnels and bridges; gyms and fitness clubs; and package holidays and amusement parks. In each of these cases, it is unlikely that the supplier can adjust capacity to meet the higher level of demand in peak periods, or reduce capacity in response to the lower level of demand in off-peak periods. Furthermore, none of these products or services is storable. It is not possible for consumers to build up stocks during off-peak periods, and then run down these stocks during peak periods. Under such conditions, the supplier faces a **peak-load pricing** problem. Specifically, two issues need to be addressed: first, what level of capacity should be installed; and second, for any given capacity what are the optimal peak period and off-peak period prices.

In order to develop a model to address these questions, it is assumed there are separate peak period and off-peak period market demand functions, denoted D_1 and D_2 respectively. In Figure 13.5, it is assumed these two demand functions are completely independent of one another: purchases made in one period do not in any way affect demand in the other period. Capacity can be installed and maintained at a constant marginal cost per unit of capacity of b, which allows the industry to operate in both the peak period and the off-peak period. Production costs in each period are directly proportional to output, so there is also a constant marginal production cost of c per unit of output.

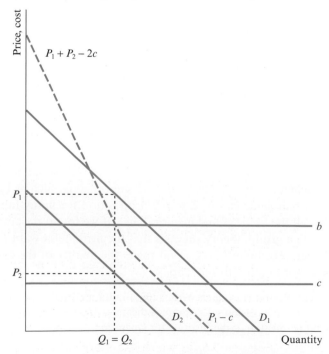

Figure 13.5 Peak-load pricing: full capacity production in both periods

In many countries, some (although not all) of the industries that are subject to the peak-load problem are either in state ownership, or in private ownership but heavily regulated. Accordingly, much of the theoretical literature on peak-load pricing is based on an assumption of social welfare maximization, rather than profit maximization. As shown in Section 3.4, the standard condition for social welfare maximization is price *equals* marginal cost. In the present case, this condition needs to be amended, because for each additional unit of capacity that is installed, one additional unit of output can be produced and sold in each of the two periods, at different prices. If the industry operates at full capacity in both periods, the equivalent condition for social welfare maximization is:

$$P_1 + P_2 = b + 2c$$

$$\text{or} \quad P_1 + P_2 - 2c = b$$

$$\text{or} \quad P_1 = b + 2c - P_2 \text{ and } P_2 = b + 2c - P_1$$

In these expressions, P_1 and P_2 are the prices charged per unit of output in the peak period and off-peak period, respectively. The first of the three expressions says the total proceeds obtained by creating an additional unit of capacity enabling the industry to produce and sell one additional unit of output in both periods, $P_1 + P_2$, *equals* the marginal cost of installing the additional capacity, b, *plus* the marginal production cost for the two additional units of output, $2c$. The second expression is a rearrangement of the first, used to identify the optimal prices and capacity in Figure 13.5. The third expression says the optimal price for each period is the total marginal cost incurred through the installation of additional capacity and the additional production in both periods, $b + 2c$, *minus* the price charged in the other period.

In Figure 13.5, the broken line shows, for each per-period output level shown on the horizontal axis, the value of $P_1 + P_2 - 2c$ implied by the two market demand functions. Over the range of output levels where $P_1 > c$ and $P_2 > c$, the broken line is constructed by summing the two demand functions vertically, and subtracting $2c$. Over the range of outputs where $P_1 > c > P_2$, the broken line is $P_1 - c$. According to the expressions for social welfare maximization, in Figure 13.5 the optimal capacity is $Q_1 = Q_2$, and the optimal values of P_1 and P_2 are obtained from the peak and off-peak demand functions (D_1 and D_2 respectively) at this point. The peak-period consumers, whose demand or willingness to pay is stronger, are charged a higher price than the off-peak consumers. However, the willingness to pay of consumers in both periods is taken into account in determining the optimal capacity, because the system operates at full capacity in both periods.

It need not always be the case that the industry operates at full capacity in both periods. If the marginal cost of installing additional capacity were lower than is shown in Figure 13.5, it might be optimal (again in terms of social welfare maximization) to operate at full capacity during the peak period, but to maintain some spare capacity in the off-peak period. This case is shown in Figure 13.6, in which the marginal cost of installing additional capacity is lowered from b to b'. For the peak period, it is now worthwhile to install capacity

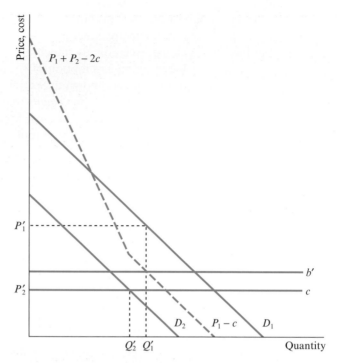

Figure 13.6 Peak-load pricing: spare capacity in off-peak period

of Q_1', and sell Q_1' units of output for a price of $P_1' = b' + c$. For the off-peak period, however, if Q_1' units of output were produced, the price would fall below the marginal production cost of c. In the off-peak period, the industry should operate below full capacity, and sell Q_2' units of output for a price of $P_2' = c$. In this case, the willingness to pay of the off-peak consumers becomes irrelevant in determining the optimal capacity, because the system only operates at capacity during the peak period.

Case study 13.4

Ofgem to crack down on unfair pricing

Ofgem, the energy regulator, is to crack down on unfair price differences, it said yesterday as it unveiled a new code of practice giving new rights to retail customers and small businesses. In particular it wants to prevent price discrimination against, often poorer, customers who use prepayment meters to pay bills rather than other payment methods preferred by suppliers such as direct debit. The regulator also proposes to give new rights to small and medium-sized businesses, including an end to the automatic rollover of fixed-term contracts, which often stop business customers securing the best deal.

It aims to stop energy suppliers charging customers different prices unless they can prove those variations are justified by differences in costs or other 'objectively justifiable' factors. Prepayment meters typically result in additional costs for suppliers of between £85 and £95 compared with direct debit. But some customers pay even more than this. Ofgem, however, has decided not to put a cap on charges. The regulator will also prevent the practice, still used by some companies, of charging more to electricity customers in the areas where they were once the monopoly supplier. However, the restriction, which would be included as a condition in the suppliers' licences, is intended to lapse after three years, by which time Ofgem hopes its new standards for the retail market will have taken effect.

The standards are intended to have the effect of 'empowering consumers' through the code of practice, which will force suppliers to provide consumers with a standard annual statement reminding them of their rights to switch suppliers; simplified information on tariffs, and written price quotations following doorstep sales. Ofgem said it could take the matter to the Competition Commission for a more detailed investigation if companies failed to agree on the proposals. The new standards follow its probe last year into the retail gas and electricity markets. Ofgem said it would consult the industry on the details of its plans, expected to take effect in the autumn.

Source: Ofgem to crack down on unfair pricing, © The Financial Times Limited. All Rights Reserved, 24 March 2009 (Pfeifer, S. and Crooks, E.).

13.5 Transfer pricing

The multi-divisional or M-form organizational structure, and the holding company or H-form structure (see Section 5.3) can raise particularly difficult issues for managers when taking pricing and production decisions. It is often the case that one division will use the output of another division as one of its inputs. In the simplest case, an M-form or H-form organization might include quasi-independent production and distribution divisions. The distribution division buys the output of the production division, and sells the product to the final consumer. The question immediately arises, at what price should the trade take place between the production division and the distribution division? In general, the M-form or H-form organization requires a system of **transfer pricing** to determine the prices of intermediate products that are produced by one division and sold to another division, when both divisions form part of the same organization (Hirschleifer, 1956).

In M-form or H-form organizations where the individual divisions are quasi-independent, the choice of transfer price can be a crucial decision, because it affects the imputed revenues of the selling division, the imputed costs of the buying division, and therefore the imputed profitability of both divisions. For example, if the transfer price is set too low, the imputed profits of the distribution division are articificially inflated, and the profits of the production division are artificially depressed. This may have implications for head office's perceptions of managerial performance or labour productivity in both divisions, which in turn may affect future investment or other internal resource allocation decisions (Eccles, 1985). Moreover, suppose the divisional managers are encouraged to operate in such a way as to minimize costs or maximize profits at divisional level. Through its effect on the divisional revenue and cost functions, the transfer price affects the divisional managers' production decisions, the volume of internal trade, the quantity of inputs purchased from outside the firm or the quantity of intermediate outputs sold outside the firm and, therefore, the profitability of the firm as a whole. As shown below, when there is internal trade within the organization, decisions taken at divisional level with a view to the maximization of divisional profits do not necessarily ensure the maximization of the total profit of the firm as a whole.

Below, profit-maximizing models of transfer pricing between the production and distribution divisions of an M-form organization are developed, for the following three cases:

■ In the first case, it is assumed all of the production division's output is passed on to the distribution division to be sold to final consumers. There is no alternative, external market in which the production division can sell its intermediate output. Similarly, the distribution division obtains its supplies only from the production division and has no alternative external sources.

■ In the second case, it is assumed there is a perfectly competitive external market, in which the production division can sell any surplus intermediate output that is not taken up by the distribution division. Similarly, the distribution division has the option of obtaining additional supplies (over and above those it obtains from the production division) through the external market.

■ In the third case, it is assumed the external market for the intermediate product is imperfectly competitive rather than perfectly competitive.

Transfer pricing with no external market for the intermediate product

Figure 13.7 presents a model of transfer pricing for trade between a production division (producer) and a distribution division (distributor) in the simplest case where there is no external market for the internally transferred product. In the left-hand diagram, MC_1 represents the producer's marginal cost function, and in the right-hand diagram D_2 and MR_2 represent the distributor's demand and marginal revenue functions. MC_2 is the marginal cost function associated with the distributor's own activities (excluding the cost of the units of output the distributor must purchase from the producer).

Suppose, initially, the distributor sets the transfer price and the producer follows price-taking behaviour in respect of this price. The distributor knows

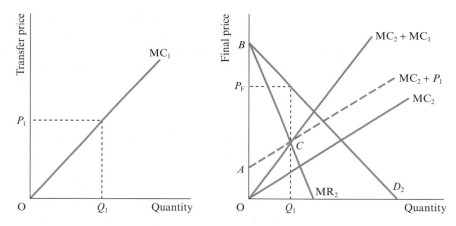

Figure 13.7 Transfer pricing: no external market for intermediate product

the chosen transfer price will be treated by the producer as the latter's marginal revenue function, and the producer will choose the output level at which the transfer price *equals* the producer's marginal cost, MC_1. In order to maximize the profit of the firm as a whole, the distributor should operate as if its total marginal cost function is $MC_2 + MC_1$, obtained by adding the value of MC_1 at each output level vertically onto MC_2. The distributor chooses the output level Q_1 at which $MC_2 + MC_1 = MR_2$. This determines the transfer price P_1, which induces the producer to produce Q_1 units of output. The distributor sells the product to the final consumers at a price of P_F.

Suppose, instead, the producer sets the transfer price, and the distributor follows price-taking behaviour. In this case, the same result is obtained. The distributor's total marginal cost function is $MC_2 + P$, where P is the transfer price chosen by the producer. The producer knows that for any value of P the producer chooses, the distributor is willing to purchase the output level at which $MC_2 + P = MR_2$. In order to maximize the profit of the firm as a whole, the producer should set a transfer price of P_1, as before.

In both cases, P_1 is the transfer price that maximizes the firm's total profit. In Figure 13.7, the area OBC represents the firm's total profit; OAC represents the profit imputed to the producer; and ABC represents the profit imputed to the distributor. However, it is interesting to note that a transfer price of P_1 does not maximize the profits of either the producer or the distributor individually. In the case where the distributor sets the transfer price, the distributor maximizes its own profit by choosing the output level at which the distributor's marginal outlay function *equals* MR_2 (see Figure 13.8). The distributor's marginal outlay function is steeper than $MC_2 + MC_1$, because it takes into account the fact that for each extra unit the distributor buys from the producer, the distributor pays not only the producer's marginal cost of producing that unit, but also an increased transfer price over all the other units the distributor was already buying. It would be in the distributor's private interest to buy a smaller quantity Q_1' at a lower transfer price of P_2, increasing the distributor's imputed profit from ABC to A'BDE in Figure 13.8. The producer's imputed profit falls from OAC to OA'E, and the firm's total profit falls from OBC to OBDE.

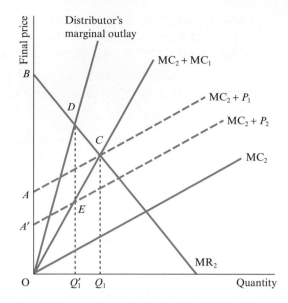

Figure 13.8 Transfer pricing: profit maximization for the distributor

Similarly, in the case where the producer sets the transfer price, the producer maximizes its own profit by choosing the ouput level at which the producer's marginal revenue function *equals* $MC_2 + MC_1$. The producer's marginal revenue function takes account of the fact that at very low output levels, the distributor would be willing to pay a high transfer price, but as output increases, the transfer price is reduced not only on the most marginal unit bought, but also over all the other units the distributor was already buying (see Figure 13.9). It would be in the producer's private interest to supply a smaller quantity Q_1'' at a higher

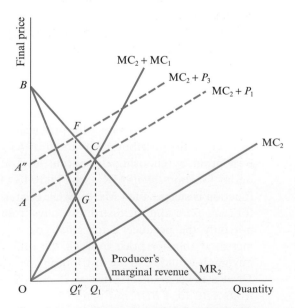

Figure 13.9 Transfer pricing: profit maximization for the producer

transfer price of P_3, increasing the producer's imputed profit from OAC to OA″FG in Figure 13.9. The distributor's imputed profit falls from ABC to A″BF, and the firm's total profit falls from OBC to $OBFG$.

Transfer pricing with a perfectly competitive external market for the intermediate product

Some intermediate products may be traded between the divisions of an M-form or H-form firm, but may also be traded between the production divisions and external buyers from outside the firm. For example, a car manufacturer might be one division of an M-form organization, which includes a separate tyre manufacturing division. The latter sells tyres not only to the car manufacturing division, but also externally to garages and car repair shops, or direct to consumers. There are many other tyre manufacturers, so the external market for tyres is highly competitive. Returning to the previous case of the production division and distribution division, if the external market is perfectly competitive the production division has the option to sell as much of the intermediate commodity as it likes on the external market at the perfectly competitive price. Similarly, the distribution division has the option to buy as much of the intermediate commodity as it likes, again at the perfectly competitive price.

Under these circumstances, the transfer price is effectively constrained to be equal to the perfectly competitive price. If the transfer price were higher than the competitive price, the distributor would prefer to make all of its purchases of the intermediate commodity on the external market; and if the transfer price were lower than the competitive price, the producer would prefer to sell all of its output on the external market. However, it is also likely that the quantity of internal trade and the quantity of production will diverge, with external trade accounting for the difference between the two. Figures 13.10 and 13.11 illustrate two possible cases.

First, in Figure 13.10 the perfectly competitive price P_C is lower than P_1 in Figure 13.7. The distributor's total marginal cost function is $MC_2 + P_C$ and the distributor selects the quantity Q_3 at which $MC_2 + P_C = MR_2$. At a price of P_C,

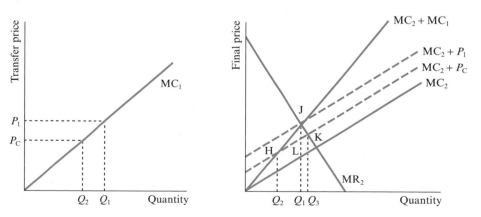

Figure 13.10 Transfer pricing: perfectly competitive external market (price below P_1)

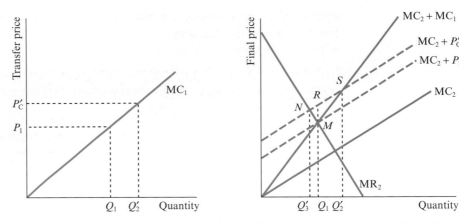

Figure 13.11 Transfer pricing: perfectly competitive external market (price above P_1)

the producer is willing to supply only Q_2 units. The distributor purchases the additional $Q_3 - Q_2$ units on the external market. In comparison with the case where the transfer price is P_1 and Q_1 units are traded, the triangle HJL represents the cost saving to the firm resulting from buying $Q_1 - Q_2$ units of the intermediate commodity on the external market rather than producing these units internally, and LJK represents the additional profit earned because the distributor's total output increases from Q_1 to Q_3 (with the extra $Q_3 - Q_1$ units also purchased on the external market).

Second, in Figure 13.11 the perfectly competitive price P'_C is higher than P_1 in Figure 13.7. The distributor's total marginal cost function is $MC_2 + P'_C$, and the distributor selects the quantity Q'_3 at which $MC_2 + P'_C = MR_2$. At a price of P'_C, the producer wishes to supply Q'_2 units. The producer sells the additional $Q'_2 - Q'_3$ units on the external market. In comparison with the case where the transfer price is P_1 and Q_1 units are traded, the triangle NRM represents the extra profit to the firm resulting from selling $Q_1 - Q'_3$ units of the intermediate commodity on the external market rather than internally, and MRS represents the additional profit earned because the producer's output increases from Q_1 to Q'_2.

The analysis shown in Figures 13.10 and 13.11 suggests that if a competitive external market exists, the firm should participate in this market. It is damaging to the firm's interests to insist that all units of the intermediate commodity used by the distributor are produced internally, if the commodity can be purchased more cheaply on the external market. And it is equally damaging to insist that the producer can only sell the intermediate commodity to the distributor, if the commodity can be produced and sold more profitably on the external market. By participating in the external market, in both cases the firm achieves an increase in its total profit. Of course, these conclusions could change if the firm had some other strategic motive for non-participation in the external market. For example, the firm might not wish to purchase externally because it seeks to prevent a competitor from selling its output, hoping to force the competitor to exit from the production industry; or similarly, the firm might not wish to sell externally because it seeks to prevent a competitor from gaining access to supplies of the intermediate commodity, hoping to force the competitor to exit from the distribution industry.

Transfer pricing with an imperfectly competitive external market for the intermediate product

A further possibility is that the intermediate product may be traded not only between the divisions of an M-form or H-form firm, but also between the production division and one or more external buyers in an imperfectly competitive market. A car manufacturer might be one division of an M-form organization, which buys inputs from a separate division which manufactures specialized electrical components. There are very few other manufacturers of similar components, so the external market for components is imperfectly competitive.

Returning to the theoretical model, with an imperfectly competitive external market, the transfer price for internal trade between the production and distribution divisions differs from the price paid by buyers in the external market. In Figure 13.12, the analysis is restricted to the case where the transfer price, denoted P_4, turns out to be higher than P_1 in Figure 13.7. This means the producer's output of Q_5 is larger than the distributor's output of Q_4, and the producer sells the surplus output of $Q_5 - Q_4$ in the imperfectly competitive external market for the intermediate product. The two left-hand diagrams in Figure 13.12 are constructed in the same way as before. The right-hand diagram shows the producer's demand function and marginal revenue function in the external market, denoted D_3 and MR_3 respectively. The optimal transfer price of P_4 is the only value that satisfies the following conditions:

- At the producer's total output level of Q_5, the producer's marginal cost *equals* the transfer price, or $MC_1 = P_4$.

- At the transfer price of P_4, the distributor's total marginal cost *equals* the distributor's marginal revenue, or $MC_2 + P_4 = MR_2$, yielding an output level for the distributor of Q_4.

- When the surplus intermediate output of $Q_5 - Q_4$ is sold in the external market, the producer's marginal revenue in the external market *equals* the

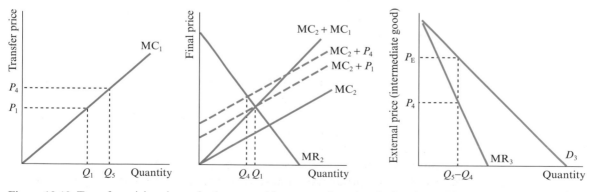

Figure 13.12 Transfer pricing: imperfectly competitive external market (price above P_1)

transfer price, or $MR_3 = P_4$. The producer's selling price in the external market is P_E, which is higher than the transfer price of P_4. Effectively, the producer practises third-degree price discrimination (see Section 13.3), by charging different prices in the segmented internal and external markets for the intermediate output.

Transfer pricing: some implications

The analysis in Section 13.5 has shown that the imputed profitability of each division is not the same as the contribution of each division to the profitability of the firm as a whole. There are several implications:

■ The rewards and incentives for divisional managers should not be based solely on the imputed profitability of their own divisions, but should reflect the implications of their decisions for the profitability of the firm as a whole. If divisional managers seek to maximize the imputed profitability of their own divisions, in the case where there is no external market for the intermediate product a situation of bilateral monopoly exists. The distributor would prefer to use its monopsony power (as sole buyer) to reduce output and reduce the transfer price (see Figure 13.8), while the producer would prefer to use its monopoly power (as sole producer) to reduce output and increase the transfer price (see Figure 13.9). However, both of these outcomes reduce the profitability of the firm as a whole.

■ Strategic decisions concerning the closure of (imputed) loss-making divisions or the expansion of profitable divisions should take account of the implications for the profitability of the firm as a whole. For example, the firm as a whole does not benefit from the closure of a loss-making production division if this decision reduces the profitability of the distribution division by more than the direct saving achieved by not producing the intermediate product in-house. If there are significant transaction costs associated with buying or selling on the external market, these should also be taken into account when assessing the viability of (imputed) loss-making divisions.

■ Transfer pricing is a particularly controversial topic in the case of multi-national firms. The fact that decisions concerning transfer prices have implications for the profits imputed to each division within the firm provides strong incentives for firms to set their transfer prices in such a way as to shift profits towards divisions located in countries with low rates of corporation tax (tax on company profits). A multinational firm may therefore declare artificially high or low transfer prices, so that its profits are declared in a way that minimizes its overall corporation tax liability. The tax authorities may attempt to impose rules or controls on transfer pricing; for example, by insisting that transfer prices are comparable with prices at which the intermediate product can be traded on the external market. However, often such controls are easily circumvented, especially in developing countries where the influence of the tax authorities over the accounting practices of large, foreign-owned multinationals may be weak.

Case study 13.5

Emerging economies toughen tax stance

Emerging economies including India and China are increasingly cracking down on multinationals' tax planning, according to a new survey that underlined the growing competition for revenues between governments. Companies are facing increased scrutiny of their 'transfer pricing' – how they divide taxable profits between the different countries they operate in. Governments across the world are scrambling to get a share of revenues and increasingly want to block businesses from shifting profits to lower tax jurisdictions. The number of companies facing government audits tripled to 12 per cent in China and nearly doubled to 11 per cent in India between 2007 and 2010, according to a survey by Ernst & Young, professional services group.

Most emerging economies have only recently introduced transfer pricing rules – under which multinationals have to justify how they split their profits between different tax domains – but some have become more assertive with inward investors, as exemplified by India's $2bn litigation with Vodafone. India wants the telecoms group to pay capital gains tax on the acquisition of an Indian business. John Hobster, a partner, said: 'We are seeing increased audit activity and evidence of increased penalties, with a particularly marked increase in audits in emerging markets such as China and India.' He urged companies to prepare for more intense and sophisticated scrutiny and to be aware of the increased availability of dispute resolution tools, such as advance pricing agreements.

The Chinese State Administration of Taxation is considering 30 per cent of companies for audit, Ernst & Young said. It is targeting companies which have significant inter-company transactions, consecutive years without taxable income, reduced profit margins and low margins relative to industry peers.

Overall, two thirds of the respondents said they had undergone a transfer pricing audit, compared with 52 per cent in a similar survey carried out in 2007. One in five audit adjustments triggered a penalty, compared with one in 25 in 2005. The survey, which questioned 877 multinationals from 25 countries, found that the increasing scrutiny means that three-quarters of tax directors believe that transfer pricing will be 'absolutely critical' or 'very important' to their organisation over the next two years.

This sentiment was strongest in Europe, followed closely by the US and Asia. There were also sector differences, with pharmaceutical and biotechnology companies far more concerned about transfer pricing than telecoms or financial services companies. In some countries, such as France, Japan and the UK, the number of audits has fallen since 2007. Mr Hobster said this did not reflect a declining emphasis on transfer pricing but a more careful selection of targets for investigation. Companies were most likely to be audited by the US, where the Internal Revenue Service has increased its workforce examining international tax issues. Transfer pricing has become an increasingly prominent issue as a result of public debate and Congressional hearings on tax avoidance through transfer pricing.

13.6 Price dispersion

In a competitive market in which an identical product or service is sold by many firms, and consumers have perfect information, firms should act as price-takers with the same price charged by all producers or retailers. If different prices are charged for the same product or service, this suggests some form of departure from the assumptions underlying the theoretical model of perfect competition. Therefore studying the extent of **price dispersion** across producers or retailers, and studying the degree to which price dispersion persists over time, may be informative as an indicator as to whether markets are competitive or uncompetitive (Pratt *et al.*, 1979; Lach, 2002).

Theory suggests that price dispersion may arise due to heterogeneity between buyers in respect of search costs, brand loyalty, frequency of repeat purchases and access to information; or heterogeneity between sellers in respect of production costs, product quality and technology (Stigler, 1961; Rothschild, 1973; Reinganum, 1979; Rosenthal, 1980; Varian, 1980; Narasimhan, 1988; Stahl, 1989; Spulber, 1995; Sorenson, 2000; Gerardi and Shapiro, 2009). If individual sellers pitch their prices at permanently low or high levels relative to their competitors, then consumer learning should lead to the elimination of high-price sellers from the market, and to the elimination of price dispersion. On the other hand, if sellers frequently vary their relative positions, then search costs may make it prohibitive for consumers to identify the lowest prices available at any particular time. It is likely that the advent of the internet had implications for the extent and persistence of price dispersion by reducing search costs.

In recent years, the development and rapid growth of online markets has made it easier for researchers to collect information on the prices charged by different retailers, either by collecting data from the websites of individual producers or retailers or by using specialized price comparison websites. Price comparison websites enable retailers to display price information, information about the attributes of the products they supply, and information about the service the retailers themselves provide, in a format that can be easily accessed by consumers (Baye and Morgan, 2001). Price comparison websites may drastically reduce the search costs that consumers would otherwise incur. Therefore it might be expected that, in markets where price comparison websites are available, the level of price dispersion should be less than in markets where such tools are unavailable.

In the academic literature on price dispersion, it is often assumed that there are two types of consumers: the informed (sometimes known as shoppers) and the uninformed (sometimes known as loyals). Informed consumers search intensively in order to obtain the lowest available prices; while uninformed consumers either do not access price data, or have preferences for particular retailers that override price considerations. This suggests price dispersion is possible, even in equilibrium. This price dispersion is likely to be persistent, with the identity of firms offering the highest and lowest prices changing over time.

In an early empirical study, Brynjolsson and Smith (2000) compare the prices of books and CDs at 41 online and traditional retailers between 1998 and 1999. Contrary to expectations, prices and price dispersion were found to be higher in online markets than in traditional markets. Subsequent US and Italian studies for books and CDs by Clay *et al.* (2002) and Ancarani and Shankar (2004) report similar findings. These studies attribute their findings to a lack of maturity in the online market.

Early studies for other products also suggest price dispersion is higher in online markets. Using US data, Erevelles *et al.* (2001) find the price of vitamins is higher online than in drug stores, supermarkets and warehouse suppliers. Scholten and Smith (2002) compare price dispersion in traditional retail markets for products such as deodorants, hairspray, aspirin and cameras in 1976, with dispersion for the same products in 2000. Price dispersion was higher in 2000 than in 1976. However, Brown and Goolsbee (2002) find the price dispersion of life insurance policies declined over the period 1992–7 as customer use of the internet increased. A hedonic regression model is used to control for differences in the terms, conditions and coverage of the policies that are compared.

Another facet of recent work is to examine whether price dispersion differs between pure play (specialist online retailers) and multi-channel retailers (bricks and mortar and non-specialist online retailers). Tang and Ting (2001) compare the levels and dispersion of prices between six online retailers and four multi-channel retailers for 51 DVD titles in Singapore. The online retailers tended to charge lower prices, and there was less price dispersion, than the multichannel retailers. Using Italian data on the prices of books and CDs, Ancarani and Shankar (2004) find multichannel retailers charged higher prices and had greater price dispersion than pure play retailers.

Several price dispersion studies use data from internet price comparison sites, where information may be updated on a weekly, daily or even hourly basis (Baye and Morgan, 2001; Baye *et al.*, 2007). For example, Baye *et al.* (2004) examine 4 million daily price observations for 1,000 consumer electronic products posted on the shopper.com website between August 2000 and March 2001, in order to determine whether price dispersion decreased as consumer usage of this website increased over the eight-month period of the study. A reduction in price dispersion over time would suggest that dispersion is a temporary, disequilibrium phenomenon. Alternatively, if there was no reduction, this would suggest that price dispersion is an equilibrium phenomenon, reflecting structural characteristics of the markets concerned. Three measures of price dispersion are used: the average percentage difference in price; the average difference between the two lowest prices; and the average coefficient of variation. There is little evidence to support the view that price dispersion was a temporary phenomenon; instead, price dispersion was persistent over time, and was dependent on structural indicators such as the number of firms listing prices for a given product. The degree of price dispersion was greater when there were fewer firms.

Pan *et al.* (2004) examine the determinants of price dispersion in online retailing, using 2000 and 2001 US data from a price comparison website on several hundred identical products. The factors that may be relevant in explaining the degree of price dispersion in the online markets for different products and services include shopping, retailer, market and product characteristics. Shopping characteristics include shopping convenience (ease of finding and evaluating products through search tools), reliability of delivery and customer service, depth of online product information, quality of shipping service and returns policy. Retailer characteristics include the timing of the retailer's market entry, degree of consumer trust and retailer branding, and consumer awareness. Market and product characteristics include the number of competing sellers, whether the product is cheap or expensive, homogeneity or heterogeneity of product characteristics and the popularity of the product among consumers. In general, variability of shopping characteristics is found to be important in explaining price dispersion, but retailer characteristics are found to be less important.

13.7 Summary

One of the earliest challenges to the neoclassical theory of the firm questioned whether in practice firms have sufficient information to apply the profit-maximizing rule marginal revenue *equals* marginal cost when setting their prices. Cost plus pricing is an alternative pricing rule, whereby price is determined by adding a percentage mark-up to average variable cost. The mark-up includes a contribution towards fixed costs, and a profit margin. Under some conditions, cost plus pricing may be simpler and less demanding in terms of its informational requirements than profit-maximizing pricing. However, the advantages of cost plus pricing are only likely to materialize if the firm's costs are stable, and if average variable cost is constant over the relevant range of output levels. If the cost plus pricing firm always selects approximately the same profit margin as a profit-maximizing firm would achieve, cost plus pricing and profit maximization are equivalent. If so, the margin must be an inverse function of the firm's price elasticity of demand. Although the use of cost plus pricing is widely reported, cost plus could just be a convenient rule-of-thumb for firms that are really profit maximizers, even if profit maximization is not explicitly acknowledged.

Firms with a degree of market power need not always set uniform prices that are identical for all consumers, and identical no matter how many units of the product each consumer buys. With a policy of price discrimination, the firm might sell at different prices to different consumers, or make the price per unit each consumer pays dependent on the number of units purchased. For price discrimination to be possible, the firm must have market power, and the market must be divisible into sub-markets with different demand conditions, so that secondary trade or resale between consumers in different sub-markets is not possible.

There are three types of price discrimination:

■ First-degree price discrimination makes the price per unit of output dependent on the identity of the purchaser and on the number of units purchased. The monopolist exploits differences in consumers' willingness to pay, by charging each consumer his or her own reservation price for each individual unit purchased. First-degree price discrimination yields a higher abnormal profit than the standard case of profit maximization with a uniform price in monopoly, because the consumer surplus in the standard case is converted into producer surplus, and deadweight loss is eliminated. The outcome under first-degree price discrimination is allocatively efficient, because price *equals* marginal cost for the most marginal unit produced and sold.

■ Second-degree price discrimination makes the price per unit of output dependent on the number of units purchased. The price does not depend on the identity of the purchaser. The monopolist designs a menu of prices and quantities such that each consumer chooses a price–quantity combination that allows the monopolist to discriminate profitably between consumers. A two-part tariff, requiring the payment of a fixed fee if the consumer wishes to make any purchases at all, plus an additional uniform price per unit purchased, is a form of second-degree price discrimination.

■ Third-degree price discrimination involves making the price per unit depend on the identity of the purchaser. The price does not depend on the number of units purchased. However, the monopolist is able to segment the market by offering different prices to different consumers. The monopolist charges a relatively high price to consumers whose demand is price inelastic, and a relatively low price to consumers whose demand is price elastic.

Forms of price discrimination used in practice include the following:

■ Intertemporal price discrimination, whereby the supplier segments the market by the point in time at which the product is purchased.

■ Branding, whereby different prices are charged for similar or identical goods differentiated solely by a brand label.

■ Loyalty discounts for regular customers, operated by airlines, supermarkets and other retailers.

■ Coupons providing price discounts that discriminate between consumers on the basis of willingness to make the effort to claim the discount.

■ Stock clearance sales involving successive price reductions which are a form of inter-temporal price discrimination.

■ Metering, involving pricing for a low profit margin on a primary product (such as movie tickets) and a high profit margin on a tied secondary product (such as popcorn).

■ Free-on-board pricing, involving the producer or distributor absorbing transport costs, and representing a form of price discrimination favouring buyers in locations where transport costs are higher.

In markets where demand varies at different times of the day or on different days of the year, but the supplier is unable to adjust capacity to meet the higher level of demand in peak periods (or reduce capacity in off-peak periods) the supplier faces a peak-load problem. If the levels of demand and costs are such that it is efficient to operate at full capacity in both periods, the social welfare maximizing price for each period is the marginal cost of installing an extra unit of capacity *plus* the marginal production cost in both periods *minus* the price charged in the other period. If it is efficient to operate at full capacity during the peak period, the willingness to pay of the off-peak consumers becomes irrelevant in determining the optimal capacity, because the system only operates at capacity during the peak period.

In multidivisional organizations, the choice of transfer prices at which intermediate products are traded internally between divisions affects the imputed profitability of the divisions involved. Decisions taken at divisional level with a view to the maximization of divisional profits do not necessarily ensure the maximization of the total profit of the firm as a whole. In this chapter, profit-maximizing models of transfer pricing have been developed for the cases where there is no external market for the intermediate product; and where the intermediate product can be traded on an external market that is either perfectly competitive or imperfectly competitive. The analysis suggests that incentives for divisional managers should not be based solely on imputed divisional profitability, but should reflect the profitability of the entire organization. Strategic decisions concerning the closure of (imputed) loss-making divisions should also take account of the implications for the profitability of the firm as a whole, including any additional transaction costs associated with trade on the external market that are not considered when calculating imputed divisional profits. The transfer pricing practices of multinational firms can raise particularly difficult policy issues in cases where firms use transfer pricing to minimize their corporation tax liabilities.

In a competitive market with perfect information and product homogeneity, economists would expect all producers or retailers to charge the same price. If there is price dispersion, this suggests some form of failure of the assumptions underlying the theoretical model of perfect competition. In recent years, the growth of online markets has allowed consumers to compare prices more easily, either from the websites of individual producers or retailers, or by using specialized price comparison websites. Product characteristics, and structural characteristics of online markets including the number of retailers, their reputation and the quality of service they offer, appear to be influential in determining the extent of price dispersion.

Discussion questions

1. For what reasons might a firm depart from a policy of pricing for profit maximization and adopt a cost plus pricing formula instead? Under what conditions do these two pricing methods produce identical outcomes?

2. What conditions must be satisfied for a producer to be able to implement a policy of price discrimination?

3. Explain carefully the distinction between the three degrees of price discrimination.

4. In the case of a monopolist, why might a policy of first-degree price discrimination produce an outcome that is preferred on social welfare criteria to a policy of setting a uniform price in order to maximize profit?

5. Consider two medium-sized English Premier League football clubs, one of which has a small stadium, which is regularly filled to capacity, while the other has a larger stadium in which often there are many empty seats. In what ways might you expect the ticket price structures of these two clubs to differ? Your answer should refer to Case Study 13.1.

6. With reference to Case Study 13.2, examine the conditions under which intertemporal price discrimination might be a profitable pricing strategy.

7. Explain why economists have interpreted supermarket (or other retailer) loyalty cards as a form of second-degree price discrimination.

8. The demand for gas and electricity varies between different times of the day and between different months of the year. What factors should be considered by a utility company when deciding how much capacity to install, and what prices to charge during peak and off-peak periods?

9. With reference to Case Study 13.3, what factors should be considered by a cinema chain in setting its ticket prices, and the prices that are charged inside the cinema for food and drinks?

10. With reference to Case Study 13.4, assess the fairness to customers of price discrimination.

11. To maximize the aggregate profits of a multidivisional firm, it is not sufficient to ask each division to attempt to maximize its own profit. Explain why not and discuss the implications for corporate governance.

12. Explain how a multidivisional firm should set its transfer price when there is an imperfectly competitive external market for the intermediate product.

13. With reference to Case Study 13.5, explain how a multinational firm can use transfer pricing to minimize its tax exposure and outline the response of the tax authorities.

14. Explain how study of the phenomenon of price dispersion can provide insights into the competitive strcture of traditional and online retail markets.

Further reading

Armstrong, M. (1999) Price discrimination by a many-product firm, *Review of Economic Studies*, 66, 151–68.

Carlton, D. (1989) The theory and facts about how markets clear, in Schmalensee, R. and Willig, R. (eds) *Handbook of Industrial Organization*, Amsterdam: Elsevier.

Courty, P. and Pagliero, M. (2012) The impact of price discrimination on revenue: evidence from the concert industry, *Review of Economics and Statistics*, 94, 359–69.

Eccles, R. (1985) *The Transfer Pricing Problem*. Lexington, MA: D.C. Heath.

Fabiani, S., Loupias, C., Martins, F. and Sabbatini, R. (2007) *Pricing Decisions in the Euro Area: How Firms Set Prices and Why*. Oxford: Oxford University Press.

Gil, R. and Hartmann, W.R. (2009) Empirical analysis of metering price discrimination: evidence from concession sales at movie theaters, *Marketing Science*, 28, 1046–62.

Marx, L.M. and Shaffer, G. (2004) Opportunism and menus of two-part tariffs, *International Journal of Industrial Organization*, 22, 1399–414.

Nayle, T. (1984) Economic foundations of pricing, *Journal of Business*, 57, 23–39.

Phlips, L. (1983) *The Economics of Price Discrimination*. Cambridge: Cambridge University Press.

Stole, L. (2007) Price discrimination in competitive environments, in Armstrong, M. and Porter, R. (eds) *Handbook of Industrial Organization*, Vol. 3. Amsterdam: Elsevier.

Learning objectives

This chapter covers the following topics:

- English and Dutch auctions, first and second price sealed bid auctions
- the pure common value model and the independent private values model
- the winner's curse
- optimal bidding strategies
- the seller's optimal reserve price, risk aversion, asymmetric bidders and affiliated valuations
- experimental and field evidence on buyer and seller behaviour in auctions

Key terms

Affiliated valuations model
Ascending bid auction
Descending bid auction
Dutch auction
English auction
First price sealed bid auction
Independent private values model

Pure common value model
Reserve price
Revenue equivalence theorem
Second price sealed bid auction
Vickrey auction
Winner's curse

14.1 Introduction

Goods have been bought and sold through auctions throughout history. The Romans, for example, auctioned slaves and property looted from their foreign conquests. Auctions are still used today for a wide variety of transactions in the modern-day economy. Houses, cars, paintings and antiques are commonly sold by auction, while farmers often use auctions to trade livestock and other agricultural produce. Governments commonly sell the rights to drill for oil or gas within a particular tract of land or sea by auction. In many countries, large sums have been raised in recent years from the auction of licences to operate mobile phone services. Governments also use auctions to sell treasury bills and other government securities. Government procurement contracts require contractors to submit tenders, with the lowest tender winning the right to become the supplier. The expansion of the internet has created new opportunities for trading by auction. For example, a huge variety and volume of goods are now traded on a daily basis through the eBay website. Even your local department store conducts a certain type of auction each time it announces a sale, in which the prices of sale items are successively reduced until all such items have been sold.

An auction is a market mechanism for converting bids from market participants into decisions concerning the allocation of resources and prices, through a specific set of rules. In general terms, auction theory raises several issues that have already been encountered in previous chapters. Specifically, auction theory is concerned with price formation under conditions of uncertainty, asymmetric information and interdependence. Auctions can be characterized by the rules for the submission of bids, for determining the identity of the winning bidder, and for determining the price the winning bidder pays. Section 14.2 describes the four basic auction formats, which provide the cornerstone for the economic theory of auctions, and which (subject to certain possible variations or embellishments) describe most auctions in practice. In auction theory, the assumptions concerning the way in which bidders assess the value of the item under auction turns out to be a crucial ingredient. Two polar cases, known as the **pure common value model** and the **independent private values model**, are introduced in this section.

Section 14.3 develops the pure common value model, in which bidders form individual estimates of the value of an item that has the same intrinsic value to all of them. This section introduces the phenomenon of the **winner's curse**: an apparent tendency for winning bidders in auctions requiring the submission of sealed bids to systematically overvalue the item in question and consequently to overbid.

Section 14.4 considers optimal bidding strategies for all four basic auction formats, in the case where bidders form independent private valuations of the item under auction. A central result in auction theory, known as **revenue equivalence**, suggests that with the independent private values model, all four basic auction formats yield the same expected price to the seller.

Section 14.5 discusses a number of extensions to the basic theory covered in the two previous sections. These include the theory governing the seller's optimal choice of **reserve price**; risk aversion, which raises the possibility that in certain auctions bidders may bid more aggressively in order to improve their chances of winning; asymmetric bidders, who can be divided into different sub-groups with different average valuations of the item under auction; and the **affiliated valuations model**, in which bidders' valuations of the item under auction contain elements of both the pure common value and the independent private values models. Finally, Section 14.6 reviews some of the empirical evidence on buyer and seller behaviour in auctions. This review is subdivided into studies based on experimental evidence and those based on field evidence.

14.2 Auction formats and models of bidders' valuations

Section 14.2 introduces the four basic auction formats which provide the cornerstone for the economic theory of auctions. Also considered in this section are the assumptions that can be used to model the way in which bidders value the item under auction. Two polar cases, known as the pure common value model and the independent private values model, are considered. This section begins, however, with a brief description of the four basic auction formats.

- The **English auction**, also known as the **ascending bid auction**, involves the price being set initially at a very low level which many bidders would be prepared to pay, and then raised successively until a level is reached which only one bidder is willing to pay. The last remaining bidder secures the item at the final price and the auction stops. This type of auction can be conducted by having the seller call out the prices continuously, with individual bidders withdrawing when the price reaches a level they are unwilling to pay, until only one bidder remains. Alternatively, the bidders themselves might be required to call out their bids; or the bids might be submitted electronically with the highest current bid posted. The English auction is widely used to sell items such as paintings, antiques and (sometimes) houses and cars. Over the years, its dramatic potential has also made it the favourite auction format of numerous movie directors.

- The **Dutch auction**, also known as the **descending bid auction**, works in the opposite way. The price is set initially at a very high level which no bidder would be prepared to pay, and is then lowered successively until a level is reached which one bidder is prepared to pay. The first bidder who is prepared to match the current price secures the item at that price and the auction stops. The Dutch auction is used in a number of countries to sell agricultural produce, including tulips in the Netherlands (the source of the name Dutch auction).

- In the **first price sealed bid auction**, each bidder independently submits a single bid, without seeing the bids submitted by other bidders. The highest bidder secures the item and pays a price equal to their winning bid. The first price sealed bid auction has been used by governments to sell drilling rights for oil and gas, and the rights to extract minerals from state-owned land. Another example of this type of auction is the English Premier League's regular auctions of the live television broadcasting rights for Premier League football.

- The **second price sealed bid auction** is also sometimes known as a **Vickrey auction**, after the author of a seminal paper on auction theory (Vickrey, 1961). The bidding process works in the same manner as a first price sealed bid auction: each bidder independently and privately submits a single bid.

Again, the highest bidder secures the item, but pays a price equal to the second-highest submitted bid. This format has a number of interesting theoretical properties, but it has only occasionally been used in practice.

Asymmetric information is a key element of most theoretical models of auctions. First, the seller typically does not have perfect information concerning the distribution of bidders' valuations of the item being auctioned. Second, the bidders themselves do not have perfect information about each others' valuations. The simplest theoretical models of auctions are based on two alternative assumptions concerning the distribution of bidders' valuations.

- In the **pure common value model**, the item has a single, intrinsic value that is the same for all bidders. However, no single bidder knows what this true value is. On the basis of private information or signals that differ between bidders, each bidder makes an independent assessment or estimate of the item's true value. For example, in an auction for the drilling rights to an oilfield, there is a certain amount of oil under the ground which determines the intrinsic value of the rights, and this value might be considered identical by all oil firms. At the time the drilling rights are auctioned, no firm knows exactly how much oil is present, although each firm has made its own private assessment based on its own survey work. In this case, one bidder's private estimate of the value would be influenced by knowledge of the estimates of other bidders. For example, if firm A initially valued the rights at £100m, but subsequently discovered that nine other firms had each carried out a similar survey that valued the rights at less than £100m, firm A would probably conclude that its own survey was overoptimistic or inaccurate and would revise its estimate downwards.

- In the **independent private values model**, each bidder knows the true value of the item to themselves personally. However, personal valuations of the item differ between bidders and there is no single, intrinsic value that all bidders can agree on. For example, my valuation of a painting might depend solely upon my personal appreciation of the item, and anyone else's opinion might be completely irrelevant to me in forming my personal valuation.

The pure common values model and the independent private values model can usefully be interpreted as theoretical, polar extremes. In practice, elements of both models may be required in order to represent the actual distribution of bidders' preferences. In the first example cited above, the value of the drilling rights might not be the same for all oil firms. Firm A might possess some specific assets (physical assets, or specialized or experienced labour) that are productive only in certain geological conditions, and which make these particular drilling rights of greater value to firm A than to any other oil firm. In the second example, your personal valuation of a painting might depend partly on your own personal tastes, but it might also depend partly on other people's tastes, which determine how much prestige you gain by becoming the painting's owner, or how much cash you expect to realize if you subsequently decide to sell. In such cases, it may be necessary to use a third model known as the **affiliated valuations model**, which includes elements of both the pure common value model and the independent private values model (Milgrom and Weber, 1982). Although the full details of the affiliated valuations model are beyond the scope of this text, this model is considered briefly in Section 14.5.

14.3 The pure common value model and the winner's curse

This section examines some of the properties of auctions when there is a single, intrinsic value of the item being auctioned that is the same for all bidders, but unknown precisely to any individual bidder. As shown in Section 14.2, the auction of the drilling rights to a particular tract of land or sea provides a classic example of an auction that may conform to the pure common values model. A second example, which has been widely used in classroom or laboratory experiments, is as follows. Your lecturer brings a jar filled with penny coins into the classroom and allows each student to take a quick look at the jar, which is sufficient for the student to form an estimate of the number of coins but insufficient to count the number of coins precisely. The lecturer then auctions the jar. In this case, the jar has an intrinsic value (determined by the actual number of coins) which is unknown to any of the students but is the same for every student; and each student forms an imperfect estimate of this intrinsic value, which may turn out to be either too high or too low.

In a classic paper on auctions of oilfield drilling rights, Capen *et al.* (1971) identify a phenomenon known as the **winner's curse**, which appears to be a rather common feature of many auctions in which bidders' valuations conform to the pure common value model. In order to describe the winner's curse, the following assumptions are made:

■ The auction format is first price sealed bid. Only this auction format is considered in the current section. Detailed consideration is given to all four basic auction formats in the discussion of the independent private values model in Section 14.4; and in Section 14.5 some consideration is given to the other three auction formats in the case where bidders' valuations conform to the pure common value model.

■ Each bidder forms an unbiased private estimate of the true value of the item being auctioned. In other words, in any particular auction each bidder is equally likely to undervalue or overvalue the item, but if there were a large number of auctions no bidder would systematically overvalue or undervalue the items on average.

■ Each bidder submits a sealed bid that is strictly increasing relative to their own private estimate of the intrinsic value. This implies the bidder with the highest private estimate always submits the highest bid and this bidder always wins the auction.

Suppose, initially, all bidders submit bids equivalent to their own private estimates. Since these private estimates are equally likely to be above or below the true value, it is very likely that the winning bidder, with the highest private estimate, has overestimated the true value of the item. Therefore, the bidder with the highest private estimate wins the auction, having submitted a bid that is very likely to turn out to be higher than the true value of the item! Paradoxically, the winning bidder is very likely to turn out to be a loser, in the sense of having overpaid for the item. The winning bidder falls victim to the winner's curse. In their analysis of auctions for oil and gas drilling rights in the Gulf of Mexico during the 1950s and 1960s, Capen *et al.* note a consistent tendency for the winning oil firms to have overestimated the true values of the rights they were successful in securing.

> In recent years, several major companies have taken a rather careful look at their record and those of the industry in areas where sealed competitive bidding is the method of acquiring leases. The most notable of these areas, and perhaps the most interesting, is the Gulf of Mexico. Most analysts turn up with the rather shocking result that, while there seems to be a lot of oil and gas in the region, the industry is not making as much return on its investment as it intended.
>
> *(Capen* et al.*, 1971, p. 641)*

In experiments replicating the second example cited above, in which a jar containing an (unknown) number of penny coins is auctioned and sold to the highest bidder, a similar tendency is observed very frequently: the winning bid often exceeds the true value of the jar and the winning bidder consequently experiences the winner's curse. Experimental and field evidence on the winner's curse is reviewed in greater detail in Section 14.6.

The paradox of the winner's curse can also be described in the following terms. In the oil firms' example, if firm A's own private valuation of the drilling rights is the only information available to A, this private valuation represents A's best estimate of the true value of the rights. However, if A also has information concerning the private valuations of other firms, this information might well cause A to revise its estimate of the true value. For example, if A's private survey produces a valuation of £100m, but A subsequently discovers that nine other firms have all (independently) valued the rights at less than £100m, A might well infer that its own valuation of £100m is likely to be an overestimate. A's best estimate of the true value, conditional on the news that its own private valuation of £100m is the highest of 10 similar private valuations, is now considerably less than £100m. If A also discovers that the other nine valuations are all within the range £50m to £95m, A might perhaps revise its estimate downwards towards the middle of this range: this would produce a revised estimate of around £75m.

Therefore, firm A has two possible estimates of the true value of the rights on which it could base its sealed bid:

- A's original private estimate of the true value of the rights, unconditional on any information about the private estimates of the other bidders.

- A's revised estimate of the true value of the rights, conditional on A's private estimate being the highest private estimate of any bidder, and A's bid therefore being the winning bid.

At the time it submits its bid, firm A has only its own original estimate to go on, but if A bases its bid on this estimate, A is very likely to experience the winner's curse if A wins. In order to avoid the winner's curse, A's sealed bid should be based on a revised estimate, conditional on A's original estimate being the highest estimate. Since A only wins if A's bid does turn out to be the highest, and A's bid is irrelevant to A if some other bidder submits a higher bid, A's revised estimate of the true value should be made conditional on the assumption that A's original estimate will turn out to be the highest, and that A's bid will therefore turn out to be the winning bid.

Using mathematical notation, the situation can be described as follows. Let V represent the true value of the item that is being auctioned. V is unknown to any of the bidders, but each bidder obtains a signal, denoted S_i for bidder i. For simplicity it is assumed that S_i is drawn randomly from a uniform distribution with a minimum value of zero and a maximum value of $2V$. In other words, if a bidder is selected at random, this bidder's private signal is equally likely to take any value between zero and $2V$, and is therefore equally likely to provide an underestimate or an overestimate of V. Therefore, each bidder's signal is an unbiased estimate of V. This implies $E(V|S_i) = S_i$, where $E(V|S_i)$ denotes the expected value of V, conditional on i's signal but unconditional on any information about the signals obtained by other bidders.

To write bidder i's estimate of the true value of the item conditional on S_i being the highest signal obtained by any bidder, and i's bid therefore being the winning bid, the following result is useful:

$$E[S_{(1)}] = \underline{v} + [N/(N + 1)](\bar{v} - \underline{v})$$

where $S_{(1)}$ denotes the highest signal obtained by any bidder, $E[S_{(1)}]$ is the expected value of $S_{(1)}$, $\underline{v}$ and $\bar{v}$ are the minimum and maximum values (respectively) that any bidder's signal can take, and N is the number of bidders. The result is derived in Appendix 1. In this case, $\underline{v} = 0$ and $\bar{v} = 2V$, so $E[S_{(1)}] = 2VN/(N + 1)$.

Let $E[V|S_i = S_{(1)}]$ denote the expected value of V, conditional on S_i being the highest signal obtained by any bidder. If the true value of the item is V, on average S_i (if it is known to be the highest signal) should be $2VN/(N + 1)$. Rearranging:

$$E[V|S_i = S_{(1)}] = (N + 1)S_i/(2N)$$

Alternatively, $E[V|S_i = S_{(1)}] = d(N)S_i$, where $d(N) = (N + 1)/(2N)$ is the discount factor that should be applied to S_i in order to obtain an expected value for V conditional on i's signal being the highest signal, or $S_i = S_{(1)}$. As Table 14.1 shows, as N (the number of bidders) increases, $d(N)$ decreases. Therefore as N increases the size of the discount increases.

Note that if bidder i is the only bidder ($N = 1$), by definition bidder i has the highest signal, so $d(N) = 1$ (there is no discount). The larger the value of N, the greater is the likelihood that by being the highest signal, S_i represents an overestimate of V. Therefore, as N increases, $d(N)$ decreases and the size of the discount increases. When the number of bidders is very large, bidder i should apply a 50 per cent discount; in other words, i's valuation conditional on S_i being the highest signal obtained by any bidder is only 50 per cent of S_i.

Table 14.1 Relationship between N, the number of bidders, and $d(N)$

N	1	2	5	10	100	1,000
$d(N)$	1	0.75	0.6	0.55	0.505	0.5005

The preceding analysis suggests that in the pure common value model, to avoid the winner's curse bidder i's submitted bid should be based on $E[V|S_i = S_{(1)}]$. This is not quite the same as saying that bidder i's submitted bid should actually *be* $E[V|S_i = S_{(1)}]$. In fact, in a first price sealed bid auction it pays to submit a bid some distance below the bidder's opinion as to the true value of the item. Therefore, when formulating their submitted bid, bidder i should apply a further discount to $E[V|S_i = S_{(1)}]$. The reasons for doing so are examined in Section 14.4, in which the formulation of optimal bidding strategies for all four basic auction formats is examined, in the context of the independent private values model.

14.4 Optimal bidding strategies and revenue equivalence in the independent private values model

This section examines some of the properties of auctions when bidders form independent private valuations of the item being auctioned. Each bidder privately and independently forms an opinion of the value of the item and, even if one bidder's opinion as to the value of the item were to be revealed, this information would be completely irrelevant to other bidders when formulating their own private valuations. This section analyzes the optimal bidding strategies for an individual bidder in each of the four basic auction formats that were introduced in Section 14.2, in an independent private values setting. The discussion of optimal bidding strategies also illustrates an important result in auction theory, known as the revenue equivalence theorem.

Optimal bidding strategies

In order to determine a bidder's optimal bidding strategy in each of the four basic auction formats, it is assumed for simplicity that all bidders' private values of the item under auction are drawn randomly from a uniform distribution, with a minimum value of zero and a maximum value of one. In other words, if a bidder is selected at random, this bidder's private value is equally likely to take any value between the lowest possible value of any bidder (equal to zero) and the highest possible value (equal to one). This choice of minimum and maximum values of zero and one is purely a scaling decision, and does not affect the generality of the results derived below. The assumption that the values are distributed uniformly is a simplifying assumption, introduced in order to keep the mathematics as simple as possible. In fact, this assumption is not required for the treatment of the first two auction formats (English and second price sealed bid) examined below, but it is required for the treatment of the other two formats (first price sealed bid and Dutch). For these two formats a more general treatment would require the use of an arbitrary probability distribution for the bidders' private values; however, the mathematics involved is beyond the scope of this text.

One other assumption introduced at this stage is that the bidders are risk neutral. The meaning of risk neutrality, and the implications of relaxing this assumption, are discussed in Section 14.5. Under these assumptions, it is a simple task to determine the optimal bidding strategies for an individual bidder in two of the four auction formats: the English (ascending bid) auction and the second price sealed bid auction. The discussion begins by considering these two cases.

The English (ascending bid) auction

In an English auction, a bidder's optimal bidding strategy is to continue bidding for as long as the price is below their private value, and to withdraw as soon as the price *equals* or exceeds this private value. If another bidder is currently offering a price that is below your own private value, it is certainly worthwhile for you to enter a revised and higher bid (as long as this bid is also below your private value) for the following reasons:

■ If your revised bid is successful, you gain a rent equal to the difference between your private value and your winning bid.

■ If your revised bid is unsuccessful, you gain and lose nothing through having entered the revised bid.

Therefore, if another bidder is currently offering a price that is below your private value, you might possibly gain something, and you certainly cannot lose anything, by entering a revised bid. It is a trivial matter to show that if another bidder is currently offering a price that is above your private value, you can only lose and you cannot possibly gain by entering a revised bid.

The second price sealed bid auction

As shown in Section 14.2, according to the rules of a second price sealed bid auction, the bidder who submits the highest bid pays a price equivalent to the second-highest entered bid. In this case, a bidder's optimal bidding strategy is to enter a bid equivalent to his or her own private value. To see why this is necessarily the optimal strategy, consider the implications of raising or lowering the submitted bid slightly, in the region of this optimal bid.

■ Suppose you raise your submitted bid so it is now slightly above your private value. This only affects the outcome of the auction if your original bid (equal to your private value) was not the highest bid but your raised bid is the highest bid. In this case, by raising your bid you must have overtaken some other bid, which now becomes the second-highest. This bid determines the price you will now pay. But this price must be higher than your private value!

Therefore, you would not wish to be the winner under these circumstances. By raising your bid, you can only lose, you cannot possibly gain.

■ Suppose you lower your submitted bid so that it is now slightly below your private value. This only affects the outcome of the auction if your original bid (equal to your private value) was the highest bid, but your lower bid is not the highest bid. In this case, by lowering your bid you must have dropped below some other bid, which now becomes the highest. This rival bid determines the price you would have paid if you had bid your private value (because the rival bid would then have been the second highest). But this price must be lower than your private value! Therefore by lowering your bid you have forfeited an opportunity to buy the item for less than your private value. As before, by lowering your bid you can only lose, you cannot possibly gain.

In both an English auction and a second price sealed bid auction, it pays to tell the truth. In an English auction each bidder's best bidding strategy is to continue bidding up to his or her private value; and in a second price sealed bid auction the best strategy is to submit a bid equivalent to this private value. This strategy is optimal no matter what other bidders decide to do. In the terminology of game theory, it is a dominant strategy (see Section 7.6). When all bidders implement this dominant strategy, a dominant strategy equilibrium is achieved.

Furthermore, at the dominant strategy equilibrium, the outcomes of the English auction and the second price sealed bid auction are the same. The bidder with the highest private value of the item always wins, and always pays a price equal to the second-highest bidder's private value. At first sight this result may seem surprising: the rules of these two auction formats appear very different, so one might expect the outcomes to differ as well. However, if bidders behave rationally there is no difference between the outcomes of these two auction formats, which can be described as strategically equivalent.

The first price sealed bid auction

Does the conclusion for the two auction formats analyzed so far, that truth-telling (bidding in accordance with your private value) pays, extend to the first price sealed bid auction? The answer is no. In a first price sealed bid auction, it pays to submit a bid that is below your own private value. Figure 14.1 illustrates why this is so. For the purposes of constructing this diagram, bidder i has a private value of V_i, and in accordance with the assumptions made at the start of this section, it is assumed $0 \leq V_i \leq 1$. Assume bidder i is considering submitting a bid of B, where $0 \leq B \leq V_i$. It is never worthwhile to submit a bid of $B > V_i$, because, if this turns out to be the winning bid, the price exceeds bidder i's private value. Assume that for each bid in the range $0 \leq B \leq V_i$, a probability that B will turn out to be the winning bid, denoted $P(B)$, can be calculated. The factors that determine $P(B)$ are considered below. At this stage, however, $P(B)$ is taken as given. The following assumptions about $P(B)$ are uncontroversial:

■ $P(0) = 0$: a submitted bid of zero will always be beaten by at least one other bidder, so the probability that a bid of zero wins the auction is zero.

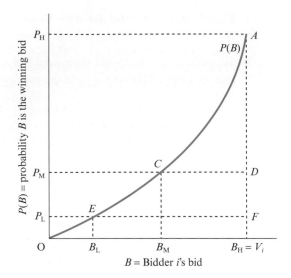

Figure 14.1 Bidding strategies: first price sealed bid auction (independent private values model)

- $P(B)$ is an increasing function of B: the higher the submitted bid, the higher the probability that the bid wins the auction.

- $P(B)$ is a decreasing function of N, the number of bidders. On the assumptions made so far, all bids lie somewhere in the range zero to one. Assume for example you intend to submit a bid of 0.8. If there is only one other bidder, the probability that this rival bid is below 0.8 and you win the auction is perhaps quite high. If there are two other bidders, the probability that *both* rival bids are below 0.8 is somewhat lower, but still reasonably high. But if there are 100 or 1,000 other bidders, the probability that these rival bids are *all* below 0.8 is extremely small.

In Figure 14.1, the curve OA represents the relationship between B and $P(B)$, drawn on the assumption that N, the number of bidders, is fixed. Three possible bids are shown on the horizontal axis: $B_H = V_i$ (high), B_M (medium) and B_L (low).

- Suppose bidder i submits the high bid of B_H, equal to their private value. The probability that B_H turns out to be the winning bid is $P(B_H)$. The expected value of the payment is $B_H \times P(B_H) = OP_HAB_H$ in Figure 14.1, and the expected value of the acquisition is $V_i \times P(B_H) = OP_HAB_H$. Therefore, if bidder i submits the high bid of B_H, the expected rent is zero, because the expected values of the payment and the acquisition are the same.

- Suppose bidder i submits the medium bid of B_M. The probability that B_M turns out to be the winning bid is $P(B_M) < P(B_H)$. The expected value of the payment is $B_M \times P(B_M) = OP_MCB_M$, and the expected value of the acquisition is $V_i \times P(B_M) = OP_MDB_H$. Therefore, if bidder i submits the medium bid of B_M, the expected rent is positive and equal to the area B_MCDB_H.

■ Finally, suppose bidder i submits the low bid of B_L. The probability that B_L turns out to be the winning bid is $P(B_L) < P(B_M) < P(B_H)$. The expected value of the payment is $B_L \times P(B_L) = OP_LEB_L$, and the expected value of the acquisition is $V_i \times P(B_L) = OP_LFB_H$. Therefore, if bidder i submits the low bid of B_L, the expected rent is positive and equal to the area B_LEFB_H.

By visual inspection of Figure 14.1, it is apparent that $B_MCDB_H > B_LEFB_H$. Therefore, in this case, it is better to submit the medium bid of B_M than the low bid of B_L. However, both B_M and B_L are better options than submitting the high bid $B_H = V_i$ (although as B_L approaches zero, the expected rent also approaches zero). By reducing the submitted bid below $B_H = V_i$, bidder i gains by committing to pay a lower price, but also loses by accepting a lower probability of winning the auction. Choosing the optimal bid involves selecting the optimal trade-off between these two effects.

The analysis in Figure 14.1 is only partial, because as yet the determination of the curve OA has not been explained. In fact, the position of this curve depends on the bidding strategies of the other bidders. Clearly, the probability that any given bid submitted by bidder i turns out to be the winning bid depends not only on the number of other bidders, but also on whether the others are bidding high (close to their own private values) or low (well below their own private values). In other words, each bidder faces a situation of interdependence. In such a situation, there is a Nash equilibrium solution to the auction. Each bidder should submit the bid that maximizes their expected rent, based on the conjectural variation assumption (which turns out to be correct at the equilibrium) that all other bidders also submit the bids that maximize their expected rents.

Under the assumptions used to develop the model to this point (uniformly distributed independent private values, and risk neutrality), it can be shown that at the Nash equilibrium the optimal bidding strategy for each bidder is to submit a bid equal to $(N - 1)/N$ *times* the bidder's own private value, where N is the number of bidders. In other words, the optimal bid of bidder i is:

$$B_i^* = b^* V_i$$

where $b^* = (N - 1)/N$ and $V_i = $ bidder i's private value. Accordingly, when there are $N = 2$ bidders, $b^* = (N - 1)/N = 1/2$, so each bidder submits a bid equivalent to one-half of their private value. When there are $N = 3$ bidders, $b^* = (N - 1)/N = 2/3$, so each bidder submits a bid equivalent to two-thirds of their private value. When there are $N = 100$ bidders, $b^* = (N - 1)/N = 99/100$, so each bidder submits a bid equivalent to 99 per cent of their private value. As the number of bidders increases, the optimal bid approaches the bidder's private value. The mathematical derivation of this result is examined in Appendix 1.

The Dutch (descending bid) auction

In a Dutch auction, a bidder's optimal bidding strategy is to wait until the price has fallen a certain amount below their private value, and then (assuming no other bidder has already done so) to call out what will instantly become the winning bid.

Why is this the optimum bidding strategy? In a Dutch auction, there is clearly no point in bidding while the price is higher than your private value, because if you do so you pay more than the item is worth to you. There is also no point in bidding when the price *equals* your private value, because if you do so you pay exactly what the item is worth to you, so you gain nothing. But if you allow the price to drop a little further: *either* another bidder will enter a bid before you, in which case you have not lost anything; *or* you will still be the first to bid, in which case you obtain the item for a price that is lower than your private value and you gain a positive rent. So, by allowing the price to drop, you can only gain and you cannot possibly lose.

How far below your private value should you allow the price to drop before entering your bid? The answer turns out to be the same as in the case of the first price sealed bid auction. Your bidding strategy should maximize your expected rent, based on the conjectural variation assumption that all other bidders' strategies also maximize their expected rents. And it turns out that the bidding strategy which satisfies this condition, and produces a Nash equilibrium, is exactly the same as in the case of the first price sealed bid auction. Under the previous assumptions (uniformly distributed independent private values and risk neutrality), bidder i should bid when the price reaches $B_i^* = b^* V_i$, where $b^* = (N-1)/N$, and $V_i =$ bidder i's private value, as before.

At the Nash equilibrium, the outcomes of the first price sealed bid auction and the Dutch auction are always the same. The bidder with the highest private value of the item always wins and always pays a price equal to $(N-1)/N$ *times* their own private value. Again, this result may seem quite surprising, because the rules of these two auction formats appear to be very different. However, in both cases the information available to bidders when they submit their bids is identical: no bidder learns anything about other bidders' willingness to pay before submitting his or her own bid. If bidders behave rationally, there is no difference between the outcomes of these two auction formats. Therefore, the first price sealed bid auction and the Dutch auction are said to be strategically equivalent.

The revenue equivalence theorem

The final stage in the analysis of the four basic auction formats (based on assumptions of uniformly distributed independent private values and risk neutrality) involves a comparison of the seller's expected proceeds in each case. This answers a very important question for the seller: which auction format is expected to yield the highest price; or, in other words, which auction format should the seller select? And the answer based on the preceding analysis, which again may seem surprising, is that it does not matter! All four auction formats are expected to yield exactly the same price to the seller on average. This powerful result in auction theory is known as the **revenue equivalence theorem**. The intuition is as follows:

■ In an English auction, bidders continue to participate until the price reaches their own private values. The auction stops when the bidder with the second-highest value drops out and, at this point, the price payable by the winning bidder is determined. Therefore, the seller's expected price is the expected value or expectation of the second-highest private value.

■ In a second price sealed bid auction, each bidder submits a bid equivalent to their own private value. Under the second price principle, the winning bidder therefore pays a price equivalent to the second-highest private value.

■ In a first price sealed bid auction, each bidder submits a bid some distance below their private value. The seller's expected price is the expected value of the highest private value *minus* the amount by which this bidder shades their bid. If all bidders behave rationally when deciding how far to shade their bids, the seller's expected price turns out to be the expectation of the second-highest private value.

■ In a Dutch auction, each bidder plans to call out when the price has fallen some distance below his private value. The seller's expected price is the expected value of the highest private value *minus* the further amount by which this bidder allows the price to drop before calling out. Again, the seller's expected price turns out to be the expectation of the second-highest private value.

When the bidders' private values are distributed randomly in the range zero to one, a general formula for the average price each of the four auction formats is expected to yield to the seller is $(N - 1)/(N + 1)$, where N is the number of bidders, as before. The mathematical derivation of this result is examined in Appendix 1. When there are $N = 2$ bidders, on average the seller expects to receive a price of $1/3 = 0.33$. When there are $N = 3$ bidders, the expected price is $2/4 = 0.5$. With $N = 4$ bidders the expected price is 0.6; with $N = 10$ the expected price is 0.82; and with $N = 100$ the expected price is 0.98. As the number of bidders increases, two factors tend to work in the seller's favour. First, in a second price sealed bid auction and in a Dutch auction, increased competition between bidders results in higher bids being entered. Second, in all four auction formats, the probability increases that some bidders will have private values very close to the maximum value of one. The higher the bidder's private value, the higher the submitted bid in all four auction cases.

Table 14.2 summarizes the results of the analysis of optimal bidding strategies and revenue equivalence for the independent private values model. It is important to remember that the revenue equivalence theorem relies heavily on the independent private values assumption. As will be shown in Section 14.5, for example, if the pure common value model applies, an English auction produces a higher expected price than a first price sealed bid auction (Milgrom and Weber, 1982).

Evidence concerning the empirical validity of the revenue equivalence theorem is rather limited. However, Lucking-Reiley (1999) describes an analysis of the secondary market for collectable cards. Cards were traded over the internet using all four basic auction formats (English, first price sealed bid, second price sealed bid and Dutch). The revenues obtained using the Dutch auction format were significantly higher than those obtained using the first price sealed bid

Table 14.2 Optimal bidding strategies and revenue equivalence for the independent private values model

Auction format	Optimal bidding strategy	Price paid by winning bidder	Seller's expected proceeds
English (ascending bid)	Be prepared to remain in the bidding until price *equals* your private value	Second-highest private value, denoted $V_{(2)}$	$E[V_{(2)}] = \dfrac{N-1}{N+1}$
Second price sealed bid	Submitted bid *equals* your private value	Second-highest private value, $V_{(2)}$	$E[V_{(2)}] = \dfrac{N-1}{N+1}$
First price sealed bid	Submitted bid *equals* $[(N-1)/N]$ *times* your private value	$[(N-1)/N]$ *times* winning bidder's private value $= [(N-1)/N]V_{(1)}$ where $V_{(1)}$ denotes the highest private value	$\left(\dfrac{N-1}{N}\right)E[V_{(1)}]$ $= \left(\dfrac{N-1}{N}\right) \times \left(\dfrac{N}{N+1}\right) = \dfrac{N-1}{N+1}$
Dutch (descending bid)	Be prepared to wait and bid when price *equals* $[(N-1)/N]$ *times* your private value	$[(N-1)/N]$ times winning bidder's private value $= [(N-1)/N]V_{(1)}$	$\dfrac{N-1}{N+1}$ (as above)

format, even though these two formats are strategically equivalent. However, revenues obtained using the English auction format were not significantly higher than those obtained in second price sealed bid auctions.

14.5 Extensions and additional topics in auction theory

The seller's optimal auction design, and the reserve price

The revenue equivalence theorem demonstrates that under the assumptions adopted in Section 14.4, all four of the basic auction formats yield the same expected price to the seller in the independent private values model. Therefore the choice between the four formats should be a matter of indifference to the seller. However, this does not mean that any (or all) of these four formats are optimal from the seller's perspective, in the sense of producing the highest expected proceeds under any possible set of rules the seller could devise.

In fact, there is one very obvious reason why these auction rules might be sub-optimal from the seller's perspective. If the item being sold has a positive private value to the seller, all four basic auction formats (as described so far) leave open the possibility that the seller ends up selling the item at a price below the seller's own private value. If the seller's private value is V_0 (assuming $0 \leq V_0 \leq 1$, as before) and $V_0 > V_{(1)}$ (where $V_{(1)}$ is the private value of the bidder with the highest private value, as before), the seller's proceeds are certainly below V_0 in all four auction formats, because no bidder ever bids more than his own private value. Even if $V_{(1)} > V_0$ but $V_0 > V_{(2)}$, in an English auction the seller's proceeds are below V_0, because the bidder with the second-highest private value drops out when the bidding reaches $V_{(2)}$. In a second price sealed bid auction the seller's proceeds are below V_0, because the bidder with $V_{(1)}$ pays a price of $V_{(2)}$. In a first price sealed bid auction or a Dutch auction, if $V_{(1)} > V_0 > V_{(2)}$ the seller's proceeds are below V_0 if the submitted bid of the bidder with $V_{(1)}$ is below V_0.

This discussion suggests the seller can always increase his expected proceeds by specifying a **reserve price**, and introducing a rule that the item is not sold if the price payable by the winning bidder does not at least match (or exceed) the reserve price. Suppose, initially, the seller sets a reserve price, denoted r, equivalent to their own private value, so $r = V_0$. (In fact, as will be shown below, the seller can do better than this by setting $r > V_0$.) In comparison with the case where there is no reserve price at all, setting $r = V_0$ can sometimes increase and can never reduce the seller's proceeds. Suppose the price paid by the winning bidder in the absence of the reserve price would have been below $r = V_0$. With the reserve price imposed, *either* the winning bidder pays a higher price of r, *or* the seller retains the item which is worth V_0 to the seller. Either way the seller is better off. Suppose instead the price paid by the winning bidder in the absence of the reserve price would have been above $r = V_0$. In this case the existence of the reserve price becomes irrelevant and the outcome is unchanged. Therefore in this case the seller is no worse off.

It can be shown mathematically that it is optimal for the seller to set a reserve price that is higher than their own private value, so $r > V_0$. It is interesting to note that this leaves open the possibility of an inefficient allocation of resources: if $r > V_{(1)} > V_0$ the seller retains the item even though there is a bidder who values the item more highly than the seller. However, as in the standard case of monopoly, an inefficient allocation of resources can be consistent with the maximization of the seller's (or monopolist's) private proceeds (or profit).

What reserve price is optimal from the seller's perspective? As the seller increases the reserve price slightly within the region $r > V_0$, there is a trade-off, which can be illustrated simply in the case of an English auction. Suppose r is already above V_0, and the seller is considering a small increase in the reserve price from r to $r + \Delta r$.

- If $V_{(1)} > r + \Delta r > r > V_0$, the price paid by the winning bidder increases by Δr. The item is still sold and seller's rent increases from $r - V_0$ to $r + \Delta r - V_0$.

- If $r + \Delta r > V_{(1)} > r > V_0$, the bidder with the highest value, who would have paid the old reserve price of r, drops out of the bidding before the new reserve price of $r + \Delta r$ is reached. The item is no longer sold and the seller loses out on a rent of $r - V_0$.

The optimal reserve price is the one that maximizes this trade-off from the seller's perspective. In the case where all private values are distributed uniformly within the range zero to one, the formula for the optimal reserve price is simple: the seller should set $r = (1 + V_0)/2$. The mathematical derivation of this result for the case of $N = 2$ bidders is shown in Appendix 1. Accordingly, even if the item has no value to the seller, the reserve price should be set at $r = 1/2$; if the seller's private value is $V_0 = 1/2$, the reserve price should be set at $r = 3/4$; if $V_0 = 0.8$, $r = 0.9$; if $V_0 = 0.9$, $r = 0.95$; and so on. It is interesting to note, and perhaps counterintuitive, that under these conditions the optimal reserve price does not depend at all on the number of bidders.

Risk averse bidders

The analysis in Section 14.4 is based on an assumption that the bidders in the auction are indifferent to risk or are risk neutral. From the bidder's perspective, the outcomes of all of the auctions examined in this chapter are binary: either the bidder wins the auction and gains some rent; or the bidder fails to win the auction and gains and loses nothing. Consider the following three auctions:

- Auction A1, in which the bidder is certain to win the auction and by doing so gains a rent of +5.

- Auction A2, in which the bidder has a probability of 0.5 of winning the auction and gains a rent of +10 if they do win.

- Auction A3, in which the bidder has a probability of 0.25 of winning the auction and gains a rent of +20 if they do win.

In A2 and A3, if the bidder fails to win the auction, they gain zero rent. The expected rent (calculated by multiplying the rent by the probability of winning) is the same in all three cases: $5 \times 1 = 10 \times 0.5 = 20 \times 0.25 = +5$. A risk-neutral bidder is indifferent between these three auctions, but a risk-averse bidder prefers A1 to A2 and A2 to A3. With A1 there is zero risk, because the bidder is certain to gain a rent of +5. A2 is more risky than A1, because the certain rent of +5 is replaced by possible rents of either +10 or 0. And A3 is riskier still, because the variance or spread in the distribution of possible outcomes is even larger: in A2 the possible outcomes are +10 or 0 but in A3 the possible outcomes are +20 or 0. This implies a risk-averse bidder would be prepared to trade a reduction in the rent gained from winning the auction for an increase in the probability of winning. If a risk-averse bidder prefers A2 to A3, for example, the same bidder might perhaps be indifferent between A2′ and A3, where A2′ also offers a probability of 0.5 of winning, but a rent of only +8 rather than +10 if the bidder does win. The expected rent is lower in A2′ than in A3, but the probability of winning is higher, which implies there is less risk.

How does risk aversion affect the optimal bidding strategies considered in Section 14.4? The answer to this question is straightforward in the cases of the English and Dutch auctions.

- In an English auction, risk aversion makes no difference to the optimal bidding strategy. The only decision the bidder has to make at each stage of the bidding is whether to remain in the bidding or drop out. By remaining, the bidder retains a chance of gaining a rent for as long as the price is below their private value but, by dropping out, the bidder is immediately certain that the rent will be zero. Therefore, as before, the bidder remains in the bidding until the price reaches their private value and then withdraws.

- In a Dutch auction, in contrast, risk aversion does affect the optimal bidding strategy. As soon as the price has fallen below the bidder's private value, and as it continues to fall further, the bidder has to trade the risk that someone else will call out first (so the opportunity of obtaining the item at a price below the bidder's private value is lost) against the possible benefit of allowing the price to fall a little further (the possibility of obtaining the item even more cheaply). From the previous discussion, it follows that a risk-averse bidder will adopt a more cautious attitude to this trade-off than a risk-neutral bidder. In other words, in a Dutch auction a risk averse bidder will call out earlier. The risk-averse bidder is prepared to trade a reduction in the rent he gains by winning the auction for a higher probability of winning.

Summarizing, risk aversion makes no difference to bidders' behaviour in an English auction, but it causes bidders to bid more aggressively (in other words, higher) in a Dutch auction. Therefore, the revenue equivalence theorem breaks down if bidders are risk averse: a Dutch auction yields a higher expected price to the seller than an English auction.

For sealed bid auctions the logic is similar:

- In a second price sealed bid auction (strategically equivalent to an English auction), risk-averse bidders submit bids equivalent to their private values. Therefore, a second price sealed bid auction yields the same expected price to the seller, regardless of whether bidders are risk neutral or risk averse.

- In a first price sealed bid auction (strategically equivalent to a Dutch auction) risk-averse bidders tend to bid closer to their private values than risk-neutral bidders. In other words, risk-averse bidders bid more aggressively (higher) than risk-neutral bidders.

Therefore, with risk-averse bidders, a first price sealed bid auction yields a higher expected price to the seller than a second price sealed bid auction; and, again, revenue equivalence breaks down. This means the seller is no longer indifferent between the four basic auction formats. With risk-averse bidders, the seller should select a Dutch auction or a first price sealed bid auction in preference to an English auction or a second price sealed bid auction.

Asymmetric bidders

In some auctions where bidders have independent private values, it may be necessary to relax the assumption that all bidders' private values are drawn from an identical probability distribution. It might be the case that bidders can be split into two (or more) groups, with members of one group systematically tending to value the item more highly than members of the other group. For example, bidders for a work of art might divide into dealers and private collectors. All dealers' valuations might be drawn from one specific probability distribution, and all collectors' valuations might be drawn from another distribution.

With asymmetric bidders, the English auction (and the second price sealed bid auction) operates in the same way as in Section 14.4. In the English auction, the second-last bidder withdraws when the bidding reaches the second-highest private value across both groups. However, the existence of asymmetric bidders complicates the analysis of the first price sealed bid auction (and the Dutch auction). In a first price sealed bid auction the bidder submits a bid below their private value. How far below depends on the optimal trade-off between the increased rent if the submitted bid still wins and the reduced probability of winning. With asymmetric bidders, however, bidders from the two groups will tend to form different assessments of this trade-off. Suppose, for example, there are four bidders in total: two dealers and two collectors. Suppose also that dealers tend to value the item more highly on average than collectors and all bidders are aware of this fact.

■ Each collector knows he is competing against two dealers and one other collector. The collector perceives the competition he faces to be quite fierce: to win the auction, he needs to outbid two dealers (who are both likely to value the item more highly than he does) and one other collector. To have any realistic chance of winning, the collector feels he must bid aggressively; in other words, he submits a bid close to his own private value.

■ Each dealer knows he is competing against one other dealer and two collectors. The dealer does not perceive the competition to be very fierce: to win the auction, he only needs to outbid one other dealer and the two collectors (who are both likely to value the item less highly than he does). The dealer feels he can afford to bid conservatively; in other words, he submits a bid that is some considerable amount below his own private value.

In this situation, it is possible that the winning bidder turns out not to be the bidder with the highest private value. Suppose dealer 1 has a higher private value than collector A, but collector A ends up submitting a higher bid than dealer 1 for the reasons outlined above. Then collector A wins the auction, despite not having the highest private value. The fact that this outcome has a non-zero probability invalidates the revenue equivalence theorem in the case of asymmetric bidders: the first price sealed bid auction (or the Dutch auction) generally yields an expected price different from that of the English auction (or the second price sealed bid auction). Which auction format yields the higher expected price depends on the precise nature of the two distributions of private values. Furthermore, the fact that the bidder with the highest private value may not always win the auction implies the first price sealed bid auction with asymmetric bidders is allocatively inefficient.

McAfee and McMillan (1987) show that the theory of optimal auction design in the case of asymmetric bidders can, in some cases, explain or justify (on strictly economic criteria) the practice whereby local government departments give preferential treatment to local suppliers for the award of procurement contracts. Suppose non-local suppliers have a cost advantage over local suppliers. Then the department might find it optimal to allow a local price preference of (say) 5 per cent; in other words, the lowest local tender wins the contract provided it is not more than 5 per cent higher than the lowest non-local tender. At any given price, the contract is worth more to a non-local supplier than it is to a local supplier, due to the former's cost advantage. The price preference policy increases the degree of competition perceived by the non-local supplier, encouraging the latter to bid more aggressively (tender more cheaply) in the hope that it might still win the contract. This tends to operate in the local government department's interest, by lowering the price it expects to pay.

Affiliated valuations and the winner's curse revisited

In the independent private values model, the individual bidders' private values of the item are completely unrelated: one bidder's opinion of the value of the item is completely irrelevant to other bidders in forming their valuations. In contrast, in the pure common value model, in which bidders independently estimate a single true value of the item that is the same for all of them, each bidder's opinion is highly relevant to other bidders. If a bidder could collect information about other bidders' valuations, he could assess the true value of the item more accurately.

As shown in Section 14.2, the independent private values model and the pure common value model are theoretical extremes, and in many cases bidders' actual valuations of an item may contain elements of both models. Section 14.2 cited the example of a painting, for which a bidder's personal valuation depends partly on their personal tastes, and partly on other people's tastes, which influence the resale value or the prestige the bidder obtains by becoming the owner. Broadly speaking, bidders are said to have affiliated valuations if the revelation that one bidder perceives the value of the item to be high would cause other bidders to increase their assessments of the value of the same item.

When bidders' valuations are affiliated, bidders tend to bid more aggressively in an English auction than they do in the other three basic auction formats. This statement is true both in the special case of the pure common value model and in the more general case of affiliated valuations. Therefore the English auction yields a higher expected price to the seller than the other three basic auction formats. This is because the bidders who remain in the bidding as an English auction progresses can observe the fact that other bidders have also remained in the bidding and can, therefore, infer that these other bidders' valuations of the item are at least as high as the current price. The acquisition of this information lessens the effect of the winner's curse. The bidder who can observe that other bidders are still interested at the current price does not have to form such a cautious estimate of the item's true value (conditional on being the winning bidder) as the bidder in the first price sealed bid auction, whose bid effectively is submitted in a 'blind' condition.

When bidders' valuations are affiliated (including the special case of the pure common value model) revenue equivalence breaks down. The seller should use an English auction in preference to any of the other three auction formats, because an English auction yields the highest expected price. It can also be shown that with affiliated valuations, a second price sealed bid auction yields the seller a higher expected price than either a first price sealed bid auction or a Dutch auction, both of which yield the same expected price (Milgrom and Weber, 1982; McAfee and McMillan, 1987).

Finally, when bidders' valuations are affiliated (including the pure common value model), the seller's optimal reserve price depends on the auction format and on the number of bidders. This also follows from the fact that in the affiliated valuations case, any bidder's valuation of the item conditional on being the winning bidder depends on the auction format and on the number of bidders. This result is in contrast to the equivalent result for the independent private values model (see Section 14.2), in which the optimal reserve price is the same for all four auction formats, and is independent of the number of bidders (Klemperer, 2002a,b).

14.6   Empirical evidence

Much of the empirical research into auctions examines cases that approximate to the pure common value model, where the true value of the item is the same for all bidders, but this value is not known to any bidder with certainty. Several studies have considered how auctions should be designed to maximize the price received by the seller. From the seller's perspective, it is important to design the auction in such as way as to maximize competition among bidders; minimize the possibility of collusion among bidders; and minimize the tendency for bidders to reduce their submitted bids in an effort to avoid falling victim to the winner's curse. Case Study 14.1 describes the auction of licences to operate third generation (3G) mobile telephone services in the UK in 2000. This section provides a selective review of empirical studies of auctions. Extended reviews can be found in McAfee and McMillan (1987), Smith (1989), Klemperer (1999, 2004), Kagel and Levin (2002) and Milgrom (2004).

Experimental evidence

Auction theory lends itself to empirical scrutiny using experimental methods, which allow the researcher the opportunity to observe buyer and seller behaviour under controlled conditions (Plott, 1989). This sub-section describes some representative examples. Bazerman and Samuelson (1983) report tests for the existence of a winner's curse that were conducted using 12 classes of postgraduate students at Boston University. Students were asked to submit sealed bids for four jars of objects containing either coins or paperclips. The true value of each jar (based on retail prices in the case of jars containing paperclips) was $8. Across 48 auctions, the average submitted bid was $5.13, but the average winning bid was $10.01. Therefore, the winning bidders fell victim to the winner's curse, realizing an average loss of $2.01.

Kagel and Levin (1986) conducted experiments in which students participate in a sequence of first price sealed bid auctions. The students are each given $10 accounts, with winning bidders' balances adjusted for their expenditure and the values of any items acquired. Losing bidders' balances remain unchanged, with no monies added or subtracted. Before submitting bids, the students were informed of a minimum and maximum possible value of each item for sale. Participants were allowed to bid until the balance in their account reached zero. Outcomes are compared with the predictions of a theoretical model that assumes risk neutrality and rational bidding. In auctions with small numbers of bidders, there was a tendency for profits to be realized on average: in auctions with three or four bidders, for example, the average profit was just over $4 per auction. Losses were realized on average in auctions with more than about six bidders. In contrast, the theoretical model predicts average profits of $7.48 and $4.82 at the Nash equilibrium, for small and large groups of bidders, respectively.

The auction of the UK 3G mobile telephone spectrum licences

The sale by auction of spectrum licences to operate third generation (3G) mobile telephone services in the UK, completed in April 2000, raised more than £22.4bn, equivalent to around 2.5 per cent of GNP. 3G technology provides mobile phone users with high-speed internet access. When the earlier second generation (2G) licences were sold, telecom firms were required to submit business plans detailing costs and timescales for the roll-out of services. Each licence was sold for as little as £40,000, plus an annual licence fee. By 2000–1 the total annual 2G licence fee had risen to about 1 per cent of the rental value implied by the 3G auction prices. Objectives which informed the design of the 3G auctions, both in the UK and elsewhere in Europe, included achieving an efficient allocation of the spectrum, promoting competition, realizing the full economic value of the licences, and enabling UK or European operators to play a leading role in the development of new technology in telecommunications (Binmore and Klemperer, 2002).

Auction design features

There is extensive evidence that incumbents are more likely to win auctions for licences in cases where incumbents have incurred sunk cost investment expenditure in the past. This was likely in the case of incumbent 2G licence holders, who had more to lose in the 3G auction than entrants (Klemperer, 2004). Furthermore, the incumbents were likely to enjoy absolute cost advantages over entrants, derived from their existing 2G infrastructure (Binmore and Klemperer, 2002). Therefore the UK government anticipated (correctly, as it turned out) that the four existing 2G licence holders would submit winning bids for 3G licences. To encourage competition from new bidders, it was decided to grant a fifth licence, guaranteeing there would be at least one successful bid from an entrant.

The five 3G licences that were auctioned (labelled A to E) were variable in size: licences A and B were both significantly larger than licences C, D and E. To give maximum opportunity to entrants, none of the four incumbents was permitted to bid for the largest licence A. The auction design involved multiple ascending bids, with full disclosure of the present state of the bidding between each bidding round. In the first round, each bidder submits a bid for one of the five licences. In subsequent rounds, any bidder who is not currently the top bidder for one of the five licences must raise one of the current top bids by at least the minimum bid increment, or withdraw. The process continues until only five bidders remain. These bidders obtain the licence for which they are the current top bidder, at their current bid price.

The design of the 3G bidding process offered several advantages from the UK government's perspective. Its simultaneous nature ensured that bidding competition would spill over from one licence to another. As in an English auction, each bidder's optimal bidding strategy was relatively simple to determine: bidders should stay in the bidding until the current prices of all licences exceed the bidder's own private valuations. And as in an English auction, publication of current bids while bidding was underway would tend to mitigate the effect of the winner's curse, enabling each bidder to see that other bidders are still involved in the bidding at the current price. The outcome of the auction should be efficient, in the sense that at the final prices no reallocation of licences among bidders could increase the rent of any bidder. Finally, because this was the first auction of its kind, the designers were confident that bidders lacked the experience to collude effectively.

Participants in the auction were TIW, Vodafone, BT, Deutsche Telecom, Orange, NTL, France Telecom, Telefonica, Worldcom, Nomura, Sonera, Global Crossing and Eircom. The bidding process took place over a six-week period from March to April 2000, and lasted for 150 rounds. The entrant TIW took licence A at a price of £4.4bn. The incumbent Vodaphone secured licence B for £6bn. The other successful incumbent bidders were BT, Deutsche Telecom and Orange, who each paid just over £4bn for the other three licences.

Other European 3G auctions

Perhaps surprisingly, the successful design of the UK auction appears to have been ignored when similar auctions were held in several other European countries (Klemperer, 2002a,b). For example, in the Netherlands five licences were auctioned to an industry comprising five dominant incumbent firms. This design feature appears to have discouraged firms other than the five incumbents from bidding, and consequently the revenue raised from the auction was disappointing. The Italian government threatened to postpone the auction and withdraw licences if no new bidders were forthcoming. In the event only one nominal bid was received from a non-incumbent, and this firm withdrew from the bidding at an early stage, raising suspicions of collusion. Eventually five licences were awarded to five incumbents, and the revenues raised were lower than expected. In Switzerland, joint bids were invited for four licences. Four relatively modest joint bids were duly submitted, with the revenues only slightly higher than the government's reserve prices. Denmark had a more successful experience. A sealed bid design was adopted, so as to minimize opportunities for collusion between bidders, and encourage bids from entrants. A new entrant displaced an incumbent to secure one of the five licences, and the total revenue was higher than expected (Klemperer, 2002b).

Was there a winner's curse?

Cable *et al.* (2002) use share price data for the successful and unsuccessful bidders in the UK 3G licence auction to assess the effect of the announcement of the outcome of the auction on the share prices or market values of the companies involved. Event-study methodology examines movements in company share prices immediately before and after some event that is expected to influence the stock market valuation of the companies involved, controlling for the company's typical response to any general stock market movement that may have occurred on the day of the event. This methodology is applied to the share price data of the winning and losing bidders, around the time of the announcement of the outcome of the auction in April 2000. One winning bidder, Orange, was excluded from the analysis due to several changes of ownership during the estimation and event periods. By the time of the auction Orange was owned by Vodaphone, which submitted a separate winning bid, thereby contravening a rule preventing ownership of more than one licence. Vodaphone was subsequently required to divest itself of Orange.

On the first trading day following the announcement, the shares of three of the successful bidders (BT, TIW, Vodaphone) increased in value, while Deutsche Telekom (One2One) declined in value. Several of the losing bidders (NTL, Worldcom, Nomura and Sonera) increased in value but a number of others (France Telecom, Telefonica, Global Crossing and Eircom) declined in value. Overall, the pattern was rather inconsistent. Over a 30-day period following the announcement, of the winning bidders only Vodafone increased in value. Among the losing firms, there was again little consistent pattern in the change in the share price over the same 30-day period.

To assess whether the successful bidders were subject to the winner's curse, cumulative returns on the combined values of portfolios of winning and losing bidders are calculated over the rest of the calendar year following the announcement of the auction result. Over a 30-day period following the announcement, the portfolio of losing firms recorded a 1 per cent loss, while the portfolio of winning firms recorded a 7 per cent loss. Subsequently, however, the performance of the two portfolios converged, and there was no lasting difference in performance. Overall, there is little systematic evidence of any winner's curse.

> There is no evidence that the outcome of the auction was anything but efficient and, further, no case for easing the regulatory stance in the industry on the grounds that the successful licence bidders paid too much.
>
> *(Cable* et al., *2002, p. 459)*

Between 2000 and 2003 most telecom firms experienced large share-price reductions. This was a global phenomenon, which affected the winners and losers in the UK's 3G auction in equal measure. With the benefit of hindsight, it seems clear that winning bidders paid far more for the licences in 2000 than they would have paid two or three years later. The auction appears to have distributed wealth from the shareholders of the winning bidders to the UK government (Klemperer, 2002c). However, it has been suggested that the winning bidders have subsequently used their ownership of the licences to impede entry and retard the rate of take-up of 3G technology, while at the same time seeking to renegotiate terms and conditions. Delaying the take-up of 3G technology has enabled these firms to extend the profitable lifetime of the older 2G technology (Ozanich *et al.*, 2004).

Case study 14.2

Dutch auctions prove viable alternative to IPOs FT

The well-received stock market debut last week of Interactive Brokers, the US broker-trader, offered further proof that a so-called Dutch auction can be a viable alternative to the traditional float managed and controlled by Wall Street. In Dutch auctions, made famous during the stock market debut of online search engine Google, investors bid for shares and the final offer price is based on the highest level at which orders for all the offered shares can be filled. The auctioneer starts out at a prohibitively high price and gradually lowers this, filling the share allocation gradually at a range of prices.

Thomas Peterffy, the maverick founder and chairman of Interactive Brokers, has said he preferred a Dutch auction process because it gave all investors an equal chance to get in on the act. One analyst said: 'He couldn't very well do the float in any other way, given the business model he preaches of easy automated access to trading venues. Using the Dutch auction process for the initial public offering is clearly the option that is most in line with this sort of thinking.'

Traditional IPOs are priced and allocated by powerful Wall Street firms, which balance the competing interests of issuers, investors, trading clients and themselves. But the success of the $1.2bn IPO of Interactive Brokers, whose shares soared as much as 14 per cent before falling back, could prompt other companies to follow suit, according to several analysts. The deal was co-lead by HSBC, only the second time the bank has led a US IPO. The other lead co-manager was WR Hambrecht, which pioneered the Dutch auction-style flotation during the dotcom bubble.

Alongside the $1bn–$2bn fund-raisings by Google and Interactive Brokers, other floats conducted by auction have been smaller and met varying degrees of success. Only three other WR Hambrecht deals raised more than $50m since 1999, while only two deals were offered by auction last year.

Critics of the process point to the fact that the widely predicted surge in use of the Dutch auctions following Google failed to materialise. At the time some blamed glitches that Google encountered during its flotation on the process it used. For example, they argue that the Dutch auction was flawed because Google at one point reset its offer range.

Others consider the ability to reset the price range to be a strength of the Dutch auction, not a weakness. Rather than forcing Google to commit to a clearing price, the process gave Google the ability to set a price based on investor demand as revealed through the bidding process.

One former US equity capital markets banker said that entrenched interests around the old methods would mean Wall Street would resist any move by companies towards more auction based offerings. 'Investment banks charge lucrative underwriting fees, and powerful traders get newly issued shares at a discount that can be cashed in on the first day, and that is a lot of power to give up,' he said.

Laboratory experiments of this kind have been subject to criticism from several directions. Kagel *et al.* (1989) and Kagel and Richard (2001) demonstrate that learning and experience gained by bidders over a series of auctions tends to reduce the impact of the winner's curse. However, even with experienced bidders, outcomes are not always fully consistent with the theoretical model's prescriptions for rational bidding behaviour. Hansen and Lott (1991) attribute the average losses realized by bidders in the Kagel and Levin study to a tendency for aggressive bidding, in a rather artificial case in which participants can lose no more than their initial balances.

Reliance upon inexperienced student volunteers might represent a significant shortcoming of many experimental studies, if there are systematic differences between the behaviour of volunteers and that of experienced professional decision makers. Dyer *et al.* (1989) report an experiment in which the behaviour of construction industry executives was compared with that of student volunteers, in a common value auction in which participants submitted tenders to become the lowest-cost supplier. Perhaps surprisingly, there was little difference in the behaviour or performance of students and executives, with both falling victim to the winner's curse.

Cox and Hayne (1998) investigate possible differences in behaviour between experiments in which bidders are organized into teams and experiments with individual bidders. The hypothesis is that team decision-making may help reduce the impact on bidding behaviour of individual judgemental errors. In experiments where individuals and teams receive one signal each, there is little difference in performance, and susceptibility to the winner's curse is mainly a function of the experience of the participants. However, in experiments with multiple signals (for example, each member of a team of five receives a separate signal, while an individual bidder receives all five signals) teams appear to handle the multiple signal data significantly less effectively than individuals.

Field evidence

Capen *et al.* (1971) are widely credited for providing the first field evidence relating to the phenomenon of the winner's curse. As noted in Section 14.3, this study examined the bidding for oil and gas drilling rights in the Gulf of Mexico during the 1950s and 1960s. In a number of auctions the winning bids were many times higher than the next-highest bids, suggesting that some form of winner's curse was operative. For example, in Alaska in 1969 the winning bids were at least twice as large as the next-highest bids in 77 per cent of all cases. In follow-up studies, Mead *et al.* (1983) found after-tax rates of return to have been below the average return on equity for US manufacturing corporations, and expressed qualified support for the existence of a winner's curse. Hendricks *et al.* (1987) report that firms granted leases between 1954 and 1969 in auctions involving more than six bidders earned low or negative returns. The bids submitted by around two-thirds of the firms investigated were significantly higher than those that would produce a Nash equilibrium in the theoretical model.

The results of the experiments indicate that a few firms did not behave optimally, and that, in at least one case, a firm [Texaco] consistently overestimated the value of the tracts. Most firms seemed aware that their valuations of tracts they win are biased upward, although a subset of the firms may have underestimated the extent of this bias.

(Hendricks et al., 1987, p. 518)

Drawing on the results of an earlier study by Cassing and Douglas (1980), Blecherman and Camerer (1998) test for the winner's curse in wage offers made to players in US major league baseball in 1990. Two groups of players were examined: players who were free agents at the time of signing (and who were eligible to sell their services to the highest bidder); and players who were already on unexpired contracts and therefore ineligible for free agent status. In the absence of a winner's curse, players' salaries should be equivalent to their marginal revenue products (MRP). MRPs are estimated for both groups of players, and compared with actual salaries. The average salary of free agents was $934,000, and the average estimated MRP of $605,000. For players without free agent status, the equivalent figures were $712,000 and $704,000. This suggests a tendency for teams that signed free agents to have overpaid and experienced the winner's curse. The contract system can be interpreted as a form of collusion between team owners who seek to avoid becoming involved in competitive bidding wars and overpaying for the services of star players.

Lee and Malmendier (2011) use a large dataset of prices paid for goods available immediately for purchase at a fixed price or via auction. They find that in the majority of auctions, the final price paid by the winning bidder is higher than the price at which an indentical product could be purchased on the same website. Overbidding is more likely in auctions with a long bidding period and a large number of participants. Interestingly the evidence suggests experienced bidders are most likely to suffer from the winner's curse.

The market for corporate takeover is another in which the possibility of a winner's curse arises. In cases where a number of bidders are competing to take over a firm and the highest offer wins, it seems likely there may be a systematic tendency for winning bidders to overbid. Assessing the evidence presented in a number of empirical studies, Roll (1986) finds acquiring firms do tend to pay a substantial premium over and above the market value of the firms they acquire. This premium cannot be explained by subsequent increases in post-acquisition performance (see Section 18.3). Many merger decisions may be driven by either peer pressure or hubris and may not be explicable in terms of rational economic calculus.

Case study 14.3

What determines the prices of goods traded in online auctions?

The growth of the internet has created new opportunities for trading by auction. A huge volume of goods is now traded daily through the eBay websites around the world. Online auctions provide a convenient low-cost environment for buyers and sellers to trade. The search engine technology underlying online auctions allows buyers and sellers to trade specialized products in liquid markets.

Founded in 1995 by Pierre Omidyar, eBay created an electronic platform for the sale of goods and services. eBay is not a traditional firm, even by the standards of the internet, because it does not hold any stock. Instead it acts as a broker to facilitate trade between buyers and sellers, by bringing them into contact with one another. In any transaction, the seller can set the opening price, a (secret) reserve price (if they wish), and the duration of the auction (between three and ten days). Bidders submit bids, which can be raised at any time within the auction period. Because the duration is fixed, many bidders post their bids during the last few hours or minutes of the auction period. When the auction closes and a winning bid is selected, the buyer and seller make contact. At this point the buyer pays for the goods via a PayPal account (an online payments system purchased by eBay in 2002); and the seller ships the goods to the buyer.

Information concerning the reliability of buyers and sellers can be obtained from published data concerning their previous trading history. Under this system, buyers and sellers rate the experience of trading with each other (following a transaction) as positive (+1), negative (−1), or neutral (0). Cumulative ratings are displayed for each trader. A rating exceeding +10 receives a star, while a rating below −4 leads to a trader being banned from further use of eBay. For the use of its services, eBay charges sellers a listing fee and a commission based on the value of the transaction.

Several academic economists have investigated the behaviour of buyers and sellers in auctions. Particular interest has focused on the impact of asymmetric information, reputation effects and the degree of trust between buyers and sellers on traders' behaviour. This literature is surveyed by Bajari and Hortacsu (2004). For example, Lucking-Reiley *et al.* (2007) analyse the determinants of the prices of 461 collectable coins (Indian Head pennies) that were traded on eBay during July and August 1999. Data were collected on the age and grade of the coin; the minimum submitted bid; the final submitted bid; the number of bids; the reserve price (if any); the seller's rating; the duration of the auction; and whether or not the auction period included a weekend. Results from the analysis included the following:

- Positive (negative) seller ratings lead to higher (lower) prices. Negative ratings have more impact on price than positive ratings.

- Longer auctions fetch higher prices.

- Reserve prices fetch higher prices (especially when only one bidder participates).

Summary

An auction is a market mechanism for converting bids from market participants into decisions concerning the allocation of resources and prices. Auctions can be characterized by the rules for the submission of bids, for determining the identity of the winning bidder, and for determining the price the winning bidder pays. There are four basic auction formats:

■ The English auction or ascending bid auction requires bids to be raised successively until a price is reached which only one bidder is willing to pay.

■ The Dutch auction or descending bid auction requires the offer price to be lowered successively until a price is reached which a bidder is prepared to pay.

■ The first price sealed bid auction requires bidders to submit sealed bids independently. The highest bidder pays a price equivalent to the winning bid.

■ The second price sealed bid auction also requires bidders to submit independent sealed bids. The highest bidder pays a price equivalent to the second-highest submitted bid.

The simplest theoretical models of auctions are based on two alternative assumptions concerning the distribution of bidders' valuations of the item under auction.

■ In the pure common value model, there is a single, intrinsic value of the item that is the same for all bidders. No single bidder knows what this true value is. Each bidder estimates the item's true value independently.

■ In the independent private values model, each bidder knows the true value of the item to him or herself personally. Personal valuations of the item differ between bidders.

The winner's curse is a common feature of auctions where the pure common value model applies, especially those conducted using the first price sealed bid format. If all bidders submit bids equivalent to their private estimates of the item's intrinsic value, it is likely the winning bidder will have overestimated the intrinsic value. To avoid the winner's curse, each bidder's sealed bid should be based on a revised estimate of this value, conditional on the original estimate being the highest estimate made by any bidder.

In the independent private values model, if risk-neutral bidders pursue optimal bidding strategies which maximize their own private rents, all four basic auction formats are expected to yield the same expected price to the seller. This result is known as the revenue equivalence theorem.

In all four basic auction formats, the seller increases their expected proceeds by specifying a reserve price, such that the item is not sold if the selling price does not at least match (or exceed) the reserve price. The optimal reserve price is usually some distance above the seller's private valuation of the item. If bidders are risk averse, the optimal bidding strategy in an English auction or a second price sealed bid auction is unaffected. Risk-averse bidders tend to bid more aggressively in a Dutch auction or a first price sealed bid auction, in an effort to reduce the risk of not winning the auction. If bidders are asymmetric (split into two groups with private values drawn from different distributions), revenue equivalence breaks down. In this situation, it is possible that the winning bidder is not the bidder with the highest private value.

The pure common values model and the independent private values model are theoretical extremes. An affiliated valuations model allows bidders' valuations to be partly dependent on the intrinsic value of the item, but also partly subjective. When bidders' valuations are affiliated, revenue equivalence breaks down. An English auction yields the highest expected price to the seller, because the bidders' ability to observe each other's behaviour while bidding is underway mitigates the effects of the winner's curse. In the UK, this result helped inform the design of the government's successful auction of licences to operate mobile phone services using 3G technology, which took place in April 2000.

Discussion questions

1. Describe the four basic auction formats.

2. Explain the distinction between the pure common value model and the independent private values model of bidder valuations.

3. In a sealed bid auction in which bidders form independent private values, why might a bidder be well advised to abstain from submitting a bid equivalent to her private estimate of the item being sold?

4. 'In a sealed bid auction, it would pay to bid more aggressively if you knew you were competing against ten other bidders than you would if you knew you were only competing against two other bidders.' Do you agree or disagree with this statement? Explain your reasoning.

5. Explain why the English auction and the second price sealed bid auction are strategically equivalent.

6. Explain why the Dutch auction and the first price sealed bid auction are strategically equivalent.

7. Why does it 'pay to tell the truth' in a second price sealed bid auction, but not in a first price sealed bid auction?

8. What are the implications of the revenue equivalence theorem for the seller's choice of auction format?

9. Under what conditions does revenue equivalence break down?

10. Assess the extent to which field evidence supports the phenomenon of the winner's curse.

11. Assess the extent to which experimental evidence supports the phenomenon of the winner's curse.

12. Referring to Case Study 14.1, assess the effectiveness of the auction designs used to sell licences to operate mobile phone services using 3G technology in the UK and elsewhere in Europe.

13. With reference to Case Study 14.2, discuss the effectiveness of Dutch auction designs in Initial Public Offerings.

14. Are bidders who use the eBay website (see Case Study 14.3) at risk of experiencing the winner's curse? Justify your answer by referring to relevant aspects of auction theory.

Further reading

Athey, S. and Haile, P. (2006) Empirical models of auctions, in Blundell, R., Newey, W.K. and Persson, T. (eds) *Advances in Economics and Econometrics: Theory and Applications*, Vol. 2. Cambridge: Cambridge University Press.

Ausubel, L.M. (2008) Auctions (theory), in Durlauf, S.N. and Blume, L.E. (eds) *New Palgrave Dictionary of Economics*, 2nd edition. London: Palgrave Macmillan.

Bajari, P. (2008) Auctions (applications), in Durlauf, S.N. and Blume, L.E. (eds) *New Palgrave Dictionary of Economics*, 2nd edition. London: Palgrave Macmillan.

Bajari, P. and Hortacsu, A. (2004) Economic insights from internet auctions, *Journal of Economic Literature*, 42, 457–86.

Bergstrom, T.C. and Miller, J.H. (2000) *Experiments with Economic Principles*, 2nd edition. New York: McGraw Hill.

Binmore, K. (2007) *Game Theory: A Very Short Introduction*. Oxford: Oxford University Press.

Binmore, K. and Klemperer, P. (2002) The biggest auction ever: the sale of the British 3G Telecom licences, *Economic Journal*, 112, C74–96.

Cohen, A. (2002) *The Perfect Store: Inside eBay*. London: Piatkus Publishers.

Hendricks, K. and Porter, R. (2007) Auctions, in Armstrong, M. and Porter, R. (eds) *Handbook of Industrial Organization*, Vol. 3. Amsterdam: Elsevier.

Klemperer, P. (1999) Auction theory: a guide to the literature, *Journal of Economic Surveys*, 13, 227–86.

Klemperer, P. (2002) How not to run auctions: the European 3G telecom auctions, *European Economic Review*, 46, 829–45.

Klemperer, P. (2004) *Auctions: Theory and Practice*. Princeton, NJ: Princeton University Press.

Krishna, V. (2010) *Auction Theory*, 2nd edition. London: Academic Press.

Lee, Y.H. and Malmendier, U. (2011) The bidder's curse, *American Economic* Review, 101, 749–87.

McAfee, R. and McMillan, J. (1987) Auctions and bidding, *Journal of Economic Literature*, 25, 699–738.

Milgrom, P. (1989) Auctions and bidding: a primer, *Journal of Economic Perspectives*, 3, 3–22.

Perrigne, I. and Vuong, Q. (2008) Auctions (empirics), in Durlauf, S.N. and Blume, L.E. (eds) *New Palgrave Dictionary of Economics*, 2nd edition. London: Palgrave Macmillan.

Thaler, R. (1991) *The Winner's Curse: Paradoxes and Anomalies of Economic Life*. Princeton, NJ: Princeton University Press.

Product differentiation

15.1 Introduction

Most markets are typified by some degree of product differentiation. There is no single homogeneous brand of car, soap powder, hotel, T-shirt or breakfast cereal. Product differentiation can be viewed as the ability of producers to create distinctions (in a physical or in a psychological sense) between goods that are close substitutes, so that consumers no longer regard them as identical or near-identical.

Chapter 15 deals with product differentiation as a topic in industrial organization in its own right for the first time. However, product differentiation has already had an important role to play in several earlier chapters; and it will do so again later in this book. For example, in Chapter 3 the degree of product differentiation was cited as one of the defining characteristics of market structure. The theoretical model of monopolistic competition refers to an industry in which a large number of firms compete to produce and sell similar but slightly differentiated products or services. In Chapters 7 and 8, product differentiation is one of the principal forms of non-price competition open to oligopolists seeking to avoid becoming embroiled in damaging price competition. In Chapter 9, the issue of market definition was seen to depend on decisions as to where to draw the dividing line between groups of products that, on the basis of degree of similarity, might be considered either as part of the same market, or as comprising separate markets. In Chapter 11, product differentiation (or brand proliferation) was cited as one of the strategies an incumbent firm can adopt in order to raise barriers to entry.

Section 15.2 begins by drawing a distinction between **vertical** and **horizontal product differentiation**, and identifying a number of natural and strategic sources of product differentiation. This section also draws a distinction between two types of economic model of product differentiation. In **representative consumer models**, consumers have tastes or preferences for goods or services, and firms compete to attract consumers by differentiating the products they offer. In **spatial** or **location models**, consumers' tastes or preferences are defined in terms of the individual characteristics that are embodied in the goods or services. Section 15.3 develops an analysis of the implications of product differentiation for social welfare in the representative consumer model of monopolistic competition. This analysis suggests that, in this model, only by accident does the degree of product differentiation at the post-entry equilibrium maximize social welfare.

The next three sections present a series of spatial or location models of product differentiation. Section 15.4 develops Lancaster's product characteristics model, in which goods are viewed as bundles of characteristics, and differentiated goods or brands contain the same characteristics in varying proportions. Section 15.5 develops Hotelling's model of spatial competition. In the original version of this model, geographic location is the characteristic that differentiates one supplier's product from another. However, the same approach has been widely used to model competition in product characteristic space. In one variant of the model, two firms choose locations on a straight line, with prices assumed fixed. An alternative variant allows for price determination with fixed locations. Finally, Section 15.6 examines Salop's adaptation of the Hotelling model, in which both firms and consumers are located around the circumference of a circle. In this case, both locations and prices are endogenous, and there is free entry. The model's solution is analogous to the post-entry equilibrium in the neoclassical (representative consumer) model of monopolistic competition.

15.2 Types of product differentiation

In the economics literature, it is customary to distinguish between vertical and horizontal product differentiation (Beath and Katsoulacos, 1991). First, **vertical product differentiation** means one product or service differs in overall quality from another. For example, one brand of fruit juice may have higher fruit content and lower sugar content than another brand, and as such is recognized as a higher-quality brand by all consumers. If the prices of the high-fruit brand and the high-sugar brand were the same, most or all consumers would purchase the high-fruit brand. Second, **horizontal product differentiation** means products or services are of the same or similar overall quality, but offer different combinations of characteristics. For example, a Ford Focus, Vauxhall Astra, Honda Civic, Volkswagen Golf and Toyota Corolla are all similar brands or models of car, but each one offers a slightly different package of attributes. Most drivers of cars in the relevant class would be able to express a preference in favour of one of these brands or models, but different drivers might well express different preferences.

It may be useful to classify the distinguishing characteristics of differentiated products and services as either natural or strategic. With **natural product differentiation**, the distinguishing characteristics arise from natural attributes or characteristics, rather than having been created through the deliberate actions of suppliers. With **strategic product differentiation**, the distinguishing characteristics are consciously created by suppliers; for example, through a decision to create a new brand and promote it by means of advertising or other types of marketing activity. Sometimes, however, the distinction between natural and strategic product differentiation is not clear-cut. For example, suppliers might attempt to reinforce or strengthen consumers' perceptions of natural product differences through strategies such as advertising or branding.

Sources of natural product differentiation include the following:

- *Geographic variation.* In this case, the location of a seller automatically differentiates a product or service in the minds of consumers. Clearly the corner shop and the out-of-town superstore offer competing services that are differentiated in the minds of consumers on the basis of location (as well as other characteristics such as choice and price). In the residential property market, houses that are identical in every other respect might be highly differentiated in terms of the town, city or region in which they are located.

- *New technology.* New technology can be used to differentiate a product; for example, through the addition of internet and email features to a mobile telephone. Procter & Gamble has been successful in differentiating many of its products through the introduction of new technological features. Examples include the *Swiffer* mop that captures dust, and the *Nutri-Delight* orange drink, which has a special formula allowing iodine to coexist with certain vitamins and minerals, and which it is claimed permits children to gain weight.

- *Brands and trademarks.* Trademarks are words or symbols used to identify particular brands. Brands and trademarks have been used throughout the history of commerce to differentiate similar products (Moore and Reid, 2008). In many cases, a firm that has developed a trademark will also hold exclusive property rights to use the trademark. Examples include a crocodile or a polo player on horseback (Lacoste or Ralph Lauren clothing). In some cases, the brand or trademark eventually becomes synonymous with the product. For example, the brand name Hoover has become widely used as a generic term for any vacuum cleaner. For many, the company name Google has become synonymous with internet search. In such cases the brand owner may eventually lose its exclusive property rights (Bryson, 1994).

- *Community or national differences.* The country or community of origin might be the defining attribute that differentiates goods and services. In other words, products and services from certain parts of the world are deemed to be different and of higher quality. Examples include Devon custard, Russian vodka, Scottish whisky, Swiss watches, curry from the Indian subcontinent, Italian designer clothes and Hollywood movies.

- *Consumer tastes and preferences.* Consumers themselves have different attributes, tastes and preferences. Consequently, the product characteristics that are most desired vary from one consumer to another. Product differentiation targeted at meeting these varied wants is often horizontal. Examples include the colour of cars and the style of clothes. Case Study 15.1 illustrates how fashion can be used to differentiate PCs and mobile phones.

Sources of strategic product differentiation include the following:

- *Additional services.* Additional services can often be used to differentiate products. Even if the same product is available from two suppliers, the conditions surrounding the sale might be different. Suppliers might differentiate their products by offering cheaper credit, faster delivery times or a more comprehensive after-sales service. By offering after-sales guarantees or warranties, the supplier sends signals to consumers that it has confidence in the quality of its product.

- *Rate of change of product differentiation.* Products with a short natural lifespan can be subjected to planned obsolescence, especially in cases where the product accounts for a relatively small proportion of most consumers' budgets. Consumers might be urged to purchase new styles or models with superficial changes in characteristics. Products such as clothing and video games are often subject to this form of strategic product differentiation. Monopolies and Mergers Commission (1966) and Schmalensee (1978) present evidence of such behaviour in the UK detergents and US ready-to-eat cereals markets, respectively.

- *Factor variations.* Factor inputs such as labour and capital are rarely homogeneous. This creates opportunities for final outputs produced using differentiated factors of production to be marketed as distinct from those of other firms. For example, a supplier might claim its employees are more highly skilled, better trained or less prone to make errors; or that its components or raw material inputs are superior to those used by rival suppliers.

■ *Consumer ignorance*. Ignorance on the part of consumers can allow firms to exaggerate the extent of differentiation of their products and services. Suppliers sometimes exploit consumer ignorance through misleading advertising. Sometimes suppliers attempt to convince consumers that higher prices reflect higher quality (Scitovsky, 1950, 1971). If such attempts are successful, the level of consumer demand might even increase as price increases. Chawla (2002) discusses the role of consumer ignorance in determining prices for health treatment in private practice. In the Egyptian private health sector in the late 1990s, patients were poorly informed and prices were relatively high as a consequence.

Case study 15.1

High-tech reaches a new age of style

When Henry Ford began mass producing the Model T Ford he famously said 'the customer can have any colour he wants, so long as it's black'. In the early days of personal computing and mobile phones, manufacturers, including Apple, IBM and Motorola adopted similarly inflexible policies. They believed, perhaps, that the new technologies were exciting enough to sell themselves. It is only in the last few years that most PC and mobile phone makers have broken out of the design straitjacket and begun to pay attention to consumer fashions and trends.

Nadine Kano, marketing director for experience computing at Microsoft, says in a recent paper – Fashion meets technology: welcome to the future of PCs – that: 'Product differentiation in the PC industry is getting harder and harder to achieve based on technical specs. People have always wanted power, speed and reliability, but these days they can get comparable disk space, processor speed, and Ram (random access memory) from many PC manufacturers. To get something unique, people are now looking for style.' Forrester Research, the US-based market research firm, predicts that between now and 2012 will be the 'Age of Style' for the consumer PC industry, with manufacturers weaving design considerations into every aspect of their business, including research and development, brand management, marketing and retailing.

'Fashion is how we express our identities,' says Ms Kano. 'Style is everywhere today . . . The shift we're seeing in consumer PCs is just as inevitable.' In addition to a variety of colour choices, from pink to brown and every hue in between, PCs are coming in a variety of materials, textures, shapes, sizes and form factors. And matching accessories, such as mice, carrying cases and music players, are becoming standard. 'People are willing to pay more for a product that expresses their personal style,' says Ms Kano. Customers for some of Dell Computer's Inspiron performance laptops can now choose from up to 12 colours while Hewlett-Packard Pavilion laptops feature a subtle swirly pattern that would not look out of place on a surfboard. HP dubs the design its 'radiance' imprint.

But Ms Kano cautions that 'painting a PC a different colour is a superficial interpretation of fashion . . . Fashion is about lifestyle as well as aesthetics.' Indeed, some laptop makers have gone further by experimenting with new materials. Asus, the Taiwan PC maker, recently unveiled a notebook PC in a bamboo case and has a best-selling line of laptops bearing the Lamborghini brand name with metallic-yellow cases and dark-leather palm rests. When you fire up the Asus Lamborghini VX3, it purrs like its automotive namesake. Similarly Canon, the Japanese electronics and digital photography company, offers its PowerShot SD1100 IS camera in five metallic finishes, with names such as 'rhythm and blue' and 'Bohemian brown'. 'We consider fashion to be important for general consumers who will be carrying or wearing the camera in their everyday lives,' says Canon. Its designers make observations in their own lives, and then make predictions based on active trend surveys and user observations. 'Previously, black and silver dominated the camera market – however, due to the recent expanding base of users and the diversification of tastes, there has been an increase in bright colour variations,' says Canon.

Other personal technology manufacturers have also hitched their wagon to fashion brands, while handset manufacturers, such as Korea's LG Electronics and Samsung, have scored big with phones bearing names such as Prada and Armani respectively (see below). 'The Prada phone has been very successful for us, particularly in Europe,' says Jeff Hwang, president of LG Electronics Mobilecomm. As mobile phone penetration has edged towards – and in some cases passed – 100 per cent, handset makers have begun to emphasise design, styling and marketing.

'Phones are very individual, personal items,' says Bill Ogle, Samsung's US marketing manager. 'The phone you carry says a lot about you.'

In the economics literature, there are two basic approaches to the specification of consumer preferences and the modelling of firm behaviour in the case of horizontal product differentiation (Waterson, 1994). First, in **representative consumer models** consumers have tastes or preferences for goods or services, and firms compete to attract consumers by differentiating the goods or services they offer. Each firm's demand is a continuous function of its own price and the prices set by competing firms. This is true even in models where competition is atomistic. In the neoclassical model of monopolistic competition, developed in Section 3.5, each firm assumes its own individual pricing decision provokes a negligible response from its rivals.

Second, in **spatial** or **location models** consumers have tastes or preferences for the characteristics embodied in goods or services. In this case, consumer demand for a particular firm's product might be highly dependent on small changes in the price set by another firm whose product embodies a very similar bundle of characteristics, but be independent of small changes in the price set by a third firm, whose product characteristics are further removed. Consider the high-street food chains McDonald's, Burger King and Pizza Hut. If Burger King implements a small price cut, this might have a significant effect on demand at

McDonald's, but if Pizza Hut does the same, this might have no effect on demand at McDonald's (or at Burger King). Only if Pizza Hut implements a large price cut would consumers who normally buy burgers consider switching to pizzas. This suggests that McDonald's' demand might be a smooth function of Burger King's price because the product characteristics are so similar, but is a discontinuous function of Pizza Hut's price because the product characteristics are further removed.

15.3 Monopolistic competition revisited: the socially optimal amount of product differentiation

This section develops an analysis of the implications of product differentiation for social welfare in the model of monopolistic competition that was developed earlier (see Section 3.5). Dixit and Stiglitz (1977) provide an extended treatment of some of the issues that are raised below.

The discussion begins by recalling the pre-entry and post-entry equilibria for a representative firm in monopolistic competition (see Figure 3.8). At the pre-entry equilibrium, the firm earns an abnormal profit equivalent to the area C_1P_1BD. This abnormal profit attracts entrants, whose presence reduces the quantity the representative firm can sell at any price, and shifts the firm's demand or average revenue function to the left. At the post-entry equilibrium, the tangency solution is attained and the representative firm's abnormal profit has disappeared.

For the purposes of examining the welfare implications of product differentiation, the pre-entry equilibrium shown earlier (see Figure 3.8) is interpreted as depicting the situation when the representative firm is the only firm in the industry. This interpretation was not used earlier (see Section 3.5), where it was simply assumed that there are fewer firms present at the pre-entry stage than at the post-entry stage. Logically, however, there is no difficulty in carrying out the pre-entry analysis for the extreme case where only one firm is present. This implies that the shift from the pre-entry to the post-entry equilibrium illustrated earlier (see Figure 3.8) can be interpreted as depicting a change in the number of firms from $N_1 = 1$ to N_2, the number of firms at the post-entry equilibrium at which each firm earns only a normal profit.

In order to establish the welfare implications of increasing product differentiation, it is necessary to determine the implications for total producer surplus or abnormal profit, and for total consumer surplus as the number of firms increases from $N_1 = 1$ to N_2. This relationship is derived in Figure 15.1. The construction is as follows:

■ The function $\pi(N)$ shows the relationship between N, the number of firms, and the abnormal profit earned by the representative firm (represented by the area C_1P_1BD in Figure 3.8 for the case $N = 1$). It is assumed that as N increases and the average revenue functions of incumbent firms start shifting to the left, their abnormal profits decrease smoothly. $\pi(N_2) = 0$ because, at the post-entry equilibrium, the representative firm earns zero abnormal profit.

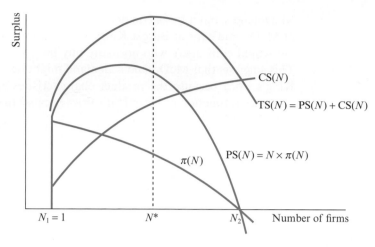

Figure 15.1 Monopolistic competition: too much product differentiation

- The function $PS(N) = N \times \pi(N)$ shows the relationship between the number of firms and the total producer surplus or abnormal profit earned by all firms collectively. Starting from $N = 1$, a second firm can enter and earn an abnormal profit that exceeds the reduction in the first firm's abnormal profit resulting from this entry decision. Therefore, total abnormal profit increases as the number of firms increases from $N = 1$ to $N = 2$. Similarly, for other small values of N, further entry causes the total abnormal profit to increase, since each entrant's abnormal profit exceeds the total loss of abnormal profit to the incumbents. Eventually, however, as N continues to increase, total abnormal profit must start to decrease. $PS(N) = N \times \pi(N)$ must attain a value of zero when the number of firms reaches N_2, since $\pi(N_2) = 0$.

- The function $CS(N)$ shows the relationship between the number of firms and the total consumer surplus. In the case $N_1 = 1$, consumer surplus was represented previously by the area P_1AB (see Figure 3.8). As the number of firms increases and each incumbent firm's average revenue function starts shifting to the left, total consumer surplus increases for two reasons: first, entry causes total industry output to increase and prices to fall; and, second, as more variety is introduced, each consumer is more likely to find a brand that matches their tastes more closely.

- Finally, the function $TS(N) = PS(N) + CS(N)$ shows the relationship between the number of firms and the total surplus, calculated as the vertical summation of $PS(N)$ and $CS(N)$. In Figure 15.1, $TS(N)$ attains its maximum value at $N = N^*$, below N_2. Therefore, in this case, there is too much product differentiation at the post-entry equilibrium. However, the opposite case is also possible. In Figure 15.2, $TS(N)$ attains its maximum value at $N = N^{**}$, above N_2. In this case there is too little product differentiation at the post-entry equilibrium.

The main conclusion that emerges from this analysis is that only by coincidence is social welfare maximized at the post-entry equilibrium in monopolistic competition. The number of firms at the post-entry equilibrium is determined by entrants examining whether or not they obtain a positive private benefit (abnormal profit)

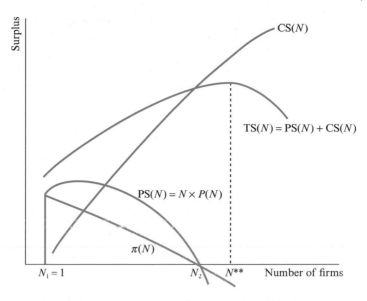

Figure 15.2 Monopolistic competition: insufficient product differentiation

if they enter. However, each entry decision also imposes costs and benefits on other parties, which are not considered by the entrant. By increasing industry output and reducing prices, entry tends to reduce the producer surplus (abnormal profits) of incumbent firms, but it also tends to increase consumer surplus. Whether the number of firms, and therefore the amount of product differentiation, at the post-entry equilibrium is too high or too low (from a social welfare maximization perspective) depends on which of these two effects dominates. If the negative producer surplus effect dominates, there is too much product differentiation; but if the positive consumer surplus effect dominates, there is too little product differentiation. Only by coincidence, if these two effects are evenly balanced, is the degree of product differentiation optimal.

15.4 Lancaster's product characteristics model

In Sections 15.4 to 15.6, the discussion switches away from the representative consumer model of monopolistic competition, towards a number of spatial or location models of product differentiation. The first model to be examined is Lancaster's (1966) product characteristics model. In this model, consumers derive utility not from the goods they consume but from the characteristics that are embodied in those goods. Goods are viewed as bundles of characteristics, and differentiated goods or brands are goods that contain the same characteristics in different proportions. For example, when you decide which car to buy, you consider an array of characteristics. Car manufacturers produce glossy brochures listing characteristics such as safety features, performance, comfort, seating, security, styling, in-car entertainment and so on. Similarly, mobile phones are marketed by product characteristics: does the phone have a camera, personal organizer, polyphonic ring tones, predictive text, vibrating alert, video capture, voice-activated dialling, FM radio and so on? The average car or mobile phone purchaser is not interested in every available model. He or she narrows the choice down to those models that come close to delivering the desired bundle or mix of characteristics. Many product markets are saturated with huge numbers of models and product types. During a visit to his local store, Schwartz (2004) counted 85 varieties of crackers, 285 varieties of cookies, 85 brands of juices, 75 iced teas, 15 flavours of bottled water, 61 varieties of sun protection products, 80 pain relievers, 40 toothpastes, 150 lipsticks, 75 eyeliners, 90 nail polishes, 116 skin creams and 360 brands of shampoo and other hair care products. Case Study 15.2 offers other examples.

Case study 15.2

Cut and pastiche

'There are simply too many notes, that's all. Just cut a few and it will be perfect.' Joseph II's friendly advice to Mozart – as presented in Peter Shaffer's screenplay for the film *Amadeus* – provokes harsh laughter from any writer who has dealt with the editor's pen. Mozart is said to have replied, 'Which few did you have in mind, Majesty?' Mozart's urbane response made the emperor look absurd. But Tyler Cowen, an economics professor at George Mason University, seems to have a similar perspective in his new book about arts funding, *Good and Plenty*: 'Mozart's Don Giovanni has musical beauty, terror, comedy and a sense of the sublime, making it a favourite of opera connoisseurs. But what if consumers draw their comedy from one work, their terror from another, their beautiful music from yet another, and so on?' Cowen knows that the idea is outrageous for Don Giovanni, but not so for lesser works.

Move away from the peaks of artistic creation and there lie many albums, books, television shows and films whose artistic qualities are unbundled, tweaked and repackaged to suit the demands of the petty emperor in all of us. Music is remixed in 'mashups' combining vocals from one source and instrumentation from another. Favourite sitcom characters gain independent life in their own shows. Films are released and re-released offering director's cuts and a choice of endings. What is more, these lesser packages of comedy and terror, not Don Giovanni, are the artistic products that most of us consume in quantity. Products are bundles of characteristics. Sometimes the characteristics are easy to spot and interchangeable, such as your MP3 player's memory, battery life and styling. Sometimes, as with Don Giovanni, part of the product's appeal is that the characteristics are perfectly balanced. But more often than we might think, we gain real satisfaction from being able to choose from products with a different range of attributes.

The man who first thought of products as bundles of valuable characteristics was the Australian economist, Kelvin Lancaster. He realised that customers do not much like 'one size fits all' and would prefer to have products that exactly matched their needs. The reason we do not all enjoy perfectly tailored products is not that the idea is absurd – although it is easy to mock 'the ultimate chill-out album' – but because of increasing returns to scale. I would like to hear U2 produce more tracks such as 'Acrobat' and

'Exit', but Bono and company do not find it profitable to write them just for me. Lancaster showed that producers can do a better job of satisfying individual customers when the market is bigger. In London I can find something close to my ideal restaurant experience because there are enough people like me to keep the restaurant afloat. In a small town a restaurant cannot survive on the passing trade of one person per decade with Tim Harford's tastes, so I have to enjoy what is there, even if it is not quite what I would have chosen myself.

The same should be true of the arts, and that is one reason why fears of global homogenisation are overstated. Given that there are more customers out there than ever before, and given that it is easier to move around goods and services too, it is now much more likely that there will be kindred spirits who share my tastes enough to encourage some entrepreneurial artist to produce exactly the products I want. I can find them too. I searched the internet for 'Don Giovanni abridged'. It turns out, incredibly, that such a work exists and was performed in New York this month. Emperor Joseph II, take note.

Source: Cut and pastiche, © The Financial Times Limited. All Rights Reserved, 19 May 2006 (Harford, T.).

In Figure 15.3, a consumer obtains utility from the consumption of two characteristics. The quantities of each characteristic are shown along the axes of the diagram and IC is the consumer's indifference curve. Indifference curves for characteristics have the usual properties: more of each characteristic is always preferred to less of the same characteristic, and the indifference curves are convex to the origin. The four rays represent the proportions of characteristics

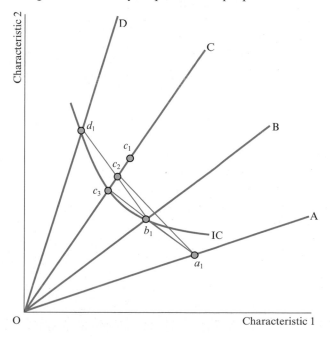

Figure 15.3 Lancaster's product characteristics model

1 and 2 that are available from brands A, B, C and D. For example, brand A offers lots of characteristic 1 but very little of characteristic 2. Brand D offers the opposite combination. Brands B and C offer more balanced combinations of characteristics 1 and 2. The following table shows some examples of products and the characteristics they might embody:

Product	Characteristic 1	Characteristic 2
Breakfast cereals	Crunchiness	Fruitiness
Curry sauces	Flavour	Hot, medium or mild
Musical acts	Beat	Melody
Cars	Spaciousness	Manoeuvrability

The consumer with indifference curve IC normally prefers the characteristics to be combined in proportions similar to those provided by Brand C. Initially, the prices of the four brands are such that for a given level of expenditure, the consumer can afford to locate at b_1 if he or she allocates all of the budget to brand B, c_1 if he or she purchases brand C, or likewise, a_1 or d_1. Faced with this set of choices, the consumer chooses brand C and locates at c_1. Utility at c_1 is higher than at b_1 or d_1, both of which are located on the same indifference curve, IC. Utility at c_1 is also higher than at a_1, which is located on a lower indifference curve than IC.

Consider the implications of an increase in the price of Brand C. Let P_1 denote the price of C that enables the consumer to locate at c_1. Suppose the price of C increases to P_2, so that, if the same budget is allocated to good C, the consumer can only attain c_2. If it is possible to achieve a desired mix of characteristics by consuming combinations of brands in varying proportions, there is another way of attaining c_2. If the quantities of brands B and D can be mixed in this way, any combination of characteristics along the arc $b_1 d_1$ is attainable. The consumer could also achieve c_2 by splitting the budget between purchases of brands B and D. If the price of C increases beyond P_2, the consumer prefers combined consumption of brands B and D to sole consumption of brand C. At prices beyond P_2, this consumer is eliminated from the market for brand C.

In practice, can a desired mix of characteristics actually be achieved by consuming different brands in varying combinations? For products such as breakfast cereals or curry sauces, it is easy to imagine purchasing two different brands and mixing them together. For musical acts or cars, it is harder to imagine consuming different brands in combination, unless perhaps alternative combinations of characteristics are required at different times of the day or week. If manoeuvrability is required for town driving during the week, but spaciousness is more important for long trips at weekends, a family might decide to run two cars.

If it is not possible to consume combinations of alternative brands in varying proportions in order to achieve a desired mix of characteristics, in Figure 15.3 the consumer would stick with brand C unless the price increases beyond P_3 (at which the point c_3 is attainable). Beyond P_3, the consumer would derive higher utility by switching altogether to either brand B or brand D.

In the case where brands can be consumed in combination, in Figure 15.3 the purchase of brand C is not ruled out altogether at prices above P_2. Consider a

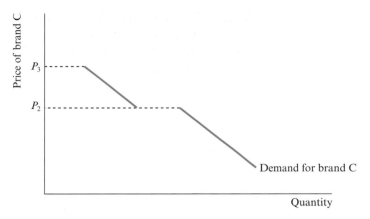

Figure 15.4 Discontinuous demand function for brand C

second consumer with a different set of indifference curves, who normally prefers the characteristics to be combined in proportions similar to those provided by brand B. If the points attainable by allocating the entire budget to one brand are a_1, b_1, c_2 and d_1, it is better to purchase a combination of brands A and C than to allocate the entire budget to brand B. In this way, a point on OB beyond b_1 is attainable. However, if the price of brand C increases beyond P_3, combined consumption of A and C is no longer preferable. In this case, the second consumer is also eliminated from the market for brand C.

This analysis suggests there are sharp discontinuities in the demand curve for brand C, illustrated in Figure 15.4. Above P_3, neither consumer purchases brand C. At P_3, however, C captures the second consumer (who normally prefers B) and there is a sudden jump in the demand for C. Similarly, at P_2, C captures the first consumer (who normally prefers C) and there is a further jump in the demand for C. Variation in the price of C also produces sharp discontinuities in the demand for C's **near-neighbour brands**, in this case brands B and D.

Discontinuous demand functions, and the interdependence between them, are likely to have major implications for competition and pricing strategy. Archibald and Rosenbluth (1975) consider the implications of variations in the number of characteristics and the number of competing brands:

- When there are many competing brands and there are many rays in Figure 15.3, small price changes cause smoother and more continuous switching between brands. The effect of a change in the price of brand C on the total demand for brand D is negligible from the viewpoint of the producers of brand D, because brand C is only one of a very large number of competitors in brand D's near-neighbourhood. In this case the Lancaster model approximates to the neoclassical model of monopolistic competition described in Section 3.5.

- In Figure 15.3, strong product differentiation produces rays that are further apart, while weak product differentiation produces rays that are closer together. If the rays are far apart, large price variations are needed to trigger switching between brands. If the rays are close together, only small price variations are needed for the same effect.

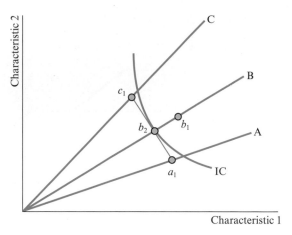

Figure 15.5 Positioning of new brand B

■ In Figure 15.3, non-substitutable characteristics make the indifference curves more L-shaped, while easily substitutable characteristics make the indifference curves flatter. If the indifference curves are L-shaped, large price variations are needed to trigger switching between brands. If the indifference curves are flat, only small price variations are needed for the same effect.

The Lancaster product characteristics model also provides insights into the decision to introduce a new brand. The market depicted in Figure 15.5 is currently occupied by Brands A and C. As before, A and C can be combined in varying proportions to produce a preferred combination of characteristics. A consumer with the indifference curve IC maximizes utility by consuming a combination of A and C at point b_2. However, the gap that exists in the product characteristic space between brands A and C represents an opportunity for the creation of a new brand B. If brand B can be priced so that the consumer can attain a position such as b_1, the consumer will switch from the combined purchase of brands A and C at b_2 to the sole purchase of brand B at b_1.

15.5   Hotelling's location model

In an early and highly influential contribution to the literature on spatial competition and product differentiation, Hotelling (1929) develops a model of competition in which geographical location is the characteristic that differentiates one supplier's product from another. The products themselves are identical, but if all firms were charging the same price, all consumers would prefer to purchase from their nearest supplier. This means each firm has a certain amount of market power. A firm that raises its price does not automatically lose all its customers to its competitors. Some customers (those located nearest to the firm concerned) are willing to pay a slightly higher price in order to continue buying locally, rather than incur the costs of travelling further afield in order to buy more cheaply.

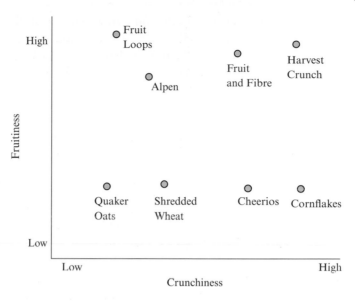

Figure 15.6 Product characteristic space for breakfast cereals

Although the original version of the Hotelling model describes competition in 'geographic space', the same model can easily be adapted to describe competition in 'product characteristic space', where the relevant attributes of different suppliers are the characteristics of their products, rather than their geographic locations. In the case of breakfast cereals, it is possible to imagine different brands as being situated at different locations on a two-dimensional plane such as Figure 15.6, in which the horizontal dimension measures one characteristic such as degree of crunchiness, and the vertical dimension measures another characteristic, degree of fruitiness. Each consumer has a preferred location on the two-dimensional plane, reflecting the consumer's ideal brand which, if it existed, would embody the consumer's preferred combination of these two characteristics. The consumer can either buy a brand that is situated close to his or her own location (which provides the highest utility), or a brand that is situated further away (which provides less utility). As before, if all firms were charging the same price, all consumers would prefer to purchase from their nearest supplier (in characteristics space). If there are significant price disparities, however, it might be worthwhile to purchase from a more distant supplier, provided the saving in price is at least sufficient to compensate for the loss of utility.

In order to develop the Hotelling location model, the examples cited below refer to competition in geographic space and competition in product characteristic space interchangeably. Initially, however, the model is developed using the geographic interpretation. Consider a town comprising one street running from west to east. The street is perfectly straight and consumers live at addresses distributed evenly (or uniformly) along the street. For simplicity, distances are standardized so that the total length of the street is 1. Each consumer's address is represented by a number between 0 and 1, with 0 denoting the address at the far west end of the street, and 1 denoting the address at the far east end. For simplicity, the model of competition in geographic space is one-dimensional: all consumers are located on a single east–west dimension. For the model of competition in product characteristic space, the equivalent condition is that there is only one relevant product characteristic: degree of crunchiness, for example, in the breakfast cereals' case. Each consumer's location, or ideal brand (in terms of degree of crunchiness), can be represented by an address number between 0 (soft) and 1 (crunchy), in the same way as before.

In the case where suppliers are differentiated by geographic location, it is assumed that every day, each consumer wishes to make a single purchase from one of two firms, both of which supply an identical product. The utility obtained by consuming a unit of the product can be standardized to a value of one. When making their daily purchase, each consumer incurs a transport cost dependent on the distance travelled. Transport cost is quadratic in distance so, as distance increases, transport cost increases at an increasing rate. Suppose initially the two firms are located at opposite ends of town: firm A at address 0 and firm B at address 1. For a consumer located at address d between 0 and 1, the utility gained and total cost incurred (purchase price *plus* transport cost) are as follows:

	Utility	Purchase price plus transport cost
Purchase from firm A	1	$P_A + kd^2$
Purchase from firm B	1	$P_B + k(1 - d)^2$

In the case where suppliers are differentiated by the characteristics of their brands, again it is assumed that, every day, each consumer wishes to make a single purchase from one of two firms. The utility that would be obtained by consuming a brand corresponding precisely to the consumer's ideal brand (if such a brand existed) is standardized to a value of one. When making his or her daily purchase of one of the two available brands, each consumer incurs a utility loss dependent on the distance between the location of the brand purchased, and the location of the consumer's ideal brand. The utility loss is quadratic in distance, so as distance increases, the utility loss increases at an increasing rate. Again, suppose initially firms A and B are located at addresses 0 and 1, respectively. For a consumer located at address d between 0 and 1, the (net) utility gained and cost incurred (just the purchase price in this case) are as follows:

	Utility (net)	Purchase price
Purchase from firm A	$1 - kd^2$	P_A
Purchase from firm B	$1 - k(1 - d)^2$	P_B

The parameter k plays a vital role in the model. In the model of competition in geographic space, a higher value of k implies a higher transport cost. In the model of competition in product characteristic space, a higher value of k implies a higher degree of consumer brand loyalty: as k increases, it costs consumers more (in terms of utility forgone) to switch from a brand situated close to the ideal brand to a brand situated further away. In both models, as k increases consumers become less likely to switch between firms A and B in response to small changes in P_A and P_B. Therefore k is a measure of the consumers' rate of substitution between firms A and B. The higher the value of k, the lower the rate of substitution and the lower the intensity of competition between firms A and B.

In both models, the consumer buys from the firm from which he or she receives the highest surplus, defined as the difference between the utility gained and the cost incurred, provided this surplus is positive:

- If $P_A + kd^2 < P_B + k(1-d)^2$ and $P_A + kd^2 \leq 1$, the consumer buys from firm A.

- If $P_A + kd^2 > P_B + k(1-d)^2$ and $P_B + k(1-d)^2 \leq 1$, the consumer buys from firm B.

Hotelling considers the case where the price is determined exogenously and is the same for both firms ($P_A = P_B = \bar{P}$), but the firms are free to choose where (in geographic space or product characteristic space) to locate. However, the model can be extended to cover a second case where the two firms' locations are fixed, but prices are endogenous and each firm is free to set its own price. A third case, in which both locations and prices are endogenous and chosen by the firms, is more complex. In fact, this third case turns out not to have a stable equilibrium solution at all. Accordingly, Section 15.5 examines only the first two cases. In both cases, for simplicity it is assumed that production costs are zero. A modified version of the Hotelling model, in which there is an equilibrium in the third case (endogenous locations and prices) is examined in Section 15.6.

Case 1: locations endogenous, price exogenous (fixed)

In this case, each firm chooses its location so as to maximize its own profit. Under the fixed price and zero cost assumptions, each firm's profit is a linear function of the number of consumers it serves. At which addresses (on the scale 0 to 1) should the two firms locate? Intuitively, it might be expected that firm A should locate at the address 0.25, and firm B should locate at the address 0.75. In this case, firm A would serve all consumers living at addresses between 0 and 0.5, and firm B would serve all consumers living at addresses between 0.5 and 1. This situation is shown in the upper section of Figure 15.7.

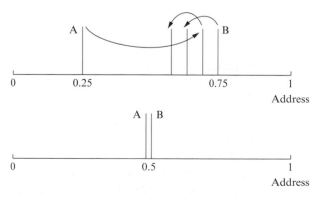

Figure 15.7 Hotelling's location model with fixed prices and endogenous locations

But is this choice of locations a Nash equilibrium? The answer is no. If firm A assumes B's location is fixed at its current address of 0.75, A can increase its market share by relocating to a point just fractionally to the west of B, say 0.749. By doing so, A now serves all consumers at addresses between 0 and 0.7495, and B's market share is reduced to consumers at addresses between 0.7495 and 1. However, this position is also unstable, and is also not a Nash equilibrium. If B now assumes A's location is fixed at its current address of 0.749, B can increase its market share by relocating to a point just fractionally to the west of A, say 0.748. By doing so, B now serves all consumers at addresses between 0 and 0.7485, and A's market share is reduced to consumers at addresses between 0.7485 and 1.

According to this reasoning, the two firms are engaged in a leap-frogging process, as each seeks to acquire more market share at the expense of its competitor. Is there ever an end to this process? The answer is yes. Notice that as leap-frogging takes place, both firms are moving in the direction of the centre of town. And when both firms are located at the very centre, at addresses just fractionally on either side of 0.5, neither is able to increase its market share (or profit) by changing its location any further. Therefore a stable Nash equilibrium is achieved when both firms locate in the same position, in the very centre of town, as shown in the lower section of Figure 15.7. All firms locating in the central position is not a property of the Nash equilibrium, in the general case with more than two firms. However, even in this case there is a tendency for bunching, whereby several firms locate together in the same position.

Is this solution simply a feature of a highly stylized and unrealistic theoretical model, or does it have any relevance in the real world? Perhaps it does. In the case of competition in geographic space, a tendency for several petrol stations to cluster together at important traffic intersections or other busy locations is often noticeable when driving around towns and cities. In the case of competition in product characteristic space, the perception that all brands of soap powder are the same has long been something of a cliché in public discussion of the role of branding and advertising in modern society. Hotelling's location model provides a plausible explanation as to why it might make sense for more than one brand of soap powder to have similar or identical characteristics.

Case study 15.3

Dear Economist [Hotelling's model]

Dear Economist

Why is it so hard for me to find a properly fitting pair of trousers on the high street? As a 33in–34in waisted, 5ft 11in male, I consider myself of average build. Yet appropriate attire always seems to be out of stock. Can economic theory shed any light on this?

Concerned Trouser Consumer

Dear Trouser Consumer,

The obvious economic analysis here is Harold Hotelling's 1929 classic on product differentiation. Hotelling imagined two ice-cream stands trying to decide where to locate on a beach. His conclusion was that they would end up side-by-side in the middle, with each customer going to the nearest stall. Similarly, major political parties tend to cluster in the centre of the political spectrum.

We do not see companies specialising in a single size of trouser – if we did, you would be swamped with pairs that fitted you well. A better explanation may be that companies are engaging in 'strategic product differentiation' to avoid competition. For Hotelling's ice-cream vendors, that would mean locating at opposite ends of the beach. For rival bus companies, it would mean one service departing on the hour and half hour, the other at quarter to and quarter past. In each case the aim is to give both companies the ability to raise prices without losing too many customers.

In your case, strategic product differentiation would mean that one clothes store offers trousers with a 32in, 36in and 40in waist. The other offers 30in, 34in and 38in. If you are shopping at the wrong store you will never be satisfied; the right store would supply clothes to fit, but prices would be higher for lack of competition. It is a bizarre economic theory, I agree. But it would explain your commonplace frustration.

Source: Dear Economist [Hotelling's model], © The Financial Times Limited. All Rights Reserved, 16 August 2007 (Harford, T.).

Case 2: locations fixed (exogenous), prices endogenous

In this case, the locations of the two firms are assumed to be fixed and each firm sets its price so as to maximize its own profit. It is assumed that the two firms are located at the opposite ends of the spectrum of addresses, with firm A at address 0 and firm B at address 1. Two models of price determination are examined:

- A collusive model, in which the two firms behave as if they were a single monopolist, and charge the price that maximizes their joint profit.

- A non-collusive model, in which the two firms set their prices independently. At the Bertrand (or Nash) equilibrium, each firm sets its price so as to maximize its own profit, treating the other firm's price as fixed at its current level.

The mathematical details of both models can be found in Appendix 1.

Collusive model: joint profit maximization

In the collusive model, the monopoly (joint profit-maximizing) price is always the same for both firms. Whenever $P_A = P_B$, the consumer located at address 0.5 is indifferent between buying from either firm. The price at which this consumer is indifferent between buying (from either firm) and withdrawing from the market is denoted $\tilde{P}$, and defined as follows:

$$\tilde{P} + kd^2 = \tilde{P} + k(1 - d)^2 = 1$$

Substituting $d = 1/2$ into this expression, it is easily shown:

$$\tilde{P} = 1 - k/4$$

When k is small, transport costs or brand loyalties are low, and the rate of substitution or the propensity for consumers to switch between suppliers is high. When k is small, $\tilde{P}$ turns out to be the joint profit-maximizing or monopoly price. The two firms' common price should be set so that the most marginal consumer is just willing to stay in the market.

However, when k is large, transport costs or brand loyalties are high, and the rate of substitution or propensity for consumers to switch between suppliers is low. When k is large, it is profitable for the two firms to set their common price higher than $\tilde{P}$. Although some consumers withdraw from the market, the firms increase their joint profit by raising the common price, and exploiting the market power that arises from the reluctance to switch of those consumers who remain in the market.

Figure 15.8 shows the determination of the monopoly (joint profit-maximizing) price for $k = 1.00$, 1.33 and 1.67. In each case, the left-hand diagram shows the total cost of buying from either firm as a function of location, represented on the horizontal axis. The right-hand diagram shows marginal revenue as a function of price: the effect on revenue (or profit in a model with zero costs) of a small increase in price. At prices below $\tilde{P}$, marginal revenue (in terms of price) is always positive and constant. The monopoly (joint profit-maximizing) price is never less than $\tilde{P}$, because in this range price can always be increased without causing any consumer to withdraw. Above $\tilde{P}$, however, marginal revenue (in terms of price) tends to be negative when k is low, but positive when k is high.

Let P_M denote the monopoly (joint profit-maximizing) price.

■ When $k = 1.00$, $P_M = \tilde{P} = 0.75$. The marginal effect on revenue or profit of a further increase in price is negative, so a further increase in price would not be profitable.

■ When $k = 1.33$, $P_M = \tilde{P} = 0.67$. The marginal effect on revenue or profit of a further increase in price is just equal to zero. Again, a further increase in price would not be profitable.

■ When $k = 1.67$, $\tilde{P} = 0.6$. In this case, the marginal effect on revenue or profit of a further increase in price is positive, so price should be increased beyond $\tilde{P}$. Joint profit maximization occurs at $P_M = 0.67$, where this marginal effect is equal to zero.

In fact, it can be shown that for any value of $k > 1.33$, $P_M = 0.67$ is the joint profit-maximizing price. When transport costs or brand loyalties are sufficiently high, each firm operates like a monopolist within its own market segment (addresses 0 to 0.5 for firm A and 0.5 to 1 for firm B). For $k > 1.33$ it is worthwhile to raise price beyond the level at which all consumers remain in the market, exploiting fully the reluctance to switch (brand loyalties) of those consumers who do remain.

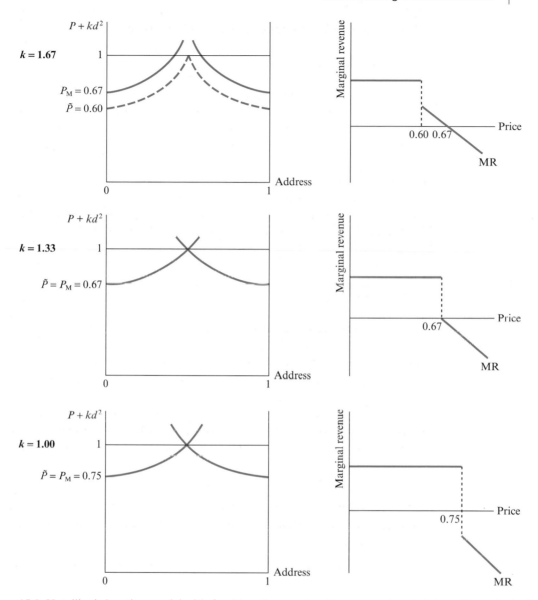

Figure 15.8 Hotelling's location model with fixed locations and endogenous prices: joint profit maximization

Non-collusive model: Bertrand (or Nash) equilibrium

The apparatus of isoprofit curves and reaction functions for firms A and B (see Chapter 7) can be used to locate the Bertrand (or Nash) equilibrium in the non-collusive model. In Section 7.3, isoprofit curves and reaction functions were derived for a quantity-adjustment duopoly model (in which two firms take profit-maximizing decisions about their output levels), with quantities shown on the horizontal and vertical axes. In the present case, isoprofit curves and reaction functions are required for a price-adjustment model, with prices rather than quantities shown on the horizontal and vertical axes.

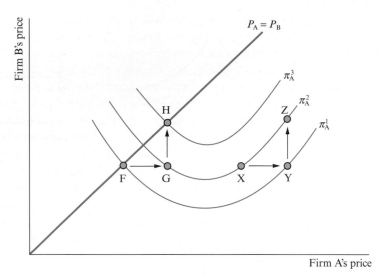

Figure 15.9 Derivation of firm A's isoprofit curves

It is assumed initially that both firms are operating at prices sufficiently low that no consumer is priced out of the market. All consumers are willing to buy from at least one of the two firms. Figure 15.9 examines the following shifts:

(i)   Both firms initially charge the same price and are located at point F in Figure 15.9. A decides to increase its price, represented by a shift from F to G.

(ii) A initially charges a higher price than B, and the firms are located at point X in Figure 15.9. A decides to increase its price, represented by a shift from X to Y.

In both (i) and (ii), there are two effects on firm A's profit, which operate in opposite directions:

■   By charging a higher price to each consumer it retains, A tends to earn more profit than before.

■   However, A also loses some business, because A's price increase causes A's most marginal consumers to switch to B. A loses the profit it was earning previously from those consumers who switch.

In (i), A's most marginal consumers who switch to B are those located at addresses close to 0.5, at the centre of town. These consumers incur relatively high transport costs in order to buy from A. For any given price increase by A, the rate at which these marginal consumers switch from A to B is low (if transport costs are a large proportion of the total cost of buying from A, a small increase in P_A makes only a small difference). The first of the two effects identified above tends to dominate, and A's profit increases due to the move from F to G.

In (ii), A's most marginal consumers who switch to B are located at addresses closer to firm A than before. These consumers incur lower transport costs than before in order to buy from A. For any further price increase by A, the rate at which these marginal consumers switch from A to B is high (if transport costs are only a small proportion of the total cost of buying from A, a small increase in P_A makes a big difference). The second of the two effects identified above tends to dominate, and A's profit decreases due to the move from X to Y.

To complete the derivation of A's isoprofit curves, suppose B now implements a small price increase, while A holds its price constant. This is represented by the shift from G to H, or from Y to Z in Figure 15.9. In both cases, some consumers switch from B to A, causing A's profit to increase. Similarly, if B cuts its price while A holds its price constant, consumers switch from A to B, causing A's profit to decrease. This establishes that A's isoprofit curves are convex to the horizontal axis, or U-shaped. Reading Figure 15.9 from the bottom to the top, each successive isoprofit curve represents a higher level of profit to firm A. Similarly, B's isoprofit curves are convex to the vertical axis.

For each value of P_B, firm A's reaction function, denoted RF_A, shows the profit-maximizing value of P_A. Accordingly, RF_A runs through the minimum points of each of A's isoprofit curves. But what is the shape of RF_A? In fact, the precise shape and location depend on the value of the parameter k. As discussed previously, this parameter determines the rate of substitution, or the rate at which consumers switch between A and B in response to a small price change by either firm.

Figure 15.10 shows a sketch of the typical shape of RF_A. RF_A is upward-sloping between points M and N; backward-bending between points N and R; and vertical between points R and S. The logic is based on an analysis of the effect of a small increase in P_B on the profit-maximizing values of P_A in different regions of Figure 15.10.

- Between M and N, P_B is relatively low and B captures most of the market. As P_B increases from point M, the most marginal consumers lost by B are located close to A. These consumers prefer to switch to A rather than drop out of the market altogether, so A's demand increases. To maximize profit, A should respond by increasing P_A, until the marginal profit gained from

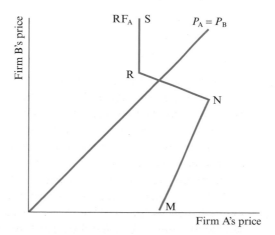

Figure 15.10 Firm A's reaction function

those consumers A retains (despite the increase in P_A) *equals* the marginal profit lost from those consumers who switch back to B (due to the increase in P_A). RF_A is upward sloping between M and N because A reacts to an increase in P_B by *increasing* P_A.

- Between N and R, P_B is higher than before. As P_B increases from point N, the marginal consumers lost by B are located further away from A than before. Also, P_A is higher than before. Accordingly, the consumers lost by B prefer to drop out of the market altogether, rather than switch to A. However, this decision is sufficiently borderline that they could be enticed back if A were to reduce P_A. A does so until the marginal profit A gains from the extra consumers enticed back matches the marginal profit lost from A's existing consumers (due to the cut in P_A). RF_A is backward bending between N and R because A reacts to an increase in P_B by *reducing* P_A.

- Finally, between R and S, P_B is higher still. As P_B increases from point R, the marginal consumers lost by B are located close to B and far away from A. They prefer to drop out of the market altogether rather than switch to A. This decision is not borderline and these consumers would not be enticed back by a small reduction in P_A. They might be enticed back by a large reduction in P_A, but it is not profitable for A to implement a sufficiently large price cut: the loss of revenue from A's existing customers would be too great. A's demand is unaffected by the increase in P_B, and the profit-maximizing value of P_A is also unaffected. RF_A is vertical between R and S because A reacts to an increase in P_B by leaving P_A *unchanged*.

Figure 15.11 shows the determination of the Bertrand (or Nash) equilibrium price for $k = 0.33$, 0.67, 1.00, 1.33 and 1.67. In each case, the left-hand diagram shows the intersection of the two firms' reaction functions, and compares the Bertrand (or Nash) equilibrium price, denoted P_N, with the monopoly (joint profit-maximizing) price, P_M. The right-hand diagram shows the total cost of buying from either firm as a function of location on the horizontal axis, when the selling price is either P_N or P_M. As before, the precise solutions depend heavily on k, or the consumers' rate of substitution between firms A and B.

Small k; high rate of substitution; intense competition

Small values of k ($k = 0.33$, 0.67) represent high rates of substitution between firms A and B. Price competition between A and B tends to be intense. The Bertrand (or Nash) equilibrium prices are located on the upward-sloping sections of RF_A and RF_B. These turn out to be $P_N = 0.33$ and $P_N = 0.67$, respectively. In fact, when the model is parameterized as assumed here, it can be shown $P_N = k$ for all $k \leq 0.67$ (see Appendix 1). In the most extreme case of price competition, when $k = 0$ and the rate of substitution between firms A and B in response to small changes in P_A and P_B is infinite, the present model becomes equivalent to one of Bertrand price competition between two duopolists selling an identical product. As shown earlier (see Section 7.4), equilibrium in the Bertrand model is reached when the prices set by the two duopolists have been

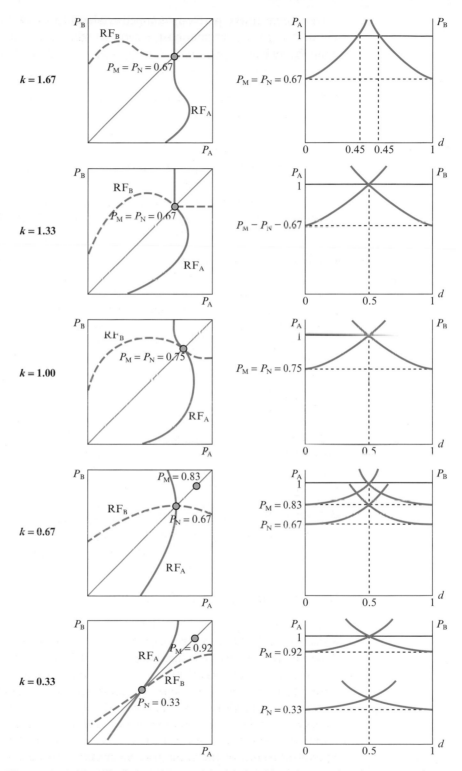

Figure 15.11 Hotelling's location model with fixed locations and endogenous prices: Bertrand (or Nash) equilibrium

driven down to the perfectly competitive level (price *equals* marginal cost). In the present case, marginal cost is zero, so when $k = 0$ the Bertrand (or Nash) equilibrium price is $P_N = 0$.

Medium k; medium rate of substitution; medium competition

Higher values of k ($k = 1.00$, 1.33) represent medium rates of substitution and less intense price competition between firms A and B. The Bertrand (or Nash) equilibrium prices are located on the backward-bending sections of RF_A and RF_B. Each firm acts as a monopolist within its own market segment, and P_N and P_M coincide, at $P_N = P_M = 0.75$ for $k = 1.00$, and at $P_N = P_M = 0.67$ for $k = 1.33$. In both cases, however, the rate of substitution is still sufficiently high that it is profitable to set prices in such a way that all consumers are served.

Large k; low rate of substitution; weak competition

Finally, the highest value of k considered in Figure 15.11 ($k = 1.67$) represents the lowest rate of substitution and the least intense price competition between firms A and B. The Bertrand (or Nash) equilibrium prices are located on the vertical sections of RF_A and RF_B. Each firm acts as a monopolist within its own market segment. For all values of $k \geq 1.33$, P_N and P_M always coincide at $P_N = P_M = 0.67$. But for $k > 1.33$, the rate of substitution is so low that it is profitable to set prices in such a way that some consumers are excluded from the market.

The results of the analysis of the collusive and non-collusive versions of the Hotelling model with fixed locations and endogenous prices are summarized in Figure 15.12, which shows the relationship between the parameter k and P_M, the joint profit-maximizing (monopoly) price and P_N, the Bertrand (or Nash) equilibrium (competitive) price. The findings can be summarized as follows:

■ Over small and medium values of k, P_M is decreasing in k. As k increases, it is worthwhile for the firms to reduce P_M in order to retain those consumers who would otherwise withdraw from the market. However, if k becomes sufficiently large, it ceases to be profitable to continue cutting P_M in order to retain the consumers from the more distant locations. Instead, it becomes more profitable to hold P_M constant and allow the most marginal consumers to withdraw.

■ In perfect competition ($k = 0$), $P_N = 0$. Any increase in k beyond $k = 0$ confers some market power on the two firms so, initially, P_N is increasing in k. Over medium values of k, the firms acquire sufficient market power to begin to act like monopolists within their own sub-markets. Consequently P_N approaches P_M, and eventually P_N and P_M become equivalent. Over high values of k, P_N (like P_M) is unaffected by further increases in k. It is interesting to note that over some values of k ($1.00 \leq k \leq 1.33$), P_N is decreasing in k: as the market becomes less competitive, the Nash equilibrium price decreases. This is because within this range, the two duopolists are already operating effectively as if they were local monopolists.

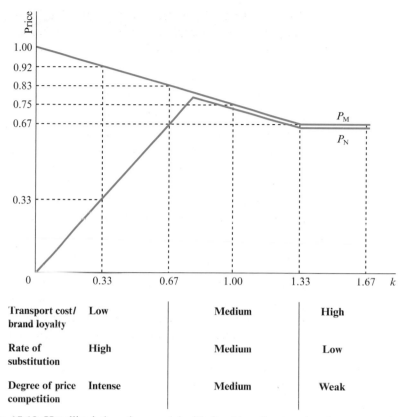

Transport cost/ brand loyalty	Low		Medium		High
Rate of substitution	High		Medium		Low
Degree of price competition	Intense		Medium		Weak

Figure 15.12 Hotelling's location model with fixed locations and endogenous prices: summary of results

15.6 Salop's location model

Salop (1979) develops a modified version of the Hotelling model, in which the firms and consumers are located around the circumference of a circle. In contrast to the Hotelling model (where the firms and consumers are located on a straight line with two end points), an equilibrium exists in the Salop model in the case where both locations and prices are endogenous. The presence of the two end points accounts for the non-existence of an equilibrium solution in Hotelling's model; and, conversely, the fact that a circle does not have any end points explains the existence of an equilibrium in Salop's model. In order to develop the Salop model, one further modification to the specification of the Hotelling model is required: non-zero production costs, including both a fixed cost and a variable cost component, are assumed.

The theoretical properties of Salop's model are quite interesting but, with reference to competition in product characteristics space, it is difficult to think of many real world examples where the characteristics of a group of differentiated products might realistically be represented in the form of a circular array. One case that might correspond to this formulation, however, is a group of rival airlines offering flights on a particular route at different hours of the day and

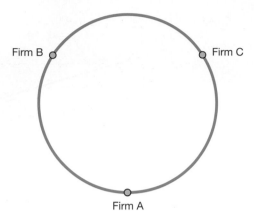

Figure 15.13 Salop's location model with three firms

night, around a 24-hour clock. Each airline offers a flight at a particular time, and each passenger has a preferred departure time, which varies between passengers (and which might be anytime, day or night). A passenger whose preferred departure time is 1100 might be indifferent between a 0900 and a 1300 departure (but with lower utility than at 1100), and indifferent between a 0700 and a 1500 departure (but with still lower utility). This passenger's least favoured departure time might be 2300.

Assuming consumers are located uniformly around the circumference of the circle, in the Salop model each firm wishes to locate as far as possible from its nearest competitors. This means it is always optimal for the firms to spread out as much as possible, locating at equidistant points around the circumference. If the length of the circumference is standardized to one, and the number of firms is N, the optimal distance between each firm is $1/N$. Figure 15.13 illustrates a three-firm version of the Salop model, in which the optimal distances between the firms are 1/3.

The formulation of each consumer's transport cost in the model of competition in geographic space, or the consumer's utility cost of consuming a product with characteristics different from the consumer's ideal characteristics, is the same as in the Hotelling model. The transport or utility cost is kd^2, where d represents distance, and the parameter k determines the consumer's rate of substitution between suppliers. The utility gained from consuming one unit of the product (the product with the ideal characteristics in the product differentiation model) is one, as before. If the firms are equidistant, the maximum distance of any consumer from their nearest supplier is $1/(2N)$. Let $\bar{P} = 1 - k/(2N)^2$ denote the price at which the most distant consumer is indifferent between buying and withdrawing from the market. If all three firms charge a price of $\bar{P}$, all three firms achieve a quantity demanded of 1/3.

Figures 15.14 and 15.15 examine the relationship between firm A's pricing decision and demand, on the assumption that firms B and C both charge a price of $\bar{P}$. In Figure 15.14, the circle has been redrawn as a straight line (but without end points). Suppose initially firm A also charges $P_1 = \bar{P}$, but A is considering either reducing its price to P_2, or increasing its price to P_3.

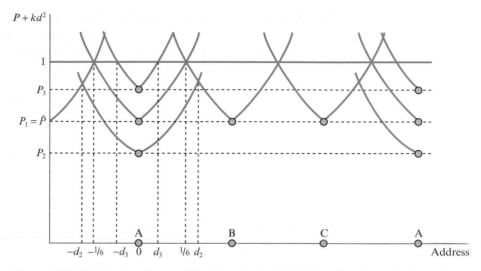

Figure 15.14 Salop's location model: effect of changes in firm A's price with three firms

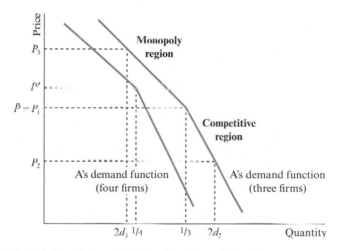

Figure 15.15 Salop's location model: firm A's demand function

■ With a price reduction below $P_1 = \bar{P}$, A acquires some consumers from B and C, so A's quantity demanded increases, from 1/3 to $2d_2$. Because consumers switch between suppliers at prices such as P_2 (below $\bar{P}$), P_2 lies within what Salop terms the *competitive region*.

■ With a price increase above $P_1 = \bar{P}$, A loses some consumers, who prefer to withdraw from the market altogether rather than switch to either B or C. A's quantity demanded decreases, from 1/3 to $2d_3$. Because A's former consumers either continue to buy from A or withdraw from the market altogether at prices such as P_3 (above $\bar{P}$), P_3 lies within the *monopoly region*.

Figures 15.14 and 15.15 show that the rate at which firm A loses consumers by increasing its price in the monopoly region exceeds the rate at which A gains consumers by reducing its price in the competitive region. Consequently, A's demand function has a kink located at price $P_1 = \bar{P}$.

What happens if a new firm is allowed to enter the market, increasing the number of firms from three to four? Assuming the three incumbent firms can relocate costlessly, the four firms will choose to arrange themselves at equal distances of 1/4 from one another. The maximum distance of any consumer from their nearest supplier is now less than before. Therefore $\bar{P}'$, the new price at which the consumer who is most distant from any firm is indifferent between buying and withdrawing, is higher than $\bar{P}$. If all four firms charge a price of $\bar{P}'$, all four firms achieve a quantity demanded of 1/4. Therefore the position of the kink in firm A's demand function shifts up and to the left, as shown in Figure 15.15.

Suppose all firms face a constant marginal cost, denoted c, per unit of output *plus* a non-zero fixed cost, denoted f. Salop shows that entry will take place until a Nash equilibrium is reached, at which no incumbent firm wishes to change its price and no outside firm wishes to enter. This equilibrium is analogous to the post-entry equilibrium in the (representative consumer) monopolistic competition model (see Section 3.5 and Figure 3.8). At the equilibrium in the Salop model, each incumbent firm earns a normal profit, and if another firm were to enter, this would cause all firms (including the entrant) to earn negative profits. The equilibrium number of firms is established using the following relationships:

Each firm's quantity demanded $= 1/N$

Each firm's price $= \bar{P} = 1 - k/(4N^2)$

Each firm's total revenue $= (1/N)[1 - k/(4N^2)]$

Each firm's total cost $= (1/N)c + f$

Each firm earns zero abnormal profit when total revenue equals total cost. Therefore the equilibrium value of N is determined by the following condition:

$$(1/N)[1 - k/(4N^2)] = (1/N)c + f$$

This condition can be rearranged to obtain a cubic equation in N, which can be solved to determine the equilibrium value of N, which in turn determines the equilibrium value of $\bar{P}$.

According to Figure 15.15, the Nash equilibrium price in the Salop model rises as the number of firms increases from three to four. This result may seem surprising: usually price is expected to fall as competition increases. But, in fact, the tendency for price to rise as the number of firms increases (due to entry) is a feature of this model throughout the entire process of adjustment towards the Nash equilibrium. As the number of firms increases, each individual firm services a smaller segment of the market, but obtains some compensation by raising its price. It is possible for the firms to do so, because as each firm's market segment becomes narrower, the preferences of the consumers the firm retains become more closely aligned with the characteristics of its own product. Although consumers pay a higher price, they obtain a product with characteristics that are closer on average to their own ideal product specification.

15.7 Summary

There are two forms of product differentiation. Vertical product differentiation means one product or service differs in overall quality from another. If the prices of both products were the same, most or all consumers would purchase the higher-quality product. Horizontal product differentiation means products or services are of the same or similar overall quality but have different attributes. Different consumers would express different preferences favouring one or other of the products. It may also be useful to classify the distinguishing characteristics of differentiated products and services as either natural or strategic. Natural product differentiation exists when the distinguishing characteristics of products or services are natural attributes. Strategic product differentiation involves the deliberate creation of real or perceived distinguishing characteristics by suppliers.

Sources of natural product differentiation include location, which might automatically differentiate a product or service in the minds of consumers; technology, which can be used to add new features to an existing product; brands and trademarks, which help differentiate products that are physically similar; associations in consumers' minds between particular products and particular countries; and consumers' own preferences for attributes such as colour or style. Sources of strategic product differentiation include the quality of factor inputs used by a supplier; variations in the conditions of sale, guarantees or after-sales service; planned obsolescence and frequent changes in design or style; and misleading advertising which exploits consumer ignorance.

In the economics literature, the two basic approaches to modelling horizontal product differentiation are: representative consumer models, in which consumers have tastes or preferences for goods or services, and firms compete to attract consumers by differentiating the goods or services they offer; and spatial or location models, in which consumers have tastes or preferences for the characteristics that are embodied in goods or services. The neoclassical model of monopolistic competition and several of the standard models of duopoly or oligopoly with product differentiation are representative consumer models. Several of the models that are introduced in Chapter 15 fall into the category of spatial or location models.

An analysis of the implications of product differentiation for social welfare in the representative consumer model of monopolistic competition suggests that only by coincidence is social welfare maximized at the post-entry equilibrium in monopolistic competition. The number of firms at the post-entry equilibrium is determined by entrants examining whether or not they obtain a positive private benefit if they enter. By increasing industry output and reducing prices, entry tends to reduce the producer surplus (abnormal profits) of incumbent firms, but it also tends to increase consumer surplus. Whether the number of firms, and therefore the amount of product differentiation, at the post-entry equilibrium is too high or too low depends upon which of these two effects dominates.

In Lancaster's product characteristics model, goods are viewed as bundles of characteristics, and differentiated goods or brands are goods that contain the same characteristics in varying proportions. The quantities of each characteristic are shown along the axes of an indifference curve diagram, and rays reflect the proportions in which the characteristics are available from competing brands. The demand functions for each brand are discontinuous functions of the brand's own price and the prices of adjacent brands. Consumers sometimes respond to small price changes by making small adjustments to the quantities of the brands they are currently consuming. However, sometimes small changes in price trigger switches between brands, in which case there are large, discrete changes in the quantities purchased.

Hotelling's model of spatial competition, in which geographic location is the characteristic that differentiates one supplier's product from another, has been widely used to model competition in product characteristic space. In the duopoly model in which price is exogenous and the firms choose where to locate along a straight line drawn in geographic or product characteristic space, an equilibrium is achieved when the firms locate in the same position, at the very centre of the straight line. In the case where locations are exogenous and the firms are free to select their own prices, it is possible to develop collusive and non-collusive versions of the model of price determination. The main conclusions are as follows:

■ When transport costs or brand loyalties are low, the collusive or joint profit-maximizing price is higher than in the case where transport costs or brand loyalties are high. In the latter case, it pays the duopolists to lower the price to some extent to prevent some consumers from withdrawing from the market altogether. If transport costs increase beyond a certain point, however, it is better to allow some withdrawals, rather than cut the price any further. In this case, both duopolists effectively operate as local monopolists within their own sub-markets.

■ The equilibrium price in the non-collusive model tends to be low when transport costs or brand loyalties are low. In this case the non-collusive model tends towards one of perfect competition. When transport costs or brand loyalties are high, it becomes profitable for the duopolists to operate as local monopolists within their own sub-markets. In this case the non-collusive and collusive models yield identical outcomes.

Finally, in Salop's adaptation of the Hotelling model, the firms and consumers are located around the circumference of a circle. In this case, it is possible to derive an equilibrium for the case where both locations and prices are endogenous, and there is free entry. The solution to the Salop model is analogous to the post-entry equilibrium in the neoclassical model of monopolistic competition. A feature of this model is that the equilibrium price rises as the number of firms increases. Each firm's market segment becomes narrower, and the preferences of the consumers each firm retains become more closely aligned with the characteristics of that firm's product. Although consumers pay a higher price, they obtain a product with characteristics closer on average to their ideal product specification.

Discussion questions

1. What is the distinction between vertical and horizontal product differentiation?

2. What is the distinction between natural and strategic product differentiation?

3. Explain the methodological difference between representative consumer models and spatial or location models of product differentiation.

4. With reference to Case Study 15.1 explain why manufacturers of PCs and laptops have turned to fashion to differentiate their products.

5. Can a free market be expected to deliver a socially optimal level of product differentiation?

6. With reference to Case Study 15.2 select an 'artistic' product and list the most important characteristics you search for. What factors may help you to get close to a desired bundle of characteristics?

7. According to Lancaster's product characteristics model, why might the demand functions for competing brands exhibit discontinuities with respect to small changes in the price of each brand?

8. What factors should be taken into account by a firm that is seeking to strengthen the loyalties of consumers to its brand?

9. Under what circumstances might it make sense for two rival bus companies to charge the same fares, and schedule identical departure times, for a daily long-distance bus service?

10. In the Hotelling model with fixed locations and endogenous prices, a decrease in the consumers' rate of substitution between competing brands might result in a decrease in the equilibrium collusive price, but an increase in the equilibrium non-collusive price. Explain why.

11. Consider Case Study 15.3. Indentify factors which may lead companies to undertake 'strategtic product differentiation'.

12. In the Salop model with endogenous locations and prices, explain why an increase in the number of competing suppliers (due to entry) might be associated with an increase in the equilibrium price for each competing brand.

Further reading

Bagwell, K. (2007) Advertising, in Porter, R. and Armstrong, M. (eds) *Handbook of Industrial Organization*, Vol. 3. Amsterdam: Elsevier.

Beath, J. and Katsoularos, Y. (1991) *The Economic Theory of Product Differentiation*. Cambridge: Cambridge University Press.

Caves, R.E. and Williamson, P.J. (1985) What is product differentiation really?, *Journal of Industrial Economics*, 34, 113–32.

Degryse, H. (1996) On the interaction between vertical and horizontal product differentiation: an application to banking, *Journal of Industrial Economics*, 44, 169–86.

Moore, K. and Reid, S. (2008) The birth of brand: 4000 years of branding history, *Business History*, 50, 419–32.

Phlips, L. and Thisse, J.-F. (1982) Spatial competition and the theory of differentiated markets, *Journal of Industrial Economics*, 31, 1–9.

Waterson, M. (1994) Models of product differentiation, in Cable, J. (ed.) *Current Issues in Industrial Economics*. London: Macmillan.

Learning objectives

This chapter covers the following topics:

- the determinants of advertising expenditures
- advertising intensity measures
- informative and persuasive advertising
- advertising and welfare
- advertising and barriers to entry
- the relationship between advertising and industry concentration and profitability
- advertising and prices

Key terms

Advertising intensity
Advertising response function
Advertising-to-sales ratio
Convenience goods
Credence goods
Dorfman–Steiner condition

Experience goods
Informative advertising
Persuasive advertising
Search goods
Shopping goods

16.1 Introduction

Advertising is a method used by producers to communicate information to consumers about the goods or services they have to sell. Advertising is perhaps the most widely used method for informing or persuading consumers of the benefits of choosing a particular product or service, or a particular brand.

Advertising can involve a number of practices including direct mail, in-store promotion, telemarketing, product placements, sponsorship and exhibitions.

> [E]xpenditure on advertisement is expenditure (over and above the costs of producing and transferring the commodity to the consumer) which is increased by the seller with a view to increasing sales of his commodity. Thus in addition to the costs of the printed advertisement, it includes expenditure on travelling salesmen, 'free offers', competitions, coupons, and on displays and other services for attracting buyers.
>
> *(Braithwaite, 1928, p. 18)*

Producers often use advertising to persuade consumers that there are genuine differences between competing brands of a product or service. Over longer periods of time, advertising can be used to construct an attractive image for a brand, and strengthen the loyalties of the brand's consumers. In the days before there was meaningful regulation of advertising, firms often made outrageous claims in promoting their products. In the US in the 1930s, for example, many products were portrayed as having miraculous properties (Bryson, 1994). One company boasted that its brand of cigarettes could cure a smoker's cough.

> Coca-Cola advertising a century ago told you that the beverage was healthful, refreshing, the preferred drink of ladies, available at any drug store. Today, the same company tells you only that 'Coke is it'.
>
> *(Kay, 2004, pp. 215–16)*

According to Tedlow (1993), large-scale marketing in the US began as long ago as the 1880s, when large industrial firms started to appear for the first time selling mass-produced and highly standardized products to the newly emerging mass market. Typical examples include Coca-Cola, Johnson & Johnson, Procter & Gamble and Heinz, all of which are still prominent in their respective industries today. The reliance upon mass-production technologies to achieve economies of scale meant marketing, like production, had to be carried out on a large scale, and tended to treat consumers as homogeneous agents.

From the 1950s onwards, the introduction and wide-scale penetration of commercial television and radio created new advertising and marketing opportunities. Advertising messages could be transmitted directly into the homes of consumers. By choosing the time of day and the type of programme within which advertisements were embedded, advertisers could segment audiences according to key demographic or socio-economic categories, such as age, sex, income, education and so on. Tedlow (1993) notes that, since the 1990s, there has been a trend toward micro-marketing, where each consumer represents a potential segment. These changes are driven by changes in production and information technologies that have given firms more flexible systems to deliver goods, services and advertising messages to consumers. For example, Dell allows consumers to order tailor-made versions of personal computer products online. However, Tedlow (1993, p. 31) acknowledges that such trends may not necessarily continue if 'confused consumers are confronted in the marketplace with scores of distinctions without differences', or if constraints in distribution networks are met. Producers can now more easily measure the effectiveness of any given advertising strategy. The increasing sophistication of advertising links on the internet means firms only have to pay each time a consumer accesses the advertisement. 'This is the equivalent of paying for junk mail only to households that read it' (*The Economist*, 2004b, p. 84). American Airlines are reported as using 'behavioural targeting', by monitoring the interest shown by readers of the online version of the *Wall Street Journal* in travel stories. It then targets the selected readers with flight offers (*The Economist*, 2004b). Evans (2009) surveys the online advertising industry.

Advertising is one of the main weapons of competition between firms. From a theoretical perspective, the importance of advertising might be expected to vary according to market structure.

■ In the theoretical model of perfect competition, there appears to be no role for advertising, because each firm faces a perfectly elastic demand function and can sell as much output as it wants at the current price, which is determined through the interaction between supply and demand across the entire market. In any case, all market participants are assumed to have perfect information, which seems to eliminate the need for firms to advertise.

■ At the other extreme, in the case of monopoly, there appears to be some scope for advertising, although the scope is perhaps limited. The monopolist faces an inelastic demand function and is insulated from competition by entry barriers. The monopolist can therefore choose the price it charges. There may be some incentive to advertise if advertising is effective in increasing total industry demand. But there is no incentive to advertise in order to tempt consumers away from competitors, since, by definition, a monopolist has no competitors.

■ Finally, in the intermediate case of oligopoly, oligopolists who recognize their interdependence may prefer to avoid price competition, and instead engage in non-price forms of competition such as advertising or research and development. There may be strong incentives to advertise, both in order to increase total industry demand, and to attract customers at the expense of competitors.

Chapter 16 discusses theoretical ideas and empirical evidence concerning the role of advertising. Section 16.2 presents some facts and figures about the economic importance of advertising in modern societies, and about patterns of advertising expenditure across different types of product and service. Section 16.3 examines the relationship between certain key attributes of products, services and brands, and the likely effectiveness of advertising. The distinction between **search goods** and **experience goods** is introduced. Section 16.4 develops an optimizing model of advertising behaviour. The relationship between market structure and the optimal level of advertising is developed more formally, under profit-maximizing assumptions.

Section 16.5 examines ways in which advertising acts as a barrier to entry. Thanks to past advertising expenditure, an incumbent firm may achieve more sales for any given level of current advertising than an entrant, leading to an absolute cost advantage. Alternatively, economies of scale in advertising may make it difficult for small-scale entrants to compete with incumbents. Section 16.6 examines the role of advertising in situations where consumers have limited information, and an informational asymmetry exists between producers and consumers. The role of informative advertising in reducing consumers' search costs is considered. A signalling model is developed in which the actual content of advertising messages is unimportant, but consumers receive useful signals about product quality from the fact that some brands are advertised more heavily than others.

Section 16.7 considers whether there is too much advertising in modern societies. Some economists have argued that advertising leads to a misallocation of resources, because advertising distorts consumer preferences. Others believe advertising improves the flow of information concerning product and service attributes, and therefore improves the allocation of resources. Finally, Section 16.8 provides a selective review of empirical evidence concerning several of the issues raised in Chapter 16.

16.2 Determinants of advertising expenditure

Advertising is a huge global business. In the UK, total expenditure on advertising increased from £121 million in 1948 to £17.3 billion in 2008 As Table 16.1 shows, the contribution of advertising to Gross Domestic Product (GDP) varies widely across countries. In 2008 advertising accounted for 1.09 per cent of GDP in the US and 1.00 per cent in the UK, while in France, Germany, Italy and Japan the corresponding percentage figures were only 0.57 per cent, 0.78 per cent, 0.58 per cent and 0.85 per cent, respectively (Advertising Association, 2009).

Many economists draw a distinction between informative and persuasive advertising. **Informative advertising** provides consumers with factual information about the existence of a product, service or brand, or about attributes such as its price, features or uses. Informative advertising aims to give consumers information with which to make informed choices that will help them maximize their (exogenously determined) utility functions, subject to their budget constraints. **Persuasive advertising**, on the other hand, makes claims which may not be objectively verifiable, aiming to change consumers' perceptions of a product, service or brand with a view to stimulating sales. Drinking a sophisticated brand of coffee will make you sexually attractive; driving a sporty car will help you become rich, glamorous or powerful; wearing a certain brand of trainers will turn you into a world champion. One interpretation of persuasive advertising is that it seeks to shift consumers' tastes and thereby change the shape of their utility functions (no longer exogenous) in a direction favouring the advertising firm.

Table 16.1 Advertising as a percentage of gross domestic product (at market prices)

Country	1996	1998	2000	2002	2004	2006	2008
Austria	0.72	0.83	0.97	0.90	0.94	0.94	1.05
Belgium	0.65	0.74	0.81	0.83	0.85	0.85	0.79
Denmark	0.82	0.87	0.77	0.68	0.77	0.77	0.72
Finland	0.87	0.91	0.93	0.90	0.92	0.92	0.81
France	0.65	0.64	0.71	0.63	0.66	0.66	0.57
Germany	0.89	0.93	1.00	0.84	0.80	0.79	0.78
Greece	0.79	0.85	1.02	0.95	0.81	0.80	0.81
Ireland	0.96	0.95	1.13	0.96	0.88	0.86	0.85
Italy	0.49	0.55	0.69	0.60	0.69	0.70	0.58
Japan	0.76	0.75	0.79	0.73	0.81	0.81	0.85
Netherlands	0.90	0.95	0.97	0.84	0.76	0.74	0.75
Norway	0.81	0.85	0.73	0.73	0.67	0.70	0.58
Portugal	0.76	0.87	1.14	1.08	1.48	1.49	1.32
Spain	0.83	0.83	0.89	0.75	0.78	0.78	0.64
Sweden	0.75	0.85	0.83	0.67	0.78	0.84	0.79
Switzerland	0.93	0.94	1.07	0.97	0.85	0.83	0.76
UK	1.16	1.24	1.30	1.12	1.23	1.18	1.00
United States	1.28	1.30	1.39	1.21	1.40	1.35	1.09

Note: Data are net of discounts. They include agency commission and press classified advertising expenditure but exclude production costs.

Sources: The European Advertising and Media Forecast, National Data Sources, NTC Publications Ltd. Reproduced from Advertising Association (2003) *Advertising Statistics Yearbook 2003*, Table 19.4, p. 183 and Advertising Association (2009) *Advertising Statistics Yearbook 2009*, Table 19.4, p. 221. Oxford: NTC Publications. Reprinted with permission.

Economists often take a positive view of informative advertising, and a more critical view of persuasive advertising. Informative advertising is 'good' because reliable information is a powerful lubricant, needed to ensure the smooth functioning of competitive markets. But persuasive advertising is 'bad' because it (perhaps deliberately) sets out to mislead or confuse, and may even tend to distort competition. In practice, however, it is often difficult to make a clear distinction between informative and persuasive advertising. Many advertisements seek to inform and persuade at the same time.

> [T]o interpret advertising effort as primarily designed to persuade consumers to buy what they really do not want, raises an obvious difficulty. It assumes that producers find it more profitable to produce what consumers do not want, and then to persuade them to buy it, with expensive selling campaigns, rather than to produce what consumers do already in fact want (without need for selling effort).

> *(Kirzner, 1997b, p. 57)*

Case study 16.1

BlackRock pushes brand awareness

BlackRock has launched an international print and online advertising campaign to position itself as a thought leader in investment and financial advice. The group's Investing for a New World campaign started last week with four full pages in the *Financial Times*, followed by advertisements in national newspapers in other targeted countries. The campaign will continue online, where a microsite has been created, as well as on social media channels, printed materials and other means of communication. BlackRock, which owns iShares, the exchange traded fund manager, wants to boost its brand awareness in nine countries and territories: Italy, Germany, the Netherlands, the US, Canada, Taiwan, Hong Kong, Australia and the UK. One former senior ranking executive at BlackRock, who did not want to be named, says such a campaign is long overdue: 'The iShares brand is very recognisable to clients, but most people continually thought I worked at Blackstone rather than BlackRock.'

This is the first time the fund manager has pursued a global multimedia campaign. BlackRock would not provide details about the cost of the campaign, but chief executive Larry Fink has previously said he would spend hundreds of millions of dollars on branding. A single full-page advert in the FT costs in the region of £150,000. Despite being the world's largest money manager, BlackRock says it is still fairly unknown by retail investors outside of the US, and that investing in its brand will help to increase assets under management. Rob Fairbairn, head of BlackRock's global client group, says: 'It's a complete reorganisation of the way BlackRock communicates with the world. We're not very well known by [retail] investors. We're a B2B business, but we want investors to know us when they talk to their advisers.' BlackRock adds that the campaign will help 'make it clear to investors large and small around the world' who it is and what it stands for.

In Europe, the US group decided against allocating a budget to campaigns in France and Spain, but will target the institutional market in the Netherlands as well as the UK's retail and institutional markets. The group says it is reaching out globally to provide 'guidance and practical advice to investors struggling to make sense of this new world of volatile markets, low yields and uncertain returns'. BlackRock's content-heavy campaign invites investors to follow five practical pieces of advice, including '[opening their] eyes to alternatives, using [their] longevity, and being active about passive'.

Mr Fink highlighted the big themes of the firm's educational campaign in a speech last week in New York. 'We must help investors adapt to the new world,' he said. 'It's in everyone's interest to bolster confidence in long-term investment. But, I'll be the first to say that the asset management industry has not done a great job of helping investors take a long-term view. We have to step up guidance and provide answers.' Last summer, Mr Fink said he wanted to 'embellish' the BlackRock name, adding that one of the biggest challenges for the group was to have the same identity all over the world.

Source: BlackRock pushes brand awareness, © The Financial Times Limited. All Rights Reserved, 4 March 2012 (Aboulian, B.).

In general, therefore, advertising seeks to either inform or persuade or do both. However, there are specific reasons why firms invest in advertising campaigns:

- *To launch a product or service.* Advertising can be used to provide potential consumers with information concerning a new product or service. Such advertising may be primarily informative rather than persuasive. For example, the UK government and firms in the financial services sector advertised heavily in order to provide the public with detailed information before and after the launch of Individual Savings Accounts (ISAs) in 1999.

- *To provide information on price and quality.* Advertising can be used to provide consumers with information concerning price and quality attributes of products and services. This is particularly important if these attributes tend to change rapidly over time, as a result of competition or technological change. Advertising may be used to provide consumers with information on the location of the firm's sales outlets. Recent estimates suggest consumers in the US are exposed to an average of 3,000 advertising messages each day (*The Economist*, 2004b).

- *To increase or protect market share.* Advertising campaigns may be designed to persuade consumers that a firm's products and services are superior to those of its competitors. In a rapidly expanding market, there may be less need for advertising of this kind, as there is a large pool of potential customers available for all firms. Where consumer demand is stagnant or decreasing, firms may tend to advertise more heavily, in an effort to protect their individual shares of a dwindling market.

- *To establish a brand's image or strengthen consumers' brand loyalties.* Advertising can be considered as a type of investment expenditure, whereby a firm seeks to create positive associations in consumers' minds with its own brand, which may yield benefits to the firm in the form of lasting consumer brand loyalty. Goodwill and positive reputation effects can act as significant entry barriers, making it difficult for outside firms to establish a presence in a market dominated by an established brand that has been heavily advertised in the past. In 2006, the furniture retailer DFS spent over £106 million in the UK promoting its brand image (Advertising Association, 2007).

Klein (2000) criticizes the use of brands by large multinationals. She argues that the power of brands has reduced consumer choice and increased the dominance of large multinational firms at the expense of their smaller competitors.

Case study 16.2

Manufacturers shift focus on branding

British manufacturers are abandoning their traditional resistance to branding and are turning to more nuanced promotional techniques to enhance their 'brand appeal', rather than relying solely on their product's technical quality. 'Companies which tried to compete purely on reputation have realised that strong brands can establish a much stronger link with the customer,' says Stephen Judge, director of Bonfire Creative Intelligence, a marketing agency in Bedfordshire that specialises in manufacturing. For small companies selling 'niche' products, it has often been hard using traditional methods to make contact with potential customers, who are split between many countries and can be hard to identify.

Frank Michaux, managing director of Spax, an Oxfordshire company that makes shock absorbers, has pushed through a 'wholesale review' of the way it brands itself. 'We had to recognise the fact that there are many competitors globally that sell similar products to ours much more cheaply. Therefore to make a difference we had to pay much more attention to the brand to convey the special nature of what we do based on quality and technology.'

Mr Michaux used a website designer in Argentina and a graphic artist in Berlin to give the company a fresh image. 'The cost of the new approach came to a few hundred thousand pounds but has paid off in spades,' he said. The company – which faced potential closure in 2000 – last year had sales of £2m with 'very healthy' profits. Another company which adopted a similar approach is Hainsworth, a family-owned textiles maker based in Leeds, which sells to a range of businesses such as makers of home furnishings and military uniforms. Rather than use 11 'sub-brands' to promote itself, the company decided to focus on its main brand – the use of the company name – in all its literature and website promotion. 'We realised that we had an incredibly strong brand, which is probably even more important to the company than our most advanced production process, if only we could learn to use it better,' says Tom Hainsworth, managing director. At Northampton-based Torquemeters, which makes instruments for monitoring rotational movement in sectors such as aerospace or chemicals production, the company has fine-tuned its website to promote the 'Torquetronic' brand more widely. 'There are probably only about 2,000 people worldwide with any detailed knowledge of what we do – but with a better use of the internet we should be able to increase this by at least 10 times,' says Craig Delves, sales manager.

Among the manufacturers that have embraced Twitter as a marketing tool is Rudd Macnamara, a Birmingham maker of small plates that are fixed to beer pumps in pubs. 'With the explosion in new microbreweries in the UK we have the possibility to sell to many more customers than we ever had before and Twitter is a good way of keeping in contact,' says Val Smith, sales manager.

More companies – among them Dortrend, a company in Worcestershire that makes specialist door handles – are using video on their websites to explain how their products work. Dortrend's biggest selling products are high-tech 'anti-ligature' door handles, designed so that people in detention centres cannot use the handles to strangle themselves. 'It's a difficult area in which to get your message across and we have found that videos are a good tool for promoting the brand worldwide,' says Philip Dean, managing director.

However, some companies say that an overenthusiastic use of new branding techniques – or websites that contain too many advertising messages as opposed to solid technical information – risk alienating long-standing customers.

'The engineering industry is intensely conservative and you have to be careful about trying to change too much,' says Chris Rea, managing director of AES Engineering, a Rotherham-based maker of industrial seals.

Table 16.2 Advertising-to-sales ratios of selected UK product groups, 2008

Product group	Advertising-to-sales ratio
Airlines	3.85
Babycare products	39.70
Bath and shower additives	1.55
Beer	0.05
Blu-ray disc	5.28
Carbonated soft drinks	8.48
Cars	0.03
Cereals	7.11
Cheese	14.95
Chocolate bars	2.43
Cinema	0.30
Coffee	3.11
Deodorants	8.64
DVD players	0.68
Hair colourants	16.48
Internet service providers	21.84
Magazines	6.66
Mobile phones	9.18
Motor insurance	8.79
Rail travel	0.97
Shampoos	2.59
Sportswear	0.26
Tea	2.49
Televisions	0.58
Vitamins	9.62

Source: Adapted from Advertising Association (2009) *Advertising Statistics Yearbook 2009*, Table 18.1, pp. 206–12, researched and compiled by WARC (http://www.warc.com).

Theoretical models of oligopoly suggest firms may prefer to engage in non-price rather than price competition. Industry advertising expenditure as a proportion of industry sales, known as **advertising intensity** or the industry's **advertising-to-sales ratio** provides an indication of the importance of advertising as a form of non-price competition. As shown in Table 16.2, the advertising-to-sales ratio varies considerably between product groups (Advertising Association, 2009). In the UK in 2008, babycare products, internet service providers and hair colourants all had relatively high advertising-to-sales ratios, 39.70 per cent, 21.84 per cent, and 16.48 per cent respectively. In contrast, sportswear, DVD players, and televisions all had much lower advertising-to-sales ratios, 0.26 per cent, 0.68 per cent, and 0.58 per cent, respectively. However, these percentages can sometimes be misleading. In some cases, absolute expenditure on advertising is huge, but sales are so large that advertising intensity turns out to be quite low. The motor industry, with an advertising-to-sales ratio of only 0.03 per cent in Table 16.2, is an obvious example. Table 16.3 identifies the UK firms that spent most on advertising in 2008, and the most heavily advertised brands.

Table 16.3 Top 10 advertisers and brands in the UK, 2008

Top advertisers in 2008	£ millions	Top brands in 2008	£ millions
COI	193.1	DFS – suite range	88.0
Procter & Gamble	181.0	Asda product range	37.7
Unilever	160.0	McDonald's restaurant chain	32.5
British Sky Broadcasting	127.0	Sainsbury's product range	29.8
Tesco	102.4	Tesco product range	29.1
Reckitt Benckiser	91.7	Skydigital – TC/Talk/Broadband	26.0
DFS Furniture	87.9	Morrisons product range	24.5
BT	87.6	Skydigital – Sky Plus system	23.8
Kellogg's	78.3	Direct Line – motor insurance	23.7
Asda	77.5	Argos – product range	23.0

Source: Adapted from Advertising Association (2009) *Advertising Statistics Yearbook* 2009, pp. 251–2, with permission of The Neilsen Company.

Case study 16.3

The serial painkiller

As Marijn Dekkers, chief executive of Bayer, presents the latest quarterly results of the German life sciences and chemicals group today, he will outline plenty of changes. But there will be one constant: a product that has remained a mainstay of the company for decades. Aspirin, the painkiller the company launched more than a century ago, was still generating €766m in sales in 2010. That made it one of just a handful of Bayer's $1bn-plus a year 'blockbuster' drugs, led by Betaferon for multiple sclerosis and the birth control pill Yaz, but it is the only one long unprotected by patents. 'It's hard to imagine Bayer without aspirin, or the other way round,' says Hemming Ornskov, head of strategic marketing at Bayer Healthcare Pharmaceuticals. 'It is an integral part of our history. I wish I could say the company set out 100 years ago to have this as a sustainable success.' Yet the story of this medicine, and Bayer's continued market dominance for aspirin – which has become the generic term for the painkiller that Bayer originally named – is the antithesis of the conventional story of a modern drug, in which a company invests substantial sums in research and development to make, patent and sell a product for a limited life before losing control to generic rivals.

Despite being based on an ancient remedy, and suffering weak intellectual property protection and intense competition, Bayer's Aspirin has survived expropriation of its name, tough regulatory action and periodic health scares to remain one of the top-selling drugs of all time. Last year a fresh, targeted marketing effort yielded double-digit sales increases. 'We had done such a good job communicating [generally] around aspirin that consumers had forgotten about its excellent efficacy for a broader range of pain,' says Jay Kolpon, vice-president of Bayer's consumer care division.

The remedy has undergone regular evolutions that were designed to keep Bayer in control. The medicinal value of the willow bark from which it derives was described by Hippocrates in 400BC, and an 18th-century English doctor used it to treat rheumatic pain. Acetylsalicylic acid, the active ingredient, was developed in 1853, and it was only in 1897 that Bayer's involvement began when its chemist Felix Hoffmann synthesised a stable form. Within two years – just as it was also commercialising heroin as a branded cough remedy – Bayer launched its branded painkiller Aspirin, which rapidly became the world's top-selling drug. The name is derived from 'a' for acetyl, 'spir' from the spiraea plant (a source of the ingredient salicin) and 'in', a common suffix for medicines at the time.

A key to its success was Bayer's consistent investment in the brand. In the UK and the US, Bayer received patents, but in many countries, including Germany, it won only registration as a trademark for Aspirin. During the first world war, the company's trademarks – Bayer and Aspirin – were expropriated in the US, France, the UK and much of the British Commonwealth, who were allies against Germany. It fought hard to retain its exclusive use of the trademark Aspirin in the rest of the world, and to regain rights where it could. It could never win back trademark protection for aspirin in the US, but it ultimately reacquired the Bayer name there in 1994. That allowed it to market 'Bayer Aspirin', and signalled the start of reinvigorated efforts to market the brand globally.

A second factor has been the regular expansion of aspirin's medical uses. Originally sold to treat rheumatism, and then lumbago and neuralgia, the drug's value has grown significantly. In the 1980s, regulators approved it to protect against repeat heart attacks and strokes. Many new applications for aspirin came through 'retrospective' analyses of widespread existing uses of the drug rather than specific 'prospective' clinical trials. Mr Ornskov says Bayer still spends more than €1m a year on testing, although one senior former executive says: 'A lot of the drive for aspirin marketing came from our consumer business. The [innovative] pharma guys are reluctant owners of the franchise.'

A third reason for Bayer's success with aspirin has been periodic reformulations – all brand-protected – to renew its appeal. Early in the 20th century, it switched aspirin's format from powder to tablets. A chewable version for children came in the 1950s. In the 1970s, Aspirin Plus C combined it with Vitamin C in effervescent form. In the 1990s, Bayer added the coated Aspirin Protect, which dissolves in the intestines to reduce the risk of stomach problems, which have become a cause for concern among physicians in recent years. Bayer's multiple formats for the drug continue to evolve, with the latest including low-dose Aspirin Cardio to protect against repeat strokes and heart attacks and Cafiaspirina, which is mixed with caffeine.

Bayer has also benefited from its persistent intensive marketing of Aspirin. Originally targeted at physicians, the drug was sold over the counter without prescription from 1915. In addition, in some countries, including the UK, it continues to be prescribed and sometimes reimbursed by health services, which adds to its medical credibility and helps justify premium prices.

Bayer's Aspirin remains widely advertised, with an emphasis on the company's high quality and the product's breadth of use. Some of Bayer's campaigns have triggered reprimands, including from the US Federal Trade Commission and Food and Drug Administration, over claimed medical uses that were not authorised by regulators.

The company has boosted its credibility by sponsoring Aspirin scientific prizes and funding bodies such as the Aspirin Foundation in the UK, which advocates for the drug's wider use. Set up in the 1970s to counter rivals' campaigns for paracetamol that warned of the dangers of Reyes syndrome, a rare but lethal condition linked to children taking aspirin, the foundation today also disseminates research suggesting the drug's potential for new applications. Even this Friday, a new academic study will analyse aspirin's potential to prevent cancer. Bayer may long ago have lost the patent and reduced its own investments in development, but as the pharmaceutical industry seeks to diversify into new, less risky products and emerging markets, it remains an anchor brand to envy.

Source: The serial painkiller, © The Financial Times Limited. All Rights Reserved, 27 October 2011 (Jack, A.).

16.3   Advertising and product characteristics

Several economists have suggested that product characteristics may be an important determinant of advertising intensity. For example, it has been suggested that goods whose attributes consumers can assess accurately before they are purchased and consumed are unlikely to be the subject of large-scale advertising campaigns. In contrast, goods whose attributes are difficult to assess may be more heavily advertised. For products that are purchased regularly, consumers are unlikely to search for detailed information prior to purchase, and are unlikely to be persuaded by advertising that the brands they consume have qualities other than those consumers can discern for themselves. For products that are purchased less frequently, consumers may be more open to persuasion through advertising prior to purchase. Consumers are more likely to search for detailed information prior to purchase of products whose price accounts for a significant proportion of a typical consumer's budget. For such products, persuasive advertising may be ineffective in swaying the consumer's eventual purchase decision. For inexpensive products or services, on the other hand, mistakes tend to matter less, and consumers may be content to be swayed by advertising messages.

Nelson (1974a,b) defines **search goods** as those whose attributes can easily be determined by inspection, either by touch or by sight, prior to purchase. Common examples include clothes, carpets, household and office furniture. **Experience goods** are those whose attributes can only be determined when they are consumed, after they have been purchased. Common examples include foods, toothpaste, washing-up liquid, cars and hi-fi systems. Nelson argues the probable effectiveness of persuasive advertising differs systematically between search goods and experience goods. There may be a role for informative advertising of search goods, to ensure consumers are aware of the product's price, capabilities or existence. But persuasive advertising of search goods is unlikely to be effective, because it is easy for consumers to assess the quality of the product for themselves before deciding whether or not to purchase. The truth (or otherwise) of advertising claims about the qualities of search goods is in any case transparent.

For experience goods, in contrast, there is likely to be a role for both informative and persuasive advertising. If consumers cannot assess the quality of the product for themselves prior to purchase, the purchase decision may be swayed by persuasive advertising. The truth (or otherwise) of advertising claims about the qualities of experience goods only becomes apparent after the consumer is already committed and purchase has already taken place. Accordingly, Nelson concludes that advertising intensity is likely to be higher for experience goods than for search goods.

Darby and Karni (1973) extend this classification to include **credence goods**; see also Mixon (1994). A credence good is one whose quality cannot easily be assessed before or after consumption, because a judgement about quality requires the consumer to have specialized knowledge of the product or service. Common examples are dental services, medical care, car repair services and (perhaps) university courses. Applying similar reasoning, both informative and persuasive advertising may be effective in the case of credence goods.

Frequency of purchase may also have implications for the effectiveness of persuasive advertising, especially in the case of experience goods. Arterburn and Woodbury (1981) use the term **convenience goods** to describe goods that are relatively cheap and that are purchased frequently. In contrast, **shopping goods** are expensive and purchased infrequently. For example, washing-up liquid and hi-fi equipment are both experience goods, because their qualities cannot easily be identified prior to purchase and consumption; but washing-up liquid is a convenience good, while hi-fi equipment is a shopping good. Bin-liners and furniture are both search goods, because their qualities can easily be assessed prior to purchase and consumption, but bin-liners are a convenience good, while furniture is a shopping good.

Suppose there are two new brands of washing-up liquid, one of which is of high quality and the other low quality. In both cases, persuasive advertising might be effective in persuading consumers to try either brand for the first time. Once consumers have had the opportunity to assess the qualities of the brands for themselves, however, only the high-quality brand is likely to attract repeat purchases. The advertising expenditure devoted to the low-quality brand is mostly wasted if this brand turns out to be incapable of attracting repeat purchases. This discussion suggests advertising might sometimes have a role to play in signalling quality to consumers. The content of the advertising message itself may be irrelevant, but the very fact that a brand is advertised heavily suggests the producer is confident that consumers who try the brand will be satisfied, and will make repeat purchases. A model of quality signalling through advertising is described in Section 16.6.

Many consumer durables, such as cars, washing machines, and audio-visual equipment, can be classified as experience goods and as shopping goods. Other things being equal, the infrequency of purchase might suggest advertising intensities for shopping goods should be higher than for convenience goods. But there is a countervailing factor. Shopping goods are expensive, and their purchase accounts for a large proportion of a typical consumer's budget. When purchasing shopping goods that are also experience goods, consumers are likely to make efforts to gather reliable information about the attributes of competing brands.

16.4 Advertising and profit maximization

Whether informative or persuasive advertising is employed, firms spend money on advertising campaigns in order to increase the demand for their products or services, in the hope that increased consumer demand will yield a higher profit. This section analyzes the firm's advertising decision within a traditional framework of profit maximization. In order to select the level of advertising expenditure that maximizes its profit, the firm advertises until the marginal benefit (in terms of increased revenue) gained from the last unit of advertising *equals* the marginal cost. Below, the problem of selecting the profit-maximizing level of advertising is considered separately for the market structures of monopoly, oligopoly and perfect competition.

Monopoly

In the case of a monopoly, only a simple extension of the neoclassical model of profit maximization is needed in order to identify the optimal level of advertising. In Figure 16.1, it is assumed that the position of a monopolist's average revenue function, which is the same as the market demand function, depends on the level of advertising expenditure. Advertising expenditures of a_1, a_2, a_3 and a_4 are shown in Figure 16.1, and it is assumed the difference between each successive level of advertising expenditure ($a_2 - a_1$, $a_3 - a_2$ and so on) is the same, and equal to Δa. It is assumed there are diminishing returns to advertising, so on each successive occasion advertising expenditure is increased by Δa, the outward shift in the average revenue function becomes smaller. For simplicity, production cost is assumed to be linear in output. The firm's total cost is the sum of its production cost and its advertising expenditure.

■ When advertising expenditure is a_1, the firm's optimal output is Q_1, where $MR_1 = MC$.

■ By increasing advertising expenditure from a_1 to a_2, the firm increases its optimal output to Q_2, where $MR_2 = MC$. The increase in operating profit (revenue *minus* production cost) of $\Delta\pi_2$ exceeds the advertising expenditure of Δa. The decision to advertise is beneficial and the shift from Q_1 to Q_2 is profitable. The firm should continue to increase its advertising expenditure until the marginal increase in operating profit is just equal to the marginal increase in advertising expenditure.

■ By increasing advertising expenditure from a_2 to a_3, the firm increases its optimal output to Q_3, where $MR_3 = MC$. The increase in operating profit of $\Delta\pi_3$ is just equal to the additional advertising expenditure of Δa. The effect of the extra advertising is neutral, and the firm is indifferent between operating at Q_3 and Q_2. If advertising is continuous ($\Delta a \to 0$) rather than discrete, there is a unique profit-maximizing level of advertising expenditure.

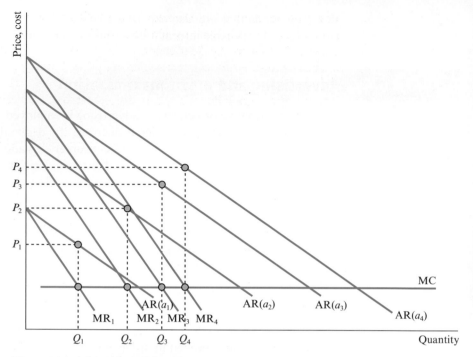

Figure 16.1 Advertising and profit maximization in monopoly

■ Finally, by increasing advertising expenditure from a_3 to a_4, the optimal output increases to Q_4, where $\mathrm{MR}_4 = \mathrm{MC}$. The increase in operating profit of $\Delta\pi_4$ is less than the additional advertising expenditure of Δa. The extra advertising is not worthwhile, and the firm should not seek to operate at Q_4.

In a seminal article, Dorfman and Steiner (1954) develop an analysis of the monopolist's optimal advertising decision using an algebraic model. Their results are insightful, and working through the formal algebraic derivation is worthwhile. The Dorfman–Steiner framework is essentially the same as in Figure 16.1, except it is assumed that advertising expenditure is continuous rather than discrete, and it is no longer assumed that the firm's demand (or average revenue) function and production costs are necessarily linear in output. The monopolist's demand (or average revenue) function is:

$$Q = Q(P, a)$$

where Q denotes quantity demanded, P denotes price and a denotes advertising expenditure. The monopolist's cost function is:

$$c = c(Q) + a$$

where Q denotes quantity produced, and c denotes cost. The monopolist's profit is:

$$\pi = \mathrm{TR} - c(Q) - a = P \times Q(P, a) - c(Q) - a$$

For profit maximization, the additional profit gained from a marginal increase in advertising expenditure should be zero. For simplicity, Dorfman and Steiner assume that when the firm changes its advertising expenditure it adjusts its quantity produced but does not alter its price. Let ΔQ, Δc and Δa denote the changes in output, cost and advertising expenditure, respectively. For profit maximization, the following relationship must hold between these quantities:

$$P\left(\frac{\Delta Q}{\Delta a}\right) - \left(\frac{\Delta c}{\Delta Q}\right)\left(\frac{\Delta Q}{\Delta a}\right) - 1 = 0 \text{ or } \left\{P - \left(\frac{\Delta c}{\Delta Q}\right)\right\}\left\{\frac{\Delta Q}{\Delta a}\right\} = 1$$

Multiply both the left-hand side and the right-hand side through by $\dfrac{a}{PQ}$ and note that $(\Delta c/\Delta Q) = \text{MC}$:

$$\left(\frac{P - \text{MC}}{P}\right)\left(\frac{\Delta Q}{\Delta a}\right)\frac{a}{Q} = \frac{a}{PQ}$$

From Chapter 2, $(P - \text{MC})/P = 1/|\text{PED}|$, where $|\text{PED}|$ is the price elasticity of demand. Furthermore, $(P - \text{MC})/P$ is the Lerner index, widely used as an indicator of market power (see Section 3.4).

Applying the general definition for any elasticity, $\left(\dfrac{\Delta Q}{\Delta a}\right)\dfrac{a}{Q} = \text{AED}$, where AED is the advertising elasticity of demand (defined as the ratio of the proportionate change in quantity demanded to the proportionate change in advertising expenditure). By substitution and re-ordering the previous expression:

$$\frac{a}{PQ} = \left(\frac{P - \text{MC}}{P}\right)\text{AED} \quad \text{or} \quad \frac{a}{PQ} = \frac{\text{AED}}{|\text{PED}|}$$

This expression is known as the **Dorfman–Steiner condition**. It implies that for profit maximization, the ratio of advertising expenditure to total revenue, or the advertising-to-sales ratio, should be proportional to the ratio of advertising elasticity of demand to price elasticity of demand. The intuition underlying this result is as follows. When the advertising elasticity is high relative to the price elasticity, it is efficient for the monopolist to advertise (rather than cut price) in order to achieve any given increase in quantity demanded. Accordingly, the monopolist spends a relatively high proportion of its sales revenue on advertising. On the other hand, when the price elasticity is high relative to the advertising elasticity, it is efficient to cut price (rather than advertise) in order to achieve any given increase in quantity demanded. Accordingly, the monopolist spends a relatively low proportion of its sales revenue on advertising.

Oligopoly

The preceding analysis refers to a monopolist, and the reactions of competing firms are therefore irrelevant. In order to apply the same kind of analysis to the case of oligopoly, the analysis needs to be extended to take account of the interdependence between the oligopolistic firms. Consider a market in which there are two duopolists: firms A and B. Assume initially, for simplicity, that firm B's advertising expenditure is fixed, and consider the profit-maximizing advertising decision of firm A. Adapting previous notation, let q_A denote firm A's quantity demanded and a_A denote firm A's advertising expenditure. Q denotes total industry demand, equal to the combined demand for firms A and B, $q_A + q_B$; m_A denotes firm A's share of industry demand, or q_A/Q; and AED_A denotes firm A's advertising elasticity of demand.

The revised expression for AED_A is as follows:

$$AED_A = \frac{a_A}{Q}\left(\frac{\Delta Q}{\Delta a_A}\right) + \frac{a_A}{m_A}\left(\frac{\Delta m_A}{\Delta a_A}\right)$$

The two terms on the right-hand-side of this expression represent the following effects of a small change in a_A on q_A. First, there is an increase in total industry demand, ΔQ, part of which goes to firm A. Second, there is an increase in firm A's share of total industry demand, m_A. The expression for AED_A justifies the idea that the advertising elasticity of demand under oligopoly should be higher than it is under monopoly. When firm A increases its advertising expenditure, it benefits not only from an increase in total industry demand (as does the monopolist) but also from an increase in its own market share. This 'market share' effect does not apply in the case of the monopolist. In other words, for a monopolist, $m_A = 1$ and $\Delta m_A = 0$, so the second term on the right-hand-side of the expression for AED_A is zero. For an oligopolist, $m_A < 1$ and $\Delta m_A > 0$, so the second term on the right-hand side of the expression for AED_A is positive.

Using the Dorfman–Steiner condition as before:

$$\frac{a_A}{P_A q_A} = \left(\frac{P_A - MC}{P_A}\right)AED_A = \left(\frac{P_A - MC}{P_A}\right)\left\{\frac{a_A}{Q}\left(\frac{\Delta Q}{\Delta a_A}\right) + \frac{a_A}{m_A}\left(\frac{\Delta m_A}{\Delta a_A}\right)\right\}$$

P_A denotes firm A's price. The advertising-to-sales ratio for an oligopolist should be higher than for a monopolist. The oligopolist has an additional incentive to advertise: not only does advertising increase total industry demand, but it also increases the advertising firm's share of industry demand.

The final extension to the analysis of firm A's profit-maximizing advertising decision under duopoly builds into the formula for AED_A an allowance for the effects of firm B's reaction to firm A's decision to increase its advertising expenditure. Firm B's advertising expenditure is denoted a_B, and the change in advertising expenditure implemented by firm B is Δa_B. The revised expression for AED_A is as follows:

$$AED_A = \frac{a_A}{Q}\left\{\left(\frac{\Delta Q}{\Delta a_A}\right) + \left(\frac{\Delta Q}{\Delta a_B}\right)\left(\frac{\Delta a_B}{\Delta a_A}\right)\right\} + \frac{a_A}{m_A}\left\{\left(\frac{\Delta m_A}{\Delta a_A}\right) + \left(\frac{\Delta m_A}{\Delta a_B}\right)\left(\frac{\Delta a_B}{\Delta a_A}\right)\right\}$$

The two terms of the right-hand side of this expression represent the same two effects of a small change in a_A on q_A as before. But as well as the direct effect of Δa_A on Q and on m_A, there are also indirect effects resulting from Δa_B, the change in firm B's advertising expenditure implemented in response to the change in firm A's advertising expenditure. Assuming $(\Delta a_B/\Delta a_A)$ is positive, firm B responds to an increase in firm A's advertising by increasing its own advertising. Firm A gains to the extent that firm B's action increases total industry demand, but firm A also loses to the extent that firm B's action reduces firm A's market share.

Using the Dorfman–Steiner condition:

$$\frac{a_A}{P_A q_A} = \left(\frac{P_A - \text{MC}}{P_A}\right)\left[\frac{a_A}{Q}\left\{\left(\frac{\Delta Q}{\Delta a_A}\right) + \left(\frac{\Delta Q}{\Delta a_B}\right)\left(\frac{\Delta a_B}{\Delta a_A}\right)\right\} + \frac{a_A}{m_A}\left\{\left(\frac{\Delta m_A}{\Delta a_A}\right) + \left(\frac{\Delta m_A}{\Delta a_B}\right)\left(\frac{\Delta m_B}{\Delta a_A}\right)\right\}\right]$$

Because $(\Delta Q/\Delta a_B) > 0$ and $(\Delta m_A/\Delta a_B) < 0$, firm A's advertising-to-sales ratio in the case where firm B reacts to firm A's actions could be either higher or lower than in the case where firm B's behaviour is fixed.

However, suppose the effect of advertising on each firm's market share generally tends to dominate the effect on total industry demand. In the most extreme case, it could be assumed $(\Delta Q/\Delta a_A) = (\Delta Q/\Delta a_B) = 0$. Suppose also each firm tends to ignore or underestimate its rival's reaction to its own advertising decisions. In the most extreme case, suppose firm A assumes $(\Delta a_B/\Delta a_A) = 0$, when in fact $(\Delta a_B/\Delta a_A) > 0$. Then, according to the previous expression, firm A will tend to set its advertising-to-sales ratio at a level too high for profit maximization. Firm A's advertising-to-sales ratio under the (false) assumption $(\Delta a_B/\Delta a_A) = 0$ is:

$$\frac{a_A}{P_A q_A} = \left(\frac{P_A - \text{MC}}{P_A}\right)\frac{a_A}{m_A}\left\{\left(\frac{\Delta m_A}{\Delta a_A}\right)\right\}$$

But firm A's (true) profit-maximizing advertising-to-sales ratio is:

$$\frac{a_A}{P_A q_A} = \left(\frac{P_A - \text{MC}}{P_A}\right)\left[\frac{a_A}{m_A}\left\{\left(\frac{\Delta m_A}{\Delta a_A}\right) + \left(\frac{\Delta m_A}{\Delta a_B}\right)\left(\frac{\Delta a_B}{\Delta a_A}\right)\right\}\right]$$

The second of these expressions is smaller than the first, because $(\Delta m_A/\Delta a_B) < 0$ and $(\Delta a_B/\Delta a_A) > 0$. Accordingly, in this case firm A tends to overspend on advertising. If firm B has a similar tendency to underestimate the size of firm A's reactions, there will be a general tendency for the firms collectively to advertise more heavily than they would if they took proper account of their interdependence.

Perfect competition

The Dorfman–Steiner condition, which states that the profit-maximizing advertising-to-sales ratio *equals* the ratio of the firm's advertising elasticity of demand to its price elasticity of demand, provides a straightforward justification for the assertion made in Section 16.1, that there is no role for advertising in perfect competition. The demand function of the perfectly competitive firm is horizontal, and the firm's price elasticity of demand is infinite. Accordingly, the ratio of the firm's advertising elasticity of demand to its price elasticity of demand is zero. The profit-maximizing advertising-to-sales ratio is also zero. If the firm can sell as much output as it likes at the current market price, there is no point in advertising.

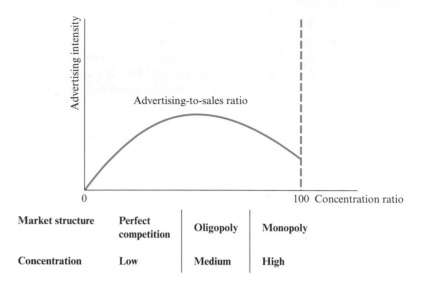

Figure 16.2 Advertising, market structure and concentration

The alternative formulation of the Dorfman–Steiner condition, which states that the profit-maximizing advertising-to-sales ratio equals the product of the Lerner index and the advertising elasticity of demand, produces the same conclusion. For the perfectly competitive firm, the Lerner index is zero because price *equals* marginal cost. Therefore the profit-maximizing advertising-to-sales ratio is also zero.

Figure 16.2 summarizes the conclusions of Section 16.4 concerning the relationship between market structure and the profit-maximizing advertising-to-sales ratio. The latter should be zero under perfect competition, positive under oligopoly and positive under monopoly, but larger under oligopoly than under monopoly. Section 16.8 includes a review of a number of empirical studies of this relationship between advertising intensity and market structure or concentration, as summarized in Figure 16.2.

16.5   Advertising as a barrier to entry

Advertising can act as a barrier to entry in several ways:

■ *The need to advertise increases start-up costs*. Entrants may need to spend heavily on advertising in order to establish name recognition and a presence in the market. This raises entrants' initial costs. It may be difficult for an entrant to raise the required finance because the returns to advertising outlays are usually uncertain (Weiss, 1963).

■ *High levels of advertising build up reputation effects*. Past advertising by incumbents creates goodwill and strengthens consumer brand loyalties. These advantages may be difficult for entrants to overcome. Reputation effects may be particularly strong for first-movers: firms that have in the past pioneered a particular product or brand. Pioneering firms are often able to shape consumer tastes in favour of their own products or brands (Glazer,

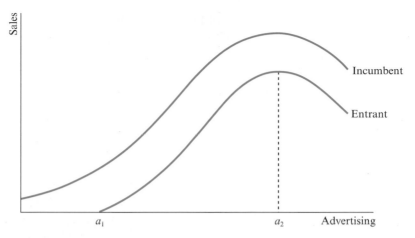

Figure 16.3 Advertising response functions

1985). Robinson *et al.* (1994) survey the sources of first-mover advantages, while Bar-Isaac and Tadelis (2008) provide an extensive analysis of the models of seller reputation.

- *Economies of scale in advertising.* According to Scherer and Ross (1990), there are two sources of economies of scale in advertising. First, firms must advertise a large number of times before advertising messages permeate the minds of consumers, and produce increased sales. Second, large-scale advertisers may pay less per unit of advertising than small-scale advertisers. Furthermore, an indirect 'distribution effect' arises when retailers increase stocks of products in response to a manufacturer's advertising campaign, in the expectation that demand will increase (*The Economist*, 2004b).

Figure 16.3 shows the possible **advertising response functions** of an incumbent firm and an entrant. These functions reflect the responsiveness of sales to the volume of advertising expenditure. For the entrant, assumed to be advertising its product or brand for the first time, a threshold level of advertising expenditure of a_1 must be achieved before its advertising begins to have any positive effect on sales. The entrant must spend at least a_1 in order for its brand to achieve name recognition among potential purchasers. Further advertising beyond a_1 increases the entrant's sales, although diminishing returns eventually set in. Saturation point is reached at an advertising expenditure level of a_2. Any further advertising beyond a_2 has a harmful effect on sales: consumers become fed up with receiving the firm's advertising messages, and stop buying the product or brand.

The incumbent is assumed to have advertised its product or brand in the past. Past advertising is assumed to have been effective in building up name recognition and consumer brand loyalty. In contrast to the entrant, the incumbent does not have to overcome an advertising threshold before it reaps any benefits from advertising: any advertising expenditure in the current period produces some increase in sales. Like the entrant, however, the incumbent is subject to diminishing returns to advertising, and may reach a saturation point beyond which further advertising has a harmful effect on sales.

Advertising response functions such as those shown in Figure 16.3 may contribute to entry barriers due to both an absolute cost advantage favouring the incumbent, and economies of scale (see Section 11.2). Thanks to its past advertising investment, the incumbent achieves more sales for any given amount of current advertising expenditure. This implies the incumbent has an absolute cost advantage over the entrant.

Furthermore, because the gradient of the advertising response function is increasing over the lower end of the range of values for a, and because the threshold level of advertising expenditure is effectively a fixed cost from the entrant's perspective, there are economies of scale in advertising. Within the relevant range of values for a, the effectiveness of each unit of advertising expenditure increases as the volume of advertising expenditure increases. If advertising costs are incorporated into the firms' total cost functions, economies of scale in advertising may change the location of the minimum efficient scale of production. This in turn may alter the extent to which the cost structure, and in particular the need to be producing on a scale sufficiently large to be cost-efficient, acts as a barrier to entry.

Scott Morton (2000) examines the extent to which the advertising of patented branded pharmaceutical products in the US immediately prior to the loss of patent protection deterred the entry of generic drugs. The sample comprises drugs that lost patent protection over the period 1986–91, while the advertising data are monthly from three years before to one year after patent expiration. There is little evidence that advertising deterred entry. Advertising response may vary not only between incumbent firms and entrants but also among incumbent firms. Fare *et al.* (2004) examine the cost-efficiency of advertising by media (television, radio, print) for a sample of six large US brewers over the period 1983–93. Only one of the six firms (Anheuser Buesch) is found to use advertising efficiently. Advertising efficiency estimates are found to be positively linked to profitability.

16.6 Advertising, information search and quality signalling

Information plays a crucial role in competition. In the perfectly competitive model, all buyers and sellers have perfect knowledge. Consequently, one price prevails, and all firms earn normal profit. However, if information is imperfect or if there is an informational asymmetry between producers and consumers, consumers may not be capable of making an informed choice about the products and services they purchase. This may have serious implications for the effectiveness of competition and the nature of market equilibrium.

Some economists have suggested that advertising improves the speed and efficiency with which consumers search for information. Consumers gather information through a search process, which imposes costs in the form of wages or leisure time forgone. From the consumer's perspective, advertising reduces the cost of obtaining this information. Equivalently, if products are heavily advertised, the consumer can obtain a given amount information more cheaply, since the information obtained from advertisements reduces the need for independent search.

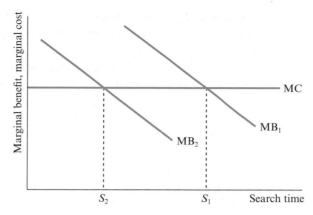

Figure 16.4 Optimal search time

In Figure 16.4, the marginal cost function MC represents the cost of each additional hour of search and is assumed to be constant. The benefit to the consumer from each additional hour of search is represented by the downward-sloping marginal benefit function MB_1. The benefit gained from spending additional time searching declines as the time already spent increases. The search process continues until the marginal benefit *equals* the marginal cost, with S_1 hours devoted to search.

The provision of information through advertising reduces the marginal benefit gained from each additional hour of information search, shifting the marginal benefit function to the left from MB_1 to MB_2. The optimal search time decreases from S_1 to S_2. If, as seems likely, information is disseminated more efficiently through advertising than it is through having large numbers of consumers searching for information independently, the sum of the product price and the search cost is likely to be lower due to advertising.

> Advertising is among other things, a method of providing potential buyers with knowledge of the identity of sellers. It is clearly an immensely powerful instrument for the elimination of ignorance – comparable in force to the use of the book instead of the oral discourse to communicate knowledge.
>
> *(Stigler, 1961, p. 182)*

Advertising also plays an important role in some signalling models, which deal with situations of asymmetric information between producers and consumers. In a classic analysis of the market for secondhand cars, Akerlof (1970) argues that sellers tend to have more information than potential buyers about the true quality of each car on the market, and a potential buyer may not be able to tell which cars that are for sale are of good quality and which ones should be avoided. In the terminology of the advertising literature, secondhand cars are an experience good. Faced with this uncertainty, the maximum price a rational buyer is willing to pay falls somewhere between the true value of a high-quality car and the true value of a low-quality car. However, if sellers of high-quality cars are unwilling to sell at a price below the true value of a high-quality car, they withdraw from the market. The market for high-quality cars collapses, and only low-quality cars are traded. The title of Akerlof's article, 'The market for lemons', refers to American slang terminology for a low-quality second-hand car.

A similar situation might exist in the market for a product with competing high-quality and low-quality brands. If the product is an experience good and potential buyers cannot distinguish between the low- and high-quality brands before purchase, there may be a tendency for high-quality brands to be driven out of the market by low-quality brands, for the reasons discussed by Akerlof. However, Kihlstrom and Riordan (1984) and Milgrom and Roberts (1986) show that if there are repeat purchases of the product, the producer of a high-quality brand may be able to use advertising as a signal of quality. The idea is that for advertising to be worthwhile, it has to persuade consumers to buy the product more than once. It is not worthwhile for a low-quality producer to advertise its brand as high quality, because consumers who are initially misled into purchasing the inferior brand discover from experience that the brand is low quality, and will not make the same mistake again. However, it is worthwhile for a high quality producer to advertise, because consumers who purchase this brand and confirm from experience that it *is* high quality, will make repeat purchases.

To demonstrate the signalling model, it is assumed that each brand of a certain product has a two-period lifetime. A low-quality brand that is known by consumers to be low-quality earns a profit of 10 per period. However, a low-quality brand can earn a profit of 30 per period, if it is mistakenly perceived by consumers to be high quality. A high-quality brand can earn a profit of 25 per period, provided consumers can distinguish between the high-quality brand and its low-quality imitators. If consumers cannot make this distinction, in each period the high-quality brand is driven out of the market by a flood of low-quality imitators, and the high-quality brand earns zero profit.

Suppose initially there is no advertising, and the low-quality producer can pretend its brand is high-quality at zero cost.

- A low-quality brand that is known to be low-quality earns a combined profit in periods 1 and 2 of 10 + 10 = 20.

- A low-quality brand that pretends to be high-quality earns a profit of 30 in period 1. However, in period 2 consumers know from experience the brand is actually low quality, so the period 2 profit is 10. The combined profit in periods 1 and 2 is 30 + 10 = 40.

Accordingly, it is profitable for low-quality producers to pretend their brands are high quality in period 1. The high-quality brand is driven out of the market and earns zero profit. In period 2, the same thing happens again. Although the low-quality brands that existed in period 1 are now perceived by consumers to be low quality, new brands appear that are actually low quality but pretend to be high quality. Again, the high-quality brand is driven out of the market and earns zero profit.

Now suppose producers of either brand can convince consumers their brand is high quality in period 1 only by advertising, at a cost of 25. No advertising is necessary in period 2, because by then consumers have established for themselves the true quality of the brand they purchased in period 1.

■ The producer of a low-quality brand that is not advertised and is known to be low quality earns a combined profit in periods 1 and 2 of $10 + 10 = 20$, as before.

■ The producer of a low-quality brand that is advertised and pretends to be high quality earns a profit of $30 - 25 = 5$ in period 1. Despite the advertising, in period 2 consumers know the brand is actually low quality, so the period 2 profit is 10. The combined profit in periods 1 and 2 is $5 + 10 = 15$.

Accordingly, it is not profitable for producers of low-quality brands to advertise and pretend to be high quality in period 1. The producer of the high-quality brand, on the other hand, does advertise, and is not driven out of the market. The period 1 profit is $25 - 25 = 0$. In period 2, however, this producer earns a profit of 25. The combined profit in periods 1 and 2 is $0 + 25 = 25$.

In the signalling model, it is not the advertising message itself that is effective in convincing consumers that the advertised brand is high quality. Rather, the simple fact that this brand is being advertised provides the necessary signal of high quality. Consumers realize the producer only advertises if it is confident of attracting repeat purchases. Similarly, the fact that the low-quality brand is not advertised provides a signal of low quality. Consumers realize that if the brand was high quality the producer would advertise; therefore the fact that the brand is not advertised signals that it is low quality.

> [If] the consumer believes that the more a brand advertises, the more likely it is to be a better buy . . . in consequence, the more advertisements of a brand the consumer encounters, the more likely he is to try the brand.
>
> *(Nelson, 1974b, p. 732)*

> It is clear that if high-quality brands advertise more and if advertising expenditures are observable (even if not perfectly so), then rational, informed consumers will respond positively to advertising even if the ads cannot and do not have much direct informational content.
>
> *(Milgrom and Roberts, 1986, p. 797)*

> Costly and wasteful advertisement demonstrates that the advertiser is also investing in the quality of the product and a continued relationship with customers, because otherwise the costly and wasteful advertising would serve no purpose.
>
> *(Kay, 2004, p. 217)*

Advertising is not necessarily the only method by which producers can send signals of quality. Hertzendorf (1993) argues that if price signalling is effective, advertising is unnecessary. Advertising is only useful if price does not provide consumers with enough information to assess quality. Fluent and Garella (2002) develop a theoretical model to examine whether firms use advertising or price to signal quality to consumers. They find that advertising is an appropriate signalling device in differentiating products when quality differences are small, but price is preferred when quality differences are large. Horstmann and MacDonald (2003) suggest advertising is an important tool in informing consumers about product quality and characteristics; but as consumer awareness increases, the need for advertising should decline. However, data from the US market for compact disc players over the period 1983–92 suggests a tendency for prices to fall and advertising intensity to increase over time.

Siegel and Vitaliano (2007) investigate whether producers of experience and credence goods spend more on corporate social responsibility (CSR) policies (see Section 6.7) than producers of search goods. For experience and credence goods, consumers rely on information supplied by the producer regarding product attributes. The hypothesis is that CSR policies are seen by consumers primarily as a signal of quality, honesty and reliability. Siegel and Vitaliano identify producers of search goods, and producers of experience or credence goods, using the KLD database. Firms selling credence services, such as financial services, are 23 per cent more likely to be involved in CSR activity than firms selling search goods. Firms selling durable experience goods such as electronic equipment are 15 per cent more likely to be involved in CSR. Firms selling experience services or non-durable experience goods are not significantly more likely to be involved in CSR activity than producers of search goods.

16.7 Is there too much advertising?

As shown above, advertising is often categorized as either informative or persuasive. Informative advertising is widely regarded as useful because it provides consumers with information, with which they can make more informed choices. Persuasive advertising, in contrast, distorts the information consumers receive, making it more difficult for them to make informed choices on the basis of objective information. Reliable information is a prerequisite for effective competition, which ensures resources are used efficiently to produce the goods and services that consumers actually want. Persuasive advertising changes the preferences of consumers and might even damage competition, if firms that have invested in building up brand loyalties exploit their market power by charging higher prices and earning abnormal profit.

The traditional view of advertising, expressed by Kaldor (1950), Bain (1956), Galbraith (1958, 1967) and Comanor and Wilson (1974), takes a critical view. Advertising tends to distort consumer preferences, by persuading consumers to buy products and services that are heavily promoted.

> Most advertising is not informative. The typical Marlboro ad, with a cowboy smoking a cigarette, or a Virginia slims ad, or a Budweiser beer ad, conveys no credible information concerning the nature of the product being sold, the price at which the product is sold, or where the

product may be obtained. Firms spend money on ads such as these because they believe it increases their profit, because such ads have an effect on demand curves.

(Stiglitz, 1991, p. 842)

The goal of persuasive advertising is to change customers' perceptions of a product. If persuasive advertising works, it means that a branded product is considered in some non-tangible way to be 'different' to its rivals. If successful, therefore, persuasive advertising may generate brand loyalty – customers may be unwilling to switch to competitors' products if they are convinced that their preferred brand offers something that no other product would be able to provide.

(Nawaz, 1997, p. 3)

Persuasive advertising interferes with the exercise of innate preferences, it alters choices away from the efficient lines that 'consumer sovereignty' would yield. Thus persuasive image instilling advertising is largely a form of economic waste.

(Shepherd, 1997, p. 111)

In one of the most famous critiques of advertising, Kaldor (1950) argues that because advertising is supplied jointly with goods and services, consumers are forced to pay for advertising they do not want, and are unwilling accomplices in a waste of resources. The amount of advertising supplied exceeds that demanded because it is provided as a 'free' service not only to purchasers, but also to consumers who will never buy the good or service under consideration. Advertisers do not charge a positive price for advertising, since to do so would result in less advertising being demanded than is required for advertisers to maximize profit. Consequently, there is an oversupply of advertising, and a waste of resources that is financed by consumers who have no choice other than to pay a higher price for the advertised goods.

The main criticisms of Kaldor's argument are as follows:

- Consumers have a choice between advertised and non-advertised goods. If consumers did not buy advertised products, there would be no market for advertising (Telser, 1966b).

- By supplying advertising jointly with goods and services, savings may be realized. Collecting separate fees for the provision of information might be more expensive than incorporating advertising costs into the price of the product or service.

- Kaldor's view is consistent with the underlying assumptions of microeconomic theory, in which a consumer with fixed tastes possesses perfect information (Koutsoyannis, 1982). In reality, however, consumers inhabit societies that are dynamic by nature. Tastes are socially and culturally conditioned, and are not exogenous. Consumers continuously acquire new information from their own experiences and through the media. The static equilibrium methodology used in consumer theory, based on assumptions of fixed tastes and perfect information, is therefore misleading (Nichols, 1985; Hoschman and Luski, 1988).

An alternative view, articulated by Stigler (1961), Telser (1964, 1966a), Littlechild (1982) and Nelson (1974a,b, 1975, 1978) is that advertising provides consumers with valuable information, allowing them to make rational choices. Under this view, advertising plays a positive role in ensuring the efficient allocation of resources. The extent to which consumers are able to make informed choices depends on the knowledge and certainty they have about the attributes of products and services. Informed consumers are unlikely to pay higher prices for any particular product or service unless 'real' differences exist. Becker and Murphy (1993) argue that advertisements should be treated as valuable complements to the goods they promote, and not as products that distort consumer tastes and preferences. In cases where advertisements appear on television and radio, these tend to lower consumer utility. However, consumers are compensated for exposure to advertising by the provision of free television and radio programmes. Advertising does not necessarily reduce utility in all forms of media. In media where consumers can easily ignore advertising, such as the print media, advertising is more likely to be informative and utility-increasing to consumers.

Evaluation of the welfare effects of advertising is made difficult by the fact that persuasive advertising changes consumer tastes and preferences. This means there is no consistent standard for making welfare comparisons before and after advertising takes place. It may be difficult to determine whether a consumer is better or worse off as a result of advertising, if the consumer has a different utility function in each case. However, Dixit and Norman (1978) suggest a method for avoiding this difficulty. If it can be shown that welfare is increased by advertising if the assessment is made using pre-advertising consumer preferences, *and* if it can also be shown that welfare is increased if the assessment is made using post-advertising consumer preferences, then it is unambiguous that welfare is increased, no matter how the comparison is made.

Dixit and Norman's analysis for the case of a monopolist is shown in Figure 16.5, drawn on the same assumptions as Figure 16.1. As before, following an advertising campaign costing $\Delta a = a_2 - a_1$, the monopolist's average revenue function shifts from $AR(a_1)$ to $AR(a_2)$, and the profit-maximizing price and quantity shift from P_1Q_1 to P_2Q_2. What are the welfare implications of this shift? As argued above, there are two possible answers, depending whether pre-advertising or post-advertising preferences are used to make the comparison.

■ Using the pre-advertising demand function $AR(a_1)$, the welfare gain from the extra production is the area between $AR(a_1)$ and MC over the range Q_1 to Q_2, *minus* the advertising expenditure. The welfare gain is $B - \Delta a$. This expression could be positive or negative.

■ Using the post-advertising demand function $AR(a_2)$, the welfare gain from the extra production is the area between $AR(a_2)$ and MC over the range Q_1 to Q_2, *minus* the advertising expenditure. The welfare gain is $B + C + D - \Delta a$. This expression could also be positive or negative.

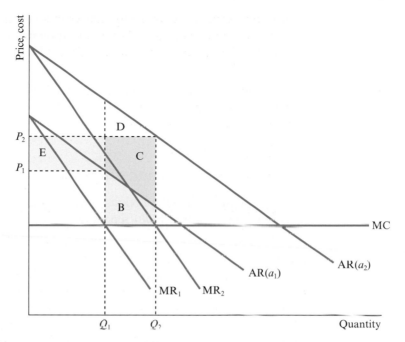

Figure 16.5 Welfare analysis of an increase in advertising expenditure in monopoly

In order to ascertain whether advertising is always welfare-enhancing if it is also profitable, one further assumption concerning Figure 16.5 is introduced at this point: it is assumed area D < area E. From the construction of Figure 16.5 it is clear that for sufficiently small changes in a, the condition D < E is very likely to be satisfied, and below it is assumed that this is the case.

The gain in monopoly profit resulting from the shift from P_1Q_1 to P_2Q_2 is B + C + E − Δa. The monopolist only advertises if B + C + E − $\Delta a \geq 0$, which is a necessary (but not a sufficient) condition for B − Δa > 0 and (assuming D < E) for B + C + D − Δa > 0. This means advertising can only be welfare-enhancing if it is also profitable. There cannot be a case in which welfare could be improved by advertising more, but the monopolist fails to increase advertising because it is not profitable to do so.

The profit-maximizing monopolist increases its advertising until B + C + E − Δa = 0. Consider the welfare effects of the last unit of advertising expenditure at the profit-maximizing equilibrium.

- Using pre-advertising preferences, the welfare effect of the last unit of advertising expenditure is B − Δa. If B + C + E − Δa = 0, B − Δa must be negative, because C and E are both positive.

- Using post-advertising preferences, the welfare effect of the last unit of advertising expenditure is B + C + D − Δa. If B + C + E − Δa = 0, B + C + D − Δa must be negative, because it is assumed D < E.

Therefore, at the profit-maximizing equilibrium, the welfare effect of the last unit of advertising expenditure is negative. From a welfare perspective the profit-maximizing monopolist tends to overspend on advertising, and a small reduction in advertising would be welfare-improving. Dixit and Norman show that similar results also hold in oligopoly and monopolistic competition.

16.8 Empirical evidence

This section provides a selective review of empirical evidence relating to issues raised in this chapter.

Information content and effectiveness of advertising

Based on data from 60 previous studies and over 90,000 advertisements, Abernethy and Franke (1996) report an average number of 'cues' of 2.04 per advertisement. Advertising 'cues' include information on price, quality, performance, component parts or contents, availability, special offers, taste, packaging or shape, guarantees or warranties, safety, nutrition, independent research, company sponsored research and new ideas. Advertisements for durable goods provided 35 per cent more cues on average than those for non-durable goods. Outdoor advertising and television advertising contain less information than magazine and radio advertising. Paton (1998) uses survey data on UK manufacturing, service and distribution firms to assess the extent to which advertisements incorporate price information. 70 per cent of the sample included no price information in their advertisements. Price information tends to be included in advertising more commonly in distribution than in manufacturing and services, and when consumers are the end-users of a product or service.

Advertising and concentration

Most empirical studies of the link between advertising and concentration test for the existence of a relationship similar to the one summarized in Figure 16.2. The methodology used to test this hypothesis is SCP-based, and accordingly most of these studies were published during the 1960s, 1970s and 1980s. Taken as a whole, the empirical evidence favouring the hypothesis that advertising intensity should be higher under oligopoly than under either perfect competition or monopoly appears to be reasonably strong and convincing (Leahy, 1997).

Some of the earliest studies test for a linear relationship between concentration and advertising intensity (Telser, 1964). Many later studies test for a non-linear relationship between concentration and advertising intensity (Leahy, 1997). If a quadratic functional form is assumed, the specification of the regression equation is as follows:

$$\left(\frac{A_i}{S_i}\right) = \alpha + \beta_1 + \beta_2 CR_i + \beta_3 CR_i^2 + u_i$$

where the dependent variable is (A_i/S_i), the advertising-to-sales ratio of industry i; and the independent variables are linear and quadratic terms in CR_i, the industry i concentration ratio, or some other suitable industry concentration measure. A necessary (but not always sufficient) condition for an inverted U-shaped relationship between concentration and advertising intensity is $\beta_2 > 0$ and $\beta_3 < 0$.

The UK and US evidence from the 1970s and 1980s on the association between concentration and advertising intensity is somewhat ambiguous (Cable, 1972; Sutton, 1974; Reekie, 1975; Weiss *et al.*, 1983; Buxton *et al.*, 1984). In an international study, Lambin (1976) examines the relationship between several variables, including price elasticity of demand and concentration, and advertising intensity. There is no systematic association between market concentration and advertising intensity. Lee (2002) uses a sample of 426 (five-digit) manufacturing industries to examine the relationship between advertising and concentration. An inverted U-shaped relationship is found for consumer goods industries, but a J-shaped relationship is observed in the case of producer goods.

Advertising and profitability

Paton and Vaughan Williams (1999) report a positive relationship between advertising expenditures and current and future profitability for a large sample of UK firms. Greuner *et al.* (2000) examine the long-run relationship between advertising and profitability for three dominant US car manufacturers (GM, Ford and Chrysler). There is little evidence that advertising influenced profitability. Notta and Oustapassidis (2001) examine the relationship between four advertising media (television, radio, newspapers and magazines) and profitability for a sample of 350 Greek food manufacturing firms. Only television advertising appears to increase profitability.

Advertising-to-sales ratios, widely used in many empirical studies, are prone to measurement error. If a firm actively pursued a strategy based on promotions other than advertising, the estimated correlation between concentration, profitability and advertising may be biased (Lambin, 1976). For diversified firms, it can be difficult to assess from company accounts which product lines are being heavily advertised. This problem can be tackled using data at the line-of-business level. Using US lines-of-business data for 258 industry categories, Ravenscraft (1983) finds no relationship between advertising expenditure and profitability.

A few methodological problems arise in empirical studies of the relationship between advertising and profitability. First, it is often difficult to determine the direction of causation between advertising and profit. Does advertising lead to increased profit, or do profitable firms advertise more? Second, size measures such as sales, assets and employment are often highly correlated. These measures are used in the denominators of both the advertising and profitability measures, leading to the possibility that spurious relationships may be identified. Third, advertising may be a useful instrument for firms wishing to adjust their reported profit for tax reasons. A high profit in any particular year, and the tax liability this would create, might be massaged and reduced by spending heavily on advertising. Finally, Bloch (1974) argues that advertising expenditures should be treated as a capital expenditure and depreciated accordingly, and not as a current expense.

Advertising and market share

In studies of the link between advertising and market share, the main hypothesis is that, if advertising promotes competition, the market shares of the top firms should be unstable; but if advertising restricts competition the opposite applies (Willis and Rogers, 1998). Eckard (1987) reports that as advertising intensity increased, the ranking of the largest firms in each industry by market share tended to change more frequently and market shares became less stable. This implies support for the view that advertising promotes competition. Vakratsas (2008) reports a positive relationship between advertising expenditures and the variability of the market shares of US Sports Utility Vehicle and Minivan producers in the US.

Advertising and product quality

Tellis and Fornell (1988) test for an empirical relationship between advertising intensity and product quality. Products are grouped into those at early stages (introductory and growth) and those at advanced stages (maturity, decline) of the product life cycle. There are strong positive relationships between product quality and each of advertising expenditure, market share and profitability for products at advanced stages of the product life cycle. Caves and Greene (1996) report a positive association between product quality and advertising intensity for experience goods and new products; and Thomas *et al.* (1998) report evidence that car producers use advertising expenditures to signal quality.

Advertising and price

One view of the effect of advertising on price is that the prices of advertised goods tend to be higher than those of non-advertised goods, due to the higher selling costs; and because advertising reduces the price elasticity of demand by inducing brand loyalty (Chioveanu, 2008). Furthermore, producers or retailers that market generic or own-brand products at a lower price may attempt to free-ride, by exploiting the information spread by the advertised goods (Porter, 1976). An alternative view, implicit in the notion of informative advertising (Stigler, 1961), suggests that an informed consumer is better able to select products at a lower price for given level of quality. Therefore advertising reduces consumer ignorance and increases the price elasticity of demand, resulting in lower prices.

On balance, much of the available empirical evidence suggests advertising appears to reduce both the level and the variability of prices. Empirical evidence for several professional service industries suggests advertising aids consumer search, and enables consumers to make more informed choices (Love and Stephen, 1996). However, the price information contained in advertisements produced by service sector firms is often low (Paton, 1998; Paton and Vaughan Williams, 1999).

16.9 Summary

This chapter has examined the role of advertising in the modern economy. Some advertising messages provide useful information about the attributes of the products, services or brands they promote, enabling consumers to make more informed choices. However, advertising which seeks to persuade consumers of the superiority of particular goods by transmitting messages whose truth (or otherwise) may be unreliable, or at least not objectively verifiable, may represent a waste of resources or may damage competition or reduce welfare. It has been shown that the effectiveness of advertising may depend on whether the product's attributes are easily identifiable prior to purchase and consumption (search and experience goods), and upon cost and frequency of purchase (convenience and shopping goods).

There are good theoretical reasons to expect that the relationship between market structure and advertising intensity should have an inverted U-shaped appearance. Advertising intensity should be zero under perfect competition, positive under both oligopoly and monopoly, but larger under oligopoly than under monopoly. A monopolist's only incentive to advertise is to try to increase total industry demand, whereas oligopolists have the additional incentive of trying to capture market share from one another. During the 1960s, 1970s and 1980s, a number of empirical studies based on the structure–conduct–performance paradigm identified evidence of a relationship of this kind between industry concentration and advertising-to-sales ratios.

Advertising can help raise barriers to entry. An incumbent firm may benefit from an absolute cost advantage in advertising if its past advertising investment has helped establish name recognition or brand loyalty among consumers. Consumer familiarity makes current advertising more effective than it is for an entrant attempting to establish a presence in the market for the first time. Economies of scale in advertising may also make it difficult for small-scale entrants to compete effectively with incumbents who are already producing and advertising on a large scale.

The competitive model relies on an assumption of perfect information, but in situations where consumers have limited information advertising may play an important role in signalling information about product quality. The content of advertising messages may be unimportant, but the fact that a producer is prepared to invest in advertising suggests the producer is confident that consumers, having made an initial purchase, will return and make repeat purchases.

Some economists believe advertising tends to mislead or distort the truth, and is usually wasteful or even damaging. Others argue advertising contributes positively to the circulation of information through society, and in any event consumers have choices and are not forced to purchase advertised goods if they do not wish to do so. Perhaps this debate will never be resolved conclusively. However, some of the empirical evidence, at least, seems to suggest that advertising has beneficial effects for competition and for consumers. For example, increased advertising appears to be associated with rapid turnover in firm-level market shares, which suggests competition is effective; advertising seems to increase price elasticity of demand as consumers become better informed; and prices appear to be lower in markets where advertising is deregulated than in those where restrictions exist. All of this is supportive of the view that some, if perhaps not all, advertising does play a positive role in transmitting useful information and stimulating competition.

Discussion questions

1. At the national level, identify factors that might be expected to influence a country's aggregate level of expenditure on advertising.

2. With reference to Case Studies 16.1, 16.2 and 16.3 compare the approaches of BlackRock, British manufacturing companies and Bayer to investment in advertising.

3. Explain the distinction between search goods and experience goods. Quote examples of goods that belong in each category.

4. Explain the distinction between convenience goods and shopping goods. What are the implications of this distinction for the likely effectiveness of persuasive advertising?

5. On theoretical grounds, explain why a higher level of advertising might be expected in an oligopoly than in either of the polar cases of perfect competition or monopoly.

6. Assess the validity of Kaldor's view that most advertising is simply a waste of resources.

7. According to the Dorfman–Steiner condition, a monopolist's optimum ratio of advertising expenditure to sales revenue is given by the ratio of the advertising elasticity of demand to price elasticity of (market) demand. Explain the intuition underlying this theoretical result. Would you give an oligopolist the same advice?

8. In what ways might a heavy advertising campaign by an incumbent firm raise barriers to entry? Illustrate your answer by drawing possible advertising response functions for an incumbent and an entrant.

9. With reference to a quality-signalling model of advertising, explain carefully why the content of the advertising message might be less important than the simple fact that the product is being advertised for consumers who are considering buying the product.

10. 'Evaluation of the welfare effects of advertising is made difficult by the fact that persuasive advertising changes consumer tastes and preferences.' Explain how Dixit and Norman (1978) avoid this difficulty. What are the main conclusions of their analysis of the social welfare implications of advertising?

11. Explain carefully how the existence of an inverted U-shaped relationship between concentration and advertising intensity might be tested empirically. Does the available empirical evidence support such a relationship?

Further reading

Albion, M.S. and Farris, P. (1981) *The Advertising Controversy*. Boston, MA: Auburn House.

Bagwell, K. (2007) The economics of advertising, in Armstrong, M. and Porter, R. (eds) *Handbook of Industrial Organization*, Vol. 3. Amsterdam: Elsevier.

Baye, M.R., Morgan, J. and Scholten, P. (2007) Information, search and price dispersion, in Hendershott, T. (ed.) *Handbook on Economics and Information Systems*. Amsterdam: Elsevier.

Bearne, A. (1996) The economics of advertising: a reappraisal, *Economic Issues*, 1, 23–38.

The Economist (2005) Target practice: advertising used to be straightforward, 2 April.

Gabszewicz, J.J., Laussel, D. and Sonnac, N. (2005) Does advertising lower the price of newspapers to consumers? A theoretical appraisal, *Economics Letters*, 87, 127–34.

Comanor, W.S. and Wilson, T. (1979) Advertising and competition: a survey, *Journal of Economic Literature*, 17, 453–76.

Evans, D.S. (2009) The online advertising industry: economics, evolution, and privacy, *Journal of Economic Perspectives*, 23, 37–60.

Kaul, A. and Wittink, D.R. (1995) Empirical generalisations about the impact of advertising on price sensitivity and price, *Marketing Science*, 14, 151–60.

Leahy, A.S. (1997) Advertising and concentration: a survey of the empirical evidence, *Quarterly Journal of Business and Economics*, 36, 35–50.

Lee, C.Y. (2002) Advertising, its determinants and market structure, *Review of Industrial Organization*, 21, 89–101.

Love, J.H. and Stephen, F.H. (1996) Advertising, price and quality in self regulating professions: a survey, *International Journal of the Economics of Business*, 3, 227–47.

Luik, J. and Waterson, M.J. (1996) *Advertising and Markets: A Collection of Seminal Papers*. Oxford: NTC Publications.

Schmalensee, R.C. (1972) *The Economics of Advertising*. Amsterdam: North-Holland.

Key terms

Creative destruction	Joint ventures	Product innovation
Diffusion	Open source technology	Schumpeterian hypothesis
Innovation	Patent	Switching costs
Invention	Process innovation	

17.1 Introduction

Technological change can be defined as the introduction of superior qualities to products or methods of production, which eventually render existing products or production processes obsolete. Invention means the development of new ideas, while innovation means the successful application of new ideas. In most studies of industrial organization, research and development (R&D) undertaken by firms is assigned a high level of importance. Technological change affects output, product quality, employment, wages and profits, and is a major driving force behind the growth of any economy and the improvement in social welfare.

This chapter begins in Section 17.2 with an examination of the relationship between market structure, firm size and the pace of technological change. A five-stage classification of the components of a successful R&D programme is introduced. Several of the key ideas of Joseph Schumpeter, perhaps still the most influential thinker in this area, are examined (see Box 1.1). The Schumpeterian hypothesis, that there is an association between innovation and monopoly, has provided the motivation for an extensive body of theoretical and empirical research. In a well-known contribution, Arrow shows that the incentive to innovate is greater under perfectly competitive conditions than it is under a monopoly. Several economists have suggested that oligopoly might be the market structure most conducive to a fast pace of technological change. The attractions for oligopolists of collusion, cooperative joint ventures and open source technology are examined. Finally, the case for a positive association between firm size and the pace of technological change is assessed.

Section 17.3 examines the decision to invest in R&D. A distinction is drawn between offensive, defensive, imitative and dependent R&D strategies. Like any other investment decision, the decision to commit resources to a R&D programme can be subjected to investment appraisal analysis. Relevant considerations include the anticipated levels of demand and costs, the marketing strategy (in the case of a new product), and the means of financing the research programme.

The rate of diffusion measures the pace at which a piece of new technology spreads from the original innovating firm to other firms for which the technology is applicable. Section 17.4 describes the Mansfield model of diffusion, which provides a benchmark for measuring and modelling the factors that influence the pace of diffusion. One such factor is the patenting system, discussed in Section 17.5. The granting of a patent to the inventor of a new product, process, substance or design confers a property right over the knowledge that is embodied in the invention. In designing a patenting system, a balance needs to be struck between providing sufficient incentives to encourage R&D on the one hand, and avoiding excessive monopolization and possible abuses of market power on the other.

Finally, Section 17.6 reviews some of the empirical literature on the economics of R&D, including studies which present evidence on a number of the issues covered in the previous sections of this chapter. Overall, the empirical research on the relationships between market structure, firm size and innovation is shown to be rather inconclusive.

17.2 Market structure, firm size and the pace of technological change

As a process, R&D can subdivided into several different stages. Different economists and management scientists have developed their own taxonomies. Probably the best-known of these, described by Stoneman (1995), is the trichotomy which identifies three stages: **invention**, **innovation** and **diffusion**. This three-stage classification was first developed by Joseph Schumpeter (1928, 1942). A more extensive five-stage classification is as follows:

■ *Basic research.* An invention is the creation of an idea and its initial implementation. Basic research corresponds to the invention stage in the Schumpeterian trichotomy. At its extreme, basic research may be carried out without any practical application in view. For example, early research in molecular physics was carried out without any foreknowledge of the use of the valve in broadcasting and communications. Industrial firms may be reluctant to undertake basic research, due to the uncertainty of outcome. Consequently, basic research is often the province of government agencies and universities.

■ *Applied research.* Unlike basic research, applied research has a stated objective. Following an investigation of the potential economic returns, research is undertaken to determine the technological feasibility of the proposed application.

■ *Development.* Generally this can be considered as the bringing of an idea or invention to the stage of commercial production. At this stage, resources are heavily committed and pilot plants or prototypes may have to be built. Although it is clear that at every stage of R&D the firm must review its progress, it is at the development stage that the selection process for the next (commercial production) stage is most important. The failure of a new product that has already entered into commercial production would be very costly to the organization.

■ *Commercial production.* This stage refers to the full-scale production of a new product or application of a new process. Regardless of the amount of R&D already undertaken, there is still a large element of risk and uncertainty. A major difference between invention and innovation arises from the level of risk involved: the main interest of the inventor is in the generation of ideas and not the production of goods and services on a commercial basis. Together, the applied research, development and commercial production stages correspond to the innovation stage in the Schumpeterian trichotomy.

■ *Diffusion.* The final stage refers to the spread of the new idea through the firm, as well as the imitation and adoption of the innovation by other firms in the same industry, or in other industries where the innovation may be applicable. There is also a spatial element to the diffusion process, as ideas spread geographically through foreign direct investment, licensing agreements or **joint ventures**.

A distinction is often drawn between product and process innovation. A **product innovation** involves the introduction of a new product. A **process innovation** involves the introduction of a new piece of cost-saving technology. However, the distinction between product and process innovation is not always clear cut. New products often require new methods of production; and new production processes often alter the characteristics of the final product. Furthermore, one firm's product innovation may be another firm's process innovation. For example, a new piece of capital equipment might be classed as product innovation by the producing firm, but, from the point of view of the user, the machine would represent a process innovation.

Schumpeter and the gale of creative destruction

At several points in this book, it is suggested that monopoly may be associated with inefficiency in production. Shielded from the full rigours of competition, the monopoly producer may tend to become complacent and fail to produce at the lowest attainable average cost. A similar case can be made to suggest that among all possible market structures, monopoly may not be the most conducive to a rapid pace of technological progress. A complacent monopoly producer that is already earning an abnormal profit may feel reasonably content with its existing production technology, even if it might be possible for the firm to realize cost savings and increase its abnormal profit by investing in R&D.

However, it has also been argued that high levels of seller concentration and market power may be associated with a fast pace of technological change. Much of the theoretical and empirical analysis of the economics of R&D and innovation is based on ideas developed by Schumpeter (1928, 1942), who saw technological change as the fundamental driving force behind the growth and development of the capitalist economy. Schumpeter coined the term **creative destruction** to describe the economic impact of technological change. The creative aspect of technological change results in new and improved goods and services being brought to market, and more cost effective technologies being used in production.

> The fundamental impulse that sets and keeps the capitalist engine in motion comes from the new consumers' goods, the new methods of production or transportation, the new markets, the new forms of industrial organization that capitalist enterprise creates.
>
> *(Schumpeter, 1942, p. 83)*

But there is also a destructive aspect to technological change. The introduction of new technologies challenges the market power of incumbent firms that remain wedded to the older, less effective technologies. The process of creative destruction simultaneously rewards successful innovators, and punishes those firms whose technologies are superseded and become obsolete. The process of creative destruction 'incessantly revolutionises the economic structure from within, incessantly destroying the old one, incessantly creating a new one. This process of creative destruction is the essential fact about capitalism' (Schumpeter, 1942, p. 83).

Successful innovators are rewarded with market power. For a time, the firm becomes a monopoly supplier of the new product; or its mastery of a new process enables it to produce at a lower cost than its rivals, and perhaps capture some or all of their market share by setting a reduced price that they are unable to match. However, the market power conferred by successful innovation is always temporary, and never permanent. The firm must continually guard against the possibility that others will encroach into its market by introducing further improvements in technology, new sources of supply, or new forms of organization.

Schumpeter claims the textbook neoclassical models of oligopoly and monopoly cannot convincingly account for the huge increases in production and consumption that took place during the late nineteenth and early twentieth centuries. The popular view of large quasi-monopolistic concerns, reducing output in order to maximize profit and thereby denying society a higher standard of living, was not a credible representation of the reality of modern capitalist economies.

> As soon as we go into details and inquire into the individual items in which progress was most conspicuous, the trail leads not to the doors of those firms that work under conditions of comparatively free competition but precisely to the doors of the large concerns which, as in the case of agricultural machinery, also account for much of the progress in the competitive sector and a shocking suspicion dawns upon us that big business may have had more to do with creating that standard of life than with keeping it down.
>
> *(Schumpeter, 1942, p. 82)*

The Schumpeterian analysis has several important implications. Perfect competition is not the ideal market structure. Large corporations that have acquired market power as a result of having been successful innovators in the past are the main drivers of technological change and economic growth. Economists should focus less on price competition and more on other forms of competition, especially product and process innovation. In one remarkable passage, Schumpeter even comes close to anticipating the theory of contestable markets by about 40 years:

> It is hardly necessary to point out that competition of the kind we now have in mind acts not only when in being but also when it is merely an ever present threat. It disciplines before it attacks. The businessman feels himself to be in a competitive situation even if he is alone in his field or if, though not alone, he holds a position such that investigating government experts fail to see any effective competition between him and any other firms in the same or a neighboring field and in consequence conclude that his talk, under examination, about his competitive sorrows is all make believe.
>
> *(Schumpeter, 1942, p. 85)*

The **Schumpeterian hypothesis**, that there is an association between innovation and monopoly, has provided the motivation for much further theoretical and empirical research. Schumpeter's approach lies beyond the confines of the neoclassical theory of the firm and the SCP paradigm, which concentrate on decisions concerning price, output or other conduct variables within a pre-determined market structure. For Schumpeter, causation lies in the opposite direction. The conduct of a successful innovator is rewarded with the creation of a (temporary) monopoly based on sole ownership of the intellectual property rights embodied in the new technology. Nevertheless, certain theoretical contributions attempt to reposition the Schumpeterian hypothesis within a neoclassical framework, by examining the relationship between market structure and the incentive to invent or innovate. Other contributions examine the closely related (but conceptually distinct) question of the relationship between firm size and the pace of technological change.

The pace of technological change: monopoly versus perfect competition

Is monopoly more conducive than perfect competition to a high level of effort being committed to R&D, or a high level of innovative activity? As suggested above, arguments pointing in either direction can be developed. In favour of monopoly, firms in highly concentrated industries may earn abnormal profits, which can be invested in risky R&D programmes. Firms in highly competitive industries may earn only a normal profit, leaving no uncommitted resources available to finance speculative investment in R&D. Furthermore, the lack of competitive pressure in a monopoly creates an environment of security, within which it is possible for the firm to undertake high-risk investment in projects whose returns may be uncertain. If the investment succeeds, there is less risk of imitation; and if the project fails, there are no rivals waiting to step in and take advantage of the firm's temporary financial difficulties (for example, by initiating a price war at a time when the firm's ability to sustain losses might be diminished). The lack of competitive pressure gives the firm the time and space it needs to develop and grow.

On the other hand, and as noted above, in the absence of competitive pressure, the managers of a monopoly might become complacent or lazy; or excessive internal bureaucracy within the firm's organizational structures might lead to a loss of managerial control, or other forms of technical inefficiency (x-inefficiency). Another line of reasoning suggests that the probability that a successful product or process invention emerges depends upon the number of research teams simultaneously working on a similar challenge. In a competitive market, there may be more teams competing to be the first to find a solution, and a higher probability that at least one team will succeed. Finally, a monopolist that owes its market power to a successful past innovation might be tied to its existing technology. To switch resources to a new product or process might be considered too costly.

A slightly more subtle variant of this final argument in favour of competition points out that if a new piece of technology displaces a monopoly firm's current technology, the monopolist's incentive to innovate is governed by the *net* effect on its profit. Under a competitive market structure, the incentive to innovate is governed by the *gross* return from the innovation. Accordingly, the incentive to innovate may be greater under competition than it is for a monopolist.

This argument is formalized by Arrow (1962), in a widely cited theoretical contribution to the debate surrounding the relationship between market structure and the pace of technological change. Arrow compares the impact of a cost-saving process innovation under market structures of perfect competition and monopoly. In both cases, constant returns to scale and horizontal LRAC and LRMC (long-run average and marginal cost) functions are assumed. The innovation causes a downward shift in the position of the LRAC (= LRMC) function. Under perfect competition, it is assumed that the inventor charges each competitive firm a royalty per unit of output for use of the cost saving technology. The inventor's return is the total value of the royalty payments. Under monopoly, it is assumed that the monopoly firm itself is the inventor. The inventor's return is the increase in abnormal (or monopoly) profit realized due to the adoption of the cost saving technology. There are two alternative versions of Arrow's analysis, covering the cases where the innovation produces a small reduction and a large reduction in the LRAC function. However, both analyses produce the same conclusion: that the incentive to invent or innovate is greater under perfect competition than it is under monopoly.

Figure 17.1 shows Arrow's analysis for the case of a small reduction in the LRAC function, from $LRAC_1$ to $LRAC_2$.

■ Before the innovation, the monopolist maximizes profit by operating at (P_1, Q_1). The monopolist's abnormal profit is $A + B$.

■ After the innovation, the monopolist maximizes profit by operating at (P_2, Q_2). The monopolist's abnormal profit is $B + C + D + E$. Therefore the monopolist's reward for the innovation is $(B + C + D + E) - (A + B) = C + D + E - A$.

■ Before the innovation, the perfectly competitive industry reaches equilibrium by operating at (P_C, Q_C). At P_C, price *equals* average cost and normal profits are earned. Q_C represents the combined output of all of the perfectly competitive firms.

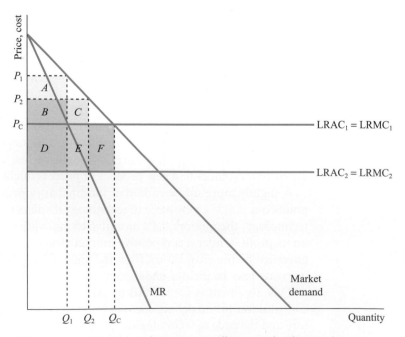

Figure 17.1 Arrow's incentive to innovate: small cost-saving innovation

- The maximum royalty per unit of output the inventor can charge for use of the technology is given by the amount of the cost saving, $LRAC_1 - LRAC_2$. Therefore, from the viewpoint of the perfectly competitive firms, nothing changes. Before the invention they incur a production cost of $LRAC_1$ per unit of output. After the invention they incur a production cost (per unit) of $LRAC_2$, and a royalty payment of $LRAC_1 - LRAC_2$, so effectively their average cost is $LRAC_1$. The industry equilibrium remains at (P_C, Q_C) and the inventor's total royalty payment is $D + E + F$.

- To show that the reward for the innovation is greater under perfect competition than it is under monopoly, the condition $D + E + F > C + D + E - A$, or $F + A - C > 0$, is required. To demonstrate this condition it is sufficient to show $A - C > 0$. Note that $A + B$ is the largest rectangle that can be constructed within the triangle formed by the market demand function and $LRAC_1$ ($A + B$ being constructed by setting $MR = LRAC_1$). Therefore $A + B > B + C \Rightarrow A > C \Rightarrow F + A - C > 0 \Rightarrow D + E + F > C + D + E - A$.

Figure 17.2 shows Arrow's analysis for the case where the shift from $LRAC_1$ to $LRAC_2$ represents a large saving in average costs.

- Before the innovation, the monopolist maximizes profit by operating at (P_1, Q_1). The monopolist's abnormal profit is A.

- After the innovation, the monopolist maximizes profit by operating at (P_2, Q_2). The monopolist's abnormal profit is B. Therefore the monopolist's reward for the innovation is $B - A$.

- Before the innovation, the perfectly competitive industry reaches equilibrium by operating at (P_3, Q_3). At P_3, price *equals* average cost and normal profits are earned. Q_3 is the combined industry output.

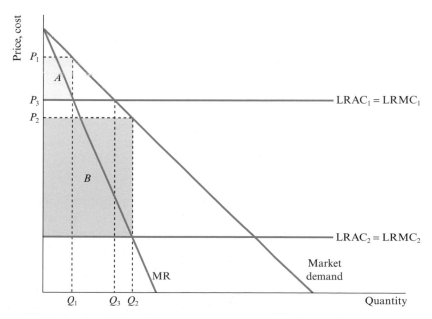

Figure 17.2 Arrow's incentive to innovate: large cost-saving innovation

■ The inventor maximizes the royalty payment by setting the charge for use of the technology in such a way as to force the perfectly competitive industry to operate as if it were a monopolist. This implies the royalty per unit of output should be set at $P_2 - \text{LRAC}_2$ (so that $\text{MR} = \text{LRMC}_2$). After the innovation, the perfectly competitive firms incur a production cost (per unit) of LRAC_2, and a royalty payment of $P_2 - \text{LRAC}_2$, so effectively their average cost is P_2. The industry equilibrium shifts to (P_2, Q_2), the firms continue to earn normal profits, and the inventor's total royalty payment is B.

■ In this case, it is obvious that the reward for the invention under perfect competition is greater than the reward under monopoly, because $B > B - A$.

Arrow's analysis is criticized by Demsetz (1969). Because the pre-innovation output levels of the perfectly competitive industry and the monopoly are different, Arrow fails to compare like with like. Arrow's comparison tends to favour the perfectly competitive industry because the benefits of the cost-saving technology are spread over a larger volume of output than in the monopoly case. In order to make a fair comparison, the usual tendency for a monopolist to produce less output than a perfectly competitive industry should be set aside. Instead, the comparison should be based on an assumption that the pre-innovation output levels are the same under both market structures. In order to achieve this effect, it is necessary to assume that the market demand function differs between the two cases. Kamien and Schwartz (1970) argue that a fair comparison between the incentives for innovation under perfect competition and monopoly should be based on a starting position at which not only the industry output levels, but also the price elasticities of demand, are the same. In the cases examined by Demsetz and Kamien and Schwartz, the incentive for innovation is stronger under monopoly than under perfect competition.

The pace of technological change: oligopoly

So far it is clear that there is no unequivocal answer to the question as to which of the two extreme market structures (monopoly or perfect competition) most favours high levels of R&D activity, high levels of innovation, and a fast pace of technological change. Some economists have suggested that the correct answer to this question is 'neither', and that oligopoly is the market structure most conducive to rapid technological change. Accordingly, an inverted u-shaped relationship between seller concentration and the level of inventive or innovative activity might be expected.

■ In perfect competition, abnormal profit is zero. Competitive firms may not have the means to invest in risky or speculative programmes. Furthermore, they might not have much incentive to do so, unless competition dictates that such investment is a necessary condition for minimizing costs and remaining in business.

■ In monopoly, abnormal profit is positive, so a monopolist has the means to invest in research if it chooses to do so. But a lack of competition may create little incentive to do so.

- In oligopoly, abnormal profit may be positive (depending on the precise form of competition that develops, given the firms' situation of rivalry and interdependence). There is also competitive pressure: the firms' recognition of their interdependence suggests that they perceive competition as being especially keen. Therefore, oligopolists have both the means and the incentive to invest in R&D. R&D is one discretionary channel (advertising being another) for the firms' competitive rivalry, that does not entail potentially destructive price competition.

The arguments for an inverted u-shaped relationship between concentration and the levels of inventive or innovative activity are of course very similar to those that suggest a similar relationship between concentration and advertising intensity (see Section 16.4).

It is important to note that the pace of technological progress may depend not only on firms' decisions on whether to embark on R&D, but also on the speed at which these programmes are implemented. In an oligopoly in which interdependence is recognized, speed may have a critical influence on the success or failure of a research project. If the research proceeds too slowly, a rival firm might develop a similar idea sooner and take out a patent. If the firm moves too fast and takes insufficient care to protect itself from imitation, it might fail to appropriate the benefits from its own investment.

Scherer (1967) develops a model which makes explicit the speed or time dimension involved in the firm's R&D decision. The model is illustrated in Figure 17.3. The curved function C represents the trade-off between development time (shown on the horizontal axis) and cost (vertical axis). A research programme can be implemented at a slow and leisurely pace, or at a fast pace, or at various speeds in between. By increasing the pace and aiming for a shorter development period, the firm incurs costs for the following reasons:

- Over a short development period, research activity may be subject to the Law of Diminishing Returns. Hiring more scientists may produce diminishing marginal returns if the quantity of equipment or the size of the laboratory is

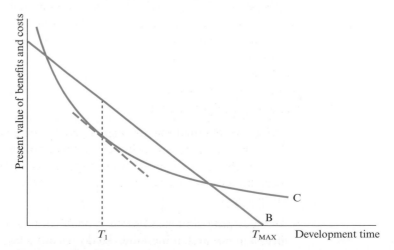

Figure 17.3 The optimal development time

fixed in the short run. Diminishing returns may set in if the firm is obliged to recruit from a finite pool of properly qualified or fully trained research staff.

■ Errors are likely to occur if researchers move from one stage of the research to the next without waiting for detailed results from tests or experiments at earlier stages.

■ In order to generate results quickly, researchers may pursue several alternative research paths simultaneously, in the hope that one or more will deliver results. Costly effort is devoted to ideas that eventually fail to materialize.

■ A slower pace of development implies a smaller up-front cost, as the total cost of the research is spread over a longer development period. Accordingly, due to the effects of discounting future values to calculate a present value, the longer the development period, the smaller the present value of the total cost.

In Figure 17.3, the function B represents the relationship between the development time and the benefit the firm receives from the innovation. B is negatively sloped for two reasons. First, early completion of the project maximizes the firm's first-mover advantage, and maximizes the period before rivals catch up by developing their own alternative technologies. The benefit function B attains a value of zero at development time T_{MAX} because, if the firm delays for too long, allowing all its rivals to precede it in introducing comparable innovations, it may receive no benefit from the research. (In contrast, the cost function C is tapered, because the present value of the future costs is non-zero and positive, however far ahead in the future the costs are incurred.) Second, earlier completion implies the benefits are less heavily discounted. As with costs, the present value of the benefits varies inversely with the duration of the development period, due to the discounting effect. The profit-maximizing firm selects the optimum development time, at which the slope of the benefits function *equals* the slope of the cost function, maximizing vertical distance between B and C in Figure 17.3. A development time of T_1 is chosen.

The shape of the cost function C is determined by the nature of technology, but the slope of the benefit function B is determined by market structure. In Figure 17.4, the benefit functions B_1, B_2 and B_3 represent monopoly, oligopoly and perfect competition, respectively. The relative slopes of B_1, B_2 and B_3 are determined by the competition the innovating firm faces under each market structure.

■ Under monopoly there are no competitors, so the innovating firm reaps the full benefit regardless of the development time. The discounting of future benefits to obtain a present value creates a negative relationship between the development time and the present value of the benefit. This value is not affected by the risk that rivals will introduce comparable innovations if the development is delayed.

■ Under oligopoly the innovating firm worries about the actions of its rivals. The number of competitors is small and entry barriers are significant, although not insurmountable. Delay will not necessarily reduce the benefit to the innovating firm to zero: with only a small number of competitors, it is unlikely that any of the firm's rivals will produce a similar innovation immediately. But the longer the delay, the more likely it is that one or more of them will do so.

■ Finally, under perfect competition there are many competitors and no entry barriers. In this case, speed is crucial. It is very likely that one or more competitor firms is already working on a similar idea. The first firm to bring the idea to fruition captures most of the benefit, so there is a steep negative relationship between development time and the present value of the benefit.

Figure 17.4 has been constructed so as to produce an inverted u-shaped relationship between seller concentration and the pace of technological change. Under monopoly, the benefit curve B_1 produces a relatively long profit-maximizing development time of T_1. Under oligopoly, the steeper benefit curve B_2 produces a shorter development time of T_2. Finally, under perfect competition, the benefit curve B_3 is so steep that it fails to exceed the cost curve C at any value of T. In this case, there is no investment at all in R&D. Accordingly, technological change proceeds at the fastest pace under oligopoly, at an intermediate pace under monopoly, and at the slowest pace under perfect competition.

This analysis can be criticized on the grounds that the theorizing underlying Figure 17.4 is intuitive, and is not based on any explicit model of conduct under alternative market structures. '[T]he results of this theoretical research are sensitive to the assumptions made, and with the appropriate constellation of assumptions, virtually anything can be shown to happen' (Scherer, 1992, p. 1419). For example, in a market containing one dominant firm and one small firm, the dominant firm faces a benefit curve similar to B_1, provided the small firm does not attempt to innovate. If the small firm does innovate, the dominant firm risks losing its position unless it quickly follows. Therefore the dominant firm's benefit curve shifts to something similar to B_2, and the dominant firm responds quickly by imitating the small firm's innovation. Netscape's initial success in developing the first internet browser proved to be short-lived once Microsoft, the dominant firm, launched its own rival product.

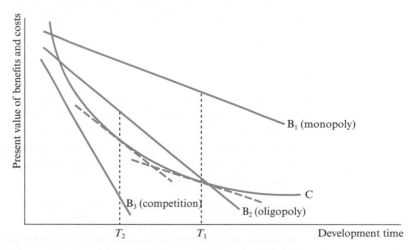

Figure 17.4 Market structure and the optimal development time

The pace of technological change: firm size

The Schumpeterian hypothesis is often interpreted in terms of an association between market structure and the pace of technological change. However, this hypothesis is also consistent with the idea that only large firms have the resources to implement the large-scale R&D that is required to generate ideas for new products and processes, and to develop these ideas so that they can be implemented commercially. In a series of books and articles published during the 1950s and 1960s, Galbraith (1958, 1967) argued more explicitly that large firms were mainly responsible for driving the process of technological change.

> Thus mention has been made of machines and sophisticated technology. These require in turn, heavy investment of capital. They are designed and guided by technically sophisticated men. They involve, also, a greatly increased elapse of time between any decision to produce and the emergence of a saleable product. From these changes come the need and the opportunity for the large business organization. It alone can deploy the requisite capital; it alone can mobilize the requisite skills. It can also do more. The large commitment of capital and organization well in advance of result requires that there be foresight and also that all feasible steps be taken to insure that what is foreseen will transpire. It can hardly be doubted that General Motors will be better able to influence the world around it – the prices and wages at which it buys and the prices at which it sells – than a man in suits and cloaks.
>
> *(Galbraith, 1967, p. 4)*

The argument that technological change is most likely to be driven by large firms rather than small firms or independent inventors is based mainly on economies of scale or scope in R&D, or in adjacent functions such as finance.

■ Modern research and laboratories are expensive to build, equip and staff. A large firm operates at the scale required to justify the purchase of sufficiently specialized equipment, or the hiring of specialist staff. If there is a minimum efficient scale (MES) for cost-effective R&D, the small firm might be unable to attain the required threshold.

■ A large firm can spread risk over several projects, reducing the damage to the firm that the failure of any one project might cause. In contrast, a small firm might be forced to place all its eggs in one basket, and bear the risk that the failure of the project could cause the firm's closure.

■ For a large diversified firm, knowledge acquired from research in one area might have applications in other areas. For a small specialized firm, such economies of scope might not be available.

■ Because investment in R&D is highly risky, it might be necessary to rely heavily on internally generated finance, rather than finance raised from capital markets. A large firm might have larger internal cash flows than a small firm. If capital markets are efficient, external finance might provide a solution for a small firm lacking the financial resources to develop a promising idea. However, in practice the small firm might still face a disadvantage: the large firm might be able to borrow more cheaply because it is perceived to be less risky, or due to its reputation. Alternatively, a group of small firms might attempt to collaborate in a joint research venture. But in this case transaction costs might arise in negotiating an agreement or monitoring compliance.

The counter-argument that technological progress is more likely to originate from outside the confines of large corporations is based on the idea that large organizations discourage creative or original thinking. An employee with a bright idea might find it difficult to appropriate the commercial rewards; or the bureaucratic nature of large organizations tends to reward behaviour that conforms with institutional norms, discouraging creativity, originality or non-conformity.

The empirical evidence for a positive association between firm size and the level of inventive or innovative activity is not particularly strong, and in some cases it may point in the opposite direction. In a widely cited study covering 61 major inventions from the period 1900–56, Jewkes *et al.* (1969) find that the majority emanated from small private inventors, rather than the research departments of large firms. However, this finding is not necessarily inconsistent with the Schumpeterian view. While private inventors might be successful as originators of new and original ideas, the resources of large firms might still be required to carry out the development work to bring these ideas to commercial fruition.

Collusion and cooperation

Price competition tends to reduce the profits of all of the firms in an oligopolistic market, and oligopolists may attempt to avoid direct competition on price. To the extent that discretionary expenditure on advertising and R&D represents a form of non-price competition, it is natural to ask whether there is a tendency for oligopolists to collude, either tacitly or explicitly, to avoid wasteful and mutually damaging competition in these areas as well.

Firms may choose to cooperate over R&D projects for several reasons. First, cooperation may help reduce spillover effects. Spillovers arise because some firms find it difficult to appropriate all of the benefits of their R&D investments. There is always a possibility that the new technology will also benefit rival firms. Second, economies of scale might be realized through cooperation, such as the joint financing of projects. Third, cooperation may generate various synergies when firms are working along similar lines of research. Finally, firms in a technologically driven environment face greater uncertainty and complexity, which may require a greater range of capabilities beyond the core competences of a single firm. Rather than attempting the internalization of more capabilities, firms may seek to pool their capabilities through cooperative ventures (Caloghirou *et al.*, 2003; Sena, 2004).

In an oligopoly comprising a small number of firms, it may be quite simple to agree a common price, but more difficult to determine an optimal level of R&D activity. The implications of a price agreement for sales and profitability may be simple to predict; in contrast, the consequences of R&D cannot easily be foreseen in advance. Prices are visible and transparent, so monitoring and punishing non-compliance is relatively straightforward. R&D is complex and opaque, so monitoring and enforcement may be more difficult.

If a price agreement breaks down, the long-run consequences may be relatively minor. If a R&D agreement breaks down, those firms that have already invested heavily tend to suffer more than those that have made a smaller commitment. If one firm is selected to carry out the research on the others' behalf, the others run the risk of subsequently being excluded from ownership of the property rights. If the research turns out to have more far-reaching applications than were originally envisaged, the firm that undertook the original research might attempt to capture all of the unanticipated benefits for itself. If the research effort is shared, it may be difficult to achieve coordination; and, given the numbers of firms involved, some firms may attempt to free-ride, allowing others to do most of the work.

Nevertheless, despite the difficulties, cooperative R&D ventures do happen. Some agreements cover the pre-competitive stage, where firms share basic scientific or technical knowledge, but continue to compete as suppliers of products based on this knowledge. In other agreements, cooperation is extended to cover the firms' activities as suppliers to the product's ultimate buyers (Hagedoorn, 2002). Different institutional and social environments lead to different levels of commitment. For example, it has been suggested that the less heavily regulated UK labour market is more conducive than the more heavily regulated German labour market to initiating joint ventures (Love and Roper, 2004; Malerba, 2007).

D'Aspremont and Jacquemin (1988) find little evidence to suggest that cooperation over R&D that aims to eliminate wasteful duplication has any adverse consequences in the form of lost output through the creation of quasi-monopolies. Therefore, the liberal attitudes of most governments to joint R&D ventures appear to be justified. Baumol (2001) takes a similar view, suggesting that with a few exceptions, the wider social benefits of joint research usually outweigh the costs.

Open source technology

The open source movement is based on principles that are in marked contrast to the usual business practice of guarding intellectual property by means of copyright and patents. **Open source technology** is made freely available to anyone who wishes to use it, under the condition that any further improvements or refinements developed by users are also made freely available to all other users. Well known open source products include the Linux operating system for computers, and the Wikipedia online encycolpaedia. The core principle is that cooperation should lead to continual improvement and refinement. Despite the absence of copyright and patenting, open source appears to be capable of generating innovative, reliable and low-cost technological progress. In the debate surrounding the relationship between firm size and the pace of technological change, open source represents an extreme challenge to the view that only the research departments of large firms have the capability to generate viable new ideas for commercial implementation.

The open source movement raises several interesting questions for economists (Lerner and Tirole, 2002, 2005; Lerner *et al.*, 2006). In the case of computer programming, why should programmers devote effort to the production of public goods, for which they receive no direct monetary remuneration? One possibility is that programmers obtain direct benefits (bug fixing or customization) for their own organizations from solving a problem that has arisen with an open source program. Another possibility is that programmers derive enjoyment or satisfaction from tackling and solving open source problems, which may be more interesting or challenging than their routine work. In the long run, a contribution to the development of open source projects may benefit a programmer professionally, by signalling talent to prospective employers or venture capital financiers. Alternatively, some programmers might be motivated by the desire for peer recognition from other programmers, rather than by prospective monetary reward.

Open source offers several other advantages. Open source projects benefit by obtaining free programmer training from schools and universities. In contrast, owners of proprietary code have to train their own programmers in-house. Suppliers of proprietary software cannot easily allow users to modify and customize their code for the user's own purposes. Because of the tendency for commercial firms to hide the visibility of their key employees from the outside world, it may be difficult for these staff to signal their talents to the outside labour market. This may create disincentive effects.

Although there have been attempts to develop open source projects in other fields, such as medical research and online publishing, there may be limits to the application of the open source model. Manufactured products require less intellectual or knowledge-based inputs and more physical capital and labour inputs than software programming. Therefore, the open source model may not be applicable. The altruistic tendencies of contributors to open source software might derive partly from a personal or socio-political stance against the dominant software firms, which may not exist in other fields. Finally, the open source model works best in the field of incremental research, and is less capable of generating revolutionary or first generation innovations.

17.3 Investment in research and development

Research and development strategies

In many cases, the decision to invest in R&D is strategic, and is not determined exclusively by considerations of short-run profit maximization. Freeman and Soete (1997) discuss a number of strategic issues that may inform or influence this investment decision.

Offensive strategy

An offensive strategy seeks to enable a firm to dominate its market through the introduction of new technology. The main focus is to generate new ideas, and protect these ideas and associated spin-offs by acquiring patents. The firm typically invests heavily in capital equipment and in developing the human capital of its research workers. Major twentieth-century innovations that were originally developed in this manner include DuPont's development of nylon (in 1928) and lycra (in 1959), IG Farben's development of PVC (in 1929), and RCA's development of colour television (in 1954). The firm might invest in basic research but not of the purest type. To stay ahead of actual or potential competitors, the firm undertakes some developmental work, and it requires a capability to design, build and test prototypes and pilot plants. Furthermore, a key element of Microsoft's innovation strategy is to ensure that new products are accompanied by investment in customer education.

Defensive strategy

For some firms, investment in R&D may be necessary for survival, in order to keep pace with product improvements or technical change in production processes initiated by competitors. If it does nothing, the firm's market share could collapse if rivals are offering more advanced products or are able to sell at a lower price because their costs are lower. A firm that adopts a defensive strategy follows the lead set by a rival whose strategy is offensive. The defensive firm may lack the technical resources needed to pursue an offensive strategy, or it may be risk averse, preferring to invest only in proven products or processes. A defensive strategy may include efforts to introduce small improvements to existing technologies, permissible within the constraints of patents. Defensive firms must have sufficient technical resources to be able to respond quickly to new ideas generated by offensive firms.

Imitative strategy

Unlike the defensive firm, the imitator does not attempt to improve on the innovations of the offensive firm. Instead it is content to copy, by acquiring a licence in the short run or exploiting free knowledge in the long run. Investment in technical resources is relatively low, but for an imitative strategy to be profitable the imitator must have some advantage that it can exploit, such as cheap labour or a captive market. As well as increased competition from alternative products, such as orlon, dacron and nylon, a major reason for DuPont's withdrawal from the US rayon market in 1960 was its inability to compete with low-cost producers. Imitators might have access to captive markets, such as their own subsidiaries or other markets that are protected by political patronage or tariff barriers. In some countries, governments actively seek to encourage imitation, in order to exploit technologies that have been developed elsewhere.

Dependent strategy

A firm that adopts a dependent strategy adopts a subservient role in relation to stronger offensive or defensive firms, perhaps as a supplier or subcontractor. Dependent firms do not themselves initiate R&D. They adopt technologies that are handed to them, often as a condition for preserving the relationship. A new technology might be accompanied by technical assistance, the loaning of skilled labour, or other forms of assistance or support. This type of relationship is common in the Japanese electronics and car industries. A dependent relationship may sometimes be a precursor towards full vertical integration, especially if the dominant firm sees this as necessary in order to protect its investment in the relevant technology.

Investment appraisal of research and development projects

Often, it is clear how a firm should apportion its R&D budget. In small firms, the direction of research often reflects the aspirations of the owner or technical director. In industries where the direction of technological change is clear, it may be straightforward for individual firms to decide the direction their research expenditures should take. However, for firms with large R&D budgets and no obvious technological priorities, there may be an element of discretion. Perhaps the main difference between investment in the replacement of capital goods and investment in R&D lies in the level of uncertainty attached to the latter. The risk attached to research effort is neither repetitive nor measurable and is therefore unlikely to be insurable. The risk tends to be less for research into the application and modification of established technology than for basic research and radical product or process development. This sub-section examines the main factors that need to be considered in the investment appraisal decision.

Demand

Perhaps the most important issue is whether the new idea meets an unsatisfied market demand. 'Demanding and adventurous consumers drive innovation by providing firms with incentives to enter new markets and creating pressures on firms to improve their products and services' (Department for Innovation, Universities and Skills, 2008, p. 16). A large proportion of R&D is stimulated by requests for product or process improvement from users (Saha, 2007). Advances in mobile phone technology have been driven by consumer demand for a wide variety of handset types and styles. The strength of competition from other incumbents or potential entrants might be another important factor.

Assessment of the growth potential of the relevant market might involve long-range forecasting, which can be highly speculative. Alternatively, the Delphi technique, developed by the RAND Corporation in the late 1960s, is based on the assessments of a number of experts or specialists. Individuals drawn from various fields of expertise are asked to present opinions as to the future of a market. Each opinion is circulated to all members of the group, who are then asked to reconsider their original opinions. Through a process of iteration, an expert consensus is eventually reached. For example, the Taiwanese information technology sector is said to have reorganized itself using this method. The Delphi technique assumes that a collective consensus is better than the views of one individual. This may not always be the case. An alternative approach to technological forecasting is trend extrapolation, using historical sales data to forecast future developments. This method is based on an assumption that the parameters remain the same in the future as they were in the past. Over a 10- or 20-year forecast period this may be a dangerous assumption.

> Almost every major innovation in [electronics and synthetic materials] was hopelessly underestimated in its early stages, including polyethylene, PVC and synthetic rubber in the material field, and the computer, the transistor, the robot and numerical control in electronics.
>
> *(Freeman and Soete, 1997, p. 249)*

Costs

Since the full costs of development projects are often uncertain and spread over relatively long durations, it is difficult to produce reliable cost estimates. The uncertainty can be reduced by concentrating on less speculative projects, but the likelihood of error remains high.

> Those firms who speak of keeping development cost estimating errors within a band of plus or minus 20 per cent are usually referring to a type of project in which technical uncertainty is minimal, for example, adapting electronic circuit designs to novel applications, but well within the boundaries of existing technology.
>
> *(Freeman and Soete, 1997, p. 246)*

Accordingly, there is a high variance attached to cost estimates for innovations involving anything more than a straightforward application of existing technology. Furthermore, there is a common tendency to underestimate costs, perhaps to a greater extent than with other types of investment. Particular interest groups within an organization might deliberately underestimate (or overestimate) costs in an attempt to influence the likelihood of a project being adopted, or at least allow their assessment to be clouded by their own interests.

Under the general heading of costs, a firm needs to evaluate the demands placed on its production capabilities when considering investment in the development of a new product or process. Does the firm has the capacity, capital, trained staff and technical expertise required to see the project through? Does a new technology require new inputs, involving the firm in new and unfamiliar supply relationships? Will the production of a new product be hindered by a capacity constraint, or is the idea of developing the product motivated by a need to exploit spare capacity that already exists?

Marketing

Several issues should be considered when devising a marketing strategy for a new product. Can the firm exploit its own reputation to promote a new product? Conservatism or suspicion on the part of consumers may disadvantage a new firm attempting to market a new product. Does the new product have distinctive marketable features? If the idea is too complex for consumers to understand, the market may never develop. Does the firm have well developed distribution channels or dealer networks, through which the new product can be promoted? The alternative is to rely on independent distributors, who may need to be persuaded or prised away from existing suppliers. Finally, what pricing strategy might be required to overcome consumer inertia or resistance? Leibenstein (1950) discusses a *taboo effect*, such that consumers are reluctant to buy a product until a large number of other consumers have already done so. In this case it might be necessary to charge a loss-making price, or perhaps even give the product away, in order to break the taboo. During the early days of satellite TV in the UK, BSkyB gave away satellite dishes in order to encourage take-up of its subscription TV services. If there are **switching costs**, the task for a competitor seeking to break into the market subsequently becomes much harder.

Finance

The returns from investment in R&D are uncertain and difficult to estimate (see Case Study 17.1). The managers initiating the research may have more information as to the likely success of the project than the financier. Therefore it may be difficult to raise finance externally and internally generated funds may be required. Consequently, research is often underfunded (Bougheas *et al.*, 2003). The venture capital market exists to fill this gap, providing external finance for risky projects. According to Kortum and Lerner (2000), increased activity in the venture capital market in the US was associated with an increase in the pace of innovation. Scellato (2007) argues that capital market imperfections in Italy tend to delay innovations, particularly by medium-sized firms.

Case study 17.1

Big pharma counts the cost of R&D

Big pharma is getting worse at R&D. This is the conclusion of a new study, which finds that returns on investment in drug development by the largest pharmaceutical companies have dropped sharply over the past year, highlighting their continued struggle with productivity. The average internal rate of return for the top dozen companies fell from 11.8 per cent in 2010 to 8.4 per cent this year, while the cost of developing a new drug rose from $830m to $1.1bn, estimates Deloitte, the accountancy and consultancy firm. The figures are not based on the companies' own internal data but on estimates calculated from publicly available information on pipelines and historical rates of costs, market potential and failure rates of drugs. But they provide further support to market scepticism of the value of the industry's pipeline of experimental medicines, which is triggering increased scrutiny by investors of efforts by the companies to boost returns. GlaxoSmithKline has already published its own calculations and targets on an internal rate of return from its pipeline, and a number of other companies are also preparing internal data although so far have proved reluctant to make it public. Julian Remnant, the Deloitte partner who co-ordinated the research, expressed surprise that more chief executives had not yet set out their own calculations. 'In the midst of a battle for capital, how R&D can make its case without a commitment to returns I don't know,' he said. The calculations, which have been made anonymously, reveal wide variations, with one of the top 12 companies showing a drop in internal rate of return from 18 per cent to minus 5 per cent, and only two which have increased the returns over the past year. Deloitte stressed that its method had limitations and the figures needed to be assessed over four or five years. It only considers returns on products before regulatory approval, with recent reductions for some companies caused by successful product launches and a corresponding drop in the number of drugs still in late-stage clinical trials. 'R&D is still performing, but it's getting harder,' said Mr Remnant. 'For most companies, the challenges go beyond simply organisational fixes. The next wave to boost productivity is more collaboration. We see an unprecedented appetite by chief executives to work with each other in non-competitive areas.'

Source: Big pharma counts the cost of R&D, © The Financial Times Limited. All Rights Reserved, 21 November 2011 (Jack, A.). Abridged.

17.4 Diffusion

The pace at which new technologies filter through into common use varies enormously from one case to another. The rate at which technological change spreads throughout the economy is known as the rate of **diffusion**. Some new technologies are adopted rapidly, and spread like wildfire among firms or consumers. Others seem to languish in oblivion for several years and then suddenly take off. Others, despite seeming to be brilliantly conceived from a scientific or technological point of view, may never succeed in challenging or superseding an established product or process.

A model of diffusion

In a seminal study, Mansfield (1961) develops a mathematical framework that provides the basis for many subsequent attempts to measure the pace of diffusion and investigate its determinants. This framework underpins both the microeconomics of technology adoption and the macroeconomic impact of technology on competitiveness and growth (Diamond, 2003). Suppose the diffusion of an innovation that is eventually adopted by all firms in an industry is observed, and the number of firms that have adopted is counted at regular time intervals. Let N_i denote the number of firms that will eventually adopt innovation i and let $n_{i,t}$ denote the number of firms that have adopted by time t. The proportion of firms that has adopted by time t is $n_{i,t}/N_i$. Figure 17.5 shows the

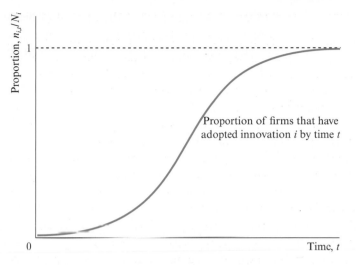

Figure 17.5 Growth over time in the proportion of firms that have adopted an innovation

expected pattern if this proportion is plotted against time. The positively sloped and elongated S-shaped curve is interpreted as follows:

- When the innovation first appears, there are very few adopters, and the pace of diffusion is slow. At this stage the costs may be high and the benefits uncertain. Only the most innovative or far-sighted firms are willing to take the decision to adopt.

- As time passes, the benefits of the innovation become clearer, and the costs of adoption start to fall. The pace of diffusion increases, as more firms take the decision to adopt.

- Eventually, however, a point is reached at which most firms have already adopted. The pace of diffusion slows down. Only the most cautious firms, or those most resistant to change, have not yet taken the decision to adopt.

How can this logic be represented in mathematical form? A suitable mathematical expression for the pace of diffusion, measured by the number of firms adopting between time t and time $t + 1$, is as follows:

$$n_{i,t+1} - n_{i,t} = k_i\left(\frac{n_{i,t}}{N_i}\right)\left(1 - \frac{n_{i,t}}{N_i}\right)$$

where k_i is a positive constant. This expression captures the logic of the previous discussion as follows:

- At the start of the diffusion process when $n_{i,t}/N_i \cong 0$, the pace of diffusion is close to zero.

- Mid-way through the diffusion process when $n_{i,t}/N_i \cong 0.5$ and $1 - n_{i,t}/N_i \cong 0.5$, the pace of diffusion is non-zero and positive.

- At the end of the diffusion process when $n_{i,t}/N_i \cong 1$ and $1 - n_{i,t}/N_i \cong 0$, the pace of diffusion again approaches zero.

Similar models are used in the natural or biological sciences, for tasks such as modelling the spread of contagious diseases among a human or animal population. By analogy, a successful innovation can be likened to a contagious disease; or even a *meme*, defined as 'good ideas, good tunes, good poems . . . Anything that spreads by imitation' (Dawkins, 1998, p. 304).

Returning to the mathematics, some manipulations can be applied to the above expression for $n_{i,t+1} - n_{i,t}$, in order to obtain expressions for the proportions of firms that have adopted and have not adopted by time t. The derivations of the following expressions are shown in Appendix 1:

$$\frac{n_{i,t}}{N_i} = \frac{1}{1 + e^{-(\alpha_i + \beta_i t)}} \quad \text{and} \quad 1 - \frac{n_{i,t}}{N_i} = \frac{N_i - n_{i,t}}{N_i} = \frac{e^{-(\alpha_i + \beta_i t)}}{1 + e^{-(\alpha_i + \beta_i t)}}$$

where α_i and β_i are constants, and e is the exponential function. It is also useful to consider the ratio of these two expressions, $n_{i,t}/(N_i - n_{i,t})$, equivalent to the ratio of adopters at time t to non-adopters at time t. Taking the natural logarithm of this ratio:

$$\log_e[n_{i,t}/(N_i - n_{i,t})] = \alpha_i + \beta_i t$$

According to this expression, the natural logarithm of the ratio of adopters to non-adopters follows a linear time trend. Using data on $n_{i,t}$ for each time period, it is possible to obtain numerical estimates of the parameters α_i and β_i. This is done quite simply, by running a regression with $\log_e[n_{i,t}/(N_i - n_{i,t})]$ as the dependent variable and a linear time trend as the independent variable. The estimate of the parameter β_i is of particular interest, because this parameter provides a direct measure of the pace of diffusion.

Using data on 12 innovations in the US coal mining, brewing, iron and steel, and railroads industries, in the first stage of his empirical analysis Mansfield obtains estimates of β_i for each of the 12 cases. He then estimates a second-stage cross-sectional regression, using data on all 12 innovations, to identify factors that influence the pace of diffusion measured by β_i. The pace of diffusion is positively related to average profitability, and negatively related to the size of the initial investment. In a follow-up study, Mansfield (1969) examines the adoption of numerical control (a process of operating machine tools via numerical instructions on cards or tape) in the US tool and die industry in the 1960s. Highly educated managers were better informed about the potential of a new technology, and younger managers were less resistant to change. Many chief executives of adopting firms were college graduates. Many chief executives of non-adopting firms were educated to high school level only, and were older. 'Judging by the interviews and other evidence, the diffusion process seems to have been slowed perceptibly by misunderstanding of the innovation and resistance to change' (Mansfield, 1969, p. 71).

Although Mansfield's methodology for measuring and modelling the pace of diffusion has been employed widely, it has been subject to criticism.

■ One objection concerns the implicit assumptions that all imitators are homogeneous, and that their number, the profitability of the investment and the technology itself are all constant over time. Adopters are seen as passive recipients, rather than active seekers, of technological change. More sophisticated models include controls for adopters' search costs, and the effects of networking on the dissemination of information (Midgley *et al.*, 1992).

- A second objection is that the Mansfield model is fundamentally demand-oriented, and ignores the role of supply-side factors. The pace of diffusion is influenced, however, by cost structures, the market structures in which suppliers operate, and supply-side technological change (Stoneman, 1989). Battisti and Stoneman (2005) find that the diffusion of Computer Numerically Controlled machine tools technology in UK engineering can be better explained by the profitability of individual firms, rather than by employing the Mansfield model.

- A final objection is that the adopting firms' costs are not properly analyzed. Adoption costs include more than just the cost of acquiring new capital equipment. The technology may require adaptation of the firm's training practices or organizational structures. 'In the limit, technology may be purpose built for a firm, in which case the study of diffusion becomes a study of customer supplier relationships' (Karshenas and Stoneman, 1995, p. 279).

The pace of diffusion

Mansfield's pioneering research in the 1960s identifies several factors that may either help or hinder the diffusion of new technologies. This sub-section details some further industry- and firm-level factors.

Communication

An important barrier to rapid diffusion is poor communication between inventors, innovators and the business community. The development of science parks and other initiatives is motivated by the wish to bring universities (the producers of new knowledge) and the immediate users, closer together. According to the definition provided by the UK Science Parks Association (1999), a science park is a business support and technology transfer initiative with the following objectives:

- To encourage and support the start-up and incubation of innovation-led, high-growth, knowledge-based businesses.

- To provide an environment in which larger and international businesses can develop specific close interactions with a particular centre of knowledge creation, for the mutual benefit of all parties concerned.

Science parks are a channel which distributes academic ideas and discovery to industry and commerce. Science parks are more likely to grow and thrive where there is an abundance of new knowledge and specific types of infrastructure. Most commentators agree that universities are influential in fostering new ideas that will eventually contribute towards technological progress (Salter and Martin,

2001; Jacobsson, 2002). This suggests that close proximity of science parks to universities increases the cross-fertilization of ideas, though this notion has been challenged by Fukugawa (2006). It is difficult to measure universities' contribution to technological progress. Pavitt (2001) suggests that only a small proportion of the scientific research carried out within universities transfers seamlessly into commercial application. Laurensen and Salter (2003) find that R&D intensity, firm size, and factors relating to the industrial environment are important in explaining the propensity of firms to develop links with universities.

The quality of communication between firms in the same industry also influences the pace of diffusion. If the firms are clustered geographically, the pace of diffusion tends to be faster (Baptista, 2000). In Aharonson *et al.*'s (2004) study of the Canadian biotechnology industry, firms that are clustered geographically are eight times more likely to innovate than firms in remote locations. In a study of the car industry in eastern Europe, Lorentzen *et al.* (2003) find the existence of networks and the presence of multinational companies are key determinants of the pace of diffusion. By contrast, Beaudry and Breschi (2003) find clustering does not guarantee a rapid pace of diffusion, because firms within clusters can be negatively influenced by the presence of non-innovating firms.

Case study 17.2

UK universities must embrace wider R&D funding links

Sir, Your analysis of why Pfizer has decided to pull out of Sandwich is spot on (reports, February 3). Talking to Pfizer executives (and other big research and development spenders) it is clear the world has changed. These organisations realise that to maximise the output from their R&D spend they need to do more work with external organisations, especially universities, and less internally.

One Pfizer business unit recently informed me that it wished to outsource $200m of its $300m R&D spend. 'Open Innovation' is not a mere management fad – it's a reality of this brave new world.

The key question now is not navel-gazing on why Pfizer and its contemporaries are changing. It is how the UK's universities and research funding infrastructure are adapting to this new model and encouraging these companies to spend their R&D funds here rather than Germany, France or China. In my experience it is not quick or radical enough.

The historical dislike of industry by UK universities has long dissipated but the focus is still on technology licensing and spin-outs rather than developing effective collaborative relationships with companies. This is not helped by a general mentality from research funders that their role is to fund basic research and then 'throw it over the wall' for commercial companies to pick up. More collaborative research funding opportunities, where the risks of projects are shared earlier but for longer, would be a great start.

Many universities also lack the experience, expertise and business development capabilities to reach out to companies especially when those companies have limited physical presence in UK.

There are examples of good practice; an executive from a large US agrochemical company with a $1bn R&D spend told me that in his dealings with Oxford University last year he found it to be one of the most professional organisations with which he has ever dealt. As a Cambridge alumnus, this is not the easiest thing for me to admit.

Source: UK universities must embrace wider R&D funding links, © The Financial Times Limited. All Rights Reserved, 4 February 2011 (Kaplan, C.).

Management inertia

The education, experience and attitudes of managers may influence the adoption of new technology at firm level. Managers who are scientifically educated to a high level, and conversant with the characteristics of current scientific and technological developments, are likely to be more imaginative, more flexible and more open to persuasion as to the commercial potential of new products or processes. Managers with a weak technical background may be reluctant to recognize the superiority of a new technology, may adopt only when their existing equipment needs replacement, and may be slow, cautious or unimaginative in seizing technical opportunities. In 1959, Pilkington, a UK glass manufacturer, developed a new process that revolutionized the production of flat glass. When attempting to patent the process in the US, the firm's management was astonished to discover that an identical patent had been in existence in the US since 1907, but no US or foreign firm had previously attempted to exploit the idea.

> The most charitable explanations are ignorance of the US patents, which would hardly be a tribute to their technical awareness, or satisfaction with the existing technology and a consequent disinclination to embark on the development work ultimately and successfully pursued by a smaller British firm.
>
> *(Blair, 1972, p. 236)*

Protecting an older technology

Reluctance to innovate need not be solely due to stubbornness, inertia or resistance to change on the part of managers. In some cases a dominant firm might wish protect its existing market share or preserve the current market structure, either by keeping new ideas secret or by denying entry to firms with a new ideas or newer technologies. The speed at which new technology replaces old is partly dependent on the age profile of the existing capital stock. Firms with a high proportion of older equipment are likely to adopt a new technology at a faster rate than those that have recently installed equipment using the old technology.

Employee or trades union resistance

Organized labour might attempt to resist the adoption of new technology, if they view it as a threat to employment. For example, in the 1970s, print unions in the UK were reluctant to accept technology which allowed journalists to electronically transfer their copy direct to the photosetting department, bypassing the composing rooms. The newspaper industry was slow in adopting technologies that were already in widespread use elsewhere.

Regulation

If an industry is subject to a cumbersome regulatory framework, perhaps requiring standards for materials, design and safety, the adoption of new technology may be sluggish. However, Hannan and McDowell (1984) find that regulation may have encouraged the rapid diffusion of automated telling machines (ATMs) by US banks. The adoption of ATMs provided a means for circumventing state-level restrictions on the number of branches a bank could operate. Giaccotto *et al.* (2005) suggest that an absence of price regulation in the US pharmaceutical industry encouraged higher R&D spending.

Risk and liquidity

A new technology may be adopted slowly or reluctantly if its introduction involves significant risk. The use of capital intensive production methods can increase a firm's vulnerability to fluctuations in demand. It might be argued that the more profitable the firm, the more able it is to generate internal funds for the development and application of new technology. It is implicit in this view that investment in new technology is risky, and it is difficult for firms to raise external finance.

17.5 Patents

The granting of a **patent** to the inventor of a new product, process, substance or design confers a property right over the knowledge that is embodied in the invention. The relevant knowledge is legally recognized as an economic asset, which can either be exploited by the patent holder, or licensed or sold by the patent holder for exploitation by others. In exchange for this legal recognition, the inventor discloses information about the existence of the invention to the public. In most countries patents are awarded for a finite period. In the UK, the lifetime of patents was increased from 16 to 20 years (the current figure at the time of writing) by the 1977 Patents Act. In most countries, to be patented an invention must meet the following criteria:

■ *The invention must be new*, in the sense that it has not been previously used, published or demonstrated in the public domain. There are certain ideas that cannot be patented, including pure scientific discoveries, mathematical formulae, mental processes and artistic creations.

■ *The invention must be non-obvious*, in the sense that it does not represent a trivial modification of something that is already known to specialists in the relevant scientific field. It must embody a genuine advance in knowledge, that would not have been obvious to a reasonably informed specialist.

■ *The invention must be capable of commercial application.* It is not possible to patent pure scientific knowledge that has no practical application.

In the UK in 2008, the application fee for a patent was £200 (£100 for search and £30 and £70 for the examinations), and the annual renewal fee (payable from the fourth year onwards) was £50, rising to £400 in the twentieth year. Other expenses may be incurred in making an application. The services of consultants (patent agents) might be required to ensure the application is drafted so as to avoid imitation around the patent and minimize the risk of litigation. It might also be necessary to take out patents in foreign countries, to prevent imitation by foreign competitors. One website estimated the total cost of a patent application to be as much as £30,000. The costs and effort can act as a deterrent, especially for small and medium-sized firms or independent inventors.

Patents exist in order to provide incentives for investment in R&D and for innovation. Granting a property right over the knowledge creates a monopoly, conferring market power upon the patent holder. Moser (2005) shows that patenting encourages innovation, and influences the direction of innovation towards countries and industries that have strong protection. Expressing this argument in other terminology, the knowledge created through successful R&D possesses the characteristics of public goods known as non-excludability and non-rivalness. In the absence of a patenting system, these characteristics reduce the incentive for investment in the acquisition of new knowledge.

■ *Non-excludability* implies that, once new knowledge has been created, it is difficult to exclude others from gaining access to the knowledge. In other words, it is difficult to establish property rights in the knowledge. This means that, without a patenting system, inventors encounter difficulties in appropriating the rewards from their investment in acquiring the knowledge.

■ *Non-rivalness* implies that making knowledge available to one person does not diminish the quantity of the same knowledge available to others. In other words, the marginal cost of disseminating knowledge to each additional person is either very small or zero. This creates a conflict between the inventor's private interest in restricting access to the knowledge, and the social objective of welfare maximization, which requires the knowledge to be disseminated as widely as possible.

Intellectual property can also be protected by copyrights. Patents are primarily viewed as protecting ideas, while copyrights protect the expression of ideas. For example, a patent can protect a new machine, and a copyright can protect the author of a book. However, some creations, such as computer software, can be seen as both ideas and the expression of ideas. Watt (2005) suggests that one solution might be to allow innovators to choose, at a price, the type of protection they prefer. Absolute secrecy might sometimes be more attractive than patenting. When a firm discloses knowledge as part of a patent application it runs the risk of imitation, and in some cases patenting may be interpreted as a means for spreading rather than withholding information (Kultti *et al.*, 2007).

In designing a patent system, policy makers need to strike a balance between providing sufficient incentives to encourage R&D on the one hand, and avoiding monopolization and the abuse of market power on the other. The dilemma is illustrated in Figure 17.6. Consider the incentive to invest in the development of a new process that has the potential to produce a large average cost saving for the firms in a perfectly competitive industry (as in Figure 17.2). The inventor's initial development cost is X. The benefits from using the process accrue over two periods:

■ *In Period 1 (the short run)*, the inventor has exclusive knowledge of the process, and can license it to the perfectly competitive firms. Imitation is not possible in the short run, so paying for the right to use the process is the only way for the firms to gain access.

■ *In Period 2 (the long run)*, if the invention is not patented imitation is possible, and any firm can use the process (without incurring the development cost). If the invention is patented, the inventor can continue to charge the licence fee or royalty.

In Figure 17.6, $LRAC_1$ represents the average cost under the old technology, and $LRAC_2$ represents the average cost using the new process. Q_1 is the industry output before the invention, and P_1 is the market price. While it is possible to control access to the process, the profit-maximizing royalty is $P_2 - LRAC_2$ per unit of output. Q_2 is the industry output, P_2 is the market price, and $D + E$ is the total royalty payment. If it is not possible to control access (because the inventor's property rights are not protected by patent), Q_3 is the industry output and P_3 is the market price.

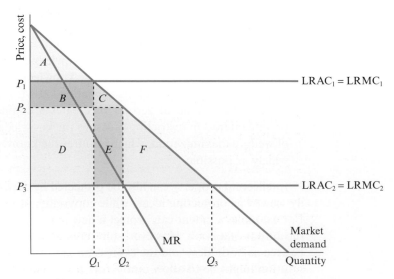

Figure 17.6 Welfare implications of patenting

Does the option for the inventor to take out a patent increase welfare by improving the inventor's incentive to proceed? Or does this option reduce welfare by conferring market power upon the inventor, which can be used to restrict output and raise the market price? In fact, either outcome is possible. Suppose initially $X < D + E$.

■ Even if there is no patenting, it is worthwhile for the inventor to proceed with the invention. The inventor's Period 1 (short run) reward of $D + E$ exceeds the development cost of X. In Period 1 industry output adjusts to Q_2. In Period 2, however, imitation takes place. The inventor receives no further return in Period 2, and industry output adjusts to Q_3. In Period 2 there is allocative efficiency, because price *equals* marginal cost. Consumer surplus is $A + B + C + D + E + F$.

■ If there is patenting, the same analysis applies in Period 1. In Period 2, however, the inventor continues to charge for the use of the process, and in Period 2 again earns a return of $(D + E)$. The inventor's total return is $2(D + E)$. Industry output remains at Q_2. In Period 2 there is allocative inefficiency because price exceeds marginal cost. Consumer surplus is $A + B + C$, and producer surplus (in the form of the royalty payment) is $D + E$.

Now suppose $D + E < X < 2(D + E)$.

■ If there is no patenting, it is not worthwhile for the inventor to proceed with the invention. The inventor's Period 1 (short run) return of $D + E$ does not repay the development cost of X, and in Period 2 the inventor receives no further reward. The invention does not take place, and industry output remains at Q_1 in Periods 1 and 2. There is allocative efficiency only in the narrow sense that price *equals* marginal cost (at the higher level). Consumer surplus is A and there is no producer surplus.

■ If there is patenting, it is worthwhile for the inventor to proceed. In Periods 1 and 2, the inventor charges for use of the process, and earns a total royalty of $2(D + E)$, which exceeds the development cost of X. Industry output is Q_2 in Periods 1 and 2. There is allocative inefficiency, because price exceeds marginal cost (at the lower level). However, consumer surplus is $A + B + C$ and producer surplus is $D + E$.

Therefore, in the case $X < D + E$, combined consumer and producer surplus in Period 2 is higher if there is no patent system. But in the case $D + E < X < 2(D + E)$, the opposite is true. In this latter case, the equilibrium of (P_2, Q_2) with patenting is a second best solution. The best outcome would be (P_3, Q_3), but this outcome is not feasible because of the problem of inappropriability. Without a patent, the inventor cannot recoup the development cost due to imitation. However, the second best outcome of (P_2, Q_2) is preferable to (P_1, Q_1), the actual outcome in the absence of patenting.

This analysis raises practical questions about the duration and coverage of patents. Clearly the duration should be long enough to enable the inventor to earn a sufficient return on the R&D investment for this investment to take place. Since every invention has a different time profile of costs and proceeds, it is difficult or impossible for policy makers to determine a patent duration that is suitable for every case. Yang and Tsou (2002) examine the propensity to patent following a change in the Taiwanese patenting system in 1994, which increased the duration of patents. Although the number of patents increased after the change, this may have been due to factors other than the change in duration.

Determining the optimal coverage or breadth of a patent is even more difficult, since the concept of breadth is difficult to measure or generalize, unlike duration which is straightforward. A new idea should differ sufficiently from any existing idea to prevent other firms inventing around the existing idea. Too broad a protection encourages firms to invest in fundamental technologies, but discourages further investment in second and third generation applications or smaller improvements (Scotchmer, 1991). Taken together, the issues of duration and breadth are complex, and it is difficult to make general recommendations (Denicolò, 1996; Takalo, 2001). O'Donoghue *et al.* (1998) define the effective life of a patent as the duration at which the idea either reaches the end of its usefulness, or is superseded by something new. The effective life of a patent is heavily dependent on the breadth of the patent.

To this point, the discussion has focused on the possibility that insufficient research may be undertaken if the patent system provides either insufficient incentive for the original inventor, or too much incentive in the form of excessive market power once the innovation has taken place, inhibiting diffusion. It is also possible to envisage situations in which too much research, or the wrong kind of research, is produced, either with or without a patenting system (Hirschleifer, 1971; Cockburn and Henderson, 1994; Hall and Ziedonis, 2001). This could arise if firms launch competitive R&D or patent races, in an effort to be the first to acquire a patent and the market power that this confers. Not only is much of the research effort duplicated, but excessive haste may lead to errors and a further waste of resources. A patenting system may produce distortions in the allocation of resources to research activity, favouring activities for which patenting is feasible. There is no reason to assume that patented work necessarily produces the greatest economic benefit. By granting monopoly status, patents might offer greater protection to innovators than to genuine inventors. Some firms might patent pre-emptively, in an effort to limit competition. Patents might tend to provide protection at the wrong stage in the process. Inventors require protection, but at the innovation stage competition is preferable, to maximize the pace of diffusion.

Several of these points are investigated in empirical research into the effects of patents on the incentives for inventive or innovative activity. Schankerman (1998) investigates patent renewals in France for four technology fields: pharmaceuticals, chemicals, mechanical engineering and electronics.

> The finding that patent rights are surprisingly less valuable in pharmaceuticals, where there is stringent price regulation in France, highlights the important point that R&D incentives are shaped not only by patent law but also other institutional constraints that affect the appropriability environment.

(Schankerman, 1998, p. 104)

Greenhalgh and Longland (2005) examine the size and durability of protection offered by patents and trademarks to a sample of UK manufacturing firms. There is evidence of productivity gains to firms that invested in R&D, but the protection offered by patents and trademarks was relatively short-lived. Firms in the most dynamic sectors need to maintain high levels of R&D investment in order to maintain their advantages over competitors.

Case study 17.3

Yahoo sues Facebook for patent infringement

Yahoo has filed suit against Facebook for patent infringement, alleging that the social network's popular and financial success is based on technology developed and owned by Yahoo. In a lawsuit filed in federal court in San Jose, California, on Monday, Yahoo claimed Facebook was 'freeriding' on its intellectual property and went as far as saying that Facebook's advertising model and 'the majority of its revenues [are] therefore dependent on technology owned by Yahoo'. Yahoo is seeking damages for the violation of 10 patents covering advertising, personalisation, privacy and social networking, and could seek to settle its claims by demanding shares in Facebook ahead of its highly anticipated initial public offering. The allegations come at a sensitive time for Facebook as it attempts to present clean financial and business records to potential investors ahead of its IPO, expected as early as May. After negotiations with federal regulators, the company added its patent dispute with Yahoo to its list of risk factors in its updated IPO filing last week. 'We're disappointed that Yahoo, a longtime business partner of Facebook and a company that has substantially benefited from its association with Facebook, has decided to resort to litigation,' Facebook said in a statement. 'We learned of Yahoo's decision simultaneously with the media. We will defend ourselves vigorously against these puzzling actions.'

Yahoo has seen a rise in traffic to its own site after integrating with Facebook's news sharing service, which allows people to easily share articles they have read on Yahoo with their friends. Traffic to Yahoo from Facebook rose 300 per cent between September and December, Yahoo said earlier.

Intellectual property battles are relatively new for Facebook, but likely to ramp up as the social network holds only 56 patents protecting its technology. It has filed more than 410 US patent applications in the past 18 months, according to M. Cam, an asset management firm. Yahoo's lawsuit echoes a similar move the web company made against Google ahead of its IPO in 2004; Yahoo won 2.7m Google shares – worth $230m – in a search patent dispute. Yahoo's litigation against Facebook reflects the drive by Scott Thompson, Yahoo's new chief executive, to boost the performance of all aspects of the company's business, according to a person familiar with the matter. 'Yahoo has invested substantial resources in research and development through the years, which has resulted in numerous patented inventions of technology that other companies have licensed,' the company said in a statement. 'Unfortunately, the matter with Facebook remains unresolved and we are compelled to seek redress in federal court. We are confident that we will prevail.'

17.6　Empirical evidence

The Schumpeterian hypothesis

As shown in Section 17.2, the Schumpeterian analysis suggests two distinct hypotheses: first, that market structure affects the quantity of inventive or innovative activity or the pace of technological change; and, second, that large firms are more likely to invest in R&D than small firms owing to economies of scale. This section examines some of the empirical evidence concerning these two hypotheses. At the outset, it is important to draw attention to some of the difficulties that confront researchers in this field.

Typically, three types of measure of the level of R&D activity are used:

■ Input-based measures, usually based on levels of R&D expenditure (the hiring of scientific personnel and spending on research equipment) reported in company accounts.

■ Output-based measures, usually based on the numbers of patents issued.

■ Lists of inventions or innovations.

Input-based measures are of limited value, for several reasons. First, all of a firm's R&D expenditure may be attributed to the firm's principal activity, whereas in fact the effort may be directed towards subsidiary activities. Second, some research activity may be located outside the firm's R&D department, for example in a design office. Third, official statistics may not reflect research undertaken by small and medium-sized firms, if these firms do not identify their research expenditures specifically in their accounts. Finally, an input-based measure is by definition a measure of effort, but not necessarily a measure of achievement.

The use of data on patent applications or patents granted offers the advantage that most patent applications are made with a view to commercial application. Nevertheless, patents are not homogeneous, and outcomes range from the commercially successful to the completely useless. A patent count of two should reflect twice as much technical output as a count of one, but clearly this is not always so. Cross-sectional comparisons (between industries) are distorted by variation in the propensity to patent from one industry to another. For example, defence contractors seldom patent their inventions, since governments are the main or sole purchasers of their products. In organic chemicals and petrochemicals, small changes to the molecular structure of compounds can have major implications for product characteristics. This creates a tendency for proliferation of manipulated molecule patenting. International studies face the further difficulty that the institutional barriers that need to be surmounted in order to secure a patent vary widely between countries.

Patel and Pavitt (1995) recommend using lists of inventions and innovations, as an alternative to patents data. With hindsight, the economic contribution of each technological advance can be assessed. However, decisions as to which innovations to include and exclude are to some degree subjective. One possibility is to identify technological innovations that are 'important enough to warrant annotation in the vast array of trade journals covering particular industries' (Scherer, 1992, p. 1423). Fortunately, input- and output-based measures of R&D activity appear to be highly correlated.

A simple test of the relationship between market structure and the level of inventive or innovative activity is based on a cross-sectional regression of a suitable input- or output-based measure against an industry seller concentration measure. However, the causation between concentration and the quantity of R&D is not necessarily all one-way. As a result of technological change, opportunities for new innovations arise. Some firms take advantage while others are slow to adapt. Over time, the more innovative firms increase their market shares, and seller concentration increases.

According to Geroski (1994), factors such as increased product differentiation, economies of scale and the tendency for seller concentration to increase over time even if growth is essentially random (see Section 10.3) made a larger contribution than innovation to the rise in seller concentration in most developed countries during the twentieth century. Geroski reports evidence in support of Blair's (1972) hypothesis that, over the long run, technological change (specifically, the advent of new materials and electronics) reduced the MES (minimum efficient scale) at plant level, and was a force for deconcentration.

Tests of the Schumpeterian hypothesis based on cross-sectional regressions of industry research activity indicators against industry concentration can be criticized on the grounds that different industries offer different technological opportunities. Technological opportunity may be an inherent product characteristic, or it may depend partly upon whether a vigorous scientific culture forms part of industry tradition. Levin *et al.* (1987) define technological opportunity on the basis of interviews which seek to measure receptiveness to scientific advance based on information flows from government, universities, suppliers and clients.

Much empirical research on innovation focuses on the twin hypotheses that firms in highly concentrated industries and large firms are most likely to invest heavily in R&D (Scherer, 1965; Kamien and Schwartz, 1982; Cohen and Levin, 1989; Scherer, 1992; Cohen, 1995). Using UK data for the period 1945–83, Geroski (1994) examines whether monopoly or competition is the market structure most conducive to innovation. There is only a limited relationship between market power and the pace of technological change. Industries that are highly concentrated and becoming more so tend to produce a slower pace of technological change than competitive industries. There is a positive relationship between expectations of abnormal profit and the pace of technological change. Industry size, export intensity and unionization are unrelated to innovative activity, and there is little or no support for a Schumpeterian association between monopoly and innovation. Alexander *et al.* (1995) report evidence of a positive relationship between firm size and the pace of technological change. R&D activity was lower in non-US-owned firms. Although there is a positive relationship between R&D expenditure and output, this relationship is subject to diminishing returns.

Geroski *et al.* (1993) examine the empirical relationship between innovation and profitability, using UK manufacturing data. There is a positive relationship between the number of innovations produced by a firm and its profitability, although this relationship is weak. Spillover effects are less important than in similar US-based research. An effort is made to distinguish between the contributions of R&D inputs and outputs to profitability, and to determine whether the correlation between innovative output and profitability reflects transitory or permanent performance differences between innovating and non-innovating firms. Permanent effects are more apparent during recessions, suggesting that innovating firms are better able to withstand cyclical downturns than non-innovating firms.

In a survey of the empirical literature on the relationship between firm size and innovation, Scherer (1992) draws several conclusions. Large firms are more likely to invest in R&D and to obtain patents. However, most manufacturing firms, even those of a modest size, appear to involved in some form of innovative activity. Traditional measures of innovation based on R&D expenditure ignore a large amount of informal activity, especially within smaller firms. There is some evidence that R&D activity and patenting tend to increase linearly with firm size. The ratio of R&D expenditure to sales at firm level varies more between industries than within industries. Large size achieved through diversification typically does not result in a higher R&D expenditure-to-sales ratio, unless diversification is pursued specifically in order to develop R&D synergies.

Although there is some empirical evidence suggesting a positive relationship between seller concentration and the level of R&D activity, this relationship appears to be weak, and becomes even more fragile if factors such as technological opportunity and appropriability are considered. Even if a positive relationship between concentration and innovation does exist, its interpretation can be problematic. Causation between market structure and innovation can run in either direction. Furthermore, and contrary to the Schumpeterian hypothesis, it is possible that the small or medium-sized firms in highly concentrated industries are primarily responsible for the positive association between concentration and R&D activity.

Using data from Korean manufacturing, Lee (2005) attempts to explain why there are so many diverse and conflicting empirical results in studies of the relationship between industry R&D intensity and market structure. Lee defines market structure using an index based on each firm's technological competence weighted by its market share, to reflect the appropriability of R&D. A negative relationship is found in those industries where market share is related to technological competence and a positive relationship is found where market share is less dependent on technological competence.

Overall, the empirical research on the relationships between firm size, market structure and innovation has failed to produce unambiguous conclusions. Many studies are based on small data sets, and many face serious problems in defining and quantifying key variables. One general conclusion that does emerge, however, is that a simplistic or mechanistic interpretation of the Schumpeterian hypothesis is not supported by the empirical evidence.

The pace of diffusion

Canepa and Stoneman (2004) examine factors that explain differences between countries in the pace of diffusion, using survey data on the take-up of new manufacturing technologies. The pace of diffusion is heavily dependent on the nature of the technology, and no country achieved a faster pace of diffusion consistently across all technologies. Adoption costs, information and learning effects, and firm or industry characteristics including size, location and competition are major influences on the pace of diffusion. Further European evidence on the pace of technological change is presented in Box 17.1.

Box 17.1

The pace of technological change: some international comparisons

Most observers would agree that productivity and competitiveness are important ingredients for economic growth and development, and that productivity and competitiveness in turn depend on the pace of technological change. For example, the UK's Department of Trade and Industry (2003) identifies several reasons why innovation is important for individual businesses and for the economy as a whole. This DTI report refers specifically to the UK, but similar points would be equally applicable to many developed economies.

- Liberalization of international markets has exposed UK firms to competition from firms with relatively low labour costs, yet high levels of technical education. For example, similar proportions of the population in the relevant age group attend university in South Korea and the UK, but average wages in South Korea are around half those in the UK.

- Reductions in transportation and communication costs have reduced barriers to international trade, making product characteristics (including the level of technology) a more significant determinant of a firm's ability to attract customers in the global market.

- The adaptation of science and technology to the development of new products and industries (such as biotechnology) is an important source of international competitive advantage.

- Service industries (including banking and financial services), which in total account for more than 70 per cent of GDP in most developed economies, have become more technology-intensive.

- Increased awareness and concern over environmental issues has increased demands for businesses to find technological solutions in order reduce harmful externalities.

The European Trend Chart on Innovation (2005) measures the comparative innovative performance of EU member states. Several measures are based on the European Innovation Scoreboard (EIS), which groups performance indicators according to five themes.

■ *Innovation drivers* (input measure): number of science and engineering graduates per 1,000 population; proportion of the working population with tertiary education; proportion of the population aged 20–24 who have completed secondary education; proportion of the working population in lifelong learning; and broadband penetration.

■ *Knowledge creation* (input measure): public R&D as a proportion of GDP; the share of high technology R&D in total manufacturing R&D; public funding to support innovation by firms in the private sector; and the share of university funding from private business.

■ *Innovation and entrepreneurship* (input measure): small and medium-sized enterprises in-house innovations; extent of joint ventures; early stage venture capital as a proportion of GDP; and information technonogy expenditure as a proportion of GDP.

■ *Application* (output measure): proportion of the labour force employed by high technology services; share of high technology products in total exports; share of new products in aggregate turnover.

■ *Intellectual property* (output measures): number of US, European or Japanese patents per one million population.

Other indicators are grouped into two further themes: domestic demand and innovation governance. It is assumed that the willingness of firms to invest in R&D depends partly on the level of demand, and on the level of government support. Table 17.1 shows the UK's rankings in 2005.

According to Table 17.1, in 2005 the UK ranked eighth in the EU, mainly due to high scores on innovation drivers, coupled with average scores for the other variables. The UK does well in terms of science and engineering graduates, venture capital provision, total innovation expenditure, information technology expenditure, employment in high technology sectors and patents. Public funding for innovation by private sector firms is

Table 17.1 UK innovation performance by EIS and other indicators, 2005

	Value	Rank	No. of EU countries
EIS indicators:			
Summary index	0.48	8	25
Innovation drivers	0.65	4	25
Knowledge creation	0.46	11	25
Innovation and entrepreneurship	0.45	10	23
Application	0.49	8	25
Intellectual property	0.36	9	25
Other indicators			
Domestic demand	0.34	20	24
Innovation governance	0.59	8	22

Source: European Trend Chart on Innovation (2005), *Innovation Strengths and Weaknesses*, MERIT December, Brussels: European Commission.

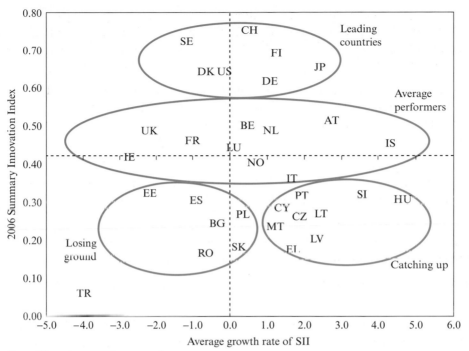

Figure 17.7 Summary innovation index (SII) and trends for EU and selected countries

AT Austria, BE Belgium, BG Bulgaria, CH Switzerland, CY Cyprus, CZ Czech Republic, DE Germany, DK Denmark, EE Estonia, EL Greece, ES Spain, FI Finland, FR France, HU Hungary, IE Ireland, IT Italy, IS Iceland, JP Japan, LT Latvia, LU Luxembourg, LV Lithuania, MT Malta, NL the Netherlands, NO Norway, PL Poland, PT Portugal, RO Romania, SE Sweden, SI Slovenia, SK Slovakia, TR Turkey, UK United Kingdom, US United States.

Source: *European Innovation Scoreboard Report* 2005, European Commission, Brussels.

a weakness. However, had tax incentives been included in the calculation, this indicator would have improved.

The report identifies a number of challenges for the UK. Private sector funding of university R&D declined from 7.3 per cent in 1998 to 5.6 per cent in 2003: a shift from 14 per cent above the European average to 11 per cent below the average. Private sector R&D is lower than for countries in the UK's peer group, although it did improve towards the end of the survey period. High technology exports are volatile, declining from 25 per cent of total exports in 2002 to 20 per cent in 2003, due primarily to declines in the aerospace and pharmaceutical sectors. The market share of new-to-market products is only 2 per cent, and below the equivalent figures for Holland (3.8 per cent), Austria (7.6 per cent), Germany (4.5 per cent), Belgium (5.1 per cent) and France (5.8 per cent). Innovation demand is low, due to low capital investment and low customer responsiveness to new products. Using a Summary Innovation Index based on EIS data, Figure 17.7 compares the innovation performance of the UK with other selected countries.

Massini (2004) examines the pace of diffusion in the UK and Italian mobile phone industries. Rapid diffusion in Italy was encouraged by handsets being made available to consumers at relatively low prices. In the UK rising real incomes were important. Sundqvist *et al.* (2005) examine the diffusion of wireless communications across 64 countries. Wealthy countries adopted earlier than poorer ones; the pattern of adoption was similar across countries deemed to have similar cultures; and the pace of diffusion was faster in countries that adopted later (lag markets) than in those that adopted early (lead markets). According to Beise (2004), lead markets that have a competitive advantage related to low-cost production, buoyant demand, intense rivalry between existing producers, and a strong export orientation, are best suited to produce innovations that are later adopted globally. The mobile phone industry conforms to the lead market hypothesis. In this case, Scandinavia took the lead in production and adoption. Eventually cellular telephony and the associated cellular mobile phone standard achieved global acceptance, displacing rival technologies such as pagers. Battisti *et al.* (2007) compare the intra- and inter-firm diffusion rates of various information and communication technologies in the UK and Switzerland. Organizational forms and managerial practices were important determinants of the pace of diffusion.

Several studies examine the pace of diffusion of new technologies in banking and financial services. Jagtiani *et al.* (1995) examine the diffusion of stand-by letters of credit, loan sales, swaps, options, futures and forwards among US banks. Regulatory changes in bank capital requirements had little effect on the rate of adoption in four of these five cases, but the rate of adoption increased for stand-by letters of credit, as banks substituted these for more traditional forms of lending. The adoption decision was not explained by the size or other measurable characteristics of the banks. For many banks, the timing of adoption appeared to be influenced by a bandwagon effect. Molyneux and Shamroukh (1996) examine the diffusion of junk bonds an note issuance facilities among European, Japanse and US banks. Adoption of junk bonds appears to have been driven by assessments of future profitability, based on market conditions. Adoption of note issuance facilities appears to have been a defensive strategy, in response to a perceived threat to traditional lending business. Fung and Cheng (2004) examine the diffusion of contingent liabilities, exchange rate contracts and interest rate contracts among Hong Kong banks. Information complementarity (using customer information to market several financial products) and individual bank creditworthiness were drivers of diffusion.

17.7 Summary

Much of the theoretical and empirical analysis of the economics of R&D and innovation is based on ideas developed by Schumpeter, who saw technological change as the main driving force for economic growth. The process of creative destruction rewards successful innovators, and punishes firms whose technologies are superseded and become obsolete. Large firms that became monopolies through successful innovation in the past are the main drivers of technological progress.

The Schumpeterian hypothesis, that there is an association between successful innovation and monopoly, has provided the motivation for an extensive body of research, including several attempts to reposition Schumpeter's approach within a neoclassical economics framework. In a well known contribution, Arrow shows that the incentive to innovate may be greater under competitive conditions than it is under a monopoly. However, Arrow's analysis has been subject to criticism for failing to present a fair comparison, based on equivalent output levels or price elasticities before the innovation takes place, in the cases of both perfect competition and monopoly. Several economists have argued for an inverted u-shaped relationship between seller concentration and the amount of R&D effort, with oligopoly being the market structure most conducive to a fast pace of technological change. An oligopolist has both the means to devote resources to R&D (being capable of earning an abnormal profit, unlike the perfect competitor); and the incentive (being subject to intense competitive pressure from rivals, unlike the monopolist).

Although the Schumpeterian hypothesis is often interpreted in terms of an association between market structure and the pace of technological change, this hypothesis is consistent with the notion of a relationship between firm size and the amount of R&D. It might be that only large firms have the resources to implement large-scale research programmes, or bear the risk. On the other hand, large organizations may fail to provide their managers or other employees with incentives for creative or original thinking. The bureaucratic nature of many large organizations might actively discourage originality and non-conformity.

In many cases, the decision to invest in R&D is strategic. A key strategic issue is the choice between an offensive strategy, whereby the firm pioneers new ideas; a defensive strategy, whereby the firm undertakes sufficient research to keep pace with competitors; an imitative strategy, copying ideas that have been developed elsewhere; or a dependent strategy, which involves borrowing or acquiring a licence to use technology that has been developed elsewhere. Like any other investment decision, the decision to commit resources to R&D can be subjected to investment appraisal analysis. Relevant considerations include the anticipated levels of demand and costs, the marketing strategy (in the case of a product innovation), and the means of financing the research.

The pace of diffusion refers to the speed at which new technology spreads from the original innovating firm to others that can also use the technology. The Mansfield model provides a benchmark for investigating factors that influence the pace of diffusion, including the following:

- Quality of communications: effective channels of communication between firms that are members of the same industry, and between firms and university researchers, are likely to produce a faster pace of diffusion.

- The education, experience and attitudes of a firm's managers may influence or determine their receptiveness to new ideas.

■ A dominant firm that hopes to maintain an entrenched position as market leader might be reluctant to experiment with new technology; so too might a firm that has only recently upgraded its capital stock based on an older technology.

■ Organized labour might have an interest in resisting the adoption of new technology, if a threat to employment is perceived.

■ A cumbersome regulatory framework may slow down the pace of adoption of new technology.

■ A new technology may be adopted slowly or reluctantly if its introduction involves high risk.

■ The design of a country's patenting system can affect the pace of diffusion in either direction.

The award of a patent to the inventor of a new product, process, substance or design confers a property right over the knowledge embodied in the invention. In most countries patents are awarded for a finite period; the current UK duration is 20 years. In order to be patented, an invention must be new, non-obvious, and capable of commercial application. Patents exist in order to provide incentives for investment in R&D and for innovation. Granting a property right over the knowledge creates a monopoly, conferring market power upon the patent holder. The opportunity to earn an abnormal profit through the exploitation of this market power may represent the main incentive for the original investment. In designing a patent system, policy makers need to strike a balance between providing sufficient incentives to encourage R&D on the one hand, and avoiding excessive monopolization and abuses of market power on the other. Determining how long patents should be issued for, and how narrow or wide their coverage should be, are difficult issues, which may have implications for the pace of technological change.

Although there is some empirical evidence to suggest a positive association between seller concentration and the amount of R&D, the relationship appears weak. If factors such as technological opportunity and appropriability are taken into account, the evidence for such a relationship becomes even more fragile. Causation between market structure and innovation can run in either direction. Overall, research on the relationships between market structure, firm size and innovation has failed to deliver unambiguous empirical results.

Discussion questions

1. Explain the distinction between the basic research, applied research, development, commercial production and diffusion stages in the commercial application of a new technology.

2. Explain the distinction between product innovation and process innovation. Quote examples of new technologies that required elements of both forms of innovation.

3. What is the distinction between the creative and destructive aspects of Schumpeter's process of creative destruction?

4. Is the level of effort devoted to research and development likely to be higher if an industry is monopolized than if it is perfectly competitive? Consider this issue with reference to the theoretical analysis of Arrow.

5. A commentator claimed, 'The most profitable companies put far more emphasis than less profitable ones on innovation in the marketplace . . . Yet there are serious disagreements between technical directors on one side and chief executives and marketeers on the other about whether innovation is primarily a technological issue or a customer issue.' Assess the contribution of marketing to the processes of innovation and technological change.

6. With reference to Case Study 17.1, what difficulties arise in evaluating research and development expenditure using investment appraisal techniques?

7. What factors are relevant to a firm in determining the speed at which it intends to execute a planned research and development programme? Why might the market structure in which the firm operates be a relevant factor in this decision?

8. Examine Case Study 17.2. Suggest specific reasons why universities and companies might cooperate over research and development.

9. For what reasons did Galbraith believe most private sector research and development in a developed economy would be carried out by large firms, rather than by small firms or independent inventors? Do you think Galbraith's arguments are correct?

10. What are the strengths and limitations of Mansfield's mathematical model of the process of diffusion? Which factors are influential in determining the pace of diffusion?

11. Distinguish between offensive, defensive, imitative and dependent research and development strategies. Give examples of organizations which follow these strategies.

12. What factors should be considered by policy makers when deciding the duration of patents? Is it possible that patents might slow the pace of technological change?

13. With reference to Case Study 17.3, suggest reasons that may explain why Facebook ran the risk of litigation by infringing Yahoo's patents.

14. Are effective arrangements for the protection of intellectual property rights always a necessary prerequisite for innovation to take place?

15. What factors might be relevant in explaining why Europe's performance in innovation may have been relatively weak compared with that of the US and Japan?

16. With reference to the most up-to-date Summary Innovation Index based on the European Innovation Scoreboard [Google SII EIS], select a country from the leading group, the average group, the catching-up group and the losing-ground group. Examine and explain any changes in the ranking for the countries selected.

Further reading

Cohen, W.M. and Levin, R.C. (1989) Empirical studies of innovation and market structure, in Schmalensee, R. and Willig, R. (eds) *Handbook of Industrial Organisation*, Vol. 2. Amsterdam: North-Holland, pp. 1059–107.

Farrell, J. and Klemperer, P. (2007) Coordination and lock-in: competition with switching costs and network effects, in Armstrong, M. and Porter, R. (eds) *Handbook of Industrial Organisation*. Amsterdam: Elsevier, pp. 1967–2072.

Freeman, C. and Soete, L. (1997) *The Economics of Industrial Innovation*, 3rd edition. London: Pinter.

Karshenas, M. and Stoneman, P. (1995) Technological diffusion, in Stoneman, P. (ed.) *Handbook of the Economics of Innovation and Technical Change*. Oxford: Blackwell, Ch. 7.

Malerba, F. (2007) Innovation and the dynamics and evolution of industries: progress and challenges, *International Journal of Industrial Organization*, 25, 675–99.

Horizontal mergers and strategic alliances

Learning objectives

This chapter covers the following topics:

- profit-maximizing motives for horizontal merger
- non-profit-maximizing motives for horizontal merger
- merger waves
- strategic alliances
- empirical evidence on horizontal merger

Key terms

Consolidation	Strategic alliance
Joint venture	Synergy
Horizontal integration	Vertical integration
Horizontal merger	Vertical merger
Conglomerate merger	

18.1 Introduction

A merger takes place when two independent companies join together in order to form a single company. Often, there is a clear distinction between the acquiring company and the acquired company. Accordingly, many mergers may be viewed as acquisitions or takeovers. In practice, however, the terms *merger*, *acquisition* and *takeover*, are often used interchangably, because it can be difficult to interpret the strategic intent of managers. Integration and consolidation are alternative terms used to describe the formation of a combined entity by bringing together two separate entities. A merger may involve the exchange of shares in the two independent companies for shares in the new company. This exchange does not necessarily involve any financial transactions. Alternatively, the acquiring company may decide to purchase some or all of the shares of the acquired company. In order to do so, it is likely that the acquiring company would need to offer to purchase the shares at a price in excess of the current market price of the shares of the acquired company.

There are three types of merger: horizontal, vertical, conglomerate. **Horizontal integration** or **horizontal merger** involves firms producing the same products and services. The large majority of mergers are of this type. Recent examples of horizontal mergers in the UK include Pendragon and Reg Vardy (car retailing) in 2006, the Portman Building Society and the Nationwide Building Society (retail banking) in 2007, and Taylor Woodrow and George Wimpey (house building) in 2007. Horizontal mergers often attract the scrutiny of the competition authorities, because any reduction in the number of firms servicing a market, and in the availability of substitute products or services, may confer enhanced market power upon any of the survivors, and upon the merged company in particular. Therefore, vigilance is required in order to ensure that there are no negative effects on consumer welfare after the merger takes place, due to abuses of market power. Even if market power is increased, however, the detrimental effects on consumer welfare might be offset by improvements in the efficiency of the merged company, which might allow lower prices and consequent gains in consumer welfare. In such cases, the merger might be viewed as part of an evolutionary process whereby efficient firms prosper and inefficient firms disappear. Horizontal merger is the principal subject of this chapter.

Vertical integration or **vertical merger** involves firms operating at different stages of the same production process. Since a vertical merger does not necessarily result in any reduction in the number of suppliers servicing a market, or in the availability of substitute products or services, any damage to consumer welfare is more complicated to assess. A vertical merger might increase market power at various stages of the supply chain, although this might follow from associated actions such as foreclosure, rather than from the merger itself. Such actions are known as vertical restraints. Vertical integration and vertical restraints are the subjects of Chapters 19 and 20.

Conglomerate merger involves firms producing different goods or services. A possible motive for conglomerate merger is the exploitation of some element of commonality, such as the sharing of raw materials, technology or retail outlets. An example is the razor manufacturer Gillette, which acquired the battery manufacturer Duracell in order to exploit its retail operations in emerging markets. Economies of scope might give a producer a crucial cost advantage, enabling it to cut prices and force its competitors out of business. Conglomerate merger is examined in Chapter 22.

This chapter proceeds as follows. Section 18.2 examines profit-maximizing motives for horizontal merger. Horizontal merger might increase profitability through either or both of two channels: through the enhanced market power of the merged firm; or through efficiency gains or reductions in average costs achieved as a result of increases in scale or internal restructuring and rationalization following the merger. Section 18.3 examines several alternative non-profit-maximizing motives for horizontal merger, some of which refer back to the alternative (managerial and behavioural) theories of the firm that were examined in Chapter 4. It has long been observed that the level of merger activity tends to follow an irregular cyclical pattern, and that merger activity might be correlated to macroeconomic conditions. Section 18.4 examines merger waves, or cyclical variation in the pattern of merger activity. Section 18.5 considers the advantages and disadvantages of **strategic alliances** between two or more companies that operate in the same market. Strategic alliances, which may take the form of licensing arrangements or **joint ventures**, are interpreted as an alternative method for achieving cooperation between producers, which stop some distance short of full-scale merger. Finally, Section 18.6 reviews some of the empirical literature related to the topic of horizontal merger.

18.2 Profit-maximizing motives for horizontal mergers

This section examines profit-maximizing motives for horizontal merger. **Synergy**, the most common justification given by senior management for horizontal merger proposals, refers to the increased market power of the merged entity, and to the potential for cost savings through the realization of average cost savings due to economies of scale. Naturally, the managers of institutions involved in mergers prefer to emphasise cost savings rather than market power in their public statements. Case studies 18.1 and 18.2 provide illustrations of a merger apparently motivated by synergy considerations, and a merger proposal in which synergy may also have played a part.

Market power

Oligopoly as a market structure is characterized by interdependence (as shown in Chapters 7 and 8). A firm's success (or lack of success) depends on how its rivals act and react to its strategies. Interdependence creates uncertainty in strategic planning. One way of reducing uncertainty is for the firms to collude, either explicitly or tacitly, over prices, output levels, the extent of product differentiation, and so on. In cases where collusion is difficult to organize or control, horizontal integration might be seen as a viable alternative strategy. This is especially true when legislation on cartels and collusion is tightened.

A horizontal merger *may* leave the newly integrated firm with a larger market share, or it may eliminate a close rival from the market. Either or both of these outcomes increases the ability of the merged firm to raise its price, without having to worry about its rivals' reactions. Furthermore, the merger may make collusion easier to achieve. With fewer firms operating in the industry, there is a better chance of being able to reach agreements and monitor compliance. These outcomes may create concerns for the competition authorities. A merger is more likely to be regarded as anticompetitive if it not only increases the degree of seller concentration, but also makes the entry of new firms more difficult. The treatment of mergers as part of competition policy is discussed in Chapter 23.

As well as increasing market power, a horizontal merger might be motivated by a desire to protect the dominance of an incumbent firm. For example, should a dominant incumbent be threatened by an entrant with a new product, it might attempt to acquire the entrant as a way of preserving the status quo. The alternative strategy might be to invest in the development of a rival product. To do so might take time and might carry a high financial risk. Acquisition of the rival firm might be a cheaper and less risky strategy, even if relatively generous terms are required for the takeover bid to be accepted. Equally, if international competition threatens the dominance of a group of domestic firms, it is possible that a process of consolidation involving mergers between the domestic firms might be pursued to fight off the challenge.

Motta (2004) identifies several factors that influence the degree of market power following a merger:

■ *Degree of seller concentration.* If the industry is fragmented, then a merger between two small firms may have little effect on the level of competition. However, if a merger were to create an effective monopoly, then there would be issues of concern. A merger might increase the potential for collusion and/ or the formation of a cartel. As the number of firms decreases, it becomes administratively easier to organize common prices and guard against cheating. The US competition authorities provide guidelines based on the Herfindhal–Hirschmann (HH) index concentration measure (see Section 9.4). The US guidelines not only focus on the level of concentration but on the *changes* in concentration brought about by the proposed merger.

■ *Productive capacity of rivals.* The ability of the merged firm to sustain a higher price is dependent on the capacity of its rivals to respond to the probable increase in their demand that follows from the higher price set by the merged firm. If they are unable to respond because they lack spare productive capacity, the market power of the merged firm is enhanced.

■ *The ease of entry.* Market power is higher where entry is more difficult. However, the merger may encourage potential entrants if they believe that industry prices may rise.

■ *Market demand.* If the price elasticity of demand is low, there is more opportunity for an increase in price, and the merged firm has more market power.

■ *The level of buyer concentration* can act as a constraint on market power. If the merged firm were to increase its price, this may encourage large buyers to bargain more aggressively for a discount, or alternatively to set up their own upstream operations.

■ *Acquisition of a failing firm.* Any merger should be assessed by drawing comparisons with the situation if the merger had not taken place. If the merger involves the acquisition of a firm that would otherwise fail, the relevant comparison for the market power of the merged firm is with the market power of the acquirer had the acquired firm exited, rather than been acquired.

Cost savings

One of the most common arguments in favour of horizontal mergers is that the combined size of two firms allows cost savings to be realized, to a greater extent than would be possible through internal expansion. The following classification of the sources of cost savings is based on Roller *et al.* (2001):

- *Rationalization.* Suppose two firms own a number of plants, each operating at a different marginal cost. The differences in marginal cost might be due to differences in the quantities of the fixed (capital) input, differences in the technologies employed, or differences in the scale of production. Following a merger, the firm can shift production from the high marginal cost plants to the low marginal cost plants. This process should continue until marginal costs in all plants are the same. It may even be possible that rationalization requires some plants to close down altogether.

- *Economies of scale* are realized when long-run average cost decreases as the scale of operation increases (see Section 2.2). In order to achieve economies of scale, it is important that the productive assets of the two firms are integrated. According to Parsons (2003), horizontal mergers in the US cable television industry during the 1990s allowed many firms to benefit from economies of scale in areas such as personnel, marketing, advertising and, importantly, the ability to exploit new fibre-optic and digital-server technologies. The trend towards merger and clustering led to many large cities being dominated by single cable companies. In the short run, however, integration involving the dismantling of existing capacity might be temporarily disruptive.

- *Research and development.* The integration of research and development activity might allow cost savings, by eliminating unnecessary duplication of effort. Diffusion of new technology may be achieved more efficiently by an integrated organization. One firm may be technologically superior in all aspects of production and marketing, and this advantage can be transferred to the merger partner. In this case, the superior firm does not benefit technologically from the merger. Alternatively, the two firms may have complementary skills and knowledge. Diffusion may take place in both directions, such that both partners realize benefits. Since a horizontal merger reduces the number of competitors, the merged firm may feel more confident in undertaking speculative R&D investment, since there is less risk of imitation by rivals. A merger could also protect a firm's technology if there is a danger that it might be appropriated by a rival. Accordingly, mergers internalize the benefits of research and development. Cassiman and Columbo (2006) examine 31 mergers since 1987, and find that the most important factors contributing to innovation were the extent of market relatedness, prior relationships and geographical location.

- *Purchasing economies.* A horizontal merger increases the bargaining power of the integrated firm, which may be able to extract lower prices from its suppliers. A merged firm may be able to secure a discount, even in the absence of bargaining power. A supplier may offer a non-linear price, such as a two-part tariff made up of a fixed fee and a price per unit (see Section 13.3). The second part of the tariff allows the firm to exercise price discrimination between high and low users. The merger increases the purchasing requirement, allowing the integrated firm to spread the fixed fee over a larger volume. In addition, the integrated firm may be able to raise finance from the capital markets at a lower cost than its constituent parts.

■ *Productive inefficiency and organizational slack.* In the absence of competitive pressure, a monopolist may fail to achieve efficiency in production (see Section 3.4). Technical inefficiency (x-inefficiency) is said to occur when a firm fails to achieve the maximum output that is technically feasible given the set of inputs it employs. Economic inefficiency occurs when a firm fails to employ the most cost-effective combination of inputs, given the current levels of factor prices. Closely related to the notion of productive inefficiency in the microeconomics literature is the idea of organizational slack in the organizational behaviour literature. By increasing the size and market power of the merged entity, a horizontal merger may reduce competitive pressure. This may increase the likelihood that the firm fails to achieve efficiency in production, or that it operates with organizational slack. On the other hand, a highly active market for corporate ownership can help impose discipline, by reducing the number of inefficient firms. A firm that fails to achieve efficiency in production (or operates with too much slack) may find its share price reduced, making it an acquisition target. Potential new owners believe they can operate the business more efficiently, increasing profits and the firm's share price (see Section 18.3).

Farrell and Shapiro (2000) suggest horizontal mergers which produce cost savings through economies of scale are relatively few in number. Where the potential exists for economies of scale, these can often be realized through internal expansion and do not require a merger. In assessing the benefits and costs of any specific merger, only merger-specific gains, which cannot be achieved in any other way, should be considered. Merger-specific gains, also known as **synergies**, include gains arising from the integration of specific, hard-to-trade assets owned by the merger partners. Some examples are as follows:

■ *Coordination of joint operations.* When two firms are linked by the joint management of a resource, such as an oil field, frequent contractual disputes might tend to increase costs. By reducing or eliminating disputes of this kind, a merger might result in cost savings.

■ *Sharing of complementary skills.* Consider a situation where one firm is more skilled in manufacturing than a rival, while the rival is more skilled in distribution. In time it might be possible for both firms to become skilled in their areas of current weakness, but a merger might enable this to happen sooner or more effectively. Similarly, one firm might own a patent that could be more fully or quickly exploited using another firm's resources.

■ *Improved interoperability.* Two firms might develop what they consider to be separate products; for example, two pieces of software that can be used interchangeably by end-users. However, because the two pieces of software were developed separately, they may be incompatible when used jointly. Moves to develop compatible software may be thwarted if there is a culture of competition between the two firms. By eliminating rivalry of this type, a horizontal merger may enable the benefits of compatibility or interoperability to be achieved more easily.

■ *Network configuration.* Suppose two firms operate a rail service between two cities, with each firm owning a single track. If each firm offers a return service, 'down' trains meet 'up' trains, so passing points have to be built, making route planning more complex and creating the potential for delays. However, if the two firms merge, the two tracks can each be used to serve traffic in one direction, resulting in a cost saving through a synergy effect.

Case study 18.1

A merger fit for world domination

News that Glencore, the world's biggest commodities trader, and Xstrata, a large mining company, are nearing a merger deal brings a long but expected courtship to an end. The business logic for combining the two groups is undeniable. Alas, much of the gains investors count on making will come at the expense of the world's consumers of commodities. Both fiancés are already behemoths by themselves. Glencore is the undisputed champion of physical commodities trading and has been busy accumulating mines on its own account. Xstrata, one of the world's largest miners, is a dominant player in thermal coal, copper, zinc, and nickel.

A union between two such giants is itself enough to raise eyebrows. But it seems that this merger is only the first step in a grand strategy. The joint group will be in a position to go on an acquisition spree for mines around the world. Raising capital for this was Glencore's prime motivation for going public last year. Both chief executives – Mick Davis of Xstrata and Ivan Glasenberg of Glencore – are thought to have their eyes on Anglo American, which will be the world's fifth-largest mining company by market capitalisation after the combined Glencore/Xstrata group. And why stop there?

The public, as well as commodity-rich states, should be concerned. The extraction of many ores is already unhealthily concentrated within a handful of producers, and this merger heralds a further consolidation. In addition, any vertical integration in the global commodity supply chain should put the world on alert.

The combined group will control about a third of the internationally traded production of thermal coal. The analogy in the oil market would be a Saudi Arabia producing three times more crude than it already does. Glencore and Xstrata have a quarter share in the world's zinc market. In copper, the combined group is in a good place to leap into first position in the world, with the market power that comes with controlling the world's marginal supply. This would be worrying in any industry and should be even more so in such crucial inputs to energy generation and manufacturing. With less competition, producers' pricing power grows, not just against the owners of the commodities – often poor countries – but also against the buyers of the ore.

Vertical integration aggravates the risk. Glencore already markets some of Xstrata's output, but now all production, trading and sales decisions can be unified. This benefits the group even if it does not manipulate commodity markets in any direct way. It could simply raise premia for physical delivery or time its production and shipping schedules to capture the highest price buyers are willing to pay.

Strikingly, however, there may be no legal avenues for opposing this merger. The EU already treats the two as a single entity, given Glencore's large shareholding in Xstrata. No doubt regulators in commodity-importing states such as Japan and South Korea will take a hard look at the merger – but there is little they can do to enforce any action they may desire. There is simply no adequate alternative available if Glencore and Xstrata tell customers to take their terms or leave them.

This exposes the inadequacy of global governance of commodities. While much attention is being paid to regulating commodity-related financial products, physical markets remain largely unregulated. Against the Opec oil cartel, the world has only diplomacy to rely on. Even that unsatisfying policy tool has little purchase on market capture by private groups.

For the two companies and their investors there is no doubt that theirs is a marriage made in heaven. For customers, the consequences of this mining mega-deal look a long way from paradise.

Source: A merger fit for world domination, © The Financial Times Limited. All Rights Reserved, 5 February 2012 (Editorial).

Drive for VW-Porsche synergies

A Volkswagen-Porsche combination could deliver greater synergies than the €700m identified, the carmakers have said, underscoring why they want to create an integrated car group, writes Chris Bryant. VW and Porsche SE, the holding group that owns half of the Porsche carmaking business and half of VW, were forced to scrap a merger attempt in September because of legal risks arising from Porsche's failed attempt to take over VW in 2008. VW has a back-up option by which it could acquire the 50 per cent of Porsche's carmaking operations that it does not already own.

But the exercise of its financial options could lead to a tax bill of €1bn unless the parties wait until 2014.

The carmakers are therefore also exploring other options via which they could form an integrated group, but are unwilling to say what these might be. The size of potential synergies could mean it makes financial sense to accelerate the combination. Currently, in spite of extensive co-operation and platform sharing, the companies are forced to operate at arm's length in areas such as purchasing and IT. About €500m in synergies are already in the works, management said. But Hans Dieter Poetsch, VW and Porsche SE chief financial officer, said of a further previously identified €200m in additional synergies, more could be achieved if the two companies were integrated.

'The [original] estimate was a bit too conservative,' he said. 'That means it is worth considering whether now the merger is not available we can find a possible path that leads somewhat earlier than 2014 to the integrated car company,' he said.

Martin Winterkorn, chief executive of the Porsche holding group, who is also head of VW, said: 'All parties involved continued to make every effort to realise the integrated automotive group at economically feasible terms and conditions . . . and I can assure you today: the integrated automotive group of Volkswagen and Porsche will be realised. We want to combine the enormous strengths of Volkswagen and Porsche. We want to leverage the strengths even more efficiently. And we want to exploit the rising synergies to the full.'

Source: Drive for VW-Porsche synergies, © The Financial Times Limited. All Rights Reserved, 15 March 2012 (Bryant, C.). Abridged.

18.3 Non-profit-maximizing motives for horizontal mergers

As shown in Section 4.3, non-profit-maximizing theories of the firm distinguish between the motives of shareholders and managers, and emphasize the strategic role of control and governance issues in the economic analysis of the firm. In accordance with this approach, a merger decision might be taken with a view to the maximization of the utility functions of a team of managers. A merger might be implemented in order to remove a team of weak or non-profit-maximizing managers, or to produce greater leverage in competitive situations. This section examines what are termed non-profit-maximizing motives for horizontal merger.

Managerial discretion

Given the assumption of a divorce of ownership from control, and the existence of a principal–agent relationship between managers and shareholders, it has been argued that managers, rather than aiming to maximize profits, have discretion in the pursuit of alternative goals. One of these goals, suggested by Marris (1964), is the growth of the firm (see Section 4.3). Growth, rather than profit, serves as a performance indicator, and the status, power, survival and remuneration of the managers depend on achieving growth subject to a minimum profit requirement to support the market valuation of the company. Rather than focus on internally generated growth, which might take time and involve risk, managers might aim for external growth through merger and acquisition.

Market for corporate control

Closely related to the managerial discretion hypothesis, Manne (1965) argues that, in an efficient capital market, managers who act against the interests of shareholders, and incompetent managers, should be removed. If the market perceives that the firm is underperforming, its market value declines, attracting the attentions of potential acquirers who believe they can use the firm's productive assets more efficiently. The threat of merger or acquisition imposes discipline on the firm's managers.

In reality, however, the importance of this constraint on the managers' actions is debatable. First, a raider would need to access information about the target firm in order to identify possible sources of slack. Second, for the raider to make a profit, the offer price for shares would have to be less than the post-merger share price. Existing shareholders might be reluctant to sell if they expect the share price to increase in the future. Third, the managers of the target firm may have developed *poison pill* strategies to frustrate a takeover raid. Examples include a deliberate increase in debt to make the firm less financially attractive; generous stock options to key employees that are cancelled in the event of acquisition; extended guarantees to customers in the event of acquisition; and staggered elections to the Board of Directors ensuring that, for a few years after the merger, the new managers face a hostile Board. This is also an important issue for the competition authorities. If competition policy is designed to make mergers difficult, the ability of the threat of acquisition to constrain the actions of underperforming or incompetent managers becomes diluted.

The threat of takeover is not the only factor that acts as a constraint on underperforming managers. First, regular market competition imposes a need for managerial efficiency to avoid bankruptcy. Second, large institutional shareholders may be able to exercise control over the managers, if they have access to information and sufficient voting power. Finally, the managers themselves may hold shares in the firm, which would help align their interests more closely with those of the owners.

The failing firm hypothesis

Dewey (1961) claims that mergers are a 'civilized alternative' to bankruptcy, providing a mechanism for the transfer of the assets of a failing firm to a successful firm. The successful firm might wish to acquire the failing firm for possible short-term financial advantage, such as using the losses of the failing firm to offset its own tax exposure (Mead, 1969). This depends on the relevant tax law. Alternatively, the merger might entail rationalization sufficient to ensure the future profitability of the industry. A few testable hypotheses are associated with the failing firm hypothesis. For example, acquiring firms should have higher profit rates than target firms. More mergers should occur during recessions, when there are more failing firms. Tremblay and Tremblay (1988) report evidence of significant differences in the performance of acquiring and acquired firms in the US brewing industry. The average growth rate over a two-year period prior to a merger was 17.6 per cent for the acquiring firms and 11.1 per cent for the acquired firms. Other studies suggest little or no difference

Table 18.1 Characteristics of acquiring and target companies, 1980–98

		Profit rates	
	Number of mergers	Acquirer	Target
USA	1,967	0.029	0.019
UK	379	0.066	0.039
Continental Europe	172	0.035	0.033
Japan	16	0.011	0.030
Australia, New Zealand, Canada	172	0.024	0.027
Rest of the World	47	0.052	0.013
All mergers	2,753	0.034	0.023

Source: Adapted from Gugler, K., Mueller, D.C., Yurtoglu, B.B. and Zulehner, C. (2003) The effects of mergers: an international comparison, *International Journal of Industrial Organisation*, 21, 625–53, with permission from Elsevier.

between the average performance of acquirers and acquired. In results summarized in Table 18.1, Gugler *et al.* (2003) report that the average profit rates of firms acquired in the US, the UK and continental Europe were lower than those of their acquirers, but the pattern was reversed in Japan, Australia, New Zealand and Canada. Buehler *et al.* (2006) find no evidence to support the failing firm hypothesis using Swiss data. Merger rates were particularly low in industries where bankruptcies were high, and merger rates tended to increase with macroeconomic growth.

The capital redeployment hypothesis

A motive for horizontal merger might exist if the owners or managers of a merged organization are able to perform the task of capital allocation within the organization more efficiently than the capital markets can when the two merger partners are separate. Under an internal system of rewards and penalties, divisional managers might be provided with incentives to reveal information that helps central management to direct funding into the most effective uses. Such incentives might be lacking in the case of an independent company raising finance from an external provider such as a bank. A provider of finance that holds the property rights in the residual value of the organization's assets has more incentive to monitor the performance of the divisions than an external provider. If one division of a merged organization performs badly, its assets can be re-assigned to the other divisions. An external provider of finance to an independent company that fails might be forced to attempt to sell the assets, and might not be able to realize their full market value (Gertner *et al.*, 1994).

The hubris hypothesis

Roll (1986) suggests that the valuation of target firms in takeover bids is often subject to *hubris* on the part of managers of the successful bidder. In other words, successful bidders tend to overestimate the value of their targets.

Suppose there are several bidders for a target firm. The winner is the firm (the managers) whose valuation of the target firm is the highest and who lodge the highest bid. As shown in the discussion of the winner's curse in Section 14.3, under rational expectations and randomly distributed bidding the average bid should be close to the true value of the firm, but the highest bid is likely to exceed the true value. Why then does anyone bid? Roll suggests most managers have few opportunities throughout their careers to be involved in the takeover of another firm. Therefore, most managers have little or no experience to draw on when attempting to judge whether their valuations of target firms are correct. Some of the empirical research is broadly supportive of the hubris hypothesis. For example, Dodd (1980) reports that acquirers suffered negative returns, while Bradley *et al.* (1983) reports significant gains for target firms. Billett and Qian (2008) attributes a tendency for some managers to be over-confident in their own judgement to a 'self-attribution bias', whereby managers tend to award themselves credit for their past successes, but attribute their past failures to bad luck.

Case study 18.3

Empire builders fall prey to their vanity

Just as confidence is vital to success, so overconfidence typically leads to downfall. And nowhere is such hubris more prevalent than when boardrooms suffer from acquisition mania.

A stunning recent example was the purchase by Cisco of Pure Digital, the parent company for the best-selling camcorder, Flip, in 2009 for $590m. Having owned the business for less than two years, Cisco announced last month that it was shutting it down – in spite of Flip's enduring popularity. Now John Chambers, Cisco's chief executive, might argue that he has grown the group from revenue of $1.2bn in 1995 to $40bn this year, and hence a write-off on the scale of the Flip debacle makes little difference to his overall achievements. Nevertheless, such an extraordinarily rapid and absolute destruction of value takes some doing – especially since Cisco has delivered much of its expansion via acquisitions. Yet the stock market appeared to approve of Cisco's high-profile exit from consumer products. All public companies must dance to the whims of institutional investors, and these gyrations distort their M&A behaviour, because too often they are bullied to buy at the top and sell at the bottom.

However, there have been many, very much bigger mistakes than Flip. Recall the catastrophic purchase by Daimler of Chrysler for $38bn, or indeed the series of terrible deals done by Ford Motor in the 1990s, including Volvo for $6.5bn, Jaguar for $2.4bn, and Kwik-Fit for $1.6bn. At the time, Ford was embracing the idea of diversifying into a services organisation. Their stagnant core business was still throwing off lots of cash, which enabled the group to squander many billions in ill-advised purchases. Kwik-Fit was subsequently almost given away to private equity house CVC for a third of its original cost, just three years after its purchase. Typically, the architect of the strategy, Jacques Nasser, then departed and new management felt less shame in taking the loss and moving on. Ford refocused, and has just delivered record first-quarter net income of $2.6bn.

I was on the other side in a similar situation. We sold a restaurant business called My Kinda Town for about £56m in cash to Capital Radio in the 1990s. As a seller, I was baffled as to why a radio company was interested in our casual dining chain but I had not led the negotiations and assumed they knew what they were doing. Shockingly, the cheerleader for this curious diversification left the broadcaster within months. It soon became apparent that the acquirer could not manage its new division. Within a few years, it had broken the business up and sold off the pieces for a fraction of the purchase price. The rationale for the merger was flawed – the compelling synergy between entertainment and eating was an illusion.

Another disaster story was the acquisition of Snapple drinks by Quaker. In 1994, it paid $1.7bn, or almost 30 times earnings, for the beverage company. The objective was to integrate the business with its Gatorade soft drink operation. But the two businesses never gelled, and Snapple fell into a $75m loss. By 1997, it had been offloaded to Triarc for just $300m. It was yet another example of a huge mistake by a corporate behemoth.

One assumes rich public companies do exhaustive research into targets, and that they use the full extent of their industry expertise to analyse the risks and opportunities. But so often all that diligence appears to be a waste of money. Empire builders rarely know when to stop. When Stagecoach bought Coach USA in 1999 for £1.2bn, did it know what it was doing? The deal almost broke Stagecoach, and most of the US business was sold off at a substantial loss.

It is scary how often deals are done for reasons of ego or narcissism. Making attractive returns from acquisitions is extremely difficult, yet momentum, vanity and impatience too often play a big part in the process, especially in bidding wars and contested takeovers. And even veteran buyers can get carried away when the desire to possess an asset becomes overwhelming.

Source: Empire builders fall prey to their vanity, Refereduced with kind permission of 3 May 2011. Reproduced with kind permission of Johnson, L.

18.4 Merger waves

The UK's economic history is peppered with 'waves' of merger activity. The twentieth-century decades of peak merger activity were the 1920s, when mergers were motivated primarily by a desire to achieve economies of scale associated with the new mass-production techniques; the late 1960s and early 1970s, when mergers were actively encouraged by the UK government; and the 1980s and 2000s, when renewed high levels of merger activity were prompted by increased globalization and changes in corporate governance. This section examines the factors that have driven past merger waves, and reviews the UK experience since the 1950s.

Many empirical studies identify cyclical patterns in the level of merger activity, and claim there is a weak correlation with macroeconomic activity and stock market prices. Gort's (1969) disturbance theory represents a natural starting point. Profit-maximizing explanations for merger (the pursuit of market power or cost savings through economies of scale) cannot adequately explain fluctuations in the *rate* of merger activity. Gort argues that the number of mergers tends to increase when individuals form differing expectations of future income streams and the associated risks. Bidders will appear, whose estimates of the value of a firm's assets exceed that of the firm's owners. Differences between individual valuations are likely to emerge when economic disturbances alter investors' expectations and make the future less predictable. Technology shocks, which render historical costs and prices redundant, thereby making future costs and prices hard to estimate, are a particularly potent source of disturbances of this kind. Other potential sources of disturbance include changes in the regulatory regime and a rising stock market. The latter creates uncertainty as to whether the increase in stock prices indicates that there has been a change in fundamentals, or whether it reflects a bubble, being driven primarily by speculation. When the stock market is rising, it becomes easier for acquirers to raise new capital with which to acquire other firms. Horizontal mergers may also be stimulated by increasing demand at the industry or sectoral level, as firms seek to acquire new capacity through merger as an alternative to relying upon internally generated growth. Industry or sector-specific merger activity can then reinforce aggregate merger activity (Andrade *et al.*, 2001; Harford, 2005).

Several *real* factors can be identified as potential drivers of increases in the level of merger activity. The growth of international markets, coupled with reductions in tariffs, has encouraged industries, often with government assistance, to rationalize their production. Improvements in information and telecommunications technologies and networks have allowed the efficient development of multidivisional corporate structures.

The growth of financial intermediation has generated greater liquidity in the market for takeovers. Investment companies, insurance companies and pension funds have been attracted to invest directly in the corporate sector, including the purchase of debt or shares issued by firms in support of a merger strategy. Consequently, *behavioural* factors arising from the psychology of stock markets may contribute to merger waves. Gugler *et al.* (2012) examine whether real or behavioural factors drive merger waves. If real factors are to explain merger waves, then listed and unlisted firms should have similar levels of merger activity. Mergers involving listed US, UK and European firms occurred mostly in periods where stock valuations were high, suggesting that behavioural factors matter more than real factors in driving merger activity.

Prior to the 1980s, external mechanisms for corporate governance were weak and rarely used. The influence of institutional investors was limited, and internal corporate governance was bureaucratic and inefficient. During the 1980s, firms turned increasingly to debt as a source of finance, which required greater financial discipline. Debt may be particularly attractive as a source of finance for mergers because interest payments are deducted from profits before taxation, reducing corporate tax exposure. In leveraged buyouts, where a substantial part

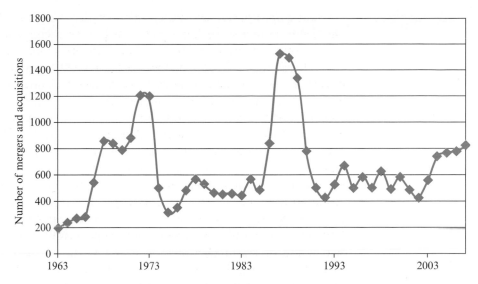

Figure 18.1 Summary of mergers and acquisitions in the UK by UK companies: by number, 1963–2007
Source: Compiled from Office for National Statistics data 2008.

of the price is paid with borrowed funds, financial sponsors will closely monitor and govern the firms they acquire. At the start of the twenty-first century, voluntary and compulsory codes of practice for corporate governance were strengthened to ensure decisions are taken in the light of full information and the absence of conflicts of interest. Rossi and Volpin (2004) find the volume of merger activity is much higher in countries enjoying higher accounting standards and shareholder protection.

Figure 18.1 presents data on aggregate merger activity in the UK for the period 1963–2007. The peaks come in the late 1960s, 1972–3, the late 1980s and 2003–7. Owen (2006) identifies three causes of the merger waves of the late 1960s and early 1970s. First, the internationalization of the world economy meant UK firms needed to achieve increases in scale in order to compete effectively with larger foreign firms, and to service larger international markets. Second, the UK government actively promoted mergers through the Industrial Reorganization Corporation, a quango with powers to exempt mergers from reference to the Monopolies and Mergers Commission (a forerunner of the present-day Competition Commission). Third, the 1956 Restrictive Trade Practices Act made cartel formation more difficult to achieve, forcing some firms to search for means of achieving rationalization other than through collusion. In contrast, the merger wave of the late 1980s had little to do with increasing the size of organizations. It was driven primarily by the perception that value could be extracted from companies by means of merger deals that entailed corporate restructuring through leverage and buy-outs, drawing heavily on techniques imported from the US and fuelled by financial deregulation and a buoyant stock market. The merger wave of the mid-2000s was driven primarily by mergers in specific industries, such as utilities, telecommunications and pharmaceuticals, aimed at realizing economies of scale and improving competitiveness in global markets.

18.5 Strategic alliances

Inter-firm alliances are commonly seen as a viable alternative to mergers. An alliance is defined as an 'organizational structure to govern an incomplete contract between separate firms and in which each firm has limited control' (Gomes-Casseres, 2001). An incomplete contract is one that does not specify every duty and every responsibility of the parties under every conceivable circumstance. A strategic alliance is an incomplete contract, involving an agreement to cooperate, that is brokered without the parties being able to foresee at the outset every detail of how their relationship will subsequently evolve. According to the transaction costs literature, incomplete contracts tend to leave both parties vulnerable to the possibility of opportunistic behaviour from the other party. Internalization of the transaction through merger represents one possible solution to this problem. In the case of a strategic alliance, however, the partners anticipate that the long-run gains of a loose and flexible arrangement outweigh the costs arising from possible opportunistic behaviour in the short run.

Gomes-Casseres (2001) argues that an efficient alliance must be less costly to implement than a merger, and must generate positive synergies. Clearly, a full-scale merger eliminates the potential transaction costs arising from the incomplete nature of the contract between the alliance partners. For an alliance to be the preferred solution, therefore, it must be less costly than a merger. In some cases a merger might be infeasible due to regulatory or political opposition (for example, in the case of the takeover of a domestic firm by a foreign firm in certain countries). Alternatively, the costs of full integration may be prohibitive. A successful takeover might require the bidder to pay more than the current market value of the target firm in order to persuade enough shareholders of the latter to sell. The costs of post-merger rationalization might be prohibitive, as all resources and capabilities have to be integrated, rather than just selected capabilities in the case of the alliance.

Positive synergies arise when the total value of the capabilities of the partners within the alliance is greater than when these capabilities were employed independently. According to Dyer *et al.* (2004), *modular synergies* arise from resources that are managed independently but whose results are pooled. For example, Hewlett-Packard and Microsoft pool their systems and their software respectively to offer customers a seamless solution to their computing needs. *Sequential synergies* are tasks which, when completed, are forwarded to partners to add further value. For example, a pharmaceutical firm might develop a new drug, but pass the responsibility for seeking government approval for its marketing campaign to a partner with more experience in dealing with government departments. *Reciprocal synergies* deliver value through an iterative process of continual customization of resources, to ensure an optimal fit.

A fundamental difference between mergers and alliances is that mergers driven by market prices are competitive, and risky in the sense that once a merger has been completed it may be either irreversible, or at least difficult and expensive for the two entities to subsequently decouple. Alliances are typically negotiated, cooperative in nature, and less risky because it is straightforward to

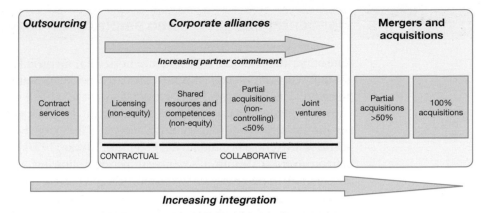

Figure 18.2 Alliances: a continuum of transactions
Source: Pekar Jr, P. and Margulis, M.S. (2003) Equity alliances take centre stage,
© London Business School [2003]. The definitive, peer reviewed and edited version
of this article is published in *Business Strategy Review* [volume 14, pages 50–65, 2003],
www.london.edu/bsr.

terminate the agreement and for the parties to go their separate ways. Alliances can be formed in many different guises, determined by the objectives of the agreement, the control of assets and the managerial structure. For example, firms might enter into a joint research and development initiative, a joint marketing programme, a licensing agreement or a jointly owned venture such as the construction of a large infrastructure project. An alliance might be formed between firms with similar capabilities, or it might seek to combine the technological skills of one firm with the marketing skills of another. Alliances can be either horizontal or vertical (discussed further in Chapter 19).

Figure 18.2 illustrates one approach to classifying alliances in terms of the level of integration (Pekar and Margulis, 2003). Outsourcing is located on the left-hand side of the diagram and merger on the right-hand side. Alliances occupy the middle ground. Moving from left to right implies an increase in integration and a decreasing reliance on contractual market transactions. The weakest form of alliance is the licensing agreement, which is governed by contract, requiring limited cooperation between the two parties. A licence is a contractual right which gives permission for one party to use an activity or property owned by another. With intellectual property rights such as software, the owner or 'licensor' charges a fee to the user or 'licensee'. Collaborative alliances include agreements over projects such as research and development programmes. Equity alliances involve some degree of common or cross-ownership of resources. Under partial acquisition, one partner holds a minority stake in the equity of another; and under partial cross-ownership each partner holds equity in the other. Joint ventures include agreements between partners to create a new entity to exploit a business opportunity, or to form a consortium to buy a company that will fill a gap in their joint competences. For example, in 2007 Sony Ericsson and Motorola formed a joint venture to develop software for mobile phones. Motorola agreed to take a 50 per cent interest in UI Holdings, which had been acquired by Sony Ericsson a few months earlier.

18.6   Horizontal mergers: some empirical evidence

The empirical evidence as to whether horizontal mergers lead to increased profitability through synergy effects of increased market power or cost savings is, on the whole, inconclusive. For example, Cosh *et al.* (1980) compare profitability during a five-year period before a number of UK mergers with profitability during the five years following the merger. The merged firms experienced an increase in average profitability. By contrast, Meeks (1977) finds that profitability fell on average during a seven-year period following a merger. Rydén and Edberg (1980) find merged Swedish firms experienced lower profitability than a control group.

Ravenscraft and Scherer (1987) examine the pre-merger profitability of 634 US target firms in the late 1960s and early 1970s. The target firms' profitability (ratio of operating income to assets) was 20 per cent, much higher than the average profitability of all firms of 11 per cent. Using a different sample, Ravenscraft and Scherer report a negative effect of merger on (post-merger) profitability. In contrast, Healy *et al.* (1992) report that while performance declined on average following the largest 50 US mergers between 1979 and 1984, it fell by less than the industry averages for the firms involved. Pesendorfer (2003) examines the effect of mergers in the US paper industry during the mid-1980s. Post-1984 (when merger guidelines were revised to allow a more liberal interpretation by the competition authorities) 31 mergers occurred. The analysis suggests that cost savings were typically realized post-merger. One way of testing the effects of merger on market power is to compare pre- and post-merger prices. In a survey of nine such studies, Weinberg (2007) finds that only a minority of mergers resulted in higher prices.

Gugler *et al.* (2003) report a large-scale study of around 15,000 mergers worldwide, over the period 1981–99. The aim is to examine whether mergers are motivated by an objective of increasing market power, reducing costs or furthering managerial aims such as growth maximization. The test for market power is based on sales and profit data. A merged firm with increased market power should increase price, moving onto a more inelastic portion of its demand function. While profits increase, sales tend to fall. The test for cost savings is based on the notion that a reduced marginal cost leads to a reduction in price and an increase in both profit and sales. If managerial objectives are dominant, neither costs nor profit need be affected in the long run, although, in the short run, costs are incurred in integrating the two organizations. Therefore both profit and sales may tend to fall. A broad conclusion is that just over half of the mergers resulted in profits greater than would have been expected had the merger not occurred. A similar proportion resulted in a fall in sales. The combination of rising profit and falling sales is consistent with the market power hypothesis.

An alternative approach to analyzing the performance of merged firms is to study the effect of merger announcements on the stock market prices of the firms involved, using an *event study*. An event study compares a company's share price immediately before and after the occurrence of an event that is expected to influence the firm's market valuation. Share prices reflect the present value of investors' estimates of potential future profits. If investors expect a merger to result in greater market power or future cost savings, the share prices of the merger partners should increase. Empirical studies focus on the share prices of the target firms, the bidding firms, or a combination of both. For example, Bradley *et al.* (1988) examine 236 US merger bids between 1963 and 1984, and find that the mean increase in share prices was 32 per cent. Schwert (1996) examines 1,814 US target firms in both successful and unsuccessful merger bids between 1975 and 1991, and calculates an average share price increase of 17 per cent. However, Jarrell *et al.* (1988) find evidence of share price reductions for bidding firms during the 1980s. Roller *et al.* (2001) report that, across a large number of studies, the average gains of target firms are around 30 per cent, while bidding firms tended to break even on average. Noting the wide divergence of results from a large number of event studies, Mueller and Sirower (2003) examine 168 mergers during the period 1978–90. They find evidence to support the managerial discretion hypothesis and the hubris hypothesis (see Section 18.3), but little evidence of synergies resulting from mergers producing increased profitability for shareholders.

Hannah and Kay (1981) find mergers played an important role in increasing seller concentration in the UK over the period 1919–69. Furthermore, if growth attributable to merger was excluded, small firms would have grown by more than large firms. Accordingly, '[m]erger has been the dominant force in increasing concentration in the UK since 1919 . . . Its role has been growing and it now accounts for essentially all of currently observed net concentration increase' (Hannah and Kay, 1981, p. 312). However, Hart (1981) suggests Hannah and Kay may have overstated the impact of mergers on concentration: 'even if all the 122 large mergers [involving over £5 million] had been prohibited, aggregate concentration would have continued to increase' (Hart, 1981, p. 318). As a cause of increasing concentration, mergers are less important than internal growth. Pautler (2003) surveys the empirical literature based on event studies, accounting data studies, structure–conduct–performance studies, which examine the impact of mergers upon competition, and case studies. The latter includes not only survey-based (interview) methods, but also studies based on the analysis of pre-merger and post-merger financial performance.

Overall, the empirical literature suggests many mergers have not succeeded in increasing the profitability of the merged organization. Perhaps there is a systematic tendency to underestimate the practical difficulties involved in linking different product and distribution systems. Merged information systems may prove to be inefficient, and senior managers may face distorted information flows for a significant period after the merger. Finally, if the two parties to a merger have separate and incompatible corporate cultures, staff from the two firms may find it difficult to integrate. The empirical evidence on the importance of horizontal merger as a factor driving trends in seller concentration also appears to be rather mixed and inconclusive.

18.7 Summary

A merger takes place when two independent companies join together in order to form a single company. There are three types of merger: horizontal, vertical and conglomerate. Horizontal integration or horizontal merger, the subject of this chapter, involves the combination of two (or more) firms producing the same products and services. Vertical and conglomerate merger are examined separately in Chapters 19 and 22, respectively.

The motives for horizontal merger are examined under the headings of profit-maximizing and non-profit-maximizing motives. Profit-maximizing motives for horizontal merger involve the pursuit of synergies, either through an enhancement of the market power of the merged entity, or through the pursuit of savings in average costs through rationalization or economies of scale. Enhanced market power may derive from the ability of the merged firm to eliminate threats from substitute producers, securing an effective monopoly position or producing suitable conditions for collusion. Cost savings are realized when a merger results in the rationalization of production, acting as a driver towards the use of more efficient technology or the exploitation of financial or purchasing economies. Mergers may also produce synergies through the integration of hard-to-trade assets, such as joint operations, the sharing of complementary skills and network configurations.

Non-profit-maximizing motives focus on the interaction of principals and agents, and the set of rules which govern their institutions. Horizontal merger might be a vehicle for the exercise of managerial discretion, for example in the case of a team of managers intent on the pursuit of growth rather than profitability. The threat of acquisition might be seen as an instrument for imposing discipline on underperforming managers in an efficiently functioning market for corporate control. Similarly, according to the failing firm hypothesis, merger might be seen as a means of transferring the assets of failing firms into more effective corporate ownership and control. The capital redeployment hypothesis emphasizes the benefits of integration for information flows within the merged organization, and the possibility that this might lead to a more efficient allocation of capital resources than capital markets themselves can achieve in the absence of perfect information. Finally, the hubris hypothesis emphasizes the tendency for successful bidders in the market for corporate control to be overly optimistic in their assessment of the potential benefits of a merger. Historically, the level of merger activity has been highly cyclical, suggesting that macroeconomic, institutional, technological and regulatory changes may all play a role in influencing the demand for integration.

Horizontal merger is only one of several ways in which strategic relationships can be developed between two or more firms. It is useful to think of a continuum of relationships, stretching from outsourcing at one extreme, via various forms of strategic alliance such as licensing, shared resources and competences, shared equity and joint ventures in the middle of the continuum, through to full-scale merger or acquisition at the opposite extreme.

On the whole, the empirical literature suggests that many mergers have not succeeded in increasing the profitability of the merged organization. A wide range of methodologies has been used to examine the impact of mergers on financial performance and on pricing and competition. These include: event studies based on stock market (share price) data; accounting data studies based on financial statement analysis; structure–conduct–performance studies which seek to measure the impact on pricing, concentration, competition and consumer welfare; and case studies based on surveys or the analysis of the pre-merger and post-merger performance in individual cases. In the absence of compelling evidence of synergy effects from a large number of studies based on several complementary methodologies, it is difficult to avoid the conclusion that many mergers have been motivated by non-profit considerations, or simple hubris on the part of decision-takers.

Discussion questions

1. With reference to media archives, give examples of recent horizontal, vertical and conglomerate mergers. In each case identify the objectives of the firms involved.

2. Given the potential for efficiency gains from mergers, why do we not end up with monopolies in all industries?

3. Explain the concept of synergy. With reference to examples, explain the advantages of *improved interoperability* and *network configuration*.

4. With reference to Case Study 18.1, speculate on the extent to which the merger between Glencore and Xstrata will benefit customers.

5. With reference to Case Study 18.2, discuss the possible motives for the Volkswagen-Porsche combination.

6. Discuss reasons why it is suggested that some managers are 'empire builders', and are therefore keen to pursue a strategy of growth maximization.

7. With reference to Case Study 18.3, discuss Roll's hubris hypothesis.

8. Quoting examples, explain how a poison pill strategy might dissuade a potential acquirer.

9. Discuss how changes in the following factors may affect the level of merger activity: national income, interest rates, stock market prices, technology, competition policy and management education.

10. If stock market returns for merged firms are positive, which motives for horizontal merger would be supported? If stock market returns were negative, which motives would be supported?

11. Identify the most important differences between a merger and a strategic alliance. In what circumstances might an alliance be preferred to a merger?

Further reading

Gregoriou, G. and Renneboog, L. (2007) *International Mergers and Acquisitions Activity Since 1990.* Oxford: Elsevier.

Martynova, M. and Renneboog, L.D.R. (2008) A century of corporate takeovers: what have we learned and where do we stand? *Journal of Banking and Finance*, 32, 2148–77.

Pautler, P.A. (2003) Evidence on mergers and acquisitions, *Antitrust Bulletin*, 48, 119–221.

Sudarsanam, S. (2010) *Creating Value from Mergers and Acquisitions*, 2nd edition. Harlow: Prentice Hall.

Weston, J.F., Mitchell, M.L. and Mulherin, J.H. (2003) *Takeovers, Restructuring, & Corporate Governance*, 4th edition. Harlow: Prentice Hall.

Vertical integration

19.1   Introduction

The topic of vertical relationships covers a wide range of issues involving firms operating at different stages of the same production process. **Vertical integration** refers to a situation where a single firm has ownership and control over production at successive stages of a production process. Activities located at the initial stages of a production process are known as *upstream* activities, and those located closer to the market for the final product are known as *downstream* activities. Therefore **upstream** (or **backward**) **vertical integration** refers to a situation where a firm gains control over the production of inputs necessary for its own operation; and **downstream** (or **forward**) **vertical integration** refers to a situation where a firm gains control over an activity that utilizes its outputs. Since capacity may differ at different stages of production, even a vertically integrated firm may have to rely on external market transactions to achieve its required capacity. Balanced vertical integration occurs if capacities at successive stages are equal.

The earliest explanations for vertical integration tended to focus on issues such as the desire to secure enhanced market power; the technological benefits of linking successive stages of production; the reduction in risk and uncertainty associated with the supply of inputs or the distribution of a firm's finished product; and the avoidance of taxes or price controls. Section 19.2 describes motives for vertical integration associated with the enhancement of market power. Section 19.3 describes motives associated with cost savings. This discussion starts by interpreting vertical integration as a strategy for reducing transaction costs (see also Section 5.3), and interprets the various opportunities for cost savings using a transaction costs framework. Section 19.4 discusses reasons why firms may consider a strategy of **vertical disintegration**, disengaging from involvement at some stages of the production process. Section 19.5 reviews some of the empirical evidence on the motivations for and consequences of vertical integration.

As an alternative to vertical integration, some firms may decide to develop vertical relationships of a looser nature than full-scale vertical integration. Advantages include the preservation of some (or all) of both parties' independence, and the avoidance of costs that might be associated with vertical integration. Examples of agency or vertical relationships that stop short of full-scale integration include franchising, involving a specific contractual agreement between a franchisor and franchisee; and networks of independent firms that are linked vertically, and establish non-exclusive contracts or other relationships with one another. Franchising and networks are examined in Section 19.6.

19.2 Motives for vertical integration: enhancement of market power

A major debate in industrial organization concerns the implications of vertical integration for market power. This section examines a number of incentives for vertical integration that raise issues concerning possible uses and abuses of market power.

Double marginalization

One of the strongest arguments in favour of vertical integration derives from an analysis of the problem of **double marginalization** or double mark-up (Spengler, 1950; Machlup and Taber, 1960; Tirole, 1988). Consider an industry in which there are two vertical stages: an upstream production stage and a downstream retail stage. The problem of double marginalization arises when the production stage is under the monopoly control of a single producer, the retail stage is under the monopoly control of a single retailer, and both the producer and the

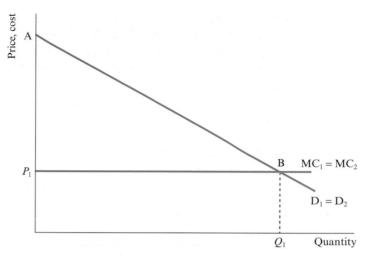

Figure 19.1 Competitive producers, competitive retailers

retailer add their own mark-ups to the price. The outcome is that price is higher and output is lower than in the case where the two stages are vertically integrated with a single monopoly producer–retailer.

Although the problem of double marginalization arises only in the case where both the production and retail stages are monopolized, in theory it is possible for both of these stages to be either competitive or monopolized. In order to develop the analysis of double marginalization, it is useful to analyze the four possible combinations of competition and monopoly that could arise. These are illustrated in Figures 19.1 to 19.4.

In Figure 19.1, D_2 is the market demand function faced by the competitive retailers and MC_1 is the marginal cost function of the competitive producers. The producers sell to the retailers at a price of P_1, equal to the producers' marginal cost, MC_1. Therefore, $P_1 = MC_1 = MC_2$ becomes the retailers' marginal cost function. The retailers sell an output of Q_1 to consumers at a price of P_1, equal to the retailers' marginal cost; therefore the market price is P_1. Producer surplus (abnormal profit) is zero, and consumer surplus is P_1AB.

In Figure 19.2, D_2 and MC_1 represent the monopoly retailer's market demand function and the competitive producers' marginal cost function, as before. MR_2 represents the retailer's marginal revenue function. The producers are competitive, so they sell to the retailer at a price of P_1, equal to the producers' marginal cost, MC_1. As before $P_1 = MC_1 = MC_2$ is the retailer's marginal cost function. In this case, however, the monopoly retailer sets $MR_2 = MC_2$, and sells an output of Q_2 to consumers at a market price of P_2. The competitive producers earn zero abnormal profits, but the monopoly retailer earns an abnormal profit of P_1P_2CD. The combined producer surplus is P_1P_2CD, and consumer surplus is P_2AC. The usual deadweight loss associated with monopoly is DCB.

In Figure 19.3, the monopoly producer knows the price it sets will become the competitive retailers' marginal cost function. The retailers will trade at a

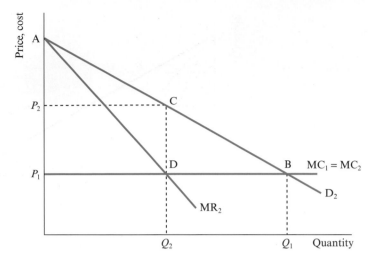

Figure 19.2 Competitive producers, monopoly retailer

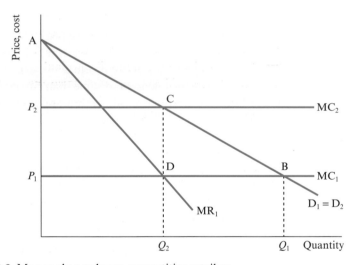

Figure 19.3 Monopoly producer, competitive retailers

price equal to their marginal cost, and will sell whatever quantity the market will bear at this price. Therefore, D_2, the market demand function facing the retailers, is also the producer's demand function, D_1. Accordingly, MR_1 is the producer's marginal revenue function. MC_1 is the producer's marginal cost function, as before. The producer sets $MR_1 = MC_1$, and sells an output of Q_2 at a price of P_2. P_2 becomes the competitive retailers' marginal cost function, MC_2, so they sell the output of Q_2 to consumers at a market price of P_2. The monopoly producer earns an abnormal profit of P_1P_2CD, but the competitive retailers earn zero abnormal profit. As before, the combined producer surplus is P_1P_2CD, and consumer surplus is P_2AC. The only difference between this case and the previous one is that in Figure 19.2 the abnormal profit of P_1P_2CD accrues to the monopoly retailer, while in Figure 19.3 the same abnormal profit accrues to the monopoly producer.

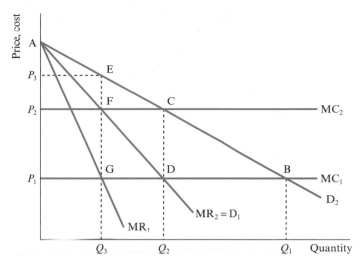

Figure 19.4 Monopoly producer, monopoly retailer

Finally, Figure 19.4 shows the case of double marginalization. The monopoly producer knows the price it sets will become the monopoly retailer's marginal cost function, and it also knows the retailer will sell a quantity such that the retailer's marginal revenue and marginal cost are equal. In other words, the quantity that is sold to consumers (also the quantity the producer can sell to the retailer) is located using the retailer's marginal revenue function MR_2. Effectively, MR_2 represents the producer's demand function, D_1. The producer maximizes profit by setting the marginal revenue associated with this demand function, MR_1, equal to the producer's marginal cost, MC_1 (as before). The producer sells an output of Q_3 at a price of P_2, which becomes the retailer's marginal cost function, MC_2. The retailer maximizes profit by setting the marginal revenue associated with the market demand function, MR_2, equal to MC_2. The retailer sells the output of Q_3 to consumers at a market price of P_3. The monopoly producer earns an abnormal profit of P_1P_2FG and the monopoly retailer earns an abnormal profit of P_2P_3EF. The combined producer surplus is P_1P_3EG, and consumer surplus is P_3AE. However, $P_1P_3EG < P_1P_2CD$, because P_1P_2CD is the maximum profit that can be earned from a market demand function of D_2 when the marginal cost function is MC_1. Moreover $P_3AE < P_2AC$, and the deadweight loss of GEB is larger in Figure 19.4 than the equivalent deadweight loss of DCB in Figures 19.2 and 19.3.

Figure 19.2 can be used again to illustrate the profit-maximizing price and output in the case where the producer and retailer are vertically integrated. In this case, MC_1 is the integrated producer–retailer's marginal cost function, and D_2 is its market demand function. The integrated firm sells an output of Q_2 to consumers at a market price of P_2. The integrated firm earns an abnormal profit (producer surplus) of P_1P_2CD, and consumer surplus is P_2AC. Both consumers and the integrated producer–retailer are better off than in the double marginalization case (Figure 19.4), and the deadweight loss is reduced from GEB (Figure 19.4) to DCB. In the double marginalization case, the problem facing the non-integrated producer is that the retailer's additional mark-up operates against the producer's interests, by reducing the output that is sold to a level below the producer's profit-maximizing output. However, there are some other possible solutions to this problem for the producer, short of full-scale vertical integration. One solution might be to impose a maximum resale price. Another might be to require the retailer to stock an output of Q_2; the alternative being that the retailer receives no supplies at all. These practices are examined in further detail in Chapter 20.

Forward vertical integration

If a monopolist supplies input A to a competitive downstream industry which produces output X, by entering the downstream industry the monopolist could use its control over the supply of inputs to become the dominant firm. But is this worthwhile? The traditional answer is that the monopolist has no incentive to integrate forward if industry X is already competitive. The monopolist cannot produce X any more cheaply. However, if industry X is not competitive and efficient in production, cost savings could be achieved through vertical integration. For example, expenditure on marketing could be reduced, or lower stock levels could be maintained.

This argument, known as the Adelman–Spengler hypothesis (Adelman, 1949; Spengler, 1950), is based on an assumption of fixed factor proportions. Suppose, however, firms in industry X can vary the proportions used of the input A and a substitute input B that is produced under competitive conditions; in other words, suppose input substitution is possible. The supplier of A might have an incentive to integrate vertically with firms in industry X (Vernon and Graham, 1971; Scherer and Ross, 1990) for the following reasons. In Figure 19.5, the isoquant x_1 shows combinations of A and B that can be used to produce x_1 units

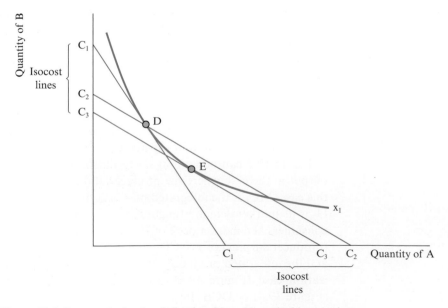

Figure 19.5 Input substitution following forward vertical integration

of the output X. Prior to vertical integration, the isocost line is C_1C_1. The relatively steep slope of C_1C_1 reflects the ratio of the monopoly price charged for A and the competitive price (equal to the marginal cost) of B. The economically efficient (lowest-cost) method of producing x_1 is represented by point D. If input A were supplied at marginal cost, the isocost line passing through D would be C_2C_2. The shallower slope of C_2C_2 reflects the ratio of the marginal cost of A to the competitive price (marginal cost) of B. The abnormal profit of the monopoly supplier of A (measured in units of B) is represented by the vertical distance C_1C_2.

If the monopoly supplier of A integrates into industry X, however, the relevant cost per unit of A is not the monopoly price, but the marginal cost of producing A. With the new relative factor prices, it is no longer economically efficient to produce x_1 units of X at point D. Instead, in order to produce x_1, the vertically integrated firm should switch to point E on the lower isocost line C_3C_3. By doing so, a further cost saving (again measured in units of B) of C_2C_3 is achieved. Furthermore, since the cost of producing X has fallen, it might be profitable to increase production of X to a higher level than x_1 (not shown in Figure 19.5). C_2C_3 is therefore a lower bound for the increase in the profit of the vertically integrated firm. If it is optimal to produce more than x_1, profit must increase by more than C_2C_3.

Backward vertical integration

Suppose an industry is monopolized by firm A. Effectively, firm A imposes a 'tax' on the users of A's output in industry B, in the form of a monopoly price. As shown in Figure 19.6, industry B firms have an incentive to vertically integrate backward. Firm B5 is able to produce an alternative input (B_A), and does so if it considers firm A's price to be excessive. The incentive only exists if firm B5 can replace A's activity at a cost lower than the price charged by A. If a monopolist feels some of its customers are actively pursuing a policy of backward vertical integration in order to avoid the 'tax', it may be willing to accommodate them with special price concessions, in order to avoid losing their custom.

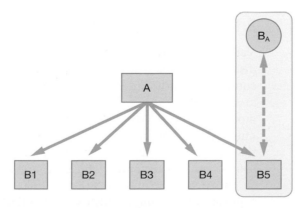

Figure 19.6 Backward vertical integration: case 1

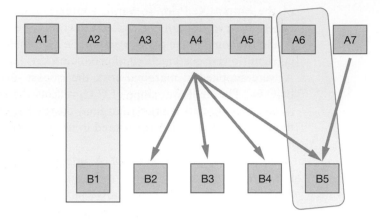

Figure 19.7 Backward vertical integration: case 2

A mid-1980s example involving forward vertical integration is News International's reluctance to use the UK's railway network to distribute its newspapers to wholesalers. News International instead used its own subsidiary TNT, a road haulage company (Monopolies and Mergers Commission, 1993). Oi and Hunter (1965) analyze the conditions under which firms might develop their own private distribution channels, rather than rely on contracting carriers through the market.

Another case in which a firm might consider backward vertical integration is illustrated in Figure 19.7. Firm B1, one of a number of firms in downstream industry B, has been seeking to secure control over an essential input produced by upstream industry A, by vertically integrating backward and acquiring firms A1 to A5. In order to prevent B1 from gaining monopoly control over the A-industry, firm B5 vertically integrates backward by acquiring firm A6. In the long run, rival suppliers such as A7 might enter in order to challenge the emerging monopoly, but in the short run it would be extremely damaging for B5 to allow A6 to go the same way as A1 to A5 and fall into B1's ownership. B5's non-integrated competitors B2, B3 and B4 are already weakened, because they have no alternative other than to buy from the A-firms that have been acquired by B1.

Price discrimination

Vertical integration could provide a means for implementing a policy of price discrimination, which might otherwise be ineffective or ruled unlawful by the competition authorities. As discussed earlier (see Section 12.3), three conditions are required for successful price discrimination. First, the supplier must exercise monopoly control over the market. Second, the price elasticities of demand must be different for different classes of buyer. Third, the supplier must ensure that no resale or seepage occurs: customers who can buy at the lower price cannot resell to customers who are charged the higher price.

The Alcoa case in the US (Perry, 1980; Stuckey, 1983) involved a monopoly supplier of aluminium, which sold to both the aircraft industry and the kitchen utensils industry (pots and pans). Many substitute materials can be used to produce pots and pans, so the price elasticity of demand is high and the price-discriminating supplier sets a low price. In the aircraft industry there are few substitutes for aluminium, so the elasticity is low and the price is high. This suggests kitchen utensils producers have an incentive to resell surplus aluminium ingots to the aircraft industry. By forward vertical integration into the kitchen-utensils industry the aluminium supplier can prevent seepage, and can perhaps more easily conceal the policy of price discrimination.

19.3	Motives for vertical integration: cost savings

Williamson (1971, 1975, 1989, 2002) argues that vertical integration may enable the integrated firm to reduce transaction costs. '[T]he firm is not a simple efficiency instrument . . . but possesses coordinating potential that sometimes transcends that of the market' (Williamson, 1971, p. 112). As shown earlier (see Sections 5.2 and 5.3), Williamson's transaction costs paradigm is based on Coase's (1937) seminal article on the nature of the firm. Coase raises the fundamental question as to why firms exist within a market economy. Coase argues that there are costs associated with the use of the price mechanism to allocate resources and coordinate economic activity. Within a firm, coordination is achieved through management direction and not through the price mechanism. The supersession of the price mechanism is the defining characteristic of the firm.

In cases where the market fails to work well, and a particular transaction proves costly to execute through the market, there may be a cost saving if the firm internalizes that transaction. In other words, the market fails in the case of any transaction involving costs that could be reduced by substituting internal organization for external market exchange. Accordingly, whenever there is a large differential between the costs of external (market) coordination and internal organization for transactions involving producers at successive stages of a production process, there is an incentive for vertical integration. Many of the cost-savings explanations for vertical integration can be located within the transaction costs framework.

Technological conditions

A familiar argument for vertical integration is that technical conditions may dictate that production should be integrated under one coordinating unit. In the steel industry, for example, blast furnaces that produce steel and the strip mills that shape and cut steel are not only controlled by the same firm, but are also located within the same plant so as to conserve heat. In general, where there are closely related or technologically complementary production processes, a vertically integrated firm may be able to achieve better planning and coordination, longer production runs and better use of capacity. In many cases, however, this justification for vertical integration does not lead to vertical merger because, if such obvious technological advantages exist, it is likely that integrated plants have been built from the outset. One might even argue that the two successive stages of production have really evolved into one stage. However, technological change may create new opportunities for integration.

Williamson (1989) suggests the technical economies realized through common ownership of technologically adjacent production processes are often exaggerated. Closely related technical processes may be integrated because the alternative of achieving coordination using market mechanisms is too expensive. For example, the costs of drawing up and monitoring a contract between an owner of a blast furnace and an owner of steel mill would be prohibitively high. Any attempted contract would probably be incomplete, because the codification of the obligations and responsibilities of both parties under all circumstances that could conceivably arise, is impossible.

Uncertainty

Uncertainty creates a number of problems affecting firms' efforts to organize production. Coordination requires foresight concerning many possible events, some of which can be predicted while others cannot. As noted earlier (see Section 4.4), Simon (1959) coins the term *bounded rationality* to describe the limited ability of economic agents to absorb and process the information needed to make optimal decisions. Helfat and Teece (1987) discuss two types of uncertainty. Primary uncertainty arises from factors external to the firm, such as technological change, change in consumer demand, and change in government policy. Secondary uncertainty arises from a lack of information available to the firm's decision makers. Vertically adjacent firms may fail to disclose information to each other; or even worse, may distort information in an attempt to gain an unfair advantage.

A vertically integrated firm may also be able to take advantage of opportunities to conceal information. When a vertically integrated firm produces goods for its own consumption, it avoids making publicly observable market transactions. In certain cases this can create uncertainty in the minds of rivals. Transactions between firms at different stages of production are subject to several forms of uncertainty. For example, raw material supplies might be affected by political instability or climatic variation, which may interfere with the smooth flow of inputs. Many prices do not adjust automatically to ensure a balance between supply and demand. The firm never knows the exact demand for its product in the short term. The adjustment of production in response to fluctuations in demand is not instantaneous; decisions often have to be taken in the absence of any clear price signal; and the firm is at risk of over- or underproducing. However, some of these uncertainties can be reduced through vertical integration. An integrated firm might obtain information about changing supply and demand conditions earlier than a non-integrated firm (Arrow, 1975; Carlton, 1979).

Another possible cause of uncertainty is the quality of the inputs. Without directly observing a supplier's production process, a firm is faced with the risk that it may be in receipt of substandard inputs. The desire to monitor the production of inputs may provide an incentive for vertical integration. In the food industry, for example, the cost of determining quality is a significant transaction cost involved in the marketing of intermediate goods (Hennessy, 1997).

Uncertainty need not always lead to vertical integration. In an industry characterized by rapid technological change, a firm might be able to manage risk and uncertainty most effectively by buying in its inputs, rather than producing them itself. Jacobson and Andréosso-O'Callaghan (1996) cite the case of major software firms such as Microsoft and Lotus, which did not publish their own users' manuals, preferring instead to use specialist firms which bore the uncertainty over the demand for manuals. In the event, the market did eventually decline, as online help functions largely superseded the printed manual.

Carlton (1979) suggests an optimal partial integration strategy might involve integrating to meet high-probability demand, while leaving low-probability demand to specialist producers. Emons (1996) considers a downstream firm whose demand for inputs varies randomly. The downstream firm can integrate vertically and produce its own inputs, or buy them through the market. If the vertically integrated firm invests in the capacity required to meet demand in good times, it incurs costs because it has spare capacity in bad times. However, when the downstream firm produces its own inputs, the market demand for inputs falls, leading to a reduction in input prices. This price effect may outweigh the costs of maintaining spare capacity.

Assured supply

Monteverde and Teece (1982) find that the higher the level of investment undertaken by engineering firms in the production of components, the greater the tendency towards vertical integration. Buyers of technologically complex and strategically important inputs can find themselves at the mercy of suppliers, and backward integration is an obvious strategy for downstream producers to ensure supplies. Similarly, Acemoglu *et al.* (2003) find that when producers are more technology intensive than their suppliers, it is more likely that the producer will integrate backward than when the opposite is the case. The implication is that interruptions to the supply of inputs could threaten the producer's investment. If this is a frequent or serious problem, the producer might consider backward integration in order to secure its own supply of inputs. However, it is important to identify the ultimate cause of the supply shortage. In industries where this may be due to factors beyond the supplier's control, such as political instability or variations in climate, backward integration does not protect the downstream producer.

Adelman (1955) and Langlois and Robertson (1989) suggest vertical integration may be linked to the industry life cycle (see also Section 10.2). In the introduction and growth stages, producers may integrate backward to develop their own supplies, and integrate forward to ensure efficient marketing and after-sales service. As the industry approaches the maturity stage, specialist supply industries and independent distribution channels evolve, allowing producers to divest themselves of upstream and downstream activities. Eventually, during the maturity and decline stages, the extent of vertical integration may increase, as incumbent firms attempt to compensate for declining consumer demand by increasing their market power.

Externalities

Externalities may arise when property rights are poorly defined. Suppose firm A discovers a new process that only firm B can develop and produce. A asks B to keep the idea a secret from A's rivals, and to sell the finished product only to A. However, once A has passed the necessary information to B, there may be no incentive for B to comply with A's original request, in which case A fails to benefit from its own discovery. In this case, A has a clear incentive to integrate with B, in order to protect its property rights in the discovery. In the US in the 1920s, the development and profitability of the automobile and petrol industries were retarded by the slow pace of innovation of petrol retailing: petrol was still sold in canisters by small cornershops. To speed up the development of retailing, petroleum producers integrated forward. The producers did not wish to invest in petrol stations *and* allow them to stay independent, because the new stations could have sold other firms' petrol. Similar examples can be found in the UK brewing, tailoring and airlines industries. Some producers argue forward integration into distribution is necessary in order to protect their investments. The final, retail stage may be too important to be left in the hands of inexperienced or inefficient independent retailers.

Case study 19.1

Stagecoach seeks more control over rail

One of Britain's biggest rail operators has called on the government to give train companies more control so they can improve reliability. Brian Souter, chief executive of Stagecoach, said further improvements to punctuality and reliability were dependent on Lord Adonis, transport minister, giving train operators more responsibility for tracks and other infrastructure currently in the hands of Network Rail. The outspoken rail boss said: 'The next step to better performance is to give operators more control over the tracks and to let them take responsibility for the day-to-day maintenance. We want more flexibility to determine the type of train used and the timetable.'

His comments will reignite the debate over whether the running of the tracks and trains should be integrated at a time when the government is keen to shore up the rail franchising system. Lord Adonis recently published plans to overhaul rail contracts, including the introduction of longer 22-year deals between train operators and the government. But the idea of 'vertical integration' of the railways has been sidelined. Mr Souter said that longer franchises were welcome but unlikely to provide a solution to failures in the rail network. 'There's a lot of motherhood and apple pie in the talk of longer franchises,' said Mr Souter. 'We would prefer an integrated model where operators have control of the tracks. What's needed is a couple of pilot schemes.'

Network Rail, which relies on the taxpayer for the majority of its funding, has come in for criticism in the past few years, most recently after a series of overhead line failures on the West Coast Mainline put a stop to train services in both directions. It also faces potential strike action after the RMT rail union said it would ballot staff in protest at 1,500 job cuts. The RMT warns that the cost-cutting plans could lead to repeated chaos and potentially precipitate a big rail disaster.

Stagecoach, which runs the West Coast franchise along with Sir Richard Branson, received £358m ($561m) in compensation from Network Rail last year after suffering a decade of disruption on the line. It also runs the South West Trains franchise out of Waterloo station, and East Midlands Trains, which runs from London's St Pancras station. Network Rail plans to invest £20bn in the railway network over the next five years, with much of the money to be spent on delivering longer and more frequent trains. Network Rail said: 'Vertical integration is a red herring that will deliver nothing for passengers except more cost.'

The transport department said: 'The Government constantly strives to makes improvements to the rail franchising model, however we believe the current overall structure of the railway is the right one. Wholesale reorganisation would be damaging to the industry and would make it more difficult to deliver the many improvements planned for next few years.'

Source: Stagecoach seeks more control over rail, © The Financial Times Limited. All Rights Reserved, 17 February 2010 (Plimmer, G.).

Complexity

When two successive stages of a production process are linked by potentially complex legal relations, it may be efficient to integrate vertically. To guarantee a more certain supply of inputs or distribution outlets, a producer may attempt to negotiate long-term contracts with its suppliers or distributors. However, if the product is non-standard, perhaps due to frequent changes in design or technology, it may be difficult to specify an exhaustive contract capable of foreseeing all possible circumstances or pre-empting all possible ambiguities that could subsequently result in expensive litigation. An alternative approach might be to negotiate only a short-term contract. However, where a long-term investment is involved, the producer might feel it requires long-term guarantees. In such cases, neither long-term nor short-term contracts are effective, and vertical integration may provide a better solution.

The production and retailing stages of the movie industry provide an example of the issue of complexity. Each movie is unique and distribution patterns for one movie never quite coincide with those for another. Issues such as pairing, regional exposure, repeat showings, television sales and degree of promotional effort determine a unique distribution strategy for every movie. This implies complex contractual relations between producers, distributors and exhibitors. Contractual agreements would also have to be monitored by a sophisticated and costly inspectorate. It may be simpler for producers to integrate forward with distributors and cinema chains, or for the latter to integrate backward.

Gil (2008) examines vertical relationships between distributors and exhibitors in the movie industry. Since contracts are inherently uncertain and subject to externalities, they are incomplete, especially as regards the length of time for which movies will be screened. It is particularly difficult to write contracts specifying the degree and effectiveness of the promotional activities supplied by the distributor and exhibitor. The distributor is generally responsible for national, regional and local promotion, while the exhibitor concentrates on point-of-sale promotion and pricing policy. The exhibitor also decides which movie to show on which screen in the cinema. Decisions taken by the exhibitor affect ancillary markets supplied by the distributor, such as the DVD and video purchase and rental markets. In addition, the exhibitor may have other sources of revenue dependent on the screening of specific movies, such as concessionary sales and on-screen advertisements. Consequently the incentives of both parties may be misaligned. In the case of the Spanish movie industry, Gil (2008) finds movies shown by vertically integrated distributor–exhibitors are screened for up to two weeks longer than movies screened by independent exhibitors. Movies of uncertain quality are more likely to be distributed by integrated firms.

Moral hazard

In general, a moral hazard problem arises when an agent lacks the incentive to work in the best interests of the principal, and the principal cannot monitor the actions of the agent. Moral hazard issues can affect contracts between firms at a different stages of a production process. Suppose a buyer of inputs arranges a contract under conditions of uncertainty. It is possible for the input supplier to bear the risk, but this requires a risk premium to be added to the supply price. The buyer might regard this premium as excessive, and might decide to bear the risk itself by offering terms under which the buyer reimburses the supplier for all costs incurred and adds a mark-up for profit. Many government contracts are structured in this manner. However, contracts of this kind provide no incentive for the supplier to control its own costs. The buyer might insist on monitoring the supplier's work, but if monitoring proves too difficult or costly, vertical integration may be a better alternative.

Asset specificity

Asset specificity occurs when two firms are dependent on each other, as a result of investments in specific physical capital, human capital, sites or brands. The specialized nature of the asset creates a situation of bilateral monopoly, in which only one firm buys and one firm sells the specialized asset or resource. Figures 19.8 and 19.9 show a microeconomic analysis of bilateral monopoly. In Figure 19.8, it is assumed there is one (monopoly) upstream seller and many downstream buyers of the specialized asset. This case corresponds to a standard model of monopoly. The upstream seller maximizes profit by producing at the point where marginal revenue *equals* marginal cost. Using the buyers' demand function to identify the corresponding price, the seller's profit maximizing price and output combination is (P_1, Q_1).

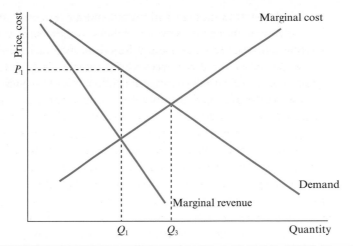

Figure 19.8 One seller, many buyers

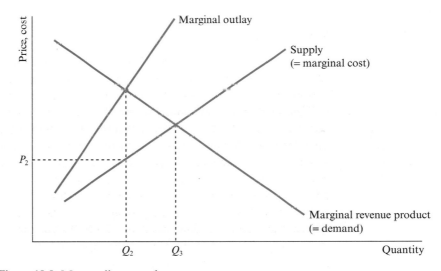

Figure 19.9 Many sellers, one buyer

In Figure 19.9 it is assumed there are many upstream sellers and one (monopsony) downstream buyer of the specialized asset. The construction is as follows:

- The downstream buyer's demand function (the same as the buyers' collective demand function in Figure 19.8) is interpreted as the downstream buyer's marginal revenue product function: the maximum amount the buyer is prepared to pay for each additional unit of the asset is the extra revenue it obtains by using the marginal unit of the asset to produce and sell more of its own product.

- The upstream sellers' collective supply function corresponds to the monopolist's marginal cost function in Figure 19.8.

■ The downstream buyer's marginal outlay function is the marginal function corresponding to the upstream sellers' supply function. The marginal outlay function lies above the supply function. For each additional unit of the specialized asset the buyer wishes to purchase, in order to induce more supply the buyer has to offer a slightly higher price, not only for the marginal unit but also for all the other units (up to the marginal unit) to which the buyer is already committed.

In Figure 19.9 the downstream buyer should buy the quantity of the specialized asset at which marginal revenue product *equals* marginal outlay. Using the sellers' supply function to identify the corresponding price, the buyer's profit maximizing price and output combination is (P_2, Q_2). P_2 in Figure 19.9 is certainly lower than P_1 in Figure 19.8: a monopsony buyer is able to impose a low price on a group of atomistic sellers, and a monopoly seller is able to extract a high price from a group of atomistic buyers. Depending on the relative slopes of the revenue and cost functions, Q_2 might be higher or lower than Q_1.

Combining the analyses in Figures 19.8 and 19.9, there is no determinate solution to the bilateral monopoly case, in which a single seller confronts a single buyer. The equilibrium price could fall anywhere between P_1 and P_2, depending on the relative negotiating or bargaining strengths of the monopoly seller and monopsony buyer of the specialized asset. However, it would be in the joint interests of both parties to agree to exchange the quantity Q_3, at which the downstream buyer's marginal revenue product *equals* the upstream seller's marginal cost. Collusion between the two parties might be one method by which this outcome could be achieved (Machlup and Taber, 1960). However, the usual difficulties of negotiating, monitoring and enforcing an agreement can be avoided if the two firms integrate vertically.

Using transaction costs terminology, the difficulties of the situation can be illustrated with reference to the following example. Suppose a shipper of antique furniture is the only firm that requires specialized padded wagons for long-distance rail transport; and in view of the low level of demand, only one firm produces such wagons. The producer and the shipper are locked in by the specific nature of the asset. Both can behave opportunistically, in an attempt to extract more favourable terms. The seller may demand a higher price, threatening a refusal to supply, knowing the buyer has no alternative source of supply. Equally, the buyer may demand a lower price, threatening to refuse to buy, knowing the supplier has no alternative market. 'Because non-redeployable specific assets make it costly to switch to a new relationship, the market safeguard against opportunism is no longer effective' (John and Weitz, 1988, p. 340). Consequently, the market transaction is characterized by expensive haggling and high contractual costs, which may propel the firms to integrate vertically.

Williamson (1985) identifies four types of asset specificity:

■ *Site specificity*. By having plants located close to one another, there is a saving on transportation, processing and inventory costs. The assets cannot be moved to other locations without increasing costs.

■ *Physical asset specificity*. Plant and machinery that is designed with a limited end use, either for use by one buyer or with one input, is specific to one market transaction. Such investments offer little or no return in alternative uses.

■ *Human asset specificity*. Human capital, in the form of specialized knowledge and experience that has been developed by a firm's managers or workers, may be essential for one supplier but irrelevant and therefore worthless elsewhere.

■ *Dedicated assets*. A firm may be forced to make large-scale investments in dedicated assets in order to meet the needs of one large buyer. If the buyer decides to go elsewhere, the firm is left with excess capacity.

Using data from ten large computer manufacturers between 1950 and 1970, Krickx (1995) tests the hypothesis that vertical integration is more likely when asset specificity is high, by analyzing three major components: receiving tubes, transistors and integrated circuits. As the specificity of the components increased, so did the tendency towards vertical integration. By the late 1960s, the top six computer producers had all vertically integrated backward into the integrated circuit industry. Bigelow and Argyres (2008) examine the make-or-buy decisions of early US automobile manufacturers during the period 1917–35. Most firms produced unique engines internally, but purchased standardized engines from independent suppliers. This suggests that the greater the degree of asset specificity, the stronger the tendency to internalize production.

Avoidance of tax or price controls

Vertical integration between downstream and upstream firms, either within or across national boundaries, can be a means of avoiding tax or price controls. A market transaction that is subject to a sales tax or price control can be replaced by an internal transaction, escaping the liability or restriction. For example, if A is liable to pay a sales tax, from which B (the next stage of production) is exempt, there is a clear incentive for A to integrate vertically with B in order to escape the tax (see Figure 19.10). Alternatively, vertical integration might enable firms to avoid minimum or maximum price controls imposed by governments or regulators.

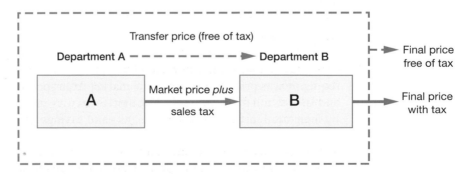

Figure 19.10 Vertical integration to avoid a sales tax

Of course, the authorities are aware of these possibilities, and may attempt to tax or regulate upstream firms as well. Scherer (1980, p. 305) shows that in the US and Europe, integrated petroleum firms reported low pre-tax profits at the refining and marketing stages of production, but much higher profits at the crude oil extraction stage, which was subject to a lower rate of tax on profits. Within the EU, there is wide variation in national rates of corporate taxation, providing an incentive for firms to locate their subsidiaries in low-tax countries (Jacobson and Andréosso-O'Callaghan, 1996).

19.4   Vertical disintegration

A relatively neglected issue is why vertically integrated firms might sometimes wish to create new intermediate markets by disengaging from parts of the supply chain and transforming themselves into more specialized organizations. Stigler (1951) suggests a theory of vertical disintegration along the following lines. Initially, when markets are small, there is a tendency for integration of the various stages of the supply chain. As markets develop and become larger, however, benefits may be obtained from specialization and economies of scale at different stages of the supply chain, and there may be a tendency towards vertical disintegration.

Chen (2005) considers Stigler's argument to be logically incomplete. Why should it be necessary for the firm to decouple its upstream operation in order for the latter to realize economies of scale? Why should a specialized upstream *division* not also benefit from economies of scale? According to Chen, the motivation for vertical disintegration originates in the nature of the horizontal competition at the downstream level. An integrated firm may find it hard to persuade its downstream competitors to purchase their inputs from its upstream division. The competitors may choose to 'boycott' the upstream supplier which is also their downstream rival, and purchase from independent suppliers. In order to retain the business of its downstream competitors as purchasers of inputs from its upstream division, the firm might need to decouple the upstream division and reconstitute the latter as an independent entity.

Jacobides (2005) presents examples of vertical disintegration. The manufacture of early prototypes of the PC (desktop) started as an integrated operation, dominated by the manufacturers of large mainframe computers such as IBM and DEC. With the advent of the PC, the industry tended to disintegrate into separate segments (component manufacturers, software and operating system developers, assemblers and retailers). Another example is the data processing function in banking. This used to be handled by the banks themselves, but subsequently was procured through the market from specialized firms such as EDS and IBM. Until the 1970s in the US, mortgages were granted, funded and serviced by integrated institutions such as banks and savings and loans associations. By 2000, mortgage lending had disintegrated into a 'collection of vertically co-specialized entities' (Jacobides, 2005, p. 468). The trend towards vertical disintegration was motiovated by the realization of economic benefits from specialization and trade, and a trend towards the standardization of the information used to evaluate the creditworthiness of borrowers across the industry.

19.5   Empirical evidence on vertical integration

The topic of vertical integration has been extensively dealt with in the theoretical industrial organization literature. In contrast, the empirical literature on the motives for vertical integration, and the impact of vertical integration on performance, is surprisingly sparse. This may be due partly to the difficulties involved in measuring vertical integration accurately. This section reviews a selection of empirical studies that tackle issues associated with vertical integration. For a comprehensive review, see Lafontaine and Slade (2007).

Spiller (1985) evaluates two competing hypotheses concerning the motives for vertical integration. The first is a neoclassical hypothesis that vertical integration increases profit by permitting savings in average costs, risk reduction, tax evasion or the imposition of price controls. The second is a transaction costs hypothesis, which emphasizes the benefits of integration arising from asset specificity. The findings from an empirical study of the share price effect of a number of US vertical mergers tend to favour the asset specificity hypothesis. John and Weitz (1988) develop a transaction costs analysis of forward vertical integration. The use of direct distribution channels implies vertical integration, while indirect channels comprise a variety of institutional structures. It is suggested that four particular factors may increase the use of direct channels: asset specificity, environmental uncertainty, behavioural uncertainty and the availability of savings in average costs. Asset specificity is discussed in Section 19.3; environmental uncertainty refers to unforeseen fluctuations in supply and demand in the markets for the firm's inputs and outputs; behavioural uncertainty refers to opportunistic behaviour on the part of one of the contracting parties in a vertical relationship; and the cost savings argument is based on the notion that integration is more likely if there is potential for savings through economies of scale or scope.

D'Aveni and Ravenscraft (1994) examine the effects of vertical integration on costs. First, vertical integration can reduce costs by reducing the number of market transactions, integrating administrative functions and allowing better access to information on upstream or downstream operations. Second, vertical integration can increase costs, through managerial diseconomies of scale (the difficulties in managing a larger organization), or an absence of competitive pressure allowing the managers to get away with technical or x-inefficiencies. Cook (1997) examines the motives for vertical integration in the UK brewing and petrol industries. The market power motive for vertical integration involves collusion at the retail level, and the creation of entry barriers. The transaction costs motive is focused on asset specificity and uncertainties due to hold-up. Asset specificity is determined by the size of the sunk cost, which is related to the minimum efficient scale. The market power motive appears to be more important in the brewing industry, and the transaction costs motive is more important in the petrol industry.

Gertner and Stillman (2001) examine vertical relationships, and the ability of firms to respond to sudden changes in their competitive environment. The response of integrated and non-integrated clothing firms to the internet is examined. In general, vertically integrated firms offered online services earlier than their non-integrated counterparts, and offered a wider product range. Kwoka (2002) examines the economies of vertical integration in the electricity generating industry in the US; Nemoto and Goto (2002) explore similar issues for Japan. Vertical integration between the power generation, transmission and distribution stages is a common feature of the electricity industry. The US industry is characterized by large vertically integrated utililies, operating alongside non-integrated generators, transmission and distribution firms. Kwoka finds the large vertically integrated utilities benefit from economies of scale in distribution, through the packaging and selling of power and the billing and servicing of accounts. Enforced deintegration would result in the loss of these vertical economies.

19.6   Agency and vertical relationships

Sections 19.2 and 19.3 examine reasons why a strategy of vertical integration might be attractive to some firms. However, vertical integration is only one of a number of possible vertical structures. This section examines some alternative vertical relationships, which fall within the general category of principal–agent relationships. For example, a producer (acting as the principal) contracts a supplying firm (the agent) to produce its inputs. The fundamental reason for developing contractually specific vertical ties is harmonization of production, processing and distribution activities. But why should firms choose this approach, rather than rely on the advantages of vertical integration? In general there are two reasons: first, to maintain some degree of independence; and, second, to avoid costs that may be associated with full-scale backward or forward vertical integration. Firms that value their independence or wish to operate only in familiar stages of production may develop vertical relationships short of full-scale integration (Harrigan, 1983; Aust, 1997; Gal-Or, 1991, 1999). Vertical separation, as opposed to vertical integration, might allow the development of sufficiently friendly relations among the principals to facilitate effective collusion (Bonanno and Vickers, 1988). This section examines two common forms of vertical relationship: **franchise agreements** and **networks**.

Franchise agreements

Franchising refers to a vertical relationship between two independent firms: a franchisor and a franchisee (OECD, 1993). The franchisor sells a proven product, process or brand to a franchisee on a contractual basis, in return for set-up fees, licence fees, royalties or other payments. The contract typically covers issues such as the prices to be charged, services offered, location and marketing effort. One of the commonest models of **franchise agreement** involves retail franchising, in which a producer develops a vertical relationship with a retailer.

Several types of franchise agreement can be identified:

■ The *business format franchise* covers not only the sale of a product or brand, but also the entire business format, comprising a marketing strategy, staff training, manuals, quality control processes, store layout and close communications between the franchisor and franchisee. Kentucky Fried Chicken, Dyno-Rod and Prontaprint operate franchises of this type.

- The *product* or *trademark franchise* allows greater independence to the franchisee and gives the franchisor less control. For example, a relationship between a car manufacturer and a car dealer may allow the dealer a large degree of independence. Car dealers supplying identical brands can differentiate their service; in contrast, Kentucky Fried Chicken outlets are characterized by their homogeneity.

- The *producer-to-wholesaler franchise* and the *wholesaler-to-retailer franchise* complete the list. As an example of the former, the wholesalers of Coca-Cola are independent bottlers who hold perpetual Coca-Cola franchises with exclusive territories. In the latter case, a wholesaler owns the franchise to supply independent retail outlets trading under their own brand names.

It is natural to ask why the relationship between the franchisor and franchisee is subject to contractual control. The fundamental reason is that decisions taken by one party concerning price, quality, service offered, quality of factor inputs employed and so on, affect the profit and performance of the other party. Furthermore, the decisions of one franchisee may well impact on rival franchisees. While individual decisions may maximize the profit of one of the parties, externalities may reduce aggregate profits for the entire vertical operation. Accordingly, contractual control is necessary in order to reduce or eliminate negative externalities. 'The crucial economic fact that underlies franchising contracts is that the incentives of the transacting parties do not always coincide' (Klein, 1995, p. 12).

Klein (1995) identifies four potential sources of conflict:

- When franchisees jointly use a common brand, a free-rider problem arises. Each franchisee has an incentive to reduce the quality of the product in order to save costs, but the consequences of any such action are borne by all franchisees. The probable future reduction in customer demand is spread across the entire market, and does not fall directly on the free-rider.

- If an initial pre-sales service is required to persuade customers to buy the product, free-riding franchisees might be able to avoid providing such a service by relying on other firms to do so. For example, online car dealers might be able to charge a lower price by selling cars over the internet, avoiding the costs of providing showrooms, test drives and sales staff to answer queries. Customers might first obtain these services from franchised outlets, and then purchase more cheaply from the free-riding online supplier.

- A franchisee may have some degree of market power in the setting of a price for the final product, perhaps because the franchisor has granted exclusive distribution rights. In this case, a case of double marginalization may arise (see Section 19.2). The higher price charged by the franchisee might not necessarily be in the franchisor's best interests.

■ If the price at which the franchisor sells the product to the franchisee exceeds the franchisor's marginal cost, there is an incentive for the franchisor to increase its output, requiring the franchisee to increase the supply of its complementary input (for example, marketing or other promotional effort). However, the amount of the complementary input a franchisee may wish to supply is not dependent on the franchisor's profit-maximizing output level. For example, suppose a franchisor sells its product at a wholesale price of £4.50, and the franchisee sells to consumers at a retail price of £5. The £0.50 mark-up covers the average distribution cost and the franchisee's normal profit. Suppose a particular buyer has a reservation price of £4, but if the buyer is exposed to marketing services costing £3, the reservation price would increase to £5. Clearly, the franchisee cannot afford to spend £3 in order to secure this sale. However, if the franchisor's marginal cost is below £1.50, it would benefit the franchisor to spend £3 in order to attract a sale worth £5. If the producer were vertically integrated with the distributor, the additional marketing service would be funded. Under a franchise agreement, the franchisor would need to subsidize the franchisee's marketing effort in order to achieve the same outcome.

Three forms of contractual control or vertical restraint can be identified, which reduce or eliminate conflict due to negative externalities:

■ Relationships can be coordinated by giving the franchisor direct control over the franchisee's decisions, such as price-setting, quality of product or service and marketing effort.

■ A structure of rewards and penalties can be designed to ensure the incentives facing both parties are properly aligned. For example, the contract could specify that the franchisee pays the franchisor a fixed fee, and buys all variable inputs at marginal cost. Under this structure, the franchisee's profit-maximizing output decision coincides with that of the franchisor.

■ To reduce competition between franchisees (intra-brand competition), a franchisor might offer exclusive territorial contracts, or fix a minimum retail price.

In practice, contracts between franchisors and franchisees may include aspects of all three forms of contractual structure. Macho-Stadler and Pérez-Castrillo (1998) view franchise contracts as a mix of centralized and decentralized decision-making. In the fast-food industry, for example, decisions such as menu selection and building design are taken centrally by the franchisor, while employee recruitment and local advertising are taken locally by the franchisees.

Under some circumstances, it might be in a franchisor's interest to give certain franchisees ownership of several units (Kalnins and Lafontaine, 2004). Multi-unit ownership may increase the franchisee's bargaining power and lead to opportunistic behaviour. A franchisor might be willing to accept this risk for several reasons. First, a franchisee might possess specialized knowledge that can be deployed productively in more than one unit. Second, franchisees might be tempted to free-ride, by using lower quality inputs or offering poor service, while enjoying the benefits of brand recognition and loyalty. This externality tends to diminish as the size of the franchisee's operation expands. Third, by concentrating franchise ownership the franchisor can prevent excessive local competition between franchisees in the same chain. Kalnins (2004) finds prices in fast-food restaurants are influenced more by the pricing strategies of competitors in the same chain than by the prices set by rival chains. Finally, multi-unit owners may benefit from economies of scale in marketing.

In some cases, a franchisor might decide to maintain centralized control by running some outlets itself. For example, the development of a new brand or product might be too important strategically to be left to franchisees, and the company might prefer to channel such strategic initiatives through its own outlets. The geographic location of outlets is a key determinant of the degree of centralization or decentralization. Outlets far from the franchisor's headquarters, outlets in rural areas and outlets close to motorways are more likely to operate with less centralized control (Macho-Stadler and Pérez-Castrillo, 1998; Dnes and Garoupa, 2005).

Informal networks

Informal networks are groups of firms linked vertically by regular contact and relationships that may eventually develop into formal relations. For example, upstream firms might train staff in downstream firms, provide technical expertise, and customize their products in order to meet specific requirements of buyers. The relationship is non-exclusive, and both parties sell to and buy from other firms. In contrast, independent firms rely solely on market transactions for standardized products, and do not develop special relationships with upstream suppliers or downstream customers. In the face of uncertain demand, it is suggested informal networks can sometimes offer better solutions than full-scale vertical integration. First, buyers reliant on multiple sourcing arrangements may be able to reduce the bargaining power of sellers. Second, firms in informal networks can make specific investments, in order to meet the needs of buyers or sellers. Accordingly, vertical integration is not the only possible solution to specificity problems. Third, the aggregate level of investment in specific assets by the network may be less than in a vertically integrated firm (Bolton and Whinston, 1993).

According to Robertson and Langlois (1995), informal networks can be located within the transaction costs paradigm, encompassing independent, market-oriented firms at one extreme, and firms that have internalized transactions through common ownership or contractual agreements at the other extreme. However, informal networks can also be analyzed within a second dimension. This approach focuses on two alternative definitions of the firm (see Sections 5.4 and 5.5). First, the firm as nexus of contracts approach (Jensen and Meckling, 1976; Cheung, 1983) characterizes the firm by the nature of its internal and external contracts. Contracts within the firm are informal, subject to revision, and need to be coordinated administratively. The essence of a firm is its ability to manage these internal contracts efficiently. Second, the property rights approach characterizes the firm by its ownership of assets. Accordingly,

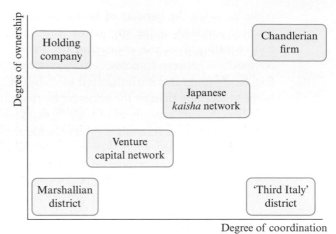

Figure 19.11 Robertson and Langlois's two dimensions of integration

vertical integration involves the ownership of successive stages of production. In order to understand vertical relationships, both definitions are useful. For example, it may be possible for two independent firms to be linked via administrative coordination, or for an integrated firm to deal with its subsidiary through the market. In Figure 19.11 these two defining characteristics, integration of coordination and integration of ownership, are represented by the horizontal and vertical axes, in order to locate the following organizational forms:

- *Marshallian district*. This refers to the most informal of all networks, based on Alfred Marshall's analysis of nineteenth-century British manufacturing firms. Groups of small firms, producing the same or similar products, tend to cluster in specific geographic areas. Being vertically separated, the firms rely on local market transactions. However, the network (or district) allows for the realization of external economies, through the development of pools of specialized labour and the rapid diffusion of new technologies.

- *'Third Italy' district*. This refers to the system developed in north-east Italy, where clusters of relatively small firms have developed into industrial districts (see also Section 10.4), often located in the vicinity of smaller towns or cities. The firms often specialize in the production of standardized products, such as ceramics or textiles. The major difference between this and the Marshallian district is the level of cooperation between the firms. Cooperation is often sponsored by government, and may involve shared accounting services, domestic and international marketing initiatives and investment in infrastructure.

- *Venture capital network*. Venture capitalists are often involved in financing small, high technology start-up businesses. Well known high-technology clusters include Silicon Valley in the US and the Cambridge Science Park in the UK. The degree of integration of coordination is low; although perhaps higher than in the Marshallian district, since some coordination is provided by venture capitalists who supply the initial finance. Venture capitalists help protect their investments by ensuring producers have at their disposal entrepreneurial and managerial expertise, as well as contacts with upstream suppliers and downstream customers. The involvement of venture capitalists implies producers cede some control to their investors, so there is an element of centralization and outside control.

- *Japanese* kaisha *network*. Where production is characterized by the availability of significant economies of scale, industrial districts comprising clusters of small firms are less likely to develop. An alternative core network model involves many small satellite firms located in the vicinity of one large firm, often an assembler. For example, US (and British) car manufacturers often rely on suppliers with relations governed through short-term contracts. The large manufacturer ensures discipline by exercising market power as a single (monopsony) buyer. If suppliers do not meet the manufacturer's requirements regarding price, quality and timing, the manufacturer buys its inputs elsewhere. The manufacturer's detached attitude towards its upstream suppliers does not inspire loyalty, and fails to provide incentives for innovation, or for any action other than sticking rigidly to the terms of the contract. However, under the *kaisha* network system, large Japanese manufacturers typically offer long-term contracts to their suppliers, and share technical and design knowledge. Japanese manufacturers often have significant ownership stakes in their suppliers. Owing to their interconnectedness, upstream and downstream firms tend to share similar business and financial goals.

- *Chandlerian firm*. Chandler (1977) describes the traditional vertically integrated firm. Successive stages of production are centrally owned, and market relationships between upstream suppliers and downstream buyers have been internalized.

- *Holding company*. This structure combines integration of ownership, with non-integration of coordination. Consequently, divisions or subsidiaries owned by the parent are allowed to operate in an independent, market-oriented manner. The development of multidivisional structures can be interpreted as a form of decentralization. Although vertically integrated, the core firm retains only very narrowly defined strategic functions, and the divisions or subsidiaries operate almost autonomously.

Case study 19.2

Outsourcing: Beware false economies

Letting a contractor deal with 'your mess for less' is the conventional attraction of outsourcing – customers save money by handing over their hardware, software, networking and even information technology staff to a third party. Clients often say they want to outsource to focus on their core business, to improve flexibility or to access skilled staff, says Neville Howard, a partner in the technology integration team at Deloitte, the business advisers. 'But I haven't seen one yet that doesn't want to save money on operating costs.'

Traditional IT outsourcing contracts last five, seven or even 10 years, and offer annual savings of about 20 per cent. Suppliers tend to lose money in the first year or two because of the investment required in taking over legacy systems. Over the long term, they save by shedding staff, streamlining systems and achieving economies of scale. In recent years, this pricing model has become harder to achieve because of a shortage of capital to borrow. Clients' discomfort with the idea of their IT being handled at long distances has also made it more difficult for suppliers to cut costs by offshoring. The advent of cloud computing and software as a service, with their pay-as-you-go pricing, has also increased the financial pressure on outsourcing suppliers. Many have made unrealistic promises to win contracts and then underinvested. 'Service levels dip and customers become frustrated. We hear that again and again,' says Mr Howard. Customers should be careful about driving a hard bargain, he says, because what looks like a lower price might end up costing more.

Martin Burvill, group vice-president of global solutions at Verizon Business, the US IT services provider, says that customers who just want to save money by outsourcing and ruthlessly drive down suppliers on price are making a big mistake. 'Suppliers try to recover their losses by charging for all the extras or cutting back resources, so there is a huge gulf between expectation and execution.'

Customers can't expect to get a cheaper service unless they are prepared to let suppliers change the operating model and methodology, Mr Burvill says. 'Without transformation, the supplier won't make money. This is pure logic, but it gets forgotten,' he says. Customers have to be prepared to adapt, he adds, and the more they can move to the outsourcing provider's systems, the greater the potential savings. Customers can often get better value for money by focusing on how the outsourcing provider can make them more competitive or help to bring out products faster, says Jonathan Cooper-Bagnall, head of outsourcing at PA Consulting. 'That might mean switching some services off or scaling them back, or shifting the speed of transition from legacy infrastructure to new customer-focused applications.' They could also request fewer estimates for new applications, which are expensive, he says.

For outsourcing providers, moving away from guaranteed returns and minimum commitments is a big step, says Mr Cooper-Bagnall. 'It fundamentally changes the way they can sell, because it's not about length of contract. They have to change the incentive structure for sales staff, and think about whether it cannibalises a service they already provide.' Nick Grossman, group business development director of 2e2, an IT services provider, suggests that customers should set challenges for outsourcing suppliers, such as reducing the time and cost of processing documents. 'With measurable targets, suppliers can be offered a share in the risks and rewards of improving business efficiency,' he says. Keeping outsourcing providers to a minimum also helps to reduce costs, says Don Herring, the New Jersey-based senior vice-president of network sourcing at AT&T, the communications company. AT&T encourages clients to engage a maximum of three suppliers to handle computing, applications and networking respectively, and to expect them to collaborate. This can result in savings of up to 35 per cent, says Mr Herring.

Having multiple suppliers can also help to keep prices low by introducing competition. It is smart to have a couple of providers for activities such as maintenance and application development, says Deloitte's Mr Howard. Then you can have a mini contest between the two. 'Otherwise,' he says, 'it's very hard to know how long they need; you might get a low hourly rate that ends up costing more than another provider that charges more but does the job quicker.' Minimising the use of consultants also saves money, says Mr Burvill at Verizon. 'Being paid by the day motivates consultants to prolong their contracts by continuously changing the specification.'

There is a lot of emotion in outsourcing, especially as it often involves transferring staff, which is upsetting and causes upheaval. This disruption is one reason why about 40 per cent of clients for which Deloitte looks at outsourcing end up keeping the service in-house. They decide there are not enough cost savings, or the risks outweigh the benefits, particularly for small and medium-sized businesses.

A number of Deloitte's clients that have tried outsourcing are bringing it back in house, Mr Howard says. 'It is a bit like marriage – there can be lots of suffering and violence, and occasionally a messy divorce.' To avoid breakdown, customers should be prepared to share the financial rewards of improved efficiency. A level of mild dissatisfaction is not unusual in customers, Mr Howard says. 'But responsibility for making it work rests as much with them as with suppliers.'

Source: Outsourcing: Beware false economies, © The Financial Times Limited. All Rights Reserved, 6 December 2011 (Bird, J.).

Britvic makes global franchise plans

Britvic, maker of Tango and Robinsons Fruit Shoot, is making plans to take its soft drinks global through franchisees. The company, which derives four-fifths of its revenues from the UK and Ireland, has begun testing the waters with its Fruit Shoot children's drinks in Australia and in the south-east of the US. Other areas of the former British empire may prove fertile ground for Britvic brands, John Gibney, chief financial officer, told Evolution Securities' investors' conference in Edinburgh. 'So the way we are thinking is how to capture that value . . . without laying down capital. And the best way is through franchising,' he said.

A pilot was launched last November in Australia with Bickford's, an Adelaide-based soft drinks company. Fruit Shoot is now available in Australia's two dominant supermarkets, Woolworths and Coles. The drink is also distributed in Alabama, Florida and Georgia through Buffalo Rock, one of the largest independent Pepsi bottlers in the US. Alabama sales, from a small base, are up 20 per cent year on year, said Mr Gibney. Britvic's overseas exposure is however largely limited to France, which accounts for the vast majority of non-UK and Ireland revenues. This leaves it vulnerable to crumbling consumer confidence and disposable income in Ireland and the competitive British market, where an estimated two-thirds of soft drinks are on promotion. UK-orientated food and drinks companies are pursuing divergent strategies. While some are considering overseas expansion, others, such as Premier Foods, are sticking with Britain and focusing on changing the product line-up.

Andrew Holland, beverages analyst at Evolution Securities, said the plans to go overseas with an international partner, thereby requiring no capital deployment, made sense. 'For a little UK company to have global ambitions, there is no way you could do that without an international partner,' he said. The downside is that profits must then be shared with the franchisee.

Mr Gibney described the putative relationships as 'almost a mirror image of what we do in the UK with Pepsi' as bottlers of the US cola drink. Britvic would provide the concentrate and the brand, while the bottler would package and distribute the drinks in its market.

Such an arrangement, he added, limits Britvic's exposure by requiring only a few staff on the ground and advertising and promotional spending.

Source: Britvic makes global franchise plans, © The Financial Times Limited. All Rights Reserved, 14 March 2011 (Lucas, L.). Abridged.

19.7 Summary

The topic of vertical relationships covers a wide range of issues involving firms operating at different stages of the same production process. Vertical integration refers to a situation where a single firm has ownership and exercises control over production at successive stages of the production process. Vertical integration may be used as a strategy for restricting competition, by either using or abusing market power. However, one of the strongest arguments in favour of vertical integration derives from an analysis of the problem of double marginalization, which arises when successive stages of a production process are under the control of independent (non-integrated) monopoly firms. For example, if a producer and retailer are both monopolists, and both add their own mark-ups to the price, the outcome is a higher price and lower output than in the case where the two firms are vertically integrated. Both producer and consumer surplus are higher if the production and retail stages are vertically integrated.

Williamson's transaction costs paradigm provides another very general and wide-ranging explanation for vertical integration. Specific sources of cost saving include the following:

■ *Technological conditions*. Vertical integration may lead to the reduction of production costs. This may occur where complementary processes are best completed together.

■ *Uncertainty*. The relationship between firms in successive stages of production is subject to uncertainty arising from incomplete information. Vertical integration can help reduce such incompleteness.

- *Assured supply*. Firms may be concerned about the risks of being let down by a supplier. Backward vertical integration may help ensure a steady supply of inputs.

- *Externalities* arise when a firm incurs additional costs brought about by the actions of its suppliers or distributors. Vertical integration may help eliminate these costs.

- *Complexity*. Vertical relationships may be characterized by complex technical and legal relations. The resulting difficulties may be reduced through vertical integration.

- *Moral hazard*. A firm's independent suppliers or retailers may have insufficient incentive to act in the firm's best interests. Within an integrated organization these disincentives may be eliminated.

- *Asset specificity* arises when a firm invests in the production or distribution of custom-made products for specific clients. High bargaining costs in a case of bilateral monopoly may be reduced or eliminated through integration.

- *Avoidance of tax or price controls* may also be possible through a strategy of vertical integration.

Empirical evidence on the impact of vertical integration on performance is surprisingly sparse, partly because of the difficulties involved in measuring vertical integration accurately. As an alternative to vertical integration, vertical relationships of a looser nature, stopping short of full-scale merger, are also possible. Examples include franchise agreements, involving a specific contractual agreement between a franchisor and franchisee; and informal networks of independent firms that are linked vertically through non-exclusive contracts or other relationships. Potential advantages of franchising or informal networks include the preservation of some (or all) of both parties' independence, and the avoidance of some of the costs that might otherwise be associated with full-scale vertical integration.

Discussion questions

1. In a certain industry, both the production stage and the distribution stage are controlled by separate monopoly firms. Why might acquisition of the distributor be an attractive proposition for the producer? Would such a takeover be likely to make consumers better off or worse off?

2. Outline the cost-saving motives for vertical integration.

3. In the market for a certain intermediate product, there exists a single seller and a single buyer. Why are the equilibrium price and quantity traded theoretically indeterminate? For what reasons might it be profitable for the buyer and the seller to integrate vertically?

4. Quote examples of firms that have vertically integrated backward in order to guarantee their sources of supply, and firms that have vertically integrated forward in order to safeguard their distribution outlets.

5. With reference to Case Study 19.1, identify the potential benefits of a return to vertical integration in railways.

6. With reference to Case Study 19.2, assess the arguments for and against outsourcing.

7. How might a strategy of vertical integration help a firm to reduce its tax exposure?

8. With reference to Case Study 19.3, identify potential benefits to franchise agreements.

9. Explain the categorization of networks of vertically related firms according to the degree of integration of coordination, and the degree of integration of ownership.

Further reading

Combs, J., Michael, S.C. and Castrogiovanni, G.J. (2004) Franchising: a review and avenues to greater theoretical diversity, *Journal of Management*, 30, 907–31.

Dobson, P.W. and Waterson, M. (1996) *Vertical Restraints and Competition Policy*. Office of Fair Trading Research Paper No. 12. London: OFT.

Jensen, M.C. (2000) *Foundations of Organizational Strategy*. Cambridge, MA: Harvard University Press.

Joskow, P.L. (2005) Vertical integration, in Menard, C. and Shirley, M.M. (eds) *Handbook of New Institutional Economics*. Berlin: Springer.

Katz, M.L. (1989) Vertical contractual relations, in Schmalensee, R. and Willig, R.D. (eds) *Handbook of Industrial Organisation*. Amsterdam: Elsevier.

Lafontaine, F. and Slade, M. (2007) Vertical integration and firm boundaries: the evidence, *Journal of Economic Literature*, 45, 629–85.

Phlips, L. (ed.) (1998) *Applied Industrial Economics*. Cambridge: Cambridge University Press, Chs 9, 15 and 21.

Scherer, F.M. and Ross, D. (1990) *Industrial Market Structure and Economic Performance*, 3rd edition. Boston, MA: Houghton Mifflin, Chs 14 and 15.

Williamson, O.E. (1971) The vertical integration of production; market failure considerations, *American Economic Review*, 61, 112–27.

Williamson, O.E. (1989) Transaction cost economics, in Schmalensee, R. and Willig, R.D. (eds) *Handbook of Industrial Organisation*. Amsterdam: Elsevier.

Vertical restraints

Learning objectives

This chapter covers the following topics:

■ motives for vertical restraints
■ resale price maintenance
■ foreclosure
■ territorial exclusivity
■ quantity-dependent pricing

Key terms

Bundling
Certification
Chicago school
Foreclosure
Non-linear pricing
Quantity-dependent pricing

Quantity forcing
Resale price maintenance
Slotting allowances
Two-part tariff
Tying
Vertical restraint

20.1 Introduction

In some cases, the cost of organizing vertical integration or monitoring other types of vertical relationship might be prohibitive. As an alternative, various forms of **vertical restraint** might be developed, in order to achieve similar outcomes. Vertical restraints are conditions and restrictions on trade imposed by firms that are linked vertically. It is perhaps unfortunate that the words 'restraint' and 'restriction' have negative connotations, because in certain cases arrangements of the kind that are examined in this chapter may have beneficial rather than harmful effects on economic welfare.

This chapter proceeds as follows. Section 20.2 considers profit-enhancing motives for the creation of vertical restraints. As before, these are subdivided into enhancement of market power and pursuit of cost savings.

Section 20.3 examines the main forms that vertical restraints may take. Resale price maintenance (RPM) is an arrangement whereby an upstream firm retains the right to control the price at which a product or service is sold downstream by a wholesaler or retailer. Foreclosure refers to the practice of refusing to supply a downstream firm, or to purchase from an upstream firm. Territorial exclusivity refers to an arrangement whereby a producer imposes territorial restrictions permitting dealers to operate only in specified locations. Finally, quantity-dependent pricing describes several arrangements such that the price per unit paid by a downstream buyer depends on the number of units purchased.

20.2 Motives for vertical restraints

In some cases, firms may find that vertical integration or other types of vertical relationship are too costly to organize or monitor. As an alternative, they may develop various forms of **vertical restraint**, in an attempt to achieve similar outcomes. Vertical restraints are conditions and restrictions on trade imposed by firms that are linked vertically. Generally speaking, vertical restraints may serve two purposes: enhancement of market power, and realization of cost savings. The principal motives for vertical restraints are discussed under these headings.

Enhancement of market power

In some cases, market power over one stage of production or distribution can be extended to an adjacent stage by means of vertical restraints. One way of extending market power is through a price or profit squeeze. An integrated monopolist can reduce the margin between the price of a raw material input and the price of the finished product.

Table 20.1 summarizes an example based on the Alcoa case of 1945 in the US, in which the Aluminium Company of America was convicted of restrictive practices involving vertical restraints (Shepherd, 1997, p. 276). Under pricing policy A, the dominant firm sells aluminium ingots to its own manufacturing division, and to other firms, at a price of 1,000 per ton, and earns a profit of 200 from ingot production. After processing at an additional cost of 500, aluminium products are sold to final consumers for 2,000 per ton. The dominant firm and the non-integrated rival both earn a profit of 500 at the manufacturing stage. The dominant firm's total profit is 700. The price of 1,000 that the dominant firm charges its division is known as a transfer price (see Section 13.5). Under pricing policy B, the dominant firm increases ingot prices to 1,490, and earns a profit of 690 from ingot production. The accounting costs of its manufacturing division rise to 1,990 and profit falls to 10, but total profit remains 700. However, the non-integrated rival experiences a profit squeeze, from 500 to 10. This might be sufficient to force the rival to withdraw from manufacturing.

Table 20.1 Enhancement of market power through a price/profit squeeze

Pricing policy	Integrated dominant firm		Non-integrated rival firm	
	A	B	A	B
Aluminium ingot production				
Cost	800	800		
Price	1,000	1,490		
Profit	200	690		
Manufacturing aluminium products				
Cost – ingots	1,000	1,490	1,000	1,490
– other	500	500	500	500
Price	2,000	2,000	2,000	2,000
Profit	500	10	500	10
Total profit	700	700	500	10

Other methods for enhancing market power through vertical restraints include:

■ *Increase in final prices and deterioration of service.* A restraint that results in customers being forced to concentrate their orders on a narrow range of suppliers results in the denial of access to alternative (more efficient) sources of supply, and access to alternative products. This can lead to a reduction in intra brand competition and inter brand competition. Unable to exploit alternative sources, consumers may face higher prices and poorer conditions of supply.

■ *Increased opportunities for collusion.* The practice of forcing distributors to resell the product at a minimum price reduces intra-brand price competition and presents opportunities for effective horizontal price-fixing. An upstream producer may be tempted to cheat on a cartel of which it is a member by undercutting the cartel price, and stealing its rivals' downstream business. This would not occur if the rivals were vertically integrated. A downstream firm would refuse to buy from the deviant cartel member, and would favour its upstream division regardless of the price offered by the deviant firm. Integrated firms would naturally prefer any profits to accrue to their own affiliates rather than to rivals. Vertical integration reduces the number of outlets through which the deviant firm can trade, making cheating less profitable and collusion more likely to succeed (Chen and Riordan, 2007; Nocke and White, 2007).

■ *Raising entrants' costs.* Vertical restraints discourage entry by raising sunk costs. Exclusive distribution agreements deny outlets to entrants, who are obliged to develop their own distribution networks. If potential rivals are denied access to cheap or high-quality inputs by an integrated firm, they face an absolute cost advantage entry barrier. Potential entrants could also be fearful about certainty of supply. An upstream firm could deny sufficient inputs to a downstream firm, frustrating its attempts to produce at the minimum efficient scale (MES). Rivals' costs as well as potential entrants' costs may be raised through increased innovative effort on the part of downstream firms (Banerjee and Lin, 2003). An innovative downstream firm benefits from reduced costs, which can be passed on to consumers in the form of lower prices, leading to increased demand. The downstream firm buys more inputs from upstream suppliers, leading to increased input prices which increase production costs, not only offsetting some of the benefits to the innovative downstream firm (a negative effect from this firm's perspective), but also increasing the costs facing the firm's rivals (a positive effect). Some forms of vertical restraint could be conducive to entry. Non-integrated producers and upstream suppliers of inputs could agree to set wholesale prices at levels above average cost, allowing downstream producers to justify setting a higher price for their outputs. Accordingly, vertical separation results in higher industry prices, which may tend to attract entry (Bonanno and Vickers, 1988; Innes, 2006).

Cost savings

Vertical restraints have the potential to produce cost savings in cases where arm's length dealing between producers and distributors via the market leads to sub-optimal outcomes. A free-rider or externality problem occurs when a retailer is willing to invest in marketing, but is deterred from doing so because it is unable to appropriate the full benefits of this effort. For example, the retailer may wish to invest in a large retail space, where customers can browse at their leisure and be advised by fully trained staff. However, a rival discount retailer could prosper by attracting customers who have already accessed the pre-sales service and undercutting the price. Consequently the service-oriented retailer may be unwilling to invest in providing the service, which damages the producer because sales are reduced if the service is not available. To prevent such an externality, the producer may refuse to supply the discount retailer, or adopt a policy of resale price maintenance (see Section 20.3).

The European Commission (1998) recommends three tests that can be used to ascertain whether the free-rider problem is a valid reason for imposing vertical restraints. First, the free-riding issue should relate to pre-sales rather than after-sales service; second, the product should be new or technically complex, so that consumers actually need information; and, third, the product should be relatively expensive, so that it would be worthwhile for a consumer to obtain information from one source but purchase elsewhere.

Other issues relating to the free-rider problem include the question of **certification**, which arises when upmarket retailers with a high reputation effectively certify the quality of a good by stocking it. This may be particularly important for new products, which require recognition of this kind in order to become established. Retailers serve their customers not only by stocking products, but also by acting as agents who search the market for goods that are attractive to their customers in terms of quality. In large measure, the reputation of a retailer may be externally defined, and the retailer may have limited influence over the independent assessments on which its reputation is based. Coupled with the costs of a damaged reputation, the fact that reputation is hard to achieve may reduce the likelihood of opportunistic behaviour on the part of a retailer that has established an upmarket reputation. However, there may be a free-rider problem, if customers subsequently switch to a downmarket retailer in order to complete the purchase at a lower price, having verified quality through the certification provided by the upmarket retailer. The upmarket retailer may not be able to charge a premium price to cover the costs of certification. A solution might be for the upstream producer to impose a larger margin upon all downstream retailers (Marvel and McCafferty, 1984; Standifird and Weinstein, 2007).

20.3 Forms of vertical restraint

This section examines the principal forms of vertical restraint.

Resale price maintenance

Resale price maintenance (RPM) is an arrangement whereby an upstream firm retains the right to control the price at which a product or service is sold by a downstream firm, usually in the retail market (Mathewson and Winter, 1998). RPM most commonly involves the fixing of a minimum price (price floor), although a maximum price (price ceiling) is also possible. RPM has been subject to criticism from two directions, one legal and the other economic. From a legal viewpoint, RPM can be interpreted as contrary to the principle of alienation, which implies that, as an individual relinquishes ownership of goods, he or she should have no further say in their use and disposal. From an economic viewpoint, the principal concern is that RPM is anticompetitive.

- *Retailer collusion.* Retailers or dealers often share information or communicate for benign reasons, although it is possible that informal contact develops subsequently into full-blown collusion. As seen earlier (see Chapter 8), any collusive agreement is potentially unstable, due to the possibility that one or more of the parties decides to take independent action. RPM may be a means by which price discipline, and therefore stability, can be achieved (Julien and Rey, 2000). Furthermore, RPM can protect the retailer cartel from entry by other retailers offering price discounts. This view is questioned by the **Chicago school** (Bork, 1978; Posner, 1981; Ornstein, 1985), who claim that retailer cartels are rare, owing to relatively low entry barriers. Furthermore, there is no reason why a producer should wish to support a retailer cartel that might work against the producer's own interests.

- *Producer collusion.* Producers wishing to collude on price might be expected to focus on the wholesale price. This policy may be effective if retailers' cost and demand conditions are stable. If these conditions vary, however, the producers may not know whether differences in the prices charged by different retailers are due to genuine differences in cost or demand conditions, or due to cheating by one or more of the colluding producers. RPM eliminates price variations, since retailers are prevented from adjusting the retail price.

Arguments in favour of RPM can be developed from both a legal and an economic perspective. From a legal perspective, it can be argued that the owner of a good has the right to offer any contract associated with the sale of the good that he or she wishes. From an economic perspective, it can be argued that RPM permits cost savings in distribution. Success in the production and marketing of a product depends on the actions of both producers and retailers. It is possible for individually rational behaviour to lead to sub-optimal outcomes for both the producer and the retailer.

One case in point arises when the demand for a product depends not only on price, but also on associated pre-sales services, such as convenient location, availability of parking space, short waiting times, displays and demonstrations, and information provided by staff. Producers have an incentive to ensure retailers provide such services. However, the free-rider problem (see Section 20.2) may explain why certain retailers are unable to provide the necessary service. For example, the UK bicycle manufacturer Raleigh argued at the Monopolies and Mergers Commission (1981) that the demand for bicycles depends on pre-delivery services such as pre-sales inspection, final assembly and adjustments, as well as post-delivery services such as advice, repairs and stock of spare parts. Raleigh argued that discount stores such as Halfords could not offer these services and sell at a discounted price (Hardt, 1995).

Historically, however, RPM has covered products such as confectionery, tobacco and clothing which perhaps do not require much pre-sales service. Butz and Kleit (2001) suggest producers often set low price floors, to limit the level of discounting without excluding it altogether. By narrowing the price differential between discount store prices and stores offering full service, producers may hope to encourage full-service stores to maximize the quality of their service.

The pre-sales service and certification arguments assume producers are unable to contract for the provision of these services directly. A contractual solution may be difficult to achieve, because of problems associated with the monitoring of contractual obligations. Klein and Murphy (1988) and Blair and Lewis (1994) suggest RPM can help provide the necessary discipline for a contractual solution to be feasible. If the producer is happy with the level of service provided, retailers earn an abnormal profit, assuming the cost of providing the service is within their margin. However, if the producer is unhappy with the service, the dealer's quasi-rents would be lost when the producer terminates the contract.

Gilligan (1986) attempts to distinguish between allocative efficiency and market power as motives for RPM, by examining the effect on the profits of firms that were subject to complaints under competition law for the use of RPM. Using share price changes as a proxy for changes in future profits, Gilligan finds share prices were affected by these challenges. This suggests RPM makes an important contribution to profit. Share price changes appear to be related to structural characteristics of the firms and their industries; this is consistent with the retailer and producer collusion hypotheses.

> [T]he findings of this study do not support the recent recommendations that RPM should enjoy benign treatment under contemporary antitrust policy . . . The results from our study of a sample of firms that were the object of antitrust adjudication clearly suggest that RPM sometimes

causes allocative distortions in manufacturing and distribution. When RPM appears to promote efficiencies in the distribution process, its use is outlived and persists only because of marketing inertia. Calls for *per se* legality of RPM must, given the findings of this study, be based on grounds other than economic efficiency.

(Gilligan, 1986, pp. 554–5)

Using a different methodology, Hersch (1994) examines the share prices of high-volume retailers and producers associated with high RPM usage, following the 1951 US Supreme Court Schwegmann verdict, which severely limited the enforcement of RPM. Hersch finds little effect on share prices, but there are significant differences in the impact of RPM based on firm and market characteristics. This conclusion lends support to the retailer collusion hypothesis. In other contributions, Deneckre *et al.* (1996) argue that producers facing uncertain demand have an incentive to resort to RPM in order to maintain adequate levels of stock, by preventing the emergence of discount stores. Wang (2004) examines the incentives for an upstream oligopoly to impose RPM.

Foreclosure

Foreclosure refers to the practice of refusing to supply a downstream firm, or to purchase from an upstream firm. Complete or absolute foreclosure occurs either when a supplier obtains control over all of the downstream outlets; or a purchaser obtains control over all of the supplying outlets. In each case, non-integrated rivals are denied a share in the relevant market. For example, vertically integrated cable operators, which make and distribute TV programmes, tend to exclude rival programmes from access to their distribution networks (Chipty, 2001; Rubinfeld and Singer, 2001).

Rey and Tirole (2007) define foreclosure as a dominant's firm refusal of access to an *essential* good or service it produces. An essential good or service is one that cannot be produced efficiently by the user. Typical examples are infrastructure projects such as ports, bridges, telecommunications and computer networks. The dominant firm extends its market power from its bottleneck segment of the market to the competitive segment. Foreclosure might be either partial, such that the dominant firm favours some competitive users over others, or complete, such that the dominant firm supplies none of the competitive users. Foreclosure can be achieved in several ways, such as setting a very high price, or creating incompatibility with the technologies of the users.

With reference to exclusive distribution and exclusive purchasing agreements, Dobson (1997) identifies three conditions for the effectiveness of foreclosure:

- A sufficient proportion of upstream or downstream firms are covered by the exclusive agreement.

- There are substantial barriers to entry or an inability to expand output internally at the upstream or downstream stage.

- The agreements are of relatively long duration.

In addition to the possible anticompetitive effects, Heide *et al.* (1998) identify a number of other factors that might influence the extent to which a firm pursues an exclusive dealing strategy. Firm size may influence the degree of exclusive dealing. Large firms may benefit from economies of scale and scope in distribution by developing exclusive dealerships, or from promotional economies which enhance the reputation of their brands. This can bring benefits to producers, retailers and customers through the coordination of sales efforts, enabling customers to make informed choices. However, exclusive dealing makes it difficult or impossible to compare different brands at one location. Customers save on search costs by shopping at outlets that carry a large selection of brands. The implication is that exclusive dealing may cause distributors to lose custom, reducing the incentive for distributors to enter into such agreements.

Does foreclosure or exclusivity damage competition? Can dominant manufacturers use exclusive contracts to deter entrants? Posner (1976) and Bork (1978) suggest the anticompetitive effects are exaggerated. Buyers will require some additional benefit for entering into an exclusive contract. Why should buyers commit themselves to being supplied by an incumbent if potential entrants may be more efficient? Motta (2004) illustrates this point using the analysis shown in Figure 20.1. Assume there is an incumbent monopolist, a more efficient potential entrant, and one downstream buyer. The monopolist's average and marginal cost is C_1, the monopoly price and output are (P_1, Q_1), and the downstream buyer's consumer surplus is A. The potential entrant's average and marginal cost is C_2. In order to capture the downstream buyer's business at a price the incumbent monopolist cannot match, the potential entrant could offer to sell an output of Q_2 at a price that is fractionally below C_1. The potential entrant realizes a profit of $E + F$, and the downstream buyer's consumer surplus is $A + B + D$. To secure the downstream buyer's business, the incumbent monopolist would need to offer a payment equivalent to the difference in consumer surplus, $B + D$. However, such a payment is not feasible because it exceeds the incumbent monopolist's profit of B.

For an exclusive contract to be feasible, there must be efficiency gains to both the seller and the buyer, perhaps in the form of reduction or elimination of the transaction costs incurred in bargaining. In this case the contract should be of no concern to the antitrust authorities (Matouschek and Ramezzana, 2007).

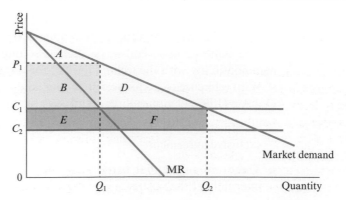

Figure 20.1 Exclusive contracts

According to the Chicago school, foreclosure is an irrelevancy; what matters is the degree of concentration in the upstream and downstream markets. Vertical integration and foreclosure are of little consequence provided horizontal markets are competitive.

On the other hand, Comanor and French (1985), Ordover *et al.* (1990) and Bolton and Whinston (1993) suggest vertical mergers may reduce competition in input markets. As a firm vertically integrates downstream, it has less incentive to compete on price with other upstream suppliers. Accordingly, the upstream rivals can also increase their prices. In the markets for hardware and software systems, there is evidence that foreclosure can lead to monopolization of the hardware market (Church and Gandal, 2000; Chen and Riordan, 2007). Bernheim and Whinston (1998) are more agnostic: under different conditions, exclusive dealing can be anticompetitive, efficiency enhancing or simply irrelevant.

Krattenmaker and Salop (1986) suggest a number of conditions that could be used to determine whether competition is harmed by foreclosure:

- *Is the ability of excluded rivals to compete reduced*? Exclusion might lead to an increase in rivals' costs in the following cases. First, if a firm gains control over the entire supply of a low-cost or high-quality input, rivals might have to acquire inputs that are more costly or of lower quality. Second, if exclusion reduces the supply of inputs available on the open market, rivals are forced to bid up the prices of the remaining inputs. However, foreclosure need not necessarily increase rivals' costs if abundant supplies are available from alternative sources.

- *Is market power increased by exclusion*? The ability to foreclose need not necessarily increase the firm's market power, if it has powerful rivals or if entry is possible. Exclusion may harm certain competitors, without necessarily damaging competition.

- *Is exclusion profitable*? Foreclosure implies some sales forgone. The increase in profit from enhanced market power might not be enough to compensate for the loss of revenue.

Case study 20.1

Ticketmaster/Live Nation

What an unpopular melody. A mooted merger between Ticketmaster and concert producer Live Nation has yet to be confirmed. The idea, though, has prompted anguished howls from around the music industry. Even Bruce Springsteen is in on the act. His objection mainly concerns the ability of the combined company to direct fans to its resale sites (with higher prices) rather than offering tickets at face value – a charge already levelled at Ticketmaster.

Nobody likes paying over the odds. And, given the general outrage, an antitrust investigation beckons, should a deal progress. There would be two broad issues. The first, concerning horizontal concentration within specific markets, is somewhat incidental. The two largely operate in separate domains. True, Ticketmaster dominates ticketing in areas such as concerts and has proved adept at defending that position. Live Nation only in January took its own ticketing inhouse, having also threatened to create more competition by courting third parties. Consumers may feel aggrieved by ticket charges – but ultimately a deal would merely reinstate the competitive landscape of last year.

The second issue (concerning vertical integration) is more knotty. A merger would combine artist management (through Ticketmaster's Front Line acquisition last year) with concert production, venues and primary and secondary ticketing. With interests from singer to stage, the company could squeeze competitors in each area, for example, a non-Ticketmaster venue seeking to attract the top talent, a process known as foreclosure. This kind of competitive threat was largely brushed aside in the name of efficiency under the Bush administration.

That Thomas Weisel Partners estimates the deal's cost savings at just 1 per cent of operating expenses reflects that vertical restraints, rather than a classic horizontal monopoly, is likely to be the hot topic. A high-profile clampdown on ticketing power by authorities may prove popular. Even more tempting, perhaps, is the opportunity to reverse the prevailing competitive wisdom of the past eight years.

Source: Ticketmaster/Live Nation, © The Financial Times Limited. All Rights Reserved, 6 February 2009 (Lex team).

Territorial exclusivity

Producers can impose territorial restrictions, which allow dealers to operate only in specified locations. In some cases, the dealer is restricted to operating in a particular territory, but can serve any customer who approaches them. Alternatively, the dealer may be obliged to serve only customers from a specified location. Katz (1989) suggests territorial agreements affect final consumers' search costs. In order to draw comparisons, consumers may have to visit a range of outlets in different locations. As a result of increased search costs, consumers may be unwilling to shop around, in which case inter-brand competition is reduced and industry profits are increased. However, territorial agreements may help foster dealer collusion, by limiting the number of dealers in a given area. This could work against the producer's interests.

Slotting allowances

Slotting allowances occur in retailing, when large buyers, such as supermarket chains, require fees or other payments from suppliers, such as food manufacturers, to place their products in prominent positions. These could be on eye-level shelves, or special displays in frequently visited parts of the store. A distributional efficiency argument suggests that manufacturers should pay for this service, as it enables them to reach their target market more effectively. The store is entitled to compensation for the costs of setting up the display, and to cover the investment risk should the product fail. On the other hand, slotting allowances may be seen as a mechanism for enhancing market power through the creation of entry barriers or foreclosure. In the UK, most grocery and related sales are channelled through four dominant supermarket chains. Planning restrictions ensure these stores are in relatively short supply, leading to high entry barriers and a shortage of shelf space. Small manufacturers that cannot afford to pay the fees set by the supermarket chains are precluded from marketing their products. Large manufacturers might be willing accomplices in paying high fees, in order to deny space to their smaller competitors (Dobson, 2005; Foros and Jarle Kind, 2008).

Quantity-dependent pricing

Quantity-dependent pricing implies the price per unit paid by a buyer depends on the quantity purchased (Katz, 1989). Several specific types of vertical restraint fall under this heading.

Quantity forcing

Quantity forcing occurs when a buyer is obliged to buy more than he or she would wish under normal circumstances. This might be achieved by forcing the buyer to make a minimum payment for purchases up to a certain level. Forcing buyers to stock and sell more than they wish may have the effect of improving service and reducing prices to final consumers. This latter effect could help overcome the problem of double marginalization (see Section 19.2).

Non-linear pricing

A **two-part tariff** (see Section 13.3) is an example of a **non-linear pricing** structure. With a two-part tariff, a buyer pays a fixed franchise fee, *plus* a price per unit. As the quantity bought increases, the average cost per unit falls. The policy of charging a fixed franchise fee for the opportunity of stocking and selling the product on top of a constant per-unit charge can also be used to eliminate double marginalization, without resorting to full-scale vertical integration. In Figure 19.4, (P_3, Q_3) is the price and quantity combination chosen by the monopoly retailer, with double marginalization. The monopoly producer earns an abnormal profit of P_1P_2FG, and the retailer earns an abnormal profit of P_2P_3EF. From the producer's perspective, a better solution would be to charge the retailer a franchise fee of P_1P_2CD, and to make the product available at a price per unit equivalent to the producer's marginal cost, MC_1. In this case, (P_2, Q_2) is the price and quantity combination chosen by the retailer. The producer's abnormal profit is provided by the franchise fee of P_1P_2CD.

Kay (1990b) suggests two reasons why a non-linear pricing structure might be attractive to a producer. First, if a retailer's profit increases more than proportionately with the total amount of business done with the producer, this should increase the incentive to promote the product. For example, an insurance company might wish independent brokers to recommend its policies above others, or a breakfast cereal producer might wish a supermarket to display its brand prominently on the shelves. A non-linear price structure should provide incentives. Second, if retailers stock only one product or a narrow range of products, the switching and search costs to consumers are increased. This policy increases the producer's market power. Mortimer (2008) examines the effect of non-linear pricing in the video rental industry in the US in the 1990s. Retail outlets paid a fixed fee to the distributor for a film, and received a share of the revenue (between 40 and 60 per cent to the retailer). The profits of both the upstream distributors and downstream retailers increased through the operation of this pricing structure.

Tying

The European Commission (1999) defines **tying** as the selling of two or more distinct products, where the sale of one good is conditional on the purchase of another. Products are distinct if, in the absence of tying arrangements, the products are purchased in separate markets. For example, the supply of shoes with laces is not generally considered as the supply of two distinct products. In contrast, if the purchase of a machine entails a contractual obligation to have the machine serviced by the producer's engineers, two distinct supply markets are tied: one for the machine and the other for servicing. Singer (1968) suggests a number of reasons why tying might be an attractive option for a supplier (producer or retailer):

■ *Evasion of price controls.* If the price a supplier can charge for one product is regulated, the supplier might force its buyers also to stock an unregulated product at a high price, effectively evading the price control.

■ *Protection of goodwill.* A supplier may wish to protect the quality of its product by insisting repairs and spare parts are supplied only by itself. The supplier might argue that to have the product serviced by non-approved engineers may cause damage and could harm the firm's reputation. Whether this argument is justified depends on whether efficient alternatives to the tying arrangement exist.

■ *Economies of distribution.* Producers may tie two or more complementary products in order to benefit from economies in distribution. In principle, assembled products such as cars involve tying many separate products such as engines, crankshafts, axles, wheels, tyres and other parts.

■ *Price discrimination.* Suppose a monopoly supplier sells colour printers (the tying product) and ink cartridges (the tied product). The supplier charges a competitive price for its printers but prices the cartridges above their marginal cost. Large customers (with a low price elasticity of demand) are forced to pay a higher price overall, since they use proportionately more of the expensive cartridges than the smaller customers. Resale is ruled out since the price of cartridges is the same for all customers. A form of price discrimination is achieved indirectly. The common practice of selling machines and expensive service contracts can be interpreted as a similar case of covert price discrimination.

- *Leverage*. A tying arrangement can extend the power of a monopolist into related markets, enhancing market power in the market for the tied product. The leverage a monopolist can exert depends on the proportion of the tied market covered by the tying arrangement, and on the effectiveness of the tying arrangement as a barrier to entry or as a means of sustaining collusion in the downstream market (Whinston, 1990; Chen and Ross, 1999; Choi and Stefanadis, 2001; Carlton and Waldman, 2002; Spector, 2007).

Bundling

Under the practice of **bundling**, a supplier offers several goods as a single package. For example, hotels offer rooms bundled with the use of facilities such as in-house gyms and swimming pools. The prices of all these additional services are included in the price of the room, whether they are used or not. Adams and Yellen (1976) show bundling is profitable since customers can be sorted into different groups with different willingness to pay, and their consumer surplus appropriated accordingly. In other words, bundling can be used as a form of price discrimination. Nalebuff (2004) shows that bundling can be an effective barrier to entry. A monopolist operating in two markets can bundle the goods, making it difficult for rivals to enter either market. An entry barrier is created without having to lower prices in either market.

With reference to the movie industry, Stigler (1963) discusses the practice of block booking, which can be interpreted as a form of bundling. Block booking refers to the practice of offering an exhibitor a collection of movies in a package, rather than making them available individually. Assume a London distributor knows the reserve prices of two exhibitors. One exhibitor owns an arthouse cinema in Hampstead, and the other owns a West End cinema which shows popular movies. The reserve prices each exhibitor is willing to pay for two movies, *Citizen Kane* and the latest *Harry Potter*, are:

Exhibitor	Harry Potter	Citizen Kane
Hampstead	7,000	4,000
West End	8,500	3,000

If each movie is sold separately and the distributor is able to prevent resale, perfect price discrimination can be achieved. The total rental is £22,500 (= 7,000 + 4,000 + 8,500 + 3,000). However, if it is not possible to prevent resale, the best the distributor can do is to charge £7,000 for *Harry Potter* and £3,000 for *Citizen Kane*. This generates a total rental of £20,000 (= 7,000 + 7,000 + 3,000 + 3,000). If the distributor practises block booking without discrimination, the two-film package can be sold for £11,000 to both exhibitors. The total rental rises to £22,000.

Reed chief hits back at critics of division

Erik Engstrom, chief executive of Reed Elsevier, said the growing academic backlash against the group's core scientific publishing division was based on 'misstatements' and 'misunderstandings', as he unveiled full-year results slightly ahead of expectations. Over the past month more than 6,000 academics across the globe have joined a boycott against Elsevier publications in what has been dubbed 'an international academic spring' by Dennis Johnson, the co-founder of US publishing house Melville House. The academics – based at institutions including Massachusetts Institute of Technology, University of Cambridge and University of Bologna – are refusing to submit or peer-review papers for Reed's scientific journals, which include the *American Journal of Medicine* and *The Surgeon*.

They believe the group's journal prices are too high and object to Reed's practice of 'bundling' journals that they believe prompts libraries of universities, whose budgets are already under pressure, to spend money on titles they may not want. Tim Leunig, editor of an Elsevier journal called *Explorations in Economic History*, said: 'I regret the fact that Elsevier charge over three times the prices prevailing in my subject area. It makes the journal less accessible and less influential than it would otherwise be.'

Reed said on Thursday that libraries were not forced to take bundled packages and that the cost of downloading articles had never been lower. Mr Engstrom said: 'We are taking the petition very seriously and we are engaging with our stakeholders to better understand and address their concerns . . . All [objections] . . . are based on misstatements or misunderstandings of the fact.'

Claudio Aspesi, analyst at Bernstein Research, questioned how 'a public relations incident of this kind could happen' and urged investors to ask Reed why the crisis management had been 'so tentative'. Elsevier contributes almost half of group profits.

Vertical restraints: anticompetitive or benign?

Are vertical restraints always anticompetitive? Or are they sometimes desirable on efficiency or welfare criteria? Or is their effect simply neutral? Much of the debate in Europe and the US has centred on the views of the Chicago school (Telser, 1960; Bork, 1978; Posner, 1981). Before the views of the Chicago school came to prominence, it was widely believed that vertical restraints, by their very nature, reduce the independence of distributors and are therefore anticompetitive. Resale price maintenance (RPM), for example, was seen as little different from horizontal price-fixing, and was banned in most countries. In contrast, the Chicago school distinguish between vertical and horizontal restraints. Competition takes place within a market, and is therefore impeded by horizontal restraints but not by vertical restraints. Producers do not normally impose restrictions downstream that would reduce the level of demand for their own products. If restrictions are imposed, it is because a potential cost saving or efficiency gain can be realized, perhaps through the elimination of externalities or opportunism (Baake *et al.*, 2004).

Since the 1970s, the tide has turned somewhat against the Chicago view (Comanor, 1985; Rey and Tirole, 1986). It is now customary to analyze vertical restraints on a case-by-case basis. Restraints may sometimes raise entry barriers or facilitate collusion, leading to a distortion of competition. For example, RPM might be used as an alternative to horizontal price-fixing, the latter being more obvious as well as illegal. However, why upstream firms should wish to cooperate in enhancing market power downstream is not always clear. Grimes (2002) analyzes the approach of the US legal system to vertical restraints. The US Supreme Court recognizes that vertical restraints can be justified as a cost-effective method for promoting an upstream supplier's brands. In some cases, vertical restraints may foster competition and blanket condemnation of such practices is unwarranted.

20.4 Summary

Vertical restraints are conditions and restrictions on trade that are imposed by firms that are linked vertically. Such restrictions may be motivated by factors similar to those that motivate other types of vertical relationship: specifically, the enhancement of market power and the potential for the realization of cost savings. Principal types of vertical restraint are as follows:

■ *Resale price maintenance* (RPM) involves a producer controlling the price at which a product or service is sold by a retailer. RPM usually involves the fixing of a minimum price, although a maximum price is also possible. RPM may eliminate disincentives for retailers to supply pre-sales service, or provide an informal quality certification service.

■ *Foreclosure* refers to the practice of refusing to supply a downstream firm, or to purchase from an upstream firm. The extent to which foreclosure damages competition is controversial; some economists argue that only horizontal competition matters, and vertical restraints of this kind are irrelevant.

■ *Territorial exclusivity* is a form of geographic foreclosure, whereby a producer requires its retailers to trade only in specified geographic locations.

■ *Quantity-dependent pricing* implies the price paid by a buyer depends on the quantity purchased. A retailer might be obliged to stock more than he or she would wish; the price the retailer pays might include a fixed component and a variable component that depends on quantity (two-part tariff); the supply of one product to a retailer might be made conditional on the retailer's willingness to stock a second product (tying); or several products might be sold together to consumers as a single package (bundling).

The many types of vertical restraints that have been examined in this chapter may help promote efficiency or economic welfare; may be anticompetitive; or may simply have a neutral effect. In the 1970s and 1980s, the views of the Chicago school, who took an essentially benign view of the implications of vertical restraints for competition, influenced the formulation of competition policy in many countries. More recent thinking suggests a more sceptical and cautious approach is appropriate. Although blanket condemnation of vertical restraints is unwarranted, it is advisable to examine the implications for competition, efficiency and welfare of each case on its own individual merits.

Discussion questions

1. What are vertical restraints? Examine the market power and cost saving motives for vertical restraints.

2. With reference to Case Study 20.1, explain why cost savings can arise from market power advantages.

3. Slotting allowances and 'pay to stay' fees are lump sum payments made by suppliers to the retail trade to ensure prime shelf locations for new lines. Assess the pro- and anti-competitive effects of these payments.

4. Setting a recommended retail price is just resale price maintenance by another name. Assess the validity of this argument.

5. Explain the distinction between the practices of tying and bundling. Using Case Study 20.2, examine why a supplier might consider adopting such practices.

6. Under what circumstances might vertical restraints be beneficial to consumer interests?

Further reading

Bork, R. (1978) *The Antitrust Paradox: A Policy at War with Itself.* New York: Basic Books.
Dobson, P.W. and Waterson, M. (1996) *Vertical Restraints and Competition Policy.* Office of Fair Trading Research Paper No. 12. London: OFT.
Motta, M. (2004) *Competition Policy, Theory and Practice.* Cambridge: Cambridge University Press, Ch. 6.
OECD (1993) *Competition Policy and Vertical Restraints: Franchising Agreements.* Paris: OECD.

Network goods and services

Learning objectives

This chapter covers the following topics:

- Network externalities
- Demand for a network product or service
- Market equilibrium under perfect competition and monopoly
- Market equilibrium under duopoly
- Competition over standards and compatibility

Key terms

Demand-side economies of scale	Installed base
Network effects	Side-payment
Network externalities	

21.1 Introduction

For some products or services, the value or utility to any user increases with the total number of users. A classic historical example is the telephone. The larger the number of users who connect to a telephone network, the larger is the number of other users with whom each user can communicate, and the greater is the value of the service to each user. Similar **network externalities** are available for other communications technologies, both old and new, including postal services, and online social networks such as *Facebook* and *Twitter*. Stock and other securities markets may feature a network externality through an increase in liquidity and a reduction in transaction costs as the number of traders increases. Similarly, the value each user derives from trading in online markets or betting exchanges such as eBay and Betfair increases with the number of other users, as auctions or the markets for bets on individual sporting events become more liquid and more competitive.

Another type of network externality arises when an increase in the number of users of a core product or service stimulates the production of complementary products or services, and the increased availability of complements increases the value to each user of the core product or service. This type of network externality characterizes many hardware-software markets. As the number of users of a particular games console increases, for example, suppliers of software are encouraged to produce more applications, and the value or utility derived from ownership of the console increases owing to the increased availability of software. Similar examples include PC operating systems and compatible software, and DVD or Blu-Ray players and compatible disks. Stock markets may feature a similar type of network externality, through an increase in vertically related services (for example, brokers or investment banking services) as the number of traders increases.

In many markets featuring network goods or services, a key feature of the market that determines the extent of the network externalities is the degree of compatibility between the products or services of different suppliers. If systems are compatible, the relevant network is the aggregate number of users of all suppliers. If systems are incompatible, the relevant network for each user is the number of other users who are connected to the same supplier. In many cases the compatibility or incompatibility of the products or services provided by two (or more) suppliers depends on the suppliers' own strategic choices.

The outcome of a battle between technologies aiming to establish supremacy as the industry standard may have far-reaching consequences for the survival and profitability of the competing suppliers. Often the coexistence of competing technologies is unstable. Small or early advantages gained in a standards battle may have decisive and far-reaching consequences, if one technology surpasses a tipping point beyond which all users would switch to the victor, through a bandwagon effect. History matters, and the preferences of early adopters may have considerable influence in shaping product characteristics.

Technically superior or cheaper products that arrive on the market later might be unable to dislodge an inferior product that arrived earlier, because users of the latter are already benefiting from a network effect that they are unwilling to forgo by switching. A first-mover advantage might prove decisive in determining the outcome of a standards battle. For example, the QWERTY keyboard was originally designed for mechanical typewriters, to slow down the speed of typing so as to prevent the keys from being jammed. It is claimed that other keyboard layouts would permit much faster typing speeds but, even when the mechanical problems had been solved, QWERTY remained the standard, because typists had invested too much in effort in learning to type using the QWERTY keyboard for a new design to be marketable. Users of a losing technology may incur switching costs, which they could have avoided if they had correctly anticipated the outcome of the standards battle. This suggests that consumer expectations of the future number of users are important in influencing the purchase decision, and suppliers may face incentives to attempt to influence or manipulate these expectations.

This chapter describes the economics of markets that exhibit network externalities. Section 21.2 examines how a network effect modifies the specification of a demand function for a network product or service. In specifying demand functions, a distinction is drawn between the stand-alone benefit each user derives from consumption of the product or service regardless of the number of other users, and the network benefit that increases in proportion to the number of other users. The properties of the demand function are examined for two cases: first, where the stand-alone benefit is the same for every user but different users attach different value to the network benefit; and second, where the stand-alone benefit differs between users but the network benefit is the same for every user. Section 21.3 examines the nature of the market equilibrium under perfect competition (large numbers of competing suppliers of the network product or service) and monopoly (a single supplier), for both sets of demand assumptions.

Section 21.4 extends the theoretical analysis to cover the case of duopoly, in which there are two competing suppliers who might prefer either compatibility or incompatibility between their own technical standards. Section 21.5 contains a less formal discussion of factors that are likely to influence the form of competition between two or more suppliers offering competing technologies. Alternative forms of competition include inter-technology competition, where the suppliers prefer incompatibility to compatibility and are willing to engage in a standards battle in an effort to establish their own technology as the industry standard; and intra-technology competition, where the suppliers prefer compatibility to incompatibility under any circumstances, but would prefer rivals to adopt their technology if they can be persuaded to do so.

21.2 Demand for a network product or service

Network externalities, also known as **network effects** or **demand-side economies of scale**, arise from the fact that the value to any user of certain products and services increases in proportion to the total number of users. In communications markets, the value comes from the ability to communicate with other users via a network. As the number of users increases, the opportunities for communication increase, and the value to each user of belonging to the network increases. As the number of users increases, there is also a stronger incentive for more individuals to join the network. In this case, the network externalities are *direct*.

Another type of network externality arises in systems markets, where value is obtained by combining several components, such as a piece of hardware and a number of compatible software applications. As the number of applications increases, the value to each user derived from ownership of the hardware increases. As the number of applications increases, there is a stronger incentive for more individuals to purchase the hardware and compatible software applications, and a stronger incentive for software designers to create further applications. In this case the network externalities are *indirect*.

Following the modelling approach adopted by Economides and Himmelberg (1995) and Economides (1996), suppose the utility obtained by the *i*-th user from belonging to the network takes the following form:

$$U_i = \tau_i + f_i(n^e)$$

where τ_i denotes the stand-alone benefit to the i-th user that is independent of the number of other users, and $f_i(\ )$ is the utility function that specifies user i's network benefit as a function of the total number of users of the network, n^e.

Different models can be derived for the determination of an equilibrium for the number of users under two alternative sets of assumptions concerning this utility function. In the first case that is considered below, it is assumed that the stand-alone benefit is homogeneous (the same for all users) and the network benefit is heterogeneous (differs between users). In the second case, conversely, it is assumed that the stand-alone benefit is heterogeneous and the network benefit is homogeneous.

In this section, price is treated as exogenously determined, and the analysis focuses on the determination of the quantity demanded at the given price. In Section 21.3 some simple cost assumptions are introduced, and the analysis focuses on the determination of the market equilibrium price and quantity under supply conditions of either perfect competition or monopoly.

Heterogeneous network benefits

In the case of homogeneous stand-alone benefits and heterogeneous network benefits, it is assumed $\tau_i = \tau$ for all i, and $f_i(n^e) = v_i n^e$, where τ is constant, and the population of consumers (all actual and potential users) has v_i distributed uniformly over the interval from 0 to 1. Accordingly, the consumer who values the network benefit the least has $v_i = 0$ and $f_i(n^e) = 0$ for any n^e. The consumer who values the network benefit the most has $v_i = 1$ and $f_i(n^e) = n^e$. The utility of the i-th consumer is

$$U_i = \tau + v_i n^e$$

Let p denote the price at which membership of the network is sold. The most marginal consumer, who is just willing to join the network at price p, has $v_i = v$ so that

$$\tau + v n^e - p = 0 \quad \text{or} \quad v = (p - \tau)/n^e$$

Any consumer with $v_i \geq v$ is willing to join the network at price p; consumers with $v_i < v$ do not join. Therefore the total demand to belong to the network is $n = 1 - v$. This expression implies $v = 1 - n$. The demand function can be derived from the expression

$$\tau + (1 - n)n^e - p = 0$$

The inverse demand function when the total network size is n^e can be written as

$$p = \tau + (1 - n)n^e$$

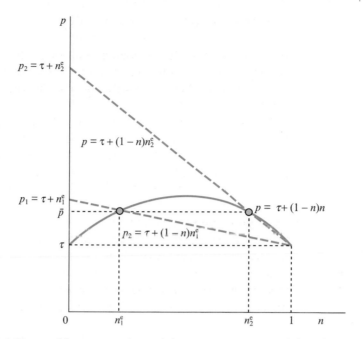

Figure 21.1 Demand for a network good, heterogeneous network benefits

In order to establish the quantity demanded at any price, a fulfilled expectations assumption can be applied. It is assumed that the total demand to belong to the network *equals* the number of network users that enters the utility function of each individual user, or $n = n^e$. By substitution into the previous expression, the market equilibrium must satisfy the condition

$$p = \tau + (1 - n)n$$

Figure 21.1 illustrates the determination of quantity demanded for a price of $\bar{p}$. The downward-sloping dotted line labelled $p = \tau + (1 - n)n_1^e$ identifies the inverse demand function constructed under the assumption that the number of network users is held constant at a relatively low level of n_1^e. In this case, the highest price that any consumer would pay to belong to the network is $p_1 = \tau + n_1^e$. At the price of p_1 (and with n_1^e network users), the consumer with $v_i = 1$ is just willing to belong. In order to persuade all consumers to belong, including the consumer with $v_i = 0$, a lower price of τ would be required.

Similarly the dotted line labelled $p = \tau + (1 - n)n_2^e$ identifies the inverse demand function constructed under the assumption that the number of network users is held constant at a higher level of n_2^e. The highest price that any consumer would pay to belong to the network is $p_2 = \tau + n_2^e$. At the price of p_2 (and with n_2^e network users) the consumer with $v_i = 1$ is again just willing to belong. To persuade all consumers to belong, including the consumer with $v_i = 0$, a lower price of τ would again be required.

In Figure 21.1, the quadratic function $p = \tau + (1 - n)n$ is interpreted as the collection of points that satisfy the condition $n = n^e$. At the price of $\bar{p}$, there are three possible solutions for quantity demanded: $n = 0$, $n = n_1^e$ and $n = n_2^e$. At $n = 0$, the price of $\bar{p}$ is above the value that all consumers place on belonging to the network when no others belong, equivalent to the stand-alone benefit of τ. Consequently, no consumer chooses to belong to the network. At both $n = n_1^e$ and $n = n_2^e$, the total level of demand is the same as the number of network users assumed in the construction of the inverse demand function. At $[\bar{p}, n_1^e]$, each consumer expects few consumers in total to belong to the network, and only those consumers with a relatively high network benefit will belong. The expectation that few consumers will belong becomes a self-fulfilling prophecy: acting on this expectation few consumers *do* choose to belong. At $[\bar{p}, n_2^e]$ by contrast, each consumer expects many other consumers to belong to the network and many consumers, including some with a relatively small network benefit, will belong. Again the expectation that many consumers will belong becomes a self-fulfilling prophecy: acting on this expectation many consumers *do* choose to belong.

The preceding analysis identifies multiple outcomes for quantity demanded, owing to the presence of the network externalities. Is any of the three outcomes either more likely or less likely to occur in practice? By imagining a disturbance in the form of a small change to the price of $\bar{p}$, the price–quantity combination $[\bar{p}, n_1^e]$ may be identified as unstable, and therefore unlikely to be sustained for a long time. By contrast, the price–quantity combination $[\bar{p}, n_2^e]$ may be identified as stable, and therefore more likely to be sustained.

To demonstrate the instability of $[\bar{p}, n_1^e]$, consider first a small and temporary increase in price that has perhaps been driven by an increase in costs. The most marginal consumers withdraw from the network because it is no longer worthwhile for them to belong. However, their withdrawal reduces the network benefit to all, resulting in a downward shift in the inverse demand function. It would now take a reduction in price larger than the original increase to restore equality between n^e and n. If the cost pressure is upward, such a price reduction is unlikely to be forthcoming. Consequently further withdrawals will occur, and the market will tend to tend to collapse in the direction of the stable price–quantity combination $[\bar{p}, 0]$.

Now consider a small and temporary reduction in price, again starting from $[\bar{p}, n_1^e]$. Some additional consumers are attracted into the market by the lower price. Their arrival increases the network benefit to all, resulting in an upward shift in the inverse demand function. It would now take an increase in price larger than the original reduction to restore equality between n^e and n. If no such increase is forthcoming, further consumers will decide to join, and the market will tend to expand in the direction of the stable price–quantity combination $[\bar{p}, n_2^e]$.

Repeating a similar analysis starting from $[\bar{p}, n_2^e]$, the stability of this price–quantity combination is easily demonstrated. A small increase in price causes a few users to withdraw, reducing the network benefit for all, and a new price–quantity combination is rapidly established at the higher price on a new (lower) inverse demand function. Similarly, a small reduction in price causes a few additional consumers to join, increasing the network benefit for all, and a new price–quantity combination is rapidly established at the lower price on a new (higher) inverse demand function.

This analysis suggests that the market for goods or services that confer network benefits will tend to settle either at a point at which there are no users, or at one with many users. The intermediate case, with a small number of users, is the least likely to be sustained. In other words, the network either gains widespread acceptance, perhaps becoming the industry standard; or it fails to gain acceptance, and withers and dies.

Clearly consumer expectations and history play an important role in determining the outcome. As noted above, the analysis is based on the fulfilled expectations assumption: the assumptions of each consumer, when deciding whether to belong to the network, concerning the total number of users, turn out to be accurate. Different assumptions about expectations could lead to different outcomes for the level of demand. History matters, because as the stability analysis shows, small disturbances to the solution $[\bar{p}, n_1^e]$ can have large consequences in either direction. There is no sure-fire mechanism to ensure that the 'successful' price–quantity combination $[\bar{p}, n_2^e]$ is always achieved, rather than the unsuccessful $[\bar{p}, 0]$. Small disturbances, especially at the critical moments in time when the network is striving to gain wider or universal acceptance, might create a bandwagon effect that could operate in either direction.

Heterogeneous stand-alone benefits

In the case of heterogeneous stand-alone benefits and homogeneous network benefits, it is assumed $f_i(n^e) = vn^e$ for all i, where v is constant, and the population of consumers (all actual and potential users) has τ_i distributed uniformly over the interval from 0 to 1. The utility of the i-th consumer is

$$U_i = \tau_i + vn^e$$

As before, let p denote the price at which membership of the network is sold. The most marginal consumer, who is just willing to join the network at price p, has $\tau_i = \tau$ so that

$$\tau + vn^e - p = 0 \quad \text{or} \quad \tau = p - vn^e$$

For prices that produce feasible values of τ such that $0 \le \tau \le 1$, any consumer with $\tau_i \ge \tau$ is willing to join the network at price p, and any consumer with $\tau_i < \tau$ does not join. The total demand is $n = 1 - \tau$. This expression implies $\tau = 1 - n$. The demand function can be derived from the expression

$$(1 - n) + vn^e - p = 0$$

If $v < 1$, the network externalities are weak. The consumer with $\tau_i = 1$ values belonging to the network when all consumers belong ($n^e = 1$) less than the stand-alone benefit. If $v > 1$, the network externalities are strong. The consumer with $\tau_i = 1$ values belonging to the network when all consumers belong ($n^e = 1$) more than the stand-alone benefit. The nature of the demand function depends upon whether the network externalities are weak or strong. These two cases are considered separately.

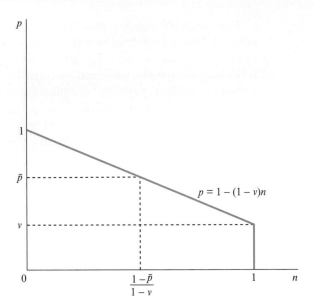

Figure 21.2 Demand for a network good, heterogeneous stand-alone benefits, weak network externalities

Weak network externalities, $v < 1$

- At the price $p = 1$, the consumer with $\tau_i = 1$ is just willing to belong to the network, even if no other members belong ($n^e = 0$). For any $p > 1$, no member is willing to belong.

- At the price $p = v$, the consumer with $\tau_i = 0$ is just willing to belong to the network, provided all other members belong ($n^e = 1$). For any $p < v$, all members are willing to belong.

- At prices in the range $v < p < 1$, the quantity demanded is determined by setting $n = n^e$ and solving $(1 - n) + vn - p = 0$, or $p = 1 - (1 - v)n$, for n. The solution is $n = (1 - p)/(1 - v)$. Accordingly, $[\bar{p}, (1 - \bar{p})/(1 - v)]$ is a feasible solution for $v < \bar{p} < 1$.

Figure 21.2 illustrates the solution for the case of weak network externalities. In the range $v < p < 1$, quantity demanded is a decreasing function of price, because $-1/(1 - v) < 0$. Intuitively, if the stand-alone benefit dominates the network benefit, the demand function is downward-sloping and similar to that for any regular (non-network) good or service (for which all of the benefit to the consumer is stand-alone). For every price, there is a unique solution for quantity demanded.

Strong network externalities, $v > 1$

- At the price $p = 1$ when $n^e = 0$, the consumer with $\tau_i = 1$ is just willing to belong to the network. For any $p > 1$ when $n^e = 0$, no member is willing to belong. Accordingly $[\bar{p}, 0]$ is a feasible solution for $\bar{p} > 1$.

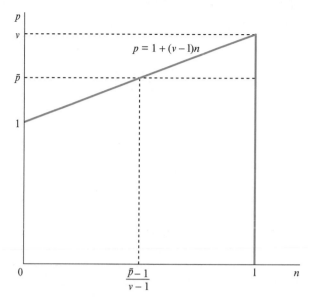

Figure 21.3 Demand for a network good, heterogeneous stand-alone benefits, strong network externalities

- At the price $p = v$ when $n^e = 1$, the consumer with $\tau_1 = 0$ is just willing to belong to the network. For any $p < v$ when $n^e = 1$, all members are willing to belong. Accordingly $[\bar{p}, 1]$ is a feasible solution for $\bar{p} < v$.

- At prices in the range $1 < p < v$, quantity demanded is determined by setting $n = n^e$ and solving $(1 - n) + vn - p = 0$, or $p = 1 + (v - 1)n$, for n. The solution is $n = (p - 1)/(v - 1)$. Accordingly, $[\bar{p}, (\bar{p} - 1)/(v - 1)]$ is a feasible solution for $1 < \bar{p} < v$.

Figure 21.3 illustrates the solution for the case of strong network externalities. In the range $1 < p < v$, quantity demanded is an increasing function of price, because $-1/(1 - v) > 0$. Intuitively, if the network benefit dominates the stand-alone benefit, the demand function is upward-sloping. As more consumers belong, the value to each consumer of belonging increases, and the willingness-to-pay of each consumer also increases. There are three possible solutions for every price, a situation resembling the position in the case of heterogeneous network benefits. In particular, the intermediate solution $[\bar{p}, (1 - \bar{p})/(1 - v)]$ is likely to be unstable, for the same reasons as before. A small increase in price would cause some marginal consumers to withdraw, leading to a reduction in the network benefit for all, and further withdrawals. The market moves in the direction of the stable solution $[\bar{p}, 0]$. A small reduction in price would cause some additional marginal consumers to join, leading to an increase in the network benefit for all, and further arrivals. The market moves in the direction of the stable solution $[\bar{p}, 1]$.

BlackBerry unveils BBM Music app

Research in Motion is attempting to bolster its popular BlackBerry Messenger service against a raft of competition from Facebook, Apple, Google and WhatsApp by bolting on a new subscription music service. BBM Music will offer tracks from all four major music labels which the BlackBerry owners can share on their 'profiles'.

BlackBerry devices already have a music store, powered by London's 7Digital, but BBM Music has a social twist: the more friends you have using the service, the more tracks you can listen to. Each subscriber can store up to 50 songs on their BBM profile, swapping out up to 25 each month, and listen to those plus whatever their friends have in their playlists. RIM hopes this will help give a viral boost to BBM Music and in the process show the way for other third-party developers to use its platform. The stand-alone app uses the same programming hooks that RIM made available to independent developers through its 'social' upgrade with BBM 6.0, released last month.

A closed beta launches on Thursday in the US, UK and RIM's native Canada with the full service going live later this year. RIM is working with Omnifone, which also powers cloud-music services from the likes of Sony and Vodafone, to build the service.

More than 45m people use BBM, giving it a strong base to build on, in spite of the competition from Apple's iMessage, Facebook Messenger, Google Plus's Huddle and WhatsApp Messenger, which is still riding high in the iPhone's App Store charts. Compared with the unlimited listening available through rival services such as Napster, Spotify and Rhapsody for $9.99, BBM Music's $4.99 monthly fee seems a touch expensive when the selection is limited by your friends' tastes. But by making the experience mobile-first and lowering the pricing towards its teenage target market, BBM Music may maintain that network effect which has kept so many kids using BlackBerrys in the UK, Middle East, Malaysia and other regions, even as older demographics switch to touch-screen Android and iPhone devices.

Source: BlackBerry unveils BBM Music app, © The Financial Times Limited. All Rights Reserved, 25 August 2011 (Bradshaw, T.).

21.3 Market equilibrium price and quantity for a network good or service: perfect competition and monopoly

The analysis of the market equilibrium price and quantity requires the super-imposition of cost and supply assumptions onto the preceding analysis of quantity demanded. In this section it is assumed that the supplier of the network product or service faces a linear total cost function, and incurs a constant marginal cost of connecting each consumer to the network, denoted c. As in the previous section, separate analyses are required for the following two demand-side cases:

first, heterogeneous network benefits (and homogeneous stand-alone benefits); and second, heterogeneous stand-alone benefits (and homogeneous network benefits).

Heterogeneous network benefits

In the case of heterogeneous network benefits, the downward-sloping segment of the curved function labelled $p = \tau + (1 - n)n$ in Figure 21.1 identifies the range of feasible and stable non-zero pairings of price and quantity demanded; and the analysis of the nature of the market equilibrium focuses on this segment. Although this function is interpreted as a collection of points, and not as a demand or average revenue function in the regular sense, from the supplier's perspective it plays the same role as an average revenue function, by identifying feasible combinations of price and quantity demanded. This means it is possible to identify a corresponding marginal revenue function, $MR = \tau + 2n - 3n^2$, which bears the same relation to the collection of feasible price–quantity combinations as does a 'regular' marginal revenue function to the corresponding average revenue. The maximum value of the 'average revenue' function $p = \tau + (1 - n)n$, located at $n = 1/2$, is $\tau + 1/4$; the value of the marginal revenue function at $n - 1/2$ is also $\tau + 1/4$; and the value of this function at $n = 1$ is $\tau - 1$. Appendix 1 contains a mathematical derivation of these results.

Figure 21.4 identifies the market equilibria for four possible values of marginal cost, denoted c_1, c_2, c_3, c_4, in the case where the supply of the network product or service is perfectly competitive. In accordance with the standard model of perfect competition, the market equilibrium is located at the point where price *equals* marginal cost, subject to the constraint that market demand cannot exceed the maximum of $n = 1$. Accordingly, the equilibrium prices are $p_j^* = c_j$ for $j = 1, \ldots, 4$. When the marginal cost is either c_1 or c_2 (where $c_1 < \tau - 1$, and

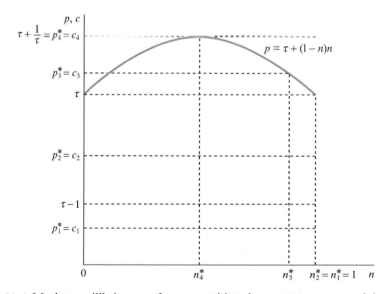

Figure 21.4 Market equilibrium, perfect competition, heterogeneous network benefits

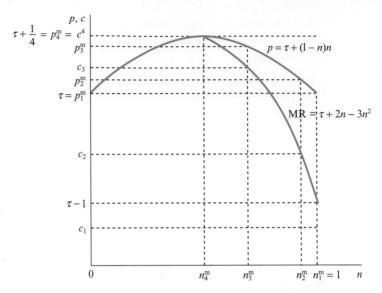

Figure 21.5 Market equilibrium, monopoly, heterogeneous network benefits

$\tau - 1 < c_2 < \tau$), the market equilibrium quantity is $n_1^* = n_2^* = 1$. When the marginal cost is c_3 (where $\tau < c_3 < \tau + 1/4$), the equilibrium quantity is n_3^* (where $1/2 < n_3^*$). When the marginal cost is $c_4 = \tau + 1/4$, the equilibrium quantity is $n_4^* = 1/2$.

Figure 21.5 illustrates a similar analysis in the case where the supplier of the network product or service is a monopolist. In accordance with the standard model of monopoly, the market equilibrium is located at the point where the derived 'marginal revenue' function *equals* marginal cost, again subject to the constraint that market demand cannot exceed the maximum of $n = 1$. The equilibrium prices are denoted p_j^m for $j = 1, \ldots, 4$. Note that $p_j^m > p_j^*$ for $j = 1, \ldots, 3$, but $p_4^m = p_4^*$. When the marginal cost is c_1, the market equilibrium quantity is $n_1^m = 1$ (the same as in the case of perfect competition). When the marginal cost is c_2, the market equilibrium quantity is $n_2^m < n_2^* = 1$. When the marginal cost is c_3, the equilibrium quantity is $n_3^m < n_3^* < 1$. Finally, when the marginal cost is c_4, the equilibrium quantity is $n_4^m = 1/2 = n_4^*$.

In summary, when the marginal cost is sufficiently low (for $c < \tau - 1$), both perfect competition and monopoly lead to full market coverage. When the marginal cost is higher (for $\tau - 1 < c < \tau + 1/4$), monopoly leads to lower coverage than perfect competition. In any of these cases (for $c < \tau + 1/4$), the monopoly price exceeds the market equilibrium price under perfect competition. In the limiting case $c = \tau + 1/4$ (above which the market would not be supplied), perfect competition and monopoly lead to identical coverage and identical prices.

Heterogeneous stand-alone benefits

Section 21.2 has noted a tendency for quantity demanded to gravitate to the extreme values of either $n = 0$ or $n = 1$ in the case of strong network externalities. In this sub-section, accordingly, the comparison of perfect competition and monopoly is limited to the case of weak network externalities.

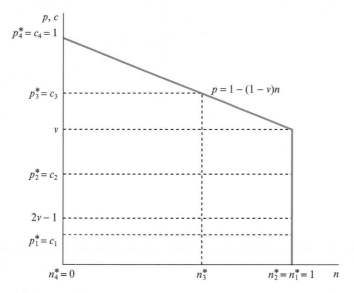

Figure 21.6 Market equilibrium, perfect competition, heterogeneous stand-alone benefits, weak network externalities

The downward-sloping segment of the function labelled $p = 1 - (1 - v)n$ in Figure 21.2 can be interpreted directly as a demand or average revenue function in the range $v < p < 1$ and $0 < n < 1$. The corresponding marginal revenue function, $MR = 1 - 2(1 - v)n$, assumes the usual position relative to this average revenue function, and at $n = 1$ attains a value of $2v - 1$ (see Appendix 1).

Figure 21.6 identifies the market equilibria for four possible values of marginal cost, denoted c_1, c_2, c_3, c_4 (but not representing the same values as in Figures 21.4 and 21.5), in the case where the supply of the network product or service is perfectly competitive. As before, the equilibrium prices are $p_j^* = c_j$ for $j = 1, \ldots, 4$. When the marginal cost is either c_1 or c_2 (where $c_1 < 2v - 1$, and $2v - 1 < c_2 < v$), the market equilibrium quantity is $n_1^* = n_2^* = 1$. When the marginal cost is c_3 (where $v < c_3 < 1$), the equilibrium quantity is $n_3^* < 1$. When the marginal cost is $c_4 = 1$, only the consumer with $\tau_i = 1$ is willing to join at a price of $p_4^* = c_4 = 1$. Under the large numbers assumption, this consumer represents a negligible portion of the entire potential market, so the equilibrium quantity is $n_4^* \cong 0$.

Figure 21.7 illustrates a similar analysis in the case where the supplier of the network product or service is a monopolist. The equilibrium prices are denoted p_j^m for $j = 1, \ldots, 4$. As before $p_j^m > p_j^*$ for $j = 1, \ldots, 3$, but $p_4^m = p_4^*$. When the marginal cost is c_1, the market equilibrium quantity is $n_1^m = 1$ (the same as in the case of perfect competition). When the marginal cost is c_2, the market equilibrium quantity is $n_2^m < n_2^* = 1$. When the marginal cost is c_3, the equilibrium quantity is $n_3^m < n_3^* < 1$. Finally, when the marginal cost is c_4, the equilibrium quantity is $n_4^m = n_4^* \cong 0$.

In summary, and with very close parallels to the heterogeneous network benefits case, when the marginal cost is sufficiently low (for $c < v$), both perfect competition and monopoly lead to full market coverage. When the marginal cost is higher (for $v < c < 1$), monopoly leads to lower coverage than perfect

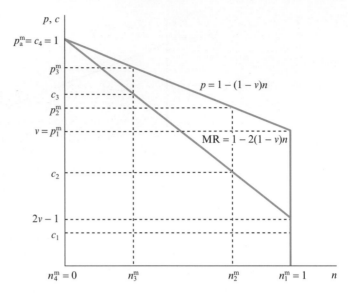

Figure 21.7 Market equilibrium, monopoly, heterogeneous stand-alone benefits, weak network externalities

competition. In all of these cases (for $c < 1$), the monopoly price exceeds the perfectly competitive price. In the limiting case $c = 1$ (above which the market would not be supplied), perfect competition and monopoly lead to identical coverage and identical prices.

Welfare properties of the perfectly competitive and monopoly equilibria, and network externalities

The finding that for marginal cost within specified ranges of values, the monopolist achieves lower coverage and charges a higher price than would be realized under a perfectly competitive structure, leads to the standard conclusion that monopoly is welfare-reducing in comparison with perfect competition. However, in the range of marginal costs for which neither perfect competition nor monopoly achieves full coverage, it can be shown that neither structure achieves the socially optimal coverage of the network good or service. Appendix 1 shows that in the models considered in this section, the socially optimal coverage is *always* full coverage with quantity supplied and demanded of $n = 1$.

Accordingly, network externalities may give rise to a form of market failure. At both the perfectly competitive equilibrium and the monopoly equilibrium, there are unexploited gains that could have been realized from further trade. When consumers decide whether to join the network, they only take account of their private benefit, and not the social benefit their decision to join confers upon other consumers. When marginal costs are sufficiently high to prevent full coverage from being achieved, the producers also fail to capture these unexploited gains from further trade. The resulting market equilibrium coverage is less than the socially optimal coverage, and allocative efficiency is not achieved.

Market equilibrium price and quantity for a network good or service: duopoly

This section presents a model of competition between two duopolists, who compete to supply a product or service with network externalities, in the case of heterogeneous stand-alone benefits. The model, originally developed by Cremer *et al.* (2000), builds on the earlier work of Katz and Shapiro (1985). A key feature of this model is that it allows for different levels of compatibility between the products or services of the two suppliers. The polar cases are perfect compatibility and complete incompatibility. With perfect compatibility a customer of either supplier can connect seamlessly with customers of both suppliers, and each customer's network benefit depends on the total number of customers. With complete incompatibility, a customer of either supplier can connect with customers of the same supplier, but not with customers of the other supplier. Each customer's network benefit depends on the number of customers of their own supplier. The model also allows for partial compatibility: the case where customers can connect with customers of the other supplier, but not seamlessly. In this case, a customer's marginal network benefit when their own supplier acquires an additional customer is larger than their marginal network benefit when the other supplier acquires an additional customer; but the latter is positive and not zero (as it is in the case of complete incompatibility).

The other change to the set-up in Sections 21.2 and 21.3 is that the two suppliers are each assumed to have a number of existing customers, who are locked in as a result of having entered into previously-signed contracts. Below, each supplier's locked-in existing customers are referred to as its **installed base**. A degree of asymmetry between the two suppliers is introduced into the model when the size of the installed base is assumed to differ between the two suppliers.

As before, for the case of heterogeneous stand-alone benefits it is assumed that the population of unconnected consumers has τ_i distributed uniformly over the interval from 0 to 1. The utility of the i-th consumer if they are supplied by firm j (for $j = $ A,B) is

$$U_i = \tau_i + v[(\beta_j + q_j^e) + \theta(\beta_k + q_k^e)]$$

where β_j is the installed base (number of existing customers) and q_j^e is the expected number of new customers of the consumer's own supplier j (for $j = $ A,B); β_k is the installed base and q_k^e is the expected number of new customers of the other supplier $k \neq j$; and $0 \leq \theta \leq 1$ is the compatibility parameter. $\theta = 0$ implies complete incompatibility, $0 < \theta < 1$ implies partial compatibility, and $\theta = 1$ implies perfect compatibility. It is assumed $\beta_A \geq \beta_B$.

Let p_j denote the price at which membership is sold by supplier j. If both networks are to attract positive numbers of new customers, p_A and p_B must be set in such a way that the most marginal customer, with $\tau_i = \tau$, is indifferent between joining either network or remaining unconnected. This condition implies

$$p_A - v[(\beta_A + q_A^e) + \theta(\beta_B + q_B^e)] = p_B - v[(\beta_B + q_B^e) + \theta(\beta_A + q_A^e)] = \tau$$

or $\quad p_A = v[(\beta_A + q_A^e) + \theta(\beta_B + q_B^e)] + \tau \quad$ and $\quad p_B = v[(\beta_B + q_B^e) + \theta(\beta_A + q_A^e)] + \tau$

Let q_j denote the actual number of new customers of each supplier j (for $j = A,B$). If the most marginal customer has $\tau_i = \tau$, then the total number of new customers is $q_A + q_B = 1 - \tau$; therefore $\tau = 1 - (q_A + q_B)$. Substituting into the two previous expressions, applying the fulfilled expectations assumption so $q_A = q_A^e$ and $q_B = q_B^e$, and rearranging, yields the following expressions for the two suppliers' inverse demand functions

$$p_A = 1 + v(\beta_A + \theta\beta_B) - (1 - v)q_A - (1 - \theta v)q_B;$$
$$p_B = 1 + v(\beta_B + \theta\beta_A) - (1 - v)q_B - (1 - \theta v)q_A$$

Let c denote the marginal cost to each supplier of connecting a new customer to the supplier's own network, assumed to be the same for both suppliers. For any given level of compatibility (treating the parameter θ as fixed), each supplier chooses q_j to maximize its own profit. The profit functions are:

$$\pi_j = (p_j - c)q_j = [1 + v(\beta_j + \theta\beta_k) - (1 - v)q_j - (1 - \theta v)q_k - c]q_j$$
for $j = A,B$, $k \neq j$

Using the two profit functions, which depend upon both q_A and q_B, it is possible to derive a Cournot–Nash equilibrium by maximizing π_A with respect to q_A while treating q_B as fixed, and simultaneously maximizing π_B with respect to q_B while treating q_A as fixed. The solutions for q_A and q_B are

$$q_A^* = \frac{1}{2}\left(\frac{2(1 - c) + v(1 + \theta)(\beta_A + \beta_B)}{2(1 - v) + (1 - \theta v)} + \frac{(1 - \theta)v(\beta_A - \beta_B)}{2(1 - v) - (1 - \theta v)}\right)$$

$$q_B^* = \frac{1}{2}\left(\frac{2(1 - c) + v(1 + \theta)(\beta_A + \beta_B)}{2(1 - v) + (1 - \theta v)} - \frac{(1 - \theta)v(\beta_A - \beta_B)}{2(1 - v) - (1 - \theta v)}\right)$$

At the Cournot–Nash equilibrium, the maximized profits of the two suppliers are $\pi_j^* = (1 - v)(q_j^*)^2$, and the consumer surplus is $S = (1/2)(q_A^* + q_B^*)^2$. Using these expressions, it is easily shown that an improvement in compatibility (an increase in θ) has two effects.

First, there is a *demand expansion effect*: total quantity demanded from the two suppliers, $q_A^* + q_B^*$, increases as θ increases. This follows from

$$q_A^* + q_B^* = \frac{2(1 - c) + v(1 + \theta)(\beta_A + \beta_B)}{2(1 - v) + (1 - \theta v)}$$

The right-hand-side expression is increasing in θ. As compatibility increases, the value to consumers of both suppliers' products or services increases. Total output increases as a consequence, and so too does consumer surplus.

Second, there is a *quality differentiation effect*: the difference between the quantities demanded from the two suppliers, $q_A^* - q_B^*$, increases as θ decreases. This follows from

$$q_A^* - q_B^* = \frac{(1 - \theta)v(\beta_A - \beta_B)}{2(1 - v) - (1 - \theta v)}$$

The right-hand-side expression is decreasing in θ. When compatibility is only partial, or if there is complete incompatibility, supplier A with the larger installed base benefits from a superior perceived quality, and becomes dominant in the market for new customers. An important result in the economics of networks follows directly from this result. Increased compatibility is less attractive for the supplier with the larger installed base.

To this point, compatibility has been treated as an exogenously determined parameter. Often, however, the compatibility or incompatibility of the network products or services provided by two (or more) suppliers is a consequence of strategic decisions taken by the suppliers. When the network externalities are large, the choice between compatibility and incompatibility may have far-reaching consequences in practice for the survival and profitability of the suppliers, both individually and collectively. The suppliers might agree or disagree over the desirability of compatibility, and whether or not compatibility is achieved might be beyond any supplier's individual control.

Katz and Shapiro (1985) highlight two possible mechanisms for achieving compatibility. First, the suppliers might reach a collective decision to adopt a common standard. If compatibility increases total profitability, but does not increase the profitability of every supplier individually, **side-payments** might be used to ensure that all suppliers benefit from the adoption of a common standard. Side-payments might take the form of licence fees, or compensation for the cost of conversion to the common standard. Second, the construction of an adapter might enable a single firm to act unilaterally to make its product or service-compatible with those of other suppliers. Based on an assumption that the costs of achieving compatibility are fixed, Katz and Shapiro demonstrate a number of propositions concerning the private and social incentives for compatibility.

Let $\Delta\pi_A$ and $\Delta\pi_B$ denote the changes in profits of suppliers A and B, and $\Delta\pi = \Delta\pi_A + \Delta\pi_B$ denote the total change in profit, as a consequence of achieving compatibility. Let ΔS denote the change in consumer surplus. Let $\Delta W = \Delta\pi + \Delta S$ denote the change in total welfare. Let F denote the fixed cost of achieving compatibility. F is assumed to be payable by both suppliers in the case where compatibility is achieved through the adoption of an industry standard; or by the supplier that constructs the adapter in the case where compatibility is achieved through the construction of an adapter.

The Katz and Shapiro analysis is based on the following two conclusions, which follow from the previous analysis of the demand expansion effect and the quality differentiation effect:

- Any move to complete compatibility is welfare-enhancing. This follows from $\Delta\pi > 0$ and $\Delta S > 0$, therefore $\Delta W > 0$.

- Other things being equal, the supplier with the smaller installed base has the stronger private incentive to achieve compatibility.

In the case where the compatibility mechanism is adoption of a common standard, the prospects of achieving compatibility depend upon whether side-payments are feasible. If side-payments are not feasible, a move to perfect compatibility requires $\Delta\pi_A > F$ and $\Delta\pi_B > F$. If side-payments are feasible, a move to perfect compatibility requires $\Delta\pi > 2F$. The former is a more stringent requirement than the latter. Even when side-payments are feasible, however, profit-maximizing suppliers might fail to achieve the welfare-maximizing outcome of perfect compatibility. In the case $\Delta\pi < 2F < \Delta W$, perfect compatibility is socially optimal, but there is insufficient private incentive for the suppliers to achieve perfect compatibility.

In the case where the compatibility mechanism is the construction of an adapter, the supplier with the smaller installed base, supplier B, has the stronger private incentive to achieve compatibility by means of an adapter. Supplier B's private incentive is $\Delta\pi_B - F$. The social incentive is $\Delta\pi_A + \Delta\pi_B + \Delta S - F$. From the previous discussion, the difference between the private incentive and the social incentive, $\Delta\pi_A + \Delta S$, might be either positive or negative. The change in consumer surplus resulting from complete compatibility, ΔS, is positive, but the change in supplier A's profit, $\Delta\pi_A$, might be negative and larger in absolute magnitude than ΔS. This implies supplier B's incentive to construct an adapter might be either too high or too low from the perspective of social welfare maximization.

Case study 21.2

Google hopes Spark ignites its social network

The irony was inescapable. A week ago, US regulators opened a formal investigation into Google's dominance of the search market. Then, within days, the world's most powerful internet company gave a vivid demonstration of its own deep insecurities about whether its grip on the web may be slipping. Tuesday's announcement of a social 'project' called Google+ is a bid for relevance in the Facebook age and the most important thing to come out of the Googleplex since the breakthrough AdWords system. And this time, the company might just fall flat on its face.

This coincidence, of the launch of an antitrust investigation with a grand defensive move, harks back to an earlier period. Microsoft was at the height of its desktop software power, but also feeling deeply under threat, when the regulators came calling in the late-1990s. The parallels should not be exaggerated. Google has not launched the sort of anticompetitive assault on Facebook that Microsoft began against Netscape. But in the grand battle that has now broken out between these and other giants of the tech world, a lot of smaller companies could get squashed.

The latest phase of the tech industry's platform wars is bringing a new convergence that could squeeze out some promising start-ups. With its forthcoming iCloud, for instance, Apple wants to venture beyond devices to supply the 'glue' that makes a user's data and media move seamlessly between its gadgets – the very services supplied by any number of 'cloud computing' start-ups.

Google is now making a bid to draw together many of its own services with a new kind of social glue.

In one fell swoop, it has added the sort of 'social feed' of updates familiar to Facebook users. These include a new 'information feed' called Spark that tries to plumb a user's interests and draw in relevant and up-to-the-minute links and information (a sort of cross between Twitter and Digg, the user generated review site); communication services like group text messaging and group video chat; and a mobile app that includes features of many of the latest photosharing services.

This headlong rush by the biggest tech companies to extend their platforms into new areas and consolidate their existing audiences is a direct threat to start-ups like Dropbox, Instagram and GroupMe. Of course, there is a clear risk here that Google is spreading itself too thin and that many of these services will later be consigned, quietly, to oblivion – as happened to the once-vaunted Google Health service last week. But at the same time, Google may find ways to consolidate its vast online audience that put others at a serious disadvantage.

One way is if it started to use its search engine power to favour its own services, to the detriment of rivals. So far, the Google+ project (so called because it is said to be an evolving series of new services that will grow over time) has not sought to harness search, though an earlier initiative, called +1, lets users vote for search results they find useful. A tighter connection may follow.

The claim that Google already unfairly favours its own services in search results – at the expense of other 'vertical', or specialised, online information services – is an issue that is already before regulators in Europe, and is also likely to feature in the wide ranging US inquiry.

The other powerful advantage concerns the vast banks of personal data that the largest internet companies have been amassing. Even if a company like Google allows its users, in principle, to take their data to other services if they wish, in practice the heavy weight of inertia makes it unlikely many will take up the offer. That data could prove invaluable in deepening the engagement of an audience. Google, for instance, hopes to apply what it knows about its users from various services, such as Gmail, to make educated guesses about what information they are interested in seeing, or which person they are most likely to want to connect with, in any particular situation. This could give the term 'social engineering' a whole new meaning – with equally sinister overtones.

A new piece of accepted wisdom in Silicon Valley holds that 'data is the new platform': that is, that the vast body of data held by companies like Google has become the substrate on which new applications and services can be built. The company with the richest body of personal data – and which best uses this to refine its services – should win. Of course, users may simply decide at the outset that there is nothing much in the new Google+ to hold their interest – particularly since their friends are already fully engaged over on Facebook. If Spark fails to catch light, or users decide not to put their heads together in Huddle (the new messaging system), all will have been for nought. Google still needs to prove that, for all its grand strategic plans, it can create some real social buzz.

Source: Google hopes Spark ignites its social network, © The Financial Times Limited. All Rights Reserved, 29 June 2011 (Waters, R.).

21.5 ## Forms of competition over standardization and compatibility

Strategies and tactics in competition between rival suppliers over compatibility or standardization are discussed by Besen and Farrell (1994), who examine the technology choices made by two suppliers A and B which could, in principle, adopt either technology 1 or technology 2. Each supplier might have a preference for one of the technologies over the other; the two technologies might previously have been developed by the two suppliers (technology 1 by supplier A, and technology 2 by supplier B), so each supplier has an interest in its 'own' technology becoming the industry standard. The technologies are incompatible, and the payoffs to each supplier depend on the adoption decisions of both suppliers, as summarized by the following payoff matrix:

		Supplier B adopts	
		Technology 1	*Technology 2*
	Technology 1	$a_{1,1}, b_{1,1}$	$a_{1,2}, b_{1,2}$
Supplier A adopts			
	Technology 2	$a_{2,1}, b_{2,1}$	$a_{2,2}, b_{2,2}$

Although the payoff matrix suggests certain analogies with game theory, Besen and Farrell suggest that this intuition should not be extended too far. It is not clear, for example, that the actions of the two suppliers are truly simultaneous, or that each supplier is unaware of the other supplier's action at the moment in time when it decides upon its own action. Instead, Besen and Farrell focus on three possible forms of competition that could emerge from the situation summarized by the payoff matrix: first, inter-technology competition or incompatibility is preferred by both suppliers; second, intra-technology competition or compatibility is preferred by both suppliers; and third, one supplier prefers inter-technology competition or incompatibility, while the other prefers intra-technology competition or compatibility.

Inter-technology competition (Tweedledee and Tweedledum)

If the off-diagonal payoffs exceed the on-diagonal payoffs, or $a_{1,2} > a_{2,2}$, $a_{2,1} > a_{1,1}$ and $b_{1,2} > b_{1,1}$ and $b_{2,1} > b_{2,2}$, then both suppliers prefer incompatibility to compatibility. This case is characterized by Besen and Farrell as 'Tweedledee and Tweedledum', after two fictional characters in an English nursery rhyme who agree to take part in a battle that never actually transpires. Tweedledee and Tweedledum also appear in Lewis Carroll's *Through the Looking Glass*.

If each supplier has 'ownership' of one of the technologies, then it is likely that each supplier will adopt its 'own' technology. This situation is likely to arise when the two suppliers are symmetric, and the battle between the two technologies to become the industry standard does not inhibit adoption by consumers (compatibility is unimportant). Possible tactics in inter-technology competition to become the industry standard include the following:

- *Building an early lead.* A technology with a large installed base is difficult to displace, even if the alternative is cheaper or technically superior. Early competition might include aggressive discounting to attract early customers, or exaggerated claims concerning the number of customers in cases where the installed base is imperfectly observable to customers.

- *Influencing the supply of complements to the supplier's own technology.* The attractiveness to consumers of a games console, for example, increases with the quantity of available compatible software products.

- *Pre-announcements of new versions or new products.* Pre-announcements might be made in order to deter consumers from adopting a rival's technology prior to the introduction of the new version or new product; though they could also have the negative consequence of deterring consumers from adopting the supplier's own current version.

- *Price commitments.* A public commitment to keep the price or subscription fee at a low level for a long period might be helpful in encouraging adoption.

Intra-technology competition (Battle of the Sexes)

If the on-diagonal payoffs exceed the off-diagonal payoffs, or $\mathbf{a_{1,1}} > \mathbf{a_{2,1}}$, $\mathbf{a_{2,2}} > \mathbf{a_{1,2}}$ and $b_{1,1} > b_{1,2}$ and $b_{2,2} > b_{2,1}$, then both suppliers prefer compatibility to incompatibility. This case is characterized as 'Battle of the Sexes'. A male–female couple always prefers being together to being apart; but he would rather they both attend a football match, while she would rather they both go shopping.

This situation is likely to arise when the suppliers are symmetric, and a battle between the two technologies to become the industry standard would inhibit adoption by consumers (compatibility is important). If both suppliers can agree as to which technology is preferable, then standardization is straightforward to achieve. On the contrary, if each supplier has 'ownership' of one of the technologies and each would prefer its 'own' technology to become the industry standard, but each would nevertheless prefer adoption of the other supplier's technology to incompatibility, then either supplier might attempt to persuade the other to adopt its 'own' technology. Tactics might include commitments and concessions. Commitments visibly reduce the payoff of the supplier concerned from adopting its rival's technology. Relevant actions might include investment in additional production capacity, or further expansion of the installed base. The following concessions are designed to make it more attractive for the rival to adopt the supplier's 'own' technology:

- Low-cost licensing of the technology.

- Creation of a hybrid standard that combines the technologies of more than one supplier.

- Commitments to cooperate in future development of the technology.

- Shifting future development to a neutral third party.

Any of the latter three concessions might be used primarily to provide reassurance to rivals that the original 'owner' of the technology will not exploit its 'ownership' to the disadvantage of its rivals once the technology has become the industry standard.

One supplier prefers inter-technology competition, the other prefers intra-technology competition (Pesky Little Brother)

If the off-diagonal payoffs exceed the on-diagonal payoffs for one supplier, or $a_{1,2} > a_{2,2}$, $a_{2,1} > a_{1,1}$, but the opposite is true for the other supplier, or $b_{1,1} > b_{1,2}$ and $b_{2,2} > b_{2,1}$, then the first supplier prefers incompatibility and the second prefers compatibility. This case is characterized as 'Pesky Little Brother': the older of two siblings prefers to play alone, while the younger prefers to play with his older sibling.

This situation is likely to arise when the two suppliers are asymmetric. As the earlier analysis of the quality differentiation effect (see Section 21.4) suggests, a dominant supplier (supplier A) with a large installed base prefers incompatibility and inter-technology competition; the same might true in other situations of asymmetry, such as one supplier having a markedly superior technology, or a powerful reputation. The smaller rival (supplier B), by contrast, prefers compatibility and intra-technology competition. If supplier A is powerless to prevent imitation, then compatibility will follow. If supplier A is able to assert property rights over its 'own' technology, however, through copyright protection or patenting, then A might be in a position to assert its preference for incompatibility. Alternatively, frequent changes of technology might be used as a tactic by a dominant supplier to make imitation more difficult or more costly.

Case study 21.3

Renewed hostilities

The platform wars have returned. The past few days have brought an outbreak of hostilities between Apple and Adobe, and tensions between Twitter and the companies that make software clients that let people tweet. The facts are different, but the underlying story is the same. Many software and internet companies aspire to be platforms for which others compete to make applications and services. Becoming a platform entrenches them and (usually) their profitability.

The most famous beneficiary of such a network effect was, of course, Microsoft, which established Windows as the biggest PC operating system, and enjoyed years of growth as a result.

For a few years, the explosive growth of the internet – the ultimate open platform – has put many such rivalries into abeyance. Now, they are rearing up again.

In Apple's case, it has launched two blows against Adobe, the company that produces Flash software for web design and animation. First, it refused to allow Flash videos to run on the iPad and then it changed the rules for iPod and iPad software developers to exclude new Adobe tools for writing applications. The best explanation can be found on John Gruber's Daring Fireball blog, which first noted a change in the iPhone developer agreement. Steve Jobs, Apple's founder, does not like Flash (there is a history of tension between the two companies) and thinks its tools would lower the quality of iPad apps. Meanwhile, Twitter has taken steps to produce official clients for people using the Twitter service, rather than letting other companies sell (or give away) their own. It has launched an official Twitter app for BlackBerry and bought Atebits, which makes the popular client Tweetie.

All this is leading to interesting debates in Silicon Valley between those who would prefer companies such as Apple to be more open and those who see the logic, in both software and business terms, of companies wielding control over their platforms.

Steven Johnson, the technology writer, contributed an interesting piece to the *New York Times* this weekend, reflecting on some of the quality advantages of closed platforms, such as Apple's, despite his sympathy for openness. Meanwhile, my colleague Richard Waters argues on the FT Tech blog that Twitter's move is a good thing for the Twitter ecosystem, and for users.

The debate over the iPad, which I wrote about in last week's column, also reflects the tension among the two camps. Whatever the rights and wrongs of the tussles, they show that the internet may have changed much, but it has not ended platform battles.

Source: © The Financial Times Limited. All Rights Reserved, 13 April 2010 (Gapper, S.).

21.6 Summary

Network externalities, also known as network effects or demand-side economies of scale, characterize products or services where the value to any user increases in proportion to the total number of users. Direct network externalities are common in communications markets, where the value to any user comes from the ability to communicate with other users via a network. Indirect network externalities are common in hardware-software markets, where an increase in the number of users of the hardware product stimulates the production of complementary software products, and the increased availability of software increases the value to each user of the hardware.

Different specifications for the demand function for a network product or service rely on different assumptions concerning the utility functions of individual users. In one of the cases examined in this chapter, it is assumed that the network benefit is heterogeneous (differs between users) and the stand-alone benefit is homogeneous (the same for all users). In another case it is assumed that the stand-alone benefit is heterogeneous and the network benefit is homogeneous.

- In the case of heterogeneous network benefits, the dependence of quantity demanded on users' expectations of the total size of the network makes multiple solutions for quantity demanded feasible for some prices. The more extreme price–quantity combinations, characterized by either a zero rate or a high rate of adoption, tend to be more stable than the intermediate combination characterized by a low but non-zero rate of adoption.

■ In the case of heterogeneous stand-alone benefits, the relationship between price and quantity demanded has a regular downward-sloping appearance in the case where the stand-alone benefit dominates the network benefit. This relationship may be upward-sloping, however, for certain prices in the case where the network benefit dominates the stand-alone benefit. In the latter case again, multiple solutions for quantity demanded are feasible for some prices.

Analysis of the profit-maximizing market equilibrium under alternative supply conditions of perfect competition and monopoly leads to the following conclusions. If marginal cost is sufficiently low, both perfect competition and monopoly lead to full market coverage. For intermediate values of marginal cost, monopoly leads to lower coverage than perfect competition. In all of these cases, the monopoly price exceeds the perfectly competitive price. For a limiting value of marginal cost, above which the market is not supplied, perfect competition and monopoly lead to identical coverage and identical prices. The standard welfare conclusion, that monopoly is welfare-reducing in comparison with perfect competition, is maintained; but there are cases for which neither perfect competition nor monopoly achieves the welfare-maximizing provision of the network good or service.

In a duopoly model that allows for different levels of compatibility between the products or services of two competing suppliers, the properties of a Cournot–Nash equilibrium shed light on the nature of competition between suppliers offering alternative networks. Through a demand-expansion effect, an increase in compatibility increases total output, and is welfare-enhancing. Through a quality-differentiation effect, however, increased compatibility is less attractive for a dominant supplier with the larger installed base than it is for a small supplier. When side-payments are feasible, the likelihood of achieving perfect compatibility is greater than it is when there are no side-payments. Even when side-payments are feasible, however, profit-maximizing suppliers might fail to achieve the welfare-maximizing outcome of perfect compatibility, because the private incentives might not be sufficiently aligned with the social incentives.

The degree of compatibility between competing technological standards is typically the outcome of strategic decisions taken by the suppliers. Forms of competition that could emerge from a situation in which suppliers have 'ownership' of separate technologies that are candidates to become the industry standard include: inter-technology competition, in the case where incompatibility is preferred by both suppliers; intra-technology competition, in the case where compatibility is preferred by both suppliers; and a hybrid case in which one (dominant) supplier prefers inter-technology competition while the other (smaller) supplier prefers intra-technology competition. In the latter case the outcome may depend on the ease with which the dominant supplier, which prefers incompatibility, can prevent imitation of its technology by the smaller supplier.

Discussion questions

1. Distinguish between direct and indirect network externalities.

2. Using a diagram illustrate the equilibrium price and quantity for a network good or service under perfect competition.

3. Using a diagram illustrate the equilibrium price and quantity for a network good or service under monopoly.

4. In the videotape format war of the 1970s the fight was between Sony's Betamax and JVC's VHS. The winner was the VHS system. On the basis of your research present reasons why JVC won the war.

5. Discuss the possible strategies a firm might follow to ensure its product becomes the industry standard.

6. With reference to Case Study 21.1 identify the strategy behind the 2011 launch of BlackBerry's BBM music app. How successful has this strategy been?

7. With reference to Case Study 21.2, discuss the importance and possible market advantages of Google's 'vast banks of personal data'.

8. Section 21.5 deals with forms of competition over standardization and compatibility. Three forms are identified, 'Tweedledee and Tweedledum', 'Battle of the Sexes' and 'Pesky Little Brother'. Explain these forms and suggest possible real-life examples.

9. With reference to Case Study 21.3 discuss the advantages and disadvantages of 'open' versus 'closed' platforms.

Further reading

Birke, D. (2009) The economics of networks: a survey of the empirical literature, *Journal of Economic Surveys*, 23, 762–93.

Economides, N. (1996) The economics of networks, *International Journal of Industrial Organization*, 16, 673–99.

Farrell, J. and Klemperer, P. (2007) Coordination and lock-in: competition with switching costs and network effects, in Armstrong, A. and Porter, R. (eds) *Handbook of Industrial Organization*, Vol. 3. Amsterdam: Elsevier, 1967–2072.

Shy, O. (2010) A short survey of network economics, *Federal Reserve Bank of Boston*, Working Paper No. 10–3.

Learning objectives

This chapter covers the following topics:

- product extension, market extension and pure diversification
- the rationale for diversification
- why firms may decide to reduce their commitment to diversification
- evidence related to the direction and determinants of diversification in the UK and Europe

Key terms

Conglomerate
Conglomerate merger
Cross-subsidization
Deconglomeration
Direction of diversification

Internal capital market
Predatory competition
Reciprocity
Tying (tie-in sale)

22.1 Introduction

A diversified firm is involved in the production of a number of different goods and services. In other words, a diversified firm is a multi-product firm. Large diversified firms which operate in many sectors of the economy are often referred to as **conglomerates**. Examples are Unilever, which produces a large array of packaged food and personal care products; BAA, which is involved in airport management services, building projects, railways, property management and consultancy services; and ABB, which is involved in various power and automotive technologies as well as oil, gas and petroleum. Large diversified firms account for a significant proportion of the total economic activity in most developed economies. Naturally, this raises questions concerning the implications of diversification for competition and performance. Chapter 22 addresses these issues.

Section 22.2 identifies three principal types of diversification: first, diversification by product extension, where a firm supplies a new product that is closely related to its existing products; second, diversification by market extension, where a firm moves into a new geographic market; and, third, pure diversification, where a firm moves into a completely unrelated field of activity. There are two ways in which a diversification strategy might be implemented: either through internally generated expansion, or through merger and acquisition. Section 22.3 examines the theories that have been developed to explain why a firm might decide to pursue a diversification strategy. These are considered under four broad headings: enhancement of market power; realization of cost savings; reduction of transaction costs, and managerial motives for diversification.

Typically, the direction of diversification is not determined randomly; instead, the products of most conglomerates tend to be related. Nevertheless, during the 1980s and 1990s there appears to have been a shift of emphasis away from diversification, and in some cases towards the divestment of unrelated activities in pursuit of increased corporate focus. Section 22.4 considers reasons why some conglomerates have been subject to a strategy of divestment or **deconglomeration**.

Section 22.5 discusses the empirical evidence on the extent and direction of diversification among UK and European conglomerates. In general the empirical evidence seems to suggest most conglomerates are rather cautious in their diversification strategies, preferring in most cases to diversify in a manner that leaves them operating relatively close to their current technological and market bases.

22.2 Types of diversification

As shown earlier (see Section 9.2), the definition of a market contains both a product dimension and a geographic dimension. The product market definition includes all products that are close substitutes for one another, either in consumption or in production. The geographic market definition involves determining whether an increase in the price of a product in one geographic location significantly affects either the demand or supply, and therefore the price, in another location. If so, both locations form part of the same geographic market. Based on this definition of markets, the US Federal Trade Commission's annual *Statistical Report on Mergers and Acquisitions* suggests a convenient three-part classification of types of diversification:

■ *Product extension*. A firm can diversify by supplying a new product that is closely related to its existing products. A sweet manufacturer that sells a milk chocolate bar may decide to produce and sell a dark chocolate bar as a product extension. Diversification by product extension could also include a move slightly further afield; for example, a chocolate bar producer might decide to supply closely related products such as ice cream or snack foods. Diversification by product extension should not be viewed as a discrete series of easily identifiable steps, but rather as part of a continuous process. Since almost all firms produce more than one product line or offer more than one service, all firms are to some extent diversified.

■ *Market extension*. Diversification by market extension involves moving into a new geographic market. For example, the sweet manufacturer that produces chocolate bars for the UK market might decide to venture further afield by marketing the same chocolate bars elsewhere in the EU.

■ *Pure diversification*. A pure diversification strategy involves movement into unrelated fields of business activity. Firms that supply unrelated products to unrelated markets are known as conglomerates. The UK conglomerate Virgin plc is a well-known example of a firm that has grown mainly through a strategy of pure diversification. Virgin began in the early 1970s as a music store, before diversifying into numerous other fields including airlines, train services, financial products, soft drinks, mobile phones, holidays, cars, wines, publishing and bridal wear. Diversification by product extension or market extension refers to a strategy based on core product specialization. Conglomerates or purely diversified firms do not specialize in this way. Pure diversification is a relatively unusual strategy. Most firms tend to diversify by entering adjacent markets, rather than totally unrelated ones. Sometimes it might appear that a firm is involved in pure diversification, but on closer examination there is a logical explanation as to why a particular direction has been chosen. For example, in 1982, Mars UK, the confectionery firm, developed marine radar, aimed at the small boat market. At first glance, this appears to be a case of pure diversification. However, Mars Electronics had developed a successful electronics business on the basis of technical expertise accumulated through its vending machine operations. Having spotted a gap in the market for a cheap and reliable radar system, the company diversified into this niche market.

There are two ways in which a diversification strategy can be implemented: first, through internally generated expansion; and, second, through merger and acquisition. **Conglomerate merger** involves the integration of firms that operate in different product markets, or in the same product market but in different geographic markets. Internally generated expansion is likely to require the simultaneous extension of the firm's plant and equipment, workforce and skills base, supplies of raw materials, and the technical and managerial expertise of its staff. A strategy of diversification through conglomerate merger may be a lot less demanding in this respect. Another important distinction is that diversification through internal expansion is likely to result in an increase in the total productive capacity in the industry concerned, while diversification through conglomerate merger involves only a transfer of ownership and control over existing productive capacity. The main requirements for the latter strategy are an ability to select an appropriate target firm; access to the financial resources required to secure a controlling interest in the target firm; and an ability to manage the integrated organization effectively after the merger has taken place.

De Jong (1993) suggests the choice of diversification strategy might depend on the stage reached in the industry life cycle (see Section 10.2). Firms operating in newer industries where rivalry is low are likely to face plentiful opportunities to extend their product lines as their markets expand. Firms operating in mature industries are likely to find their opportunities for new product developments constrained by slow growth in market demand and more intense rivalry. Diversification through conglomerate merger rather than through internally generated expansion may be a more attractive strategy, especially since, as noted above, it avoids increasing the industry's total productive capacity. During the late 1940s, 1950s and 1960s, when most European economies were still undergoing reconstruction following the Second World War, diversification in Europe was typically implemented through internally generated expansion, while diversification by conglomerate merger was more common in the US (Chandler, 1990; Jacobson and Andréosso-O'Callaghan, 1996). During the post-war reconstruction phase, most European industries were at an earlier stage of their life cycles than the equivalent US industries. Furthermore, Chandler (1990) suggests the ability of European firms to finance conglomerate mergers was constrained by the small size and lack of flexibility of European capital markets relative to their US counterparts.

22.3 Motives for diversification

Section 22.3 examines a number of theories that have been developed to explain why a firm might decide to pursue a strategy of diversification. The discussion begins by examining motives related to the enhancement of the firm's market power, and motives related to the potential for cost savings. Theories of diversification based on some of the alternative theories of the firm introduced in Chapter 4 are also examined.

Enhancement of market power

The diversified firm which operates in a number of separate geographic and product markets may enjoy a competitive advantage over a specialized firm, because it can draw on resources from its full range of operations in order to fight rivals in specific markets. Furthermore, a firm that already has significant market power in one market might be reluctant to expand further within the same market, for fear of alerting the competition authorities. A superior and less confrontational strategy might be to move into other related or unrelated markets. There are several specific anti-competitive consequences of diversification.

Cross-subsidization and predatory competition

Through a policy of **cross-subsidization**, the diversified firm may be in a strong position to compete against a specialized rival in the rival's own market, drawing on cash flows or profits earned elsewhere within the organization to cover the costs of engaging the rival in either price or non-price forms of **predatory competition** (Aron, 1993; Myers, 1994). Predatory competition involves diverting resources from one operation in order to fight elsewhere. Under a predatory pricing strategy, for example, the diversified firm might undercut the specialized firm's price in an attempt to force it out of the market (see also Section 11.3). Once the rival has withdrawn, the price is reset to the original level or a higher level. In order for this strategy to succeed, the predator must have a deeper pocket than its rival (OECD, 1989; Scherer and Ross, 1990). A predatory pricing strategy is only likely to be profitable if there are barriers to entry. Otherwise the sacrifice of profit in the short run may be in vain. 'Predatory competition is an expensive pastime, undertaken only if monopoly and its fruits can be obtained and held' (Adelman, 1959, p. 369). However, by signalling commitment, the predator may develop a reputation as a willing fighter, which itself serves as an entry barrier (Milgrom and Roberts, 1982; Chen, 1997).

There may be limits to the usefulness of a predatory competition strategy for a diversified firm. The specialized rival might turn out to be a more effective fighter, as it would be fighting for its very survival. For any firm wishing to eliminate rivalry, there may be alternative, less costly strategies than predatory competition, such as collusion or acquisition (McGee, 1958; Telser, 1966a). Although the diversified firm might have the capability to carry out a predatory competition strategy, it might refrain from doing so if this places its other operations at risk. For example, one of Rockefeller's associates remarked that Standard Oil 'gained or lost on a titan's scale while our opponents did so on a pygmy's' (Nevins, 1953, p. 65).

Gabrielsen (2003) suggests the takeover of an independent firm might be a disguised vertical merger, rather than a strategy for diversification. A firm targets the independent firm for its distribution network, which might otherwise be used by potential entrants, for whom the development of a distribution network would be costly, time-consuming and risky. Acquiring a firm with a distribution network already in place might be a cost-effective means of achieving entry. Therefore, by acquiring the firm with the distribution network, the incumbent achieves market power through effective foreclosure on the potential entrant. Although the same result could be achieved by simply acquiring the entrant, antitrust authorities typically view horizontal mergers with greater scepticism than mergers that only have implications for vertical relations.

Reciprocity and tying

Reciprocity involves an agreement that firm A purchases inputs from firm B, on condition that firm B also purchases inputs from firm A. In other words, reciprocity is 'the practice of basing purchases upon the recognition of sales to the other party, rather than on the basis of prices and product quality' (Weston, 1970, p. 314). It can be argued that, in effect, all economic transactions involve an element of reciprocity; and, in the extreme case of barter, transactions are based solely on reciprocal arrangements. Reciprocity becomes anticompetitive if one of the parties is forced to take part in a reciprocal transaction in which it would not participate voluntarily.

A specialized firm has only a limited range of input demands, whereas a diversified firm has a much wider spread of purchasing requirements. Therefore, the diversified firm is in a stronger position. The US Federal Trade Commission argues that reciprocal trade increases existing entry barriers or creates new barriers if entrants are effectively excluded as a result of reciprocal trade arrangements (Utton, 1979). For example, Wall Street and Technology (2006) reports that the investment bank Morgan Stanley encouraged its IT department to purchase technology inputs from a subsidiary of a major client. Much of the evidence on reciprocity draws on anecdotal evidence based on cases that were brought before the courts. Needham (1978) argues that reciprocity is just one method by which a firm can exploit its existing market power, rather than a strategy for extending market power. Consequently, the practice itself should not be viewed as particularly damaging to competition.

Tying involves the linked selling of two distinct products, in order to purchase good X, the buyer must also purchase good Y (see also Section 20.3). This practice may be an attractive strategy for a diversified firm that is seeking to generate sales across a number of distinct product lines.

Cost savings

In theory, a diversification strategy can result in cost savings in three ways: first, through the realization of economies of scope; second, by reducing risk and uncertainty; and, third, by reducing the firm's tax exposure.

Economies of scope

As shown earlier (see Section 2.2), economies of scale are realized when the firm reduces its long-run average cost by increasing its scale of production, while economies of scope are realized when long-run average cost savings are achieved by spreading costs over the production of several goods or services. Douma and Schreuder (1998) quote a farming example. A fruit-grower must leave enough space between the trees to allow access for labour and farm equipment. This land can be used to graze sheep. The farmer uses one input, land, to produce two products, fruit and wool. However, the availability of cost savings through economies of scope does not necessarily imply the fruit-grower must diversify into sheep farming. Instead the land could be rented to a sheep farmer. This market transaction delivers the same outcome as the diversification strategy. However, if the market transaction costs are too high, diversification might be the more cost-effective approach.

Needham (1978) expresses scepticism as to the importance of economies of scope as a motivating factor for a diversification strategy. First, if economies of scope are achieved by spreading the costs of indivisible inputs over a wider range of outputs, the specialized firm could realize similar cost savings through economies of scale, by increasing its scale of production. Second, the inputs must be non-specific and capable of being spread over different activities. This requirement might only be satisfied by certain inputs, such as the marketing or finance functions.

Reduction of risk and uncertainty

All firms are vulnerable to adverse fluctuations in demand, and increased competition in their product markets. The more products a firm develops, the lower is this vulnerability. According to Penrose (1995), the unpredictability of demand creates uncertainty, which in turn might motivate a diversification strategy:

> Except for seasonal variations, it is rarely possible accurately to predict fluctuations in demand. The less accurate the firm feels its predictions are, the more uncertain are profit expectations; consequently the firm will give more weight to the possibilities of obtaining a more complete utilization of its resources and a more stable income stream and less weight to the possible restriction on its ability to meet fully the peak demand for its existing product.

(Penrose, 1995, p. 140)

A diversification strategy can help smooth out seasonal fluctuations in cash flows, if the firm is able to establish a presence in markets with different seasonal peaks. Examples of offsetting activities include Walls' ice cream and meat products; Valor Gas's heating and gardening equipment product ranges; and the newsagent W.H. Smith's involvement in travel agency services.

The ability to manage risk through diversification may help the firm to raise finance at a lower cost. From the point of view of the lender, however, it is not immediately obvious why a diversified firm should receive more advantageous terms than a specialized firm. A lender can manage his or her own risk by spreading a diversified portfolio of investments across a number of specialized firms. It could be argued that for a small investor, in particular, holding shares in one diversified firm might be more attractive than holding a diversified portfolio of investments in many firms. For the small investor, the transaction costs incurred in making multiple investments and the cost of monitoring their performance might be onerous. However, vehicles such as unit trusts exist in order to channel funds from small-scale investors into managed diversified portfolios, reducing their investors' exposure to risk.

Obi (2003) examines whether the diversification of US bank holding companies into non-bank activities reduced the amount of unsystematic risk. Unsystematic risk is specific to the individual firm. This is in contrast to systematic or market risk, which affects all firms equally and cannot be managed through a strategy of diversification. Fifty financial institutions that moved from traditional banking business into areas such as life insurance, share dealing and real estate, between 1984 and 1995, are examined. The results suggest unsystematic risk was reduced through diversification, although market risk appears to have increased over the same period. Stiroh (2009) suggests that in recent years banks have refocused away from volatile capital market business back toward more stable retail banking business.

Reduction of tax exposure

Under some taxation regimes, diversification can enable a firm to reduce its tax liability. Profits in one activity can be offset against losses in another.

A specialized firm which makes a loss pays no tax on profit, but the tax payable by other profitable specialized firms is not reduced. A diversified firm might make greater use of debt rather than equity finance. If interest payments on loans are tax deductible, the overall effect might be a reduction in the firm's taxable profit (Needham, 1978). These arguments were tested by Berger and Ofek (1995), who express scepticism as to whether such factors are significant in most diversification or divestment decisions:

> Two potential benefits of diversification are increased interest tax shields resulting from higher debt capacity and the ability of multi-segment firms to immediately realize tax savings by offsetting losses in some segments against profits in others. Our estimate of tax saving, however, is only 0.1 per cent of sales, far too small to offset the documented value loss.
>
> *(Berger and Ofek, 1995, p. 60)*

Diversification as a means of reducing transaction costs

Motives for diversification or conglomerate merger can also be identified using the transaction costs approach. Below, these are considered under three headings: the conglomerate as an **internal capital market**, the conglomerate as a vehicle for the exploitation of specific assets, and the ability of a conglomerate to deliver services.

The conglomerate as an internal capital market

In theory, the financial or capital markets should always reward efficient management by increasing the market value of the firm. In practice, however, investors may be unable to access accurate information in order to judge the performance of management, especially since managers are likely to exercise influence or control over the flow of information. It would require a great deal of altruism for managers to pass on information which might reflect badly on their own performance. Information impactedness (Williamson, 1971) creates a transaction cost that frustrates the efficient allocation of investment funds.

With an M-form corporate structure (Williamson, 1975), the headquarters of the conglomerate performs the task of allocating funds for investment between a number of divisions (see Section 5.3). The managers of the divisions have autonomy in their day-to-day decision-making. In this coordinating role, the M-form headquarters has two advantages over the capital market. First, the divisional managers are subordinates to the senior managers, and can be ordered to provide reliable information. An implicit disciplinary threat can be used to encourage compliance (Harris and Raviv, 1996). It might be easier for divisional managers to share confidential information with senior managers than with external investors. Second, the headquarters can conduct internal audits to guard against mismanagement at divisional level. Effectively, the conglomerate acts as a miniature capital market, but enjoys better access to information and is able to monitor performance at divisional level more effectively. Of course, as the conglomerate grows larger, limits may be reached to the ability of the senior managers to monitor and coordinate effectively. There is also an opposing view, that the managers of a large diversified conglomerate might perform the task of allocating funds less efficiently than the capital markets. The managers might be excessively willing to prop up ailing divisions at the expense of the profitable ones. Divisions within a conglomerate bargain for funds and the bargaining power of a division might be enhanced by investments that do not benefit the organization as a whole. The head office might buy the cooperation of divisions by diverting investment funds in their direction (Berger and Ofek, 1995; Scharfstein, 1998; Berlin, 1999).

Van Oijen and Douma (2000) elaborate on the factors that determine whether or not central management can exercise effective control over the divisions of a large, diversified conglomerate. Diversification eventually presents a challenge to the control exercised by central management in the following areas:

- *Planning*. A corporate strategy identifies the portfolio of industries and geographic markets in which the firm will be involved. This is distinct from a business strategy, which concerns individual divisions in different industries and countries. The centre is responsible for corporate strategy, but the extent of its involvement in business strategy depends on the level of diversification. The greater the participation of the centre in business strategy, the greater the likelihood that decisions benefit the corporation, rather than the individual division. If the divisions are to benefit from synergies in marketing and distribution, some central coordination is required. Central coordination is easier to achieve if the level of diversification is relatively low.

- *Evaluation*. The centre allocates funds to the individual divisions and must monitor the subsequent use of funds. Traditional accounting rates of return may be too crude to measure the true contribution of individual divisions to the corporation as a whole. For example, division A may be instructed to send resources to division B, but if this were likely to compromise division A's financial performance, A's cooperation might not be forthcoming. A more sophisticated method of evaluation may be required, recognizing each division's total contribution to the corporation's performance.

- *Selection*. This reflects the ability of the corporation to select managers who are sympathetic to its strategies, ideals and culture. Effective selection is easiest when the level of diversification is relatively low and the centre is informed about of the specific needs of individual divisions.

- *Rotation*. The rotation of resources, especially management, helps spread best practice and develops networks. Rotation encompassing all aspects of the corporation's activities is more difficult in large diversified conglomerates.

- *Motivation*. In large conglomerates, financial criteria tend to determine incentives, since the centre may be unable to access other information. In less diversified corporations, it may be easier to develop incentive structures based not only on financial criteria, but also on strategic criteria reflecting the performance of the entire organization.

- *Coordination.* Coordination of joint activities among divisions tends to be easier in less diversified corporations. In highly diversified conglomerates, central coordination may be impeded if it is seen as damaging to the interests of the individual division and consequently resisted by its management.

- *Support.* Functions such as human resources, research and development, and legal services can be organized centrally, but the level of diversification is likely to influence the extent of central provision. There is less scope for central provision in a corporation with a diversified range of activities.

Summarizing these arguments, Van Oijen and Douma anticipate that, as the level of diversification increases, the centre becomes less involved in planning business strategies and in the day-to-day management of the divisions; relies more on financial criteria when evaluating performance; becomes less involved in the selection of staff; reduces the level of staff rotation; tends to rely increasingly on financial incentives; and offers fewer centralized services.

Doukas and Kan (2008) report that diversified firms that generate higher returns from their non-core business than from their core business tend to favour diversifying mergers, while those that generate lower returns from their non-core activities tend to favour non-diversifying mergers. Accordingly, it appears that the profitability of the core business of the conglomerate plays an important role in the decision to diversify. A conglomerate that reallocates capital from a less profitable core activity to a more profitable non-core activity contributes to an improvement in the efficiency of capital allocation

The conglomerate as a vehicle for the exploitation of specific assets

Penrose (1995) suggests firms' opportunities for growth derive from their possession of resources and assets that can be exploited in other markets. If these resources could be sold to other firms through the market, the rationale for diversification would disappear. Specific assets include new technologies, trade secrets, brand loyalty, managerial experience and expertise (Gorecki, 1975; Sutton, 1980; Teece, 1982; Markides and Williamson, 1994). In the management science literature, assets of this kind are termed core competences by Prahalad and Hamel (1990) and core capabilities by Stalk *et al.* (1992). In order to capitalize on its specific assets, the firm can either sell the assets in the market, or diversify into the relevant industry and exploit the asset itself. The decision whether to sell or diversify depends on the presence of market imperfections which increase the transaction costs incurred by selling the assets in the market.

- A market may not exist because the property rights in the asset cannot be protected. Basic knowledge which is non-patentable is an example of a specific asset of this kind.

- It may be too difficult to transfer a specific asset independently of its owner. A team of managers or a group of skilled workers may be uniquely loyal to an owner and unwilling to transfer to another organization.

- The transaction costs of transferring the asset may be too high. For example, if the technology is complex, it might not be possible to find a buyer with the skills and facilities needed to exploit the asset. It might be necessary to transfer not only the blueprints and recipes for a new product or process, but also skills that are learnt through experience. This would require the training of staff in the buying firm, whose technical background may be unsuitable.

■ Market transactions may be subject to externalities. For example, if B purchases A's brand or trademark, but B is unable to maintain A's standards of service, A's reputation and profitability may suffer. Negotiations between a seller and a buyer may reveal production methods and strategies sufficient for the buyer to contemplate entry into the seller's industry, even if the sale and purchase are not completed. To guard against externalities or spillovers of these kinds, strict and complex contractual relations, perhaps involving high monitoring and policing costs, would be required.

In view of these market imperfections and the associated transaction costs, firms might find it more beneficial to diversify than to trade their specific assets in the market. For example, Gillette's acquisition of the battery manufacturer Duracell in 1996 can be interpreted in terms of the exploitation of specific assets. At first glance there appears to be no obvious potential for economies of scope. Capital equipment and technology are very different for the two products. Douma and Schreuder (1998) suggest Gillette wished to exploit its marketing and sales operations in emerging markets such as Brazil, China and India by selling batteries as well as razors.

Montgomery and Wernerfelt (1988) see diversification as a means for extracting rents in related activities. Rents are the returns or rewards to owners of unique factors. Potential diversifiers have excess capacity in their factor inputs, which can be exploited beyond their current use. As a firm diversifies it transfers this excess capacity to the adjacent market which yields the highest rents. Should any spare capacity remain, the firm diversifies into markets further afield, until the marginal rents disappear. Davis and Devinney (1997) suggest three ways in which the desire to make better use of specific assets might propel firms towards diversification. First, supply conditions relate to the potential for economies of scale and scope, created by the possibility of spreading the costs of production, marketing and distribution over a greater number of activities. Second, synergies are created by various customer switching costs. For example, if a firm has built up brand loyalty, and consumers perceive the brand as representing high quality, then this perception can be exploited in other markets. Third, and perhaps most importantly, is the exploitation of managerial skills, such as technical expertise, the ability to marshal skilled labour and knowledge of the workings of supply industries.

The delivery of services

The role of diversification as a means for eliminating transaction costs may be applicable to the delivery of services. Unlike physical products, services are intangible and therefore have the characteristics of experience goods (see Section 16.3). Furthermore, services involve interactions between customers and suppliers. These characteristics create difficulties for customers in comparing the services offered by different suppliers, which give rise to switching costs. Diversified organizations, which supply both goods and services, may therefore have an advantage over specialized suppliers of goods only. Based on an analysis of US data for the period 1998–2000, Skaggs and Droege (2004) report that manufacturers that had diversified into services performed better, with less risk, than specialized manufacturers.

Managerial motives for diversification

As shown earlier (see Section 4.3), an important characteristic of the large corporation is the separation of ownership from control. According to Marris's (1964) managerial theory of the firm, diversification is the principal method by which growth in demand is achieved in the long run. Similarly, Mueller (1969) suggests conglomerate merger is a strategy that may be pursued by managers more concerned with the maximization of growth than with the maximization of shareholder value. If the regulatory authorities make it difficult for firms to expand horizontally or vertically, conglomerate merger may represent the best available alternative strategy.

There may be several reasons why the managers (the agents) might wish to pursue growth at a faster rate than would be chosen by the owners or shareholders (the principals). First, the managers' power, status and remuneration might be related to the growth of the organization. Second, diversification into new activities might complement the talents and skills of the managers, increasing their value to the organization. Third, unlike shareholders, who are able to reduce risk by diversifying their portfolios, the managers' job security depends on the fortunes of the firm. Diversification might provide a means of reducing the risk of failure facing the firm and its managers. Income from employment represents a large proportion of the managers' remuneration, and this income is correlated with the firm's performance. The risks to the managers' income are closely related to the risks facing the firm. Since their employment risk cannot easily be reduced by diversifying their personal portfolios, managers diversify their employment risk by supporting strategies of diversification or conglomerate merger. Amihud and Lev (1981) find manager-controlled firms are more likely to pursue conglomerate merger than owner-controlled firms.

Any firm that wishes to grow within its existing markets is eventually likely to find these markets incapable of expanding sufficiently quickly. Investment opportunities in new markets may offer better prospects than those in existing markets. These opportunities may reflect not just changes in prices, tastes and other market conditions, but also the development of skills and knowledge within the firm (Penrose, 1995). Furthermore, the firm might find expansion within its existing markets triggers increasing rivalry from its competitors.

In a survey of US firms, Rose and Shepard (1997) find managers' salaries were 13 per cent higher in diversified firms than those in similar specialized firms. However, some caution is required in interpreting this finding. Perhaps diversified firms are more complex to manage and require managers with more ability. Incumbent managers who pursue diversification strategies are not necessarily rewarded with higher salaries; instead, newly appointed managers of diversified firms might be paid more than managers of specialized firms because the job is more demanding.

Foreign competition and globalization

Does an increase in foreign competition propel domestic firms towards diversification into foreign markets? Foreign competition in a domestic market can increase through either the import of foreign-produced goods, or direct competition from foreign-owned subsidiaries. The latter may pose the greater threat to domestic firms, as it is based on specific organizational and location capabilities. Foreign competition might force domestic firms to become more competitive by, for example, investing in capital intensive methods of production. Firms that adapt to this new competitive environment might themselves decide to exploit their new capabilities at the global level (Wiersema and Bowen, 2007).

There may also be a tendency for the organization or the entire industry to become global, perhaps driven by increased standardization or homogeneity of consumer demand worldwide. This presents opportunities for the realization of economies of scale in production, marketing and research and development. The degree to which the domestic firm is already diversified might impact negatively on international diversification. To some extent, domestic (product) diversification and geographic diversification are conflicting strategies. Both paths create costs for management in achieving coordination and control. If a firm has already chosen a path of product diversification, it may face higher costs of coordination when contemplating geographical diversification.

Case study 22.1

Quercus looks to life after Larsson

Quercus plans to further expand its international presence and boost digital book sales, as the UK publisher adapts its business model to 'life after Larsson'. The Plus Market-traded publishing house scored a major coup in 2007 when it secured the English language print and digital rights to Stieg Larsson's 'Millennium series', the Swedish detective trilogy that became a global bestseller with 55m sales internationally, including 4.6m in the UK. The boost to Quercus's turnover that stemmed from the series' success – revenues near-tripled from £10.9m in 2008 to £31.8m in 2010 – has given the group sufficient cash to diversify its portfolio.

In a sign diversification is working, Quercus on Monday reported that turnover from 'non-Larsson' titles rose by 83 per cent year-on-year and now comprises an estimated 80 per cent of total revenues. Full results will not be released until later in the year. Ebook sales rose from 3 per cent to 11 per cent of total revenues in 2011, and Quercus plans to further boost digital sales to more than one-third of total turnover within the next three years. It has poached senior staff from rivals including HarperCollins,

Penguin, Orion and Little Brown Book Group, to diversify into areas including cookery, science fiction and literature for women. 'We are bringing people in to take us into different areas that we weren't in previously,' said Mark Smith, the Australian who established Quercus in 2004 with Wayne Davies, his former colleague at Orion. Mr Smith acknowledged that the *The Girl with the Dragon Tattoo* 'put Quercus on the map', and coupled with lucrative profit-sharing remuneration packages, the publishing house's enhanced reputation has helped it poach staff who he believes will ensure the future success of the company.

'After Larsson, we have been offered things from the author and agent community that we only could have dreamed of beforehand,' he said. 'It has given us the financial resources to grow the company. It has raised our profile with authors, agents and potential staff members.'

New senior staff include Jo Fletcher, a science fiction expert from Gollancz Publishing, and Jenny Heller, an expert on TV brands and cookery publishing, and the group's headcount has risen by nearly half to 65 over the past year. 'The group has made remarkable progress in building a sustainable post-hit business, attracting the calibre of editors and authors well above that implied by its size and maturity,' Fiona Orford-Williams, an analyst at Edison Investment Research said.

However, the later-than-expected promotion for the English-language film adaptation of *The Girl with the Dragon Tattoo* – starring Daniel Craig and Rooney Mara – delayed sales for the tie-in book, prompting Edison's Ms Orford-Williams to cut her full-year revenue estimates by 10 per cent to £20.7m for 2011 and by the same percentage to £24.1m for 2012.

Mr Smith is eager to move Quercus's geographic focus away from the UK, which accounts for two-thirds of turnover. 'Geographic expansion is on the top of my list,' said Mr Smith. 'We have already enhanced our business in Australia with a partnership with Pan Macmillian, and we have a foot in the water with a fiction joint venture in the US and we will expand our presence there.

'The US is the top of our agenda – it's the biggest market in the world and [we] need to be there.'

Mr Smith, who was named Entrepreneur of the Year at the Grant Thornton Growth Company Awards in 2011, holds no misapprehensions that the Millennium series' success can be repeated in the near future, hence the diversification. Quercus' situation echoes that of Bloomsbury, the British publishing house that was launched to prominence through JK Rowling's Harry Potter series of seven global bestsellers. The group's larger rival dealt with the dearth of Potter novels from 2009 onwards by expanding into academic and professional publishing in an effort to avoid the volatility that comes from fiction and non-fiction book sales.

'Our diversification gives us a lot less reliance on Larsson,' said Mr Smith. 'And our what we call our "non-Larsson business" is well up on last year. Where you see Bloomsbury diversifying into education, we are firmly on the consumer side of things and will remain so.'

Source: Quercus looks to life after Larsson, © The Financial Times Limited. All Rights Reserved, 30 January 2012 (Wembridge, M.).

Samsung diversification going awry   **FT**

Samsung Group's new businesses appear to be going awry. Samsung Electronics, the group's flagship company, is considering taking over its light-emitting diode (LED) joint venture with affiliate Samsung Electro-Mechanics as the LED business suffers from slowing demand for TVs.

The news comes after Samsung Electronics said in May it would unload its solar cell business to its affiliate Samsung SDI, after a disappointing start in the new business. 'They seem to be putting expansion of new businesses on hold as market conditions deteriorate,' said Jae Lee, an analyst at Daiwa Securities. Samsung has spread into new businesses such as renewable energy and healthcare after its chairman Lee Kun-hee predicted last year that most of the group's current businesses and products would disappear in 10 years.

Samsung has identified five businesses – solar cells, rechargeable batteries for hybrid cars, LED technology, biopharmaceuticals and medical equipment – as its future growth drivers and pledged to invest about $21bn to generate $44bn of annual sales by 2020. But analysts say most of the new businesses are not making much headway as prices of solar cells have plunged this year amid oversupply and LED demand growth stalled amid the global economic slowdown. The group's solar cell business reportedly posted about Won30bn of losses even under the control of Samsung SDI. The future of its LED business has been thrown into doubt as the South Korean government recently designated LED as a business suitable for small and mid-sized companies.

The only bright spot among the new businesses seems to be medical equipment manufacturing. Analysts say Samsung was able to make rapid inroads into the healthcare market through acquisitions. This month, Samsung Electronics bought Nexus, a US company making cardiac testing solutions. It follows acquisitions of Medison, a leading domestic medical equipment maker, and another local firm Ray, an X-ray machine manufacturer. Samsung also entered a joint venture with US biopharmaceutical company Quintiles earlier this year, pledging to invest Won2,100bn in the burgeoning sector. But the business has not yet contributed much to the group's earnings.

Still, analysts say Samsung has little choice but to diversify its businesses from computer chips, flat screens and mobile phones to secure stability in its revenue streams. 'Its portion of cyclical businesses is so high that steady growth is not warranted. It needs to break into new businesses in order to reduce the earnings volatility and seek secular growth,' said Lee at Daiwa.

22.4 | Corporate focus and deconglomeration

In the management science literature, the term corporate focus refers to the extent to which a firm specializes in its core activity. In a study of 33 large US firms over the period 1950–86, Porter (1987) notes most had divested more acquisitions than they had retained; in other words, most had become increasingly focused. Similar conclusions are drawn by Scharfstein (1998), who analyzes a US sample of 165 conglomerates that were diversified into at least one other unrelated activity in 1979. By 1994, 55 of these firms had become focused on their core activity; 57 firms that had not become more focused had been acquired by other firms; and only 53 firms still existed as conglomerates in 1994.

Why did many large conglomerates tend to divest activities during the 1980s and 1990s? The fundamental reason is that, in many cases, firms that had become increasingly diversified also became less profitable. Conversely, average profitability often tended to increase among firms that became more focused. There is some evidence of a tendency for the stock market prices of parent firms that divested some activities to have risen (Daley *et al.*, 1997). Furthermore, this tendency was more pronounced for firms that sold unrelated activities than for firms that sold related activities. In a study of 1,449 US firms in the 1980s, Lang and Stulz (1994) find Tobin's q (the ratio of the market value of a firm to its replacement cost of assets) was greater for specialized firms than for diversified firms.

If the share prices of diversified firms are consistently lower than those of specialized firms (relative to the underlying value of assets), it appears that shareholders tend to penalize diversified firms. This might suggest that unrelated diversification is a strategy intended to benefit managers and not shareholders. Analyzing the profitability of the parent firms that divested themselves of their acquisitions, as well as the units that were divested, Daley *et al.* (1997) find that profitability increased for both types of organization. This appears to justify the observed tendency for capital markets to be optimistic about firms that have become more focused.

The issue of focus is approached from a different angle in Siggelkow's (2003) study of US mutual fund providers. Some providers offer a broad range of funds, including specialized equity, bond and index funds; while others focus on a narrower range of funds. Using data for the period 1985–96, Siggelkow finds the mutual funds of focused providers outperformed those of diversified providers. Similar findings are reported by Ravenscraft and Scherer (1987), Kaplan and Weisbach (1992), Comment and Jarrell (1995) and Haynes *et al.* (2002). Martin and Sayrak (2003) survey the literature on diversification and shareholder value.

Berger and Ofek (1995) test for the existence of a diversification discount, measured by comparing the performance of individual divisions of a conglomerate with that of specialized firms in the same industry. The diversification discount is the difference between the sum of the hypothetical stand-alone market values of each constituent division of the conglomerate and the actual market value. The stand-alone values exceeded the market values by about 15 per cent on average.

Agreement as to the existence and magnitude of the diversification discount is not universal. Hyland (2003) tests the hypothesis that a diversification discount may already exist before a firm decides to diversify. A firm that diversifies may have a relatively low value of Tobin's q for reasons other than diversification, such as inferior management. Accordingly, Hyland examines the diversification discount over the three years before and the three years after the diversification decision. On average, Tobin's q tends to fall in the first year after diversification, but the value for the subsequent two years is not lower than that for the preceding three years. In an international study, Lins and Servaes (1999) find evidence of a diversification discount for Japan and the UK but not for Germany. It is suggested the different results might reflect different levels of concentration of ownership.

Nevertheless, the consensus seems to be that a diversification discount does exist and, if the discount is as large as some studies suggest, it is perhaps unsurprising that shareholders have encouraged managers to implement strategies of divestment or **deconglomeration**. Haynes *et al.* (2002) suggest the following reasons for improved performance following divestment from diversified activities. First, the diversified firm may be overstretched in so far as its organizational structure is unable to cope with the complex demands of its divisions. Second, if diversification was originally undertaken in order to realize managerial objectives such as growth or sales revenue maximization, then divestment may enable the firm to regain previous levels of profitability performance. Third, for an underperforming firm, a divestment announcement may signal that management are addressing the problem and that changes are imminent. The stock market may view such an announcement in a positive light. Finally, if the divesting firm is acquired by a new owner, the potential for cost savings may generate gains which flow to the vendors via a higher purchase price. An improvement in performance is therefore linked with divestment.

Mair and Moschieri (2006) view deconglomeration as beneficial when there is a clash of cultures between the divisions of a conglomerate. Central management might have a vested interested in the retention of the non-core divisions, but culture clashes may tend to consume scarce resources, such as managerial time and effort, and create barriers to internal capital mobility. Following divestment, resources are freed for reinvestment in the core activity. The divested unit might still benefit from the support of its former parent, through access to capital, expertise and reputation. For example, the electronics manufacturer Philips operates a Technology Incubator, which develops new ideas, with a view to selling them when they are able to attract their own customers, strategic partners and venture capital finance.

Porter (1990) suggests another reason for poor performance: the neglect of innovation in the divisions of the conglomerate. Innovation stems from focus and commitment to sustained investment in a specific activity. In contrast:

> Unrelated diversification, particularly through acquisition, makes no contribution to innovation. Unrelated diversification almost inevitably detracts from focus, commitment and sustained investment in the core industries, no matter how well-intentioned management is at the outset.

Acquired companies, where there is no link to existing businesses, often face short-term financial pressures to justify their purchase price. It is also difficult for corporate managers of a diversified firm to be forward-looking in industries they do not know.

(Porter, 1990, p. 605)

I will continue to hold the view that management too often underestimates the problems in carrying through mergers, especially of companies in unrelated fields. It has indeed been one of the more welcome developments of recent years that companies have been increasingly concentrating on their core activities, divesting themselves of some of the enterprises they have acquired in earlier diversifications. It is the very pressures of competition I referred to earlier that have forced so many companies to re-examine their structure.

(John Bridgeman, Director-General of Fair Trading, speech to the European Policy Forum, 30 January 1996)

In the light of most of this evidence, it is natural to wonder why companies ever diversified into unrelated activities, and why some still do. One possibility is that the diversification discount may once have been lower than it subsequently became (Matsusaka, 1993; Servaes, 1996). The increasing scope and efficiency of capital markets may have reduced the need for the conglomerate to act effectively as an internal capital market. In the US and UK in particular, the refocusing of many conglomerates during the 1980s and 1990s was made possible by leveraged buyouts, in which unsecured junk bonds and loans were used to buy up large diversified conglomerates. Typically, the less profitable parts of the target firm would be sold off, leaving only the more profitable core activities. The receipts from the sale of unrelated activities would be used to service and repay the unsecured loans. An example of this type of buyout was Hoylake's attempt to buy British and American Tobacco, which, in 1989, was the ninth largest company in Europe. In another case, Hanson's purchase of a 2.8 per cent share in ICI was interpreted by the markets as a prelude to a full takeover bid. Investors inferred that to finance the takeover, Hanson would be forced to sell off some ICI divisions, and refocus the remaining activities. ICI fought back by splitting into two independent companies: one (ICI) concentrating on chemicals, and the other (Zeneca) on pharmaceuticals and agriculture. As a result of this strategy, the profitability and share prices of both companies increased.

22.5 Empirical evidence

This section examines some of the empirical evidence concerning the reasons for diversification and its direction. The discussion starts by examining the measurement of the degree of diversification.

In a technical sense, the measures of the extent of diversification are quite similar to the measures of concentration reviewed earlier (see Section 9.4).

Concentration measures reflect the number and relative sizes of the firms operating in an industry. Diversification measures reflect the number of industries in which one firm is involved, and the relative scale of its involvement in each case (Gollop and Monahan, 1991; Lacktorin and Rajan, 2000). Some of the most widely used diversification measures are as follows:

- *A count of activities.* One possibility is to simply count the number of three- or four-digit Standard Industrial Classification (SIC) activities in which the firm is involved. This is perhaps too simple for most purposes: one would naturally wish to discount or disregard activities in which the firm's involvement is very small.

- *Ratio of non-primary activities to all activities.* A simple measure of the extent of diversification is the ratio DR = B/(A + B), where A represents the firm's primary activity and B represents all other non-primary activities. A and B might be measured in terms of sales or employees. A specialized firm has DR = 0; and the greater the extent of diversification, the closer is DR to its maximum value of one. However, DR does not reflect the relative importance of each of the non-primary activities.

- *Herfindahl index of specialization, H(S).* This index is based on a weighted sum of the share of each activity in the total of all of the firm's activities (Berry, 1971, 1974). It is defined in the same way as the Herfindahl–Hirschman (HH) index of concentration (see Section 9.4). For a firm involved in N activities, let x_i denote the share of sales or employment in activity i in the firm's total sales or employment. The H(S) index is calculated as follows:

$$H(S) = \sum_{i=1}^{N} x_i^2$$

The index is influenced by both the number of activities and their relative importance. The more specialized the firm, the greater is H(S). As in the case of the HH index of concentration, a numbers equivalent of the H(S) index is defined as 1/H(S). The numbers equivalent is an inverse measure of diversification. For a firm with N activities (and using a sales-based measure), the minimum possible value of the numbers equivalent is 1/H(S) = 1, when virtually all of the firm's sales are derived from one activity, with a negligible proportion split between the other $N - 1$ activities. The maximum possible value is 1/H(S) = N, when the firm's sales are split equally between the N activities.

Using 1963 UK manufacturing data, Gorecki (1975) examines the direction and determinants of diversification. Measurement of the **direction of diversification** distinguishes between diversification within and outside a firm's two-digit industry group. To measure direction, Gorecki calculates the extent of participation of diversified firms in other industries within a broadly defined industry, known as an order. An order roughly corresponds to a two-digit industry group. Gorecki's data set comprises 14 orders and 51 industries. The measure of direction is the T-value, the summation of the total number of enterprises that own establishments in each of the other industries within the same order, divided by the summation of the total number of enterprises that own establishments in any other manufacturing industry.

The actual T-value can be compared with the T-value expected if diversification occurs randomly across the other 50 industries. In the majority of cases examined by Gorecki, the actual T-value was greater than the expected T-value. In only a handful of cases, including building materials, footwear and furniture, was the actual value less than the expected value. Gorecki's overall conclusion, that the direction of diversification was not random, is unequivocal.

In a regression model that seeks to identify the determinants of the decision to diversify, Gorecki's dependent variable is the ratio of employment in non-primary activities to total employment. Two types of independent variable are used to explain diversification. The first covers activities determined by the firm, such as advertising and research and development, which produce specific assets (brands, trademarks, innovation) that can be exploited through diversification. Advertising is measured using an advertising-to-sales ratio, and research and development is measured using the number of research employees. Dummy variables control for differences between consumer and non consumer goods industries. The second category of variables covers environmental factors, such as industry growth and concentration. Firms in low-growth industries are more likely to diversify in order to exploit their specific assets; therefore a negative relationship between growth and the extent of diversification is expected (although this relationship might be offset if firms in declining industries are unable to finance diversification). Firms in highly concentrated industries face higher costs of further expansion within the same industries. Firms in more highly concentrated industries are therefore expected to be more likely to diversify.

The estimation results do not support all of the hypotheses advanced above. The results are consistent with the hypothesis that diversification and research and development expenditure are positively related. However, the coefficient on the advertising-to-sales ratio is negative and not positive as expected. Gorecki suggests firms in consumer goods industries characterized by heavy advertising might vertically integrate forwards in order to protect their brands, and this type of strategy might be at the cost of diversification. The coefficients on industry growth and concentration are both statistically insignificant.

Writing from a strategic management perspective, Luffman and Reed (1984) examine diversification by UK firms during the 1970s, using a four-category methodology suggested by Rumelt (1974):

- In a single business, more than 95 per cent of sales are accounted for by one product.

- In a dominant firm, between 70 per cent and 95 per cent of sales are accounted for by one product.

- In a related firm, no one product accounts for more than 70 per cent of sales, but all products are related.

- In an unrelated firm, no one product accounts for more than 70 per cent of sales, and the products are unrelated.

Luffman and Reed find there was a trend towards increased diversification during the 1970s, although the trend was not as strong as in the decades immediately after the Second World War. There was significant movement into unrelated (conglomerate) activities.

Rondi *et al.* (1996) measure the extent of diversification among major firms producing within the EU, and attempt to identify the major determinants of diversification. Their sample is based on the five leading EU firms in each manufacturing industry. Although both EU and non-EU firms are considered, any production activity located outside the EU is ignored. The diversification measures used are those described at the start of this section: first, a simple count of different industry involvement, N; second, the ratio of secondary production to total production, DR; and, third, the Berry (1971, 1974) index, $D = 1 - H(S)$. All three measures are calculated at the two-digit and three-digit levels, to allow a distinction to be drawn between product extension (related) and pure (unrelated) diversification. Production outside the two-digit level implies pure diversification.

Table 22.1 summarizes the results. The average firm is involved in almost five three-digit industries, and almost three two-digit industries. Around 28 per cent of output is produced outside the primary two-digit industry, and 17 per cent is produced within the primary two-digit industry. By country, the highest levels of diversification at the three-digit level were for the UK and the Netherlands, and the lowest levels were for Italy and Germany.

In examining the determinants of diversification, Rondi *et al.* (1996) focus on three theories of diversification. The first, attributed to Marris (1964) and Penrose (1959), suggests managers seek to maximize the growth of the firm. The exploitation of specific assets such as marketing skills and technical expertise in other industries provides a convenient vehicle for the pursuit of a growth objective. The second theory, attributed to Bain (1959), focuses on the conditions that make entry possible or attractive. These include industry-level characteristics such as average profitability, growth and concentration, as well as barriers to entry. The third theory, attributed to Rumelt (1984) and Williamson (1975), focuses on relatedness between industries that makes diversification attractive. Relatedness refers to similarities between technologies, markets and organizational structures.

Table 22.1 Measures of diversification, large EU manufacturing enterprises

	Two-digit industry definition	Three-digit industry definition
Average number of industries, N	2.9	4.9
% Production outside primary industry, DR	17.1	28.3
Berry index, $D = 1 - H(S)$	0.23	0.37

Source: Adapted from Rondi, L., Sembenelli, A. and Ragazzi, E. (1996) Determinants of diversification patterns, in Davies, S. and Lyons, B. (eds) *Industrial Organisation in the European Union*. Oxford: Oxford University Press, p. 171.

Rondi *et al.*'s empirical model is:

$$P(F, P, S) = f\{W(F), X(P), Y(S), Z(P,S)\}$$

The dependent variable $P(F, P, S)$ is the probability that firm F with primary activity P diversifies into secondary activity S. The independent variables are $W(F)$, a vector of characteristics of firm F; $X(P)$, a vector of characteristics of primary activity P; $Y(S)$, a vector of characteristics of secondary activity S; and $Z(P, S)$, a vector reflecting the degree of relatedness between P and S.

The vector $W(F)$ includes a firm size measure, to reflect the ease with which a firm can acquire resources; a measure of the size of the firm's domestic market, to reflect the opportunities for growth; and dummy variables to capture relevant characteristics of each country's capital markets. $X(P)$ includes indicators of advertising intensity, research and development, human resources and capital intensity, to reflect the firm's specific assets. $Y(S)$ includes measures of the attractiveness of secondary industries and the height of entry barriers, captured using industry growth, profitability, advertising intensity, research and development, human resources and capital intensity indicators. $Z(P,S)$ includes measures of the relatedness of each secondary and primary industry, also based on advertising, research and development, human resources and capital intensity indicators.

The estimation results suggest firm size matters. Large firms are more likely to diversify than small firms. Firms originating from countries where there is a separation of ownership from control (proxied by capital market characteristics) are more likely to diversify. However, the size of the domestic market has no effect on the probability of diversification. Diversification is more likely if levels of advertising, research and development and specific human capital skills are high in both the primary and secondary activities. Specific assets play an important role in determining the rate and direction of diversification, as does the degree of relatedness: diversification often involves entry into secondary industries with characteristics similar to the primary industry. The coefficients on capital intensity are negative, supporting the notion that entry barriers influence the direction of diversification.

Altunbaş and Marqués (2008) examine diversification through merger in the EU banking industry. Does diversification into new financial services and diversification into geographical areas yield benefits including economies of scale and scope, reduction of risk, increased use of specific assets and improved access to low-cost (internal) finance? Alternatively, does diversification produce diseconomies of scale as the organization becomes too complex to manage efficiently? Does the degree of organizational and strategic similarity between the merger partners influence their subsequent performance? Broad similarities between the merging firms are found to improve post-merger performance. However, there are differences in the pattern between different types of merger (domestic or international), and between mergers involving different strategies regarding loans and deposits, capitalization, technology and innovation.

Using a dataset comprising the entire range of US financial intermediaries, Schmid and Walter (2012) investigate whether geographic diversification is value-enhancing or value-destroying in the financial services sector. The results indicate that geographic diversification is not associated with a valuation discount in financial intermediaries. However, when accounting for the firms' main activities, there is evidence of a significant discount associated with geographic diversification in securities firms, and a premium in credit intermediaries and insurance companies.

Santalo and Becerra (2008) examine the effects of diversification on performance, taking account of industry characteristics. Most empirical studies measure the average effect of diversification on performance on the assumption either that this effect is homogeneous across industries, or that it varies randomly. There is evidence of a diversification discount when a diversified firm competes in an industry dominated by specialized producers. Conversely, there is evidence of a diversification premium when the diversified firm faces only a few specialized competitors, whose share of the relevant market is small.

In general, the empirical evidence on the direction and determinants of diversification in the UK and Europe suggests firms tend to be relatively cautious in their diversification strategies, preferring in most cases to remain close to their technological and market bases. Perhaps the single most important motive for diversification is the opportunity to exploit specific assets within related industries.

22.6   Summary

Chapter 22 has examined the topic of diversification. There are three basic types of diversification. Diversification by product extension implies a firm supplies a new product that is closely related to its existing products. Diversification by market extension implies a firm supplies its existing product in a new geographic market. Finally, pure diversification involves a movement into a completely unrelated field of activity. There are two ways in which a diversification strategy can be implemented: first, through internally generated expansion; and, second, through conglomerate merger. While diversification through internal expansion leads to an increase in the total productive capacity in the industry concerned, diversification through conglomerate merger involves only a transfer of ownership and control over existing productive capacity.

Several theories have been developed to explain why a firm might decide to pursue a diversification strategy:

■ *Enhancement of market power.* The diversified firm may be in a strong position to compete against a specialized rival by drawing on cash flows or profits earned elsewhere within the organization, effectively cross-subsidizing the costs of engaging the rival in either price or non-price forms of competition. Reciprocity and tying may be attractive strategies for a diversified firm that is seeking to generate sales across several distinct product lines.

■ *Cost savings.* Diversification can result in cost savings in three ways. First, economies of scope are realized when the costs of indivisibilities are spread over the production of several goods or services, or when the diversified producer is able to realize other types of average cost saving. Second, diversification reduces the firm's exposure to adverse fluctuations in demand in any one of its product markets. The ability to manage risk through diversification may reduce the firm's cost of raising finance. Third, by offsetting profits earned from one activity against losses in another, a diversified firm may be able to reduce its tax exposure.

■ *Reduction of transaction costs.* If investors are unable to access reliable information in order to judge the performance of managers, the efficient allocation of investment funds may be impeded. Within a diversified firm or conglomerate, central managers at head office undertake the task of allocating funds between the divisions of the conglomerate. Effectively, the conglomerate acts as a miniature capital market, but enjoys better access to information and is able to monitor performance more effectively. Most firms possess specific assets that are of value if exploited in other markets. If the transaction costs incurred in trading specific assets through the market are high, it may be better for the firm to exploit the assets itself by implementing a diversification strategy.

■ *Managerial motives for diversification.* According to several of the early managerial theories of the firm, diversification is the principal method by which growth in demand is achieved in the long run. Managers might target growth rather than profit because their compensation and prestige are related to the size or growth of the organization. Diversification might increase the managers' value to the organization, and it might enhance their job security by reducing risk.

During the 1980s and 1990s there was a shift of emphasis away from diversification, and in some cases towards the divestment of unrelated activities in pursuit of increased focus. There is some empirical evidence of a diversification discount: a tendency for conglomerates to underperform relative to specialized firms in terms of profitability and stock market valuation. This may explain why shareholders encouraged managers to implement a strategy of divestment or deconglomeration.

There are several reasons why a diversified firm might underperform, or why a policy of divestment might be expected to bring about an improvement in performance. First, some conglomerates may simply be too large and their organizational structures overstretched. Second, if diversification was originally undertaken in pursuit of non-profit objectives, divestment might enable the firm to recover previous levels of profitability. Third, a divestment announcement may signal to the stock market that the problems of an underperforming conglomerate are being addressed. Finally, in the more market-oriented environment of the late twentieth and early twenty-first centuries, the economic rationale for the existence of large, highly diversified conglomerates is perhaps less persuasive than it may have been during the decades up to the 1970s, when the trend towards corporate diversification was apparently at its strongest.

Discussion questions

1. Explain the distinction between diversification through product extension, diversification through market extension, and pure diversification.

2. With reference to Case Studies 22.1 and 22.2, examine the features of successful and unsuccessful diversification strategies.

3. For what reasons might a firm's choice of diversification strategy depend on the stage achieved in the industry life cycle?

4. In what ways might a strategy of diversification enhance the market power exercised by a conglomerate in some of its product markets?

5. The argument that diversification benefits a firm through the realization of economies of scale by spreading the costs of indivisible inputs over a larger output is of limited appeal, according to some economists. Explain why.

6. Williamson argues that a common motive for conglomerate merger is the opportunity to take over inefficiently managed and undervalued firms. Owing to information impactedness, capital markets and shareholders may be unable to discipline weak management effectively. Why might a cadre of corporate managers be better positioned than shareholders to exercise effective control over an unsuccessful firm?

7. For what reasons might a non-profit-maximizing firm be expected to diversify at a faster rate than a profit-maximizing firm?

8. In what ways might a strategy of continued diversification eventually weaken the control exercised by central management over the divisions of a large conglomerate?

9. Describe the methods that can be used to measure the extent of diversification.

10. Strategies of deconglomeration have become more fashionable than the strategy of continued diversification for many large conglomerates. Examine why.

Further reading

Blackstone, E.A. (1972) Monopsony power, reciprocal buying, and government contracts: the General Dynamic case, *Antitrust Bulletin*, 17, 445–66.

Gorecki, P. (1975) An inter-industry analysis of diversification in the UK manufacturing sector, *Journal of Industrial Economics*, 24, 131–46.

Luffman, G.A. and Reed, R. (1984) *The Strategy and Performance of British Industry*, 1970–80. London: Macmillan.

Martin, J.D. and Sayrak, A. (2003) Corporate diversification and shareholder value: a survey of recent literature, *Journal of Corporate Finance*, 9, 37–57.

Utton, M.A. (1979) *Diversification and Competition*. Cambridge: Cambridge University Press.

23.1 Introduction

Chapter 23 examines competition policy. There are strong associations between competition and the theoretical notions of productive and allocative efficiency (see Section 3.4). Firms operating in competitive markets may be compelled to achieve full efficiency in production, or face the prospect of being driven out of business by more efficient competitors. The long-run market equilibrium in perfect competition is also consistent with allocative efficiency, since the industry operates at the point where price *equals* marginal cost. Accordingly, the economic case for competition policy rests largely on the theoretical arguments for and against perfect competition and monopoly. These arguments are examined in Section 23.2.

The idea that competition is always preferable to monopoly has not gone unchallenged. If the monopolist is able to operate on a lower average or marginal cost function than the firms comprising a perfectly competitive industry, then social welfare could be higher under monopoly than under perfect competition. The theories of natural monopoly and price discrimination can also be used to make a case for monopoly based on social welfare criteria. The Schumpeterian hypothesis suggests that market power and monopoly status may be interpreted as a reward for successful past innovation.

Section 23.3 discusses some of the more practical aspects of competition policy. Competition policy deals with three principal areas: monopoly, restrictive practices and merger. The implementation of **monopoly**, **restrictive practices** and **merger policy** requires a practical method for measuring market power. Seller concentration and market share measures are obvious candidates. Issues of product and geographic market definition have major implications for the measurement of market power using concentration or market share measures. The notion of **workable competition**, which may provide a more realistic target than the theoretical ideal of perfect competition, is examined.

At the time of writing, competition policy in the UK is the responsibility of the Office of Fair Trading and the Competition Commission. One of the objectives of the most recent competition policy legislation, especially the Competition Act 1998 and the Enterprise Act 2002, was to harmonize the UK's arrangements with those effective at EU level. Section 23.4 describes the competition policy regimes of the US, the EU and the UK. A major objective of EU competition policy is the promotion of competition within the European Single Market. The cornerstones are Articles 101 and 102 of the Treaty of Lisbon, which came into force in 2009, replacing earlier competition policy provisions within the Treaty of Rome. This chapter concludes in Section 23.5 with an assessment of the strengths and weaknesses of current competition policy arrangements.

23.2 Competition policy: theoretical framework

According to the structure–conduct–performance (SCP) paradigm, perfect competition is the market structure with the most favourable efficiency and welfare properties. In much of the theoretical and policy debate, there is an implicit assumption that competition is good and monopoly bad. This section examines the economic case for and against monopoly in some detail. Several of the arguments have already been rehearsed in previous chapters of this book. As has been shown previously, not all economists agree that monopoly is necessarily a worse state of affairs than competition.

Abnormal profit, allocative and productive inefficiency

A comparison between the models of perfect competition and monopoly in the neoclassical theory of the firm was developed early on in this book (see Section 3.4). The case was made for perfect competition and against monopoly, on the grounds of allocative and productive efficiency (see Figures 3.5 and 3.6). The monopolist and the perfectly competitive industry were assumed both to face the same horizontal LRAC (long-run average cost) and LRMC (long-run marginal cost) function (see Figure 3.5). Some of the consumer surplus achieved under perfect competition is converted into producer surplus (abnormal profit) under monopoly; and the rest becomes deadweight loss. Therefore, monopoly is allocatively inefficient. It was further assumed that a complacent monopolist, shielded from competitive pressure emanating either from rival firms or from actual or potential entrants, operates on a higher LRAC and LRMC function than it would if it were fully efficient in production (see Figure 3.6). This leads to a further increase in the deadweight loss. The main findings of this analysis can be summarized as follows:

■ Under monopoly, market price is higher and output is lower than under perfect competition. If LRAC is U-shaped or L-shaped, the monopolist typically fails to produce at the MES (minimum efficient scale), and therefore fails to produce at the lowest attainable long-run average cost (LRAC). In contrast, the perfectly competitive firm produces at the MES in long-run equilibrium. The monopolist earns an abnormal profit in the long run, while the perfectly competitive firm earns only a normal profit.

■ Under monopoly, there is allocative inefficiency because price exceeds marginal cost. This implies the value society would place on an additional unit of output (measured by the price the most marginal consumer is prepared to pay) exceeds the cost of producing that unit. Therefore, industry output is too low and welfare could be increased by producing more output. In contrast, under perfect competition there is allocative efficiency because price *equals* marginal cost.

■ Under monopoly, there may also be productive inefficiency, if a lack of competitive pressure enables the monopolist to become complacent or lazy. A complacent monopolist may fail to make the most efficient use of its factor inputs (technical inefficiency), or it may fail to employ the most cost-effective combination of inputs (economic inefficiency). Under perfect competition, intense competitive pressure compels all firms to be efficient in production, since any firm that fails to minimize its LRAC will realize a loss and be forced out of business.

■ The sum of consumer surplus and producer surplus is lower under monopoly than it is under perfect competition. Therefore, under monopoly, there is a deadweight loss, due to industry output being lower than it is under perfect competition. The existence of a deadweight loss is a corollary of the monopolist's preference to produce an output level at which price exceeds marginal cost (allocative inefficiency). The size of the deadweight loss is increased if the monopolist is also inefficient in production.

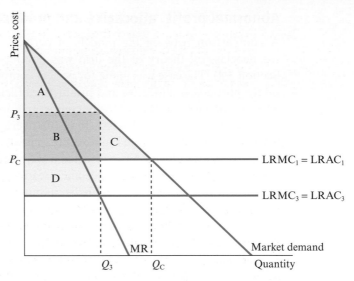

Figure 23.1 Consumer and producer surplus: perfect competition versus a monopolist with a cost advantage

However, a further possibility (not considered in Figures 3.5 and 3.6) is that the monopolist could operate on a *lower* LRAC and LRMC function than the firms comprising the perfectly competitive industry. For example, by exploiting economies of scale in research and development, the monopolist might be able to gain access to a production technology that is not available to a group of perfectly competitive firms. This argument is developed by Williamson (1968a,b), and has often been used in support of large firms seeking to merge horizontally, despite the fact that the merged entity would acquire enhanced market power. This efficiency defence for mergers forms part of the US Department of Justice Merger Guidelines.

Figure 23.1 considers prices, costs and output under conditions of monopoly and perfect competition, in the case where the monopolist's costs are below those of the firms under perfect competition. The perfect competitors' cost functions are $LRMC_1 = LRAC_1$, and the monopolist's cost functions are $LRMC_3 = LRAC_3$. The perfectly competitive industry operates at (P_C, Q_C) (as in Figure 3.5). Consumer surplus is A + B + C and producer surplus (abnormal profit) is zero. The monopolist operates at (P_3, Q_3). Consumer surplus is A and producer surplus is B + D. Comparing the sum of consumer surplus and producer surplus in the two cases, welfare is higher under monopoly than it is under perfect competition if D > C. Whether this condition is satisfied depends on the size of the difference between $LRMC_1 = LRAC_1$ and $LRMC_3 = LRAC_3$: the larger the difference, the more likely it is that welfare is higher under monopoly than it is under perfect competition.

Overall, the theoretical evidence as to whether monopoly leads to a reduction in efficiency and social welfare is inconclusive. Consequently, the case for and against the continuation of any particular monopoly must be assessed on an individual basis.

The regulatory problems posed by dominant positions in the private sector can be brought into focus by considering the distinction between technical efficiency and allocative efficiency. In many markets the need of technical efficiency may threaten allocative efficiency by allowing firms to attain dominance due to economies of large size to bolster their position by restrictive or exclusionary practices. Success in this respect may then also create x-inefficiency and thus reduce welfare still further.

(Utton, 1986, p. 135)

Harberger (1954) estimates that the welfare loss from monopolization accounted for 0.1 per cent of US gross national product over the period 1921–8. Kamerschen (1966) reports a much larger estimate of almost 6 per cent of national income for the period 1956–61. Cowling and Mueller (1978) evaluate several measures of welfare loss for the US (1963–6) and the UK (1968–9). They find that in the former case, welfare losses arising from monopoly range from 4 per cent to 13.1 per cent of national income. In the latter, they range from 3.9 per cent to 7.2 per cent. Jenny and Weber (1983) report welfare losses for France ranging from 0.14 per cent to 8.9 per cent for the period 1967–74. Hay and Morris (1991) point out that many of these studies were carried out at national level, and so provide little information concerning the welfare effects of monopoly at industry level. Littlechild (1981) argues that monopoly profits are a temporary phenomenon, and short-run welfare losses should not be overemphasized.

Natural monopoly

As shown earlier (see Section 3.4), a **natural monopoly** is a market in which LRAC is decreasing as output increases over the entire range of outputs that could conceivably be produced, given the location of the market demand function. (This case is illustrated in Figure 3.7.) There is insufficient market demand for any firm to exploit all possible opportunities for savings in average costs through economies of scale; in other words, there is insufficient market demand for any firm to attain the MES (minimum efficient scale) of production. In a natural monopoly, monopoly is always more cost-effective than competition. LRAC is lower if one firm services the entire market than if two (or more) firms share the market between them. In a natural monopoly, fixed costs tend to constitute a large proportion of total costs. The utilities (water, gas, electricity) and telecommunications are the most obvious examples of industries that tend to conform, to some extent, to the textbook case of natural monopoly. Competition would tend to lead to wasteful duplication of infrastructure and delivery systems. The regulation of utilities is examined in Chapter 24.

Price discrimination

As discussed earlier, a monopolist can practise price discrimination in several ways (see Section 13.3). Under **first-degree** (perfect) **price discrimination**, the price per unit of output depends on the identity of the purchaser and on the number of units purchased. Under **second-degree price discrimination**, the price per unit of output depends on the number of units purchased, but not on the identity of the purchaser. All consumers who buy a particular number of units pay the same price per unit. Under **third-degree price discrimination**, the price per unit of output depends on the identity of the purchaser, but not on the number of units purchased. Any consumer can buy as many or as few units as he or she wishes at the same unit price. In each case, the market for the product must be divisible into sub-markets, within which there are different demand conditions (or different price elasticities of demand). These sub-markets must be physically separate either in space or time, so that secondary trade or resale between consumers in different sub-markets is not possible. For example, according to the European Commission (1995), European car manufacturers have practised a form of price discrimination that has resulted in large price disparites between different countries.

Perhaps surprisingly, however, price discrimination should not always be judged pejoratively. The monopolist who adopts a policy of first-degree price discrimination earns an even higher abnormal profit than the monopolist who charges a uniform price, but, on allocative efficiency criteria, the outcome in the former case is preferable. Total output is higher under first-degree price discrimination than under monopoly with uniform pricing, and in the former case the last unit of output produced is sold at a price equivalent to its marginal cost. In the less extreme but more realistic cases of second- and third-degree price discrimination, it is not possible to generalize about the social welfare implications, which can be either positive or negative.

Entry barriers and vertical restraints

Various strategies that a monopolist might adopt in an attempt to raise entry barriers and deter potential entrants were examined earlier (see Section 11.3). These might include limit pricing, predatory pricing and product differentiation or brand proliferation. For example, Myers (1994) suggests predatory pricing in the deregulated UK bus industry led to a decline in the number of bus operators. Another example involves a case brought by the European Commission against Deutsche Post in 2001, in which the company was alleged to have used its monopoly profit from mail delivery to subsidize its prices in the business parcel service market, where it was exposed to competition from United Parcel Services (UPS). The commission found the company had failed to cover its costs in parcel delivery for five years, suggesting a form of predatory pricing.

As shown earlier (see Chapter 20), vertical restraints are conditions and restrictions on trade that are imposed by firms that are linked vertically. Principal forms of vertical restraint include retail price maintenance, foreclosure, territorial exclusivity and quantity dependent pricing (tying or bundling).

Technological progress

According to the **Schumpeterian hypothesis**, market power and monopoly status should be interpreted as the reward for successful innovation (see Section 17.2). For a time, the successful innovating firm becomes a monopoly supplier of a new product; or its mastery of a new process enables it to produce at a lower cost than its rivals, perhaps capturing some or all of their market share by setting a price they are unable to match. However, the market power conferred by successful innovation is always temporary, because in time the new technology will itself be superseded by further technological progress. Successful innovation brings benefits to society, in the form of new products or more efficient production processes. In the past, the competition authorities have often tended to take a benign or favourable view of firms that are perceived to invest heavily in research and development.

Case study 23.1

The Microsoft monopoly in the US

In 1998, the US Department of Justice launched an investigation that accused the Microsoft Corporation of operating a monopoly in the computer industry. Specifically, Microsoft was accused of:

- Operating a monopoly in operating systems in the personal computer industry.

- Using its market power to distort competition in other markets by preventing firms from offering applications that could run on the Microsoft Windows operating system.

- Using its market power to prevent rival firms from developing alternative operating systems

- Engaging in vertical restraints to trade by bundling software products (such as its Internet Explorer application) with operating systems licenced to third-party users.

Microsoft's market power was due to its position as a vertically integrated firm that supplied not only the Windows operating system, but also thousands of applications which ran on this system. Any firm wishing to compete with Microsoft by producing a rival operating system would have to produce a huge number of applications compatible with the alternative operating system. These were described by the Department of Justice as 'applications barriers to entry'. On the supply side, competitors faced barriers to entry due to the cost of capital, while on the demand side competitors faced difficulties in persuading consumers to switch from the numerous established Microsoft products to alternatives.

Microsoft argued that due to the fast pace of technological change in the computing industry, its dominance had arisen naturally, as the outcome of fair competition. Microsoft pointed to the success of other companies in developing rival software systems. It defended itself against charges of bundling by arguing that adding Internet Explorer to Windows represented a technological advance, resulting in the availability of an improved product for end-users. However, the Department of Justice contended that such a strategy had enabled Microsoft to displace the former market leader for internet browsers, Netscape Navigator, by anticompetitive means.

In 2000, Microsoft was found guilty of operating a monopoly in the operating systems market, of using this position to restrain competition, and of the effective monpolization of the internet browser market (by bundling Internet Explorer with Windows). However, the remedies and penalties were not determined immediately. Possible remedies were structural and conduct based. Structural remedies would influence the market structure of the computing industry. Conduct-based remedies would impose limits on Microsoft's business activities. Specific remedies suggested at the time included the following:

■ Breaking the company into two parts: first, an operating systems company to supply the Windows system; and, second, a software applications company. However, this would still leave the operating systems company with a monopoly position in its own market.

■ Breaking Microsoft into several smaller vertically integrated companies that would provide competing operating systems and software applications. However, whether these companies would actually compete is questionable. There would be obvious incentives for collusion. Furthermore, opportunities to exploit technical and learning economies of scale and scope might be lost; or, if there was genuine competition, this might result in wasteful duplication of effort.

■ Force Microsoft to publish or provide details of the Windows code to software producers wishing to develop applications to run on Windows.

■ Force Microsoft to license Windows to any company wishing to buy it, and allow licensees to alter or improve the software as they see fit. This option might lead to a fall in standards and a fragmentation of operating systems.

■ Impose limits on the ways in which Microsoft conducts its business, for example by preventing the extension of its monopoly position into other areas of the computing business. However, this option could prove costly to monitor and enforce.

Microsoft argued that breaking the company into smaller companies would reduce efficiency and stifle future innovation in the computing industry. Talks between a mediator (Judge Richard Posner) and Microsoft, regarding a suitable remedy, broke down in April 2000. Subsequently, Judge Jackson ruled that Microsoft should split its Windows operating systems division from its software applications division. Microsoft appealed against this decision and, in 2001, the Court of Appeal declared the initial judgment was too severe. While Microsoft was guilty of some anticompetitive practices, such as bundling, these should be assessed on a *rule of reason* basis, weighing the benefits to consumers (an efficient, integrated browsing system), against the costs imposed by the lack of effective competition. In November 2002, the Court of Appeal reversed the verdict concerning monopolization of the internet browser market, on the grounds that the relevant market had not been properly defined in the initial judgment. However, Microsoft would be required to remove many of the restrictions preventing competitors from offering applications that would run on Windows. Microsoft would also be required to provide more flexible conditions to third-party users wishing to offer alternative configurations of Windows. Microsoft was also asked to disclose certain technical information to allow rival applications to run on the Window platform.

Source: Various issues of *The Economist* throughout 1999–2002 provide details of the Microsoft case, as does the US Department of Justice website www.usdoj.com. Useful overviews of the economics of the Microsoft case can be found in Evans, D. (2000) An analysis of the government's economic case in US v Microsoft, *Antitrust Bulletin*, 46: 2, 163–251; Fisher, F.M. and Rubinfield, D. (2001) US v Microsoft, *Antitrust Bulletin*, 46, 1–69; Gilbert, R. and Katz, M. (2001) An economist's guide to US v Microsoft, *Journal of Economic Perspectives*, 15, 25–44.

Case study 23.2

Anglo-Lafarge tie-up concerns regulator

Anglo American's planned joint venture with Lafarge to create a £1.8bn building materials group was thrown into question on Tuesday after the Competition Commission warned that it could increase the risk of prices being rigged. The commission is now considering whether to block the deal or force asset sales, with a final report due on May 1. With the UK cement market already in the hands of just four companies, the regulator said it was concerned that further consolidation could squeeze supplies and force prices higher. The competition commission said that although it had not found evidence of collusion, cement prices and profit margins have not been affected in the way it would have anticipated following a drop in cement demand over the past few years.

'We have not reached a view on whether or not there has been co-ordination in the bulk cement market,' said Roger Witcomb of the competition commission. 'But we are concerned that the proposed tie-up would increase the susceptibility of this market to co-ordination.'

Despite the findings, both companies and analysts said they were confident the two companies would be able to avoid an outright cancellation of the merger. 'Whilst this is a setback for the proposed tie-up, the Competition Commission has compiled a list of remedies, therefore this is not a fatal block,' said analysts at Liberum Capital in a note. 'We expect disposals should appease the regulator, noting Lafarge's response that "findings can be remedied".'

The two companies proposed a 50/50 merger of their UK operations in February 2011 with the aim of trimming £60m of annual costs from a joint business that would generate £1.8bn of sales a year.

Four large companies – Lafarge, Heidelberg, Cemex and Anglo American – account for more than 90 per cent of the cement market, 75 per cent of aggregates sales and 70 per cent of ready-mix concrete production in the UK. Despite this the industry is seeking further economies of scale as it grapples with a downturn in public and private sector building.

Anglo American, one of the world's largest mining companies, has been looking to sell Tarmac since 2007 as part of a wider strategy to dispose of non-core business. The deal with Lafarge is believed to create considerable synergies. Anglo American, which trades in Britain through Tarmac, brings a record in aggregates and road building, while Lafarge offers expertise in cement and research.

The commission said it will accept comments on its provisional findings until March 13 and possible remedies until March 6.

Source: Anglo-Lafarge tie-up concerns regulator, © The Financial Times Limited. All Rights Reserved, 21 February 2012 (Plimmer, G. and Jones, A.).

FTC opens formal probe against Google

The US government has opened a formal investigation into the influence over the internet that Google has amassed as a result of its dominance of the search business. The move marks Washington's most significant antitrust intervention in the technology industry since its case against Microsoft more than a decade ago. It caps a widening series of regulatory probes of the search group on both sides of the Atlantic. Google revealed the investigation, launched by the Federal Trade Commission, in a blog post on Friday. 'It's still unclear exactly what the FTC's concerns are, but we're clear about where we stand,' wrote Amit Singhal, the engineer in charge of Google's algorithms, which determine where other sites appear in the company's search rankings. 'Since the beginning, we have been guided by the idea that if we focus on the user, all else will follow.'

Google has been the subject of an investigation by Brussels since last autumn, after complaints that the company had harmed some websites by deliberately pushing them down its search rankings and that it had abused its dominance of search advertising. Complaints have followed more recently that Google puts its own services ahead of those of other web companies, robbing rivals of internet traffic. The US Department of Justice recently cleared Google's acquisition of travel service ITA, despite claims from rivals that it would let the company dominate what has become the largest sector in online commerce.

The FTC has been gathering information from rivals and other companies that believe they have been harmed by Google's search practices, said people familiar with the discussions.

On Friday, Google said it had 'received formal notification' of the agency's review. Washington does not announce antitrust investigations, but such studies become formal when the regulators issue subpoenas, known as civil investigative demands, under which they can start gathering evidence under oath.

Google's defence is likely to rest heavily on the benefits it brings to internet users and advertisers, said antitrust lawyers. 'The FTC has got a significant burden of finding that consumers are harmed by Google's conduct,' said David Balto, a former antitrust attorney at the FTC and senior fellow at American Progress. 'Just because there is a chorus of complaining by competitors doesn't mean that consumers are harmed.' The attorneys-general of California, New York and Ohio have also joined Texas in launching their own enquiries, the Financial Times reported this week. 'We respect the FTC's process and will be working with them [as we have with other agencies] over the coming months to answer questions about Google and our services,' Google's Mr Singhal wrote.

Source: FTC opens formal probe against Google, © The Financial Times Limited. All Rights Reserved, 24 June 2011 (Waters, R. and Kennard, M.).

23.3 Elements of competition policy

Competition policy aims to promote competition and control or eliminate abuses of market power. More specifically, competition policy may seek to increase efficiency, promote innovation, or improve consumer choice.

> Competition policy has its central economic goal as the preservation and promotion of the competitive process, a process which encourages efficiency in the production and allocation of goods and services over time, through its effects on innovation and adjustment to technological change, a dynamic process of sustained economic growth.
>
> *(OECD, 1984, para. 232)*

> The role of competition policy is to ensure that competition is indeed effective. To this end, competition policy stops, penalizes and deters anti-competitive actions by suppliers. It extends also to the unnecessary restrictions on competition stemming from government laws and regulation. And a full effective competition policy also embraces measures to make markets work more competitively by enhancing the power of consumer choice.
>
> *(Vickers, 2002, p. 8)*

Competition policy deals with three principal areas: monopoly, merger and restrictive practices. First, **monopoly policy** addresses existing monopolies. If a firm has sufficient market power, its dominant position may enable it to pursue policies detrimental to competition or the wider public interest. The competition authorities must weigh this danger against the possible benefits (such as cost savings through economies of scale) of large-scale operation.

Second, **merger policy** deals with situations where two or more firms propose a merger that may create a dominant position in the market for the newly merged entity. Merger policy considers whether the increased concentration of market power arising from a merger is in the public interest. For example, the possible benefits of rationalization must be weighed against the possible cost in terms of potential abuse of market power. Merger policy should not be so restrictive as to provide inefficient management with complete protection from the threat of being taken over. The threat of merger or takeover can, in some cases, act as a spur to managerial efficiency (see Section 18.3).

Third, **restrictive practices policy** examines cases where a firm or a group of firms is involved in restrictive practices of one type or another that may prove damaging to competition or the wider public interest. Such practices might include price-fixing agreements, predatory pricing and vertical restraints (Pickering, 1982). As shown earlier (see Chapter 8), an agreement to collude might be either formal (explicit) or informal (implicit or tacit). **Horizontal agreements** involve firms in the same industry, and are primarily aimed at reducing competition. Examples include common pricing policies, production quotas, market allocation, or sharing of information on prices, output and quality. **Vertical agreements** involve firms operating at successive stages of production or distribution, such as exclusive dealing contracts and resale price maintenance.

> If companies seek to eliminate or at least to reduce competition between themselves, they will normally try to do so by some form of agreement or concerted practice; these are classified as horizontal since they are made by undertakings operating at a similar level, for example as manufacturers or retailers. By contrast vertical agreements are those where relationships of the parties are complementary, for example when a supplier makes a distribution agreement with a dealer or a patent owner enters into a licence agreement with a licensee.
>
> *(Goyder, 2003, pp. 11–12)*

The implementation of monopoly, restrictive practices and merger policy requires a practical method for measuring market power. Seller concentration and market share measures are the most obvious candidates (see Section 9.4). According to Shepherd (1997), abuses of market power are most likely to take place in industries with four-firm concentration ratios (CR_4) exceeding 60 per cent and the attentions of the competition authorities should be focused on such cases. Of course, the market share of an individual firm is also highly relevant as an indicator of market power. As a rule-of-thumb, a firm with a market share exceeding 30 per cent has at many times been assumed by the UK competition authorities to be dominant. However (as shown in Section 11.5) according to the contestable markets approach of Baumol *et al.* (1982), provided entry barriers are not insurmountable and markets are contestable, the threat of entry and competition constrains the pricing policy of a firm that might appear to have market power according to a standard seller concentration measure, perhaps even to the extent that only a normal profit can be earned. In assessing the degree of market power, it is therefore relevant to ask questions concerning the ease of entry.

In order to assess whether an abuse of market power is taking place, it is first necessary to define the extent of the relevant market. Naturally, this decision has major implications for the values of the market power indicators mentioned above, seller concentration and market share. If a narrow market definition is employed, market power may be overstated. Conversely, if a wide market definition is employed, market power may be understated and genuine abuses might not even be investigated. The definition of any market contains both a product dimension and a geographic dimension (see Section 9.2). The product market definition should include all products that are close substitutes for one another, both in consumption and in production. In practice, however, it is not usually straightforward to decide which products to include within this definition. Budweiser lager might be included in the same market as Stella Artois, but do other beers (bitter and real ale) belong in the same product market? Should other beverages, such as soft drinks, tea, coffee, wines and spirits, be included? Geographic market definitions present similar problems. Is the relevant geographic market defined at a local, regional, national or international level? The market definition should reflect the true competitive situation. If it fails to do so, competition policy decisions will be biased. In practice, the competition authorities in the UK and elsewhere tend to rely on a range of market definitions. Recent exchanges between antitrust economists in the US have begun to question whether market definitions should be calculated at all (Kaplow, 2010; Werden, 2012).

It is also relevant to note that market definitions are not static, but are subject to change over time due to changes in technology or consumer tastes. Therefore, in some cases, it might be appropriate to incorporate a dynamic element into market definitions. For example, in 2002, Tetra (a carton packaging firm with a world market share of around 80 per cent) sought to merge with Sidel (a plastics packaging firm with a world market share of around 60 per cent). While the European Commission concluded the relevant markets were separate, it was likely they would tend to converge over time. Therefore the proposed merger would reduce competition in the long run.

Most economists would recognize that perfect competition is a theoretical ideal, which is highly unlikely to prevail in practice (Clark, 1940; Sosnick, 1958; Reid, 1987). Therefore, a more realistic objective for competition policy might be to foster **workable competition**. This approach searches for aspects of structure and conduct that can be adjusted in order to bring about a favourable performance outcome. In other words, competition policy should start from a definition of good performance, and aim to bring into being the forms of industry structure and conduct that are most likely to produce good performance.

The workable competition approach has several drawbacks. First, the weights that should be attached to each dimension of performance are not specified. Second, any definition of favourable performance is subjective to some extent. There is scope for disagreement as to the appropriate criteria for the implementation of competition policy based on the concept of workable competition. Stigler (1968) criticizes the workable competition approach for its serious ambiguity. According to the Austrian school, 'departures from the optimality conditions of perfectly competitive equilibrium are not a threat to any relevant notion of economic efficiency. Equilibrium is not an attainable ideal, nor are perfect or "near perfect" competition attainable' (Kirzner, 1997b, p. 59).

23.4 Implementation of competition policy

The United States

The modern framework for antitrust or competition law in the US was established by the Sherman Act of 1890, the Clayton Act of 1914 and the Federal Trade Commission Act of 1914. These pieces of legislation codified previous American and English common law concerning restraint of trade. The term antitrust originated in the formation by US corporations in the late nineteenth century of trusts to conceal the nature of their restrictive practices. Section 1 of the Sherman

Act prohibits restraints on trade in the form of 'contracts, combinations and conspiracies'. Section 2 of the Act deals with monopolies, monopolization and conspiracies to monopolize. The Act prescribes criminal penalties in the form of fines or imprisonment for violators.

Enforcement of the Sherman Act was patchy during the years immediately following its enactment. However, US Supreme Court rulings in 1911 against two major trusts, Standard Oil and American Tobacco, signalled the introduction of a tougher approach. The Standard Oil case is perhaps the most famous in the history of US antitrust policy. Formed in Ohio in 1870 by the industrialist John D. Rockefeller with partners including his brother William, Standard Oil rapidly achieved a position of dominance in the embryonic US oil industry through a series of questionable business practices. By 1890 Standard Oil controlled 88 per cent of refined oil flows in the US. Although its market share had fallen to 64 per cent by 1911, the Supreme Court declared Standard Oil to be an unreasonable monopoly. It was adjudged guilty of a number of forms of unfair practice, including predatory pricing through localized price-cutting, and vertical restraints achieved through acquisitions of distribution networks (pipelines and railroads). The Court ordered the break-up of Standard Oil into 34 independent companies, several of which themselves became dominant players in the global oil industry throughout the twentieth century and beyond. For example, Standard Oil Company of New Jersey eventually became Exxon, Standard Oil Company of New York became Mobil, and Standard Oil of California became Chevron. Shortly after the Standard Oil case, the Supreme Court passed a similar verdict against American Tobacco, which had engaged in even more aggressive predatory pricing practices than Standard Oil in its campaign to control the market for chewing tobacco. In the 1911 Standard Oil case the Supreme Court also developed the **rule of reason** doctrine which specified that only monopolies and contracts which restrained trade *unreasonably* were subject to action under the Sherman Act. The possession of monopoly or market power was not illegal in itself.

The Sherman Act covers monopoly, price-fixing and other forms of restrictive practice on the part of independent firms, but it does not provide for the scrutiny or prohibition of mergers. Therefore, independent firms wishing to collude had the option of merging in order to place themselves beyond the reach of the legislation. The Clayton Act extended antitrust policy to cover mergers that were deemed capable of damaging competition, and introduced provisions covering a number of other forms of restrictive practice that were originally excluded from the Sherman Act. These included price discrimination in cases where the effect is a reduction in competition or the creation of a monopoly, exclusive dealings and tying, and interlocking directorships in competing companies. The Federal Trade Commission Act established the Federal Trade Commission (FTC) as the agency charged with enforcement of the Clayton Act. The FTC was awarded powers to intervene in a wide range of situations involving very broadly defined 'unfair methods of competition'. Both the FTC and the US Department of Justice can initiate actions under the US antitrust legislation. Most cases are precipitated by a complaint from a competitor, a report in the press or a report from a government agency.

The legislative framework for US antitrust policy that was established in the late nineteenth and early twentieth centuries has remained intact subsequently, subject to modifications such as the Robinson-Patman Act of 1936, which extended the provisions for dealing with price discrimination; and the Celler-Kefauver Act of 1950, which extended the coverage of the Clayton Act to mergers involving the acquisition of assets, as well as those involving stock acquisition. However, the interpretation and strength of enforcement has varied over time with political and intellectual trends, and with changes to the structure of the economy. For example, by acquitting US Steel of conspiring to fix prices in a case brought in 1920, the Supreme Court established a precedent that considerably weakened the interpretation of Section 2 of the Sherman Act for the next 25 years. US Steel had been charged with cooperating with its competitors through trade meetings and the notorious 'dinners' hosted by Judge Elbert Gary, the company president, at which discussions took place with competitors over matters related to pricing. The Supreme Court ruled that because US Steel needed to cooperate with its competitors, it could not be held to constitute a monopoly.

A further landmark ruling came with the Alcoa case of 1945, in which the Aluminium Company of America (Alcoa) was charged with monopolizing the market for aluminium ingots. Issues of market definition were key to the outcome of the Alcoa case. The District Court, which had originally acquitted Alcoa, defined the company's market share in 1937 as 33 per cent, by including secondary ingot (produced from scrap aluminium) in the same market as primary ingot. However, the New York Court of Appeals, which overturned the District Court's ruling, ruled that Alcoa's dominance of primary ingot production gave it indirect control over the market for secondary ingots, and an overall market share in 1937 of 90 per cent. Although there was little evidence of predatory pricing or other aggressive anti-competitive practice on the part of Alcoa (in contrast to Standard Oil and American Tobacco), the Court of Appeal ruled that an overwhelming market share was in itself a violation of Section 2 of the Sherman Act, unless there were economies of scale such that the industry would take the form of a natural monopoly.

The Alcoa case signalled the onset of a relatively stringent and aggressive phase in the implementation of antitrust policy in the US, which continued from the mid-1940s until the mid- to late 1970s. Several academic economists and lawyers connected to the Chicago school became increasingly vocal in their criticism of the interventionist nature of antitrust policy during this phase, arguing that there was a tendency for the implementation of policy to be biased towards favouring certain groups and harming others, and therefore subject to influence through political lobbying. Others argued that the potential efficiency gains associated with large-scale and vertical integration should carry greater weight in determining the outcome of merger cases brought under the antitrust legislation. As US manufacturers struggled to maintain competitiveness in world export markets during the 1970s, this efficiency argument attracted increasing levels of sympathy. At the start of the 1980s, the incoming administration of President Ronald Reagan was highly receptive to the anti-interventionist economic philosophy of the Chicago school.

During the 1980s and 1990s, a less interventionist and more 'hands-off' approach to antitrust policy was informed by the view that market forces should be allowed to select the most efficient firms, unless there were compelling reasons otherwise. It became more difficult to secure a judgment against a firm on antitrust grounds, especially in cases involving monopolization or vertical restraints. In 1977, a total of 1,611 private antitrust cases were filed in the US District Courts, but by 1989 this total had fallen to 638 (Motta, 2004). More recently, there have been signs of a partial reversion towards a more stringent and interventionist approach once again, with the current approach having been characterized as lying 'somewhere between the interventionism of the 60s and the laissez faire of the 80s' (Motta, 2004, p. 9). An important development in the prosecution of cases involving cartels or other forms of collusion during the 2000s has been the imposition by the courts of lengthy prison sentences in several high-profile cases, and an increased willingness to enter into plea-bargaining or grant amnesties to whistle-blowers.

The European Union

During the first half of the twentieth century, the authorities in many European countries took a more tolerant view of monopoly and restrictive practices than those in the US. Although competition was seen as desirable, considerations of scale and efficiency often took precedence. In countries such as France, Germany and the UK, the suspicions of Americans concerning big business and collusion were often felt to be overblown, and incompatible with their own national institutions and traditions. Since the Second World War, however, there has been a progressive strengthening of antitrust legislation throughout Europe. Although some important differences remain between the American and European models, in many respects European provision has converged towards the American model. Ironically, by the start of the twenty-first century the European approach could be characterized as more stringent than that of the US in some respects. Many European governments were instinctively hostile towards the laissez-faire, non-interventionist approach that had been influential or dominant in the US since the 1980s. They were also sceptical of the view that market forces should be allowed to select the most efficient firms unless there were compelling reasons to the contrary.

The stated objective of EU competition policy is the promotion of competition within the European Single Market. The cornerstones of EU competition policy are Articles 101 and 102 of the Treaty of Lisbon, which was concluded in 2007 and came into force in early 2009. These articles incorporate Articles 85 and 86 of the earlier Treaty of Rome. In accordance with the principle of subsidiarity, the scope of Articles 101 and 10 is confined to firms based in EU member states that trade in other EU states. These articles do not apply to the activities of domestic firms trading within the domestic market. Cases are investigated and the articles are enforced by the Competition Directorate-General IV, which has the power to fine companies up to 10 per cent of their annual worldwide turnover. The Directorate-General IV Leniency programme offers reductions in fines of between 10 per cent and 100 per cent for cooperation or provision of information relating to violations of Article 101.

Article 101 deals with restrictive practices, prohibiting agreements between firms from EU member states that prevent or restrict competition. The prohibition covers both horizontal and vertical agreements. For example, agreements to fix prices, production quotas or to share markets are all deemed illegal. However, exemptions are available if it can be shown the benefits outweigh the costs to consumers. For example, an agreement might be exempt if it led to higher production, resulting in economies of scale, improvements in efficiency in distribution, or technological progress, with consumers ultimately benefiting from lower prices or improvements in quality. Block exemptions are also available, typically with respect to vertical agreements between firms at different stages of the supply chain, in cases where the parties involved do not exercise significant market power. For example, it is accepted that agreements between a manufacturer and a distributor do not necessarily reduce competition. At the end of 2000, a block exemption covering distribution agreements permitted agreements between firms at different stages of the supply chain, as long as the seller (buyer) does not account for at least 30 per cent of the relevant seller (buyer) market. Agreements covering market partitioning, price fixing and resale price maintenance remain illegal.

Article 102 regulates possible abuses of monopoly power, such as monopoly pricing, predatory pricing and price discrimination. An individual firm occupies a dominant position if it can prevent competition, behave independently of competitors, and exercise control over production and prices. In practice, an investigation is triggered if a single firm has a 40 per cent share of the relevant market. Price-fixing, the restriction of production or technical development to the detriment of consumers, a refusal to trade with certain customers, and the imposition of unfair terms or restrictions are recognized forms of abuse of a dominant position. A landmark case in 1978 involved the prices charged for bananas by the United Brands company to distributors in EU countries. Higher prices charged to distributors in Denmark and Germany than to those in Ireland, Belgium, the Netherlands and Luxembourg were found to be unjustifiable on criteria such as cost or risk. In contrast to Article 101, there are no provisions for exemptions from Article 102. Figure 23.2 shows the number of cartel and antitrust decisions over the period 2005–10.

Mergers are regulated by Regulation 139/2004, which came into force in May 2004, covering mergers, acquisitions and joint mergers. A horizontal merger qualifies for investigation if it has a fundamental effect on competition within the EU. Regulation 139/2004 is intended to streamline and improve the transparency of merger investigations. It contains guidelines for the assessment of mergers based on economic indicators, and guidelines for firms concerning their rights in the event of a merger being disallowed. The Merger Task Force, which previously had responsibility for investigating proposed mergers, was disbanded.

Lyons (2003) suggests that these changes were motivated by increased recognition of the usefulness of economic analysis in informing competition policy, and a need to streamline procedures following the accession of ten new member states to the EU in May 2004. Lyons cites three successful appeals (Airtours/First Choice; Schneider/Le Grand; and Tetra/Sidel) against decisions taken under the pre-2004 arrangements. In each case the Merger Task Force was criticized

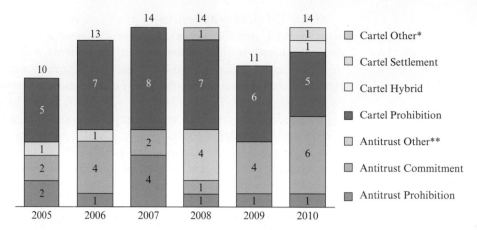

Figure 23.2 Number of antitrust and cartels enforcement decisions per year and type, 2005–10

* Rejection of complaint

**Rejection of complaint, procedural infringement, penalty payment

Source: DG Competition, Eurostat.

for using inappropriate economic theory, failing to take account of changing industry conditions and misinterpreting documentary evidence.

Notification of any merger should be made to Competition Directorate-General IV not more than one week after a bid is placed or a deal announced. Failure to notify may result in a fine. The Directorate reviews any proposed merger in two phases. Phase I, the initial investigation, is completed within one month, and may or may not trigger a more detailed Phase II investigation. Phase II, which is normally completed within four months, examines the implications of the proposed merger for competition (based on the dominance test) and the single market. The investigation invites views and written submissions from customers, suppliers and competitors. The Directorate-General IV takes the final decision as to whether an investigation takes place and whether a merger is permitted to proceed. Figure 23.3 shows the number of merger decisions over the period 2005–10.

Most merger investigations weigh the implications for competition and the single market against any possible benefits, which might include scale economies or technological advance. It is unusual for a merger to be allowed to proceed if it creates or strengthens a dominant position. However, any investigation will take account of the extent to which buyer power acts as a countervailing force against the competitive dominance brought about by the proposed merger. If a merger is disallowed, the parties involved can appeal to the Court of First Instance and, ultimately, to the European Court of Justice.

Control over state aid is a further important strand of EU competition policy, regulated by Article 107 of the Treaty of Lisbon. Article 107 establishes a member state's right to deliver public services, but requires that public service providers should otherwise be subject to the same rules on collusion and abuses of market power as firms in the private sector. The Article specifies rules precluding the deployment of state aid or subsidies in a manner that distorts

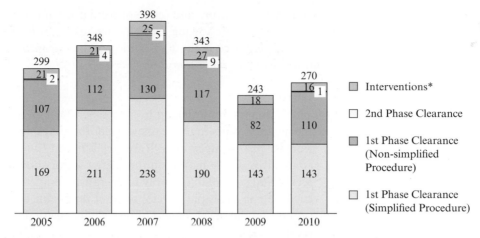

Figure 23.3 Number of merger final decisions per year and type, 2005–10

* Includes one prohibition in 2007

Source: DG Competition, Eurostat.

competition, but also grants exemptions in a number of cases where state intervention is necessary to maintain the smooth functioning of the economy. For example, aid targeted at research and development, the promotion of SMEs, and regional economic development, is normally permitted. EU rules on state aid control permit a failing company to be rescued once subject to approval, which requires the articulation of a feasible and coherent plan to restore the firm's long-term viability. Figure 23.4 shows the evolution of total state aid in the EU over the period 2004–9.

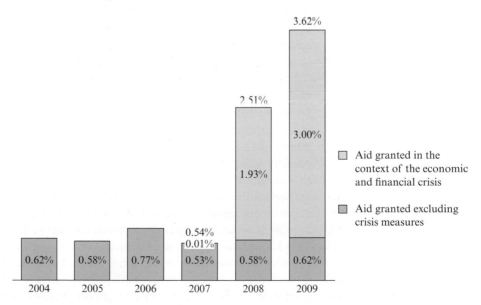

Figure 23.4 Evolution of total state aid granted by Member States as % of GDP in the EU, 2004–9

Source: DG Competition, Eurostat.

To illustrate the nature and scope of regulatory intervention under EU competition policy, the following extracts are taken from a summary of sector developments reported in the 2010 edition of the European Commission's (2011) annual *Report on Competition Policy*.

Energy

The Commission presented in November 2010 its energy strategy for the next ten years in the framework of the Flagship Initiative of the Europe 2020 strategy on a 'Resource Efficient Europe'. An open and competitive single market in the energy sector should contribute to a secure and sustainable supply of energy at competitive prices by encouraging the rapid development of renewable energies and by promoting the development of new environmentally friendly technologies.

Financial services

The financial crisis that began in 2007 has continued to affect the financial sector in most EU countries until the time of writing in 2012. The temporary regulatory framework established in 2008 was further extended to 2011 under tightened conditions. Its implementation was the main focus of competition enforcement, in particular in the field of restructuring of supported financial institutions.

The Single Euro Payments Area (SEPA) has continued to be an important focus of antitrust policy in financial services, in particular through informal dialogue with the European Payments Council. For instance it was clarified that SEPA compliant card schemes do not need to cover all 32 States of the SEPA territory, giving new schemes a real chance of entering the market. The Commission adopted a proposal on establishing technical requirements for credit transfers and direct debits in Euros in December 2010.

Information technology

In spring 2010, the Commission launched two parallel preliminary investigations into business practices by Apple relating to the iPhone. Apple had made its warranty repairs service available only in the country where the iPhone was bought, which could have potentially led to a partitioning of the EEA market. Apple had also restricted the terms and conditions of its licence agreement with independent developers of applications requiring the use of Apple's native programming tools and approved software languages to the detriment of third-party software. This could have closed off competition from applications developed for running on other mobile platforms. After Apple decided in September 2010 to introduce cross-border iPhone warranty repair services within the EEA, and to relax the restrictions on development tools for iPhone apps, the Commission decided to close both investigations.

Media

The Commission continued to approve state financing for public service broadcasters where both the public service remit and the financing are determined in full transparency and where state funding does not exceed what is necessary to fulfil the public service mission. On 20 July 2010, the Commission closed with a positive decision the formal investigations into the new financing system for public service broadcasters in France and Spain, and closed the investigation into the existing financing regime for the Dutch public service broadcasters, following amendments and formal commitments by the Netherlands

Automotive industry

On 27 May 2010, the Commission adopted new competition rules for agreements between vehicle manufacturers and their authorised dealers, repairers and spare parts distributors. The new framework applies the general Vertical Block Exemption Regulation adopted in April 2010 to such agreements from 2010 as regards second-hand markets, and 2013 as regards the markets for the sale of new vehicles. In addition, the Commission adopted Regulation 461/2010157, which sets out three supplementary hardcore clauses relating to spare parts distribution, and a detailed set of supplementary guidelines for assessing vertical agreements. The new rules represent a flexible and proportionate response to the differing intensities of competition on the primary and second-hand markets, and broadly align the rules applicable to agreements between car manufacturers and their authorised dealers, repairers and spare-parts distributors with the general regime.

Transport

The Commission put an end to a major antitrust case under Article 101 in the air transport sector by making legally binding commitments offered by British Airways, American Airlines and Iberia in response to the competition concerns stemming from their agreement to coordinate prices, capacity, schedules, marketing and sales and to share revenues on transatlantic routes. To address the identified competition concerns, the three airline companies committed to release seven slot pairs at London Heathrow or London Gatwick airports on four routes, to offer combined fares and special pro-rate agreements and provide competitors access to the parties' frequent flyer programmes. This decision will entail significant benefits for European consumers by strengthening competition on transatlantic flights, in particular from London.

Postal services

The Commission continued in 2010 its investigation opened in 2007 into the alleged overcompensation of Deutsche Post AG for carrying out its universal service obligations from 1989 to 2007. Following the confirmation of the annulment of the 2002 Commission decision by the Court of Justice, the ongoing investigation follows, as demanded by the Court of Justice, a comprehensive approach including all universal services provided by Deutsche Post.

The United Kingdom

Before 1998 in the UK, regulation of monopoly and the scrutiny of merger proposals was the responsibility of the Monopolies and Mergers Commission (MMC), originally established in 1948 and reconstituted in 1965. Restrictive practices were policed by the Restrictive Practices Court (RPC), originally established in 1956. The Competition Act 1998 and the Enterprise Act 2002 are the two principal pieces of legislation that established the current framework for the conduct of competition policy in the UK. The Competition Act of 1998 rationalized and consolidated competition policy, bringing it into line with EU norms. The Act dissolved the Restrictive Practices Court, and set up a new Competition Commission to take over the responsibilities of the Monopolies and Mergers Commission. Competition policy in the UK is the responsibility of the Office of Fair Trading (OFT) and the Competition Commission. The OFT investigates complaints of anticompetitive practices and, if these complaints are upheld, refers the findings to the Competition Commission. In May 2012, the UK Government's Enterprise and Regulatory Reform Bill signalled the creation of a new Competition and Markets Authority, which consolidates the Competition Commission and the Office of Fair Trading into a single regulatory authority.

The Competition Act consists of two main components, known as chapter prohibitions. The **Chapter I prohibition** deals with anticompetitive (restrictive) practices, and the **Chapter II prohibition** deals with abuses of dominant (or monopoly) positions. Both chapters are concerned with promoting competition. Section 60 requires the enforcement of the act and any investigations to be consistent with EU competition policy.

The Chapter I prohibition applies to (formal or informal) agreements between firms which prevent, distort or otherwise affect trade within the UK. Agreements which fall under the remit of the act include:

■ agreements to fix buying or selling prices;

■ agreements to share markets;

■ agreements to limit production;

■ agreements relating to collusive tendering;

■ agreements involving the sharing of information.

Exemptions can be granted if the agreement improves the production or distribution of goods and services, or promotes technological progress, leading to substantial benefits for consumers.

The Chapter I prohibition is closely related to **Article 101** of the EU's Treaty of Lisbon. In cases of investigative overlap under the terms of Chapter I and the equivalent Article 101, the Competition Directorate-General IV takes charge of the investigation. An exemption granted under Article 101 automatically implies a parallel exemption from the Chapter I prohibition. However, an exemption from the Chapter I prohibition does not automatically lead to an exemption from Article 101.

The Chapter II prohibition is based on **Article 102** of the Treaty of Lisbon, and deals with the possible abuse of market power by monopolies. The investigation of a dominant position comprises a two-stage test, to assess whether the firm is dominant in the relevant market and, if so, whether the firm is abusing its position. Practices that constitute abuse include charging an excessive price, price discrimination, various forms of predatory competition, vertical restraints and refusals to supply. For example, in 2001 Napp Pharmaceuticals was fined £3.2m for overcharging NHS hospitals and pharmacies for the supply of morphine. Napp was convicted of charging between 33 per cent and 67 per cent more than other firms that were selling similar products in other markets. Section 36 of the Act specifies the penalties for violation of either of the chapter prohibitions. The maximum penalty is 10 per cent of annual turnover for each year that the violation takes place, up to a maximum of 3 years.

The Enterprise Act 2002 strengthened the regulatory framework for UK competition policy. The act established the OFT as a legal entity, and provided guidelines with respect to the OFT's day-to-day running, investigative powers, and operating and reporting procedures. The act sought to improve the use of quantitative and qualitative analysis in reaching expert and independent decisions.

The act also introduced a new merger policy which is based on economic analysis of the likely effects on competition (via the substantial lessening of competition, (SLC) test), rather than vague public interest concerns. In cases of disallowed mergers, firms have the right to appeal to the Competition Appeals Tribunal (CAT). The process of investigation and enforcement has been made more transparent, in line with EU practice. The act also strengthened the punishment regime for managers convicted of anticompetitive practice. Harsh penalties (up to five years imprisonment) can be imposed on managers found guilty of price fixing and related offences.

Evaluation of UK and EU competition policy

For most of the post-war period, the policy approach of the UK authorities towards the regulation of monopoly and merger has been relatively cautious, and has been implemented on a case-by-case basis. The question posed by regulators is not whether a firm has monopoly power, but whether or not this power is used in a way that is detrimental to the wider public interest. In contrast, the approach taken towards the regulation of restrictive practices has usually been more stringent in principle, although it has encountered difficulties in its execution.

It seems likely that tacit forms of collusion have been widespread, and difficult for the authorities to uncover (Rees, 1993a,b). For most of the post-war period, the risk of detection was small and penalties in the event of detection were light (Utton, 2000). For example, prior to the Competition Act 1998, there were no fines for first offenders: 'it is as though the police having captured a bank robber red-handed, inform him that he has broken the law and should not do it again, but then let him go with the fruits of his crime' (Williams, 1993, cited in Utton, 2000, p. 276).

In an extensive evaluation of the pre-1998 competition policy arrangements in the UK, Davies *et al.* (1999) investigate the determinants of MMC decisions against monopolies. The MMC ruled against roughly two-thirds of the 73 cases examined in the study. Of these cases, 36 referred to pricing issues (monopoly pricing, predatory pricing and collusion), and 37 referred to vertical restraints (vertical integration, resale price maintenance, tie-in sales, exclusivity in distribution and purchasing). Among the cases where the MMC ruled against the firms, recommendations included the termination of a restrictive practice (34 cases), price controls (nine cases) and divestment of assets (nine cases).

Davies *et al.* use a statistical model to identify the factors most likely to influence the probability of the MMC ruling against a firm or group of firms. Explanatory variables include indicators of market structure, such as concentration, rates of entry and market shares; indicators of conduct covering areas such as vertical integration, exclusive purchasing, exclusive distribution, monopoly, predatory pricing, price discrimination and collusion; and variables to allow for changes in the MMC's decisions over time, and to identify whether or not the investigation was a repeat referral. The estimated model suggests the greater the market share of the biggest firm in the industry, the more likely it was that the MMC would rule against the monopoly practice. The MMC was more likely to rule against in cases involving exclusive dealing, but less likely to do so in cases involving vertical restraints. The MMC was more likely to rule against in the 1970s and 1980s than in the 1990s.

It is often easier to prevent an increase in seller concentration by preventing a merger before it takes place than by breaking up an incumbent firm that already occupies a dominant position. Weir (1992, 1993) analyzes MMC decisions on referred mergers using a sample of 73 published reports covering the period 1974–90. The sample is split into two groups: cases where the MMC thought the merger would reduce competition; and cases where the MMC thought the merger would have no effect on competition. Regression analysis is used to identify the factors that influence the judgment as to whether a merger was in the public interest. Factors investigated include the effects of the merger on prices, market shares, profits, product quality, efficiency, research and development expenditure and the UK balance of payments. The analysis distinguishes between horizontal, vertical and conglomerate mergers. Unsurprisingly, mergers were more likely to be permitted in cases where the MMC thought competition would increase. Expectations of lower prices, cost savings, increased expenditure on research and development, or a benefit to the balance of payments increased the likelihood of a positive verdict.

In 2001, the DTI commissioned Price Waterhouse to carry out an assessment of UK competition policy, in comparison with other EU and OECD countries including the US, Germany, Australia, France, Italy, Ireland, the Netherlands, Spain, Sweden and Switzerland (Department of Trade and Industry, 2001). Experts (including senior officials from competition authorities, multinational companies, competition lawyers, academic economists and representatives of consumer bodies) were asked to assess a number of factors relating to the effectiveness of competition policy, including:

- clarity of policy objectives;

- competence of economic and legal analysis;

- political independence;

- quality of leadership within competition authorities;

- transparency of procedures;

- communication with the general public.

The experts were also invited to suggest improvements to the UK's arrangements. Each country was assigned a score relative to an EU benchmark. The UK was deemed to have a competition policy regime less effective than the US and Germany, but more effective than the average for the other OECD countries included in the study. The UK was praised for its economic analysis, transparency of procedures and speed of decision-making in investigations of monopolies. However, relative to the EU, UK merger policy was criticized as being less politically independent, providing a lower quality of legal analysis, and slower in taking decisions. The report suggested abandoning the vague notion of public interest in favour of a competition-based test for the assessment of proposed mergers. Follow-up reports (Department of Trade and Industry, 2004, 2007) indicate UK merger policy has improved relative to the EU since 2001. This may be partly as a consequence of difficulties experienced by the EU, in the form of successful appeals by the firms involved in several high-profile merger cases (Lyons, 2003). While UK monopoly policy was rated as strong, policy towards cartels still lacks some clarity; although the introduction of the Competition Appeals Tribunal has improved transparency. Further simplification of procedures and speeding up decisions would improve the performance of the competition regime further

A report commissioned by the OFT (2007) examines the extent to which UK competition policy arrangements deterred anticompetitive behaviour. Face-to-face and telephone interviews with lawyers, economists and company executives were used to ascertain the extent to which OFT scrutiny constrained behaviour. Merger proposals were less likely to proceed if there had been a recent Competition Commission (CC) inquiry into the sector concerned. Lawyers and economists perceived that infringement rulings under the Competition Act concerning anticompetitive practices had a greater deterrent effect on firms operating in the same sector as the subject of the ruling, than on firms operating in other sectors. However, company executives did not share this perception.

Davies (2010) conducts an in-depth analysis to examine impact estimation methodologies utilised by UK competition authorities. He concludes '. . . no other Competition Authority worldwide takes impact estimation more seriously . . .' and 'much of OFT's work in this area is well-founded in up-to-date appropriate academic literatures' (Davies, 2010, p. 37).

Overall, the UK's 1998 and 2002 legislation, together with the stricter provisions that are effective at EU level, has strengthened the UK's competition policy regime significantly. Emphasis is placed on serving the needs of consumers and enhancing the productivity and competitiveness of UK industry. OFT (2007) recommends further improvement through increased publicity and education, faster decision-taking and an increased willingness to initiate criminal prosecutions in cases involving cartels.

At EU level, a study by the EU Directorate-General for Competition (2005) examines the types of remedy imposed if competition was deemed to be restricted. Of the 96 remedies examined, 80 per cent were within an industry (horizontal competition concerns, such as monopoly pricing). Fourteen per cent of remedies involved a combination of both within and across industry (vertical concerns such as foreclosure), and 6 per cent involved pure vertical concerns. Resolution of horizontal, and the combination of horizontal and vertical concerns, was most commonly achieved through a transfer of market share. Vertical concerns were often addressed by commitments to grant access to suppliers or networks.

Several studies have presented statistical analyses of the regulatory treatment of merger proposals at EU level. For example, Bergman *et al.* (2005) examine the factors that influence the probability of an in-depth investigation of a merger proposal taking place, and the probability that the merger is prohibited. These probabilities increase when the market shares are high and when entry barriers are high. No significant evidence of political interference is found. Similarly, Bougette and Turolla (2006) find the market power, size and sectoral affiliation of the acquiring firm are all signifcant factors in determining whether an in-depth investigation of a proposed merger takes place. Aktas *et al.* (2007) find there is a higher probability of intervention in merger proposals where the bidding firm is foreign, lending some support to the allegation that EU merger policy is protectionist.

Duso *et al.* (2007) assess whether the stock market anticipated that merger proposals would be pro-competitive (indicated by a decline in rival firms' stock prices) or anticompetitive (indicated by an increase in rival firms' stock prices). Mergers the stock market identified as pro-competitive that were prohibited or had remedies imposed are classed as Type I errors; and mergers identified as anticompetitive that were allowed to proceed are classed as Type II errors. Of 167 merger proposals examined in the study, 28 per cent resulted in Type I errors and 23 per cent resulted in Type II errors. The pattern is partially explained by country and industry effects.

23.5　Summary

The economic basis for competition policy rests in large measure on the theoretical case for and against monopoly. According to the neoclassical theory of the firm, under monopoly, market price is higher and output is lower than under perfect competition. The monopolist typically fails to produce at the minimum efficient scale, and therefore fails to produce at the lowest attainable average cost. The monopolist earns an abnormal profit in the long run, while the perfectly competitive firm earns only a normal profit. Under monopoly, there is allocative inefficiency because price exceeds marginal cost. Industry output is too low, and welfare could be increased by producing more output. Under monopoly, there may also be productive inefficiency, if a lack of competitive pressure implies a monopolist becomes complacent or lazy, failing to achieve full technical or economic efficiency. Monopoly produces a deadweight loss, and the sum of consumer surplus and producer surplus is lower than it is under perfect competition.

On the other hand, if the monopolist is able to operate on a lower average or marginal cost function than the firms comprising a perfectly competitive industry, social welfare could be higher under monopoly than under perfect competition. Overall, the theoretical evidence as to whether monopolies lead to a reduction in efficiency and social welfare is inconclusive.

A natural monopoly is a market in which average cost decreases as output increases over the entire range of realistic output levels. In natural monopoly, monopoly is always more cost-effective than competition. In this case, it is not at all obvious that competition is a more desirable state of affairs than monopoly. On theoretical grounds, a policy of price discrimination practised by a monopolist should not always be judged pejoratively. Although in this way the monopolist earns an even higher abnormal profit than is possible by charging a uniform price, total output is higher and the last unit of output produced is sold at a price equivalent to its marginal cost. Therefore a policy of first-degree price discrimination may be consistent with social welfare maximization. With other forms of price discrimination, it is not possible to generalize about the social welfare implications.

An incumbent monopolist might pursue various strategies in an attempt to raise entry barriers and deter potential entrants. Monopolists might also seek to impose vertical restraints on other firms that are vertically linked (suppliers of the monopolist's inputs or purchasers of its outputs). Such practices might be expected to attract the attention of the competition authorities. According to the Schumpeterian hypothesis, market power and monopoly status should be interpreted as the reward for successful past innovation. Successful innovation brings benefits to society, in the form of new products or more efficient production processes. In the past, the competition authorities have often taken a benign or favourable view of firms that are perceived to invest heavily in research and development.

Competition policy deals with three principal areas: monopoly, restrictive practices and merger. The implementation of monopoly, restrictive practices and merger policy requires a practical method for measuring market power. Seller concentration and market share measures are obvious candidates. However, provided entry barriers are not insurmountable and markets are contestable, the threat of entry and competition may constrain a monopolist's pricing policy. It is therefore relevant to ask questions concerning the likelihood of entry. Issues of product and geographic market definition have major implications for the measurement of market power using concentration or market share indicators. Most economists recognize that perfect competition is a theoretical ideal, which is unlikely to be attainable in practice. A more realistic objective for competition policy might be to foster workable competition, which seeks to create aspects of structure and conduct that are most likely to deliver good performance.

At the time of writing, competition policy in the UK is the responsibility of the OFT (Office of Fair Trading) and the Competition Commission. The OFT investigates complaints of anticompetitive practices, and if these complaints are upheld, refers the findings to the Competition Commission. The Competition Act 1998 and the Enterprise Act 2002 consolidated current arrangements for the conduct of competition policy, and harmonized the UK's arrangements with those operative at EU level. The Chapter I prohibition deals with restrictive practices, and corresponds to Article 101 of the EU's Treaty of Lisbon. The Chapter II prohibition deals with abuses of dominant (or monopoly) positions and corresponds to Article 102 of the Treaty of Lisbon. In UK competition policy, the current emphasis is on the examination of the consequences of anticompetitive behaviour, rather than the form taken by any particular agreement or restrictive practice. The most recent legislation, together with the provisions operative at EU level, has strengthened the UK's competition policy regime considerably, in comparison with previous decades.

Discussion questions

1. Compare the long-run equilibrium values of output, price and average cost under perfect competition and monopoly, assuming cost structures are identical in both cases. What conclusions can be drawn concerning productive and allocative efficiency?

2. With reference to Q1, is the assumption of identical cost structures reasonable? If a monopolist operates on a lower long-run average cost function than a perfectly competitive industry, what are the implications for the comparison between the productive and allocative efficiency properties of perfect competition and monopoly?

3. What factors should be taken into account by the competition authorities in determining whether a particular market is under monopoly control?

4. With reference to Case Study 23.1, outline the key components of the US Department of Justice Case against Microsoft.

5. With reference to Case Study 23.2 what factors must regulators consider when assessing proposed mergers?

6. With reference to Case Study 23.3, why is Google causing concern for the regulation of competition in Europe and the US?

7. What is workable competition, and what are its implications for competition policy?

8. Outline the relationship between the chapter prohibitions contained in the UK Competition Act 1998, and Articles 101 and 102 of the EU Treaty of Lisbon.

9. To what extent has competition policy legislation in the UK provided an effective deterrent to anticompetitive behaviour?

Further reading

Audretsch, D., Baumol, W.J. and Burke, A. (2001) Competition policy in a dynamic economy, *International Journal of Industrial Organization*, 19, 613–34.

Beverley, L. (2008) Stock market event studies and Competition Commission inquiries, *CCP Working Paper* 08–16.

Clarke, R. and Morgan, E.J. (2006) *New Developments in UK and EU Competition Policy*. Cheltenham: Edward Elgar.

Lyons, B. (2008a) *Cases in European Competition Policy: The Economics Analysis*. Cambridge: Cambridge University Press.

Lyons, B. (2008b) An economic assessment of EC Merger Control: 1957–2007, CCP Working Paper 08–17.

Goyder, D.G. (2003) *EC Competition Law: Text and Cases*. London: Oxford University Press.

Hoi, J. (2007) Competition law and policy indicators for the OECD countries, *OECD Economic Department Working Papers*, No. 568.

Kwoka, J.E. and White, L.J. (2008) *The Anti-trust Revolution*, 5th edition. London: Oxford University Press.

Mateus, A.M. and Moreira, T. (2010) (eds) *Competition Law and Economics: Advances in Competition Policy Enforcement in the EU and North America*. Cheltenham: Edward Elgar.

Motta, M. (2004) *Competition Policy: Theory and Practice*. Cambridge: Cambridge University Press.

Office of Fair Trading (OFT) (1999) *Quantitative Techniques in Competition Analysis*. London: OFT.

Whish, R. (2003) *Competition Law*, 4th edition. London: Butterworth.

White, L.J. (2013) Market power: how does it arise? How is it measured? in Thomas, C.R. and Shughart, W.F. (eds) *Oxford Handbook of Managerial Economics*. Oxford: Oxford University Press

24

Regulation

Learning objectives

This chapter covers the following topics:

- the rationale for government regulation
- resource allocation under conditions of natural monopoly
- public ownership and privatization
- price cap and rate of return regulation
- regulation of UK privatized industries
- regulation of the banking industry
- franchise agreements
- compulsory competitive tendering and best value

Key terms

Compulsory competitive tendering
Conduct regulation
Franchising
Natural monopoly
Price cap regulation

Privatization
Rate of return regulation
Regulatory capture
Structural regulation

24.1 Introduction

Chapter 24 examines government or public sector involvement in the provision of goods and services. Government provision is often motivated by a desire to correct various types of market failure. More specifically, this chapter examines the relative merits of organizing production in the private and public sectors, particularly in cases where average costs tend to fall over the entire range of industry output; in other words, when the industry operates under cost conditions that give rise to a **natural monopoly**. Advantages sometimes attributed to organizing production within the public sector include the elimination of wasteful competition, and the exploitation of the full potential for economies of scale and scope. Disadvantages include a lack of competitive discipline or incentive to minimize costs and maximize productivity. With these and other factors in mind, during the 1980s and 1990s the pendulum swung away from state ownership and towards **privatization** in many countries. If privatization involves the break-up of monopolies into smaller units, an element of competition may be introduced automatically. In cases where this is not feasible, regulation may be required in order to ensure outcomes mimicking those that may have occurred under (hypothetical) competitive conditions.

The chapter begins in Section 24.2 with a review of the policy issues raised by natural monopolies, including an overview of the range of options open to policy makers seeking to reduce or eliminate the scope for a natural monopolist to abuse its market power. These options are examined in more detail in the next four sections. Section 24.3 discusses the policy of nationalization, which involves taking an industry into state ownership. Section 24.4 considers the reverse policy of privatization, whereby state-owned enterprises are transferred to private ownership and control. These two sections discuss the economic case for and against nationalization and privatization, and review the empirical evidence concerning the performance of state-owned enterprises, and those that have been transferred to private ownership during their pre- and post-privatization stages.

In cases of natural monopolies in particular, privatization often does not involve the creation of a competitive market structure. In such cases, regulation of the newly privatized industry provides an alternative method for avoiding various forms of market failure, and achieving outcomes that might have resulted had the introduction of competition been a feasible option. Section 24.5 examines regulation, and draws comparisons between the types of regulatory regime most widely used in the US and in Europe. These are known as **rate of return regulation** and **price cap regulation**, respectively. Section 24.6 describes the arrangements for regulation of selected UK industries that were privatized during the 1980s and 1990s: telecommunications, gas and electricity, water and rail. Section 24.7 examines the regulation of the banking industry. Section 24.8 cites some empirical evidence on the extent to which regulation or, where appropriate, deregulation, has improved the functioning of markets, and helped boost productivity and economic growth. Finally, Section 24.9 discusses the policy of **franchising**, involving the allocation of exclusive rights to supply certain goods and services. Consideration is also given to the widespread local government practice of competitive tendering, under which in-house public sector providers compete against private contractors to retain or acquire the rights to provide public services.

24.2   The problem of natural monopoly

One of the main arguments in favour of the regulation of industry is based on the notion that some industries are natural monopolies. As shown earlier (see Section 3.4), a **natural monopoly** exists when production at the minimum possible long-run average cost can take place only if one firm controls the industry's total production; or in other words, when the minimum efficient scale (MES) is roughly equivalent to (or larger than) the total market size.

In the case of a natural monopoly with a large fixed cost, entry may well be uneconomic. Suppose, for example, a water company supplies an entire geographic region through a network of pipes. It might well be uneconomic for an entrant to set up its own infrastructure and start supplying a segment of the same market, because the entrant would have difficulty in claiming a sufficient share of the market to cover its fixed cost. In the UK 'a degree of scepticism of the merits of competition developed, particularly in relation to water and gas, as the duplication of facilities funded by major capital outlays and often surplus capacity, was perceived to be wasteful' (Ogus, 1996, p. 265).

If a natural monopolist is abusing its market power, there are several possible solutions. The first is public ownership, which normally involves granting statutory rights to a single firm. In doing so, the firm can be required to price its products in a competitive manner. A second solution is to open up the relevant market to competition. In many countries, the privatization of previously nationalized industries, involving the transfer of state-owned assets to the private sector, has been accompanied by efforts to create more competitive post-privatization market conditions. A final solution is to allow temporary monopoly rights through the granting of a franchise. In this case, competition takes place prior to the award of the franchise during the bidding process, with stipulations concerning matters such as price and quality of service written into the successful bidder's contract. The merits of these three approaches have been summarized as follows:

> First, the firm can be publicly owned . . . , the expectation being that the mechanics of political direction and accountability will be sufficient to meet public interest goals. Secondly, the firm may remain in, or be transferred to, private ownership but be subjected to external constraints in the form of price and quality regulation . . . Thirdly, firms desiring to obtain a monopoly right may be forced to compete for it . . . As part of their competitive bid, they are required to stipulate proposed conditions of supply, relating especially to prices and quality; and those conditions then become terms of the licence or franchise under which they exercise the monopoly right.
>
> *(Ogus, 1996, p. 5)*

In Sections 24.3 to 24.6, each of these solutions to the problem of natural monopoly is examined in turn.

24.3 Nationalization

In most cases, nationalization involves the creation of a statutory monopoly owned and controlled by the government. Usually, competition is prohibited: other firms cannot enter and compete with the established monopolist. Domberger and Piggott (1986) suggest there is a strong case for public ownership of natural monopolies. By assuming ownership, the government can instruct the firm to pursue certain objectives or adopt certain policies. The aim is to correct market failures associated with market power, externalities and asymmetric information, and to satisfy the necessary conditions for allocative efficiency. In practice, however, allocative efficiency may be difficult to achieve, if a marginal cost pricing policy causes the natural monopolist to realize a loss (see Section 3.4, Figure 3.7). Therefore second-best policies are sometimes pursued: the firm might adopt average cost pricing; or the government might provide a subsidy to cover the losses entailed by marginal cost pricing (Lipsey and Lancaster, 1956).

Nationalization involving the creation of a statutory monopoly may result in the elimination of wasteful competition, or it may allow the full exploitation of economies of scale. In some cases, nationalization may be justified in terms of social objectives, such as the provision of services that would otherwise be deemed uneconomic by the private sector: for example, postal or telephone services to rural areas.

However, the public provision of goods and services does raise a number of difficult issues. Nationalized firms are generally shielded from the rigours of competition. Therefore there is little or no threat of bankruptcy, as losses are effectively underwritten or recovered by means of government subsidy. Nationalized firms are also protected from the threat of being taken over. Consequently, there may be little or no incentive for the managers of nationalized firms to achieve full productive efficiency, especially if the managers' remuneration is not directly linked to the organization's performance. In many cases, conflict between political and economic objectives has made nationalized firms difficult to manage. Nationalized firms may be instructed to follow non-commercial objectives, in pursuit of policy objectives concerning employment, procurement and trade.

Foster (1992) suggests political objectives gained precedence over objectives relating to economic efficiency in the management of nationalized industries in the UK. Rees (1984) suggests the efforts of UK nationalized industries to pursue commercial objectives were stifled by excessive trade union power in the labour market. Bos (1991, 2003) suggests underperformance was due to various imperfections in the structure of ownership and control; for example, lack of clarity concerning objectives, financial constraints on borrowing and investment, inadequate incentives for efficient performance, and excessive interference by politicians. However, empirical evidence concerning the performance of the UK's nationalized industries is rather more varied than the views of some critics might suggest. Below, a selection of empirical studies is reviewed briefly.

Pryke (1981, 1982) examines trends in productivity in nine nationalized industries over the period 1968–78. In industries subject to rapid technological change, including airlines and telecoms, labour or total factor productivity increased. The rate of increase was slower in utilities such as gas and electricity. However, productivity in several nationalized industries, including steel, coal, postal services, bus and rail services declined.

> What public ownership does is to eliminate the threat of takeover and ultimately of bankruptcy and the need, which all private undertakings have from time to time, to raise money from the market. Public ownership provides a comfortable life and destroys commercial ethic.
>
> *(Pryke, 1982, p. 81)*

Molyneux and Thompson (1987) report a similar analysis for the same nine nationalized industries for the period 1978–85, and find productivity increased in all nine cases. The improvement is attributed to greater workforce flexibility, tighter controls over subsidy (which stimulated cost savings), increased investment, technological progress, rationalization and learning economies of scale. Millward (1990) compares the productivity of nationalized firms with privately owned firms in the gas, electricity, water and transport industries. Over the period 1956–86, in many cases productivity measures for publicly owned firms increased faster than those for privately owned firms. Finally, Lynk (1993) examines productivity differences between private and publicly owned water companies, prior to privatization in 1989. The publicly owned companies were found to be more productive. Overall, the empirical evidence provides a rather mixed view of the productivity and performance of the UK's nationalized industries.

24.4 Privatization

There is some confusion surrounding the use of the term **privatization**. This term has been widely used to refer to (at least) three distinct policies: denationalization, deregulation and franchising.

- *Denationalization.* This involves the transfer and sale of assets from the public to the private sector. The transfer of assets may or may not be accompanied by a process of deregulation (or market liberalization). Where capital markets are developed, the transfer of assets can be implemented by means of a sale of shares to financial institutions and the general public.

- *Deregulation and market liberalization.* Policies of deregulation and market liberalization aim to increase competition (Winston, 1993, 1998). This may involve altering the market structure, perhaps by reducing or eliminating barriers to entry. Some re-regulation might be required, in order to control the behaviour of incumbent firms towards new entrants. Advantages of deregulation are that inefficient firms, previously protected from competition, may eventually be superseded by more efficient competitors (Saal, 2003). However, Winston (1998) notes that this is by no means an instantaneous process.

It is not surprising that deregulated (or partially deregulated) industries are slow to achieve maximum efficiency. When regulatory restrictions on pricing, operations and entry (especially from new firms), has been enforced for decades, managers and employees of regulated firms settle into patterns of inefficient production and missed opportunities for technological advance and entry into new markets . . . [I]t takes firms a long time to tear down decades-old barriers to efficiency and to adopt more efficient production and marketing practices.

(Winston, 1998, pp. 89–90)

- The negative effects of deregulation are experienced if the process results in the transfer of surplus from consumers to producers (see *The Economist*, 2002, for an extended discussion). For example, Crandell (2003) discusses the recent deregulation of the electricity industry in California.

In 2000–2001, California's failed approach to deregulation allowed generators to exploit the short term scarcity of power created by natural forces, such as shortfall in precipitation and a rise in fossil fuel prices, because California forbade utilities to enter into long term contracts. The result was an increase in the state's electricity bill of approximately $12 billion per year.

(Crandell, 2003, p. 78)

- *Franchising.* This involves the contracting out to private contractors (often by means of some form of auction) of services that were previously provided from within the public sector. Franchising is often used in cases where direct competition is deemed impossible or undesirable. In the UK, examples include local bus services and commercial passenger train services. The aim is to increase competition indirectly, by encouraging firms to bid competitively for contracts and licences to provide the relevant goods or services.

In the UK, denationalization, deregulation and franchising were all policies implemented with enthusiasm by the Conservative goverments led by Margaret Thatcher (1979–90) and John Major (1990–7). This chapter reserves use of the term **privatization** to describe the first of these three policies: denationalization, or the transfer of state-owned assets to the private sector. The policy of privatization is examined in Section 24.4.

Table 24.1 lists a selection of the UK's largest privatizations. In total, the UK's privatization programme transferred assets exceeding £100bn from public to private ownership (Helm and Jenkinson, 1997). The policy of privatization was motivated partly by a desire to widen share ownership among the general public. Between 1979 and 1988, the proportion of adults in the UK holding shares increased from 7 per cent to 21 per cent (Fraser, 1988). The sale of state-owned assets also provided windfall gains to the Treasury, which helped finance tax cuts. In cases where the sale of state-owned assets involved the break-up of

Table 24.1 Selected UK privatizations by industry and year of first sale

Enterprise	Industry	Year privatized
British Aerospace	Aerospace	1981
Cable & Wireless	Telecommunications	1981
Britoil	Oil	1982
National Freight Corporation	Transport	1982
Associated British Ports	Ports	1983
British Telecom	Telecommunications	1984
British Leyland (Austin–Rover)	Cars	1984
Jaguar	Cars	1984
British Gas	Gas	1986
National Bus Company	Buses	1986
British Airports Authority	Airports	1987
British Airways	Airlines	1987
British Steel	Steel	1988
Water authorities (10 companies)	Water	1989
Electricity distribution (12 companies)	Electricity	1990
Electricity generation	Electricity	1991
British Rail (Railtrack)	Railways	1995
British Energy	Nuclear energy	1996

nationalized industries into smaller constituent parts, an element of competition was introduced. In several industries where direct competition is not feasible, such as rail services, a relatively tough regulatory regime has been introduced (Parker, 2003a). In contrast, deregulation has been implemented in a number of industries where competition prevails (such as telecommunications services).

The perceived success of the UK privatization programme persuaded many other industrialized countries to follow suit (Megginson and Netter, 2001). Telecommunications and financial intermediation account for approximately half of all privatization proceeds. Privatization proceeds in OECD countries reached a peak of US$100.6bn in 1998; but subsequently the proceeds fell sharply. Notoriously in 2002, the UK government placed Railtrack, the country's rail network operator, into receivership, prior to effective renationalization. Plans to privatize the UK's postal services, one of the few remaining state-owned industries, have been repeatedly postponed. Since 2007, numerous banks worldwide have been transferred partially or entirely into state ownership.

The following points contribute to the economic case for privatization:

■ *Increased competition.* Privatization may encourage firms that were previously in state ownership to search for methods of reducing costs and eliminating x-inefficiencies for several reasons. If privatization is accompanied by a change in market structure, perhaps through the break-up of a previously state-owned monopoly into a number of competing units, the resulting competitive pressure may dictate that the newly privatized firms engage vigorously in the search for cost savings (Moore, 1983, Price Waterhouse, 1989). Increased competition may help deliver lower prices, improved product or service quality, and greater choice for consumers.

In the 1980s, when utility privatizations were being driven through by the conservative governments, the objectives were fairly simple and straightforward. Privatisation was to undo the inefficiencies of public ownership bringing in commercial management incentivised by the carrot of profits, and controlled by the stick of competition. Competition was to gradually take up the slack from regulation, which was always a second best, and over time regulation would wither away for many – and perhaps most – of the utilities. Where natural monopoly remained, the takeover mechanism would challenge management, and regulation would cap prices, mimicking a competitive market in which all firms are price takers.

(Helm, 2005, p. 2)

- *Increased capital market discipline.* Following privatization, the creation of a tier of profit-motivated shareholders may force management to attach higher priority to objectives related to profitability. Therefore, pressure from shareholders may also motivate the search for methods of reducing costs, through the elimination of bureaucracy, waste and inefficiency (Wolfram, 1998). In privatized firms, the shareholder is the principal and the manager is the agent. Reward and incentive structures can be created to encourage managers to perform well.

    Efficiency gains from privatization arise essentially out of the interaction of product and capital market pressures. Competition in product markets means that the persistent underperformance will ultimately lead to bankruptcy. Competitive capital markets mean that if management is not successful in averting a downward performance trend, it will be displaced through takeover well before the company has reached the point of no return.

    (Domberger and Piggott, 1986, p. 150)

In nationalized industries, the government is the principal and the manager is the agent. This principal–agent relationship is mediated through a complex bureaucracy. Direct communication between principal and agent is difficult, and information flows tend to be distorted. Direct incentives for the manager to maximize performance, and penalties in the event of underperformance, tend to be weak. The capital market discipline that threatens underachieving managers with the possibility of takeover is absent in the case of state-owned enterprises. In contrast, by the end of 1997, 10 of the UK's 12 privatized regional electricity distribution firms had been acquired by domestic or foreign rivals (Helm and Jenkinson, 1997).

- *Reduction in government borrowing.* During the 1980s and 1990s, the UK's privatization programme had the intended side-effect of reducing the national debt. The total borrowing requirement of the nationalized industries shifted from a deficit of £1.1bn in 1984 to a surplus of £1.35bn in 1987 (Foster, 1992).

This contributed to a reduction in the overall public sector borrowing requirement (PSBR), making the conduct of monetary and fiscal policy easier than it would otherwise have been. For example, the availability of privatization proceeds increased the scope for the large cuts in income tax rates that were implemented in successive budgets between 1986 and 1988.

■ *Elimination of government controls.* Nationalized enterprises are subject to various controls over their operations or financing, which may be eliminated through privatization. For example, borrowing by nationalized enterprises in the UK contributed to the PSBR, and accordingly was subject to public sector borrowing rules. Privatized enterprises have the same freedom to raise finance via the capital markets as any other companies.

There are several counter-arguments against privatization. If privatization simply leads to the transfer of a monopoly from public to private ownership, with the privatized firm free to exploit its market power in pursuit of shareholder profit, then this is likely to work against the interests of consumers. On the other hand, if privatization involves the break-up of a state-owned monopoly into smaller components, costs might increase if the smaller units are unable to realize the full benefits of economies of scale or scope. The use of privatization proceeds to finance current government spending or tax cuts can also be criticized. The proceeds from the sale of a state-owned assets are effectively the capitalized value of the future profit flows those assets are expected to yield. There is an element of short-termism in the policy of using such windfall gains to finance current expenditure, which is likely to lead to a gap appearing in the public finances in future years when no further saleable assets remain.

There is an extensive literature on the impact of privatization. Parker (1991) examines the performance of several privatized firms over the period 1987–90. Profitability increased for British Gas, British Telecom and Rolls-Royce, but declined for Associated British Ports, Jaguar and Enterprise Oil. Bishop and Thompson (1992) examine changes in productivity and profitability over the period 1970–90 for nine privatizations: British Airports Authority, British Airways, British Telecom, British Coal, electricity supply, British Gas, Post Office, British Rail and British Steel. While productivity and profitability improved, there is no direct evidence that the privatizations were solely or primarily responsible. Price and Weyman-Jones (1993) identify increases in productivity for British Gas between the late 1970s (several years before privatization in 1984) and the early 1990s.

Parker (1994) examines the effects of privatization on the performance of BT (formerly British Telecom). Performance indicators include price changes, service quality indicators, employment, research and development and productivity measures. Prices fell by 11 per cent on average, but there was considerable variation in price changes across BT's full range of products and services. The reliability of network equipment and quality of installation improved. Employment increased during the late 1980s, but decreased subsequently as the firm searched for cost savings. Profitability increased but investment in research and development declined post-privatization. This latter trend may be due to short-term pressure to maximize profit.

Parker and Martin (1995) measure the trend in labour and total factor productivity for 11 privatized firms. Labour productivity is measured by changes in output in response to changes in labour inputs. Similarly, total factor productivity is measured by changes in output in response to changes in various inputs, including capital, raw materials, energy and labour. There was typically a substantial improvement in performance during the lead-up to privatization. However, performance did not always continue to improve after privatization, especially for privatizations that preceded the recession of the early 1990s, and in cases where there was intense competition or underinvestment in the privatized firm's capital assets.

Parker and Wu (1998) assess the performance of British Steel before and after privatization in 1988. Labour and total factor productivity indicators, and profitability, are used as performance measures. Performance improved immediately before privatization, but the rate of improvement slowed considerably after privatization. Comparisons between British Steel and the steel industries of Australia, Canada, France, Germany, Japan and the US suggest that, before privatization, British Steel was more efficient than several of its international competitors, but this position had been reversed by the early 1990s. Dewenter and Malatesta (2001) compare the performance of a number of large state-owned and privately owned firms in 1975, 1985 and 1995. The privately owned firms were generally more profitable and more efficient than the state-owned firms.

Overall, the empirical evidence seems to suggest the productivity and profitability of some, but not all, privatized firms improved as a result of privatization. In some cases, productivity gains achieved in the run-up to privatization exceeded any further improvements post-privatization. In most cases, it is difficult to determine whether some or all of the improvements would have taken place anyway, without the transfer of ownership from the public to the private sector.

> In practice, the effects of privatization have been complex. There have been significant reductions in costs. Staffing levels have fallen, in some cases dramatically, and with these reductions in operating costs, prices have typically fallen too. Some of these reductions have been due to incentives created by regulation, some by new management practices, some by the reduction in union power, and some by the application of the new information technologies, which were particularly relevant to networks. It is impossible to estimate with much precision how great the changes would have been in the state sector if privatization had not taken place.
>
> *(Helm, 2001, p. 299)*

Privatisation defined Thatcher era   FT

Enthusiasm for privatisation under Margaret Thatcher was close to its apogee when British Gas made its stock market debut 25 years ago on Thursday. About 1.5m people, lured by a fast profit and the notorious 'tell Sid' advertising campaign, took part in the record £5.6bn flotation.

Some 800m shares changed hands, the highest volume the London market had seen for an entire day, as the partly-paid share price rose from 50p to 67p, ending at $62\frac{1}{2}$p.

In the event, Mrs Thatcher's hope of a share-owning democracy never really took off – the frenzy for cheap shares was already starting to fade – but privatisation went on to become a global phenomenon from Russia to New Zealand, seen by many as the defining idea of the Thatcher era.

By the time of her tearful departure from office in 1990, more than 40 UK state-owned businesses employing 600,000 workers had been privatised. The drive continues today, with the coalition preparing to sell or float Royal Mail – a step too far even for the Iron Lady.

Frequently privatisation proved controversial. On the day of the gas flotation, Tony Blair, then a Labour Treasury spokesman, complained that taxpayers had lost at least £600m through the underpricing of the issue. Later, as prime minister, he extended privatisation to areas where the Conservatives feared to go during their 18 years in power, such as air traffic control.

The Thatcher era is in people's minds at the moment, not least because of the hype over the film *The Iron Lady*, starring Meryl Streep. Other echoes include the resurgence of public sector strikes and the coalition's extension of the right to buy public housing, a popular Thatcher policy.

Some contrast her big idea with David Cameron's supposed lack of one, but in reality Mrs Thatcher came to the policy only slowly before it took off in her second term. Privatisation did not feature in the 1979 Tory manifesto and her first term brought only small-scale sell-offs such as Amersham International, the medical diagnostics group.

Nor was it wholly new. The term was coined in the 1930s to describe aspects of Nazi Germany's economic policy (Reprivatisierung). Winston Churchill denationalised the UK steel industry and road freight in the 1950s after Labour's nationalisations in the 1940s. James Callaghan's Labour government sold 17 per cent of BP in May 1977 to keep the International Monetary Fund happy.

Mrs Thatcher embraced it initially as a way to reduce public debt after the 1980–81 recession. It was only when the £4bn flotation of British Telecom in 1984 proved hugely successful – with the offer almost 10 times subscribed – that she seized on its political possibilities for rolling back socialism.

In 1987 came the flotations of British Airways, Rolls-Royce and British Airports Authority, followed later by steel (which had been renationalised by Labour in the 1960s), water and electricity. John Major's government sold off the remains of the coal industry and the railways.

For the most part, privatisation has been seen as delivering benefits to consumers, especially where there is competition. The fragmented rail sell-off has been the most troubled, resulting in the 2002 replacement of Railtrack, the infrastructure owner, by Network Rail, nominally in the private sector but with no shareholders and its borrowing guaranteed by government.

In energy, the need to encourage investment is driving a more 'planned' approach, revising some elements of the strategy of Nigel Lawson, energy secretary in the early 1980s, who rejected central planning and set out a competitive vision for a market that paved the way for privatisation.

'Private ownership radically changed the incentives, but it was not the panacea its architect imagined,' said Dieter Helm, professor of energy policy at Oxford university. 'What was gradually recognised was that privatised industries needed regulating, and serious regulatory failings, as well as badly designed reforms of the market after privatisation, are at the root of many of the problems that persist.'

Chris Huhne, energy secretary, proposes a market that gives incentives to low-carbon forms of generation, aimed at encouraging new entrants and investors. Now the coalition aims to sell off Royal Mail, which even Mrs Thatcher balked at because she was 'not prepared to have the Queen's head privatised'. The government has passed an act, but privatisation may not happen before 2013. Some say it may even have missed the boat because of the loss of letters traffic to email. The outcome could be a part-sale to private equity followed by flotation later — precisely the format that caused a storm over Qinetiq, the defence research group, when it resulted in huge windfalls for bosses. Ministers are already pondering how to sell this to the public.

Source: Privatisation defined Thatcher era, © The Financial Times Limited. All Rights Reserved, 7 December 2011 (Groom, B. and Pfeifer, S.).

24.5   Forms of regulation

Regulation may be required when one or more forms of market failure leads to allocative inefficiency. Possible causes of market failure include the following:

- *Market power*. Under perfect competition firms set prices equal to marginal cost and there is allocative efficiency: no one can be made better off without making someone else worse off. At the opposite end of the competitive spectrum, the monopolist restricts output and charges a price higher than marginal cost and there is allocative inefficiency. Therefore there is a case for regulation to prevent or curb the exercise of market power.

- *Asymmetric information*. Asymmetric information arises when buyers and sellers have access to different information. For example, regulation of sellers through licensing or certification might be required to provide buyers with assurances concerning the quality of the product or service.

■ *Externalities.* An externality exists when a transaction confers benefits or costs on parties other than the buyer or seller, who are not compensated under the terms of the transaction. There is likely to be overproduction of goods that produce negative externalities (such as pollution), and underproduction of goods that produce positive externalities (such as education, training or research and development). In both cases there is allocative inefficiency, and a case for regulation to alter behaviour in a way that results in an efficient allocation of resources.

■ *Public goods.* The non-exclusivity characteristic of services such as policing, fire protection and street lighting makes it difficult to charge directly for their provision. If the service is provided at all, it is provided to everyone regardless of willingness to pay. Consequently, private contractors are unlikely to provide such services, unless there is some form of regulatory intervention.

The potential for market failure due to the exercise of market power has raised particular concerns in the case of privatizations (in the sense of denationalization) of state-owned monopolies. While privatization may create incentives for cost savings, this will not guarantee allocative efficiency unless there is also competition. In cases where the introduction of genuine competition may be infeasible (perhaps because cost conditions approximate to those of natural monopoly), a stringent regulatory regime may be required to deliver outcomes that mimic those that would hypothetically be achieved under competition.

> The first phase of privatization is associated with regulating the incumbent monopoly; a second stage involves policing the developing competition and establishment and monitoring infrastructure access rules to ensure that the dominant firm does not crush new entrants to the industry; and a third stage is concerned within maintaining the effective competition that eventually develops.
>
> *(Parker, 2003b, p. 548)*

In the US, the utilities have traditionally been in private ownership, and there is a long regulatory tradition. In the UK, where the utilities were in state ownership prior to privatizations during the 1980s and 1990s, the regulation of utilities is a more recent phenomenon. Accordingly, the state has moved from being primarily concerned with production towards a greater emphasis on regulation (Helm, 1994). Kay and Vickers (1990) characterize regulation with reference to principal–agent theory. The regulator can be regarded as a principal, and the regulated firms are the agents that are expected to follow the principal's instructions in pursuit of the principal's objectives. However, the regulated firms also have their own objectives, which differ from those of the regulator. The firms are likely to have more information than the regulator, making it difficult for the latter to construct a suitable framework to ensure its objectives are met.

Furthermore, over time, the regulator's objectives are influenced by the actions of regulated firms. Ultimately this process may lead to the regulator representing the interests of the industry rather than those of consumers.

Regulated firms tend to be better organized than consumers. Often, regulators are themselves industry insiders, who may have worked in the industry previously or who may hope to do so again in the future (Asch and Seneca, 1985). Consequently, regulated firms are able to influence the regulator, leading to **regulatory capture** (Dal Bo, 2006). For these reasons, Stigler (1971) and Peltzman (1976, 1989) suggest regulation tends to distort, more than it promotes competition. Becker (1983) suggests regulators will tend to respond to lobbying by the regulated firms, as long as the gains arising from the resulting changes in regulation are not outweighed by the possible loss of votes from consumers or others who lose out as a result. Regulatory capture may be less likely if the regulatory framework and objectives are clear, consistent and transparent. For legitimacy, regulation should be proportional to the extent of any perceived distortion in competition, and accountable to the various interest groups, especially consumers (Parker, 2003b).

At a general level, there are two basic types of regulation: structural and conduct regulation. **Structural regulation** focuses on market structure. Measures include the functional separation of firms into complementary activities (for example, electricity generators and distributors), restrictions on entry and rules regarding the operation of foreign firms. Structural regulation may tend to make entry difficult, and may tend to protect incumbent firms from competitive pressure. In contrast, **conduct regulation** seeks to influence the behaviour of firms, through measures such as price controls, regulated fees and commissions, controls on the levels of advertising or research and development expenditure, or restrictions on the rate at which distribution networks can be expanded. '[Structural regulation] aims to create a situation in which the incentives or opportunities for undesirable behaviour are removed, while [conduct regulation] addresses not the underlying incentives, but the behaviour that they would otherwise induce' (Kay and Vickers, 1990, p. 233).

For regulation to be effective, the regulator requires information on changes in costs and market conditions. In a stable market, this requirement is relatively straightforward. In a dynamic market, where conditions tend to change rapidly, it may be difficult to maintain an accurate picture. The robust design and implementation of regulatory policies is therefore paramount.

The main regulatory regimes adopted in the US and UK are **rate of return regulation** and **price cap regulation**, respectively.

Rate of return (or cost plus) regulation

In the US, rate of return regulation is the main regulatory regime. The regulator fixes a required rate of return on capital, denoted R^*, as follows:

$$R^* = \frac{\text{Total revenue} - \text{total cost}}{\text{Capital employed}}$$

Under rate of return regulation, the regulator allows the firm to set a price that covers costs and allows a mark-up for profit. Price reviews can be carried out frequently. However, there may be little incentive for the firm to minimize its costs, given that the rate of return on assets is effectively guaranteed, and in the event of an increase in costs the firm can simply apply to be allowed to increase price. The frequency of contact between the regulator and the regulated firms makes it likely that a relationship will develop over time. This increases the likelihood of regulatory capture, which may create opportunities for the firm's managers to maximize their own utility, for example by spending on pet projects. US regulators have sought to address this problem by creating a time-lag between any request for a price change and its implementation. In this case, a firm that fails to control its costs is penalized by earning a reduced return during the waiting period. Similarly, if costs were to fall, the firm would earn a return exceeding the required rate during the waiting period. Therefore a regulatory lag provides an incentive for firms to exercise effective cost control.

Another drawback with rate of return regulation is that if the required rate of return is set at an inappropriate level, this can encourage either over- or under-investment in assets (Averch and Johnson, 1962). A required rate of return that is set too high encourages overinvestment, since the more capital the firm employs, the more profit is required in order to achieve the required rate of return. Klevorick (1966) suggests that this tendency can be avoided by reducing the required rate of return in cases where the firm's capital base has recently been increased dramatically. However, this may simply introduce other distortions into the way in which firms use their factors of production (Sherman, 1985). If the required rate of return is set too low, firms may seek economies (perhaps by reducing the quality of their inputs or outputs) in order to earn an adequate return.

Rate of return regulation is often problematic because regulators find it difficult to value the firm's capital employed. For example, should capital be valued on a historical cost basis, or should it be calculated as the replacement cost of assets? Technical decisions on matters affecting the calculation of the firm's declared rate of return for regulatory purposes may have major implications for the firm's true profitability.

Price cap regulation

In the UK and most other European countries, price cap regulation is the most widely practised regulatory regime. Price cap regulation imposes a specific limit on the prices firms are permitted to charge. In the UK, price changes are commonly determined by a formula of the form RPI *minus* an X-factor, where RPI denotes the change in the retail price index, and the X-factor allows for productivity gains and other factors affecting costs. Therefore, if inflation is expected to be 5 per cent, but productivity gains of 3 per cent are expected over the same period, a price rise of 2 per cent would be permitted. In the UK and many other European countries, price caps are generally reviewed every four or five years. In addition to price cap regulation, there may be a need for regulation of the quality of products or services, especially if the search for cost savings creates a temptation to compromise on product or service quality. In the UK, the Competition and Service Utilities Act 1992 represents an attempt to extend the scope of regulation to cover quality as well as price.

Price cap regulation seeks to ensure cost savings are passed on to consumers in the form of lower prices. In the short run there is an incentive for the firm to minimize costs, if profitability is boosted by savings that were unanticipated by the regulator at the time of the last price review. In the long run, however, the regulator may simply increase the X-factor in order to incorporate the cost saving, in which case the firm fails to benefit. In this case, there may be disincentives for long-run investment in cost saving technologies 'RPI *minus* X regulation encouraged a management style based upon cost minimization rather than investment' (Helm, 2001, p. 300). Critics argue that, in some countries, price cap regulation has resulted in a tendency for long-term underinvestment in the infrastructure of network industries such as rail, water and energy.

Factors influencing the regulator's decision when setting the X-factor include the firm's cost structure and capital structure, its investment plans, expected productivity gains and expected changes in market demand, and the implications of the chosen X-factor for competition. It may be necessary to set the initial value of X at the time of privatization, when the firm is still state-owned and before competition has been introduced. In cases where there is likely to be public opposition to the privatization decision, there may be a temptation to allow consumer interests to weigh heavily in determining the initial value of X; however, successful privatization requires the expected profitability of the newly privatized firm to be sufficient to attract private shareholder investment. Similarly, in reviewing the X-factor after privatization, the regulator must strike a balance between consumer and shareholder interests. If a state-owned monopoly has been broken up into smaller components, the impact of competition on prices may provide useful information for the regulator in determining the appropriate price cap during the post-privatization phase (Shleifer, 1985).

Littlechild's (1983) study of the UK telecommunications industry was influential in determining the UK's approach to regulation. Littlechild analyzes five possible types of regulation: no interference; rate of return regulation (as in the US); profit ceilings; an output-related profit levy (firms producing low output are unlikely to be operating at the minimum efficient scale, and are subject to a high levy in order to encourage expansion); and price cap regulation. Each regulatory regime is evaluated regarding its ability to protect consumers from abuses of market power; to promote cost savings and increase productivity; to promote competition; and ease of implementation. Littlechild concludes in favour of price cap regulation with an RPI *minus* X pricing formula, because it provides greater incentives for firms to search for cost savings than the other regulatory regimes, and because it is both simple to operate and transparent.

In the UK, separate Acts of Parliament have created agencies responsible for the regulation of newly privatized and formerly state-owned industries. In general, these agencies are responsible for:

■ collecting and publishing information on competitive conditions;

■ advising the Office of Fair Trading or Competition Commission of possible abuses of market power or anticompetitive practices;

■ enforcing competition law;

■ setting price and quality levels and investigating complaints;

■ specifying conditions under which individual firms are licensed to trade.

Helm and Jenkinson (1997) characterize the UK regulatory approach as one of contracts and discretion. Effectively, firms are contracted to operate within price and quality guidelines imposed by the regulator, who retains the discretion to intervene in order to promote competitive outcomes. Under free competition, entry and exit would normally ensure profit rates gravitate towards competitive levels in the long run. In privatized industries, this process does not always happen spontaneously, and it is the regulator's responsibility to ensure compliance, not necessarily with the process, but with the consequences of competition. '[I]n principle, the regulator can intervene to lower prices or increase costs to keep the actual rate of return at or around the normal level – to mop up excess returns' (Helm, 1994, p. 25).

Beesley and Littlechild (1997) point out a number of key differences between US-style rate of return regulation and European-style price cap regulation:

■ Under price cap regulation, if X is set for a defined period, the firm faces an element of risk over this period. Under rate of return regulation, the firm can apply for a price review at any time if its rate of return falls below the required rate.

■ With rate of return regulation, calculations are based on historic costs, revenues and capital valuations. Cost savings are likely to lead to price reductions being imposed quickly. In contrast, price cap regulation incorporates assumptions concerning the firm's future trading conditions. Cost savings in excess of those built into the X-factor can be appropriated by the firm between reviews.

■ With price cap regulation, the regulator can exercise greater discretion, by selecting assumptions concerning any of the variables thought to affect the X-factor.

■ In Europe, the X-factor is often set by the regulator without much consultation. In contrast, the more legalistic US approach demands explicit justification for the regulator's decisions.

■ With price cap regulation as widely practised in Europe, the firm exercises discretion over the prices charged for individual products, provided the average price of the firm's portfolio of products complies with the price cap (Armstrong *et al.*, 1994, p. 168). With rate of return regulation as practised in the US, the prices of individual products require regulatory approval.

24.6 Regulation of UK privatized industries

Section 24.6 describes the arrangements for regulation of selected UK industries that were privatized during the 1980s and 1990s: telecommunications, gas and electricity, water and rail.

Telecommunications

Telecommunications was the first major privatization in the UK during the 1980s. The incumbent, British Telecom or BT, was privatized in 1984 as a single entity. Initially, the post-privatization market structure was a duopoly in telephone networks, consisting of BT and Mercury Communications, an entrant which was given permission to use parts of the BT network. However, Mercury failed to achieve sufficient scale to compete effectively with BT. An alternative competitive regime was introduced in the early 1990s, which focused on competition in call services, rather than networks. By 1998, there were more than 200 call service operators. Regulation has been most active in the areas of national and international calls, and fixed line rentals (Butler, 1998). Television broadcasters have been encouraged to develop network services, using their own communications networks. Since privatization, competition in the telecommunications industry has become much more intense, with a rapid pace of technological change creating numerous opportunities for innovation and the provision of new products and services.

The post-privatization regulatory regime was established in the 1984 Telecommunications Act, which assigned responsibility for regulation to the newly created Office of Telecommunications (Oftel). Oftel was superseded by the Office of Communications (Ofcom) in 2003. The X-factor for the purposes of price cap regulation of the form 'RPI *minus* X' for the basic services used by the lowest 80 per cent of BT customers by average bill size (such as call charges and line rental) was initially set at 3 per cent for the period 1984–9; in other words, the maximum price increase was 3 per cent below inflation. X was subsequently increased to 4.5 per cent (1989–91), 6.25 per cent (1991–3) and 7.5 per cent (1993–7), before being progressively reduced prior to the abolition of price cap regulation on basic services in 2006. However, BT remains subject to network price regulation, to control the prices BT can charge other operators via interconnection agreements. The cap is also set using the 'RPI *minus* X' formula, with X varying from year to year and between different services, depending on Ofcom's assessment of the degree of competition BT is likely to face.

Case study 24.2

Competitive markets show limitations

Competitive markets have their limits. This economic principle has been demonstrated this week by both telecom operators in the US and a regulator in the UK.

Deutsche Telekom is selling out its US mobile operations to the larger AT&T because 34m customers is too few to compete successfully. But when the old American Telephone and Telegraph Corporation was broken up in 1984, the whole idea was that smaller companies would drive the industry forward.

It did not work out that way. The eight new telecom operators and their start-up rivals soon started merging. The industry is now heading towards an effective duopoly. And analysts whisper that users would be better served with a single national network for the next generation of mobile phone technology. The huge economies of scale in capital investment and marketing make this network look like what economists call a natural monopoly.

The fervour for freer markets also inspired the 1990 break-up of the UK electricity industry (traditionally regulated as a natural monopoly), but mighty market forces were not unleashed. As Monday's report from Ofgem, the UK energy regulator, pointed out, the six big companies still give lazy customers a bad deal. More fundamentally, several rejigs of the pricing system have left the country with inadequate investments in large power plants. That should not be surprising. At any instant, competitive markets set fair prices, but they can give few hints about many crucial issues: safety, pollution, diversification of power sources, national self-sufficiency and carbon emissions. These are topics for technical and political debate. Complex regulation is inevitable.

So the new structures in the US telecoms and UK electricity industries did not work as proponents hoped; but the shake-ups were not necessarily in vain. They spurred managers to improve services and abandon outmoded practices. Sometimes regulatory changes can do the work of markets.

Source: Competitive markets show limitations, © The Financial Times Limited. All Rights Reserved, 22 March 2011 (Lex team).

Gas and electricity

The Office of Gas and Electricity Markets (Ofgem) is responsible for regulation of energy markets in the UK, under the terms of the Gas Act (1986), Electricity Act (1998) and Utilities Act (2000). In conjunction with Energywatch, an independent organization set up in 2000, Ofgem aims to promote competition and protect consumers.

British Gas was privatized under the terms of the Gas Act of 1986 as an integrated firm, with operations in exploration and in the production and supply of gas. The Office of Gas Supply (Ofgas), a forerunner of Ofgem, was the original regulator. Price cap regulation was implemented through an 'RPI *minus* X *plus* Y' formula, in which an additional variable Y-factor allowed for changes in cost conditions which could be passed on to consumers. The X-factor was set at 2 per cent (1987–92), 5 per cent (1992–7), 4 per cent (1997–2002) and 2 per cent (2003–7). The Y-factor was dropped from the formula for 2003–7.

An element of competition was introduced in 1992, when other suppliers were permitted to use British Gas's distribution network to supply large customers (consuming more than 2,500 therms per year). Between 1991 and 1996, British Gas's share of this market fell dramatically, from 91 per cent to 29 per cent. The Gas Act of 1995 extended competition to the rest of the market. Other firms were allowed to use pipeline systems, for the shipping and supply of gas. Charges for the use of British Gas's pipelines were capped at RPI *minus* 5 per cent (1995–7) and RPI *minus* 6.5 per cent (1997–2001). By 1998, around 70 new suppliers had obtained a combined market share of more than 70 per cent. Following a 1996 Monopolies and Mergers investigation, in 1997 British Gas voluntarily split its operations into a gas supply company (British Gas, comprising Transco and several other units) and an exploration and production company (Centrica). In 2000 Transco was sold, and became the major constituent of a new supply company, the Lattice Group. Ofgem assumed responsibility for regulation in 1998. Between 1986 and 2002, prices had fallen by 37 per cent in real terms, and price cap regulation was eventually abandoned in 2002.

The electricity industry in England and Wales was privatized in the 1989 Electricity Act. This unbundled the Central Electricity Generating Board (which had previously operated generation and transmission, with 12 area boards responsible for distribution) into separate units responsible for generation, transmission and regional distribution. In Scotland, the two electricity providers were privatized as fully integrated firms. The Office of Electricity Regulation (Offer) was the original regulator, before being superseded by Ofgem in 1998. Post-privatization, the National Grid Company assumed responsibility for transmission, while generation was under the control of a duopoly, comprising National Power and Powergen.

The wholesale market for electricity used the electricity pool after privatization. Electricity suppliers purchased electricity at wholesale prices from the pool, while the generators sold electricity to it. The National Grid Company set prices so as to balance the demand and supply of electricity Within each day, demand was estimated for half-hour periods. Generators were then asked to submit bids, stating how much electricity each of their power stations would produce and at what price. The bids were arranged in ascending order, until demand was satisfied. If demand exceeded supply, the generators were required to increase production. Concern over alleged abuses of market power by the generators (making low-cost generating plants unavailable; claiming emergency maintenance programmes) led to enforced sales of power stations to new entrants or distributors. In 2001, the New Electricity Trading Arrangements (NETA) came into force. Electricity is traded forward in bilateral contracts between buyers and sellers. Prices are agreed today for quantities of electricity to be purchased in future. NETA has led to a further reduction in prices. In transmission, price cap regulation of the form 'RPI *minus* X' has been used. The X-factor was set at 0 per cent (1990–2), 3 per cent (1992–6), 20 per cent (1996–7) and 4 per cent (1997–2000). By April 2002, most price controls in the retail market were removed.

Over time and on some measures, competition appears to have increased in the retail gas and electricity markets (Littlechild, 2003). This is evidenced by the high levels of consumer switching between suppliers. In 2005, for example, more than 13 per cent of all UK consumers switched between electricity suppliers (Littlechild, 2007). However, the retail pricing of gas and electricity was a politically charged issue in the UK throughout the 2000s, with large swathes of public and media opinion being convinced that regulation of the privatized energy industry was fundamentally flawed, and that consumers were being fleeced by profit-hungry energy companies.

Water

Privatization of the water industry involved the creation of ten regional companies, responsible for water supplies and sewage. The Water Industry Act of 1991 set up the Office of Water Services (Ofwat) to oversee regulation. In 2006 the Office of Water services was replaced by the Water Services Regulation Authority, but the name 'Ofwat' is still used. The Competition and Service Utilities Act of 1992 allowed rival firms to supply domestic customers from outside their original regions, and competition was extended to large corporate customers. In the period 1989–94, price cap regulation was based on an 'RPI *plus* Y *plus* K' formula, where the Y-factor allowed for cost increases and the K-factor allowed for expenditure on the maintainance, renewal or expansion of the distribution network. From 1995 an 'RPI *minus* X' formula was adopted. The Water Industry Act of 1999 introduced new consumer protection measures, and a one-off 10 per cent price cut was imposed by Ofwat in 2000. Ofwat sets price limits for each water company by forecasting the revenue it is likely to need to operate efficiently. This is compared with the revenue the company is expected to generate, in order to determine the price limit after allowing for inflation. The price limits are reviewed every five years. Ofwat also specifies the minimum services the water companies are required to deliver, but the companies decide for themselves how to meet these targets.

Case study 24.3

Industry price controls hit Severn Trent

A new industry pricing regime and higher costs hit full-year results at Severn Trent, the water company that serves eight million customers across a region stretching from mid-Wales to the Humber. Severn Trent Water reduced prices 0.7 per cent last year, the first year of a new regulatory period, to comply with a requirement from Ofwat, the industry regulatory, that it reduce prices by an average of 0.9 per cent per year over five years. However, increased consumption by domestic customers and businesses helped to offset the effect of this price effect on revenues.

An underlying pre-tax profit of £288.6m was 14.7 per cent lower in 2010 and fractionally below the consensus forecast of £292.5m. But the results were overshadowed by confirmation that two managers suspended last October over concerns over deficiencies identified by the Drinking Water Inspectorate at water testing in Bridgend, south Wales, had left the company.

Severn Trent took a charge of £3.8m following an audit into the operations of the Bridgend plant while it was also hit by a further £3.9m overhead charge connected with a request from Ofwat, the industry watchdog, for information over a Competition Act probe into its laboratories division.

Tony Wray, Severn Trent chief executive, said problems at the plant were being dealt with and the company, was co-operating with investigations. In 2008, Severn Trent was fined £35.8m for overcharging customers after admitting two charges relating to the misreporting of water leakage data.

The group also blamed the coldest December on record for falling behind on upgrading water infrastructure as well as missing a target to repair leaking pipes set by Ofwat, the industry regulator. It was the first time in four years that the target had been missed, said Mr Wray, Severn Trent chief executive, who added performance on leaks was broadly in line with that of competitors.

'We have reduced leakage significantly since the winter and have plans in place to achieve our targets in 2012. We have taken into account recent experiences and have already commenced with plans to improve the resilience of the network,' he added. The group, which covers a region stretching from the Bristol Channel to the Humber, said it had experienced 'unseasonably dry' conditions, and that it was not ruling out usage restrictions such as a hosepipe ban.

Source: Industry price controls hit Severn Trent, © The Financial Times Limited. All Rights Reserved, 27 May 2011 (Child, A. and Kavanagh, M.). Abridged.

Rail

The Railways Act of 1993, the Transport Act of 2000, *Transport 2010* (Department of the Environment, Transport and the Regions, 2000) and the Railways Act of 2005 established the framework for the past and future regulation of the UK's rail industry. Privatization was a highly complex operation, involving the division of the state-owned British Rail into a number of separate components. A single firm, Railtrack, owned and operated the rail network, with responsibilities for the track, stations and the coordination of timetables. Responsibility for the supply of rolling stock was split between three firms. Train services are provided by a number of operators, which compete with one another to secure franchises to operate specific routes on an exclusive basis. The nature of the bidding process depends on the expected profitability of the route: lump-sum payments are required for profitable routes, while subsidies are available for loss-making routes. Subject to various commitments on service quality, the firm offering the highest lump-sum payment or requiring the lowest subsidy secures the franchise. Fares are set by the individual train service operators.

Railtrack was regulated by the Office of Rail Regulation (ORR). Railtrack charged individual operators for use of its network. These charges were subject to an 'RPI *minus* X' formula. The X-factor was set at 8 per cent (1995–6) and 2 per cent (1996–2001). However, with Railtrack on the verge of financial collapse, in October 2002 its assets and responsibilities were transferred to a new not-for-profit body, Network Rail. This decision amounted to effective renationalization of the network operation. Meanwhile, regulation of the privately owned (but in several cases heavily subsidized) train operating franchises was the responsibility of the Strategic Rail Authority (SRA). SRA monitored the performance of franchise operators, and had the power to levy fines for failure to meet the terms of their contracts. In November 2002, as part of the UK government's *Transport 2010* initiative, the SRA announced a package of measures aimed at improving quality of service. The Rail Review and Railways Act of 2005 effectively repealed the Transport Act 2000 and abolished the SRA, transferring its powers to Network Rail and the Department of Transport. Responsibility for safety was transferred from the Health and Safety Executive to ORR.

Rail privatization makes a strong claim to be considered the UK's least successful privatization of the 1980s and 1990s. A lack of clarity in the formulation of policy, the division of decision-making authority between bodies with overlapping responsibilities, unrealistic targets for the network provider and the train operators, a lack of investment, and a series of highly publicized accidents, were factors that contributed to the post-privatization difficulties of the UK's railway industry (Glaister, 2003).

24.7   Regulation of the banking industry

Banks play a critical role in every economy. Banks operate the payments system, are the major source of credit, and (normally) act as a safe haven for depositors' funds. The banking system (via the intermediation process) reallocates resources from those members of society in surplus (depositors) to those in deficit (borrowers), by transforming (typically) small liquid deposits into larger illiquid loans. If the intermediation process is efficient, then the demands of both depositors and borrowers can be satisfied at low cost, while mobilizing funds for investment that offers the potential to deliver enhanced economic growth.

In recent years, changes in the economic environment, structural and conduct deregulation and prudential regulation, along with technological and financial innovation, have transformed the banking industry. The largest banks in many countries are multi-product financial service conglomerates, offering a range of services including retail banking, asset management, brokerage, insurance, investment banking and wealth management. Deregulation has removed barriers to competition in traditional and new (non-banking) services, and has reduced the geographical barriers to competition.

Bank failures create negative externalities. Although each bank may be acting rationally in pursuit of its own objectives, a negative externality arises if there is insufficient incentive for each bank to take into account the effect of its own actions on the banking system as a whole. The failure of one bank may lead to the failure of others, and ultimately a loss of confidence in the financial system. This form of market failure creates the need for the supervision and regulation of individual banks.

Regulation can help strengthen solvency, by requiring banks to accumulate reserve assets or capital. In addition to structural regulation and conduct regulation, banks are also subject to prudential regulation. Feasible structural regulation measures might include the functional separation of banks into different activities (for example, the separation of commercial banking from investment banking), or the creation of entry barriers through minimum capital requirements or restrictions on the types of business banks can transact. The regulatory authorities might seek to limit the number of banks, by placing restrictions on the number of bank licences granted. Structural regulation tends to make entry into banking markets difficult, allowing incumbent banks the opportunity to exercise market power, and perhaps the opportunity to become even larger. Conduct regulation operates on the strategic or operational policies or decisions of banks. Controls might be imposed on the level of interest rates, the volume of loans granted, or the expansion of branch networks.

Prudential regulation seeks to safeguard the stability of banks and protect consumer interests. Relevant measures might include participation in deposit insurance schemes, and provisions for the central bank to act as lender-of-last-resort. Such regulations seek to promote the efficiency of banks and protect consumers; but they can have damaging consequences. For example, a flawed deposit insurance system might cause more harm than good, if moral hazard results in excessive risk-taking or other reckless behaviour on the part of banks. Banks may become willing to undertake more risky investments, safe in the knowledge that they will be bailed out if these investments subsequently fail. Depositors are attracted to risky banks that offer high returns, despite the risk, because they know they are protected if things go wrong. Possible remedies include interest rate controls, minimum liquidity requirements and restrictions on the permissible volumes of investment in any single activity.

As banking business has become increasingly complex, the usefulness of the traditional tools of supervision (which often rely on historical data) in monitoring risk-taking by banks has been called into question. Consequently, the role of market discipline in monitoring and constraining banks' activities has been the subject of attention (Flannery, 2012). Forward-looking, market-based information, embodied in a bank's share price, debt instruments and ratings, can help inform bank supervision, and provide advance warning of a need for supervisory corrective action.

Regulation and supervision are no panacea for every form of market failure that might afflict the banking industry. Effectiveness depends crucially upon the extent to which the broader economic, legal and political environment provides the right incentives for the governance of banks (Barth *et al.*, 2006). Kane (2012) views the regulation and supervision of the banking industry as a repeated game of move and counter-move, with the regulatory and supervisory agencies usually playing catch-up with the banks they are charged with regulating.

Measured in terms of implications for the stability of the financial system, the comparison between a regime of deregulation and increased competition, and one of strict regulation and limited competition, is by no means clear cut. The competition-fragility (charter or franchise value) view suggests banks earn monopoly profits in less competitive markets, resulting in higher charter values and accumulation of capital in the form of retained profits. This places a bank in a stronger position to withstand demand- or supply-side shocks, and discourages excessive risk-taking (Allen and Gale, 2004). By contrast, the competition-stability view suggests competition leads to less fragility. If the banking industry is highly concentrated, any abuse of market power by incumbent banks produces higher interest rates for borrowers, either increasing the risk of default, or increasing the incentive for borrowers to accept greater risk in their investments or other activities in search of a return sufficient to service the original loan. All of this tends to make the financial system less stable (Boyd and DeNicolo, 2005).

The largest banks have been characterized as too big to fail, too interconnected to fail or too complex to fail. Widespread recognition that the government would always intervene to prevent the failure of important banks, owing to their size, interconnectedness or complexity, provides an implicit public insurance or safety-net guarantee (O'Hara and Shaw, 1990; Mishkin, 2006). This raises severe moral hazard issues: the banks concerned may tend to take on excessive risk; or their depositors and investors may fail to carry out their monitoring or control responsibilities with adequate diligence.

Individual bank failures and systemic crises typically disrupt lending, leading to reduced investment and a decline in the overall level of economic activity. Stricter regulation and supervision of the banking industry often follows a financial crisis. In the US, for example, the Glass-Steagall Act (1933), which separated the commercial and investment banking arms of privately owned banks and created the Federal Deposit Insurance Corporation (FDIC) as a vehicle for insuring bank deposits, was passed in response to widespread bank failures in the aftermath of the Wall Street Crash of 1929.

More recently, the financial crisis of 2007–9 has heightened public awareness of regulatory issues. Factors that have been cited as causes of the financial crisis include inappropriate monetary policy, misaligned incentives for investors, banks and credit rating agencies, weak financial disclosure and accounting rules, lax lending standards, loopholes in regulation and supervision, and outright fraud. In particular, excessively risky lending in the US residential property mortgage market, to low-income 'subprime' borrowers without a strong credit history, led to a sharp increase in the rate of default on mortgage loans, and a decline in the value of asset-backed securities that had been created by bundling together anticipated streams of interest payments on residential mortgages. The complex nature of asset-backed securities, and the lack of transparency of the off-balance-sheet vehicles created by the banks in order to transact such business, made it impossible to value these assets or assess the exposure of individual banks to the risk of default. Banks became wary of lending to each other, culminating in a liquidity freeze in inter-bank lending markets. Declines in property prices led to further declines in the value of securitized mortgage products, and in the value of the banks' own loans portfolios. Numerous banks became insolvent, forcing the intervention of central banks and governments.

Initial responses to the crisis included government purchase of distressed assets, changes in rules surrounding assets accepted as collateral, nationalization or part-nationalization of banks and other financial institutions considered too big, complex or interconnected to fail, strengthening of provisions for government guarantees of consumer deposits and other bank liabilities, and improvements in financial disclosure and transparency. Over the longer term, a complete overhaul of the architecture of the regulatory arrangements for banks and the financial system is in progress, over a period of years. Key principles include a more realistic assessment of risk with greater emphasis on simple capital and liquidity ratios, greater transparency and the curtailment of opaque business models, enhanced consumer protection, and the development of effective early-warning systems and procedures for intervention in cases of financial distress on the part of individual institutions or at a system-wide level. Specific actions include the extension of coverage of bank regulation based on economic substance rather than legal form, strengthened capital provisioning requirements and moves towards counter-cyclical capital provisioning, enhanced supervision of credit rating agencies, new codes of conduct for executive compensation and benefits, improved arrangements for regulation of cross-border banks, reform of accounting disclosure rules, and the creation of new consumer protection agencies.

24.8 Evaluation of regulation and deregulation

Regulation or, where appropriate, deregulation, can improve the functioning of markets, and lead to increased productivity and economic growth. Competitive pressure forces firms to improve the efficiency of their useage of factor inputs and eliminate x-inefficiencies. The reduction of entry and exit barriers leads to the reallocation of market share from inefficient to efficient firms. Over the longer term, the adoption of new technologies produces favourable shifts the production possibility frontier (Ahn, 2001, 2002; Conway *et al.*, 2006).

OECD (2005) sets a number of benchmarks for effective regulation and regulatory reform:

- Adoption of regulatory reform programmes with clear objectives and plans for implementation.

- Regular assessments of the impact of regulation to ensure that intended objectives are met.

- Mechanisms to ensure that regulations and regulatory institutions are transparent.

- Review and strengthening of competition policy in areas of the economy where market power is prevalent.

- Design of regulations to stimulate competition and efficiency.

- Elimination of unnecessary regulatory barriers to trade and investment.

- Identification of linkages with other micro- and macroeconomic policy objectives.

The assumption is that efficient regulation, and the removal of unnecessary regulation, yields identifiable benefits to the economy in the form of increased productivity and economic growth (Djankov *et al.*, 2006; Malyshev, 2006; Schiantarelli, 2008). A number of databases examine the burden of regulation facing business in developed and developing economies. For example, the World Bank *Doing Business Database* produces annual rankings of countries showing the ease with which firms can conduct business. The regulatory environment is characterized by regulation in ten specific areas: starting a business; dealing with construction permits; employing workers; registering property; obtaining credit; protecting investors; paying taxes; trading across borders; enforcing contracts; and closing a business. The 2011 rankings are listed in Table 24.2. The World Bank sees the OECD countries as having the most business-friendly regulations, followed by countries in Eastern Europe and Central Asia; East Asia and the Pacific; the Middle East and North Africa; Latin America; and South Asia. Sub-Saharan Africa has the least business-friendly regulatory environment.

Much of the early empirical evidence on the impact of the regulatory environment on productive efficiency is indirect, focusing on the relationship between competition and productivity, rather than on the direct link between product market regulation or deregulation and productivity (Green and Mayes, 1991). Later studies using EU data find strong evidence that product market reforms implemented as part of the EU single market programme led to increased productive efficiency, particularly among firms in public ownership (Griffith, 2001; Nicodeme and Sauner-Leroy, 2007). There is evidence that liberalization with respect to entry conditions is linked to improvements in firm-level productivity (Nicoletti and Scarpetta, 2003; Brandt, 2004). Finally, most of the empirical evidence suggests there is an inverted U-shaped relationship between innovation and competition, and a positive relationship between innovation and growth in productivity (Griffith *et al.*, 2004; Griffith and Harrison, 2004).

However, Helm (2006) strikes a note of caution by pointing out that the accepted market failure and efficiency justifications for regulation are based on normative judgements.

> Why regulate? What is the rationale for regulation? The usual answer is that there is some identifiable market failure considered to be so great that intervention to correct it will be efficient, in the sense that the costs of intervention will be lower than the costs of failure. This conventional answer is a normative one: it assumes that the objective of policy is efficiency, and that the reason why regulation arises is to address this objective. However, there are other objectives, including equity and freedom, and many of the justifications for intervention are for non-efficiency reasons. . . . Regulation exists to . . . prevent discrimination on gender and race grounds . . . Concern for future generations motivates environmental law, with the concept of sustainable development requiring non-decreasing utility over time.

(Helm, 2006, p. 171)

Table 24.2 Doing Business ranking for 2011

Economy	Ease of Doing Business rank	Economy	Ease of Doing Business rank	Economy	Ease of Doing Business rank	Economy	Ease of Doing Business rank	Economy	Ease of Doing Business rank
Singapore	1	Bahrain	38	St. Vincent & Gren.	75	El Salvador	112	Algeria	148
Hong Kong SAR, China	2	Chile	39	Vanuatu	76	Argentina	113	Gambia, The	149
New Zealand	3	Cyprus	40	Fiji	77	Guyana	114	Burkina Faso	150
United States	4	Peru	41	Namibia	78	Kiribati	115	Liberia	151
Denmark	5	Colombia	42	Maldives	79	Palau	116	Ukraine	152
Norway	6	Puerto Rico (U.S.)	43	Croatia	80	Kosovo	117	Bolivia	153
United Kingdom	7	Spain	44	Moldova	81	Nicaragua	118	Senegal	154
Korea, Rep.	8	Rwanda	45	Albania	82	Cape Verde	119	Equatorial Guinea	155
Iceland	9	Tunisia	46	Brunei Darussalam	83	Russian Federation	120	Gabon	156
Ireland	10	Kazakhstan	47	Zambia	84	Costa Rica	121	Comoros	157
Finland	11	Slovak Republic	48	Bahamas, The	85	Bangladesh	122	Suriname	158
Saudi Arabia	12	Oman	49	Mongolia	86	Uganda	123	Mauritania	159
Canada	13	Luxembourg	50	Italy	87	Swaziland	124	Afghanistan	160
Sweden	14	Hungary	51	Jamaica	88	Bosnia & Herzegovina	125	Cameroon	161
Australia	15	St. Lucia	52	Sri Lanka	89	Brazil	126	Togo	162
Georgia	16	Mexico	53	Uruguay	90	Tanzania	127	São Tomé & Príncipe	163
Thailand	17	Botswana	54	China	91	Honduras	128	Iraq	164
Malaysia	18	Armenia	55	Serbia	92	Indonesia	129	Lao PDR	165
Germany	19	Montenegro	56	Belize	93	Ecuador	130	Uzbekistan	166
Japan	20	Antigua & Barbuda	57	Morocco	94	West Bank and Gaza	131	Côte d'Ivoire	167
Latvia	21	Tonga	58	St. Kitts & Nevis	95	India	132	Timor-Leste	168
Macedonia, FYR	22	Bulgaria	59	Jordan	96	Nigeria	133	Burundi	169
Mauritius	23	Samoa	60	Guatemala	97	Syrian Arab Rep.	134	Djibouti	170
Estonia	24	Panama	61	Vietnam	98	Sudan	135	Zimbabwe	171
Taiwan, China	25	Poland	62	Yemen, Rep.	99	Philippines	136	Angola	172
Switzerland	26	Ghana	63	Greece	100	Madagascar	137	Niger	173
Lithuania	27	Czech Rep.	64	Papua New Guinea	101	Cambodia	138	Haiti	174
Belgium	28	Dominica	65	Paraguay	102	Mozambique	139	Benin	175
France	29	Azerbaijan	66	Seychelles	103	Micronesia, Fed. Sts.	140	Guinea-Bissau	176
Portugal	30	Kuwait	67	Lebanon	104	Sierra Leone	141	Venezuela, RB	177
Netherlands	31	Trinidad &Tobago	68	Pakistan	105	Bhutan	142	Congo, Dem. Rep.	178
Austria	32	Belarus	69	Marshall Islands	106	Lesotho	143	Guinea	179
United Arab Emirates	33	Kyrgyz Republic	70	Nepal	107	Iran, Islamic Rep.	144	Eritrea	180
Israel	34	Turkey	71	Dominican Rep.	108	Malawi	145	Congo, Rep.	181
South Africa	35	Romania	72	Kenya	109	Mali	146	Central African Republic	182
Qatar	36	Grenada	73	Egypt, Arab Rep.	110	Tajikistan	147	Chad	183
Slovenia	37	Solomon Islands	74	Ethiopia	111				

Source: From www.doingbusiness.org/economyrankings/ (data from Doing Business 2011), with permission of The World Bank.

Furthermore, in democratic countries there is a tendency for politicians to respond to calls for regulation in order to maximize votes. Even if politics is removed from the regulatory process, excessive regulation can occur.

> Regulatory bodies have a direct incentive to over-supply regulation. Institutions have budgets and missions; their staff have salaries and careers. The former are related to the latter: in general, the bigger the budget, the greater the pay, non-pecuniary benefits, and scope for promotion. In the UK, the chairmen and chief executives of large regulatory bodies also tend to attract public recognition through the honours system.
>
> *(Helm, 2006, p. 173)*

24.9 Franchising and competitive tendering

As shown earlier (see Section 19.6), **franchising** involves the allocation of exclusive rights to supply certain types of goods and services. This right or licence protects the franchisee from competition for the duration of the contract. Governments sometimes award franchises in cases where there are efficiency or welfare grounds for doing so. For example, restrictions on entry might be needed to allow an incumbent the opportunity to realize the full benefits of economies of scale. An example is the practice of franchising the rights for sole provision of passenger train services on specific routes or sections of the rail network to individual firms.

Franchises can be characterized as *ownership* or *operating*. Ownership franchises grant the holder control over an asset in perpetuity. Operating franchises grant the holder temporary control, for a limited period of time. Both types of franchise shield the holder from competition while the franchise is effective, but in the case of an operating franchise this benefit is of limited duration. It has been argued that operating franchises discourage long-term investment, because the franchise holder is aware of the risk that the franchise will not be renewed when it expires. For example, it has been suggested this factor has discouraged long-term investment by passenger train service operators on the UK rail network. Winston (1993, 1998) argues that by eliminating entry barriers, franchising tends to make markets contestable. To win a contract, the future monopoly provider has to charge a competitive price for its services. A successful bid overcomes what was previously a government-imposed entry barrier.

Once the franchise has been awarded, the franchisor retains an element of control, either by threatening that the franchise might not be renewed when it expires; or, in extreme cases, by retaining the right to revoke the franchise in the event of the franchisee's non-compliance with the terms and conditions. Although the franchisee is shielded from competition once the franchise has been awarded, competition during the bidding process may be intense (Demsetz, 1968). If the franchise is expected to be profit-making, bidders are invited to pay to secure the franchise. Conversely, if the franchise is expected to be loss-making, bidders are invited to state the payment or subsidy they would require to supply the product or service. As shown earlier (see Chapter 14), the design of the auction under which the franchise is to be awarded may have significant implications for the size of the proceeds the franchisor can expect to realize from the auction.

There are several ways in which bids for a franchise contract might be invited (McAfee and McMillan, 1987; Milgrom, 1989):

■ *Bidding by the lowest cost per unit*. In this case, the winning bidder is the one that offers to perform the service at the lowest average cost. Competition in the bidding process may cause the price to reach a level at which the franchisee can earn only a normal profit. Certain problems can arise under this bidding method. First, if cost savings are achieved after the award of the franchise, perhaps due to technological advance, consumers do not necessarily see any benefit in the form of lower prices. Second, if the franchise covers several products or services, it may be difficult to determine which bid is the lowest overall. Third, in order to secure the franchise, a firm may submit a bid below its average cost. After the award of the franchise, the franchisee may claim that costs have risen, and attempt to renegotiate the agreement.

■ *Bidding by the lowest lump-sum subsidy*. In this case, the winning bidder is the one that offers to perform the service for the lowest lump-sum subsidy. Some privatized industries were loss-making before privatization, and were expected to remain so afterwards. Private contractors would therefore require a subsidy in order to provide the service.

■ *Bidding by lump-sum payment*. In this case, bidders offer a lump-sum payment to secure the franchise. This method of franchise allocation is often used in cases of natural monopoly, where it is likely an abnormal profit will be earned, but breaking the industry up into constituent parts is not feasible. Effectively, this system allows the franchisor the opportunity to appropriate some of the abnormal profit the successful bidder expects to earn once it becomes the monopoly supplier. If potential franchisees can be induced to submit bids equivalent to or near to the full value of the abnormal profit they expect to earn, all or most of the abnormal profit may revert to the franchisor. In the short term, the lump-sum payment provides funds for the government, but if the franchisee secures the right to exploit its market power over the duration of the franchise, this may work against the interests of consumers. Regulation may be required to avoid this outcome; although bidders who know they will be subject to stringent regulation are unlikely to bid aggressively to secure the franchise.

Issues that arise when inviting bids for the award of franchises include the following:

■ *Setting the length of the contract*. This may be important in determining the degree of competition at the bidding stage. On the one hand, if the duration of the contract is too short, bidders may be deterred; but on the other hand, short-term contracts offer the franchisor greater control over the franchisee's activities. Long-term contracts may attract more bidders, but they may also allow the winning bidder the opportunity to abuse its market power, or to underperform for a long period.

■ *Collusion among bidders*. Bidders may decide to collude to ensure the contract goes to a particular firm, or to maximize the financial benefit to the winning bidder by limiting competition among bidders. The gains from collusion might be split between the colluding firms. Collusion is more likely when the duration of a contract is short, and when sealed bids are required, leaving the winning bidder at greater risk of experiencing the winner's curse (Schmalensee, 1979); see also Section 14.3.

■ *The level of fixed investment*. If the franchisee needs to incur significant sunk cost investment expenditure in order to operate the franchise, bidding is likely to be discouraged, especially if this investment is non-recoverable in the event of non-renewal of the franchise. To avoid this difficulty, the franchisor might need to make arrangements for the transfer of ownership of industry-specific assets at the end of the contract. However, this might prove difficult in cases where the assets are also firm-specific.

■ *Asymmetric information between bidders*. If the bidding is for the renewal of an existing franchise, an incumbent franchisee's specialized knowledge may place it at an unfair advantage relative to other bidders, making it difficult for the latter to displace the incumbent.

■ *Measuring quality of product or service*. In cases where the franchisor is concerned about quality as well as cost, it may be possible to invite bids based on price–quality combinations. In this case, an 'RPI *minus* X' price cap might be amended to 'RPI *minus* X *plus* ΔQ', where ΔQ represents quality improvements. Effectively, the franchisee is permitted to charge for introducing improvements in quality. In practice, however, measurement of quality can be problematic (Rovizzi and Thompson, 1995; Baldwin and Cave, 1998).

Compulsory competitive tendering (CCT) is a practice similar to franchising. In this case, existing local government (in-house) providers and private contractors are invited to tender for contracts to provide services for local government (Lavery, 1997). For provision to remain in-house, the local government department has to demonstrate it can provide the service more cheaply than any alternative private contractor (UK Cabinet Office, 1996). CCT was introduced under the terms of the 1988 Local Government Act; though many local authorities had practised some form of competitive tendering previously (Wilson, 1994; Domberger, 1999). The 1988 Act covered service provision in areas such as catering (schools, hospitals, residential care centres), cleaning (of local authority buildings, hospitals, schools) and refuse collection. Following the election of the Labour government in the UK in 1997, CCT was replaced by a new system known as *Best Value* (DETR, 1998). Best Value placed greater emphasis than CCT on quality, as well as cost criteria, in determining the provision of local government services.

It has been suggested CCT represents 'a convenient halfway house between public production and private ownership by retaining public sector control over the activity whilst simultaneously introducing commercial discipline through a formal contracting process' (Domberger and Rimmer, 1994, p. 441). The debate surrounding CCT focuses on the following issues:

- In-house teams or private contractors may perceive increased incentives to strive for cost savings and productivity improvements, due to the threat of losing the contract on the next occasion it is renewed.

- By helping to trim local government expenditure on the services concerned, CCT may provide opportunities for increased spending elsewhere, tax cuts, or a reduction in the public sector borrowing requirement (Domberger and Jenson, 1997).

- CCT encourages flexible working practices such as part-time work, job sharing and casualization. However, this may be interpreted as a euphemism for a deterioration in the working conditions of local government employees (Ascher, 1987).

- Substantial transaction costs are involved in specifying the terms of the contract, the method of bidding, and monitoring the contract after it has been awarded. Contracting out should only be considered if the expected cost saving exceeds these transaction costs (Domberger and Hall, 1995). Monitoring costs may tend to be higher for contracts awarded to private contractors. The latter are more profit-motivated than their in-house counterparts, and may seek to minimize costs at the expense of quality (Prager, 1994).

Case study 24.4

Threat to outsourced workers' benefits

The government is 'minded' to scrap an informal code guaranteeing public sector benefits for thousands of outsourced private sector jobs, threatening a confrontation with unions. The proposal, aimed at reducing the cost of outsourcing swaths of government business from cleaning and catering to information technology, health and waste management, provoked opposition from union representatives on Tuesday. It also brought only a guarded welcome from employers, who said individuals doing the same job in the same company could receive different rates of pay and benefits.

Under European legislation, workers transferred to the private sector have much of their employment terms and conditions protected. But under a voluntary two-tier workforce code agreed between the unions, employers and the Labour government in 2003, new recruits are offered terms that overall are 'no less favourable' than those of transferred employees. Francis Maude, the Cabinet Office minister, told the Financial Times that 'we are minded to abolish it [the code]'.

He plans to address the issue through a working group via the Public Services Forum, which represents unions and outsource employers. Requiring employers to pay new recruits the same as transferred workers 'distorts the market when we are trying to encourage new entrants into the outsourced [services] market', worth £80bn ($125bn) a year, Mr Maude said. The Trades Union Congress said: 'We would be opposed. This is no more than an attempt to drive down the living standards for low-paid workers.' The CBI employers organisation and the Business Services Association, which represents outsourcers, gave the move a cautious welcome.

Beginning with the slash and burn of the 1980s – when the previous Conservative government first imposed compulsory competitive tendering on local government – the outsourcing of public services has over the years become big business. Three decades ago, cowboy operators often won contracts for bin emptying and street cleaning by scything through the pay and conditions of ex-council staff. Since then, the public services industry has become a much more sophisticated operation. More than a third of all public services – not just cleaning, catering and security, but IT, health, legal and construction services, welfare to work and elements of defence – are now delivered by the private and voluntary sectors. The industry employs more than 1m people. And while by no means all have been transferred from the public sector – some contracts are entirely new business, and many staff are new recruits – a chunk of them are former public sector employees.

As the coalition government seeks to extract 'more for less' from public spending, it is likely to outsource more – so this £80bn-a-year market looks set to grow, in spite of looming cuts.

In recent years, the industry has been largely free of strife – in part, though only in part, because of a voluntary code that stipulates that new recruits should be paid on terms that overall are 'no less favourable' than those enjoyed by staff whose terms are broadly protected when they are transferred to a private sector employer.

When Labour agreed the 'two-tier workforce' code with the unions back in 2003, the industry's reaction was nuanced. At the time, Norman Rose, then director-general of the Business Services Association that represents many of the outsourcers, accused the government of 'capitulating to trade union pressure'. But he acknowledged that it salved a running sore – staff in the same company being paid different terms for identical jobs – and said the sector could now concentrate on 'delivery, quality, productivity and innovation'.

The TUC seized on that point on Tuesday in its response to Mr Maude's disclosure that he wanted to scrap the code. It said: 'The private sector claims they can deliver things more efficiently. But in our view more efficiently does not include reducing the terms and conditions of workers. That is not efficiency, it is attacking the living standards of often low-paid people – and it will increase inequality.' Mark Fox, the BSA's current director, said his members had not lobbied for the scrapping of the code, while adding that they would not oppose its abolition. The bigger outsourcers had managed to live with it, he said. But he argued that abandoning the code would make the market more accessible for smaller and medium companies that could not afford to match public sector terms – one reason Mr Maude cited for wanting to get rid of it.

There is no doubt that the code added to costs. While it is hard to gauge how much the taxpayer might save from its abolition, the health department calculated when it signed up that the code would add £75m a year to the outsourced contracts for cleaning, catering and laundry that about a third of NHS hospitals then held. Susan Anderson, head of public services for the CBI, said it was clear 'that we are in different times' and 'that some firms cannot afford to compete on the existing pay packages'. In addition, she said, 'what this has tended to do is ossify terms and conditions when we need more flexibility about how we do things'. Given the fiscal position 'we can't have business as usual', she said. Unions, however, said abolishing the code would produce 'chaos', and 'strife' between colleagues. Unison, which has members in outsourced health and local government services, said 'having people doing the same job on different rates of pay is not a recipe for a motivated and happy workforce'.

Source: Threat to outsourced workers' benefits, © The Financial Times Limited. All Rights Reserved, 27 July 2010 (Pickard, J. and Timmins, N.).

24.10 Summary

Chapter 24 has examined regulation, in particular the regulation of natural monopolies. If a natural monopolist is abusing its market power, there are several possible solutions. The first is public ownership, which normally involves granting statutory rights to a single firm. In doing so, the firm can be required to price its products in a competitive manner. A second solution is to open up the relevant market to competition. In many countries, particularly in the UK, the privatization of previously nationalized industries, involving the transfer of state-owned assets to the private sector, has often been accompanied by efforts to create more competitive post-privatization market conditions. Regulation may be viewed as a substitute for competition in cases where competition is impractical. A final solution is to allow temporary monopoly rights through the granting of a franchise. In this case, competition takes place prior to the award of the franchise during the bidding process, with stipulations concerning matters such as price and quality of service written into the successful bidder's contract.

In most cases, nationalization involves the creation of a statutory monopoly owned and controlled by the government. By assuming ownership of a natural monopoly, the government can instruct the firm to pursue certain objectives or adopt certain policies. The aim is to correct market failure and satisfy the necessary conditions for allocative efficiency. Nationalization may eliminate wasteful competition, or it may allow the full exploitation of economies of scale. Nationalization may be motivated by social objectives, such as the provision of services that would be deemed uneconomic by the private sector. However, without a profit motive, and in the absence of competitive discipline, incentives to operate efficiently may be lacking. Confusion or conflict between economic and non-economic objectives has often made nationalized firms difficult to manage. Overall, the empirical evidence presents a rather mixed picture of the performance of the UK's nationalized industries before most of them were privatized during the 1980s and 1990s.

The economic case for privatization, in the sense of the sale or denationalization of state-owned enterprises, rests on the following arguments.

■ Privatization accompanied by the introduction of competition may help deliver lower prices, improved product or service quality and greater consumer choice, as firms subject to competitive pressure search for cost savings and productivity gains.

■ The creation of a tier of profit-motivated shareholders, and increased capital market discipline, may force management to attach higher priority to objectives related to profitability.

■ In the short term, privatization proceeds make a positive contribution to the public finances, creating new options for increasing public expenditure, cutting taxes or reducing borrowing.

■ Privatized firms have the same freedom to raise finance from capital markets as any other private sector firms. In contrast, state-owned firms may be subject to public sector borrowing constraints.

On the other hand, if privatization simply leads to the transfer of a state-owned monopoly into private ownership, this may work against the interests of consumers. Following a privatization involving the break-up of a state-owned monopoly into smaller components, costs might increase if the smaller units fail to realize the full benefits of economies of scale or scope. The use of proceeds from the sale of capital assets to finance current expenditure or tax cuts suggests unsound management of the public finances. In general, the benefits and costs of privatizations are difficult to evaluate. In some cases, staffing levels, costs and prices have fallen, sometimes dramatically. However, in several cases, privatization has been accompanied by rapid and far-reaching technological progress. It is usually difficult or impossible to estimate with any certainty what might have happened had the enterprises concerned remained in state ownership.

Regulation is an option when one or more types of market failure result in allocative inefficiency. Sources of market failure include the abuse of market power, asymmetric information between buyers and sellers, various types of externality and the non-exclusivity characteristic of public goods. The potential for market failure due to the exercise of market power has raised particular concerns in the case of privatized natural monopolies. In several cases a stringent regulatory regime has been introduced, in an attempt to deliver outcomes that mimic those that would (hypothetically) be achieved under competitive conditions. Structural regulation includes the functional separation of firms into complementary activities, restrictions on entry, and rules regarding the operation of foreign firms. Conduct regulation seeks to influence the regulated firms' behaviour, through measures such as controls on price, or product or service quality, or other conduct variables.

The main regulatory regime used in the US is rate of return regulation. The regulator specifies a required rate of return on capital, and allows regulated firms to set their prices accordingly, subject to frequent price reviews. In the UK and most other European countries price cap regulation is widely used, especially in the case of privatized companies supplying products or services such as telecommunications, energy, water and transport, which were formerly in public ownership. Price changes are dictated by an 'RPI *minus* X' formula, where X can be adjusted to allow for productivity savings or improvements in quality. Reviews of the price cap usually take place at intervals several years apart. Price cap regulation may provide stronger incentives for firms to search for cost savings than other regulatory regimes, because the firm keeps the saving (at least until the next review). Effective regulation requires clear policy objectives, accurate information and accountability. Although regulation or, where appropriate, deregulation, can produce gains in productivity and economic growth, in the long term any regulatory regime is subject to the possibility of regulatory capture: a tendency for the regulated firms to exercise undue influence over the regulator's decisions.

The financial crisis of 2007–9 has heightened public awareness of regulatory issues involving the banking industry. The failure of one bank may lead to a loss of confidence in the financial system, and a negative externality is created when there is insufficient incentive for each bank to consider the implications of its own actions for the stability of the system as a whole. Many large banks have been characterized as too big to fail. Widespread recognition that governments would always intervene to prevent the failure of key banks raises severe moral hazard issues: the banks themselves, which benefit from an implicit public insurance subsidy, may accept excessive risk, or their depositors and investors may fail monitor their activities diligently. Post-crisis, a fundamental overhaul of the regulatory arrangements for banks and the financial system is underway, involving greater emphasis on simple risk measures based on capital and liquidity ratios, more transparency and less reliance on opaque business models, enhanced consumer protection, and the development of effective early-warning systems and resolution procedures in the event of financial distress.

Franchising involves the allocation of exclusive rights to supply a particular good and service. Bidders may be invited to pay to secure a profit-making franchise; or to state the minimum subsidy they would require to run a loss-making franchise. Although the franchisee is shielded from competition once the franchise has been awarded, competition to secure the franchise may be intense. After the award the franchisor retains an element of control, by threatening non-renewal when the present franchise expires, or by terminating the franchise in the event of non-compliance with the terms and conditions. Competitive tendering is a practice similar to franchising, in which in-house local government providers and private contractors are invited to tender for contracts to provide services for local government. There is evidence that compulsory competitive tendering has produced substantial cost savings in some cases, although there are concerns about the implications for quality and standards of service, as well as the pay and employment conditions of local government employees and those hired by private contractors.

Discussion questions

1. If a natural monopolist is suspected of abusing its market power, what remedies short of full-scale nationalization might be available?

2. Describe the evolution of regulation and competition policy in the UK since the 1980s.

3. Assess the arguments for and against the public ownership of key industries.

4. With reference to Case Study 24.1, on what economic grounds can the policy of privatization be justified?

5. What are the linkages between the arrangements for financing the investment and operating activities in the privatized utilities, and the performance of the utilties in delivering investment and competitive prices to consumers?

6. It is often argued that regulation is justified in cases where some form of market failure would otherwise create an inefficient allocation of resources. Identify possible sources of market failure that might give rise to a need for regulation.

7. What is meant by regulatory capture?

8. Distinguish between structural and conduct regulation. With reference to regulation in the UK or elsewhere, provide specific examples of each of these forms of regulation.

9. Explain the difference between rate of return (cost plus) regulation and price cap regulation, and assess the advantages and disadvantages of each.

10. With reference to Case Studies 24.2 and 24.3, compare and contrast the UK's approach to the regulation of the following privatized industries: telecommunications, energy and water.

11. Explain the rationale for the regulation of banks, and describe how regulatory arrangements for the banking industry have evolved since the financial crisis of 2007–9.

12. What are the main issues an intending franchisor should consider when framing the bidding rules and drafting the terms and conditions under which the franchise will be awarded?

13. Assess the effectiveness of compulsory competitive tendering and best value initiatives in improving efficiency and quality in public services.

14. With reference to Case Study 24.4, explain why outsourcing may reduce the welfare of workers.

Further reading

Armstrong, M. and Sappington, D.E.M. (2007) Recent developments in regulation, in Armstrong, M. and Porter, R. (eds) *Handbook of Industrial Organization*, Vol. 3. Amsterdam: Elsevier.

Ball, A., Broadbent, J. and Moore, C. (2002) Best value and the control of local government: challenges and contradictions, *Public Money and Management*, 22, 9–16.

Barth, J.R., Caprio, G. and Levine, R. (2006) *Re-thinking Bank Regulation: Till Angels Govern*. Cambridge: Cambridge University Press.

Beck, T., Coyle, D., Dewatripoint, M., Freixas, X. and Seabright, P. (2010) *Bailing out the Banks: Reconciling Stability and Competition*. London: Centre for Economic Policy Research.

Beesley, M.E. (ed.) (1997) *Privatization, Regulation and Deregulation*, 2nd edition. London: Routledge.

Domberger, S. and Hall, C. (1995) *The Contracting Casebook: Competitive Tendering in Action*. Canberra: Australian Government Publishing Service.

Green, R. (1999) Checks and balances in utility regulation: the UK experience, *Public Policy for the Private Sector*, May. Washington, DC: World Bank.

Helm, D. and Jenkinson, T. (1997) The assessment: introducing competition into regulated industries, *Oxford Review of Economic Policy*, 13, 1–14.

Kay, J.A., Mayer, C. and Thompson, D. (eds) (1986) *Privatization and Regulation: The UK Experience*. Oxford: Clarendon Press.

Megginson, W.L. and Netter, J.M. (2001) From state to market: a survey of empirical studies on privatization, *Journal of Economic Literature*, 39, 321–89.

Newberry, D. (2000) *Privatisation, Restructuring and Regulation of Network Utilities*. Cambridge, MA: MIT Press.

Nicodeme, G. and Saunder-Leroy, J.-B. (2007) Product market reforms and productivity: a review of the theoretical and empirical literature on the transmission channels, *Journal of Industry, Competition and Trade*, 7, 53–72.

Parker, D. (2000) *Privatization and Corporate Performance*. Cheltenham: Edward Elgar.

Schiantarelli, F. (2008) Product market regulation and macroeconomic performance: a review of cross country evidence, *Boston College Working Papers in Economics*, No. 623.

Vickers, J. and Yarrow, G. (1988) *Privatization: An Economic Analysis*. Cambridge, MA: MIT Press.

Wilson, J. (1994) Competitive tendering and UK public services, *Economic Review*, April, 12, 31–5.

Winston, C. (1993) Economic deregulation: days of reckoning for microeconomists, *Journal of Economic Literature*, 31, 1263–89.

Winston, C. (1998) US industry adjustment to economic deregulation, *Journal of Economic Perspectives*, 12, 89–110.

Analytical Tools

Mathematical methods

Appendix 1 contains mathematical derivations of selected results from chapters of this book. To follow these derivations, a knowledge of elementary calculus is required. The section numbers and headings containing each result are identified at the start of each derivation.

2.3 Demand, revenue, elasticity and profit maximization

This section demonstrates the relationship between marginal revenue and price elasticity of demand.

Symbols
P = price
Q = output
TR = total revenue
MR = marginal revenue
PED = price elasticity of demand

The formal definition of price elasticity of demand is:

$$\text{PED} = \frac{dQ}{dP} \times \frac{P}{Q}$$

where $\dfrac{dQ}{dP}$ is the derivative of the market demand function with respect to price.

The definition of total revenue is:

$$\text{TR} = PQ$$

Using calculus, the definition of marginal revenue is the derivative of TR with respect to Q.

According to the Product Rule, if $y = uv$, $\dfrac{dy}{dx} = u\dfrac{dv}{dx} + v\dfrac{du}{dx}$.

Let $y = \text{TR}$, $x = Q$, $u = P$ and $v = Q$.

$$\text{MR} = \frac{d\text{TR}}{dQ} = P\frac{dQ}{dQ} + Q\frac{dP}{dQ}$$

$$\text{MR} = P + Q\frac{dP}{dQ}, \text{ because } \frac{dQ}{dQ} = 1$$

Multiplying top and bottom of the second term on the right-hand-side by P:

$$\text{MR} = P + P\left(\frac{dP}{dQ} \times \frac{Q}{P}\right)$$

$$\text{MR} = P + P\frac{1}{\left(\dfrac{dQ}{dP} \times \dfrac{P}{Q}\right)} = P\left(1 + \frac{1}{\text{PED}}\right) = P\left(1 - \frac{1}{|\text{PED}|}\right)$$

3.3 Theory of perfect competition and monopoly

This section derives the long-run profit-maximizing equilibrium in monopoly for the case where the market demand function is linear, and the long-run average cost (LRAC) and long-run marginal cost (LRMC) functions are horizontal (constant returns to scale production technology).

Symbols
P = price
Q = output
c = marginal cost
TR = total revenue
π = profit

The market demand function (in inverse form) is:

$$P = a - bQ$$

By definition, total revenue is:

$$\text{TR} = PQ = (a - bQ)Q = aQ - bQ^2$$

Total cost is:

$$\text{TC} = cQ$$

By definition, profit is total revenue *minus* total cost:

$$p = \text{TR} - \text{TC} = aQ - bQ^2 - cQ$$
$$p = (a - c)Q - bQ^2$$

To find the value of Q at which π is maximized, differentiate π with respect to Q, set the derivative to zero, and solve the resulting equation for Q.

$$\frac{\partial \pi}{\partial Q} = (a - c) - 2bQ$$

$$(a - c) - 2bQ = 0$$

Therefore the profit-maximizing output level is:

$$Q = \frac{a - c}{2b}$$

The profit-maximizing price and profit are as follows:

$$P = a - bQ = a - b\left(\frac{a - c}{2b}\right) = \frac{a + c}{2}$$

$$\pi = PQ - cQ = (P - c)Q = \left(\frac{a + c}{2} - c\right)\left(\frac{a - c}{2b}\right) = \left(\frac{a - c}{2}\right)\left(\frac{a - c}{2b}\right) = \frac{(a - c)^2}{4b}$$

7.3 Models of output determination in duopoly

This section provides an algebraic derivation of the Cournot–Nash, joint profit maximization and Stackelberg equilibria for a two-firm (duopoly) model and an N-firm (oligopoly) model. It is assumed the firms produce identical products, the market demand function is linear, and the long-run average cost (LRAC) and long-run marginal cost (LRMC) functions are horizontal (constant returns to scale production technology).

Symbols
P = price
q_i = output of firm i
$Q = \sum_i q_i$ = total output of all firms
c = marginal cost
TR_i = total revenue of firm i
π_i = profit of firm i

Two-firm model (firms A and B)

The market demand function (in inverse form) is:

$$P = a - bQ$$

Substituting for Q in the market demand function, we can write:

$$P = a - b(q_A + q_B)$$

Therefore:

$$\text{TR}_A = Pq_A = [a - b(q_A + q_B)]q_A = aq_A - bq_A^2 - bq_Aq_B$$
$$\text{TR}_B = Pq_B = [a - b(q_A + q_B)]q_B = aq_B - bq_Aq_B - bq_B^2$$
$$p_A = \text{TR}_A - cq_A = aq_A - bq_A^2 - bq_Aq_B - cq_A = (a - c)q_A - bq_A^2 - bq_Aq_B$$
$$p_B = \text{TR}_B - cq_B = aq_B - bq_Aq_B - bq_B^2 - cq_B = (a - c)q_B - bq_Aq_B - bq_B^2$$

Reaction functions

To derive the expression for firm A's reaction function: take the partial derivative of π_A with respect to q_A (holding q_B constant, in accordance with the zero conjectural variation assumption), set this partial derivative to zero, and solve the resulting expression for q_A.

$$\frac{\partial \pi_A}{\partial q_A} = (a - c) - 2bq_A - bq_B$$

$$(a - c) - 2bq_A - bq_B = 0$$

Therefore firm A's reaction function is:

$$q_A = \frac{a - c}{2b} - \frac{q_B}{2}$$

Firm B's reaction function is derived in the same way:

$$q_B = \frac{a - c}{2b} - \frac{q_A}{2}$$

Cournot–Nash equilibrium

The Cournot–Nash equilibrium occurs at the intersection of the two firms' reaction functions. To locate the Cournot–Nash equilibrium, substitute the expression for q_B from firm B's reaction function into firm A's reaction function, and solve the resulting expression for q_A. Let q_A^* and q_B^* denote the Cournot–Nash equilibrium values of q_A and q_B.

$$q_A = \frac{a - c}{2b} - \frac{1}{2}\left[\frac{a - c}{2b} - \frac{q_A}{2}\right] \Rightarrow q_A = \frac{a - c}{4b} + \frac{q_A}{4} \Rightarrow \frac{3q_A}{4} = \frac{a - c}{4b}$$

$$q_A^* = \frac{a - c}{3b}$$

Substituting q_A^* into firm B's reaction function:

$$q_A = \frac{a - c}{2b} - \frac{a - c}{6b}$$

$$q_B^* = \frac{a - c}{3b}$$

The equilibrium total output and price are:

$$Q_n = q_A^* + q_B^* = \frac{2(a-c)}{3b}$$

$$P_n = a - bQ_n = a - \frac{2(a-c)}{3} = \frac{a-2c}{3}$$

If $a = b = 1$ and $c = 0$, $q_A^* = q_B^* = \frac{1}{3}$, $Q_n = \frac{2}{3}$ and $P_n = \frac{1}{3}$, as in Section 7.3.

Joint profit maximization

Let $q_A^M = q_B^M = \frac{Q}{2}$, where Q is total output, shared equally between firms A and B under joint profit maximization.

Let $\pi = \pi_A + \pi_B$ denote joint profits:

$$\pi = PQ - cQ = (a - bQ)Q - cQ = (a - c)Q - bQ^2$$

To find the value of Q that maximizes joint profits, differentiate π with respect to Q, set the derivative to zero, and solve for Q.

$$\frac{\partial \pi}{\partial Q} = (a - c) - 2bQ$$

$$(a - c) - 2bQ = 0$$

The equilibrium total output and price are:

$$Q_M = \frac{a-c}{2b}$$

$$P_M = a - bQ_M = a - \frac{a-c}{2} = \frac{a+c}{2}$$

Let q_A^M and q_B^M denote the corresponding values of q_A and q_B:

$$q_A^M = q_B^M = \frac{a-c}{4b}$$

If $a = b = 1$ and $c = 0$, $q_A^M = q_B^M = \frac{1}{4}$, $Q_M = \frac{1}{2}$ and $P_M = \frac{1}{2}$, as in Section 7.3.

Stackelberg equilibrium

Let firm A be the Stackelberg leader, and firm B be the follower. Firm A chooses q_A to maximize π_A, subject to the constraint that (q_A, q_B) must lie on firm B's reaction function. From the above, the relevant functions are firm A's profit function and firm B's reaction function:

$$\pi_A = (a - c)q_A - bq_A^2 - bq_Aq_B$$

$$q_B = \frac{a - c}{2b} - \frac{q_A}{2}$$

Substitute firm B's reaction function for q_B in firm A's profit function:

$$\pi_A = (a - c)q_A - bq_A^2 - bq_A\left(\frac{a - c}{2b} - \frac{q_A}{2}\right)$$

$$\pi_A = \left(\frac{a - c}{2}\right)q_A - \frac{bq_A^2}{2}$$

To find the value of q_A that maximizes π_A subject to the constraint that firm B must operate on firm B's reaction function, differentiate π_A with respect to q_A, set the derivative to zero, and solve for q_A.

$$\frac{d\pi_A}{dq_A} = \frac{a - c}{2} - bq_A$$

$$\frac{a - c}{2} - bq_A = 0$$

Let q_A^L and q_B^F denote the equilibrium output levels of firms A and B as Stackelberg leader and follower respectively.

$$q_A^L = \frac{a - c}{2b}$$

To find q_B^F, substitute q_A^L for q_A in firm B's reaction function:

$$q_B = \frac{a - c}{2b} - \frac{a - c}{4b}$$

$$q_B^F = \frac{a - c}{4b}$$

The equilibrium total output and price are:

$$Q_S = q_A^L + q_B^F = \frac{3a - c}{4b}$$

$$P_S = a - bQ_S = \frac{a + 3c}{4}$$

If $a = b = 1$ and $c = 0$, $q_A^L = \frac{1}{2}$, $q_B^F = \frac{1}{4}$, $Q_S = \frac{3}{4}$, and $P_S = \frac{1}{4}$, as in Section 7.3.

N-*firm model* (firms 1 . . . N)

As before, substituting for Q in the market demand function:

$$P = a - b\sum_{j=1}^{N} q_j$$

Therefore for firm i:

$$\text{TR}_i = Pq_i = \left(a - b\sum_{j=1}^{N} q_j\right)q_i = aq_i - bq_i^2 - bq_i\sum_{j\neq i} q_j$$

$$\pi_i = \text{TR}_i - cq_i = aq_i - bq_i^2 - bq_i\sum_{j\neq i} q_j - cq_i = (a - c)q_i - bq_i^2 - bq_i\sum_{j\neq i} q_j$$

Reaction functions

To derive the expression for firm i's reaction function:

$$\frac{\partial \pi_i}{\partial q_i} = (a - c) - 2bq_i - b\sum_{j\neq 1} q_j$$

$$\frac{\partial \pi_i}{\partial q_i} = 0 \Rightarrow (a - c) - 2bq_i - b\sum_{j\neq 1} q_j = 0$$

Therefore firm i's reaction function is:

$$q_i = \frac{a - c}{2b} - \frac{\sum_{j\neq 1} q_j}{2}$$

Cournot–Nash equilibrium

The Cournot–Nash equilibrium occurs at the intersection of the reaction functions of all N firms. Let q_i^* denote the Cournot–Nash equilibrium value of q_i. Since all firms are identical, q_i^* is the same for all N firms. Therefore it is possible to solve for q_i^* by substituting for q_i and q_j in the expression for firm i's reaction function:

$$q_i^* = \frac{a - c}{2b} - \frac{(N - 1)q_i^*}{2}$$

$$\frac{(N + 1)q_i^*}{2} = \frac{a - c}{2b}$$

$$q_i^* = \frac{a - c}{(N + 1)b}$$

The equilibrium total output and price are:

$$Q_n = Nq_i^* = \frac{N(a-c)}{(N+1)b}$$

$$P_n = a - bQ_n = a - \frac{N(a-c)}{N+1} = \frac{a - Nc}{N+1}$$

Note that the perfectly competitive output level at which price *equals* marginal cost, denoted Q_C, is given by the following expression:

$$P = a - bQ \Rightarrow Q_C = \frac{a-c}{b}$$

Accordingly:

$$Q_n = \left(\frac{N}{N+1}\right)Q_C$$

Joint profit maximization

Let $q_i^M = \dfrac{Q}{N}$, where Q is total output, shared equally between all N firms under joint profit maximization.

As before, the equilibrium total output and price are:

$$Q_M = \frac{a-c}{2b}, \quad P_M = a - bQ_M = \frac{a+c}{2}$$

Therefore for each firm:

$$q_i^M = \frac{a-c}{2Nb}$$

Stackelberg equilibrium

Let firm i be the Stackelberg leader, and let the other firms be followers. Firm i chooses q_i to maximize π_i, subject to the constraint that all other firms must be located on their own reaction functions. Firm i's profit function and firm j's reaction function are as follows:

$$\pi_i = (a-c)q_i - bq_i^2 - bq_i\sum_{j\neq1}q_j$$

$$q_j = \frac{a-c}{2b} - \frac{q_i}{2} - \frac{\sum\limits_{k\neq i,j}q_k}{2}$$

Since all of the followers are identical, firm j's reaction function can be written as follows:

$$q_j = \frac{a-c}{2b} - \frac{q_i}{2} - \frac{(N-2)q_j}{2}$$

$$\frac{Nq_j}{2} = \frac{a-c}{2b} - \frac{q_i}{2}$$

$$q_j = \frac{a-c}{Nb} - \frac{q_i}{N}$$

Substitute into firm i's profit function:

$$\pi_i = (a-c)q_i - bq_i^2 - bq_i(N-1)q_j$$

$$\pi_i = (a-c)q_i - bq_i^2 - \frac{(N-1)(a-c)q_i}{N} + \frac{(N-1)bq_i^2}{N}$$

As before, differentiate π_i with respect to q_i, set the derivative to zero, and solve for q_i:

$$\frac{d\pi_i}{dq_i} = (a-c) - 2bq_i - \frac{(N-1)(a-c)}{N} + \frac{(N-1)2bq_i}{N}$$

$$(a-c) - 2bq_i - \frac{(N-1)(a-c)}{N} + \frac{(N-1)2bq_i}{N} = 0$$

$$\frac{a-c}{N} = \frac{2bq_i}{N}$$

Let q_i^L and q_j^F denote the equilibrium output levels of the leader and each of the followers, respectively:

$$q_i^L = \frac{a-c}{2b}$$

$$q_j^F = \frac{a-c}{Nb} - \frac{a-c}{2Nb} = \frac{a-c}{2Nb}$$

The equilibrium total output and price are:

$$Q_S = q_i^L + (N-1)q_j^F = \frac{(2N-1)(a-c)}{2Nb}$$

$$P_S = a - bQ_S = \frac{a + (2N-1)c}{2N}$$

13.3 Price discrimination

This section derives the profit-maximizing equilibrium under third-degree price discrimination for the case of two sub-markets, and demonstrates that the total profit under third-degree price discrimination exceeds the total profit under uniform monopoly pricing.

Symbols
Q_1, Q_2 = quantities sold in sub-markets 1 and 2, respectively
P_1, P_2 = prices in sub-markets 1 and 2
Q = total quantity under uniform monopoly pricing
P = uniform monopoly price
c = marginal cost
TR_1, TR_2 = total revenues in sub-markets 1 and 2
π_1, π_2 = profits in sub-markets 1 and 2
π = profit under uniform monopoly pricing

The sub-market demand functions (in inverse form) are as follows:

$$P_1 = a_1 - b_1 Q_1 \qquad\qquad P_2 = a_2 - b_2 Q_2$$

Therefore the total revenue and profit functions for each sub-market are:

$$TR_1 = a_1 Q_1 - b_1 Q_1^2 \qquad TR_2 = a_2 Q_2 - b_2 Q_2^2$$
$$\pi_1 = (a_1 - c)Q_1 - b_1 Q_1^2 \qquad \pi_2 = (a_2 - c)Q_2 - b_2 Q_2^2$$

For profit maximization:

$$\frac{d\pi_1}{dQ_1} = (a_1 - c) - 2b_1 Q_1 \qquad \frac{d\pi_2}{dQ_2} = (a_2 - c) - 2b_2 Q_2$$

$$a_1 - c - 2b_1 Q_1 = 0 \qquad\qquad a_2 - c - 2b_2 Q_2 = 0$$

$$Q_1 = \frac{a_1 - c}{2b_1} \qquad\qquad Q_2 = \frac{a_2 - c}{2b_2}$$

The prices and profits in each sub-market are as follows:

$$P_1 = (a_1 - b_1)\left(\frac{a_1 - c}{2b_1}\right) = \frac{a_1 + c}{2}$$

$$P_2 = (a_2 - b_2)\left(\frac{a_2 - c}{2b_2}\right) = \frac{a_2 + c}{2}$$

$$\pi_1 = P_1 Q_1 = c Q_1$$

$$\pi_1 = \left(\frac{a_1 + c}{2}\right)\left(\frac{a_1 - c}{2b_1}\right) - c\left(\frac{a_1 - c}{2b_1}\right) = \frac{(a_1 - c)^2}{4b_1}$$

Similarly, $\pi_2 = \left(\dfrac{a_2 - c}{4b_2}\right)$.

To show that the total profit under third-degree price discrimination exceeds the total profit under uniform monopoly pricing, begin by rearranging the sub-market demand functions:

$$Q_1 = \frac{a_1}{b_1} - \frac{P_1}{b_1} \qquad Q_2 = \frac{a_2}{b_2} - \frac{P_2}{b_2}$$

Let P denote the uniform monopoly price, and Q denote the total quantity:

$$Q = Q_1 + Q_2 = \frac{a_1}{b_1} + \frac{a_2}{b_2} - \left(\frac{1}{b_1} + \frac{1}{b_2}\right)P = \frac{a_1 b_2 + a_2 b_1}{b_1 b_2} - \left(\frac{b_1 + b_2}{b_1 b_2}\right)P$$

Therefore the inverse demand function is:

$$P = \frac{a_1 b_2 + a_2 b_1}{b_1 + b_2} - \left(\frac{b_1 b_2}{b_1 + b_2}\right)Q = \alpha - \beta Q$$

where $\alpha = \dfrac{a_1 b_2 + a_2 b_1}{b_1 + b_2}$, $\beta = \dfrac{b_1 b_2}{b_1 + b_2}$.

The total revenue and profit functions are:

$$TR = \alpha Q - \beta Q^2$$
$$\pi = (\alpha - c)Q - \beta Q^2$$

For profit maximization:

$$\frac{d\pi}{dQ} = (\alpha - c) - 2\beta Q$$

$$\alpha - c - 2\beta Q = 0$$

$$Q = \frac{\alpha - c}{2\beta} \quad \Rightarrow \quad P = \frac{\alpha + c}{2}; \quad \pi = \frac{(\alpha - c)^2}{4\beta}$$

The condition for profit under third-degree price discrimination to exceed profit under uniform monopoly pricing is:

$$\frac{(a_1 - c)^2}{4b_1} + \frac{(a_2 - c)^2}{4b_2} - \frac{(\alpha - c)^2}{4\beta} > 0$$

$$\frac{a_1^2 - 2a_1 c + c^2}{4b_1} + \frac{a_2^2 - 2a_2 c + c^2}{4b_2} - \frac{\alpha^2 - 2\alpha c + c^2}{4\beta} > 0$$

It is trivial to show the following:

$$-\frac{2a_1 c}{4b_1} - \frac{2a_2 c}{4b_2} + \frac{2\alpha c}{4\beta} = 0; \qquad \frac{c^2}{4b_1} + \frac{c^2}{4b_2} - \frac{c^2}{4\beta} = 0$$

Therefore it is sufficient to show:

$$\frac{a_1^2}{4b_1} + \frac{a_2^2}{4b_2} - \frac{\alpha^2}{4\beta} > 0$$

$$\frac{a_1^2}{4b_1} + \frac{a_2^2}{4b_2} = \left(\frac{1}{4b_1 b_2}\right)(b_2 a_1^2 + b_2 a_2^2)$$

$$\frac{\alpha^2}{4\beta} = \frac{(a_1 b_2 + a_2 b_1)^2}{4b_1 b_2 (b_1 + b_2)} = \left(\frac{1}{4b_1 b_2}\right)\left[\left(\frac{b_2}{b_1 + b_2}\right)b_2 a_1^2 + \left(\frac{b_1}{b_1 + b_2}\right)b_1 a_2^2 + \frac{2a_1 a_2 b_1 b_2}{b_1 + b_2}\right]$$

Therefore:

$$\frac{a_1^2}{4b_1} + \frac{a_2^2}{4b_2} - \frac{\alpha^2}{4\beta} = \left(\frac{1}{4b_1 b_2}\right)\left[\left(\frac{b_1}{b_1 + b_2}\right)b_2 a_1^2 + \left(\frac{b_2}{b_1 + b_2}\right)b_1 a_2^2 - \frac{2a_1 a_2 b_1 b_2}{b_1 + b_2}\right]$$

$$= \frac{a_1^2 + a_2^2 - 2a_1 a_2}{4(b_1 + b_2)} = \frac{(a_1 - a_2)^2}{4(b_1 + b_2)} > 0$$

14.3 The pure common value model and the winner's curse

This section discusses the derivation of the expected value of the highest signal obtained by any bidder in the pure common value model.

Symbols

N = number of bidders

$S_{(1)}$ = highest signal obtained by any bidder

$E[S_{(1)}]$ = expected value of $S_{(1)}$

$\underline{v}$, $\bar{v}$ = minimum and maximum values (respectively) any bidder's signal can take

Section 14.3 makes use of the following result: if the bidders' signals are distributed uniformly over the interval $\underline{v}$ to $\bar{v}$:

$$E[S_{(1)}] = \underline{v} + [N/(N + 1)](\bar{v} + \underline{v})$$

Below and with reference to independent private values model, we prove the result $E[V_{(1)}] = N/(N + 1)$ for the cases $N = 2$ and $N = 3$, where $E[V_{(1)}]$ is the expected value of the highest private valuation, and bidders' private valuations are distributed uniformly over the interval 0 to 1. This proof is equivalent to the proof required in the present case (simplified, but unaffected in any important way, by setting $\underline{v} = 0$ and $\bar{v} = 1$).

14.4 Optimal bidding strategies and revenue equivalence in the independent private values model

Optimal bidding strategies

This section derives a bidder's optimal bidding strategy in a first price sealed bid auction in the independent private values model.

Symbols

V_i = independent private valuation of bidder i
B_i = submitted bid of bidder i
b_i = ratio of bidder i's submitted bid to bidder i's private valuation
R_i = bidder i's economic rent
N = number of bidders

Two bidders

Bidder 1's economic rent is:

$$R_1 = (V_1 - B_1) \times \text{Probability that bidder 1's bid is the winning bid}$$

$$R_1 = V_1(1 - b_1) \times P(B_1 > B_2)$$

$$R_1 = V_1(1 - b_1) \times P(b_1 V_1 > b_2 V_2) = V_1(1 - b_1) \times P\left(V_2 < \frac{b_1 V_1}{b_2}\right)$$

$$R_1 = V_1(1 - b_1)\frac{b_1 V_1}{b_2} = \frac{V_1^2}{b_2}(b_1 - b_1^2)$$

To find the value of b_1 that maximizes R_1, take the partial derivative of R_1 with respect to b_1, set this derivative to zero, and solve for b_1.

$$\frac{\partial R_1}{\partial b_1} = \frac{V_1^2}{b_2}(1 - 2b_1)$$

$$\frac{V_1^2}{b_2}(1 - 2b_1) = 0$$

$$b_1 = \frac{1}{2}\left(= \frac{N-1}{N} \text{ with } N = 2\right)$$

Similarly, it can be shown that the value of b_2 that maximizes R_2 is $b_2 = \frac{1}{2}$.

N bidders

Bidder 1's economic rent is:

$$R_1 = V_1(1 - b_1) \times P(B_1 > B_2) \times \cdots \times P(B_1 > B_N)$$

$$R_1 = V_1(1 - b_1) \times P(b_1 V_1 > b_2 V_2) \times \cdots \times P(b_1 V_1 > b_N V_N)$$

$$R_1 = V_1(1 - b_1) \times P\left(V_2 < \frac{b_1 V_1}{b_2}\right) \times \cdots \times P\left(V_N < \frac{b_1 V_1}{b_N}\right)$$

$$R_1 = V_1(1 - b_1)\frac{(b_1 V_1)^{N-1}}{b_2 \cdots b_N} = \frac{V_1^N}{b_2 \cdots b_N}(b_1^{N-1} - b_1^N)$$

$$\frac{\partial R_1}{\partial b_1} = \frac{V_1^N}{b_2 \cdots b_N}[(N-1)b_1^{N-2} - Nb_1^{N-1}]$$

$$\frac{V_1^N}{b_2 \cdots b_N}[(N-1)b_1^{N-2} - Nb_1^{N-1}]$$

$$\frac{V_1^N}{b_2 \cdots b_N}[(N-1)b_1^{N-2} - Nb_1^{N-1}] = 0$$

$$b_1 = \frac{N-1}{N}$$

Similarly (or by symmetry), $b_2 = \cdots = b_N = \dfrac{N-1}{N}$.

The revenue equivalence theorem

This section demonstrates the revenue equivalence theorem in the independent private values model for the cases where the number of bidders is two or three, and the private valuations are distributed uniformly over the interval zero to one.

Symbols
V_i = independent private valuation of bidder i
$V_{(1)}$ = highest private valuation of any bidder
$V_{(2)}$ = second-highest private valuation of any bidder
$E(V_{(1)})$, $E(V_{(2)})$ = expected values of $V_{(1)}$ and $V_{(2)}$
N = number of bidders
x_i = possible values of V_i over which integrals are evaluated.

To demonstrate the results summarized in Table 14.2, it is necessary to demonstrate (i) $E(V_{(1)}) = \dfrac{N}{N+1}$; (ii) $E(V_{(2)}) = \dfrac{N-1}{N+1}$. Below, these results are derived for the cases $N = 2$ and $N = 3$.

Two bidders

$$E(V_{(1)}) = \int_{x_1=0}^{1} \int_{x_2=0}^{x_1} x_1 dx_2 dx_1 + \int_{x_1=0}^{1} \int_{x_2=0}^{1} x_2 dx_2 dx_1$$

$$E(V_{(1)}) = \int_{x_1=0}^{1} [x_1 x_2]_0^{x_1} + \int_{x_1=0}^{1} [x_2^2/2]_{x_1}^{1} = \int_{x_1=0}^{1} (x_1^2 + 1/2 - x_1^2/2)dx_1$$

$$E(V_{(1)}) = \int_{x_1=0}^{1} (x_1^2/2 + 1/2)dx_1 = [x_1^3/6 + x_1/2]_0^1 = 1/6 + 1/2 = 2/3$$

$$F(V_{(2)}) = \int_{x_1=0}^{1} \int_{x_2=0}^{x_1} x_2 dx_2 dx_1 + \int_{x_1=0}^{1} \int_{x_2=0}^{x_1} x_1 dx_2 dx_1$$

$$E(V_{(2)}) = \int_{x_1=0}^{1} [x_2^2/2]_0^{x_1} + \int_{x_1=0}^{1} [x_1 x_2]_{x_1}^{1}(x_1^2/2 + x_1 - x_1^2)dx_1$$

$$E(V_{(2)}) = \int_{x_1=0}^{1} (x_1 - x_1^2/2)dx_1 = [x_1^2/2 - x_1^3/6]_0^1 = 1/2 - 1/6 = 1/3$$

Three bidders

$$E(V_{(1)}) = \int_{x_1=0}^{1} \int_{x_2=0}^{x_1} \int_{x_3=0}^{x_2} x_1 dx_3 dx_2 dx_1 + \int_{x_1=0}^{1} \int_{x_2=0}^{x_1} \int_{x_3=x_2}^{x_1} x_1 dx_3 dx_2 dx_1$$

$$+ \int_{x_1=0}^{1} \int_{x_2=0}^{x_1} \int_{x_3=x_1}^{1} x_3 dx_3 dx_2 dx_1 + \int_{x_1=0}^{1} \int_{x_2=x_1}^{1} \int_{x_3=0}^{x_1} x_2 dx_3 dx_2 dx_1$$

$$+ \int_{x_1=0}^{1} \int_{x_2=x_1}^{1} \int_{x_3=x_1}^{x_2} x_2 dx_3 dx_2 dx_1 + \int_{x_1=0}^{1} \int_{x_2=x_1}^{1} \int_{x_3=x_2}^{1} x_3 dx_3 dx_2 dx_1$$

Evaluating the innermost integrals only:

$$[x_1 x_3]_0^{x_2} + [x_1 x_3]_{x_2}^{x_1} + [x_3^2/2]_{x_1}^1 = x_1^2/2 + 1/2$$

$$[x_2 x_3]_0^{x_1} + [x_2 x_3]_{x_1}^{x_2} + [x_3^2/2]_{x_2}^1 = x_2^2/2 + 1/2$$

$$E(V_{(1)}) = \int_{x_1=0}^{1} \int_{x_2=0}^{x_1} (x_1^2/2 + 1/2)dx_2 dx_1 + \int_{x_1=0}^{1} \int_{x_2=x_1}^{1} (x_2^2/2 + 1/2)dx_2 dx_1$$

Evaluating the innermost integrals only:

$$[x_1^2 x_2/2 + x_2/2]_0^{x_1} + [x_2^3/6 + x_2/2]_{x_2}^1 = 2/3 + x_1^3/3$$

$$E(V_{(1)}) = \int_{x_1=0}^1 (2/3 + x_1^3/3)dx_1 = [2x_1/3 + x_1^4/12]_0^1 = 2/3 + 1/12 = 3/4$$

$$E(V_{(2)}) = \int_{x_1=0}^1 \int_{x_2=0}^{x_1} \int_{x_3=0}^{x_2} x_2 dx_3 dx_2 dx_1 + \int_{x_1=0}^1 \int_{x_2=0}^{x_1} \int_{x_3=x_2}^{x_1} x_3 dx_3 dx_2 dx_1$$

$$+ \int_{x_1=0}^1 \int_{x_2=0}^{x_1} \int_{x_3=x_1}^1 x_1 dx_3 dx_2 dx_1 + \int_{x_1=0}^1 \int_{x_2=x_1}^1 \int_{x_3=0}^{x_1} x_1 dx_3 dx_2 dx_1$$

$$+ \int_{x_1=0}^1 \int_{x_2=x_1}^1 \int_{x_3=x_1}^{x_2} x_3 dx_3 dx_2 dx_1 + \int_{x_1=0}^1 \int_{x_2=x_1}^1 \int_{x_3=x_2}^1 x_2 dx_3 dx_2 dx_1$$

Evaluating the innermost integrals only:

$$[x_2 x_3]_0^{x_2} + [x_3^2/2]_{x_2}^{x_1} + [x_1 x_3]_{x_1}^1 = x_1 - x_1^2/2 + x_2^2/2$$

$$[x_1 x_3]_0^{x_1} + [x_3^2/2]_{x_1}^{x_2} + [x_2 x_3]_{x_2}^1 = x_2 + x_1^2/2 - x_2^2/2$$

$$E(V_{(2)}) = \int_{x_1=0}^1 \int_{x_2=0}^{x_1} (x_1 - x_1^2/2 + x_2^2/2)dx_2 dx_1 + \int_{x_1=0}^1 \int_{x_2=x_1}^1 (x_2 + x_1^2/2 - x_2^2/2)dx_2 dx_1$$

Evaluating the innermost integrals only:

$$[x_1 x_2 - x_1^2 x_2/2 + x_2^3/6]_0^{x_1} + [x_2^2/2 + x_1^2 x_2/2 - x_2^3/6]_{x_1}^1 = 1/3 + x_1^2 - 2x_1^3/3$$

$$E(V_{(2)}) = \int_{x_1=0}^1 (1/3 + x_1^2 - 2x_1^3/3)dx_1 = [x_1/3 + x_1^3/3 - 2x_1^4/12]_0^1$$

$$= 1/3 + 1/3 - 2/12 = 1/2$$

14.5 Extensions and additional topics in auction theory

This section derives the formula for the optimal reserve price in the independent private values model, for the case of an English auction with two bidders, where the bidders' private valuations are distributed uniformly over the interval zero to one.

Symbols

r = seller's reserve price
V_0 = seller's private valuation
R_0 = seller's economic rent
$E(R_0)$ = expected value of R_0
V_1, V_2 = private values of bidders 1 and 2
x_1, x_2 = possible values of V_1 and V_2 over which integrals are evaluated.

The optimal reserve price is the value of r that maximizes $E(R_0)$.

If $r > V_1 > V_2$ or $r > V_2 > V_1$, both bidders drop out before the reserve price is attained. No sale takes place, so the seller retains the item worth V_0.

If $V_1 > r > V_2$ or $V_2 > r > V_1$, one bidder drops out before the reserve price is attained, but one bidder remains. A sale takes place at the reserve price, r.

If $V_1 > V_2 > r$ or $V_2 > V_1 > r$, both bidders remain when the reserve price is attained. Bidding continues until the bidder with the lower private valuation drops out. A sale takes place, with the remaining bidder paying a price equivalent to the lower of the two private valuations.

$$E(R_0) = \int_{x_1=0}^{r} \int_{x_2=0}^{x_1} V_0 dx_2 dx_1 + \int_{x_1=0}^{r} \int_{x_2=x_1}^{r} V_0 dx_2 dx_1 + \int_{x_1=0}^{r} \int_{x_2=r}^{1} r dx_2 dx_1$$

$$+ \int_{x_1=r}^{1} \int_{x_2=r}^{x_1} x_2 dx_2 dx_1 + \int_{x_1=r}^{1} \int_{x_2=0}^{r} r dx_2 dx_1 + \int_{x_1=r}^{1} \int_{x_2=x_1}^{1} x_1 dx_2 dx_1$$

Evaluating the innermost integrals only:

$$[V_0 x_2]_0^{x_1} + [V_0 x_2]_{x_1}^{r} + [r x_2]_r^1 = V_0 r + r - r^2$$

$$[x_2^2/2]_1^{x_1} + [r x_2]_0^r + [x_1 x_2]_{x_1}^1 = x_1^2/2 + r^2/2 + x_1 - x_1^2$$

$$E(R_0) = \int_{x_1=0}^{r} (V_0 r + r - r^2) dx_1 + \int_{x_1=r}^{1} (x_1^2/2 + r^2/2 + x_1 - x_1^2) dx_1$$

$$E(R_0) = [V_0 r x_1 + r x_1 - r^2 x_1]_0^r + [x_1^3/6 + r^2 x_1/2 + x_1^2/2 - x_1^3/3]_r^1$$

$$E(R_0) = (1 + V_0)r^2 - 4r^3/3 + 1/3$$

To find the value of r that maximizes $E(R_0)$, differentiate $E(R_0)$ with respect to r, set the derivative to zero, and solve for r.

$$\frac{dE(R_0)}{dr} = 2(1 + V_0)r - 12r^2/3$$

$$2(1 + V_0)r - 4r^2 = 0$$

$$r = \frac{1 + V_0}{2}$$

15.5 Hotelling's location model

This section derives the equilibrium prices in the collusive and non-collusive versions of the Hotelling model with fixed locations and endogenous prices.

Symbols
P_A, P_B = prices charged by firms A and B
P = common price charged by both firms (where applicable)
TR = total revenue
d = consumers' addresses, measured on a scale of $d = 0$ to $d = 1$
k = parameter reflecting magnitude of transport cost (per unit of distance), or degree of substitution between the products of firms A and B
$\tilde{p}$ = price at which the consumer located at address $d = 0.5$ is indifferent between buying from either firm

Collusive model: joint profit maximization

$\tilde{P} = 1 - k/4$ denotes the price at which the consumer located at address $d = 0.5$ is indifferent between buying from either firm or withdrawing from the market. Let $P = P_A = P_B$ represent the common price charged by firms A and B under a policy of joint profit maximization. We examine the implications for joint total revenue (and therefore joint profit) of variations in P around $\tilde{P}$.

For $0 \leq P < \tilde{P}$, firms A and B each supply one half of the market. Total quantity demanded = 1, and total revenue = P.

For $\tilde{P} \leq P < 1$, firm A supplies consumers at addresses d such that $P + kd^2 \leq 1$.

The consumer at address $d = \sqrt{\dfrac{1-P}{k}}$ is indifferent between buying from firm A or withdrawing from the market.

Therefore firm A's quantity demanded = $\sqrt{\dfrac{1-P}{k}}$. By symmetry, firm B's quantity demanded is given by the same expression.

Total quantity demanded = $2\sqrt{\dfrac{1-P}{k}}$, and total revenue = TR = $2P\sqrt{\dfrac{1-P}{k}}$.

To find the value of P that maximizes TR, differentiate TR with respect to P, set the derivative to zero, and solve for P.

$$TR = \frac{2}{\sqrt{k}}P(1-P)^{1/2}$$

To differentiate TR with respect to P, use both the Product Rule and the Chain Rule. It can be shown:

$$\frac{d\,TR}{dP} = \frac{2}{\sqrt{k}}\left(-\frac{P}{2(1-P)^{1/2}} + (1-P)^{1/2}\right)$$

$$\frac{2}{\sqrt{k}}\left(-\frac{P}{2(1-P)^{1/2}}+(1-P)^{1/2}\right)=0$$

$$(1-P)^{1/2}=\frac{P}{2(1-P)^{1/2}}\Rightarrow 1-P=\frac{P}{2}\Rightarrow 1=\frac{3P}{2}$$

$$P=2/3$$

When $\tilde{P}\geq\frac{2}{3}$ or $k\leq\frac{4}{3}=1.33$, total revenue is maximized by setting $P=\tilde{P}=1-k/4$.

When $\tilde{P}<\frac{2}{3}$ or $k\geq\frac{4}{3}=1.33$, total revenue is maximized by setting $P=\frac{2}{3}$.

Non-collusive model: Bertrand (or Nash) equilibrium

For the mathematical derivation of the Bertrand (or Nash) equilibrium, we assume both firms' prices arc sufficiently low that no consumer is priced out of the market.

The address at which a consumer is indifferent between purchasing from firm A or from firm B is d such that:

$$P_A+kd^2=P_B+k(1-d)^2$$

To solve for d:

$$P_A+kd^2=P_B+k(1-2d+d^2)$$

$$P_A-P_B-k=-2kd$$

$$d=\frac{P_B-P_A+k}{2k}$$

This expression represents firm A's quantity demanded. Therefore firm A's total revenue is:

$$TR_A=\frac{P_AP_B-P_A^2+kP_A}{2k}$$

Similarly, firm B's total revenue is:

$$TR_B=\frac{P_AP_B-P_B^2+kP_B}{2k}$$

To determine the Bertrand (or Nash) equilibrium, at which each firm sets its price to maximize its own profit treating the other firm's price as fixed: take the partial derivatives of TR_A and TR_B with respect to P_A and P_B respectively, set the partial derivatives to zero, and solve the resulting simultaneous equations for P_A and P_B.

$$\frac{\partial TR_A}{\partial P_A}=\frac{P_B-2P_A+k}{2k}\qquad\frac{\partial TR_B}{\partial P_B}=\frac{P_A-2P_B+k}{2k}$$

From the expression for: $\dfrac{\partial TR_A}{\partial P_A}$

$$\frac{P_B - 2P_A + k}{2k} \Rightarrow 2P_A = P_B + k$$

$$P_A = \frac{P_B + k}{2}$$

Substituting P_A into the expression for $\dfrac{\partial TR_B}{\partial P_B}$ and multiplying through by $2k$:

$$\frac{P_A - 2P_B + k}{2k} = 0 \Rightarrow \frac{P_B + K}{2} - 2P_B + K = 0$$

$$P_B + k - 4P_B + 2k = 0$$

$$P_B = k$$

$$P_A = k$$

Therefore the Bertrand (or Nash) equilibrium is $P_A = P_B = k$. As noted above, this result is based on the assumption that no consumer is priced out of the market altogether at the Bertrand (or Nash) equilibrium. For the consumer located at $d = 0.5$, this assumption is valid under the following condition:

$$k + kd^2 \le 1 \Rightarrow k + \frac{k}{4} \le 1 \Rightarrow \frac{5k}{4} \le 1 \Rightarrow k \le \frac{4}{5} = 0.8$$

For $k > 0.8$, both firms operate as local monopolists, and their quantities demanded are not dependent on the other firm's price. Each firm maximizes profit within its own market. The solution is the same as in the collusive model. Therefore the full set of solutions (see also Figure 15.12) is as follows:

For $k \le 0.8$, $P_A = P_B = k$

For $0.8 < k \le 1.33$, $P_A = P_B = 1 - k/4$

For $k > 1.33$, $P_A = P_B = 2/3$

17.4 Diffusion

With reference to the Mansfield model, this section demonstrates the equivalence between the following expressions:

Pace of diffusion: $n_{i,t+1} - n_{i,t} = k_i\left(\left(\frac{n_{i,t}}{N_t}\right)\left(1 - \frac{n_{i,t}}{N_i}\right)\right)$

Solution for $\dfrac{n_{i,t}}{N_i}$: $\dfrac{n_{i,t}}{N_i} = \dfrac{1}{1 + e^{-(\alpha_i + \beta_i t)}}$

Symbols

N_i = total number of firms that will eventually adopt innovation i

$n_{i,t}$ = number of firms that have adopted by time t

k_i, α_i, β_i = constants

To simplify the notation, drop the subscripts on all variables and coefficients, and define the time-dependent variable y as follows:

$$y = \frac{n_{i,t}}{N_i} = \frac{1}{1 + e^{-(\alpha+\beta t)}}$$

$n_{i,t+1} - n_{i,t}$ is interpreted as the rate of change of y with respect to time, $\dfrac{dy}{dt}$.

Therefore the original expression for the pace of diffusion can be rewritten as follows:

$$\frac{dy}{dt} = ky(1 - y)$$

The equivalence between the two previous expressions is shown by demonstrating that when

$$y = \frac{1}{1 + e^{-(\alpha+\beta t)}}, \frac{dy}{dt} = ky(1 - y)$$

To differentiate $y = \dfrac{1}{1 + e^{-(\alpha+\beta t)}}$ with respect to t, use the Chain Rule.

In general, if $y = f[g(t)]$, $\dfrac{dy}{dt} = f'[g(t)]g'(t)$, where $f[\ ]$ and $g(\ )$ are functions, and $f'[\ ]$ and $g'(\ )$ are the derivatives of $f[\ ]$ and $g(\ )$.

In this case, $g(t) = (1 + e^{-(\alpha+\beta t)})$ and $f[g(t)] = (1 + e^{-(\alpha+\beta t)})^{-1}$:

$$f'[g(t)] = -(1 + e^{-(\alpha+\beta t)})^{-2}$$

$$g'(t) = -\beta e^{-(\alpha+\beta t)}$$

Applying the Chain Rule:

$$\frac{dy}{dt} = \frac{\beta e^{-(\alpha+\beta t)}}{(1 + e^{-(\alpha+\beta t)})^2}$$

This expression is equivalent to $ky(1 - y)$ if $k = \beta$:

$$\frac{dy}{dt} = ky(1 - y) = k\left(\frac{1}{1 + e^{-(\alpha+\beta t)}}\right)\left(1 - \frac{1}{1 + e^{-(\alpha+\beta t)}}\right)$$

$$= k\left(\frac{1}{1 + e^{-(\alpha+\beta t)}}\right)\left(\frac{e^{-(\alpha+\beta t)}}{1 + e^{-(\alpha+\beta t)}}\right)$$

$$\frac{dy}{dt} = ky(1 - y) = \frac{ke^{-(\alpha+\beta t)}}{(1 + e^{-(\alpha+\beta t)})^2}$$

Market equilibrium price and quantity for a network good or service: perfect competition and monopoly

This section derives the marginal revenue functions, and demonstrates that the socially optimal coverage is always full coverage.

Symbols

n = total number of users ($0 \leq n \leq 1$)

p = price

τ = stand-alone benefit parameter (constant in the case of heterogeneous network benefits, distributed uniformly over $0 \leq \tau \leq 1$ in the case of heterogeneous stand-alone benefits)

v = network benefit parameter (constant in the case of heterogeneous stand-alone benefits, distributed uniformly over $0 \leq v \leq 1$ in the case of heterogeneous network benefits)

Heterogeneous network benefits

The function $p = \tau + n(1 - n)$ plays a role in the model equivalent to an average revenue function.

The corresponding total revenue function is

$$\text{TR} = pn = \tau n + n^2 - n^3$$

The corresponding marginal revenue function is

$$\text{MR} = \frac{d\text{TR}}{dn} = \tau + 2n - 3n^2$$

When $n = 1/2$, $p = \tau + 1/4$, and $\text{MR} = \tau + 1/4$

When $n = 1$, $p = \tau$ and $\text{MR} = \tau - 1$

Substituting $n = n^e$, the utility of consumer i is $\tau + v_i n$, for $1 - n \leq i \leq 1$

Social welfare is the sum of consumer surplus and producer surplus.

$$\text{Consumer surplus} = \int_{v=1-n}^{n} (\tau + vn - p)dv = \left[\tau v + \frac{v^2 n}{2} - pv \right]_{1-n}^{1}$$

$$= \tau + \frac{n}{2} - p - \tau(1 - n) - \frac{(1-n)^2 n}{2} + p(1 - n)$$

$$= (\tau - p)n + n^2 - \frac{n^3}{2}$$

$$\text{Producer surplus} = n(p - c)$$

$$\text{Social welfare} = W = (\tau - c)n + n^2 - \frac{n^3}{2}$$

To show that welfare is always increasing in n, differentiate W with respect to n.

$$\frac{dW}{dn} = \tau - c + 2n - \frac{3n^2}{2} > 0$$

Heterogeneous stand-alone benefits

The function $p = 1 - (1 - v)n$ plays a role in the model equivalent to an average revenue function.

The corresponding total revenue function is

$$TR = pn = n - (1 - v)n^2$$

The corresponding marginal revenue function is

$$MR = \frac{dTR}{dn} = 1 - 2(1 - v)n$$

When $n = 0$, $p = 1$, and $MR = 1$
When $n = 1$, $p = v$, and $MR = 1 - 2(1 - v)$
Substituting $n = n^e$, the utility of consumer i is $\tau_i + vn$, for $1 - n \le i \le 1$
Social welfare is the sum of consumer surplus and producer surplus.

$$\text{Consumer surplus} = \int_{\tau=1-n}^{n} (\tau + vn - p)d\tau = \left[\frac{\tau^2}{2} + vn\tau - p\tau \right]_{1-n}^{1}$$

$$= \frac{1}{2} + vn - p - \frac{(1-n)^2}{2} - vn(1-n) + p(1-n)$$

$$= n - \frac{n^2}{2} + vn^2 - pn$$

Producer surplus $= n(p - c)$

Social welfare $= W = n - \dfrac{n^2}{2} + vn^2 - cn$

To show that welfare is always increasing in n, differentiate W with respect to n.

$$\frac{dW}{dn} = 1 - c - n + 2vn > 0$$

Econometric methods

Introduction

Several chapters in this book refer to empirical studies, which examine whether economic hypotheses based on theoretical reasoning are supported empirically using data from the real world. In many cases, this evidence is obtained by applying regression analysis to industrial organization data. Appendix 2 provides a brief survey of the essentials of regression analysis at an introductory and non-technical level. Any reader requiring a comprehensive treatment of this topic is advised to consult one (or more) of the following textbooks:

Greene, W. (2011) *Econometric Analysis*, 7th edition. Englewood Cliffs, NJ: Prentice Hall.
Gujarati, D. and Porter, D. (2009) *Basic Econometrics*, 5th edition. New York: McGraw Hill.
Stock, J.H. and Watson, M.W. (2012) *Introduction to Econometrics*, 3rd edition. Harlow: Pearson Education.
Studenmund, A.H. (2011) *Using Econometrics: A Practical Guide*, 6th edition, International edition. Harlow: Pearson Education.
Vogelvang, B. (2005) *Econometrics: Theory and Applications with E-views*. Harlow: Financial Times Prentice Hall.

Types of industrial organization data set

Data sets used for empirical research in industrial organization may have been compiled by government agencies or commercial organizations. There are two basic types of data set: time series and cross-sectional.

- A time-series data set contains observations on a specific 'unit' over a number of time periods, which might be days, months or years. The 'unit' might be a single firm, or a particular industry.

- A cross-sectional data set contains observations on a number of 'units' at one particular point in time. The 'units' might be a group of firms classified as members of one industry, or a number of industries that comprise a larger grouping, such as an entire manufacturing or service sector.

Some data sets include both a time-series and a cross-sectional dimension. For example, there might be several time-series observations on each member of a group of firms or industries. This type of data set is known as pooled cross-sectional time-series data, or alternatively as panel data.

The two-variable linear regression model

Most empirical studies seek to explain observed facts about the real world. One of the most important questions that can be investigated using appropriate data is whether there is empirical evidence of a relationship between some specific economic variables. For example, if we have cross-sectional data on the levels of advertising expenditure and the sales revenues of a number of firms in the same year, we can investigate whether the data reveals any evidence of a relationship between advertising and sales revenue.

More generally, a two-variable linear regression model takes the following form:

$$y_i = \beta_1 + \beta_2 x_i + u_i$$

The definitions of variables and symbols are as follows:

y_i is the dependent variable
x_i is the independent or explanatory variable
u_i is the error term
β_1, β_2 are the regression coefficients

The dependent variable y_i is the variable whose behaviour the model seeks to explain. The independent variable x_i is a variable thought to influence or determine y_i. The coefficient β_2 identifies the impact on y_i of a small change in the value of x_i. For example, if x_i increases by one unit, the numerical adjustment to the value of y_i is given by the coefficient β_2. The coefficient β_1 can be interpreted as the expected value of the dependent variable y_i when the independent variable x_i *equals* zero. Finally the error term u_i allows for any variation in the dependent variable that is not accounted for by corresponding variation in the independent variable. In most regression models, the error term is assumed to be purely random. For purposes of statistical inference (see below) it is often useful to assume the error term is drawn from some specific probability distribution, such as the normal distribution.

So far, everything we have said refers to what is known as the 'population' or 'true' regression model. β_1 and β_2 are unknown parameters which describe the true relationship between x_i and y_i. In order to know β_1 and β_2, we would need complete information about every member of the population of firms or industries. In practice we do not have this much information. However, we can take a random sample of observations of y_i and x_i, and use it to obtain estimates of β_1 and β_2. If we take a random sample and using only these observations, fit a line as best we can through them, we obtain the sample regression line.

Because no sample is ever perfectly representative of the population from which it is drawn, the sample regression line will never coincide precisely with the (true but unknown) population regression line: we will always slightly over- or underestimate β_1 and β_2.

The sample regression model is specified as follows:

$$y_i = \hat{\beta}_1 + \hat{\beta}_2 x_i + e_i$$

In the sample (estimated) model, $\hat{\beta}_1$ and $\hat{\beta}_2$ are the sample estimators of β_1 and β_2. e_i is the sample estimator of u_i, known as the estimated error term or residual. $\hat{y}_i = \hat{\beta}_1 + \hat{\beta}_2 x_i$ are known as the estimated values or fitted values of the dependent variable, y_i.

Consider the following table, which records the levels of advertising expenditure and sales revenue for a sample of nine firms, observed in 2012:

Firm	y_i = Sales revenue of firm i, 2012, £m	x_i = Advertising expenditure of firm i, 2012, £m
A	14	8
B	4	1
C	12	8
D	14	6
E	6	2
F	16	9
G	12	7
H	10	5
I	10	4

These data can be plotted on a graph, with y_i = sales revenue shown on the vertical axis, and x_i = advertising expenditure shown on the horizontal axis. The resulting graph is shown as Figure A.1.

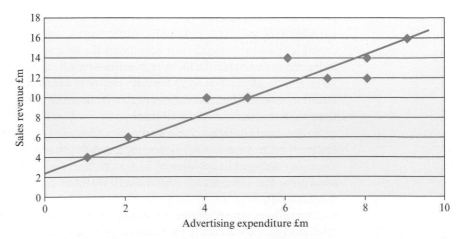

Figure A.1 Sample regression line for advertising–sales model

The simplest way of thinking about regression analysis is in terms of using a ruler to draw a 'line-of-best-fit' through the centre of the set of plotted points. The estimation technique known as Ordinary Least Squares (OLS) is the mathematical method that is used to locate the line-of-best-fit precisely. Numerical estimates of the regression coefficients β_1 and β_2 can be obtained from any computer package that includes OLS estimation. The estimation results are shown below.

	Coefficient	**Standard error**	***t*-statistic**
Intercept β_1	3.607	1.102	3.27
Advertising β_2	1.311	0.179	7.21
N = number of observations = 9			
Total variation, $\sum(y_i - \bar{y})^2 = 120.9$			
Explained variation, $\sum(\hat{y}_i - \bar{y})^2 = 106.9$			
Unexplained variation, $\sum e_i^2 = 14.0$			
R-square = 0.884 (= 106.9/120.9)			

Therefore the fitted regression model is:

$$\hat{y}_i = 3.607 + 1.311 x_i$$

In many empirical studies, it is standard practice to write down an estimated regression model using a slightly different notational convention, in which the dependent and independent variables are identified by names (which are often abbreviated). Therefore we might use SALES to denote sales revenue and ADVERT to denote advertising expenditure. Using this alternative notation, the same fitted regression model would be written:

$$SALES = 3.607 + 1.311 \text{ ADVERT}$$

Statistical inference

Once a regression model has been estimated, the signs and numerical magnitudes of the estimated coefficients convey information about the direction and strength of the relationship between the independent variable and the dependent variable. Because the estimated coefficients are based on a limited sample of data, there is always a suspicion of imprecision or unreliability attached to them. For this reason, estimation methods for regression coefficients provide a standard error for each estimated coefficient. The standard error reflects the reliability of the estimated coefficient: the smaller the standard error, the greater the reliability.

The ratio of an estimated coefficient to its standard error, usually known as a t-statistic or z-statistic (depending on precisely which type of regression model is being fitted), provides a convenient method for assessing whether the estimation has succeeded in identifying a relationship between variables that is reliable in a statistical sense. This is one of the main tasks of statistical inference. The t-statistic (or z-statistic) for the estimated coefficient $\hat{\beta}_2$ is calculated as $t = \hat{\beta}_2/se(\hat{\beta}_2)$, where $se(\hat{\beta}_2)$ is the standard error of $\hat{\beta}_2$. If the absolute value of the t-statistic exceeds a certain critical value, we say that $\hat{\beta}_2$ is statistically significant or significantly different from zero. This means we have sufficient statistical evidence to reject the hypothesis that the true value of the coefficient β_2 is zero.

Whenever a hypothesis test is carried out, it is usual to quote an accompanying significance level, such as 1, 5 or 10 per cent. This expresses the probability that the test may cause us to draw a wrong inference, by rejecting a hyothesis that is actually true. With a significance level of 5 per cent, if β_2 really were zero, the test would run a 5 per cent risk of incorrectly concluding that β_2 is non-zero. The smaller the significance level, the greater the degree of confidence we can have in any decision to reject the hypothesis that the true value of the coefficient is zero.

In the advertising–sales example, suppose we wish to test the hypothesis that advertising has no effect on sales revenue. This is equivalent to testing the hypothesis that the true value of the unknown coefficient β_2 *equals* zero. We will use a significance level of 5 per cent.

■ The t-statistic is $\hat{\beta}_2/se(\hat{\beta}_2) = 1.311/0.179 = 7.21$.

■ The critical value for the test is taken from statistical tables for the t-distribution with $n - k = 7$ degrees of freedom, where $n = 9$ is the number of observations used to estimate the model, and $k = 2$ is the number of estimated regression coefficients. For a test at the 5 per cent significance level, this critical value is 2.365.

■ If the t-statistic is numerically smaller than the critical value, we accept the hypothesis we are testing. If the t-statistic is numerically greater than the critical value, we reject the hypothesis.

■ In this case, the t-statistic of 7.21 exceeds the critical value of 2.365. Therefore we reject the hypothesis that the true value of the coefficient β_2 *equals* zero. We infer β_2 is non-zero, and advertising does therefore have a significant effect on sales revenue.

Multiple regression

The two-variable linear regression model that is described above can easily be extended to allow for cases where there is more than one independent variable. We might wish to expand the model that seeks to explain the variation in sales, by adding more independent variables. For example, we might believe that for any particular firm, sales will depend not only on the firm's own advertising expenditure, but also on a number of other factors such as price, product quality, or rivals' pricing and advertising decisions.

For a multiple regression, the population or 'true' model is defined as follows:

$$y_i = \beta_1 + \beta_2 x_{2i} + \beta_3 x_{3i} + \cdots + \beta_k x_{ki} + u_i$$

The definitions of variables and symbols are as follows:

y_i is the dependent variable;
$x_{2i}, x_{3i}, \ldots, x_{ki}$ are the independent or explanatory variables;
u_i is the error term;
$\beta_1, \beta_2, \beta_3, \ldots, \beta_k$ are the regression coefficients.

As before, the dependent variable y_i is the variable whose behaviour the model seeks either to explain or to predict. The independent variables $x_{2i}, x_{3i}, \ldots, x_{ki}$ are other variables thought to influence or determine y_i. The coefficients $\beta_2, \beta_3, \ldots, \beta_k$ identify the impact on y_i of small changes in the values of each of $x_{2i}, x_{3i}, \ldots, x_{ki}$, respectively.

The sample/estimated model is written as follows:

$$y_i = \hat{\beta}_1 + \hat{\beta}_2 x_{2i} + \hat{\beta}_3 x_{3i} + \cdots + \hat{\beta}_k x_{ki} + e_i$$

This type of regression cannot be presented graphically, but computer software can be used to obtain estimated regression coefficients denoted $\beta_1, \beta_2, \ldots, \beta_k$, as well as their standard errors and t-statistics.

So far, we have assumed the dependent variable, y_i, is influenced by a number of independent variables, $x_{2i} \ldots x_{ki}$, which are quantitative (measurable) in nature. However, in some cases we might also want to incorporate certain non-quantitative or qualitative information as well.

With reference to our earlier example of a model for the sales revenues of firms in 2012, it might be the case that some of the firms have introduced a new model in 2012, while others are continuing to sell an old model. For each firm, the information as to whether or not a new model has been introduced can be captured by defining a 0–1 dummy variable d_i:

$d_i = 1$ if firm i introduced a new model in 2012
$d_i = 0$ if firm i did not introduce a new model in 2012

In our earlier example, suppose firms A, D, F and I introduced new models in 2012, while firms B, C, E, G and H continued to sell old models. The extended data set is as follows:

Firm	y_i = Sales revenue of firm i, 2012, £m	x_i = Advertising expenditure of firm i, 2012, £m	d_i = Dummy variable identifying firms that introduced a new model in 2012
A	14	8	1
B	4	1	0
C	12	8	0
D	14	6	1
E	6	2	0
F	16	9	1
G	12	7	0
H	10	5	0
I	10	4	1

Running a multiple regression, in which the dependent variable is y_i and the independent variables are x_i and d_i, the estimation results (presented in the same format as before) are as follows:

	Coefficient	Standard error	t-statistic
Intercept, $\hat{\beta}_1$	3.567	0.680	5.25
Advertising, $\hat{\beta}_2$	1.138	0.121	9.40
New model, $\hat{\beta}_3$	2.254	0.640	3.52
N = number of observations = 9			
Total variation, $\Sigma(y_i - \bar{y})^2 = 120.9$			
Explained variation, $\Sigma(\hat{y}_i - \bar{y})^2 = 116.3$			
Unexplained variation, $\Sigma e_i^2 = 4.6$			
R-square = 0.962 (= 116.3/120.9)			

Therefore the fitted regression model is:

$$\hat{y}_i = 3.567 + 1.138x_i + 2.254d_i$$

Using the alternative notation, and letting NEW denote the new product dummy variable, the same fitted regression model would be written:

$$\text{SALES} = 3.567 + 1.138 \text{ ADVERT} + 2.254 \text{ NEW}$$

Suppose we now wish to test the hypothesis that the introduction of a new model has no effect on sales revenue. This is equivalent to testing the hypothesis that the true value of the unknown coefficient β_3 *equals* zero. As before, we will use a significance level of 5 per cent.

■ The t-statistic is $\hat{\beta}_3/se(\hat{\beta}_3) = 2.254/0.640 = 3.52$.

■ The critical value for the test is taken from statistical tables for the t-distribution with $n - k = 6$ degrees of freedom (there are $n = 9$ observations and $k = 3$ estimated regression coefficients). For a test at the 5 per cent level, this critical value is 2.447.

■ The t-statistic of 3.52 exceeds the critical value of 2.447. Therefore we reject the hypothesis that the true value of the coefficient β_3 is zero. We infer the introduction of a new model does have a significant effect on sales revenue.

Coefficient of determination, R^2

When we fit a regression model using a sample of data, we are attempting to explain as much as possible of the variation in y_i (the dependent variable). The variation in y_i is explained by corresponding variation in x_i (the independent variable). However, not all of the variation in y_i can be explained by variation in x_i. This is why we have an error term, u_i, which allows for all other (random) influences on y_i.

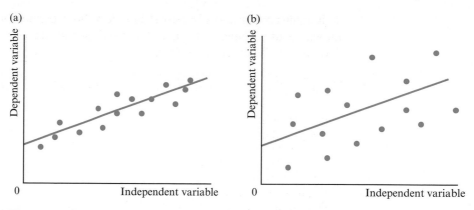

Figure A.2 Regression models with different degrees of explanatory power

Consider Figures A.2a and A.2b. In both cases, the same regression line has been fitted. Both lines have the same intercept and the same slope. However, it is clear that the regression line in Figure A.2a fits the data more accurately than the one in Figure A.2b, because in the latter case the data are more widely dispersed around the fitted regression line. It is natural to ask what proportion of the total variation in y_i is explained by x_i, and what proportion is left unexplained.

In the case of a multiple regression, the estimated model may be written:

$$y_i = \hat{y}_i + e_i \quad \text{where} \quad \hat{y}_i = \hat{\beta}_1 + \hat{\beta}_2 x_{2i} + \hat{\beta}_3 x_{3i} + \cdots + \hat{\beta}_k x_{ki}$$

Subtracting the sample mean of the dependent variable $\bar{y}$, denoted, from both sides we can write:

$$(y_i - \bar{y}) = (\hat{y}_i - \bar{y}) + e_i$$

For the i-th observation, we can interpret the components of this expression as follows:

$y_i - \bar{y}$ = total variation in the i-th observation of the dependent variable (difference between the actual value and the sample mean).

$\hat{y}_i - \bar{y}$ = explained variation in the i-th observation (difference between the fitted value and the sample mean).

e_i = unexplained variation (error, or difference between the actual and fitted values).

It can be shown that a similar relationship exists between the sums (over all observations in the sample) of squares of these terms. By squaring, we make all the terms positive and therefore comparable with each other. By summing we obtain measures of variation over the entire sample.

$$\Sigma(y_i - \bar{y})^2 \quad = \quad \Sigma(\hat{y}_i - \bar{y})^2 \quad + \quad \Sigma e_i^2$$

Total variation in y_i = Explained variation + Unexplained variation

This relationship allows us to define R^2 ('R-square') or goodness-of-fit, also known as the coefficient of determination, as follows:

$$R^2 = \frac{\text{Explained variation}}{\text{Total variation}}$$

$$R^2 = \frac{\Sigma(\hat{y}_i - \bar{y})^2}{\Sigma(y_i - \bar{y})^2}$$

R^2 must lie between 0 and 1. As we have seen, its interpretation is quite simple: R^2 is the proportion of the variation in y_i that is explained by the model.

For the first of our two fitted regression models,
SALES = 3.607 + 1.311 ADVERT:

$$\Sigma(\hat{y}_i - \bar{y})^2 = 106.9 \quad \text{and} \quad \Sigma(y_i - \bar{y})^2 = 120.9 \Rightarrow R^2 = 0.882.$$

For the second of our two models, SALES = 3.567 + 1.138 ADVERT + 2.254 NEW:

$$\Sigma(\hat{y}_i - \bar{y})^2 = 116.3 \quad \text{and} \quad \Sigma(y_i - \bar{y})^2 = 120.9 \Rightarrow R^2 = 0.962.$$

Therefore, advertising expenditure by itself is capable of explaining 88.2 per cent of the variation in sales revenue. When the information about which firms are selling new models is added to the data set, the proportion of the variation in sales revenue that is explained by the model increases to 96.2 per cent.

Difficulties and pitfalls in the interpretation of regression results

In practice, various statistical issues can create difficulties or cloud the interpretation of an estimated regression model. This survey concludes with a brief discussion of a few of the issues that arise most frequently.

■ *The direction of causation.* Although regression analysis may be able to confirm the existence of significant relationships between economic variables, it may be unable to determine the direction of causation. For example, one might find evidence of a positive relationship between research and development and the level of seller concentration. However, it might still be difficult to decide whether high concentration leads to high research and development expenditure, or whether a high level of research and development expenditure tends to create a highly concentrated industry structure.

■ *Multicollinearity.* Multicollinearity describes the case where some or all of the independent variables included in a multiple regression model are highly correlated with one another. Collectively, the independent variables are successful in explaining the variation in the dependent variable, but the estimation is unable to pinpoint the individual relationships between each independent variable and the dependent variable. For example, suppose the quantity demanded of a firm's product depends on its own price, and on a rival's price (as well as other variables). If the two firms always tend to change their prices in the same direction at the same time, it becomes difficult for the regression model to isolate the separate effects of each of the two prices on the quantity demanded.

■ *Autocorrelation*. Autocorrelation or serial correlation arises when the assumption of a random error term is violated. This problem commonly arises in regression models estimated using time-series data. The randomness assumption requires that all random disturbances affect the dependent variable for one time period only, and then disappear completely. However, this requirement may not be satisfied in practice. For example, the demand for a particular product may be affected by many factors that change slowly through time, such as lifestyles, tastes, customs, habits. If these factors are not captured explicitly among the model's independent variables, their effects will be incorporated into the error term. Because these factors change slowly over time, the values of the error term in successive periods will be correlated, violating the randomness assumption. If uncorrected, autocorrelation may result in *t*-statistics and *R*-square giving an exaggerated impression of the precision of a fitted regression model.

■ *Heteroskedasticity*. If the amount of variation in the random error term (measured by its variance) changes as the values of the independent variables change, there is a problem of heteroskedasticity. Heteroskedasticity is a common problem in regression models estimated using cross sectional data. For example, over a large cross-section of firms, one might expect to find greater variation in growth rates at the lower end of the firm size distribution than at the upper end. Starting from a very low base, a successful small firm might record a year-on-year growth rate of several hundred per cent, whereas an unsuccessful small firm might just as easily shed most of its sales or assets in any one year. It is unlikely that proportionately, a very large firm would experience such a large (positive or negative) year-on-year growth rate. Therefore a cross-sectional regression model using growth as a dependent variable might be subject to a heteroskedasticity problem, if the variation in the dependent variable feeds through into similar variation in the error term. If uncorrected, heteroskedasticity can lead to incorrect inferences being drawn from hypothesis tests.

■ *Misspecification*. Misspecification errors arise when independent variables that actually have no effect the dependent variable are included in a multiple regression model, or when variables that do have an effect are omitted. Another possible source of misspecification error is the selection of an incorrect functional form for the estimated equation. For example, if the true relationship between seller concentration and advertising expenditure is quadratic, but a linear specification is estimated instead, misleading inferences about the existence or nature of this relationship may be obtained. In practice, finding the correct specification for a regression model is often a difficult task. There are hundreds of economic variables, many of which are interrelated to a greater or lesser extent. Researchers may need to estimate and compare many different versions of a model before a final specification is accepted.

Glossary

Abnormal profit. The return in excess of the minimum required to prevent the owner from closing the firm down, equivalent to revenue *minus* accounting costs *minus* **normal profit**.

Absolute cost advantage entry barrier. An incumbent incurs a lower long-run average cost than a potential entrant at any output level.

Accounting profitability approach. An indirect method of testing for economies of scale, based on the correlation between firm size and accounting profitability.

Accounting rate of profit. A profit measure based on company accounts data. Normally calculated as the ratio of profit to assets (return on capital), equity (return on equity) or sales revenue (return on sales).

Adverse selection. Arises when a principal is unable to verify an agent's claims concerning the agent's own ability or productivity.

Advertising elasticity of demand. A measure of the sensitivity of quantity demanded to changes in advertising expenditure. Measured as the ratio of the proportionate change in quantity demanded to the proportionate change in advertising expenditure.

Advertising intensity. See **advertising-to-sales ratio**.

Advertising response function. Measures the responsiveness of sales revenue to the volume of advertising expenditure.

Advertising-to-sales ratio. The ratio of advertising expenditure to sales revenue.

Affiliated valuations model. In auction theory, the case where information about one bidder's valuation of the item would influence other bidders' valuations. Represents an intermediate case between the **independent private values model** and the **pure common value model**.

Agency theory. The study of relationships between principals and agents. For example, a manufacturing firm, acting as principal, contracts a supplying firm, the agent, to produce its inputs.

Aggregate concentration. The share of the largest firms in total sales, assets or employment (or other appropriate size measure) for the economy as a whole.

Allocative efficiency. Describes an allocation of resources such that no possible reallocation could make one agent (producer or consumer) better off without making at least one other agent worse off.

Article 101. In EU competition policy Article 101 deals with restrictive practices; prohibiting agreements between firms from EU member states that prevent or restrict competition.

Article 102. In EU competition policy Article 102 regulates possible abuses of monopoly power, such as monopoly pricing, predatory pricing and price discrimination.

Ascending bid auction. See **English auction**.

Asset specificity. An asset that is specific to a contractual relationship, and which has little or no value outside that relationship.

Asset-stripping. The practice of buying a company with the intention of transferring funds or assets to another company but leaving the liabilities behind.

Austrian school. A school of thought originally identified with the University of Vienna. Views competition as a dynamic process, driven by the acquisition of new information. Tends to be hostile to government intervention.

Average cost. The ratio of total cost to output.

Average fixed cost. The ratio of total fixed cost to output.

Average product of labour. The ratio of total output to the number of workers employed.

Average revenue. The ratio of total revenue to quantity demanded, equivalent to price.

Average variable cost. The ratio of total variable cost to output.

Backward vertical integration. Expansion upstream into an activity at an earlier stage of a production process (further away from the final market). For example, a manufacturer starts producing its own inputs. Also known as **upstream vertical integration**.

Bargain-then-ripoff pricing. A pricing strategy that involves offering new customers a low price in order to attract their business, and charging existing customers a high price in order to extract increased revenue or profit.

Barometric price leadership. One firm announces a price change, which is followed by other firms in the same industry. The leader is not necessarily a dominant firm and does not necessarily have market power.

Barrier to entry. Any factor which makes the average cost of a would-be entrant higher than that of an incumbent or that impedes entry in any other way.

Barrier to exit. Any cost incurred by an incumbent wishing to exit from an industry.

Bertrand model. A duopoly model in which each firm sets its own price treating its rival's price as fixed at its current level (zero **conjectural variation**). Each firm sells as much output as it can at its chosen price.

Best value. Has recently replaced **compulsory competitive tendering** as a method for determining the provision of local government services in the UK. Local government departments are expected to demonstrate that provision is efficient.

Bounded rationality. Recognizes that decision-making takes place within an environment of incomplete information and uncertainty.

Bundling. The practice of selling several goods together as a single package.

Business ethics. An analysis of moral issues seen from the perspective of companies and other forms of business organization. It is a practical application of ethics in the domain of business firms.

Business unit effects. The component of profitability that derives from a particular division or line of business within a firm.

Buyer concentration. A measure of the number and size distribution of buyers, reflecting the degree of market power on the demand side.

Call option. A call option on any asset gives the holder the right, but not the obligation, to purchase the asset at a pre-determined price on a specified future date.

Cartel. A group of firms that acts collectively, often in order to increase their joint profitability by exploiting their (collective) market power.

Certification. Retailers with reputations for selling high-quality goods provide a 'quality certification' for their products. Discounters enjoy the benefits of such certification without incurring any cost.

Chairman–CEO duality. Under a board structure of chairman–CEO duality, the CEO is also the chairman of the board. In other cases, chairman of the board and CEO are separate roles.

Chapter I prohibition. Part of the UK's 1998 Competition Act dealing with restrictive practices. Closely related to Article 101 of the EU's Treaty of Amsterdam.

Chapter II prohibition. Part of the UK's 1998 Competition Act dealing with abuses of monopoly power. Closely related to Article 102 of the EU's Treaty of Amsterdam.

Chicago school. A school of thought originally identified with the University of Chicago. Tends to view high profitability as a reward for superior efficiency, rather than symptomatic of abuses of market power. Argues government intervention in the form of active competition policy tends to lead to less rather than more competition.

Cluster. A group of interdependent firms that are linked through close vertical or horizontal relationships, located within a well defined geographic area.

Collusion. Firms agree, either tacitly or explicitly, to limit competition through the coordination of price, output or other decisions.

Collusion hypothesis. The view that a positive association between concentration and profitability constitutes evidence of the abuse of market power in an effort to enhance profitability.

Committed incumbent. A firm that signals intent to resist entry by increasing its own sunk cost expenditure.

Complements. Goods with a negative cross-price elasticity of demand: an increase in the price of one good leads to an decrease in the demand for the other good.

Compulsory competitive tendering. In-house providers and private contractors tender for contracts to provide services to local government.

Concentration measures. Measures of the number and size distribution of the firms in an industry. Size is usually measured using data on sales, assets, employees or output.

Concentration ratio. The share of an industry's n largest firms in a measure of total industry size, for some specific value of n.

Conduct regulation. Regulation designed to influence firms' behaviour directly, through measures such as price controls, regulated fees and commissions, controls on advertising, or restrictions on the expansion of distribution networks.

Conglomerate. A firm that produces a number of unrelated products or operates in a number of unrelated markets.

Conglomerate merger. A merger between firms that produce unrelated products or operate in unrelated markets.

Conjectural variation. The assumption one firm makes about its rivals' reactions to its own decisions, often with respect to decisions on price or output.

Consolidation. The bringing together of separate companies into a single corporate entity.

Constant returns to scale. If the use of all inputs increases by k per cent, output also increases by k per cent. Long-run average cost is constant with respect to changes in output.

Constant-sum game. In game theory, a game in which the sum of the payoffs to all players is always the same, whatever actions are chosen.

Consumer surplus. The difference between the maximum price a consumer would be willing to pay and the market price.

Contestable market. A market with free entry and exit conditions. An outside firm can enter temporarily, and cover its costs when it subsequently exits. Consequently, the behaviour of incumbents is constrained not only by actual competition but also by potential competition.

Contractual incompleteness. Firms are unable to conclude contracts that specify outcomes under every possible contingency, due to incomplete information.

Convenience goods. Goods that are relatively cheap and purchased frequently.

Core competences. Firm-specific skills deriving from specialized knowledge, and the manner in which this knowledge is employed by the firm.

Corporate effects. The component of profitability that derives from membership of a larger corporate group.

Corporate governance. Corporate governance refers to the systems by which companies are directed and controlled. More specifically, corporate governance describes the arrangements that ensure the company operates in accordance with the objectives of its own stakeholders, and the mechanisms that deal with conflicts of interest between various stakeholder groups.

Corporate social responsibility. A formulation and implementation of explicit policies designed to satisfy stakeholder expectations and fulfil social responsibilities beyond the narrow pursuit of increasing shareholder value.

Cost plus pricing. The firm calculates or estimates its average variable cost, and sets its price by adding a percentage mark-up to average variable cost. The mark-up includes a contribution towards firm's fixed cost, and a profit margin.

Cournot–Nash equilibrium. A duopoly or oligopoly equilibrium in which all firms make their output decisions based on a zero **conjectural variation** assumption: each firm optimizes assuming its rivals' actions are given or fixed.

Creative destruction. Term coined by Schumpeter to describe the economic impact of technological change. The creative aspect results in new and improved goods and services being brought to market, and cost-saving technologies being used in production. The destructive aspect refers to the displacement of obsolete goods, services and technologies.

Credence goods. Goods whose qualities cannot easily be assessed before or after consumption, because a judgement about quality requires specialized knowledge.

Cross-price elasticity of demand. A measure of the sensitivity of the quantity demanded of Good A to changes in the price of Good B. Measured as the ratio of the proportionate change in quantity demanded of Good A to the proportionate change in price of Good B.

Cross-subsidization. The practice of using revenue or profit earned from one activity to support or subsidize another activity.

Deadweight loss. The loss of social welfare (the sum of **consumer surplus** and **producer surplus**) attributable to the fact that an industry is monopolized, or to some other source of market failure or misallocation of resources.

Deconglomeration. Cessation of production of some products by a conglomerate, in order to focus more on its core products.

Decreasing returns to scale. If the use of all inputs increases by k per cent, output increases by less than k per cent. Long-run average cost is increasing with respect to an increase in output. See also **diseconomies of scale**.

Degrees of collusion. Measures of the strength and effectiveness of collusion.

Demand-side economies of scale. See **network externalities**.

Descending bid auction. See **Dutch auction**.

Diffusion. The imitation and adoption of new technologies (products or processes) by firms other than the original innovating firm.

Direction of diversification. Describes whether a firm diversifies within the same (broadly defined) industry, or into an unrelated industry.

Diseconomies of scale. Long-run average cost is increasing with respect to an increase in output. See also **decreasing returns to scale**.

Distinctive capabilities. A firm's unique or specialized competences.

Dominant price leadership. The dominant firm acts as leader by setting the market price. Firms on the competitive fringe adopt **price-taking behaviour** with respect to the price set by the dominant firm.

Dominant strategy. In game theory, a strategy which always produces the best outcome for one player, no matter what strategies are selected by other players.

Dominant strategy equilibrium. In game theory, the outcome that is achieved if each player has a dominant strategy and each player follows their own dominant strategy.

Dorfman–Steiner condition. The profit-maximizing advertising-to-sales ratio *equals* the ratio of **advertising elasticity of demand** to **price elasticity of demand**.

Double marginalization. Two stages of the same production process are both under the control of monopoly producers, and each producer adds its own monopoly mark-up to the price. The price of the finished product is higher than it would be if the two producers were vertically integrated.

Downstream vertical integration. See **forward vertical integration**

Dumping. The practice of charging a lower price in poorer countries than in richer countries for the same product.

Duopoly. A market that is supplied by two firms. A special case of oligopoly.

Dutch auction. An auction in which the price is lowered successively until a level is reached which a bidder is prepared to pay. Also known as a **descending bid auction**.

Economic efficiency. A firm is economically efficient if it has selected the combination of factor inputs that enable it to produce its current output level at the lowest possible cost, given prevailing factor prices.

Economies of scale. Long-run average cost is decreasing with respect to an increase in output. See also **increasing returns to scale**.

Economies of scale entry barrier. An incumbent incurs a lower long-run average cost than an entrant by virtue of producing at a larger scale, and benefiting from economies of scale.

Economies of scope. Long-run average cost when two or more goods are produced together is lower than long-run average cost when the goods are produced separately.

Edgeworth model. A duopoly model of price competition with a production capacity constraint. The model predicts there is no stable equilibrium.

Efficiency hypothesis. The view that a positive association between concentration and profitability derives from a tendency for the most efficient firms to dominate their own industries.

Elasticity. A measure of the responsiveness of one economic variable to a small change in another variable. See **price elasticity of demand**, **price elasticity of supply**, **cross-price elasticity of demand**, **advertising elasticity of demand**.

Empire-building. The pursuit of growth for its own sake, rather than growth that is targeted at increasing shareholder value. An example of agency problems that arise from the principal–agent relationship between shareholders and managers.

Engineering cost approach. Method for estimating a production function or cost function based on hypothetical rather than actual data. Expert (engineering) estimates are used to quantify relationships between inputs and outputs.

English auction. An auction in which the price is raised successively until a level is reached which only one bidder is willing to pay. Also known as an **ascending bid auction**.

Entropy coefficient. Concentration measure based on a weighted sum of market shares: the weights are the natural logarithms of the reciprocals of market shares.

Entry-deterring strategy. Any action that is taken by an established firm to discourage potential entrants from entering the market.

Executive compensation. Executive compensation packages are a key determinant of the extent to which the incentives of top managers are either aligned or misaligned with shareholder interests. In addition to the basic salary and any employee benefits and perquisites, executive compensation packages may include cash bonuses related to company performance, share ownership and call options.

Experience goods. Goods whose qualities can only be ascertained when they are consumed, and not by inspection prior to purchase and consumption.

Experimental economics. A branch of economics which uses laboratory experiments to test economic theories.

Explicit collusion. Collusion that is organized through a formal, explicit contract or other agreement between the colluding parties.

First-degree price discrimination. Price depends on the number of units purchased and on the identity of the buyer. Also known as **perfect price discrimination**.

First-mover advantage. An advantage that rewards a firm for being the first to enter a market or the first to take some other strategic action.

First price sealed bid auction. An auction in which each bidder independently submits a single bid, without seeing the bids submitted by other bidders. The highest bidder secures the item and pays a price equivalent to their winning bid.

Five forces model. A model used by Porter (1980) to describe competition. The five forces are: the extent and intensity of direct competition; the threat of entrants; the threat of substitute products and services; the power of buyers; and the power of suppliers.

Fixed cost. Cost that does not vary with the quantity of output produced.

Foreclosure. The practice of refusing to supply downstream firms or to purchase from upstream firms.

Forms of collusion. Organizational structures, as well as custom and practice, which characterize collusive agreements.

Forward vertical integration. Expansion downstream into an activity at a later stage of a production process (closer to the final market). For example, a manufacturer starts selling its own products direct to consumers. Also known as **downstream vertical integration**.

Franchise agreement (franchising). The allocation of exclusive rights to supply a particular good or service. The franchisee is protected from competition for the duration of the franchise.

Game theory. A theory of decision-making under conditions of uncertainty and interdependence. Components of a game include players, strategies, actions, payoffs, outcomes and an equilibrium.

Geographic concentration. Measures whether a large share of an industry's total output is produced in a small number of countries or regions, or whether the industry is widely dispersed geographically.

Geographic market definition. Involves determining whether an increase in the price of a product in one geographic area significantly affects either demand or supply, and therefore price, in another area. If so, both areas are in the same geographic market.

Geographic entry barrier. Any entry barrier affecting foreign firms attempting to enter a domestic market. Examples include tariffs, quotas, frontier controls, national standards, regulations and exchange controls.

Gibrat's law. Describes the implications for industry concentration if the growth rate of each firm is random, or more specifically, unrelated to the current size of the firm. If firm sizes are subject to random growth, the firm size distribution becomes increasingly skewed and concentration increases over time. Also known as the **Law of Proportionate Effect**.

Gini coefficient. A measure of inequality based on the **Lorenz curve**, which can be applied to data on firm sizes or market shares.

Governance. Describes the manner in which an organization manages its contractual relationships between shareholders, managers, employees and other relevant parties.

Hannah and Kay index. Generalization of the **Herfindahl–Hirschman index**, based on the sum of market shares raised to some exponent, for all member firms of an industry.

Herfindahl–Hirschman index. Concentration measure based on the sum of the squared market shares of all member firms of an industry.

Hit-and-run entry. A situation in which an entrant has sufficient time to sell its product profitably and withdraw before the incumbent has time to react.

Horizontal agreement. An agreement between firms in the same industry, which may result in reduced competition. Subjects of such agreements may include common pricing policies, production quotas or information sharing.

Horizontal integration. See **horizontal merger**.

Horizontal merger. A merger between two firms that produce the same or similar products, also known as **horizontal integration**.

Horizontal product differentiation. Products or brands are of the same or similar overall quality, but offer different combinations of characteristics, and may be valued differently by different consumers.

Imperfect competition. Market structures that fall between the polar cases of perfect competition and monopoly. Includes **monopolistic competition** and **oligopoly**.

Incomplete contracts. A contract for which the parties cannot identify in advance every possible contingency which might affect their contractual relationship. Most contracts are incomplete contracts.

Increasing returns to scale. If the use of all inputs increases by k per cent, output increases by more than k per cent. Long-run average cost is decreasing with respect to an increase in output. See also **economies of scale**.

Independent action. Competing firms take decisions without consulting one another, or colluding in any other way.

Independent private values model. In an auction, each bidder independently forms an opinion of the value of the item to themself. These private valuations differ between bidders, and there is no single, intrinsic valuation that all bidders can agree on.

Industrial district. A geographic area containing a number of firms producing similar products, including firms operating at different stages of a production process.

Industry concentration. Measure of importance of the largest firms in an industry. See also **seller concentration**.

Industry effects. The component of profitability that derives from involvement in a particular industry.

Industry life cycle. Describes the long-run evolution of an industry and its constituent firms through the introduction, growth, maturity and decline phases of the life cycle.

Informative advertising. Advertising that provides consumers with factual information about the existence, attributes or price of a product, service or brand.

Installed base. A number of existing customers, who are locked in as a result of having entered into previously signed service contracts.

Innovation. Bringing a new idea or invention to the stage of commercial application, through the applied research, development and commercial production stages.

Interdependence. A situation in which the outcome for each firm depends not only on its own actions, but also on the actions of its rivals. A defining characteristic of the market structure of **oligopoly**.

Internal capital market. An organization's procedures for allocating investment funds internally, between departments or divisions that are competing for access to such funds.

Internal rate of return. In investment appraisal, the discount rate at which the net present value of all cash flows associated with the project under consideration *equals* zero.

Intertemporal price discrimination. Price depends on the point in time when a good is sold, but production costs do not depend on the point in time when the good is produced and sold.

Invention. The creation of an idea and its initial implementation, through basic research.

Isocost. All combinations of two-factor inputs which produce an identical total cost.

Isoprofit curve. All combinations of quantities produced or prices charged by two firms which produce an identical profit for one of the firms.

Isoquant. All combinations of two factor inputs which produce an identical level of output.

Joint profit maximization. Two or more firms set their combined output level and price as if they were a single monopolist. The firms share the resulting monopoly profit among themselves.

Joint venture. A form of **strategic alliance**, in which two or more independent firms enter into an agreement to cooperate over a specific project.

Junk bond. A bond which carries a high risk of default and thus doesn't reach an investment 'grade' by bond-rating agencies. To attract buyers such bonds offer higher yields.

Kinked demand curve. An **oligopoly** model that explains price rigidity, arguing that a firm in a situation of **interdependence** may be reluctant either to raise or lower its price, because in both cases it expects its rivals to react in a way that reduces its own profit.

Law of Diminishing Returns. As the use of a variable factor input increases progressively while the use of other factor inputs is fixed, beyond some point successive increases in output become smaller.

Law of Proportionate Effect. See **Gibrat's law**.

Legal entry barrier. Any entry barrier created by government, for example through franchised state-sponsored monopolies, patents and registration, certification or licensing requirements.

Lerner index. Price *minus* marginal cost expressed as a proportion of price. The extent to which price exceeds marginal cost can be interpreted as a measure of market power.

Limit pricing. A pricing strategy by an incumbent firm intended to prevent entry. The incumbent sacrifices some profit by setting a price sufficiently low to make it impossible for an entrant to operate profitably.

Location model. A model of product differentiation in which consumers' tastes or preferences are expressed in terms of the characteristics embodied in goods or services. Also known as a **spatial model**.

Long run. A time period of sufficient duration that the quantities of all factor inputs used in production can be varied.

Lorenz curve. When plotted using firm size or market share data, shows the cumulative sizes or market shares of all firms up to firm n, for n 1 ... N (where N is the total number of firms), when the firms are numbered in descending size or market share order.

Managerial utility. Managerial satisfaction.

Marginal cost. The additional cost of producing one extra unit of output.

Marginal product of labour. The additional output obtained by employing one extra unit of labour.

Marginal revenue. The additional revenue obtained by selling one extra unit of output.

Mark-up test. A test suggested by Bresnahan (1982, 1989) and Lau (1982), which involves estimating a structural model incorporating demand and cost equations, and drawing inferences about the nature of competition by observing each firm's **conjectural variation** under an assumption of profit maximization.

Market concentration. See **seller concentration** and **industry concentration**.

Market demand function. The relationship between market price and the number of units of a product or service consumers wish to buy at that price.

Market equilibrium. At the equilibrium or market-clearing price, quantity demanded *equals* quantity supplied.

Merger policy. A branch of competition policy dealing with mergers. Examines whether a merger should be permitted, or prevented on the grounds that it may lead to abuses of market power.

Merger waves. Cyclical peaks in the level of merger activity across the entire corporate sector.

Metering. The practice of charging a low price for a primary product, and a high price for a secondary product that is tied to the primary product.

Minimum efficient scale. The output level beyond which the firm can achieve no further saving in long-run average cost by means of further expansion of production.

Minimum profit constraint. In managerial theories of the firm, a minimum profit level demanded by shareholders, which limits managers' discretion to pursue objectives such as sales revenue, growth or managerial utility.

Mixed strategy. In game theory, a player adopts a mixed strategy by choosing their actions randomly, using fixed probabilities.

Monopolistic competition. A market structure with a large number of firms producing similar but not identical products, and with free entry. Falls between the polar cases of perfect competition and monopoly.

Monopoly. A market structure with a single firm, producing a unique product and protected from competition by insurmountable entry barriers.

Monopoly policy. A branch of competition policy dealing with abuses of market power when a single firm or group or firms has a large market share.

Moral hazard. Arises when an agent has the opportunity to act in their own private interests but against the principal's interests, in contravention of the terms of the contract between the two parties. It is difficult for the principal to detect and punish opportunistic behaviour on the part of the agent.

Multiple-period game. In game theory, a game that is repeated a number of times. Also known as a **repeated game**.

Nash equilibrium. In game theory, all players maximize their own actual or expected payoffs, subject to a zero **conjectural variation** constraint: each player takes the other players' current strategies as given. No player can improve their actual or expected payoff given the strategies currently chosen by the other players. See also **Cournot–Nash equilibrium**.

Natural monopoly. An industry in which long-run average cost is decreasing in output over all the output levels the market is capable of absorbing. The definition depends on both the cost structure and the position of the **market demand function**.

Natural product differentiation. The distinguishing characteristics of products or services derive from their inherent or natural attributes.

Near-neighbour brands. Brands with similar characteristics.

Network effects. See **network externalities**.

Network externalities. The effect that one user of a product or service has on the value of the same product or service to other users. Also known as **network effects** or **demand-side economies of scale**.

New empirical industrial organization. An approach which attempts to draw inferences about market structure and competitive conditions from direct observation of conduct at firm level.

New industrial organization. Theories of industrial organization which focus primarily on strategy and conduct at firm level, rather than on market or industry structure.

Non-constant-sum game. In game theory, the sum of the gains and losses of all players depends on the actions chosen by the players.

Non-linear pricing. See **quantity-dependent pricing**.

Normal profit. The minimum return a firm's owner must earn to prevent the owner from closing the firm down, equivalent to the **opportunity cost** of running the firm.

Numbers equivalent. An inverse measure of concentration, which compares the structure of an observed N-firm industry to a hypothetical industry comprising N equal-sized firms.

Oligopoly. A market structure with a small number of firms, whose products may be identical or differentiated, and where there are barriers to entry. The firms recognize their **interdependence**.

Open source technology. A technology that is freely available, on condition that improvements or refinements developed by users are also made freely available to other users.

Opportunity cost. The cost of allocating scarce resources to some economic activity, measured as the return that could be earned by allocating the same resources to the next best available alternative activity.

Organizational slack. In the behavioural theory of the firm, resources held by the organization which permit **side-payments** in excess of the minimum required to prevent individuals or groups withdrawing from the organization.

Passive incumbent. A firm that does not signal intent to resist entry.

Patent. The award of a patent to the inventor of a new product, process, substance or design confers a property right over the knowledge that is embodied in the invention.

Payoff. In game theory, a player's return, which is dependent on the strategies and actions chosen by all players.

Peak load pricing. Demand varies over time for a good which cannot be stored, but production capacity does not vary over time. The peak-period price charged by the producer exceeds the off-peak period price.

Pecuniary economies of scale. Economies of scale arising when large firms find it easier or cheaper than small firms to obtain or purchase inputs or raise finance.

Perfect competition. A market structure with a large number of firms producing identical products and with free entry.

Perfect price discrimination. See **first-degree price discrimination**.

Perquisites. Perquisites refer to the diversion of resources of the firm to support on-the-job consumption by the managers, through means such as luxury offices, expense accounts and foreign travel.

Persistence of profit. The extent to which profits or losses above or below average levels tend to be sustained, either in the short run or long run.

Persuasive advertising. Advertising that aims to change consumers' perceptions of a product, service or brand with a view to stimulating sales. May include claims that are not objectively verifiable.

Porter's Diamond Model. A model of the determinants and dynamics of competitive advantage, based on analysis of competitive rivalry, factor and demand conditions, and the existence of related and supporting industries.

Predatory competition. A dominant firm engages in certain aggressive forms of price or non-price competition, aiming to force a weaker competitor to withdraw from the market.

Predatory pricing. A dominant firm adopts price-cutting as an instrument of **predatory competition**.

Price cap regulation. Regulation in the form of a specific limit on the price a firm is permitted to charge.

Price–cost margin. The ratio of profit to sales revenue, or price *minus* average cost to price.

Price dispersion. Variation in the prices charged by competing sellers for the same product or services.

Price elasticity of demand. A measure of the sensitivity of quantity demanded to changes in price. Measured as the ratio of the proportionate change in quantity demanded to the proportionate change in price.

Price elasticity of supply. A measure of the sensitivity of quantity supplied to changes in price. Measured as the ratio of the proportionate change in quantity supplied to the proportionate change in price.

Price leadership. See **barometric price leadership** and **dominant price leadership**.

Price rigidity. A tendency for oligopolists to avoid frequent changes of price, perhaps preferring instead non-price forms of competition.

Price taking behaviour. Each firm's market share is sufficiently small that the firm believes its output decision has no bearing on the market price. Therefore, the firm treats the market price as being beyond its control.

Principal–agent problem. Agency theory emphasizes the conflicts that can arise between principals and agents. The principal–agent problem refers to the difficulties that arise when a principal hires an agent, due to imperfect information.

Prisoner's dilemma. In game theory, refers to a case in which players select their dominant strategies and achieve an equilibrium in which they are worse off than they would be if they could all agree to select an alternative (non-dominant) strategy.

Privatization. The sale and transfer of assets from the public sector to the private sector.

Process innovation. The commercial application of a new piece of cost-saving technology.

Producer surplus. The difference between the market price and the minimum price a producer would be willing to accept.

Product differentiation. The practice of making close substitutes appear different, so that customers no longer regard them as similar or identical.

Product differentiation entry barrier. Arises when a potential entrant incurs advertising or other marketing costs in order to achieve a viable market share, because consumers are loyal to the established brands of incumbents. Both **natural** and **strategic product differentiation** may give rise to entry barriers.

Product innovation. Production of a new product on a commercial basis.

Product market definition. Includes all products that are close substitutes for one another, both in consumption and in production.

Production function. A technological relationship between the quantities of inputs and the level of output.

Productive efficiency. A firm is efficient in production if it has achieved both **technical efficiency** and **economic efficiency**.

Profit maximization. The output level where marginal revenue equals marginal cost.

Pure common value model. In auction theory, there is a single, intrinsic value of the item being sold, that is the same for all bidders.

Pure strategy. In game theory, a strategy whereby one player always chooses a certain action, regardless of the actions chosen by other players.

Quantity-dependent pricing. The price per unit depends on the number of units purchased. Also known as **non-linear pricing**.

Quantity forcing. A seller with market power forces buyers to purchase more units of a good than they would wish if they had the choice.

Quasi-rent. Rent arising from the creation of an asset that is specific to some particular relationship, but with little or no value outside that relationship.

Rate of return regulation. Regulation in the form of a limit on the rate of return on capital a firm is permitted to earn. Price must be set so that the target rate of return is achieved.

Reaction function. Shows the profit-maximizing response of one firm to a price or output decision taken by a rival firm, treating the rival's decision as fixed.

Real economies of scale. Economies of scale arising from technological relationships between inputs and output embodied in a firm's long-run production function.

Reciprocity. An agreement whereby firm A purchases inputs from firm B, on condition that firm B also purchases inputs from firm A.

Regional concentration. See **geographic concentration**.

Regulatory capture. A tendency for lobbying by a regulated firm to succeed in influencing the regulator in the regulated firm's favour.

Repeated game. See **multiple-period game**.

Representative consumer model. A model of product differentiation in which consumers' tastes or preferences are expressed in terms of goods or services (rather than characteristics), and firms compete to attract buyers by differentiating the goods or services they offer.

Resale price maintenance. A practice whereby an upstream firm sets a minimum (or possibly a maximum) price to be charged in a downstream (usually retail) market.

Reserve price. In auction theory, a minimum bid that must be registered for the sale of the item to proceed.

Residual rights (to control). Rights to whatever resources are left after a firm's contractual obligations have been satisfied and all **specific rights** to the firm's resources have been assigned.

Restrictive practices policy. A branch of competition policy dealing with single firms or groups or firms that engage in practices that may be detrimental to consumer welfare, such as price fixing, output quotas, predatory pricing and vertical restraints.

Returns to scale. See **increasing returns to scale** and **decreasing returns to scale**.

Revenue equivalence theorem. In auction theory, in the case where bidders form independent private valuations of the item that is for sale, all four basic auction types (English, Dutch, first price sealed bid and second price sealed bid) yield the same expected proceeds to the seller.

Revenue test. A test proposed by Rosse and Panzar (1977), which examines whether firm conduct is in accordance with the models of perfect competition, imperfect competition or monopoly, based on observation of the impact of variations in factor prices on profit-maximizing firm-level revenues.

Rule of reason. The principle that competition policy should be concerned with the practical consequences for competition and welfare of specific abuses of market power or other restrictive practices, rather than with the structural characteristics of markets which might, in theory, create opportunities for anticompetitive practice.

Sample selection bias. Bias arising in statistical analysis if the data has been chosen non-randomly. For example, if five years' data is required for each firm, and only those firms that traded continuously for five years are included, a non-random sample of survivors is obtained, excluding all firms that entered and exited during the five-year period. This specific form of sample selection bias is known as **survivorship bias**.

Satisficing. In the behavioural theory of the firm, a firm aims for a satisfactory profit but does not necessarily maximize profit.

Schumpeterian hypothesis. Describes the view that a fast pace of innovation is more likely to be associated with monopoly than with competition.

Search goods. Goods whose qualities can be ascertained by inspection prior to purchase and consumption.

Second-degree price discrimination. The price per unit of output depends on the number of units purchased, but not on the identity of the buyer. All buyers who purchase a given number of units pay the same price per unit.

Second price sealed bid auction. An auction in which each bidder independently and privately submits a single bid. The highest bidder secures the item, but pays a price equal to the second-highest submitted bid. Also known as a **Vickrey auction**.

Seller concentration. A measure of the number and size distribution of sellers, reflecting the degree of market power on the supply side. May refer either to **aggregate concentration** (for the economy as a whole) or to **industry concentration** (for one particular industry).

Semi-collusion. Firms collude over certain areas of activity (for example, pricing or production), but compete in other areas in which it may be more difficult to specify, conclude or enforce an agreement (for example, research and development).

Sequential game. In game theory, players choose their actions sequentially (in turn). A player who moves later knows which actions were chosen by players who moved earlier.

Shopping goods. Goods that are expensive and are purchased infrequently.

Short run. A time period during which only one factor input used in production can be varied, while other factor inputs are fixed.

Side-payment. In the behavioural theory of the firm, a payment in excess of the minimum required to prevent an individual or group from withdrawing from the organization.

Simultaneous game. In game theory, all players choose their actions simultaneously. When choosing, no player knows the actions chosen by other players.

Slotting allowances. These occur in retailing, when large buyers, such as supermarket chains, require fees or other payments from suppliers, such as food manufacturers, to place their products in prominent positions.

Spatial model. See **location model**.

Specialization. Refers to the extent to which a country's production is composed mainly of a small number of products or services, or is more widely dispersed.

Specific rights. Rights that are specified explicitly in the terms of a contract.

Stackelberg equilibrium. A solution to a **duopoly** or an **oligopoly** model, in which one firm anticipates its rivals' tendencies to act in accordance with a zero **conjectural variation** assumption, and exploits this awareness to increase its own profit.

Stakeholder. The broadest stakeholder definition includes any group that has the capability to influence or exert pressure on the company's management.

State-sponsored collusion. Collusion that is encouraged or dictated by government. The justification might be to promote rationalization, or to assure a steady supply.

Strategic alliance. A form of cooperation between producers that stops short of a full-scale merger, such as a licensing arrangement or a **joint venture**.

Strategic group. A group of firms from the same industry, whose conduct is similar and that tend to view other firms from the same group as their main competitors.

Strategic product differentiation. The distinguishing characteristics of products are consciously created by suppliers, for example through advertising or other types of marketing campaign.

Strategy. In game theory, a set of rules defining which action a player should choose under each possible set of circumstances that might exist at any stage in the game.

Structural regulation. Regulation that seeks to influence market structure. Measures include the functional separation of firms into complementary activities, restrictions on entry, and restrictions on the operation of foreign firms.

Structure–conduct–performance paradigm. A methodological approach for research in industrial organization, in which the structural characteristics of industries are assumed to influence or dictate the conduct and performance of the industry's member firms. More sophisticated models allow for feedback effects, whereby conduct and performance variables help shape the industry's future structure.

Substitutes. Goods with a positive cross-price elasticity of demand: an increase in the price of one good leads to an increase in demand for the other good.

Sunk cost. Expenditure on items such as advertising and research and development that is non-recoverable in the event that the firm exits from the industry.

Survivorship bias. See **sample selection bias**.

Switching costs. Costs associated with switching from one supplier to another.

Synergy. Synergies exist when two companies merge and the combined sum in value is greater than the sum of the individual values.

Tacit collusion. Collusion that is not organized through a formal, explicit contract or other specific agreement between the colluding parties.

Tangency solution. Long-run equilibrium under **monopolistic competition**, at which each firm's average revenue function is tangential to its average cost function. Accordingly, each firm earns only a normal profit.

Technical efficiency. A firm is technically efficient if it is producing the maximum quantity of output that is technologically feasible, given the quantities of the factor inputs it employs. A technically efficient firm operates on (and not within) its own production function. Also known as **x-efficiency**.

Third-degree price discrimination. Price depends on the identity of the buyer but not on the number of units purchased. Any buyer is offered as many or as few units as he or she wishes at a constant price.

Tie-in sale. See **tying**.

Tit-for-tat. In game theory, a strategy whereby one player punishes another for non-cooperation in a previous period.

Tobin's q. The ratio of a firm's stock market value to the replacement cost of its capital.

Total cost. Variable cost *plus* fixed cost.

Total revenue. Price *times* quantity sold.

Tournament theory. The theory suggests that high CEO remuneration is a 'prize'. This provides incentives for junior executives on much lower salaries to compete against each other. The winner then becomes eligible for promotion to the rank of CEO. The larger the firm, the greater the pay disparity.

Trade association. An organization that represents the interests of the member firms of an industry. It usually differs from a cartel in that it has no monopolistic intent.

Transaction costs. Costs incurred when using the market to allocate resources, arising from the acquisition of information or the negotiation, monitoring and enforcement of contracts.

Transfer pricing. The pricing of intermediate products traded internally between the divisions of a single firm.

Two-part tariff. A price structure requiring the payment of a fixed fee (mandatory if any purchases are to be made) and an additional uniform price for each unit purchased.

Tying. A firm with market power in the market for Good X requires buyers also to purchase Good Y in order to obtain Good X. Also known as a **tie-in sale**.

Type 1 industry. An industry in which growth in the size of the market leads to fragmentation of industry structure and deconcentration (Sutton, 1991). The level of sunk cost investment expenditure is determined exogenously, by product characteristics and technological conditions.

Type 2 industry. An industry in which growth in the size of the market leads to growth in the size of the largest firms, and no tendency for fragmentation of industry structure or deconcentration (Sutton, 1991). The level of sunk cost investment expenditure is determined endogenously, by incumbent firms' decisions on advertising and research and development.

Upstream vertical integration. See **backward vertical integration**.

Valuation ratio. The ratio of the firm's stock market value to the book value of its assets.

Value chain. A technique devised to disaggregate a firm into its strategically relevant activities, in order to appraise each activity's contribution to the firm's performance.

Variable cost. The component of total cost that varies with output.

Variance decomposition analysis. A statistical technique involving the decomposition of the variation in a firm's profitability into components deriving from the industries in which the firm operates, and from each division or business unit within the firm.

Vertical agreement. Agreements between firms operating at successive stages of a production process, such as exclusive dealing contracts and resale price maintenance.

Vertical disintegration. A corporate strategy of disengaging from an involvement in one or more stages of the production process.

Vertical integration. See **vertical merger**.

Vertical merger. A merger between two firms that produce at different stages of a production process, also known as **vertical integration**.

Vertical product differentiation. One product, service or brand differs from another in terms of overall quality. If the prices were the same, all consumers would choose the superior product.

Vertical restraint. Conditions or restrictions on trade between firms that are linked vertically.

Vickrey auction. See **second price sealed bid auction**. Due to Vickrey (1961).

Welfare. A measure of well-being based on alternative allocations of scarce resources.

Winner's curse. A tendency for the winning bid to exceed the intrinsic value of the item being auctioned, common in sealed bid auctions.

Workable competition. An approach to competition policy which seeks to adjust aspects of structure and conduct in order to bring about a favourable performance outcome.

X-efficiency. See **technical efficiency**.

Zero-sum game. A constant sum game in which the sum of the gains and losses of all players is always zero.

Bibliography

Aaronovitch, S. and Sawyer, M.C. (1975) Mergers, growth and concentration, *Oxford Economic Papers*, 27, 136–55.

Abernethy, A. and Franke, G.R. (1996) The information content of advertising: a meta-analysis, *Journal of Advertising*, 25, 1–17.

Acemoglu, D., Aghion, P., Griffiths, R. and Zilibotti, F. (2003) Vertical integration and technology, theory and evidence, *National Bureau of Economic Research Working Paper*, 10997.

Acs, Z.J. and Audretsch, D.B. (1990) *Innovation and Small Firms*. Cambridge: Cambridge University Press.

Adams, R. and Ferreira, D. (2009) Women in the boardroom and their impact on governance and performance, *Journal of Financial Economics*, 94, 291–309.

Adams, R. and Mehran, H. (2003) Is corporate governance different for bank holding companies? *Economic Policy Review*, 123–42.

Adams, R. and Mehran, H. (2008) Corporate performance, board structure and its determinants in the banking industry. *Federal Reserve Bank of New York, Staff Report*, Number 330.

Adams, R., Hermalin, B. and Weisbach, M. (2010) The role of boards of directors in corporate performance: a conceptual framework and survey, *Journal of Economic Literature*, 48, 58–107.

Adams, W.J. and Yellen, J. (1976) Commodity bundling and the burden of monopoly, *Quarterly Journal of Economics*, 90, 475–98.

Adelman, M.A. (1949) Integration and antitrust policy, *Harvard Law Review*, 63, 27–77.

Adelman, M.A. (1955) Concept and statistical measurement of vertical integration, in Stigler, G.J. (ed.) *Business Concentration and Price Policy*. Princeton, NJ: Princeton University Press.

Adelman, M.A. (1959) *A & P: A Study in Price–Cost Behaviour and Public Policy*. Cambridge, MA: Harvard University Press.

Adner, R. and Helfat, C.E. (2003) Corporate effects and dynamic managerial capabilities, *Strategic Management Journal*, 24, 1011–25.

Advertising Association (2003) *Advertising Statistics Yearbook 2003*. Oxford: NTC Publications.

Advertising Association (2007) *Advertising Statistics Yearbook 2007*. Oxford: NTC Publications.

Advertising Association (2009) *Advertising Statistics Yearbook 2009*. Oxford: NTC Publications.

Aguilera, R.V. and Jackson, T. (2003) The cross-national diversity of corporate governance: dimensions and determinants, *Academy of Management Review*, 28, 447–66.

Aharonson, B.S., Baum, J.A.C. and Feldman, M.P. (2004) Industrial clustering and the returns to inventive activity: Canadian biotechnology fims, 1991 2000, DRUID Working Paper No. 03-16, www.druid.dk/wp/pdf_files/04-03.pdf.

Ahn, S. (2001) Firm dynamics and productivity growth: a review of micro evidence from OECD countries, *OECD Economics Department Working Papers*, No. 297.

Ahn, S. (2002) Competition, innovation and productivity growth: a review of theory and evidence, *OECD Economics Department Working Papers*, No. 317.

Aiginger, K. (1999) Do industrial structures converge? A survey of empirical literature on specialization and concentration of industries, WIFO, mimeograph. Vienna: WIFO.

Aiginger, K. and Davies, S.W. (2000) Industrial specialization and geographic concentration: two sides of the same coin? Not for the European Union. Department of Economics Working Paper 23/2000, University of Luiz.

Aitchison, J. and Brown, J.A.C. (1966) *The Lognormal Distribution*. Cambridge: Cambridge University Press.

Akerlof, G.A. (1970) The market for lemons: quality uncertainty and the market mechanisms, *Quarterly Journal of Economics*, 39, 489–500.

Aktas, N., de Bodt, E. and Roll, R. (2007) Is European M&A regulation protectionist?, *Economic Journal*, 117, 1096–121.

Alchian, A.A. (1963) Reliability and progress curves in airframe production, *Econometrica*, 31, 679–93.

Alchian, A.A. (1965) The basis of some recent advances in the theory of management of the firm, *Journal of Industrial Economics*, 14, 30–41.

Alchian, A.A. and Demsetz, H. (1972) Production, information costs, and economic organisation, *American Economic Review*, 62, 777–95.

Alexander, D.L., Flynn, J. and Linkins, L. (1995) Innovation, and global market share in the pharmaceutical industry, *Review of Industrial Organisation*, 10, 197–207.

Allen, F. and Gale, D. (2000) Corporate governance and competition, in Vives, X. (ed.) *Corporate Governance: Theoretical and Empirical Perspectives*. Cambridge: Cambridge University Press.

Allen, F. and Gale, D. (2004) Competition and financial stability, *Journal of Money, Credit, and Banking*, 36, 433–80.

Altunbaş, Y. and Marqués, D. (2008) Mergers and acquisitions and bank performance in Europe: the role of strategic similarities, *Journal of Economics & Business*, 60, 204–22.

Álvarez, L.J. and Hernando, I. (2005) The price setting behaviour of Spanish firms: evidence from survey data, *Banco de España Working Paper*, No. 0537.

Álvarez, L.J. and Hernando, I. (2006) Competition and price adjustment in the euro area, *Bank of Spain Working Paper*, No. 0629.

Amato, L. and Wilder, R.P. (1990) Firm and industry effects in industrial economics, *Southern Economic Journal*, 57, 93–105.

Amihud, Y. and Lev, B. (1981) Risk reduction as a managerial motive for conglomerate mergers, *Bell Journal of Economics*, 12, 605–17.

Amiti, M. (1997) Specialisation patterns in Europe, *Centre for Economic Policy Research, Discussion Paper*, No. 363.

Amiti, M. (1998) New trade theories and industrial location in the EU: a survey of the evidence, *Oxford Review of Economic Policy*, 14, 45–53.

Ancarani, F. and Shankar, V. (2004) Price levels and price dispersion within and across multiple retailer types: further evidence and extensions, *Journal of the Academy Marketing Science*, 32, 176–84.

Andrade, G., Mitchell, M. and Stafford, E. (2001) New evidence and perspectives on mergers, *Journal of Economic Perspectives*, 15, 103–20.

Arbatskaya, M., Hviid, M. and Shaffer, G. (2006) On the use of low-price guarantees to discourage price cutting, *International Journal of Industrial Organisation*, 24, 1139–56.

Archibald, G.C. and Rosenbluth, G. (1975) The new theory of consumer demand and monopolistic competition, *Quarterly Journal of Economics*, 89, 569–90.

Armentano, D.T. (1975) Price fixing in theory and practice, in Brozen, Y. (ed.) *The Competitive Economy*. Morristown, NJ: General Learning Press.

Armstrong, M. (1999) Price discrimination by a many-product firm, *Review of Economic Studies*, 66, 151–68.

Armstrong, M. and Sappington, D.E.M. (2007) Recent developments in regulation, in Armstrong, M. and Porter, R. (eds) *Handbook of Industrial Organization*, Vol. 3. Amsterdam: Elsevier.

Armstrong, M., Cowan, S. and Vickers, J. (1994) *Regulatory Reform: Economic Analysis and British Experience*. Oxford: Oxford University Press.

Aron, D.J. (1993) Diversification as a strategic preemptive weapon, *Journal of Economics and Management*, 2, 41–70.

Arrow, K.J. (1962) Economic welfare and the allocation of resources for invention, in *The Rate and Direction of Inventive Activity*. National Bureau of Economic Research Conference Report. Princeton, NJ: Princeton University Press, 609–25.

Arrow, K.J. (1975) Vertical integration and communication, *Rand Journal of Economics*, 6, 173–83.

Arterburn, A. and Woodbury, J. (1981) Advertising, price competition and market structure, *Southern Economic Journal*, 47, 763–75.

Asad. D. and Hoje, J. (2010) Corporate governance and the fall of Enron, *Review of Business Research*, 10, 13–24.

Asch, P. (1969) Collusive oligopoly: an antitrust quandary, *Antitrust Law and Economic Review*, 2, 53–68.

Asch, P. and Seneca, J. (1975) Characteristics of collusive firms, *Journal of Industrial Economics*, 23, 223–37.

Asch, P. and Seneca, J. (1976) Is collusion profitable?, *Review of Economics and Statistics*, 58, 1–10.

Asch, P. and Seneca, J. (1985) *Government and the Market Place*. New York: Dryden.

Ascher, K. (1987) *The Politics of Privatisation: Contracting Out Public Services*. London: Macmillan.

Athey, S, and Haile, P. (2006) Empirical models of auctions, in Blundell, R., Newey, W.K. and Persson, T. (eds) *Advances in Economics and Econometrics: Theory and Applications*, Vol. 2. Cambridge: Cambridge University Press, 1–45.

Aubert, C., Rey, P. and Kovacic, W.E. (2006) The impact of leniency and whistle-blowing programs on cartels, *International Journal of Industrial Organization*, 24, 1241–66.

Aucremanne, L. and Druant, M. (2005) Price-setting behaviour in Belgium: what can be learned from an ad hoc survey? *ECB Working Paper*, No. 448.

Audretsch, D.B., Baumol, W.J. and Burke, A. (2001) Competition policy in a dynamic economy, *International Journal of Industrial Organization*, 19, 613–34.

Audretsch, D.B., Klomp, L., Santarelli, E. and Thurik, A.R. (2004) Gibrat's Law: are the services different? *Review of Industrial Organization*, 24, 301–24.

Aust, P. (1997) An institutional analysis of vertical co-ordination versus vertical integration: the case of the US broiler industry, Department of Agricultural Economics, Michigan State University Staff Paper, 97–124.

Ausubel, L.M. (2008) Auctions (theory), in Durlauf, S.N. and Blume, L.E. (eds) *New Palgrave Dictionary of Economics*, 2nd edition. London: Palgrave Macmillan.

Averch, H. and Johnson, L.L. (1962) Behaviour of the firm under regulatory constraint, *American Economics Review*, 52, 1052–69.

Ayres, I. (1987) How cartels punish: a structural theory of self enforcing collusion, *Columbia Law Review*, 87, 295.

Azer, A. (2002) The ethics of corporate social responsibility: management trend of the new millennium? *Sheldon Chumir Foundation*, http://www.chumirethics foundation.ca/files/pdf/azeralison1.pdf Accessed 10 January 2012.

Baake, P., Kamecke, U. and Norman, H. (2004) Vertical foreclosure versus downstream competition with capital precommitment, *International Journal of Industrial Organisation*, 22, 185–92.

Bagwell, K. (2002) Advertising, in Armstrong, M. and Porter, R. (eds) *Handbook of Industrial Organization*, Vol. 3. Amsterdam: Elsevier.

Bagwell, K. (2007) The economics of advertising, in Armstrong, M. and Porter, R. (eds) *Handbook of Industrial Organization*, Vol. 3. Amsterdam: Elsevier.

Bagwell, K. and Staiger, R.W. (1997) Collusion over the business cycle, *Rand Journal of Economics*, 28, 82–106.

Bailey, D. and Boyle, S.E. (1971) The optimal measure of concentration, *Journal of the American Statistical Association*, 66, 702–6.

Bain, J.S. (1951) Relation of profit rate to industry concentration: American manufacturing, 1936–1940, *Quarterly Journal of Economics*, 65, 293–324.

Bain, J.S. (1956) *Barriers to New Competition*. Cambridge, MA: Harvard University Press.

Bain, J.S. (1959) *Industrial Organisation*. New York: John Wiley.

Bain, J.S. (1960) Price leaders, barometers, and kinks, *Journal of Business of the University of Chicago*, 33, 193–203.

Bajari, P. (2008) Auctions (applications), in Durlauf, S.N. and Blume, L.E. (eds) *New Palgrave Dictionary of Economics*, 2nd edition. London: Palgrave Macmillan.

Bajari, P. and Hortacsu, A. (2004) Economic insights from internet auctions, *Journal of Economic Literature*, 42, 457–86.

Balachandran, S., Kogut, B. and Harnal, H. (2011) The probability of default, excessive risk, and executive compensation: a study of financial services firms from 1995 to 2008, Columbia Business School Discussion Paper.

Baldwin, J.R. and Gorecki, P.K. (1987) Plant creation versus plant acquisition: the entry process in Canadian manufacturing, *International Journal of Industrial Organisation*, 5, 27–41.

Baldwin, R. and Cave, M. (1998) *Understanding Regulation*. Oxford: Oxford University Press.

Ball, A., Broadbent, J. and Moore, C. (2002) Best value and the control of local government: challenges and contradictions, *Public Money and Management*, 22, 9–16.

Banerjee, S. and Lin, P. (2003) Downstream R&D, raising rivals' costs, and input price contracts, *International Journal of Industrial Organisation*, 21, 79–96.

Baptista, R. (2000) Do innovations diffuse faster within geographical clusters? *International Journal of Industrial Organization*, 18, 515–35.

Bar-Isaac, H. and Tadelis, S. (2008) Seller reputation, *Foundations and Trends in Microeconomics*, 4, 273–351.

Barney, J.B. (1991) Firm resources and sustained competitive advantage, *Journal of Management*, 17, 99–120.

Barney, J.B. and Hoskisson, R.E. (1990) Strategic groups: untested assertions and research proposals, *Managerial and Decision Making Economics*, 11, 187–98.

Barth, J.R., Caprio, G. and Levine, R. (2006) *Re-thinking Bank Regulation: Till Angels Govern*. Cambridge: Cambridge University Press.

Bartlett, F.C. (1932) *Remembering*. New York: Cambridge University Press.

Battisti, G. and Stoneman, P. (2005) The intra-firm diffusion of new process technologies, *International Journal of Industrial Organization*, 23, 1–22.

Battisti, G., Hollenstein, H., Stoneman, P. and Woerter, M. (2007) Inter and intra firm diffusion of

ICT in the United Kingdom (UK) and Switzerland (CH): an internationally comparative study based on firm-level data, *Economics of Innovation & New Technology*, 16, 669–87.

Baudry, L., Le Bihan, H., Sevestre, P. and Tarrieu, S. (2004) Price rigidity in France – evidence from consumer price micro-data. *ECB Working Papers Series*, No. 384.

Baumol, W. (1959) *Business Behaviour, Value and Growth*. New York: Harcourt Brace Jovanovich.

Baumol, W.J. (1962) On the theory of the expansion of the firm, *American Economic Review*, 52, 1078–87.

Baumol, W.J. (1991) (Almost) perfect competition (contestability) and business ethics, in Baumol, W.J. with Blackman, S.A.B. (eds) *Perfect Markets and Easy Virtue: Business Ethics and the Invisible Hand*. Cambridge, MA: Blackwell Publishers, 1–23.

Baumol, W.J. (2000) *The Free Market Innovation Machine: Analyzing the Growth Miracle of Capitalism*. Princeton, NJ: Princeton University Press.

Baumol, W.J. (2001) When is inter-firm coordination beneficial? The case of innovation, *International Journal of Industrial Organization*, 19, 727–37.

Baumol, W.J., Panzer, J. and Willig, R.D. (1982) *Contestable Markets and the Theory of Industry Structure*. New York: Harcourt Brace Jovanovich.

Baye, M. and Morgan, J. (2001) Information gatekeepers on the internet and the competitiveness of homogeneous product markets, *Amercian Economic Review*, 91, 454–74.

Baye, M.R., Morgan, J. and Scholten, P.A. (2004) Price dispersion in the small and in the large: evidence from an internet price comparison site, *Journal of Industrial Economics*, 52, 463–96.

Baye, M.R., Morgan, J. and Scholten, P. (2007) Information, search and price dispersion, in Hendershott, T. (ed.) *Handbook on Economics and Information Systems*. Amsterdam: Elsevier.

Bazerman, M.H. and Samuelson, W.F. (1983) I won the auction, but I don't want the prize, *Journal of Conflict Resolution*, 27, 618–34.

Bearne, A. (1996) The economics of advertising: a reappraisal, *Economic Issues*, 1, 23–38.

Beath, J. and Katsoulacos, Y. (1991) *The Economic Theory of Product Differentiation*. Cambridge: Cambridge University Press.

Beaudry, C. and Breschi, S. (2003) Are firms in clusters really more innovative?, *Economics of Innovation and New Technology*, 12, 325–42.

Becattini, G., Bellandi, M., Dei Ottati, G. and Sforzi, F. (2003) *From Industrial Districts to Local Development*. Cheltenham: Edward Elgar.

Beck, T., Demirguc-Kunt, A. and Maksimovic, V. (2005) Financial and legal constraints to growth: does firm size matter?, *Journal of Finance*, 60, 137–77.

Beck, T., Coyle, D., Dewatripoint, M., Freixas, X. and Seabright, P. (2010) *Bailing out the Banks: Reconciling Stability and Competition*. London: Centre for Economic Policy Research.

Becker, G. (1983) A theory of competition among pressure groups for political influence, *Quarterly Journal of Economics*, 98, 371–400.

Becker, G. and Murphy, K.M. (1993) A simple theory of advertising as a good or bad, *Quarterly Journal of Economics*, 108, 941–64.

Beder, S. (1998) Is planned obsolescence socially responsible?, *Engineers Australia*, November, 52.

Beesley, M.E. (ed.) (1997) *Privatization, Regulation and Deregulation*, 2nd edition. London: Routledge.

Beesley, M.E. and Littlechild, S.C. (1997) The regulation of privatised monopolies in the United Kingdom, in Beesley, M.E. (ed.) *Privatisation, Regulation and Deregulation*, 2nd edition. London: Routledge.

Beise, M. (2004) Lead markets: country-specific drivers of the global diffusion of innovations, *Research Policy*, 33, 997–1018.

Bell, G.G. (2005) Clusters, networks and firm innovativeness, *Strategic Management Journal*, 26, 287–95.

Beltratti, A. and Stulz, R.M. (2012) The credit crisis around the globe: why did some banks perform better? *Journal of Financial Economics*, 105, 1–17.

Bergenstock, D.J., Deily, M.E. and Taylor, L.W. (2006) A cartel's response to cheating: an empirical investigation of the De Beers diamond empire, *Southern Economic Journal*, 73, 173–89.

Berger, A.N. (1995) The profit–structure relationship in banking: tests of market power and efficient structure hypotheses, *Journal of Money, Credit and Banking*, 27, 404–31.

Berger, A.N. and Dick, A.A. (2007) Entry into banking markets and the early-mover advantage, *Journal of Money, Credit, and Banking*, 39, 775–807.

Berger, A.N. and Hannan, T.H. (1998) The efficiency cost of market power in the banking industry: a test of the quiet life and related hypotheses, *Review of Economics and Statistics*, 80, 454–65.

Berger, A., Kick, T. and Schaeck, K. (2012) Executive board composition and risk taking, mimeograph.

Berger, P.G. and Ofek, E. (1995) Diversification's effect on firm value, *Journal of Financial Economics*, 37, 39–65.

Bergman, M., Jakobsson, M. and Razo, C. (2005) An econometric analysis of the European Commission's merger decisions, *International Journal of Industrial Organization*, 23, 717–37.

Bergstrom, T.C. and Miller, J.H. (2000) *Experiments with Economic Principles*, 2nd edition. New York: McGraw Hill.

Berle, A.A. and Means, G.C. (1932) *The Modern Corporation and Private Property*. London: Macmillan.

Berlin, M. (1999) Jack of all trades? Product diversification in nonfinancial firms, *Federal Reserve Bank of Philadelphia Business Review*, May, 15–29.

Bernheim, B. and Whinston, M. (1998) Exclusive dealing, *Journal of Political Economy*, 106, 64–103.

Berry, C.H. (1971) Corporate growth and diversification, *Journal of Law and Economics*, 14, 371–83.

Berry, C.H. (1974) Corporate diversification and market structure, *Rand Journal of Economics* (formerly the *Bell Journal of Economics and Management Science*), 5, 196–204.

Berry, S. and Reiss, P. (2007) Empirical models of entry and market structure, in Armstrong, M. and Porter, R. (eds) *Handbook of Industrial Organization*, Vol. 3. Amsterdam: Elsevier.

Bertrand, J. (1883) Théorie mathématique de la richesse sociale, *Journal des Savants*, 67, 499–508.

Besen, S. and Farrell, J. (1994) Choosing how to compete: Strategies and tactics in standardization, *Journal of Economic Perspectives*, 8, 117–31.

Beverley, L. (2008) Stock market event studies and Competition Commission inquiries, *CCP Working Paper 08-16*.

Bigelow, L.S. and Argyres, N.S. (2008) Transaction costs, industry experience and make-or-buy decisions in the population of early US auto firms, *Journal of Economic Behaviour & Organization*, 66, 791–807.

Billett, M.T. and Qian, Y. (2008) Are overconfident CEOs born or made? Evidence of self-attribution bias from frequent acquirers, *Management Science*, 54, 1037–51.

Bils, M. and Klenow, P. (2004) Some evidence on the importance of sticky prices, *Journal of Political Economy*, 112, 947–85.

Binmore, K. (2007) *Game Theory: A Very Short Introduction*. Oxford: Oxford University Press.

Binmore, K. and Klemperer, P. (2002) The biggest auction ever: the sale of the British 3G Telecom licences, *Economic Journal*, 112, C74–96.

Bird, R., Hall, A.D., Momente, F. and Reggiani, F. (2007) What corporate social responsibility activities are valued by the market?, *Journal of Business Ethics*, 76, 189–206.

Birke, D. (2009) The economics of networks: a survey of empirical literature, *Journal of Economic Surveys*, 23, 762–93.

Bishop, M. and Thompson, D. (1992) Regulatory reform and productivity growth in the UK's public utilities, *Applied Economics*, 24, 1181–90.

Bishop, S. and Walker, C. (2002) *The Economics of EC Competition Law*, 2nd edition. London: Sweet & Maxwell.

Blackstone, E.A. (1972) Monopsony power, reciprocal buying, and government contracts: the General Dynamic case, *Antitrust Bulletin*, 17, 445–66.

Blair, B.F. and Lewis, T.R. (1994) Optimal retail contracts with asymmetric information and moral hazard, *Rand Journal of Economics*, 25, 284–96.

Blair, J.M. (1972) *Economic Concentration*. New York: Harcourt Brace Jovanovich.

Blaug, M. (2001) Is competition such a good thing? Static efficiency versus dynamic efficiency, *Review of Industrial Organization*, 19, 37–48.

Blecherman, B. and Camerer, C.F. (1998) Is there a winner's curse in the market for baseball players? New York: Brooklyn Polytechnic University, mimeograph.

Blinder, A.S., Cannetti, E.R.D., Lebow, E.D. and Rudd, J.B. (1998) *Asking About Prices: A New Approach to Understanding Price Stickiness*. New York: Russell Sage.

Bloch, II. (1974) Advertising and profitability: a re-appraisal, *Journal of Political Economy*, 82, 267–86.

Blonigen, B.A. and Tomlin, K. (2001) Size and growth of Japanese plants in the United States, *International Journal of Industrial Organization*, 19, 931–52.

Boerner, C.S. and Macher, J.T. (2001) Transaction cost economics: an assessment of empirical research in the social sciences. Georgetown University Working Paper.

Bolton, P. and Scharfstein, D.S. (1998) Corporate finance, the theory of the firm and organisations, *Journal of Economic Perspectives*, 12, 95–114.

Bolton, P. and Whinston, M. (1993) Incomplete contracts, vertical integration, and supply assurances, *Review of Economic Studies*, 60, 121–48.

Bolton, P., Mehran, H. and Shapiro, J. (2010) Executive compensation and risk taking, *Federal Reserve Bank of New York Staff Report*, Number 456.

Bonanno, G. and Vickers, J. (1988) Vertical separation, *Journal of Industrial Economics*, 36, 257–65.

Bork, R. (1978) *The Antitrust Paradox: A Policy at War with Itself*. New York: Basic Books.

Bornstein, S. and Netz, J. (2000) Why do all flights leave at 8am? Competition and departure differentiation in the airline markets, *International Journal of Industrial Organization*, 17, 611–40.

Bos, D. (1991) *Privatisation: A Theoretical Treatment*. Oxford: Clarendon Press.

Bos, D. (2003) Regulation: theory and concepts, in Parker, D. and Saal, D. (eds) *International Handbook on Privatization*. Cheltenham: Edward Elgar.

Bougette, P. and Turolla, S. (2006) Merger remedies at the European Commission: a multinomial logit analysis, mimeograph.

Bougheas, S., Holger Görg, H. and Strobl, E. (2003) Is R&D financially constrained? Theory and evidence from Irish manufacturing, *Review of Industrial Organization*, 22, 159–74.

Bourlakis, C.A. (1997) Testing the competitive environment and the persistence of profits hypotheses, *Review of Industrial Organization*, 12, 203–18.

Bowman, E.H. and Helfat, C.E. (2001) Does corporate strategy matter? *Strategic Management Journal*, 22, 1–23.

Boyd, J. and DeNicolo, G. (2005) The theory of bank risk taking revisited, *Journal of Finance*, 60, 1329–43.

Bradley, M., Desai, A. and Kim, E.H. (1983) The rationale behind interfirm tender offers: information or synergy, *Journal of Financial Economics*, 11, 183–206.

Bradley, M., Desai, A. and Kim, E.H. (1988) Synergistic gains from corporate acquisitions and their division between the stockholders of target and acquiring firms, *Journal of Financial Economics*, 21, 3–40.

Bragues, G. (2009) Adam Smith's vision of the ethical manager, *Journal of Business Ethics*, 90, 447–60.

Braithwaite, D. (1928) The economic effects of the advertisement, *Economic Journal*, 38, 16–37.

Brammer, S. and Millington, A. (2005) Profit maximisation vs. agency: An analysis of charitable giving by UK firms, *Cambridge Journal of Economics*, 29, 517–34.

Brandt, N. (2004) Business, dynamics, regulation and performance, *OECD Directorate for Science Technology and Industry Working Paper*, 2004/3.

Brenkert, G.G. and Beauchamp, T.L. (2010) *The Oxford Handbook of Business Ethics*. Oxford: Oxford University Press.

Bresnahan, T.F. (1982) The oligopoly solution identified, *Economics Letters*, 10, 87–92.

Bresnahan, T.F. (1989) Empirical studies of industries with market power, in Schmalensee, R. and Willig, R.D. (eds) *Handbook of Industrial Organization*, Vol. 2. Amsterdam: Elsevier, 1011–58.

Bresnahan, T. (1992) Sutton's sunk costs and market structure: price competition, advertising and the evolution of concentration. Review article, *Rand Journal of Economics*, 23, 137–52.

Bresnahan, T. and Reiss, P.C. (1991) Entry and competition in concentrated markets, *Journal of Political Economy*, 99, 997–1009.

Bresnahan, T.F. and Reiss, P.C. (1994) Measuring the importance of sunk costs, *Annals of Economics and Statistics*, 34, 181–217.

Bresnahan, T.F. and Schmalensee, R.C. (1987) The empirical renaissance in industrial economics: an overview, *Journal of Industrial Economics*, 35, 371–8.

Briggs, H. (1996) Optimal cartel trigger strategies and the number of firms, *Review of Industrial Organisation*, 11, 551–61.

Brod, A. and Shivakumar, R. (1999) Advantageous semi-collusion, *Journal of Industrial Economics*, 47, 221–30.

Bronfenbrenner, M. (1940) Applications of the discontinuous oligopoly demand, *Journal of Political Economy*, 48, 420–7.

Brown, J. and Goolsbee, A. (2002) Does the internet make markets more competitive: evidence from the life insurance industry, *Journal of Political Economy*, 110, 481–507.

Brozen, Y. (1971) Bain's concentration and rates of return revisited, *Journal of Law and Economics*, 13, 279–92.

Brozen, Y. (1975) *The Competitive Economy*. Morristown, NJ: General Learning Press.

Brulhart, M. (1998) Economic geography, industry location and trade: the evidence, *World Economy*, 21, 775–801.

Brunnermeier, M.K. (2009) Deciphering the liquidity and credit crunch 2007–08, *Journal of Economic Perspectives*, 23, 77–100.

Brush, T.H. and Bromiley, P. (1997) What does a small corporate effect mean? A variance components simulation of corporate and business effects, *Strategic Management Journal*, 18, 10, 825–35.

Brynjolsson, E. and Smith, M. (2000) Frictionless commerce? A comparison of internet and conventional retailers, *Management Science*, 46, 563–85.

Bryson, B. (1994) *Made in America*. London: Minerva.

Buch, C. and DeLong, G. (2009) Banking globalization: international consolidation and mergers in banking, in Berger, A., Molyneux, P. and Wilson, J.O.S. (eds) *Oxford Handbook of Banking*. Oxford: Oxford University Press.

Buehler, S., Kaiser, C. and Jaeger, F. (2006) Merge or fail? The determinants of mergers and bankruptcies in Switzerland, 1995–2000, *Economics Letters*, 90, 88–95.

Bunch, D.S. and Smiley, R. (1992) Who deters entry? Evidence on the use of strategic entry deterrence, *Review of Economics and Statistics*, 74, 509–21.

Burton, B.K. and Goldsby, M.G. (2009) The moral floor: a philosophical examination of the connection between ethics and business, *Journal of Business Ethics*, 91, 145–54.

Butler, J. (1998) Regulating telecommunications: lessons from the UK, in Vass, P. (ed.) *Network Industries in Europe*. London: CIPFA.

Button, K. and Stough, R. (2000) *Air Transport Networks*. Cheltenham: Edward Elgar.

Butz, D.A. and Kleit, A.N. (2001) Are vertical restraints pro- or anticompetitive? Lessons from 'Interstate Circuit', *Journal of Law and Economics*, 44, 131–59.

Buxton, A.J., Davies, S.W. and Lyons, S.R. (1984) Concentration and advertising in consumer and producer markets, *Journal of Industrial Economics*, 32, 451–64.

Cable, J. (1972) Market structure, advertising policy and intermarket differences in advertising intensity, in Cowling, K. (ed.) *Market Structure and Corporate Behaviour: Theory and Empirical Analysis of the Firm*. London: Gray Mills.

Cable, J. and Schwalbach, J. (1991) International comparisons of entry and exit, in Geroski, P. and Schwalbach, J. (eds) *Entry and Market Contestability*. Oxford: Blackwell.

Cable, J., Henley, A. and Holland, K. (2002) Pot of gold or winner's curse? An event study of the auctions of 3G telephone licences in the UK, *Fiscal Studies*, 23, 447–62.

Cabral, L.M.B. (2008) Barriers to entry, in Durlauf, S.N. and Blume, L.E. (eds) *The New Palgrave Dictionary of Economics*, 2nd edition. London: Palgrave Macmillan.

Cabral, L.M.B. and Mata, J. (2003) On the evolution of the firm size distribution: facts and theory, *American Economic Review*, 93, 1075–90.

Cabral, L.M.B. and Ross, T.W. (2008) Are sunk costs a barrier to entry?, *Journal of Economics and Management Strategy*, 17, 97–112.

Cadbury Report (1992) *Report of the Committee on the Financial Aspects of Corporate Governance*. London: Gee.

Call, G.D. and Keeler, T.E. (1985) Airline deregulation, fares and market behaviour: some empirical evidence, in Daugherty, A.H. (ed.) *Analytical Studies in Transport Economics*. Cambridge: Cambridge University Press.

Caloghirou, Y., Ionnides, S. and Vonortas, N.S. (2003) Research joint ventures, *Journal of Economic Surveys*, 17, 541–70.

Campbell, J.R. and Hopenhayn, H.A. (2005) Market size matters, *Journal of Industrial Economics*, 53, 1–25.

Canepa, A. and Stoneman, P. (2004) Comparative international diffusion: patterns, determinants and policies, *Economics of Innovation and New Technology*, 13, 279–98.

Capen, E.C., Clapp, R.V. and Campbell, W.M. (1971) Competitive bidding in high risk situations, *Journal of Petroleum Technology*, 23, 641–53.

Caprio, G., Laeven, L. and Levine, R. (2007) Governance and bank valuation, *Journal of Financial Intermediation*, 16, 584–617.

Carlton, D. (1979) Vertical integration in competitive markets under uncertainty, *Journal of Industrial Economics*, 27, 189–209.

Carlton, D. (1986) The rigidity of prices, *American Economic Review*, 76, 637–58.

Carlton, D. (1989) The theory and facts about how markets clear, in Schmalensee, R.C. and Willig, R.D. (eds) *Handbook of Industrial Organization*, Vol. 2. Amsterdam: Elsevier.

Carlton, D.W. (2004) Why barriers to entry and barriers to understanding, *American Economic Review*, 94, 466–70.

Carlton, D.W. (2005) Barriers to entry, *National Bureau of Economic Research Working Paper 11645*.

Carlton, D.W. and Waldman, M. (2002) The strategic use of tying to preserve and create market power in evolving industries, *Rand Journal of Economics*, 33, 194–220.

Carranza, J.E. (2008) Concentration measures, in Durlauf, S.N. and Blume, L.E. (eds) *The New Palgrave Dictionary of Economics*, 2nd edition. London: Palgrave Macmillan.

Carroll, A. (1979) A three-dimensional conceptual model of corporate social performance, *Academy of Management Review*, 4, 497–505.

Carroll, A. (1991) The pyramid of corporate social responsibility: toward the moral management of organizational stakeholders, *Business Horizons*, 34, 39–48.

Cassiman, B. and Colombo, M.G. (eds) (2006) *Mergers and Acquisitions, The Innovation Impact*. Cheltenham: Edward Elgar.

Cassing, J. and Douglas, R.W. (1980) Implications of the auction mechanism in baseball's free agent draft, *Southern Economic Journal*, 47, 1110–21.

Casson, M. (1982) *The Entrepreneur: An Economic Theory*. Oxford: Oxford University Press.

Caves, R.E. (1986) *American Industry: Structure, Conduct and Performance*, 6th edition. Englewood Cliffs, NJ: Prentice Hall.

Caves, R.E. (1998) Industrial organization and new findings on the turnover and mobility of firms, *Journal of Economic Literature*, 36, 1947–82.

Caves, R.E. (2007) In praise of the old I.O. *International Journal of Industrial Organization*, 25, 1–12.

Caves, R.E. and Greene, D.P. (1996) Brands, quality levels and advertising outlays, *International Journal of Industrial Organization*, 14, 29–52.

Caves, R.E. and Porter, M.E. (1977) From entry barriers to mobility barriers: conjectural decisions and contrived deterrence to new competition, *Quarterly Journal of Economics*, 91, 241–62.

Caves, R.E. and Williamson, P.J. (1985) What is product differentiation really?, *Journal of Industrial Economics*, 34, 113–32.

Chamberlin, E. (1933) *The Theory of Monopolistic Competition*. Cambridge, MA: Harvard University Press.

Chandler, A.D., Jr (1977) *The Visible Hand: The Managerial Revolution in American Business*. Cambridge, MA: Harvard University Press.

Chandler, A.D. (1990) *Scale and Scope: The Dynamics of Industrial Capitalism*. Cambridge, MA: Harvard University Press.

Chang, H.J. and Singh, A. (2000) Corporate and industry effects on business unit competitive position, *Strategic Management Journal*, 21, 739–52.

Chawla, M. (2002) Estimating the extent of patient ignorance of the health care market, *World Bank Economists' Forum*, 2, 3–24.

Chen, Y. (1997) Multidimensional signalling and diversification, *Rand Journal of Economics*, 28, 168–87.

Chen, Y. (2005) Vertical disintegration, *Journal of Economics & Management Strategy*, 14, 209–29.

Chen, Y. and Riordan, M.H. (2007) Vertical integration, exclusive dealing, and expost cartelization, *Rand Journal of Economics*, 38, 1–21.

Chen, Z. and Ross, T.W. (1999) Refusals to deal and orders to supply in competitive markets, *International Journal of Industrial Organisation*, 17, 399–418.

Chen, C.R., Steiner, T.L. and Whyte, A.M. (2006) Does stock option-based executive compensation induce risk-taking? An analysis of the banking industry, *Journal of Banking & Finance* 30, 915–45.

Cheng, I.H., Hong, H. and Scheinkman, J. (2009) Yesterday's heroes: compensation and creative risk-taking, Princeton University Working Paper.

Chih, H., Chih, H. and Chen, T. (2010) On the determinants of corporate social responsibility: international evidence on the financial industry, *Journal of Business Ethics*, 93, 115–35.

Chesher, A. (1979) Testing the law of proportionate effect, *Journal of Industrial Economics*, 27, 403–11.

Cheung, S.N. (1983) The contractual nature of the firm, *Journal of Law and Economics*, 26, 386–405.

Chioveanu, I. (2008) Advertising, brand loyalty and pricing, *Games and Economic Behaviour*, 64, 68–80.

Chipty, T. (2001) Vertical integration, market foreclosure, and consumer welfare in the cable television industry, *American Economic Review*, 91, 428–53.

Choi, J.P. and Stefanadis, C. (2001) Tying investment, and dynamic leverage theory, *Rand Journal of Economics*, 32, 52–71.

Church, J. and Gandal, N. (2000) Systems competition, vertical merger and foreclosure, *Journal of Economics and Management Strategy*, 9, 25–51.

Church, J. and Ware, R. (2000) *Industrial Organization: A Strategic Approach*. New York: McGraw Hill.

Clanton, D.A. (1977) Trade associations and the FTC, *Antitrust Bulletin*, 22, 307.

Clark, J.B. (1899) *The Distribution of Wealth*. London: Macmillan.

Clark, J.M. (1940) Towards a concept of workable competition, *American Economic Review*, 30, 241–56.

Clarke, R. (1979) On the lognormality of firm and plant size distribution: some UK evidence, *Applied Economics*, 11, 415–33.

Clarke, R. (1985) *Industrial Economics*. Oxford: Blackwell.

Clarke, R. (1993) Trends in concentration in UK manufacturing, 1980–9, in Casson, M. and Creedy, J. (eds) *Industrial Concentration and Economic Inequality*. Aldershot: Edward Elgar.

Clarke, R. and Morgan, E.J. (2006) *New Developments in UK and EU Competition Policy*. Cheltenham: Edward Elgar.

Clarke, R., Davies, S. and Waterson, M. (1984) The profitability–concentration relation: market power or efficiency?, *Journal of Industrial Economics*, 32, 435–50.

Claver, E., Molina, J. and Tari, J. (2002) Firm and industry effects on firm profitability: a Spanish empirical analysis, *European Management Journal*, 20, 321–8.

Clay, K., Krishnan, R., Wolff, E. and Fernandes, D. (2002) Retail strategies on the web: price and non-price competition in the online book industry, *Journal of Industrial Economics*, 50, 351–67.

Clerides, S.K. (2002) Book value: intertemporal pricing and quality discrimination in the US market for books, *International Journal of Industrial Organization*, 20, 1385–408.

Clowes, J. and Clements, N. (2003) An examination of discriminatory ticket pricing practice in the English football Premier League, *Managing Leisure*, 8, 105–20.

Coad, A. (2007) A closer look at serial growth rate correlation, *Review of Industrial Organization*, 31, 69–82.

Coad, A. (2009) The growth of firms: a survey of theory and evidence. Cheltenham: Edward Elgar.

Coase, R.H. (1937) The nature of the firm, *Economica*, 4, 386–405.

Coase, R.H. (1960) The problem of social cost, *Journal of Law and Economics*, 3, 1–44.

Coase, R.H. (1972) Durability and monopoly, *Journal of Law and Economics*, 15, 143–9.

Coase, R.H. (1991) The nature of the firm: meaning, in Williamson, O.E. and Winter, S.G. (eds) *The Nature of the Firm, Origins, Evolution and Development*. Oxford: Oxford University Press.

Coate, M.B. (1989) The dynamics of price–cost margins in concentrated industries, *Applied Economics*, 21, 261–72.

Cockburn, I. and Henderson, R. (1994) Racing to invest? The dynamics of competition in the ethical drugs market, *Journal of Economics and Management Strategy*, 3, 481–519.

Cockerill, T. and Johnson, P. (2003) Industry in the EU: trends and policy issues, in Johnson, P. (ed.) *Industries in Europe*. Cheltenham: Edward Elgar.

Cohen, A. (2002) *The Perfect Store: Inside eBay*. London: Piatkus Publishers.

Cohen, K.J. and Cyert, R.M. (1965) *Theory of the Firm*. Englewood Cliffs, NJ: Prentice Hall.

Cohen, W.M. (1995) Empirical studies of innovative activity, in Stoneman, P. (ed.) *Handbook of the Economics of Innovation and Technical Change*, Oxford: Blackwell, Ch. 8.

Cohen, W.M. and Levin, R.C. (1989) Empirical studies of innovation and market structure, in Schmalensee, R. and Willig, R. (eds) *Handbook of Industrial Organisation*, Vol. 2. Amsterdam: North-Holland, 1059–107.

Collins, N.R. and Preston, L.E. (1966) Concentration and price–cost margins in food manufacturing industries, *Journal of Industrial Economics*, 15, 271–86.

Comanor, W.S. (1985) Vertical price-fixing, vertical market restrictions, and the new antitrust policy, *Harvard Law Review*, 98, 983–1002.

Comanor, W.S. and Frech, H.E., III (1985) The competitive effects of vertical agreements, *American Economic Review*, 75, 539–46.

Comanor, W.S. and Leibenstein, H. (1969) Allocative efficiency, X-efficiency and the measurement of welfare losses, *Economica*, 36, 304–9.

Comanor, W.S. and Wilson, T. (1967) Advertising, market structure and performance, *Review of Economics and Statistics*, 49, 423–40.

Comanor, W.S. and Wilson, T. (1974) *Advertising and Market Power*. Cambridge, MA: Harvard University Press.

Comanor, W.S. and Wilson, T. (1979) Advertising and competition: a survey, *Journal of Economic Literature*, 17, 453–76.

Combs, J., Michael, S.C. and Castrogiovanni, G.J. (2004) Franchising: a review and avenues to greater theoretical diversity, *Journal of Management*, 30, 907–31.

Comment, R. and Jarrell, G. (1995) Corporate focus and stock returns, *Journal of Financial Economics*, 37, 67–87.

Competition Commission (2001) *A Report on the Acquisition by Interbrew SA of the Brewing Interests of Bass Plc*. London: HMSO.

Competition Commission (2006) *Home Credit*. London: HMSO.

Compte, O., Jenny, F. and Rey, P. (2002) Capacity constraints, mergers and collusion, *European Economic Review*, 46, 1–29.

Conlin, M. and Kadiyali, V. (2006) Entry-deterring capacity in the Texas lodging industry, *Journal of Economics and Management Strategy*, 15, 167–85.

Conner, K.R. and Prahalad, C.K. (1996) A resource-based theory of the firm: knowledge versus opportunism, *Organization Science*, 7, 477–501.

Contini, B. and Revelli, R. (1989) The relationship between firm growth and labour demand, *Small Business Economics*, 1, 309–14.

Conway, P., Janod, V. and Nicoletti, G. (2006) Product market regulation in OECD countries: 1998 to 2003, *OECD Economics Department Paper*, No. 419.

Cook, G. (1997) A comparative analysis of vertical integration in the UK brewing and petrol industries, *Journal of Economic Studies*, 24, 152–66.

Cornett, M., McNutt, J.J. and Tehranian, H. (2010) The financial crisis: corporate governance and performance of publicly-traded US Bank holding companies, Boston College Discussion Paper.

Cosh, A., Hughes, A. and Singh, A. (1980) The causes and effects of takeovers in the United Kingdom: an empirical investigation for the late 1960s at the micro-economic level, in Mueller, D.C. (ed.) *The Determinants and Effects of Mergers: An International Comparison*. Cambridge, MA: Oelgeschlager, Gun & Hanin.

Cournot, A. (1838) Recherches sur les principes mathématiques de la théorie des richesses, published in Cournot, A. (ed.) *Researches into the Mathematical Principles of the Theory of Wealth*. London: Macmillan, 1897.

Coursey, D., Isaac, M.R. and Smith, V.L. (1984) Market contestability in the presence of sunk costs, *Rand Journal of Economics*, 15, 69–84.

Cowling, K. and Mueller, D.C. (1978) The social costs of monopoly power, *Economic Journal*, 88, 727–48.

Cowling, K. and Sugden, P. (1998) The essence of the modern corporation: markets, strategic decision-making and the theory of the firm, *The Manchester School*, 66, 1, 59–86.

Cox, J.C. and Hayne, S. (1998) Group versus individual decision making in strategic market games, mimeograph. Tucson, AZ: Arizona University.

Crandell, R.W. (2003) An end to economic regulation?, in Robinson, C. (ed.) *Competition and Regulation in Utility Markets*. Cheltenham: Edward Elgar.

Crane, A., Matten, D., McWilliams, A., Moon, J. and Siegel, D. (2008) *The Oxford Handbook of Corporate Social Responsibility*, Oxford: Oxford University Press.

Cremer, J., Ray, P. and Tirole, J. (2000) Connectivity in the commercial internet, *Journal of Industrial Economics*, 48, 433–72.

Croteau, J.T. (1963) *The Economics of the Credit Union*. Detroit, MI: Wayne State University Press.

Cuaresma, J.C. and Gschwandtner, A. (2008) Tracing the dynamics of competition: evidence from company profits, *Economic Inquiry*, 46, 208–13.

Cubbin, J.S. and Geroski, P.A. (1990) The persistence of profits in the United Kingdom, in Mueller, D.C. (ed.) *The Dynamics of Company Profits: An International Comparison*. Cambridge: Cambridge University Press.

Curry, B. and George, K. (1983) Industrial concentration: a survey, *Journal of Industrial Economics*, 31, 203–55.

Cuthbert, N. and Black, W. (1959) Restrictive practices in the food trades, *Journal of Industrial Economics*, 8, 33–57.

Cyert, R. and March, J.G. (1964) *A Behavioural Theory of the Firm*. Englewood Cliffs, NJ: Prentice Hall.

Dal Bo, E. (2006) Regulatory capture: a review, *Oxford Review of Economic Policy*, 22, 203–25.

Daley, L., Mahotra, V. and Sivakumar, R. (1997) Corporate focus and value creation: evidence from spinoffs, *Journal of Financial Economics*, 45, 257–81.

D'Aspremont, C. and Jacquemin, A. (1988) Joint R&D ventures, cooperative and non-cooperative R&D in duopoly with spillovers, *American Economic Review*, 78, 1133–7.

D'Aspremont, C., Jacquemin, A., Gabszowiez, J. and Weymark, J. (1983) On the stability of collusive price-leadership, *Canadian Journal of Economics*, 16, 17–25.

D'Aveni, R. and Ravenscraft, D. (1994) Economies of integration versus bureaucracy costs: does vertical integration improve performance?, *Academy of Management Journal*, 37, 1167–206.

Darby, M. and Karni, E. (1973) Free competition and optimal amount of fraud, *Journal of Law and Economics*, 16, 67–88.

Darrel, R. and Zook, C. (2002) Open market innovation, *Harvard Business Review*, 80, 80–9.

Daughety, A.F. (2008) *The New Palgrave Dictionary of Economics*, Durlauf, S. and Blume, L. (eds), 2nd edition. London: Palgrave Macmillan.

Davidson, K. (1983) The competitive significance of segmented markets, *California Law Review*, 71, 445–63.

Davies, S.W. (1979) Choosing between concentration indices: the iso-concentration curve, *Economica*, 46, 67–75.

Davies, S.W. (1989) Concentration, in Davies, S. and Lyons, B. (eds) *The Economics of Industrial Organisation*. London: Longman.

Davies, S. (2010) *A Review of OFT's Impact Estimation Methods*. London: Office of Fair Trading.

Davies, S.W. and Geroski, P.A. (1997) Changes in concentration, turbulence and the dynamics of market shares, *Review of Economics and Statistics*, 79, 383–91.

Davies, S.W. and Lyons, B.R. (1982) Seller concentration: the technological explanation and demand uncertainty, *Economic Journal*, 92, 903–19.

Davies, S.W. and Lyons, B.R. (1996) *Industrial Organisation in the European Union*. Oxford: Clarendon Press.

Davies, S.W., Driffield, N.L. and Clarke, R. (1999) Monopoly in the UK: what determines whether the MMC finds against the investigated firms, *Journal of Industrial Economics*, 47, 263–83.

Davies, S.W., Rondi, L. and Sembenelli, A. (2001) European integration and the changing structure of EU manufacturing, 1987–1993, *Industrial and Corporate Change*, 10, 37–75.

Davis, J. and Devinney, T. (1997) *The Essence of Corporate Strategy: Theory for Modern Decision Making*. Sydney, St Leonards, NSW: Allen & Unwin.

Davis, L.E. (1974) Self-regulation in baseball 1909–71, in Noll, R.G. (ed.) *Government and the Sports Business*. Washington, DC: Brookings Institute.

Davis, M. (2007) The dynamics of daily retail gasoline prices, *Managerial and Decision Economics*, 28, 713–22.

Dawkins, R. (1998) *Unweaving the Rainbow, Science, Delusion and the Appetite for Wonder*. London: Penguin.

De Bandt, O. and Davis, E.P. (1999) Competition, contestability and market structure in European banking sectors on the eve of EMU, *Journal of Banking and Finance*, 24, 1045–66.

Degryse, H. (1996) On the interaction between vertical and horizontal product differentiation: an application to banking, *Journal of Industrial Economics*, 44, 169–86.

De Jong, H.W. (ed.) (1993) *The Structure of European Industry*. Dordrecht: Kluwer Academic.

Demmert, H.H. (1973) *The Economics of Professional Team Sports*. Lexington, MA: D.C. Heath.

Demsetz, H. (1968) Why regulate utilities?, *Journal of Law and Economics*, 11, 55–65.

Demsetz, H. (1969) Information and efficiency: another viewpoint, *Journal of Law and Economics*, 12, 1–22.

Demsetz, H. (1973) Industry structure, market rivalry and public policy, *Journal of Law and Economics*, 16, 1–9.

Demsetz, H. (1974) Two systems of belief about monopoly, in Goldschmid, H.J., Mann, H.M. and Weston, J.F. (eds) *Industrial Concentration: The New Learning*. Boston, MA: Little, Brown.

Demsetz, H. (1982) Barriers to entry, *American Economic Review*, 72, 47–57.

Donoekre, R., Marvel, H.P. and Peck, J. (1996) Demand uncertainty, inventories and resale price maintenance, *Quarterly Journal of Economics*, 111, 885–913.

Denicolò, V. (1996) Patent races and optimal patent breadth and length, *Journal of Industrial Economics*, 44, 249–65.

Dennis, P.T. (1992) Practical approaches: an insider's look at the new horizontal merger guidelines, *Antitrust Bulletin*, 6, 6–11.

Department of the Environment, Transport and the Regions (DETR) (1998) *Modern Local Government: In Touch with the People* (Best value White Paper). London: DETR.

Department of the Environment, Transport and the Regions (DETR) (2000) *Transport 2010 – The Ten-year Plan*. London: Department of the Enviroment, Transport and the Regions.

Department for Innovation, Universities and Skills (2008) *Innovation*, HMSO, Cmd 7345.

Department of Trade and Industry (2001) *Peer Review of Competition Policy*. London: Department of Trade and Industry.

Department of Trade and Industry (2003) *Innovation Report: Competing in the Global Economy: The Innovation Challenge*. London: HMSO.

Department of Trade and Industry (2004) *Peer Review of Competition Policy*. London: Department of Trade and Industry.

Department of Trade and Industry (2007) *Peer Review of Competition Policy*. London: Department of Trade and Industry.

Deutsch, L. (1984) An examination of industry exit patterns, *Review of Industrial Organisation*, 1, 60–8.

Deutsche Welle (2009) http://www.dw.de/dw/article/0,,4917610,00.html. Accessed 24 February 2012.

DeYoung, R., Peng, E.Y. and Yan. M. (2012) Executive compensation and business policy choices in US Commercial banks, *Journal of Financial and Quantitative Analysis*, forthcoming.

Dewenter, K. and Malatesta, P.H. (2001) State owned and privately owned enterprises: an empirical analysis of profitability, leverage and labor intensity, *American Economic Review*, 91, 320–34.

Dewey, D. (1961) Mergers and cartels: some reservations about policy, *American Economic Review*, 52, Papers and Proceedings, 255–62.

Diamond, A.M. (2003) Edwin Mansfield's contributions to the economics of technology, *Research Policy*, 32, 1607–17.

Dias, M., Dias, D. and Neves, P. (2004) Stylised features of price setting behaviour in Portugal: 1992–2001. *ECB Working Paper Series*, No. 332.

Dick, A. (1996) Identifying contracts, combinations and conspiracies in restraint of trade, *Managerial and Decision Economics*, 17, 203–16.

Dick, A.A. (2007) Market size, service quality and competition in banking, *Journal of Money, Credit, and Banking*, 39, 49–81.

Disney, R., Haskel, J. and Heden, Y. (2003) Entry, exit and establishment survival in UK manufacturing, *Journal of Industrial Economics*, 51, 91–112.

Dixit, A.K. (1982) Recent developments in oligopoly theory, *American Economic Review, Papers and Proceedings*, 72, 12–17.

Dixit, A.K. and Norman, G. (1978) Advertising and welfare, *Bell Journal of Economics*, 9, 1–17.

Dixit, A.K. and Stiglitz, J.E. (1977) Monopolistic competition and optimum product diversity, *American Economic Review*, 67, 297–308.

Djankov, S., McLeish, C. and Ramalho, R. (2006) Regulation and growth, *Economics Letters*, 92, 395–401.

Djankov, S. (2009) The regulation of entry: a survey, *The World Bank Research Observer*, 24, 183–203.

Dnes, A. and Garoupa, N. (2005) Externality and organizational choice in franchising, *Journal of Economics and Business*, 57, 139–49.

Dobson, P. (1997) The EC green paper on vertical restraints: an economic comment, *Competition and Regulation Bulletin, London Economics*, No. 7.

Dobson, P. (2005) Exploiting buyer power: lessons from the British grocery trade, *Antitrust Law Journal*, 72, 529–62.

Dobson, P.W. and Waterson, M. (1996) *Vertical Restraints and Competition Policy*, Office of Fair Trading Research Paper No. 12. London: OFT.

Dobson, S. and Goddard, J. (2011) *The Economics of Football*, 2nd edition. Cambridge: Cambridge University Press.

Dodd, P. (1980) Merger proposals, managerial discretion and stockholder wealth, *Journal of Financial Economics*, 8, 105–38.

Domberger, S. (1999) *The Contracting Organization: A Strategic Guide to Outsourcing*. Oxford: Oxford University Press.

Domberger, S. and Fiebig, D.G. (1993) The distribution of price changes in oligopoly, *Journal of Industrial Economics*, 41, 295–313.

Domberger, S. and Hall, C. (1995) *The Contracting Case-book: Competitive Tendering in Action*. Canberra: Australian Government Publishing Service.

Domberger, S. and Jenson, P. (1997) Contracting out by the public sector: theory, evidence, prospects, *Oxford Review of Economic Policy*, 13, 67–78.

Domberger, S. and Piggott, S. (1986) Privatisation policies and public enterprise: a survey, *Economic Record*, 62, 145–62.

Domberger, S. and Rimmer, S. (1994) Competitive tendering and contracting in the public sector: a survey, *International Journal of the Economics of Business*, 1, 439–53.

Domberger, S., Meadowcroft, S. and Thompson, D. (1986) Competitive tendering and efficiency: the case of refuse collection, *Fiscal Studies*, 7, 69–87.

Donsimoni, M.P., Economides, N.S. and Polemarchakis, H.M. (1986) Stable cartels, *International Economic Review*, 27, 317–27.

Dorfman, R. and Steiner, P.O. (1954) Optimal advertising and optimal quality, *American Economic Review*, 44, 826–36.

Dosi, G., Malerba, F., Marsila, O. and Orsenigo, L. (1997) Industrial structures and dynamics: evidence interpretations and puzzles, *Industrial and Corporate Change*, 6, 3–24.

Doukas, J.A. and Kan, O.B. (2008) Investment decisions and internal capital markets: evidence from acquisitions, *Journal of Banking & Finance*, 32, 1484–98.

Douma, S. and Schreuder, H. (1998) *Economic Approaches to Organisations*, 2nd edition. Hemel Hempstead: Prentice Hall.

Dowell, G., Han, S. and Young, B. (1999) Do corporate global environmental standards create or destroy market value? *Management Science*, 46, 1059–74.

Droucopoulos, V. and Lianos, T. (1993) The persistence of profits in the Greek manufacturing industry, 1963–1988, *International Review of Applied Economics*, 7, 163–76.

Dunne, P. and Hughes, A. (1994) Age, size, growth and survival: UK companies in the 1980s, *Journal of Industrial Economics*, 42, 115–40.

Dunne, T., Roberts, M.J. and Samuelson, L. (1988) Patterns of firm entry and exit in US manufacturing industries, *Rand Journal of Economics*, 19, 495–515.

Duso, T., Neven, D. and Roeller, L.H. (2007) The political economy of European merger control: evidence using stock market data, *Journal of Law and Economics*, 50, 455–89.

Dyer, D., Kagel, J.H. and Levin, D. (1989) A comparison of naive and experienced bidders in common value offer auctions: a laboratory analysis, *Economic Journal*, 99, 108–15.

Dyer, J.H., Kale, P. and Singh, H. (2004) When to ally and when to acquire, *Harvard Business Review*, 82, 108–15.

Eccles, R. (1985) *The Transfer Pricing Problem*. Lexington, MA: D.C. Heath.

Eckard, E.W. (1987) Advertising, competition and market share instability, *Journal of Business*, 60, 539–52.

Eckard, E.W. (1995) A note on the profit–concentration relation, *Applied Economics*, 27, 219–23.

The Economist (1998) The economics of antitrust, 18 May.

The Economist (2002) Coming home to roost: privatization in Europe, 29 June.

The Economist (2004a) Just as mobile phones have changed dramatically in recent years, the industry that makes them is being transformed too, 29 April.

The Economist (2004b) The future of advertising, 26 June.

The Economist (2005) Target practice: advertising used to be straightforward, 2 April.

Economides, N. (1996) The economics of networks, *International Journal of Industrial Organization*, 16, 673–99.

Economides, N. and Himmelberg, C. (1995) Critical mass and network size with application to the US FAX market, Discussion paper EC-95-11, Stern School of Business, NYU.

Edgeworth, F. (1897) La teoria pura del monopolio, *Giornale degli Economisti*, 15, 13–31. Reprinted as The pure theory of monopoly, in *Papers Relating To Political Economy*, London: Macmillan, 1925.

Efroymson, C.W. (1955) The kinked demand curve reconsidered, *Quarterly Journal of Economics*, 69, 119–36.

Einav, L. and Levin, J. (2010) Empirical industrial organization: a progress report, *Journal of Economic Perspectives*, 24, 145–62.

Elango, B. and Sambharya, R.B. (2004) The influence of industry structure on the entry mode choice of overseas entrants in manufacturing industry, *Journal of International Management*, 10, 107–24.

Ellison, G. (1994) Theories of cartel stability and the Joint Executive Committee, *Rand Journal of Economics*, 25, 37–57.

Ellison, G. (2005) A model of add-on pricing, *Quarterly Journal of Economics*, 120, 585–637.

Elyasiani, E. and Jia, J. (2008) Institutional ownership stability and BHC performance, *Journal of Banking & Finance*, 32, 1767–81.

Elzinga, K.G. and Hogarty, T.F. (1973) The problem of geographic delineation in anti-merger suits, *Antitrust Bulletin*, 18, 45–81.

Elzinga, K.G. and Hogarty, T.F. (1978) The problem of geographic delineation revisited: the case of coal, *Antitrust Bulletin*, 23, 1–18.

Emons, W. (1996) Good times, bad times, and vertical upstream integration, *International Journal of Industrial Organisation*, 14, 465–81.

Enright, M.J. (1998) Regional clusters and firm strategy, in Chandler, A., Hagstrom, P. and Sovell, O. (eds) *The Dynamic Firm: the Role of Technology Strategy, Organizations and Regions*. New York: Oxford University Press.

Enright, M.J. (2000) The globalization of competition and the localization of competitive advantage, in Hood, N. and Young, S. (eds) *Globalization of Multinational Enterprise Activity and Economic Development*. London: Macmillan.

Erevelles, S., Rolland, E. and Srinivasan, S. (2001) Are prices really lower on the internet? An analysis in the vitamin industry. Working Paper, University of California, Riverside, CA.

Erickson, W.B. (1969) Economics of price fixing, *Antitrust Law and Economic Review*, 2, 82–122.

Erkens, D., Hung, M. and Matos, P. (2012) Corporate governance in the 2007–2008 financial crisis: evidence from financial institutions worldwide. *Journal of Corporate Finance* 18, 389–411.

EU Directorate General Competition (2005) *Merger Remedies Study*. Brussels: European Commission.

Eucaouna, D. and Geroski, P.A. (1986) Price dynamics and competition in five countries, *OECD Economic Studies*, 6, 47–74.

European Commission (1985) *Completing the Internal Market* (White Paper), COM(85)310, 14 June 1985.

European Commission (1995) *Car Price Differentials in the European Union on 1 May 1995*, IP/95/768. Brussels: European Commission.

European Commission (1997a) Competition issues, *The Single Market Review*, Subseries 5, vol. 3. London: Kogan Page.

European Commission (1997b) Economies of scale, *The Single Market Review*, Subseries 5, vol. 4. London: Kogan Page.

European Commission (1998) *Communication from the Commission on the Application of the Community Competition Rules to Vertical Restraints*, COM(98)544.

European Commission (1999) *Draft Guidelines on Vertical Restraints*, http://europa.eu.int/comm/ dg04/antitrust/others/vertical_restraints/reform/ consultation/draft_guidelines_en.pdf.

European Commission (2000) *Panorama of EU Business*. Luxembourg: Office for Official Publications of the European Communities.

European Commission (2002) Regional clusters in Europe, *Observatory of European SMEs*, No. 3. Luxembourg: Enterprise Publications.

European Commission (2003a) *EU Business: Facts and Figures*. Luxembourg: Office for Official Publications of the European Communities.

European Commission (2003b) *High-speed Internet*, Press release July 2003, IP/03/1025.

European Commission (2005) *European Innovation Scoreboard Report*. Brussels: European Commission.

European Commission (2007a) *EU Business. Facts and Figures*. Luxembourg: Office for Official Publications of the European Communities.

European Commission (2007b) *Report on Competition Policy 2007*. Luxembourg: Office for Official Publications of the European Communities.

European Commission (2011) *Report on Competition Policy* 2010. Luxembourg: Office for Official Publications of the European Communities.

European Trend Chart on Innovation (2005) *Innovation Strengths and Weaknesses*, MERIT December. Brussels: European Commission.

Eurostat (2009) *European Business Facts and Figues*. Luxembourg: Office for Official Publications of the European Communities.

Eurostat (2011) *Key Figures on European Business*. Luxembourg: Office for Official Publications of the European Communities.

Evans, D.S. (1987a) Tests of alternative theories of firm growth, *Journal of Political Economy*, 95, 657–74.

Evans, D.S. (1987b) The relationship between firm growth, size and age: estimates for 100 manufacturing industries, *Journal of Industrial Economics*, 35, 567–81.

Evans, D.S. (2000) An analysis of the government's economic case in the US v. Microsoft, *Antitrust Bulletin*, 46, 2, 163–251.

Evans, D.S. (2009) The online advertising industry: economics, evolution, and privacy, *Journal of Economic Perspectives*, 23, 37–60.

Evely, R. and Little, I.M.D. (1960) *Concentration in British Industry*. Cambridge: Cambridge University Press.

Fabiani, S., Druant, M., Hernando, I., Kwapil, C., Landau, B., Loupias, C., Martins, F., Matha, T., Sabbatini, R., Stahl, H. and Stokman, A. (2006) What firms' surveys tell us about price-setting behavior in the euro area, *International Journal of Central Banking*, 2, 3–47.

Fabiani, S., Loupias, C., Martins, F. and Sabbatini, R. (2007) *Pricing Decisions in the Euro Area: How Firms Set Prices and Why*. Oxford: Oxford University Press.

Fabra, N. (2006) Collusion with capacity constraints over the business cycle, *International Journal of Industrial Organization*, 24, 69–81.

Fahlenbrach, R. and Stulz, R. (2011) Bank CEO incentives and the credit crisis. *Journal of Financial Economics*, 99, 11–26.

Fare, R., Grosskopf, S., Seldon, B.J. and Tremblay, V.J. (2004) Advertising efficiency and the choice of media mix: a case of beer, *International Journal of Indusrial Organization*, 22, 503–22.

Farrell, J. and Klemperer, P. (2007) Coordination and lock-in: competition with switching costs and network effects, in Armstrong, A. and Porter, R. (eds) *Handbook of Industrial Organisation*, Vol. 3. Amsterdam: Elsevier, 1967–2072.

Farrell, J. and Shapiro, C. (2000) Scale economies and synergies in horizontal merger analysis, *Competition Policy Center Working Paper CPC00-015*.

Fellner, W.J. (1965) *Competition Among the Few*. London: Frank Cass.

Ferguson, C. and McKillop, D. (1997) *The Strategic Development of Credit Unions*. Chichester: John Wiley.

Financial Reporting Council (2010) *The UK Corporate Governance Code*, The Financial Reporting Council Limited, June 2010.

Fisher, F.M. and Rubinfeld, D. (2001) US v. Microsoft, *Antitrust Bulletin*, 46, 1, 1–69.

Flannery, M.J. (2012). Market discipline in bank supervision, in Berger, A.N., Molyneux, P. and Wilson, J.O.S. (eds) *Oxford Handbook of Banking*. Oxford: Oxford University Press.

Fluent, C. and Garella, P.G. (2002) Advertising and prices as signals of quality in a regime of price rivalry, *International Journal of Industrial Organization*, 20, 965–94.

Fog, B. (1956) How are cartel prices determined?, *Journal of Industrial Economics*, 5, 16–23.

Foros, Ø. and Jarle Kind, H. (2008) Do slotting allowances harm retail competition?, *Scandinavian Journal of Economics*, 110, 367–84.

Fortune (1969) See how judgment came for plumbing conspirators, December, 96.

Foss, N.J. (2003) The strategic management and trans-action cost nexus: past debates, central questions, and future research possibilities, *Strategic Organization*, 1, 139–69.

Foss, N.J. and Eriksen, B. (1995) Competitive advantage and industry capabilities, in Montgomery, C.A. (ed.) *Resource-based and Evolutionary Theories of the Firm: Towards a Synthesis*. Dordrecht and Boston, MA: Kluwer Academic, 43–69.

Foster, C.D. (1992) *Privatisation, Public Ownership and the Regulation of Natural Monopoly*. Cambridge: Cambridge University Press.

Fraas, A.G. and Greer, D.F. (1977) Market structure and price collusion: an empirical analysis, *Journal of Industrial Economics*, 26, 21–44.

Fraser, R. (ed.) (1988) *Privatisation: The UK Experience and International Trends*. Cambridge: Cambridge University Press.

Frederiksen, C.S. (2010) The relation between policies concerning corporate social responsibility (CSR) and philosophical moral theories: an empirical investi-gation, *Journal of Business Ethics*, 93, 357–71.

Freedman, C. (1995) The economist as mythmaker – Stigler's kinky transformation, *Journal of Economic Issues*, 29, 175–96.

Freeman, C. and Soete, L. (1997) *The Economics of Industrial Innovation*, 3rd edition. London: Pinter.

Freeman, R.E. (1984) *Strategic Management: A Stakeholder Approach*. Boston, MA: Pitman.

Freeman, R.E., Wicks, A.C. and Parmar, B. (2004) Stakeholder theory and the corporate objective revisited. *Organization Science*, 15, 364–69.

Friedman, M. (1953) *Essays in Positive Economics*. Chicago, IL: Chicago University Press.

Friedman, M. (1962) *Capitalism and Freedom*. Chicago, IL: Chicago University Press.

Friedman, M. (1970) The social responsibility of business is to increase its profits, *New York Times Magazine*, 13 September 1970.

Frydman, C. and Jenter, D. (2010) CEO compensation, *Annual Review of Financial Economics*, 2, 75–102.

Fukugawa, N. (2006) Science parks in Japan and their value-added contributions to new technology based firms, *International Journal of Industrial Organ-ization*, 24, 381–400.

Fung, M.K. and Cheng, A.C.S. (2004) Diffusion of off balance sheet financial innovations: information complementarity and market competition, *Pacific Basin Finance Journal*, 12, 525–40.

Furman, J.L. (2000) Does industry matter differently in different places? A comparison of industry, corporate parent, and business segment effects in four OECD countries. *Working Paper No. 4121*. Boston, MA: MIT Sloan School of Management.

Gabrielsen, T.S. (2003) Conglomerate mergers: vertical mergers in disguise?, *International Journal of the Economics of Business*, 10, 1–16.

Gabszewicz, J.J., Laussel, D. and Sonnac, N. (2005) Does advertising lower the price of newspapers to consumers? A theoretical appraisal, *Economics Letters*, 87, 127–34.

Galbraith, J.K. (1958) *The Affluent Society*. Boston, MA: Houghton Mifflin.

Galbraith, J.K. (1967) *The New Industrial Estate*. Boston, MA: Houghton Mifflin.

Gal-Or, E. (1991) Optimal franchising in oligopolistic markets with uncertain demand, *International Journal of Industrial Organisation*, 9, 343–64.

Gal-Or, E. (1999) Vertical integration or separation of the sales function as implied by competitive forces, *International Journal of Industrial Organisation*, 17, 641–62.

Genovese, D. (2003) The nominal rigidity of apartment rents, *Review of Economics and Statistics*, 85, 844–53.

Gerardi, K.S. and Shapiro, A.H. (2009) Does competition reduce price dispersion? New evidence from the airline industry, *Journal of Political Economy*, 117, 1–37.

Geroski, P.A. (1990) Modelling persistent profitability, in Mueller, D.C. (ed.) *The Dynamics of Company Profits: An International Comparison*. Cambridge: Cambridge University Press.

Geroski, P.A. (1991a) *Market Dynamics and Entry*. Oxford: Blackwell.

Geroski, P.A. (1991b) Domestic and foreign entry in the United Kingdom, in Geroski, P.A. and Schwalbach, J. (eds) *Entry and Market Contestability: An International Comparison*. Oxford: Blackwell.

Geroski, P. (1994) *Market Structure, Corporate Performance and Innovative Activity*. Oxford: Clarendon Press.

Geroski, P.A. (1995) What do we know about entry?, *International Journal of Industrial Organization*, 13, 421–40.

Geroski, P.A. (2003) *The Evolution of New Markets*. Oxford: Oxford University Press.

Geroski, P.A. and Jacquemin, A. (1988) The persistence of profits: a European comparison, *Economic Journal*, 98, 375–89.

Geroski, P.A. and Mazzucato, M. (2001) Learning and the sources of corporate growth, mimeograph. London: London Business School.

Geroski, P.A., Machin, S. and Van Reenen, J. (1993) The profitability of innovating firms, *Rand Journal of Economics*, 24, 198–211.

Geroski, P.A., Lazarova, S., Urga, G. and Walters, C.F. (2003) Are differences in firm size transitory or permanent? *Journal of Applied Econometrics*, 18, 47–59.

Gertner, R. and Stillman, R. (2001) Vertical integration and internet strategies in the apparel industry, *Journal of Industrial Economics*, 49, 415–40.

Gertner, R.H., Scharfstein, D.S. and Stein, J.C. (1994) Internal versus external capital markets, *Quarterly Journal of Economics*, 109, 1211–30.

Ghemawat, P. (2002) Competition and business strategy in historical perspective, *Business Strategy Review*, 76, 37–74.

Ghemawat, P. (2003) Semiglobalization and international business strategy, *Journal of International Business Studies*, 34, 138–52.

Giaccotto, C., Santerre, R.E. and Vernon, J.A. (2005) Drug prices and research and development investment bahaviour in the pharmaceutical industry, *Journal of Law and Economics*, 48, 195–214.

Gibrat, R. (1931) *Les Inégalités economiques*. Paris: Sirey.

Gil, R. (2008) Revenue sharing distortions and vertical integration in the movie industry, *Journal of Law, Economics and Organization*, Research Paper 1983.

Gil, R. and Hartmann, W. (2008) Empirical analysis of metering price discrimination: evidence from concession sales at movie theaters, *Marketing Science*, 28, 1046–62.

Gilbert, B.A., McDougall, P.P. and Audretsch, D.B. (2008) Clusters, knowledge spillovers and new venture performance: an empirical examination, *Journal of Business Venturing*, 23, 405–22.

Gilbert, R. and Katz, M. (2001) An economist's guide to US v Microsoft, *Journal of Economic Perspectives*, 15, 25–44.

Gillan, L. (2006) Recent developments in corporate governance: an overview, *Journal of Corporate Finance*, 12, 381–402.

Gilligan, T.W. (1986) The competitive effects of resale price maintenance, *Rand Journal of Economics*, 17, 544–56.

Gilo, D., Moshe, Y. and Spiegel, Y. (2006) Partial cross ownership and tacit collusion, *Rand Journal of Economics*, 37, 81–99.

Gini, C. (1912) *Variabilità e Mutabilità*. Bologna: Tipographia di Paolo Cuppini.

Glaister, S. (2003) UK Transport policy, 1997–2001, in Robinson, C. (ed.) *Competition and Regulation in Utility Markets*. Cheltenham: Edward Elgar.

Glazer, A. (1985) The advantages of being first, *American Economic Review*, 75, 473–80.

Glen, J., Lee, K. and Singh, A. (2001) Persistence of profitability and competition in emerging markets: a time series analysis, *Economic Letters*, 72, 247–53.

Glen, J., Lee, K. and Singh, A. (2003) Corporate profitability and the dynamics of competition in emerging markets: a time series analysis, *Economic Journal*, 113, F465–84.

Goddard, J. and Wilson, J.O.S. (1996) Persistence of profits for UK manufacturing and service sector firms, *Service Industries Journal*, 16, 105–17.

Goddard, J. and Wilson, J.O.S. (1999) Persistence of profit: a new empirical interpretation, *International Journal of Industrial Organisation*, 17, 663–87.

Goddard, J. and Wilson, J.O.S. (2009) Competition in banking: a disequilibrium approach, *Journal of Banking and Finance*, 33, 2282–92.

Goddard, J., Blandon, P. and Wilson, J.O.S. (2002a) Panel tests of Gibrat's law for Japanese manufacturing, *International Journal of Industrial Organization*, 20, 415–33.

Goddard, J., McKillop, D.G. and Wilson, J.O.S. (2002b) The growth of US credit unions, *Journal of Banking and Finance*, 22, 2327–56.

Goddard, J., McMillan, D.G. and Wilson, J.O.S. (2006) Do firm sizes and profit rates converge? Evidence on Gibrat's law and the persistence of profits in the long run, *Applied Economics*, 38, 267–78.

Goddard, J., Molyneux, P. and Wilson, J.O.S. (2009) Banking in the European Union, in Berger, A., Molyneux, P. and Wilson, J.O.S. (eds) *Oxford Handbook of Banking*. Oxford: Oxford University Press.

Goddard, J., Molyneux, P., Wilson, J.O.S. and Tavakoli, M. (2007) European banking: an overview, *Journal of Banking & Finance*, 31, 1911–35.

Goddard, J., Tavakoli, M. and Wilson, J.O.S. (2009) Sources of variation in company profitability and growth, *Journal of Business Research*, 64, 495–508.

Goergen, M. (2012) *International Corporate Governance*. Harlow: Pearson.

Gollop, F.M. and Monahan, J.L. (1991) A generalised index of diversification: trends in US manufacturing, *Review of Economics and Statistics*, 73, 318–30.

Gomes-Casseres, B. (2001) Alliances (inter-firm), in Jones, R.J.B. (ed.) *Routledge Encyclopedia of International Political Economy*. London: Routledge.

Gompers, P., Ishii, J. and Metrick, A. (2003) Corporate governance and equity prices, *Quarterly Journal of Economics*, 118, 107–55.

Goolsbee, A. and Syberson, C. (2008) How do incumbents respond to the threat of entry? Evidence from the major airlines, *Quarterly Journal of Economics*, 123, 1611–33.

Gorecki, P. (1975) An inter-industry analysis of diversification in the UK manufacturing sector, *Journal of Industrial Economics*, 24, 131–46.

Gort, M. (1962) *Diversification and Integration in American Industry*. Princeton, NJ: Princeton University Press.

Gort, M. (1969) An economic disturbance theory of mergers, *Quarterly Journal of Economics*, 83, 624–42.

Goyder, D.G. (2003) *EC Competition Law: Text and Cases*. London: Oxford University Press.

Grabowski, H. and Mueller, D. (1970) Industrial organization: the role and contribution of econometrics, *American Economic Review*, 60, 100–4.

Graham, D.R., Kaplan, D.P. and Sibley, R.S. (1983) Efficiency and competition in the airline industry, *Bell Journal of Economics*, 14, 118–38.

Grant, R.M. (1991) The resource-based theory of competitive advantage: implications for strategy formulation, *California Management Review*, 33, 114–35.

Grant, R.M. (1996) Toward a knowledge-based theory of the firm, *Strategic Management Journal*, 17, 109–22.

Green, A. and Mayes, D.G. (1991) Technical efficiency in manufacturing industries, *Economic Journal*, 101, 523–38.

Green, E.J. and Porter, R.H. (1984) Non-cooperative collusion under imperfect price information, *Econometrica*, 52, 87–100.

Green, R. (1999) Checks and balances in utility regulation: the UK experience, *Public Policy for the Private Sector*, May. Washington, DC: World Bank.

Greene, W. (2011) *Econometric Analysis*, 7th edition. Englewood Cliffs, NJ: Prentice Hall.

Greenbury Report (1995) *Directors Remuneration: Report of a Study Group Chaired by Sir Richard Greenbury*. London: Gee.

Greenhalgh, C. and Longland, M. (2005) Running to stand still? The value of R&D, patents and trade marks in innovating manufacturing firms, *International Journal of the Economics of Business*, 12, 307–28.

Gregoriou, G. and Renneboog, L. (2007) *International Mergers and Acquisitions Activity Since 1990*, Oxford: Elsevier.

Greuner, M.R., Kamerschen, D.R. and Klein, P.G. (2000) The competitive effects of advertising in the

US automobile industry, 1970–1994, *International Journal of the Economics of Business*, 7, 245–61.

Griffith, R. (2001) Product market competition, efficiency and agency costs: an empirical analysis, *Institute for Fiscal Studies*, Working Paper, 01/12.

Griffith, R. and Harrison, R. (2004) The link between product market reform and macroeconomic performance, *European Economy*, Paper No. 209.

Griffith, R., Redding, S. and Van Reenan, J. (2004) Mapping the two faces of R&D: productivity growth in a panel of OECD manufacturing industries, *Review of Economics and Statistics*, 86, 883–95.

Grimes, W.S. (2002) GTE Sylvania and the future of vertical restraint law, *Antitrust Magazine*, Fall, 27–31.

Grossman, S. and Hart, O. (1986) The costs and benefits of ownership: a theory of vertical and lateral integration, *Journal of Political Economy*, 94, 691–719.

Grout, P.A. and Sonderegger, S. (2005) Predicting cartels, *Office of Fair Trading* OFT773.

Growiec, J., Pammolli, F., Riccaboni, M. and Stanley, E.H. (2008) On the size distribution of business firms. *Economics Letters*, 98, 207–12.

Gugler, K., Mueller, D.C., Yurtoglu, B.B. and Zulehner, C. (2003) The effects of mergers: an international comparison, *International Journal of Industrial Organisation*, 21, 625–53.

Gugler, K., Mueller, D.C. and Weichselbaumer, M. (2012) The determinants of merger waves: an international perspective, *International Journal of Industrial Organization*, 30, 1–15.

Gujarati, D. and Porter, D. (2009) *Basic Econometrics*, 5th edition. New York: McGraw Hill.

Haan, M.A. (2003) Vaporware as a means of entry deterrence, *Journal of Industrial Economics*, 51, 345–58.

Haan, M.A. (2007) Cartel prohibition may increase prices, *The Manchester School*, 75, 557–68.

Hagedoorn, J. (2002) Interfirm R&D partnerships – an overview of major trends and patterns since 1960, *Research Policy*, 31, 477–92.

Hall, B.H. (1987) The relationship between firm size and firm growth in the US manufacturing sector, *Journal of Industrial Economics*, 35, 583–606.

Hall, B.H. and Ziedonis, R.H. (2001) The patent paradox revisited: an empirical study of patenting in the US semiconductor industry, 1979–1995, *Rand Journal of Economics*, 32, 101–28.

Hall, R.L. and Hitch, C.J. (1939) Price theory and business behaviour, *Oxford Economic Papers*, 2, 12–45.

Hall, S., Walsh, M. and Yates, T. (1996) How do UK companies set prices?, *Bank of England Quarterly Bulletin*, 36, 180–92.

Hall, S., Walsh, M. and Yates, T. (2000) How do UK companies set prices?, *Oxford Economic Papers*, 52, 425–46.

Hallett, M. (2000) Regional specialisation and concentration in the EU, European Commission Working Paper, No. 141.

Haltwanger, J. and Harrington, J. (1991) The impact of cyclical demand movement on collusive behavior, *Rand Journal of Economics*, 22, 89–106.

Hamberg, D. (1966) *Essays in the Economics of Research and Development*. New York: Random House.

Hamel, G. and Prahalad, C.K. (1994) *Competing for the Future*. Boston, MA: Harvard Business School Press.

Hampel Report (1998) *Committee on Corporate Governance: Final Report*. London: Gee.

Hannah, L. and Kay, J.A. (1977) *Concentration in Modern Industry*. London: Macmillan.

Hannah, L. and Kay, J.A. (1981) The contribution of mergers to concentration growth: a reply to Professor Hart, *Journal of Industrial Economics*, 29, 305–13.

Hannan, T.H. and McDowell, J.M. (1984) The determinants of technology adoption: the case of the banking firm, *Rand Journal of Economics*, 15, 328–35.

Hansen, R.G. and Lott, J.R. (1991) Winner's curse and public information in common value auctions: comment, *American Economic Review*, 75, 156–9.

Hanson, W. (1992) The dynamics of cost-plus pricing, *Managerial and Decision Economics*, 12, 149–61.

Harberger, A.C. (1954) Monopoly and resource allocation, *American Economic Review, Papers and Proceedings*, 44, 77–87.

Harbord, D. and Hoehn, T. (1994) Barriers to entry and exit in European competition policy, *International Review of Law and Economics*, 14, 411–35.

Hardt, M. (1995) Market foreclosure without vertical integration, *Economic Letters*, 47, 423–9.

Harford, J. (2005) What drives merger waves?, *Journal of Financial Economics*, 77, 529–60.

Harrigan, K.R. (1983) A framework for looking at vertical integration, *Journal of Business Strategy*, 3, 30–7.

Harrington, J.E. (1989) Collusion among asymmetric firms: the case of different discount factors, *International Journal of Industrial Organization*, 7, 289–307.

Harrington, J.E. (1991) The determination of price and output quotas in a heterogeneous cartel, *International Economic Review*, 32, 767–92.

Harrington, J.E. (2004) Cartel pricing dynamics in the presence of an antitrust authority, *Rand Journal of Economics*, 35, 651–73.

Harrington, J.E. (2008) Detecting cartels, in Buccirossi, P. (ed.) *Handbook of Antitrust Economics*. Cambridge: MIT Press.

Harris, M. and Raviv, A. (1996) The capital budgeting process: incentives and information, *Journal of Finance*, 51, 1139–74.

Harrison, B., Kelley, M. and Gant, J. (1996) Innovative firm behaviour and local milieu: exploring the intersection of agglomeration, firm effects, industrial organization and technical change, *Economic Geography*, 72, 233–58.

Hart, O. (1995a) *Firms, Contracts and Financial Structure*. Oxford: Oxford University Press.

Hart, O. (1995b) Corporate governance: some theory and implications, *Economic Journal*, 105, 678–89.

Hart, O. and Moore, J. (1990) Property rights and the nature of the firm, *Journal of Political Economy*, 98, 1119–58.

Hart, P.E. (1962) The size and growth of firms, *Economica*, 29, 29–39.

Hart, P.E. (1981) The effects of mergers on industrial concentration, *Journal of Industrial Economics*, 29, 315–20.

Hart, P.E. and Clarke, R. (1980) *Concentration in British Industry: 1935–1975*. Cambridge: Cambridge University Press.

Hart, P.E. and Oulton, N. (1996) The size and growth of firms, *Economic Journal*, 106, 1242–52.

Hart, P.E. and Oulton, N. (1999) Gibrat, Galton and job generation, *International Journal of the Economics of Business*, 6, 149–64.

Hart, P.E. and Prais, S.J. (1956) The analysis of business concentration: a statistical approach, *Journal of the Royal Statistical Society*, Series A, 119, 150–91.

Hart, R.A., Hutton, J. and Sharot, T. (1975) A statistical analysis of Association Football attendances, *Applied Statistics*, 24, 17–27.

Hartley, K. (2003) Defence industries, in Johnson, P. (ed.) *Industries in Europe*. Cheltenham: Edward Elgar.

Haskel, J. and Scaramozzino, P. (1997) Do other firms matter in oligopolies?, *Journal of Industrial Economics*, 45, 27–45.

Hawawini, G., Subramanian, V. and Verdin, P. (2003) Is performance driven by industry or firm-specific factors? A new look at the evidence, *Strategic Management Journal*, 24, 1–16.

Hay, D. and Morris, D. (1991) *Industrial Economics and Organization*, 2nd edition. Oxford: Oxford University Press.

Haynes, M., Thompson, S. and Wright, M. (2002) The impact of divestment on firm performance: empirical evidence from a panel of UK companies, *Journal of Industrial Economics*, 50, 173–96.

Healy, P.M., Palepu, K. and Ruback, R.S. (1992) Does corporate performance improve after mergers? *Journal of Financial Economics*, 31, 135–75.

Heffernan, M. (2011) *Wilful blindness: Why We Ignore the Obvious at Our Peril*. New York: Walker Publishing.

Heide, J.B., Dutta, S. and Bergen, M. (1998) Exclusive dealing and business efficiency: evidence from industry practice, *Journal of Law and Economics*, 41, 387–407.

Helfat, C.E. and Teece, D.J. (1987) Vertical integration and risk reduction, *Journal of Law, Economics and Organisation*, 3, 47–68.

Helm, D. (1994) British utility regulation: theory, practice and reform, *Oxford Review of Economic Policy*, 10, 17–39.

Helm, D. (2001) The assessment: European networks – competition, interconnection, and regulation, *Oxford Review of Economic Policy*, 17, 297–312.

Helm, D. (2005) The future of infrastructure regulation, *OXERA Discussion Paper*.

Helm, D. (2006) Regulatory reform, capture, and the regulatory burden, *Oxford Review of Economic Policy*, 22, 169–85.

Helm, D. and Jenkinson, T. (1997) The assessment: introducing competition into regulated industries, *Oxford Review of Economic Policy*, 13, 1–14.

Hendricks, K. and Porter, R. (2007) Auctions, in Armstrong, M. and Porter, R. (eds) *Handbook of Industrial Organization*, Vol. 3. Amsterdam: Elsevier.

Hendricks, K., Porter, R.H. and Boudreau, B. (1987) Information, returns, and bidding behavior in OCS auctions: 1954–1969, *Journal of Industrial Economics*, 35, 517–42.

Hennessy, D.A. (1997) Information asymmetry as a reason for vertical integration, in Caswell, J.A. and Cotterill, R.W. (eds) *Strategy and Policy in the Food System: Emerging Issues*, Proceedings of NE-165 Conference, Washington, DC.

Herfindahl, O.C. (1950) Concentration in the US steel industry. Unpublished PhD thesis, Berkeley, CA: University of California.

Hersch, P.L. (1994) The effects of resale price maintenance on shareholder wealth: the consequences of Schwegmann, *Journal of Industrial Economics*, 42, 205–16.

Hertzendorf, M.N. (1993) I'm not a high quality firm, but I play one on TV, *Rand Journal of Economics*, 24, 236–47.

Higgs, D. (2003) *Review of the role and effectiveness of non-executive directors*. London: Department for Business, Enterprise and Regulatory Reform.

Hirschleifer, J. (1956) On the economics of transfer pricing, *Journal of Business*, 29, 172–84.

Hirschleifer, J. (1971) The private and social value of information and the reward of inventive activity, *American Economic Review*, 61, 561–74.

Hirschman, A.O. (1945) *National Power and the Structure of Foreign Trade*. Berkeley, CA: University of California Bureau of Business and Economic Research.

Hoffmann, J. and Kurz-Kim, J.-R. (2005) Consumer price adjustment under the microscope: Germany in a period of low inflation, *Deutsche Bundesbank*, mimeograph.

Hoi, J. (2007) Competition law and policy indicators for the OECD countries, *OECD Economic Department Working Papers*, No. 568.

Holahan, W.L. (1978) Cartel problems: comment, *American Economic Review*, 68, 942–6.

Horstmann, I. and MacDonald, G. (2003) Is advertising a signal of product quality? Evidence from the compact disc player market, 1983–1992, *International Journal of Industrial Organization*, 21, 317–45.

Hoschman, J. and Luski, I. (1988) Advertising and economic welfare: comment, *American Economic Review*, 78, 290–6.

Hotelling, H. (1929) Stability in competition, *Economic Journal*, 39, 41–57.

Houston, J. and James, C. (1995) CEO compensation and bank risk: is compensation in banking structured to promote risk taking? *Journal of Monetary Economics*, 36, 405–31.

Huck, S., Normann, H. and Oechssler, J. (2001) Two are few and four are many: number effects in experimental oligopolies, *Bonn Econ Discussion Papers* bgse12_2001, University of Bonn, Germany. ideas.repec.org/p/bon/bonedp/bgse12_2001.html. Accessed 19 April 2004.

Hughes, J. (2008) Andersen's collapse results in a fee bonus for Big Four rivals, *Financial Times*, 29 April.

Hunter, A. (1954) The Monopolies Commission and price fixing, *Economic Journal*, 66, 587–602.

Hurdle, G.J., Johnson, R.L., Joskow, A.S., Werden, G.J. and Williams, M.A. (1989) Concentration, potential entry, and performance in the airline industry, *Journal of Industrial Economics*, 38, 119–39.

Hyland, D.C. (2003) The effect of diversification on firm value: a pre- and post-diversification analysis, *Studies in Economics and Finance*, 21, 22–39.

Hymer, S. and Pashigian, P. (1962) Firm size and rate of growth, *Journal of Political Economy*, 52, 556–69.

Innes, R. (2006) Entry deterrence by non-horizontal merger, *Journal of Industrial Economics*, 54, 369–95.

International Joint Project on Co-Operative Democracy (1995) *Making Membership Meaningful: Participatory Democracy In Co-Operatives*. Saskatoon: Centre For The Study Of Co-Operatives.

Jacobides, M.G. (2005) Industry change through vertical disintegration: how and why markets emerged in mortgage banking, *Academy of Management Journal*, 48, 465–98.

Jacobson, D. and Andréosso-O'Callaghan, B. (1996) *Industrial Economics and Organisation: A European Perspective*. Maidenhead: McGraw-Hill.

Jacobsson, S. (2002) *Universities and Industrial Transformation: An Interpretative and Selective Literature Study with Special Emphasis on Sweden*. Brighton, UK: SPRU – Science and Technology Policy Research.

Jacquemin, A. and Slade, M.E. (1989) Cartels, collusion and horizontal merger, in Schmalensee, R. and Willig, R.D. (eds) *Handbook of Industrial Organization*. Cambridge, MA: MIT Press.

Jagtiani, J., Saunders, A. and Udell, G. (1995) The effect of bank capital requirements on bank off balance sheet financial innovations, *Journal of Banking and Finance*, 19, 647–58.

Janssen, M.A. (2008) Evolution of cooperation in a one-shot prisoner's dilemma based on recognition of trustworthy and untrustworthy agents, *Journal of Economic Behaviour and Organization*, 65, 458–71.

Jarrell, G.A., Brickley, J.A. and Netter, J.M. (1988) The market for corporate control: the empirical evidence since 1980, *Journal of Economic Perspectives*, 2, 49–68.

Jenny, F. and Weber, A.P. (1983) Aggregate welfare loss due to monopoly power in the French economy: some tentative estimates, *Journal of Industrial Economics*, 32, 113–30.

Jenny, F. and Weber, A.P. (1990) The persistence of profits in France, in Mueller, D.C. (ed.) *The Dynamics of Company Profits: An International Comparison*. Cambridge: Cambridge University Press.

Jensen, M. and Meckling, W. (1976) Theory of the firm: managerial behaviour, agency costs, and capital structure, *Journal of Financial Economics*, 3, 305–60.

Jensen, M.C. (2000) *Foundations of Organizational Strategy*. Cambridge, MA: Harvard University Press.

Jeon, Y. and Miller, S.M. (2007) Births, deaths and marriages in the US Commercial Banking Industry, *Economic Inquiry*, 45, 325–41.

Jevons, W.S. (1871) *The Theory of Political Economy*, 5th edition. New York: Kelley & Macmillan (1957).

Jewkes, J., Sawers, D. and Stillerman, R. (1969) *The Sources of Invention*, 2nd edition. London: Macmillan.

John, G. and Weitz, B.A. (1988) Forward integration into distribution: an empirical test of transaction cost analysis, *Journal of Law, Economics and Organisation*, 4, 337–56.

John, K. and Qian, Y. (2003) Incentive features in CEO compensation in the banking industry. *New York Federal Reserve Economic Policy Review*, 9, 109–21.

John, K., Litov, L. and Yeung, B. (2008) Corporate governance and risk taking, *Journal of Finance*, 63, 1679–728.

John, K., Mehran, H. and Qian, Y. (2010) Outside monitoring and CEO compensation in the banking industry, *Journal of Corporate Finance*, 16, 383–99.

Johnson, P.S. (2003) Air transport, in Johnson, P. (ed.) *Industries in Europe*. Cheltenham: Edward Elgar.

Jonker, N., Blijenberg, H. and Folkertsma, C. (2004) Empirical analysis of price setting behaviour in the Netherlands in the period 1998–2003 using micro data. *ECB Working Paper*, No. 413.

Joskow, A.S., Werden, G.J. and Johnson, R.L. (1994) Entry, exit and performance in airline markets, *International Journal of Industrial Organization*, 12, 457–71.

Joskow, P.L. (2005) Vertical integration, in Menard, C. and Shirley, M.M. (eds) *Handbook of New Institutional Economics*. Berlin: Springer.

Julien, B. and Rey, P. (2000) Resale price maintenance and collusion, CEPR Discussion Paper No. 2553. London: Centre for Economic Policy Research.

Kagel, J.H. and Levin, D. (1986) The winner's curse and public information in common value auctions, *American Economic Review*, 76, 894–920.

Kagel, J.H. and Levin, D. (2002) *Common Value Auctions and the Winner's Curse*, Princeton, NJ: Princeton University Press.

Kagel, J.H. and Richard, J.F. (2001) Super-experienced bidders in first price auctions: rules of thumb, Nash equilibrium bidding and the winner's curse, *Review of Economics and Statistics*, 83, 408–19.

Kagel, J.H., Levin, D., Battalio, R. and Meyer, D.J. (1989) First price common value auctions: bidder behavior and winner's curse, *Economic Inquiry*, 27, 241–58.

Kaldor, N. (1950) The economic aspects of advertising, *Review of Economic Studies*, 18, 1–27.

Kalnins, A. (2004) Hamburger prices and spatial econometrics: implications for firm strategy and public policy, *Journal of Economics and Management Strategy*, 12, 591–616.

Kalnins, A. and Lafontaine, F. (2004) Multi-unit ownership in franchising: evidence from the Texan fast food industry, *Rand Journal of Economics*, 35, 747–61.

Kamerschen, D.R. (1966) An estimation of the 'welfare losses' from monopoly in the American economy, *Western Economic Journal*, 4, 221–36.

Kamien, M. and Schwartz, N. (1970) Market structure, elasticity of demand and incentive to invent, *Journal of Law and Economics*, 13, 241–52.

Kamien, M. and Schwartz, N. (1982) *Market Structure and Innovation*. Cambridge: Cambridge University Press.

Kane, E.J. (2012) Regulation and supervision: an ethical perspective, in Berger, A.N., Molyneux, P. and Wilson, J.O.S. (eds) *Oxford Handbook of Banking*. Oxford: Oxford University Press.

Kantzenbach, E., Kottman, E. and Krüger, R. (1995) New industrial economics and experiences from European merger control – new lessons about collective dominance?, *European Commission*. Luxembourg: Office for Official Publications of the European Communities.

Kaplan, S. and Weisbach, M. (1992) The success of acquisitions: evidence from divestitures, *Journal of Finance*, 47, 107–38.

Kaplan, S., Schenkel, A., von Krogh, G. and Weber, C. (2001) Knowledge-based theories of the firm in strategic management: a review and extension. MIT Sloan Working Paper 4216–01, www-management. wharton.upenn.edu/kaplan/documents/KBV-Sloan WP-4216-01.pdf/.

Kaplow, L. (2010) Why (ever) define markets? *Harvard Law Review*, 124, 438–517.

Karshenas, M. and Stoneman, P. (1995) Technological diffusion, in Stoneman, P. (ed.) *Handbook of the Economics of Innovation and Technical Change*. Oxford: Blackwell, Chapter 7.

Kashyap, A. (1995) Sticky prices: new evidence from retail catalogues, *Quarterly Journal of Economics*, 110, 245–74.

Katz, M.L. (1989) Vertical contractual relations, in Schmalensee, R. and Willig, R.D. (eds) *Handbook of Industrial Organization*, Vol. 2. Amsterdam: Elsevier.

Katz, M. and Shapiro, C. (1985) Network externalities, competition and compatibility, *American Economic Review*, 75, 424–40.

Kaul, A. and Wittink, D.R. (1995) Empirical generalisations about the impact of advertising on price sensitivity and price, *Marketing Science*, 14, 151–60.

Kay, J.A. (1990a) Identifying the strategic market, *Business Strategy Review*, 1/2, 2–24.

Kay, J.A. (1990b) Vertical restraints in European competition policy, *European Economic Review*, 34, 551–61.

Kay, J.A. (1993) *Foundations of Corporate Success*. Oxford: Oxford University Press.

Kay, J.A. (1999) Mastering strategy, *Financial Times*, 27 September.

Kay, J.A. (2003) A brief history of business strategy, in Kay, J. (ed.) *Economics of Business Strategy*. Cheltenham: Edward Elgar.

Kay, J.A. (2004) *The Truth about Markets: Why Some Nations are Rich, but Most Remain Poor*. London: Penguin.

Kay, J.A. and Vickers, J. (1990) Regulatory reform: an appraisal, in Majone, G. (ed.) *Deregulation or Reregulation? Regulatory Reform in Europe and the United States*. London: Pinter.

Keating, B. (1991) An update on industries ranked by average rates of return, *Applied Economics*, 23, 897–902.

Khanna, T. and Rivkin, J.W. (2001) Estimating the performance of business groups in emerging market, *Strategic Management Journal*, 22, 45–74.

Khemani, R.S. and Shapiro, D.M. (1990) The persistence of profitability in Canada, in Mueller, D.C. (ed.) *The Dynamics of Company Profits: An International Comparison*. Cambridge: Cambridge University Press.

Kihlstrom, R.E. and Riordan, M.A. (1984) Advertising as a signal, *Journal of Political Economy*, 92, 427–50.

King, A. and Lennox, M. (2001) Does it pay be to be green? Accounting for strategy selection in the relationship between environmental and financial performance, *Journal of Industrial Ecology*, 5, 105–16.

Kirzner, I. (1973) *Competition and Entrepreneurship*. Chicago, IL: Chicago University Press.

Kirzner, I. (1997a) Entrepreneurial discovery and the competitive market process: an Austrian approach, *Journal of Economic Literature*, 35, 60–85.

Kirzner, I. (1997b) *How Markets Work: Disequilibrium, Entrepreneurship and Discovery. IEA Hobart Paper No. 133*. London: Institute of Economic Affairs.

Klapper, L., Laeven, L. and Rajan, R. (2004) Business environment and firm entry: evidence from international data, *World Bank Research Paper*, No. 3232.

Klein, B. (1995) The economics of franchise contracts, *Journal of Corporate Finance*, 2, 9–37.

Klein, B. (2000) Fisher – General Motors and the nature of the firm, *Journal of Law and Economics*, 37, 105–41.

Klein, B. and Murphy, K. (1988) Vertical restraints as contract enforcement mechanisms, *Journal of Law and Economics*, 31, 265–97.

Klein, B., Crawford, R. and Alchian, A. (1978) Vertical integration, appropriable rents, and the competitive contracting process, *Journal of Law and Economics*, 21, 297–326.

Kleit, A.N. and Palsson, H.P. (1999) Horizontal concentration and anticompetitive behavior in the central Canadian cement industry; testing arbitrage cost hypothesis, *International Journal of Industrial Organisation*, 17, 1189–202.

Klemperer, P. (1987) Markets with consumer switching costs, *Quarterly Journal of Economics*, 102, 375–94.

Klemperer, P. (1995) Competition when consumers have switching costs, *Review of Economic Studies*, 62, 515–39.

Klemperer, P. (1999) Auction theory: a guide to the literature, *Journal of Economic Surveys*, 13, 227–86.

Klemperer, P. (2002a) What really matters in auction design, *Journal of Economic Perspectives*, 16, 169–89.

Klemperer, P. (2002b) How not to run auctions: the European 3G telecom auctions, *European Economic Review*, 46, 829–45.

Klemperer, P. (2002c) The wrong culprit for telecom trouble, *Financial Times*, 26 November.

Klemperer, P. (2004) *Auctions: Theory and Practice*. Princeton, NJ: Princeton University Press.

Klemperer, P. (2008) Network effects and switching costs, in Durlauf, S.N. and Blume, L.E. (eds) *The New Palgrave Dictionary of Economics*, 2nd edition. London: Palgrave Macmillan.

Klepper, S. (1997) Industry life cycles, *Industrial and Corporate Change*, 6, 145–81.

Klevorick, A.K. (1966) The graduate fair return: a regulatory proposal, *American Economic Review*, 56, 477–84.

Klimenko, M.M. (2004) Competition, matching, and geographical clustering at early stages of the industry life cycle, *Journal of Economics and Business*, 56, 177–95.

Knight, F. (1921) *Uncertainty and Profit*, Boston, MA: Houghton Mifflin.

Kogut, B. and Zander, U. (1992) Knowledge of the firm, combinative capabilities and the replication of technology, *Organization Science*, 3, 383–97.

Koller, R.H. (1975) On the definiton of predatory pricing, *Antitrust Bulletin*, 20, 329–37.

Kolstad, I. (2007) Why firms should not always maximise profits, *Journal of Business Ethics*, 76, 137–45.

Koppl, R. (2000) Fritz Machlup and behavioralism, *Journal of Industrial and Corporate Change*, 9, 4.

Kortum, S. and Lerner, J. (2000) Assessing the contribution of venture capital to innovation, *Rand Journal of Economics*, 31, 674–92.

Koutsoyannis, A. (1982) *Non-price Decisions, The Firm in a Modern Context*. London: Macmillan.

Krattenmaker, T.G. and Salop, S.C. (1986) Anti-competitive exclusion: raising rivals' cost to achieve power over price, *Yale Law Journal*, 96, 209–93.

Krickx, G.A. (1995) Vertical integration in the computer main frame industry: a transaction cost interpretation, *Journal of Economic Behaviour and Organisation*, 26, 75–91.

Krishna, V. (2010) *Auction Theory*, 2nd edition. London: Academic Press.

Krugman, P. (1991) *Geography and Trade*. Cambridge, MA: MIT Press.

Krugman, P. (2000) Where in the world is the new economic geography?, in Clark, G.L., Feldman, M.P. and Gertler, M.S. (eds) *Oxford Handbook of Economic Geography*. Oxford: Oxford University Press.

Kuehn, D.A. (1975) *Takeovers and the Theory of the Firm*. London: Macmillan.

Kuhlman, J.M. (1969) Nature and significance of price fixing rings, *Antitrust Law and Economic Review*, 2, 69–82.

Kultti, K., Takalo, T. and Toikka, J. (2007) Secrecy versus patenting, *RAND Journal of Economics*, 38, 22–42.

Kumar, M.S. (1985) Growth, acquisition activity and firm size: evidence from the United Kingdom, *Journal of Industrial Economics*, 33, 327–38.

Kurucz, E., Colbert, B.A. and Wheeler, D. (2008) The business case for corporate social responsibility, in A. Crane (ed.) *The Oxford Handbook of Corporate Social Responsibility*. Oxford: Oxford University Press, 83–112.

Kwoka, J.E. (1981) Does the choice of concentration measure really matter?, *Journal of Industrial Economics*, 29, 445–53.

Kwoka, J.E. (2002) Vertical economies in electric power: evidence on integration and its alternatives, *International Journal of Industrial Organisation*, 20, 653–71.

Kwoka, J.E. and White, L.J. (2008) *The Anti-trust Revolution*, 5th edition. London: Oxford University Press.

Lach, S. (2002) Existence and persistence of price dispersion, *Review of Economics and Statistics*, 84, 433–44.

Lacktorin, M. and Rajan, M. (2000) A longitudinal study of corporate diversification and restructuring activities using multiple measures, Academy of Business and Administrative Sciences Conference, July, Prague, Czech Republic.

Laeven, L. and Levine, R. (2009) Bank governance, regulation and risk taking. *Journal of Financial Economics*, 93, 259–75.

Lafontaine, F. and Slade, M. (2007) Vertical integration and firm boundaries: the evidence, *Journal of Economic Literature*, 45, 629–85.

Lambin, J.J. (1976) *Advertising, Competition and Market Conduct in Oligopoly over Time*. Amsterdam: Elsevier.

Lancaster, K. (1966) A new approach to consumer theory, *Journal of Political Economy*, 74, 132–57.

Lang, L.H. and Stulz, R.M. (1994) Tobin's q, corporate diversification, and firm performance, *Journal of Political Economy*, 102, 1248–80.

Langinier, C. (2004) Are patents strategic barriers to entry?, *Journal of Economics and Business*, 56, 5, 349–61.

Langlois, R.N. and Foss, N.J. (1997) Capabilities and governance: the rebirth of production in the theory of economic organization, *DRUID Working Paper*, No. 97–2.

Langlois, R.N. and Robertson, P.L. (1989) Explaining vertical integration: lessons from the American automobile industry, *Journal of Economic History*, 49, 361–75.

Larner, R.J. (1966) Ownership and control in the 200 largest non-financial corporations, 1929 and 1963, *American Economic Review*, 56, 777–87.

Lau, L. (1982) On identifying the degree of competitiveness from industry, price and output data, *Economics Letters*, 10, 93–9.

Laurensen, K. and Salter, A. (2003) Searching low and high: what types of firm use universities as a source of innovation? *DRUID Working Paper No. 03–16*.

Lavery, K. (1997) *Smart Contracting for Local Government Services: Processes and Experience*. Westport, CT: Praeger.

Lawler, K. and Lee, K.-P. (2003) Brewing, in Johnson, P. (ed.) *Industries in Europe*. Cheltenham: Edward Elgar.

Layson, S. (1994) Third degree price discrimination under economies of scale, *Southern Economic Journal*, 61, 323–7.

Leahy, A.S. (1997) Advertising and concentration: a survey of the empirical evidence, *Quarterly Journal of Business and Economics*, 36, 35–50.

Lee, C. (2002) Advertising, its determinants, and market structure, *Review of Industrial Organization*, 21, 89–101.

Lee, C. (2005) A new perspective on industry R&D and market structure, *Journal of Industrial Economics*, 53, 101–22.

Lee, Y.H. and Malmendier, U. (2011) The bidder's curse, *American Economic Review*, 101, 749–87.

Leech, D. and Leahy, J. (1991) Ownership structure, control type classifications and the performance of large British companies, *Economic Journal*, 101, 1418–37.

Leibenstein, H. (1950) Bandwagon, snob, and Veblen effects in the theory of consumers' demand, *Quarterly Journal of Economics*, 64, 183–207.

Leibenstein, H. (1966) Allocative efficiency versus X-efficiency, *American Economic Review*, 56, 392–415.

Lerner, A.P. (1934) The concept of monopoly and the measurement of monopoly power, *Review of Economic Studies*, 1, 157–75.

Lerner, J. and Tirole, J. (2002) Some simple economics of open source, *Journal of Industrial Economics*, 52, 197–234.

Lerner, J. and Tirole, J. (2005) The economics of technology sharing: open source and beyond, *Journal of Economic Perspectives*, 19, 99–120.

Lerner, J., Pathak, P.A. and Tirole, J. (2006) The dynamics of open-source contributors, *American Economic Review*, 96, 114–18.

Levenstein, M.C. (1996) Do price wars facilitate collusion? A study of the bromine cartel before World War I, *Explorations in Economic History*, 33, 107–37.

Levenstein, M.C. (1997) Price wars and the stability of collusion: a study of the pre-World War I bromine industry, *Journal of Industrial Economics*, 45, 117–37.

Levenstein, M. and Suslow, V. (2006) What determines cartel success?, *Journal of Economic Literature*, 44, 43–95.

Levin, R.C., Klevorick, A.K., Nelson, R.R. and Winter, S.G. (1987) Appropriating the returns from industrial R&D, *Brookings Papers on Economic Activity*, 3, 783–820.

Levine, P. and Aaronovitch, S. (1981) The financial characteristics of firms and theories of merger activity, *Journal of Industrial Economics*, 30, 149–72.

Levine, R. (2004) The corporate governance of banks: a concise discussion of concepts and evidence, *World Bank Policy Research Working Paper*, No. 3404.

Levy, D. (1987) The speed of the invisible hand, *International Journal of Industrial Organisation*, 5, 79–92.

Levy, D., Bergen, M., Dutta, S. and Venable, R. (1997) The magnitude of menu costs: direct evidence from large supermarket chains, *Quarterly Journal of Economics*, 112, 791–825.

Liebeskind, J.P. (1996) Knowledge, strategy, and the theory of the firm, *Strategic Management Journal*, 17, 93–107.

Liefmann, R. (1932) *Cartels, Concerns and Trusts*. London: Methuen.

Lins, K. and Servaes, H. (1999) International evidence on the value of corporate diversification, *Journal of Finance*, 54, 2215–39.

Lipczynski, J. (1994) Selected aspects of cartel stability. Unpublished PhD thesis, London School of Economics.

Lipsey, R. and Lancaster, K. (1956) The general theory of second best, *Review of Economic Studies*, 24, 11–32.

Littlechild, S. (1981) Misleading calculations of the social costs of monopoly power, *Economic Journal*, 91, 348–63.

Littlechild, S. (1982) *The Relationship between Advertising and Price*. London: Advertising Association.

Littlechild, S. (1983) *Regulation of British Telecommunications' Profitability*. London: HMSO.

Littlechild, S. (2003) Electricity: developments worldwide, in Robinson, C. (ed.) *Competition and Regulation in Utility Markets*. Cheltenham: Edward Elgar.

Littlechild, S.C. (2007) Beyond regulation, in Robinson, C. (ed.) *Utility Regulation in Competitive Markets*. Cheltenham: Edward Elgar.

Lorentzen, J., Møllgaard, P. and Rojec, M. (2003) Host-country absorption of technology: evidence from automotive supply networks in eastern Europe, *Industry and Innovation*, 10, 415–32.

Lorenz, M.O. (1905) Methods of measuring the concentration of wealth, *American Statistical Association Journal*, 9, 209–19.

Lotti, F., Santarelli, E. and Vivarelli, M. (2001) The relationship between size and growth: the case of Italian newborn firms, *Applied Economics Letters*, 8, 451–4.

Lotti, F., Santarelli, E. and Vivarelli, M. (2003) Does Gibrat's law hold among young, small firms? *Journal of Evolutionary Economics*, 13, 213–35.

Love, J.H. and Roper, S. (2004) The organization of innovation: collaboration and multifunctional groups in the UK and German manufacturing, *Cambridge Journal of Economics*, 28, 379–95.

Love, J.H. and Stephen, F.H. (1996) Advertising, price and quality in self regulating professions: a survey, *International Journal of the Economics of Business*, 3, 227–47.

Lucking-Reiley, D. (1999) Using field experiments to test equivalence between auction formats: magic on the internet, *American Economic Review*, 81, 1063–80.

Lucking-Reiley, D., Bryan, D., Prasad, N. and Reeves, D. (2007) Pennies from eBay: the determinants of price in online auctions, *Journal of Industrial Economics*, 55, 223–33.

Luffman, G.A. and Reed, R. (1984) *The Strategy and Performance of British Industry, 1970–80*. London: Macmillan.

Luik, J. and Waterson, M.J. (1996) *Advertising and Markets*: *A Collection of Seminal Papers*. Oxford: NTC Publications.

Lundvall, B. and Johnson, B. (1994) The learning economy, *Journal of Industry Studies*, 1, 23–42.

Lynk, E. (1993) Privatisation, joint production and the comparative efficiencies of private and public ownership: the UK water case, *Fiscal Studies*, 14, 98–116.

Lyons, B.R. (1996) Empirical relevance of efficient contract theory: inter-firm contracts, *Oxford Review of Economic Policy*, 12, 27–52.

Lyons, B.R. (2003) Reform of European merger policy, *Centre for Competition and Regulation, Working Paper 03-05*. Norwich: University of East Anglia.

Lyons, B. (2008a) *Cases in European Competition Policy: The Economics Analysis*. Cambridge: Cambridge University Press.

Lyons, B. (2008b) An economic assessment of EC Merger Control: 1957–2007, *CCP Working Paper 08-17*.

Lyons, B.R., Matraves, C. and Moffatt, P. (1997) Industrial concentration and market integration in the European Union, *Wissenschaftszentrum Berlin für Sozialforschung*, Discussion Paper FSIV, 97–21.

MacGregor, D.H. (1906) *Industrial Combination*. London: Bell & Sons.

Machlup, F. (1946) Marginal analysis and empirical research, *American Economic Review*, 36, 519–54.

Machlup, F. (1952a) *The Economics of Sellers' Competition*. Baltimore, MD: Johns Hopkins University Press.

Machlup, F. (1952b) *The Political Economy of Monopoly*. Baltimore, MD: Johns Hopkins University Press.

Machlup, F. (1967) Theories of the firm: marginalist, behavioural, managerial, *American Economic Review*, 57, 1–33.

Machlup, F. and Taber, M. (1960) Bilateral monopoly, successive monopoly and vertical integration, *Economica*, 27, 101–19.

Macho-Stadler, I. and Pérez-Castrillo, J.D. (1998) Centralised and decentralised contracts in a moral hazard environment, *Journal of Industrial Economics*, 46, 489–510.

Mahajan, S. (2005) Concentration ratios for business by industry in 2003, *Economic Trends*, 624, 52–62.

Mahajan, S. (2006) Concentration ratios for business by industry in 2004, *Economic Trends*, 635, 25–47.

Mair, J. and Moschieri, C. (2006) Unbundling frees business takeoff, *Financial Times*, 19 October.

Malerba, F. (2007) Innovation and the dynamics and evolution of industries: progress and challenges, *International Journal of Industrial Organization*, 25, 675–99.

Malmendier, U. and Tate, G. (2009) The superstar CEOs, *Quarterly Journal of Economics*, 124, 1593–38.

Malyshev, N. (2006) Regulatory policy: OECD experience and evidence, *Oxford Review of Economic Policy*, 22, 274–99.

Manne, H. (1965) Mergers and the market for corporate control, *Journal of Political Economy*, 73, 110–20.

Mansfield, E. (1961) Technical change and the rate of imitation, *Econometrica*, 29, 741–66.

Mansfield, E. (1962) Entry, Gibrat's law, innovation, and the growth of firms, *American Economic Review*, 52, 1023–51.

Mansfield, E. (1968) *Industrial Research and Technological Innovation*. New York: Norton.

Mansfield, E. (1969) Industrial research and development: characteristics, costs and diffusion results, *American Economic Review, Papers and Proceedings*, 59, 65–79.

Marayuma, N. and Odagiri, H. (2002) Does the persistence of profits persist? A study of company profits in Japan, 1964–1997, *International Journal of Industrial Organization*, 20, 1513–33.

Marion, B.W. (1998) Competition in grocery retailing: the impact of a new strategic group on BLS price increases, *Review of Industrial Organization*, 13, 381–99.

Markham, J.W. (1951) The nature and significance of price leadership, *American Economic Review*, 41, 891–905.

Markides, C. and Williamson, P.J. (1994) Related diversification, core competencies and corporate performance, *Strategic Management Journal*, 15, 149–65.

Markusen, A. (1996) Sticky places in slippery space, a typology of industrial districts, *Economic Geography*, 72, 293–313.

Marris, R. (1964) *The Economic Theory of Managerial Capitalism*. London: Macmillan.

Marshall, A. (1870) *Industry and Trade*. New York: Cosimo (2006).

Marshall, A. (1890) *Principles of Economics*, 8th edition. London: Macmillan (1920).

Marshall, A. (1892) *Elements of Economics of Industry*, 3rd edition. London: Macmillan (1964).

Marshall, A. (1920) *Principles of Economics*, 8th edition. London: Macmillan.

Marshall, R.C., Marx, L.M. and Raiff, M.E. (2007) Cartel price announcements: the vitamins industry,

International Journal of Industrial Organisation, 26, 762–802.

Martin, J.D. and Sayrak, A. (2003) Corporate diversification and shareholder value: a survey of recent literature, *Journal of Corporate Finance*, 9, 37–57.

Martin, R. and Sunley, P. (1997) Paul Krugman's geographical economics and its implications for regional theory, *Regional Studies*, 77, 259–92.

Martin, S. (2002) *Advanced Industrial Economics*, 2nd edition. Cambridge, MA: Blackwell.

Martin, S. (2008) Limit pricing, in Durlauf, S.N. and Blume, L.E. (eds) *The New Palgrave Dictionary of Economics*, 2nd edition. London: Palgrave Macmillan.

Martynova, M. and Renneboog, L.D.R. (2008) A century of corporate takeovers: What have we learned and where do we stand? *Journal of Banking and Finance*, 32, 2148–77.

Marvel, H. and McCafferty, K. (1984) Resale price maintenance and quality certification, *Rand Journal of Economics*, 15, 346–59.

Marx, L.M. and Shaffer, G. (2004) Opportunism and menus of two-part tariffs, *International Journal of Industrial Organization*, 22, 1399 414.

Mason, E.S. (1939) Price and production policies of large scale enterprise, *American Economic Review*, 29, 61–74.

Mason, E.S. (1949) The current state of the monopoly problem in the United States, *Harvard Law Review*, 62, 1265–85.

Massini, S. (2004) The diffusion of mobile telephony in Italy and the UK: an empirical investigation, *Economics of Innovation and New Technology*, 13, 251–77.

Mata, J. (2008) Gibrat's Law, in Durlauf, S.N. and Blume, L.E. (eds) *New Palgrave Dictionary of Economics*. London: Palgrave Macmillan.

Mateus, A.M. and Moreira, T. (2010) (eds) *Competition Law and Economics: Advances in Competition Policy Enforcement in the EU and North America*. Cheltenham: Edward Elgar.

Mathewson, F. and Winter, R.A. (1998) The law and economics of resale price maintenance, *Review of Industrial Organisation*, 13, 57–84.

Matouschek, N. and Ramezzana, P. (2007) The role of exclusive contracts in facilitating market transactions, *Journal of Industrial Economics*, 55, 347–71.

Matsui, A. (1989) Consumer-benefited cartels under strategic capacity investment competition, *International Journal of Industrial Organisation*, 7, 451–70.

Matsusaka, J.G. (1993) Takeover motives during the conglomerate merger wave, *Rand Journal of Economics*, 24, 357–79.

Matten, D. and Moon, J. (2008) 'Implicit' and 'explicit' CSR: a conceptual framework for a comparative understanding of corporate social responsibility, *Academy of Management Review* 33, 404–24.

Maurizi, A., Moore, R.L. and Shepard, L. (1981) The impact of price advertising: the California eyewear market after one year, *Journal of Consumer Affairs*, 15, 290–300.

McAfee, R. and McMillan, J. (1987) Auctions and bidding, *Journal of Economic Literature*, 25, 699–738.

McAfee, R.P., Mialon, H. and Williams, W. (2004) What is a barrier to entry?, *American Economic Review*, 94, 461–5.

McCloughan, P. (1995) Simulation of industrial concentration, *Journal of Industrial Economics*, 43, 405–33.

McGahan, A.M. (1999) The performance of US corporations: 1981–1994, *Journal of Industrial Economics*, 47, 373–98.

McGahan, A.M. (2000) How industries evolve, *Business Strategy Review*, 11, 1–16.

McGahan, A.M. and Porter, M.E. (1997) How much does industry matter really?, *Strategic Management Journal*, 18, 15–30.

McGahan, A.M. and Porter, M.E. (1999) The persistence of shocks to profitability, *Review of Economics and Statistics*, 81, 143–53.

McGahan, A.M. and Porter, M.E. (2002) What do we know about the variance in accounting profitability?, *Management Science*, 48, 834–51.

McGahan, A.M. and Porter, M.E. (2003) The emergence and sustainability of abnormal profits, *Strategic Organization*, 1, 79–108.

McGee, J.S. (1958) Predatory price cutting: the Standard Oil (NJ) case, *Journal of Law and Economics*, 1, 137–69.

McGee, J. and Thomas, H. (1986) Strategic groups: theory, research and taxonomy, *Strategic Management Journal*, 7, 141–60.

Mead, W.S. (1969) Instantaneous merger profit motive, *Western Economic Journal*, 7, 295–306.

Mead, W.J., Moseidjord, A. and Sorensen, P. (1983) The rate of return earned by energy leases under cash bonus bidding in OCS oil and gas leases, *Energy Journal*, 4, 37–52.

Meeks, G. (1977) *Disappointing Marriage: A Study of the Gains from Merger*. Cambridge: Cambridge University Press.

Megginson, W.L. and Netter, J.M. (2001) From state to market: a survey of empirical studies on privatization, *Journal of Economic Literature*, 39, 321–89.

Megginson, W.L. and Netter, J.M. (2003) History and methods of privatization, in Parker, D. and Saal, D. (eds) *International Handbook on Privatization*. Cheltenham: Edward Elgar.

Mehran, H. and Rosenberg, J. (2008) The effects of employee stock options on bank investment choice, borrowing, and capital, *Federal Reserve Bank of New York Staff Reports* no. 305.

Mehran, H., Morrison, A. and Shapiro, J. (2011) Corporate governance and banks: what have we learned from the financial crisis? *Federal Reserve Bank of New York Staff Reports*, No. 502.

Melitz, J. (1965) Friedman and Machlup on testing economic assumptions, *Journal of Political Economy*, 73, 37–60.

Midgley, D.F., Morrison, P.D. and Roberts, J.H. (1992) The effect of network structure in industrial diffusion processes, *Research Policy*, 21, 533–52.

Milgrom, P. (1989) Auctions and bidding: a primer, *Journal of Economic Perspectives*, 3, 3–22.

Milgrom, P. (2004) *Putting Auction Theory To Work*. Cambridge: Cambridge University Press.

Milgrom, P. and Roberts, J. (1982) Predation, reputation, and entry deterrence, *Journal of Economic Theory*, 27, 280–312.

Milgrom, P. and Roberts, J. (1986) Price and advertising signals of product quality, *Journal of Political Economy*, 94, 796–821.

Milgrom, P. and Roberts, J. (1988) Economic theories of the firm: past, present, and future, *Canadian Journal of Economics*, 21, 444–58.

Milgrom, P. and Weber, R.J. (1982) A theory of auctions and competitive bidding, *Econometrica*, 50, 1485–527.

Miller, D. and Shamsie, J. (1996) The resource-based view of the firm in two environments: the Hollywood Film Studios from 1936 to 1965, *Academy of Management Journal*, 39, 519–43.

Millward, R. (1990) Productivity in the UK services sector: historical trends 1956–1985 and comparisons with the USA, *Oxford Bulletin of Economics and Statistics*, 52, 423–35.

Minehart, D. and Neeman, Z. (1999) Termination and coordination in partnerships, *Journal of Economics and Management Strategy*, 8, 191–221.

Mishkin, F.S. (2006) How big a problem is too big to fail? A review of Gary Stern and Ron Feldman's Too big to fail: the hazards of bank bailouts, *Journal of Economic Literature*, 44, 988–1004.

Mixon, F.G. (1994) The role of advertising in the market process: a survey, *International Journal of Advertising*, 13, 15–23.

Molyneux, P. and Shamroukh, N. (1996) Diffusion of financial innovations: the case of junk bonds and note issuance facilities, *Journal of Money, Credit and Banking*, 28, 502–22.

Molyneux, P. and Wilson, J.O.S. (2007) Developments in European banking, *Journal of Banking and Finance*, 31, 1906–10.

Molyneux, P., Lloyd-Williams, M. and Thornton, J. (1994) Competitive conditions in European banking, *Journal of Banking and Finance*, 18, 445–59.

Molyneux, R. and Thompson, D. (1987) Nationalised industry performance, *Fiscal Studies*, 8, 48–82.

Monbiot, G. (2011) The 1% are the very best destroyers of wealth the world has ever seen, The *Guardian*, 7 November 2011, http://www.guardian.co.uk/commentisfree/2011/nov/07/one-per-cent-wealth-destroyers.

Monopolies and Mergers Commission (1966) *Household Detergents: A Report on the Supply of Household Detergents*. London: HMSO.

Monopolies and Mergers Commission (1968) *Supply of Man-Made Cellulose Fibres*. London: HMSO.

Monopolies and Mergers Commission (1981) *Bicycles: A Report on T.I. Raleigh Industries*. London: HMSO.

Monopolies and Mergers Commission (1993) *A Report on the Supply of National Newspapers in England and Wales*, December 1993, Cm 2422.

Monopolies and Mergers Commission (1997) *London Clubs International and Capital Corporation PLC: A Report on the Merger Situation*. London: HMSO.

Monteverde, K. and Teece, D. (1982) Supplier switching costs and vertical integration in the automobile industry, *Bell Journal of Economics*, 13, 206–13.

Montgomery, C.A. and Wernerfelt, B. (1988) Diversification, Ricardian rents, and Tobin's q, *Rand Journal of Economics*, 19, 623–32.

Moore, J. (1983) Why privatise?, in Kay, J., Mayer, C. and Thompson, D. (eds) *Privatisation and Regulation: The UK Experience*. Oxford: Clarendon Press.

Moore, K. and Reid, S. (2008) The birth of brand: 4000 years of branding history, *Business History*, 50, 419–32.

Moore, T.G. (1986) US airline deregulation: its effect on passengers, capital and labour, *Journal of Law and Economics*, 29, 1–28.

Morosini, P. (2004) Industrial clusters, knowledge integration and performance, *World Development*, 32, 305–26.

Morrison, S.A. and Winston, C. (1987) Empirical implications of the contestability hypothesis, *Journal of Law of Economics*, 30, 53–66.

Mortimer, J.H. (2008) Vertical contracts in the video rental industry, *Review of Economic Studies*, 75, 165–99.

Moser, P. (2005) Do patent laws influence innovation? Evidence from nineteenth-century World's Fairs, *American Economic Review*, 95, 1214–36.

Moss, S. (1984) The history of the theory of the firm from Marshall to Robinson and Chamberlin: the source of positivism in economics, *Economica*, 51, 307–18.

Motta, M. (2004) *Competition Policy: Theory and Practice*. Cambridge: Cambridge University Press.

Mueller, D.C. (1969) A theory of conglomerate mergers, *Quarterly Journal of Economics*, 84, 643–59.

Mueller, D.C. (1977) The persistence of profits above the norm, *Economica*, 44, 369–80.

Mueller, D.C. (1986) *Profits in the Long Run*. Cambridge: Cambridge University Press.

Mueller, D.C. (1990) The persistence of profits in the United States, in Mueller, D.C. (ed.) *The Dynamics of Company Profits: An International Comparison*. Cambridge: Cambridge University Press.

Mueller, D.C. and Sirower, M.L. (2003) The causes of mergers: tests based on the gains to acquiring firms' shareholders and the size of premia, *Managerial and Decision Economics*, 24, 373–416.

Mund, V.A. and Wolf, R.H. (1971) *Industrial Organisation and Public Policy*. New York: Appleton-Century-Crofts.

Myers, G. (1994) *Predatory Behaviour in UK Competition Policy*, Office of Fair Trading, Research Paper 5. London: Office of Fair Trading.

Myers, S.C. (1977) Determinants of corporate borrowing, *Journal of Financial Economics*, 5, 147–75.

Myners, P. (2001) *Institutional Investment in the United Kingdom: A Review*. London: HM Treasury.

Myners, P. (2010) Break up Britain's uncompetitive big banks, *Financial Times*, 12 December.

Nalebuff, B. (2004) Bundling as an entry barrier, *Quarterly Journal of Economics*, 119, 159–87.

Narasimhan, C. (1988) Competitive promotional strategies, *Journal of Business*, 61, 427–49.

Nash, J.F. (1950) The bargaining problem, *Econometrica* 18, 155–62.

Nathan, A. and Neave, E.H. (1989) Competition and contestability in Canada's financial system: empirical results, *Canadian Journal of Economics*, 22, 576–94.

National Economic Research Associates (NERA) (1992) Market Definition in UK Competition Policy, *Office of Fair Trading Research Paper*, No. 1. London: Office of Fair Trading.

National Economic Research Associates (NERA) (2003) Switching costs. Part one: economic models and policy implications. *Office of Fair Trading Economic Discussion Papers*, No. 5. London: OFT.

Nawaz, M. (1997) The power of the puppy – does advertising deter entry? *London Economics – Competition and Regulation Bulletin*, 6, 1–7 April.

Nayle, T. (1984) Economic foundations of pricing, *Journal of Business*, 57, 23–39.

Needham, D. (1976) Entry barriers and non-price aspects of firms' behaviour, *Journal of Industrial Economics*, 25, 29–43.

Needham, D. (1978) *The Economics of Industrial Structure Conduct and Performance*. Edinburgh: Holt, Rinehart & Winston.

Nelson, M.N. (1922) *Open Price Associations*. Urbana, IL: University of Illinois.

Nelson, P. (1974a) The economic value of advertising, in Brozen, Y. (ed.) *Advertising and Society*. New York: New York University Press.

Nelson, P. (1974b) Advertising as information, *Journal of Political Economy*, 82, 729–54.

Nelson, P. (1975) The economic consequences of advertising, *Journal of Business*, 48, 213–41.

Nelson, P. (1978) Advertising as information once more, in Tuerck, D.C. (ed.) *Issues in Advertising: The Economics of Persuasion*. New York: New York University Press.

Nemoto, J. and Goto, M. (2002) Technological externalities and economics of vertical integration in the electric utility industry, *International Journal of Industrial Organisation*, 22, 67–81.

Neuberger, D. (1998) Industrial organization of banking: a review, *International Journal of the Economics of Business*, 5, 97–118.

Neumann, J. von and Morgenstern, O. (1944) *The Theory of Games and Economic Behaviour*. Princeton, NJ: Princeton University Press.

Neven, D.J. (1989) Strategic entry deterrence: recent developments in the economics of industry, *Journal of Economic Surveys*, 3, 213–33.

Nevins, A. (1953) *Study in Power: John D. Rockefeller*. New York: Scribner's.

Newberry, D. (2000) *Privatisation, Restructuring and Regulation of Network Utilities*. Cambridge, MA: MIT Press.

Newman, H.H. (1978) Strategic groups and the structure–performance relationship, *Review of Economics and Statistics*, 60, 417–27.

Nichols, L. (1985) Advertising and economic welfare, *American Economic Review*, 75, 213–18.

Nicodeme, G. and Sauner-Leroy, J.-B. (2007) Product market reforms and productivity: a review of the theoretical and empirical literature on the transmission channels, *Journal of Industry, Competition and Trade*, 7, 53–72.

Nicoletti, G. and Scarpetta, S. (2003) Regulation, productivity and growth: OECD evidence, OECD Economics Department Working Paper 347.

Nightingale, P. (2003) Pharamceuticals, in Johnson, P. (ed.) *Industries in Europe*. Cheltenham: Edward Elgar.

Noam, E. (2003) The media concentration debate, *Financial Times*, 31 July.

Nocke, V. and White, L. (2007) Do vertical mergers facilitate upstream collusion?, *American Economic Review*, 97, 1321–39.

Noll, R.G. (1974) Attendance and price setting, in Noll, R.G. (ed.) *Government and the Sports Business*. Washington, DC: Brooking Institution.

Notta, O. and Oustapassidis, K. (2001) Profitability and media advertising in Greek food manufacturing industries, *Review of Industrial Organization*, 18, 115–26.

Nyman, S. and Silbertson, A. (1978) The ownership and control of industry, *Oxford Economic Papers*, 30, 74–101.

Obi, C.P. (2003) Bank holding company expansion into nonbank functions: is the rise in systematic risk rewarded?, *Managerial Finance*, 29, 9–22.

Öberseder, M., Schlegelmilch, B.B. and Gruber, V. (2011) 'Why don't consumers care about CSR?': A qualitative study exploring the role of CSR in consumption decisions, *Journal of Business Ethics*, 104, 449–60.

O'Brien, D.P. and Swann, D. (1969) *Information Agreements, Competition and Efficiency*. London: Macmillan.

Odagiri, H. and Yamawaki, H. (1990) The persistence of profits in Japan, in Mueller D.C. (ed.) *The Dynamics of Company Profits: An International Comparison*. Cambridge: Cambridge University Press.

O'Donoghue, T., Scotchmer, S. and Thisse, J. (1998) Patent breadth, patent life, and the pace of technological progress, *Journal of Economics and Management Strategy*, 7, 1–32.

O'Hara, M., and Shaw, W. (1990) Deposit insurance and wealth effects: The benefit of being too big to fail, *Journal of Finance* 45, 1587–600.

OECD (1965) Glossary of terms relating to restrictive business practices, B-2. Paris: OECD.

OECD (1984) *Competition and Trade Policies*. Paris: OECD.

OECD (1989) *Predation*, www.oecd//dat/clp/Publications/PREDA.PDF, Paris.

OECD (1993) *Competition Policy and Vertical Restraints: Franchising Agreements*. Paris: OECD.

OECD (1998) *Report to the OECD on Corporate Governance: Improving Competitiveness and Access to Capital in Global Markets*. Paris: Business Sector Advisory Group, OECD.

OECD (2004) *Principles of Corporate Governance*. Paris: OECD.

OECD (2005) *OECD Guiding Principles for Regulatory Policy and Governance*. Paris: OECD.

OECD (2009) *Corporate Governance and the Financial Crisis: Key Findings and Main Messages*. Paris: OECD.

Office of Fair Trading (OFT) (1994) *Predatory Behaviour in UK Competition Policy*, Research Paper No. 5. London: Office of Fair Trading.

Office of Fair Trading (OFT) (1999) *Quantitative Techniques in Competition Analysis*. London: Office of Fair Trading.

Office of Fair Trading (OFT) (2002a) *BSkyB: The Outcome of the OFT's Competition Act Investigation, December 2002*, OFT62. London: Office of Fair Trading.

Office of Fair Trading (OFT) (2002b) *Predation by Aberdeen Journals Limited*, CE/127-02. London: Office of Fair Trading.

Office of Fair Trading (OFT) (2003) *The Control of Entry Regulations and Retail Pharmacy Services in the UK*. London: Office of Fair Trading.

Office of Fair Trading (2007) *The Deterrent Effect of Competition Enforcement by the OFT*, OFT962, London: Office of Fair Trading.

Office of Fair Trading (2010) *Review of Barriers to Entry, Expansion and Exit in Retail Banking*. London: HMSO.

Ogus, A.I. (1996) *Regulation: Legal Form and Economic Theory*. Oxford: Oxford University Press.

Oi, W.Y. (1971) A Disneyland dilemma: two-part tariffs for a Mickey Mouse monopoly, *Quarterly Journal of Economics*, 85, 77–96.

Oi, W.Y. and Hunter Jr, A.P. (1965) *Economics of Private Truck Transportation*. New York: William C. Brown.

Ordover, J.A. (2008) Predatory pricing, in Durlauf, S.N. and Blume, L.E. (eds) *The New Palgrave Dictionary of Economics*, 2nd edition. London: Palgrave Macmillan.

Ordover, J., Saloner, G. and Salop, S. (1990) Equilibrium vertical foreclosure, *American Economic Review*, 80, 127–42.

Orlitzky, M., Schmidt, F.L. and Rynes, S.L. (2003) Corporate social and financial performance: a meta-analysis. *Organization Studies*, 24, 403–41.

Ornstein, S.I. (1985) Resale price maintenance and cartels, *Antitrust Bulletin*, 30, 401–32.

Orr, D. (1974) The determinants of entry: a study of the Canadian manufacturing industries, *Review of Economics and Statistics*, 56, 58–65.

Orts, E.W. and Strudler, A. (2009) Putting a stake in stakeholder theory, *Journal of Business Ethics*, 88, 605–15.

Osborne, D.K. (1976) Cartel problems, *American Economic Review*, 66, 835–44.

Oster, S.M. (1999) *Modern Competitive Analysis*, 3rd edition. New York: Oxford University Press.

Owen, S. (2006) The history and mystery of merger waves: a UK and US perspective, School of Banking and Finance, University of New South Wales, Working Paper No. 2006-02.

Ozanich, G.W., Hsu, C-W. and Park, H.W. (2004) 3G wireless auctions as an economic barrier to entry: the western European experience, *Telmatics and Informatics*, 21, 225 35.

Pakes, A. (2003) Common sense and simplicity in empirical industrial organization, *Review of Industrial Organization*, 23, 193–213.

Pan, X., Ratchford, B.T. and Shankar, V. (2004) Price dispersion on the internet: a review and directions for future research, *Journal of Interactive Marketing*, 18, 116–35.

Panthan, S. (2009) Strong boards, CEO power and bank risk taking, *Journal of Banking & Finance*, 33, 1340–50.

Panzar, J.C. and Rosse, J.N. (1982) Structure, conduct and comparative statistics, *Bell Laboratories Economics Discussion Paper*. Stanford, CA: Bell Laboratories.

Panzar, J.C. and Rosse, J.N. (1987) Testing for monopoly equilibrium, *Journal of Industrial Economics*, 35, 443–56.

Parker, D. (1991) Privatisation ten years on, *Economics*, 27, 155–63.

Parker, D. (1994) A decade of privatisation: the effect of ownership change and competition on British Telecom, *British Review of Economic Issues*, 16, 87–115.

Parker, D. (2000) *Privatization and Corporate Performance*. Cheltenham: Edward Elgar.

Parker, D. (2003a) Privatization in the European Union, in Parker, D. and Saal, D. (eds) *International Handbook on Privatization*. Cheltenham: Edward Elgar.

Parker, D. (2003b) Privatization and the regulation of public utilities: problems and challenges for developing economies, in Parker, D. and Saal, D. (eds) *International Handbook on Privatization*. Cheltenham: Edward Elgar.

Parker, D. and Martin, S. (1995) The impact of UK privatisation on labour and total factor productivity, *Scottish Journal of Political Economy*, 42, 201–20.

Parker, D. and Wu, H.L. (1998) Privatisation and performance: a study of the British Steel industry under public and private ownership, *Economic Issues*, 3, 31–50.

Parsons, P. (2003) Horizontal integration in the cable television industry: history and context, *Journal of Media Economics*, 16, 23–40.

Patel, P. and Pavitt, K. (1995) Patterns of technological activity: their measurement and interpretation, in Stoneman, P. (ed.) *Handbook of the Economics of Innovation and Technical Change*. Oxford: Blackwell.

Patinkin, D. (1947) Multiple-plant firms, cartels, and imperfect competition, *Quarterly Journal of Economics*, 61, 173–205.

Paton, D. (1998) Who advertises prices? A firm level study based on survey data, *International Journal of the Economics of Business*, 5, 57–75.

Paton, D. (2008) Advertising as an entry deterrent: evidence from UK firms, *International Journal of the Economics of Business*, 15, 63–83.

Paton, D. and Vaughan Williams, L. (1999) Advertising and firm performance: some evidence from UK firms, *Economic Issues*, 4, 89–105.

Pautler, P.A. (2003) Evidence on mergers and acquisitions, *Antitrust Bulletin*, 48, 119–221.

Pavitt, K.L.R. (2001) Public policies to support basic research: what can the rest of the world learn from US theory and practice? (And what they should not learn), *Industrial and Corporate Change*, 10, 761–79.

Pekar Jr, P. and Margulis, M.S. (2003) Equity alliances take center stage, *Business Strategy Review*, 14, 50–62.

Peltzman, S. (1976) Toward a more general theory of regulation, *Journal of Law and Economics*, 2, 211–40.

Peltzman, S. (1989) The economic theory of regulation after a decade of deregulation, *Brooking Papers on Economic Activity: Microeconomics*, 5, 1–41.

Peltzman, S. (2000) Prices rise faster than they fall, *Journal of Political Economy*, 108, 466–502.

Penrose, E. (1959) *The Theory of the Growth of the Firm*, London: Basil Blackwell.

Penrose, E. (1995) *The Theory of the Growth of the Firm*, 3rd edition. Oxford: Oxford University Press.

Perrigne, I. and Vuong, Q. (2008) Auctions (empirics), in Durlauf, S.N. and Blume, L.E. (eds) *New Palgrave Dictionary of Economics*, 2nd edition. London: Palgrave Macmillan.

Perry, M.K. (1980) Forward integration by Alcoa: 1888–1930, *Journal of Industrial Economics*, 29, 37–53.

Pesendorfer, M. (2003) Horizontal mergers in the paper industry, *Rand Journal of Economics*, 34, 495–515.

Peston, M.H. (1959) On the sales maximisation hypothesis, *Economica*, 26, 128–36.

Phelan, S.E. and Lewis, P. (2000) Arriving at a strategic theory of the firm, *International Journal of Management Reviews*, 2, 305–23.

Phillips, A. (1962) *Market Structure, Organisation and Performance*. Cambridge, MA: Harvard University Press.

Phillips, A. (1972) An econometric study of price-fixing, market structure and performance in British industry in the early 1950s, in Cowling, K. (ed.) *Market Structures and Corporate Behaviour: Theory and Empirical Analysis of the Firm*. London: Gray Mills, 177–92.

Phillips, A. (1976) A critique of empirical studies of relations between market structure and profitability, *Journal of Industrial Economics*, 24, 241–9.

Phlips, L. (1983) *The Economics of Price Discrimination*. Cambridge: Cambridge University Press.

Phlips, L. (ed.) (1998) *Applied Industrial Economics*. Cambridge: Cambridge University Press, Sections II and III.

Phlips, L. and Thisse, J.-F. (1982) Spatial competition and the theory of differentiated markets, *Journal of Industrial Economics*, 31, 1–9.

Pickering, J.F. (1982) The economics of anticompetitive practices, *European Competition Law Review*, 3, 253–74.

Pigou, A.C. (1920) *Economics of Welfare*. London: Macmillan.

Pindyck, R.S. (1977) Cartel pricing and the structure of the world bauxite market, *Rand Journal of Economics*, 8, 343–60.

Pinkston, T.S. and Carroll, A.B. (1994). Corporate citizenship perspectives and foreign direct investment in the US, *Journal of Business Ethics*, 13, 157–69.

Piotrowski, R. (1932) *Cartels and Trusts*. London: Allen & Unwin.

Pissaris, S., Jeffus, W. and Gleaso, K. (2010) The joint impact of executive pay disparity and corporate governance on corporate performance, *Journal of Managerial Issues*, 22, 306–29.

Plender, J. (2003) Restoring trust after the bubble, *Business Economics*, 38, 21–4.

Plott, C.R. (1989) An updated review of industrial organization: applications to experimental methods, in Schmalensee, R.C. and Willig, R. (eds) *Handbook of Industrial Organization*, Vol. 2. Amsterdam: Elsevier.

Porter, M.E. (1976) Interbrand choice, media mix and market performance, *American Economic Review*, 66, 398–406.

Porter, M.E. (1979a) How competitive forces shape strategy, *Harvard Business Review*, July–August, 1–10.

Porter, M.E. (1979b) The structure within industries and companies performance, *Review of Economics and Statistics*, 61, 214–27.

Porter, M.E. (1980) *Competitive Strategy: Techniques for Analysing Industries and Competitors*. New York: The Free Press.

Porter, M.E. (1985) *Competitive Advantage: Creating and Sustaining Superior Performance*. New York: The Free Press.

Porter, M.E. (1987) From competitive advantage to corporate strategy, *Harvard Business Review*, May–June, 43–59.

Porter, M.E. (1990) *The Competitive Advantage of Nations*. New York: The Free Press.

Porter, M.E. (1996) What is strategy?, *Harvard Business Review*, 74, 61–78.

Porter, M.E. (1998a) Locations, clusters and company strategy, in Clark, G.L., Feldman, M.P. and Gertler, M.S. (eds) *Oxford Handbook of Economic Geography*. Oxford: Oxford University Press.

Porter, M.E. (1998b) Clusters and the new economics of competition, *Harvard Business Review*, 76, 77–90.

Porter, M.E. (2001) Regions and the new economics of competition, in Scott, A.J. (ed.) *Global-city Regions: Trends, Theory, Policy*. Oxford: Oxford University Press.

Porter, M.E. and Kramer, M.R. (2006) Strategy and society: the link between competitive advantage and corporate social responsibility, *Harvard Business Review*, 84, 78–92.

Porter, M.E. and Sovall, O. (1998) The role of geography in the process of innovation and the sustainable competitive advantage of firms, in Chandler, A., Hagstrom, P. and Sovell, O. (eds) *The Dynamic Firm: The Role of Technology Strategy, Organizations and Regions*. New York: Oxford University Press.

Porter, R.H. (1983) A study of cartel stability: the Joint Executive Committee, 1880–1886, *Bell Journal of Economics*, 14, 301–14.

Posner, R.A. (1976) *Antitrust Law – An Economic Perspective*. Chicago, IL: University of Chicago Press.

Posner, R.A. (1979) The Chicago school of antitrust analysis, *University of Pennsylvania Law Review*, 127, 925–48.

Posner, R.A. (1981) The next step in the antitrust treatment of restricted distribution – per se legality, *University of Chicago Law Review*, 48, 6–26.

Prager, J. (1994) Contracting out government services: lessons from the private sector, *Public Administration Review*, 54, 176–84.

Prahalad, C.K. and Hamel, G. (1990) The core competence of the corporation, *Harvard Business Review*, 68, 79–91.

Prais, S. (1976) *The Evolution of Giant Firms in Britain*, National Institute of Economic and Social Research, Economic and Social Studies, 30. Cambridge: Cambridge University Press.

Pratt, J., Wise, D. and Zechauser, R. (1979) Price differences in almost competitive markets. *Quarterly Journal of Economics*, 93, 189–211.

Pratten, C.F. (1988) A survey of the economies of scale, in *Research on the Costs of Non-Europe*, Vol. 2. Luxembourg: Office for Official Publications of the European Communities.

Price, C. and Weyman-Jones, T.G. (1993) *Malmquist Indices of Productivity Change in the UK Gas Industry Before and After Privatisation*, Department of Economics, Research Paper 93/12, Loughborough University.

Price Waterhouse (1989) *Privatization: Learning the Lessons from the UK Experience*. London: Price Waterhouse.

Prokop, J. (1999) Process of dominant-cartel formation, *International Journal of Industrial Organisation*, 17, 241–57.

Pryke, R. (1981) *The Privatised Industries: Policies and Performance since 1968*. Oxford: Martin Robertson.

Pryke, R. (1982) The comparative performance of public and private enterprise, *Fiscal Studies*, 3, 68–81.

Pryor, F.L. (2001a) New trends in US industrial concentration, *Review of Industrial Organization*, 18, 301–26.

Pryor, F.L. (2001b) Dimensions of the worldwide merger boom, *Journal of Economic Issues*, 35, 825–40.

Pryor, F.L. (2002) News from the monopoly front: changes in industrial concentration, 1992–1997, *Review of Industrial Organization*, 20, 183–5.

Quandt, R.E. (1966) On the size distribution of firms, *American Economic Review*, 56, 416–32.

Radice, H.K. (1971) Control type, profitability and growth in large firms: an empirical study, *Economic Journal*, 81, 547–62.

Ravenscraft, D.J. (1983) Structure–profit relationships at the line of business and industry level, *Review of Economics and Statistics*, 65, 22–31.

Ravenscraft, D.J. and Scherer, F. (1987) *Mergers, Sell Offs and Economic Efficiency*. Washington, DC: The Brookings Institution.

Reder, M.W. (1982) Chicago economics: permanence and change, *Journal of Economic Literature*, 20, 1–38.

Reekie, W.D. (1975) Advertising and market structure: another approach, *Economic Journal*, 85, 156–64.

Rees, R. (1984) *Public Enterprise Economics*. London: Weidenfeld & Nicolson.

Rees, R. (1993a) Collusive equilibrium in the great salt duopoly, *Economic Journal*, 103, 833–48.

Rees, R. (1993b) Tacit collusion, *Oxford Review of Economic Policy*, 9, 27–40.

Reid, G.C. (1987) *Theories of Industrial Organization*. Oxford: Blackwell.

Reid, G.C. (1992) *Small Firm Growth and its Determinants*, Department of Economics Discussion Paper No. 9213. University of St Andrews.

Reinganum, J. (1979) A simple model of price dispersion, *Journal of Political Economy*, 87, 851–8.

Rey, P. (2002) Collective dominance in the telecommunications industry, University of Toulouse, mimeograph, http://europa.eu.int/comm/competition/antitrust/others/telecom/collective_dominance.pdf.

Rey, P. and Tirole, J. (1986) The logic of vertical restraints, *American Economic Review*, 76, 921–39.

Rey, P. and Tirole, J. (2007) A primer on foreclosure, in Armstrong, M. and Porter, R.H. (eds) *Handbook of Industrial Organization*, Vol. 3. Amsterdam: Elsevier.

Robbins, L. (1932) *An Essay on the Nature and Significance of Economic Science*. New York: New York University Press.

Roberts, B. and Thompson, S. (2003) Entry and exit in a transition economy: the case of Poland, *Review of Industrial Organization*, 22, 225–43.

Roberts, P. and Eisenhardt, K. (2003) Austrian insights on strategic organization: from market insights to implications for firms, *Strategic Organization*, 1, 345–52.

Robertson, D.H. (1930) *Control of Industry*, Cambridge Economic Handbooks, 4. London: Nisbet.

Robertson, P.L. and Langlois, R.L. (1995) Innovation, networks, and vertical integration, *Research Policy*, 24, 543–62.

Robinson, J. (1933) *The Economics of Imperfect Competition*. London: Macmillan.

Robinson, J. (1969) *The Economics of Imperfect Competition*, 2nd edition. London: Macmillan.

Robinson, W.T. and Chiang, J. (1996) Are Sutton's predictions robust? Empirical insights into advertising, R&D and concentration, *Journal of Industrial Economics*, 44, 389–408.

Robinson, W.T., Kalyanaram, G. and Urban, G.L. (1994) First-mover advantages from pioneering new markets: a survey of empirical evidence, *Review of Industrial Organisation*, 9, 1–23.

Roll, R. (1986) The hubris hypothesis of corporate takeovers, *Journal of Business*, 59, 197–216.

Roller, L. and Steen, F. (2006) On the workings of a cartel: evidence from the Norwegian cement industry, *American Economic Review*, 96, 321–38.

Roller, L., Stennek, J. and Verboven, F. (2001) Efficiency gains from mergers, Centre for Economic Policy Research, Report for EC Contract II/98/003. London: Centre for Economic Policy Research.

Rondi, L., Sembenelli, A. and Ragazzi, E. (1996) Determinants of diversification patterns, in Davies, S. and Lyons, B. (eds) *Industrial Organisation in the European Union*. Oxford: Oxford University Press, Ch. 10.

Roquebert, J.A., Phillips, R.L. and Westfall, P.A. (1996) Markets versus management: what drives profitability?, *Strategic Management Journal*, 17, 653–64.

Rose, N.L. and Shepard, A. (1997) Firm diversification and CEO compensation: managerial ability or executive entrenchment?, *Rand Journal of Economics*, 28, 489–514.

Rosen, S. and Rosenfield, A. (1997) Ticket pricing, *Journal of Law & Economics*, 40, 351–76.

Rosenthal, R.W. (1980) A model in which an increase in the number of sellers leads to an increase in price, *Econometrica*, 48, 1575–80.

Ross, T.W. (1992) Cartel stability and product differentiation, *International Journal of Industrial Organisation*, 10, 1–13.

Rosse, J. and Panzar, J. (1977) *Chamberlin versus Robinson: An Empirical Test of Monopoly Rents, Studies in Industry Economics*, Research Paper No. 77. Stanford, CA: Stanford University Press.

Rossi, S. and Volpin, P.F. (2004) Cross-country determinants of mergers and acquisitions, *Journal of Financial Economics*, 74, 277–304.

Rotemberg, J.J. and Saloner, G. (1986) A supergame-theoretic model of price wars during booms, *American Economic Review*, 76, 390–407.

Roth, A.E. (1991) Game theory as a part of empirical economics, *Economic Journal*, 101, 107–14.

Rothschild, K. (1947) Price theory and oligopoly, *Economic Journal*, 57, 299–302.

Rothschild, M. (1973) Models of market organization with imperfect information: a survey, *Journal of Political Economy*, 81, 1233–308.

Rothschild, R. (1981) Cartel problems: a note. *American Economic Review*, 71, 179–81.

Rothschild, R. (1999) Cartel stability when costs are heterogeneous, *International Journal of Industrial Organisation*, 17, 717–34.

Rothwell, G. (1980) Market coordination by the uranium oxide industry, *Antitrust Bulletin*, 25, 233–68.

Rotwein, E. (1962) On the methodology of positive economics, *Quarterly Journal of Economics*, 73, 554–75.

Rovizzi, L. and Thompson, D. (1995) The regulation of product quality in public utilities, in Bishop, M., Kay, J. and Mayer, C. (eds) *The Regulatory Challenge*. Oxford: Oxford University Press.

Rubinfeld, D.I. and Singer, H.J. (2001) Vertical foreclosure on broadband access? *Journal of Industrial Economics*, 49, 299–318.

Rudholm, N. (2001) Entry and the number of firms in the Swedish pharmacuticals market, *Review of Industrial Organization*, 19, 351–64.

Ruefli, T.W. and Wiggins, R.R. (2003) Industry, firm and business unit effects on performance: a non-parametric approach, *Strategic Management Journal*, 24, 861–79.

Rumelt, R.P. (1974) *Strategy, Structure and Economic Performance*. Boston, MA: Harvard Business School.

Rumelt, R.P. (1984) Towards a strategic theory of the firm, in Lamb, R.B. (ed.) *Competitive Strategic Management*. Englewood Cliffs, NJ: Prentice Hall, 556–70.

Rumelt, R.P. (1991) How much does industry matter?, *Strategic Management Journal*, 12, 167–86.

Rydén, B. and Edberg, J. (1980) Large mergers in Sweden, 1962–1976, in Mueller, D.C. (ed.) *The Determinants and Effects of Mergers: An International Comparison*. Cambridge, MA: Oelgeschlager, Gun & Hanin.

Saal, D. (2003) Restructuring, regulation and the liberalization of privatised utilities in the UK, in Parker, D. and Saal, D. (eds) *International Handbook on Privatization*. Cheltenham: Edward Elgar.

Saha, S. (2007) Consumer preferences and product and process R&D, *RAND Journal of Economics*, 38, 250–68.

Salop, S. (1979) Monopolistic competition with outside goods, *Bell Journal of Economics*, 10, 141–56.

Salop, S. and Stiglitz, J.E. (1977) Bargains and ripoffs: a model of monopolistically competitive price dispersion, *Review of Economic Studies*, 44, 493–510.

Salter, A. and Martin, B.R. (2001) The economic benefits of publicly funded basic research: a critical review, *Research Policy*, 30, 509–32.

Salvanes, K.G., Steen, F. and Sorgard, L. (2004) Hotelling in the air? Flight departures in Norway, *Regional Science and Urban Economics*, 35, 193–213.

Samuals, J.M. (1965) Size and growth of firms, *Review of Economic Studies*, 32, 105–12.

Samuals, J.M. and Chesher, A.D. (1972) Growth, survival, and size of companies, 1960–69, in Cowling, K. (ed.) *Market Structure and Corporate Behaviour*. London: Gray–Mills.

Sandy, R., Sloane, P.J. and Rosentraub, M.S. (2004) *The Economics of Sport: An International Perspective*. Basingstoke: Palgrave Macmillan.

Santalo, J. and Becerra, M. (2008) Competition from specialized firms and the diversification–performance linkage, *Journal of Finance*, 63, 851–83.

Sargent, F.P. (1933) *The Logic of Industrial Organization*. London: Kegan Paul.

Sargent, F.P. (1961) *Ownership, Control and Success of Large Companies*. London: Sweet and Maxwell.

Sawyer, M.C. (1985) *The Economics of Industries and Firms*, 2nd edition. London: Croom-Helm.

Scellato, G. (2007) Patents, firm size and financial constraints; an empirical analysis for a panel of Italian manufacturing firms, *Cambridge Journal of Economics*, 31, 55–72.

Schaeck, K., Čihák, M., Maechler, A. and Stolz, S. (2012) Who disciplines bank managers? *Review of Finance*, 16, 197–243.

Schankerman, M. (1998) How valuable is patent protection? Estimates by technology field, *Rand Journal of Economics*, 29, 77–107.

Scharfstein, D.S. (1998) *The Dark Side of Internal Capital Markets*, 2, NBER Working Paper No. 6352.

Schary, M.A. (1991) The probability of exit, *Rand Journal of Economics*, 22, 339–53.

Scherer, F.M. (1965) Firm size, market structure, opportunity and the output of patented inventions, *American Economic Review*, 55, 1097–125.

Scherer, F.M. (1967) Research and development resource allocation under rivalry, *Quarterly Journal of Economics*, 81, 359–94.

Scherer, F.M. (1980) *Industrial Market Structure and Economic Performance*, 2nd edition. Chicago, IL: Rand McNally.

Scherer, F.M. (1992) Schumpeter and plausible capitalism, *Journal of Economic Literature*, 30, 1416–33.

Scherer, F.M. and Ross, D. (1990) *Industrial Market Structures and Economic Performance*, 3rd edition. Boston, MA: Houghton Mifflin.

Schiantarelli, F. (2008) Product market regulation and macroeconomic performance: a review of cross country evidence, *Boston College Working Papers in Economics*. No. 623.

Schmalensee, R.C. (1972) *The Economics of Advertising*. Amsterdam: North-Holland.

Schmalensee, R.C. (1978) Entry deterrence in the ready-to-eat cereal industry, *Bell Journal of Economics*, 9, 305–27.

Schmalensee, R.C. (1979) *The Control of Natural Monopolies*. Lexington, MA: DC Heath.

Schmalensee, R. (1981) Monopolistic two-part pricing arrangements, *Bell Journal of Economics*, 12, 445–66.

Schmalensee, R.C. (1982) Antitrust and the new industrial economics, *American Economic Review*, Papers and Proceedings, 72, 24–8.

Schmalensee, R.C. (1985) Do markets differ much? *American Economic Review*, 74, 341–51.

Schmalensee, R.C. (1987) Competitive advantage and collusive optima, *International Journal of Industrial Organization*, 5, 351–67.

Schmalensee, R.C. (1988) Industrial economics: an overview, *Economic Journal*, 98, 643–81.

Schmalensee, R.C. (1989) Inter-industry studies of structure and performance, in Schmalensee, R.C. and Willig, R.D. (eds) *Handbook of Industrial Organization*, Vol. 2. Amsterdam: North-Holland, Ch. 16.

Schmalensee, R.C. (1990) Empirical studies of rivalrous behaviour, in Bonanno, G. and Brandolini, D. (eds) *Industrial Structure in the New Industrial Economics*. Oxford: Clarendon Press.

Schmalensee, R.C. (1992) Sunk costs and market structure: a review article, *Journal of Industrial Economics*, 40, 125–34.

Schmid, M. and Walter, I. (2012) Geographical diversification and firm value in the financial sector, *Journal of Empirical Finance*, 19, 109–22.

Schohl, F. (1990) Persistence of profits in the long-run: a critical extension of some recent findings, *International Journal of Industrial Organisation*, 8, 385–403.

Scholten, P. and Smith, M. (2002) Price dispersion then and now: evidence from retail and e-tail markets, *Advances in Microeconomics: Economics of the Internet and e-Commerce*, 11, 63–88.

Scholtens, B. and L. Dam. (2007) Banking on the Equator. Are banks adopting the Equator principles different from non-adoptors? *World Development*, 35, 1307–28.

Schumpeter, J. (1928) The instability of capitalism, *Economic Journal*, 30, 361–86.

Schumpeter, J. (1942) *Capitalism, Socialism, and Democracy*. New York: HarperCollins.

Schwalbach, J. (1991) Entry, exit, concentration and market contestability, in Geroski, P.A. and Schwalbach, J. (eds) *Entry and Market Contestability: An International Comparison*. Oxford: Blackwell.

Schwalbach, J., Grasshoff, V. and Mahmood, T. (1989) The dynamics of corporate profits, *European Economic Review*, 33, 1625–30.

Schwartz, B. (2004) *The Paradox of Choice: Why More is Less*. New York: HarperCollins.

Schwartz, M. (1986) The nature and scope of contestability theory, *Oxford Economic Papers* (Special Supplement), 38, 37–57.

Schwartz, M. and Reynolds, R. (1983) Contestable markets: an uprising in industry structure: comment, *American Economic Review*, 73, 488–90.

Schwartzman, D. (1963) Uncertainty and the size of the firm, *Economica*, 30, 287–96.

Schwed, F. (1955) *Where are the Customers' Yachts?* New York: John Wiley.

Schwert, W.G. (1996) Markup pricing in mergers and acquisitions, *Journal of Financial Economics*, 29, 153–92.

Scitovsky, T. (1950) Ignorance as a source of monopoly power, *American Economic Review*, 40, 48–53.

Scitovsky, T. (1971) *Welfare and Competition* (revised edition). London: Allen & Unwin.

Scotchmer, S. (1991) Standing on the shoulders of giants: cumulative research and the patent law, *Journal of Economic Perspectives*, 5, 29–41.

Scott, J.T. and Pascoe, G. (1986) Beyond firm and industry effects on profitability in imperfect markets, *Review of Economics and Statistics*, 68, 284–92.

Scott Morton, F.M. (2000) Barriers to entry, brand advertising, and generic entry in the US pharmaceutical industry, *International Journal of Industrial Organization*, 18, 1085–104.

Sedgewick, J. (2002) Product differentiation at the movies: Hollywood, 1946 to 1965, *Journal of Economic History*, 62, 676–705.

Sen, A. (1993) Does business ethics make economic sense, *Business Ethics Quarterly*, 3, 45–54.

Sena, V. (2004) The return of the Prince of Denmark: a survey on recent developments in the economics of innovation, *Economic Journal*, 114, 312–32.

Servaes, H. (1996) The value of diversification during the conglomerate merger wave, *Journal of Finance*, 51, 1201–25.

Shaffer, S. (1982) A non-structural test for competition in financial markets, in *Bank Structure and Competition*, Conference Proceedings. Chicago, IL: Federal Reserve Bank.

Shaffer, S. (2001) Banking conduct before the European single banking license: a cross country comparison, *North American Journal of Economics and Finance*, 12, 79–104.

Shaffer, S. and DiSalvo, J. (1994) Conduct in a banking duopoly, *Journal of Banking and Finance*, 18, 1063–82.

Shaw, W.H. (2009) Marxism, business ethics and corporate social responsibility, *Journal of Business Ethics*, 84, 565–76.

Shelanski, H.A. and Klein, P.G. (1995) Empirical research in transaction cost economics: a review and assessment, *Journal of Law, Economics and Organisation*, 11, 335–61.

Shen, C.-H. and Chang, Y. (2012) Corporate social responsibility, financial performance and selection bias: Evidence from TWSE-listing banks of Taiwan, in Barth, J.R., Lin, C. and Whilborg, C. (eds) *Research Handbook for Banking and Governance*, Cheltenham: Edward Elgar Publishing.

Shepherd, W.G. (1972) Structure and behaviour in British industries with US comparisons, *Journal of Industrial Economics*, 20, 35–54.

Shepherd, W.G. (1997) *The Economics of Industrial Organisation*. Englewood Cliffs, NJ: Prentice Hall.

Sherman, R. (1977) Theory comes to industrial organisation, in Jacquemin, A. and de Jong, H.W. (eds) *Welfare Aspects of Industrial Markets*. Amsterdam: Martinus Nijhoff.

Sherman, R. (1985) The Averch and Johnson analysis of public utility regulation twenty years later, *Review of Industrial Organization*, 1, 178–91.

Shipley, D. (1981) Primary objectives in British manufacturing industry, *Journal of Industrial Economics*, 29, 4, 429–43.

Shleifer, A. (1985) A theory of yardstick competition, *Rand Journal of Economics*, 16, 319–27.

Shleifer, A. and Vishny, R.W. (1997) A survey of corporate governance, *Journal of Finance*, 52, 737–83.

Shy, O. (2010) A short survey of network economics, *Federal Reserve Bank of Boston Working Paper No. 10–3*.

Siegel, D. and Vitaliano, D.F. (2007) An empirical analysis of the strategic use of corporate social responsibility, *Journal of Economics & Management Strategy*, 16, 773–92.

Siegfried, J.A. and Evans, L. (1994) Empirical studies of entry and exit: a survey of the evidence, *Review of Industrial Organisation*, 9, 121–55.

Siggelkow, N. (2003) Why focus? A study of intra-industry focus effects, *Journal of Industrial Economics*, 51, 121–50.

Silberman, I.H. (1967) On lognormality as a summary measure of concentration, *American Economic Review*, 57, 807–31.

Simon, H.A. (1947) *Administrative Behavior*. New York: Macmillan.

Simon, H.A. (1959) Theories of decision-making in economics and behavioural science, *American Economic Review*, 49, 253–83.

Simon, H.A. and Bonini, C.P. (1958) The size distribution of business firms, *American Economic Review*, 48, 607–17.

Simpson, W.G. and Kohers, T. (2002) The link between corporate social and financial performance: evidence from the banking industry, *Journal of Business Ethics*, 35, 97–109.

Singer, E.M. (1968) *Antitrust Economics*. Englewood Cliffs, NJ: Prentice Hall.

Singh, A. (1971) *Takeovers*. Cambridge: Cambridge University Press.

Singh, A. and Whittington, G. (1975) The size and growth of firms, *Review of Economic Studies*, 42, 15–26.

Singh, S., Utton, M.A. and Waterson, M. (1998) Strategic behaviour of incumbent firms in the UK, *International Journal of Industrial Organization*, 16, 229–51.

Skaggs, B.C. and Droege, S.B. (2004) The performance effects of service diversification by manufacturing firms, *Journal of Managerial Issues*, 16, 396–407.

Slade, M. (2004) Competing models of firm profitability, *International Journal of Industrial Organization*, 22, 289–308.

Sleuwaegen, L. and Dehandschutter, W. (1991) Entry and exit in Belgian manufacturing, in Geroski, P.A. and Schwalbach, J. (eds) *Entry and Market Contestability: An International Comparison*. Oxford: Blackwell.

Smiley, R. (1988) Empirical evidence on strategic entry deterrence, *International Journal of Industrial Organisation*, 6, 167–80.

Smirlock, M., Gilligan, T.W. and Marshall, W. (1984) Tobin's q and the structure–performance relationship, *American Economic Review*, 74, 1051–60.

Smith, A. (1759) *The Theory of Moral Sentiments*, http://files.libertyfund.org/files/192/0141-01_Bk.pdf. Accessed 25 January 2012.

Smith, A. (1776) *An Inquiry into the Nature and Causes of the Wealth of Nations*. New York: Modern Library (1937).

Smith, N.C., Read, D. and López-Rodríguez, S. (2010) Consumer perceptions of corporate social responsibility: The CSR halo effect, INSEAD Working Papers Collection 16, p1–22.

Smith, R. (2003) *Audit Committees: Combined Code Guidance*. London: Financial Reporting Council.

Smith, V. (1989) Theory, experiment and economics, *Journal of Economic Perspectives*, Winter, 2, 151–69.

Snow, D. (2008) Beware of old technologies' last gasp, *Harvard Business Review*, 86, 17–18.

Snyder, C.M. (1996) A dynamic theory of countervailing power, *Rand Journal of Economics*, 27, 747–69.

Solberg, E.J. (1992) *Microeconomics for Business Decisions*. Lexington, MA: D.C. Heath.

Sorenson, A.T. (2000) Equilibrium price dispersion in retail markets for prescription drugs, *Journal of Political Economy*, 108, 833–50.

Sosnick, S.H. (1958) A critique of concepts of workable competition, *Quarterly Journal of Economics*, 72, 380–423.

Spanos, Y., Zaralis, G. and Lioukas, S. (2004) Strategy and industry effects on profitability: evidence from Greece, *Strategic Management Journal*, 25, 139–65.

Spector, D. (2007) Bundling, tying and collusion, *International Journal of Industrial Organization*, 25, 575–81.

Spence, M. (1981) The learning curve and competition, *Bell Journal of Economics*, 12, 49–70.

Spengler, J.J. (1950) Vertical integration and antitrust policy, *Journal of Political Economy*, 68, 347–52.

Spiller, P.T. (1985) On vertical mergers, *Journal of Law, Economics and Organisation*, 1, 285–312.

Spulber, D.F. (1992) Economic analysis and management strategy, a survey, *Journal of Economics and Management Strategy*, 1, 535–74.

Spulber, D.F. (1994) Economic analysis and management strategy, a survey continued, *Journal of Economics and Management Strategy*, 3, 355–406.

Spulber, D.F. (1995) Bertrand competition when rivals' costs are unknown, *Journal of Industrial Economics*, 43, 1–11.

Spulber, D.F. (2003) Entry barriers and entry strategies, *Journal of Strategic Management Education*, 1, 55–80.

Sraffa, P. (1926) The laws of returns under competitive conditions, *Economic Journal*, 36, 535–50.

Stackelberg, H. von (1934) *Marktform und Gleichgewicht*, Vienna: Julius Springer. Trans. A. Peacock, *Theory of the Market Economy*. New York: Oxford University Press (1952).

Stahl, D.O. (1989) Oligopolistic pricing with sequential consumer search, *American Economic Review*, 79, 700–12.

Stalk, G., Evans, P. and Shulman, L.E. (1992) Competing on capabilities, resources and the concept of strategy, *Harvard Business Review*, March–April, 57–69.

Standifird, S. and Weinstein, M. (2007) The transaction cost economics of market-based exchange: the impact of reputation and external verification agencies, *International Journal of the Economics of Business*, 14, 409–31.

Stanley, M.H.R., Buldyrev, S.V., Havlin, S., Mantegna, R.N., Salinger, M.A. and Stanley, H.E. (1995) Zipf plots and the size distribution of firms, *Economics Letters*, 49, 453–7.

Steen, F. and Sørgard, L. (1999) Semicollusion in the Norwegian cement market, *European Economic Review*, 43, 1775–96.

Steiner, M. (2002) Clusters and networks – institutional setting and strategic perspectives, in McCann, P. (ed.) *Industrial Location Economics*. Cheltenham: Edward Elgar.

Stigler, G.J. (1947) The kinky oligopoly demand curve and rigid prices, *Journal of Political Economy*, 55, 432–47.

Stigler, G.J. (1951) The division of labor is limited by the extent of the market, *Journal of Political Economy*, 59, 185–93.

Stigler, G.J. (1955) *Business Concentration and Price Policy*. Princeton, NJ: Princeton University Press.

Stigler, G.J. (1957) Perfect competition, historically contemplated, *Journal of Political Economy*, 65, 1–17.

Stigler, G.J. (1961) The economics of information, *Journal of Political Economy*, 69, 213–25.

Stigler, G.J. (1963) United States v. Loew's Inc.: a note on block booking, *Supreme Court Review*, 152–7.

Stigler, G.J. (1964) A theory of oligopoly, *Journal of Political Economy*, 72, 44–61.

Stigler, G.J. (1966) *The Theory of Price*. New York: Macmillan.

Stigler, G.J. (1968) *The Organisation of Industry*. Holmwood, IL: Irwin.

Stigler, G.J. (1971) The theory of economic regulation, *Bell Journal of Economics*, 2, 3–21.

Stigler, G.J. (1978) The literature of economics: the case of the kinked oligopoly demand curve, *Economic Inquiry*, 16, 185–204.

Stigler, G.J. and Sherwin, R.A. (1985) The extent of the market, *Journal of Law and Economics*, 28, 555–86.

Stiglitz, J. (1991) Imperfect information in the product market, *Handbook of Industrial Organization*, Vol. 1. Amsterdam: Elsevier.

Stiroh, K. (2009) Diversification in banking, in Berger, A., Molyneux, P. and Wilson, J.O.S. (eds) *Oxford Handbook of Banking*. Oxford: Oxford University Press.

Stock, J.H. and Watson, M.W. (2012) *Introduction to Econometrics*, 3rd edition. Harlow: Pearson Education.

Stole, L. (2007) Price discrimination in competitive environments, in Armstrong, M. and Porter, R. (eds) *Handbook of Industrial Organization*, Vol. 3. Amsterdam: Elsevier.

Stoneman, P. (1989) Technological diffusion, and vertical product differentiation, *Economic Letters*, 31, 277–80.

Stoneman, P. (1995) *Handbook of the Economics of Innovation and Technical Change*. Oxford: Blackwell.

Strassmann, D.L. (1990) Potential competition in the deregulated airlines, *Review of Economics and Statistics*, 72, 696–702.

Stuckey, J. (1983) *Vertical Integration and Joint Ventures in the Aluminium Industry*. Cambridge: Cambridge University Press.

Studenmund, A.H. (2011) *Using Econometrics: A Practical Guide*, 6th edition, International edition. Harlow: Pearson Education.

Sudarsanam, S. (2010) *Creating Value from Mergers and Acquisitions*, 2nd edition. Harlow: Prentice Hall.

Sundqvist, S., Frank, L. and Puumalainen, K. (2005) The effects of country characteristics, cultural similarity and adoption timing on the diffusion of wirless communication, *Journal of Business Research*, 58, 107–10.

Sutton, C.J. (1980) *Economics and Corporate Strategy*. Cambridge: Cambridge University Press.

Sutton, J. (1974) Advertising, concentration and competition, *Economic Journal*, 84, 56–69.

Sutton, J. (1991) *Sunk Costs and Market Structure*. London: MIT Press.

Sutton, J. (1997) Gibrat's legacy, *Journal of Economic Literature*, 35, 40–59.

Sutton, J. (1998) *Technology and Market Structure*. London: MIT Press.

Sweezy, P. (1939) Demand under conditions of oligopoly, *Journal of Political Economy*, 47, 568–73.

Sylos-Labini, P. (1962) *Oligopoly and Technical Progress*. Boston, MA: Harvard University Press.

Symeonides, G. (1999) Cartel stability in advertising-intensive and R&D-intensive industries, *Economics Letters*, 62, 121–9.

Symeonides, G. (2003) In which industries is collusion more likely? Evidence from the UK, *Journal of Industrial Economics*, 51, 45–74.

Takalo, T. (2001) On the optimal patent policy, *Finnish Economic Papers*, 14, 33–40.

Tang, F. and Ting, X. (2001) Will the growth of multi-channel retailing diminish the pricing efficiency of the web?, *Journal of Retailing*, 77, 319–33.

Tedlow, R.S. (1993) The fourth phase of marketing: marketing history and the business world today, in Tetlow, R.S. and Jones, G. (eds) *The Rise and Fall of Mass Marketing*. London: Routledge.

Teece, D.J. (1982) Toward an economic theory of the multiproduct firm, *Journal of Economic Behaviour and Organisation*, 3, 39–63.

Tellis, G.J. and Fornell, C. (1988) The relationship between advertising and product quality over the product life cycle: a contingency theory, *Journal of Marketing Research*, 25, 64–71.

Telser, L. (1960) Why should manufacturers want fair trade?, *Journal of Law and Economics*, 3, 86–105.

Telser, L. (1964) Advertising and competition, *Journal of Political Economy*, 72, 537–62.

Telser, L. (1966a) Cut throat competition and the long purse, *Journal of Law and Economics*, 9, 259–77.

Telser, L. (1966b) Supply and demand for advertising messages, *American Economic Review*, 56, 457–66.

Thaler, R. (1991) *The Winner's Curse: Paradoxes and Anomalies of Economic Life*. New York: Princeton University Press.

Thomas, L.A., Shane, S. and Weigett, K. (1998) An empirical examination of advertising as a measure of product quality, *Journal of Economic Behaviour and Organization*, 37, 415–30.

Tirole, J. (1988) *Theory of Industrial Organization*. Cambridge: Cambridge University Press.

Tremblay, V.J. and Tremblay, C.H. (1988) The determinants of horizontal acquisitions: evidence from the US brewing industry, *Journal of Industrial Economics*, 37, 21–45.

Turker, D. (2009) Measuring corporate social responsibility: a scale development study, *Journal of Business Ethics*, 85, 411–27.

Turnbull, N. (1999) *Internal Control: Guidance for Directors on the Combined Code*. London: ICAEW.

UK Cabinet Office (1996) *Competing for Quality Policy Review: An Efficiency Unit Scrutiny*. London: HMSO.

UK Science Parks Association (UKSPA) (1999) www.ukspa.org.uk/htmfiles/aboutus.htm.

Utton, M.A. (1970) *Industrial Concentration*. Harmondsworth: Penguin.

Utton, M.A. (1972) Mergers and the growth of large firms, *Bulletin of Oxford University Institute of Economics and Statistics*, 34, 189–97.

Utton, M.A. (1979) *Diversification and Competition*. Cambridge: Cambridge University Press.

Utton, M.A. (1982) Domestic concentration and international trade, *Oxford Economic Papers*, 34, 479–97.

Utton, M.A. (1986) *Profits and the Stability of Monopoly*. Cambridge: Cambridge University Press.

Utton, M.A. (2000) Fifty years of UK competition policy, *Review of Industrial Organization*, 16, 267–85.

Vakratsas, D. (2008) The effects of advertising, prices and distribution on market share volatility, *European Journal of Operational Research*, 18, 283–93.

Vanlommel, E., de Brabander, B. and Liebaers, D. (1977) Industrial concentration in Belgium: empirical comparison of alternative seller concentration measures, *Journal of Industrial Economics*, 26, 1–20.

Van de Ven, B. (2005) Human rights as a normative basis for stakeholder legitimacy, *Corporate Governance*, 5, 48–59.

Van Oijen, A. and Douma, S. (2000) Diversification strategy and the roles of the centre, *Long-Range Planning*, 33, 560–78.

Varian, H. (1980) A model of sales, *American Economic Review*, 70, 651–59.

Veblen, T. (1923) *Absentee Ownership and Business Enterprise in Recent Times*. New York: B.W. Huebsch.

Vernon, J.M. and Graham, D.A. (1971) Profitability of monopolisation in vertical integration, *Journal of Political Economy*, 79, 924–5.

Veronese, G., Fabiani, S., Gattulli, A. and Sabbatini, R. (2005) Consumer price behaviour in Italy: evidence from micro CPI data. *ECB Working Paper*, No. 449.

Vickers, J. (2002) Competition is for consumers, *Fair Trading Magazine*, May, 32, 6–8.

Vickers, J. and Yarrow, G. (1988) *Privatization: An Economic Analysis*. Cambridge, MA: MIT Press.

Vickrey, W. (1961) Counterspeculation, auctions and competitive sealed tenders, *Journal of Finance*, 16, 8–37.

Villalonga, B. (2004) Intangible resources, Tobin's q and sustainability of performance differences, *Journal of Economic Behavior and Organization*, 54, 205–30.

Vogelvang, B. (2005) *Econometrics: Theory and Applications with E-views*. Harlow: Financial Times Prentice Hall.

Vogel, D.J. (2005) *The Market for Virtue: The Potential and Limits of Corporate Social Responsibility*, Washington, DC: Brookings Institution Press.

Vyas, A. (2011) The timeliness of write-downs by U.S. financial institutions during the financial crisis of 2007–2008, *Journal of Accounting Research*, 49, 823–60.

Wagner, J. (1992) Firm size, firm growth and the persistence of chance, *Small Business Economics*, 4, 125–31.

Wall Street Journal (1962) Collusion among electrical equipment manufacturers, 10 January.

Wall Street & Technology (2006) Money, power and principle, 15 May, www.wallstreetandtech.com/showArticle.jhtml?articleID=187203258.

Wang, H. (2004) Resale price maintenance in an oligopoly with uncertain demand, *International Journal of Industrial Organisation*, 22, 389–411.

Waring, G.F. (1996) Industry differences in the persistence of firm-specific returns, *American Economic Review*, 78, 246–50.

Waterson, M. (1987) Recent developments in the theory of natural monopoly, *Journal of Economic Surveys*, 1, 59–80.

Waterson, M. (1994) Models of product differentation, in Cable, J. (ed.) *Current Issues in Industrial Economics*. London: Macmillan.

Watt, R. (2005) A unifying theory of copyrights and patents, *International Journal of the Economics of Business*, 12, 389–402.

Weinberg, M. (2007) The price effects of horizontal mergers: a survey, CEPS Working Paper No. 140.

Weir, C. (1992) The Monopolies and Mergers Commission merger reports and the public interest: a probit analysis, *Applied Economics*, 24, 27–34.

Weir, C. (1993) Merger policy and competition: an analysis of the Monopolies and Mergers Commission's decisions, *Applied Economics*, 25, 57–66.

Weiss, L.W. (1963) Factors in changing concentration, *Review of Economics and Statistics*, 45, 70–7.

Weiss, L.W. (1974) The concentration–profits relationship and antitrust, in Goldschmid, H., Mann, H.M. and Weston, J.F. (eds) *Industrial Concentration: The New Learning*. Boston, MA: Little, Brown, 183–233.

Weiss, L.W. (1989) *Concentration and Price*. Boston, MA: MIT Press.

Weiss, L.W., Pascoe, G. and Martin, S. (1983) The size of selling costs, *Review of Economics and Statistics*, 65, 668–72.

Werden, G.J. and Froeb, L.M. (1993) Correlation, causality and all that jazz: the inherent shortcomings of price tests for antitrust markets, *Review of Industrial Organization*, 8, 329–53.

Werden, G. (2012) Why (ever) define markets? An answer to Professor Kaplow, available at: http://papers.ssrn.com/sol3/papers.cfm?abstract_id=2004655.

Wernerfelt, B. (1984) A resource-based view of the firm, *Strategic Management Journal*, 5, 171–80.

Wernerfelt, B. and Montgomery, C.A. (1988) Tobin's *q* and the importance of focus in firm performance, *American Economic Review*, 78, 246–50.

Weston, J.F. (1970) Conglomerate firms, *St John's Law Review*, 44, 66–80, reprinted in Yamey, B.S. (ed.) (1973) *Economics of Industrial Structure*. London: Penguin, 305–21.

Weston, J.F., Mitchell, M.L. and Mulherin, J.H. (2003) *Takeovers, Restructuring, & Corporate Governance*, 4th edition. Harlow: Prentice Hall.

Whinston, M. (1990) Tying, foreclosure and exclusion, *American Economic Review*, 80, 837–59.

Whish, R. (2003) *Competition Law*, 4th edition. London: Butterworth.

White, L.J. (2013) Market power: how does it arise? How is it measured? in Thomas, C.R. and Shughart, W.F. (eds.) *Oxford Hanbook of Managerial Economices*. Oxford: Oxford University Press.

Wiersema, M.F. and Bowen, H.P. (2007) Corporate diversification: the impact of foreign competition, industry globalization, and product diversification, *Strategic Management Journal*, 29, 115–32.

Wilcox, C. (1960) *Public Policy Toward Business*, Homewood, IL: Irwin.

Williams, M. (1993) The effectiveness of competition policy in the United Kingdom, *Oxford Review of Economic Policy*, 9, 94–112.

Williamson, O.E. (1963) Managerial discretion and business behaviour, *American Economic Review*, 53, 1032–57.

Williamson, O.E. (1967) Hierarchical control and optimum firm size, *Journal of Political Economy*, 75, 123–38.

Williamson, O.E. (1968a) Economies as an anti-trust defence: the welfare trade-offs, *American Economic Review*, 58, 18–36.

Williamson, O.E. (1968b) Economies as an anti-trust defence: correction and reply, *American Economic Review*, 58, 1372–6.

Williamson, O.E. (1971) The vertical integration of production; market failure considerations, *American Economic Review*, 61, 112–27.

Williamson, O.E. (1975) *Markets and Hierarchies*. New York: The Free Press.

Williamson, O.E. (1985) *The Economic Institutions of Capitalism*. New York: The Free Press.

Williamson, O.E. (1989) Transaction cost economics, in Schmalensee, R. and Willig, R.D. (eds) *Handbook of Industrial Organization*, Vol. 2, Amsterdam: Elsevier.

Williamson, O.E. (2002) The theory of the firm as governance structure: from choice to contract, *Journal of Economic Perspectives*, 16, 171–95.

Williamson, O.E. (2005) The economics of governance, *American Economic Review*, 95, 1–18.

Willis, M.S. and Rogers, R.T. (1998) Market share dispersion among leading firms as a determinant of advertising intensity, *Review of Industrial Organization*, 13, 495–508.

Wilson, J. (1994) Competitive tendering and UK public services, *Economic Review*, April, 12, 31–5.

Wilson, J.O.S. and Morris, J.E. (2000) The size and growth of UK manufacturing and service firms, *Service Industries Journal*, 20, 25–38.

Wilson, J.O.S. and Williams, J.M. (2000) The size and growth of banks: evidence from four European countries, *Applied Economics*, 32, 1101–9.

Winston, C. (1993) Economic deregulation: days of reckoning for microeconomists, *Journal of Economic Literature*, 31, 1263–89.

Winston, C. (1998) US industry adjustment to economic deregulation, *Journal of Economic Perspectives*, 12, 89–110.

Winter, S.G. (2003) Understanding dynamic capabilities, *Strategic Management Journal*, 24, 991–5.

Wolfram, C. (1998) Increases in executive pay following privatization, *Journal of Economics and Management Strategy*, 7, 327–61.

Yamawaki, H. (2002) Price reactions for new competition: a study of the US Luxury car market, 1986–1997, *International Journal of Industrial Organization*, 20, 19–39.

Yamey, B.S. (1970) Notes on secret price cutting in oligopoly, in Kooy, M. (ed.) *Studies in Economics and Economic History in Honour of Prof. H.M. Robertson*. London: Macmillan, 280–300.

Yamey, B.S. (1972) Predatory price cutting: notes and comments, *Journal of Law and Economics*, 15, 137–47.

Yamey, B.S. (1973) Some problems of oligopoly, Paper presented to International Conference on International Economy and Competition Policy, Tokyo, Japan.

Yamey, B.S. (1974) Monopolistic price competition and economic welfare, *Journal of Law and Economics*, 17, 377–80.

Yang, C. and Tsou, T. (2002) Do stronger patents in length induce more patents? Evidence from Taiwan's 1994 patent reform, Paper presented to the Second International Conference of the Japanese Economic Policy Association, Nagoya, Japan.

Yoon, S. (2004) A note on the market structure and performance in Korean manufacturing industries, *Journal of Policy Modelling*, 26, 733–46.

Young, G., Smith, K.G. and Grimm, C.M. (1996) Austrian and industrial organization perspectives on firm-level activity and performance, *Organization Science*, 7, 243–54.

Youssef, M.I. (1986) Global oil price war is expected to affect the industry for years, *Wall Street Journal*, 18 February.

Index